The Humanities
Volume II

The Humanities

Cultural Roots and Continuities

Fourth Edition

Volume II

The Humanities and the Modern World

Mary Ann Frese Witt
North Carolina State University at Raleigh

Charlotte Vestal Brown
North Carolina State University at Raleigh

Roberta Ann Dunbar
University of North Carolina at Chapel Hill

Frank Tirro
Yale University

Ronald G. Witt
Duke University

With the collaboration of

Ernest D. Mason
North Carolina Central University

John R. Kelly
North Carolina State University at Raleigh

D. C. Heath and Company
Lexington, Massachusetts Toronto

Address editorial correspondence to:

D. C. Heath and Company
125 Spring Street
Lexington, MA 02173

Acquisitions Editor: Paul Smith
Developmental Editor: Linda Bieze
Production Editor: Martha Wetherill
Designer: Henry Rachlin
Photo Researcher: Sharon Donahue
Production Coordinator: Richard Tonachel
Permissions Editor: Margaret Roll

Drawings by Eugene Wilson Brown, A.I.A.

For permission to use copyrighted materials, grateful acknowledgment is made to the copyright holders listed on pages 545–546, which are hereby considered an extension of this copyright page.

Published simultaneously in Canada.

Printed in the United States of America.

International Standard Book Number: 0-669-27576-X

Library of Congress Catalog Number: 92-81649

10 9 8 7 6 5 4 3

Preface

Changes in this Edition

The fourth edition of *The Humanities: Cultural Roots and Continuities* has benefited from the suggestions of readers, professors, and teachers from a wide variety of geographical locations and teaching situations, as well as from our own rethinking of the problems involved in presenting the humanities and cultural roots. Although the format and the spirit of the book remain basically the same, we have made some important changes.

The most significant of these involves an expansion of the concept of "roots." Although the book still reflects our conviction that the Greco-Roman and Judeo-Christian traditions form the basis of the Western humanities, the addition of new Chapters 1 and 2 on Mesopotamia and Egypt highlights the fact that these Western traditions have their own roots in more ancient civilizations. In an effort to emphasize somewhat more the influence of non-Western cultures on Western cultures, we have expanded the medieval section to include a new Chapter 9 on Byzantium and Islam. These new chapters feature many works of art and reading selections, including portions of the *Epic of Gilgamesh,* the "Negative Confession" from the *Egyptian Book of the Dead,* Egyptian love poetry, selections from Justinian's *The Digest,* and portions of the Islamic *Quran.*

In part because of these additions, and because of requests from readers, the present Volume II begins with the Italian Renaissance instead of with the seventeenth century. Also because of these changes, we have consolidated some of the chapters in Volume II. In addition, readings have been added to both volumes, often at the request of readers. New selections include Book 11 of Homer's *Odyssey,* the story of Pygmalion and Galatea from Ovid's *Metamorphoses,* texts from early Church fathers St. Jerome and St. Augustine, sonnets of Petrarch, the Seneca Falls "Declaration of Rights and Sentiments," Franz Kafka's "A Country Doctor," the Prologue from Ralph Ellison's *Invisible Man,* excerpts from Roland Barthes's "The Death of the Author," and Ishmael Reed's "beware: do not read this poem."

The content of all the chapters—and particularly of Chapter 35 dealing with the contemporary world—has been thoroughly reviewed and revised when necessary. For greater accessibility, we have grouped all of the readings at the end of each chapter.

Focus of the Book

Our commitment to a truly interdisciplinary introduction to the humanities through the concept of "cultural roots" remains the same. We feel that in an introductory humanities course the student's personal growth should take place on three levels—historical, aesthetic, and philosophical. The overall purpose of the two volumes can best be described by breaking it down into these three categories.

The Historical Level

We stress the concept of "cultural roots" because one cannot understand the culture in which one lives without some notion of what went into its making. Therefore, we have made every effort here to link the "roots" discussed to aspects of the contemporary American cultural environment. This can be a knotty problem because such links can sometimes be too facile, and we also would like students to discover that cultures remote in time or space can be worth studying simply for themselves. We do not in any way claim to present, let alone discuss, all of the myriad cultural roots that compose the background of today's students. Such a claim would be far beyond the scope of a single introductory humanities course.

Volume I focuses on three traditions—Greco-Roman, Judeo-Christian, and West African—while also exploring *their* roots in the ancient civilizations of Mesopotamia and Egypt and looking briefly at some other influences, such as that of Islam. African culture, a long-neglected field, is now studied more as a significant root of African-American art and thought. The cultures of Africa and the West have intertwined and influenced each other for many centuries. In addition, the study of African culture offers the opportunity to study some fundamental aspects of the humanities in a truly interdisciplinary context, often in contrast to their counterparts in the West.

In our examination of these three cultural roots, we have attempted to focus on certain periods and monuments rather than to survey everything. For example, the focus for the Greco-Roman root is on Athens during the fifth century B.C. This means that some significant works of classical Greek drama, sculpture, and architecture can be examined rather extensively, in relation to each other, while archaic Greece and the entire civilization of Rome receive a briefer treatment. Similarly, in our treatment of West Africa, we have chosen to focus on the culture of the Yoruba people, rather than to survey all of the cultures from this part of the world. While we study the "root" of the Judeo-Christian tradition in the Bible, with selections from the Old and New Testaments, we focus on the relations of arts and thought in the Gothic cathedral, with the specific example of Chartres, during the European Middle Ages. The addition of the chapter on Byzantium and Islam helps to clarify the context of this focal culture.

If we pursue the same metaphor, Volume II might be called "stems, leaves, and flowers." Here, too, we have attempted to focus and spread out more than to survey and spread thin. In our exploration of the Renaissance and Reformation periods we emphasize the fusion of the Greco-Roman and Judeo-Christian roots and focus on the development of humanism in fifteenth-century Italy and its diffusion in the north. The court of Louis XIV in the seventeenth century, the Enlightenment in France and America, the romantic movement, the Industrial Revolution, the modernist movement, and the controversial notion of postmodernism all provide centers around which the many interrelated facets of the humanities can be discussed. As in previous editions, our choice of texts and art works reflects a commitment to recognize the contributions of women, African-Americans, and Hispanic-Americans to the Western humanities.

The Aesthetic Level

On the whole, we follow the same "focal" principle in the aesthetic domain. In presenting music, we operate on the assumption that a student will retain more from listening to and analyzing an entire work than from reading music history and theory and hearing snippets. In the presentation of major works of literature and art in the focal periods, we assume that it is more useful for a student to look at the whole of Chartres cathedral than to skim the history of medieval art, and to read all of *Oedipus Rex* rather than bits and summaries from several Greek tragedies. With lengthy works, such as epics and novels, this is, of course, not possible. We have thus chosen portions of the *Iliad,* the *Aeneid,* and *The Divine Comedy* that are significant in themselves and representative of the whole.

Dance, an often-neglected art form, is given more extensive treatment here than in other humanities texts. Entire dance compositions can, of course, be appreciated only in live performance or film, and we suggest that instructors exploit those resources as much as possible. Although some art forms may seem unfamiliar to students at the beginning, it has been our experience that a long introductory chapter on how to look, listen, and read is largely wasted; therefore, we cover such matters in the introductions to individual works. Questions on the nature of genre are considered in the cultural context in which they originated, notably in ancient Greece. We place much importance on study questions that require the student to read, look, and listen carefully.

Although we try to avoid jargon, we feel that some knowledge of the technical vocabulary of criticism in the art is essential for literate discussion. Difficult or unfamiliar terms appear in italics the first time they are used in any given chapter, indicating that they are defined in the Glossary.

The Philosophical Level

It may well be objected that we compromise the focal method in our presentation of philosophy, because no entire philosophical works appear in the book. This is largely due to considerations of space; but it is also true that, when dealing with a work in terms of certain fundamental ideas rather than in terms of aesthetic wholeness, the "snippet" method is not objectionable. Beginning humanities students are probably not ready to read Aristotle's *Ethics* in its entirety, but they should be able to see how Aristotle's ideas are essential to the cultural roots of the modern world.

The student's personal growth in the philosophical area means, however, something much broader than his or her contact with formal philosophy. The (ideal) student—whose historical awareness is increased by an understanding of cultural roots and whose aesthetic sensitivity is heightened by personal confrontation with a variety of works of art—should also be able to grow intellectually through contact with diverse ideas. A humanities course should enable students to refine their thinking on the basic questions that affect all human beings, to formulate more clearly their personal values, and to discuss these with intellectual rigor rather than in vaporous "bull" sessions. Instructors should welcome debates that might arise from comparing Genesis and African mythology, the issue of women's role in society in Aristophanes's *Lysistrata* and in John Stuart Mill's *The Subjection of Women,* or the relative merits of realistic and abstract art or tonal and atonal music. They and their students will find many more such issues for debate.

Individual instructors will decide which aspect of the humanities they wish to emphasize. We believe that this book offers enough flexibility to be useful for a variety of approaches.

Supplements to the Text

To facilitate teaching and study, we provide a package of supplements available to all who adopt this text. It includes an *Instructor's Guide* with advice for using this text and suggestions for approaching the study of various art forms, a *Study Guide* for each volume for students to reinforce their learning of the text's content, a *Test Item File* for instructors to use in building their own chapter tests and examinations, and a set of slides that includes many of the works of fine art discussed in the text to facilitate class discussion. A single-volume Brief Version of the text is also available. It contains the same instructional text, illustrations, and chapter organization of the two-volume edition, excluding only the primary-source reading selections. It is well suited for one-semester courses.

Mary Ann Frese Witt
Charlotte Vestal Brown
Roberta Ann Dunbar
Frank Tirro
Ronald G. Witt

Acknowledgments

Many people have contributed time, work, ideas, and encouragement to the creation of this book. Gratitude is due, first of all, to those who provided their own research and writing: In Volume I, Professor emeritus Herbert Bodman of the University of North Carolina at Chapel Hill wrote the material on Byzantium and Islam, and Professor Edmund Reiss wrote the sections on courtly love and on medieval English poetry. In Volume II, Professor Ernest Mason of North Carolina Central University wrote the introduction to Freud as well as the material on African-American culture, and Professor John Kelly of North Carolina State University wrote the sections on Latin American culture. Professor emeritus Alan Gonzalez of North Carolina State University wrote the material on the Spanish baroque.

The plan for the first (1980) edition of *The Humanities* grew out of the four years I spent initiating and directing an interdisciplinary humanities program at North Carolina Central University in Durham. It would not have been possible without the stimulation and aid of my students and colleagues there. The late Professor Charles Ray and Dean Cecil Patterson provided me with the time, encouragement, and wherewithal to create the program. The professors who worked closely with me—Elizabeth Lee, Phyllis Lotchin, Ernest Mason, Norman Pendergraft, Earl Sanders, Winifred Stoelting, and Randolph Umberger—have all left their mark on this book. The generous support of the Kenan Foundation, which provided the humanities program with a four-year grant, enabled me to research and compile much of the material. The Kenan Foundation also gave me the opportunity to attend numerous conferences on the humanities. The workshops given at North Carolina Central university by Clifford Johnson, of the Institute for Services to Education, also provided inspiration.

The fourth edition manuscript benefited greatly from readings and criticisms by experts and users. The authors wish to thank Dr. John Brinkman and Dr. Emily Teeter of the Oriental Institute of the University of Chicago for their careful work with the chapters on Mesopotamia and Egypt.

We are also grateful to the instructors who reviewed all of or portions of this book: Henry C. Allan, Jr., Moraine Valley Community College; Lawrence Aufderheide, Lakeland Community College; H. Guy Bensusan, Northern Arizona University; Dion K. Brown, Polk Community College; Thomas J. Cleman, Northern Arizona University; Paula A. Drewek, Macomb Community College; Gunar Freibergs, Los Angeles Valley College; Ann M. Green, Jackson Community College; Mark Hawkins, Foothill College; Mary Kay Kramp, Alverno College; Rodney Oakes, Los Angeles Harbor College; Christine E. Oliver, Savannah State College; Helen C. Othow, Saint Augustine's College; Cornelius A. Page, San Diego Mesa College; William A. Pasch, Clayton State College; Joan Sevick, Nassau Community College; Robert Williams, Bethune-Cookman College. Thanks are due also to Bruce McNair for his painstaking assistance in updating the *Instructor's Guide.*

The authors are especially grateful to Linda Bieze of D. C. Heath for her scrupulous and insightful editing as well as her patience, Martha Wetherill of D. C. Heath for her careful work with the publishing process, and Shira Eisenman for her helpful assistance. The guidance of Paul Smith of D. C. Heath has been essential to the conception and the completion of this new edition.

My collaborating authors deserve many thanks for their fine work and their support over the years.

Mary Ann Frese Witt

Contents

COLOR ILLUSTRATIONS

MAPS

Chronicle of Events

	EGYPT	MESOPOTAMIA-SYRIA-PALESTINE	GREECE
3200 B.C.			
3100	Union of North and South Egypt (3150)		
3000			
2900		Sumerian city-states	
2800		Successive waves of Semites occupy Palestine	
2700			
2600	Old Kingdom (2686–2182)		
2500	Pyramids of Cheops, Chephren, and Mycerinus	Gilgamesh of Uruk	
2400			
2300	Settlement of Kerma	Agade dynasty established by Sargon (2340)	
2200			
2100	Intermediate Period (2181–2134) Middle Kingdom (2134–1782)	*Epic of Gilgamesh* (?)	
2000			Minoan Palace construction begins on Island of Crete
1900		Phoenician (Canaanite) city culture	
1800			
1700	Second Intermediate Period (1782–1570)	Babylonian Dynasty established: Hammurabi (1792)	
1600	New Kingdom (1570–1070)		High point of Minoan civilization (1600–1400)
1500		Hittites destroy Babylon	
1400	Hatshepsut (1498–1483)		
1300	Amenophis IV (Akhenaton) (1350–1334)	Phoenicians develop alphabet Hebrews enter Palestine	Destruction of Minoan palace Mycenaean expansion
1200		Phoenicians flourish (1200–900)	
1100			Traditional date for sack of Troy (1184)
1000	Third Intermediate Revival (1070–664)	Early biblical books written Saul made King of Hebrews (1025)	Greek colonies on Aegean Coast and Greek colonies in Asia Minor established

	AFRICA	MESOPOTAMIA-SYRIA-PALESTINE	ROME	GREEK POLITICAL EVENTS	GREEK CULTURAL EVENTS	
		Biblical texts written				
1000 B.C.		David King of Hebrews (1000–961) Assyrian empire begins Solomon (961–922) Hebrew kingdom divides into Israel and Judah (922)				
900		Assyria conquers Phoenicians and Israel (876–605)			Homer?	
800	Napata rules Kush (800–270) Kushite kings of Egypt (780–656)		Traditional date for founding of Rome (753)	Beginning of *polis*		
700		Nineveh falls (612) Neo-Babylonian Empire of Nebuchadnezzar (604–562)				*Archaic Age (750–480)*
600	Persia conquers Egypt (525)	Jews taken captive to Babylon (586) Persians take Babylon (539) Jews return home (538) Darius of Persia (521–486)	Kings expelled and Republic created (509)		Sappho (c. 600) Beginning of Drama and Panathenian Festivals Aeschylus (525–456)	*Archaic Age (750–480)*
500				Persian Wars (499–479) Pericles (498–427) Peloponnesian War (431–404)	Euripides (480–406) Thucydides (470–400) Socrates (470–399) Building of Parthenon (447–432) Plato (427–347) Aristophanes's *Lysistrata* (411) Sophocles's *Oedipus* (406)	*Classical Age (480–350)*
400	Alexander conquers Egypt (332) Greek dynasty rules (331–304)		Vigorous program of Roman conquest of Italy begins (343)	Philip of Macedon (382–336) Alexander of Macedon (the Great) (356–323)	Aristotle (384–322) Epicurus (342–270) Zeno (336–264) and founding of Stoic school	*Classical Age (480–350)* / *Hellenistic Age (350–150)*
300	Meroe rules Kush (270 B.C.–350 A.D.)		I Punic War (264–241) Sardinia and Corsica annexed (238) II Punic War (218–201)			*Hellenistic Age (350–150)*

	AFRICA	MESOPOTAMIA-SYRIA-PALESTINE	ROME	GREEK POLITICAL EVENTS	GREEK CULTURAL EVENTS
200	Nok civilization at its height (200 B.C.–200 A.D.) Carthage sacked (146) Rome conquers North Africa		Terence (195–159) III Punic War (149–146) Cicero (106–43) Caesar (100–44)	Rome begins conquest of Greece	
100		Occupation of Israel by Romans (63) Reign of Herod the Great in Palestine (37 B.C.–4 A.D.)	Lucretius (99–55) Horace's *Satires* (35–29) Virgil's *Aeneid* (29–19) Augustus begins reign (27)		

	AFRICA	ROMAN EMPIRE
A.D.		Birth of Jesus Christ Death of Augustus (14) Conquest of Britain (43–51) Death of Paul (c. 62–64) Persecution of Christians by Nero (64) Sack of Jerusalem (70)
100		Juvenal's *Satires* (c. 100) Roman Pantheon built (188–125)
200		Plotinus (205–270) and Neo-Platonism Period of disorder (235–284)
300		Reforms of Diocletian (285–305)

	AFRICA	WESTERN EUROPE	EASTERN EUROPE AND MIDDLE EAST
400		Augustine, *Confessions* Alaric sacks Rome (410) Vandals sack Rome (455) Traditional date for end of Western Empire (476) Franks invade Gaul (486)	Byzantium consolidates hold on area
500		Lombards invade Italy (568)	Justinian (483–555) extends empire in East and temporarily conquers part of Italy, Africa and Spain—codifies Roman Law
600	Moslem conquest of Africa		Muhammad begins preaching (610) Muhammad dies (632) Dome of the Rock (completed 692)
700	Empire of Ghana (700–1230)		

	AFRICA	WESTERN EUROPE	EASTERN EUROPE AND MIDDLE EAST
700		Moslem conquest of Spain (711) Defeat of Moslems at Poitiers (732) Charlemagne (768–814)	Iconoclasts begin century-long campaign against images Abbasid Calephate established (750–1258) at Baghdad Spanish amirate establishes independence at Cordova (756)
800		Second period of invasions (c. 800–950): Northmen, Hungarians, and Saracens	Final restoration of images (843)
900	Beginnings of Benin	Northmen establish Normandy (911) Otto I founds German Empire (962) First systematic teaching of Aristotle's *Logic* (975) Hugh Capet King of France (987) Great mosque of Cordoba completed	
1000		Building of St. Sernin—Romanesque (11th and 12th centuries)	Spanish amirate splinters (1031) into small kingdoms
1050		Norman invasion of England (1066) St. Bernard (1090–1153) First Crusade (1095)	East-West schism (1054)
1100		*Play of Daniel* (12th century) Rebuilding of St. Denis on new lines—early Gothic	
1150		Bernart de Ventadorn (late 12th century) Marie de France (late 12th century) Chartres Cathedral begun (1194)	Saladin, Kurdish ruler, captures Jerusalem from crusaders (1187)
1200	Revolt of Mande peoples against Ghana (c. 1200) and rise of Mali Empire	Mongol invasion of Russia European embassy sent to China St. Louis (1214–1270) Aquinas (1225–1274)	Conquest of Constantinople by Fourth Crusade (1204) Fall of Latin kingdom (1211)
1250		Giotto (1276–1337)	
1300	Mansa Musa pilgrimage to Mecca (1324) Exploration of Canaries (1330s and 1340s)	Dante's *Divine Comedy* (1300–1321) Petrarch (1304–1374) Boccaccio (1310–1375) Hundred Years War begins (1337) First appearance of Black Death (1348–1350)	Expansion of Ottoman Turks in Greece and elsewhere in Balkans (1308–1337)
1350		The Alhambra (c. 1354–1391) Bruni (1370–1444) Brunelleschi (1377–1446) Chaucer's *Canterbury Tales* (1390–1400)	Unsuccessful siege of Constantinople by Turks (1397–1402)
1400		Masaccio (1401–1428) Henry the Navigator founds navigation school at Sagres (1419) Piero della Francesca (1420–1492) Jeanne d'Arc burned (1431) Medici dominate Florence (1434) Alberti's *On Painting* (1435) Leonardo da Vinci (1442–1519) Botticelli (1444–1510) Lorenzo il Magnifico (1449–1492)	
1450	John Affonso d'Aveiro visits Benin (1485–1486)	Pico della Mirandola (1463–1494) Isaac's *On the Death of Lorenzo* Erasmus (1466?–1536) Spanish Inquisition established (1478) Columbus reaches America (1492) DaGama sails for India (1497)	Fall of Constantinople (1453)

Romanesque Style (11th and 12th centuries) (1000–1200)

Gothic Style (12th–15th centuries) (1100–1500)

Renaissance Style (15th and 16th centuries) (1400–1500)

	AFRICA	EUROPE	EUROPEAN CULTURE	NEW WORLD
1500	Duarte Pacheco Pereira's *Esmeraldo de situ orbis* (1507) Benin at the height of its power (16th and 17th centuries)		Michelangelo's *David* (1504) Raphael's *School of Athens* (1510–1511) Machiavelli's *Prince* (1513) First edition of Erasmus's *Colloquies* (1516) Luther publishes German *New Testament* (1521)	First black slaves in New World (1505) Magellan circumnavigates the globe (1519) Cortez in Mexico (1519–1521) Verrazano establishes French claims in North America (1524)
1525		Peasants' Revolt in Germany (1525) Henry VIII declares himself head of Church of England (1534) Jesuit Order founded (1540) Council of Trent (1545–1563)	First edition of Calvin's *Institutes* (1536) Copernicus's *Revolution of Heavenly Bodies* (1543) *Renaissance Style (15th and 16th centuries)*	
1550		Peace of Augsburg legalizes Lutheranism in Germany (1555) Reign of Queen Elizabeth I of England (1558–1603) Wars of Religion begin in France (1561) Massacre of French Protestants (1572)	Titian (1477–1576) Bruegel (1520–1569)	Building of St. Augustine in Florida (1565)
1575		Defeat of Spanish Armada (1588) Edict of Nantes (1598)	First edition of Montaigne's *Essays* (1580–1588) Shakespeare (1564–1616) Kepler (1571–1630) Caravaggio's *Calling of St. Matthew* (1599–1600)	
1600		Thirty Years War begins (1618)	Rubens's *Raising of the Cross* (1609–1610) Giambattista Marino (1569–1625) John Donne (1572–1631) Descartes (1596–1650) Corneille (1606–1684) Bacon's *Novum Organum* (1620)	Settlement at Jamestown (1607) Founding of Quebec (1608) First slaves in Virginia (1619) Plymouth colony established (1620)
1625		Civil War in England begins (1643) Peace of Westphalia in Germany (1648)	Harvey demonstrates circulation of blood (1628) French Academy founded (1635) Tirsa de Molina's *The Trickster of Seville* (1635) Galileo's *Discourse on Two New Sciences* (1638) Richard Crashaw (1612–1649)	
1650				

	AFRICA	EUROPE	EUROPEAN CULTURE	NEW WORLD
1650		Restoration of English Monarchy (1660) Louis XIV (1638–1715) Louis revokes Edict of Nantes (1685)	Hobbes' *Leviathan* (1651) Rome's Cornaro Chapel (1645–1652) Rembrandt (1606–1669) Milton (1609–1674) Lully (1632–1687) Royal Society of London created (1662) Construction of Versailles begins (1669) Molière's *Le Bourgeois Gentilhomme* (1670) Robert Boyle (1627–1691) Newton publishes *Mathematical Principles* (1687) Locke's *An Essay Concerning Human Understanding* (1690)	New York City taken by English from Dutch (1664) Salem Witch Trials (1692)
1700	Foundation of Ashanti Confederacy (1701)	Union of Scotland and England (1707) War of Spanish Succession (1701–1713) Hanover (Windsor) dynasty begins in England (1714)	Darby cokes coal (1709) Johann Sebastian Bach (1685–1750)	
1725		War of Austrian Succession (1740–1748)	Building of Hôtel Soubise (1732) Kay's Flying Shuttle (1733) English repeal laws against witchcraft (1736) Great Awakening (1730s) Handel's *Messiah* (1742) Montesquieu's *Spirit of the Laws* (1748)	Georgia, last of original thirteen colonies, founded (1733)
1750		Death of George II (1760) Accession of Louis XVI (1774)	Volume I of the *Encyclopédie* (1751) Mozart (1756–1791) Rousseau's *On the Origins of Inequality* (1755) Voltaire's *Candide* (1759) First blast furnace (1761) Rousseau's *Social Contract* (1762) Watt patents steam engine (1769) Schiller (1759–1805)	French and Indian War (1754–1763) English take Quebec (1759) English acquire Canada by Treaty of Paris (1763) Boston Massacre (1770) Revolutionary War begins (1775)
1775		Meeting of Estates General (May, 1789) Taking of Bastille (July, 1789) Fall of Robespierre (1794) Napoleon's coup d'état (1799)	Goethe's *Werther* (1787) Wollstonecraft's *Vindication of Rights of Women* (1792)	Treaty of Paris ends war (1783) Constitution goes into effect (1789) Washington dies (1799)
1800	Rise of Fulani Empire (19th century) Britain abolishes slave trade (1807)	Napoleon Consul for life (1802) Napoleon crowned Emperor (1804) End of Holy Roman Empire (1806)	David (1748–1825) Madame de Staël (1766–1817) Wordsworth (1770–1850) Constable (1776–1837)	Jefferson elected President (1801)
1810				

	AFRICA	EUROPE	EUROPEAN CULTURE	NEW WORLD
1810	France abolishes slave trade (1815)	Defeat of Napoleon and Congress of Vienna (1815) Industrialization of England (1815–1850)	Stephenson's locomotive (1814) Byron (1788–1824) Goya *Executions of the 3rd of May* (1814) Blake (1757–1827)	War of 1812 (1812–1814) Founding of *North American Review* (1815)
1820	Liberia established (1832)	Greek War of Independence (1821–1829)	Beethoven's *Ninth Symphony* (1824) Heine (1797–1856)	
1830	France annexes Algeria (1830)	Revolutions in France, Germany, Italy, Belgium, and Poland (1830) Industrialization of France and Belgium (1830–1860) Industrialization of Germany (1840–1870)	Delacroix (1799–1863) Dickens's *Old Curiosity Shop* (1840)	Emerson (1803–1882) Poe (1809–1849)
1840		Revolutions in France, Italy, Germany, and Austria (1848)	*Giselle* (1841) Chopin (1810–1849) Turner's *Rain, Steam, and Speed* (1845) Marx-Engels's *Communist Manifesto* (1848)	Seneca Falls convention (1844) Mexican War (1846–1848) Gold discovered in California (1848)
1850	Livingstone at Victoria Falls (1853–1856)	Second Empire founded in France (1852) Crimean War (1855)	Crystal Palace (1851) Millet (1814–1875) Courbet's *Manifesto* (1855) Baudelaire (1821–1867) Darwin's *Origin of Species* (1859)	Walt Whitman (1819–1892)
1860	Opening of Suez Canal (1869)	Foundation of Kingdom of Italy (1860) Emancipation of serfs in Russia (1861) Creation of Dual Monarchy Austria-Hungary (1867)	Mill's *On Subjection of Women* (1861) Ford Maddox Brown's *Work* (1862–1863) van Gogh (1853–1890)	Civil War (1861–1865) Emily Dickinson (1830–1886) Period of Reconstruction (1867–1877)
1870	Brazza explores Lower Congo (1875)	Franco-Prussian War (1870–1871) German Empire and Third French Republic created (1871) Dual Alliance: Germany and Austria-Hungary (1879)	Nietzsche (1844–1900) Monet's *Impressions: Sunrise* (1873) Gauguin (1848–1903)	Stephen Crane (1871–1900)
1880	France occupies Tunisia (1881) Britain occupies Egypt (1882) Germans in Togo and Cameroon (1886) Gold found in South Africa (1886) Rhodes establishes Rhodesia (1889–1891)	Triple Alliance: Germany, Austria-Hungary, and Italy (1882) German-Russian Reinsurance Treaty (1887)	Dostoevsky's *Brothers Karamazov* (1880) Mallarmé (1842–1898) Verlaine (1844–1896) Rimbaud (1854–1891)	William Dean Howells (1837–1920) Henry James (1843–1916)
1890				

	AFRICA	INTERNATIONAL POLITICS	EUROPEAN CULTURE	AMERICAN CULTURE
1890	French annex Guinea and Ivory Coast (1893)	Industrialization of Russia (1890–1914) Franco-Russian Alliance (1894)	Cézanne (1839–1906) Matisse (1869–1954)	Reliance Building (1891) Spanish-American War (1898) Chesnutt's *The Conjure Woman* (1899)
1900	British conquest of N. Nigeria (1900–1903)	Entente Cordiale: France and Great Britain (1902) First Russian Revolution (1905)	Apollinaire (1880–1918) Picasso's *Les demoiselles d'Avignon* (1907)	Louis H. Sullivan (1856–1924)
1910	Morocco becomes French protectorate (1912) Conquest of German colonies (1914–1915)	Balkan Wars (1912–1913) First World War (1914–1918) Russian Revolution (1917) Treaty of Versailles (1919) German Weimar Republic created (1919)	Duchamp's *Nude Descending a Staircase* (1912) Mondrian (1872–1944) Kandinsky's *On the Spiritual in Art* (1912) Stravinsky's *Rite of Spring* (1913) Kirchner's *Street* (1914) Bauhaus founded (1919)	Armory Show (1913) U.S. declares war on Germany and Austria-Hungary (1917) Harlem Renaissance (1919–1932)
1920		Irish Free State (1922) Mussolini establishes Fascism in Italy (1922) Great Depression begins (1929)	Kafka (1883–1924) Nijinsky (1890–1950) Hitler's *Mein Kampf* (1925–1926) Spengler's *Decline of the West* (1926–1928) Lipchitz' *Figure* (1926–1928) Brancusi's *Bird in Space* (1928)	W. E. B. Du Bois (1868–1963) Mariano Azuela (1873–1952) Davis's *Egg Beater No. 1* (1927) Stock Market Crash (1929)
1930	Nigerian youth movement begins (early 1930s) Italy conquers Ethiopia (1936)	Hitler rises to power (1933) Official rearmament of Germany (1935) Spanish Civil War (1936–1939) Second World War begins (1939)	Freud's *Civilization and Its Discontents* (1930) Le Corbusier's *Villa Savoye* (1929–1930) Malraux's *La Condition humaine* (1933) James Joyce (1882–1941) Virginia Woolf (1882–1941) Picasso's *Guernica* (1937)	Shahn's *Passion of Sacco and Vanzetti* (1930) New Deal begins (1933) Louis Armstrong (1900–1971) Claude McKay (1890–1948) Jean Toomer (1894–1967) Georgia O'Keeffe (1887–1986)
1940	Ethiopia liberated (1941) Léopold Sédar Senghor (b. 1903) Léon Damas (1912–1987) Aimé Césaire (b. 1913)	Formation of United Nations (1945) Fourth French Republic established (1945) Communist takeover in E. Europe (1946–1948) China becomes communist (1949)	Giacometti (1901–1966) Sartre (1905–1980) Simone de Beauvoir (1908–1986)	Welles's *Citizen Kane* (1941) Japanese attack Pearl Harbor (1941) Albert Einstein (1879–1955) T. S. Eliot (1888–1965) E. E. Cummings (1894–1962) Richard Wright (1908–1960) Jackson Pollock (1912–1956) Charley Parker (1920–1955)
1950	Algerian War begins (1954) Morocco and Tunisia freed (1955) Ghana first colony to gain independence (1957) Guinea independent (1958) Frantz Fanon (1925–1961) David Diop (1927–1960)	Korean War (1950–1953) Russian Sputnik (1957) Common Market (1957) de Gaulle's Fifth Republic (1958)	Camus (1913–1960) Charlie Chaplin (1889–1977) Arrabal's *Picnic on the Battlefield* (1952) Beckett's *Endgame* (1957) Primo Levi *If This Is a Man* (1958)	Frank Lloyd Wright (1869–1959) Ezra Pound (1885–1972) Langston Hughes (1902–1967) Duke Ellington (1899–1974) Martha Graham (1895–1991) Jorge Luis Borges (1899–1986)
1960				

	AFRICA	INTERNATIONAL POLITICS	EUROPEAN CULTURE	AMERICAN CULTURE
1960	Nigeria and most French colonies independent (1960) Algeria and Tanganyika freed (1962) Dennis Brutus (b. 1924)	Berlin Wall (1961) Beginning of Russia-China split (1962) Great Cultural Revolution in China (1966)	Jean Genet (1910–1985) Roland Barthes (1915–1980)	Ralph Ellison (b. 1914) Katherine Dunham (b. 1919) Kurt Vonnegut, Jr. (b. 1922) James Baldwin (1924–1987) Miles Davis (1926–1991) Ornette Coleman (b. 1930)
1970	Amin gains power in Uganda (1971) Breakdown of Portuguese African Empire (1974) Wathiong'O Ngugi (b. 1938) Soweto Uprising (1976)	Withdrawal of U.S. from Vietnam (1972) Oil prices rise (1973) Shah leaves Iran and Khomeini takes power (1979) Russian troops sent to Afghanistan (1979)	Michel Foucault (1926–1984) Jacques Derrida (b. 1930)	Adrienne Rich (b. 1929) Andy Warhol (1931–1987) Alvin Ailey (1931–1992) LeRoi Jones (b. 1934) Nikki Giovanni (b. 1943) Judy Chicago's *The Dinner Party* (1979)
1980	Rhodesia becomes Zimbabwe (1980) Prolonged famine (1981) Liberation struggles continue in Africa (1988)	Polish solidarity movement repressed (1981) Marcos ousted in Philippines (1986) Chernobyl nuclear explosion (1986) USA-USSR agreement on medium-range strategic force (1988) Berlin Wall falls (1989)	Salman Rushdie (b. 1947)	Ernesto Cardenal (b. 1925) John Barth (b. 1930) Alice Walker (b. 1944) Leonard Bernstein (1918–1990)
1990	South Africa repeals all racial laws (1991)	Gulf War (1991) Commonwealth of independent states replaces USSR (1991)		
2000				

PART FIVE

Renaissance and Reformation: Fusion of the Roots

16

Humanism and the Early Italian Renaissance

Beginnings of the Modern World

o historical change of great magnitude occurs abruptly, nor is a complete break ever made with the past. The modern Western world was hundreds of years in the making, and depending on what one considers the chief features of modernity to be, its beginnings can be dated at any time between 1300 and 1650. In this book we have chosen to date the modern world from the beginning of the Renaissance in the fourteenth century because in these years new conceptions of God, humanity, and nature emerge, along with new forms of art and behavior that are generally recognizable as modern.

This chapter focuses on Italy because, although northern Europe shared with Italy some of the responsibility for developing new ideas about God, humanity, and nature, the transformation in thought and culture in Italy was much more profound and widespread. Indeed, historians generally recognize that the Renaissance was largely limited to Italy until the late fifteenth century, when northern Europe began to respond to Italian influence.

An Italian Phenomenon

Whereas the center of medieval culture was located in northern France and southern Germany, the Renaissance from 1350 to 1500 was dominated by Italy. Throughout the previous two centuries Italy had been the leading commercial power of Europe, and by 1300 the peninsula became the center of industry as well. Italy was far more urbanized than the North: in 1300 half a dozen cities of more than fifty thousand people dotted the Italian landscape, whereas north of the Alps only Paris could boast of a population above that number. Although lay literacy was relatively high in urbanized sections of the peninsula, education before 1300 had largely been oriented toward practical goals, primarily medicine and law. The figure of Dante, coming at the end of the thirteenth century, therefore, is an exception and harbinger of great things to come. In contrast to its secondary role in medieval culture, Italy dominated in the Renaissance.

The Crisis of the Fourteenth Century

The fourteenth century was a time of trouble for Europe. By 1300 western Europe was overpopulated for the technological level of the society. The costs of food and food-bearing land were high, wages were low, and a good percentage of the population was undernourished. When a terrible famine, the worst of the Middle Ages, struck the subcontinent between 1314 and 1318, about 10 percent of the people died and the losses were not made up. Beginning in 1348 the Black Death struck repeatedly over a wide area for the next fifty years. By 1400 Europe had only about 60 percent of the population that it had in 1300. The population was to remain at this low level until the last decades of the century, when a spectacular rise in population began. This great human loss resulted in an economic contraction, a rise in labor costs, and a drop in rents and food prices. The overall effect on the upper classes of Europe who earned their income from trade or agriculture was adverse.

Although, like the rest of Europe, Italy was affected by the plague and the economic contraction, it remained the commercial and industrial center and did not suffer economic stagnation to the same degree as the North. Indeed, it appears that an imbalance in trade favorable to Italy existed in the fourteenth and fifteenth centuries. Quantities of gold and silver flowed into the peninsula from the North in exchange for luxury goods that Italians produced or imported from the East. The drain from the North could not go on forever, and as purchases of Italian goods by northerners slowed down, investment opportunities in business narrowed in Italy.

The effect of the economic contraction in Italy, however, was not all negative. Some of the Italian stocks of surplus precious metals, with no profitable outlet available, were subsequently funneled into culture; they paid for architecture, art objects, and patronage to scholars and writers. Both in Italy and in the North, business people learned to rationalize their production, rendering their operations more efficient to compete in a diminished market. Modern business practices such as double-entry bookkeeping and holding companies appeared. The rapid diffusion of the mechanical clock from the fourteenth century enhanced the tendency toward greater efficiency: time is, after all, money.

Humanism

The response of the best minds in Italy to the crisis of the fourteenth century brought about the intellectual movement known as humanism. On the whole, the humanists were hostile to scholasticism because they felt that elaborate philosophical and theological systems were unnecessary. The major object of intellectual labor should be to guide human conduct in this world. At the same time they argued that even if speculation on God and nature were important, the mystifying reign of death and destruction in the fourteenth century testified to the futility of such investigation.

Besides divine revelation, the only sure source of human knowledge for the humanists was their own experience and history, that is, the experience of other human beings in past times. Human beings can learn from their history because, unlike nature, history is their own creation. Thus, the humanists reasoned, the study of the successes and failures of those who preceded us would teach us how to conduct our lives. The humanists, moreover, were very clear on what history they considered to be the proper source for help. For the Italian humanists of the fourteenth to the sixteenth centuries, the ancient Romans and—after 1400, when they began to learn Greek—the ancient Greeks furnished the best examples of human conduct because their societies had reached the pinnacle of worldly achievement in all aspects of human endeavor.

In fact, the Italian humanists of the fourteenth century set out to create patterns of behavior that accorded better with their way of life than did inherited medieval ethical forms. These traditional standards still fitted northern European society, which was essentially rural and socially hierarchical, with learning a preserve of the clergy. On the other hand, by the fourteenth century, Italy—like ancient Rome and Greece—was urban, with a high degree of social mobility and widespread Latin literacy among the laity. Similar to ancient society, moreover, Italy was organized around city-states with an intense political life. Consequently, in search of a morality compatible with their evolving urban society, Italian humanists turned for guidance to the ancient orators, moralists, and historians.

Essentially, the humanists were literary scholars interested in Greek and Latin literature, grammar, history, and ethics. These subjects, therefore, constituted the *studia humanitatis*—that is, the disciplines that made human beings truly human. For the humanist, the capacity to express oneself in words distinguished the human race from all other species. If this was the basic human characteristic, those who best expressed themselves in words were the most human. Among human beings, however, they were usually concerned only with men. The humanists also assumed that outer speech was a reflection of one's inner state. If the inner man was calm and in harmony with his nature, then his speech would be fluent and harmonious. True eloquence stemmed from a fine soul, just as the highest degree of moral virtue was closely tied to eloquence. Of course, one could be virtuous and still stutter, but virtue could be realized only by helping others to become virtuous as well. The individual Christian had a responsibility to others to help them to be good Christians; this could best be done by eloquent speech that inspired the will and heart to do the right.

Since the humanists considered the ancient pagan writers to have achieved excellence in speaking and writing, they believed that the study of Greek and Roman literature could best teach effective oral and written expression. They also thought that the writings of the pagans contained moral teachings urged with such forcefulness that they could not but influence their readers to become virtuous. In reading these writings, therefore, the humanists sharpened their moral sensibilities as well as their literary technique. They, in turn, would use their eloquence and virtue to persuade and train others.

Admittedly, the truth as found in the pagan authors—fragmentary and based on reason—had to be interpreted in the context of the overarching truths of Christianity. The humanists, however, saw no incompatibility between what the Bible taught about God and about the nature of the human soul and the moral lessons taught by the ancient writers. The eloquence and learning of the ancients, consequently, coupled with the greater vision provided by divine revelation, could be a tremendous force for Christian reform.

One of the humanists' major criticisms of the scholastics was that their language was too technical and awkward. Such a style could never inspire human beings to improve their lives. There was an enormous difference between knowing the truth and carrying out its lessons in practice. Eloquent speech was the means of making truth active in the world.

Humanism was clearly an outgrowth of the urban culture of central and northern Italy. Dante had already shown the creative vigor present in this maturing urban society, but he had written in medieval Latin as well as in Tuscan. This new movement, as we have seen, took the ancients and their Latin as its models. Once initiated, imitation of the ancient Romans seemed natural to Italians.

The Use of Classical Authors Because ancient eloquence was central to their scheme of education, the humanists from the fourteenth century on devoted enormous energy not only to recovering lost ancient writings but also to preparing good editions of those inherited from the Middle Ages. In the more than eleven or twelve hundred years since ancient Roman times, the works of the pagans, especially the most popular ones, had been copied thousands of times by thousands of scribes; thus texts were terribly corrupted. It fell to the humanists to restore as fully as possible the words and phrases of the pagan writers by a systematic comparison of surviving manuscripts. If ancient eloquence was to serve as a basis of inspiration to the present generation, the texts must be restored to their original purity.

Medieval writers used the classics as a kind of quarry from which to borrow words and ideas in order to adorn and support their own schemes of thought. On the other hand, although concerned with using the ancient writers for their own purposes, the humanists were also interested in defining the personalities of the great people of antiquity. Rather than attribute attitudes and ideas to pagan writers on a piecemeal basis, they tried to form an integrated picture of their thought and personalities by a careful analysis of all of an individual writer's works. Because of the similarities between their own and the ancient culture, they were able to appreciate the thoughts and actions of the ancients as the Middle Ages never could. This awareness of an interest in the totality of a personality, moreover, motivated their approach not merely to historical personages but also to people of their own time.

Furthermore, all the comparison of words and phrases in the effort to obtain accurate texts taught the humanists a concept not well understood in the Middle Ages: languages change; they have a history. The same is true of institutions, customs, and ideas. Thus the scholarly endeavors of the humanists led them gradually to develop a sense of change and development, of historicity. This deepened their appreciation of the nature of human personality, permitting them to see the extent to which individuals were conditioned by circumstances of time and place. It also led them to a growing awareness that people are responsible for their history in large part and, subsequently, for their future as well. They came to see human beings as doers and makers, endowed with the godlike powers of reason and will to create their own culture.

Humanism and Science While not completely discarding the medieval ethos, which emphasized compassion, suffering, and humility, humanism in its essential tendencies moved toward a reevaluation of the human predicament by accenting the active, dynamic aspect of human nature. Originally biased against the natural sciences because of their focus on nature rather than human beings, the humanists nonetheless furnished the scientists with better texts of antiquity on which to base their investigations. By the sixteenth century they were largely responsible for providing a vision of human creative capacities that encouraged scientific inquiry. Through the joint efforts of humanism and natural science, the task of improving human life materially as well as spiritually through a better understanding of individuals and their environment became increasingly viewed as a primary goal of learning.

Petrarch Francesco Petrarca (1304–1374) is generally considered the first of the Italian humanists. Although he was Florentine by descent and his first teacher was an exiled Tuscan like his own father, Petrarch grew to manhood in France, not Italy. In the second half of his life, which he spent primarily in Italy, Petrarch saw the city of his ancestors only twice on brief visits. Petrarch's pioneering achievement was to formulate the basic humanistic conception of the intimate connection between ethics and eloquence just described and to develop an appreciation for ancient life and thought in its historical context.

In certain respects, however, Petrarch was still closely linked to medieval traditions. Medieval thinkers were fully committed to the belief that the contemplative life was the best form of human existence and that monarchy was the best form of government. Like these thinkers, Petrarch, who spent most of his mature life in proximity to the new princely courts of northern Italy, considered the life of the citizen—the married man with business and civic responsibilities—unquestionably inferior to that of the solitary scholar or monk, who devoted his energies to the contemplation of divine truth. Moreover, like them he believed that monarchy was the ideal political constitution and that the Roman emperors had been established by God to replace the decaying Roman Republic.

Whereas Petrarch's scholarly contemporaries and Petrarch himself believed that his principal claim to enduring fame lay in his Latin writings (he was made poet laureate for his Latin epic poem *Africa*), subsequent generations have been most influenced by the poems he wrote in Tuscan Italian, the *Rime sparse.* These include both longer poems and sonnets, and it is especially as master of the *sonnet* form that Petrarch influenced all European poetry. Petrarch's sonnets were inspired by those of Dante and the poets of the *dolce stil nuovo* (see Chapter 11). Like Dante's theme in the *Vita nuova,* Petrarch's major theme in his sonnets is the poet's love for a beautiful and inaccessible lady, and like Dante, he writes of this love both during her lifetime and after her death. But Petrarch's Laura, often pictured in nature, among spring flowers, is less symbolic and medieval than Dante's Beatrice. Although there is no hard evidence for her actual existence, most scholars assume that she was a married French noblewoman whom Petrarch encountered while living in the south of France. In his poetry, Petrarch not only speaks of Laura's beauty but also analyzes the whole range of his emotions as a lover, from elation to despair. It is this interest in the problems of human nature and in the individual that differentiates Petrarch from medieval writers. Although Petrarch sometimes strives to present Laura as the transcendental ideal in imitation of Dante's Beatrice, this effort is constantly undercut by an ambivalent mixture of the sacred and the erotic.

Civic Humanism: Salutati and Bruni

By 1400 Florence was one of a dwindling number of cities still governed by republican methods. Whereas the republican form had been common in northern and central portions of the peninsula in the thirteenth century, in the course of the next century many popular regimes had been replaced by the rule of one person or one family. Even in Florence the sphere of active citizens had by 1400 been narrowed to less than a hundred families. Hundreds of other families shared the more than two thousand public offices that had to be filled annually in the Florentine state, but a narrower group of families controlled the key positions.

Nonetheless, republican institutions were still strong enough in Florence to inspire Coluccio Salutati (1331–1406), humanist and chancellor of the city, to challenge the medieval theory of the superiority of monarchy. Both in his official work as Florentine chancellor, or secretary of state, and in his more scholarly writings, Salutati began to elaborate an argument for republicanism. His disciple Leonardo Bruni (1370–1444), however, was primarily responsible for formulating a theory of republican government that was to remain a living force down to the nineteenth century and beyond. He considered the rule of one person harmful to the common good. Since people realize themselves to the fullest in serving the state, republican government is natural and inherently stronger than monarchy. Rome reached its highest power under the Republic, not under the emperors; in fact, although some emperors might have been personally good men, as a group they destroyed Rome. Florence, founded in the days of the Roman Republic, inherited that tradition of liberty, and in contemporary Italy it served as the leader in the struggle of free people against *tyranny.*

The origins of Bruni's theory can be traced to the writings of Aristotle and Cicero. But Bruni's capacity to sense the republican spirit of these writers, which his predecessors had not perceived, stems from his personal experience as a part of a living republican society. His arguments rested both on his understanding of human nature and on the lessons he believed were found in history. The first European to formulate republican ideas with such clarity, he was followed over the next hundred years by a whole succession of writers, mainly Florentine, urging similar views.

Bruni was also one of the first of the humanists to learn Greek. Eminent Latin scholars like Petrarch and Salutati in the previous century did not know the other classical language. Aristotle's works had been translated hundreds of years before into Latin, but Bruni's knowledge of Greek gave him access to the rest of extant Greek literature.

The Medici; Neoplatonism

In the last decade of Bruni's life Florence came under the control of the Medici family and their supporters. An old Florentine banking family, the Medici, by the early fifteenth century were the richest family in the city. In the early 1430s the head of the family, Cosimo, quarreled with the other leading members of the Florentine government and was sent into exile in 1433. The following year, when his enemies in the government proved themselves clearly incompetent, they were driven out and Cosimo was recalled. Although the republican institutions continued to function and Cosimo remained a private citizen, for all practical purposes he and his close friends were usually able to control both the internal and external policies of the republic.

When Cosimo died in 1466, his son, Piero the Gouty, inherited the authority; and when three years later Piero died, he in turn was succeeded by his two sons, Lorenzo and Giuliano, then twenty and eighteen respectively. After the assassination of Giuliano in 1478, Lorenzo alone directed the political life of the city until his own death in 1492. The years of Lorenzo's domination in Florence were also years of some of the highest cultural achievements in the city. Because of his exquisite taste and personal talents, Lorenzo became known in his own lifetime as Lorenzo the Magnificent.

The rise of the Medici and their political control over Florentine institutions rendered Bruni's emphasis on the active life of the citizen unrealistic. Although a republican current persisted in the city, the mood was generally one of political quietism. Not by chance, the second half of the fifteenth century marked the progress of a movement usually labeled Florentine Platonism.

As we have already seen, Greek studies were introduced in Florence at the beginning of the fifteenth century and reinforced by the arrival of Greek scholars from Byzantium in the middle decades of that century. One of the first goals of Greek scholars was to translate the complete works of Plato. Whereas Aristotle had been translated into Latin in the thirteenth century, until this time only a handful of Plato's writings were in that language. Now, along with Plato's works, writings of Plato's ancient followers were also put into Latin. The most famous of these followers was Plotinus, an Egyptian of the second century A.D., who had given Plato's philosophy a clearly mystical bent. Plotinus stressed that through proper training the soul, whose true home was beyond this world, could at times in this life return by a mystic ascent to the world of the Ideas. The ultimate step was to merge totally with the Platonic One or Idea of the Good. Besides those of Plotinus, other Platonic writings, many of them of a magical nature, became popular with late-fifteenth-century intellectuals. This kind of literature fitted an age that was no longer interested in active participation in politics.

Rather than focus on politics as the civic humanists had done earlier, the Florentine Platonists stressed the potentialities of the human being for making contact while in this life with God and angels, the highest forms of reality. Because humans existed midway on a chain of being between the lowest material objects and God, the whole range of reality was potentially accessible to those who had received training in Platonic philosophy. One thinker, Giovanni Pico della Mirandola (1463–1494), went even further by arguing that human beings had no determined nature and that by acts of their will they could fall to the lowest depth of creation or rise to a position above that of the angels. No other thinker of the Renaissance surpassed Pico in his conception of human freedom and power.

Reading Selections

Francesco Petrarch

From the *Rime Sparse*

Petrarch explores the possibilities of symmetry and contrast in the formal aspects of the sonnet with great ingenuity. The octave usually presents a situation, event, image, or generalization, and the sestet a reflection, result, or application. The first sonnet printed below exemplifies Petrarch's love of technical ingenuity, his artificiality. He puns on each syllable of Laura's name in two forms (Laureta and Laure). Note, too, the classical reference, frequent in Petrarch, to the myth of Apollo and the laurel tree. Another sonnet plays with the word *aura* (breeze) and its relation to Laura. Although some of Petrarch's sonnets seem natural in their use of imagery, others, such as the one that develops the complex metaphor of the prison, are highly ingenious in their attempt to portray the sufferings and joys of love. To show the rhyme scheme and play on words, we have included the first sonnet (number 5 in Petrarch's collection) in the original Italian, with a literal translation by Robert M. Durling.[1] The other translations, which rhyme in English, although not always in the original scheme, are by Anna Maria Armi.

5

Quando io movo i sospiri a chiamar voi
e'l nome che nel cor mi scrisse Amore,
LAU-dando s'incomincia udir di fore
il suon de' primi dolci accenti suoi;

vostro stato RE-al che 'ncontro poi
raddoppia a l'alta impresa il mio valore;
ma "TA-ci," grida il fin, "ché 'farle onore
e d'altri omeri soma che da' tuoi."

Cosi LAU-dare et RE-verire insegna
la voce stessa, pur ch' altri vi chiami,
o d'ogni reverenza et d'onor degna;

se non che forse Apollo si disdegna
ch'a parlar de' suoi sempre verdi rami
lingua mor-TA-l presuntuosa vegna.

5

When I move my sighs to call you and the name that Love wrote on my heart, the sound of its first sweet accents is heard without in LAU-ds.

Your RE-gal state, which I meet next, redoubles my strength for the high enterprise; but "TA-lk no more!" cries the ending, "for to do her honor is a burden for other shoulders than yours."

Thus the word itself teaches LAU-d and RE-verence, whenever anyone calls you, O Lady worthy of all reverence and honor;

except that perhaps Apollo is incensed that any mor-TA-l tongue should come presumptuous to speak of his eternally green boughs.

76

Love with his promises and flattery
Directed me again to my old prison,
And gave the keys to that same enemy
Who keeps me locked, divided from my reason.

I noticed it, alas! only when I
Was in their power; and now in agony
(Who will believe it, though I will not lie?)
And weary I return to liberty.

Like to a true, afflicted captive, now
I carry a great number of my chains,
And my heart is imprinted on my brow.

---

[1] *Petrarch's Lyric Poems* (Cambridge, Mass.: Harvard University Press, 1976), pp. 40–41.

When you observe how all my colour wanes,
You will say:—If I can judge from his head,
He has not far to go before he's dead.—

90

The golden hair was loosened in the breeze
That in many sweet knots whirled it and reeled,
And the dear light seemed ever to increase
Of those fair eyes that now keep it concealed:

And the face seemed to colour, and the glance
To feel pity, who knows if false or true;
I who had in my breast the loving cue,
Is it surprising if I flared at once?

Her gait was not like that of mortal things,
But of angelic forms; and her words' sound
Was not like that which from our voices springs;

A divine spirit and a living sun
Was what I saw; if such it is not found,
The wound remains, although the bow is gone.

227

Aura that fold her blond and curly hair,
And move it softly and are moved by it,
And scatter that sweet gold as you think fit,
Then gather it and bind in knots so fair,

You fill her eyes from where some loving wasp
Stings me so that I feel it here, and grumble,
And, wavering, my treasure seek to clasp,
Like animals that often shy and stumble.

I think I have it, and I realize
That I am far from it, and fall and rise
Seeing now what I wish, now what is true.

Happy air, stay with the ray of her look,
Life-giving, fair. And you, clear running brook,
Why can I not change my journey with you?

228

Love with his right hand opened my left side
And planted in the middle of my heart
A laurel green that by its colour's art
Would cause every emerald to hide.

Ploughshare of pen with sighing of the breast,
And the pouring of sweet rain from the eyes,
Adorned it so that a scent reached the skies
Such as no other leaves ever expressed.

Fame, honour, virtue and enchantment,
A chaste beauty in heavenly array,
Are the roots from which rises the great bay.

Such I find it in me, no matter where
I am, my lovely load; and with deep prayer
I worship and revere it as a saint.

QUESTIONS

1. Note the divisions between octave and sestet in each poem. What are the advantages and disadvantages of the sonnet as a poetic form? In what respect do Petrarch's sonnets differ from Dante's?
2. How does Petrarch develop images such as the prison and the laurel tree? How do they acquire meaning?
3. How would you define the Petrarchan concept of love? of woman?

GIOVANNI PICO DELLA MIRANDOLA

FROM THE *Oration on the Dignity of Man*

I have read, O venerable fathers, in the records of the Arabs that Abdala the Saracen,[1] when asked what he believed was the most admirable thing on the stage of this world, as it were, replied that there was nothing more admirable than man. Hermes Trismegistus supported this opinion when he said, "O Asclepius, man is a great miracle!" Yet when I consider the grounds for such sayings, the many justifications, given by many, for the outstanding qualities of human nature do not satisfy me: that man is intermediary between the creatures, a friend of the higher powers, king of the lower regions; capable of understanding nature with the sharpness of his senses, the penetration of his reason, and the light of his intelligence; the space between unchanging eternity and the flux of time, and (as the Persians say) the bond of the world, nay rather, its marriage bond, and, as David testifies, only less than the angels.[2] Indeed these are great qualities but not the

[1] Abdala was presumably the cousin of Mohammed.
[2] Psalm 8:5.

principal ones, that is, those which rightly serve as the basis for such extraordinary admiration. But why should we not admire the very angels and the blessed chorus of the heavens more? At length I seemed to myself to have understood why man is the most fortunate animal and therefore worthy of universal admiration and what his place in the order of the universe is that makes him an object of envy not only by brutes or by the stars, but even by minds beyond this world. It is an unbelievable and wonderful thing. Why should it not be? For on this account man is properly said to be a great miracle and a wondrous being. But now hear, Fathers, what it is and out of your kindness lend me your full attention.

The supreme Father, God the architect, had already fabricated this house of the world which we see, the most illustrious temple of the divinity, according to the laws of His secret wisdom. He had adorned the place above the heavens with minds and animated the heavenly spheres with eternal souls; He had filled the excrementary and filthy places of the lower world with all manner of animals. But, with the work finished, the artisan wanted there to be someone who could contemplate the nature of so great a work, love its beauty and admire its magnitude. For this reason with all these things finished (as Moses and Timaeus[3] bear witness) only then did He think of creating man. But there was nothing among the archetypes from which He could model a new creature, nor in His treasuries was there an inheritance to bestow on His new son, nor was there any place left in the whole world where this contemplator of the universe could sit. Everything was already full; everything in the highest, middle, and lowest orders of being was already given out. But it was not in the Father's nature to fail as if worn out in this last creation; nor was His wisdom to waver without a plan in such a serious situation. Nor was it a part of His loving kindness that He, who would praise divine liberality in others, would condemn Himself for His lack of it. At length the consummate artificer decreed that the creature whom He could endow with no properties of its own should share in all those which the others possessed individually for themselves. Therefore, He took man, a creation of indeterminate form, and placing him at the midpoint of the world spoke to him in this way: "I have given you no fixed abode, no form of your own, no gifts peculiarly yours, O Adam, so that you might have and possess the abode, form and gifts you yourself desire according to your will and judgment. The defined nature of other beings is confined by laws which I have prescribed. You, compelled by no limitations, according to your free choice in whose hands I have placed you, shall prescribe your own limits. I have set you in the center of the world, that you might more easily observe whatever there is in the world. We have made you neither heavenly nor terrestrial, neither mortal nor immortal, so that, free of constraint and more honorable as your own moulder and maker, you might give yourself whatever form you prefer. You can degenerate toward lower beings, which are brutes, or, if you will, you can be reborn among higher beings, which are divine."

Oh, the magnificent generosity of God the Father! Oh, the extraordinary and wondrous felicity of man, who was given the power to be that which he wanted! Brutes as soon as they are born bring with them from the mother's womb everything they are to have. The highest spiritual beings either from the beginning or soon thereafter are that which they will be for eternity. In the case of man, the Father bestowed on him at birth manifold seeds and germs of every kind of life. Whichever ones he cultivates will grow and bear their fruit in him. If he cultivates vegetative seeds, then he becomes a plant; if sensual ones, then a brute; if rational seeds, then he becomes a heavenly being. If intellectual ones, then he will be an angel and son of God. And if, unhappy with being a creature of any sort, he draws into the center of his own unity, his spirit will be made one with God, and in the solitary darkness of the Father, Who is above all things, he will distinguish himself beyond all things. Who does not admire this our chameleon? Could anything else be more an object of wonder?

[3]Plato, *Timaeus.*

QUESTIONS

1. What different sources does Pico appear to use in establishing the dignity of man?
2. Compare Pico's account of man's creation with that in Genesis (Chapter 8). To what extent does he remain within the Judeo-Christian tradition, and how does he differ?
3. What is the basis for man's dignity? In what respect is man more wonderful than the angels?
4. Compare Pico's glorification of man to that of Sophocles in the choral ode from *Antigone* (see the section "Humanism and Tragedy" in Chapter 5).

17

Art, Architecture, and Music in Florence

Innovation Based on Antiquity

In 1436 when Leon Battista Alberti published the Italian version of his Latin treatise *On Painting* (1435), he added a prologue praising the great Florentine artists Donatello, Ghiberti, and Masaccio, and the architect Brunelleschi. These individuals, says Alberti, are responsible for returning to the study of nature as the source of art and have consequently brought great fame to Florence. In a passage that parallels Pericles's *Funeral Oration,* Alberti compares Florentine accomplishments in art to those of the ancients, reserving the greatest praise for the Florentines, since they had to create by first discovering the knowledge that the ancients had already attained.

This point of view stresses the sense of departure from the immediate past and that of courageous experiment and exploration which, to Alberti and his contemporaries, must have seemed characteristic of Florence in the mid-fifteenth century. Wealth, power, and the association of free people had produced the republic; these same conditions fostered the new forms and conventions in art and architecture.

Similarly, the successful artists of the fifteenth century had roots in Roman antiquity. Brunelleschi, Florence's architect, is reported to have visited Rome in the early 1400s, studying and measuring the remains of the Forum. He returned to create a conspicuously new architecture. Alberti, who knew Brunelleschi, was also an architect who studied ancient texts; he wrote about the ideals and intentions that made Roman and fifteenth-century architecture so different from that of the Middle Ages. His theory and Brunelleschi's practice were, as we will see, representative of the changes taking place in Florence and were largely responsible for the transmission of new ideas to the future.

The City of Florence

It is difficult to imagine the events of the fifteenth century without some feeling for the physical setting of Florence itself (Color Plate I). In the center of Italy, the city sits in a plain at the foothills of the Apennine Mountains, bisected by the Arno River. From almost any vantage point outside or within the city, one's view is dominated by the red-tiled octagonal dome of Saint Mary of the Flowers, or the *Duomo*, the cathedral of the city. The feeling created by this cathedral and its place within the city is vastly different from that of Notre Dame at Chartres. The *Duomo* sits in its own square *(piazza)* but within a city of other squares that belong to equally important old Christian churches or civic and mercantile enterprises. The *Palazzo Vecchio* (the old city hall) with its battlements and tower reminds one of the Gothic period (Fig. 17-1). It dominates the square where Michelangelo's *David* was originally placed.

The city has many centers of activity; there are distinguishable quarters for artisans, and the *Ponte Vecchio* (the old bridge) spanning the Arno still carries the many shops for luxury items that were there in the 1400s. Florence bustles with business activity—with the precious industries of gold, silver, silk, and leather still practiced today. The great food market near San Lorenzo and the small street stalls give the city an air of tantalizing fecundity.

Florence is dominated by narrow cobbled streets and the thick walls of the palaces, banks, and apartments that rise three and four stories, keeping the blistering summer sun from the streets. In the winter the reds, yellows, browns, and tans of marble, stone, stucco, and brick glow wetly, contrasting with the black and white, gray, or green marble of the facades of many of the churches (Fig. 17-2). The city has a this-worldly intensity, a presence of now that is surely both a condition and creation of its fifteenth-century efflorescence.

17-1 *Palazzo Vecchio, Florence. (Alinari/Art Resource, NY)*

17-2 *Baptistry, Santa Maria degli Fiore, Florence. (Alinari/Art Resource, NY)*

17-3 *Interior, San Lorenzo, Florence. (Alinari/Art Resource, NY)*

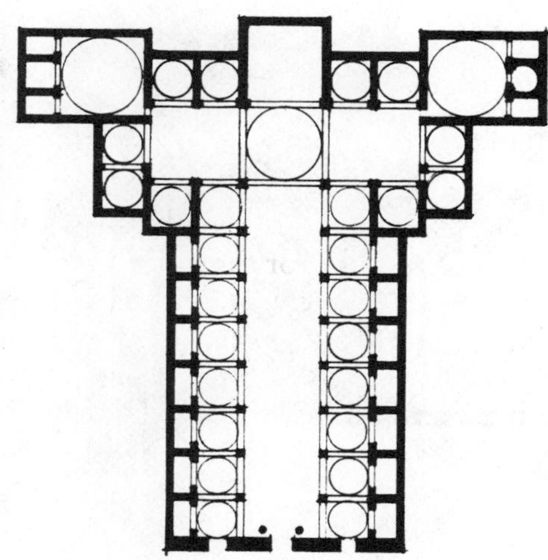

17-4 *Groundplan, San Lorenzo, Florence.*

Florentine Architecture

The cathedral dome that dominates Florence was designed by Filippo Brunelleschi (1377–1446), who won a competition for the commission. Although not the most significant of Brunelleschi's accomplishments, it introduces the scientist, inventor, and designer that Brunelleschi had become. Technically, he employed a system that suspended an interior shell from the exterior structure of ribs and concealed buttresses that originated in Roman and Gothic technology. Of almost equal importance to the city fathers were the machines and devices that Brunelleschi invented to erect the dome without an enormous quantity of wooden centering (see Roman and Gothic architecture). The *lantern* (cupola) based on his design was put in place after his death. Brunelleschi's influence on architecture was enormous. We can better appreciate some of the new ideas and vitality he gave to the art by considering two other works: the interior of San Lorenzo and the Pazzi Chapel.

The Church of San Lorenzo

Brunelleschi designed a sacristy for the Medici family to be added to San Lorenzo, an essentially Gothic church. The Medici were so delighted with it that he was then commissioned to remodel the interior of the church (Fig. 17-3), a project that began in 1421 and went on for many years. San Lorenzo's great simplicity and directness emphasize the contrast between the Renaissance and the Middle Ages. The interior seems almost early Christian, but with a substantial difference. Imposed on the traditional plan of *nave* and aisles (Fig. 17-4) is a sense of mathematical harmony, the repetition of sizes and shapes that derive from, but achieve a form different from, those of Gothic or Roman buildings.

Perhaps the most significant obvious difference is the sense of definite measured units of space, individual and independent. The nave is separated from the aisles by arcades of smooth Corinthian columns that carry semicircular arches. Above the arches is an *entablature* marking off the *clerestory* walls that are broken by arched windows centered above the arches. The columns, arches, and entablature are all in a gray stone that contrasts sharply with the smooth white plaster walls. The aisles are roofed by shallow *vaults*, and shallow side chapels line the walls. These have semicircular arched openings with a decorative *keystone* and are also flanked by pilasters with Corinthian capitals, thus repeating the column-arch combination of the nave arcade. The aisles are lit by small round windows, one centered above each side chapel (Fig. 17-5).

The division of the wall planes of the aisles and the nave arcade is reinforced by the pavement, which is arranged in squares (see plan, Fig. 17-4)—thus, two squares form a *bay* of the nave and equal the height of a column; one square equals a bay of the aisle and one-half square a chapel. The *transept* is made of four large squares that are approximately equal to four square

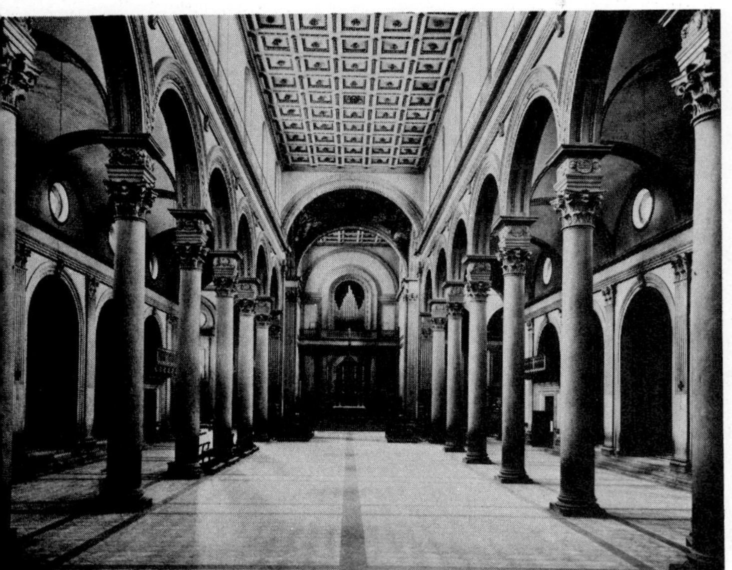

17-5 *Nave, San Lorenzo, Florence. (Alinari/Art Resource, NY)*

bays of the aisles. The nave roof is flat and decorated with square coffers.

Space in San Lorenzo is clear and limited, strongly directional but ordered into a rigorous sequence of bays. Each column, perfectly articulated, marks the beginning and end of a bay, a space. The light is dim but not mysterious. The transept is a specific and different space, as is the square *apse* at the east end. The feeling is one of intellectual control, not mystic transcendence.

Alberti, the architectural theorist, wrote that a church should induce contemplation through order and harmony, reflecting the mathematical perfection of the universe. It should, he said, be plain and encourage one to focus inward on control of the self for the attainment of right, Christian actions. Windows should be high, so that one could see only the sky and not be distracted by the external world. Brunelleschi seems to have anticipated these ideals.

The Pazzi Chapel

The Pazzi Chapel was commissioned by the wealthy Pazzi family for their own use and for the use of the monastery of which it is a part. Located in the cloister of Santa Croce, it forms a strong contrast to the church that is one of the few Gothic buildings in Florence. The façade, with its columns and portico, clearly recalls Roman architecture (Fig. 17-6).

Structurally, the interior of the chapel is familiar also (Fig. 17-7). Brunelleschi has used a *post and lintel* and load-bearing wall system to carry barrel vaults and an arrangement of domes. The plan shows two major axes; that formed by the domical space of the *portico* (which is repeated in the dome over the apse) and that formed by the rectangular spaces of the barrel vaults that support the central dome (Fig. 17-8). The directional quality of each axis is resolved under the great dome of the hall. The resultant feeling is one of quiet serenity reinforced by the articulation of the wall planes, windows, door, and apse opening. Applied pilasters rising from a base carry an entablature on which rest the arches of the vaults. These members, like the other decorative elements (the blind arches opposite the windows, for example), are made of *pietra serena,* the gray stone that is also used on the interior surfaces of San Lorenzo. They form a strong contrast with the white plastered walls and the terra cotta plaques, which are predominantly blue and white. The impression of the interior is one of cool elegance, for each element is paired, or repeated, except for the central dome, which in its singularity acts to arrest all motion. Does the chapel remind you of Roman buildings that we have seen? How does it differ from a Greek temple? A Roman one? Can you compare this building with San Lorenzo? With Chartres?

It is easy to understand how Brunelleschi's work must have appeared to his colleagues. With its order, clarity, and use of elements from the antique, it must have seemed like Rome revived. Yet it is not based on simply copying from ruins that Brunelleschi had seen, or from later uses of antique forms in early Christian and Romanesque buildings. Like Gothic art and architecture, the art and architecture of fifteenth-century Florence depend for their forms and ideals on a structure of knowledge and value, on a society that was not ignorant of the meaning to be found in building. Alberti's Latin treatise *On Architecture* presents some of the ideas and principles that he certainly believed capable of communication in building. The model for his treatise was the text by Vitruvius, the first-century B.C. Roman architect and engineer, but the book itself was very much the product of Alberti and fifteenth-century Florentine thought. It is another important way to understand the art and architecture of that century.

Leon Battista Alberti (1404–1472) and the Theory of Architecture

Alberti wrote that the architecture and the planning of cities should be based on a rational analysis of problems, needs, site, and climate. The city, he felt, would

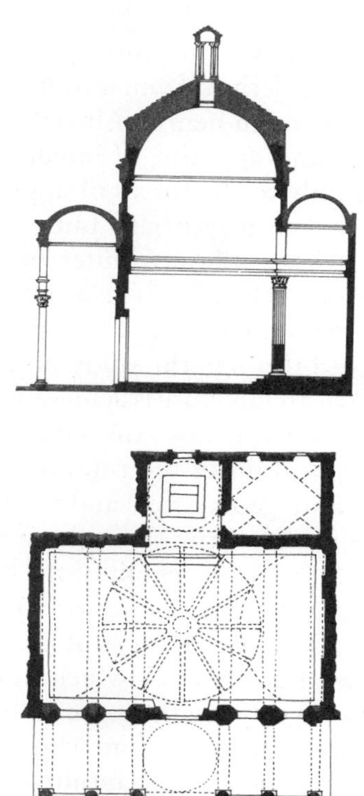

inspire its citizens through its propriety, order, harmony, and control. Buildings should be considered in a hierarchy based on significance. The ornaments of a city should be its churches. Of secondary importance are buildings of civic and mercantile nature, like guild halls, bridges, and squares; finally, one should consider housing. Private dwellings should constitute a self-effacing background for the public monuments to Christian and civic virtues.

Alberti not only advocated public housing for the lower classes but also admonished the city fathers to prevent conspicuous consumption. Rich people, he said, should not be permitted to call attention to themselves by the creation of lavish, individual buildings but should live in houses only somewhat better than the less fortunate city dwellers. Wealth should be used to create buildings that all could share, and buildings would contribute to the public good.

These ideas are consistent with Bruni's concept of a person as a civic being whose ambitions and skills, intellect and passion, should be turned to the benefit of the republic. Moreover, there is almost a parallel between the humanists' belief that eloquence should be cultivated to speak and persuade for the truth of

17-6 *Above left. Pazzi Chapel, exterior, Cloister of Santa Croce, Florence. (Alinari/Art Resource, NY)*

17-7 *Above right. Groundplan and cross section, Pazzi Chapel, Florence.*

17-8 *Below. Interior, Pazzi Chapel, Florence. (Alinari/Art Resource, NY)*

Christian virtue and Alberti's idea that eloquent architecture, based on the great principles of nature, will enable a person to discover and lead a harmonious life.

In Alberti's text we find these proposals for eloquent architecture derived from a study of nature and of the antique. Human beings, Alberti says, are creatures of reason and appetite, of intellect and will. If they succumb only to the forces of appetite and will, they may enjoy their lives briefly but will not achieve goodness and virtue, the attributes of greatness. In fact, he says, it is only by use of reason and intellect that people can know how to act. These tools are sharpened and trained through the study of nature.

Perfection in architecture is achieved for Alberti by emulation of perfect forms—the square and circle—and by the application of the rules of harmony that govern music. Both geometrical and musical forms are divine in origin and occur throughout the universe. Beauty, says Alberti, is the result of the correct observation and application of rules of proportion derived from Pythagoras' system of musical harmony. Beauty is the creation of a whole to which nothing can be added and from which nothing can be subtracted without the destruction of that whole. Our minds, understanding that perfection intuitively, respond to harmony and order, producing actions that will grace life as monuments grace a city.

The belief that good buildings can make a good life is highly debatable. What cannot be denied is that the application of reason to art was one of the most powerful forces in the Renaissance. This will emerge more clearly as we study the other arts.

17-9 *Donatello,* Saint George, *from Orsanmichele, Florence (where it has been replaced by a bronze copy), c. 1415–16, marble, height 6'10", Museo Nazionale, Florence. (Alinari/Art Resource, NY)*

Sculpture in Florence in the Fifteenth Century

Sculpture, like architecture, was considered a preeminent manifestation of civil and religious pride. As in the case of other artists, sculptors of this period drew inspiration from antiquity, nature, and thirteenth- and fourteenth-century achievements in their medium. There are many whose work might be considered—Brunelleschi, Ghiberti, Nanno di Banco, Luca della Robbia—but, as with painters, no single sculptor represents all the energy and accomplishment of this period. Donatello (1386–1466), however, created a body of work that covers the range of sculptural possibilities—low relief to freestanding sculpture in the round, carved marble and cast bronze, and a variety of subjects that provided enormous intellectual and psychological challenge. Because he was a powerful individual creator in his own right, Donatello was a natural forebear to Michelangelo.

Among his earliest commissions were two sculptures of saints, George and Mark, for niches on the exterior of a church, Orsanmichele (Fig. 17-9). These larger-than-life figures have the vitality and presence of particular, individual human beings. This effect is achieved through Donatello's clear articulation of the body under its clothing and the definite sense of personality carved in the face. These two elements are combined in the total composition of the body and its attire.

Donatello's skill and innovative ability are no better exhibited than in his gilded bronze relief for the baptismal font of the cathedral of Siena, executed in

17-10 *Donatello,* Feast of Herod, *c. 1425, gilded bronze relief, 23⅝ × 23⅝", baptismal font, Cathedral of Siena. (Alinari/Art Resource, NY)*

1425. In *The Feast of Herod,* Donatello makes use of a new formal tool—one-point perspective—which will also be used by Masaccio and other painters and sculptors to render the illusion of three-dimensional space (Fig. 17-10). Organized in an architectural setting, which provides the diminution in space that creates the illusion of light and distance, this dramatic moment is presented in all its emotional horror and intensity. In the center of the composition is a vacuum, created as people scatter before the presentation of the severed head of the Baptist. Donatello's observations of the human body in movement, of drapery, of emotion, are all demonstrated here.

Achievements like these surely convinced the Florentines of the dynamism of their own time and gave them a particular consciousness of their accomplishments and their shortcomings.

New Developments in Painting

Painting and sculpture in the Middle Ages depended on formulas and conventions for the presentation of visual equivalents of important ideas and beliefs. The makers of stained glass increased the size of significant persons in their glass and ignored any illusions of weight or volume in the representation of figures. The illuminators who made manuscript plates emphasized intense color, flat surfaces, complex linear patterns, and stylized gestures to create their pictures. Also, the size and location of figures were determined by their importance. Rarely do we feel that the rules for making—the formal conventions—are inappropriate to or detract from the information to be conveyed. Fifth-century-B.C. Athenians considered ideal representation of the human body the best means of commemorating or perpetuating important events and beliefs. The sculptors of the Royal Portal at Chartres subordinated the visible world to symmetry, pattern, flatness, and distortion to teach and inform viewers of Christian dogma. At times the rules and their results may seem strange to us, but it is the successful marriage of means and ends that makes great art and architecture. In the art of fifteenth-century Florence we meet a new set of rules, of conventions for making, that were arrived at experimentally through trial and error, as were the other conventions we have studied. Alberti wrote about painting, describing the rules for making successful pictures. Giorgio Vasari (1511–1574), who was among the first biographers of artists and architects of the Renaissance, was also an important critic of the intentions and development of their art. Like Alberti, he praised artists for their return to, and successful conquest of, the representation of nature.

Giotto (1267?–1337)

If we follow the example of Vasari, the first artist who must be considered in the development of painting in Renaissance Florence is not a fifteenth-century painter at all but Giotto, who, as Dante noted in the *Purgatorio,* eclipsed Cimabue (1271–1302), who was considered the best painter of his day.

> In painting Cimabue thought indeed
> To hold the field; now Giotto has the cry,
> So that the fame of the other few now heed.
>
> *(Canto 11, 94–96)*

Legend has it that Cimabue saw the poor young shepherd Giotto drawing on a rock with a stone and was so impressed by his talent that he brought him to Florence, where he was apprenticed to a painter. In Florence, Giotto found himself in the cultural and artistic center of Europe, and after absorbing all he needed, he rose to fame as the inventor of a new style of painting.

There was much for Giotto to absorb. In addition to the established late medieval art of Florence, there were ideas from the East, from Christian Byzantium, and from the flowering of Gothic art in France. The many different approaches and realizations of Mary, which we have seen in sculptures and glass at Chartres, and the figures from Reims are indicative of the many ways in which artists were conveying ideas and meanings. What Giotto seemed particularly successful in achieving, however, was a sense of drama, a moment stopped in real time, which the observer could then participate in for all time. Giotto combined a keen observation of human movement, gesture, and expression with a growing ability to depict figures whose weight, form, and pose convey a sense of space in which a drama is acted out.

When one first sees work by Giotto, the impact of his formal innovations is not immediately apparent. The *Madonna and Child Enthroned* (Fig. 17-11), painted (c. 1310) for the Church of the Ognissanti in Florence, has the kinds of discrepancies in scale that one expects in medieval painting. For example, the angels are one size, Mary and Jesus are another. The figures are placed in front of a traditional gold ground, long used by both Byzantine artists and many medieval illuminators and painters. But a closer examination shows that Mary and the Child occupy a gothic throne that sits heavily in space. Mary *sits;* her knees show under the folds of her robe, and the Baby, although not exactly a baby, is not a little old man, either. He is round and firm, and his cheeks are the fat cheeks of babyhood. This Mary and Child are quite different from the frontal, hierarchical Madonna and Child of the right portal of the West Porch at Chartres (Fig. 10-14).

Vasari tells us that Giotto's accomplishments were based on his observation of nature and his abandonment of the existing formal language of tradition. Whether a result of nature, the influence of French art, or a combination of these, Giotto's achievement in the Arena Chapel cycle is evident.

17-11 *Giotto,* Madonna and Child Enthroned, *tempera on panel, 10′8″ × 6′8¼″, from the Church of the Ognissanti, Florence, c. 1310, Galleria degli Uffizi, Florence. (Alinari/Art Resource, NY)*

The Arena Chapel in Padua is decorated with scenes from the life of the Virgin and the life of Christ, both traditional themes. The scenes painted in fresco on the walls are "living" tableaux, acted out in shallow constricted spaces, but they are spaces that are nonetheless based on observation of the experienced world. The participants, presented in simple drapery—the density of which seems to emphasize weight, gravity, and the physical body underneath—gesture, move, and give expression to the changing emotional content of each scene. The composition of each scene seems accidental—as if seen at a glance, and yet studied—as if designed to emphasize the significant action of the moment. In *The Lamentation* (Color Plate II) the action falls from the right to the lower left corner, where the Virgin cradles the head and shoulders of her dead Son on her knees. The actions and gestures of each of the figures and the shape of the landscape reinforce the movement into the corner, a movement that is both a visual and psychological decline and dead end. The mourners have the self-contained and controlled gestures of disbelieving grief, from the woman who tenderly holds Jesus' feet, to the stylized gesture of the standing figure (Saint John), whose arms fly back, to the onlooker who stands in the right corner, hands mutely folded. This exposition of the stages of grief acted out by heavy, somewhat lumpy figures is extraordinarily eloquent. Grief is presented as painful, timeless, and almost silent; yet the faces and hands tell us that folded into these bodies that cluster around the dead Christ is soft, muffled weeping. Then, looking into the sky, the viewer sees the angels who give themselves up to grief, wailing and keening. It is impossible to see these paintings and not be deeply moved. The stories of the Virgin and Christ are given a new humanity and power that transcends this world by being so clearly of it.

The simple intensity and power of Giotto's work disguises the monumental effort required to break with tradition and to create new formal conventions. He is still far from using the paint, color, line, light, and shade one associates with the art of fifteenth- and sixteenth-century Florence. His paintings reveal his limited knowledge of the rules of perspective, and his landscapes are as stylized as those of the older schools. None of his paintings has a secular theme. Nevertheless, no one can differ seriously with the judgment of Vasari, who traced the artistic revival that culminated in his day back to Giotto two hundred and fifty years before, for it was he who led art back to "a path which may be called the true one." Although the path is not a direct one, his work is a major basis for the art of Masaccio.

Masaccio (1401–1428?)

Giotto's accomplishment, which filled his contemporaries with admiration, was dependent on the success with which he captured the human presence through bodily form, gesture, and emotion. A few visual clues placed the scenes in the experienced world, but his technique did not extend to creating a convincing facsimile of the light, shade, and space of the three-dimensional world in which people live. This was to be the accomplishment of the many painters of fifteenth-century Florence.

One of those painters was Masaccio, who painted expressive human bodies in palpable space. The work for which he is most famous is the series of *frescoes* for the Brancacci Chapel in Santa Maria delle Carmine in Florence. Recently cleaned and restored, these works reveal Masaccio's close observation of nature and of the human form. The *Expulsion from Eden* (Fig. 17-12) on a side wall of the chapel presents a powerfully human, sorrowful, nude Adam and Eve as they leave paradise. Adam covers his face, but Eve seems to wail. Their muscular, substantial bodies are depicted through contrasts of light, shade, and shadow. These figures have the presence of the nudes of antiquity.

The central painting of the chapel, *The Tribute Money,* recounts a story from Christ's life as told in Matthew 17:24–27 (Color Plate III and detail, Fig. 17-13). A tax collector has approached Jesus, who then instructs Peter to catch a fish from the Sea of Galilee; in its mouth will be a coin sufficient for the tax to be paid. The action of the story is stretched out in the painting. Compare Giotto's *Lamentation* (Color Plate II) with this work. What are the major differences between Masaccio's fresco and that of Giotto? Is there a greater illusion of space around the figures and in which the figures move? What role does the landscape play? Is it day or night? Are weather conditions important? What is important to conveying the action? Do the figures casting shadows that fall around each other, on faces, and on hands focus our attention? Where is Masaccio's light source? Does light seem to come into the space of the painting from the sky, or does it seem to originate outside the painting? What kind of people are the disciples? Do they have personalities, or are they simply twelve images who stand for the Twelve? What has happened to enable Masaccio to delineate so easily a world similar to the one we see?

Masaccio, it would seem, has transformed the wall plane into a transparent curtain that reveals a stage space in which he can present a dramatic event. We see into the space where people move; light falls from the sky; figures cast shadows; people have personalities and are therefore like us, like the visible world of experienced reality. These people are also not self-conscious actors but are convincing as Adam and Eve, who notice neither angel nor audience in the pain of their degradation. As in Donatello's sculpture *David* (Fig. 17-14), the human body is expressive, sensuous, and filled with life.

Masaccio and Donatello both had the use of a new artistic language, which had been developed by Brunelleschi, the cathedral architect. *Linear perspective* is a tool for the accurate translation of three-dimensional space onto the two-dimensional plane of paper, panel, or wall (Fig. 17-15). Masaccio, learning from Giotto the importance of gesture and the feeling of weight, combined the two with his own ideas about shade and shadow, volume and location, to create his dramatic scenes. Obviously, Masaccio did not achieve this in one day (equally obviously, he was not alone in his endeavors), but he gives us scenes that seem suddenly familiar to us. His work both transforms and presents a series of new conventions, which we will explore further.

There is a close parallel between the development of perspective in painting and sculptural relief and the humanists' growing sense of the historical past. The fifteenth-century humanists were coming to understand the past as composed of a group of successive

17-12 *Above left. Masaccio,* Expulsion from Eden, *fresco, c. 1425, Brancacci Chapel, Florence. (Alinari/Art Resource, NY)*

17-13 *Above right. Detail of Masaccio,* The Tribute Money, *Brancacci Chapel, Florence. (Alinari/Art Resource, NY)*

17-14 *Right. Donatello,* David, *c. 1430–32. Bronze, height 62¼", Museo Nazionale, Florence. (Alinari/Art Resource, NY)*

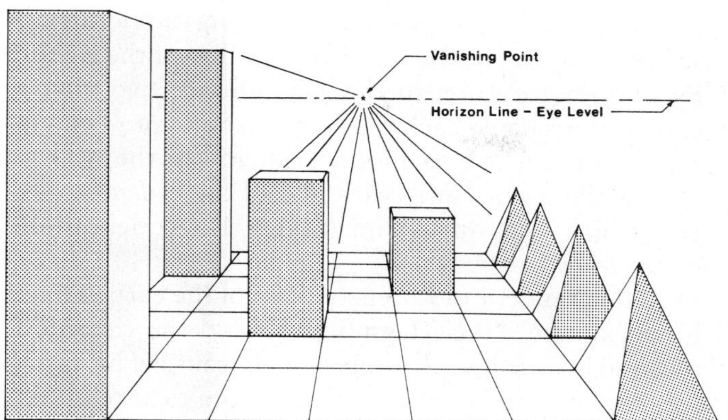

17-15 *Simplified single-point perspective (after Brunelleschi).*

societies leading down to their own time. Increasingly, they became aware of the differences between pagan Roman society and Christian Rome and of the changes that had occurred in thinking in the Middle Ages located between their own time and antiquity. In a sense they viewed history as a series of temporal planes corresponding to the spatial planes defined by the linear perspective. Just as artists objectified space from the point of view of their eyes, so humanists defined the past in relationship to their own time. Similarly, the humanists used this objectified time for their own purposes, in their case the improvement of the present and the shaping of the future.

It is not enough, however, that we celebrate the conquest of illusion. To assume that this was the goal of Renaissance painting is to miss the point of this artistic development. Just as Brunelleschi and Alberti wanted to learn the principles of antique architecture in order to create new forms in response to new ideas, so perspective was a principle, a tool, to enhance the purpose of Christian art. The purpose of creating art with Christian subjects was to teach, enlighten, and persuade people in the ways of right moral action. Viewers are therefore expected not merely to *observe* an event but to be moved by it toward repentance and salvation. The illusion of weight and volume, and of the visible world itself, and the creation of splendid individuals, all serve this purpose.

Piero della Francesca (1420–1492)

To fully appreciate the extent to which painters, sculptors, and other artisans served the church and their faith through their art, it is necessary to consider the work of other painters and the ways in which they explored the new ideas. Such a painter was Piero della Francesca. Born in southeastern Tuscany, he came to Florence as a painter's apprentice. He left a few years later, never to return, but worked in the vicinity of his birth, Arezzo, Borgo San Sepolcro, and finally in Urbino, a small but wealthy mountain principality. The origins of his art lie in Masaccio, but his intellectual capacity and artistic study created an art of severe harmony, clarity, and cool detachment.

Piero's *Resurrection* fresco (Color Plate IV), painted for the town hall in Borgo San Sepolcro in the late 1450s, presents an unforgettable image of the resurrected Christ. This Christ is a heroic figure of powerful proportions. He stands, one bare foot inside the other on the front edge of the sepulcher, a shroud covering one arm, the other bare and muscular, holding the flag of the church triumphant. He confronts the viewer directly and seems to see beyond. There is little emotional drama here; the four soldiers sleep on in the tight, constricted, but perfectly articulated space between the picture plane and the sarcophagus. Light is cool and even, revealing a body whose wounds no longer bleed but are simply shown for our contemplation. The hush of morning fills the stony Italian landscape. To the right of Christ the trees are foliage-covered; to the left there is barrenness; and at the center, the focus of our salvation and eternal resurrection. The powerful emotional energy of Masaccio's Adam and Eve (Fig. 17-12) contrasts with the still psychological drama Piero presents.

Piero did many drawings for this and every work. His investigations led to a treatise in which he demonstrated the uses of perspective to delineate bodies and architectural forms. These he reduced to their most abstract geometrical components, seeing forms as variations on or combinations of spheres, cylinders, cones, cubes, and pyramids. Like Alberti, he sought nature's perfect forms, and like Leonardo after him, he learned much from that study.

Botticelli (1444–1510)

Sandro Botticelli was more interested in the expressive possibilities of a graceful and energetic line than in the structural problems of perspective. He had been apprenticed to an engraver, and from his experiences with those conventions came his reliance on draftsmanship. The favorite painter of the Medici family, Botticelli was very much interested in the ideas of humanism and Neoplatonism prevailing in the intellectual circles around Lorenzo. He was one of the first Florentine painters to represent subjects from classical mythology. Just as the humanists attempted to fuse

Greco-Roman myths and ideas with Christian theology, Botticelli endowed his pagan subjects with a spirituality that derives from medieval painting and sculpture.

The large painting called *Primavera* (*Springtime*) or *The Realm of Venus* is an *allegory* of the rebirth of nature in spring under the power of love (Color Plate V). In the center stands Venus, who looks more like a madonna than a Greek love goddess. The fusion of the pagan goddess and the Christian saint would not have surprised the Neoplatonists, who believed that both could aid the soul in its ascent to God. Venus appears to give her blessing to the three Graces, who are dancing in a circle to her right. The rhythmical line for which Botticelli was so well known is nowhere more apparent than here. The folds of flowing drapery make one feel the movement of the dance. The seminude bodies are another classical inspiration—they could never have appeared in medieval art. Next to the Graces stands Mercury, raising his wand to the skies. To the viewer's right is Flora, in a dress abundantly covered with flowers, and another almost-nude nymph representing springtime, who is about to be seized by a young man personifying Zephyr, the wind. Above everyone flies the blindfolded Cupid with his bow and arrow. What about the setting of this painting? Although the flowers are exact copies of flowers that grow around Tuscany, Botticelli has certainly not portrayed a realistic natural setting. What kind of nature is he portraying, and what is he attempting to suggest by it? How would you characterize the colors? Make a schematic drawing to show how the *composition* works. Are the various elements of the painting held together in some way? Does the right side of the painting convey a different sort of feeling from that conveyed by the left side? How? Compare your reactions to this painting to your reactions to Piero della Francesca's paintings.

Primavera is a work that seems to state in visual terms the spirit of the Florentine Renaissance under Lorenzo de' Medici. Botticelli was inspired by a poem on the subject written by one of the Medici friends, Angelo Poliziano, and the painting decorated the Medici palace. It celebrates youth, beauty, and love, but with an underlying melancholy reminding the viewer that such joys are transitory.

Lorenzo de' Medici's Carnivals

During the fifteenth century the city of Florence developed a tradition of outdoor public celebrations, feasts that probably had their intellectual origins in the pre-Christian pagan festivals celebrating the victory of spring over winter, the returning fertility of the earth. By the time of Lorenzo the Magnificent, two major carnivals occurred each year—a season of pre-Lenten revelry (which has its modern version in the Mardi Gras activities of New Orleans) and the *Calendimaggio,* which was an extended May Day celebration (from May 1 to June 24!).

The grandeur of Lorenzo's style of life earned him his nickname, "the Magnificent," and the carnivals received his strong encouragement because of his taste for opulence and probably also for political reasons. The Medicis' love of pageantry is represented by Gozzoli's mural *Journey of the Magi* (Color Plate VI). Carnivals kept the populace happy. Lorenzo, an accomplished poet and an ardent lover of music and display, hired a musician from Flanders of international reputation, Heinrich Isaac, as his court composer and as tutor of his children.

Torchlight processions in which decorated wagons were pulled through the streets were the main feature of the carnivals. The wagons, or *carri,* were decorated by some of the best artists of the time in a manner similar to today's parade floats, and the themes of the decorations often represented stories from classical antiquity and popular legends. The usual themes associated with the "triumphs" depicted on the carnival floats were love, pleasure, and the enjoyment of life, but among them there was always a macabre "triumph of death," a terrifying float including men dressed as skeletons drawn by a team of black oxen. Thus during a part of the gaiety people were urged to repent—the Renaissance fascination with death amid a proclamation of joy in life on earth is also evident here.

Music for the Death of Lorenzo

During the same year that Columbus made his first voyage to the New World, Lorenzo de' Medici died. He had been the ideal Renaissance prince: a consummate diplomat, intellectual leader, and connoisseur and patron of the arts. His loss was felt deeply and personally by those poets and musicians who knew and worked for him and also loved and respected him.

One of the most beautiful and moving musical compositions written in the last years of the fifteenth century, the beginning of the High Renaissance in music, was Heinrich Isaac's *threnody,* a dirge or funeral song, in the Italian style on Angelo Poliziano's Latin verse lamenting the death of Lorenzo, *Quis dabit capiti meo aquam.*

Isaac's genius and sensitivity created a *motet* (a *polyphonic* composition for unaccompanied chorus based on a Latin sacred text) of moving solemnity, a four-voice composition scored in a low register to dramatize its function as a dirge. An intimate bond between word and tone was the goal of Renaissance composers working in the company of the Italian humanists, and Isaac masterfully sculpted his sounds in this musical elegy. To make the opening statement incisive, to be certain the listener could understand every word, Isaac declaimed the text of the beginning syllabically in slow-moving chords, at first in hollow *open fifths,* all voices enunciating the syllables at the same time—"Who will give my head . . ." Then, as the singers reach the word "water," the chords dissolve into flowing polyphonic lines, a musical gesture symbolizing the text being set. He begins the second phrase in like manner but sets the "fountain of tears" with a base of three chordal notes (the solid base of an actual fountain comes to mind) over which, or out of which, flows a curving, almost liquid, soprano melodic line.

Harmonic modulation, as we know it today, was not a part of the composer's art in the late fifteenth century; but Renaissance *chromaticism,* the use of accidentals (flats and sharps) to displace the music slightly out of the regular *tonal* order of the style, was an expressive device reserved for moments of intense emotion. Isaac's harmonic progression from A to F to C and then B-flat strains and wrings the phrase *Sic cygnus moriens solet* ("Thus [mourns] the dying swan").

Although the motet begins with four vocal parts, the second section of the work beginning *Laurus impetu fulminis* ("The laurel, struck [suddenly] by a thunderbolt") uses only three vocal parts. However, in the original Renaissance choirbook in which this work is notated, a space with no notes is set aside in which is written *Laurus tacet* ("The Laurel is silent"). Lorenzo's absence, therefore, was painted graphically in music by a device detectable primarily by the composer and the singers but also by those who were trained and skilled in detecting the subtleties of Renaissance tone painting. Four-voice music and three-voice music have distinctive qualities that are identifiable aurally, and the absence of a part could be felt by those in attendance who heard the change in *texture* and comprehended the meaning of the words.

At the same time that the texture of the piece drops from four to three parts, the lowest voice is given a part to sing whose words are neither the same as those being sung by the other singers nor from the text of Poliziano's poem. Instead, Isaac composed an insertion referring to the requiem service of the church, *Et requiescamus in pace* ("And let us rest in peace"). The composer took this phrase, set it to a short bass melody, and slowly repeated it over and over as an *ostinato,* one step lower each time it enters—a certain symbolic representation of Lorenzo descending step by step into the grave. The emotion of the event, the words, and the music are focused and concentrated into a dramatic setting of intense grief.

When, in the third and final section of the motet, the fourth voice reenters, it is no longer a regular part but a single, unmoving note (which is held for eighteen measures in the modern edition), quite likely an aural *image* of death in a tomb. When finally this note is given a rest (literally a rest in the music), the other three parts sing of Phoebus Apollo's sweet-sounding voice, a godly song whose magic, according to Greek mythology, could give peace and healing to those in the underworld. Then, "Now all is silent, Now all is deaf," and the motet ends.[1]

Renaissance people experienced their world passionately, proclaiming themselves in control of all they could touch, taste, see, and hear. Although Poliziano and Isaac voiced the bitterness of death in *Quis dabit capiti meo aquam,* they did not portray the fear of judgment and punishment ever present in the creations of medieval artists. It was the sadness of loss of life, of parting from the pleasures of this world, that stirred the Renaissance soul to anguish. In different ways both Botticelli's painting and Isaac's funeral dirge both celebrate the joys of life and lament the end that comes all too quickly.

---

[1]Two excellent, but different, recordings of Isaac's motet are available: *Ceremonial Music of the Renaissance* (Das alte Werk, SAWT 9524-B) and *Fifteenth-Century Netherlands Masters* (Decca DL 79413). The former employs chorus and antique instruments; the latter performs the work with voices only.

Reading Selection

Angelo Poliziano (1454–1494)

Quis Dabit Capiti

Quis dabit capiti meo aquam?
Quis oculis meis fontem lachrimarum dabit?
Ut nocte fleam,
Ut luce fleam?

Sic turtur viduus solet,
Sic cygnus moriens solet,
Sic luscinia conqueri.
Heu miser, miser,
O dolor, dolor!

Laurus impetu fulminis
Illa illa jacet subito,
Laurus omnium celebris
Musarum choris,
Nympharum choris.

Sub cuius patula coma
Et Phebi lira blandius,
Nunc muta omnia,
Nunc surda omnia.

Who will give my head water?
Who will give my eyes a fountain of tears?
That I may weep by night,
That I may weep by day?

Thus the lonely turtle-dove mourned,
Thus the dying swan,
Thus the nightingale.
Ah wretched, wretched me,
Oh grief, oh grief.

The laurel [Lorenzo] lies there,
Lies there, struck suddenly by a thunderbolt,
The laurel honored by the choir
Of all the Muses,
And all the nymphs.

Beneath whose spreading branches
The lyre of Phoebus more charmingly
Sounds and his voice more sweetly sings.
Now all is silent,
Now all is deaf.

QUESTIONS

1. In what ways is the polyphonic funeral motet more or less expressive than the monophonic *Play of Daniel* or the troubadour song *Be m'an perdut?* (See Chapters 10–11.)
2. How might the change in society with an emerging middle class affect the role of the composer?
3. Scientific advances of the Renaissance had an effect on music. What would the invention of printing do for composers? How might this affect the music they wrote?

18

The End of the Florentine Renaissance: Machiavelli, Leonardo, Michelangelo, and Raphael

The death of Lorenzo the Magnificent in 1492 came in a very troubled time not only for Florence but for the whole of Italy (see map). In 1495 the French invaded Italy, sweeping the length of the peninsula with their powerful armies. This was only the first of a whole series of foreign invasions over the next fifty years, during which time Italy became the battleground between the two rising national monarchies, France and Spain. The Medici were toppled from power with the arrival of the French in 1495, and a republic under French rule was established. But the waning of French influence over Italy in the following decade spelled the doom of the new regime, and the Medici returned to power in 1512. Except for a brief three-year interruption (1527–1530), they were to remain rulers of Tuscany down to the eighteenth century.

Already by Lorenzo's last years, Florence was sharing its position of cultural dominance with Rome. From the early decades of the sixteenth century, moreover, France and northern Europe began to rival Italy's position of cultural leadership. The Florentine efflorescence was to be given new forms in art, architecture, and political thought. Four individuals—Niccolò Machiavelli, Leonardo da Vinci, Michelangelo Buonarotti, and Raffaello Sanzio—represent aspects of the transformation of the confidence of the fifteenth century into the doubt of the sixteenth century, when Italy was invaded and the papacy came under siege from Martin Luther and the princes of northern Europe.

Niccolò Machiavelli (1469–1527)

The ease with which the Italians succumbed to Spanish and French arms shocked Italian thinkers and caused them to seek explanations. Many focused on the chaotic political structure of the peninsula as the major factor

in Italian weakness. This atmosphere of questioning produced one of the greatest political theorists of all time, the Florentine Niccolò Machiavelli. Born in Florence in 1469, Machiavelli rose to a position of prominence in the republican government established in the city after 1495. Closely associated with that regime, Machiavelli fell into disfavor after the reestablishment of Medici power in 1512. He spent most of the last fifteen years of his life as a private citizen, composing his works on history and political theory.

At heart a republican, Machiavelli faced squarely the problem that confronts any political thinker, the conflict between liberty and order. To what extent can individuals be given freedom without disrupting authority? Although he would have liked to see Florence and other Italian states republican, he recognized that, given the corruption of Italian society, only a strong ruler was capable of establishing order; until order had been established, there was no hope of reforming the people to make them capable of self-government. He realized the risk: the kind of ruler ruthless enough to establish order was not likely to be the kind of prince willing to train the people in self-government. But in a peninsula divided into fifty to a hundred power centers, a prey to foreign invasions, strong authority had priority. Thus, although raised in the tradition of Florentine civic humanism derived from Bruni, Machiavelli gave first place to political realities.

Machiavelli's most famous work, *The Prince,* written in 1513, was designed to give lessons in statecraft to a prince with an eye to creating an authority capable of driving out the invaders and bringing peace to Italy. Although throughout the work Machiavelli appeals to the selfish desire of the prince for power, in the final chapter Machiavelli's own altruistic motives on behalf of Italian unity become manifest. *The Prince* is intended to be a revolutionary "mirror of the prince," based on a medieval form of literature designed to instruct the prince on how to be a good ruler. However, whereas the traditional mirror of the prince endeavored to make the prince conform to common principles of Christian morality in his rule, the thesis of *The Prince* is that the morality of the successful ruler is unlike that of the private citizen; indeed, the conduct required of a prince would frequently be reprehensible in a private individual. Nevertheless, in the long run actions that would be immoral in an ordinary citizen may very well be the best means for achieving a goal that serves the common good.

When Machiavelli came to sketch the character of the ideal prince, he defined *virtù* as his essential quality. Not to be confused with virtue, the term was defined by Machiavelli as "the ability to measure oneself." At points in *The Prince* he appears to consider the prince as a kind of artist imposing a form (his particular regime) on matter (the people). The quality of *virtù* will help the prince to understand the nature of the particular matter he is working with and thus know the limits of what can be done with it. Realization of political ends, however, is not merely a product of executing a rationally determined course of action. The ability to measure oneself also entails taking account of the whims of fortune. Against its unpredictability, the prince can only construct dikes to protect himself when it rages. This does not mean that cautiousness is the best policy; rather, Machiavelli urges a bold attitude, modified by self-restraint.

That Machiavelli considered the ruthless Cesare Borgia (1475–1507), bastard son of Alexander VI, something approaching the ideal prince shocked many in his own generation, as it does in ours. But the fascination of Machiavelli remains, for he is telling us something that might be true but that we cannot bear to hear. This is especially true for Americans, who have always nourished the belief that at some point public morality can be forced to coincide with private morality, that leaders can be judged by the same standards as average citizens. What Machiavelli tells us is that this will never be the case, nor ought it to be; there is a fundamental difference between the rules of the game of politics and those of ordinary life.

In Machiavelli's view the state was not a product of undirected growth of authority; rather, it was a work of art, the creation of the prince who skillfully imposed a form of political order on the people, who served as the matter for his work. This kind of imagery indeed reflects the Renaissance preoccupation with defining the nature of the artist and his or her activity. It was in this period that people first began to take the word *artist* seriously and to look on the artist with respect.

The Renaissance Artist

Who is an artist? Is the artist a maker, a thinker, a craftsperson, a technician, a manipulator of emotions, a teacher? Is he or she a worldly, extroverted, confident, sophisticated personality, or lonely, introverted, filled with self-doubt and scorn? These questions were asked by writers and artists in the Renaissance, and it is to them that we owe concepts of the artist and architect, as well as the inclusion of these arts in the "fine" or "liberal" as opposed to the mechanical arts. Not only theory but also the works of the artists themselves produced these ideas. In the contrasts between two of the greatest figures of Italian Renaissance art, we find two very different images of the artist.

Leonardo da Vinci (1452–1519)

Both Leonardo and Michelangelo were Florentine, near contemporaries, and undeniable geniuses. Leonardo was splendidly handsome; Michelangelo was at times obsessed with his ugliness. When Leonardo offered his services to the duke of Milan, he gave primacy to his qualifications as a military and hydraulic engineer, architect, and sculptor, mentioning painting last. When Pope Julius II commanded Michelangelo to paint the frescoes on the ceiling of the Sistine Chapel (in the Vatican Palace), he replied that he was not a painter but a sculptor. Nevertheless, he fulfilled the commission and later became noted for his genius not only in painting and sculpture, but also in architecture. Both individuals seem to possess enormous ego and incredible versatility. In both we find characteristics that have contributed to our idea of the "Renaissance man"—a person of broad learning and skill.

Although Leonardo viewed painting as the least of his talents, until recently we knew him principally as painter and courtier. Now, since the discovery and publication of his notes and drawings, begun in the late nineteenth century, we can call him a scientist with equal correctness. Perhaps, above all, Leonardo was an investigator of nature through observation and practice. He was an architect, engineer, botanist, and musician; he studied hydraulics, geology, and human anatomy. The pages of his notebooks reveal a person obsessed with nature's beauty, power, and functional complexity. He sought answers to his questions neither in the church nor in antiquity but in nature—that which was observable—and in the mind—that which asked and imagined. He studied the motion of water to capture its power to operate engines, but his drawings also reveal his respect for its awesome natural power in a flood or storm. He dissected bodies to understand human anatomy, which then became the source for the mighty bodies in a drawing or painting. But muscles were abstracted into the ropes of levers and pulleys (Fig. 18-1). He drew the fetus in the womb and anticipated Harvey's discovery of the circulation of the blood. His botanical drawings created a style for scientific illustration, and the plants reappear, lovingly delineated, in his pictures. It is as if Leonardo could not satisfy a longing to know, to understand the principles of life—birth, transformation, change, and decay—operating in the natural world. It is as if what he saw constantly assailed him with its incredible diversity, beauty, simplicity, and ugliness; and he sought rationally to control, order, and understand the vast potentialities open to human experience. He *attended* to *his* world; he wanted nothing to escape that questing, loving eye.

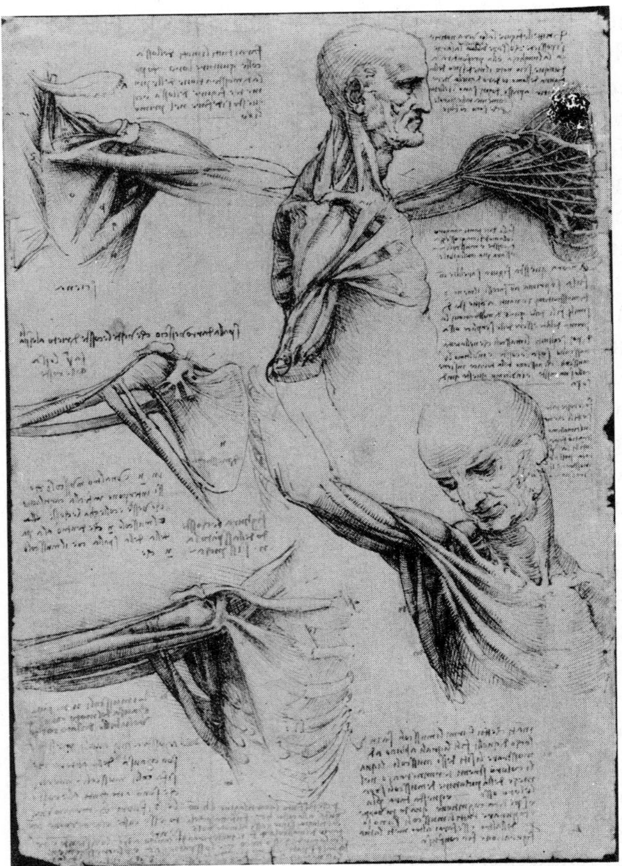

18-1 *Leonardo da Vinci, drawing:* Anatomy of a Shoulder, Transformation into Levers. *(Royal Library, Windsor Castle. Copyright 1992 Her Majesty Queen Elizabeth)*

In his lifetime Leonardo finished few paintings. The *Mona Lisa* (or *La Gioconda*), a portrait of the enigmatic lady of the sublime smile, is perhaps the most familiar. Even more enigmatic to many is *The Madonna of the Rocks* (1483) in the Louvre—a soft, slightly mist-filled representation of the Virgin with the Christ Child, who, supported by an angel, blesses the kneeling John the Baptist presented by the Virgin (Color Plates VII and VIII).

The Madonna of the Rocks Set in a curious cavelike opening on a ledge in a rocky landscape, the four figures interact with each other; yet the viewer is hard pressed to define the interaction. The light is soft and vague, the landscape shadowy and moist. The edges of the figures, their drapery, and their expressions lack clear definition. We do not doubt their presence in space, for the figures have a weight and volume that originated with Masaccio; yet there is a sense of fragility that is shared with Botticelli's *Primavera.* Nor do these figures possess Piero's intense abstraction—we are not sure what to look at in them. We seem forced by gesture and glance to look from face to face. The landscape itself is ambivalent, rocky, yet filled with beautiful plants and flowers. Light penetrates from behind and falls in the foreground. Where are we? Precisely what do we see? Academically, we know the picture may deal with the doctrine of the virgin birth of Christ, but that knowledge does not begin to explain the picture. Rather it is almost a sacred conversation—a moment suspended in time that alludes to events years hence. Or is time, in a chronological sense, of any consequence? This is a picture rich in ambivalences. Its brilliant *illusionism* is dependent on the experienced world, and on a technical mastery of the creation of subtle nuances of shade and shadow that was one of Leonardo's great accomplishments. Similarly, it is a knowledge of anatomy, the study of faces and gestures, of falling light, of air suffused with light, that makes the vision possible. But technical expertise cannot account for the experience of the picture—a profound religious silence—where children who are touchingly childlike imitate the roles of their adulthood, and a mother's protective gesture reaches all of us. This splendid vision is so rich in nuance and idea that it is ever fresh to the eye and imagination. This is the end attained by the means that the fifteenth-century Florentines made possible—an end so filled with resonances that we are still compelled to discuss the picture and we struggle to know the painter's mind.

The Madonna of the Rocks is one of the few almost finished paintings by Leonardo. It is because of such a painting that we study the complex, unfinished *Adoration of the Magi* or the ruined *Last Supper,* hoping to reconstruct not just the means but also the purpose of an artist who presents both a final statement and a vision of potentiality, of transformation. The vision is complete by Alberti's definition, but also ever ready, like nature itself, to provide a new experience, to stimulate the imagination with fresh questions. It is as if reason, finally, is not enough. One can control the will, guide intuition, define problems, comprehend mathematical harmonies, and draw the structure of the body; but one cannot determine the source of the life force or define the power of experience. Nor can one rule the imagination as it seeks knowledge of the work through the world. In this capacity, humanity is godlike and transcendent, free of everything except death.

Leonardo's art raises some problems that are still with us. What is it in the combination of nature, imagination, skill, and communication that creates a successful or a great painting or, for that matter, any work of art? How does a work of art evoke resonance and sympathy in the viewer? We may agree that a particular painting moves us, yet not on why that happens. With Masaccio's paintings, it may be the still drama, enacted in a space that we share. Piero della Francesca certainly presents clarified images, harmonized in a world that he has made both more abstract and orderly. Botticelli speaks to our sensitivities with delicate color and linear harmonies. The powerful visual experience evoked by *The Madonna of the Rocks* is more difficult to define precisely. Leonardo's predecessors and peers reinstated the nude, the portrait, and the landscape; moreover, they created conventions of form and technique to achieve the presentation of Christian and pagan themes for personal edification. The possibilities for the artist must have seemed unlimited to them, maybe frightening in their limitlessness. Perhaps, in Leonardo's mind, it was the limits imposed by sculpture that made this art seem inferior, yet it was his greatest peer, Michelangelo, who defined limits so wide and so demanding that they changed the course of sculpture.

Michelangelo Buonarotti (1475–1564)

In contrast to Leonardo, the handsome, graceful courtier with polished manners and mellifluous voice, Michelangelo seems like a difficult child. He was secretive, rude, dirty, and offensive. Leonardo passionately embraced nature, whereas Michelangelo seems to have embraced his own genius, then God, as the path to immortality (both concerns far removed from Leonardo's elevation of the artist to the status of the gentleman). But both artists shared the power to imagine, make, and move. Both used nature—the visible world—but they transformed it, filling the objects made with immediate and universal meaning.

David The squares of Florence were decorated by some of the city's great sculptors. The Loggia dei Lanzi, a great open porch to the right of the Palazzo Vecchio, is still filled with sculpture. To the left is the Neptune fountain, whose splashing water invigorates the humid summer air. Directly in front, on the raised terrace before the Palazzo, is a copy of Michelangelo's *David* (the original was moved inside a museum in 1873). Light is intense in the square, and the high walls and tower of the Palazzo Vecchio intensify the experience. The figure silently commands the busy space and challenges your passage into the palace.

The *David* is marble, over thirteen feet tall (Fig. 18-2). The figure is completely nude; the limbs and torso, now aged by rain and sun, once had a smoothness that remains only on the surface of the face. Never painted or decorated, unlike the statuary of former times, its first impact is of intractable stone formed into a superhuman figure. But what is the boy like? The *Kritios Boy* (Fig. 4-8) and *The Spearbearer* (Fig. 4-12) are obvious idealizations of the human figure. How is *David* different from these two? Compare his face with that of Augustus and with a prophet from the doors at Chartres. Is this *David* an idealization of youth? His face is not symmetrical, the hands are enormous, and the arms and legs are too long. The body is awkward, like that of a tough youth, streetwise and confident. The brooding face is reticent but filled with a fierce courage. The body turns, a knee flexed; does the boy search the horizon for Goliath? The muscles of the neck and torso are tense, standing forth under the skin. The veins in arms, elbows, and hands rise to enliven the surface of the skin. The toes on one foot grasp the ground, and the toes of the other play over the rocky ledge. Has the stone been thrown, or does it lie in his curved fingers? Does he ready the sling, or does it lie on his shoulder, no longer useful, but used?

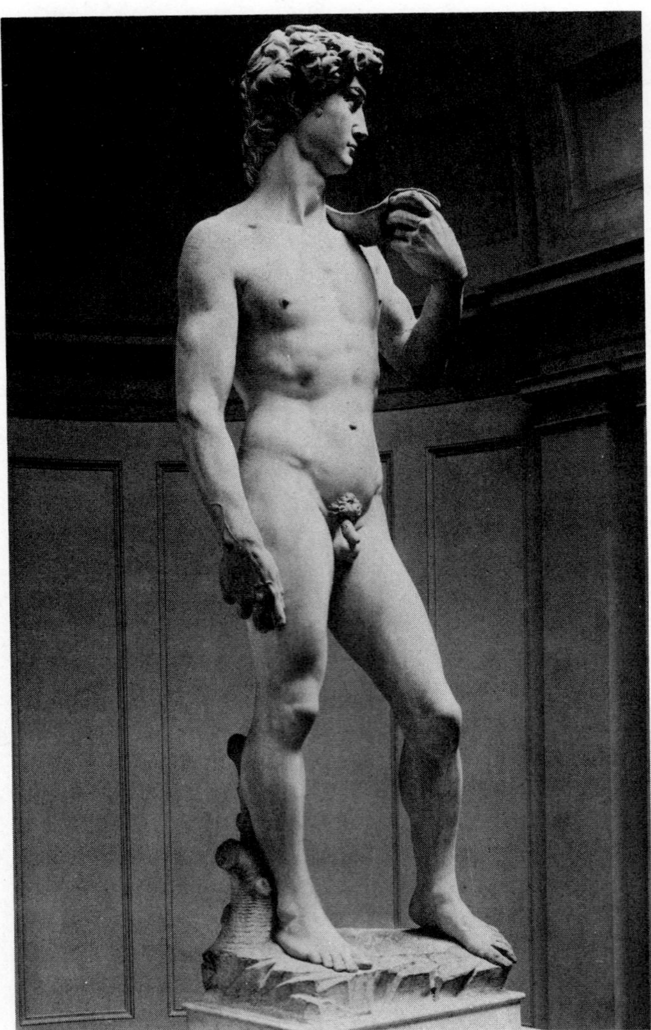

18-2 *Michelangelo,* David. *Accademia della Belle Arts, Florence. (Alinari/Art Resource, NY)*

18-3 *Michelangelo,* Captive Slave. *Louvre, Paris. (Copyright PHOTO Réunion des Musées Nationaux)*

If you are unable to decide the precise moment or motivation, you have begun to experience the *David*—an experience deriving its power from ambiguity. He is splendidly beautiful without being idealized. The torso and limbs flow into his pose with ease and grace, yet show the tension of movement. He is youthful but confident, brooding but able to act. His face has an intellectual intensity, and his body is its physical complement. Over all lies a feeling of potential—to make, do, dream, and be—to live in the world, to challenge with mind and body the limits of our human nature. That is the enemy—not the giant Goliath but the struggle between intellect and will, self-interest and unselfishness, love and hate.

The *David* was placed before the entrance to the Florentine city hall in 1504, during the restoration of the Republic, as a visible sign of courage and purpose—qualities that had made the Republic possible. After the ascendancy of the Medici, it might have been a reminder of what had been and might be again. The shepherd boy became king, only to be destroyed by his pride.

Michelangelo populated Florence and Rome with giants like this one. He loved the stone that was his medium and hated the demands that it made. In his sonnets he writes of the conflict between his art with its glorification of the human body and his personal quest for the salvation of his soul, a quest that he felt his art contradicted. The great commissions produced in the sixty years after the *David* reflect stages not only in his art but also in the bent of his mind. There were the great papal commissions like the unfinished tomb for Julius II and the frescoes for the Sistine Chapel ceiling (1508–1512) and *The Last Judgment* (1536–1541) behind its high altar. Although he became the architect for the new Saint Peter's, redesigned the Capitoline Hill, and executed other architectural and painted commissions, his greatest vehicle for expression was the human body. In some figures he was able to attain a classicism almost Greek (Color Plate IX). In other figures, like the unfinished *Captive Slave* (1527–1528), whose body is still contained in the block, the imperfect stone seems expressive of those faults that must fall away if humanity is to become good and filled with grace (Fig. 18-3).

Other Works There was no artistic convention that Michelangelo could not turn to his use. He was capable of making architecture as evocative as sculpture and painting. In the entry corridor to the Laurentian Library (Fig. 18-4), the walls push out between the paired columns and the columns seem to float above the ground, separated from a base or plinth by the *molding* and the *volutes,* which break out beneath them; thus the supporting members appear decorative and the decorative members structural. Similarly, the stairway denies the feeling of ascension by heavy curving steps that seem to ooze downward. Michelangelo deliberately transforms familiar elements of classical architecture not only to expand their potential meaning but also to change the viewer's perception of their value and importance as elements of building. He was a writer as well as an artist, and used the sonnet form to express some of his artistic concerns.

18-4 *Michelangelo, Vestibule of the Laurentian Library, Florence. (Alinari/Art Resource, NY)*

18-5 *Michelangelo,* Brutus. *(Alinari/Art Resource, NY)*

In his unfinished works, like those of Leonardo, we sense the skill needed to manipulate the medium and the potential of the object for interpretations that reach beyond the accepted meaning. The bust of Brutus (the assassin of Julius Caesar), although made after 1537 (thus after the final demise of the Republic and return of the Medici to power), seems to carry on the spirit of republican Florence (Fig. 18-5). The head and face are unfinished, the drape completed by one of Michelangelo's assistants. Compare it with similar works that we have seen. The ridges left by the chisel do not detract from the strong, heavy face. The folds of flesh that extend from the nostrils to the small but sensuous mouth, as well as the hollows of the cheeks, give the face a tension and purpose that come with age. The deep hollows of the simplified eyes hold shadow; they contrast with the broad ridge of the nose. This face could be that of any person with courage who has known fear, with purpose who has known discouragement. He is neither the purely detached imperial Augustus (Fig. 7-2) nor the political Arringatore (Fig. 7-1). He asks questions and seeks answers. He loves life but knows that death will come. He wants salvation but knows that it comes from sacrifice. Our responses to this face are varied, rich, and resonant. In it are recorded the marks of life and the need for meaning.

Raphael (1483–1520)

Raffaello Sanzio (anglicized as Raphael) is the youngest of these four individuals whose ideas were born and matured in the intensely creative, confident atmosphere of late-fifteenth-century Florence. Taught by his father, then by the painter Perugino in sophisticated, worldly Urbino, Raphael traveled to Florence, then to Rome. Raphael's vision of the nature of painting seems to have been founded on a desire to make paintings that presented an ideal and harmonious moment in which time and change are suspended. This vision contrasts sharply with the ideas of Michelangelo and Leonardo, but its presence emphasizes the rich possibilities inherent in Florentine art. Just as Giotto and Simone Martini represented alternatives in the fourteenth century, Raphael, with Leonardo and Michelangelo, presented alternatives that artists explored well into the nineteenth century.

Among Raphael's first important works, *The Marriage of the Virgin* (Fig. 18-6) was painted for the church in Città di Castello about 1504. Before a circular, domed templelike building, a group of young men and women stand in the foreground of a spacious, light-filled piazza. The paving pattern on the ground connects the foreground to the background as it diminishes in the distance.

18-6 *Raphael,* Marriage of the Virgin, *panel painting, 1504. Pinacoteca di Brera, Milan. (Alinari/Art Resource, NY)*

The arch of the frame, almost touching the dome of the temple, is one curve in a repeating pattern of curves and rectangles, which focus attention on Joseph, who places a ring on the finger of the Virgin. Their bodies and heads incline inward toward each other, as do all the figures. Everything in the work quietly conspires to concentrate on this precise moment in time. The principal characters stand as silently as their attendants; their elegant profiles and the curves of their rich drapery repeat each other. The light in the piazza is clear and golden; figures in the middle distance and background move easily through this spacious, ordered world.

The successful marriage of figures with their setting was and remains a problem for the artist. The setting must reinforce the motif of the painting, but it must not be so contrived as to be incredible. Raphael's painting *The School of Athens* (Color Plate X), executed for the Stanza della Segnatura in the papal apartments in Rome (1510–1511), presents another solution and one that should be compared with Michelangelo's Sistine ceiling frescoes (Color Plate IX).

In *The School of Athens,* Raphael places the great philosophers of antiquity in a barrel-vaulted and domed hall lined with sculpture in niches, open to the air, light filled. Plato and Aristotle are framed by the central arches as they stand in the sunlight at the top of steps, between groups of auditors. In the upper left, Socrates holds the attention of some youths; in the lower left, Pythagoras computes on a slate, and Euclid, lower right, draws a geometrical demonstration.

The groups of figures form a circle in the space and color, and gesture and overlapping figures move the eye around the composition in an even rhythm. In spite of all the movement, discussion, and implied noise, the painting seems to portray a dream of antiquity concentrated in a golden moment of time. The figures and the architecture are idealizations, like the subject itself, an occasion that could never have occurred.

On the opposite wall of the apartment, Raphael placed the complex *Disputation of the Sacrament,* an exposition of the doctrine of the Eucharist. These two subjects seem to symbolize Renaissance thought, which sought to reconcile antiquity and Christianity.

At the same time that Raphael was executing these frescoes, Michelangelo was working in the Sistine

Chapel on the ceiling decorations that were to tell the story of Creation. These paintings are directly overhead, at quite a distance from the viewer. Michelangelo was faced with a problem. What could be seen—figures, setting, both? Discarding any but the barest architectural framework, the barest landscape, Michelangelo concentrated all his effort on creating a series of idealized, heroic figures, a canopy of giants. The ceiling is given over to the human body, which is the sole carrier of meaning. These are the figures of a sculptor, translated into painting. But the difference is more than one of the physical location of the work. Raphael was more interested in attaining a completely harmonious moment in a harmonized world, whereas Michelangelo was more interested in the human power of the narrative. (The cleaning of the Sistine Chapel frescoes, a massive project that has aroused controversy in the art world, has revealed Michelangelo's work in an entirely new light.)

Raphael, like Michelangelo, could not ignore the realities of this world, or the people in it. His stunning portrait of Pope Leo X (Color Plate XI), painted about 1517, presents this Renaissance prelate in all his corpulent power. A shrewd man, given to worldly things, Leo excommunicated Martin Luther in 1520. There was no golden moment to capture here, but there was the reality of earthly power. Raphael's ability to see this, along with the ideal, gave his art its lasting vitality.

Reading Selections

Niccolò Machiavelli

From *The Prince*

Translation by Ninian Hill Thompson

Chapter XV

Of the qualities in respect of which men, and most of all Princes, are praised or blamed

It now remains for us to consider what ought to be the conduct and bearing of a Prince in relation to his subjects and friends. And since I know that many have written on this subject, I fear it may be thought presumptuous in me to write of it also; the more so, because in my treatment of it I depart widely from the views that others have taken.

But since it is my object to write what shall be useful to whosoever understands it, it seems to me better to follow the real truth of things than an imaginary view of them. For many Republics and Princedoms have been imagined that were never seen or known. It is essential, therefore, for a Prince who would maintain his position, to have learned how to be other than good, and to use or not to use his goodness as necessity requires.

Laying aside, therefore, all fanciful notions concerning a Prince, and considering those only that are true, I say that all men when they are spoken of, and Princes more than others from their being set so high, are noted for certain of those qualities which attach either praise or blame. Thus one is accounted liberal, another miserly (which word I use, rather than *avaricious,* to denote the man who is too sparing of what is his own, *avarice* being the disposition to take wrongfully what is another's); one is generous, another greedy; one cruel, another tender-hearted; one is faithless, another true to his word; one effeminate and cowardly, another high-spirited and courageous; one is courteous, another haughty; one lewd, another chaste; one upright, another crafty; one firm, another facile; one grave, another frivolous; one devout, another unbelieving; and the like. Every one, I know, will admit that it would be most laudable for a Prince to be endowed with all of the above qualities that are reckoned good; but since it is impossible for him to possess or constantly practise them all, the conditions of human nature not allowing it, he must be discreet enough to know how to avoid the reproach of those vices that would deprive him of his government, and, if possible, be on his guard also against those which might not deprive him of it; though if he cannot wholly restrain himself, he may with less scruple indulge in the latter. But he need never hesitate to incur the reproach of those vices without which his authority can hardly be preserved; for if he well consider the whole matter, he will find that there may be a line of conduct having the appearance of virtue, to follow which would be his ruin, and that there may be another course having the appearance of vice, by following which his safety and well-being are secured.

Chapter XVII

Of Cruelty and Clemency, and whether it is better to be Loved or Feared

Passing to the other qualities above mentioned, I say that every Prince should desire to be accounted merciful and not cruel. Nevertheless, he should be careful not to abuse this quality of mercy. Cesare Borgia was reputed cruel, yet his cruelty restored Romagna, united it, and brought it to order and obedience; so that if we look at things in their true light, it will be seen that he was in reality far more merciful than the people of Florence, who, to avoid the imputation of cruelty, suffered Pistoia to be destroyed by factions.[1]

[1] Florence attempted to govern Pistoia by encouraging the disputes between the two major factions. When in 1501–1502 it attempted finally to end the civil conflict, it caused untold bloodshed and destruction.

A Prince should therefore disregard the reproach of cruelty where it enables him to keep his subjects united and faithful. For he who quells disorder by a very few signal examples will in the end be more merciful than he who from excessive leniency suffers things to take their course and so result in rapine and bloodshed; for these hurt the entire State, whereas the severities of the Prince injure individuals only.

And for a new Prince, above all others, it is impossible to escape a name for cruelty, since new States are full of dangers. Wherefore Virgil, by the mouth of Dido:—

> "Res dura et regni novitas me talia cogunt
> Moliri, et late fines custode tueri."[2]

Nevertheless, the new Prince should not be too ready of belief, nor too easily set in motion; nor should he himself be the first to raise alarms; but should so temper prudence with kindliness that too great confidence in others shall not throw him off his guard, nor groundless distrust render him insupportable.

And here comes in the question whether it is better to be loved rather than feared, or feared rather than loved. It might be answered that we should wish to be both; but since love and fear can hardly exist together, if we must choose between them, it is far safer to be feared than loved. For of men it may generally be affirmed that they are thankless, fickle, false, studious to avoid danger, greedy of gain, devoted to you while you confer benefits upon them, and ready, as I said before, while the need is remote, to shed their blood, and sacrifice their property, their lives, and their children for you; but when it comes near they turn against you. The Prince, therefore, who without otherwise securing himself builds wholly on their professions, is undone. For the friendships we buy with a price, and do not gain by greatness and nobility of character, though fairly earned are not made good, but fail us when we need them most.

Moreover, men are less careful how they offend him who makes himself loved than him who makes himself feared. For love is held by the tie of obligation, which, because men are a sorry breed, is broken on every prompting of self-interest; but fear is bound by the apprehension of punishment which never loosens its grasp.

Nevertheless a Prince should inspire fear in suchwise that if he do not win love he may escape hate. For a man may very well be feared and yet not hated, as will always be the case so long as he does not intermeddle with the property or with the women of his citizens and subjects. And if constrained to put any one to death, he should do so only when there is manifest cause or reasonable justification. But, above all, he must abstain from the property of others. For men will sooner forget the death of their father than the loss of their patrimony. Moreover, pretexts for confiscation are never to seek, and he who has once begun to live by rapine always finds reasons for taking what is not his; whereas reasons for shedding blood are fewer, and sooner exhausted.

But when a Prince is with his army, and has many soldiers under his command, he must entirely disregard the reproach of cruelty, for without such a reputation in its Captain, no army can be held together or kept ready for every emergency. Among other things remarkable in Hannibal[3] this has been noted, that having a very great army, made up of men of many different nations and brought to serve in a foreign country, no dissension ever arose among the soldiers themselves, nor any mutiny against their leader, either in his good or in his evil fortunes. This we can only ascribe to the transcendent cruelty, which, joined with numberless great qualities, rendered him at once venerable and terrible in the eyes of his soldiers; for without this reputation for cruelty his other virtues would not have effected the like results.

Unreflecting writers, indeed, while praising his achievements, have condemned the chief cause of them; but that his other merits would not by themselves have been so efficacious we may see from the case of Scipio,[4] one of the greatest Captains, not of his own time only but of all times whereof we have record, whose armies rose against him in Spain from no other cause than his excessive leniency in allowing them freedoms inconsistent with military discipline. With which weakness Fabius Maximus[5] taxed him in the Senate House, calling him the corrupter of the Roman soldiery. Again, when the Locrians were shamefully outraged by one of his lieutenants, he neither avenged them, nor punished the insolence of his

[2] "A fate unkind, and newness in my reign/Compel me thus to guard a wide domain."

[3] Hannibal (247–183 B.C.) almost succeeded in destroying Rome in the Second Carthaginian War. Machiavelli often uses him as an example of efficacious cruelty. He is compared with Scipio (236–184 B.C.), the Roman general, whose humanity was equally successful.

[4] Scipio (see note above) defeated Hannibal decisively at Zama in 202 B.C.

[5] Fabius Maximus, called the Delayer, wore Hannibal's army out by delaying tactics in 217 B.C., but, knowing his army was weak, refused to do open battle with him.

officer;[6] and this from the natural easiness of his disposition. So that it was said in the Senate by one who sought to excuse him, that there were many who knew better how to refrain from doing wrong themselves than how to correct the wrong-doing of others. This temper, however, must in time have marred the name and fame even of Scipio, had he continued in it, and retained his command. But living as he did under the control of the Senate, this hurtful quality was not merely veiled, but came to be regarded as a glory.

Returning to the question of being loved or feared, I sum up by saying, that since his being loved depends upon his subjects, while his being feared depends upon himself, a wise Prince should build on what is his own, and not on what rests with others. Only, as I have said, he must do his best to escape hatred.

Chapter XIX

That a Prince should seek to escape Contempt and Hatred

Having now spoken of the chief of the qualities above referred to, the rest I shall dispose of briefly with these general remarks, that a Prince, as has already in part been said, should consider how he may avoid such courses as would make him hated or despised; and that whenever he succeeds in keeping clear of these, he has performed his part, and runs no risk though he incur other reproaches.

A Prince, as I have said before, sooner becomes hated by being rapacious and by interfering with the property and with the women of his subjects, than in any other way. From these, therefore, he should abstain. For so long as neither their property nor their honour is touched, the mass of mankind live contentedly, and the Prince has only to cope with the ambition of a few, which can in many ways and easily be kept within bounds.

A Prince is despised when he is seen to be fickle, frivolous, effeminate, pusillanimous, or irresolute, against which defects he ought therefore to guard most carefully, striving so to bear himself that greatness, courage, wisdom, and strength may appear in all his actions. In his private dealings with his subjects his decisions should be irrevocable, and his reputation such that no one would dream of over-reaching or cajoling him.

The Prince who inspires such an opinion of himself is greatly esteemed, and against one who is greatly esteemed conspiracy is difficult; nor, when he is known to be an excellent Prince and held in reverence by his subjects, will it be easy to attack him. For a Prince is exposed to two dangers, from within in respect of his subjects, from without in respect of foreign powers. Against the latter he will defend himself with good arms and good allies, and if he have good arms he will always have good allies; and when things are settled abroad, they will always be settled at home, unless disturbed by conspiracies; and even should there be hostility from without, if he has taken those measures, and has lived in the way I have recommended, and if he never despairs, he will withstand every attack; as I have said was done by Nabis the Spartan.[7]

As regards his own subjects, when affairs are quiet abroad, a Prince has to fear they may engage in secret plots; against which he best secures himself when he escapes being hated or despised, and keeps on good terms with his people; and this, as I have already shown at length, it is essential he should do. Not to be hated or despised by the body of his subjects, is one of the surest safeguards that a Prince can have against conspiracy. For he who conspires always reckons on pleasing the people by putting the Prince to death: but when he sees that instead of pleasing he will offend them, he cannot summon courage to carry out his design. For the difficulties that attend conspirators are infinite, and we know from experience that while there have been many conspiracies, few of them have succeeded.

He who conspires cannot do so alone, nor can he assume as his companions any save those whom he believes to be discontented; but so soon as you impart your design to a discontented man, you supply him with the means of removing his discontent, since by betraying you he can procure for himself every advantage; so that seeing on the one hand certain gain, and on the other a doubtful and dangerous risk, he must either be a rare friend to you, or the mortal enemy of the Prince, if he keep your secret.

To put the matter shortly, I say that on the side of the conspirator there are distrust, jealousy, and dread of punishment to deter him, while on the side of the

[6]Locri, a Greek colony in southern Italy, was bled white by its supposed governor, Quintus Pleminus. Scipio, although knowing of his misdeeds, did nothing to punish his subordinate.

[7]He was tyrant of Sparta, 205–192 B.C.

Prince there are the laws, the majesty of the throne, the protection of friends and of the government to defend him; to which if the general goodwill of the people be added, it is hardly possible that any should be rash enough to conspire. For while in ordinary cases, the conspirator has ground for fear only before the execution of his villainy, in this case he has also cause to fear after, since he has the people for his enemy, and is thus cut off from all hope of shelter.

Of this, endless instances might be given, but I shall content myself with one that happened within the recollection of our fathers. Messer Annibale Bentivoglio, Lord of Bologna and grandsire of the present Messer Annibale, was conspired against and slain by the Canneschi, leaving behind none belonging to him save Messer Giovanni, then an infant in arms. Immediately upon the murder, the people rose and put all the Canneschi to death. This resulted from the goodwill then generally felt towards the House of the Bentivogli in Bologna; which feeling was so strong, that when upon the death of Messer Annibale no one was left who could govern the State, there being reason to believe that a descendant of the family (who up to that time had been thought to be the son of a smith) was living in Florence, the citizens of Bologna went there to fetch him, and entrusted him with the government of their city; which he retained until Messer Giovanni was old enough to govern.

To be brief, a Prince has little to fear from conspiracies when his subjects are well affected towards him; but when they are hostile and hold him in abhorrence, he has then reason to fear everything and every one. And well ordered States and wise Princes have provided with extreme care that the nobility shall not be driven to desperation, and that the commons shall be kept satisfied and contented; for this is one of the most important matters that a Prince has to look to.

Among the well ordered and governed Kingdoms of our day is that of France, wherein we find an infinite number of wise institutions, upon which depend the freedom and security of the King, and of which the most important are the Parliament and its authority. For he who gave its constitution to this Realm, knowing the ambition and arrogance of the nobles, and judging it necessary to bridle and restrain them, and on the other hand knowing the hatred, originating in fear, entertained against them by the commons, and desiring that they should be safe, was unwilling that the responsibility for this should rest on the King; and to relieve him of the ill-will which he might incur with the nobles by favouring the commons, or with the commons by favouring the nobles, appointed a third party to arbitrate, who without committing the King, might depress the nobles and uphold the commons. Nor could there be any better or wiser remedy than this, nor any surer safeguard for the King and Kingdom. And hence we may draw another notable lesson, namely, that Princes should devolve on others those matters which entail responsibility, and reserve to themselves those that relate to grace and favour. And again I say that a Prince should esteem the great, but must not make himself odious to the people....

Chapter XXV

What Fortune can effect in human affairs, and how she may be withstood

I am not ignorant that many have been and are of the opinion that human affairs are so governed by Fortune and by God, that men cannot alter them by any prudence of theirs, and indeed have no remedy against them; and for this reason have come to think that it is not worth while to labour much about anything, but that they must leave everything to be determined by chance.

Sometimes when I turn the matter over, I am in part inclined to agree with this opinion, which has had the readier acceptance in our own times from the great changes in things which we have seen, and every day see, happen contrary to all human expectation. Nevertheless, that our free will be not wholly set aside, I think it may be the case that Fortune is the mistress of one half our actions, and yet leaves the control of the other half, or a little less, to ourselves. And I would liken her to one of those wild torrents which, when angry, overflow the plains, sweep away trees and houses, and carry off soil from one bank to throw it down upon the other. Every one flees before them, and yields to their fury without the least power to resist. And yet, though this be their nature, it does not follow that in seasons of fair weather, men cannot, by constructing weirs and moles, make such provision as will cause them when again in flood to pass off by some artificial channel, or at least prevent their course from being so uncontrolled and destructive. And so it is with Fortune, who displays her might where there is no prepared strength to resist her, and directs her onset where she knows there is neither barrier nor embankment to confine her.

And if you look at Italy, which has been at once the seat of these changes and their cause, you will perceive that it is a field without embankment or barrier. For if, like Germany, France, and Spain, it had been guarded with sufficient skill, this inundation, if it ever came upon us, would never have wrought the violent changes we have witnessed.

This I think enough to say generally touching resistance to Fortune. But confining myself more closely to the matter in hand, I note that one day we see a Prince prospering and the next overthrown, without detecting any change in his nature or conduct. This, I believe, comes chiefly from a cause already dwelt upon, namely, that the Prince who rests wholly on Fortune is ruined when she changes. Moreover, I believe that he will prosper most whose mode of acting best adapts itself to the character of the times; and conversely that he will be unprosperous, with whose mode of acting the times do not accord. For we see that men in those matters which lead to the end each has before him, namely, glory and wealth, proceed by different ways, one with caution, another with impetuosity, one with violence, another with subtlety, one with patience, another with its contrary; and that by one or other of these different courses each may succeed.

Again, of two who act cautiously, you shall find that one attains his end, the other not, and that two of different temperament, the one cautious, the other impetuous, are alike successful. All which happens from no other cause than that the character of the times accords or does not accord with their methods of acting. And hence it comes, as I have already said, that two operating differently arrive at the same result, and two operating similarly, the one succeeds, the other not. On this likewise depend the shifts of Fortune. For if to one who conducts himself with caution and patience, time and circumstance are propitious, so that his method of acting is good, he goes on prospering; but if these change he is ruined, because he does not change his method of acting.

For no man is found prudent enough to adapt himself to these changes, both because he cannot deviate from the course to which nature impels him, and because, having always prospered while pursuing one path, he cannot be persuaded that it would be well for him to leave it. And so when occasion requires the cautious man to act impetuously, he cannot do so and is undone: whereas, had he changed his nature with time and circumstances, his fortune would have been unchanged.

Pope Julius II acted with impetuosity in all his affairs, and found time and circumstance in such harmony with his mode of acting that he always obtained happy results. Witness his first expedition against Bologna, when Messer Giovanni Bentivoglio was yet living.[8] The Venetians were not favourable to the enterprise; nor was the King of Spain. Negotiations respecting it with France were still open. Nevertheless, the Pope with his wonted hardihood and impetuosity marched in person on the expedition, and by this movement brought the King of Spain and the Venetians to a stay, the latter through fear, the former from his eagerness to recover the entire Kingdom of Naples; at the same time, he dragged after him the King of France, who, desiring to have the Pope for an ally in humbling the Venetians, and finding him already in motion, saw that he could not refuse him his soldiers without openly offending him. By the impetuosity of his movements, therefore, Julius effected what no other Pontiff endowed with the highest human prudence could. For had he, as any other Pope would have done, put off his departure from Rome until terms had been settled and everything duly arranged, he never would have succeeded. For the King of France would have found a thousand pretexts to delay him, and the others would have menaced him with a thousand alarms. I shall not touch upon his other actions, which were all of a like character, and all of which had a happy issue, since the shortness of his life did not allow him to experience reverses. But if times had overtaken him, rendering a cautious line of conduct necessary, his ruin must have ensued, since he never would have deviated from those methods to which nature inclined him.

To be brief, I say that since Fortune changes and men stand fixed in their old ways, they are prosperous so long as there is congruity between them, and unprosperous when there is not. Of this, however, I am well persuaded, that it is better to be impetuous than cautious. For Fortune is a woman who to be kept under must be beaten and roughly handled; and we see that she suffers herself to be more readily mastered by those who so treat her than by those who are more timid in their approaches. And always, like a woman, she favours the young, because they are less scrupulous, and fiercer, and command her with greater audacity.

Chapter XXVI

An Exhortation to liberate Italy
from the Barbarians

Turning over in my mind all the matters which have above been considered, and debating with myself whether in Italy at the present hour the times are such

---

[8]Pope Julius attacked in 1506.

as might serve to win honour for a new Prince, and whether fit opportunity now offers for a prudent and valiant leader to bring about changes glorious for himself and advantageous for the whole Italian people, it seems to me that so many conditions combine to further such an enterprise, that I know of no time so favourable to it as now. And if, as I have said, it was necessary in order to display the valour of Moses that the children of Israel should be slaves in Egypt, to know the greatness and courage of Cyrus that the Persians should be oppressed by the Medes,[9] and to illustrate the excellence of Theseus[10] that the Athenians should be scattered and divided, so at this hour, to prove the worth of some Italian hero, it was required that Italy should be brought to her present abject condition, to be more enslaved than the Hebrews, more oppressed than the Persians, more disunited than the Athenians, without a head, without order, beaten, spoiled, torn in pieces, overrun and abandoned to destruction in every shape.

For although, heretofore, glimmerings may have been discerned in this man or that, whence it might be conjectured that he was ordained by God for her redemption, nevertheless it has afterwards been seen at the very height of his career that Fortune has disowned him; so that our country, left almost without life, still waits to know who it is that is to heal her bruises, to put an end to the devastation and plunder of Lombardy, to the exactions and imposts of Naples and Tuscany, and to stanch those wounds of hers which long neglect has changed into running sores.

We see how she prays God to send some one to rescue her from these barbarous cruelties and oppressions. We see, too, how ready and eager she is to follow any standard were there only some one to raise it. But at present we see no one except in your illustrious House (preeminent by its virtues and good fortune, and favoured by God and by the Church whose headship it now holds), who could assume the part of a deliverer.[11]

But for you this will not be too hard a task, if you keep before your eyes the lives and actions of those whom I have named above. For although these men were singular and extraordinary, after all they were but men, not one of whom had so great an opportunity as now presents itself to you. For their undertakings were not more just than this, nor more easy, nor was God more their friend than yours. The justice of the cause is conspicuous; for that war is just which is necessary, and those arms are sacred wherein lies our only hope. Everywhere there is the strongest disposition to engage in this enterprise; and where the disposition is strong the difficulty cannot be great, provided you follow the methods observed by those whom I have set before you as models.

Moreover, we see here extraordinary and unexampled proofs of Divine favour. The sea has been divided; the cloud has attended you on your way; the rock has flowed with water; the manna has rained from heaven; everything has concurred to promote your greatness. What remains to be done must be done by you; since not to deprive us of our free will and such share of glory as belongs to us, God will not do everything himself.

Nor is it to be marvelled at if none of those Italians I have spoken of has been able to effect what we hope to see effected by your illustrious House; or that amid so many revolutions and so many warlike movements it should always seem as though the military virtue of Italy were spent; for this comes from her old system being defective, and from no one being found among us who has known to strike out anew. Nothing confers such honour on a new ruler, as do the new laws and institutions he devises; for these when they stand on a solid basis and have a greatness in their scope, make him admired and venerated. And in Italy material is not wanting for improvement in every form. If the head be weak the limbs are strong, and we see daily in single combats, or where few are engaged, how superior are the vigour, dexterity, and intelligence of Italians. But when it comes to armies, they are nowhere, and this from no other reason than the defects of their leaders. For those who know are not obeyed, and every one thinks he knows, since hitherto we have had none among us so raised by merit or by fortune above his fellows that they should recognize him as their superior. Whence it happens that for the long period of twenty years, during which so many wars have taken place, whenever there has been an army purely Italian it has always been beaten. To this testify, first Taro, then Alessandria, Capua, Genoa, Vaïla, Bologna, Mestri.[12]

If, then, your illustrious House should seek to follow the example of those great men who have delivered their country in past ages, it is before all things

[9]Cyrus (559–529 B.C.) was king of the Medes.

[10]Theseus was a mythological figure who became king of Athens after slaying the Minotaur of Crete.

[11]*The Prince* is dedicated to Lorenzo de' Medici (1492–1519), whose grandfather was Lorenzo the Magnificent.

[12]The battle of Fornovo on the Taro occurred in 1496; that of Alessandria in 1499; of Capua in 1501; of Genoa in 1507; of Vaila, or Agnadello, in 1509; of Bologna in 1511; and of Mestri in 1513.

necessary, as the true foundation of every such attempt, to be provided with national troops, since you can have no braver, truer, or more faithful soldiers; and although every single man of them be good, collectively they will be better, seeing themselves commanded by their own Prince, and honoured and maintained by him. That you may be able, therefore, to defend yourself against the foreigner with Italian valour, the first step is to provide yourself with an army such as this.

And although the Swiss and the Spanish infantry are each accounted formidable,[13] there are yet defects in both, by reason of which troops trained on a different system might not merely withstand them, but be confident of defeating them. For the Spaniards cannot resist cavalry, and the Swiss will give way before infantry if they find them as resolute as themselves at close quarters. Whence it has been seen, and may be seen again, that the Spaniards cannot sustain the onset of the French men-at-arms, and that the Swiss are broken by the Spanish foot. And though of this last we have no complete instance, we have yet an indication of it in the battle of Ravenna,[14] where the Spanish infantry confronted the German companies, who have the same formation as the Swiss; on which occasion the Spaniards by their agility and with the aid of their bucklers forced their way over the pikes, and stood ready to close with the Germans, who were no longer in a position to defend themselves; and had they not been charged by cavalry, they must have put every German to the sword. Knowing, then, the defects of each of these kinds of troops, you can train your men on some different system, to withstand cavalry and not to fear infantry. This will be effected by the use of other weapons, and a change in the order of battle. And these are matters in reforming which the new Prince acquires reputation and importance.

This opportunity, then, for Italy at last to look on her deliverer, ought not to be allowed to pass away. With what love he would be received in all those Provinces which have suffered from the foreign inundation, with what thirst for vengeance, with what fixed fidelity, with what devotion, and what tears, no words of mine can declare. What gates would be closed against him? What people would refuse him obedience? What jealousy would stand in his way? What Italian but would yield him homage? This barbarian tyranny stinks in all nostrils.

Let your illustrious House therefore take upon itself this charge with all the courage and all the hopes with which a just cause is undertaken; so that under your standard this our country may be ennobled, and under your auspices be fulfilled the words of Petrarch:

> Brief will be the strife
> When valour arms against barbaric rage;
> For the bold spirit of a bygone age
> Still warms Italian hearts with life.[15]

---

13 The Swiss mercenaries fought for whoever would pay them but primarily for the French. The Spanish infantry was a national army.

14 The Battle of Ravenna was fought in April 1512 between the French under Gaston of Foix and the Spanish under Raimondo of Cardona.

15 Petrarch, Canzone beginning: "Italia mia, benchè 'l parlar sia indarno."

QUESTIONS

1. Do you consider Machiavelli's advice immoral or merely practical?
2. What is the author's opinion of human nature?
3. Why should the prince not fear being feared but avoid being hated?
4. To what extent can the prince conquer fortune?
5. To what motives does Machiavelli appeal to encourage Lorenzo to drive out the "barbarians"?

MICHELANGELO BUONAROTTI

Sonnets

Translation by Dante Gabriel Rossetti

Michelangelo's sonnets use the traditional form for concerns beyond those of Dante and Petrarch. The following two sonnets express his belief that there is a sphere in which love and art become one. The sculptor's art is to release the power already contained in the stone, as beautiful forms on earth express the eternal beauty of God.

The Lover and the Sculptor

The best of artists hath no thought to show
 Which the rough stone in its superfluous shell
 Doth not include: to break the marble spell
 Is all the hand that serves the brain can do.

The ill I shun, the good I seek, even so
 In thee, fair lady, proud, ineffable,
 Lies hidden: but the art I wield so well
 Works adverse to my wish, and lays me low.

Therefore not love, nor thy transcendent face,
  Nor cruelty, nor fortune, nor disdain,
  Cause my mischance, nor fate, nor destiny;

Since in thy heart thou carriest death and grace
  Enclosed together, and my worthless brain
  Can draw forth only death to feed on me.

Irreparable Loss (After the Death of Vittoria Colonna)

When my rude hammer to the stubborn stone
  Gives human shape, now that, now this, at will,
  Following his hand who wields and guides it still,
  It moves upon another's feet alone:

But that which dwells in heaven, the world doth fill
  With beauty by pure motions of its own;
  And since tools fashion tools which else were
    none,
  Its life makes all that lives with living skill.

Now, for that every stroke excels the more
  The higher at the forge it doth ascend,
  Her soul that fashioned mine hath sought the
    skies:

Wherefore unfinished I must meet my end,
  If God, the great artificer, denies
  That aid which was unique on earth before.

19

The Northern Renaissance and the Protestant Reformation

By 1500 humanism had northern European adherents. Generally speaking, northern humanism differed from the Italian variety in directing its attention to the ancient texts of the Christian religion rather than to the writings of Roman and Greek antiquity. Humanist philological techniques developed in preparing editions of Cicero, Plato, and others were now applied to editing the Bible and the writings of the Latin and Greek Church Fathers. Thus the humanists in the North were responsible for directing the attention of learned people to the early history of Christianity and the sources of the Christian faith.

Erasmus (1463–1536)

The leading northern humanist and doubtless the most important humanist of his generation was Desiderius Erasmus. Although born in the Low Countries, Erasmus lived most of his mature life in France, England, and Switzerland. Like his Italian humanist predecessors, he believed that ethics was more important than elaborate systems of philosophy and theology. Coupled with his extremely critical attitude toward current Church abuses, this insistence on the primacy of moral action became a powerful weapon for the reform of Christian life.

In Erasmus' opinion, the Church had overemphasized rituals and outward manifestations of piety. It had made too sharp a distinction between the status of a cleric and that of a layperson. The central focus of Christianity should be on the spirit, on the cultivation of deep religious feeling, rather than depending on its ceremonies. Although not attacking the principle of monasticism as evil, he nevertheless maintained that the lay life, doing God's work in the world, was just as effective in serving Christ as was the life of the cloistered monk. Moreover, the laity, too, needed and had the right to read and discuss the sources of their faith. In short, as Erasmus himself said at one point, "The world has become my monastery."

Like the texts of pagan antiquity, those of Christian antiquity were highly defective. Erasmus chose as his first task the preparation of a new edition of the Greek New Testament with Latin translation, which he published in 1516. It was a courageous task to undertake. Over a thousand years of Christian scholarship had been based on the Vulgate, composed of early translations of the books of the Bible; now Erasmus showed that some of the key passages on which countless interpretations had been made were not actually in the Greek original or were mistranslated. In the same year he published his nine-volume edition of the works of Saint Jerome. This was one of the first humanist editions of the complete works of a Church Father, but many were to follow.

Erasmus was the first great European writer to make use of an important invention, the printing press. Although printing had been developed before his time—the Gutenberg Bible first appeared in 1455—the earlier books were primarily luxury items. Erasmus distributed his editions and his polemical pamphlets throughout Europe. Writing in Latin, he could be read by educated people in all countries; thus he helped to create a culture of the printed word that has since dominated Western intellectual life.

Erasmus firmly believed that if all the sources of Christian truth could be published in an accurate form, the eloquence of the words, as they were originally written under the inspiration of the Holy Spirit, could not fail to move people to become better Christians. The goal of Erasmus' Christian scholarship was therefore to reform both individual Christians and the Church itself. He did not attack the dogma of the Church, but he did attack the effort of theologians to elaborate on the dogma and to claim certainty for their deductions. For him there were only a few absolutely certain principles in the Bible, and these were all people needed to believe in order to be saved. What was important for him was that Christian belief be reflected in one's life. True Christians acted like Christians. This was Erasmus' "philosophy of Christ" in essence. Accordingly, he was exceedingly tolerant of differing views of theology but severely critical of evil conduct.

Erasmus remained a Catholic despite every effort of the Lutherans to convince him to join their sect. Nonetheless, the sweeping criticism he made of abuses in the Church had a devastating effect and has led some scholars to say that "Erasmus laid the egg that Luther hatched."

The Protestant Reformation

The reform tendencies present in Erasmus and other northern humanists were not unique to them. Rather, by 1500 in northern Europe a broad spirit of Christian reform prevailed, of which humanism was only one reflection. Intensive efforts were under way to reform monastic orders, and new orders were founded devoted to strict enforcement of the monastic vows. Pietistic movements like the Brethren of the Common Life, which included both laity and clerics, aimed at infusing in the daily life of all Christians a deep spirit of devotion. Against this background the Lutheran reform could be interpreted as only another manifestation of a universal concern. Martin Luther (Fig. 19-1) was different from the other reformers, however, in that he attacked not only abuses but doctrines as well.

Martin Luther (1483–1546)

For Luther, the Church for the past thousand and more years had distorted the truth found in the Bible. In practice the Church had exalted the pronouncements of Church councils, popes, and learned individuals to a level equal to that of Scripture. For him these "truths" were human ones; human beings made mistakes and only the Bible was unquestionably true. Hence, he rejected the authoritative interpretations that the Church had placed on each passage of the Bible as concealing rather than revealing the Word of God found therein. Each person should have the power of coming to the text and reading it according to the dictates of his or her own conscience. When in 1521 Luther was called before the Catholic emperor, Charles V of Germany, at Augsburg to renounce his deviation from Catholic truth, he exalted the majesty of the individual human conscience in refusing:

> Since then Your Majesty and your lordships desire a simple reply, I will answer without horns and without teeth. Unless I am convicted by Scripture and plain reason—I do not accept the authority of popes and councils, for they have contradicted each other—my conscience is captive to the Word of God. I cannot and I will not recant anything, for to go against conscience is neither right nor safe. God help me. Amen.

By this, however, he did not mean that everyone's opinion about religion should be respected. The truth

19-1 *Lucas Cranach, the Elder,* Portrait of Luther as a Dominican Friar, *engraving, 13.4 × 9.5 cm, 1520. (Courtesy of the Harvard University Art Museums. Francis Calley Gray Collection of Engravings)*

on important issues of the faith was so evident for Luther that no fair-minded person could differ with his interpretation. Accordingly, he was perfectly willing to persecute others who did not share his understanding of the basic principles found in the Bible.

A dominant tradition of the medieval Church had been, as we have seen, the belief that people could cooperate with God's grace in earning their own salvation. Through a succession of good works, product of the joint efforts of human will and grace, the individual could build up enough merits to earn a place in heaven. The sacraments controlled by the Church hierarchy were viewed as the channels through which life-giving grace poured to believers. The clerics (the priests who administered the sacraments and had care of souls) and the monks and friars (who had taken special vows to devote their life to God) were considered as a group to be on a higher spiritual level than were the laity. Their average chances for entering heaven were considered better than those of non-clerics; they were more likely to build up merits because of their profession.

Luther attacked the central thesis of this belief. No human being can cooperate with God in his or her own salvation. Mortals are too sinful. God predestines some individuals from all eternity to salvation. These men and women know who they are because they have faith that Christ's merits have been imputed to them for their salvation. They themselves did absolutely nothing to win this salvation; it was a free gift of God. In saying this, Luther firmly believed that he was truly interpreting the words of Christ and Paul. Therefore, gone was the need for pilgrimages, penances, masses for the dead, and all the other rituals of the medieval Church designed to build up a sum of the good works requisite for salvation. Only after people are justified and know that Christ is their savior can they really begin to do good works. Yet these count nothing for salvation: they are merely the fruits of knowing that God has already chosen one to be saved. The good works pour out as a product of love for God and one's fellow mortals because Christ is at work in the depths of the soul.

Consequently, no one is saved because of what he or she does. From this it follows that a shoemaker has just as good a chance of being saved as does the pope. In Luther's view, the whole spiritual hierarchy with the bishops, archbishops, cardinals, and pope was a human construction. He denied that Christ in committing the keys to Peter intended to make the bishop of Rome the head of the whole Church. The present hierarchical Church was a work of humanity, not God; and since it was loaded with corruption and led by blind people, the edifice had to be destroyed. Luther's solution was that the territorial prince in each area should be the governor of the territorial Church.

The sources for Luther's thought, in addition to the Bible, included Saint Augustine and northern European critics of medieval scholasticism. Unlike Thomas Aquinas, Luther had little faith in the ability of human reason to establish truths about the divine nature. Luther's God was primarily Will, and people had no power to know anything more of him than the Bible conveyed. The reformer's insistence on the importance of the inner life as opposed to ceremonies was perhaps in part an inheritance from northern mysticism, but humanists like Erasmus also exercised an influence here. To humanism Luther also owed his training in the three major ancient languages, Latin, Greek, and Hebrew, and his confidence in his critical powers when confronted with a text. Humanism placed at his disposal a set of philological tools and a tradition of independent judgment; Luther fearlessly

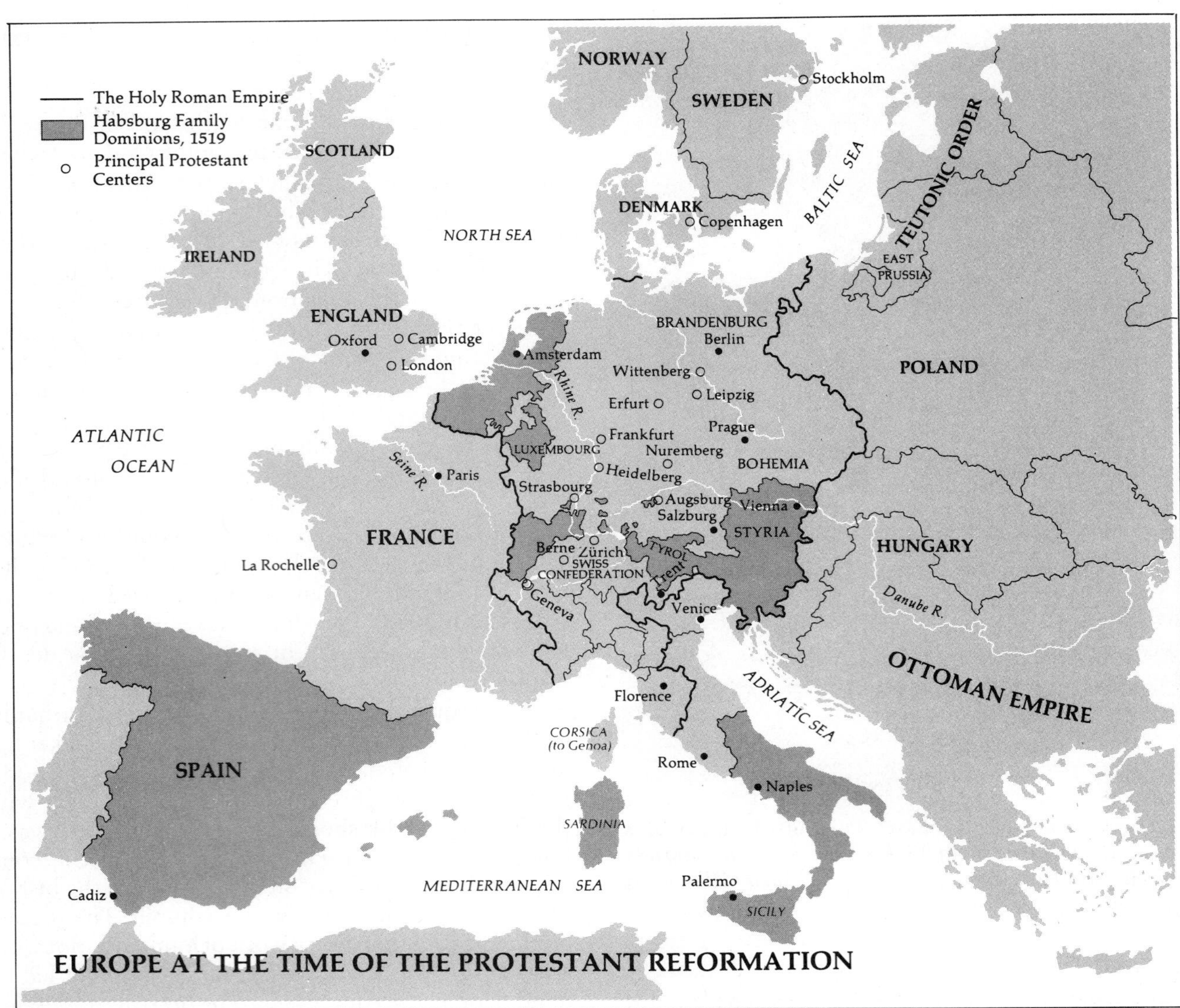

EUROPE AT THE TIME OF THE PROTESTANT REFORMATION

applied these in an examination of the whole body of Christian doctrine.

Like Erasmus, Luther made extensive use of the medium of printing to distribute his ideas. The impact of his message was much greater, however, because whereas Erasmus wrote only in Latin, Luther championed his appeal to reform in eloquent German. To make the Bible more accessible to the layperson, he translated the whole of the Old and New Testaments, a translation that served as the basis for the modern German language. A musician and poet, Luther composed literally hundreds of hymns, thus establishing the Protestant tradition of hymn singing in church. Through music and the popular word, Luther's thought had a widespread and profound influence.

Whereas Luther embraced the doctrine of the freedom of conscience to interpret the Bible—confident that the Bible clearly supported his views—other reformers, using the same principle, held very different positions with similar certainty. For more than ten centuries the holy book of the Christian faith had been protected by authoritative commentaries on key words and phrases. And now Luther proclaimed a doctrine of interpretation that, contrary to his intention, encouraged religious anarchy.

John Calvin (1509–1564)

Next to the Lutherans the single most important Protestant group were the Calvinists. John Calvin, a

Frenchman, came to Geneva in Switzerland after the city had already converted from Catholicism; after 1540 under his able direction the city became the center of that variety of Protestantism bearing his name. A second-generation reformer, Calvin believed with Luther in God's predestination of the human soul either to heaven or to hell and in the uselessness of humanity's good works for salvation. But whereas Luther's preoccupation had been with the salvation of the sinner and its consequences for the individual, Calvin focused on the duty of the "elect" to glorify God in all their actions as instruments of God's work. The result of the difference was that, whereas Lutherans stressed the need of the saved to live as Christians in their daily lives, Calvinists viewed themselves as charged with responsibility to reform society so as to make it acceptable in the Lord's eyes. As exemplified in Geneva, Calvinism was against taverns, whorehouses, elaborate clothing, and any form of behavior that would detract from God's glory. For the same reason Calvinists proved much more active missionaries than did Lutherans. Moreover, although Calvin himself was politically conservative, his followers were born revolutionaries in countries where rulers were not Calvinists. After the founder's death, Calvinism was rapidly diffused in France and England as well as in eastern Europe, especially Poland.

There is no place here to discuss the multitude of more radical Protestant sects that sprang up in the sixteenth century along with Lutheranism and Calvinism. Suffice it to say that throughout the century Catholics and Protestants, conservative Protestants and radical Protestants, tortured and killed one another in the name of their religious convictions. Religious toleration would come in the next century only because most of the European population was tired of civil wars and of anarchy created by religious struggle.

Cultural Relativism and Skepticism

Surely part of the reason for the massive participation of Europeans in the religious wars of the sixteenth century can be traced to the economic development of the subcontinent in that century and to the enormous population increases. The only previous European-wide religious phenomenon to match it was that of the Crusades in the twelfth and thirteenth centuries, the last great age of general economic boom and population increase. As in the earlier case, the vigor felt in the expanding society of the sixteenth century found an outlet to an extent in religious warfare, this time within Europe itself.

Economic Expansion

The causes of the economic expansion were various. Certainly the population increase itself was a major factor. But one element that cannot be discounted was the enormous increase in bullion stocks, which multiplied the currency of Europe, causing a price rise and stimulating production. From the early fourteenth century the Spanish and the Portuguese had been exploring the coast of Africa. By the end of the fifteenth century they managed to round the dangerous Cape of Good Hope and establish contact with the Far East. By the second half of that century significant supplies of gold were being imported into Europe from the gold mines south of the Sahara.

Through the voyages of Christopher Columbus from 1492 on, the crown of Castile laid claim to a whole new world beyond the Atlantic Ocean. In the sixteenth century the New World provided an almost unlimited stream of precious metals for Europe, raising prices and fueling the economy. Both agricultural and industrial production expanded. Although most of the industrial goods were still produced in homes and small shops, an increasing number of people were involved in their manufacture. In a few areas such as paper, glass, and cannon making, the mining of coal, shipbuilding, and printing, significant investment was made in the modes of production. The forerunners of modern factories were constructed.

The new discoveries in Africa, Asia, and the Americas had profound cultural as well as economic effects on Europeans. Contact with different systems of religion, thought, government, and new customs challenged their view of what was "natural" to human nature. In short, exploration encouraged cultural relativism.

Montaigne (1533–1592)

The writings of one of the great minds of the late sixteenth century show the effects both of the geographical discoveries and of the religious wars. Michel de Montaigne came to doubt not only the possibility of establishing any certitude in religion, but also the power of reason to establish laws of nature and society in the world. He was one of the few thinkers in history up to his time who seriously raised the question *What do I know?*

Son of a Catholic father and a Protestant-Jewish mother, Montaigne served for a time as the mayor of the modest French city of Bordeaux, but he preferred to remain away from the centers of power. His favorite place for his major activities—reading, writing, and thinking—was his book-lined study located in a tower. There he not only read and commented on classical philosophers but also, in a more modern vein, looked inward in an attempt to understand himself. He did this not because he considered himself an exceptional individual but because he thought that an understanding of oneself could lead to an understanding of the human predicament. He certainly had no intention of establishing laws for human beings. Reason could not do that; people were each one different from the other. But, at least by the last years of his life, he came to believe that nature through pain and pleasure gives us some guidance in the conduct of our lives. Although he relished his own peculiarities, he felt a kinship with other humans and a need to communicate his thoughts to them: "Every man bears the whole form of the human condition."

Montaigne called his writings essays, meaning "trials" or "experiences." He does not claim to impose a lesson but rather to invite the reader to participate in his "tryouts," his observations, his experiences. The essays might be called the journal of a man seeking wisdom. Although each one has a definite subject, Montaigne does not hesitate to go off on tangents when his reflections so lead him. The subjects he chooses may be philosophical, personal, or social. A relativist in philosophical as well as in social matters, Montaigne was one of the first Europeans to understand and portray the cultural relativism that the new travels and discoveries made possible.

Montaigne's *Essays* were translated into English in 1603 by an Englishman of Italian extraction named John Florio. They were then widely read in England, most notably by Shakespeare, who quoted from them in at least one of his plays. Florio's English has the robust, somewhat rambling quality of Montaigne's French. It is essentially the English of Shakespeare and the King James Bible.

William Shakespeare (1564–1616) and the Late Renaissance

The world of Montaigne, fraught with religious dissension, stimulated and enlarged by travels and discoveries, was also fundamentally the world of Shakespeare, although England under the reign of Queen Elizabeth I had a dynamic culture very much its own. More has been written about Shakespeare than about any other writer, and with good reason. The universality of his genius is such that it is difficult not to fall into what Bernard Shaw called "bardolatry" when discussing him. There are writers whose works are more unified, more even, certainly more "classical" than Shakespeare's; but the dramatic power, the philosophical depth, and the superb characterization in Shakespeare's major plays have never been equaled. For English-speaking people, the way in which his poetry has enriched and amplified our language assures his place in our cultural roots. His language may seem difficult to us today; but as we read Shakespeare, we become aware of his enormous impact on our everyday speech and writing.

Shakespeare remains a writer for all times, but he was also very much a man of his time. Many of the cultural and intellectual trends that we have seen developing throughout the Renaissance are synthesized in this playwright of Elizabethan England. He shares Montaigne's skeptical and relativistic view of the human condition, and he often displays a deep pessimism and doubt that would have been impossible under the more unified, God-centered culture of the Middle Ages. Yet he had also been influenced by the earlier humanists' glorification of human beings. This passage from one of Hamlet's soliloquies illustrates the two tendencies:

> What a piece of work is a man! how noble in reason! how infinite in faculty! in form and moving how express and admirable! in action how like an angel! in apprehension how like a god! the beauty of the world! the paragon of animals! And yet, to me, what is this quintessence of dust? Man delights not me.

The whole span of Renaissance-Reformation culture is found in Shakespeare: the early humanistic confidence in human powers, bolstered by the revival of classical texts, and the doubt, deepened by the Reformation, that human endeavors amounted to very much at all.

Shakespeare's Sonnets

Shakespeare's vision of the human condition may be approached through his collection of 142 sonnets. In the wake of Petrarch (see Chapter 16) and the school of poets influenced by him in France, sonnet-writing came into vogue in England during the sixteenth century. Many of these "sonneteers," as they were called, wrote in a derivative manner, writing sterile imitations of love poems to imaginary golden-haired ladies resembling Laura. In Shakespeare's hands, however, the sonnet became an original and vital English form. Not only did he ridicule the conventional Petrarchan lover in his sonnets, proposing another, more earthly vision of love for a "dark lady" instead of an elusive blonde; he also used the sonnet form for meditations of a philosophical nature, most notably on the passage of time.

Shakespeare and the Theater

It is, of course, because of his plays that Shakespeare is now considered the greatest English writer in history. The era in which he lived, Elizabethan England, was a time in which broad interests and creativity could flourish. Although Elizabeth, the Protestant daughter of Henry VIII, came to the throne when there was great rivalry between Protestant and Catholic factions, she was beloved by her subjects and proved to be a powerful and able ruler. Under the reign of Elizabeth, England changed from an island kingdom to an expanding empire that controlled the seas after the naval defeat of the greatest European power, Spain. England grew rich through trade. Sixteenth-century English citizens traveled to the New World and to Africa. Music, dance, poetry, painting, and architecture flourished; but the art form in which Elizabethan England surpassed the rest of Europe (except perhaps Spain) was the theater.

To understand the development of this theater, we should go back for a moment to the discussion of medieval drama in Volume I, Chapter 10. There we saw that the theater, which had practically disappeared from Europe after the Roman Empire, was revived as a part of the church service. As the plays representing stories from the Bible grew more elaborate, they moved to the exterior of the church. No longer a part of the service, the "mystery plays," as they were called, responded to popular taste by adding more and more comical elements, often gross ones. In England these were sponsored by various trade guilds and presented on stage-wagons that went from place to place. When the mystery plays began to lose their appeal, they were replaced by "morality" plays that had allegorical characters (such as Fellowship, Good Deeds, Beauty, Death) and always taught a moral. The best of these, *Everyman,* shows how one should prepare for death and God's judgment. Farces and clowning of various sorts continued alongside this more serious theater. In Italy these grew into the *commedia dell'arte,* an improvisational form with stock characters that would greatly influence the development of modern comedy.

The impact of the humanist resurrection of classical texts on the theater was great. Humanists in Italy translated Latin and Greek plays; then they wrote their own tragedies and comedies in the classical manner, first in Latin and later, by the sixteenth century, in Italian. French, German, and Spanish writers turned to the classical models. In England schools and universities began to produce comedies and tragedies by Plautus, Terence, and Seneca. In spite of a contemporary's remark that Shakespeare knew "a little Latin and less Greek," he was well grounded in the classical humanities through his own reading as well as through formal education. Certainly, he knew the Roman tragedies of Seneca and the comedies of Plautus, which served as models for his own drama. In characteristic Renaissance fashion, his interests ranged beyond book learning to practical knowledge of military strategy, seafaring, business affairs, and the new geographical discoveries, all evident in his plays.

Writers associated with the universities in England began to write plays in English that combined classical and medieval, Roman and English elements. Companies of "strolling players" who had specialized in morality plays began to stage the new plays. Professional actors, who had been viewed by English society as little better than vagrants or criminals, gradually came under the protection of the nobility. Licensed theater companies were formed; Shakespeare belonged to one of these, where in addition to his writing he acquired a wide experience in acting and theater management.

The theater grew in popularity, despite disapproval by the Puritans and others. Public theaters were built not inside the city limits but just outside, along with the brothels, taverns, and other places of entertainment. Theaters in Elizabethan England, like theaters in ancient Greece, were patronized by all social classes. The Globe Theatre, built in 1599, where many of Shakespeare's plays were performed, had a platform stage jutting out into a central courtyard. The audience sat around three sides of this platform—the lower-class people (who each paid a penny) in the "pit" and the wealthier spectators in the galleries above. The orchestra was on stage, because music was usually a significant part of the production. It is important to keep in mind as one reads the script that the *spectacle*—the costumes, scenery, singing, playing, and dancing, as well as the acting—was (and of course still is) essential to the total show. There was no lighting, however; plays were performed in the afternoon. Shakespeare knew his audience: his theater is addressed not just to the elite and educated but to all segments of society.

Shakespeare's plays have been classified in four categories: comedies, histories, tragedies, and romances. None of these is a "pure" form. The tragedies, for example, nearly all contain elements of history and comedy. We will concentrate here on Shakespeare's use of the tragic form in one of his major works, *Othello, the Moor of Venice,* which was first produced in 1604.

Tragedy in the Renaissance One question often asked by literary historians is: what permitted tragedy, a dead form in the Middle Ages, to revive in the Renaissance? In the scheme of Judeo-Christian values, tragedy is hardly possible. The story of Adam and Eve's fall is basically tragic, but the believer sees it as part of a greater whole, a promise of redemption. Isaac's sacrifice is almost tragic, but Jahweh intervenes just in time. The passion of Jesus would be tragic without the knowledge of God's design. The literary work closest to tragedy in the Bible is the Book of Job, but it was amended by later authors to have a happy ending. *The Play of Daniel* is typical of medieval art: it portrays a near catastrophe that is averted by the power of God. It is not by accident that the greatest literary work of the Middle Ages was called *The Divine Comedy.* It is a "comedy" not because it is funny but because it ends in happiness, in fact in paradise.

Renaissance culture, as we have seen, remained basically Christian; but with the revival of Greco-Roman elements, one often perceives in it a tension between the two sets of values. Shakespeare, for example, refers to Christian doctrines and symbols but at times almost seems to believe in something like the classical Fate. In any case, he was able to write of the fall of his heroes without reference to their possible redemption. *Othello,* although it contains references to religion, takes place in a secular scheme of things. Some commentators have argued that Shakespeare was without any religious belief, or at least was as skeptical toward religion as was Montaigne. His audience, in a theater freed from attachment to the Church, accepted non-Christian tragedy.

The sources of Shakespeare's plays range from classical history to contemporary romances. Like the Greek dramatists, he did not make up the basic plots himself but shaped those he found for his own purposes. The source that he used for *Othello* is a rather badly told tale by an Italian writer named Cinthio. Because Renaissance Italy interested Shakespeare greatly, as it did the English in general, many of his plays are set there. *Othello* had an even more exotic element for the English audience: a black man as its hero. To understand the background of the tragedy, it will be helpful to know something about Venice and about Moors.

Venice Venice was an independent Italian city-state that reached the height of its power in the fifteenth century. It was ruled by a duke (*doge*) with a senate. Its colonies included Crete, the Dalmatian coast (now part of Yugoslavia), and the island of Cyprus, in which most of *Othello* is set. The Venetians were frequently at war with the Turks, who finally captured their colonies. Venice as a trade center was full of people from faraway lands; it was a center of culture as well, especially noted for its painting. Italy, and Venice in particular, seemed to the English a place of luxuriousness, corruption, and subtle political intrigue. It is no surprise that Iago, the most intelligent and the most evil of Shakespeare's villains, is a Venetian.

Europeans and Africans Renaissance Europeans called the people of North Africa "tawny Moors" and the people of sub-Saharan Africa "black Moors." Othello is clearly one of the latter. By the time Shakespeare wrote his tragedy, black people were not uncommon on the streets of London. Several English citizens had been to Africa; various European travel accounts had found their way to England. Most of these are a mixture of fantasy and reality. There are tales of "headless men," descriptions of the legendary kingdom of Prester John, and what seem to be fairly accurate accounts of the splendor of the court of Benin (see Volume I, Chapter 12). Some of the stereotypes that would inflame prejudices are present in these accounts: black Moors, or Negroes, were said to be "naked," "without religion," "uncivilized," "cruel." They were thought to be hot-blooded and highly sexed because they lived so near the sun. In addition, the term *black* in the English language already had strong connotations of unclean, evil, and ugly, contrasted with the pure and ideally beautiful white.[1]

These associations and stereotypes served the Elizabethan dramatists who created the Moor as something of a stage type. Usually the Moor was portrayed as a villain, lusty and cruel.[2] Cinthio, Shakespeare's source, emphasizing Othello's "hot-bloodedness" and weakness, moralizes that blacks should not marry whites.

Shakespeare's Use of Black and White It was then something of a feat for Shakespeare, and a testimony to his genius, to present a black man as the hero of a

---

[1]See Winthrop D. Jordan, *White Over Black* (Chapel Hill: University of North Carolina Press, 1968), Chapter 1.

[2]See Eldred Jones, *Othello's Countrymen* (London: Oxford University Press, 1965).

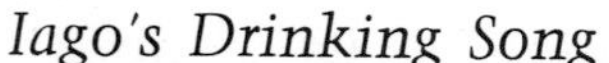

tragedy. Playing on his audience's preconceptions, Shakespeare makes an original, rich use of black and white symbolism throughout the play. It is the black man who is inwardly pure, and it is a seemingly honest white man (and a soldier, a type usually portrayed as genuinely honest) who is inwardly evil. The difficulty of distinguishing being from seeming is a major theme in the play, brought out in part by the black-white symbolism. The alleged supersexuality of Africans also figures in the play: Iago calls Othello the "lusty Moor," describing him with images of animal sexuality. Once again, the popular stereotype is turned around. Othello loves his Venetian wife Desdemona (although by no means platonically) with romantic devotion; Iago is totally unable to understand that love is not simple lust. Othello's overriding concern with sex appears only when he has been infected by Iago's "poison" (another important type of image in the play). This gradual mental and emotional poisoning of Othello by Iago is the motivating force of the tragedy.

Othello as Tragic Hero Othello, a typical tragic figure, moves from a position of power and good fortune to a degraded state in which he can no longer endure his life. Like Oedipus he experiences a powerful revelation of truth and self-knowledge; like Oedipus he turns his own hand on himself. But the combination of fate and character that caused Oedipus' tragedy is here replaced by the combination of Othello's character and the carefully plotted malignancy carried out by Iago. *Othello,* very tightly constructed, is in many ways the most classical of Shakespeare's tragedies, yet it differs substantially from Greek tragedy.

Poetic Form The poetic form of most of this tragedy is *blank verse,* the verse line introduced in the sixteenth

The Willow Song

century and still considered the most natural to the English language. It consists of unrhymed lines in *iambic pentameter,* that is, five strong stresses and five weak stresses. For example:

> It is the cause, it is the cause, my soul,—
> Let me not name it to you, you chaste stars!

Not all of *Othello* is in blank verse, however; Shakespeare uses prose and rhyming verse for various purposes in the play.

Music in *Othello* Music in Shakespeare's drama had many uses: military fanfare and pageantry, accompaniment to dance, an enhancement to a social setting, a part of an intimate lyrical mood. In *Othello,* the instrumental music is associated with the world of action; the vocal music (folk ballads rather than art songs), with the inner world of character. Two examples of the latter are Iago's drinking song, "And let me the cannakin clinke" (Act II, scene iii); and Desdemona's ballad, "The Willow Song" (Act IV, scene iii). Iago's song, like most of what he says, seems to be something that it is not and serves his purpose. Creating an atmosphere of drunken gaiety, the song is really intended to inebriate Cassio. Desdemona's ballad, once sung by a maid called Barbary (the name recalls Africa) who loved a man who went mad, allows her to express her subconscious forebodings of imminent death. The song's sad rhythms tell more vividly than Desdemona would in her speech of a deep love that somehow went wrong. It creates in the spectator a moment of agonized suspense over what will come next.

Reading Selections

Desiderius Erasmus

From the *Colloquies*

Translation by Craig R. Thompson

The *Colloquies* were originally conceived by Erasmus as a device to teach children the art of Latin conversation, but he soon realized that the dialogue form could be an effective means for teaching his reform program. The following colloquy, "The Shipwreck," is one of the most popular. A skillful satire of superficial piety and religious superstition, the work delighted most of its readers. Conservative theologians, however, criticized Erasmus as impious in what they felt was his mockery of the invocation of saints and of the Virgin Mary. In his defense Erasmus argued that he was only satirizing extravagant abuses of traditional religious practices. His critics remained unconvinced.

The Shipwreck

Antony Terrible tales you tell! That's what going to sea is like? God forbid any such notion should ever enter *my* head!

Adolph Oh, no, what I've related up to this point is mere sport compared with what you'll hear now.

Antony I've heard more than enough of disasters. When you're recalling them I shudder as if I myself were sharing the danger.

Adolph To me, on the contrary, troubles over and done with are enjoyable.—On that same night something happened which in large part robbed the skipper of his hope of safety.

Antony What, I beseech you?

Adolph The night was partially clear, and on the topmast, in the "crow's-nest" (as I think they call it), stood one of the crew, looking out for land. Suddenly a fiery ball[1] appeared beside him—a very bad sign to sailors when it's a single flame, lucky when it's double. Antiquity believed these were Castor and Pollux.[2]

Antony What's their connection with sailors? One was a horseman, the other a boxer.

Adolph This is the poets' version. The skipper, who was by the helm, spoke up: "Mate"—that's what sailors call one another—"see your company alongside there?" "I see it," the man replied, "and I hope it's good luck." Soon the blazing ball slid down the ropes and rolled straight up to the skipper.

Antony Wasn't he scared out of his wits?

Adolph Sailors get used to marvels. After stopping there a moment, it rolled the whole way round the ship, then dropped through the middle hatches and disappeared. Toward noon the storm began to rage more and more. Ever seen the Alps?

Antony Yes, I've seen them.

Adolph Those mountains are warts compared with the waves of the sea. Whenever we were borne on the crest, we could have touched the moon with a finger; whenever dipped, we seemed to plunge through the gaping earth to hell.

Antony What fools they are who trust themselves to the sea!

Adolph Since the crew's struggle with the storm was hopeless, the skipper, pale as a ghost, at last came up to us.

Antony His pallor forebodes some great disaster.

Adolph "Friends," he says, "I'm no longer master of my ship; the winds have won. The only thing left to do is to put our hope in God and each one prepare himself for the end."

Antony Truly a Scythian[3] speech.

Adolph "But first of all," he says, "the ship must be unloaded. Necessity, a stern foe, demands it. Better to save life at the cost of goods than for both to

[1]Saint Elmo's fire.

[2]Famous twins in Greek mythology.

[3]Blunt, harsh.

perish together." This was undeniable. A lot of luggage filled with costly wares was tossed overboard.

ANTONY This was sacrificing for sure!

ADOLPH On board was a certain Italian who had served as legate to the King of Scotland. He had a chest full of silver plate, rings, cloth, and silk robes.

ANTONY He didn't want to come to terms with the sea?

ADOLPH No, instead he wanted to go down with his beloved treasures or else be saved along with them. So he protested.

ANTONY What did the skipper do?

ADOLPH "We're quite willing to let you perish alone with your goods," said he, "but it's not fair for all of us to be endangered because of your chest. What's more, we'll throw you and the chest together into the sea."

ANTONY True sailor's lingo!

ADOLPH So the Italian, too, threw his goods overboard, cursing away by heaven and hell because he had entrusted his life to so barbarous an element.[4]

ANTONY I recognize the Italian accent.

ADOLPH Soon afterward the winds, unappeased by our offerings, broke the ropes and tore the sails to pieces.

ANTONY Catastrophe!

ADOLPH At that moment the skipper comes to us again.

ANTONY To make a speech?

ADOLPH "Friends"—he begins by way of greeting—"the hour warns each of us to commend himself to God and prepare for death." Questioned by some who were ignorant of seamanship as to how many hours he thought he could keep the ship afloat, he replied that he couldn't promise anything, but not more than three hours.

ANTONY This speech was even sterner than the first one.

ADOLPH After saying this, he orders all the shrouds to be slashed and the mast sawn off down to its socket and thrown into the sea, together with the spars.

ANTONY Why this?

ADOLPH With the sail ruined or torn, the mast was a useless burden. Our whole hope was in the tiller.

ANTONY What about the passengers meanwhile?

ADOLPH There you'd have seen what a wretched plight we were in: the sailors singing *Salve Regina*,[5] praying to the Virgin Mother, calling her Star of the Sea, Queen of Heaven, Mistress of the World, Port of Salvation, flattering her with many other titles the Sacred Scriptures nowhere assign to her.[6]

ANTONY What has she to do with the sea? She never went voyaging, I believe.

ADOLPH Formerly Venus was protectress of sailors, because she was believed to have been born of the sea. Since she gave up guarding them, the Virgin Mother has succeeded this mother who was not a virgin.

ANTONY You're joking.

ADOLPH Prostrating themselves on the deck, some worshiped the sea, pouring whatever oil they had on the waves, flattering it no differently from the way we do a wrathful sovereign.

ANTONY What did they say?

ADOLPH "O most merciful sea, O most kind sea, O most splendid sea, O most lovely sea, have pity on us! Save us!" Many songs of this kind they sang to the sea—which was deaf.

ANTONY Absurd superstition! What did the rest do?

ADOLPH Some did nothing but get sick. Many made vows. There was an Englishman who promised heaps of gold to the Virgin of Walsingham[7] if he reached shore alive. Some promised many things to the wood of the Cross at such and such a place; others, again, to that in some other place. The same with respect to the Virgin Mary, who reigns in many places; and they think the vow worthless unless you specify the place.

ANTONY Ridiculous! As if saints don't dwell in heaven.

ADOLPH Some pledged themselves to become Carthusians. There was one who promised to journey to St. James at Compostella[8] barefoot, bareheaded, clad only in a coat of mail, begging his bread besides.

---

[4]As Erasmus remarks in his *Praise of Folly,* everything foreign was "barbarous" to Italians.

[5]Latin for "Hail Queen."

[6]Erasmus' ecclesiastical and academic enemies denounced this and other passages in "The Shipwreck" as impious. Erasmus retorted that he was attacking superstitions *(Opera Omnia,* Leiden edition, IX, 942C–943F, 1086C–F, 1163C–E).

[7]On the gold at the shrine of Walsingham, and the wood of the Cross, see Erasmus' colloquy "A Pilgrimage for Religion's Sake," in *The Ten Colloquies of Erasmus,* trans. Craig R. Thompson (New York: Macmillan, 1957).

[8]In northwestern Spain. One of the favorite places of pilgrimage in the Middle Ages.

ANTONY Did nobody remember Christopher?[9]

ADOLPH I couldn't help laughing as I listened to one chap, who in a loud voice (for fear he wouldn't be heard) promised a wax taper as big as himself to the Christopher in the tallest church in Paris—a mountain rather than a statue. While he was proclaiming this at the top of his lungs, insisting on it again and again, an acquaintance who chanced to be standing by nudged him with his elbow and cautioned: "Be careful what you promise. Even if you sold all your goods at auction, you couldn't pay for it." Then the other, lowering his voice—so St. Christopher wouldn't overhear him, of course!—said, "Shut up, you fool. Do you suppose I'm serious? If I once touch land, I won't give him a tallow candle."

ANTONY O stupid! I suspect he was a Batavian.[10]

ADOLPH No, but he was a Zeelander.

ANTONY I'm surprised nobody thought of the Apostle Paul, who was once shipwrecked himself, and when the ship broke, jumped overboard and reached land.[11] No stranger to misfortune, he knew how to help those in distress.

ADOLPH Paul wasn't mentioned.

ANTONY Did they pray all the while?

ADOLPH Strenuously. One chanted *Salve Regina,* another *Credo in Deum.*[12] Some had certain queer beads,[13] like charms, to ward off danger.

ANTONY How devout men are made by suffering! In prosperity the thought of God or saint never enters their heads. What were you doing all this time? Making vows to any of the saints?

ADOLPH Not at all.

ANTONY Why?

ADOLPH Because I don't make deals with saints. For what else is that but a bargain according to the form "I'll give this if you do that" or "I'll do this if you'll do that"; "I'll give a taper if I can swim"; "I'll go to Rome if you save me."

ANTONY But you called on some saint for help?

ADOLPH Not even that.

ANTONY But why?

ADOLPH Because heaven's a large place. If I entrust my safety to some saint—St. Peter, for example, who perhaps will be the first to hear, since he stands at the gate—I may be dead before he meets God and pleads my cause.

ANTONY What did you do, then?

ADOLPH Went straight to the Father himself, reciting the Pater Noster. No saint hears sooner than he, or more willingly grants what is asked.

ANTONY But didn't your conscience accuse you when you did this? Weren't you afraid to entreat the Father, whom you had offended by so many sins?

ADOLPH To speak frankly, my conscience did deter me somewhat. But I soon recovered my spirits, thinking to myself, "No father is so angry with his son that, if he sees him in danger in a stream or lake, he won't grasp him by the hair and pull him out." Of all the passengers, none behaved more calmly than a certain woman who was suckling a baby.

ANTONY What did she do?

ADOLPH She was the only one who didn't scream, weep, or make promises; she simply prayed in silence, clasping her little boy. While the ship was continually battered by the sea, the skipper undergirded it with ropes both fore and aft, for fear it might break to pieces.

ANTONY Miserable protection!

ADOLPH Meantime an old priest, a man of sixty named Adam, jumped up. Stripped to his underclothes, and with his shoes and leggings removed, he urged us all to prepare likewise for swimming. And standing so in the middle of the ship, he preached to us a sermon from Gerson[14] on the five truths concerning the benefit of confession. He urged everyone to be ready both for life and for death. A Dominican was there, too. Those who wished confessed to these two.

ANTONY What did you do?

ADOLPH Seeing everything in an uproar, I confessed silently to God, condemning my unrighteousness before him and imploring his mercy.

ANTONY Where would you have gone if you had died in that condition?

ADOLPH That I left to God the judge, for I was unwilling to be judge of my own cause; nevertheless a strong hope possessed my mind the whole time. While all this is going on, the captain tearfully returns to us. "Get ready," says he, "because the ship will be useless to us in a quarter of an hour."

---

[9]Patron saint of travelers. The statue mentioned a few lines later once stood in the entrance of the Church of Notre Dame.

[10]Erasmus enjoyed a joke at the expense of his fellow Hollanders, but note his remark, at the end of the colloquy, about their character.

[11]Acts 27:9–44.

[12]Latin for "I believe in God."

[13]Rosaries.

[14]The great churchman and chancellor of the University of Paris (1363–1429); famous as a theologian and preacher.

For it was already shattered in some places, and was drawing water. Soon afterwards a sailor reports seeing a church tower in the distance, and beseeches us to appeal to whichever saint took that church under his protection. Everyone falls to his knees and prays to the unknown saint.

ANTONY Had you invoked him by name, he might have heard.

ADOLPH We didn't know his name. As much as he could, meantime, the skipper steered the ship in that direction. It was already breaking up, taking in water everywhere and clearly about to fall to pieces if it hadn't been undergirded with ropes.

ANTONY A bad state of affairs!

ADOLPH We were carried far enough in for the inhabitants of the place to see our plight. Groups of them rushed to the shore, and taking off hats and coats and sticking them on poles, urged us towards themselves, and by lifting their arms to heaven indicated their pity for our lot.

ANTONY I'm waiting to hear what happened.

ADOLPH The whole ship was filled with water now, so that thereafter we would be no safer in ship than in sea.

ANTONY At that moment you had to fall back on your last hope.

ADOLPH On suffering, rather. The crew released the lifeboat and lowered it into the sea. Everyone tried to hurl himself into it, the sailors protesting in the uproar that the lifeboat would not hold such a crowd, but everybody should grab what he could and swim. The situation did not allow leisurely plans. One person snatched an oar, another a boathook, another a tub, another a bucket, another a plank; and, each relying on his own resources, they committed themselves to the waves.

ANTONY What happened during this time to that poor little woman who alone did not weep and wail?

ADOLPH She was the first of them all to reach shore.

ANTONY How could she do that?

ADOLPH We put her on a curved plank and tied her in such a way that she couldn't easily fall off. We gave her a small board to use as a paddle, and, wishing her luck, shoved her off into the waves, pushing with a pole to get her clear of the ship, where the danger lay. Holding her baby in her left hand, she paddled with the right.

ANTONY Brave woman!

ADOLPH Since nothing else remained, one man seized a wooden statue of the Virgin Mother, now rotten and mouse-eaten, and, putting his arms around it, began to swim.

ANTONY Did the lifeboat come through safely?

ADOLPH The first to go down. And thirty people had thrown themselves into it.

ANTONY What mishap caused that?

ADOLPH Before it could get away it was overturned by the lurching of the big ship.

ANTONY A cruel business! What then?

ADOLPH While looking out for others, I nearly perished myself.

ANTONY How so?

ADOLPH Because there was nothing left for me to swim on.

ANTONY Cork would have been useful there.

ADOLPH In that emergency I would rather have had plain cork tree than golden candlestick. Casting about, I finally thought of the stump of the mast. Since I couldn't pry it loose by myself, I enlisted the help of another man. Supporting ourselves on this, we put to sea, I holding on to the right end and he to the left. While we were tossing about in this way, that priest who preached on board threw himself in our midst—on our shoulders. Big fellow, too. "Who's the third?" we yell. "He'll be the death of us all." He, on the other hand, says calmly, "Cheer up, there's plenty of room. God will help us."

ANTONY Why was he so late in starting to swim?

ADOLPH Oh, he was to be in the lifeboat along with the Dominican (for everybody conceded this much honor to him), but although they had confessed to each other on the ship, nevertheless some condition—I don't know what—had been forgotten. There on the edge of the ship they confess anew, and each lays his hand on the other. While they're doing this, the lifeboat goes down. Adam told me this.

ANTONY What became of the Dominican?

ADOLPH According to Adam, after entreating the aid of the saints he threw off his clothes and began to swim.

ANTONY Which saints did he invoke?

ADOLPH Dominic, Thomas, Vincent, and I don't know which Peter, but first and foremost he placed his trust in Catherine of Siena.

ANTONY Christ didn't come to mind?

ADOLPH This is what the priest told me.

ANTONY He'd have swum better if he hadn't thrown off his sacred cowl. With that put aside, how could Catherine of Siena recognize him? But go on with what happened to you.

ADOLPH While we were still tossing beside the ship, which was rolling from side to side at the will of the waves, the broken rudder smashed the thigh of the man who was holding on to the left end of the stump. So he was torn away. The priest, saying a prayer *Requiem aeternam* for him, took his place, urging me to keep hold of my end with confidence and kick my feet vigorously. We were swallowing a lot of salt water all this while. Thus Neptune saw to it that we had not only a salty bath but even a salty drink, though the priest showed us a remedy for that.

ANTONY What, please?

ADOLPH Every time a wave came rushing upon us, he turned the back of his head to it and kept his mouth closed.

ANTONY A doughty old fellow you tell me of.

ADOLPH When we'd made some progress after swimming a while, the priest, who was very tall, said, "Cheer up, I'm touching bottom!" I didn't dare hope for such great luck. "We're too far from shore to hope for bottom." "Oh, no," he replied, "I feel land with my feet." "Maybe it's something from the chests that the sea has rolled this way." "No," he said, "I feel land plainly by the scraping of my toes." After we had swum a while longer in this direction and he again touched bottom, "Do what you think best," he said, "I'm giving up the whole mast to you and trusting myself to the bottom"; and thereupon, after waiting for the waves to subside, he went on foot as fast as he could. When the waves overtook him again, he resisted by clasping his knees with his hands and putting his head under water, as divers and ducks do; when the waves receded, up he popped and rushed on. When I saw he was successful at this, I imitated him. Standing on the coast were men—hardy fellows, and used to the water—who by means of extremely long poles, held out from one to the other, braced themselves against the force of the waves; so that the one farthest out held his pole to the swimmer. When this was grasped, all heaved toward shore and the swimmer was hauled safely to dry land. A number were rescued by this device.

ANTONY How many?

ADOLPH Seven, but two of these died when brought to a fire.

ANTONY How many were you in the ship?

ADOLPH Fifty-eight.

ANTONY O cruel sea! At least it might have been satisfied with a tenth,[15] which is enough for priests. From so large a number how few returned!

ADOLPH We were treated with wonderful kindness by the people there, who looked after our needs with astonishing eagerness: lodging, fire, food, clothing, money for travel.

ANTONY What people were they?

ADOLPH Hollanders.

ANTONY No people could be more kindly, though they do have savage neighbors. I guess you won't visit Neptune very soon again after this.

ADOLPH No, not unless God takes my reason from me.

ANTONY And I for my part would rather hear such tales than experience the events at first hand.

[15] This refers to the tithe. A tenth of all goods produced—normally agricultural in nature—was to be given to the Church for its support.

QUESTIONS

1. What role does the description of Saint Elmo's fire at the beginning of the colloquy play?
2. How, according to Adolph, did the Virgin Mary, who "never went voyaging," become the protectress of sailors? Why might Erasmus' enemies consider the passage irreverent?
3. How did Adolph's comportment during the storm compare with that of most of the other passengers? Why did these others hesitate to pray directly to God the Father? Why is Erasmus ridiculing the invocation of the saints?
4. How might Erasmus be seen as criticizing the rite of confession? How could Erasmus defend himself against this charge?
5. Why is Erasmus in the conclusion so generous in his praise of the Hollanders who rescued some of the ship's company?

MICHEL DE MONTAIGNE

FROM THE *Essays*

Montaigne's essay on cannibals represents one of his most daring social critiques. He uses a society from a newly discovered land—Indians in Brazil—to comment on the false sense of moral superiority in his own compatriots, or in Europeans in general. The translation is by John Florio, with spelling modernized and a few phrases simplified.

Of Cannibals

When King Pyrrhus came into Italy, after he had surveyed the marshalling of the army which the Romans sent against him, he said: "I know not what barbarous men these are" (for so the Greeks called all foreign nations) "but the disposition of this army, which I see, is nothing barbarous." ... Thus should a man take heed, lest he follow vulgar opinions, which should be measured by the rule of reason, and not by the common report. I have had for a long time dwelling with me a man, who for the space of ten or twelve years had dwelt in that other world, which in our age was lately discovered in those parts where Villegaignon first landed, and surnamed Antarctic France.[1] The discovery of so infinite and vast a country seems worthy of great consideration. ... [2]

This servant I had was a simple and rough-hewn fellow, a condition fit to yield a true testimony. For subtle people may indeed ... observe things more exactly, but they amplify and gloss them, the better to persuade ... they never represent things truly, but fashion and mask them according to the visage they saw them in. ... I would have every man write what he knows, and no more. ...

Now (to return to my purpose) I find (as far as I have been informed) there is nothing in that nation, that is either barbarous or savage, unless men call that barbarism which is not common to them. As indeed, we have no other measure of truth and reason, than the example and idea of the opinions and customs of the country we live in. There is ever the perfect religion, the perfect government, perfect and complete customs in all things. We call people savage, as we call fruits wild, which nature has produced by herself. Indeed, however, we should rather term savage those which we ourselves have altered by our artificial devices and diverted from their common order. In the former are the true and most profitable virtues, and natural properties most lively and vigorous, which in the latter we have bastardized, applying them to the pleasure of our corrupted taste. And if notwithstanding we find that the fruits of those lands that were never tilled are still more excellent, compared to ours, there is no reason why art should win the point of honor over our great and powerful mother nature. We have so much by our inventions surcharged the beauties and riches of her works that we have altogether overchoked her: yet wherever her purity shines, she makes our vain and frivolous enterprises wonderfully ashamed. ... All our endeavor or wit cannot so much as represent the nest of the least little bird, its contexture, beauty, profit and use, nor even the web of a frail spider. "All things" (says Plato) "are produced, either by nature, by fortune, or by art. The greatest and fairest by one or other of the two first, the least and imperfect by the last."

Those nations therefore seem to me barbarous thus: they have received very little fashioning from human ingenuity, and are yet near their original natural state. The laws of nature do yet command them, but little bastardized by ours, and that with such purity, that I am sometimes grieved that the knowledge of it no sooner came to light, when men better than we could have judged of it. I am sorry that Lycurgus and Plato had it not, for it seems to me that what in those nations we see by experience ... exceeds all the pictures with which poetry has embellished the golden age. ... They could not imagine a genuineness so pure and simple as we see by experience, nor ever believe our society might be maintained by so little art and human combination. It is a nation, I would answer Plato, that has no kind of traffic, no knowledge of letters, no intelligence of numbers, no name of magistrate, nor of political superiority, no use of service, of riches or of poverty; no contracts, no successions, no partitions, no occupation but idle, no kinship but common, no apparel but natural, no manuring of lands, no use of wine, corn or metal. The very words that import lying, falsehood, treason, dissimulations, covetousness, envy, belittling and pardon were never heard of amongst them. How different would he find his imaginary commonwealth from this perfection: *Men but recently born of the gods.*[3]

Furthermore, they live in a country of so exceeding pleasant and temperate situation, that as my testimonies have told me, it is very rare to see a sick body amongst them; and they have further assured me they never saw any man there, either shaking with the palsy, toothless, with eyes dropping, or crooked and stooped with age. They are situated along the sea coast. ... They have great abundance of fish and flesh, that have no resemblance at all with ours, and eat them without any sauces, or skill of cookery, but plain boiled or broiled. The first man that brought a horse thither, although he had in many other voyages conversed with them, bred so great a horror in the land, that before they could take notice of him, they slew him with arrows. ... They spend the whole day dancing. Their young men go hunting after wild beasts with bows and arrows. Their women busy themselves meanwhile with warming their drink—that is their main occupation. Some of their old men, in the morn-

[1]Villegaignon landed in Brazil in 1557.

[2]In the passage omitted here, Montaigne recounts Plato's account of the "lost continent," Atlantis, and wonders if the "new world" could once have been connected with the old.

[3]Seneca, *Epistles,* XC, 44. Montaigne uses many classical quotations in this essay (as in his others), some of which are omitted here.

ing before they go to eat, preach in common to all the household, walking from one end of the house to the other, repeating the same sentence many times.... The preacher commends but two things to his listeners: first, courage against their enemies, and second, lovingness to their wives.... They are shaven all over, much closer and cleaner than we are, with no other razors than of wood and stone. They believe their souls to be eternal, and those that have deserved well of their gods to be placed in that part of heaven where the sun rises, and the cursed ones toward the west. They have certain prophets and priests which normally live in the mountains and very seldom show themselves to the people. When they do come down, a great feast is prepared.... The prophet speaks to the people in public, exhorting them to embrace virtue and follow their duty. All their moral discipline contains but these two articles: first an undaunting resolution in war, and second an inviolable affection to their wives....

They war against the nations that lie beyond their mountains, to which they go naked, having no other weapons than bows, or wooden swords, sharp at one end as our broaches are. It is an admirable thing to see the constant resolution of their combats, which never end but by effusion of blood and murder, for they know not what fear and routs are. Every victor brings home the head of the enemy he has slain as a trophy of his victory, and fastens it to the entrance of his dwelling. After they have treated their prisoners well for a long time, with all commodities, the master of them summons together a great assembly of his acquaintance, ties a cord to one of the prisoner's arms, by the end of which he holds him fast, though at some distance, for fear of being hurt. He then gives the other arm, bound in like manner, to his dearest friend, and both in the presence of all the assembly kill him with swords. This done, they roast and then eat him in common, and send some slices of him to their friends who are absent. It is not, as some imagine, to nourish themselves with it (as anciently the Scythians[4] used to do), but to represent an extreme revenge. We can prove it thus: some of them saw the Portuguese, who had allied themselves with their adversaries, use another kind of death when they took them prisoners, which was to bury them up to the middle, and shoot arrows against the upper part of the body, and then when they were almost dead to hang them. They supposed that these people of the other world, they who had sowed the knowledge of many vices among their neighbors, and were much more cunning in all kinds of evil and mischief, did not undertake this manner of revenge without cause, and that consequently it was more painful and cruel than theirs. Thereupon they began to leave their old fashion to follow this one.

I am not sorry that we note the barbarous horror of such an action, but grieved that in prying so narrowly into their faults we are so blinded in ours. I think there is more barbarism in eating men alive than to feed upon them being dead; to mangle by tortures and torments a body full of lively sense, to roast him in pieces, to make dogs and swine gnaw and tear him (as we have not only read, but seen very recently, not among ancient enemies, but among our neighbors and fellow citizens, and what is worse, under the pretext of piety and religion)[5] than to roast and eat him after he is dead. Chrysippus and Zeno, arch-pillars of the Stoic sect, thought that there was no harm at all, in time of need, to make use of our carrion bodies, and to feed upon them, as did our forefathers, who being besieged by Caesar in the City of Alexia, resolved to sustain the famine of the siege with the bodies of old men, women, and other persons unserviceable and unfit to fight.

> Gascons (as fame reports)
> Liv'd with meats of such sorts.[6]

...We may then well call these people barbarous in respect to the rules of reason, but not in respect to ourselves, who exceed them in all kinds of barbarism.

Their wars are noble and generous, and have as much excuse and as much beauty as this human infirmity can: they aim at nothing but rivalry in valor. They do not contend for the gaining of new lands, for to this day they still enjoy that natural abundance and fruitfulness which without laboring toil furnishes them in plenteous abundance with all necessary things so that they need not enlarge their limits. They are still in that happy state of desiring no more than their natural necessities: anything beyond is superfluous to them.

Those that are about the same age call each other brethren, those that are younger are called children, and the aged are esteemed as fathers to the rest. They leave full possession of goods in common, without division, to their heirs, and no other claim or title but

[4]An ancient, nomadic, and warlike people who lived in southeastern Europe and Asia.

[5]Montaigne refers to the tortures inflicted by both Protestants and Catholics on their enemies.

[6]Juvenal, *Satires,* XV, 93–94. The Gascons were a people of southwestern France (Montaigne's own region).

that which nature gives to all creatures as she brings them into the world.

If their neighbors chance to come over the mountains to invade them and are victorious over them, the victors' conquest is glory and the advantage to be and remain superior in valor and virtue. Otherwise, they have nothing to do with the goods and spoils of the vanquished, and so return to their country where they are not lacking in any necessary thing, and know how to enjoy their condition happily and be content with what nature supplies them. The others do the same when their turn comes. They require no other ransom of their prisoners but an acknowledgement and confession that they are vanquished. But it is impossible to find one in a whole century who would not rather embrace death than either by word or countenance yield one jot from the grandeur of an invincible courage. There is not one who would not rather be slain and devoured than to beg for his life or show any fear....

The reputation and worth of a man consists in his heart and will: therein lies true honor. Valor is in the strength, not of arms and legs, but of mind and courage; not in the spirit and courage of our horse, nor of our arms, but in our own. He who falls persistent in his courage, "If he slip or fall, he fights upon his knee."[7] He who, in danger of imminent death, is in no way daunted in his assuredness, he that in yielding up his ghost beholds his enemy with a scornful and fierce look, he is vanquished, not by us but by fortune; he is slain, but not conquered. The most valiant are often the most unfortunate. So are there triumphant losses that rival victories....

To return to our story, the prisoners, no matter how they are dealt with, are so far from yielding that during the two or three months they are kept they always keep cheerful and urge and defy their keepers to hasten their trial. They upbraid them with their cowardliness and with the number of battles they have lost. I have a song made by a prisoner which contains this clause: "Let them boldly come together and flock in multitudes to feed on him; for with him they shall feed upon their fathers and grandfathers that heretofore have served his body for food and nourishment. These muscles, this flesh, these veins, are your own; fools that you are, know you not that the substance of your forefathers' limbs is still tied to ours? Taste them well, for in them you shall find the relish of your own flesh." This is an invention that shows no barbarism. Those who describe them dying say that when they are put to execution, the prisoners spit in their executioners' faces and scowl at them. Truly, as long as breath is in their body, they never cease to brave and defy them, both in speech and countenance. Surely, in respect to us these are very savage men, for either they must be so or we must be so. There is a wondrous difference between their style and ours.

Their men have many wives; the more valiant they are reputed to be, the greater the number. The manner and beauty of their marriages is wondrously strange and remarkable. Just as our wives jealously try to keep us from the love and affection of other women, theirs try to obtain it. Being more concerned for their husbands' honor than for anything else, they endeavor to have as many rivals as they possibly can, since that is a testimony to their husbands' valor. Our women would count it a wonder, but it is not so. It is a properly matrimonial virtue, of the highest kind. In the Bible, Leah, Rachel, Sarah, and Jacob's wives brought their fairest maidservants to their husbands' beds.... And lest anyone should think that this is done out of simple and servile duty to custom,... or because they are so blockish and dull spirited... I must cite an example of their abilities. Besides what I have said of one of their war songs, I have a love song which begins like this: "Adder stay, stay good adder, that my sister may by the pattern of thy many-colored coat draw the fashion and work of a rich lace for me to give unto my love; so may thy beauty, thy nimbleness and disposition be ever preferred before all other serpents." The first couplet is the refrain of the song. I am familiar enough with poetry that I may judge that this invention has no barbarism at all in it, but is altogether Anacreontic.[8] Their language is a kind of pleasant speech, and has a pleasing sound, and some affinity with Greek in its endings.

Three of that nation, ignorant of how costly the knowledge of our corruptions will one day be to their repose, security and happiness, and how their ruin shall proceed from this commerce, which I imagine is already well advanced (miserable as they are to have let themselves be so deceived by a desire for new-fangled novelties and to have left the calmness of their climate to come and see ours) were at Rouen at the time of our late King Charles the ninth,[9] who talked with them a great while. They were shown our fashions, our pomp,

[7]Seneca, *On Providence,* II.

[8]Anacreon was a Greek lyric poet who lived about a century later than Sappho (c. 610–c. 580 B.C.).

[9]King Charles IX was only about twelve years old at the time of the incident related here.

and the way a beautiful city looks. Afterwards, some demanded their opinion, and wished to know of them what noteworthy and admirable things they had observed among us. They answered three things, the last of which I have forgotten, and am very sorry for it, the other two I yet remember. They said that first they found it very strange that so many tall men with long beards, strong and well armed, around the person of the king (very likely they meant his Swiss guards) would submit themselves to obey a beardless child, and they wondered why we did not rather choose one among them to command the rest. Secondly, (they have a way of speaking whereby they call men "halves" of one another) they had perceived that there were men among us full gorged with all sorts of commodities, and others which hunger-starved, and bare with need and poverty, begged at their gates, and they found it strange that these needy "halves" could endure such an injustice, and that they did not take the others by the throat or set fire to their houses.

I talked a good while with one of them but had such a bad interpreter who understood my meaning so badly and was so foolish in his conceptions of my ideas, that I did not learn a great deal from him. When I asked him what good he received from the superior position he had among his countrymen (for he was a captain and our sailors called him king) he told me that it was to march foremost in any war charge. When I asked him how many men followed him, he showed me a space of ground to signify as many as might be contained there which I guessed to be about four or five thousand men. Moreover, I asked, when all wars were ended, did his authority expire? He answered that only this much was left, that when he visited the villages dependent on him, the inhabitants prepared paths across the hedges of their woods for him to pass through at ease. All this is not very bad, but what of that? They wear no kind of breeches nor hose.

QUESTIONS AND COMMENTS

1. What does Montaigne seem to mean by "nature"? Would a modern anthropologist agree with his observations on people in a "natural" state?
2. Montaigne uses a great deal of irony in contrasting the cannibals' "natural" state with the European "civilized" one. Point out some specific examples of irony.
3. What criticisms, implicit and explicit, does Montaigne make of his own culture? How does he convince the reader that cannibalism is a relative value rather than an absolute "barbarous" evil?
4. What seem to be Montaigne's positive values? His views on morality and religion? Would you call Montaigne a humanist?
5. Montaigne's references to Greek and Roman events or thinkers often have the effect of allying the ancients with the Brazilian Indians against Europeans of his own day, to the detriment of the latter. Show how this is done. Why would this be an effective technique for Montaigne's readers?
6. What is the impact of the last sentence of the essay?
7. Is the main subject of the essay really the cannibals? What would you say it is?
8. With Montaigne, we have obviously come a long way from Pico della Mirandola and Erasmus, with their faith in the achievements and potential of humanity in general and of European culture in particular. What specific differences can you point out between Montaigne and these earlier thinkers?

WILLIAM SHAKESPEARE

FROM THE *Sonnets*

The first two sonnets reprinted here are meditations on time; the third is a meditation on love and lust; and the fourth, an anti-Petrarchan sonnet using a series of comparisons to describe the poet's ladylove. In reading these sonnets, compare Shakespeare's rhyme scheme and his use of the octave and the sestet to those of Petrarch.

15

When I consider everything that grows
Holds in perfection but a little moment,
That this huge stage presenteth nought but shows
Whereon the stars in secret influence comment;
When I perceive that men as plants increase,
Cheerèd and checked even by the selfsame sky,
Vaunt in their youthful sap, at height decrease,
And wear their brave state out of memory;
Then the conceit of this inconstant stay
Sets you most rich in youth before my sight,
Where wasteful Time debateth with Decay
To change your day of youth to sullied night;
  And, all in war with Time for love of you,
  As he takes from you, I ingraft you new.

60

Like as the waves make towards the pebbled shore,
So do our minutes hasten to their end;
Each changing place with that which goes before,
In sequent toil all forwards do contend.
Nativity, once in the main of light,
Crawls to maturity, wherewith being crowned,
Crookèd eclipses 'gainst his glory fight,
And Time that gave doth now his gift confound.
Time doth transfix the flourish set on youth
And delves the parallels in beauty's brow,
Feeds on the rarities of nature's truth,
And nothing stands but for his scythe to mow;
And yet to times in hope my verse shall stand,
Praising thy worth, despite his cruel hand.

129

Th' expense of spirit in a waste of shame
Is lust in action; and, till action, lust
Is perjured, murd'rous, bloody, full of blame,
Savage, extreme, rude, cruel, not to trust;
Enjoyed no sooner but despisèd straight;
Past reason hunted, and no sooner had,
Past reason hated, as a swallowed bait
On purpose laid to make the taker mad;
Mad in pursuit, and in possession so;
Had, having, and in quest to have, extreme;
A bliss in proof—and proved, a very woe;
Before, a joy proposed; behind, a dream.
All this the world well knows; yet none knows well
To shun the heaven that leads men to this hell.

130

My mistress' eyes are nothing like the sun;
Coral is far more red than her lips' red;
If snow be white, why then her breasts are dun;
If hairs be wires, black wires grow on her head.
I have seen roses damasked, red and white,
But no such roses see I in her cheeks;
And in some perfumes is there more delight
Than in the breath that from my mistress reeks.
I love to hear her speak, yet well I know
That music hath a far more pleasing sound.
I grant I never saw a goddess go:
My mistress when she walks treads on the ground;
And yet by heaven I think my love as rare
As any she belied with false compare.

QUESTIONS

1. What concept of time does Shakespeare express in these sonnets? How is it conveyed poetically?
2. How do paradox and contradiction function in Sonnet 129? What is its subject?
3. In what respects is Sonnet 130 anti-Petrarchan? (See Chapter 16.)

WILLIAM SHAKESPEARE

Othello, the Moor of Venice[1]

CHARACTERS

DUKE OF VENICE
BRABANTIO, [*a senator*], *father to Desdemona*
[*Other*] *Senators*
GRATIANO, [*brother to Brabantio*] } two noble Venetians
LODOVICO, [*kinsman to Brabantio*] } two noble Venetians
OTHELLO, *the Moor* [*in the military service of Venice*]
CASSIO, *an honourable lieutenant*
IAGO, [*an ensign*], *a villain*
RODERIGO, *a gulled gentleman*
MONTANO, *governor of Cyprus* [*before Othello*]
CLOWN, [*servant to Othello*]
DESDEMONA, [*daughter to Brabantio and*] *wife to Othello*
EMILIA, *wife to Iago*
BIANCA, *a courtezan*
Gentlemen of Cyprus, Sailors [*Officers, Messenger, Herald, Musicians, and Attendants*]

[SCENE: *Venice; a sea-port in Cyprus*]

ACT ONE

Scene 1. [*Venice. A street.*][2]

Enter RODERIGO *and* IAGO.

RODERIGO. [Tush]! never tell me! I take it much unkindly
That thou, Iago, who hast had my purse

---

[1]"The text of the present edition [of *Othello*] is based upon the Folio [1623], with deference to the Quarto [1622] where a better reading can be supplied." In the notes, passages from the Folio are designated with a capital F, from the Quarto with a capital Q. Lines have been renumbered for this volume.

[2]"Stage directions, if modern, are enclosed in [brackets]; when they are substantially those of editions not later than 1623, they are unbracketed, or are set aside by a single bracket only, or, when occurring within a line, are enclosed in (parentheses)." (Neilson and Hill, p. v.)

Act I, Scene i, line 1. [*Tush*] Q. Omitted in F.

As if the strings were thine, shouldst know of this.
IAGO. ['Sblood], but you'll not hear me.
If ever I did dream of such a matter,
Abhor me.
RODERIGO. Thou told'st me thou didst hold him in thy hate.
IAGO. Despise me if I do not. Three great ones of the city,
In personal suit to make me his lieutenant,
Off-capp'd to him; and, by the faith of man,
I know my price; I am worth no worse a place.
But he, as loving his own pride and purposes,
Evades them with a bombast circumstance
Horribly stuff'd with epithets of war,
[And, in conclusion,]
Nonsuits my mediators; for, "Certes," says he,
"I have already chose my officer."
And what was he?
Forsooth, a great arithmetician,
One Michael Cassio, a Florentine,
(A fellow almost damn'd in a fair wife)
That never set a squadron in the field,
Nor the division of a battle knows
More than a spinster, unless the bookish theoric,
Wherein the [toged] consuls can propose
As masterly as he. Mere prattle without practice
Is all his soldiership. But he, sir, had th' election;
And I, of whom his eyes had seen the proof
At Rhodes, at Cyprus, and on other grounds
Christen'd and heathen, must be be-lee'd and calm'd
By debitor and creditor; this counter-caster,
He, in good time, must his lieutenant be,
And I—[God] bless the mark!—his Moorship's ancient.
RODERIGO. By heaven, I rather would have been his hangman.
IAGO. Why, there's no remedy. 'Tis the curse of service,
Preferment goes by letter and affection,
And not by old gradation, where each second
Stood heir to th' first. Now, sir, be judge yourself
Whether I in any just term am affin'd
To love the Moor.
RODERIGO. I would not follow him then.
IAGO. O, sir, content you;
I follow him to serve my turn upon him.
We cannot all be masters, nor all masters
Cannot be truly follow'd. You shall mark
Many a duteous and knee-crooking knave
That, doting on his own obsequious bondage,
Wears out his time, much like his master's ass,
For nought but provender, and when he's old, cashier'd.
Whip me such honest knaves. Others there are
Who, trimm'd in forms and visages of duty,
Keep yet their hearts attending on themselves,
And, throwing but shows of service on their lords,
Do well thrive by them and, when they have lin'd their coats,
Do themselves homage. These fellows have some soul;
And such a one do I profess myself. For, sir,
It is as sure as you are Roderigo,
Were I the Moor, I would not be Iago.
In following him, I follow but myself;
Heaven is my judge, not I for love and duty,
But seeming so, for my peculiar end;
For when my outward action doth demonstrate
The native act and figure of my heart
In compliment extern, 'tis not long after
But I will wear my heart upon my sleeve
For daws to peck at. I am not what I am.
RODERIGO. What a full fortune does the thick-lips owe,
If he can carry't thus!
IAGO. Call up her father,
Rouse him. Make after him, poison his delight,
Proclaim him in the streets. Incense her kinsmen,
And, though he in a fertile climate dwell,
Plague him with flies. Though that his joy be joy,
Yet throw such [changes] of vexation on't,
As it may lose some colour.
RODERIGO. Here is her father's house; I'll call aloud.
IAGO. Do, with like timorous accent and dire yell
As when, by night and negligence, the fire
Is spied in populous cities.

---

3. *this:* Desdemona's elopement. 4. [*'Sblood*] Q. Om. F. Profane exclamations in brackets, such as this and that in I.i.33, were omitted in F on account of the act of 1605 against swearing. Frequently *Heaven* was substituted for *God.* 13. *circumstance:* discourse. 15. [*And . . . conclusion*] Q. Om. F. 23. *division:* array. 25. [*toged*] Q. wearing a toga. *tongued* F. 31. *counter-caster:* accountant. 33. [*God*] Q. Om. F. 36. *letter:* i.e., of recommendation. 37. *old gradation:* seniority.

39. *affin'd:* bound. 48. *cashier'd:* dismissed. 50. *visages:* semblances. 60. *peculiar:* private. 63. *compliment extern:* external show. 66. *thick-lips:* i.e., the Moor. *owe:* own. 72. [*changes*] Q. *chances* F. 75. *timorous:* terrifying.

RODERIGO. What, ho, Brabantio! Signior Brabantio, ho!
IAGO. Awake! what, ho, Brabantio! thieves! thieves!
Look to your house, your daughter, and your bags!
Thieves! thieves!

BRABANTIO [*appears*] *above, at a window.*

BRABANTIO. What is the reason of this terrible summons?
What is the matter there?
RODERIGO. Signior, is all your family within?
IAGO. Are your doors lock'd?
BRABANTIO. Why, wherefore ask you this?
IAGO. ['Zounds], sir, you're robb'd! For shame, put on your gown.
Your heart is burst, you have lost half your soul;
Even now, now, very now, an old black ram
Is tupping your white ewe. Arise, arise!
Awake the snorting citizens with the bell,
Or else the devil will make a grandsire of you.
Arise, I say!
BRABANTIO. What, have you lost your wits?
RODERIGO. Most reverend signior, do you know my voice?
BRABANTIO. Not I. What are you?
RODERIGO. My name is Roderigo.
BRABANTIO. The worser welcome;
I have charg'd thee not to haunt about my doors.
In honest plainness thou hast heard me say
My daughter is not for thee; and now, in madness,
Being full of supper and distemp'ring draughts,
Upon malicious [bravery] dost thou come
To start my quiet.
RODERIGO. Sir, sir, sir,—
BRABANTIO. But thou must needs be sure
My spirits and my place have in their power
To make this bitter to thee.
RODERIGO. Patience, good sir.
BRABANTIO. What tell'st thou me of robbing? This is Venice;
My house is not a grange.
RODERIGO. Most grave Brabantio,
In simple and pure soul I come to you.
IAGO. ['Zounds], sir, you are one of those that will not serve God, if the devil bid you. Because we come to do you service and you think we are ruffians, you'll have your daughter cover'd with a Barbary horse; you'll have your nephews neigh to you; you'll have coursers for cousins, and gennets for germans.
BRABANTIO. What profane wretch art thou?
IAGO. I am one, sir, that comes to tell you your daughter and the Moor are [now] making the beast with two backs.
BRABANTIO. Thou art a villain.
IAGO. You are—a senator.
BRABANTIO. This thou shalt answer; I know thee, Roderigo.
RODERIGO. Sir, I will answer anything. But, I beseech you,
If't be your pleasure and most wise consent,
As partly I find it is, that your fair daughter,
At this odd-even and dull watch o' th' night,
Transported, with no worse nor better guard
But with a knave of common hire, a gondolier,
To the gross clasps of a lascivious Moor,—
If this be known to you and your allowance,
We then have done you bold and saucy wrongs;
But if you know not this, my manners tell me
We have your wrong rebuke. Do not believe
That, from the sense of all civility,
I thus would play and trifle with your reverence.
Your daughter, if you have not given her leave,
I say again, hath made a gross revolt,
Tying her duty, beauty, wit, and fortunes
In an extravagant and wheeling stranger
Of here and everywhere. Straight satisfy yourself.
If she be in her chamber or your house,
Let loose on me the justice of the state
For thus deluding you.
BRABANTIO. Strike on the tinder, ho!
Give me a taper! Call up all my people!
This accident is not unlike my dream;
Belief of it oppresses me already.
Light, I say! light! [*Exit* [*above*].
IAGO. Farewell; for I must leave you.
It seems not meet, nor wholesome to my place,
To be produc'd—as, if I stay, I shall—
Against the Moor; for, I do know, the state,
However this may gall him with some check,
Cannot with safety cast him, for he's embark'd

---

90. *snorting:* snoring. 99. *distemp'ring:* intoxicating. 100. [*bravery*] Q: swaggering. *knavery* F. 101. *start:* startle. 106. *grange:* isolated farm.

112. *nephews:* grandsons. 113. *gennets:* Spanish horses. 114. *germans:* relatives. 117. [*now*] Q. Om. F. 124. *odd-even:* midnight. *dull:* dead. 128. *your allowance:* has your approval. 132. *from:* contrary to. 137. *extravagant:* vagabond. *wheeling:* roving. 149. *check:* rebuke. 150. *cast:* dismiss.

With such loud reason to the Cyprus wars,
Which even now [stand] in act, that, for their souls,
Another of his fathom they have none
To lead their business; in which regard,
Though I do hate him as I do hell-pains,
Yet, for necessity of present life,
I must show out a flag and sign of love,
Which is indeed but sign. That you shall surely find him,
Lead to the Sagittary the raised search;
And there will I be with him. So, farewell.

[*Exit. Enter* [*below,*] Brabantio *in his night-gown, and* Servants *with torches.*

Brabantio It is too true an evil; gone she is;
And what's to come of my despised time
Is nought but bitterness. Now, Roderigo,
Where didst thou see her? O unhappy girl!
With the Moor, say'st thou? Who would be a father!
How didst thou know 'twas she? O, she deceives me
Past thought! What said she to you? Get moe tapers;
Raise all my kindred. Are they married, think you?

Roderigo. Truly, I think they are.

Brabantio. O heaven! How got she out? O treason of the blood!
Fathers, from hence trust not your daughters' minds
By what you see them act. Is there not charms
By which the property of youth and maidhood
May be abus'd? Have you not read, Roderigo,
Of some such thing?

Roderigo. Yes, sir, I have indeed.

Brabantio. Call up my brother.—O, would you had had her!—
Some one way, some another.—Do you know
Where we may apprehend her and the Moor?

Roderigo. I think I can discover him, if you please
To get good guard and go along with me.

Brabantio. Pray you, lead on. At every house I'll call;
I may command at most. Get weapons, ho!
And raise some special officers of [night].
On, good Roderigo; I'll deserve your pains.

[*Exeunt.*

152. [*stand*] *stands* QF. 153. *fathom:* capacity.
159. *Sagittary:* an inn (with a centaur on its sign). It has also been proposed that the word is a translation of *Frezzaria*, the Street of the Arrow-makers in Venice. 161. S.D. *night-gown:* dressing gown. 173. *property:* nature. 174. *abus'd:* deceived. 183. [*night*] Q. *might* F. 184. *deserve:* reward.

Scene 2. [*Another street.*]

Enter Othello, Iago, *and* Attendants *with torches.*

Iago. Though in the trade of war I have slain men,
Yet do I hold it very stuff o' th' conscience
To do no contriv'd murder. I lack iniquity
Sometimes to do me service. Nine or ten times
I'd thought to have yerk'd him here under the ribs.

Othello. 'Tis better as it is.

Iago. Nay, but he prated,
And spoke such scurvy and provoking terms
Against your honour
That, with the little godliness I have,
I did full hard forbear him. But, I pray you, sir,
Are you fast married? Be assur'd of this,
That the magnifico is much belov'd,
And hath in his effect a voice potential
As double as the Duke's. He will divorce you,
Or put upon you what restraint or grievance
The law, with all his might to enforce it on,
Will give him cable.

Othello. Let him do his spite;
My services which I have done the signiory
Shall out-tongue his complaints. 'Tis yet to know,—
Which, when I know that boasting is an honour,
I shall promulgate—I fetch my life and being
From men of royal siege, and my demerits
May speak unbonneted to as proud a fortune
As this that I have reach'd; for know, Iago,
But that I love the gentle Desdemona,
I would not my unhoused free condition
Put into circumscription and confine
For the sea's worth. But, look! what lights come yond?

Enter Cassio, *with lights,* Officers, *and torches.*

Iago. Those are the raised father and his friends.
You were best go in.

Othello. Not I; I must be found.
My parts, my title, and my perfect soul
Shall manifest me rightly. Is it they?

Iago. By Janus, I think no.

Othello. The servants of the Duke, and my lieutenant.
The goodness of the night upon you, friends!
What is the news?

Scene ii, 5. *yerk'd:* stabbed. 14. *double:* strong.
22. *siege:* rank. *demerits:* deserts. 23. *unbonneted:* without taking my hat off, on equal terms. 26. *unhoused:* unconfined. 31. *perfect soul:* clear conscience.

CASSIO. The Duke does greet you, general,
And he requires your haste-post-haste appearance,
Even on the instant.
OTHELLO. What is the matter, think you?
CASSIO. Something from Cyprus, as I may divine;
It is a business of some heat. The galleys
Have sent a dozen sequent messengers
This very night at one another's heels,
And many of the consuls, rais'd and met,
Are at the Duke's already. You have been hotly call'd
for;
When, being not at your lodging to be found,
The Senate hath sent about three several quests
To search you out.
OTHELLO. 'Tis well I am found by you.
I will but spend a word here in the house.
And go with you. [*Exit.*
CASSIO. Ancient, what makes he here?
IAGO. Faith, he to-night hath boarded a land
carack.
If it prove lawful prize, he's made for ever.
CASSIO. I do not understand.
IAGO. He's married.
CASSIO. To who?

[*Re-enter* OTHELLO.]

IAGO. Marry, to—Come, captain, will you go?
OTHELLO. Have with you.
CASSIO. Here comes another troop to seek for you.

Enter BRABANTIO, RODERIGO, *and* Officers *with torches and weapons.*

IAGO. It is Brabantio. General, be advis'd;
He comes to bad intent.
OTHELLO. Holla! stand there!
RODERIGO. Signior, it is the Moor.
BRABANTIO. Down with him, thief!

[*They draw on both sides.*]

IAGO. You, Roderigo! come, sir, I am for you.
OTHELLO. Keep up your bright swords, for the dew
will rust them.
Good signior, you shall more command with
years
Than with your weapons.
BRABANTIO. O thou foul thief, where hast thou
stow'd my daughter?
Damn'd as thou art, thou hast enchanted her;
For I'll refer me to all things of sense,
If she in chains of magic were not bound,
Whether a maid so tender, fair, and happy,
So opposite to marriage that she shunn'd
The wealthy curled darlings of our nation,
Would ever have, t' incur a general mock,
Run from her guardage to the sooty bosom
Of such a thing as thou—to fear, not to delight.
Judge me the world, if 'tis not gross in sense
That thou hast practis'd on her with foul charms,
Abus'd her delicate youth with drugs or minerals
That weakens motion. I'll have 't disputed on;
'Tis probable, and palpable to thinking.
I therefore apprehend and do attach thee
For an abuser of the world, a practiser
Of arts inhibited and out of warrant.
Lay hold upon him; if he do resist,
Subdue him at his peril.
OTHELLO. Hold your hands,
Both you of my inclining, and the rest.
Were it my cue to fight, I should have known it
Without a prompter. [Where] will you that I go
To answer this your charge?
BRABANTIO. To prison, till fit time
Of law and course of direct session
Call thee to answer.
OTHELLO. What if [I] do obey?
How may the Duke be therewith satisfi'd,
Whose messengers are here about my side
Upon some present business of the state
To bring me to him?
OFFICER. 'Tis true, most worthy signior.
The Duke's in council; and your noble self,
I am sure, is sent for.
BRABANTIO. How! the Duke in council!
In this time of the night! Bring him away;
Mine's not an idle cause. The Duke himself,
Or any of my brothers of the state,
Cannot but feel this wrong as 'twere their own;
For if such actions may have passage free,
Bond-slaves and pagans shall our statesmen be.

[*Exeunt.*

---

40. *galleys:* i.e., officers of the galleys. 50. *carack:* large trading ship.

72. *gross in sense:* perfectly clear. 75. *motion:* will power. *disputed on:* argued legally. 77. *attach:* arrest.
79. *inhibited:* prohibited. *out of warrant:* unjustifiable.
82. *inclining:* party. 84. [*Where*] Q. *Weather* F. *Whither* F_2.
86. *course…session:* due course of law. 87. [*I*] Q. Om. F.

Scene 3. [*A council-chamber.*]

The DUKE *and* SENATORS *set at a table, with lights;* Officers *attending.*

DUKE. There is no composition in [these] news
That gives them credit.
FIRST SENATOR. Indeed, they are disproportion'd;
My letters say a hundred and seven galleys.
DUKE. And mine, a hundred forty.
SECOND SENATOR. And mine, two hundred!
But though they jump not on a just account,—
As in these cases, where the aim reports,
'Tis oft with difference—yet do they all confirm
A Turkish fleet, and bearing up to Cyprus.
DUKE. Nay, it is possible enough to judgement.
I do not so secure me in the error.
But the main article I do approve
In fearful sense.
SAILOR (*within*). What, ho! what, ho! what, ho!

Enter a SAILOR.

OFFICER. A messenger from the galleys.
DUKE. Now, what's the business?
SAILOR. The Turkish preparation makes for Rhodes;
So was I bid report here to the state
By Signior Angelo.
DUKE. How say you by this change?
FIRST SENATOR. This cannot be,
By no assay of reason; 'tis a pageant,
To keep us in false gaze. When we consider
Th' importancy of Cyprus to the Turk,
And let ourselves again but understand
That, as it more concerns the Turk than Rhodes,
So may he with more facile question bear it,
For that it stands not in such warlike brace,
But altogether lacks th' abilities
That Rhodes is dress'd in; if we make thought of this,
We must not think the Turk is so unskilful
To leave that latest which concerns him first,
Neglecting an attempt of ease and gain
To wake and wage a danger profitless.
DUKE. Nay, in all confidence, he's not for Rhodes.
OFFICER. Here is more news.

Enter a MESSENGER.

MESSENGER. The Ottomites, reverend and gracious,
Steering with due course towards the isle of Rhodes,
Have there injointed them with an after fleet.
FIRST SENATOR. Ay, so I thought. How many, as you guess?
MESSENGER. Of thirty sail; and now they do restem
Their backward course, bearing with frank appearance
Their purposes toward Cyprus. Signior Montano,
Your trusty and most valiant servitor,
With his free duty recommends you thus,
And prays you to believe him.
DUKE. 'Tis certain, then, for Cyprus.
Marcus Luccicos, is not he in town?
FIRST SENATOR. He's now in Florence.
DUKE. Write from us to him; post-post-haste dispatch.
FIRST SENATOR. Here comes Brabantio and the valiant Moor.

Enter BRABANTIO, OTHELLO, CASSIO, IAGO, RODERIGO, *and* Officers.

DUKE. Valiant Othello, we must straight employ you
Against the general enemy Ottoman.
[*To* BRABANTIO.] I did not see you; welcome, gentle signior;
We lack'd your counsel and your help to-night.
BRABANTIO. So did I yours. Good your Grace, pardon me;
Neither my place nor aught I heard of business
Hath rais'd me from my bed, nor doth the general care
Take hold on me; for my particular grief
Is of so flood-gate and o'erbearing nature
That it engluts and swallows other sorrows
And it is still itself.
DUKE. Why, what's the matter?
BRABANTIO. My daughter! O, my daughter!
SENATOR. Dead?
BRABANTIO. Ay, to me;
She is abus'd, stol'n from me, and corrupted
By spells and medicines bought of mountebanks;
For nature so prepost'rously to err,
Being not deficient, blind, or lame of sense,
Sans witchcraft could not.
DUKE. Whoe'er he be that in this foul proceeding
Hath thus beguil'd your daughter of herself
And you of her, the bloody book of law
You shall yourself read in the bitter letter

Scene iii, 1. *composition:* consistency. [*these*] Q. *this* F. 5. *jump:* agree. *just:* exact. 6. *the...reports:* the reports are conjectural. 10. *so...error:* take such assurance from the disagreement. 11. *approve:* assent to. 18. *pageant:* pretense. 23. *with...it:* capture it more easily. 24. *brace:* defense.

35. *after:* i.e., sent after. 55. *particular:* personal.

After your own sense, yea, though our proper son
Stood in your action.
BRABANTIO. Humbly I thank your Grace.
Here is the man,—this Moor, whom now, it seems,
Your special mandate for the state affairs
Hath hither brought.
ALL. We are very sorry for't.
DUKE. [*to* OTHELLO. What, in your own part, can you say to this?
BRABANTIO. Nothing, but this is so.
OTHELLO. Most potent, grave, and reverend signiors,
My very noble and approv'd good masters,
That I have ta'en away this old man's daughter,
It is most true; true, I have married her:
The very head and front of my offending
Hath this extent, no more. Rude am I in my speech,
And little bless'd with the soft phrase of peace;
For since these arms of mine had seven years' pith
Till now, some nine moons wasted, they have us'd
Their dearest action in the tented field,
And little of this great world can I speak
More than pertains to feats of broils and battle,
And therefore little shall I grace my cause
In speaking for myself. Yet, by your gracious patience,
I will a round unvarnish'd tale deliver
Of my whole course of love—what drugs, what charms,
What conjuration, and what mighty magic,
(For such proceeding I am charg'd withal,)
I won his daughter.
BRABANTIO. A maiden never bold;
Of spirit so still and quiet that her motion
Blush'd at herself; and she, in spite of nature,
Of years, of country, credit, everything,
To fall in love with what she fear'd to look on!
It is a judgment maim'd and most imperfect
That will confess perfection so could err
Against all rules of nature, and must be driven
To find out practices of cunning hell,
Why this should be. I therefore vouch again
That with some mixtures powerful o'er the blood,
Or with some dram conjur'd to this effect,
He wrought upon her.
[DUKE.] To vouch this is no proof,
Without more wider and more overt test
Than these thin habits and poor likelihoods
Of modern seeming do prefer against him.

90. *round:* plain. 95. *motion:* impulses. 106. [DUKE] Q. Om. F. 108. *thin habits:* slight semblances.
109. *modern:* ordinary, trivial.

[FIRST] SENATOR. But, Othello, speak.
Did you by indirect and forced courses
Subdue and poison this young maid's affections?
Or came it by request and such fair question
As soul to soul affordeth?
OTHELLO. I do beseech you,
Send for the lady to the Sagittary,
And let her speak of me before her father.
If you do find me foul in her report,
The trust, the office I do hold of you,
Not only take away, but let your sentence
Even fall upon my life.
DUKE. Fetch Desdemona hither.

[*Exeunt two or three.*

OTHELLO. Ancient, conduct them; you best know the place.

[*Exit* IAGO.]

And, till she come, as truly as to heaven
I do confess the vices of my blood,
So justly to your grave ears I'll present
How I did thrive in this fair lady's love,
And she in mine.
DUKE. Say it, Othello.
OTHELLO. Her father lov'd me; oft invited me;
Still question'd me the story of my life
From year to year, the battles, sieges, fortunes,
That I have pass'd.
I ran it through, even from my boyish days
To the very moment that he bade me tell it;
Wherein I spoke of most disastrous chances,
Of moving accidents by flood and field,
Of hair-breadth scapes i' th' imminent deadly breach,
Of being taken by the insolent foe
And sold to slavery, of my redemption thence
And portance in my travel's history;
Wherein of antres vast and deserts idle,
Rough quarries, rocks, [and] hills whose heads touch heaven,
It was my hint to speak,—such was my process,—
And of the Cannibals that each other eat,
The Anthropophagi, and men whose heads
[Do grow] beneath their shoulders. These to hear
Would Desdemona seriously incline;
But still the house-affairs would draw her thence,

139. *portance:* behavior. 140. *antres:* caves. *idle:* barren. 141. [*and*] Q. Om. F. 142. *hint:* occasion.
145. [*Do grow*] Q. *Grew* F. *These* Q_2. *These things* F.

Which ever as she could with haste dispatch,
She'd come again, and with a greedy ear
Devour up my discourse: which I observing,
Took once a pliant hour, and found good means
To draw from her a prayer of earnest heart
That I would all my pilgrimage dilate,
Whereof by parcels she had something heard,
But not [intentively]. I did consent,
And often did beguile her of her tears
When I did speak of some distressful stroke
That my youth suffer'd. My story being done,
She gave me for my pains a world of [sighs].
She swore, in faith, 'twas strange, 'twas passing strange,
'Twas pitiful, 'twas wondrous pitiful.
She wish'd she had not heard it; yet she wish'd
That Heaven had made her such a man. She thank'd me,
And bade me, if I had a friend that lov'd her,
I should but teach him how to tell my story,
And that would woo her. Upon this hint I spake:
She lov'd me for the dangers I had pass'd,
And I lov'd her that she did pity them.
This only is the witchcraft I have us'd.
Here comes the lady; let her witness it.

Enter DESDEMONA, IAGO, *and* Attendants.

DUKE. I think this tale would win my daughter too.
Good Brabantio,
Take up this mangled matter at the best;
Men do their broken weapons rather use
Than their bare hands.

BRABANTIO. I pray you, hear her speak.
If she confess that she was half the wooer,
Destruction on my head if my bad blame
Light on the man! Come hither, gentle mistress.
Do you perceive in all this noble company
Where most you owe obedience?

DESDEMONA. My noble father,
I do perceive here a divided duty.
To you I am bound for life and education;
My life and education both do learn me
How to respect you; you are the lord of duty;
I am hitherto your daughter. But here's my husband;
And so much duty as my mother show'd
To you, preferring you before her father,
So much I challenge that I may profess
Due to the Moor, my lord.

BRABANTIO. God be with you! I have done.
Please it your Grace, on to the state-affairs.
I had rather to adopt a child than get it.
Come hither, Moor.
I here do give thee that with all my heart
Which, but thou hast already, with all my heart
I would keep from thee. For your sake, jewel,
I am glad at soul I have no other child;
For thy escape would teach me tyranny,
To hang clogs on them. I have done, my lord.

DUKE. Let me speak like yourself, and lay a sentence,
Which, as a grise or step, may help these lovers
[Into your favour].
When remedies are past, the griefs are ended
By seeing the worst, which late on hopes depended.
To mourn a mischief that is past and gone
Is the next way to draw new mischief on.
What cannot be preserv'd when fortune takes,
Patience her injury a mock'ry makes.
The robb'd that smiles steals something from the thief;
He robs himself that spends a bootless grief.

BRABANTIO. So let the Turk of Cyprus us beguile
We lose it not, so long as we can smile.
He bears the sentence well that nothing bears
But the free comfort which from thence he hears,
But he bears both the sentence and the sorrow
That, to pay grief, must of poor patience borrow.
These sentences, to sugar or to gall
Being strong on both sides, are equivocal.
But words are words; I never yet did hear
That the bruis'd heart was pierced through the ear.
I humbly beseech you, proceed to the affairs of state.

DUKE. The Turk with a most mighty preparation makes for Cyprus. Othello, the fortitude of the place is best known to you; and though we have there a substitute of most allowed sufficiency, yet opinion, a sovereign mistress of effects, throws a more safer voice on you. You must therefore be content to slubber the gloss of your new fortunes with this more stubborn and bois'trous expedition.

OTHELLO. The tyrant custom, most grave senators,
Hath made the flinty and steel couch of war

---

151. *pliant:* convenient. 155. [*intentively*] Q: attentively. *instinctively* F. 159. [*sighs*] Q. *kisses* F. 166. *hint:* opportunity (not consciously given). Cf. 1.142.

199. *like yourself:* as you should. 200. *grise:* degree.
201. [*Into... favour*] Q. Om. F. 216. *sentences:* maxims.
217. *equivocal:* equal. 222. *fortitude:* strength, fortification.
224. *allowed:* admitted. 225. *sovereign* Q. *more sovereign* F.
227. *slubber:* sully.

My thrice-driven bed of down. I do agnize
A natural and prompt alacrity
I find in hardness, and do undertake
These present wars against the Ottomites.
Most humbly therefore bending to your state,
I crave fit disposition for my wife,
Due reference of place and exhibition,
With such accommodation and besort
As levels with her breeding.

DUKE. [If you please,
Be 't at her father's.]

BRABANTIO. I'll not have it so.

OTHELLO. Nor I.

DESDEMONA. Nor I; [I would not] there reside,
To put my father in impatient thoughts
By being in his eye. Most gracious Duke,
To my unfolding lend your prosperous ear;
And let me find a charter in your voice
To assist my simpleness.

DUKE. What would you, Desdemona?

DESDEMONA. That I [did] love the Moor to live with him,
My downright violence and storm of fortunes
May trumpet to the world. My heart's subdu'd
Even to the very quality of my lord.
I saw Othello's visage in his mind,
And to his honours and his valiant parts
Did I my soul and fortunes consecrate.
So that, dear lords, if I were left behind,
A moth of peace, and he go to the war,
The rites for [which] I love him are bereft me,
And I a heavy interim shall support
By his dear absence. Let me go with him.

OTHELLO. Let her have your voice.
Vouch with me, Heaven, I therefore beg it not
To please the palate of my appetite,
Nor to comply with heat, the young affects
In my defunct and proper satisfaction,
But to be free and bounteous to her mind;
And Heaven defend your good souls, that you think
I will your serious and great business scant
When she is with me. No, when light-wing'd toys
Of feather'd Cupid seel with wanton dullness
My speculative and offic'd instruments
That my disports corrupt and taint my business,
Let housewives make a skillet of my helm,
And all indign and base adversities
Make head against my estimation!

DUKE. Be it as you shall privately determine,
Either for her stay or going. Th' affair cries haste,
And speed must answer it.

FIRST SENATOR. You must away to-night.

[DESDEMONA. To-night, my lord?

DUKE. This night.]

OTHELLO. With all my heart.

DUKE. At nine i' th' morning here we'll meet again.
Othello, leave some officer behind,
And he shall our commission bring to you,
And such things else of quality and respect
As doth import you.

OTHELLO. So please your Grace, my ancient;
A man he is of honesty and trust.
To his conveyance I assign my wife,
With what else needful your good Grace shall think
To be sent after me.

DUKE. Let it be so.
Good-night to every one. [*To* BRABANTIO.] And, noble signior,
If virtue no delighted beauty lack,
Your son-in-law is far more fair than black.

FIRST SENATOR. Adieu, brave Moor; use Desdemona well.

BRABANTIO. Look to her, Moor, if thou hast eyes to see;
She has deceiv'd her father, and may thee.

[*Exeunt* [DUKE, Senators, Officers, *etc.*].

OTHELLO. My life upon her faith! Honest Iago,
My Desdemona must I leave to thee.
I prithee, let thy wife attend on her;
And bring them after in the best advantage.
Come, Desdemona; I have but an hour
Of love, of worldly matters and direction,
To spend with thee. We must obey the time.

[*Exeunt* OTHELLO *and* DESDEMONA.]

RODERIGO. Iago,—

---

232. *thrice-driven:* thoroughly sifted. *agnize:* acknowledge. 238. *reference:* assignment. *exhibition:* provision. 239. *besort:* company. 240. *levels with:* befits. 240–241. [*If...father's*] Q. *Why at her Fathers?* F. 242. [*I...not*] Q. *would I* F. 245. *prosperous:* propitious. 246. *charter:* privilege. 249. [*did*] Q. Om. F. 250. *My...fortunes:* my precipitate assault upon my fortunes. 258. [*which*] Q. *why* F. 265. *defunct:* The modern meaning is here excluded, and no convincing explanation has been found. 267. *defend:* forbid.

270. *seel:* blind (from falconry) 271. *My...instruments:* my faculties whose office is to perceive. 274. *indign:* unworthy. 275. *estimation:* reputation. 279. [DESDEMONA. *To-night...night*] Q. Om. F. 284. *import:* concern. 290. *delighted:* delightful. 298. *advantage:* opportunity.

IAGO. What say'st thou, noble heart?

RODERIGO. What will I do, think'st thou?

IAGO. Why, go to bed and sleep.

RODERIGO. I will incontinently drown myself.

IAGO. If thou dost, I shall never love thee after. Why, thou silly gentleman!

RODERIGO. It is silliness to live when to live is torment; and then have we a prescription to die when Death is our physician.

IAGO. O villainous! I have look'd upon the world for four times seven years; and since I could distinguish betwixt a benefit and an injury, I never found man that knew how to love himself. Ere I would say I would drown myself for the love of a guinea-hen, I would change my humanity with a baboon.

RODERIGO. What should I do? I confess it is my shame to be so fond, but it is not in my virtue to amend it.

IAGO. Virtue! a fig! 'tis in ourselves that we are thus or thus. Our bodies are our gardens, to the which our wills are gardeners; so that if we will plant nettles or sow lettuce, set hyssop and weed up thyme, supply it with one gender of herbs or distract it with many, either to have it sterile with idleness or manured with industry, why, the power and corrigible authority of this lies in our wills. If the [balance] of our lives had not one scale of reason to poise another of sensuality, the blood and baseness of our natures would conduct us to most preposterous conclusions; but we have reason to cool our raging motions, our carnal stings, our unbitted lusts, whereof I take this that you call love to be a sect or scion.

RODERIGO. It cannot be.

IAGO. It is merely a lust of the blood and a permission of the will. Come, be a man! Drown thyself? drown cats and blind puppies! I have profess'd me thy friend, and I confess me knit to thy deserving with cables of perdurable toughness; I could never better stead thee than now. Put money in thy purse; follow thou the wars; defeat thy favour with an usurp'd beard. I say, put money in thy purse. It cannot be long that Desdemona should continue her love to the Moor,—put money in thy purse,—nor he his to her. It was a violent commencement in her, and thou shalt see an answerable sequestration. Put but money in thy purse. These Moors are changeable in their wills—fill thy purse with money;—the food that to him now is as luscious as locusts, shall be to him shortly as bitter as coloquintida. She must change for youth; when she is sated with his body, she will find the error of her choice; [she must have change, she must:] therefore put money in thy purse. If thou wilt needs damn thyself, do it a more delicate way than drowning. Make all the money thou canst. If sanctimony and a frail vow betwixt an erring barbarian and a super-subtle Venetian be not too hard for my wits and all the tribe of hell, thou shalt enjoy her; therefore make money. A pox of drowning thyself! it is clean out of the way. Seek thou rather to be hang'd in compassing thy joy than to be drown'd and go without her.

RODERIGO. Wilt thou be fast to my hopes, if I depend on the issue?

IAGO. Thou art sure of me. Go, make money. I had told thee often, and I re-tell thee again and again, I hate the Moor. My cause is hearted; thine hath no less reason. Let us be conjunctive in our revenge against him. If thou canst cuckold him, thou dost thyself a pleasure, me a sport. There are many events in the womb of time which will be delivered. Traverse! go, provide thy money. We will have more of this to-morrow. Adieu.

RODERIGO. Where shall we meet i' th' morning?

IAGO. At my lodging.

RODERIGO. I'll be with thee betimes.

IAGO. Go to; farewell. Do you hear, Roderigo?

[RODERIGO. What say you?

IAGO. No more of drowning, do you hear?

RODERIGO. I am chang'd;] I'll sell all my land. [*Exit.*

IAGO. Thus do I ever make my fool my purse;
For I mine own gain'd knowledge should profane
If I would time expend with such a snipe
But for my sport and profit. I hate the Moor;
And it is thought abroad that 'twixt my sheets
He has done my office. I know not if 't be true;
But I, for mere suspicion in that kind,
Will do as if for surety. He holds me well;

---

306. *incontinently:* straightway. 325. *hyssop:* fragrant herb. 326. *gender:* kind. 329. *corrigible authority:* corrective power. 330. [*balance*] Q. *braine* F. 334. *motions:* appetites. 336. *sect or scion:* cutting or off shoot. 342. *perdurable:* eternal. 344. *defeat thy favour:* disguise thy face.

350. *sequestration:* separation. 353. *locusts:* the fruit of the carob tree. 354. *coloquintida:* a bitter fruit. 356–357. [*she...she must*] Q. Om. F. 367–368. *depend...issue:* rely on the outcome. 371. *hearted:* heartfelt. 372. *conjunctive:* united. 376. *Traverse:* forward. 382–384. [RODERIGO. *What...chang'd*] Q. Om. F. 387. *snipe:* woodcock, a silly bird.

The better shall my purpose work on him.
Cassio's a proper man: let me see now:
To get his place and to plume up my will
In double knavery—How, how?—Let's see:—
After some time, to abuse Othello's ear
That he is too familiar with his wife.
He hath a person and a smooth dispose
To be suspected, fram'd to make women false.
The Moor is of a free and open nature,
That thinks men honest that but seem to be so,
And will as tenderly be led by th' nose
As asses are.
I have't. It is engend'red. Hell and night
Must bring this monstrous birth to the world's light.

[*Exit.*

ACT TWO

Scene 1. [*A sea-port in Cyprus. An open place near the quay.*]

Enter MONTANO *and two* Gentlemen.

MONTANO. What from the cape can you discern at sea?
FIRST GENTLEMAN. Nothing at all; it is a high-wrought flood.
I cannot, 'twixt the heaven and the main,
Descry a sail.
MONTANO. Methinks the wind hath spoke aloud at land;
A fuller blast ne'er shook our battlements.
If it hath ruffian'd so upon the sea,
What ribs of oak, when mountains melt on them,
Can hold the mortise? What shall we hear of this?
SECOND GENTLEMAN. A segregation of the Turkish fleet.
For do but stand upon the foaming shore,
The chidden billow seems to pelt the clouds;
The wind-shak'd surge, with high and monstrous mane,
Seems to cast water on the burning Bear
And quench the guards of th' ever-fixed Pole.
I never did like molestation view
On the enchafed flood.
MONTANO. If that the Turkish fleet
Be not enshelter'd and embay'd, they are drown'd;
It is impossible to bear it out.

Enter a third Gentleman.

THIRD GENTLEMAN. News, lads! our wars are done.
The desperate tempest hath so bang'd the Turks,
That their designment halts. A noble ship of Venice
Hath seen a grievous wreck and sufferance
On most part of their fleet.
MONTANO. How! is this true?
THIRD GENTLEMAN. The ship is here put in.
A Veronese, Michael Cassio,
Lieutenant to the warlike Moor Othello,
Is come on shore; the Moor himself at sea,
And is in full commission here for Cyprus.
MONTANO. I am glad on't; 'tis a worthy governor.
THIRD GENTLEMAN. But this same Cassio, though he speak of comfort
Touching the Turkish loss, yet he looks sadly
And prays the Moor be safe, for they were parted
With foul and violent tempest.
MONTANO. Pray heavens he be;
For I have serv'd him, and the man commands
Like a full soldier. Let's to the seaside, ho!
As well to see the vessel that's come in
As to throw out our eyes for brave Othello,
Even till we make the main and th' aerial blue
An indistinct regard.
THIRD GENTLEMAN. Come, let's do so;
For every minute is expectancy
Of more arrivance.

Enter CASSIO.

CASSIO. Thanks, you the valiant of this warlike isle,
That so approve the Moor! O, let the heavens
Give him defence against the elements,
For I have lost him on a dangerous sea.
MONTANO. Is he well shipp'd?
CASSIO. His bark is stoutly timber'd, and his pilot
Of very expert and approv'd allowance;
Therefore my hopes, not surfeited to death,
Stand in bold cure.

[*Within,* "A sail, a sail, a sail!" *Enter a* [*fourth* Gentleman].

---

394. *proper:* handsome. 395–396. *plume...In:* brace myself to. 399. *dispose:* disposition.

Act II, Scene i, 9. *hold the mortise:* hold their joints together. 10. *segregation:* dispersion. 15. *guards:* stars in the Little Bear in line with the polestar.

23. *sufferance:* disaster. 26. *A Veronese:* In I.i.20 Cassio is called a Florentine. 49. *approv'd allowance:* tested repute. 50–51. *my hopes...cure:* The sense seems to be "My hopes, though far from being nourished to excess, yet stand a good chance of being fulfilled."

CASSIO. What noise?
[FOURTH] GENTLEMAN. The town is empty; on the brow o' th' sea
Stand ranks of people, and they cry, "A sail!"
CASSIO. My hopes do shape him for the governor.

[*A shot.*

SECOND GENTLEMAN. They do discharge their shot of courtesy.
Our friends at least.
CASSIO. I pray you, sir, go forth,
And give us truth who 'tis that is arriv'd.
SECOND GENTLEMAN. I shall. [*Exit.*
MONTANO. But, good Lieutenant, is your General wiv'd?
CASSIO. Most fortunately. He hath achiev'd a maid
That paragons description and wild fame;
One that excels the quirks of blazoning pens,
And in th' essential vesture of creation
Does tire the [ingener].

Re-enter second Gentleman.

How now! who has put in?
SECOND GENTLEMAN. 'Tis one Iago, ancient to the general.
CASSIO. He has had most favourable and happy speed.
Tempests themselves, high seas, and howling winds,
The gutter'd rocks and congregated sands,
Traitors ensteep'd to enclog the guiltless keel,
As having sense of beauty, do omit
Their mortal natures, letting go safely by
The divine Desdemona.
MONTANO. What is she?
CASSIO. She that I spake of, our great captain's captain,
Left in the conduct of the bold Iago,
Whose footing here anticipates our thoughts
A se'nnight's speed. Great Jove, Othello guard,
And swell his sail with thine own powerful breath,
That he may bless this bay with his tall ship,
Make love's quick pants in Desdemona's arms,
Give renew'd fire to our extincted spirits,
[And bring all Cyprus comfort!]

Enter DESDEMONA, EMILIA, IAGO, RODERIGO [*and* Attendants].

O, behold,
The riches of the ship is come on shore!
You men of Cyprus, let her have your knees.
Hail to thee, lady! and the grace of heaven,
Before, behind thee, and on every hand,
Enwheel thee round!
DESDEMONA. I thank you, valiant Cassio.
What tidings can you tell [me] of my lord?
CASSIO. He is not yet arriv'd; nor know I aught
But that he's well and will be shortly here.
DESDEMONA. O, but I fear—How lost you company?
CASSIO. The great contention of sea and skies
Parted our fellowship.—But, hark! a sail.

[*Within,* "A sail, a sail!" [*Guns heard.*]

SECOND GENTLEMAN. They give [their] greeting to the citadel.
This likewise is a friend.
CASSIO. See for the news.

[*Exit* Gentleman.]

Good ancient, you are welcome. [*To* EMILIA.] Welcome, mistress.
Let it not gall your patience, good Iago,
That I extend my manners; 'tis my breeding
That gives me this bold show of courtesy. [*Kissing her.*]
IAGO. Sir, would she give you so much of her lips
As of her tongue she oft bestows on me,
You'd have enough.
DESDEMONA. Alas, she has no speech.
IAGO. In faith, too much;
I find it still, when I have [list] to sleep.
Marry, before your ladyship, I grant,
She puts her tongue a little in her heart,
And chides with thinking.
EMILIA. You have little cause to say so.
IAGO. Come on, come on; you are pictures out of door,
Bells in your parlours, wild-cats in your kitchens,
Saints in your injuries, devils being offended,

62. *paragons:* excels. 63. *quirks:* flourishes. *blazoning:* praising. 64. *essential...creation:* i.e., just as she is, in her essential quality. 65. [*ingener*] (conjecture): inventor (of praise). *Ingeniver* F. For *tire the* [*ingener*] Q reads *beare an excellency.* 69. *gutter'd:* furrowed, jagged. 70. *ensteep'd:* submerged. 72. *mortal:* deadly. 82. [*And...comfort*] Q. Om. F.

88. [*me*] Q. Om. F. 94. [*their*] Q. *this* F. 104. [*list*] Q: inclination. *leave* F. 107. *with thinking:* i.e., without words. 109–112. *Come...beds.* So Q. Prose in F. 110. *Bells:* i.e., clanging tongues. 111. *Saints...injuries:* i.e., you offend sanctimoniously.

Players in your housewifery, and housewives in your beds.

DESDEMONA. O, fie upon thee, slanderer!

IAGO. Nay, it is true, or else I am a Turk.
You rise to play and go to bed to work.

EMILIA. You shall not write my praise.

IAGO. No, let me not.

DESDEMONA. What wouldst thou write of me, if thou shouldst praise me?

IAGO. O gentle lady, do not put me to't;
For I am nothing if not critical.

DESDEMONA. Come on, assay.—There's one gone to the harbour?

IAGO. Ay, madam.

DESDEMONA. I am not merry; but I do beguile
The thing I am by seeming otherwise.—
Come, how wouldst thou praise me?

IAGO. I am about it; but indeed my invention
Comes from my pate as birdlime does from frieze;
It plucks out brains and all. But my Muse labours,
And thus she is deliver'd:
If she be fair and wise, fairness and wit,
The one's for use, the other useth it.

DESDEMONA. Well prais'd! How if she be black and witty?

IAGO. If she be black, and thereto have a wit,
She'll find a white that shall her blackness fit.

DESDEMONA. Worse and worse.

EMILIA. How if fair and foolish?

IAGO. She never yet was foolish that was fair;
For even her folly help'd her to an heir.

DESDEMONA. These are old fond paradoxes to make fools laugh i' th' alehouse. What miserable praise hast thou for her that's foul and foolish?

IAGO. There's none so foul and foolish thereunto,
But does foul pranks which fair and wise ones do.

DESDEMONA. O heavy ignorance! thou praisest the worst best. But praise couldst thou bestow on a deserving woman indeed, one that, in the authority of her merit, did justly put on the vouch of very malice itself?

IAGO. She that was ever fair and never proud,
Had tongue at will and yet was never loud,
Never lack'd gold and yet went never gay,
Fled from her wish and yet said, "Now I may";
She that being ang'red, her revenge being nigh,
Bade her wrong stay and her displeasure fly;
She that in wisdom never was so frail
To change the cod's head for the salmon's tail;
She that could think and ne'er disclose her mind,
See suitors following and not look behind,
She was a wight, if ever such wights were,—

DESDEMONA. To do what?

IAGO. To suckle fools and chronicle small beer.

DESDEMONA. O most lame and impotent conclusion! Do not learn of him, Emilia, though he be thy husband. How say you, Cassio? Is he not a most profane and liberal counsellor?

CASSIO. He speaks home, madam. You may relish him more in the soldier than in the scholar.

IAGO. [*aside*]. He takes her by the palm; ay, well said, whisper. With as little a web as this will I ensnare as great a fly as Cassio. Ay, smile upon her, do; I will gyve thee in thine own courtship.—You say true; 'tis so, indeed.—If such tricks as these strip you out of your lieutenantry, it had been better you had not kiss'd your three fingers so oft, which now again you are most apt to play the sir in. Very good; well kiss'd! an excellent curtsy! 'Tis so, indeed. Yet again your fingers to your lips? Would they were clyster-pipes for your sake!

(*Trumpet within.*)

—The Moor! I know his trumpet.

CASSIO. 'Tis truly so.

DESDEMONA. Let's meet him and receive him.

CASSIO. Lo, where he comes!

Enter OTHELLO *and* Attendants.

OTHELLO. O my fair warrior!

DESDEMONA. My dear Othello!

OTHELLO. It gives me wonder great as my content
To see you here before me. O my soul's joy!
If after every tempest come such calms,
May the winds blow till they have waken'd death!
And let the labouring bark climb hills of seas
Olympus-high, and duck again as low
As hell's from heaven! If it were now to die,
'Twere now to be most happy; for, I fear,
My soul hath her content so absolute
That not another comfort like to this
Succeeds in unknown fate.

DESDEMONA. The heavens forbid

---

112. *Players:* triflers. *housewives:* hussies. 125–128. *I am…deliver'd:* So Q. Prose in F. 131. *black:* brunette.
133. *white:* with a pun on *wight* (person).
146. *put…vouch:* compel the testimony.

155. *To…tail:* to take the worthless in exchange for the worthy.
160. *chronicle small beer:* i.e., to keep petty accounts.
164. *liberal:* free-spoken. 167. *well said:* well done.
170. *gyve:* fetter, entangle. *courtship:* courtesy.
174. *sir:* gentleman. 177. *clyster-pipes:* syringes.

But that our loves and comforts should increase,
Even as our days do grow!

OTHELLO. Amen to that, sweet powers!
I cannot speak enough of this content;
It stops me here; it is too much of joy.
And this, and this, the greatest discords be [*Kissing her.*
That e'er our hearts shall make!

IAGO [*aside*]. O, you are well tun'd now!
But I'll set down the pegs that make this music,
As honest as I am.

OTHELLO. Come, let us to the castle.
News, friends: our wars are done, the Turks are drown'd.
How does my old acquaintance of this isle?
Honey, you shall be well desir'd in Cyprus;
I have found great love amongst them. O my sweet,
I prattle out of fashion, and I dote
In mine own comforts. I prithee, good Iago,
Go to the bay and disembark my coffers.
Bring thou the master to the citadel;
He is a good one, and his worthiness
Does challenge much respect. Come, Desdemona,
Once more, well met at Cyprus.

[*Exeunt* OTHELLO, DESDEMONA [*and* Attendants.]

IAGO. Do thou meet me presently at the harbour.—Come [hither]. If thou be'st valiant,—as, they say, base men being in love have then a nobility in their natures more than is native to them,—list me. The lieutenant to-night watches on the court of guard;—first, I must tell thee this: Desdemona is directly in love with him.

RODERIGO. With him! why, 'tis not possible.

IAGO. Lay thy finger thus, and let thy soul be instructed. Mark me with what violence she first lov'd the Moor, but for bragging and telling her fantastical lies. To love him still for prating,—let not thy discreet heart think it. Her eye must be fed; and what delight shall she have to look on the devil? When the blood is made dull with the act of sport, there should be, [again] to inflame it and to give satiety a fresh appetite, loveliness in favour, sympathy in years, manners, and beauties; all which the Moor is defective in. Now, for want of these requir'd conveniences, her delicate tenderness will find itself abus'd, begin to heave the gorge, disrelish and abhor the Moor. Very nature will instruct her in it and compel her to some second choice. Now, sir, this granted,—as it is a most pregnant and unforc'd position—who stands so eminent in the degree of this fortune as Cassio does? a knave very voluble; no further conscionable than in putting on the mere form of civil and humane seeming, for the better compassing of his salt and most hidden loose affection? Why, none; why, none; a slipper and subtle knave, a finder of occasion, that has an eye can stamp and counterfeit advantages, though true advantage never present itself; a devilish knave. Besides, the knave is handsome, young, and hath all those requisites in him that folly and green minds look after; a pestilent complete knave, and the woman hath found him already.

RODERIGO. I cannot believe that in her; she's full of most bless'd condition.

IAGO. Bless'd fig's-end! The wine she drinks is made of grapes. If she had been bless'd, she would never have lov'd the Moor. Bless'd pudding! Didst thou not see her paddle with the palm of his hand? Didst not mark that?

RODERIGO. Yes, that I did; but that was but courtesy.

IAGO. Lechery, by this hand; an index and obscure prologue to the history of lust and foul thoughts. They met so near with their lips that their breaths embrac'd together. Villainous thoughts, Roderigo! When these [mutualities] so marshal the way, hard at hand comes the master and main exercise, th' incorporate conclusion. Pish! But, sir, be you rul'd by me; I have brought you from Venice. Watch you to-night; for the command, I'll lay 't upon you. Cassio knows you not. I'll not be far from you. Do you find some occasion to anger Cassio, either by speaking too loud, or tainting his discipline; or from what other course you please, which the time shall more favourably minister.

RODERIGO. Well?

IAGO. Sir, he's rash and very sudden in choler, and haply may strike at you. Provoke him, that he may; for even out of that will I cause these of Cyprus to mutiny, whose qualification shall come into no true taste again but by the displanting of Cassio. So shall you have a shorter journey to your desires by the means I shall then have to prefer them; and the impediment most profitably

---

204. *desir'd:* beloved. 209. *master:* ship's master.
214. [*hither*] Q. *thither* F. 228. [*again*] Q. *a game* F.
233–234. *heave the gorge:* be nauseated.

237. *pregnant:* evident. 240. *conscionable:* conscientious.
242. *salt:* lewd. 243. *slipper:* slippery. 252. *condition:* character. 263. [*mutualities*] Q: exchanges. *mutabilities* F.
277. *qualification:* appeasement.

removed, without the which there were no expectation of our prosperity.

RODERIGO. I will do this, if you can bring it to any opportunity.

IAGO. I warrant thee. Meet me by and by at the citadel; I must fetch his necessaries ashore. Farewell.

RODERIGO. Adieu. [*Exit.*

IAGO. That Cassio loves her, I do well believe 't;
That she loves him 'tis apt and of great credit;
The Moor, howbeit that I endure him not,
Is of a constant, loving, noble nature,
And I dare think he'll prove to Desdemona
A most dear husband. Now, I do love her too;
Not out of absolute lust, though peradventure
I stand accountant for as great a sin,
But partly led to diet my revenge,
For that I do suspect the lusty Moor
Hath leap'd into my seat; the thought whereof
Doth, like a poisonous mineral, gnaw my inwards;
And nothing can or shall content my soul
Till I am even'd with him, wife for [wife];
Or failing so, yet that I put the Moor
At least into a jealousy so strong
That judgement cannot cure. Which thing to do,
If this poor trash of Venice, whom I [trash]
For his quick hunting, stand the putting on,
I'll have our Michael Cassio on the hip,
Abuse him to the Moor in the [rank] garb—
For I fear Cassio with my night-cap too—
Make the Moor thank me, love me, and reward me
For making him egregiously an ass
And practising upon his peace and quiet
Even to madness. 'Tis here, but yet confus'd;
Knavery's plain face is never seen till us'd. [*Exit.*

Scene 2. [*A street.*]

Enter OTHELLO'S Herald, *with a proclamation* [People *following.*]

HERALD. It is Othello's pleasure, our noble and valiant general, that, upon certain tidings now arriv'd importing the mere perdition of the Turkish fleet, every man put himself into triumph; some to dance, some to make bonfires, each man to what sport and revels his [addiction] leads him; for, beside these beneficial news, it is the celebration of his nuptial. So much was his pleasure should be proclaimed. All offices are open, and there is full liberty of feasting from this present hour of five till the bell have told eleven. [Heaven] bless the isle of Cyprus and our noble general Othello!

[*Exeunt.*

Scene 3. *A hall in the castle.*]

Enter OTHELLO, DESDEMONA, CASSIO, *and* Attendants.

OTHELLO. Good Michael, look you to the guard to-night.
Let's teach ourselves that honourable stop,
Not to outsport discretion.

CASSIO. Iago hath direction what to do;
But, notwithstanding, with my personal eye
Will I look to't.

OTHELLO. Iago is most honest.
Michael, good-night; to-morrow with your earliest
Let me have speech with you. [*To* DESDEMONA.]
Come, my dear love,
The purchase made, the fruits are to ensue;
That profit's yet to come 'tween me and you.
Good-night.

[*Exeunt* [OTHELLO, DESDEMONA, *and* Attendants.]
Enter IAGO.

CASSIO. Welcome, Iago; we must to the watch.

IAGO. Not this hour, Lieutenant; 'tis not yet ten o' th' clock. Our general cast us thus early for the love of his Desdemona; who let us not therefore blame. He hath not yet made wanton the night with her; and she is sport for Jove.

CASSIO. She's a most exquisite lady.

IAGO. And, I'll warrant her, full of game.

CASSIO. Indeed, she's a most fresh and delicate creature.

IAGO. What an eye she has! Methinks it sounds a parley to provocation.

CASSIO. An inviting eye; and yet methinks right modest.

IAGO. And when she speaks, is it not an alarum to love?

---

291. *apt:* natural. *of...credit:* most credible. 303. [*wife*] Q. *wist* F. 307. *trash:* worthless fellow. [*trash*] (Steevens): check. *trace* F. *crush* Q. 308. *putting on:* inciting. 310. [*rank*] Q: gross. *right* F. *garb:* manner. 314. *practising upon:* plotting against.

Scene ii, 3. *mere:* utter.

6. [*addiction*] Q_2: inclination. *addition* F. *minde* Q. 9. *offices:* kitchens, etc. 11. [*Heaven*] Q. Om. F.

Scene iii, 14. *cast:* dismissed.

CASSIO. She is indeed perfection.

IAGO. Well, happiness to their sheets! Come, lieutenant, I have a stoup of wine; and here without are a brace of Cyprus gallants that would fain have a measure to the health of black Othello.

CASSIO. Not to-night, good Iago. I have very poor and unhappy brains for drinking; I could well wish courtesy would invent some other custom of entertainment.

IAGO. O, they are our friends. But one cup; I'll drink for you.

CASSIO. I have drunk but one cup to-night, and that was craftily qualified too, and, behold, what innovation it makes here. I am unfortunate in the infirmity, and dare not task my weakness with any more.

IAGO. What, man! 'tis a night of revels. The gallants desire it.

CASSIO. Where are they?

IAGO. Here at the door; I pray you, call them in.

CASSIO. I'll do't; but it dislikes me. [*Exit.*

IAGO. If I can fasten but one cup upon him,
With that which he hath drunk to-night already,
He'll be as full of quarrel and offence
As my young mistress' dog. Now, my sick fool Roderigo,
Whom love hath turn'd almost the wrong side out,
To Desdemona hath to-night carous'd
Potations pottle-deep; and he's to watch.
Three [lads] of Cyprus, noble swelling spirits
That hold their honours in a wary distance,
The very elements of this warlike isle,
Have I to-night fluster'd with flowing cups,
And they watch too. Now, 'mongst this flock of drunkards
Am I to put our Cassio in some action
That may offend the isle. But here they come.

Re-enter CASSIO; *with him* MONTANO *and* Gentlemen [Servants *follow with wine.*]

If consequence do but approve my dream,
My boat sails freely, both with wind and stream.

CASSIO. 'Fore [God], they have given me a rouse already.

MONTANO. Good faith, a little one; not past a pint, as I am a soldier.

IAGO. Some wine, ho! [*Sings.*]
"And let me the canakin clink, clink;
And let me the canakin clink.
A soldier's a man;
O, man's life's but a span;
Why, then, let a soldier drink."
Some wine, boys!

CASSIO. 'Fore [God], an excellent song.

IAGO. I learn'd it in England, where, indeed, they are most potent in potting; your Dane, your German, and your swag-belli'd Hollander—Drink, ho!—are nothing to your English.

CASSIO. Is your Englishman so exquisite in his drinking?

IAGO. Why, he drinks you, with facility, your Dane dead drunk; he sweats not to overthrow your Almain; he gives your Hollander a vomit ere the next pottle can be fill'd.

CASSIO. To the health of our general!

MONTANO. I am for it, Lieutenant; and I'll do you justice.

IAGO. O sweet England!
"King Stephen was and-a worthy peer,
His breeches cost him but a crown;
He held them sixpence all too dear,
With that he call'd the tailor lown.

"He was a wight of high renown,
And thou art but of low degree.
'Tis pride that pulls the country down;
And take thy auld cloak about thee."
Some wine, ho!

CASSIO. Why, this is a more exquisite song than the other.

IAGO. Will you hear 't again?

CASSIO. No; for I hold him to be unworthy of his place that does those things. Well, [God's] above all; and there be souls must be saved, and there be souls must not be saved.

IAGO. It's true, good Lieutenant.

CASSIO. For mine own part—no offence to the general, nor any man of quality—I hope to be saved.

IAGO. And so do I too, Lieutenant.

CASSIO. Ay, but, by your leave, not before me; the Lieutenant is to be saved before the ancient. Let's have no more of this; let's to our affairs.—[God] forgive us our sins!—Gentlemen, let's look to our business. Do not think, gentlemen, I am drunk. This is my ancient; this is my right hand, and this

---

40. *craftily qualified:* slyly diluted. 48. *it dislikes me:* I don't want to. 55. *pottle-deep:* to the bottom of the tankard. 56. [*lads*] Q. *else* F. 57. *hold...distance:* i.e., are quick to quarrel. 58. *very elements:* true representatives. 65. *rouse:* bumper.

84. *Almain:* German. 93. *lown:* fellow, rascal.

is my left. I am not drunk now; I can stand well enough, and I speak well enough.
GENTLEMEN. Excellent well.
CASSIO. Why, very well then; you must not think then that I am drunk. [*Exit.*
MONTANO. To the platform, masters; come, let's set the watch.
IAGO. You see this fellow that is gone before:
He is a soldier fit to stand by Caesar
And give direction; and do but see his vice.
'Tis to his virtue a just equinox,
The one as long as th' other; 'tis pity of him.
I fear the trust Othello puts him in,
On some odd time of his infirmity,
Will shake this island.
MONTANO. But is he often thus?
IAGO. 'Tis evermore his prologue to his sleep.
He'll watch the horologe a double set
If drink rock not his cradle.
MONTANO. It were well
The general were put in mind of it.
Perhaps he sees it not; or his good nature
Prizes the virtue that appears in Cassio,
And looks not on his evils. Is not this true?

Enter RODERIGO.

IAGO [*aside to him*]. How now, Roderigo!
I pray you, after the lieutenant; go.

[*Exit* RODERIGO.

MONTANO. And 'tis great pity that the noble Moor
Should hazard such a place as his own second
With one of an ingraft infirmity.
It were an honest action to say
So to the Moor.
IAGO. Not I, for this fair island.
I do love Cassio well; and would do much
To cure him of this evil.—But, hark! what noise?

[*Cry within:* "Help! help!"] *Re-enter* CASSIO, *pursuing* RODERIGO.

CASSIO. 'Zounds, you rogue! you rascal!
MONTANO. What's the matter, Lieutenant?
CASSIO. A knave teach me my duty!
I'll beat the knave into a twiggen bottle.
RODERIGO. Beat me!
CASSIO. Dost thou prate, rogue? [*Striking* RODERIGO.]

125. *equinox:* counterpart, equivalent. 131. *horologe...set:* clock twice around. 149. *twiggen:* wicker-covered.

MONTANO. Nay, good Lieutenant [*staying him*];
I pray you, sir, hold your hand.
CASSIO. Let me go, sir, or I'll knock you o'er the mazzard.
MONTANO. Come, come, you're drunk.
CASSIO. Drunk!

[*They fight.*

IAGO [*aside to* RODERIGO]. Away, I say; go out, and cry a mutiny.

[*Exit* RODERIGO.

Nay, good Lieutenant,—[God's will], gentlemen;—
Help, ho!—Lieutenant,—sir,—Montano,—[sir];—
Help, masters!—Here's a goodly watch indeed!

[*Bell rings.*

Who's that which rings the bell?—Diablo, ho!
The town will rise. Fie, fie, Lieutenant, [hold]!
You will be sham'd for ever.

Re-enter OTHELLO *and* Attendants.

OTHELLO. What is the matter here?
MONTANO. ['Zounds], I bleed still;
I am hurt to the death. He dies!
OTHELLO. Hold, for your lives!
IAGO. Hold, ho! Lieutenant,—sir,—Montano,—gentlemen,—
Have you forgot all [sense of place] and duty?
Hold! the general speaks to you; hold, for shame!
OTHELLO. Why, how now, ho! from whence ariseth this?
Are we turn'd Turks, and to ourselves do that
Which Heaven hath forbid the Ottomites?
For Christian shame, put by this barbarous brawl
He that stirs next to carve for his own rage
Holds his soul light; he dies upon his motion.
Silence that dreadful bell; it frights the isle
From her propriety. What is the matter, masters:
Honest Iago, that looks dead with grieving,
Speak, who began this? On thy love, I charge thee.
IAGO. I do not know. Friends all but now, even now,
In quarter, and in terms like bride and groom
Devesting them for bed; and then, but now—
As if some planet had unwitted men—
Swords out, and tilting one at other's breast,
In opposition bloody. I cannot speak

155. *mazzard:* head. 159. [*God's will*] Q. *Alas* F. 160. [*sir*] Q. Om. F. 163. [*hold*] Q. Om. F. 168. [*sense of place*] (Hanmer). *place of sense* QF. 174. *carve...rage:* act on his own impulse. 181. *quarter:* peace.

Any beginning to this peevish odds;
And would in action glorious I had lost
Those legs that brought me to a part of it!
OTHELLO. How comes it, Michael, you are thus forgot?
CASSIO. I pray you, pardon me; I cannot speak.
OTHELLO. Worthy Montano, you were wont to be civil;
The gravity and stillness of your youth
The world hath noted, and your name is great
In mouths of wisest censure. What's the matter
That you unlace your reputation thus,
And spend your rich opinion for the name
Of a night-brawler? Give me answer to it.
MONTANO. Worthy Othello, I am hurt to danger.
Your officer, Iago, can inform you—
While I spare speech, which something now offends me—
Of all that I do know; nor know I aught
By me that's said or done amiss this night,
Unless self-charity be sometimes a vice,
And to defend ourselves it be a sin
When violence assails us.
OTHELLO. Now, by heaven,
My blood begins my safer guides to rule;
And passion, having my best judgement collied,
Assays to lead the way. If I once stir
Or do but lift this arm, the best of you
Shall sink in my rebuke. Give me to know
How this foul rout began, who set it on;
And he that is approv'd in this offence,
Though he had twinn'd with me, both at a birth,
Shall lose me. What! in a town of war,
Yet wild, the people's hearts brimful of fear,
To manage private and domestic quarrel,
In night, and on the court and guard of safety!
'Tis monstrous. Iago, who began 't?
MONTANO. If partially affin'd, or leagu'd in office,
Thou dost deliver more or less than truth,
Thou art no soldier.
IAGO. Touch me not so near.
I had rather have this tongue cut from my mouth
Than it should do offence to Michael Cassio;
Yet, I persuade myself, to speak the truth
Shall nothing wrong him. [Thus] it is, General:
Montano and myself being in speech,
There comes a fellow crying out for help;
And Cassio following him with determin'd sword
To execute upon him. Sir, this gentleman
Steps in to Cassio and entreats his pause;
Myself the crying fellow did pursue,
Lest by his clamour—as it so fell out—
The town might fall in fright. He, swift of foot,
Outran my purpose; and I return'd the rather
For that I heard the clink and fall of swords,
And Cassio high in oath; which till to-night
I ne'er might say before. When I came back—
For this was brief—I found them close together,
At blow and thrust; even as again they were
When you yourself did part them.
More of this matter cannot I report.
But men are men; the best sometimes forget.
Though Cassio did some little wrong to him,
As men in rage strike those that wish them best,
Yet surely Cassio, I believe, receiv'd
From him that fled some strange indignity
Which patience could not pass.
OTHELLO. I know, Iago,
Thy honesty and love doth mince this matter,
Making it light to Cassio. Cassio, I love thee;
But never more be officer of mine.

Re-enter DESDEMONA, *attended.*

Look, if my gentle love be not rais'd up!
I'll make thee an example.
DESDEMONA. What's the matter, dear?
OTHELLO. All's well [now], sweeting;
Come away to bed. Sir, for your hurts,
Myself will be your surgeon.— Lead him off. [*To* MONTANO, *who is led off.*]
Iago, look with care about the town,
And silence those whom this vile brawl distracted.
Come, Desdemona; 'tis the soldiers' life
To have their balmy slumbers wak'd with strife.

[*Exeunt all but* IAGO *and* CASSIO.

IAGO. What, are you hurt, Lieutenant?
CASSIO. Ay, past all surgery.
IAGO. Marry, God forbid!
CASSIO. Reputation, reputation, reputation! O, I have lost my reputation! I have lost the immortal part of myself, and what remains is bestial. My reputation, Iago, my reputation!
IAGO. As I am an honest man, I thought you had received some bodily wound; there is more sense

---

186. *peevish odds:* stupid quarrel. 194. *censure:* judgment. 196. *opinion:* reputation. 200. *offends:* pains. 207. *collied:* darkened. 212. *approv'd:* found guilty. 216. *manage:* carry on. 219. *partially affin'd:* biased because of ties. 225. [*Thus*] Q. *This* F.

253. [*now*] Q. Om. F. 267. *thought* Q. *had thought* F.

in that than in reputation. Reputation is an idle and most false imposition; oft got without merit, and lost without deserving. You have lost no reputation at all, unless you repute yourself such a loser. What, man! there are more ways to recover the general again. You are but now cast in his mood, a punishment more in policy than in malice; even so as one would beat his offenceless dog to affright an imperious lion. Sue to him again, and he's yours.

CASSIO. I will rather sue to be despis'd than to deceive so good a commander with so slight, so drunken, and so indiscreet an officer. Drunk? and speak parrot? and squabble? swagger? swear? and discourse fustian with one's own shadow? O thou invisible spirit of wine, if thou hast no name to be known by, let us call thee devil!

IAGO. What was he that you follow'd with your sword? What had he done to you?

CASSIO. I know not.

IAGO. Is't possible?

CASSIO. I remember a mass of things, but nothing distinctly; a quarrel, but nothing wherefore. O [God], that men should put an enemy in their mouths to steal away their brains! That we should, with joy, pleasance, revel, and applause, transform ourselves into beasts!

IAGO. Why, but you are now well enough. How came you thus recovered?

CASSIO. It hath pleas'd the devil drunkenness to give place to the devil wrath. One unperfectness shows me another, to make me frankly despise myself.

IAGO. Come, you are too severe a moraler. As the time, the place, and the condition of this country stands, I could heartily wish this had not befallen; but since it is as it is, mend it for your own good.

CASSIO. I will ask him for my place again; he shall tell me I am a drunkard! Had I as many mouths as Hydra, such an answer would stop them all. To be now a sensible man, by and by a fool, and presently a beast! O strange! Every inordinate cup is unbless'd and the ingredient is a devil.

IAGO. Come, come, good wine is a good familiar creature, if it be well us'd; exclaim no more against it. And, good Lieutenant, I think you think I love you.

CASSIO. I have well approved it, sir. I drunk!

IAGO. You or any man living may be drunk at a time, man. [I'll] tell you what you shall do. Our general's wife is now the general;—I may say so in this respect, for that he hath devoted and given up himself to the contemplation, mark, and [denotement] of her parts and graces;—confess yourself freely to her; importune her help to put you in your place again. She is of so free, so kind, so apt, so blessed a disposition, she holds it a vice in her goodness not to do more than she is requested. This broken joint between you and her husband entreat her to splinter; and, my fortunes against any lay worth naming, this crack of your love shall grow stronger than it was before.

CASSIO. You advise me well.

IAGO. I protest, in the sincerity of love and honest kindness.

CASSIO. I think it freely; and betimes in the morning I will beseech the virtuous Desdemona to undertake for me. I am desperate of my fortunes if they check me [here].

IAGO. You are in the right. Good-night, Lieutenant; I must to the watch.

CASSIO. Good-night, honest Iago. *Exit.*

IAGO. And what's he then that says I play the villain?
When this advice is free I give and honest,
Probal to thinking and indeed the course
To win the Moor again? For 'tis most easy
Th' inclining Desdemona to subdue
In any honest suit; she's fram'd as fruitful
As the free elements. And then for her
To win the Moor, [were't] to renounce his baptism,
All seals and symbols of redeemed sin,
His soul is so enfetter'd to her love,
That she may make, unmake, do what she list,
Even as her appetite shall play the god
With his weak function. How am I then a villain
To counsel Cassio to this parallel course,
Directly to his good? Divinity of hell!
When devils will the blackest sins put on,
They do suggest at first with heavenly shows,
As I do now; for whiles this honest fool
Plies Desdemona to repair his fortune
And she for him pleads strongly to the Moor,
I'll pour this pestilence into his ear,
That she repeals him for her body's lust;
And by how much she strives to do him good,

---

273. *recover:* regain favor with. 282. *parrot:* nonsense.
283. *fustian:* nonsense.

317. [*I'll*] Q. *I* F. 320–321. [*denotement*] Q_2. *devotement* QF. 327. *splinter:* bind with splints. 328. *lay:* wager.
336. [*here*] Q. Om. F. 342. *Probal:* probable.
345. *fruitful:* generous. 347. [*were't*] Q. *were* F.
352. *function:* mental faculties. 355. *put on:* incite.

She shall undo her credit with the Moor.
So will I turn her virtue into pitch,
And out of her own goodness make the net
That shall enmesh them all.

Re-enter RODERIGO.

How now, Roderigo!

RODERIGO. I do follow here in the chase, not like a hound that hunts, but one that fills up the cry. My money is almost spent; I have been tonight exceedingly well cudgell'd; and I think the issue will be, I shall have so much experience for my pains; and so, with no money at all and a little more wit, return again to Venice.

IAGO. How poor are they that have not patience.
What wound did ever heal but by degrees?
Thou know'st we work by wit, and not by witch-
craft;
And wit depends on dilatory time.
Does't not go well? Cassio hath beaten thee,
And thou, by that small hurt, hast cashier'd Cassio.
Though other things grow fair against the sun,
Yet fruits that blossom first will first be ripe.
Content thyself a while. In troth, 'tis morning;
Pleasure and action make the hours seem short.
Retire thee; go where thou art billeted.
Away, I say; thou shalt know more hereafter.
Nay, get thee gone.

[*Exit* RODERIGO.]

Two things are to be done:
My wife must move for Cassio to her mistress;
I'll set her on;
Myself a while to draw the Moor apart,
And bring him jump when he may Cassio find
Soliciting his wife. Ay, that's the way;
Dull not device by coldness and delay. [*Exit.*

ACT THREE

Scene 1. [*Cyprus before the castle.*]

Enter CASSIO, *with* Musicians.

CASSIO. Masters, play here; I will content your pains;
Something that's brief; and bid "Good morrow, general."

[*They play. Enter* CLOWN.

CLOWN. Why, masters, have your instruments been in Naples, that they speak i' th' nose thus?

FIRST MUSICIAN. How, sir, how?

CLOWN. Are these, I pray you, wind-instruments?

FIRST MUSICIAN. Ay, marry, are they, sir?

CLOWN. O, thereby hangs a tail.

FIRST MUSICIAN. Whereby hangs a tale, sir?

CLOWN. Marry, sir, by many a wind-instrument that I know. But, masters, here's money for you; and the General so likes your music, that he desires you, for love's sake, to make no more noise with it.

FIRST MUSICIAN. Well, sir, we will not.

CLOWN. If you have any music that may not be heard, to't again; but, as they say, to hear music the General does not greatly care.

FIRST MUSICIAN. We have none such, sir.

CLOWN. Then put up your pipes in your bag, for I'll away. Go, vanish into air, away!

[*Exeunt* Musicians.

CASSIO. Dost thou hear mine honest friend?

CLOWN. No, I hear not your honest friend; I hear you.

CASSIO. Prithee, keep up thy quillets. There's a poor piece of gold for thee. If the gentlewoman that attends the [General's wife] be stirring, tell her there's one Cassio entreats her a little favour of speech. Wilt thou do this?

CLOWN. She is stirring, sir. If she will stir hither, I shall seem to notify unto her.

CASSIO. [Do, good my friend.]

[*Exit* CLOWN. *Enter* IAGO.

In happy time, Iago.

IAGO. You have not been a-bed, then?

CASSIO. Why, no; the day had broke
Before we parted. I have made bold, Iago,
To send in to your wife. My suit to her
Is that she will to virtuous Desdemona
Procure me some access.

IAGO. I'll send her to you presently;
And I'll devise a mean to draw the Moor
Out of the way, that your converse and business
May be more free.

CASSIO. I humbly thank you for't.

[*Exit* IAGO.]

I never knew a Florentine more kind and honest.

Act III, Scene i, 1. *content:* requite.

21. *hear* Q. *hear me* F. 24. *quillets:* quibbles.
26. [*General's wife*] Q. *general* F. 31. [*Do...friend*] Q. Om. F.

Enter EMILIA.

EMILIA. Good morrow, good Lieutenant. I am sorry
For your displeasure; but all will sure be well.
The General and his wife are talking of it,
And she speaks for you stoutly. The Moor replies
That he you hurt is of great fame in Cyprus
And great affinity, and that in wholesome wisdom
He might not but refuse you; but he protests he loves you,
And needs no other suitor but his likings
[To take the safest occasion by the front]
To bring you in again.

CASSIO. Yet, I beseech you,
If you think fit, or that it may be done,
Give me advantage of some brief discourse
With Desdemon alone.

EMILIA. Pray you, come in.
I will bestow you where you shall have time
To speak your bosom freely.

CASSIO. I am much bound to you.

[*Exeunt.*

Scene 2. [*A room in the castle.*]

Enter OTHELLO, IAGO, *and* Gentlemen.

OTHELLO. These letters give, Iago, to the pilot;
And by him do my duties to the Senate.
That done, I will be walking on the works;
Repair there to me.

IAGO. Well, my good lord, I'll do't.

OTHELLO. This fortification, gentlemen, shall we see't?

GENTLEMEN. We'll wait upon your lordship.

[*Exeunt.*

Scene 3. [*The garden of the castle.*]

Enter DESDEMONA, CASSIO, *and* EMILIA.

DESDEMONA. Be thou assur'd, good Cassio, I will do
All my abilities in thy behalf.

EMILIA. Good madam, do. I warrant it grieves my husband
As if the cause were his.

DESDEMONA. O, that's an honest fellow. Do not doubt, Cassio,
But I will have my lord and you again
As friendly as you were.

CASSIO. Bounteous madam,
Whatever shall become of Michael Cassio,
He's never anything but your true servant.

DESDEMONA. I know't; I thank you. You do love my lord;
You have known him long; and be you well assur'd
He shall in strangeness stand no farther off
Than in a politic distance.

CASSIO. Ay, but, lady,
That policy may either last so long,
Or feed upon such nice and waterish diet,
Or breed itself so out of circumstances,
That, I being absent and my place supplied,
My general will forget my love and service.

DESDEMONA. Do not doubt that; before Emilia here
I give thee warrant of thy place. Assure thee,
If I do vow a friendship, I'll perform it
To the last article. My lord shall never rest;
I'll watch him tame, and talk him out of patience;
His bed shall seem a school, his board a shrift;
I'll intermingle everything he does
With Cassio's suit. Therefore be merry, Cassio;
For thy solicitor shall rather die
Than give thy cause away.

Enter OTHELLO *and* IAGO.

EMILIA. Madam, here comes my lord.

CASSIO. Madam, I'll take my leave.

DESDEMONA. Why, stay, and hear me speak.

CASSIO. Madam, not now; I am very ill at ease,
Unfit for mine own purposes.

DESDEMONA. Well, do your discretion.

[*Exit* CASSIO.

IAGO. Ha! I like not that.

OTHELLO. What dost thou say?

IAGO. Nothing, my lord; or if—I know not what.

OTHELLO. Was not that Cassio parted from my wife?

IAGO. Cassio, my lord! No, sure, I cannot think it,
That he would steal away so guilty-like,
Seeing your coming.

OTHELLO. I do believe 'twas he.

DESDEMONA. How now, my lord!
I have been talking with a suitor here,
A man that languishes in your displeasure.

OTHELLO. Who is't you mean?

43. *displeasure:* disgrace. 47. *affinity:* connections.
50. [*To...front*] Q. Om. F. *front:* forelock.

Scene ii, 3. *works:* fortification.

Scene iii, 12. *strangeness:* aloofness. 19. *doubt:* fear.
23. *watch him tame:* keep him awake till he gives in.
24. *shrift:* confessional.

DESDEMONA. Why, your lieutenant, Cassio. Good my lord,
If I have any grace or power to move you,
His present reconciliation take;
For if he be not one that truly loves you,
That errs in ignorance and not in cunning,
I have no judgement in an honest face.
I prithee, call him back.
OTHELLO. Went he hence now?
DESDEMONA. Yes, faith; so humbled
That he hath left part of his grief with me
To suffer with him. Good love, call him back.
OTHELLO. Not now, sweet Desdemon; some other time.
DESDEMONA. But shall't be shortly?
OTHELLO. The sooner, sweet, for you.
DESDEMONA. Shall't be to-night at supper?
OTHELLO. No, not to-night.
DESDEMONA. To-morrow dinner, then?
OTHELLO. I shall not dine at home;
I meet the captains at the citadel.
DESDEMONA. Why, then, to-morrow night; on Tuesday morn;
On Tuesday noon, or night; on Wednesday morn.
I prithee, name the time, but let it not
Exceed three days. In faith, he's penitent;
And yet his trespass, in our common reason—
Save that, they say, the wars must make example
Out of [their] best—is not almost a fault
T' incur a private check. When shall he come?
Tell me, Othello. I wonder in my soul
What you would ask me that I should deny,
Or stand so mamm'ring on. What! Michael Cassio,
That came a-wooing with you, and so many a time,
When I have spoke of you dispraisingly,
Hath ta'en your part,—to have so much to do
To bring him in! Trust me, I could do much.
OTHELLO. Prithee, no more; let him come when he will,
I will deny thee nothing.
DESDEMONA. Why, this is not a boon.
'Tis as I should entreat you wear your gloves,
Or feed on nourishing dishes, or keep you warm,
Or sue to you to do a peculiar profit
To your own person. Nay, when I have a suit
Wherein I mean to touch your love indeed,
It shall be full of poise and difficult weight
And fearful to be granted.
OTHELLO. I will deny thee nothing.
Whereon, I do beseech thee, grant me this,
To leave me but a little to myself.
DESDEMONA. Shall I deny you? No. Farewell, my lord.
OTHELLO. Farewell, my Desdemona; I'll come to thee straight.
DESDEMONA. Emilia, come.—Be as your fancies teach you;
Whate'er you be, I am obedient.

[*Exeunt* DESDEMONA *and* EMILIA.

OTHELLO. Excellent wretch! Perdition catch my soul,
But I do love thee! and when I love thee not,
Chaos is come again.
IAGO. My noble lord,—
OTHELLO. What dost thou say, Iago?
IAGO. Did Michael Cassio, when [you] woo'd my lady,
Know of your love?
OTHELLO. He did, from first to last. Why dost thou ask?
IAGO. But for a satisfaction of my thought;
No further harm.
OTHELLO. Why of thy thought, Iago?
IAGO. I did not think he had been acquainted with her.
OTHELLO. O, yes; and went between us very oft.
IAGO. Indeed!
OTHELLO. Indeed! ay, indeed. Discern'st thou aught in that?
Is he not honest?
IAGO. Honest, my lord?
OTHELLO. Honest! ay, honest.
IAGO. My lord, for aught I know.
OTHELLO. What dost thou think?
IAGO. Think, my lord?
OTHELLO. Think, my lord!
[By heaven, he echoes] me,
As if there were some monster in [his] thought
Too hideous to be shown.—Thou dost mean something.
I heard thee say even now, thou lik'st not that,
When Cassio left my wife. What didst not like?
And when I told thee he was of my counsel
[In] my whole course of wooing, thou criedst, "Indeed!"

66. [*their*]. *her* QF. *not almost*: hardly. 70. *mamm'ring:* hesitating. 74. *bring...in:* i.e., into your favor. 82. *poise:* weight.

94. [*you*] Q. *he* F. 106. [*By...echoes*] Q. *Alas, thou eccho'st* F. 107. [*his*] Q. *thy* F. 112. [*In*] Q. *of* F.

And didst contract and purse thy brow together,
As if thou then hadst shut up in thy brain
Some horrible conceit. If thou dost love me,
Show me thy thought.
IAGO. My lord, you know I love you.
OTHELLO. I think thou dost;
And, for I know thou'rt full of love and honesty,
And weigh'st thy words before thou giv'st them breath,
Therefore these stops of thine fright me the more;
For such things in a false disloyal knave
Are tricks of custom; but in a man that's just
They're close dilations, working from the heart
That passion cannot rule.
IAGO. For Michael Cassio,
I dare be sworn I think that he is honest.
OTHELLO. I think so too.
IAGO. Men should be what they seem;
Or those that be not, would they might seem none!
OTHELLO. Certain, men should be what they seem.
IAGO. Why, then, I think Cassio's an honest man.
OTHELLO. Nay, yet there's more in this.
I prithee, speak to me as to thy thinkings,
As thou dost ruminate, and give thy worst of thoughts
The worst of words.
IAGO. Good my lord, pardon me.
Though I am bound to every act of duty,
I am not bound to that all slaves are free to.
Utter my thoughts? Why, say they are vile and false;
As where's that palace where into foul things
Sometimes intrude not? Who has that breast so pure
[But some] uncleanly apprehensions
Keep leets and law-days and in sessions sit
With meditations lawful?
OTHELLO. Thou dost conspire against thy friend, Iago,
If thou but think'st him wrong'd and mak'st his ear
A stranger to thy thoughts.
IAGO. I do beseech you—
Though I perchance am vicious in my guess,
As, I confess, it is my nature's plague
To spy into abuses, and [oft] my jealousy
Shapes faults that are not—that your wisdom yet,
From one that so imperfectly conceits,
Would take no notice, nor build yourself a trouble
Out of his scattering and unsure observance.
It were not for your quiet nor your good,
Nor for my manhood, honesty, and wisdom,
To let you know my thoughts.
OTHELLO. What dost thou mean?
IAGO. Good name in man and woman, dear my lord,
Is the immediate jewel of their souls.
Who steals my purse steals trash; 'tis something, nothing;
'Twas mine, 'tis his, and has been slave to thousands;
But he that filches from me my good name
Robs me of that which not enriches him,
And makes me poor indeed.
OTHELLO. [By heaven,] I'll know thy thoughts.
IAGO. You cannot, if my heart were in your hand;
Nor shall not, whilst 'tis in my custody.
OTHELLO. Ha!
IAGO. O, beware, my lord, of jealousy!
It is the green-ey'd monster which doth mock
The meat it feeds on. That cuckold lives in bliss
Who, certain of his fate, loves not his wronger;
But, O, what damned minutes tells he o'er
Who dotes, yet doubts, suspects, yet soundly loves!
OTHELLO. O misery!
IAGO. Poor and content is rich, and rich enough;
But riches fineless is as poor as winter
To him that ever fears he shall be poor.
Good heavens, the souls of all my tribe defend
From jealousy!
OTHELLO. Why, why is this?
Think'st thou I'd make a life of jealousy,
To follow still the changes of the moon
With fresh suspicions? No! to be once in doubt
Is [once] to be resolv'd. Exchange me for a goat
When I shall turn the business of my soul
To such exsufflicate and [blown] surmises,
Matching thy inference. 'Tis not to make me jealous
To say my wife is fair, feeds well, loves company,
Is free of speech, sings, plays, and dances [well];
Where virtue is, these are more virtuous.
Nor from mine own weak merits will I draw
The smallest fear or doubt of her revolt;
For she had eyes, and chose me. No, Iago;
I'll see before I doubt; when I doubt, prove;
And on the proof, there is no more but this,—
Away at once with love or jealousy!
IAGO. I am glad of this, for now I shall have reason
To show the love and duty that I bear you

---

123. *close dilations:* secret (i.e., unconscious) expressions.
139. *[But some]* Q. *Wherein* F. 140. *leets:* court-days.
147. *[oft]* Q. *of* F. *jealousy:* suspicion. 151. *scattering:* random.

173. *fineless:* unlimited. 180. *[once]* Q. Om. F.
182. *exsufflicate:* inflated. *[blown]* Q. *blowed* F.
185. *[well]* Q. Om. F.

With franker spirit; therefore, as I am bound,
Receive it from me. I speak not yet of proof.
Look to your wife; observe her well with Cassio;
Wear your eyes thus, not jealous nor secure.
I would not have your free and noble nature,
Out of self-bounty, be abus'd; look to't.
I know our country disposition well;
In Venice they do let Heaven see the pranks
They dare not show their husbands. Their best conscience
Is not to leave 't undone, but keep 't unknown.
OTHELLO. Dost thou say so?
IAGO. She did deceive her father, marrying you;
And when she seem'd to shake and fear your looks,
She lov'd them most.
OTHELLO. And so she did.
IAGO. Why, go to then.
She that, so young, could give out such a seeming,
To seel her father's eyes up close as oak—
He thought 'twas witchcraft—but I am much to blame.
I humbly do beseech you of your pardon
For too much loving you.
OTHELLO. I am bound to thee for ever.
IAGO. I see this hath a little dash'd your spirits.
OTHELLO. Not a jot, not a jot.
IAGO. Trust me! I fear it has.
I hope you will consider what is spoke
Comes from [my] love. But I do see you're mov'd.
I am to pray you not to strain my speech
To grosser issues nor to larger reach
Than to suspicion.
OTHELLO. I will not.
IAGO. Should you do so, my lord,
My speech should fall into such vile success
Which my thoughts aim'd not at. Cassio's my worthy friend,—
My lord, I see you're mov'd.
OTHELLO. No, not much mov'd.
I do not think but Desdemona's honest.
IAGO. Long live she so! and long live you to think so!
OTHELLO. And yet, how nature erring from itself,—
IAGO. Ay, there's the point; as—to be bold with you—
Not to affect many proposed matches
Of her own clime, complexion, and degree,
Whereto we see in all things nature tends—
Foh! one may smell in such, a will most rank,
Foul disproportions, thoughts unnatural.
But pardon me; I do not in position
Distinctly speak of her; though I may fear
Her will, recoiling to her better judgement,
May fall to match you with her country forms,
And happily repent.
OTHELLO. Farewell, farewell!
If more thou dost perceive, let me know more;
Set on thy wife to observe. Leave me, Iago.
IAGO [*going*]. My lord, I take my leave.
OTHELLO. Why did I marry? This honest creature doubtless
Sees and knows more, much more, than he unfolds.
IAGO. [*returning*]. My lord, I would I might entreat your honour
To scan this thing no farther; leave it to time.
Although 'tis fit that Cassio have his place,
For, sure, he fills it up with great ability,
Yet, if you please to [hold] him off a while,
You shall by that perceive him and his means.
Note if your lady strain his entertainment
With any strong or vehement importunity;
Much will be seen in that. In the mean time,
Let me be thought too busy in my fears—
As worthy cause I have to fear I am—
And hold her free, I do beseech your honour.
OTHELLO. Fear not my government.
IAGO. I once more take my leave. [*Exit.*
OTHELLO. This fellow's of exceeding honesty,
And knows all [qualities], with a learn'd spirit,
Of human dealings. If I do prove her haggard,
Though that her jesses were my dear heartstrings,
I'd whistle her off and let her down the wind
To prey at fortune. Haply, for I am black
And have not those soft parts of conversation
That chamberers have, or for I am declin'd
Into the vale of years,—yet that's not much—
She's gone. I am abus'd: and my relief
Must be to loathe her. O curse of marriage,
That we can call these delicate creatures ours,
And not their appetites! I had rather be a toad
And live upon the vapour of a dungeon
Than keep a corner in the thing I love

198. *secure:* careless. 200. *self-bounty:* inherent generosity. 217. [*my*] Q. *your* F. 222. *success:* consequence. 225. *honest:* chaste.

232, 236. *will:* desire, appetite. 232. *rank:* foul. 234. *position:* i.e., conviction. 248. [*hold*] Q. Om. F. 250. *strain his entertainment:* press his reappointment. 255. *free:* guiltless. 256. *government:* management. 259. [*qualities*] Q. *quantities* F. 260. *haggard:* wild. 261. *jesses:* strings by which hawks were held. 264. *parts of conversation:* social graces. 265. *chamberers:* gallants.

For others' uses. Yet, 'tis the plague [of] great ones;
Prerogativ'd are they less than the base.
'Tis destiny unshunnable, like death.
Even then this forked plague is fated to us
When we do quicken. Look where she comes:

Re-enter DESDEMONA *and* EMILIA.

If she be false, [O, then heaven mocks] itself!
I'll not believe 't.

DESDEMONA. How now, my dear Othello!
Your dinner, and the generous islanders
By you invited, do attend your presence.

OTHELLO. I am to blame.

DESDEMONA. Why do you speak so faintly?
Are you not well?

OTHELLO. I have a pain upon my forehead here.

DESDEMONA. Why, that's with watching; 'twill away again.
Let me but bind it hard, within this hour
It will be well.

OTHELLO. Your napkin is too little [*he puts the handkerchief from him; and it drops*];
Let it alone. Come, I'll go in with you.

DESDEMONA. I am very sorry that you are not well.

[*Exeunt* [OTHELLO *and* DESDEMONA].

EMILIA. I am glad I have found this napkin;
This was her first remembrance from the Moor.
My wayward husband hath a hundred times
Woo'd me to steal it; but she so loves the token,
For he conjur'd her she should ever keep it,
That she reserves it evermore about her
To kiss and talk to. I'll have the work ta'en out
And give 't Iago. What he will do with it
Heaven knows, not I;
I nothing but to please his fantasy.

Re-enter IAGO.

IAGO. How now! what do you here alone?

EMILIA. Do not you chide; I have a thing for you.

IAGO. A thing for me? It is a common thing—

EMILIA. Ha!

IAGO. To have a foolish wife.

EMILIA. O, is that all? What will you give me now
For that same handkerchief?

IAGO. What handkerchief?

EMILIA. What handkerchief!
Why, that the Moor first gave to Desdemona;
That which so often you did bid me steal.

IAGO. Hast stol'n it from her?

EMILIA. No, [faith;] she let it drop by negligence,
And, to th' advantage, I, being here, took 't up.
Look, here it is.

IAGO. A good wench; give it me.

EMILIA. What will you do with 't, that you have been so earnest
To have me filch it?

IAGO [*snatching it*]. Why, what is that to you?

EMILIA. If it be not for some purpose of import,
Give 't me again. Poor lady, she'll run mad
When she shall lack it.

IAGO. Be not acknown on't; I have use for it.
Go, leave me.

[*Exit* EMILIA.

I will in Cassio's lodging lose this napkin,
And let him find it. Trifles light as air
Are to the jealous confirmations strong
As proofs of holy writ; this may do something.
The Moor already changes with my poison.
Dangerous conceits are, in their natures poisons,
Which at the first are scarce found to distaste,
But with a little act upon the blood
Burn like the mines of sulphur. I did say so.

Re-enter OTHELLO.

Look, where he comes! Not poppy, nor mandragora,
Nor all the drowsy syrups of the world
Shall ever medicine thee to that sweet sleep
Which though ow'dst yesterday.

OTHELLO. Ha! ha! false to me?

IAGO. Why, how now, General! no more of that.

OTHELLO. Avaunt! be gone! thou hast set me on the rack
I swear 'tis better to be much abus'd
Than but to know 't a little.

IAGO. How now, my lord!

OTHELLO. What sense had I [of] her stol'n hours of lust?
I saw 't not, thought it not, it harm'd not me.
I slept the next night well, fed well, was free and merry;

---

273. [*of*] Q. *to* F. 276. *forked plague:* curse of cuckold's horns. 277. *quicken:* begin to live. 278. [*O . . . mocks*] Q. *Heaven mock'd* F. 280. *generous:* noble.
287. *napkin:* handkerchief. 288. *it:* i.e., his forehead.
296. *work . . . out:* pattern copied.

311. [*faith*] Q. *but* F. 312. *to th' advantage:* opportunely.
319. *acknown:* aware. 328. *act:* action.
330. *mandragora:* a soporific. 333. *ow'dst:* hadst.
338. [*of*] Q. *in* F.

I found not Cassio's kisses on her lips.
He that is robb'd, not wanting what is stolen,
Let him not know 't, and he's not robb'd at all.
IAGO. I am sorry to hear this.
OTHELLO. I had been happy, if the general camp,
Pioners and all, had tasted her sweet body,
So I had nothing known. O, now, for ever
Farewell the tranquil mind! farewell content!
Farewell the plumed troops and the big wars
That make ambition virtue! O, farewell!
Farewell the neighing steed and the shrill trump,
The spirit-stirring drum, th' ear-piercing fife,
The royal banner, and all quality,
Pride, pomp, and circumstance of glorious war!
And, O you mortal engines, whose rude throats
Th' immortal Jove's dread clamours counterfeit,
Farewell! Othello's occupation's gone!
IAGO. Is 't possible, my lord?
OTHELLO. Villain, be sure thou prove my love a whore;
Be sure of it. Give me the ocular proof;
Or, by the worth of mine eternal soul,
Thou hadst been better have been born a dog
Than answer my wak'd wrath!
IAGO. Is 't come to this?
OTHELLO. Make me to see 't; or, at the least, so prove it
That the probation bear no hinge nor loop
To hang a doubt on; or woe upon thy life!
IAGO. My noble lord,—
OTHELLO. If thou dost slander her and torture me,
Never pray more; abandon all remorse;
On horror's head horrors accumulate;
Do deeds to make heaven weep, all earth amaz'd;
For nothing canst thou to damnation add
Greater than that.
IAGO. O grace! O Heaven forgive me!
Are you a man? Have you a soul or sense?
God buy you; take mine office. O wretched fool,
That lov'st to make thine honesty a vice!
O monstrous world! Take note, take note, O world,
To be direct and honest is not safe.
I thank you for this profit; and from hence
I'll love no friend, sith love breeds such offence.
OTHELLO. Nay, stay. Thou shouldst be honest.
IAGO. I should be wise, for honesty's a fool
And loses that it works for.
OTHELLO. By the world,
I think my wife be honest and think she is not;
I think that thou are just and think thou art not.
I'll have some proof. [Her] name, that was as fresh
As Dian's visage, is now begrim'd and black
As mine own face. If there be cords, or knives,
Poison, or fire, or suffocating streams,
I'll not endure it. Would I were satisfied!
IAGO. I see, [sir], you are eaten up with passion;
I do repent me that I put it to you.
You would be satisfied?
OTHELLO. Would! nay, I will.
IAGO. And may; but, how? How satisfied, my lord?
Would you, the [supervisor], grossly gape on—
Behold her topp'd?
OTHELLO. Death and damnation! O!
IAGO. It were a tedious difficulty, I think,
To bring them to that prospect; [damn] them then,
If ever mortal eyes do see them bolster
More than their own! What then? How then?
What shall I say? Where's satisfaction?
It is impossible you should see this,
Were they as prime as goats, as hot as monkeys,
As salt as wolves in pride, and fools as gross
As ignorance made drunk. But yet, I say,
If imputation and strong circumstances
Which lead directly to the door of truth
Will give you satisfaction, you might have't.
OTHELLO. Give me a living reason she's disloyal.
IAGO. I do not like the office;
But, sith I am ent'red in this cause so far,
Prick'd to't by foolish honesty and love,
I will go on. I lay with Cassio lately;
And, being troubled with a raging tooth,
I could not sleep.
There are a kind of men so loose of soul,
That in their sleeps will mutter their affairs;
One of this kind is Cassio.
In sleep I heard him say, "Sweet Desdemona,
Let us be wary, let us hide our loves";
And then, sir, would he gripe and wring my hand,
Cry, "O sweet creature!" then kiss me hard,
As if he pluck'd up kisses by the roots
That grew upon my lips; then lay his leg
Over my thigh, and sigh, and kiss; and then
Cry, "Cursed fate that gave thee to the Moor!"
OTHELLO. O monstrous! monstrous!
IAGO. Nay, this was but his dream.

346. *Pioners:* the lowest rank of soldiers. 375. *buy:* be with. 376. *lov'st* F. *livest* Q.

386. [*Her*] Q. *My* F. 391. [*sir*] Q. Om. F. 393. *nay* Q. *Nay, and* F. 395. [*supervisor*] Q. *supervision* F. 398. [*damn*] Q. Om. F. 399. *bolster:* lie on a bolster (together). 403. *prime:* lecherous. 404. *pride:* heat.

OTHELLO. But this denoted a foregone conclusion.
'Tis a shrewd doubt, though it be but a dream.
IAGO. And this may help to thicken other proofs
That do demonstrate thinly.
OTHELLO. I'll tear her all to pieces.
IAGO. Nay, [but] be wise; yet we see nothing done.
She may be honest yet. Tell me but this,
Have you not sometimes seen a handkerchief
Spotted with strawberries in your wife's hand?
OTHELLO. I gave her such a one; 'twas my first gift.
IAGO. I know not that; but such a handkerchief—
I am sure it was your wife's—did I to-day
See Cassio wipe his beard with.
OTHELLO. If it be that,—
IAGO. If it be that, or any [that] was hers,
It speaks against her with the other proofs.
OTHELLO. O, that the slave had forty thousand lives!
One is too poor, too weak for my revenge.
Now do I see 'tis true. Look here, Iago;
All my found love thus do I blow to heaven.
'Tis gone.
Arise, black vengeance, from the hollow hell!
Yield up, O love, thy crown and hearted throne
To tyrannous hate! Swell, bosom, with thy fraught,
For 'tis of aspics' tongues!
IAGO. Yet be content.
OTHELLO. O, blood, blood, blood!
IAGO. Patience, I say; your mind [perhaps] may change,
OTHELLO. Never, Iago. Like to the Pontic Sea,
Whose icy current and compulsive course
Ne'er [feels] retiring ebb, but keeps due on
To the Propontic and the Hellespont,
Even so my bloody thoughts, with violent pace,
Shall ne'er look back, ne'er ebb to humble love,
Till that a capable and wide revenge
Swallow them up. Now, by yond marble heaven,
In the due reverence of a sacred vow [*kneels*]
I here engage my words.
IAGO. Do not rise yet.
Witness, you ever-burning lights above,
You elements that clip us round about, [*kneels*]
Witness that here Iago doth give up
The execution of his wit, hands, heart,
To wrong'd Othello's service! Let him command,
And to obey shall be in me remorse,
What bloody business ever.

[*They rise.*]

OTHELLO. I greet thy love,
Not with vain thanks, but with acceptance bounteous,
And will upon the instant put thee to't:
Within these three days let me hear thee say
That Cassio's not alive.
IAGO. My friend is dead; 'tis done at your request.
But let her live.
OTHELLO. Damn her, lewd minx! O, damn her! damn her!
Come, go with me apart; I will withdraw
To furnish me with some swift means of death
For the fair devil. Now art thou my lieutenant.
IAGO. I am your own for ever.

[*Exeunt.*

Scene 4. [*Before the castle.*]

Enter DESDEMONA, EMILIA, *and* CLOWN.

DESDEMONA. Do you know, sirrah, where Lieutenant Cassio lies?

CLOWN. I dare not say he lies anywhere.

DESDEMONA. Why, man?

CLOWN. He's a soldier, and for me to say a soldier lies, 'tis stabbing.

DESDEMONA. Go to! Where lodges he?

CLOWN. To tell you where he lodges, is to tell you where I lie.

DESDEMONA. Can anything be made of this?

CLOWN. I know not where he lodges, and for me to devise a lodging and say he lies here or he lies there, were to lie in mine own throat.

DESDEMONA. Can you inquire him out, and be edified by report?

CLOWN. I will catechize the world for him; that is, make questions, and by them answer.

DESDEMONA. Seek him, bid him come hither. Tell him I have mov'd my lord on his behalf, and hope all will be well.

CLOWN. To do this is within the compass of man's wit; and therefore I will attempt the doing it.

[*Exit.*

428. *foregone conclusion:* earlier act. 429. *shrewd doubt:* strong reason for suspicion. 432. [*but*] Q. *yet* F. 440. [*that*]. *it* QF. 449. *fraught:* burden. 450. *aspics':* asps'. 452. [*perhaps*] Q. Om. F. 453. *Pontic Sea:* Black Sea. 455. [*feels*] Q_2. *keeps* F. 459. *capable:* comprehensive. 464. *clip:* embrace. 466. *execution:* action.

468. *remorse:* obligation.

Scene iv, 2. *lies:* lodges.

DESDEMONA. Where should I lose the handkerchief, Emilia?
EMILIA. I know not, madam.
DESDEMONA. Believe me, I had rather have lost my purse
Full of crusadoes; and, but my noble Moor
Is true of mind and made of no such baseness
As jealous creatures are, it were enough
To put him to ill thinking.
EMILIA. Is he not jealous?
DESDEMONA. Who, he? I think the sun where he was born
Drew all such humours from him.
EMILIA. Look, where he comes.

Enter OTHELLO.

DESDEMONA. I will not leave him now till Cassio
Be call'ed to him.—How is't with you, my lord?
OTHELLO. Well, my good lady. [*Aside.*] O, hardness to dissemble!—
How do you, Desdemona?
DESDEMONA. Well, my good lord.
OTHELLO. Give me your hand. This hand is moist, my lady.
DESDEMONA. It [yet] hath felt no age nor known no sorrow.
OTHELLO. This argues fruitfulness and liberal heart;
Hot, hot, and moist. This hand of yours requires
A sequester from liberty, fasting and prayer.
Much castigation, exercise devout;
For here's a young and sweating devil here
That commonly rebels. 'Tis a good hand,
A frank one.
DESDEMONA. You may, indeed, say so;
For 'twas that hand that gave away my heart.
OTHELLO. A liberal hand. The hearts of old gave hands;
But our new heraldry is hands, not hearts.
DESDEMONA. I cannot speak of this. Come now, your promise.
OTHELLO. What promise, chuck?
DESDEMONA. I have sent to bid Cassio come speak with you.
OTHELLO. I have a salt and sorry rheum offends me;
Lend me thy handkerchief.
DESDEMONA. Here, my lord.
OTHELLO. That which I gave you.
DESDEMONA. I have it not about me.
OTHELLO. Not?
DESDEMONA. No, indeed, my lord.
OTHELLO. That's a fault. That handkerchief
Did an Egyptian to my mother give;
She was a charmer, and could almost read
The thoughts of people. She told her, while she kept it
'Twould make her amiable and subdue my father
Entirely to her love, but if she lost it,
Or made a gift of it, my father's eye
Should hold her loathed and his spirits should hunt
After new fancies. She, dying, gave it me
And bid me, when my fate would have me wiv'd,
To give it her. I did so; and take heed on't;
Make it a darling like your precious eye.
To lose't or give't away were such perdition
As nothing else could match.
DESDEMONA. Is't possible?
OTHELLO. 'Tis true; there's magic in the web of it.
A sibyl, that had numb'red in the world
The sun to course two hundred compasses,
In her prophetic fury sew'd the work;
The worms were hallowed that did breed the silk;
And it was dy'd in mummy which the skilful
Conserv'd of maidens' hearts.
DESDEMONA. Indeed! is't true?
OTHELLO. Most veritable; therefore look to't well.
DESDEMONA. Then would to [God] that I had never seen 't!
OTHELLO. Ha! wherefore?
DESDEMONA. Why do you speak so startingly and rash?
OTHELLO. Is't lost? Is't gone? Speak, is't out o' th' way?
DESDEMONA. [Heaven] bless us!
OTHELLO. Say you?
DESDEMONA. It is not lost; but what an if it were?
OTHELLO. How?
DESDEMONA. I say, it is not lost.
OTHELLO. Fetch 't, let me see 't.
DESDEMONA. Why, so I can, [sir,] but I will not now.
This is a trick to put me from my suit.
Pray you, let Cassio be receiv'd again.
OTHELLO. Fetch me the handkerchief; my mind misgives.
DESDEMONA. Come, come;
You'll never meet a more sufficient man.
OTHELLO. The handkerchief!

---

26. *crusadoes:* Portuguese coins stamped with a cross. 37. [*yet*] Q. Om. F. 40. *sequester:* separation. 48. *our new heraldry:* Probably a topical allusion. 52. *sorry:* distressing.

57. *Egyptian:* gypsy. 58. *charmer:* sorcerer. 60. *amiable:* lovable. 75. *mummy:* embalming fluid. 76. *Conserv'd:* prepared. 87. [*sir*] Q. Om. F.

[DESDEMONA. I pray, talk me of Cassio.
OTHELLO. The handkerchief!]
DESDEMONA. A man that all his time
Hath founded his good fortunes on your love,
Shar'd dangers with you,—
OTHELLO. The handkerchief!
DESDEMONA. In sooth, you are to blame.
OTHELLO. ['Zounds!] [*Exit.*
EMILIA. Is not this man jealous?
DESDEMONA. I ne'er saw this before.
Sure, there's some wonder in this handkerchief;
I am most unhappy in the loss of it.
EMILIA. 'Tis not a year or two shows us a man.
They are all but stomachs, and we all but food;
They eat us hungerly, and when they are full
They belch us.

Enter CASSIO *and* IAGO.

Look you, Cassio and my husband!
IAGO. There is no other way, 'tis she must do't;
And, lo, the happiness! Go, and importune her.
DESDEMONA. How now, good Cassio! What's the news with you?
CASSIO. Madam, my former suit. I do beseech you
That by your virtuous means I may again
Exist, and be a member of his love
Whom I with all the office of my heart
Entirely honour. I would not be delay'd.
If my offence be of such mortal kind
That nor my service past, nor present sorrows,
Nor purpos'd merit in futurity
Can ransom me into his love again,
But to know so must be my benefit;
So shall I clothe me in a forc'd content,
And shut myself up in some other course,
To fortune's alms.
DESDEMONA. Alas, thrice-gentle Cassio!
My advocation is not now in tune.
My lord is not my lord; nor should I know him
Were he in favour as in humour alter'd.
So help me every spirit sanctified
As I have spoken for you all my best
And stood within the blank of his displeasure
For my free speech! You must a while be patient.
What I can do I will; and more I will
Than for myself I dare. Let that suffice you.
IAGO. Is my lord angry?
EMILIA. He went hence but now,
And certainly in strange unquietness.
IAGO. Can he be angry? I have seen the cannon
When it hath blown his ranks into the air,
And, like the devil, from his very arm
Puff'd his own brother:—and is he angry?
Something of moment then. I will go meet him.
There's matter in't indeed, if he be angry. [*Exit* IAGO.
DESDEMONA. I prithee, do so. Something, sure, of state,
Either from Venice, or some unhatch'd practice
Made demonstrable here in Cyprus to him,
Hath puddled his clear spirit; and in such cases
Men's natures wrangle with inferior things,
Though great ones are their object. 'Tis even so;
For let our finger ache, and it indues
Our other, healthful members even to a sense
Of pain. Nay, we must think men are not gods,
Nor of them look for such observancy
As fits the bridal. Beshrew me much, Emilia,
I was, unhandsome warrior as I am,
Arraigning his unkindness with my soul;
But now I find I had suborn'd the witness,
And he's indicted falsely.
EMILIA. Pray Heaven it be state-matters, as you think,
And no conception nor no jealous toy
Concerning you.
DESDEMONA. Alas the day! I never gave him cause.
EMILIA. But jealous souls will not be answer'd so;
They are not ever jealous for the cause,
But jealous for they're jealous. It is a monster
Begot upon itself, born on itself.
DESDEMONA. Heaven keep the monster from Othello's mind!
EMILIA. Lady, amen.
DESDEMONA. I will go seek him. Cassio, walk hereabout;
If I do find him fit, I'll move your suit
And seek to effect it to my uttermost.
CASSIO. I humbly thank your ladyship.

[*Exeunt* [DESDEMONA *and* EMILIA]. *Enter* BIANCA.

BIANCA. Save you, friend Cassio!
CASSIO. What make you from home?
How it is with you, my most fair Bianca?
Indeed, sweet love, I was coming to your house.
BIANCA. And I was going to your lodging, Cassio.
What, keep a week away? seven days and nights?

93–94. [DESDEMONA. *I... handkerchief*] Q. Om. F.
99. [*'Zounds*] Q. *Away* F. 109. *happiness:* luck.
112. *virtuous:* effective. 126. *favour:* appearance.
129. *blank:* target; strictly, the white spot in the center.

142. *practice:* plot.

Eightscore eight hours? and lovers' absent hours,
More tedious than the dial eightscore times?
O weary reck'ning!

CASSIO. Pardon me, Bianca.
I have this while with leaden thoughts been press'd;
But I shall, in a more continuate time,
Strike off this score of absence. Sweet Bianca [*giving her* DESDEMONA'*s handkerchief*],
Take me this work out.

BIANCA. O Cassio, whence came this?
This is some token from a newer friend;
To the felt absence now I feel a cause,
Is't come to this? Well, well.

CASSIO. Go to, woman!
Throw your vile guesses in the devil's teeth,
From whence you have them. You are jealous now
That this is from some mistress, some remembrance.
No, in good troth, Bianca.

BIANCA. Why, whose is it?

CASSIO. I know not, [sweet]; I found it in my chamber.
I like the work well; ere it be demanded—
As like enough it will—I'd have it copied.
Take it, and do't; and leave me for this time.

BIANCA. Leave you! Wherefore?

CASSIO. I do attend here on the General;
And think it no addition, nor my wish,
To have him see me woman'd.

BIANCA. Why, I pray you?

CASSIO. Not that I love you not.

BIANCA. But that you do not love me.
I pray you, bring me on the way a little,
And say if I shall see you soon at night.

CASSIO. 'Tis but a little way that I can bring you,
For I attend here; but I'll see you soon.

BIANCA. 'Tis very good; I must be circumstanc'd.

[*Exeunt.*

ACT FOUR

Scene 1. [*Cyprus. Before the castle.*]

Enter OTHELLO *and* IAGO.

IAGO. Will you think so?

OTHELLO. Think so, Iago!

IAGO. What,
To kiss in private?

OTHELLO. An unauthoriz'd kiss.

IAGO. Or to be naked with her friend in bed
An hour or more, not meaning any harm?

OTHELLO. Naked in bed, Iago, and not mean harm!
It is hypocrisy against the devil.
They that mean virtuously, and yet do so,
The devil their virtue tempts, and they tempt heaven.

IAGO. If they do nothing, 'tis a venial slip;
But if I give my wife a handkerchief,—

OTHELLO. What then?

IAGO. Why, then, 'tis hers, my lord; and, being hers,
She may, I think bestow 't on any man.

OTHELLO. She is protectress of her honour too;
May she give that?

IAGO. Her honour is an essence that's not seen;
They have it very oft that have it not:
But, for the handkerchief,—

OTHELLO. By heaven, I would most gladly have forgot it.
Thou said'st—O, it comes o'er my memory,
As doth the raven o'er the infectious house,
Boding to all—he had my handkerchief.

IAGO. Ay, what of that?

OTHELLO. That's not so good now.

IAGO. What
If I had said I had seen him do you wrong?
Or heard him say,—as knaves be such abroad,
Who having, by their own importunate suit,
Or voluntary dotage of some mistress,
Convinced or suppli'd them, cannot choose
But they must blab—

OTHELLO. Hath he said anything?

IAGO. He hath, my lord; but be you well assur'd,
No more than he'll unswear.

OTHELLO. What hath he said?

IAGO. Why, that he did—I know not what he did.

OTHELLO. What? what?

IAGO. Lie—

OTHELLO. With her?

IAGO. With her, on her; what you will.

OTHELLO. Lie with her! lie on her! We say lie on her, when they belie her. Lie with her! ['Zounds,] that's fulsome!—Handkerchief—confessions—handkerchief!—To confess, and be hang'd for his labour;—first to be hang'd, and then to confess.—I tremble at it. Nature would not invest herself in such shadowing passion without some instruction. It is not words that shakes me thus. Pish!

---

179. *continuate:* uninterrupted. 189. [*sweet*] Q. *neither* F. 195. *addition:* credit. 202. *circumstance'd:* reconciled.

Act IV, Scene i, 40–42. *invest...instruction:* i.e., create such imaginings unless to teach me.

Noses, ears, and lips.—Is't possible?—Confess—
handkerchief!—O devil! [*Falls in a trance.*
IAGO. Work on,
My medicine, work! Thus credulous fools are caught;
And many worthy and chaste dames even thus,
All guiltless, meet reproach.—What, ho! my lord!
My lord, I say! Othello!

Enter CASSIO.

How now, Cassio!
CASSIO. What's the matter?
IAGO. My lord is fall'n into an epilepsy.
This is his second fit; he had one yesterday.
CASSIO. Rub him about the temples.
IAGO. [No, forbear;]
The lethargy must have his quiet course;
If not, he foams at mouth and by and by
Breaks out to savage madness. Look, he stirs.
Do you withdraw yourself a little while;
He will recover straight. When he is gone,
I would on great occasion speak with you.

[*Exit* CASSIO.

How is it, General? Have you not hurt your head?
OTHELLO. Dost thou mock me?
IAGO. I mock you not, by heaven.
Would you would bear your fortune like a man!
OTHELLO. A horned man's a monster and a beast.
IAGO. There's many a beast then in a populous city,
And many a civil monster.
OTHELLO. Did he confess it?
IAGO. Good sir, be a man;
Think every bearded fellow that's but yok'd
May draw with you. There's millions now alive
That nightly lie in those unproper beds
Which they dare swear peculiar; your case is better.
O, 'tis the spite of hell, the fiend's arch-mock,
To lip a wanton in a secure couch,
And to suppose her chaste! No, let me know;
And knowing what I am, I know what she shall be.
OTHELLO. O, thou art wise; 'tis certain.
IAGO. Stand you a while apart;
Confine yourself but in a patient list.
Whilst you were here o'erwhelmed with your grief—
A passion most [unsuiting] such a man—
Cassio came hither. I shifted him away,
And laid good 'scuse upon your ecstasy;
Bade him anon return and here speak with me,
The which he promis'd. Do but encave yourself,
And mark the fleers, the gibes, and notable scorns
That dwell in every region of his face;
For I will make him tell the tale anew,
Where, how, how oft, how long ago, and when
He hath, and is again to cope your wife.
I say, but mark his gesture. Marry, patience;
Or I shall say you're all in all in spleen,
And nothing of a man.
OTHELLO. Dost thou hear, Iago?
I will be found most cunning in my patience;
But—dost thou hear?—most bloody.
IAGO. That's not amiss;
But yet keep time in all. Will you withdraw?

[OTHELLO *retires.*]

Now will I question Cassio of Bianca,
A housewife that by selling her desires
Buys herself bread and clothes. It is a creature
That dotes on Cassio, as 'tis the strumpet's plague
To beguile many and be beguil'd by one.
He, when he hears of her, cannot [refrain]
From the excess of laughter. Here he comes.

Re-enter CASSIO.

As he shall smile, Othello shall go mad;
And his unbookish jealousy must [conster]
Poor Cassio's smiles, gestures, and light behaviors
Quite in the wrong. How do you, Lieutenant?
CASSIO. The worser that you give me the addition
Whose want even kills me.
IAGO. Ply Desdemona well, and you are sure on't.
[*Speaking lower.*] Now, if this suit lay in Bianca's [power],
How quickly should you speed!
CASSIO. Alas, poor caitiff!
OTHELLO. Look how he laughs already!
IAGO. I never knew woman love man so.
CASSIO. Alas, poor rogue! I think, indeed, she loves me.
OTHELLO. Now he denies it faintly, and laughs it out.
IAGO. Do you hear, Cassio?
OTHELLO. Now he importunes him
To tell it o'er. Go to; well said, well said.
IAGO. She gives it out that you shall marry her.

---

53. [*No, forbear*] Q. Om. F. 55. *by and by:* straightaway.
65. *civil:* civilized. 69. *unproper:* not exclusively their own.
70. *peculiar:* their own. 72. *secure:* supposed safe from others. 76. *a patient list:* the bounds of patience.
78. [*unsuiting*] Q. *resulting* F.

80. *ecstasy:* trance. 89. *spleen:* anger, passion.
99. [*refrain*] Q. *restraine* F. 102. [*conster*] Q: construe. *conserve* F. 108. [*power*] Q. *dowre* F.

Do you intend it?

CASSIO. Ha, ha, ha!

OTHELLO. Do ye triumph, Roman? Do you triumph?

CASSIO. I marry [her]!! What? a customer! Prithee, bear some charity to my wit; do not think it so unwholesome. Ha, ha, ha!

OTHELLO. So, so so, so; they laugh that win.

IAGO. Why, the cry goes that you [shall] marry her.

CASSIO. Prithee, say true.

IAGO. I am a very villain else.

OTHELLO. Have you scor'd me? Well.

CASSIO. This is the monkey's own giving out. She is persuaded I will marry her, out of her own love and flattery, not out of my promise.

OTHELLO. Iago [beckons] me; now he begins the story.

CASSIO. She was here even now; she haunts me in every place. I was the other day talking on the seabank with certain Venetians; and thither comes the bauble, and, falls me thus about my neck—

OTHELLO. Crying, "O dear Cassio!" as it were; his gesture imports it.

CASSIO. So hangs, and lolls, and weeps upon me; so shakes and pulls me. Ha, ha, ha!

OTHELLO. Now he tells how she pluck'd him to my chamber. Oh, I see that nose of yours, but not that dog I shall throw it to.

CASSIO. Well, I must leave her company.

IAGO. Before me! look, where she comes.

Enter BIANCA.

CASSIO. 'Tis such another fitchew! Marry, a perfum'd one.—What do you mean by this haunting of me?

BIANCA. Let the devil and his dam haunt you! What did you mean by that same handkerchief you gave me even now? I was a fine fool to take it. I must take out the work?—A likely piece of work, that you should find it in your chamber, and know not who left it there! This is some minx's token, and I must take out the work? There; give it your hobbyhorse. Wheresoever you had it, I'll take out no work on't.

CASSIO. How now, my sweet Bianca! how now! how now!

OTHELLO. By heaven, that should be my handkerchief!

BIANCA. If you'll come to supper to-night, you may; if you will not, come when you are next prepar'd for.

[*Exit.*

IAGO. After her, after her.

CASSIO. [Faith,] I must; she'll rail in the streets else.

IAGO. Will you sup there?

CASSIO. Yes, I intend so.

IAGO. Well, I may chance to see you; for I would very fain speak with you.

CASSIO. Prithee, come; will you?

IAGO. Go to; say no more.

[*Exit* CASSIO.

OTHELLO [*advancing*] How shall I murder him, Iago?

IAGO. Did you perceive how he laugh'd at his vice?

OTHELLO. O Iago!

IAGO. And did you see the handkerchief?

OTHELLO. Was that mine?

IAGO. Yours, by this hand. And to see how he prizes the foolish woman your wife! She gave it him, and he hath given it his whore.

OTHELLO. I would have him nine years a-killing. A fine woman! a fair woman! a sweet woman!

IAGO. Nay, you must forget that.

OTHELLO. Ay, let her rot, and perish, and be damn'd to-night; for she shall not live. No, my heart is turn'd to stone; I strike it, and it hurts my hand. O, the world hath not a sweeter creature! She might lie by an emperor's side and command him tasks.

IAGO. Nay, that's not your way.

OTHELLO. Hang her! I do but say what she is. So delicate with her needle! an admirable musician! O! she will sing the savageness out of a bear. Of so high and plenteous wit and invention!

IAGO. She's the worse for all this.

OTHELLO. O, a thousand thousand times. And then, of so gentle a condition!

IAGO. Ay, too gentle.

OTHELLO. Nay, that's certain. But yet the pity of it, Iago! O Iago, the pity of it, Iago!

IAGO. If you are so fond over her iniquity, give her patent to offend; for if it touch not you, it comes near nobody.

OTHELLO. I will chop her into messes. Cuckold me!

IAGO. O, 'tis foul in her.

OTHELLO. With mine officer!

IAGO. That's fouler.

---

121. [*her*] Q. Om. F. *customer:* harlot. 125. [*shall*] Q. Om. F. 128. *scor'd*: branded. 132. [*beckons*] Q. *becomes* F. 147. *fitchew:* polecat.

204. *messes:* portions of food.

OTHELLO. Get me some poison, Iago; this night. I'll not expostulate with her, lest her body and beauty unprovide my mind again. This night, Iago.

IAGO. Do it not with poison; strangle her in her bed, even the bed she hath contaminated.

OTHELLO. Good, good; the justice of it pleases; very good.

IAGO. And for Cassio, let me be his undertaker. You shall hear more by midnight.

[*A trumpet. Enter* LODOVICO, DESDEMONA, *and* Attendants.

OTHELLO. Excellent good. What trumpet is that same?

IAGO. I warrant, something from Venice. 'Tis Lodovico, this, comes from the Duke. See, your wife's with him.

LODOVICO. Save you, worthy General!

OTHELLO. With all my heart, sir.

LODOVICO. The Duke and Senators of Venice greet you. [*Gives him a letter.*]

OTHELLO. I kiss the instrument of their pleasures. [*Opens the letter, and reads.*]

DESDEMONA. And what's the news, good cousin Lodovico?

IAGO. I am very glad to see you, signior;
Welcome to Cyprus.

LODOVICO. I thank you. How does Lieutenant Cassio?

IAGO. Lives, sir.

DESDEMONA. Cousin, there's fall'n between him and my lord
An unkind breach; but you shall make all well.

OTHELLO. Are you sure of that?

DESDEMONA. My lord?

OTHELLO [*reads*]. "This fail you not to do, as you will."—

LODOVICO. He did not call; he's busy in the paper. Is there division 'twixt my lord and Cassio?

DESDEMONA. A most unhappy one. I would do much
T' atone them, for the love I bear to Cassio.

OTHELLO. Fire and brimstone!

DESDEMONA. My lord?

OTHELLO. Are you wise?

DESDEMONA. What, is he angry?

LODOVICO. May be the letter mov'd him;
For, as I think, they do command him home,
Deputing Cassio in his government.

DESDEMONA. Trust me, I am glad on't.

OTHELLO. Indeed!

DESDEMONA. My lord?

OTHELLO. I am glad to see you mad.

DESDEMONA. Why, sweet Othello,—

OTHELLO [*striking her*]. Devil!

DESDEMONA. I have not deserv'd this.

LODOVICO. My lord, this would not be believ'd in Venice
Though I should swear I saw 't. 'Tis very much.
Make her amends: she weeps.

OTHELLO. O devil, devil!
If that the earth could teem with woman's tears,
Each drop she falls would prove a crocodile.
Out of my sight!

DESDEMONA. I will not stay to offend you. [*Going.*]

LODOVICO. Truly, [an] obedient lady:
I do beseech your lordship, call her back.

OTHELLO. Mistress!

DESDEMONA. My lord?

OTHELLO. What would you with her, sir?

LODOVICO. Who, I, my lord?

OTHELLO. Ay; you did wish that I would make her turn.
Sir, she can turn, and turn, and yet go on,
And turn again; and she can weep, sir, weep;
And she's obedient, as you say, obedient,
Very obedient. Proceed you in your tears.
Concerning this, sir,—O well-painted passion!—
I am commanded home.—Get you away;
I'll send for you anon.—Sir, I obey the mandate,
And will return to Venice.—Hence, avaunt!—

[*Exit* DESDEMONA.]

Cassio shall have my place. And, sir, to-night
I do entreat that we may sup together.
You are welcome, sir, to Cyprus.—Goats and monkeys! [*Exit.*

LODOVICO. Is this the noble Moor whom our full Senate
Call all in all sufficient? Is this the nature
Whom passion could not shake? whose solid virtue
The shot of accident nor dart of chance
Could neither graze nor pierce?

IAGO. He is much chang'd.

LODOVICO. Are his wits safe? Is he not light of brain?

IAGO. He's that he is; I may not breathe my censure
What he might be. If what he might he is not,
I would to heaven he were!

LODOVICO. What, strike his wife!

---

215. *undertaker:* dispatcher. 238. *atone:* reconcile.

250. *teem:* breed. 254. [*an*] Q. Om. F.

IAGO. Faith, that was not so well; yet would I knew
That stroke would prove the worst!
LODOVICO. Is it his use?
Or did the letters work upon his blood
And new-create [this] fault?
IAGO. Alas, alas!
It is not honesty in me to speak
What I have seen and known. You shall observe him,
And his own courses will denote him so
That I may save my speech. Do but go after,
And mark how he continues.
LODOVICO. I am sorry that I am deceiv'd in him.

[*Exeunt.*

Scene 2. [*A room in the castle.*]

Enter OTHELLO *and* EMILIA.

OTHELLO. You have seen nothing then?
EMILIA. Nor ever heard, nor ever did suspect.
OTHELLO. Yes, you have seen Cassio and she together.
EMILIA. But then I saw no harm, and then I heard
Each syllable that breath made up between them.
OTHELLO. What, did they never whisper?
EMILIA. Never, my lord.
OTHELLO. Nor send you out o' th' way?
EMILIA. Never.
OTHELLO. To fetch her fan, her gloves, her mask, nor nothing?
EMILIA. Never, my lord.
OTHELLO. That's strange.
EMILIA. I durst, my lord, to wager she is honest,
Lay down my soul at stake. If you think other,
Remove your thought; it doth abuse your bosom.
If any wretch have put this in your head,
Let Heaven requite it with the serpent's curse!
For, if she be not honest, chaste, and true,
There's no man happy; the purest of their wives
Is foul as slander.
OTHELLO. Bid her come hither; go.

[*Exit* EMILIA.

She says enough; yet she's a simple bawd
That cannot say as much. This is a subtle whore,
A closet lock and key of villainous secrets;
And yet she'll kneel and pray; I have seen her do't.

[*Enter* DESDEMONA *with* EMILIA.

DESDEMONA. My lord, what is your will?

283. [*this*] Q. *his* F.

OTHELLO. Pray, chuck, come hither.
DESDEMONA. What is your pleasure?
OTHELLO. Let me see your eyes;
Look in my face.
DESDEMONA. What horrible fancy's this?
OTHELLO [*to* EMILIA]. Some of your function, mistress;
Leave procreants alone and shut the door;
Cough, or cry "hem," if anybody come.
Your mystery, your mystery; nay, dispatch.

[*Exit* EMILIA.

DESDEMONA. Upon my knee, what doth your speech import?
I understand a fury in your words,
[But not the words.]
OTHELLO. Why, what art thou?
DESDEMONA. Your wife, my lord; your true
And loyal wife.
OTHELLO. Come, swear it, damn thyself,
Lest, being like one of heaven, the devils themselves
Should fear to seize thee; therefore be double damn'd,
Swear thou art honest.
DESDEMONA. Heaven doth truly know it.
OTHELLO. Heaven truly knows that thou art false as hell.
DESDEMONA. To whom, my lord? With whom? How am I false?
OTHELLO. Ah, Desdemon! Away! away! away!
DESDEMONA. Alas the heavy day! Why do you weep?
Am I the motive of these tears, my lord?
If haply you my father do suspect
An instrument of this your calling back,
Lay not your blame on me. If you have lost him,
[Why,] I have lost him too.
OTHELLO. Had it pleas'd Heaven
To try me with affliction; had they rain'd
All kind of sores and shames on my bare head,
Steep'd me in poverty to the very lips,
Given to captivity me and my utmost hopes,
I should have found in some place of my soul
A drop of patience; but, alas, to make me
The fixed figure for the time of scorn
To point his slow and moving finger at!

Scene ii, 24. *Pray* Q. *Pray you* F. 30. *mystery:* trade. 33. [*But...words*] Q. Om. F. 47. [*Why*] Q. Om. F. 54. *time of scorn:* scorn of the age. 55. *slow and moving:* slowly moving. Q reads *slow unmoving.*

Yet could I bear that too, well, very well;
But there, where I have garner'd up my heart,
Where either I must live or bear no life;
The fountain from which my current runs
Or else dries up; to be discarded thence!
Or keep it as a cistern for foul toads
To knot and gender in! Turn thy complexion there,
Patience, thou young and rose-lipp'd cherubin,
[Ay, there] look grim as hell!

DESDEMONA. I hope my noble lord esteems me honest.

OTHELLO. O, ay; as summer flies are in the shambles,
That quicken even with blowing. O thou weed,
Who art so lovely fair and smell'st so sweet
That the sense aches at thee, would thou hadst ne'er been born!

DESDEMONA. Alas, what ignorant sin have I committed?

OTHELLO. Was this fair paper, this most goodly book,
Made to write "whore" upon? What committed!
Committed! O thou public commoner!
I should make very forges of my cheeks,
That would to cinders burn up modesty,
Did I but speak thy deeds. What committed!
Heaven stops the nose at it, and the moon winks;
The bawdy wind, that kisses all it meets,
Is hush'd within the hollow mine of earth
And will not hear it. What committed!
[Impudent strumpet!]

DESDEMONA. By heaven, you do me wrong.

OTHELLO. Are not you a strumpet?

DESDEMONA. No, as I am a Christian.
If to preserve this vessel for my lord
From any other foul unlawful touch
Be not to be a strumpet, I am none.

OTHELLO. What, not a whore?

DESDEMONA. No, as I shall be sav'd.

OTHELLO. Is't possible?

DESDEMONA. O, Heaven forgive us!

OTHELLO. I cry you mercy, then.
I took you for that cunning whore of Venice
That married with Othello. [*Raising his voice.*]—You, mistress,

Re-enter EMILIA.

That have the office opposite to Saint Peter,
And keeps the gate of hell! You, you, ay, you!
We have done our course; there's money for your pains.
I pray you, turn the key and keep our counsel. [*Exit*

EMILIA. Alas, what does this gentleman conceive?
How do you, madam? How do you, my good lady?

DESDEMONA. Faith, half asleep.

EMILIA. Good madam, what's the matter with my lord?

DESDEMONA. With who?

EMILIA. Why, with my lord, madam.

DESDEMONA. Who is thy lord?

EMILIA. He that is yours, sweet lady.

DESDEMONA. I have none. Do not talk to me, Emilia;
I cannot weep, nor answers have I none
But what should go by water. Prithee, tonight
Lay on my bed my wedding sheets, remember;
And call thy husband hither.

EMILIA. Here's a change indeed! [*Exit.*

DESDEMONA. 'Tis meet I should be us'd so, very meet.
How have I been behav'd, that he might stick
The small'st opinion on my least misuse?

Re-enter EMILIA *with* IAGO.

IAGO. What is your pleasure, madam? How is't with you?

DESDEMONA. I cannot tell. Those that do teach young babes
Do it with gentle means and easy tasks.
He might have chid me so; for, in good faith,
I am a child to chiding.

IAGO. What's the matter, lady?

EMILIA. Alas, Iago, my lord hath so bewhor'd her,
Thrown such despite and heavy terms upon her,
That true hearts cannot bear it.

DESDEMONA. Am I that name, Iago?

IAGO. What name, fair lady?

DESDEMONA. Such as she said my lord did say I was.

EMILIA. He call'd her whore. A beggar in his drink
Could not have laid such terms upon his callet.

IAGO. Why did he so?

DESDEMONA. I do not know; I am sure I am none such.

IAGO. Do not weep, do not weep. Alas the day!

EMILIA. Hath she forsook so many noble matches,
Her father and her country and her friends,
To be call'd whore? Would it not make one weep?

---

62. *Turn thy complexion:* change thy color. 64. [*Ay, there*] *I here* FQ. 67. *quicken…blowing:* come to life as soon as impregnated. 73. *commoner:* harlot. 77. *winks:* shuts her eyes. 81. [*Impudent strumpet*] Q. Om. F.

104. *go by water:* be rendered by tears. 109. *opinion:* censure. *misuse:* misconduct. 121. *callet:* whore.

DESDEMONA. It is my wretched fortune.
IAGO. Beshrew him for't!
How comes this trick upon him?
DESDEMONA. Nay, Heaven doth know.
EMILIA. I will be hang'd if some eternal villain,
Some busy and insinuating rogue,
Some cogging, cozening slave, to get some office,
Have not devis'd this slander. I'll be hang'd else.
IAGO. Fie, there is no such man; it is impossible.
DESDEMONA. If any such there be, Heaven pardon him.
EMILIA. A halter pardon him! and hell gnaw his bones!
Why should he call her whore? Who keeps her company?
What place? what time? what form? what likelihood?
The Moor's abus'd by some most villainous knave,
Some base notorious knave, some scurvy fellow.
O heavens, that such companions thou'dst unfold,
And put in every honest hand a whip
To lash the rascals naked through the world
Even from the east to th' west!
IAGO. Speak within door.
EMILIA. O, fie upon them! Some such squire he was
That turn'd your wit the seamy side without,
And made you to suspect me with the Moor.
IAGO. You are a fool; go to.
DESDEMONA. Alas, Iago,
What shall I do to win my lord again?
Good friend, go to him; for, by this light of heaven,
I know not how I lost him. Here I kneel:
If e'er my will did trespass 'gainst his love,
Either in discourse of thought or actual deed,
Or that mine eyes, mine ears, or any sense
Delighted them [in] any other form;
Or that I do not yet, and ever did,
And ever will—though he do shake me off
To beggarly divorcement—love him dearly,
Comfort forswear me! Unkindness may do much:
And his unkindness may defeat my life,
But never taint my love. I cannot say "whore."
It does abhor me now I speak the word;
To do the act that might the addition earn
Not the world's mass of vanity could make me.
IAGO. I pray you, be content; 'tis but his humour.
The business of the state does him offence,
[And he does chide with you.]
DESDEMONA. If 'twere no other,—
IAGO. It is but so, I warrant.

[*Trumpets within.*]

Hark, how these instruments summon to supper!
The messengers of Venice stay the meat.
Go in, and weep not; all things shall be well.

[*Exeunt* DESDEMONA *and* EMILIA. *Enter* RODERIGO.

How now, Roderigo!

RODERIGO. I do not find that thou deal'st justly with me.

IAGO. What in the contrary?

RODERIGO. Every day thou daff'st me with some device, Iago; and rather, as it seems to me now, keep'st from me all conveniency than suppliest me with the least advantage of hope. I will indeed no longer endure it, nor am I yet persuaded to put up in peace what already I have foolishly suff'red.

IAGO. Will you hear me, Roderigo?

RODERIGO. I have heard too much, and your words and performances are no kin together.

IAGO. You charge me most unjustly.

RODERIGO. With nought but truth. I have wasted myself out of my means. The jewels you have had from me to deliver Desdemona would half have corrupted a votarist. You have told me she hath receiv'd them and return'd me expectations and comforts of sudden respect and acquaintance, but I find none.

IAGO. Well; go to; very well.

RODERIGO. Very well! go to! I cannot go to, man; nor 'tis not very well. Nay, I think it is scurvy, and begin to find myself fopp'd in it.

IAGO. Very well.

RODERIGO. I tell you 'tis not very well. I will make myself known to Desdemona. If she will return me my jewels, I will give over my suit and repent my unlawful solicitation; if not, assure yourself I will seek satisfaction of you.

IAGO. You have said now.

RODERIGO. Ay, and said nothing but what I protest intendment of doing.

IAGO. Why, now I see there's mettle in thee, and even from this instant do build on thee a better opinion than ever before. Give me thy hand, Roderigo. Thou hast taken against me a most just exception;

---

132. *cogging:* lying. *cozening:* cheating. 141. *unfold:* expose. 153. *discourse:* course. 155. [*in*] Q_2. *or* F. 160. *defeat:* destroy. 167. [*And...you*] Q. Om. F.

170. *stay the meat:* wait to dine. 175. *daff'st me:* puttest me off. 188. *votarist:* nun. 190. *sudden respect:* speedy notice. 195. *fopp'd:* duped.

but yet, I protest, I have dealt most directly in thy affair.

RODERIGO. It hath not appear'd.

IAGO. I grant indeed it hath not appear'd, and your suspicion is not without wit and judgement. But, Roderigo, if thou hast that in thee indeed, which I have greater reason to believe now than ever, I mean purpose, courage, and valour, this night show it. If thou the next night following enjoy not Desdemona, take me from this world with treachery and devise engines for my life.

RODERIGO. Well, what is it? Is it within reason and compass?

IAGO. Sir, there is especial commission come from Venice to depute Cassio in Othello's place.

RODERIGO. Is that true? Why, then Othello and Desdemona return again to Venice.

IAGO. O, no; he goes into Mauritania and taketh away with him the fair Desdemona, unless his abode be ling'red here by some accident; wherein none can be so determinate as the removing of Cassio.

RODERIGO. How do you mean, removing him?

IAGO. Why, by making him uncapable of Othello's place; knocking out his brains.

RODERIGO. And that you would have me to do?

IAGO. Ay, if you dare do yourself a profit and a right. He sups tonight with a harlotry, and thither will I go to him; he knows not yet of his honourable fortune. If you will watch his going thence, which I will fashion to fall out between twelve and one, you may take him at your pleasure. I will be near to second your attempt, and he shall fall between us. Come, stand not amaz'd at it, but go along with me; I will show you such a necessity in his death that you shall think yourself bound to put it on him. It is now high supper-time, and the night grows to waste. About it.

RODERIGO. I will hear further reason for this.

IAGO. And you shall be satisfi'd.

[*Exeunt.*

Scene 3. [*Another room in the castle.*]

Enter OTHELLO, LODOVICO, DESDEMONA, EMILIA, *and* Attendants.

LODOVICO. I do beseech you, sir, trouble yourself no further.

OTHELLO. O, pardon me; 'twill do me good to walk.

219. *engines:* plots.

LODOVICO. Madam, good-night; I humbly thank your ladyship.

DESDEMONA. Your honour is most welcome.

OTHELLO. Will you walk, sir?
O,—Desdemona,—

DESDEMONA. My lord?

OTHELLO. Get you to bed on th' instant; I will be return'd forthwith.
Dismiss your attendant there. Look 't be done.

DESDEMONA. I will, my lord.

[*Exeunt* [OTHELLO, LODOVICO, *and* Attendants.]

EMILIA. How goes it now? He looks gentler than he did.

DESDEMONA. He says he will return incontinent;
And hath commanded me to go to bed,
And bid me to dismiss you.

EMILIA. Dismiss me!

DESDEMONA. It was his bidding; therefore, good Emilia,
Give me my nightly wearing, and adieu.
We must not now displease him.

EMILIA. I would you had never seen him!

DESDEMONA. So would not I. My love doth so approve him
That even his stubbornness, his checks, his frowns,—
Prithee, unpin me,—have grace and favour [in them].

EMILIA. I have laid those sheets you bade me on the bed.

DESDEMONA. All's one. Good [faith], how foolish are our minds!
If I do die before, prithee, shroud me
In one of these same sheets.

EMILIA. Come, come, you talk.

DESDEMONA. My mother had a maid call'd Barbary;
She was in love, and he she lov'd prov'd mad
And did forsake her. She had a song of "Willow";
An old thing 'twas, but it express'd her fortune,
And she died singing it. That song to-night
Will not go from my mind; I have much to do
But to go hang my head all at one side
And sing it like poor Barbary. Prithee, dispatch.

EMILIA. Shall I go fetch your night-gown?

DESDEMONA. No, unpin me here.
This Lodovico is a proper man.

EMILIA. A very handsome man.

DESDEMONA. He speaks well.

Scene iii, 20. *stubbornness:* roughness. 21. [*in them*] Q. Om. F. 23. [*faith*] Q. *Father* F.

EMILIA. I know a lady in Venice would have walk'd barefoot to
Palestine for a touch of his nether lip.

DESDEMONA [*singing*].
"The poor soul sat [sighing] by a sycamore tree,
Sing all a green willow;
Her hand on her bosom, her head on her knee,
Sing willow, willow, willow.
The fresh streams ran by her, and murmur'd her moans;
Sing willow, willow, willow;
Her salt tears fell from her, and soft'ned the stones;
Sing willow"—
Lay by these;—
[*Singing.*] "—willow, willow";—
Prithee, hie thee; he'll come anon;—
[*Singing.*] "Sing all a green willow must be my garland.
Let nobody blame him, his scorn I approve,"—
Nay, that's not next.—Hark! who is't that knocks?

EMILIA. It's the wind.

DESDEMONA [*Singing*].
"I call'd my love false love; but what said he then?
Sing willow, willow, willow.
If I court moe women, you'll couch with moe men."—
So, get thee gone; good-night. Mine eyes do itch;
Doth that bode weeping?

EMILIA. 'Tis neither here nor there.

DESDEMONA. I have heard it said so. O, these men, these men!
Dost thou in conscience think,—tell me, Emilia,—
That there be women do abuse their husbands
In such gross kind?

EMILIA. There be some such, no question.

DESDEMONA. Wouldst thou do such a deed for all the world?

EMILIA. Why, would not you?

DESDEMONA. No, by this heavenly light!

EMILIA. Nor I neither by this heavenly light;
I might do't as well i' th' dark.

DESDEMONA. Wouldst thou do such a deed for all the world?

EMILIA. The world's a huge thing; it is a great price
For a small vice.

DESDEMONA. In troth, I think thou wouldst not.

EMILIA. In troth, I think I should; and undo't when I had done. Marry, I would not do such a thing for a joint-ring, nor for measures of lawn, nor for gowns, petticoats, nor caps, nor any petty exhibition; but, for all the whole world,—['ud's pity], who would not make her husband a cuckold to make him a monarch? I should venture purgatory for't.

DESDEMONA. Beshrew me, if I would do such a wrong
For the whole world.

EMILIA. Why, the wrong is but a wrong i' th' world; and having the world for your labour, 'tis a wrong in your own world, and you might quickly make it right.

DESDEMONA. I do not think there is any such woman.

EMILIA. Yes, a dozen; and as many to th' vantage as would store the world they play'd for.
But I do think it is their husbands' faults
If wives do fall. Say that they slack their duties
And pour our treasures into foreign laps,
Or else break out in peevish jealousies,
Throwing restraint upon us; or say they strike us,
Or scant our former having in despite;
Why, we have galls, and though we have some grace,
Yet have we some revenge. Let husbands know
Their wives have sense like them; they see and smell
And have their palates both for sweet and sour
As husbands have. What is it that they do
When they change us for others? Is it sport?
I think it is. And doth affection breed it?
I think it doth. Is't frailty that thus errs?
It is so too. And have not we affections,
Desires for sport, and frailty, as men have?
Then let them use us well; else let them know,
The ills we do, their ills instruct us so.

DESDEMONA. Good-night, good-night. Heaven me such uses send
Not to pick bad from bad, but by bad mend.

[*Exeunt.*

ACT FIVE

Scene 1. [*Cyprus. A street.*]

Enter IAGO *and* RODERIGO.

IAGO. Here, stand behind this [bulk]; straight will he come.

---

40. [*sighing*] Q_2 *singing* F. 74. *joint-ring:* ring made in separable halves.

75–76. *exhibition:* allowance. 76. [*'ud's pity*] Q: God's pity. *Why* F. 87. *to th' vantage:* more, to boot. 91. *peevish:* silly. 93. *having:* allowance. 94. *galls:* spirits to resent injury.

Act V, Scene i, 1. [*bulk*] Q: jutting part of a building. *barke* F.

Plate I
S. Buonsignori, Map of Florence called "della Catena." Museo di Firenze com'era.
(Scala/Art Resource, NY)

Plate II
Giotto, *Lamentation*. Scrovegni Chapel, Padua.
(Scala/Art Resource, NY)

Plate III
Masaccio, *Tribute Money*, Brancacci Chapel, Florence.
(Scala/Art Resource, NY)

Plate IV
Piero della Francesca, *Resurrection*. Pinacoteca Comunale, Sansepolcro.
(Scala/Art Resource, NY)

Plate V
Sandro Botticelli, *Primavera*. Galleria degli Uffizi, Florence.
(Scala/Art Resource, NY)

Plate VI
Benozzo Gozzoli,
Entry of the Magi into Bethlehem with Lorenzo the Magnificent.
Palazzo Medici-Riccardi, Florence.
(Scala/Art Resource, NY)

Plate VII
Leonardo da Vinci,
The Madonna of the Rocks.
The Louvre, Paris.
(Giraudon/Art Resource, NY)

Plate VIII
Leonardo da Vinci,
The Madonna of the Rocks
(detail). The Louvre, Paris.
(Giraudon/Art Resource, NY)

Plate IX
Michelangelo, *Creation of Adam*. Ceiling, Sistine Chapel, Vatican.
(Scala/Art Resource, NY)

Plate X
Raphael, *School of Athens*. Stanze di Raffaello, Vatican.
(Scala/Art Resource, NY)

Plate XI
Raphael, *Pope Leo X with Cardinals Giulio de' Medici and Luigi de' Rossi*. Panel Painting, c. 1517. Galleria degli Uffizi, Florence.
(Scala/Art Resource, NY)

Wear thy good rapier bare, and put it home.
Quick, quick; fear nothing; I'll be at thy elbow.
It makes us, or it mars us; think on that,
And fix most firm thy resolution.

RODERIGO. Be near at hand; I may miscarry in't.

IAGO. Here, at thy hand; be bold, and take thy stand. [*Retires.*]

RODERIGO. I have no great devotion to the deed,
And yet he hath given me satisfying reasons.
'Tis but a man gone. Forth, my sword: he dies.

IAGO. I have rubb'd this young quat almost to the sense,
And he grows angry. Now, whether he kill Cassio,
Or Cassio him, or each do kill the other,
Every way makes my gain. Live Roderigo,
He calls me to a restitution large
Of gold and jewels that I bobb'd from him
As gifts to Desdemona;
It must not be. If Cassio do remain,
He hath a daily beauty in his life
That makes me ugly; and, besides, the Moor
May unfold me to him; there stand I in much peril.
No, he must die. But so; I heard him coming.

Enter CASSIO.

RODERIGO. I know his gait, 'tis he.—Villain, thou diest! [*Makes a pass at* CASSIO.]

CASSIO. That thrust had been mine enemy indeed,
But that my coat is better than thou know'st.
I will make proof of thine. [*Draws, and wounds* RODERIGO.]

RODERIGO. O, I am slain.

[IAGO *from behind wounds* CASSIO *in the leg, and exit.*]

CASSIO. I am maim'd for ever. Help, ho! murder! murder! [*Falls.*

Enter OTHELLO.

OTHELLO. The voice of Cassio! Iago keeps his word.

RODERIGO. O, villain that I am!

OTHELLO. It is even so.

CASSIO. O, help, ho! light! a surgeon!

OTHELLO. 'Tis he!—O brave Iago, honest and just,
That hast such noble sense of thy friend's wrong!
Thou teachest me. Minion, your dear lies dead,
And your unblest fate hies; strumpet, I come.
[Forth] of my heart those charms, thine eyes, are blotted;
Thy bed, lust-stain'd, shall with lust's blood be spotted. [*Exit.*

Enter LODOVICO *and* GRATIANO.

CASSIO. What, ho! no watch? no passage? Murder! murder!

GRATIANO. 'Tis some mischance; the voice is very direful.

CASSIO. O, help!

LODOVICO. Hark!

RODERIGO. O wretched villain!

LODOVICO. Two or three groan. 'Tis heavy night,
These may be counterfeits; let's think 't unsafe
To come in to the cry without more help.

RODERIGO. Nobody come? Then shall I bleed to death.

Re-enter IAGO, *with a light.*

LODOVICO. Hark!

GRATIANO. Here's one comes in his shirt, with light and weapons.

IAGO. Who's there? Whose noise is this that cries on murder?

LODOVICO. We do not know.

IAGO. Do not you hear a cry?

CASSIO. Here, here! for Heaven's sake, help me!

IAGO. What's the matter?

GRATIANO. This is Othello's ancient, as I take it.

LODOVICO. The same indeed; a very valiant fellow.

IAGO. What are you here that cry so grievously?

CASSIO. Iago? O, I am spoil'd, undone by villains!
Give me some help.

IAGO. O me, Lieutenant! what villains have done this?

CASSIO. I think that one of them is hereabout
And cannot make away.

IAGO. O treacherous villains!
What are you there?—Come in, and give some help.
[*To* LODOVICO *and* GRATIANO.]

RODERIGO. O, help me there!

CASSIO. That's one of them.

IAGO. O murd'rous slave! O villain! [*Thrusts* [RODERIGO] *in.*

RODERIGO. O damn'd Iago! O inhuman dog!

IAGO. Kill men i' th' dark!—Where be these bloody thieves?—

---

11. *quat:* pimple. *the sense:* the quick. 16. *bobb'd:* cheated, swindled. 25. *coat:* i.e., of mail (worn under outer clothing). 33. *Minion:* hussy.

35. [*Forth*] Q. *For* F. 37. *passage:* passers-by. 42. *heavy:* dark.

How silent is this town!—Ho! murder! murder!—
What may you be? Are you of good or evil?
LODOVICO. As you shall prove us, praise us.
IAGO. Signior Lodovico?
LODOVICO. He, sir.
IAGO. I cry you mercy. Here's Cassio hurt by villains.
GRATIANO. Cassio!
IAGO. How is't, brother!
CASSIO. My leg is cut in two.
IAGO. Marry, heaven forbid!
Light, gentlemen! I'll bind it with my shirt.

Enter BIANCA.

BIANCA. What is the matter, ho? Who is't that cried?
IAGO. Who is't that cried!
BIANCA. O my dear Cassio! my sweet Cassio!
O Cassio, Cassio, Cassio!
IAGO. O notable strumpet! Cassio, may you suspect
Who they should be that have thus mangled you?
CASSIO. No.
GRATIANO. I am sorry to find you thus; I have been to seek you.
IAGO. Lend me a garter. So. O, for a chair,
To bear him easily hence!
BIANCA. Alas, he faints! O Cassio, Cassio, Cassio!
IAGO. Gentlemen all, I do suspect this trash
To be a party in this injury.
Patience a while, good Cassio. Come, come;
Lend me a light. Know we this face or no?
Alas, my friend and my dear countryman
Roderigo! No:—yes, sure:—yes, 'tis Roderigo.
GRATIANO. What, of Venice?
IAGO. Even he, sir; did you know him?
GRATIANO. Know him! ay.
IAGO. Signior Gratiano? I cry your gentle pardon;
These bloody accidents must excuse my manners
That so neglected you.
GRATIANO. I am glad to see you.
IAGO. How do you, Cassio? O, a chair, a chair!
GRATIANO. Roderigo!
IAGO. He, he, 'tis he.

[*A chair brought in.*]

O, that's well said; the chair.
Some good man bear him carefully from hence;
I'll fetch the General's surgeon. [*To* BIANCA.] For you, mistress,
Save you your labour. He that lies slain here, Cassio,
Was my dear friend. What malice was between you?
CASSIO. None in the world; nor do I know the man.
IAGO [*To* BIANCA]. What, look you pale? O, bear him out o' th' air.

[CASSIO *and* RODERIGO *are borne off.*]

Stay you, good gentlemen. Look you pale, mistress?
Do you perceive the gastness of her eye?
Nay, if you stare, we shall hear more anon.
Behold her well; I pray you, look upon her.
Do you see, gentlemen? Nay, guiltiness will speak.
Though tongues were out of use.

Enter EMILIA.

EMILIA. Alas, what's the matter? What's the matter, husband?
IAGO. Cassio hath here been set on in the dark
By Roderigo and fellows that are scap'd.
He's almost slain, and Roderigo quite dead.
EMILIA. Alas, good gentleman! alas, good Cassio!
IAGO. This is the fruits of whoring. Prithee, Emilia,
Go know of Cassio where he supp'd to-night.
[*To* BIANCA.] What, do you shake at that?
BIANCA. He supp'd at my house; but I therefore shake not.
IAGO. O, did he so? I charge you, go with me.
EMILIA. Oh, fie upon thee, strumpet!
BIANCA. I am no strumpet, but of life as honest
As you that thus abuse me.
EMILIA. As I? Fie upon thee!
IAGO. Kind gentlemen, let's go see poor Cassio dress'd.
Come, mistress, you must tell 's another tale.
Emilia, run you to the citadel,
And tell my lord and lady what hath happ'd.
Will you go on afore? [*Aside.*] This is the night
That either makes me or fordoes me quite.

[*Exeunt.*

Scene 2. [*A bedchamber in the castle.*]

DESDEMONA *in bed* [*asleep*]. *Enter* OTHELLO *with a light.*

OTHELLO. It is the cause, it is the cause, my soul,—
Let me not name it to you, you chaste stars!—
It is the cause. Yet I'll not shed her blood,
Nor scar that whiter skin of hers than snow,
And smooth as monumental alabaster.
Yet she must die, else she'll betray more men.

82. *chair:* sedan chair.

107. *gastness:* ghastliness. 130. *fordoes:* destroys.

Put out the light, and then put out the light.
If I quench thee, thou flaming minister,
I can again thy former light restore,
Should I repent me; but once put out thy light,
Thou cunning'st pattern of excelling nature,
I know not where is that Promethean heat
That can thy light relume. When I have pluck'd the rose
I cannot give it vital growth again,
It needs must wither. I'll smell [it] on the tree. [*Kisses her.*
Oh, balmy breath, that dost almost persuade
Justice to break her sword! One more, one more.
Be thus when thou art dead, and I will kill thee
And love thee after. One more, and that's the last;
So sweet was ne'er so fatal. I must weep,
But they are cruel tears. This sorrow's heavenly;
It strikes where it doth love. She wakes.

DESDEMONA. Who's there? Othello?

OTHELLO. Ay, Desdemona.

DESDEMONA. Will you come to bed, my lord?

OTHELLO. Have you pray'd to-night, Desdemon?

DESDEMONA. Ay, my lord.

OTHELLO. If you bethink yourself of any crime
Unreconcil'd as yet to Heaven and grace,
Solicit for it straight.

DESDEMONA. Alack, my lord, what may you mean by that?

OTHELLO. Well, do it, and be brief; I will walk by.
I would not kill thy unprepared spirit;
No; heavens forfend! I would not kill thy soul.

DESDEMONA. Talk you of killing?

OTHELLO. Ay, I do.

DESDEMONA. Then Heaven
Have mercy on me!

OTHELLO. Amen, with all my heart!

DESDEMONA. If you say [so], I hope you will not kill me.

OTHELLO. Hum!

DESDEMONA. And yet I fear you; for you're fatal then
When your eyes roll so. Why I should fear I know not,
Since guiltiness I know not; but yet I feel I fear.

OTHELLO. Think on thy sins.

DESDEMONA. They are loves I bear to you.

OTHELLO. Ay, and for that thou diest.

DESDEMONA. That death's unnatural that kills for loving.
Alas, why gnaw you so your nether lip?
Some bloody passion shakes your very frame.
These are portents; but yet I hope, I hope,
They do not point on me.

OTHELLO. Peace, and be still!

DESDEMONA. I will so. What's the matter?

OTHELLO. That handkerchief which I so lov'd and gave thee
Thou gav'st to Cassio.

DESDEMONA. No, by my life and soul!
Send for the man, and ask him.

OTHELLO. Sweet soul, take heed,
Take heed of perjury; thou art on thy deathbed.

DESDEMONA. Ay, but not yet to die.

OTHELLO. [Yes], presently:
Therefore confess thee freely of thy sin;
For to deny each article with oath
Cannot remove nor choke the strong conception
That I do groan withal. Thou art to die.

DESDEMONA. O, Heaven, have mercy on me!

OTHELLO. I say, amen.

DESDEMONA. And have you mercy too! I never did
Offend you in my life; never lov'd Cassio
But with such general warranty of heaven
As I might love; I never gave him token.

OTHELLO. By heaven, I saw my handkerchief in 's hand.
O perjur'd woman! thou dost stone my heart,
And makes me call what I intend to do
A murder, which I thought a sacrifice.
I saw the handkerchief.

DESDEMONA. He found it then;
I never gave it him. Send for him hither;
Let him confess a truth.

OTHELLO. He hath confess'd.

DESDEMONA. What, my lord?

OTHELLO. That he hath us'd thee.

DESDEMONA. How? unlawfully?

OTHELLO. Ay.

DESDEMONA. He will not say so.

OTHELLO. No, his mouth is stopp'd;
Honest Iago hath ta'en order for't.

DESDEMONA. O! my fear interprets. What, is he dead?

OTHELLO. Had all his hairs been lives, my great revenge
Had stomach for them all.

DESDEMONA. Alas! he is betray'd and I undone.

Scene ii, 12. *Promethean heat:* divine fire. 15. [*it*] Q. *thee* F. 35. [*so*] Q. Om. F.

52. [*Yes*] Q. Om. F. 55. *conception:* purpose.

OTHELLO. Out, strumpet! weep'st thou for him to my face?
DESDEMONA. O, banish me, my lord, but kill me not!
OTHELLO. Down, strumpet!
DESDEMONA. Kill me to-morrow; let me live to-night!
OTHELLO. Nay, if you strive,—
DESDEMONA. But half an hour!
OTHELLO. Being done, there is no pause.
DESDEMONA. But while I say one prayer!
OTHELLO. It is too late. [*He smothers her.*
EMILIA (*at the door*). My lord, my lord!
What, ho! my lord, my lord!
OTHELLO. What noise is this? Not dead? not yet quite dead?
I that am cruel am yet merciful;
I would not have thee linger in thy pain.
So, so.
EMILIA (*within*). What, ho! my lord, my lord!
OTHELLO. Who's there?
EMILIA (*within*). O, good my lord, I would speak a word with you!
OTHELLO. Yes:—'tis Emilia.—By and by.—She's dead.
'Tis like she comes to speak of Cassio's death.
The noise was high. Ha! no more moving?
Still as the grave. Shall she come in? Were't good?—
I think she stirs again:—no. What's best to do?
If she come in, she'll sure speak to my wife.
My wife! my wife! what wife? I have no wife.
O, insupportable! O heavy hour!
Methinks it should be now a huge eclipse
Of sun and moon, and that th' affrighted globe
Did yawn at alteration.
EMILIA (*within*). I do beseech you
That I may speak with you, O, good my lord!
OTHELLO. I had forgot thee. O, come in, Emilia.
Soft; by and by.—Let me the curtains draw.—
Where art thou? [*Unlocks the door.*]

Enter EMILIA.

What's the matter with thee now?
EMILIA. O, my good lord, yonder's foul murders done!
OTHELLO. What, now?
EMILIA. But now, my lord.
OTHELLO. It is the very error of the moon;
She comes more nearer earth than she was wont,
And makes men mad.
EMILIA. Cassio, my lord, hath kill'd a young Venetian
Call'd Roderigo.
OTHELLO. Roderigo kill'd!
And Cassio kill'd!
EMILIA. No, Cassio is not kill'd.
OTHELLO. Not Cassio kill'd! Then murder's out of tune,
And sweet revenge grows harsh.
DESDEMONA. O, falsely, falsely murder'd!
EMILIA. O Lord, what cry is that?
OTHELLO. That! what?
EMILIA. Out, and alas! that was my lady's voice.
Help! help, ho! help! O lady, speak again!
Sweet Desdemona! O sweet mistress, speak!
DESDEMONA. A guiltless death I die.
EMILIA. O, who hath done this deed?
DESDEMONA. Nobody; I myself. Farewell!
Commend me to my kind lord. O, farewell! [*Dies.*
OTHELLO. Why, how should she be murd'red?
EMILIA. Alas, who knows?
OTHELLO. You heard her say herself, it was not I.
EMILIA. She said so; I must needs report the truth.
OTHELLO. She's like a liar gone to burning hell.
'Twas I that kill'd her.
EMILIA. O, the more angel she,
And you the blacker devil!
OTHELLO. She turn'd to folly, and she was a whore.
EMILIA. Thou dost belie her, and thou art a devil.
OTHELLO. She was false as water.
EMILIA. Thou art rash as fire to say
That she was false: O, she was heavenly true!
OTHELLO. Cassio did top her; ask thy husband else.
O, I were damn'd beneath all depth in hell
But that I did proceed upon just grounds
To this extremity. Thy husband knew it all.
EMILIA. My husband!
OTHELLO. Thy husband.
EMILIA. That she was false to wedlock?
OTHELLO. Ay, with Cassio. Had she been true,
If Heaven would make me such another world
Of one entire and perfect chrysolite,
I'd not have sold her for it.
EMILIA. My husband!
OTHELLO. Ay, 'twas he that told me on her first.
An honest man he is, and hates the slime
That sticks on filthy deeds.
EMILIA. My husband!
OTHELLO. What needs this iterance, woman? I say thy husband.

109. *error:* aberration.

145. *chrysolite: a precious stone.*

150. *iterance:* repetition.

EMILIA. O mistress, villainy hath made mocks with love!
My husband say [that] she was false!
OTHELLO. He, woman;
I say thy husband; dost understand the word?
My friend, thy husband, honest, honest Iago.
EMILIA. If he say so, may his pernicious soul
Rot half a grain a day! He lies to the heart.
She was too fond of her most filthy bargain.
OTHELLO. Ha!
EMILIA. Do thy worst!
This deed of thine is no more worthy heaven
Than thou wast worthy her.
OTHELLO. Peace, you were best.
EMILIA. Thou hast not half that power to do me harm
As I have to be hurt. O gull! O dolt!
As ignorant as dirt! Thou hast done a deed—
I care not for thy sword; I'll make thee known
Though I lost twenty lives.—Help! help, ho! help!
The Moor hath kill'd my mistress! Murder! murder!

Enter MONTANO, GRATIANO, IAGO, *and others.*

MONTANO. What is the matter? How now, general!
EMILIA. O, are you come, Iago? You have done well,
That men must lay their murders on your neck.
GRATIANO. What is the matter?
EMILIA. Disprove this villain, if thou be'st a man.
He says thou told'st him that his wife was false.
I know thou didst not, thou'rt not such a villain.
Speak, for my heart is full.
IAGO. I told him what I thought, and told no more
Than what he found himself was apt and true.
EMILIA. But did you ever tell him she was false?
IAGO. I did.
EMILIA. You told a lie, an odious, damned lie;
Upon my soul, a lie, a wicked lie.
She false with Cassio!—did you say with Cassio?
IAGO. With Cassio, mistress. Go to, charm your tongue.
EMILIA. I will not charm my tongue; I am bound to speak.
My mistress here lies murdered in her bed,—
ALL. O heavens forfend!
EMILIA. And your reports have set the murderer on.
OTHELLO. Nay, stare not, masters; it is true, indeed.
GRATIANO. 'Tis a strange truth.
MONTANO. O monstrous act!
EMILIA. Villainy, villainy, villainy!
I think upon't,—I think I smell't,—O villainy!
I thought so then,—I'll kill myself for grief—
O villainy, villainy!
IAGO. What, are you mad? I charge you, get you home.
EMILIA. Good gentlemen, let me have leave to speak;
'Tis proper I obey him, but not now.
Perchance, Iago, I will ne'er go home.
OTHELLO. O! O! O! [*He falls on the bed.*
EMILIA. Nay, lay thee down and roar;
For thou hast kill'd the sweetest innocent
That e'er did lift up eye.
OTHELLO [*rising*]. O, she was foul!
I scarce did know you, uncle; there lies your niece,
Whose breath, indeed, these hands have newly stopp'd.
I know this act shows horrible and grim.
GRATIANO. Poor Desdemon! I am glad thy father's dead.
Thy match was mortal to him, and pure grief
Shore his old thread in twain. Did he live now,
His sight would make him do a desperate turn,
Yea, curse his better angel from his side,
And fall to reprobance.
OTHELLO. 'Tis pitiful; but yet Iago knows
That she with Cassio hath the act of shame
A thousand times committed. Cassio confess'd it;
And she did gratify his amorous works
With that recognizance and pledge of love
Which I first gave her. I saw it in his hand;
It was a handkerchief, an antique token
My father gave my mother.
EMILIA. O [God]! O heavenly [God]!
IAGO. ['Zounds,] hold your peace.
EMILIA. 'Twill out, 'twill out! I peace!
No, I will speak as liberal as the north,
Let Heaven and men and devils, let them all,
All, all, cry shame against me, yet I'll speak.
IAGO. Be wise, and get you home.
EMILIA. I will not.

[*Iago offers to stab* EMILIA.]

GRATIANO. Fie!
Your sword upon a woman?
EMILIA. O thou dull Moor! that handkerchief thou speak'st of
I found by fortune and did give my husband;
For often, with a solemn earnestness,

---

152. [*that*] Q_2. Om. F.

192. *I...then.* See IV.ii. 130–133. 209. *reprobance:* damnation. 218. [*God*]...[*God*] Q. *Heaven...Powers* F. 219. ['*Zounds*] Q. *Come* F. 220. *liberal:* freely.

More than indeed belong'd to such a trifle,
He begg'd of me to steal't.
IAGO. Villainous whore!
EMILIA. She give it Cassio! No, alas! I found it,
And I did give't my husband.
IAGO. Filth, thou liest!
EMILIA. By heaven, I do not, I do not, gentlemen.
O murd'rous coxcomb! what should such a fool
Do with so good a wife?
OTHELLO. Are there no stones in heaven
But what serves for the thunder?—Precious villain!

[*He runs at* IAGO: IAGO *kills* EMILIA.

GRATIANO. The woman falls; sure, he hath kill'd his wife.
EMILIA. Ay, ay! O, lay me by my mistress' side.

[*Exit* IAGO.

GRATIANO. He's gone, but his wife's kill'd.
MONTANO. 'Tis a notorious villain. Take you this weapon
Which I have [here] recover'd from the Moor.
Come, guard the door without; let him not pass,
But kill him rather. I'll after that same villain,
For 'tis a damned slave.

[*Exeunt* MONTANO *and* GRATIANO.

OTHELLO. I am not valiant neither,
But every puny whipster gets my sword.
But why should honour outlive honesty?
Let it go all.
EMILIA. What did thy song bode, lady?
Hark, canst thou hear me? I will play the swan,
And die in music. [*Singing.*] "Willow, willow, willow!"—
Moor, she was chaste; she lov'd thee, cruel Moor;
So come my soul to bliss, as I speak true;
So speaking as I think, alas, I die. [*Dies.*
OTHELLO. I have another weapon in this chamber;
It was a sword of Spain, the ice-brook's temper,—
O, here it is. Uncle, I must come forth.
GRATIANO. (*within*). If thou attempt it, it will cost thee dear:
Thou hast no weapon, and perforce must suffer.
OTHELLO. Look in upon me then and speak with me,
Or, naked as I am, I will assault thee.

[*Re-enter* GRATIANO.]

GRATIANO. What is the matter?
OTHELLO. Behold, I have a weapon;
A better never did itself sustain
Upon a soldier's thigh. I have seen the day
That, with this little arm and this good sword,
I have made my way through more impediments
Than twenty times your stop. But, O vain boast!
Who can control his fate? 'tis not so now.
Be not afraid though you do see me weapon'd;
Here is my journey's end, here is my butt
And very sea-mark of my utmost sail.
Do you go back dismay'd? 'Tis a lost fear;
Man but a rush against Othello's breast
And he retires. Where should Othello go?
Now, how dost thou look now? O ill-starr'd wench!
Pale as thy smock! when we shall meet at compt,
This look of thine will hurl my soul from heaven,
And fiends will snatch at it. Cold, cold, my girl!
Even like thy chastity. O cursed, cursed slave!
Whip me, ye devils,
From the possession of this heavenly sight!
Blow me about in winds! roast me in sulphur!
Wash me in steep-down gulfs of liquid fire!
O Desdemon! dead, Desdemon! dead!
Oh! Oh!

Enter LODOVICO, MONTANO, CASSIO *carried in a chair, and* Officers, *with* IAGO [*prisoner*].

LODOVICO. Where is this rash and most unfortunate man?
OTHELLO. That's he that was Othello; here I am.
LODOVICO. Where is that viper? Bring the villain forth.
OTHELLO. I look down towards his feet; but that's a fable.
If that thou be'st a devil, I cannot kill thee. [*Wounds* IAGO.]
LODOVICO. Wrench his sword from him.
IAGO. I bleed, sir; but not kill'd.
OTHELLO. I am not sorry neither. I'd have thee live;
For, in my sense, 'tis happiness to die.
LODOVICO. O thou Othello, that [wast] once so good,
Fall'n in the practice of a cursed slave,
What shall be said to thee?
OTHELLO. Why, anything.
An honourable murderer, if you will;

---

234. *stones:* bolts. 240. [*here*] Q. Om. F.
244. *whipster:* term of contempt. 253. *ice-brook's temper:* its steel tempered in icy water. 258. *naked:* unarmed.

264. *stop:* power to stop. 267. *butt:* goal. 273. *compt:* accounting, i.e., Judgment Day. 286. *I...feet:* i.e., to see if they are cloven. 291. [*wast*] *was* F. *wert* Q.
292. *practice:* plot.

For nought I did in hate, but all in honour.
LODOVICO. This wretch hath part confess'd his villainy.
Did you and he consent in Cassio's death?
OTHELLO. Ay.
CASSIO. Dear General, I never gave you cause.
OTHELLO. I do believe it, and I ask your pardon.
Will you, I pray, demand that demi-devil
Why he hath thus ensnar'd my soul and body?
IAGO. Demand me nothing; what you know, you know.
From this time forth I never will speak word.
LODOVICO. What not to pray?
GRATIANO. Torments will ope your lips.
OTHELLO. Well, thou dost best.
LODOVICO. Sir, you shall understand what hath befall'n,
Which, as I think, you know not. Here is a letter
Found in the pocket of the slain Roderigo,
And here another. The one of them imports
The death of Cassio to be undertook
By Roderigo.
OTHELLO. O villain!
CASSIO. Most heathenish and most gross!
LODOVICO. Now here's another discontented paper,
Found in his pocket too; and this, it seems,
Roderigo meant t' have sent this damned villain;
But that, belike, Iago in the interim
Came in and satisfi'd him.
OTHELLO. O thou pernicious caitiff!—
How came you, Cassio, by that handkerchief
That was my wife's?
CASSIO. I found it in my chamber,
And he himself confess'd but even now
That there he dropp'd it for a special purpose
Which wrought to his desire.
OTHELLO. O fool! fool! fool!
CASSIO. There is besides in Roderigo's letter,
How he upbraids Iago, that he made him
Brave me upon the watch, whereon it came
That I was cast; and even but now he spake,
After long seeming dead, Iago hurt him,
Iago set him on.
LODOVICO. You must forsake this room and go with us.
Your power and your command is taken off,
And Cassio rules in Cyprus. For this slave,
If there be any cunning cruelty
That can torment him much and hold him long,
It shall be his. You shall close prisoner rest,
Till that the nature of your fault be known
To the Venetian state. Come, bring away.
OTHELLO. Soft you; a word or two before you go.
I have done the state some service, and they know't.
No more of that. I pray you, in your letters,
When you shall these unlucky deeds relate,
Speak of me as I am; nothing extenuate,
Nor set down aught in malice. Then must you speak
Of one that lov'd not wisely but too well;
Of one not easily jealous, but, being wrought,
Perplex'd in the extreme; of one whose hand,
Like the base [Indian], threw a pearl away
Richer than all his tribe; of one whose subdu'd eyes,
Albeit unused to the melting mood,
Drops tears as fast as the Arabian trees
Their medicinal gum. Set you down this;
And say besides, that in Aleppo once,
Where a malignant and a turban'd Turk
Beat a Venetian and traduc'd the state,
I took by th' throat the circumcised dog,
And smote him—thus. [*Stabs himself.*
LODOVICO. O bloody period!
GRATIANO. All that's spoke is marr'd.
OTHELLO. I kiss'd thee ere I kill'd thee: no way but this,
Killing myself, to die upon a kiss. [*Falls on the bed, and*] *dies.*
CASSIO. This did I fear, but thought he had no weapon;
For he was great of heart.
LODOVICO. [*to* IAGO.] O Spartan dog,
More fell than anguish, hunger, or the sea!
Look on the tragic loading of this bed;
This is thy work. The object poisons sight;
Let it be hid. Gratiano, keep the house,
And seize upon the fortunes of the Moor,
For they succeed on you. To you, Lord Governor,
Remains the censure of this hellish villain;
The time, the place, the torture. O, enforce it!
Myself will straight aboard, and to the state
This heavy act with heavy heart relate.

[*Exeunt.*

Curtain

---

321. *but* Q. *it but* F.

346. *Perplex'd:* distraught. 347. [*Indian*] Q. *Indean* F. The allusion has not been identified. 357. *period:* end. 361. *Spartan dog:* bloodhound. 366. *seize upon:* take legal possession of. 368. *censure:* sentencing.

COMMENTS AND QUESTIONS

1. For what different purposes does Shakespeare use blank verse, prose, rhymed verse, and music?
2. In what ways do the dramatic purposes of the music for *Othello* differ from those of *The Play of Daniel* (see Chapter 10)?
3. What effect do the songs have on you? Would you include them in a modern production of the play?
4. How do you interpret the character of Iago? The English Romantic writer and critic Coleridge described the evil in Iago as a "motiveless malignancy." Others have called him a kind of devil, a totally evil figure. Some argue that he has (in his own mind) real motives for hating Othello. What are these motives, and which are believable?
5. How does Iago manipulate Roderigo? Cassio? Othello?
6. What is the role and the significance of the handkerchief?
7. To what extent does racial prejudice influence Iago and the other characters?
8. Describe the character of Othello. What qualifies him as a tragic hero? What is Othello's social position as a black man in a white society? Does this contribute to his insecurity and to his jealousy?
9. Does Othello at any point apply racial stereotypes to himself? Is this Iago's doing?
10. Do you think that Othello's final assessment of himself, in the speech just before his suicide, is accurate? How do you think this scene should be acted?
11. What is Desdemona's role and character? Do you have the impression that she and Othello know each other well? To what extent is the love between her and Othello endangered by their society, and to what extent is its destruction a result of Iago's manipulation?
12. Language, particularly images, plays an important part in *Othello*. We have mentioned images of black and white, animal images, and images related to poison. What effects do these have in the play? What other types can you find?
13. Do you find that *Othello* is a "depressing" tragedy, as some readers do, or that it ends on a note of redemption, as does *Oedipus Rex* (see Chapter 5)?
14. Compare Oedipus and Othello as tragic figures.
15. To what extent does Shakespeare's tragedy exemplify the humanist belief in the dignity of humanity, and to what extent does it show late Renaissance skepticism?
16. What does the play tell you about European perceptions of Africa and Africans?
17. In what ways does *Othello* seem relevant to our own time?

Renaissance and Reformation

The death and dislocation of fourteenth-century Europe served as a catalyst for the birth of the modern age. The century of crisis tended to privilege certain intellectual tendencies that led over time to the formation of a new culture distinct from that of the Middle Ages. In the section on the Italian Renaissance we focused on its beginnings in the fourteenth and fifteenth centuries rather than on its "high" (early-sixteenth-century) phase in Rome. It is in Florence in this early period that we can best witness the radical departures from medieval mentality; the innovations in art, life, and thought; and the new fusion of Christian and classical traditions that laid the basis for much of our modern art, thought, and institutions. The roots of the humanities as we know them are certainly there. We have seen how Florentine humanism spread to northern Europe, influencing the development of a literature at least equal to its own, and how its original self-confidence underwent a crisis that is still with us.

Individualism

"The discovery of the individual was made in early fifteenth-century Florence," proclaims Kenneth Clark in his *Civilization* series. "Nothing can alter that fact." Certainly, when one looks at the portraits of Renaissance Florentines (the art of the portrait had been lost in Europe since Roman times!), or when one reads about their lives or views the different styles of each artist, one senses an individuality that was not present in the more collective and symbolic arts of the Middle Ages. The development of a more naturalistic way of portraying individual characters and their natural surroundings is part of this trend—we see its beginnings in the fourteenth century with Giotto.

Civic Sense

If fifteenth-century Florentines were highly conscious of themselves as individuals, they were also very much aware of being part of a community. Florence in many ways resembled a Greek city-state; and like the ancient Athenians, the Florentines believed that participation in the affairs of state was essential for the realization of one's full humanity. But the people of the Renaissance needed to justify this classical value in Christian terms. Whereas medieval people believed that the contemplative life, or the life devoted to God, was of highest value, the fifteenth-century Florentines believed that Christian ideals could be served just as well in a secular, active life. Their political ideal of republicanism, rule by a body of citizens, has served as a basis for modern political theory. Although the modern state developed out of the medieval monarchies, since the nineteenth century these states have been on the whole republican.

By the last half of the fifteenth century, Florence came under the more autocratic rule of the Medici family. An ardent republican, Machiavelli nevertheless saw that by this time the ideal form of government was no longer practical for Florence. Yet through the early sixteenth century the spirit of republicanism, as seen in Michelangelo's *David*, with his proud, youthful defiance of tyranny, and his *Brutus*, the defender of Roman liberty, remained identified with the city. Republicanism was a part of the civic humanism of which Florentines were proud. The Florentines, with their urban-centered lifestyle, created a city whose physical aspect expressed their values. The architecture and sculpture, which even today give Florence its distinctive character, reflect a sense of beauty and proportion keyed to the measure of humankind. City planning as we know it today was born in Florence with the treatises of Leon Battista Alberti.

Visual and Verbal Eloquence

Beautiful architecture was for the practitioner Brunelleschi and the theoretician Alberti what beautiful speech was for the Florentine humanists. Visual and verbal eloquence were means of using newly rediscovered classical values in the service of Christian truth. Brunelleschi and (after him) Michelangelo observed closely the remains of Roman buildings and statues; Petrarch, Salutati, and Bruni edited and studied Latin, and eventually Greek, texts. The use of language was for the humanists the art that made people most truly human; consequently, the studies that they called the humanities focused on literature.

Historical and Visual Perspective

In their study of ancient rhetoric, the humanists observed a truth that the medieval mind seemed not to realize: language and other human customs, institutions, and ideas change; they have a history. The notion of seeing oneself and one's culture in historical perspective, as part of a continuum of time, has become a habit with us; it has its origins in the humanists' new way of thought.

Intimately connected with this sense of historical perspective was the humanists' awareness that humanity constructed its own history. This led them to view the past, particularly the ancient pagan and early Christian past, as providing cultural alternatives to their contemporary world. This helps to explain the humanist concern for introducing moral, political, and religious reforms into their society. Their efforts were predicated on the belief that it was possible to bring society back to better and purer times. This same commitment to the idea that human beings can shape the future has come to characterize the modern world. Now, however, the models we use are rarely drawn from societies that have actually existed but rather from those we envision in our mind's eye.

The ability to see with the perspective of time has its artistic parallel in the ability to see, and to draw, with the perspective of space. There is no doubt that the technical development permitting artists to give the illusion of three dimensions on the flat surface of a canvas was a major step in the history of art. Renaissance painters established a formal visual language for their art that remained until recently the official standard of all Western art academies. Yet *perspective*, it must be remembered, was a means, not an end in itself. It permitted artists to represent what they observed, rather than to create symbols of the unseen. The sources of their observation were primarily two: nature (inanimate, animate, and human) and antiquity. From these they derived an art centered on the human being and the here-and-now; yet, like the humanists, they wished to put these new modes of expression to the service of Christian values. Leonardo, who stressed the scientific nature of painting and its worthiness to be placed among the liberal arts, created one of the most mystical Virgins ever painted.

Practicality

Leonardo was also a creator of tools and devices by which human beings could control their natural surroundings. In this he reflects the tendency in the Renaissance for the theoretical to become increasingly united with the practical. The great scientific advances of the seventeenth century would have been impossible without the creation of better instrumentation with which to measure, view, and manipulate the material world. Incidentally, as we will explain in the discussion of the Scientific Revolution, the development of Neoplatonism in the fifteenth century led to a new concern with mathematics, which also made a fundamental contribution to new approaches in natural science.

Developments in Music

In music, too, nature and antiquity were sources that helped new forms to flourish. Renaissance composers were not acquainted with the actual musical works of the Greeks and Romans, but they read their musical theory and were interested in the ways in which music could be wedded to words. We have seen how this was done in the Isaac composition; we have also seen how nature (such as the flowing fountain) and human emotion are "tone painted" in this piece. Today's composer would write different sounds to depict a fountain or to express grief and anguish, but the concept of musical sound affecting human emotions stretches continuously back through history to classical Greece. Much of Renaissance music was religious, but secular music gained prominence at this time. Isaac's death lament for Lorenzo and Poliziano's poem lament the passing of this life but do not refer to the next one, and the only god mentioned in the piece is Phoebus Apollo!

Non-Christian Subject Matter

The use of pagan, classical subjects in painting, sculpture, music, and literature represents a radical break with medieval culture. Much of this "pagan" art developed under the influence of Lorenzo de' Medici and the circle of Neoplatonic scholars around him. The lyrical Venuses and nymphs of Botticelli represent joy in this world but also an underlying melancholy. One senses in them a spiritual world beyond the visible forms. Similarly, Lorenzo's carnivals adopted themes from classical mythology to urge people to enjoy life in the present—before it slips away. The medieval focus on the salvation of the immortal soul has shifted.

Human Dignity

One of Lorenzo's Neoplatonic acquaintances, Pico della Mirandola, made what is considered by many to be the most extreme Renaissance statement on human dignity and grandeur. Pico's success at fusing the Judeo-Christian and Greco-Roman ways of thinking is problematic: although he recognized Christianity as the truest of all religions, he nonetheless endowed humanity with creative powers exceeding those of celestial beings, thus sounding a note that had not been heard since antiquity. Yet, when this brilliant, handsome prince of Mirandola died in Florence of fever at the age of thirty-one, he met death wrapped in the robes of a Dominican friar.

Northern Humanism

When Italian humanism spread to northern Europe, its Christian aspect was emphasized more than its pagan one. Humanists such as Erasmus read and delighted in the classical authors but turned their attention toward the study and editing of Greek and Latin Christian texts. Erasmus believed strongly in the value of reading and study: through knowledge and the development of inner piety, individual Christians could help to reform the ignorance and emphasis on externals that pervaded the Church, especially its monasteries.

Northern Europe made its greatest contribution to our culture through the printed word. Ever since the development of printing we have relied on communications media for the circulation of news and ideas. Radio and television have, of course, speeded up the process enormously, and film has come to fuse visual with literary statements; but we still rely heavily on books for the dissemination of intellectual developments and for knowledge of the past. Books, such as those published by Erasmus, enabled more people to form intelligent opinions and thus to question authority. Humanistic educators still share Erasmus' faith in the printed word's capacity to aid in the process of creating well-informed, soundly reasoning, independently thinking human individuals.

Reformation

Martin Luther pushed Erasmus' emphasis on the study of texts and rejection of authority to what Erasmus considered a radical extreme. Trained in humanistic methods, Luther used his extensive knowledge of Hebrew, Greek, and Latin to study the Bible directly, without the official interpretations of the Church, and to translate it into German, thus making it available to his fellow citizens. Luther's studies led him to believe that the original message of Christ had been distorted over the centuries. Given this insight, he felt compelled to reject "on conscience" certain doctrines and practices of the Church and, with many other contributing factors, launched the Reformation. Although Luther became as doctrinaire as the authorities he had rejected, the impetus he gave to thinking independently of authority has had far-reaching influences on the culture of the modern world. There is a direct line from Luther to the twentieth-century individual's sense of isolation, lack of direction, and need, in a tangle of conflicting values, to find himself or herself.

Cultural Relativism

Religious wars between Catholics and Protestants raged throughout Europe in the sixteenth century. Paradoxically, this period of religious troubles coincided with a tremendous economic boom, fueled in part by the importation of gold and silver from the New World. Swift economic change, population increase, and rapidly rising prices, however, probably added to the unsettling atmosphere created by religious controversy. At the intellectual level individuals such as Montaigne reflect a new and very modern feeling that truth and belief are, after all, relative matters.

Cultural relativism became during the sixteenth century a corollary to relativism in matters of opinion. In this era of travel and exploration, Europeans discovered in America, Africa, and Asia people who lived with customs and institutions very different from theirs. Just as Mediterranean peoples had once viewed Europeans as barbaric, many Europeans now thought the newly discovered cultures uncivilized, vastly inferior to their own. Intelligent observers such as Montaigne used the different cultural values to reflect what was corrupt and unjust in European society. Cultural relativism has served self-criticism and social satire ever since.

Shakespeare

The travels of Europeans in Africa led whites to reflect on the existence of black people. Prejudice was reinforced by a black/white symbolism already built into European languages, with black generally representing evil and white good. Shakespeare used this symbolism in English for his original purposes and, in Othello, created the first black hero of the European stage.

William Shakespeare embodies nearly all of the currents that we have witnessed in the Renaissance-Reformation period. Like Leonardo, Michelangelo, and Luther, he was a giant in an age of geniuses—one who discovered and mastered new worlds of thought and expression. His characters demonstrate a range of feeling from the early humanists' confidence in humanity's abilities and powers to late Renaissance skepticism and relativism and the Reformation's doubt that human beings can accomplish much of anything on their own. Shakespeare combined the medieval and the classical traditions to lay the basis for the modern theater. His Othello, conqueror and noble warrior, yet prey to unconscious passions, black in a white society, is both a hero of the late Renaissance and a representative modern individual.

PART SIX

Science and Splendor: The Seventeenth Century

20

The Consolidation of Modernity

Many of the tendencies we recognize as modern, the beginnings of which we have identified in preceding centuries, become embodied in institutions and daily life by 1650. By this time religious issues had ceased to be matters of life and death, religion had become detached from politics, and life was secular six days a week. Literature, painting, and sculpture increasingly depicted secular subjects by this time; the palace and the theater exerted immense influence on the architectural, artistic, and ceremonial forms of the churches.

The centralized state resting on a bureaucracy, a standing army, and a system of taxation developed into the dominant form of European government in the seventeenth century. These relatively stronger governments (which had their roots in the Middle Ages) endeavored to control and expand the economic life of their respective countries, fostering in the process the conception of a national economy in competition with other national economies for the world's riches. Importation of gold and spices from other continents had been important for European commerce before 1600, and the development of the plantation system in the Americas (tied to the African slave trade and the establishment of elaborate networks of trading posts on the coasts of Africa and Asia) reflects the existence of a worldwide market by the late seventeenth century. To meet the demands of such expanded economic horizons, Europeans devised financial and business institutions such as the joint-stock company and the national bank that characterize modern commercial life. At the same time that Europe set out to dominate the rest of the world through its stronger political and economic structures, its scientists turned their attention as never before to mastering nature for human use. This attitude, which was born in the so-called

Scientific Revolution, has eventually made possible immense material improvements in the human condition and has become the dominant goal—for good or ill—not only of Europeans but of the rest of the world as well.

Reform and Counter-Reform

By 1550 an objective observer of the European scene would perhaps have predicted the ultimate triumph of Protestantism over the old religion. England, which had broken with the Roman Church in 1534 primarily for political motives, was by this time a Protestant power. The Lutherans had gained half of Germany and were advancing; theirs had become the dominant religion in the Scandinavian peninsula. Calvinism was spreading rapidly in areas such as France, the Low Countries, and Poland.

Such a prophet, however, would have misjudged the determination of the most powerful country in Europe—Spain—and the continued vitality of the Catholic Church. After centuries of campaigning to drive the Moslems from the Iberian peninsula, the Spanish, after their final victory at Grenada in 1492, could at last play a role on the European scene. By the mid-sixteenth century, through a series of wars and accidents of birth and death, the king of Spain ruled an empire much greater in area than that of Rome at its height. Charles V was, at the time of his abdication in 1553, king of the combined monarchies of Castile and Aragon, inherited from his grandparents Ferdinand and Isabella. The Spanish inheritance included lands claimed by Castile in South, Central, and North America. As Holy Roman Emperor, he also governed Germany, the Low Countries, Austria, Bohemia, and Moravia, as well as large areas of France and more than half of Italy. The wealth of the silver mines of the New World allowed him to maintain the largest, most powerful army in Europe. Whereas Spain's nearest competitor, France, was riven by religious dissension, Charles and his immediate successors presided over a people whose Catholic faith had been successfully tested by centuries of crusading against the Spanish Muslims. The Spanish monarchs throughout the sixteenth and early seventeenth centuries were unquestionably the major champions of the faith throughout western Europe.

The success of the Catholic counteroffensive was not, however, simply built on the power of the Spanish infantry. The Council of Trent, the church council that met at Trent in northern Italy at various times between 1545 and 1563, laid the groundwork for a great church reform. The basic results of the Council of Trent were to define clearly what Catholics should believe, to make some crucial administrative reforms, and to provide for the creation of seminaries for the education of the clergy. Henceforth Catholics could no longer fall into heresy because they were not aware of the orthodox doctrines. The administrative reforms made the Church less vulnerable to criticism, and the steps to raise the educational level of the clergy resulted after decades in a new respect by laity for their priests. Therefore, while establishing a platform on which to base an attack on the Protestants, Trent also provided a program of reforms that would attract individual Christians back to the faith.

The new agencies of the Church (the Jesuit order founded in 1540 and the Holy Office of the Roman Inquisition established in 1542) played an extremely important part in seconding these efforts. Heresy or false belief had always been regarded as a disease that not only destroyed the soul of the heretic but also, if diffused, could corrupt the immortal souls of others. Once identified by a commission of experts, the *Inquisition*, the heretic was expected to abjure the errors for the good of the immortal soul. If he or she did not, or first abjured and then returned to the errors, the duty of the Inquisition was to have the person executed to prevent further infecting the community of believers.

The Inquisition

There had been various forms of inquisitions established over the centuries, mostly at the level of the bishopric or archbishopric. The most famous of all, however, was the Spanish Inquisition. It was set up in 1478 by Ferdinand and Isabella of Spain as a department of their government to ferret out *conversos*, converted Jews and Moors who, although professing Christianity, remained faithful to Judaism or Islam. Independent of the papacy, this inquisition was introduced into North America along with the Spanish conquistadors. By contrast, the Holy Office of the Roman Inquisition represented an effort of the papacy to concentrate investigation of heresy throughout the Catholic world at Rome. From that vantage point heresy could be pursued even among the princes of Europe and the Church. In the decades after its foundation more than one cardinal, for example, was forced to renounce a heretical or dangerous belief under threat of death or imprisonment. The efficiency of the new organization had the desired effect of preventing the diffusion of Protestantism as well as of more exotic beliefs among Catholic populations.

The Jesuits

Recognized as an order by the papacy in 1540, the Jesuits, founded by the Spanish knight Ignatius Loyola, were to become the right arm of the pope in the Counter-Reformation. Like previous religious orders, the Jesuits took a vow of poverty, chastity, and obedience, but in their case the last vow included a promise of complete obedience to the papacy at all times. As Loyola wrote: "If we wish to proceed securely in all things, we must hold fast to the following principle: What seems to be white, I will believe black if the hierarchical Church so defines."

The Jesuits formed an elitist body, composed of men admitted because of their intelligence, finesse, physical stamina, and deep commitment. Given a superb university education, they were capable of holding their own in any situation or discussion. They actively promoted papal policies on the international level as diplomats. More humble, but perhaps more important in the long run was their role as the prime educators of the middle and upper classes of Catholic Europe through the hundreds of schools that they established over the next century.. Everywhere they diffused the brand of spirituality developed by their founder. In his effort to bring the believer to a higher state of religious awareness, Loyola focused on training and disciplining the will. All sorts of appeals were made, at least in the initial stages of development, to the senses, emotions, and imagination. As we will see, this type of spirituality was intimately related to the evolution of the artistic styles called *baroque* in Catholic countries.

Having in a sense experienced a revival of heart and conviction through the Council of Trent, resting on two powerful instruments for orthodoxy, the Inquisition and the Jesuits, and backed by the military power of the greatest European monarchy, the Church in the last forty years of the sixteenth century set off on its campaign to drive the Protestant menace back and eventually to destroy its heresies. By 1600 Poland had all but completely returned to the Catholic camp; in France the French Calvinists, the Huguenots, had already reached their maximum membership and their power was on the wane. In Germany as well, the Protestant advance was by this date turning into a retreat. The Catholic reform, relying there on two powerful German states, Austria and Bavaria, was meeting success in converting one city after another back to the old faith. Everywhere the Jesuits were leaders in the campaign.

Religious Wars

This German Catholic campaign, however, was to precipitate one of the bloodiest wars in modern times. We have already discussed in the Reformation section of Volume I the thirty-year period of French religious wars that ended in 1594. In terms of the extent of destruction and the numbers of people killed, the German Thirty Years' War between 1618 and 1648 dwarfed its earlier French counterpart. This war began directly as a response of Bohemian Protestants to the efforts of their Catholic king (who was also the ruler of Austria) to suppress the Protestant faith in their country. After the Bohemians revolted, the war gradually spread to the whole empire; no one could safely remain neutral. The war was fought on both sides by large mercenary armies over which the German princes had little control. These armies had no interest in peace; wherever they went they brought death and devastation. Moreover, after the first few years the war in Germany became the focus for international rivalries, and the provinces of the empire served as a battlefield for invading armies of Denmark, Sweden, Spain, and France.

By 1648, when peace was finally signed at Westphalia, Germany was ruined from one end to the other. In effect the peace treaty reestablished the religious policy that had dominated Germany in the seventy years prior to the war: each German prince had the right to determine the religion of his state. The advance of the Counter-Reformation was, for all practical purposes, stopped. Spain, the bulwark of the Catholic offensive, was financially exhausted and in the grip of a serious demographic decline, and from 1648 on ceased to play a central role in European politics.

The Thirty Years' War, at least in the beginning a religious struggle, constitutes the last major European war fought for motives of religion. Europe had had its orgy of religious passion; now both sides sensibly recognized the sphere of influence held by the other. The lines separating Catholics in southern Europe from Protestants in the northern areas have remained fairly stable from that time to this. Although religious persecution of minorities might continue within individual countries, even at this level a new sense of

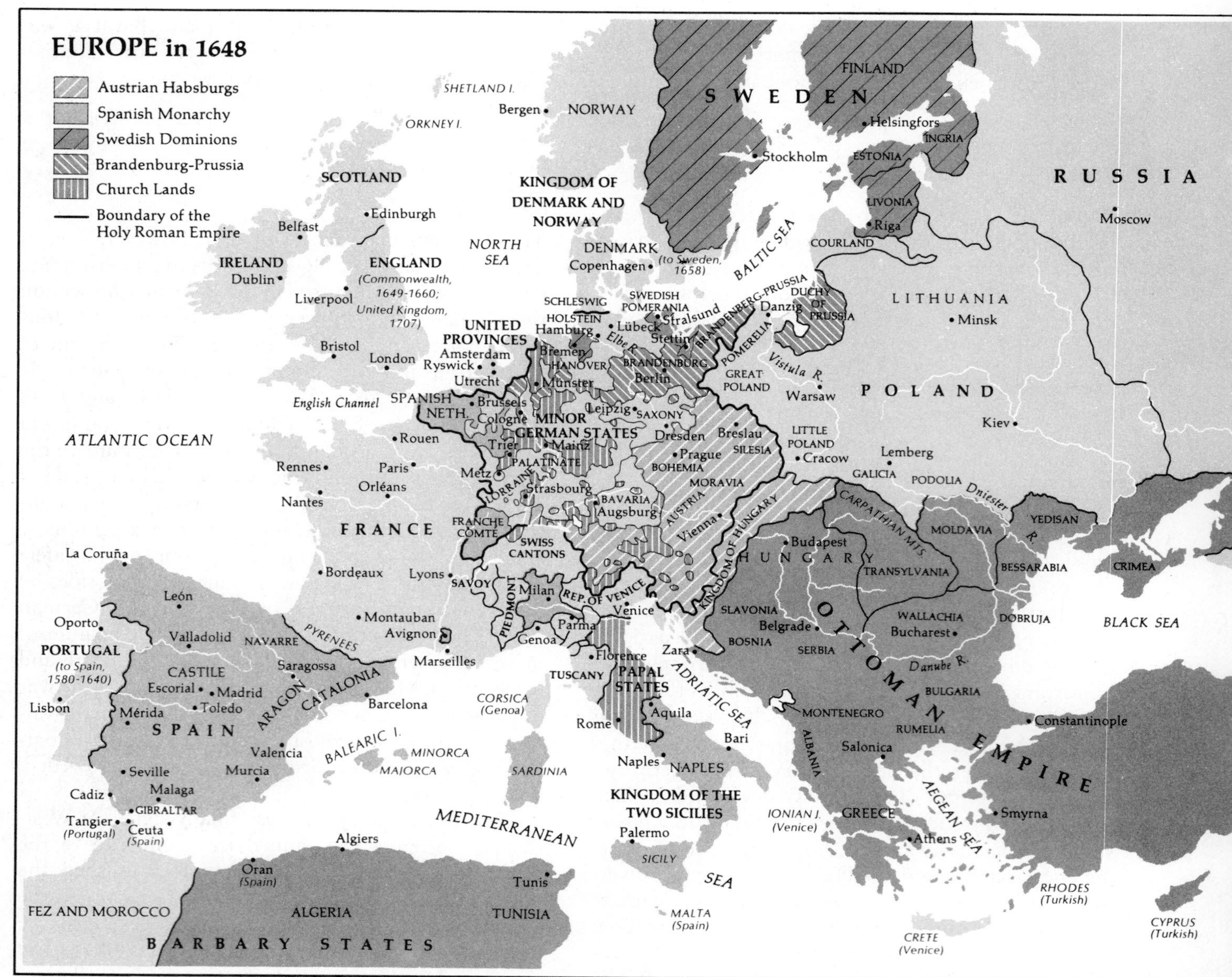

toleration was developing. King Louis XIV's revocation of the Protestant rights to worship in 1685 and his expulsion of Protestants from France were perhaps the last grand gestures of the Counter-Reformation.

By the end of the Thirty Years' War Europeans generally realized the senselessness of such struggles and the misery that they produced. But beneath the apparent tolerance of religious dissent also lay a growing religious indifference. Europeans on the whole no longer felt the need to judge their experience and to set their goals within a Christian frame of reference. Well might the student of European culture after 1650 ask: "What happened to God?"

The Scientific Revolution

So enormous and dazzling was the progress made in the course of the seventeenth century toward the understanding of the human body, the earth, and the heavens that it is not too much to say that by 1700 a radical change was taking place in the attitude of Europeans toward the interrelationship among humanity, God, and nature. At least in its initial stages this progress consisted in a rejection of the "commonsense" approach of ancient and medieval science. The European view of the universe in 1500 was substantially the same as that of Dante in 1300. The earth was at rest in the center, just as it appears, and the heavens rotated around it. These heavens—beginning with the moon, the sun, the planets out to the fixed stars—were either nine or ten in number. Beyond the outermost heaven, or the "first mover" that gave motion to everything in the universe, lay the region of God and the blessed. This universe was finite. God made the earth of heavy inferior substance, placing the finer heavenly bodies above the earth in ascending order of perfection. Since ancient times, however, astronomers had recognized a good deal of irregularity in the movement of the heavens. To make this conception fit the appearances, the astronomers had to add a whole series of special movements for individual bodies.

Although medieval and early Renaissance scholars were often very dedicated to the investigation of nature, they worked within the shadow of the ancients. The diffusion of knowledge of Greek in the fifteenth century, moreover, made available to Europeans a great number of ancient scientific writings not hitherto known, and this new scientific literature had to be absorbed. By the beginning of the sixteenth century, however, that process was completed. The translated works of Plato and his followers provided Europeans with the idea that all physical objects could be reduced to numbers and that mathematics was the key to understanding nature. This approach differed considerably from the medieval conception of science that investigated nature in terms of qualities: heavy or light, colored or transparent, voluntary or natural in movement, and the like. The increased cooperation during the Renaissance between workers skilled with their hands and scholars laid the basis for a joint effort in making new instruments for observing and calculating nature's operations. The methodology of ancient philosophers could be useful, but their authority now had to be tested against experience.

Copernicus and Kepler

The first fruit of the new concern with mathematics and experimentation was the work of the Polish priest and astronomer Nicholas Copernicus (1473–1543), who in fact had no intention of making an aggressive attack on the received ideas of his day. In his *On the Revolution of the Heavenly Bodies,* published in 1543 and dedicated to the pope, Copernicus generally accepted the traditional conception of a finite universe characterized by a series of heavens, the moon, the planets, and the fixed stars. Copernicus' innovation was to substitute the sun for the earth at the center of the universe. For him the earth became one of the planets and, like other bodies, circulated around the center.

Copernicus' primary reason for switching the position of the sun and earth was that this conception furnished a better explanation of the observed motions of the heavens, reducing the need to ascribe exceptional movements to individual bodies as in the earth-centered theory. According to the deeply religious Copernicus, the ability of his sun-centered theory to explain the appearances and to show heavenly motion to be simple and regular magnified the perfection of the divine creator.

Copernicus presented his ideas as a hypothesis; but over succeeding decades, as new observations were recorded and found to support it, some thinkers came to insist that the theory was proved. The ancient picture of the universe gradually disintegrated. Although embracing the finitude of the universe, Copernicus' theory laid the foundation for the idea of the infinite nature of God's creation. Whereas the earth-centered view of the universe maintained an absolute up and down, potentially Copernicus' theory suggested that space was relative. Even though the Copernican earth circulated around the sun, heavy bodies still fell to the earth. If the sun, which all agreed was a nobler body than the earth, was at the center of the universe, then the old view (that, beginning with the earth, other heavenly bodies increased in perfection as they came nearer to the outermost sphere) made no sense at all. Finally, the fact that mathematics played such a primary role in Copernicus' original analysis and in subsequent efforts to test it made mathematics appear as a key to scientific truth.

It fell to the mathematician-astronomer Johann Kepler (1571–1630) to discover that the orbit of the planets around the sun, including that of the earth, took the form of an ellipse. Kepler worked out a single set of mathematical formulas that could be applied to every planet. Although he could not say why the planets moved in this way, he was finally able to make sense of the appearance of planetary motion with his simple equations.

Galileo (1564–1642)

An aggressive publicist of the Scientific Revolution and one of its greatest contributors was a Florentine, Galileo Galilei. Both Copernicus and Kepler had worked with the naked eye. Galileo, informed of a new optical instrument developed in the Netherlands, the telescope, constructed one for himself and turned it toward the heavens. Through the lens of the fantastic instrument he was the first human being to see that Jupiter had moons like the earth's, and that the earth's own moon was made of material similar to that found on earth. The momentous conclusion was that heavenly bodies were not made of more perfect material. Rather, they resembled the earth and were governed by the same laws.

Galileo's conclusions were equally revolutionary when he turned to consider the behavior of bodies in motion. Traditional theories of dynamics, geared to the assumption that the natural state of a body was at rest, attempted to explain what caused motion to occur. For Galileo there was no "natural" motion of the body; rather, if a body was in motion, it would continue in a straight line at the same speed forever unless deflected, quickened, or retarded by another force—illustrating the principle of inertia. Thus what concerned Galileo was not why things move but why changes in motion occur and how one describes these changes mathematically. His formula for the acceleration of a freely falling body in terms of time and space represents the kind of solutions he had in mind.

A magnificent stylist, courageous to the point of rashness, Galileo trumpeted his discoveries in a series of eloquent works that brought him to the attention of the Inquisition. The Inquisition found his teachings dangerous in that they not only reduced the eternal heavens to the level of the earth but specifically contradicted passages of Scripture. After a period of imprisonment Galileo was forced to live under house arrest in Florence until his death. Although he was forbidden to work on astronomy, he was allowed to continue his researches on motion. In 1638 his *Discourse on Two New Sciences*, which provided the foundation for modern physics, was published in the Dutch republic.

Bacon (1561–1626)

Like his contemporary Galileo, the Englishman Francis Bacon was a gifted writer. Recognized as an outstanding essayist, Bacon has also been curiously designated by some scholars as the true author of the plays attributed to William Shakespeare. An ambitious and unscrupulous politician, he was lord chancellor of England between 1618 and 1621, under James I of England. Convicted of accepting bribes, he was dismissed and died in disgrace. Bacon is perhaps best remembered, however, as an early propagandist for the Scientific Revolution. His *New Organon* (1620), designed to replace Aristotle's logical works collectively called the *Organon*, called for a new approach to the study of nature. Science for Bacon was the means by which human beings could gain power over nature and use it for their own purposes. To do this, they needed a new instrument, a new method of approach. This new method was *empiricism*.

As far back as Aristotle, scholars had discussed the inductive method, but Bacon gave it a systematic presentation and is generally credited with being the founder of empiricism. The empirical method, which has profoundly influenced English and American thought ever since, relies on observation and experience as the roads to truth. Bacon held that we must begin by closer observation of nature, because every generalization has to be controlled by reference to specific instances.

The great shortcomings of Bacon's conception of science were his failure to appreciate the need to establish hypotheses in research and the value of mathematics. Although his methodology would ultimately prove effective in areas such as biology and chemistry, it was of little use in the fields of physics and astronomy, in which the most spectacular advances were made in the seventeenth century. Closer observation furnished data in these fields, but scientists employed mathematics for their interpretation of the data, thus they were essentially working by deduction. Nevertheless, Bacon's far-reaching criticism of contemporary natural science, his reliance on the independent judgment of the scientist based on personal observation, and his vision of the enormous benefits accruing to humanity from the scientific enterprise proved fundamental in the formation of a new attitude toward the study of nature.

Newton (1642–1727)

Bacon himself made no significant scientific discoveries, but another Englishman, Isaac Newton, accomplished the most dazzling scientific feat of the seventeenth century. This was to bring together Galileo's laws of inertia and falling bodies, Kepler's laws of celestial mechanics, and his own theory of gravitational force into a monumental system of physical principles and mathematical formulas by which every physical movement in the universe could potentially be described. Newton came to see that every body in the universe attracted every other body with a force proportional to the product of the two masses and inversely proportional to the square of the distance between them. Galileo's law that a moving body would fly off in a straight line unless affected by an external force held true for the heavens as for the earth. A planet moved in an elliptical motion around the sun and the moon in similar fashion around the earth because the mutual attraction of the two bodies drew the smaller in toward the larger and deflected the motion of the smaller into an orbit. The shape of the orbit and its velocity could be described by Galileo's formula for falling bodies.

Other Scientific Discoveries and Their Effects

Newton's findings, published in his *Mathematical Principles of Natural Philosophy* in 1687, marked the high point of the scientific revolution of the seventeenth century. But, if less spectacular, the discoveries in other areas of science were nonetheless important. In 1628 William Harvey (1578–1657) demonstrated the circulation of the blood, and at mid-century Anton van Leeuwenhoek (1632–1723) had developed the microscope, thus revealing a whole world hidden from the naked eye. Scientists such as Robert Boyle (1627–1691) were in subsequent decades involved in investigation of the action of gases.

No longer working in isolation, the scientists of this "revolution" developed communities. Societies like the Royal Society of London, founded in 1662, not only helped the diffusion of information among scientists but also brought their work to the attention of an educated public. For many, there were great expectations of a new era when, through the use of reason and new instruments, the human race would gradually eliminate the area of the unknown. But if the new discoveries brought confidence to some, others felt uncertain and confused. The Inquisition had justifiably regarded Galileo's doctrines as dangerous: people now had to deal with an order of truth appearing to contradict the Bible at several points. More than this, whereas the God of the Christian Middle Ages had been a God intimately connected with the human world, scientists such as Galileo and Newton approached the universe as if, after creating it, God had stepped aside and let nature run itself. The French philosopher Blaise Pascal phrased it: "The eternal silence of infinite spaces terrifies me."

Economic Life

Historians tend to date the birth of modern capitalism to the late sixteenth and early seventeenth centuries, but to understand what actually occurred an important distinction must be made. There are basically two types of capitalism: commercial and industrial. In commercial capitalism the capitalist is usually a merchant who invests money both in buying the raw material and in marketing the finished product once produced. In the case of wool cloth, for example, the merchant buys the raw wool; then either the merchant or an agent carries the wool to artisans who spin, weave, and dye it in their shops or homes. They usually work by the piece and own or rent their equipment. When the cloth is finished, the merchant then sells the product; the merchant's profit lies in the difference between what the cloth cost to produce and market and the purchase price of the finished goods.

This form of capitalism, with the merchant as the capitalist, began in the Middle Ages and remained the dominant form for the production of industrial goods down to the eighteenth century. The economic boom of the sixteenth century did not significantly affect the way that goods were produced; what did change was the number of people engaged in producing. The production of industrial goods significantly increased in the sixteenth century because so many more independent producers were working for the merchant.

Industrial capitalism, on the other hand, refers to investment in the modes or means of production. In this case the capitalist is not the merchant but the factory or mine owner. Investment in machines means more productivity per worker and more variety in products. To print books at all, for example, a significant investment must be made in a printing press. In the sixteenth century a rapid surge in the amount of investment in machinery occurred in areas such as metalworking, glass making, paper production, coal mining, and firearms manufacture. Although the output of goods provided by industrial capitalism climbed significantly after 1550, still down to the end of the eighteenth century commercial capitalism was responsible for most of the industrial production of Europe.

By 1550, European observers demonstrate an awareness of a long-term rise in prices that had begun by the end of the fifteenth century. Initially, the price rise came mainly in food products, testifying to the beginnings of a population increase after a century of demographic stagnation. But clearly the price rise was reinforced by the tremendous quantities of bullion pouring into Europe from the Spanish silver mines in the New World. In the long-term price rise, so favorable for investment, is to be found the major cause of the tremendous economic development that took place in most of Europe by the mid-sixteenth century.

In Spain, however—the prime source for the bullion—an expensive policy of conquest and an oppressive taxation policy falling on all but the upper classes combined to strangle both commercial and economic development. In an increasingly stratified society, the military, government service, and religion became the only valued professions. Spanish silver became diffused throughout Europe in the sixteenth century, partly through Spain's military expenditures abroad but also through its exportation to pay for imported goods its own investment-starved economy could not provide and to settle its ever-growing debts to foreign bankers.

In contrast with Spain's experience, the sixteenth century had proven highly profitable for Italy, the other major southern European country and the traditional economic center of Europe. The seventeenth century, however, witnessed a definitive movement of that center to the North Atlantic countries: France, England, and Holland. The two latter countries, both dominated by Protestants, were the leading seapowers of Europe. Both were also advanced in developing organizational forms of business capable of collecting large amounts of capital. The rest of Europe was characterized by family businesses until the nineteenth century, but these two countries used the joint-stock company to attract money into business ventures. Amsterdam was the center of a thriving stock exchange. In England and especially in Holland, banking arrangements so developed that businesses and private individuals were able to borrow large sums of money on credit.

These relatively enormous financial assets available for commercial investment meant that the Dutch and English would play a preponderant role in business ventures overseas. The plantation economy of the New World was in large part a product of this flow of capital that brought the slaves from Africa; purchased the sugar, rice, coffee, tobacco, and other commodities that the slaves produced; and marketed the goods in Europe. Even French, Spanish, and Portuguese planters depended for their survival on Dutch willingness to extend credit on purchases from harvest to harvest, a convenience not provided in their own countries.

The Age of Absolutism

The last half of the seventeenth century and most of the eighteenth has come to be recognized as the age of "absolute" monarchs. Although the king or queen had all sorts of practical limitations on what could be done without provoking a rebellion, he or she was absolute in the sense that there were no legal restraints or alternative constitutional institutions that could block the monarch's will. Of course, even in France, the ideal absolute monarchy, there were law courts and some provincial assemblies that could lawfully impede the royal decrees for a time; but eventually, if the king was willing to pay the price for publicizing the opposition, he could have his way.

By 1650 such investment of power in the royal office appeared to most observers the only way that the centralized state could advance against forces of decentralization such as the great nobility, the provincial government, and the autonomous cities. The two notable exceptions to this situation were the Dutch and the English. The fact that the Dutch had a small country, densely populated, with good communications and a weak nobility made its republican government feasible. The development of constitutional monarchy in England must be explained in the light of its small size and its early centralization and development of Parliament.

Whereas the English Parliament had established a tradition of consultation with the monarch, assemblies in France, Spain, Germany, and elsewhere brought together forces of localism opposed to concentration of power. Since the Middle Ages these were the elements that, in moments when the monarchy was weak, seized the opportunity to destroy the carefully accumulated powers of the state over its territories. The religious wars of the sixteenth and early seventeenth centuries had created an ideal situation for subjects of one religion to revolt against their king who had another. For instance, the revolt of some of the highest French nobility in the sixteenth century, although done in the name of the Protestant faith, was unquestionably also motivated by political ambitions. Consequently, monarchs and their advisers came to believe that only by taking legal authority out of the hands of cities, provinces, and the nobility and instead centering it in the monarch's hands could their countries ever experience domestic peace. In large part this policy was also supported by intellectuals and by the common people who had to choose between this or institutionalized anarchy.

Yet the monarch could not make a frontal attack on political privileges without provoking massive revolt. Basically, the European social structure was divided into three general classes: the nobility, the peasants (both in the countryside), and the bourgeoisie in the towns and cities. The latter class included groups as far apart as humble shoemakers and wealthy bankers. Consequently, we must distinguish the upper bourgeoisie, who controlled the cities, from the lower bourgeoisie, who often were economically not superior to the peasants.

From the sixteenth century in Spain and France and a century later in other parts of the continent, the monarchy developed a policy of compromise with the privileged middle classes in the cities and with the nobility. In return for sanctioning the political domination of the monarch and accepting the extension of his authority, the powerful interest groups were promised exemption from many of the burdens entailed. The king guaranteed the nobility and the upper bourgeoisie that they would not have to pay many of the new taxes and that the heaviest impositions would fall on the poor. Besides, the king acknowledged the monopoly of the nobility over the officer corps in the army and over the great ceremonial posts at court. By dazzling the bourgeoisie with the prospect of offices in the expanded central bureaucracy, the absolute monarch of the seventeenth century had the means to incorporate families of new wealth into the establishment and thus to render them supporters of the system; otherwise they would have constituted a disgruntled and potentially subversive bourgeois leadership.

Farther to the east, in countries such as Brandenburg-Prussia and Austria, the monarchies had emerged from the Middle Ages much weaker and more unstable than those in the west; as a result, eastern rulers were forced to go even further to obtain absolute political power. They granted the nobility (the middle class was insignificant in numbers) the right to reduce the local rural populations to the status of serfs. In Brandenburg-Prussia, moreover, the *Junkers*, or nobility, were made the only class legally allowed to own land.

As a result of these different compromises across Europe, the class structure in the various countries became more clearly defined: each had a legal relationship with the central government. At the same time the king became the sole judge of who would be admitted to the privileged classes, especially to the nobility. This right proved a great financial asset to the royal treasury, as most offices in the government were sold at a fixed price. The buyer earned only a small yearly salary from the government but was expected to make profits from those who needed the buyer's services in that position. Some of the higher government offices—and naturally the most expensive—carried with them a patent of nobility, ennobling forever the buyer and the buyer's descendants. This system permitted humble people who had money to put their families into the upper class. If an unlikely way to staff a bureaucracy, the method proved a good means of permitting social mobility.

But the concentration of power in the hands of kings, although affording domestic peace, had a different effect on international relations. More powerful monarchs with money to spend presided over larger armies and more far-ranging wars. In the Middle Ages and Renaissance, war was fought with troops raised for short periods of time; even the Hundred Years' War between France and England primarily consisted of a long series of summer campaigns spread out over more than a century. With the greater taxing power of the seventeenth-century monarchies, however, kings could afford to keep an army in the field for years at a time and to do so at a distance from the sources of supply. Consequently, there was a danger that one country might try to take over the whole of Europe, and kings felt it vital to their interests to know what their colleagues were about. This led to the increasing importance of diplomacy and to wars fought on the basis of international alliances.

Furthermore, as Europe became a political system based on a balance-of-power concept, in this century Europeans spread their rivalries to the rest of the world: to the Americas, Africa, and Asia. An important consequence of the increase in royal power was that the central government assumed the responsibility of regulating the economic life of the country and a commitment to fostering its development. Thus, more than ever before, hostilities between European powers appeared to be dictated by economic concerns: having influence in other areas of the world was regarded as significant for prosperity at home.

Hobbes (1588–1679)

The *Leviathan* of Thomas Hobbes was the first attempt to develop a political theory that examined the dominant tendencies of the Scientific Revolution. Despite what contemporary scientists said, Hobbes saw that they approached nature as if it were a purely mechanical system in which all could be explained by applying mathematics to the movements of bodies relative to one another. Taking geometry as his mathematical model, he started by examining the simplest elements and, by using self-evident principles, moved forward to the analysis of problems of greater complexity. He believed that each human being, like the rest of the universe, consisted of a series of motions. The center of each series was the heart, the source of vital motion in the body. Increases and decreases in this vital motion were transmitted through the sense organs, giving rise to two basic emotions, desire and aversion—movement toward that which heightened vitality and retreat from that which threatened it. The movement of other bodies stimulated one emotion or the other, depending on whether they favored or menaced the life force. Thus Hobbes's analysis rises from the study of the movement of bodies (physics) to that of the psychology and physiology of human beings.

The basic instinct of all people is the maintenance and, if possible, the heightening of the vital force. The desire for self-preservation leads to the pursuit of power, because one can never be secure enough:

> I put for a general inclination of all mankind, a perpetual and restless desire of power after power, that ceases only in death . . . because he [man] cannot assure the power and means to live well, which he hath present, without the acquisition of more.

Humanity existing in the state of nature, before the existence of government, experienced almost constant war. In a phrase that was to become classic, Hobbes described the human condition in this state as "solitary, poor, nasty, brutish, and short." It is improbable that Hobbes believed that there ever had been such a time, but consistent with his geometrical model, he (and subsequent philosophers) used the conception of a state of nature to get a clear focus on what *human* nature was like. Hobbes viewed people as essentially isolated, selfish beings. Given the misery of their circumstances, they could live in peace only after surrendering their freedom to an artificially created unitary will (Leviathan) with absolute power to rule. With the creation of Leviathan, both government and civil society came into existence.

Hobbes wrote his book in the belief that his theories would bolster the cause of monarchical absolutism, but he and his ideas were shunned by those he meant to defend. Whereas seventeenth-century monarchs justified their power as based on divine right, Hobbes considered it deriving from utilitarian needs: the alternative to royal absolutism was anarchy. His materialism, atheism, and denial that there was any absolute right or wrong also shocked his generation and earned him the epithet the Monster of Malmesbury.

Reading Selection

Francis Bacon

From the *New Organon*

Aphorisms

[Book One]

I

Man, being the servant and interpreter of Nature, can do and understand so much and so much only as he has observed in fact or in thought of the course of nature. Beyond this he neither knows anything nor can do anything.

II

Neither the naked hand nor the understanding left to itself can effect much. It is by instruments and helps that the work is done, which are as much wanted for the understanding as for the hand. And as the instruments of the hand either give motion or guide it, so the instruments of the mind supply either suggestions for the understanding or cautions.

III

Human knowledge and human power meet in one; for where the cause is not known the effect cannot be produced. Nature to be commanded must be obeyed.

IV

Toward the effecting of works, all that man can do is to put together or put asunder natural bodies. The rest is done by nature working within.

V

The study of nature with a view to works is engaged in by the mechanic, the mathematician, the physician, the alchemist, and the magician; but by all (as things now are) with slight endeavor and scanty success.

VI

It would be an unsound fancy and self-contradictory to expect that things which have never yet been done can be done except by means which have never yet been tried.

VIII

Moreover, the works already known are due to chance and experiment rather than to sciences; for the sciences we now possess are merely systems for the nice ordering and setting forth of things already invented, not methods of invention or directions for new works.

XI

As the sciences which we now have do not help us in finding out new works, so neither does the logic which we now have help us in finding out new sciences.

XII

The logic now in use serves rather to fix and give stability to the errors which have their foundation in commonly received notions than to help the search after truth. So it does more harm than good.

XVIII

The discoveries which have hitherto been made in the sciences are such as lie close to vulgar notions, scarcely beneath the surface. In order to penetrate into the inner and further recesses of nature, it is necessary that both notions and axioms be derived from things by a more sure and guarded way, and that a method of intellectual operation be introduced altogether better and more certain.

XIX

There are and can be only two ways of searching into and discovering truth. The one flies from the senses and particulars to the most general axioms, and from these principles, the truth of which it takes for settled and immovable, proceeds to judgment and to the discovery of middle axioms. And this way is now in fashion. The other derives axioms from the senses and particulars, rising by a gradual and unbroken ascent, so that it arrives at the most general axioms last of all. This is the true way, but as yet untried.

XXIV

It cannot be that axioms established by argumentation should avail for the discovery of new works, since the subtlety of nature is greater many times over than the subtlety of argument. But axioms duly and orderly formed from particulars easily discover the way to new particulars, and thus render sciences active.

XXXVI

One method of delivery alone remains to us which is simply this: we must lead men to the particulars themselves, and their series and order; while men on their side must force themselves for a while to lay their notions by and begin to familiarize themselves with facts.

XXXVII

The doctrine of those who have denied that certainty could be attained at all has some agreement with my way of proceeding at the first setting out; but they end in being infinitely separated and opposed. For the holders of that doctrine assert simply that nothing can be known. I also assert that not much can be known in nature by the way which is now in use. But then they go on to destroy the authority of the senses and understanding; whereas I proceed to devise and supply helps for the same.

XXXVIII

The idols and false notions which are now in possession of the human understanding, and have taken deep root therein, not only so beset men's minds that truth can hardly find entrance, but even after entrance is obtained, they will again in the very instauration of the sciences meet and trouble us, unless men being forewarned of the danger fortify themselves as far as may be against their assaults.

XXXIX

There are four classes of Idols which beset men's minds. To these for distinction's sake I have assigned names, calling the first class *Idols of the Tribe;* the second, *Idols of the Cave;* the third, *Idols of the Market Place;* the fourth, *Idols of the Theater.*

XLI

The Idols of the Tribe have their foundation in human nature itself, and in the tribe or race of men. For it is a false assertion that the sense of man is the measure of things. On the contrary, all perceptions as well of the sense as of the mind are according to the measure of the individual and not according to the measure of the universe. And the human understanding is like a false mirror, which, receiving rays irregularly, distorts and discolors the nature of things by mingling its own nature with it.

XLII

The Idols of the Cave are the idols of the individual man. For everyone (besides the errors common to human nature in general) has a cave or den of his own, which refracts and discolors the light of nature, owing either to his own proper and peculiar nature; or to his education and conversation with others; or to the reading of books, and the authority of those whom he esteems and admires; or to the differences of impressions, accordingly as they take place in a mind preoccupied and predisposed or in a mind indifferent and settled; or the like. So that the spirit of man (according as it is meted out to different individuals) is in fact a thing variable and full of perturbation, and governed as it were by chance. Whence it was well observed by Heraclitus that men look for sciences in their own lesser worlds, and not in the greater or common world.

XLIII

There are also Idols formed by the . . . association of men with each other, which I call Idols of the Market Place, on account of the commerce and consort of men there. For it is by discourse that men associate, and words are imposed according to the apprehension of the vulgar. And therefore the ill and unfit choice of words wonderfully obstructs the understanding. Nor do the definitions or explanations wherewith in some things learned men are wont to guard and defend themselves, by any means set the matter right. But words plainly force and overrule the understanding, and throw all into confusion, and lead men away into numberless empty controversies and idle fancies.

XLIV

Lastly, there are Idols which have immigrated into men's minds from the various dogmas of philosophies, and also from wrong laws of demonstration. These I call Idols of the Theater, because in my judgment all the received systems are but so many stage plays, representing worlds of their own creation after an unreal and scenic fashion. Nor is it only of the systems now in vogue, or only of the ancient sects and philosophies, that I speak; for many more plays of the same kind may yet be composed and in like artificial manner set forth; seeing that errors the most widely different have nevertheless causes for the most part alike. Neither again do I mean this only of entire systems, but also of many principles and axioms in science, which by tradition, credulity, and negligence have come to be received.

LXXXI

Again there is another great and powerful cause why the sciences have made but little progress, which is this. It is not possible to run a course aright when the goal itself has not been rightly placed. Now the true and lawful goal of the sciences is none other than this: that human life be endowed with new discoveries and powers. But of this the great majority have no feeling, but are merely hireling and professorial; except when it occasionally happens that some workman of acuter wit and covetous of honor applies himself to a new invention, which he mostly does at the expense of his fortunes. But in general, so far are men from proposing to themselves to augment the mass of arts and sciences, that from the mass already at hand they neither take nor look for anything more than what they may turn to use in their lectures, or to gain, or to reputation, or to some similar advantage. And if any one out of all the multitude court science with honest affection and for her own sake, yet even with him the object will be found to be rather the variety of contemplations and doctrines than the severe and rigid search after truth. And if by chance there be one who seeks after truth in earnest, yet even he will propose to himself such a kind of truth as shall yield satisfaction to the mind and understanding in rendering causes for things long since discovered, and not the truth which shall lead to new assurance of works and new light of axioms. If then the end of the sciences has not as yet been well placed, it is not strange that men have erred as to the means.

COMMENTS AND QUESTIONS

1. What does Bacon mean by "instruments of the mind"? What is their purpose?
2. Explain: "Nature to be commanded must be obeyed."
3. Why had there been so few scientific discoveries up to Bacon's time?
4. Why does Bacon define the four classes of idols?
5. Why does he feel it necessary to declare the goal of science? What is its objective?

21

The Baroque Style in the Arts

The social, religious, intellectual, and economic upheavals that characterized the late sixteenth and early seventeenth centuries were accompanied by a new style in the arts. The High Renaissance conventions of human beauty expressed in ideal proportions seemed to lead to a dead end. Luther and Calvin took to task the whole Catholic tradition of visual art in the service of religion, and they found Italian religious painting of the sixteenth century completely pagan. In literature and in music too Protestant doctrine demanded an art form less tied to classical antiquity and formal standards and more suitable to individualistic piety. Some of the best poetry and music of seventeenth-century Protestant Europe took the form of hymns. Catholics, zealous to defend their faith after the Council of Trent, found High Renaissance art inadequate for other reasons. In contrast to the Protestants, they vigorously reaffirmed the importance of rich visual and auditory imagery in churches and worship rituals. The intellectual and classical qualities of Renaissance art were found wanting in emotional appeal. Catholics wanted art that could enrapture the viewer, listener, or reader, appealing to the spirit through the senses and serving as an instrument of conversion.

Political and economic changes also had their effect on the development of new artistic forms. If the Protestant capitalists discouraged the decoration of churches, they encouraged paintings of themselves and the material objects surrounding them. Absolutist monarchy created a style of its own. Catholic monarchs liked to be shown in opulence and splendor, thus also encouraging a sensuous exploration of reality. One of the persistent characteristics of the new style in visual arts, literature, and music was a heightened sensuality combined with spirituality. Perhaps the long-lived disasters of the religious wars gave human beings zest for a life that seemed precarious and, at the same time, fervor for the life to come. Expanded trade and colonization in Africa and the New World gave artists wealth, more exotic themes, and an enlarged sense of space. The scientific and philosophical revolutions inevitably influenced artists' portrayals of reality. The shift from an authoritarian view of nature to an experimental one also encouraged artists to portray what they actually saw.

On the other hand, the new knowledge that the earth was not the center of the universe led artists to seek a depiction of enlarged space in contrast to the ordered, limited space suggested by Renaissance conventions. Seventeenth-century church architects and painters loved to give illusions of infinite space; musicians enlarged their tonal space to echo an illusion of infinity; poets and playwrights became preoccupied with the idea that life on earth is transient and precarious, or as the title of Calderón de la Barca's famous play states, *La vida es sueño;* life is a dream, an illusion. An English poet of the new age, John Donne, captured something of the effect of the Scientific Revolution on men's minds and spirits in a poem called "An Anatomie of the World."

> And new Philosophy calls all in doubt,
> The element of fire is quite put out;
> The Sun is lost, and th'earth, and no man's wit
> Can well direct him where to looke for it.
> And freely men confess that this world's spent,
> When in the Planets, and the Firmament
> They seeke so many new; they see that this
> Is crumbled out againe to his Atomies.
> 'Tis all in peeces, all coherence gone;
> All just supply, and all Relation.

The sense of being on a little planet in space rather than on firm earth is accompanied by a kind of breathless vertigo that is characteristic of much of seventeenth-century art. Yet the sense of earthly life as an illusion often appears along with a realistic depiction of it. This is one of the many contradictions of the period.

Historians of Spanish, Dutch, French, and sometimes English culture call the seventeenth century the "great century" or the "golden century." The power attained by these countries was accompanied by a great cultural outpouring in all fields. Italy, although waning in prominence, took an early lead in architecture, painting, music, and poetry, and Germany, toward the end of the century, produced the period's greatest musicians. Yet this period of rich productivity in the arts shows a diversity of style that makes it hard to classify. The stylistic terms most often used now to describe all of the arts in this century are taken from the vocabulary of visual arts: *baroque* and *neoclassical.*

Some cultural historians like to divide the century into two neat parts: the first, until roughly 1680, politically and religiously chaotic, is characterized as baroque, and the late part, a period of relative stability, as neoclassical. This may be approximately true of literature and art in most western countries, but the great period of baroque music did not end until the middle of the eighteenth century, and in the Slavic countries the baroque style in all the arts continued through that period. Even in France, where neoclassicism as a doctrine prevailed during the late-seventeenth-century reign of Louis XIV, certain elements of the baroque can still be found in the arts. We will focus on the reign of the "sun king" in Chapter 23. For now we will attempt to define some aspects of the baroque in the late sixteenth and early seventeenth centuries in the visual arts and poetry and in the seventeenth and early eighteenth centuries in music.

Baroque in the Visual Arts

The rather strange word *baroque* (from Italian *barocco*) originally meant a logical process that was contorted or involuted. In Portuguese, *perola barroca* was a term used by jewelers to designate a rough or irregularly shaped pearl. The French, by the eighteenth century, used the word *baroque* to mean "a painting ... in which the rules of proportion are not observed and everything is represented according to the artist's whim." All of these meanings were, like "Gothic," originally pejorative. What these definitions share in common is the sense of divergence from an established, accepted ideal. As art history and criticism evolved and the seventeenth century was revalued, *baroque* appeared to be the opposite of *classical,* in reference either to antiquity or to the High Renaissance. In this sense the term suggested art that was naturalistic rather than ideal, and emotional rather than rational. Translated visually, this would produce an art of movement, vitality, and brilliant color. Subjects could be chosen from daily life, as well as antiquity and the Bible, and presented to achieve maximum emotional impact or intense, detached observation.

Baroque Painting

Italian artists fashioned a new vision of the world that created an artistic revolution in the fifteenth century. This new way of seeing and painting inspired artists all

21-1 *Pieter Brueghel (the Elder),* Landscape with the Fall of Icarus, *c. 1554–55. Panel painting transferred to canvas, 29′ × 44′1/8″. (Copyright A.C.L.—Bruxelles; Institut Royal du Patrimoine Artistique)*

over Europe. The artistic accomplishments of the Italians were disseminated north and west, where they married with the explorations, ideas, and traditions of other countries. Artists in the Netherlands, Spain, France, and England gave their art a particular flavor drawn from their place and its expectations. For example, many Dutch and German artists painted scenes from daily life—farmers, skaters, hunters, village celebrations—subjects absent from the work of most Italian artists of the sixteenth century. Pieter Brueghel the Elder (born in Flanders, c. 1525–1569), who painted *Hunters in the Snow* and *The Harvest* (1565) (Color Plate XII), created a substantial body of work dealing with classical myths and Christian subjects. His human subjects, however, frequently appear subsumed by his sublime rendering of the natural world. In *Landscape with the Fall of Icarus* (Fig. 21-1) (1554–1555) the drowning young man seems an afterthought in this scene of spring plowing. Icarus' naked legs and his gesticulating father in the lower right midground of the painting are far less interesting than the sunlit world of coast, farm, and sky.

In contrast, the work of El Greco (born Domenikos Theotokopoulos in Crete, 1541–1614), a student in Italy and a successful artist in Spain at the end of the sixteenth century, seems both courtly and intensely mystical. The *Burial of Count Orgaz* (1586) (Fig. 21-2) uses a vocabulary of form and color whose sources are Italian painting but whose feeling is uniquely El Greco's. The interment of the saintly Orgaz, being laid to rest by priests and friends, fills the lower half of the large canvas; the upper half is aswirl with saints, angels, Christ, and the Virgin, who welcome his soul to heaven. The expressive faces of the noblemen who attend Orgaz, the glittering surface of objects rendered vividly, have a life and energy far different from work by Raphael and his peers. By 1600, when El Greco painted his *View of Toledo* (Color Plate XIII), sky, earth, and air take on unearthly tones of light and movement that seem to be the product of an intensely personal experience and artistic language. El Greco's painting speaks of an independent vision, an individual soul.

By the end of the sixteenth century, the artistic vocabulary of Europe had expanded to create masterpieces removed both visually and emotionally from the art of the preceding one hundred years. It was this legacy, a vast body of paintings, prints, sculpture, and architecture, that provided the artists of the seventeenth century with unlimited resources for their own personal development. And the general term *baroque*, which is used to characterize their work, must always be qualified by reference to time, artist, and place of its production. Painters from France, Italy, the Netherlands, and Spain created works that demonstrate both the diversity and the shared characteristics of painting in the seventeenth century.

Caravaggio (1573–1610)

Born Michelangelo Merisi, Caravaggio took the name of his hometown in Lombardy. He arrived in Rome during his late teens. There he lived like a rebel, was constantly in trouble for fighting and other violence, killed a man over a tennis match, and fled the city around 1606. His intense anger spilled over into his

21-2 *El Greco,* Burial of Count Orgaz, *1586, oil on canvas, 16′ × 11′10″, S. Tomé, Toledo, Spain. (Alinari/Art Resource, NY)*

painting. Caravaggio seems to have deliberately sought to shock people with his art. He produced pictures that seem to dwell on the harsh and brutal reality of daily life—his painting of Christ's mother's corpse (Fig. 21-3) portrays a dead, bloated old woman. But these realities were a means of triggering the intense internal reality of conflicting feelings that Christ and his message brought to sinful men.

The Calling of Saint Matthew (1599–1600) (Color Plate XIV), one of three scenes from the apostle's life painted by Caravaggio to decorate the Contarelli Chapel in a church in Rome, demonstrates the psychological reality Caravaggio could draw from a simple scene. The event takes place in a Roman tavern; filtered light falls from the oiled paper in the window onto the bare walls and floor. Another, stronger light slashes across the top third of the canvas. This light reveals the face and uplifted hand of Jesus, who, with Peter, steps into the room. Matthew the publican is seated at a table with three somewhat rustic, tacky youths. An older man leans over Matthew's shoulder, and Matthew himself, who looks up somewhat surprised, shows with his face and gesture the eternal "Who, me?" even as he draws away from Christ.

What has Caravaggio done to make this such a revolutionary picture? He has located this event in a specific, real setting—a tavern populated with figures who are certainly not idealized in any way. They seem to lounge casually around the table, turning away from the event and the viewer, heightening a sense of irony. Peter and Christ seem like momentary intruders who bring with them an unexpected, uncomfortable, revealing light. The viewer, who knows more than Matthew, stands very close indeed, almost in the scene. Nothing separates the real from the painted, and the objects in the painting itself are rendered with hard, firm edges and substantial, varied textures, eliciting a powerful tactile response in the viewer. How could a spiritual event be portrayed with such earthy power? The contrasts reinforce the power of Christ's gesture that makes the earthly divine.

21-3 *Caravaggio,* The Death of the Virgin. *(Alinari/Art Resource, NY)*

21-4 *Peter Paul Rubens,* The Raising of the Cross *(center panel of a triptych), 1609–10, 15′2″ × 11′2″, Cathedral of Antwerp. (Copyright A.C.L.—Bruxelles; Institut Royal du Patrimoine Artistique)*

Peter Paul Rubens (1577–1640)

Rubens was the son of a wealthy Antwerp Protestant who fled to Germany to avoid persecution by the Catholics seeking control of the Netherlands. After his father's death, his family returned to Antwerp, and Rubens grew up a Catholic. Amiable, handsome, and energetic, he was already a successful painter when he journeyed to Italy in 1600. He remained there until 1608, assimilating the art of the High Renaissance and ancient Rome, and the revolutionary naturalism of Caravaggio. From these sources he created his own distinctive, optimistic, and visually rich view of the world.

When Rubens returned to Flanders he was made court painter to the Spanish regent, and commissions began to flow into his workshop. He married well and lived in a magnificent townhouse in Antwerp that housed his collections of sculptures, paintings, antique coins, and gems, and his personal library. His studio was soon filled with assistants who transferred his sketches onto large canvases. Even when he was absent on diplomatic and professional visits to France, England, or Spain, work was still produced to await his final approval and finishing touches.

The Raising of the Cross (Fig. 21-4), painted in 1609–1610, is the central panel of a *triptych,* a three-part altarpiece executed for the cathedral in Antwerp. It is a splendid example of the new style that emerged from his Italian sojourn. The athletic, muscular figure of Christ on the cross is placed on a diagonal away from the front plane established by the surface of the canvas. Massive, muscular figures struggle to raise the cross. The background is a dark one, where leaves are silhouetted against a stormy sky. The light, falling from right to left, is a dramatic stage light that picks out faces and limbs. The physical stress and earthy faces of the soldiers contrast with Christ's upward-turned eyes and sagging body. The body types owe much to Michelangelo, and the essentially triangular *composition* is based on a similar Renaissance device. But the energy and vitality of the figures, the movement back into deep space, and the dramatic lighting contrast with the order and symmetry of Renaissance painting. There is a loving attention to the color and textures of flesh, armor, and other objects—such as the curly, soft coat of the agitated dog in the lower foreground—that heightens our awareness of this event. *Colors* themselves are strong, and the paint surface is a smooth, rich one, which enables paint to be seen as paint as well as the delineator of form and surface. Rubens has used naturalistic details, but how do they differ in effect from those of Caravaggio?

Rubens received many important commissions, but surely one of the most important was for a series of twenty-one canvases to celebrate the career of Marie de' Medici, widow of Henry IV and regent of France during the minority of her son, Louis XIII. These canvases transform an inglorious, occasionally unscrupulous, and not too beautiful individual into a woman of splendor through the unity of myth, fact, history, and allegory. For example, Marie's arrival at Marseilles (Fig. 21-5) shows her greeted by helmeted France, attended by Fame and Neptune, whose court rises from the water to celebrate her safe voyage. Marie, at the center right, is only a part of the rather glorious assemblage, which is beautiful for its rich colors, textures, and vitality of light and movement. We realize that the paintings for Marie were commissioned not only for self-glorification but also for the glorification of the French monarchy and its increasing power. Baroque art could serve to glorify the absolute monarchy as well as the Church Militant.

Rubens was adept at this kind of commission; indeed, his portraits of kings and queens, prelates and

21-5 *Peter Paul Rubens,* Arrival of Marie de Medici at Marseilles, *Louvre, Paris. (Art Resource, NY)*

courtiers, depict the brilliant world of the first half of the seventeenth century. But it is important to remember that this great master could render not only memorable scenes of both spiritual and temporal power but also those of his own life and of the world of persons and objects that he loved.

Garden of Love, painted in 1638 and inspired by Rubens's second marriage, demonstrates the earthly love whose divine counterpart was the impetus for his great paintings of Christian subjects (Color Plate XV). Rubens and his young wife, Helene, the couple at the far left, are shown in a garden, about to join a group of obviously loving couples—husbands and wives or friends and lovers, it is hardly important. The fantastic fountain house from the artist's garden in Antwerp provides background. A statue of Venus and mischievous cupids complete this vision. The colors are soft and warm, light, gay, ripe, and sensuous. The figures—who stand, sit, lean, talk, and gaze—melt into each other in a soft, flowing rhythm. Velvet and satin, soft skin and hair, sparkling eyes, and rosy lips seduce us with a vision of the joy of life and love that is suspended in this spring garden. The courtly man in the broad-brimmed hat introduces us to a world that will be, more and more, the subject of art—a golden time without pain or anxiety.

Rembrandt van Rijn (1606–1669)

Born in Leiden, near Amsterdam, Rembrandt spent his life in the Protestant society of Holland. This society appears sober and restrained, in contrast to that of Rubens's patrons. The Calvinists did not permit the painting of images, and the churches were not great patrons of the arts. But the country of the Dutch Calvinists and Lutherans was prosperous. These industrious, democratic antiroyalists established a worldwide commercial empire that brought wealth and power to many people. The land of tulips was also a country in which, for the first time, many people actively sought to buy and own art to adorn their own homes. Travelers in Holland in the seventeenth century noted that almost every family owned at least one original work of art. And for the first time, many painters made their livelihood in a free market. Paintings and prints of the flat country of land and water, with its huge, tumultuous sky, the rich and lovely interiors of private homes, as well as sumptuous still-life pictures, were popular. *The Three Trees*, an etching made by Rembrandt about 1643 (Fig. 21-6) depicts the Dutch landscape. His great portraits, subjects from the Bible and mythology, adorned the interiors that his pictures celebrate as they also celebrate the material world, personal success, and pietistic faith of the independent Dutch.

Seated around a table covered with a magnificent red oriental rug, attended by a servant, the black-coated *Syndics of the Drapers' Guild* discuss the affairs of the guild (Color Plate XVI). Yet the moment is not altogether public, for they seem to have been caught in a quiet conversation. One man rises from his seat to greet someone who has come into the room, and all eyes focus on that person. The intruder is, of course, the viewer, and this is one of the qualities that give the picture its life. The men, who seem completely unposed, become the focus of our attention through their glances, their alert faces, the direction of light, and their white collars and broad-brimmed hats. Each is an individual; each face exhibits age, experience, and reserve. The surface textures, contours of form, and features of faces and hair are all rendered with soft, easily flowing brushstrokes. The firm clarity that is present in much of Rubens's work is absent here, but

21-6 *Rembrandt,* The Three Trees, *etching, 1643. (The Metropolitan Museum of Art, bequest of Mrs. H. O. Havemeyer, 1929. The H. O. Havemeyer Collection. 29.107.31)*

the painting exhibits a softness derived from suffused light more comparable to that in *The Garden of Love.*

Rembrandt's sympathy with his patrons and their view of life grew from his own experience. His subject is always humankind, and the face, costume, and demeanor become a means to explore the internal life, with its pain, power, and pride. Thus, in his self-portraits, his own face becomes a vehicle for exploring the changes that life leaves on the body and the soul. One can follow his transformation from a foppish, well-dressed young man in the *Self-Portrait with Saskia* (his first wife) (Fig. 21-7), painted about 1635, to a mature, introspective man (Fig. 21-8), to a balding and turbaned artist holding his palette (Color Plate XVII).

Rembrandt's genius, like Rubens's, lay in the unity of composition achieved by light and by the revelation of surface features, textures, and colors in light. Renaissance painting developed conventions in which light was generally clear, even, and uniformly revealing. Masaccio, Piero, Botticelli, Raphael, and Leonardo all employed a representation of light that is not intrusive. It is a steady light that has been studied in nature but controlled in the studio. It may be slightly *warm*—that is, tending to emphasize the warm reds, yellows, and oranges of the spectrum—or it may be *cool*—emphasizing the cool blues, greens, and purples of the spectrum—but, above all, it is consistent. Along with this convention of uniform light, the Renaissance painters used another by designating *shade* or *shadow* with gray, brown, or black layers of paint. This is not the way that shades and shadows are colored in nature, but it is the way that they were conventionally depicted. Without shade and shadow there is little or no sense of volume and space. Showing shade and shadow as an absence of color gives a great sense of uniformity to a picture, particularly uniformity of light.

Just as Caravaggio used light in a new way, so, too, did Rubens and Rembrandt, who experimented with and elaborated on the conventions that had defined the way light would be rendered in fifteenth- and sixteenth-century painting. Rubens, like Caravaggio, used light dramatically to reveal and focus on objects, but unlike Caravaggio, whose light usually revealed the harsh reality of things, Rubens used light to reveal color and texture and to enliven and enhance objects. Rembrandt used light to create much sharper contrasts between figures and objects in space. In deep shadows and shadowed faces we find that same mystery of life and death, pain and joy. Although these themes were present in Rubens's work, Rembrandt portrays them without explosive theatricality. The drama becomes more personal and introspective; it is not something that we witness, but rather something that we experience. The contrast is indicative of the difference in emphasis between the theatricality of Counter-Reformation Catholicism and the individual piety of the Protestant north.

21-7 *Rembrandt,* Self-Portrait with Saskia. *(Staatliche Kunstsammlungen, Dresden)*

Return of the Prodigal Son (c. 1669) (Color Plate XVIII) is such a shadowed, almost soundless picture. The warm light falling on figures and faces reinforces the general warmth of the picture that is derived from gesture as well as from color scheme. The faces that witness this reunion seem observed in light reflected from the two major figures. There is no boisterous welcome but instead tender, loving forgiveness. This is earthly love raised to a divine power by the simplicity of composition. The paint itself seems thin except in the figures of father and son, where heavy *impastoed* layers, creating form and shadow, allude to textures. Unlike the uniformly smooth surface of Renaissance pictures, these contrasting layers of paint tell, as they do in Rubens's work, of the expansion of another Renaissance convention.

Jan Vermeer (1632–1675)

The ability to make paint give the illusion of reality has almost no limits. The Dutch landscape painters of the sixteenth century created a means of capturing a feeling of space and light, of movement, air, and color that created remarkable windows onto the world. But the size of the picture itself, as well as its careful, studio-produced composition, always checks the viewer's feeling that it is the natural world observed. Vermeer of Delft, the third great northern painter of the seventeenth century, took his experiences in the natural world and refined them to create visions that seem to be nothing so much as fragmentary moments of real time captured in a painting. His apparently simple subjects are very much in the tradition of painting in Holland and the Low Countries. Domestic scenes like *Woman with a Lute* (Fig. 21-9) had been popular for many generations. But in the work of Vermeer, these transient moments are rendered permanent.

In *The Kitchenmaid* (Color Plate XIX) a maidservant stands before a window pouring milk from a pitcher into a basin. The light from the window is cool and subdued; the colors of her sleeves, apron, and the tablecloth are also cool. The pottery basin and bowl, the cut bread, the basket, the gold of her bodice, and the red of her skirt challenge the cool, quiet northern light that falls from the window above her head. The woman is unself-conscious and unremarkable, solid and three-dimensional; her weight and volume act as a fulcrum for all the objects in the room. The milk falls of its own weight into the basin.

21-8 *Rembrandt,* Self-Portrait, *1658. (The Frick Collection, New York)*

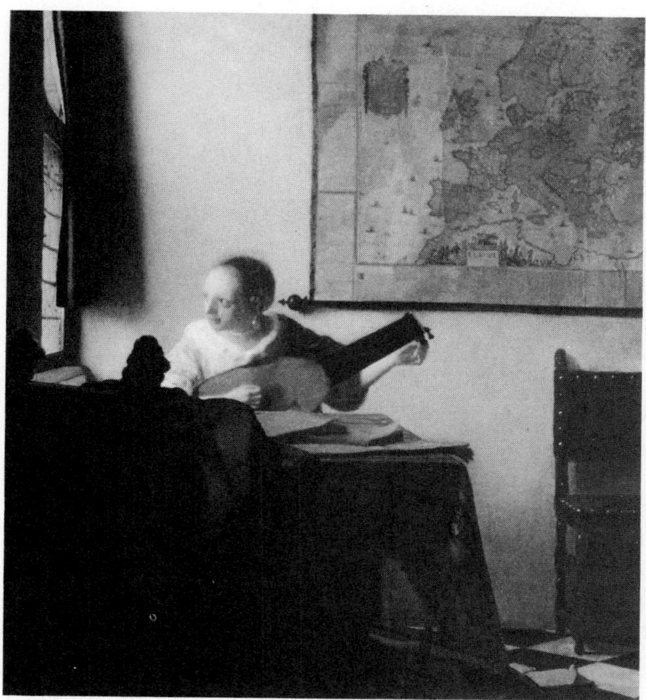

21-9 *Vermeer,* Woman with a Lute. *Oil on canvas. (The Metropolitan Museum of Art, bequest of Collis P. Huntington, 1900)*

What is so remarkable about this painting? The original, more than a reproduction, emits an incredible transparency and glow. It is possible to imagine that, should the light be gone from the room, the painting itself would provide light—so natural and convincing is its revelation of every surface, fold, and wrinkle. The colors themselves vibrate; shadows and folds are not rendered in gray, brown, or black but in thin layers of color itself—deeper blue in her apron, deeper golden red on the basin.

Light, of course, is the most essential and most recalcitrant element in all painting that seeks to render an account of nature as we perceive it. Artists have captured it by conventionalizing its representation. Raphael's even harmonious light, Rubens's dramatic spotlight effects, and Rembrandt's reflected light are some examples of the different ways to render light convincingly without absolute fidelity to light as it is experienced naturally. Vermeer, however, by confining his subjects almost exclusively to figures before windows, proclaims his interest in the transient, cool light that comes from outside and is therefore subject to immediate change. Yet change never occurs, and that is what delights: it is "real" and it is not! We know that *The School of Athens* and *Primavera* are rendered through knowledge of the behavior of light, but there is no attempt to cajole us into thinking that it is "real" or experienced light—not so with Vermeer. Moreover, a woman weighing gold, a girl reading a letter, or a geographer in his study are all intimate revelations of transience where light reveals and suggests the brevity of life and the ephemeral pleasure of things.

As we experience these pictures by Vermeer, we add another layer to our perception of the seventeenth century. Here is a vision very different from that of a Rubens or a Rembrandt. In its realism it is more like Caravaggio, but its order recalls Piero and Raphael. Above all, however, Vermeer's study of light and delineation of space is uniquely his own, as individual and personally centered as he could make it.

Diego Rodríguez de Silva y Velázquez (1599–1660)

It is perhaps curious that of all the acknowledged masters of the seventeenth century, a painter at the court of Philip IV, in the period of Spain's decline, could have created a highly original and personal style based on pure sensibility and perceptual experience. During the same years that Rubens executed great religious paintings, and Ribera and Zurbarán, Spanish contemporaries of Velázquez, made deeply moving and powerful religious pictures for Spanish patrons and the Church, the court painter (he had joined the court in 1623, remained there, and was made court chamberlain in 1652) produced few religious subjects. Rather, his fame grew from his stunning portraits and scenes of classical allegory and myth. Visiting Italy twice provided inspiration but did not essentially alter his manner. Velázquez's manner is most comparable to that of Vermeer. Like Vermeer, he was fascinated by light on objects, the light that reveals and conceals the images the artist sees and reproduces. Thus the actual surfaces of Velázquez's paintings reveal an elegant and systematic brushwork that depicts objects as fragments of light and shade, of colors placed side by side. The edges of objects are slightly indeterminate; the surface is never harsh or crisp but rather seems perpetually modulated by the movement of air and light. The most telling experience is to see a painting by Velázquez and to stalk it silently in an attempt to discover the precise moment at which the surface dissolves into the fragments, layers, and dots that constitute the source of the painted image. This is difficult, however, for the moment of dissolution is so close to the moment of seeing the image as a complete whole.

This kind of painting seems to lend itself to speculations about kinds of reality—the reality of image, of surface, of object. Yet like Vermeer's paintings, Velázquez's works do not suggest speculation; rather, they seem truly to depict reality. His most famous work, *Las Meninas* (The Ladies-in-Waiting), painted in 1656, typifies his greatest work (Color Plate XX).

In the center of the large canvas, near the front edge, stands the five-year-old princess who has come to visit the painter in his studio. To the left stands Velázquez, a very large canvas on his easel. The ladies-in-waiting attend the princess, and to the right are two dwarfs, whose plainness plays against the glitter of royalty. A dog lies quietly in the foreground, a court official enters a lighted doorway at the back of the room. It is then that the viewer sees, or is shown, the images of the king and queen, reflected by a mirror at the back of the room. They, too, have come to the studio of their painter, who must be working on a painting of the royal family.

The light in this painting seems to fall into the room from an unseen window to the left. It lights the figures, the foreground, and the king and queen, who stand where the viewer might be. As with Vermeer's painting, it is possible to imagine that one could see into the painting in the dark, because it seems to contain its own light. The surface is fairly smooth, but rich with the paints that so carefully re-create the varying surfaces of hair, skin, fabric, fur, embroidery, jewelry. It is a remarkable achievement; the painting seems to breathe with a life drawn from experienced reality, captured on canvas.

Rubens, Rembrandt, and Caravaggio, each in his own way, explore human emotions with power, drama, and sometimes the rhetoric of experience. Vermeer and Velázquez, on the other hand, seem to explore the experienced world in a direct and candid way, sacrificing nothing to give an account of the essentials of seeing, yet creating an extraordinary series of masterpieces that are, in fact, as carefully considered, composed, and conceptualized as the work of their predecessors or their peers.

Baroque Architecture and Sculpture in Rome

It was in a Rome dominated by the papacy and the militant Counter-Reformation that the baroque style in architecture began. In the late sixteenth century the popes began to transform the city. A system of wide thoroughfares and squares united the major churches and sites of the pilgrim processional. There was innovative accommodation for wheeled and pedestrian traffic. There was also a sense of order to the city, recalling that produced by the ancient Forum. The pope's cathedral, Saint Peter's, was begun in the early sixteenth century (Fig. 21-10), the dome and east end, carried forth under Michelangelo, was brought to completion and aggrandized by a succession of powerful popes. Gian Lorenzo Bernini, the greatest sculptor of the seventeenth century, was commissioned to finish the interior. He designed the great canopy that stands over the high altar; the enormous elevated throne, the Chair of Saint Peter, in the east end (Fig. 21-11); and the magnificent staircase that connects the papal apartments with the west front of the church.

All these features seem like sets for a grand spectacle, but none more so than the great plaza and colonnade set before the church to provide the necessary vista for a view of the great hovering dome of Saint Peter's. The arms of the Tuscan Doric colonnade reach down from the ends of the church façade, compress slightly, and then swell into the curved arms of the oval that welcomes the pilgrim to Saint Peter's (Fig. 21-12). The architectural vocabulary is that of Rome and the Renaissance but employed on a massive, monumental scale. The colonnade, for example, is four columns deep. Decorated with fountains and an Egyptian obelisk, this piazza—and others like it opened in Rome and decorated by Bernini and his peers—became important in the development of urban planning. Rome itself was adorned with new churches and palaces. In their interiors are still found paintings and sculptures that represent persuasive, powerful propaganda for the faith.

In contrast to the vast adornments of Saint Peter's, Bernini planned other, more intimate decorative schemes that were focused on his magnificent sculptures. Such a scheme is the Cornaro Chapel at Santa Maria della Vittoria in Rome (1645–1652) (Fig. 21-13). An anonymous eighteenth-century painting of the chapel gives us the best idea of the ensemble, whose subject is the ecstasy of Saint Teresa. Teresa of Ávila was a sixteenth-century Spanish nun whose writings on her ecstatic vision particularly appealed to the sensibility of the seventeenth century. The ceiling of the vaulted chapel seems to disappear as angels greet the dove of the Holy Spirit in a burst of divine, heavenly light. The architectural frame swells out to create a stage for the cloud with its burden of a limp, sagging Saint Teresa and a beautiful, smiling angel who holds an arrow in his upraised hand and with the other gently raises her habit to reveal her heart. In her autobiography Saint Teresa had described this vision in which an angel with a flaming golden arrow pierced her heart. "The pain was so great that I screamed aloud, but simultaneously felt such infinite sweetness

21-10 *Saint Peter's, Rome, aerial view. (Alinari/Art Resource, NY)*

21-11 *Bernini, Chair of Saint Peter, St. Peter's, Rome. (Alinari/Art Resource, NY)*

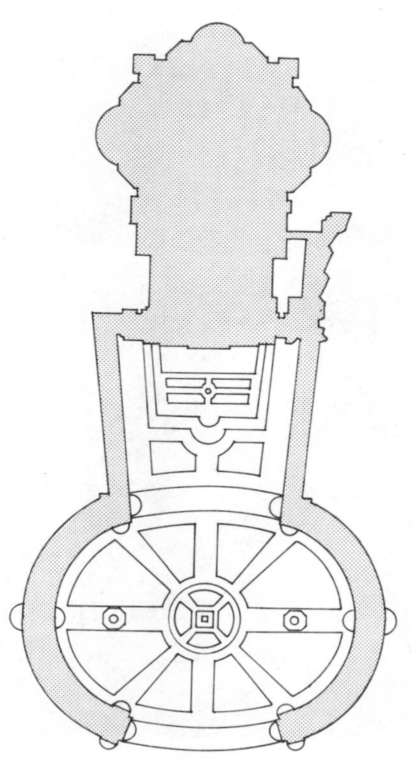

21-12 *Groundplan. Saint Peter's Square.*

that I wished the pain to last eternally. It was the sweetest caressing of the soul by God." The saint's mouth is open, as if to cry out, but the movement of her complex drapery contrasts with her thrown-back head and arm so that she seems to move both away from and toward this awesome divine love (Fig. 21-14). There is a distinctly erotic tone to pose and gesture, which is enhanced by the realistic rendition of hands, feet, and face of the saint and the angel's soft feathered wings and curls. The bronze rays falling behind the group reinforce the real light, and the marble paneling of the wall is continuous with that in the rest of the chapel. We observe from the ground, but members of the Cornaro family are in boxes on either side—these are also part of the total ensemble of sculpted and painted decoration, for the figures are marble reliefs. It is significant that many Catholics, including Bernini, practiced exercises of prayer and self-denial that were designed to induce suffering and delight comparable to that of Christ and the saints.

21-14 *Bernini,* The Ecstasy of Saint Theresa, *c. 1645–52, marble, height of group 11′6″, Cornaro Chapel, Santa Maria della Vittoria, Rome. (Art Resource, NY)*

21-13 *Anonymous,* The Cornaro Chapel, *18th-century painting. (Staatliches Museum, Schwerin, Germany)*

It was in Rome, then, that some of the greatest monuments of the seventeenth century were produced. It was from Rome also that the baroque was carried to other artistic centers. Baroque in the visual arts thus includes a rich diversity of styles and cultural patterns from the Catholic south to the Protestant north.

Literary Baroque

Although some scholars still dispute its usage, the term *baroque* has in recent decades been applied to literature as well as to the other arts. Late-sixteenth- and early-seventeenth-century drama and poetry, as well as some fiction, in all European languages do indeed show some characteristics similar to those we have seen in the visual arts: conflict, paradox and contrast, metaphysical concern, and a heightened spirituality, combined with a lively sensuality and ultrarealism. Like the baroque style in art, literary baroque also had Catholic and Protestant representatives. German Lutheran hymns, Spanish Catholic devotional poetry, Italian erotic verse, and English "metaphysical poetry" all display aspects of this multifaceted style.

Here we will limit our examples to a few poems from the country that produced the earliest and perhaps the greatest baroque writers, Spain, and to an important group of early-seventeenth-century poets in England.

The Baroque Style in Spain

The names of the novelist and playwright Miguel de Cervantes (1547–1616), the dramatists Pedro Calderón de la Barca (1600–1681) and Lope de Vega (1562–1635), and the poet Luis de Góngora y Argote (1561–1627) remind us that the seventeenth century was Spain's "golden age," a time that produced writers that were to have an impact on world literature comparable to the impact of Spanish civilization on the New World. To understand the flowering of the Spanish baroque, it is important to look at some late-sixteenth-century precursors.

The widespread sense of disillusionment felt in late-sixteenth-century Spain was in part a manifestation of the widening gap between the ideals of a great Catholic power and reality. Ambitious military enterprises such as that of the Armada forced the monarchy to live from hand to mouth and to declare periodic bankruptcies. Religious conformity discouraged independent thinking and encouraged hypocrisy. The aristocratic values of the society tended to divide the population into masters and servants.

As early as 1554, the tale of Lazarillo de Tormes presents a revealing picture of this world. In a short first-person narrative, the anonymous author vents a constant aggressiveness against the prevailing social values in a realistic style that contrasts sharply with the idealized approach of the then-popular sentimental novels and romances of chivalry. It is an irreverent work, antiestablishment, anticlerical, bitterly satirical, attacking religious orthodoxy, purity of blood, aristocratic "virtue."

The story of Lazarillo, whose parents are members of the very lowest social stratum, is one of corruption in which the hero, or more accurately the antihero, rises in the social scale as the prevailing social values force him to sink progressively into personal and moral degradation. This tale poses unambiguously the aesthetic values of what will years later become the very basis of baroque literature—that is, the dialectical relation between appearance and reality, between *engaño* (illusion) and its opposite, *desengaño,* which is not disillusionment but rather the process of arriving at the acceptance of truth, which is usually bitter and at odds with conventional wisdom.

Saint John of the Cross (1542–1591)

Chronologically closer to the full-fledged baroque are the poet-mystics who flourished in the second half of the sixteenth century. Undoubtedly, the Spanish mystics must have been influenced by the same weariness with conflict and turmoil that had caused the satirical outbursts in *Lazarillo.* In opting for a life of seclusion, a contemplative rather than an active life, they were expressing both their disdain for worldly ambition and their condemnation of the ideological oppression and the corruption that had gripped Spanish society. Many of them, including the Carmelite nun and mystical writer Saint Teresa of Ávila (see pp. 140, 145) and the poet Saint John of the Cross, fell foul of the Inquisition.

Born Juan de Yepes and canonized in 1726, Saint John of the Cross provides us with some of the most exalted mystic poetry ever written. He was a friend and disciple of Saint Teresa's, and also a Carmelite. After being imprisoned by the Inquisition in 1577, he escaped and took refuge in a monastery, from which he soon emerged to continue an active life as a reformer of the Carmelite order. His poetic production was small but intense, as well as of great originality. Mysticism, in its strictest sense, is the experience of the union of the soul with God. It transcends human reference and cannot therefore be rationally explained. The uniqueness of Saint John lies in recording that experience directly, without attempting any intellectual explanation or exegesis. Love being the basis of the relation between God and his creatures, Saint John uses the language of love and expresses divine union in terms of human love and eroticism. The human soul is the Bride; God, the Bridegroom.

The full flowering of Spanish baroque comes in the early seventeenth century. The term *barroco* denotes, in Spanish life, literature, and fine arts, a clearly defined attitude to the external world as well as a stage in artistic development. It is an attitude conditioned by the concept of *desengaño.* In a world in which all values were found to be inconstant and deceptive, the nature of life itself was subjected to constant questioning. That is the quandary of Segismundo, a sort of Everyman in Calderón's play *Life Is a Dream.* He expresses it at the end of Act II: "We are in such a singular world that to live is but to dream; I have learned, in my experience, that, in living, man but dreams what he is until he wakes." There is, of course, no knowing when the awakening will come.

This view of the deceptive nature of human experience gave rise to a preoccupation with death on the one hand and with corruptible human flesh on the other. Artists resorted to overornamentation to extract from nature the beauty that seemed (as in the painting of Velásquez) to dissolve and disappear precisely as the artist struggled to record it. Nature has lost out, they seem to be saying, and meaning has to be sought in the painful and painstaking accumulation of artifice. The most disparate notions are brought together by violence to create a new kind of aesthetic. The paintings of El Greco (Spanish for "the Greek"), although not considered baroque by all art historians, demonstrate the expressive distortion of human anatomy and of spatial relations and the violent emotion characteristic of the period (see p. 133). In literature, particularly in the style of Góngora (1561–1627), this takes the form of the use of all kinds of extravagant metaphors, violent paradoxes, and an abstruse and learned vocabulary.

Sor Juana Inés de la Cruz (1651–1695)

Góngora found many followers in the overseas Spanish possessions. The viceregal courts of Mexico and Lima, for instance, were known as sophisticated centers of learning, in which writing and the fine arts flourished. Juana de Asbaje had become known at an early age in Mexico for her unusual aptitude and thirst for learning. Society, however, frowned on learned women. It is probably correct, as historians say, that in taking vows at the age of nineteen in the order of Saint Jerome, assuming the name of Sor (Sister) Juana Inés de la Cruz, she was led by the sincere belief that in withdrawing from the secular world, in which she found herself "sought as a beautiful woman and unhappy in her wisdom," she would be able to pursue a life of study and contemplation. As she found out, she was only partly right. Nonetheless, she managed to leave a remarkable written record as poet, playwright, and essayist. We can appreciate her tender lyricism in some of her early love poems—her "Redondillas" (Quatrains) in defense of women is probably her best-known work—but it is to her mature poetry that we must turn to see the depth of her talent. Although inspired by the style of Góngora, she found her own voice to express her disdain for the vanity of life.

Don Quixote *and* Don Juan

The most justly famous of all of the literary works of Spain's golden age is Cervantes's *Don Quixote,* published in 1605. The adventures of the country gentleman who tries to impose an outmoded code of chivalry on the modern world play with the baroque themes of reality and illusion and have delighted millions of readers. But another *don* (a Spanish form of address denoting a high social status) conceived in the baroque era has had an even greater effect on the Western imagination: the figure of Don Juan.

The original Don Juan Tenorio may or may not have been a real person but was certainly a figure in Andalusian legend and oral literature when Tirso de Molina (1571?–1648) composed the first literary work about him, *El burlador de Sevilla y su convidado de piedra (The Trickster of Seville and His Guest of Stone),* around 1630. Tirso's Don Juan is a spoiled child of privilege, an overweening young aristocrat who, confident in his social status, consciously sets out to break all rules of conduct, divine as well as human, to gratify his insatiable desire to seduce women. It is not love, and not even lust, that prompts him so much as the game itself, the desire for conquest. Don Juan replaces the courtly adoration of the lady with a cynical and mocking belief in the fallibility of woman. He shows cavalier disregard for polity and morality, trusting to a distant day of reckoning as well as to God's infinite and all-encompassing grace. Catholic Spain, however, believed not in predestination but in humanity's proving itself worthy of salvation through the exercise of free will. Don Juan fails the test. His life is cut short and he is therefore condemned to eternal damnation. In his own way, Don Juan thus became one of the most compelling symbols of this period of despair as well as of the intense sensory and religious experience that was the Spanish baroque. We will study the most famous incarnation of Don Juan in Mozart's opera *Don Giovanni* in Chapter 26.

English "Metaphysical" Poetry

The group of poets in mid-seventeenth-century England, including John Donne, George Herbert, Richard Crashaw, and Andrew Marvell, was disparagingly dubbed "metaphysical" by the critic Dryden. Although inadequate to describe this school of poetry, the term has stuck. In recent years, however, continental critics and even some English critics have begun to see affinities between this school of poets and the baroque sensibility that prevailed throughout Europe. Frank Kermode, while granting that "metaphysical" may be a subdepartment of "baroque," urges caution:

> ... When we think of metaphysical, we do not think at once of St. Ignatius or Bernini or Marino, though we may do so a little later. We think first of a special moment in English poetry, a moment of

> plain but witty magniloquence, of a passionate poetry ballasted with learning and propelled by a skeptical ingenuity that may strike us as somehow very modern.[1]

This succinct definition does express the most salient qualities of "metaphysical" poetry. We shall briefly discuss here two of these poets who combined the spiritual with the sensual in ways that relate them to continental baroque poets and artists.

Crashaw (1612–1649) Perhaps the most baroque of all the seventeenth-century English poets was Richard Crashaw. Crashaw was raised in the Puritan tradition—his father was a preacher—but he converted to Roman Catholicism and spent the last years of his life in Rome. He was greatly attracted to mysticism and especially to female saints; three of his best-known poems are on Saint Teresa of Ávila. Although it is unlikely that Crashaw saw Bernini's famous statue before writing the poems, they share its spirit. In the last part of the third poem in the series, entitled "The Flaming Heart," Crashaw criticizes conventional pictorial representations of the saint (where she usually appears as a rather placid nun). He then describes how she should be represented. First, he says that she, not the seraphim beside her, should hold the dart. He then concedes to the angel "the bravery of all those Bright things," including "the radiant dart," and asks that Teresa be left only "the flaming heart."

Donne (1572–1631) In contrast to Crashaw, John Donne was brought up as a Catholic but became an Anglican. He became, in fact, one of the most successful preachers of his age, and his sermons are still read for their force and brilliant style. At the same time, Donne was a worldly man, fond of women and involved in several passionate love affairs. He was thus suited to the baroque combination of the ardently religious and the ardently erotic; his best poems successfully combine the two. His "holy sonnets" are often like prayers, comparable to Bernini's and to Crashaw's Saint Teresa in their use of erotic and violent imagery to describe mystic experience. The famous poem "To His Mistress Going to Bed" is frankly erotic, but in it the poet speaks of the bed as "love's hallowed temple" and of women as angels and "mystic books." Another type of poem, "The Flea," is set up as an argument for seduction. Centered around a tiny, apparently insignificant object (a flea), it makes use of extreme detail to portray matters of larger significance; in this sense it is more comparable to the Dutch than to the Italian baroque style in art.

Baroque Music

The baroque style in music, like that in the visual arts and in literature, had its origins in late Renaissance Italy. Humanism, the same cultural and intellectual movement that used the ideas and ideals of Greece and Rome as models for contemporary artistic creation (and to a great degree gave rise to the Renaissance itself), was also largely responsible for creating a new or "second practice" at the height of the Renaissance period.

Well before the end of the sixteenth century, musicians in Italy tried to resurrect the affective power of Greek drama: they began to experiment with *dramma per musica,* theatrical genres that developed and were later named opera and oratorio. A whole theory of *affects* became a doctrine of the baroque, a method whereby a composer could invoke specific emotional responses in an audience by employing specific musical devices. As Plato's Dorian mode stirred manly feelings in the youth of Greece, Bach's and Handel's D-major trumpet parts evoked victorious martial responses in the listeners of the eighteenth, nineteenth, and twentieth centuries.

As in the other arts, baroque music had both a Catholic and Protestant form. The Church of Rome partook in the new musical developments during the late Renaissance. The Reformation of Luther was evidently successful in winning converts through music that was particularly attractive and meaningful to laity—vernacular texts, simple settings, and short, "catchy" melodies, and the Catholic Church's Counter-Reformation thus experimented with similarly appealing music. One discovers that Saint Philip Neri's congregation of secular priests sang *laude spirituali* (spiritual songs of praise) in the oratory (a large room for public discussions) of his church in Rome. His group of followers was named after the room (*Congregazione del'Oratorio*), and the baroque musical form (oratorio) was likewise named after this place of origin. A loosely connected historical line binds together a development or metamorphosis from the *laude spirituali* to spiritual dialogues and early oratorios with biblical characters to the mature oratorio of the late baroque.

Attractive dramatic music became fairly common throughout Italy at the end of the sixteenth century,

[1] Frank Kermode, ed., *The Metaphysical Poets* (New York: Fawcett, 1969), p. 32.

and we see that Andrea Gabrieli composed choruses for a presentation of a revived Greek drama, *Oedipus Rex,* at Vicenza in 1585; Orazio Vecchi presented his madrigal comedy *L'Amfiparnaso* in Modena in 1594; and the Florentines Jacopo Corsi, Ottavio Rinuccini, and Jacopo Peri produced an entire dramatic pastoral in a representational style inspired by antique models, *Dafne,* in Corsi's palace in 1598.

By this time musicians were calling Renaissance music old, and this music of the "second practice" new or modern. The key stylistic feature of the best music of the High Renaissance was its marvelous *counterpoint,* the smooth and complex interweaving of several melodies into a unified, organic whole. In contrast, the most distinctive feature of the new music of the early baroque was the declamatory style, a technique that might use chordal declamation by several singers or a sung recitation by a soloist to a harmonic accompaniment, a device named recitativo or *recitative.* (See the following examples.)

Although a straightforward declamation of text is the most obvious feature of these works to the musical layperson, most musicians identify the new baroque style by its harmonic characteristics. The counterpoint of Renaissance music was clothed by *modal* sonorities—the distinctive scales or *modes* of the melodies and the coincidental blending of the various musical parts sounding simultaneously. Baroque music was produced within a new system of tonal harmonies, music that was composed with chords and chord relationships in mind. Regardless of what individual lines in a baroque composition might do, a progression of chord changes leads the ear from beginning to end, from level to level, forming the basic framework of the piece. *Harmonic* organization forms the basis of music from this period and, in fact, of all European music from the seventeenth through the twentieth centuries. The seventeenth-century composer writing in the new dramatic style notated a melodic line and a bass line—the upper and lower limits of sound for the piece—and filled in the middle by composing or improvising chords indicated with figures over the bass notes. Although this generalization oversimplifies a bit, it serves to illustrate an essential element of baroque musical style. This bass part with numbers and signs over the notes was called *continuo, thorough bass,* or *figured bass.* Since this musical and notational feature was pervasive in baroque music, several music historians have suggested that the period ought to be called after the musical device. Be that as it may, the important fact for our understanding of the music of this period is its shift from melodic to harmonic thinking and its new approach to text setting that signaled a change from one musical style to the next.

ORAZIO VECCHI

L'Amfiparnaso

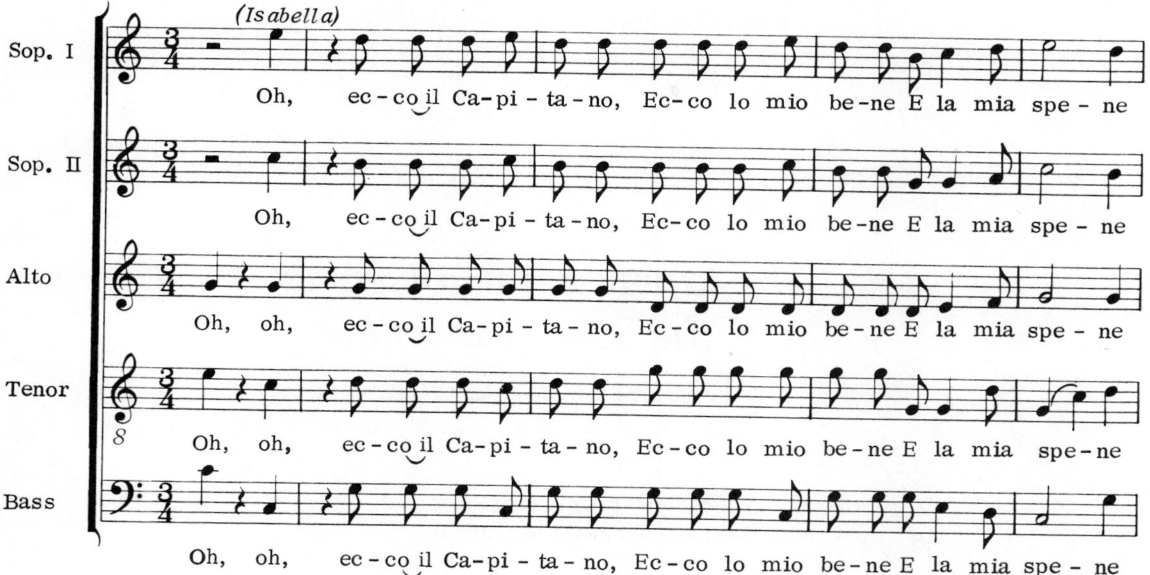

Chordal declamation.

JACOPO PERI

Euridice

Recitative.

Reading Selections

Saint John of the Cross

From *The Living Flame of Love: Songs of the Soul in Intimate Union with God*

Translation by Alan Gonzalez

As with other short poems throughout this volume, we have retained the original.

Liama de Amor Viva

Canciones que hace el alma
en la intima unión en Dios

¡Oh, llama de amor viva,
que tiernamente hieres
de mi alma en el más profundo centro!

Pues ya no eres esquiva,
acaba ya, si quieres;
rompe la tela de este dulce encuentro.

¡Oh cauterio suave!
¡Oh regalada llaga!
¡Oh mano blanda! ¡Oh toque delicado!
que a vida eterna sabe,
y toda deuda paga;
matando, muerte en vida la has trocado.

¡Oh lámparas de fuego,
en cuyos resplandores
las profundas cavernas del sentido,
que estaba oscuro y ciego,
con extraños primores
calor y luz dan junto a su querido!

Cuán manso y amoroso
recuerdas en mi seno

Living Flame of Love

Songs of the Soul in Intimate Union with God

O living flame of love
tenderly wounding my soul
in its very deepest core!

No longer coy,
close now, if it's your wish;
rend the fabric of this sweet encounter.

O softest searing burn!
O welcome ulcer!
O tender hand! O subtle touch
of life eternal tasting
and every debt redeeming;
in slaying, all death to life you've turned.

O lanterns of fire,
in whose resplendent rays
the deepest caverns of sense,
erstwhile dark and blind,
warmth, with curious care,
and light together give to its beloved.

How gentle and how loving
you wake up on my breast,

donde secretamente solo moras,
y en tu aspirar sabroso
de bien y gloria lleno
cuán delicadamente me enamoras!

where secretly alone you dwell,
and with your tempting breath,
goodness and glory filled,
how delicately my love you inflame!

QUESTIONS

1. Which images in this poem seem to blend erotic with spiritual experience? What is the effect of this?
2. Which characteristics of fire does the poet use metaphorically?

SOR JUANA INÉS DE LA CRUZ

Soneto sobre un retrato de sí misma

Translation by Alan Gonzalez

Este,[1] que ves, engaño colorido,
que del arte ostentando los primores,
con falsos silogismos de colores
es cauteloso engaño del sentido;

éste, en quien la lisonja ha pretendido
excusar de los años los horrores
y, venciendo del tiempo los rigores,
triunfar de la vejez y del olvido,

es un vano artificio del cuidado,
es una flor al viento delicada,
es un resguardo inútil para el hado;

es una necia diligencia errada,
es un afán caduco y, bien mirado,
es cadáver, es polvo, es sombra, es nada.

Sonnet on a Portrait of Herself

This,[1] that you see, polychromed deception
that, vaunting exquisite artifice,
in deceptive syllogisms of color
equivocates the sensed perception;

this, where flattery has attempted
to ignore the ravages of years
and, overcoming of time the rigor,
to triumph over age and oblivion,

is but artifice vain and counterfeit,
frail bloom to the harsh wind exposed,
'tis a futile protection against fate;

it is a mindless, aberrant pursuit,
failing obsession and, correctly viewed,
it is a corpse, a shadow, dust, a very nothing.

QUESTIONS

1. How would you characterize Sor Juana's attitude toward her portrait? What spiritual truth does this attitude represent?
2. What differences in tone and meaning are there between the *octave* and the *sestet* of this sonnet?

[1]The portrait of herself.

RICHARD CRASHAW

FROM *The Flaming Heart*

(Spelling modernized)

Leave Her alone The Flaming Heart.
Leave her that; and thou shalt leave her
Not one loose shaft but love's whole quiver.
For in love's field was never found
A nobler weapon than a Wound.
Love's passives are his activ'st part.
The wounded is the wounding heart.
O Heart! the equal poise of love's both parts
Big alike with wounds and darts.
Live in these conquering leaves; live all the same;
And walk through all tongues one triumphant
Flame.
Live here, great Heart; and love and die and kill;
And bleed and wound; and yield and conquer still.
Let this immortal life where'er it comes
Walk in a crowd of loves and Martyrdoms.
Let mystic Deaths wait on it; and wise souls be
The love-slain witnesses of this life of thee.
O sweet incendiary! show here thy art,
Upon this carcass of a hard, cold hart,
Let all thy scatter'd shafts of light, that play
Among the leaves of thy large books of day,
Combin'd against this Breast at once break in
And take away from me my self and sin,
This gracious Robbery shall thy bounty be;
And my best fortunes such fair spoils of me.
O thou undaunted daughter of desires!
By all thy dower of Lights and Fires;
By all the eagle in thee, all the dove;
By all thy lives and deaths of love;
By thy large draughts of intellectual day,
And by thy thirsts of love more large than they;
By all thy brim-fill'd Bowls of fierce desire
By thy last Morning's draught of liquid fire;
By the full kingdom of that final kiss
That seiz'd thy parting Soul, and seal'd thee his;
By all the heav'ns thou hast in him
(Fair sister of the Seraphim!)
By all of Him we have in Thee;
Leave nothing of my Self in me.
Let me so read thy life, that I
Unto all life of mine may die.

COMMENTS AND QUESTIONS

1. Baroque poets, like baroque artists, loved extreme contrasts; they expressed these with the rhetorical figures known as *oxymoron* (the juxtaposition of words with opposing meanings) and *antithesis* (the balance of parallel word groups conveying opposing ideas). An example of oxymoron here is the phrase "sweet incendiary." An example of antithesis is "Love's passives are his activ'st part./ The wounded is the wounding heart." What other examples of these figures can you find? How do they serve the poet's purpose here?
2. Another characteristic of baroque poetry is the extended use of *metaphor.* Renaissance poets tended to make more use of the *simile,* which makes a comparison between two things on an intellectual level; but the baroque sensibility preferred the more emotional fusion and identification that the metaphor provided. In this poem the poet does not compare himself to a deer but suddenly *becomes* "this carcass of a hard, cold hart." (Plays on words like *heart/hart* were also dear to baroque poets.) What other metaphors does Crashaw use here?
3. Baroque poems often tend to have a cumulative effect, comparable to the rich profusion of matter in baroque art. One way of achieving this is through the rhetorical device of *anaphora* (the repetition of the same word to introduce two or more clauses or lines). Notice here the number of lines that begin with "By all." What is the effect of this device?
4. How would you describe Crashaw's interpretation of the mystic experience of Saint Teresa? Compare it with Bernini's statue, *The Ecstasy of Saint Teresa.*
5. Do this style and sensibility appeal to you? What in your own personality makes you answer negatively or positively?

JOHN DONNE

FROM *Holy Sonnets*

(Spelling modernized)

Sonnet 14

Batter my heart, three-personed God; for you
As yet but knock, breathe, shine, and seek to mend;
That I may rise, and stand, o'erthrow me, and bend
Your force, to break, blow, burn, and make me new.
I, like an usurped° town, to another due,

[5]Captured.

Labor to admit you, but Oh, to no end,
Reason your viceroy° in me, me should defend,
But is captived, and proves weak or untrue.
Yet dearly I love you, and would be loved fain,°
But am betrothed unto your enemy:
Divorce me, untie, or break that knot again,
Take me to you, imprison me, for I
Except you enthral me, never shall be free,
Nor ever chaste, except you ravish me.

7Representative.

9Gladly.

QUESTIONS

1. How do the characteristics of contrast and repetition appear in this poem?
2. Are there extreme contrasts in the rhythm of the lines as well? How is this achieved?
3. How are the war metaphor and the sexual metaphor worked in together?
4. Compare Donne's expression of union with God to that of Saint John of the Cross.

FROM *Elegies*

(Spelling modernized)

Elegy XIX To His Mistress Going to Bed

Come, madam, come, all rest my powers defy,
Until I labor, I in labor lie.
The foe oft-times having the foe in sight,
Is tired with standing though he never fight.
Off with that girdle,° like heaven's zone glistering,
But a far fairer world encompassing.
Unpin that spangled breastplate which you wear,
That th' eyes of busy fools may be stopped there.
Unlace yourself, for that harmonious chime
Tells me from you that now it is bed time.
Off with that happy busk,° which I envy,
That still can be, and still can stand so nigh.
Your gown, going off, such beauteous state reveals,
As when from flowry meads th' hill's shadow steals.
Off with that wiry coronet and show
The hairy diadem which on you doth grow:
Now off with those shoes, and then safely tread
In this love's hallowed temple, this soft bed.
In such white robes, heaven's angels used to be
Received by men; thou, Angel, bring'st with thee
A heaven like Mahomet's Paradise,° and though
Ill spirits walk in white, we easily know
By this these angels from an evil sprite:
Those set our hairs, but these our flesh upright.
License my roving hands, and let them go
Before, behind, between, above, below.
O my America! my new-found-land,
My kingdom, safeliest when with one man manned,
My mine of precious stones, my empery,
How blest am I in this discovering thee!
To enter in these bonds is to be free;
Then where my hand is set, my seal shall be.
Full nakedness! All joys are due to thee,
As souls unbodied, bodies unclothed must be
To taste whole joys. Gems which you women use
Are like Atalanta's balls,° cast in men's views,
That when a fool's eye lighteth on a gem,
His earthly soul may covet theirs, not them.
Like pictures, or like books' gay coverings made
For lay-men, are all women thus arrayed;
Themselves are mystic books, which only we
(Whom their imputed grace will dignify)
Must see revealed. Then, since that I may know,
As liberally as to a midwife, show
Thyself: cast all, yea, this white linen hence,
There is no penance due to innocence.
To teach thee, I am naked first; why then,
What needst thou have more covering than a man?

5Belt.

11Undergarment worn over the breast.

21The Muslim idea of paradise includes beautiful women.

36Atalanta agreed to marry Hippomenes if he could defeat her in a foot race. As she was about to overtake him, he cast in her path three golden apples given to him by Venus. Distracted by their beauty, Atalanta stopped to retrieve them, and Hippomenes won the race.

QUESTIONS

1. Why does Donne spend so much time describing each article of clothing that he wants the woman to take off? What is the effect of this "slow motion"?
2. Could you compare the enumeration here to the numbers of sensuously depicted objects in baroque painting?
3. What use does Donne make here of the "new world" discoveries? What is the effect of this metaphor?

FROM *Songs and Sonnets*

(Spelling modernized)

The Flea

Mark but this flea, and mark in this,
How little that which thou deny'st me is;
It sucked me first, and now sucks thee,
And in this flea our two bloods mingled be;°
Thou know'st that this cannot be said
A sin, nor shame, nor loss of maidenhead;
Yet this enjoys before it woo,
And pampered swells with one blood made of two,
And this, alas, is more than we would do.

O stay, three lives in one flea spare,
Where we almost, yea, more than married are.
This flea is you and I, and this
Our marriage bed and marriage temple is;
Though parents grudge, and you, we are met
And cloistered in these living walls of jet.
Though use° make you apt to kill me,
Let not to that, self-murder added be,
And sacrilege, three sins in killing three.

Cruel and sudden, hast thou since
Purpled thy nail in blood of innocence?
Wherein could this flea guilty be,
Except in that drop which it sucked from thee?
Yet thou triumph'st and say'st that thou
Find'st not thyself nor me the weaker now;
'Tis true, then learn how false fears be:
Just so much honor, when thou yield'st to me,
Will waste, as this flea's death took life from thee.

COMMENTS AND QUESTIONS

1. Donne begins this poem almost as if he were beginning a sermon, using the flea as an object lesson. He then begins a series of arguments on the *carpe diem* ("seize the day," or "let's make love now before it's too late") theme. What arguments does he use? Are they meant to be logical?
2. Notice that the poem is set up like a three-act drama. What is supposed to have happened after stanza 1 and after stanza 2?
3. What is the effect of externalizing the lover's desire in the flea?

[4]It was believed at this time that conception occurred through the mixing of the man's blood with the woman's.

[16]Habit, custom.

22

Two Masterpieces of Baroque Music: Handel's Messiah *and Bach's* Christmas Oratorio

The artistic skies of the seventeenth and eighteenth centuries were spangled with musical lights of great magnitude: Monteverdi, Corelli, Alessandro Scarlatti, and Vivaldi in Italy; Domenico Scarlatti in Spain; Rameau, Lully, and Couperin in France; Purcell in England; Schütz, Buxtehude, and Johann Sebastian Bach in Germany; and a figure of international fame and travels, George Frederick Handel.

The centuries have taught us that the latter two composers—Bach and Handel—rise above all the others. Each has left us a vast store of musical riches that span the compass from small to large, easy to difficult, sacred to secular, instrumental to vocal, incidental to monumental. No single work can adequately represent either of these musical geniuses, but two have retained their universal appeal over the centuries: Bach's *Christmas Oratorio* and Handel's English masterpiece, *Messiah.*

George Frederick Handel (1685–1759)

Handel began his career in Germany, traveled and worked in Italy, and eventually emigrated to London. Although this German musician first established his reputation in England as a composer of Italian operas, the masterwork from his pen that has endeared him to the hearts of all English-speaking Christians is his sacred oratorio *Messiah,* a work created in response to an invitation from the duke of Devonshire, the Lord Lieutenant of Ireland, to present some concerts for the benefit of the Charitable Musical Society of Dublin. Composed in twenty-four days, it was first performed in Dublin in 1742 and was an immediate artistic and popular success. According to popular legend, the tradition of standing for the Hallelujah Chorus began with the first London performance in 1743 when King

George II, wakened from a nap by the opening chords of the chorus, rose to his feet—followed, of course, by all his subjects. *Messiah* was, and remains, popular with people from all walks of life. Although written more than 250 years ago, *Messiah* is available to most Americans through live performance or live broadcast at least twice a year, at Christmas and Easter. Universal recognition is not the only criterion for greatness in music, but it is clear that no other musical composition has captured the sincere affection of the English-speaking world more completely. In every aspect of its existence—concept, design, scale, quality—it is a monumental work, a superb pinnacle of artistic creation, a masterpiece that brought tears to the eyes of the composer himself and caused him to say, "I did think I did see all Heaven before me and the great God Himself." In spite of all the technical accounts of how this grand work was organized and composed with borrowed material and practical concerns for particular singers' voice ranges and abilities, nothing can detract from the fact that it was an inspired work completed in feverish haste by a musical genius of the first rank.

Messiah speaks to modern ears with the same honesty of religious expression that has stirred fervent emotions in listeners for more than two centuries. It is one of the greatest expressions of the Protestant baroque. It is not enough to deal with this *oratorio* as a musical composition only, for it is first and foremost a religious piece, a remarkable setting of biblical texts dealing with the redemption of humanity from sin through the intervention of the Messiah. The *libretto* is a compilation of verses from the Bible, a selection that draws from both the Old and the New Testaments. The organization and unity of the work is primarily text-centered, for, like three acts of an opera, the three large divisions of the oratorio reveal the following plan: PART I. A messianic prophecy, the coming and birth of Christ. The revelation of God's plan to save humankind by the coming of the Messiah. PART II. The suffering and death of Christ; the defeat of humanity, who reject God's offer; and the spread of his doctrine. PART III. The redemption of humanity through faith, the final overthrow of death, and a hymn of thanksgiving.

With this large framework in mind, Handel fleshed out a massive construct for soloists, chorus, and orchestra by using standard forms that were second nature to him and were a regular part of the fully developed operatic style of the baroque era. He sets the spell for the entire work by opening with an orchestral overture with the same characteristics as the French overture developed by Lully decades before: a slow, majestic first movement in jagged *rhythms*, duple *meter*, and *chordal texture*, followed by a lively, *fugal*

second movement with an impressive *contrapuntal* display.[1]

The *fugue* impresses the listener because the composer successfully takes a melody and uses it against itself, or in conjunction with itself, to create logical and beautiful harmonies. Exquisite fugues are a hallmark of the baroque masters, who displayed their melodic inventiveness through this process of imitating short and distinctive melodies in succession. We can see three successive entrances of the same tune (very slightly altered) in measures 1, 5, and 9 of the fugue, and we might compare their identity by playing them simultaneously:

The fugal process was one of the most compelling in the repertoire of the baroque composers, for although its texture is lighter in "weight" than most *chordal,* or *homophonic,* compositions, it has a forward-driving rhythm and additive layering-of-melody effect that propels the listener to the final release of the closing chords. Handel was a master of this mature form of the late baroque, and we can see its dramatic effect in the vocal fugues that he favors for climactic moments.

The overall design of the first part of *Messiah* can be seen in the chart at the top of the following page. The regularity or symmetry and the simplicity of the design are in fact *classical,* and we must keep in mind that Handel was working at the culmination of an age, a period in which the influence of new ideas in opposition to the norms of the baroque were beginning to make themselves felt. Simplicity of design is of great advantage in the function of a work that depends heavily upon text, for unnecessary complexity detracts by drawing attention to itself. No one was more aware of this than Handel himself, for he understood better than any other composer of his time how to employ the operatic forms of recitative and *aria* to communicate the inner message of the text.

A *recitative* is a musical form that has almost no melodic interest; consequently, a great store of information can be related to the listener in a short time. Those points in the narrative where several ideas await telling, where people need adequate introduction, where details of plot need to be unfolded quickly, and in general where there are a great many words to be dealt with are the proper domain of the recitative. Still, within that general plan, certain points need emphasis; there Handel uses chord change and chord selection as well as slight *melodic elaboration* to achieve these ends.

Other devices are available to him too, such as *orchestration,* but the essential concept that the recitative should be used to carry a high volume of words per unit of time is not disturbed. In the last example (c) we see a typical Handelian affective device. On the statement of the word "shake," Handel literally shakes the music. He takes the notes and rapidly wiggles them back and forth, a visual effect for the performer and an aural effect for the listener. As the chorus sings "All we like sheep have gone astray" the melodic lines diverge; with "we have turned," a

[1]Any number of excellent recordings of the complete *Messiah* are available, but the reader is advised to find a recent recording that seeks to approximate Handel's original scoring for small orchestra and modest chorus. The loss in dramatic power supplied by a romantic orchestra and gigantic chorus is amply compensated for by the increased clarity of line and decreased ponderosity.

Subject	Sinfonia	God's Promise			Distance Between God and Man			Message of Joy			Fulfillment Through Christ's Birth		
Selection Number	1	2	3	4	5	6	7	7a	8	8a	9	10	11
Form	0	R	A	C	R	A	C	R	A	C	R	A	C

Subject	Pifa	Christmas Story					Rapture at the Lord's Coming			
Selection Number	12	12a	13	13a	14	15	16	16a	17	18
Form	0	R	A	R	R	C	A	R	AA	C

O = Orchestra; R = Recitative; A = Air; AA = Air (Duet); C = Chorus

Messiah, PART I. Overall design.

quickly twisting and turning figure is introduced, and with "every one to his own way" a single note is stubbornly repeated.

The *aria* or "air" has a purpose almost diametrically opposed to that of the recitative. An aria usually contains two ideas often expressed in two sentences. It is an opportunity for the soloist (or composer) to wax eloquent, to spin out gradually a thought that grows fuller in meaning as the music progresses. It is usually somewhat introspective, personal to the character of the person portrayed by the soloist. The second idea is related to the first, but it casts a slightly different light on the subject or adds to it in some contrasting way. Most Handelian airs are cast in the mold of the *da capo aria,* the *ABA* form that returns to the beginning to reiterate the message of the first idea in the new light of the second statement. The bass aria "But who may abide" is a demonstration of this principle. The soloist asks the questions "But who may abide the day of His coming, and who shall stand when He appeareth?" In response, the listener might ask "Why does he ask, for would we not all stand to greet the Lord?" In the B section of the aria, the soloist states the difficulty: "For He is like a refiner's fire." God is judge and he will separate the righteous from the sinful. He is like the refiner who smelts metal from ore and separates the gold or silver from the rock. When the bass returns to his initial question of who shall stand, the listener might reconsider whether he dares be among those who rise to meet God eyeball to eyeball. And the mighty chorus, like impartial observers from another world, responds in a frightening tone, "And He shall purify the sons of Levi, that they may offer unto the Lord an offering in righteousness." Thus the plan of the specific recitative-aria-chorus combination serves as the model for all the subsections of the entire work: develop an idea rapidly (recitative), elaborate a single aspect (aria), and hammer the message home (chorus). After four exact repetitions of the plan, Handel, of course, varies the scheme by omitting, inverting, or repeating the three basic elements—recitative, aria, and chorus—but the affective function of each always remains the same. Thus listeners gear their expectations to the type of music offered.

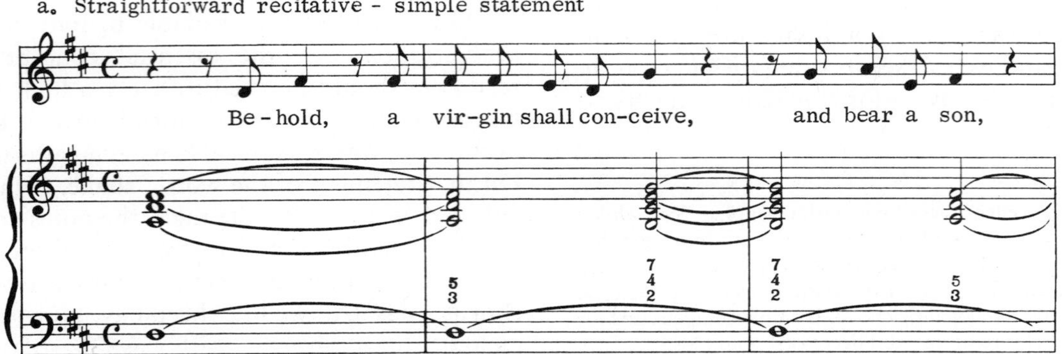
a. Straightforward recitative - simple statement
Be-hold, a vir-gin shall con-ceive, and bear a son,
5
3
7
4
2
7
4
2
5
3

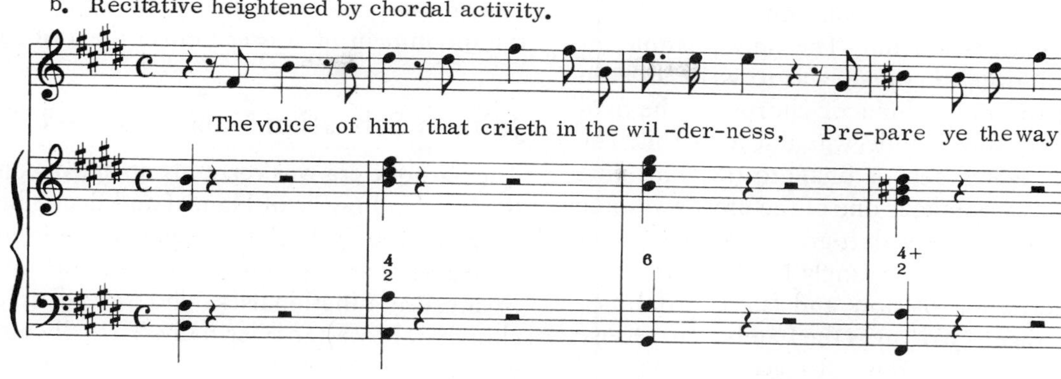

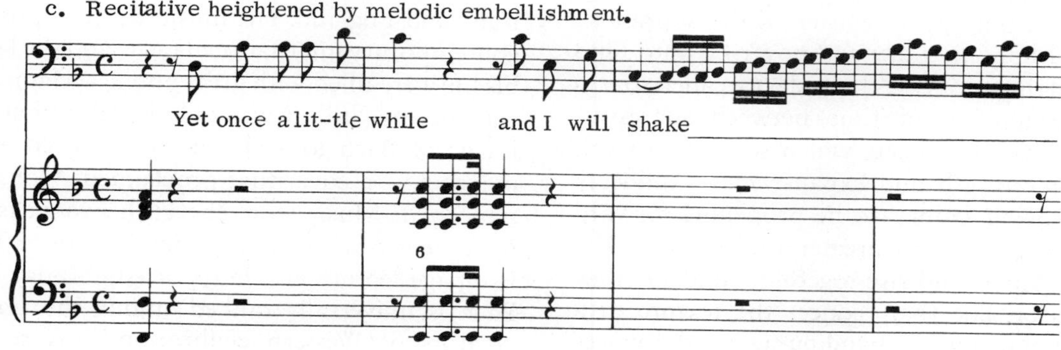

The second and third parts of the *oratorio* are naturally similar in format to that of the first. The tone of the second part is sorrowful, for it accompanies the music of the Passion and, only toward the end, Easter. The libretto tells vividly how Christ was despised: "He hid not His face from shame and spitting"; "He was bruised for our iniquities"; "All they that see Him laugh Him to scorn"; "He was cut off out of the land of the living." This intense, doleful atmosphere is relieved briefly with words and music promising the Resurrection: "But Thou didst not leave His soul in hell" and "Lift up your heads . . . the King of Glory shall come in"; but it quickly returns to a drama of death and fear when the people are reminded of their shortcomings: "Why do the nations so furiously rage together?" and "He that dwelleth in heaven shall laugh them to scorn." In other words, a religious drama is taking place; the listeners are no longer observers but participants. They do not have to identify with characters on stage as they would at the theater or opera house; they are being explicitly identified themselves as the words of the Bible preach to them. And when the words are completely damning and reduce the attentive listener to dust—"Thou shalt break them with a rod of iron, Thou shalt dash them in pieces like a potter's vessel"—then Handel steps in and saves the victory with one of the most exultant choruses of all time: "Hallelujah! for the Lord God Omnipotent reigneth." The Hallelujah Chorus alone would have brought fame to George Frederick Handel, for it is one of those resounding strokes of genius that is able in itself to embody the concept of a victorious Lord.

The Hallelujah Chorus creates a problem for the composer. In it he achieves an artistic peak, making material that follows necessarily anticlimactic. But the oratorio is not yet over. In this hurried world of the twentieth century, one still finds *Messiah* concerts that cut off the work at this point. Musically, one comes to a satisfactory conclusion at the end of the Hallelujah Chorus, but spiritually one has missed the message of the text if the portion dealing with individual redemption through faith is left out. The only possible, or impossible, solution, of course, was to write an even more stirring and more climactic chorus for the final portion; unbelievably, Handel was able to do this. The Amen Chorus, which acts as finale to the third part and the work as a whole, is one of the most awesome choral fugues ever conceived. It grows and swells, piling layer on layer in a surprisingly brief sprint to the finish. An alternation of slow and fast chordal passages sets the stage: "Worthy is the Lamb . . . to receive power . . . worthy is the Lamb . . . to receive power. . . ." This introduction is followed by a fugue whose vocal entrances rise successively from the low range of the men's voices to the upper register of the sopranos': "Blessing and honour, glory and pow'r be unto Him that sitteth on the throne." A fugal device called *stretto* collapses the interval of time between successive entrances so that the music, which seemed to work only at greater length and expansiveness, suddenly feels to be moving faster—to be propelling forward with less caution but no greater recklessness. The voices begin to pair and rise together; suddenly they join in a unison line that reduces the texture to a penetrating knife edge. Expanding again, the voices move into a series of high, sustained chords that virtually teeter on the brink of a musical chasm. Then, at last, the voices begin to move and gain momentum in the final *fugue* to the single word "Amen." The sense of completion is achieved; the restoration of balance is accomplished; the work is consummated.

Strangely enough, *Messiah* was not composed for a church service. Handel was a bankrupt impresario-composer who was currently out of favor as a local opera composer. He seized an opportunity to perform "some of his choicest Musick" for the benefit of Mercer's Hospital in Dublin. On April 12, 1742, he performed his new oratorio in public for the first time. With its baroque harmonies and standardized forms, it reflected ideas seen emerging out of the past with a steady linkage back to the Renaissance through the operas of Lully to the congregational sacred music of Saint Philip Neri in Rome. In its expansiveness and classical balance, in its communication with a growing middle class, and in its seeming power to attract listeners from all walks of life in the modern world, it is a searching tendril that stretches upward to the future. Many works of art seem to be understood fully only within the context of the age in which they were created. Handel's *Messiah* is an exception to this rule, for it seems to have had an immediacy and direct impact on musicians and laity alike from its origin in 1742 to the present day. It is perhaps the most substantial monument of Western musical art of all time.

Johann Sebastian Bach (1685–1750)

The baroque era was certainly an age of contrast, and the lives and music of Handel and Bach illustrate this principle vividly. Bach led a relatively uneventful musical career that saw him employed as one of a number of musical functionaries who served at court and church in Protestant Germany. Virtually his entire life was spent within sixty miles of his birthplace. Handel, on the other hand, developed his profession in the company of the leading musical patrons of Germany, Italy, and England. His music was composed for the contemporary international taste, and the last years of his life were filled with great public acclaim and financial success. Still, it was only in 1968 that a painted image of Bach looked out from the cover of *Time* magazine—a cover that proclaimed, "Johann Sebastian Bach: Music from the Fifth Evangelist." Media hype or a truth worthy of investigation? Inside, the five-page feature article reported, "Today, of course, Bach is universally ranked among the transcendent creators of Western civilization."[2] A transcendent creator, not just of western *music* but of western *civilization!* What, then, is the magic of the composer from Eisenach?

Bach, although well known as a virtuoso organist, saw few of his works published during his lifetime, and his music found almost total neglect immediately after his death. However, great composers of subsequent generations would not allow his music to die. Haydn owned a copy of the Mass in B Minor, Mozart studied his motets and *The Art of Fugue,* and Mendelssohn resurrected his music for the larger public with his revival of the *St. Matthew Passion* in 1829, seventy-nine years after the composer's death. Regardless of his provincial life, and regardless of the superlative creations of other masters, including his famous contemporary Handel, Bach's surviving works are so various, inventive, intellectual, and beautiful that it is difficult to name his equal among composers of any age! Today, Bach societies and Bach choirs thrive throughout the world. Organists know his music as the principal repertoire for the instrument, and violinists and cellists learn his solo sonatas, partitas, and suites as the

[2]"A Composer for All Seasons (But Especially for Christmas)," *Time* (December 27, 1968), p. 35.

tests that separate professional from beginner, master from novice. All serious keyboard players learn with the Inventions, mature with *The Well-Tempered Clavier,* and strive for the Goldberg Variations and the *Chromatic Fantasia and Fugue.* And today's composers study and marvel at the sheer genius displayed in the contrapuntal intricacies of *The Art of Fugue* and the *Musical Offering.* But the master composer's profound religious convictions come triumphantly to light in his vocal compositions, especially those for chorus, soloists, and orchestra in combination—cantatas, passions, Masses, Magnificat settings, and oratorios.

For the last twenty-seven years of his life, Bach was a Lutheran church musician in Leipzig. For the Christmas services of 1734, he composed a mammoth work in six parts, the *Christmas Oratorio.* Written for the six feast days or Sundays of the holiday season (1734–35)—the three days of Christmas (December 25–27), New Year's Day, the Sunday after New Year, and Epiphany (the manifestation of the Savior to the gentiles, or the coming of the Magi), each part is like a complete cantata in itself and lasts about thirty minutes. An unusual feature of the first performance was the publication of the entire libretto in advance, so that members of the congregation could not only understand the words more readily but also see the totality of the work. Because only one of the six portions was performed at each of the six services, it was important for the congregation to review the significance of the day's setting within the context of the whole.

The first three parts are built on the story of Christmas as reported in the Gospel of Luke; the fourth deals with the circumcision and naming of Jesus; the fifth tells of the flight into Egypt; and the sixth deals with the story of the Three Wise Men from the East. Unlike Handel's *Messiah,* Bach's *Christmas Oratorio* places great emphasis on reflection and downplays the dramatic element. In addition to using German prose from Luther's translation of the Bible, Bach combines introspective poetry from an unknown librettist, possibly Picander (Friedrich Henrici). Like Handel and most of the other composers of his day, Bach reused much musical material he had composed earlier, but he constantly strove for a unified total work that was true and complete unto itself, a work that displayed perfect craftsmanship in every element.

The oratorio is a collection of biblical texts and poetic meditations underscored by sixty-four separate musical movements. Bach's composition and orchestration are superlative, and he avails himself of a rich palette of musical resources, an orchestra of organ, strings, flutes, oboes, oboes *d'amore,* oboes and horns *da caccia,*[3] bassoon, trumpets, and timpani; a chorus; and four solo voices. A tenor assumes the role of the Evangelist and narrates the Bible story. The other three—soprano, alto, and bass—sometimes sing the role of a biblical character—Herod, Angel—and sometimes merely elaborate and reflect on a text. There is ample opportunity for virtuosic display by both singer and instrumentalist, but the use of this and every other musical device is always subordinated to the primary purpose of underscoring the meaning of the text, never of seeking to impress a concert audience. The music was created to help a congregation join professional musicians in musical worship.

Fourteen times in the course of the six services a chorale is inserted into the musical tapestry, and these are the congregational hymns that Bach's Lutheran parishioners knew, loved, and felt with deep emotion.

The first-used chorale tune, "Herzlich tut mich Verlangen" (My Heart Is Filled with Longing), piece #5 of the sixty-four, is also the chorale that closes the entire cycle, piece #64. In Bach's day it was known as the Passion Chorale, "O Haupt voll Blut und Wunden" (O Sacred Head Sore Wounded). Bach had used several settings of this chorale in his *St. Matthew Passion* five years earlier, and its use here, with the Christmas texts, #5 ("How Best Can I Receive Thee?") and #64 ("Now Christ Will Avenge Our Satanic Foes"), can also be interpreted as Bach's way of suggesting that the birth of Christ must also be interpreted as a foreshadowing of his death on the cross, if it is to have religious significance as well as musical or other artistic significance.

The musical forms and techniques displayed in this work are as diverse as the orchestral and vocal resources already mentioned, but the size and complexity of the *Christmas Oratorio* prevents detailed analysis in a limited space. However, some important and obvious features will help interpretation and understanding. Similarities to Italian and French opera, as well as to Handel's *Messiah,* exist in the recitatives and arias. The same principles of exposition of text in recitatives and reflection on one or two thoughts in an aria hold true. The same principles of tonal organization for individual pieces, daily sections,

[3]The oboe *d'amore,* or oboe of love, was a baroque oboe whose tone was considered sweeter than the regular soprano oboe. The horns *da caccia,* or hunting horns, were valveless natural horns that had, in the early eighteenth century, a more trumpetlike sound.

and the complete work operate here to give formal unity and variety to each part:

THE ORATORIO COMPLETE

The six days:	I	II	III	IV	V	VI
Keys of each part:	D	G	D	F	A	D

The key of D establishes the base or tonic of the entire work. The keys of G and A are closely related to D (subdominant and dominant) and provide variety with a sense of belonging. The key of F is somewhat more distantly related, but placed in the center, after the reaffirmation of the tonic, it allows greater exploration and development, and more intense contrast, within the safe framework or confines of the surrounding parts.

At the next level, the individual service, we see the same principles at work. For example,

DAY ONE
CHRISTMAS DAY

Pieces:	1	2	3	4	5	6	7	8	9
Key of each:	D	to E	A	a	a	to D	G	D	D

The tonic is D, and it is firmly established at beginning and ending. The keys of A and G are the dominant and subdominant, respectively, as mentioned above, and are the most closely related keys. A-minor (pieces #4 and #5) is the minor dominant and gives some variety. Pieces #2 and #6 are recitatives that prepare the entrance to their arias (#3 and #7) by moving to the dominant of their related piece. Because this is the first of the six major sections of the oratorio, the tonal exploration and development are not as great as they will become later in the work, but the related variety is sufficient for the composer to sustain the congregation's attention for a long duration without interruption. For the nonmusician, the exposition of these keys and their relationships may seem meaningless, but to all listeners these key relationships have their effect, whether or not the listener is consciously aware of their presence or technically competent to describe their intricacies. Bach knew this, and he assumed even more. He believed that D major had affective power on his listener, that it instilled a sense of joy and exuberance that was absolute and intrinsic to the sound itself. Therefore, to set the Christmas story with its joyful opening

> Praise, joy and gladness be blended in one!
> Tell what the Father Almighty has done!

in the key of D was almost a requirement of the doctrine of affections that governed baroque composition. We respond to the jubilant trumpets, the energetic voices, the rush of notes, and the instrumental colors, but Bach also believed that we would react to D major, the key of gladness and strength.

The *Christmas Oratorio* can be listened to in one sitting, of course, but the composer's original intent was to provide music for services spanning two weeks. Therefore, let us study and listen to the music for December 25, Christmas Day, as one complete unit. The opening chorus is a massive three-part structure in *da capo* format. Using the full resources of the orchestra and chorus, it has a monumental grandeur. In contrapuntal style, the forces pile one on the other, creating an effect of both solidity and motion. The basic melodic motive is embellished, and it appears over and over in a series of fugal entries. The orchestra leads the way,

and the voices proclaim the message "Praise, joy, and gladness be blended in one!"

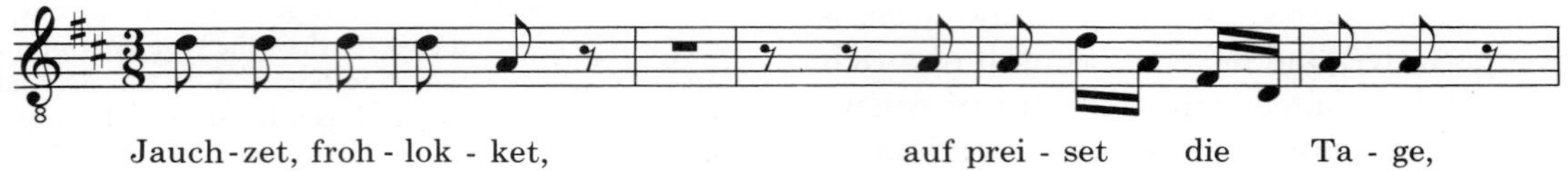

There is a middle, contrasting section. Its hushed tones reflect the awe of the singers as they say, "Worship the Highest and fall down before him."

The music gradually builds again, and the *da capo* returns us to the beginning for a repeat of the entire first section.

Pieces #2 and #3 are both recitatives, but they are quite different. The first is unaccompanied except by continuo (keyboard and a bass instrument or two), and the tenor sings the biblical prose from Luke, "And it came to pass in those days, that there went out a decree from Caesar Augustus. . . ."

The second recitative, #3, is accompanied by two oboes *d'amore,* and it almost has the quality of an arioso. The alto sings the words of the poet,

Behold the Bridegroom, Love Divine,
Behold the hope of David's line. . . .

She then sings her aria in A minor, which, even though it is structured in the *da capo* format, is composed as a trio sonata, a contrapuntal work for three equal melodic lines, usually for two melodic instruments and continuo. The first melodic line is played by violin and oboe *d'amore* in unison; the second melodic line is sung by the alto; and the third line is performed by continuo—keyboard (organ), cello, and bassoon doubling the bass melody. It was also standard practice for the keyboard player to improvise a simple chordal accompaniment with the right hand while the left hand or pedal played the bass melody. This aria is typical of one aspect of Bach's idiom. The structure is clear and balanced, the counterpoint is obvious and fascinating, and the music moves along relentlessly through the persistent baroque rhythm. Even though it has these features of master craftsmanship, the work is tender and expressive. The master craftsman oversteps neither the artist nor the devout Lutheran.

4. Aria
16
Alto
Be - rei - te dich, Zi - on, mit zärt - li - chen Trie - ben,
89
Alto
Dei - ne Wan - gen müs - sen heut viel schö - ner pran - gen,

The choir and instruments respond with a simple setting of the chorale usually associated with the Crucifixion. Its tentative, inconclusive ending on the dominant (E in the key of A minor) might be attributed to the composer's supposed attempt to express a foreshadowing of future tragedy, or it might simply be the result of a modal melody that begins and ends on E. Either way, the Lutheran congregation cannot help but respond sympathetically to its depth and beauty.

5. Choral
Wie soll ich dich emp - fan - gen und wie be - gegn' ich dir?
O al - ler Welt Ver - lan - gen, o mei - ner See - len Zier!

The Evangelist returns with the biblical text "And she brought forth her firstborn Son . . .,"

6. Evangelista
Recitativo
Tenor
Und sie ge - bar ih - ren er - sten Sohn
6
5
Continuo

and this is immediately followed by an accompanied chorale setting in which the bass soloist intersperses devotional, meditative statements in recitative style. This time the chorale is not harmonized but sung as a unison line by the sopranos (normally boys). This melody, less familiar to us today than it was to Lutherans in 1734, is set against the melodic layers of the two oboes *d'amore.*

A final aria shifts the mood from contemplation to one of celebration as the sounds of the opening return to continue the birthday celebration. The syncopation between trumpet and orchestra is a prominent feature of this opening, and the bass enters to proclaim

Sovereign Lord and King Almighty,
Savior dear, behold how lightly
Holdest Thou all pride and state.

Finally, the chorus returns singing to the tune of the Christmas chorale, "Vom Himmel hoch" (From Heaven High), the words "Ah, my dearest Jesus child..."

Two centuries before Bach labored as a church musician in his beloved homeland, Martin Luther had chosen the chorale as the most appropriate vehicle for the congregation's communal expression of faith. Early in his career, Bach stated his goal of creating "a well-regulated church music to the honor of God." Like a preacher, he interpreted the texts he compiled with all the craft and art at his disposal. Taking the Lutheran chorale as his *cantus prius factus,* his preexistent sacred melody, and coupling it with his skill, genius, and pious dedication, he composed works expressive of his age and for ours. Why he was held in no great esteem as a composer during his lifetime is a mystery that may never be solved, but it matters little to those of us today who have the opportunity of sharing his music in a way not possible at any other time in history. The *Christmas Oratorio* is both typical and unique, an example of his sacred music and an incomparable masterpiece.

23

The Arts at the Court of Louis XIV

ecause the high point of baroque music came in the early eighteenth century, later than that of the other arts, we have temporarily stepped out of chronological order. We now return to France in the late seventeenth century to examine aspects of a culture that fused the baroque aesthetic with an espousal of reason, order, and clarity, as found in classical (Greco-Roman) art, a culture that came to be called *neoclassical.*

Louis XIV (1638–1715) and Absolutism

The most populous country in western Europe, reunited after the divisive religious wars of the late sixteenth century, sharing with England and Holland in the flourishing Atlantic trade, France was the most powerful country in Europe from the mid-seventeenth to the early nineteenth century. Under Louis XIV, France became dominant not only in politics but in cultural life as well. It was, however, a culture with a narrow base, created by and for the aristocracy and upper bourgeoisie, always oriented around the monarch (contrast the cultures of ancient Athens, the Middle Ages, and Africa), but one that impressed people from all social classes. This culture developed from the king's lifestyle at his court.

Absolutism as a form of government (manifested as absolute monarchy) began to take shape under Louis's predecessors, Henry IV and Louis XIII, but Louis XIV made it an unchangeable fact. He managed to transform France's traditionally restless, independent nobles into fawning courtiers eager to catch the smile of their king. As a child, Louis had witnessed the evils that seditious upper classes could inflict on society; now the central aim of his life was to transform these elements into loyal servants of the crown. A

23-1 *Andrea Palladio, Villa Rotonda, Vicenza. (Alinari/Art Resource, NY)*

master showman, he created around him such an aura of grandeur that he became known as the Great Monarch. The upper nobility were expected to live at court, rather than in their own castles on their own lands. Louis moved his court from the palace of the Louvre in Paris to Versailles, twelve miles outside. There he built up a somewhat insulated world where he could entertain the nobles and keep an eye on them. Members of the bourgeoisie, eager to buy their way into the nobility and to be presented at court, were not likely to cause any trouble; and the peasants and lower classes were so heavily taxed that they remained in an almost feudal state of dependence. Louis saw to it that the monarchy became the primary source of privilege and honor in the society so that people would look to him as to the light. The "Sun King" was extolled as the center and source of all power, just as the sun was the center of the universe.

Versailles

The art and architecture of Versailles provided the setting for the spectacle of the monarchy of Louis XIV. It remains as the example of a place designed and refined to enhance the ideal of kingship and power.

The transformation of the medieval castle, secure from attack with its high walls and battlements, into an open palace tells the story of the transformation from a feudal way of life to the ascendancy of one ruler. When the court had an urban location, the rich and powerful built in the city. By the sixteenth century, however, in both Italy and France wealthy nobility and gentry had begun to build splendid country houses. In Italy the Venetian architect Andrea Palladio was the greatest designer of this type of residence (Fig. 23-1). In France sixteenth-century palatial architecture tended to grow from the local traditions with some influence from Renaissance Italy.

23-2 *Louis Le Vau, Villa Vaux-le-Vicomte. (Giraudon/Art Resource, NY)*

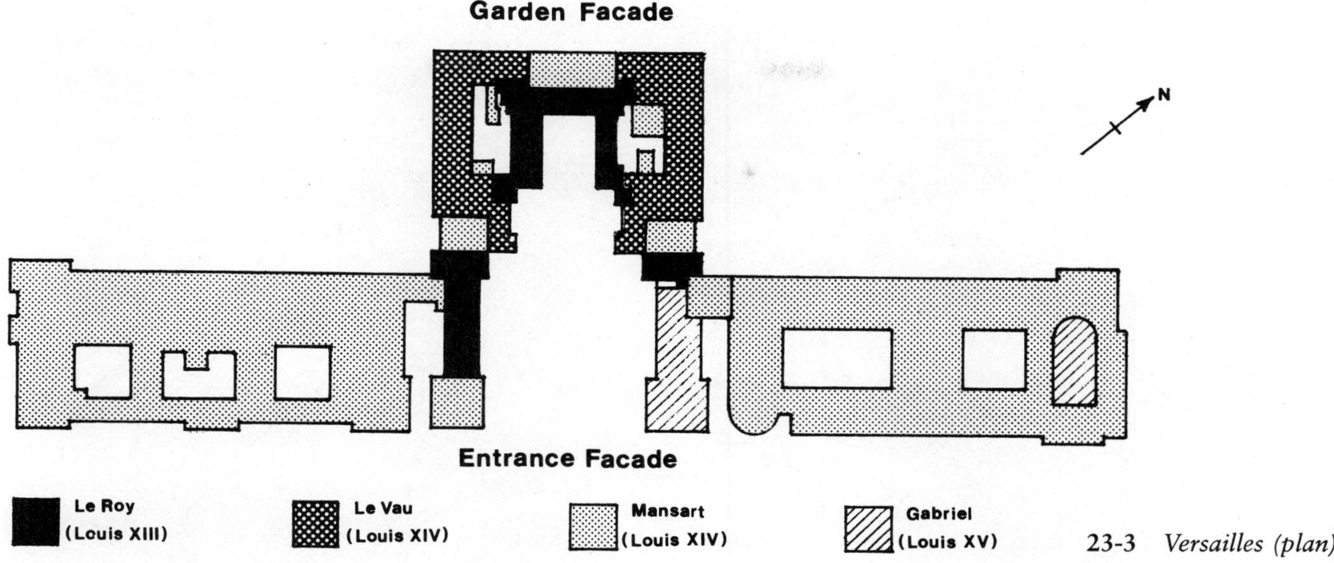

23-3 *Versailles (plan)*

By the early seventeenth century the great country house, the château, had become a magnificent retreat for the summer; for hunting, games, and entertainments; and for escape from life at the royal court. Louis XIII and his ministers had established a pattern that Louis XIV accepted and transformed. Vaux-le-Vicomte (1657–1661), built by Louis Le Vau for one of Louis's ministers, was the most splendid and sumptuous of these residences (Fig. 23-2). With this (and the beautiful Louise de la Vallière) in mind, Louis XIV decided to enlarge the small hunting lodge at Versailles that had served Louis XIII. This extravaganza is based on the adaptation of the architectural language of Rome and the Renaissance.

The palace of Versailles was begun in 1669 by Le Vau, who incorporated the old brick and stone lodge into the new designs. Originally, the building was a three-sided rectangle with the chief entrance on the east and the garden façade on the west with its courtyard (Fig. 23-3). Le Vau extended the wings east to create a courtyard on the entrance side; on the west garden façade he encased the building in the same pale, warm marble of the other sides, centering the courtyard with a six-columned portico and the ends of the flanking wings with smaller porticoes with paired columns. When Le Vau died in 1670, he was replaced by Jules Hardouin Mansart. It was Mansart who gave the palace its present scale.

On the east side Mansart focused attention on the entrance by the convergence of three great avenues (Fig. 23-4). In the angles were the horseshoe-shaped stables. He also added the long flanking wings that run north and south. On the garden façade (Fig. 23-5) Mansart joined the wings with the Hall of Mirrors, and the façade became an unbroken expanse, punctuated by a central portico, like the original one.

As the garden façade was meant as the principal view, it is appropriate to examine it more closely. The ground floor has a deep substantial base and round arches for the windows. The masonry is fairly smooth, but deep grooves run parallel to the ground and break to create the curved *voussoirs* of the arches. The only other decoration is on the *keystones* of the arches; each has the relief of a head; the sequence depicts the ages of humanity. On the next level, which is slightly taller than the first, the arched windows are repeated and are separated by Ionic *pilasters* on bases that support the *entablature.* Each window is also framed by other pilasters and a profiled molding with decorative keystone. The central portico and those on either side have Ionic columns and freestanding sculpture above the entablature. The masonry is smooth, the joints filled even with the surface. The third, attic story is lower in height; its rectangular windows with simple molding, pilaster, and balustrade with urns and sculpture act as a *cornice,* weighing down the whole flat-roofed block. All the details are familiar from the Greek, Roman, and Renaissance vocabularies. Their elaborate combination gives the wall rhythm and interest but only begins to suggest the complexity of weight, load, and plan that lies behind. In its strict continuity and order it also disguises scale. It is difficult to know how big the building is, how tall, wide, or long. One cannot easily relate to its size, which is even

23-4 *Versailles, aerial view. (French Government Tourist Office)*

23-5 *Versailles, garden façade. (Giraudon/Art Resource, NY)*

23-6 *Versailles, Fountain of Apollo. (Giraudon/Art Resource, NY)*

more impressive as one walks around it. The exterior detailing is essentially continuous, and if one walks from long end to end, the distance is some six hundred yards or six football fields. From his bedroom on the east, facing the rising sun, the Sun King had an unimpeded view of three miles.

Begun with the work on the palace, the gardens were designed as its setting. André Le Notre, their designer, combined plantings, ponds, canals, fountains, and falls to enhance and repeat the symmetry and order of the palace. The long tree-lined or hedged walks and the intricately planted beds of brilliantly colored flowers provided the vistas, reflections, and light of outdoor rooms. Everywhere the court's formality was recalled in the total subjugation of nature to order and design, a formality that showed absolute control. Everywhere the Sun King's magnificence was proclaimed. The garden façade faced two great fountains: one featured the ancestors of Apollo; the other, on axis with the Hall of Mirrors and the long canal, was dedicated to Apollo himself, the god of light and sun (Fig. 23-6).

The Hall of Mirrors, which fills the central block of the west side, was the gathering place for the court and the site for balls and other performances (Fig. 23-7). Its great windows drew light from the expansive open vistas, and its mirrors reflected that light. At night, filled with candles, it glittered icily. On either end of this opulent vast room are the Salons of War and Peace. The ceilings and walls are decorated with allegorical paintings celebrating the deeds of Louis XIV. Le Brun, chief painter at the court, was responsible for this and for all the interior decoration. The paintings themselves, executed by swarms of assistants, are a bit mechanical and cold. Rather the rich marble paneled walls, inlaid floors, and gilded pilasters and moldings attract our attention.

The Royal Chapel, added by Mansart between 1689 and 1710, gives us another experience of the palace (Fig. 23-8). Already the Sun King's power was waning; battles were lost, treasure spent. In his old age, when religion became more important to him, Louis abandoned all building except for this light, very beautiful chapel. Its great height (lower floor for the court, gallery level for royalty) recalls the Gothic style, although the architectural members and details have their origin in antiquity and the Renaissance. Compare this with Brunelleschi's interior at San Lorenzo. (See Chapter 17.) What are the most significant departures from his ideals? Compare this with the Cornaro chapel.

The marble, gilded, painted, and paneled rooms of Versailles echoed with the feet of courtiers, ambassadors, and kings of France until the French Revolution, but no one was truly accommodated except Louis

23-7 *Versailles, Hall of Mirrors. (Giraudon/Art Resource, NY)*

23-8 *Jules Hardouin-Mansart, Royal Chapel, Palace of Versailles. (Giraudon/Art Resource, NY)*

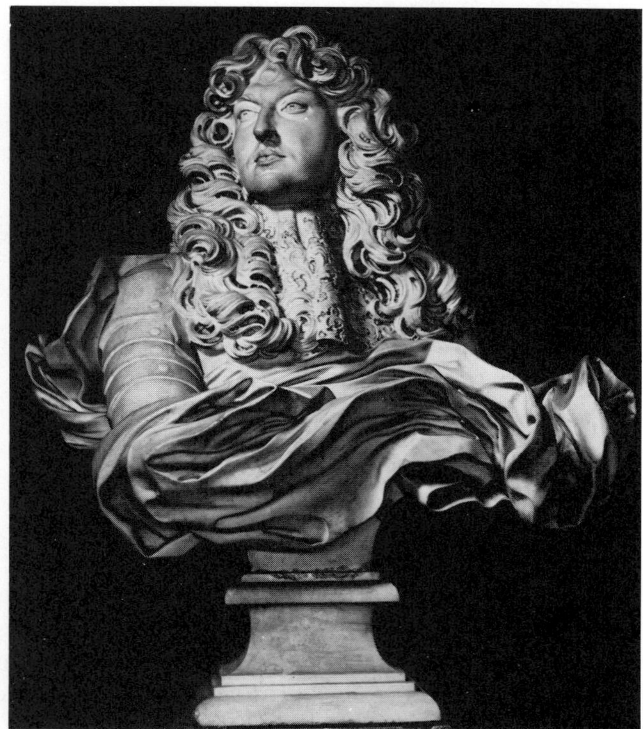

23-9 *Bernini,* Louis XIV, *Versailles. (Alinari/Art Resource, NY)*

23-10 *Hyacinthe Rigaud,* Portrait of Louis XIV, *1701, oil on canvas, 9′2″ × 7′10¾″ (detail), Louvre, Paris. (Alinari/Art Resource, NY)*

XIV. A portrait bust by Bernini shows him shortly after his ascension (Fig. 23-9). The sensuous hair and mouth, the sharp-eyed gravity, the swirling drapery reveal the youthful, virile Sun King. The later portrait by Hyacinthe Rigaud gives us a better idea of the pomp and ceremony that defined the formal court (Fig. 23-10). The face is older, strong but sagging. The sweeping blue, gold, and ermine robes of state almost obscure the Sun King.

The overwhelming feeling at Versailles is domination: domination by order, symmetry, balance, and repetition; domination achieved by forcing grass, flowers, hedges, and trees into intricate patterns and by channeling water into pools, fountains, and falls, subduing nature itself to Louis's ego. This architectural complex created by the classical vocabulary contradicts the intent of the vocabulary by its vast scale and its disregard for restraint and simplicity. In a similar way there is a conflict in our response to Versailles. It vacillates between respect for, and delight in, the intricate workmanship and a kind of horrified awe at the vast scale and richness, at this complex produced at great expense to the people of France. We sense that the glittering spectacle could not endure or be endured. Art and architecture had to become more and more accessible and essential to the rising bourgeoisie.

French Court Ballet and the Origins of Modern Theatrical Dancing

The showy, dramatic qualities of the palace at Versailles were appropriate to the highly theatrical rituals constituting life at court. Central to this life were the great festivals given in the gardens and halls at Versailles, where the nobles staged their own shows. It is then hardly surprising that in this world theatrical spectacles were the favorite form of entertainment and that the arts of ballet, opera, tragedy, and comedy reached new heights in France in the reign of Louis XIV.

Around the same time that baroque opera was developing in Italy, another new baroque art form was taking shape in France. The *ballet de cour* (court ballet) developed at the French court in the early seventeenth century but had its most splendid age under Louis XIV, who was himself an excellent dancer and took the starring role in a number of performances. The court ballet, although a short-lived art form, is nonetheless a crucial one because it is one of the important roots of both our social and our theatrical dancing. It demonstrates not only another facet of seventeenth-century art but also something of the nature of dance itself.

Why do people dance? The urge springs from the same desire to express that motivates the other arts, but the medium is the most accessible—the human body. Dancing is in a sense "body language." We have all felt the need to express fear, sorrow, anger, love, and joy with gesture and with movement. This kind of expression is both preverbal and postverbal—one can express an emotion in movement before it can be put into words and also gesture feelings beyond the limits of words. Yet no real dancing is simply an acting out of feelings. It is related to body language as poetry is to conversation; that is, it is more concentrated and more stylized.

We have seen something of the function of dance and its relation to the other arts in the cultures studied in Volume I. Dancing in ancient Greece served a ceremonial or religious function that was incorporated into tragedy and comedy at the festival of Dionysus. King David, according to the Bible, "danced before the Lord," and dance enhanced medieval Christianity in religious dramas such as *The Play of Daniel.* It is certain, too, that medieval Europeans had secular folk dances to celebrate festivities such as harvest time. During the Renaissance, dance became less religious in function but remained linked with ceremony and festival, as Lorenzo de' Medici's carnivals show. Nearly all African cultures place great value on dance, which remains a highly developed art form in modern Africa. We saw in the African section of Volume I how dance in Africa influences all the arts and how dance expresses dramatic and religious feeling in ceremonies such as the Gelede. Although all of these cultures have had a direct or indirect impact on the way that we dance today, it is in seventeenth-century Europe that we find the origins of stage dancing as we know it.

Court ballet, the first theatrical dancing, evolved from court dances, many of which were themselves influenced by folk dances. Court dancing as a form of entertainment probably began in Italy. Manuals by dancing masters published in the fifteenth and sixteenth centuries make it clear that dancing was considered an essential social grace for courtiers. Since the young nobles spent so much of their time learning to dance well, there was little need to hire professional dancers for entertainment. Nobles entertained each other with "dinner ballets"—great feasts of several courses with a dance between each course. Balls became popular in all the courts of Europe, and nobles raged to learn the latest dances from Italy. A few, like "La Volta," scandalous to many because the gentleman lifted his lady in the air (but nonetheless danced by Queen Elizabeth), were couple dances (Fig. 23-11). Most, however, were dances for couples in large groups, intended to be danced as processions or in circles, lines, or other formations.

When Catherine de' Medici, great-granddaughter of Lorenzo, became queen of France through her marriage to Henry II, she brought many aspects of Italian culture to her new country. She was especially fond of dancing and feasts. Dancing masters at Catherine's court discovered that they could make dancers move in geometric patterns; they also experimented with imitative dances that mimed dramatic actions. As musicians, poets, and stage designers worked with dancing masters, the lavish spectacles known as court ballets were born.

Histories of theatrical dancing often open with *The Comic Ballet of the Queen,* a spectacle staged by Catherine's dancing master, Balthasar de Beaujoyeulx, at the Salle Bourbon in the Louvre palace in 1581. Like an all-star gala, it lasted from ten in the evening until three in the morning. It included drama, music, poetry,

23-11 *Lord de L'Isle,* Queen Elizabeth I Dancing with Robert Dudley, Earl of Leicester. *(Reproduced by permission of Viscount de L'Isle, VC, KG, from his private collection)*

extravagant costumes, and an elaborate baroque stage set, as well as dance. The ballet had a mythological subject but a political purpose: it was intended to impress on the French people the triumph of reason and order (in the person of the king) over chaos and disorder. This and most of the court ballets following it were, like the palace at Versailles, excellent examples of the adoption of the French baroque style to the ideal of absolutism.

The theme of order and harmony that appears in many of the ballets was not, however, a mere political expedient. Dancing masters (or *choreographers,* as they came to be called) made high theoretical claims for their art, as Leonardo had done for painting. Dance, which united all the arts in the court ballet, was said to establish harmony among them. It reflected not only the unity of the arts but the grand design of nature as well. One choreographer concluded, "The Author of the Universe is the greatest Master of ballet."

The court ballet continued to grow in appeal throughout the seventeenth century. The prime minister under Louis XIII and Louis XIV, Cardinal Mazarin, used this popularity for political purposes by impressing on the court the royal authority of the young Louis XIV through his performances. At the age of fifteen, Louis made his most celebrated appearance in the role of Apollo, the sun god, in *The Royal Ballet of Night* (1653). This is a typical piece of baroque theater in its mixtures of tones and genres, its extravagant scenery and costumes, its use of machines and surprises, and its ballet within a ballet, similar to a play within a play. The *entrées* (the term comes from the dinner ballet) included serious mythology, magical allegory, court dances, and comic and burlesque characters. A loose plot concerned with the events of a night holds it together. In the end the political purpose is manifest, for Louis appears to dance as the rising sun while the cast sings the glories of his realm. His title of Sun King derived from this role and the splendid costume that he wore (Fig. 23-12) while playing it.

As he grew to maturity, Louis continued both to dance himself and to encourage the production of more ballets. He was also an accomplished guitar player and fond of poetry and drama, but dance was his favorite of the arts. His dancing master was Pierre Beauchamps; his court musician, the former Florentine Jean-Baptiste Lully. They collaborated on some opera-ballets, but eventually these two arts separated. In 1661 Louis founded the Royal Academy of Dance and in 1669 the Royal Academy of Music, which became the Paris Opera. The dance academy was primarily for noble amateurs, but in 1672 Louis founded a school to train professional dancers; this date marks the beginning of stage dancing as we know it today. Beauchamps codified the five positions and other steps still taught in ballet classes. Dance in the ballroom and

23-12 *Louis XIV as the Sun King in the* Ballet de la Nuit. *(Bibliothèque Nationale, Paris)*

dance in the theater from then on went their separate ways.

Beauchamps and Lully did collaborate with the actor-director-playwright Molière in another type of production that flourished at the end of the century. The "comedy-ballet," exemplified by *Le Bourgeois Gentilhomme,* represented a more impressive unity of the arts than did the court ballet. Molière, as we will see, is justly considered the father of modern comedy. To understand this art form, we must know something about drama in seventeenth-century France.

French Neoclassical Tragedy

Drama in France, in the early part of the seventeenth century, resembled the court ballet in its mixture of genres (tragedy, comedy, pastoral, and so on), its extravagant and complicated plots, and its sometimes unwieldly length. Later in the century, however, theoreticians and practitioners of the theater reacted against what they viewed as unbridled exuberance and attempted, in conformity with the reigning political absolutism, to impose universal standards on drama. Yet as in the palace at Versailles, classical standards of clarity, order, and harmony were often used in the service of qualities such as extremes of emotion, extravagance, *grandeur,* and high-flown rhetoric that we might call baroque.

Classicism as an aesthetic first appeared in tragedy and in theories of tragedy. Basing their ideas on the Italian humanists' revival and imitations of Greek and Roman tragedy, French writers found rules that they believed must be followed to produce good tragedy. The rules that they set down became a kind of standard doctrine after they were accepted by the French Academy, founded in 1635. The academy, still in operation today, was charged with putting together theoretical works of importance to the French language: dictionaries, grammars, and treatises on rhetoric and poetics. It became in fact a kind of watchdog over matters of style and usage. Its members standardized the rules for tragedy when they pronounced judgment on the first important tragedy by Pierre Corneille, based on a Spanish work, entitled *Le Cid* (1637). The members of the academy found the tragedy basically a good one but lacking in certain points. What were the standards by which they judged?

Most important to the "classical" ideal of tragedy were the so-called three unities: unity of time, place, and action. The tragedy was to take place in no more than twenty-four hours, in the same setting, and was to have only one plot. Related to these three basic unities was unity of tone—tragedy and comedy were not to appear in the same play. The characters of tragedy were to be nobles, kings and queens, who would speak in a dignified manner. No vulgar realism and no violent action could appear on the stage: such events necessary to the plot could be related by a messenger. Also, the events and characters could not be contemporary: they had to be far away either in time or in space. In fact, most of the French classical tragedies were based on Greek or Roman history or mythology. And yet the plots were to follow the rule of *verisimilitude.* They were not to be fantasies but to seem as if they could actually happen.

One can see how these rules might be applied to a Greek tragedy such as *Oedipus Rex,* but the French were in fact stricter than the Athenians; many Greek tragedies do not fit these standards. Certainly, every play by Shakespeare would fail the French Academy's test. It is hard for us to understand now how such strict rules could be effectively applied to art; but French classicism did produce two great tragedians: Pierre

Corneille (1606–1684), who admittedly did have some trouble with the rules; and Jean Racine (1639–1699), whose pure, compressed works seem to have benefited by the limits imposed on them. The grandeur and magnificence characteristic of all art in the era of Louis XIV is evident in the tragedies of these two writers.

Corneille and Racine were (and are) considered by many to be the glories of their age; but when the influential literary critic Boileau was asked by Louis XIV to name the greatest contemporary writer, he replied, "Molière, Sire." Most people today would concur with that judgment, for although the two tragedians seem particularly French, the comedy writer Molière is universal. Yet Molière, too, was obliged to write in conformity with the standards of his day and, especially, for the pleasure of the king.

Molière (1622–1673), A Genius of Comedy

Jean-Baptiste Poquelin, who later assumed the stage name of Molière, was born to a solidly bourgeois Parisian family. After receiving a good education, he abandoned a possible career in law to pursue two passions—the theater and the actress Madeleine Béjart. Molière and Mlle. Béjart together founded a company of actors, the *Illustre Théâtre,* in 1643. During the years in which the company toured France, Molière gained valuable experience as an actor, director, and manager. He also wrote and produced two of his own comedies, heavily influenced by the Italian *commedia dell'arte,* with its improvisations on stock characters, which he often saw during his travels. Like Shakespeare, Molière was not just a writer but a complete man of the theater.

The great breakthrough for the *Illustre Théâtre* came when the company pleased the king, performing before him at the Louvre. Louis then offered them a theater to play in, the Petit Bourbon, which they were to share with an Italian company. From then on, Molière turned more seriously to writing, although he continued to act in his own comedies throughout his lifetime (in fact, he died during a performance). Continuing to enjoy the protection and interest of the king, Molière staged his comedies not only at the Louvre but also at the palace at Versailles and at other castles. He thus became intimately involved in the atmosphere of festivity surrounding the court of Louis XIV, but his comedies reached a much wider audience. Common people as well as bourgeois and nobles attended them with great enthusiasm when they played in Paris. Molière was accused by certain purists of catering to the vulgar element of the audience, but it is exactly his wide human experience and his refusal to become too refined that helped to make him a great writer of comedy.

Molière's comedies range from rather gross farces, based on the stock character of the ridiculous dupe and almost slapstick effects, to subtle analyses of human character that are close to serious drama. His greatest originality lay in his ability to observe keenly the society and the people around him and to create from them characters both of their time and for all times and places. On the whole his comedies observe the classical three unities originally laid down for tragedy, as well as other classical canons such as simplicity and verisimilitude, yet Molière did not hesitate to deviate from the rules when it suited his purposes. The only really important rule, he maintained, was to *please.* Audiences, not theoreticians, were the best judges. It was necessary, too, to please the king. Luckily, Louis was not a person of narrow tastes.

One of Molière's greatest comedies was written for a great festival at Versailles called "The Pleasures of the Enchanted Island" (Fig. 23-13) in 1664. The title character of the play *Tartuffe* is a religious hypocrite, and the proposed moral clearly favors good common sense against fanaticism. The play so shocked the religious elements of the court that the archbishop used his influence to persuade Louis to ban it; not until five years later was Molière free to produce it. Another of his most admired plays, *The Misanthrope,* is about a man who hates the pretensions and superficiality of upper-class society but is in love with a girl who accepts them fully. Both of these plays are centered around a complex character and are satirical studies of human life in society.

Le Bourgeois Gentilhomme, or *The Would-Be Gentleman,* is not Molière's most complex or most literary play, but it remains a favorite on stage. The king himself suggested part of the subject of this spectacle, created for festivities at the royal hunting castle at Chambord in 1670. The preceding year Louis had established diplomatic relations with the Ottoman empire, receiving an ambassador from the Grand Turk Suleiman. This exotic embassy had so impressed the French court that Louis wanted a spectacle with a Turkish ceremony in it. He left the assignment and the actual planning to the musician Lully, the dancing master Beauchamps, and the comedian Molière.

The three had collaborated before on "comedy-ballets," but this was their most successful production. At first glance it seems an unlikely combination: what has the gross realism of comedy to do with the courtly

23-13 *Staging for an outdoor ballet at Versailles,* Alcina's Island. *(By courtesy of the Board of Trustees of the Victoria and Albert Museum)*

and imaginary world of ballet? And yet it is just this contrast between solid reality and make-believe that is the subject of the comedy-ballet. As usual, Molière's comedy is centered around a character through whom he depicts a whole society. Monsieur Jourdain, the main figure here, comes from the most everyday, "prosaic" milieu possible, the Parisian bourgeoisie. He is the very type of the self-made man—obviously shrewd and practical enough to have made himself a great deal of money. And yet this solid merchant has a dream: he senses that there is a world of ideas, art, culture, and refinement out beyond his experience, and he longs to enter into it. For him, the dream world is summed up by one word, *gentleman,* which at that time meant a member of a particular social class, the nobility. The gentlemen are those with titles, taste, fine clothes, fine educations, and exquisite ladies—and Monsieur Jourdain feels that he now has the money to buy all these things. But Jourdain also has very common human defects: pretentiousness, vanity, and egotism. These qualities receive the full force of Molière's satire; yet many readers and spectators feel a great deal of sympathy for this man with a dream. The dream world itself (as seen by Molière and the spectator, not by Jourdain) is hardly admirable: Molière's satiric comedy hits the cynicism and complacency of the petty nobility and the foppery of the artists and teachers as hard as it hits the bourgeois. (Naturally, the king and the powerful nobles around him, Molière's patrons, are not attacked!) The only people with good sense, bourgeois and servants, are rather limited as characters.

The comedy-ballet combination admirably demonstrates the two realms of real world/dream world. At the end of the first act the music master and dance master put on a show that represents the world of culture to which Jourdain aspires. At the end of the second act the tailors who have brought the bourgeois "dream" clothes perform a dance. Song and dance accompany the dinner that Jourdain gives for his dream lady, the marquise, at the end of Act III. The "Turkish" ceremony at the end of Act IV brings Jourdain, now a complete dupe, into a fantasy world, and the entire play dissolves into fantasy with the long ballet at the end. It may be argued that the solid, clear, "real-seeming" prose comedy constitutes the classical element of the play and the fantasy-ballets its baroque element.

Lully's Music from Le Bourgeois Gentilhomme

Modern audiences view Molière's text of the play as the most important element of this comedy-ballet, but the seventeenth-century audience thought of it as "a ballet composed of six *entrées* accompanied by comedy."[1] The music and dance were thus highly significant elements. The composer Jean-Baptiste Lully (1632–1687) enjoyed at the time a greater prestige than did Molière. He dominated French music from the time of his appointment as superintendent of Music of the Chamber in 1661 until his death in 1687, and his taste for magnificence is reflected in his compositions for the king: theater pieces with acting, dance, orchestra, costumes, and elaborate scenery. He directed two string orchestras—the Grande Bande, or "The King's 24 Violins," and the Petite Bande. Of course he wrote other music, but his operas and ballets stand out as the most characteristic of the types of music enjoyed at court at this time. In his comedy-ballets, Lully perfected all the elements of his mature style: appropriately pompous overtures for string orchestra; massive and spectacular choruses; rhythmically attractive dances that reflected the tastes of the French court; and musical recitatives suited to the French language.

Le Bourgeois Gentilhomme begins with a "French overture," an instrumental form established by Lully for the introduction of large works—operas and ballets. It was also used as an independent composition and as an opening movement of an instrumental *suite, sonata,* or *concerto.* These compositions for the *24 Violons du Roi* are composed in two parts: the first section in duple *meter,* jagged *rhythm, homophonic* or *chordal texture,* and slow, majestic movement; the second section in triple meter, sprightly rhythm, and *fugal* or *contrapuntal texture.*

In listening to the opening section, one hears not only the jagged or dotted rhythm of the melodies but also an underlying pulse or beat of steady eighth notes, a stylistic feature of the period that some have referred to as the "baroque motor rhythm." This new sense of beat, like the jazz drummer's sense of time, pervades the music and infuses it with life and motion.

A clever baroque device occurs immediately after the conclusion of the overture. The play opens with a play within the play. We discover the composer at work at his harpsichord preparing music for the *comédie-ballet* to follow.

We see and hear him trying phrases, accepting and rejecting passages, humming and strumming, and otherwise reworking a number heard later in its polished

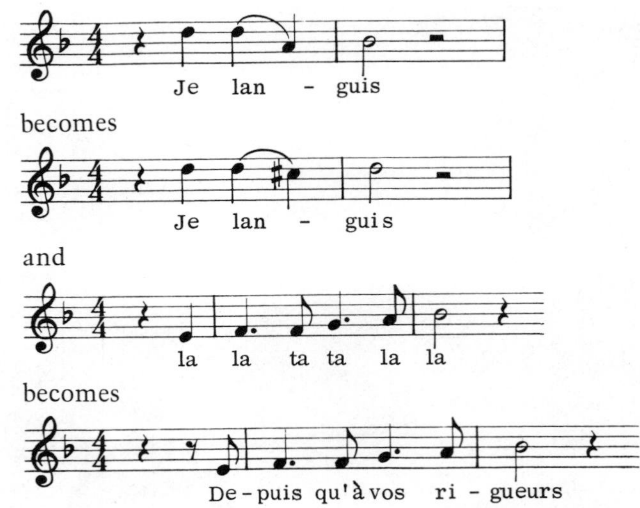

form, *"Je languis nuit et jour"* ("I pine night and day"). Actually, Lully is not giving us a true glimpse into the composer's workshop, for the unfinished version is as complete, correct, and baroque as the shorter final song; but he gives the impression of something not real, and that is very characteristic of French baroque theater. It delighted Louis XIV and is capable of delighting audiences today.

Molière's story line, of course, outlines the formal structure of the entire comedy-ballet, but, according to taste, Lully inserts favorite court dances throughout. Here are some examples:

[1]The music and the entire play in French can be heard on London Records, LL 1447.

Turkish March

Both Lully and Louis took music seriously. For political reasons, the court composer had to do his best to please his sovereign, as inferior performance was rewarded harshly. On the other hand, for political reasons too Louis XIV took his court entertainments most seriously. Besides satisfying his vanity and love of pleasure, they helped to perpetuate the mystique of absolutist monarchy. Keeping the nobles and even the bourgeoisie pleasantly entertained was another way of keeping them in their place.

Jean-Baptiste Lully

Le Bourgeois Gentilhomme

(Beginning of the Overture)

Violin I

Violin II

Viola I

Viola II

Cello

Piano reduction

A reduction demonstrating homophonic character and jagged rhythm

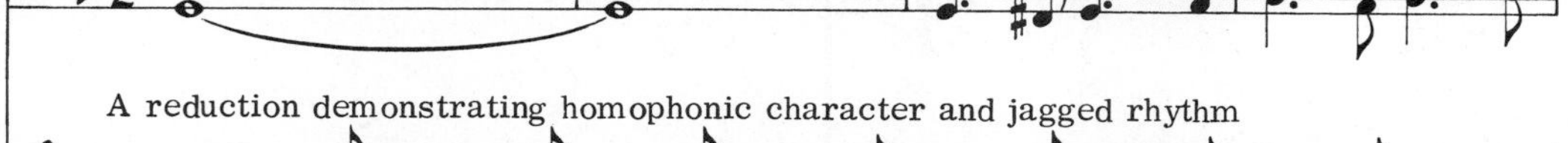

(Beginning of the second section of the Overture)

Reading Selections

From The *Memoirs of Louis de Rouvroy, Duc de Saint-Simon*

Translation by Bayle St. John

A noble from a once-powerful family—not at all pleased with the new absolutism—has left us a sometimes scathing but nonetheless vivid and penetrating portrayal of Louis and his court. The memoirs of the duke of Saint-Simon, although written in the last years of the Sun King's reign, are the best record that we have of what went on throughout.

Versailles

He early showed a disinclination for Paris. The troubles that had taken place there during the minority[1] made him regard the place as dangerous; he wished, too, to render himself venerable by hiding himself from the eyes of the multitude; all these considerations fixed him at St. Germain[2] soon after the death of the Queen, his mother. It was to that place he began to attract the world by fêtes and gallantries, and by making it felt that he wished to be often seen.

His love for Madame de la Vallière,[3] which was at first kept secret, occasioned frequent excursions to Versailles, then a little card castle, which had been built by Louis XIII... the King, his son, slept there, so that he might be more in private with his mistress, pleasures unknown to the hero and just man, worthy son of Saint Louis, who built the little château.

These excursions of Louis XIV by degrees gave birth to those immense buildings he erected at Versailles; and their convenience for a numerous court, so different from the apartments at St. Germain, led him to take up his abode there entirely shortly after the death of the Queen. He built an infinite number of apartments, which were asked for by those who wished to pay their court to him; whereas at St. Germain nearly everybody was obliged to lodge in the town, and the few who found accommodation at the château were strangely inconvenienced.

The frequent fêtes, the private promenades at Versailles, the journeys, were means on which the King seized in order to distinguish or mortify the courtiers, and thus render them more assiduous in pleasing him. He felt that of real favours he had not enough to bestow; in order to keep up the spirit of devotion, he therefore unceasingly invented all sorts of ideal ones, little preferences and petty distinctions, which answered his purpose as well.

He was exceedingly jealous of the attention paid him. Not only did he notice the presence of the most distinguished courtiers, but those of inferior degree also. He looked to the right and to the left, not only upon rising but upon going to bed, at his meals, in passing through his apartments, or his gardens of Versailles, where alone the courtiers were allowed to follow him; he saw and noticed everybody; not one escaped him, not even those who hoped to remain unnoticed. He marked well all absentees from the court, found out the reason of their absence, and never lost an opportunity of acting towards them as the occasion might seem to justify. With some of the courtiers (the most distinguished), it was a demerit not to make the court their ordinary abode; with others 'twas a fault to come but rarely; for those who never or scarcely ever came it was certain disgrace. When their names were in any way mentioned, "I do not know them," the King would reply haughtily. Those who presented themselves but seldom were thus characterised: "They are people I never see"; these decrees were irrevocable. He could not bear people who liked Paris.

[1]The "Fronde," a revolt of nobles against the power of the king.

[2]Another palace outside of Paris.

[3]Louis XIV's first mistress.

On Dancing

On Mardi Gras, there was a grand toilette of the Duchesse de Chartres, to which the King and all the Court came; and in the evening a grand ball, similar to that which had just taken place, except that the new Duchesse de Chartres was led out by the Duc de Bourgogne. Every one wore the same dress, and had the same partner as before.

I cannot pass over in silence a very ridiculous adventure which occurred at both of these balls. A son of Montbron, no more made to dance at Court than his father was to be chevalier of the order (to which, however, he was promoted in 1688), was among the company. He had been asked if he danced well; and he had replied with a confidence which made every one hope that the contrary was the case. Every one was satisfied. From the very first bow, he became confused, and he lost step at once. He tried to divert attention from his mistake by affected attitudes, and carrying his arms high; but this made him only more ridiculous, and excited bursts of laughter, which, in despite of the respect due to the person of the King (who likewise had great difficulty to hinder himself from laughing), degenerated at length into regular hooting. On the morrow, instead of flying the Court or holding his tongue, he excused himself by saying that the presence of the King had disconcerted him, and promised marvels for the ball which was to follow. He was one of my friends, and I felt for him. I should even have warned him against a second attempt, if the very different success I had met with had not made me fear that my advice would be taken in ill part. As soon as he began to dance at the second ball, those who were near stood up, those who were far off climbed wherever they could to get a sight; and the shouts of laughter were mingled with clapping of hands. Every one, even the King himself, laughed heartily, and most of us quite loud, so that I do not think any one was ever treated so before. Montbron disappeared immediately afterwards, and did not show himself again for a long time. It was a pity he exposed himself to this defeat, for he was an honourable and brave man.

Every action of the day at court was performed with such ceremony and ritual that life must have seemed like a continuous formal ballet. Courtiers were present and assisted at *le lever du roi* and *le coucher du roi,* the king's getting up in the morning and going to bed at night. (The same words in French are used for the rising and setting of the sun.) Here is Saint-Simon's description of the king's rising:

Le Lever du Roi

At eight o'clock the chief valet de chambre on duty, who alone had slept in the royal chamber, and who had dressed himself, awoke the King. The chief physician, the chief surgeon, and the nurse (as long as she lived), entered at the same time. The latter kissed the King; the others rubbed and often changed his shirt, because he was in the habit of sweating a great deal. At the quarter, the grand chamberlain was called (or, in his absence, the first gentleman of the chamber), and those who had, what was called the *grandes entrées.* The chamberlain (or chief gentleman) drew back the curtains which had been closed again, and presented the holy water from the vase, at the head of the bed. These gentlemen stayed but a moment, and that was the time to speak to the King, if any one had anything to ask of him; in which case the rest stood aside. When, contrary to custom, nobody had aught to say, they were there but for a few moments. He who had opened the curtains and presented the holy water, presented also a prayer-book. Then all passed into the cabinet of the council. A very short religious service being over, the King called, they re-entered. The same officer gave him his dressing-gown; immediately after, other privileged courtiers entered, and then everybody, in time to find the King putting on his shoes and stockings, for he did almost everything himself and with address and grace. Every other day we saw him shave himself; and he had a little short wig in which he always appeared, even in bed, and on medicine days. He often spoke of the chase, and sometimes said a word to somebody. No toilette table was near him; he had simply a mirror held before him.

As soon as he was dressed, he prayed to God, at the side of his bed, where all the clergy present knelt, the cardinals without cushions, all the laity remaining standing; and the captain of the guards came to the balustrade during the prayer, after which the King passed into his cabinet.

QUESTIONS

1. On the basis of these passages, what was Saint-Simon's attitude toward Louis XIV?
2. Besides vanity, what other motivation might Louis XIV have had for wanting the most important nobles at his court?

MOLIÈRE

The Would-Be Gentleman

Translation by John Watts

CHARACTERS

M. JOURDAIN, *a self-made man*
MME JOURDAIN, *his wife*
LUCILE, *their daughter*
NICOLE, *their maid*
CLÉONTE, *a suitor to Lucile*
COVIELLE, *his valet, suitor to Nicole*
DORANTE, *a courtier*
DORIMÈNE, *a marchioness, widowed*
MUSIC MASTER AND PUPIL
DANCING MASTER
FENCING MASTER
PHILOSOPHY MASTER
MASTER TAILOR
JOURNEYMAN TAILORS
SINGERS AND MUSICIANS
PAGES AND LACKEYS

ACT I

THE SCENE MUSIC MASTER, *a* PUPIL *of the Music Master (composing at a table in the middle of the stage), a* WOMAN SINGER, *and two* MEN SINGERS; *a* DANCING MASTER *and* DANCERS

MUSIC MASTER (*to the musicians*) Here, step into this hall, and sit there till he comes.

DANCING MASTER (*to the dancers*) And you too, on this side.

MUSIC MASTER (*to his pupil*) Is it done?

PUPIL Yes.

MUSIC MASTER Let's see.... 'Tis mighty well.

DANCING MASTER Is it anything new?

MUSIC MASTER Yes, 'tis an air for a serenade, which I set him to compose here while we wait till our gentleman's awake.

DANCING MASTER May one see what it is?

MUSIC MASTER You will hear it, with the dialogue, when he comes. He won't be long.

DANCING MASTER We have no want of business, either of us, at present.

MUSIC MASTER 'Tis true. We have found a man here, just such a one as we both of us want. This same Monsieur Jourdain is a sweet income, with his visions of nobility and gallantry which he has got into his noddle, and it would be well for your capers and my crotchets, were all the world like him.

DANCING MASTER Not altogether so well; I wish, for his sake, that he were better skilled than he is in the things we give him.

MUSIC MASTER It is true he understands 'em ill, but he pays for 'em well. And that's what our art has more need of at present than of anything else.

DANCING MASTER For my part, I own it to you, I regale a little upon glory. I am sensible of applause, and think it a very grievous punishment in the liberal arts to display one's self to fools and to expose our compositions to the barbarous judgment of the stupid. Talk no more of it, there is a pleasure in working for persons who are capable of relishing the delicacies of an art, who know how to give a kind reception to the beauties of a work, and, by titillating approbation, regale you for your labour. Yes, the most agreeable recompense one can receive for the things one does is to see them understood, to see 'em caressed with an applause that does you honour. There's nothing, in my opinion, which pays us better than this for all our fatigues. And the praises of connoisseurs give an exquisite delight.

MUSIC MASTER I grant it, and I relish them as well as you. There is nothing certainly that tickles more than the applause you speak of, but one cannot live upon this incense. Sheer praises won't make a man easy. There must be something solid mixed withal, and the best method of praising is to praise with the open hand. This indeed is one whose understanding is very shallow, who speaks of everything awry, and cross of the grain, and never applauds but in contradiction to sense. But his money sets his judgment right. He has discernment in his purse. His praises are current coin; and this ignorant commoner is more worth to us, as you see, than that grand witty lord who introduced us here.

DANCING MASTER There's something of truth in what you say; but I find you lean a little too much towards the pelf. And mere interest is something so base that an honest man should never discover an attachment to it.

MUSIC MASTER For all that, you decently receive the money our spark gives you.

DANCING MASTER Certainly; but I don't place all my happiness in that: and I wish that, with his fortune, he had also some good taste of things.

MUSIC MASTER I wish the same; 'tis what we both labour at as much as we can. But, however, he gives us the opportunity of making ourselves known in the world; and he'll pay for others what others praise for him.

DANCING MASTER Here he comes.

(*Enter* M. JOURDAIN *in a nightgown and cap, and two* LACKEYS)

M. JOURDAIN Well, gentlemen? What have you there? Will you let me see your little drollery?

DANCING MASTER How? What little drollery?

M. JOURDAIN Why the—how do you call that thing? your prologue, or dialogue of songs and dancing.

DANCING MASTER Ha, ha!

MUSIC MASTER You see we are ready.

M. JOURDAIN I have made you wait a little, but 'tis because I am to be dressed out to-day like your people of quality;[1] and my hosier has sent me a pair of silk stockings which I thought I should never have got on.

MUSIC MASTER We are here only to wait your leisure.

M. JOURDAIN I desire you'll both stay till they have brought me my clothes, that you may see me.

DANCING MASTER As you please.

M. JOURDAIN You shall see me most exactly equipped from head to foot.

MUSIC MASTER We don't doubt it.

M. JOURDAIN I have had this Indian thing made up for me.

DANCING MASTER 'Tis very handsome.

M. JOURDAIN My tailor tells me that people of quality go thus in a morning.

MUSIC MASTER It fits you to a miracle.

M. JOURDAIN Why, ho! Fellow there! both my fellows!

FIRST LACKEY Your pleasure, sir?

M. JOURDAIN Nothing! 'Tis only to try whether you hear me readily. (*to the* MUSIC *and* DANCING MASTERS) What say you of my liveries?

DANCING MASTER They are magnificent.

M. JOURDAIN (*half-opens his gown and reveals a tight pair of breeches of scarlet velvet, and a green velvet jacket*) Here again is a kind of dishabille to perform my exercises in a morning.

MUSIC MASTER 'Tis gallant.

M. JOURDAIN Lackey!

FIRST LACKEY Sir?

M. JOURDAIN T'other lackey!

SECOND LACKEY Sir?

M. JOURDAIN (*taking off his gown*) Hold my gown. (*to the* MUSIC *and* DANCING MASTERS) Do you like me so?

DANCING MASTER Mighty well; nothing can be better.

M. JOURDAIN Now for your affair a little.

MUSIC MASTER I should be glad first to let you hear an air (*pointing to his pupil*) he has just composed for the serenade which you gave me orders about. He is one of my pupils, who has an admirable talent for these sort of things.

M. JOURDAIN Yes, but that should not have been put to a pupil to do; you were not too good for that business yourself.

MUSIC MASTER You must not let the name of pupil impose upon you, sir. These sort of pupils know as much as the greatest masters, and the air is as good as can be made. Hear it only.

M. JOURDAIN (*to his servants*) Give me my gown that I may hear the better.—Stay, I believe I shall be better without the gown.—No, give it me again, it will do better.

MUSICIAN

I languish night and day, nor sleeps my pain,
Since those fair eyes imposed the rigorous chain;
But tell me, Iris, what dire fate attends
Your enemies, if thus you treat your friends?

M. JOURDAIN This song seems to me a little upon the dismal; it inclines one to sleep; I should be glad you could enliven it a little here and there.

MUSIC MASTER 'Tis necessary, sir, that the air should be suited to the words.

M. JOURDAIN I was taught one perfectly pretty some time ago. Stay—um—how is it?

DANCING MASTER In good troth, I don't know.

M. JOURDAIN There's lamb in it.

DANCING MASTER Lamb?

M. JOURDAIN Yes—Ho!

I thought my dear Namby
As gentle as fair-o:
I thought my dear Namby
As mild as a lamb-y.
Oh dear, oh dear, oh dear-o!
For now the sad scold is a thousand times told,
More fierce than a tiger or bear-o.

Isn't it pretty?

MUSIC MASTER The prettiest in the world.

DANCING MASTER And you sing it well.

M. JOURDAIN Yet I never learnt music.

MUSIC MASTER You ought to learn it, sir, as you do dancing. They are two arts which have a strict connection one with the other.

DANCING MASTER And which open the human mind to see the beauty of things.

M. JOURDAIN What, do people of quality learn music too?

MUSIC MASTER Yes, sir.

M. JOURDAIN I'll learn it then. But I don't know how

---

[1]Jourdain's concern with dress is representative of the importance that he now gives to *appearance*. He judges something to be good or bad according to whether "people of quality" (the nobility) appear to have it or not.

23-14 *Scene from Act I of* Le Bourgeois Gentilhomme *(1951 Comèdie Française production) with Louis Seigneur and Jacques Charon. (Lipnitzki/Viollet, Paris)*

I shall find time. For, besides the fencing master who teaches me, I have also got me a philosophy master, who is to begin this morning.

MUSIC MASTER Philosophy is something; but music, sir, music—

DANCING MASTER Music and dancing—music and dancing, that is all that's necessary.

MUSIC MASTER There's nothing so profitable in a state as music.

DANCING MASTER There's nothing so necessary for men as dancing.

MUSIC MASTER A state cannot subsist without music.

DANCING MASTER Without dancing, a man can do nothing.

MUSIC MASTER All the disorders, all the wars one sees in the world, happen only from not learning music.

DANCING MASTER All the disasters of mankind, all the fatal misfortunes that histories are replete with, the blunders of politicians, the miscarriages of great commanders, all this comes from want of skill in dancing.

M. JOURDAIN How so?

MUSIC MASTER Does not war proceed from want of concord amongst men?

M. JOURDAIN That's true.

MUSIC MASTER And if all men learnt music, would not that be a means of keeping them better in tune, and of seeing universal peace in the world?

M. JOURDAIN You're in the right.

DANCING MASTER When a man has been guilty of a defect in his conduct—be it in the affairs of his family, or in the government of the state, or in the command of an army—don't we always say, such a one has made a false step in such an affair?

M. JOURDAIN Yes, we say so.

DANCING MASTER And can making a false step proceed from anything but not knowing how dance?

M. JOURDAIN 'Tis true, and you are both in the right.[2]

DANCING MASTER This is to let you see the excellence and advantage of dancing and music.

M. JOURDAIN I now comprehend it.

MUSIC MASTER Will you see each of our compositions?

M. JOURDAIN Yes.

MUSIC MASTER I have told you already that this is a slight essay which I formerly made upon the different passions that may be expressed by music.

M. JOURDAIN Very well.

MUSIC MASTER (*to the musicians*) Here, come forward. (*to* M. JOURDAIN) You are to imagine with yourself that they are dressed like shepherds.

M. JOURDAIN Why always shepherds? One sees nothing but such stuff everywhere.

MUSIC MASTER When we are to introduce persons as speaking in music, 'tis necessary to probability that we give in to the pastoral way. Singing has always been appropriated to shepherds; and it is by no means natural in dialogue that princes or citizens should sing their passions.

M. JOURDAIN Be it so, be it so. Let's see.

(*Dialogue in music between a* WOMAN *and two* MEN)

WOMAN *The heart that must tyrannic love obey,*
A thousand fears and cares oppress.
Sweet are those sighs and languishments,
they say;
Say what they will for me,
Nought is so sweet as liberty.

[2]Molière mocks the pretentiousness of the two teachers here, but beneath the comedy is some serious contemporary thought on the benefits of the arts, with which Molière probably agreed. Jourdain, however, must be convinced by a strictly utilitarian argument that distorts the theory.

FIRST MAN *Nothing so sweet as love's soft fire,*
Which can two glowing hearts inspire
With the same life, the same desire.
The loveless swain no happiness can prove.
From life take soothing love,
All pleasure you remove.

SECOND MAN *Sweet were the wanton archer's sway,*
Would all with constancy obey;
But, cruel fate!
No nymph is true:
The faithless sex more worthy of our hate,
To love should bid eternally adieu.

FIRST MAN *Pleasing heat!*

WOMAN *Freedom blest!*

SECOND MAN *Fair deceit!*

FIRST MAN *O how I love thee!*

WOMAN *How I approve thee!*

SECOND MAN *I detest!*

FIRST MAN *Against love's ardour quit this mortal hate.*

WOMAN *Shepherd, myself I bind here,*
To show a faithful mate.

SECOND MAN *Alas! but where to find her?*

WOMAN *Our glory to retrieve,*
My heart I here bestow.

SECOND MAN *But, nymph, can I believe*
That heart no change will know?

WOMAN *Let experience decide,*
Who loves best of the two.

SECOND MAN *And the perjured side*
May vengeance pursue.

ALL THREE *Then let us kindle soft desire,*
Let us fan the amorous fire.
Ah! how sweet it is to love,
When hearts united constant prove!

M. JOURDAIN Is this all?

MUSIC MASTER Yes.

M. JOURDAIN I find 'tis very concise, and there are some little sayings in it pretty enough.

DANCING MASTER You have here, for my composition, a little essay of the finest movements, and the most beautiful attitudes with which a dance can possibly be varied.

M. JOURDAIN Are they shepherds too?

DANCING MASTER They're what you please. (*to the dancers*) Hola!

(*Four dancers execute all the different movements and steps that the dancing master commands. This dance constitutes the first "intermission."*)

ACT II

THE SCENE MONSIEUR JOURDAIN, MUSIC MASTER, DANCING MASTER

M. JOURDAIN This is none of your stupid things, and these same fellows flutter it away bravely.

MUSIC MASTER When the dance is mixed with the music, it will have a greater effect still, and you will see something gallant in the little entertainment we have prepared for you.

M. JOURDAIN That's however for by and by; and the person for whom I have ordered all this, is to do me the honour of dining with me here.

DANCING MASTER Everything's ready.

MUSIC MASTER But in short, sir, this is not enough, 'tis necessary such a person as you, who live great and have an inclination to things that are handsome, should have a concert of music at your house every Wednesday, or every Thursday.

M. JOURDAIN Why so? Have people of quality?

MUSIC MASTER Yes, sir.

M. JOURDAIN I'll have one then. Will it be fine?

MUSIC MASTER Certainly. You must have three voices, a treble, a counter-tenor, and a bass, which must be accompanied with a bass-viol, a theorbolute, and a harpsichord for the thorough-bass, with two violins to play the symphonies.

M. JOURDAIN You must add also a trumpet-marine. The trumpet-marine is an instrument that pleases me, and is very harmonious.

MUSIC MASTER Leave us to manage matters.

M. JOURDAIN However, don't forget by and by to send the musicians to sing at table.

MUSIC MASTER You shall have everything you should have.

M. JOURDAIN But above all, let the entertainment be fine.

MUSIC MASTER You will be pleased with it, and, amongst other things, with certain minuets you will find in it.

M. JOURDAIN Ay, the minuets are my dance; and I have a mind you should see me dance 'em. Come, master.

DANCING MASTER Your hat, sir, if you please.

(M. JOURDAIN *takes off his foot-boy's hat, and puts it on over his own nightcap; upon which his* MASTER *takes him by the hand and makes him dance to a minuet-air which he sings*)

Tol, lol, lol, lol, lol, lol,
Tol, lol, lol,
twice;

Tol, lol, lol; tol, lol.
In time, if you please,
Tol, lol,
the right leg.
Tol, lol, lol.
Don't shake your shoulders so much.
Tol, lol, lol, lol, lol.
Why, your arms are out of joint.
Tol, lol, lol, lol, lol.
Hold up your head. Turn out your toes.
Tol, lol, lol.
Your body erect.[1]

M. JOURDAIN Heh?

MUSIC MASTER Admirably well performed.

M. JOURDAIN Now I think of it, teach me how I must bow to salute a marchioness; I shall have occasion for it by and by.

DANCING MASTER How you must bow to salute a marchioness?

M. JOURDAIN Yes, a marchioness whose name is Dorimène.

DANCING MASTER Give me your hand.

M. JOURDAIN No. You need only to do it, I shall remember it easily.

DANCING MASTER If you would salute her with a great deal of respect, you must first of all make a bow and fall back, then advancing towards her, bow thrice, and at the last bow down to her very knees.

M. JOURDAIN Do it a little. (*after the* DANCING MASTER *has made three bows*) Right.

(*Enter a* LACKEY *holding two foils*)

LACKEY Sir, your fencing master is here.

M. JOURDAIN Bid him come in that he may give me a lesson. (*to the* MUSIC *and* DANCING MASTERS) I'd have you stay and see me perform.

(*Enter a* FENCING MASTER)

FENCING MASTER (*taking the two foils out of the* LACKEY'S *hand, and giving one to* M. JOURDAIN) Come, sir, your salute. Your body straight. A little bearing upon the left thigh. Your legs not so much a-straddle. Your feet both on a line. Your wrist opposite to your hip. The point of your sword overagainst your shoulder. Your arm not quite so much extended. Your left hand on a level with your eye. Your left shoulder more square. Hold up your head. Your look bold. Advance. Your body steady. Beat carte, and push carte. One, two. Recover. Again with it, your foot firm. One, two. Leap back. When you make a pass, sir, 'tis necessary your sword should disengage first, and your body make as small a mark as possible. One, two. Come, beat tierce, and push the same. Advance. Your body firm. Advance. Quit after that manner. One, two. Recover. Repeat the same. One, two. Leap back. Parry, sir, parry.

(*The* FENCING MASTER *gives him two or three home-thrusts, crying, "Parry"*)

M. JOURDAIN Ugh!

MUSIC MASTER You do wonders.

FENCING MASTER I have told you already—the whole secret of arms consists but in two things, in giving and not receiving. And as I showed you t'other day by demonstrative reason, it is impossible you should receive if you know how to turn your adversary's sword from the line of your body; which depends only upon a small motion of your wrist, either inward, or outward.

M. JOURDAIN At that rate therefore, a man without any courage is sure to kill his man and not to be killed.

FENCING MASTER Certainly. Don't you see the demonstration of it?

M. JOURDAIN Yes.

FENCING MASTER By this one may see of what consideration such persons as we should be esteemed in a state, and how highly the science of arms excels all the other useless sciences, such as dancing, music, and—

DANCING MASTER Soft and fair, Monsieur *Sa, sa.* Don't speak of dancing but with respect.

MUSIC MASTER Pray learn to treat the excellence of music in a handsomer manner.

FENCING MASTER You're merry fellows, to pretend to compare your sciences with mine.

MUSIC MASTER Do but see the importance of the creature!

DANCING MASTER The droll animal there, with his leathern stomacher!

FENCING MASTER My little master skipper, I shall make you skip as you should do. And you, my little master scraper, I shall make you sing to some tune.

DANCING MASTER Monsieur Tick-tack, I shall teach you your trade.

M. JOURDAIN (*to the* DANCING MASTER) Are you bewitched to quarrel with him, who understands tierce and carte, who knows how to kill a man by demonstrative reason?

---

[1]The minuet was the favorite social dance at court at this time, and continued to be so throughout the eighteenth century (both George Washington and Thomas Jefferson were very good at it). It is usually done in couples, with a bit of flirtation, and requires a good deal of precision and balance.

DANCING MASTER I laugh at his demonstrative reason, and his tierce and his carte.

M. JOURDAIN (*to the* DANCING MASTER) Softly, I say.

FENCING MASTER (*to the* DANCING MASTER) How? Master Impertinence!

M. JOURDAIN Nay, my dear fencing master!

DANCING MASTER (*to the* FENCING MASTER) How? You great dray-horse!

M. JOURDAIN Nay, my dancing master.

FENCING MASTER If I lay my—

M. JOURDAIN (*to the* FENCING MASTER) Gently.

DANCING MASTER If I lay my clutches on you—

M. JOURDAIN Easily.

FENCING MASTER I shall curry you with such an air—

M. JOURDAIN (*to the* FENCING MASTER) For goodness' sake.

DANCING MASTER I shall drub you after such a manner—

M. JOURDAIN (*to the* DANCING MASTER) I beseech you.

MUSIC MASTER Let us teach him a little how to speak.

M. JOURDAIN (*to the* MUSIC MASTER) Lack-a-day, be quiet.

(*Enter a* PHILOSOPHY MASTER)

Hola, Monsieur Philosopher, you are come in the nick of time with your philosophy. Come, and make peace a little amongst these people here.

PHILOSOPHY MASTER What's to do? What's the matter, gentlemen?

M. JOURDAIN They have put themselves into such a passion about the preference of their professions as to call names, and would come to blows.

PHILOSOPHY MASTER O fie, gentlemen, what need was there of all this fury? Have you not read the learned treatise upon anger, composed by Seneca? Is there anything more base and shameful than this passion, which makes a savage beast of a man? And should not reason be master of all our commotions?

DANCING MASTER How, sir? Why he has just now been abusing us both, in despising dancing which is my employment, and music which is his profession.

PHILOSOPHY MASTER A wise man is above all foul language that can be given him, and the grand answer one should make to all affronts is moderation and patience.

FENCING MASTER They had both the assurance to compare their professions to mine.

PHILOSOPHY MASTER Should this disturb you? Men should not dispute about vainglory and rank; that which perfectly distinguishes one from another is wisdom and virtue.

DANCING MASTER I maintained to him that dancing was a science to which one cannot do sufficient honour.

MUSIC MASTER And I, that music is one of those that all ages have revered.

FENCING MASTER And I maintained against 'em both that the science of defence is the finest and most necessary of all sciences.

PHILOSOPHY MASTER And what becomes of philosophy, then? You are all three very impertinent fellows, methinks, to speak with this arrogance before me; and impudently to give the name of science to things that one ought not to honour even with the name of art, that can't be comprised but under the name of a pitiful trade of gladiator, ballad-singer, and morris-dancer.

FENCING MASTER Out, ye dog of a philosopher.

MUSIC MASTER Hence, ye scoundrel of a pedant.

DANCING MASTER Begone, ye arrant pedagogue.

(*The* PHILOSOPHER *falls upon them, they all three lay him on*)

PHILOSOPHY MASTER How? Varlets as you are—

M. JOURDAIN Monsieur Philosopher!

PHILOSOPHY MASTER Infamous dogs! Rogues! Insolent curs!

M. JOURDAIN Monsieur Philosopher!

FENCING MASTER Plague on the animal!

M. JOURDAIN Gentlemen!

PHILOSOPHY MASTER Impudent villains!

M. JOURDAIN Monsieur Philosopher!

DANCING MASTER Deuce take the pack-saddled ass!

M. JOURDAIN Gentlemen!

PHILOSOPHY MASTER Profligate vermin!

M. JOURDAIN Monsieur Philosopher!

MUSIC MASTER The devil take the impertinent puppy!

M. JOURDAIN Gentlemen!

PHILOSOPHY MASTER Knaves! Ragamuffins! Traitors! Impostors!

M. JOURDAIN Monsieur Philosopher! Gentlemen! Monsieur Philosopher! Gentlemen! Monsieur Philosopher!

(*The four* MASTERS *beat each other out*)

Nay, beat your hearts out if you will, I shall neither meddle nor make with you, I shan't spoil my gown to part you. I should be a great fool to thrust myself among them, and receive some blow that might do me a mischief.[2]

(*Enter the* PHILOSOPHY MASTER)

PHILOSOPHY MASTER (*setting his band right*) Now to our lesson.

M. JOURDAIN Ah! Sir, I'm sorry for the blows they have given you.

PHILOSOPHY MASTER 'Tis nothing at all. A philosopher knows how to receive things in a proper manner; and I'll compose a satire against 'em, in the manner of Juvenal, that shall cut 'em most gloriously. Let that pass. What have you a mind to learn?

M. JOURDAIN Everything I can, for I have all the desire in the world to be a scholar, and it vexes me that my father and mother had not made me study all the sciences when I was young.

PHILOSOPHY MASTER 'Tis a very reasonable sentiment. *Nam, sine doctrina vita est quasi mortis imago.* You understand that, and are acquainted with Latin, without doubt?

M. JOURDAIN Yes; but act as if I were not acquainted with it. Explain me the meaning of that.

PHILOSOPHY MASTER The meaning of it is, that without learning, life is as it were an image of death.[3]

M. JOURDAIN That same Latin's in the right.

PHILOSOPHY MASTER Have you not some principles, some rudiments of science?

M. JOURDAIN Oh! yes, I can read and write.

PHILOSOPHY MASTER Where would you please to have us begin? Would you have me teach you logic?

M. JOURDAIN What may that same logic be?

PHILOSOPHY MASTER It's that which teaches us the three operations of the mind.

M. JOURDAIN What are those three operations of the mind?

PHILOSOPHY MASTER The first, the second, and the third. The first is to conceive well, by means of universals. The second, to judge well, by means of categories. The third, to draw the conclusion right, by means of figures: Barbara, Celarent, Darii, Ferio, Baralipton, etc.

M. JOURDAIN These words are too crabbed. This logic does not suit me by any means. Let's learn something else that's prettier.

PHILOSOPHY MASTER Will you learn morality?

M. JOURDAIN Morality?

PHILOSOPHY MASTER Yes.

M. JOURDAIN What means morality?

PHILOSOPHY MASTER It treats of happiness, teaches men to moderate their passions, and—

M. JOURDAIN No, no more of that. I'm as choleric as the devil, and there's no morality holds me; I will have my belly full of passion whenever I have a mind to it.

PHILOSOPHY MASTER Would you learn physics?

M. JOURDAIN What is it that physics treat of?

PHILOSOPHY MASTER Physics are what explain the principles of things natural and the properties of bodies; which discourse of the nature of elements, of metals, of minerals, of stones, of plants, and animals, and teach us the cause of all the meteors; the rainbow, *ignes fatui,* comets, lightnings, thunder, thunder-bolts, rain, snow, hail, winds, and whirlwinds.

M. JOURDAIN There's too much hurly-burly in this, too much confusion.

PHILOSOPHY MASTER What would you have me teach you then?

M. JOURDAIN Teach me orthography.

PHILOSOPHY MASTER With all my heart.

M. JOURDAIN Afterwards you may teach me the almanack, to know when there's a moon, and when not.

PHILOSOPHY MASTER Be it so. To pursue this thought of yours right and treat this matter like a philosopher, we must begin, according to the order of things, with an exact knowledge of the nature of letters and the different manner of pronouncing them. And on this head I am to tell you that letters are divided into vowels, called vowels because they express the voice: and into consonants, so called because they sound with the vowels and only mark the different articulations of the voice. There are five vowels or voices, A, E, I, O, U.

M. JOURDAIN I understand all that.

PHILOSOPHY MASTER The vowel A is formed by opening the mouth very wide, A.

M. JOURDAIN A, A. Yes.

PHILOSOPHY MASTER The vowel E is formed by drawing the under-jaw a little nearer to the upper, A, E.

[2]Jourdain here shows solid middle-class sense, opposed to his "masters." How does each defend his art? Is there anything serious beneath their foolishness? Can you think of any modern equivalents to this squabble (college departments?)?

[3]How has this philosopher contradicted the image of the philosopher that he expounds? Here, again, Molière quotes something that he believes in while ridiculing the person who says it. What do you think of the philosophy master's teaching methods? Why is Jourdain so intimidated that he pretends to know Latin? How could you use this scene to illustrate the difference between a humanist and a pedant?

M. JOURDAIN A, E. A, E. In troth it is. How pretty that is!

PHILOSOPHY MASTER And the vowel I, by bringing the jaws still nearer one to the other, and stretching the two corners of the mouth towards the ears, A, E, I.

M. JOURDAIN A, E, I, I, I, I. 'Tis true. Long live learning!

PHILOSOPHY MASTER The vowel O is formed by re-opening the jaws and drawing the lips near at the two corners, the upper and the under, O.

M. JOURDAIN O, O. There's nothing more just, A, E, I, O, I, O. 'Tis admirable! I, O, I, O.

PHILOSOPHY MASTER The opening of the mouth makes exactly a little ring, which resembles an O.

M. JOURDAIN O, O, O. You're right, O. How fine a thing it is but to know something!

PHILOSOPHY MASTER The vowel U is formed by bringing the teeth near together without entirely joining them, and pouting out both your lips, bringing them also near together without absolutely joining 'em, U.

M. JOURDAIN U, U. There's nothing more true, U.

PHILOSOPHY MASTER Your two lips pout out, as if you were making faces. Whence it comes that if you would do that to anybody and make a jest of him, you need say nothing to him but U.

M. JOURDAIN U, U. It's true. Ah! why did not I study sooner, that I might have known all this!

PHILOSOPHY MASTER To-morrow we shall take a view of the other letters, which are the consonants.

M. JOURDAIN Is there anything as curious in them, as in these?

PHILOSOPHY MASTER Doubtless. The consonant D, for example, is pronounced by clapping the tip of your tongue above the upper teeth, DE.

M. JOURDAIN DE, DE. 'Tis so. Oh! charming things! charming things!

PHILOSOPHY MASTER The F, in leaning the upper teeth upon the lower lip, EF.

M. JOURDAIN EF, EF. 'Tis truth. Ah! father and mother o' mine, how do I owe you a grudge!

PHILOSOPHY MASTER And the R, in carrying the tip of the tongue up to the roof of your mouth; so that being grazed upon by the air which bursts out with a force, it yields to it, and returns always to the same part, making a kind of trill, R, ra.

M. JOURDAIN R, r, ra. R, r, r, r, r, ra. That's true. What a clever man are you! And how have I lost time! R, r, r, ra.

PHILOSOPHY MASTER I will explain to you all these curiosities to the bottom.

M. JOURDAIN Pray do. But now, I must commit a secret to you. I'm in love with a person of great quality, and I should be glad you would help me to write something to her in a short *billet-doux,* which I'll drop at her feet.

PHILOSOPHY MASTER Very well.

M. JOURDAIN That will be very gallant, won't it?

PHILOSOPHY MASTER Without doubt. Is it verse that you would write to her?

M. JOURDAIN No, no, none of your verse.

PHILOSOPHY MASTER You would only have prose?

M. JOURDAIN No, I would neither have verse nor prose.

PHILOSOPHY MASTER It must be one or t'other.

M. JOURDAIN Why so?

PHILOSOPHY MASTER Because, sir, there's nothing to express one's self by, but prose, or verse.

M. JOURDAIN Is there nothing then but prose, or verse?

PHILOSOPHY MASTER No, sir, whatever is not prose, is verse; and whatever is not verse, is prose.

M. JOURDAIN And when one talks, what may that be then?

PHILOSOPHY MASTER Prose.

M. JOURDAIN How? When I say, Nicole, bring me my slippers, and give me my nightcap, is that prose?

PHILOSOPHY MASTER Yes, sir.

M. JOURDAIN On my conscience, I have spoken prose above these forty years without knowing anything of the matter;[4] and I have all the obligations in the world to you for informing me of this. I would therefore put into a letter to her: Beautiful marchioness, your fair eyes make me die with love; but I would have this placed in a gallant manner; and have a gentle turn.

PHILOSOPHY MASTER Why, add that the fire of her eyes has reduced your heart to ashes: that you suffer for her night and day all the torments—

M. JOURDAIN No, no, no, I won't have all that—I'll have nothing but what I told you. Beautiful marchioness, your fair eyes make me die with love.

PHILOSOPHY MASTER You must by all means lengthen the thing out a little.

M. JOURDAIN No, I tell you, I'll have none but those very words in the letter: but turned in a modish way, ranged handsomely as they should be. I desire you'd show me a little, that I may see the different manners in which one may place them.

PHILOSOPHY MASTER One may place them first of

---

[4]M. Jourdain's realization that he has been speaking prose all his life is cited in various contexts more often than anything else in the play. Why do you think this is so?

all as you said: Beautiful marchioness, your fair eyes make me die for love. Or suppose: For love die me make, beautiful marchioness, your fair eyes. Or perhaps: Your eyes fair, for love me make, beautiful marchioness, die. Or suppose: Die your fair eyes, beautiful marchioness, for love me make. Or however: Me make your eyes fair die, beautiful marchioness, for love.

M. JOURDAIN But of all these ways, which is the best?

PHILOSOPHY MASTER That which you said: Beautiful marchioness, your fair eyes make me die for love.

M. JOURDAIN Yet at the same time, I never studied it, and I made the whole of it at the first touch. I thank you with all my heart, and desire you would come in good time to-morrow.

PHILOSOPHY MASTER I shall not fail.

(*Exit* PHILOSOPHY MASTER)

M. JOURDAIN (*to his* LACKEY) What? Are my clothes not come yet?

LACKEY No, sir.

M. JOURDAIN This cursed tailor makes me wait unreasonably, considering it's a day I have so much business in. I shall go mad. A quartan ague wring this villain of a tailor. D—l take the tailor. A plague choke the tailor. If I had him but here now, this detestable tailor, this dog of a tailor, this traitor of a tailor, I—

(*Enter a* MASTER TAILOR *and a* JOURNEYMAN TAILOR *bringing a suit of clothes for* M. JOURDAIN)

Oh! You're there. I was going to be in a passion with you.

MASTER TAILOR I could not possibly come sooner, and I set twenty fellows to work at your clothes.

M. JOURDAIN You have sent me a pair of silk hose so tight that I had all the difficulty in the world to get 'em on, and there are two stitches broke in 'em.

MASTER TAILOR They'll grow rather too large.

M. JOURDAIN Yes, if I break every day a loop or two. You have made me a pair of shoes too, that pinch me execrably.

MASTER TAILOR Not at all, sir.

M. JOURDAIN How, not at all?

MASTER TAILOR No, they don't pinch you at all.

M. JOURDAIN I tell you they do hurt me.

MASTER TAILOR You fancy so.

M. JOURDAIN I fancy so because I feel it. There's a fine reason indeed.

MASTER TAILOR Hold, stay, here's one of the handsomest suits at court, and the best-matched. 'Tis a masterly work to invent a grave suit of clothes that should not be black, and I'll give the cleverest tailor in town six trials to equal it.

M. JOURDAIN What a deuce have we here? You have put the flowers downwards.

MASTER TAILOR Why, you did not tell me you would have 'em upwards.

M. JOURDAIN Was there any need to tell you of that?

MASTER TAILOR Yes, certainly. All the people of quality wear 'em in that way.

M. JOURDAIN Do people of quality wear the flowers downwards?

MASTER TAILOR Yes, sir.

M. JOURDAIN Oh, 'tis very well, then.

MASTER TAILOR If you please I'll put 'em upwards.

M. JOURDAIN No, no.

MASTER TAILOR You need only say the word.

M. JOURDAIN No, I tell you, you have done right. Do you think my clothes will fit me?

MASTER TAILOR A pretty question! I defy a painter with his pencil to draw you anything that shall fit more exact. I have a fellow at home who, for fitting a pair of breeches, is the greatest genius in the world; another who, for the cut of a doublet, is the hero of the age.

M. JOURDAIN Are the peruke[5] and feather as they should be?

MASTER TAILOR Everything's well.

M. JOURDAIN (*looking earnestly at the* TAILOR'S *clothes*) Ah, hah! Monsieur Tailor, here's my stuff of the last suit you made for me. I know it very well.

MASTER TAILOR The stuff appeared to me so handsome, that I had a mind to cut a coat out of it for myself.

M. JOURDAIN Yes, but you should not have cabbaged it out of mine.

MASTER TAILOR Will you put on your clothes?

M. JOURDAIN Yes, give 'em me.

MASTER TAILOR Stay; the matter must not go so. I have brought men along with me to dress you to music; these sort of suits are put on with ceremony. Soho? come in there, you.

(*Enter four* JOURNEYMEN TAILORS, *dancing*)

Put on this suit of the gentleman's, in the manner you do to people of quality.

(*Two of the tailors pull off his straight breeches made for his exercises, and two others his waistcoat; then they put on his new suit to music, and* M. JOURDAIN *walks amongst them to show them his clothes to see whether they fit or no*)

---

[5]Wig.

JOURNEYMAN TAILOR My dear gentleman, please to give the tailor's men something to drink.

M. JOURDAIN How do you call me?

JOURNEYMAN TAILOR My dear gentleman.

M. JOURDAIN "My dear gentleman!" See what it is to dress like people of quality. You may go clothed like a commoner all your days, and they'll never call you "my dear gentleman." (*gives them something*) Stay, there's for "my dear gentleman."

JOURNEYMAN TAILOR My lord, we are infinitely obliged to you.

M. JOURDAIN My lord! Oh, ho! My lord! Stay, friend; "my lord" deserves something, "my lord" is none o' your petty words. Hold, there, "my lord" gives you that.

JOURNEYMAN TAILOR My lord, we shall go drink your grace's health.

M. JOURDAIN Your grace! oh, oh, oh! stay, don't go. Your grace, to me! (*aside*) I'faith if he goes as far as highness, he'll empty my purse. (*aloud*) Hold, there's for "my grace."

JOURNEYMAN TAILOR My lord, we most humbly thank your grace for your liberality.

M. JOURDAIN He did very well; I was going to give him all.

(*The four* JOURNEYMAN TAILORS *perform a dance that constitutes the second intermission.*)

ACT III

THE SCENE MONSIEUR JOURDAIN *and his two* LACKEYS

M. JOURDAIN Follow me, that I may go and show my clothes a little through the town; and especially take care, both of you, to walk immediately at my heels, that people may plainly see you belong to me.

LACKEYS Yes, sir.

M. JOURDAIN Call me Nicole, that I may give her some directions. You need not go—here she comes.

(*Enter* NICOLE)

Nicole?

NICOLE Your pleasure, sir?

M. JOURDAIN Harkee.

NICOLE (*laughing*) Ha, ha, ha, ha, ha.

M. JOURDAIN Who do ye laugh at?

NICOLE Ha, ha, ha, ha, ha, ha.

M. JOURDAIN What does this slut mean?

NICOLE Ha, ha, ha. How you are bedizened! Ha, ha, ha.

M. JOURDAIN How's that?

NICOLE Oh! oh! my stars! ha, ha, ha, ha, ha.

M. JOURDAIN What a jade is here! What! do ye make a jest of me?

NICOLE No, no, sir, I should be very sorry to do so. Ha, ha, ha, ha, ha, ha.

M. JOURDAIN I shall give ye a slap o' the chops, if you laugh any more.

NICOLE Sir, I cannot help it. Ha, ha, ha, ha, ha, ha.

M. JOURDAIN Won't ye have done?

NICOLE Sir, I ask your pardon; but you are so comical, that I cannot hold from laughing. Ha, ha, ha.

M. JOURDAIN Do but see the insolence!

NICOLE You are so thoroughly droll there! Ha, ha.

M. JOURDAIN I shall—

NICOLE I beg you would excuse me. Ha, ha, ha, ha.

M. JOURDAIN Hold, if you laugh again the least in the world, I protest and swear I'll give ye such a box o' the ear as ye never had in your life.

NICOLE Well, sir, I have done; I won't laugh any more.

M. JOURDAIN Take care you don't. You must clean out against by and by—

NICOLE Ha, ha.

M. JOURDAIN You must clean out as it should be—

NICOLE Ha, ha.

M. JOURDAIN I say, you must go clean out the hall, and—

NICOLE Ha, ha.

M. JOURDAIN Again?

NICOLE (*tumbles down with laughing*) Hold, sir, beat me rather, and let me laugh my belly-full, that will do me more good. Ha, ha, ha, ha.[1]

M. JOURDAIN I shall run mad!

NICOLE For goodness' sake, sir, I beseech you let me laugh. Ha, ha, ha.

M. JOURDAIN If I take you in hand—

NICOLE Si-ir, I shall bu-urst, if I do—not laugh. Ha, ha, ha.

M. JOURDAIN But did ever anybody see such a jade as that, who insolently laughs in my face, instead of receiving my orders!

NICOLE What would you have me do, sir?

M. JOURDAIN Why, take care to get ready my house for the company that's to come by and by.

NICOLE (*getting up*) Ay, i'fakins, I've no more inclination to laugh; all your company makes such a litter here that the very word's enough to put one in an ill humour.

---

[1]Here is a comic portrayal of Molière's deep belief in the therapeutic value of laughter for all human beings.

M. JOURDAIN What! I ought to shut my doors against all the world for your sake?

NICOLE You ought at least to shut it against certain people.

(*Enter* MME JOURDAIN)

MME JOURDAIN Ah, hah! Here's some new story. What means this, husband, this same equipage? D'ye despise the world, that you harness yourself out in this manner? Have you a mind to make yourself a laughing-stock wherever ye go?

M. JOURDAIN None but fools, wife, will laugh at me.

MME JOURDAIN In truth, people have not stayed thus long to laugh; 'tis a good while ago that your ways have furnished all the world with a laugh.

M. JOURDAIN Who is that "all the world," pray?

MME JOURDAIN That "all the world" is a world perfectly in the right, and much wiser than yourself. For my part, I am shocked at the life you lead. I don't know what to call our house. One would swear 'twere carnival here all the year round; and from break o' day, for fear there should be any respite, there's nothing to be heard here but an uproar of fiddles and songsters which disturb the whole neighbourhood.

NICOLE Madame says right. I shall never see my things set to rights again for that gang of folks that you bring to the house. They ransack every quarter of the town with their feet for dirt to bring here; and poor Frances is e'en almost slaved off her legs with scrubbing of the floors, which your pretty masters come to daub as regularly as the day comes.

M. JOURDAIN Hey-day! our maid Nicole! you have a pretty nimble tongue of your own for a country-wench.

MME JOURDAIN Nicole's in the right, and she has more sense than you have. I should be glad to know what you think to do with a dancing master, at your age?

NICOLE And with a lubberly fencing master, that comes here with his stamping to shake the whole house, and tear up all the pavement of the hall.

M. JOURDAIN Peace, our maid, and our wife.

MME JOURDAIN What! will you learn to dance against the time you'll have no legs?

NICOLE What! have you a mind to murder somebody?

M. JOURDAIN Hold your prate; I tell you you are ignorant creatures, both of you, and don't know the advantage of all this.

MME JOURDAIN You ought much rather to think of marrying your daughter, who is of age to be provided for.

M. JOURDAIN I shall think of marrying my daughter when a suitable match presents itself; but I shall think too of learning the *belles sciences.*

NICOLE I've heard say further, madame, that to pin the basket, he has got him a philosophy master today.

M. JOURDAIN Very well. I've a mind to have wit, and to know how to reason upon things with your genteel people.

MME JOURDAIN Won't you go to school one of these days, and be whipped at your age?

M. JOURDAIN Why not? Would I were whipped this very instant before all the world, so I did but know what they learn at school!

NICOLE Yes, forsooth, that would be a mighty advantage t'ye.

M. JOURDAIN Without doubt.

MME JOURDAIN This is all very necessary to the management of your house.[2]

M. JOURDAIN Certainly. You talk, both of you, like asses, and I'm ashamed of your ignorance. (*to* MME JOURDAIN) For example, do you know, you, what it is you now speak?

MME JOURDAIN Yes, I know that what I speak is very right, and that you ought to think of living in another manner.

M. JOURDAIN I don't talk of that. I ask you what the words are that you now speak?

MME JOURDAIN They are words that have a good deal of sense in them, and your conduct is by no means such.

M. JOURDAIN I don't talk of that, I tell you. I ask you, what is that I now speak to you, which I say this very moment?

MME JOURDAIN Mere stuff.

M. JOURDAIN Pshaw, no, 'tis not that. That which we both of us say, the language we speak this instant?

MME JOURDAIN Well?

M. JOURDAIN How is it called?

MME JOURDAIN 'Tis called just what you please to call it.

M. JOURDAIN 'Tis prose, you ignorant creature.

MME JOURDAIN Prose?

M. JOURDAIN Yes, prose. Whatever is prose, is not verse; and whatever is not verse, is prose. Now, see what it is to study. And you, (*to* NICOLE) do you

[2]Madame Jourdain, the voice of the middle class and Nicole, the voice of the lower class, represent good sense and honesty as opposed to Monsieur Jourdain's pretentiousness and the nobles' dishonesty. And yet, are they entirely in the right? Typically, Madame Jourdain can see no benefit in the arts unless they are directly *useful.*

know very well how you must do to say U?

NICOLE How?

M. JOURDAIN Yes. What is it you do when you say U?

NICOLE What?

M. JOURDAIN Say U a little, to try.

NICOLE Well, U.

M. JOURDAIN What is it you do?

NICOLE I say U.

M. JOURDAIN Yes, but when you say U, what is it you do?

NICOLE I do as you bid me.

M. JOURDAIN O! what a strange thing it is to have to do with brutes! You pout out your lips, and bring your under-jaw to your upper, U, d'ye see? I make a mouth, U.

NICOLE Yes, that's fine.

MME JOURDAIN 'Tis admirable!

M. JOURDAIN 'Tis quite another thing, had but you seen O, and DE, DE, and EF, EF.

MME JOURDAIN What is all this ridiculous stuff?

NICOLE What are we the better for all this?

M. JOURDAIN It makes one mad, to see these ignorant women.

MME JOURDAIN Go, go, you should send all these folks apacking with their silly stuff.

NICOLE And especially that great lubberly fencing master, who fills all my house with dust.

M. JOURDAIN Hey-day! This fencing master sticks strangely in thy stomach. I'll let thee see thy impertinence presently.

(*He orders the foils to be brought, and gives one to* NICOLE)

Stay, reason demonstrative, the line of the body. When they push in carte one need only do so; and when they push in tierce one need only do so. This is the way never to be killed; and is not that clever to be upon sure grounds, when one has an encounter with anybody? There, push at me a little, to try.

NICOLE Well, how?

(NICOLE *gives him several thrusts*)

M. JOURDAIN Gently! Hold! Oh! Softly; deuce take the hussy.

NICOLE You bid me push.

M. JOURDAIN Yes, but you push me in tierce before you push in carte, and you have not patience while I parry.

MME JOURDAIN You are a fool, husband, with all these whims, and this is come to you since you have taken upon you to keep company with quality.

M. JOURDAIN When I keep company with quality, I show my judgment; and that's much better than herding with your bourgeoisie.

MME JOURDAIN Yes, truly, there's a great deal to be got by frequenting your nobility; and you have made fine work with that count you are so bewitched with.

M. JOURDAIN Peace, take care what you say. Do you well know, wife, that you don't know whom you speak of when you speak of him? He's a man of more importance than you think of; a nobleman of consideration at court, who speaks to the king just for all the world as I speak to you. Is it not a thing that does me great honour, that you see a person of that quality come so often to my house, who calls me his dear friend and treats me as if I were his equal? He has more kindness for me than one would ever imagine, and he caresses me in such a manner before all the world that I myself am perfectly confounded at it.

MME JOURDAIN Yes, he has a great kindness for you, and caresses you; but he borrows your money of you.

M. JOURDAIN Well, and is it not a great honour to me to lend money to a man of that condition? And can I do less for a lord who calls me his dear friend?

MME JOURDAIN And what is it this lord does for you?

M. JOURDAIN Things that would astonish you if you did but know 'em.

MME JOURDAIN And what may they be?

M. JOURDAIN Peace, I can't explain myself. 'Tis sufficient that if I have lent him money, he'll pay it me honestly, and that before 'tis long.

MME JOURDAIN Yes, stay you for that.

M. JOURDAIN Certainly. Did he not tell me so?

MME JOURDAIN Yes, yes, and he won't fail to disappoint you.

M. JOURDAIN He swore to me on the faith of a gentleman.

MME JOURDAIN A mere song.

M. JOURDAIN Hey! You are mighty obstinate, wife of mine; I tell you he will keep his word with me, I am sure of it.

MME JOURDAIN And I am sure that he will not, and all the court he makes to you is only to cajole you.

M. JOURDAIN Hold your tongue. Here he comes.

MME JOURDAIN That's all we shall have of him. He comes perhaps to borrow something more of you; the very sight of him gives me my dinner.

M. JOURDAIN Hold your tongue, I say.

(*Enter* DORANTE)

DORANTE My dear friend, Monsieur Jourdain, how do you do?

M. JOURDAIN Very well, sir, to do you what little service I can.

DORANTE And Madame Jourdain there, how does she do?

MME JOURDAIN Madame Jourdain does as well as she can.

DORANTE Hah! Monsieur Jourdain, you're dressed the most genteelly in the world!

M. JOURDAIN As you see.

DORANTE You have a very fine air with that dress, and we have ne'er a young fellow at court that's better made than you.

M. JOURDAIN He, he.

MME JOURDAIN (*aside*) He scratches him where it itches.

DORANTE Turn about. 'Tis most gallant.

MME JOURDAIN (*aside*) Yes, as much of the fool behind as before.

DORANTE 'Faith, Monsieur Jourdain, I was strangely impatient to see you. You're the man in the world I most esteem, and I was talking of you again this morning at the king's levee.[3]

M. JOURDAIN You do me a great deal of honour, sir. (*to* MME JOURDAIN) At the king's levee!

DORANTE Come, be covered.[4]

M. JOURDAIN Sir, I know the respect I owe you.

DORANTE Lack-a-day, be covered; no ceremony, pray, between us two.

M. JOURDAIN Sir—

DORANTE Put on your hat, I tell you, Monsieur Jourdain; you are my friend.

M. JOURDAIN Sir, I am your humble servant.

DORANTE I won't be covered, if you won't.

M. JOURDAIN (*puts on his hat*) I choose rather to be unmannerly than troublesome.

DORANTE I am your debtor, you know.

MME JOURDAIN (*aside*) Yes, we know it but too well.

DORANTE You have generously lent me money upon several occasions; and have obliged me, most certainly, with the best grace in the world.

M. JOURDAIN You jest, sir.

DORANTE But I know how to repay what is lent me, and to be grateful for the favours done me.

M. JOURDAIN I don't doubt it, sir.

DORANTE I'm willing to get out of your books, and came hither to make up our accounts together.

M. JOURDAIN (*aside to* MME JOURDAIN) Well, you see your impertinence, wife.

DORANTE I'm one who loves to be out of debt as soon as possible.

M. JOURDAIN (*aside to* MME JOURDAIN) I told you so.

DORANTE Let's see a little what 'tis I owe you.

M. JOURDAIN (*aside to* MME JOURDAIN) You there, with your ridiculous suspicions.

DORANTE Do you remember right all the money you have lent me?

M. JOURDAIN I believe so. I made a little memorandum of it. Here it is. Let you have at one time two hundred louis d'or.

DORANTE 'Tis true.

M. JOURDAIN Another time, six-score.

DORANTE Yes.

M. JOURDAIN And another time a hundred and forty.

DORANTE You are right.

M. JOURDAIN These three articles make four hundred and sixty louis d'or, which come to five thousand and sixty livres.

DORANTE The account is very right. Five thousand and sixty livres.

M. JOURDAIN One thousand eight hundred and thirty-two livres to your plume-maker.

DORANTE Just.

M. JOURDAIN Two thousand seven hundred and four-score livres to your tailor.

DORANTE 'Tis true.

M. JOURDAIN Four thousand three hundred and seventy-nine livres, twelve sols, and eight deniers to your tradesman.

DORANTE Very well. Twelve sols, eight deniers. The account is just.

M. JOURDAIN And a thousand seven hundred and forty-eight livres, seven sols, four deniers to your saddler.

DORANTE 'Tis all true. What does that come to?

M. JOURDAIN Sum total, fifteen thousand eight hundred livres.

DORANTE The sum total, and just. Fifteen thousand and eight hundred livres. To which add two hundred pistoles, which you are going to lend me, that will make exactly eighteen thousand francs, which I shall pay you the first opportunity.

MME JOURDAIN (*aside to* M. JOURDAIN) Well, did I not guess how 'twould be!

M. JOURDAIN (*aside to* MME JOURDAIN) Peace.

DORANTE Will it incommode you to lend me what I tell you?

---

[3]The king's levee—the ceremony of the king's morning rising, which courtiers attended (see Saint-Simon on p. 180).

[4]Put your hat back on.

M. JOURDAIN Oh! no.

MME JOURDAIN (*aside to* M. JOURDAIN) This man makes a mere milch cow of you.

M. JOURDAIN (*aside to* MME JOURDAIN) Hold your tongue.

DORANTE If this will incommode you, I'll seek it elsewhere.

M. JOURDAIN No, sir.

MME JOURDAIN (*aside to* M. JOURDAIN) He'll ne'er be satisfied till he has ruined you.

M. JOURDAIN (*aside to* MME JOURDAIN) Hold your tongue, I tell you.

DORANTE You need only tell me if this puts you to any straits.

M. JOURDAIN Not at all, sir.

MME JOURDAIN (*aside to* M. JOURDAIN) 'Tis a true wheedler.

M. JOURDAIN (*aside to* MME JOURDAIN) Hold your tongue then.

MME JOURDAIN (*aside to* M. JOURDAIN) He'll drain you to the last farthing.

M. JOURDAIN (*aside to* MME JOURDAIN) Will you hold your tongue?

DORANTE I've a good many people would be glad to lend it me, but as you are my very good friend, I thought I should wrong you if I asked it of anybody else.

M. JOURDAIN 'Tis too much honour, sir, you do me. I'll go fetch what you want.

MME JOURDAIN (*aside to* M. JOURDAIN) What! going to lend him still more?

M. JOURDAIN (*aside to* MME JOURDAIN) What can I do? Would you have me refuse a man of that rank, who spoke of me this morning at the king's levee?

MME JOURDAIN (*aside to* M. JOURDAIN) Go, you're a downright dupe.

(*Exit* M. JOURDAIN)

DORANTE You seem to me very melancholy. What ails you, Madame Jourdain?

MME JOURDAIN My head's bigger than my fist, even if it is not swelled.

DORANTE Where is Mademoiselle your daughter that I don't see her?

MME JOURDAIN Mademoiselle my daughter is pretty well where she is.

DORANTE How does she go on?

MME JOURDAIN She goes on her two legs.

DORANTE Won't you come with her, one of these days, and see the ball, and the play that's acted at court?

MME JOURDAIN Yes, truly, we've a great inclination to laugh, a great inclination to laugh have we.

DORANTE I fancy, Madame Jourdain, you had a great many sparks in your younger years, being so handsome and good-humoured as you were.

MME JOURDAIN Tredame, sir! what, is Madame Jourdain grown decrepit, and does her head totter already with a palsy?

DORANTE Odso, Madame Jourdain, I ask your pardon. I was not thinking that you are young. I'm very often absent. Pray excuse my impertinence.

(*Enter* M. JOURDAIN)

M. JOURDAIN (*to* DORANTE) Here's two hundred pieces for you, hard money.

DORANTE I do assure you, Monsieur Jourdain, I am absolutely yours; and I long to do you service at court.

M. JOURDAIN I'm infinitely obliged to you.

DORANTE If Madame Jourdain inclines to see the royal diversion, I'll get her the best places in the ballroom.

MME JOURDAIN Madame Jourdain kisses your hand.

DORANTE (*aside to* M. JOURDAIN) Our pretty marchioness, as I informed you in my letter, will be here by and by to partake of your ball and collation; I brought her, at last, to consent to the entertainment you design to give her.

M. JOURDAIN Let us draw to a distance a little, for a certain reason.

DORANTE 'Tis eight days since I saw you, and I gave you no tidings of the diamond you put into my hands to make her a present of, as from you; but the reason was, I had all the difficulty in the world to conquer her scruples, and 'twas no longer ago than to-day, that she resolved to accept of it.

M. JOURDAIN How did she like it?

DORANTE Marvellously; and I am much deceived if the beauty of this diamond has not an admirable effect upon her.

M. JOURDAIN Grant it, kind Heaven!

MME JOURDAIN (*to* NICOLE) When he's once with him, he can never get rid of him.

DORANTE I made her sensible in a proper manner of the richness of the present and the strength of your passion.

M. JOURDAIN These kindnesses perfectly overwhelm me; I am in the greatest confusion in the world to see a person of your quality demean himself on my account as you do.

DORANTE You jest sure. Does one ever stop at such sort of scruples among friends? And would not you do the same thing for me, if occasion offered?

M. JOURDAIN Oh! certainly, and with all my soul.

MME JOURDAIN (*aside to* NICOLE) How the sight of him torments me!

DORANTE For my part, I never mind anything when a friend is to be served; and when you imparted to me the ardent passion you had entertained for the agreeable marchioness, with whom I was acquainted, you see that I made an immediate offer of my service.

M. JOURDAIN 'Tis true, these favours are what confound me.

MME JOURDAIN (*to* NICOLE) What! will he never be gone?

NICOLE They are mighty great together.

DORANTE You've taken the right way to smite her. Women, above all things, love the expense we are at on their account; and your frequent serenades, your continual entertainments, that sumptuous firework she saw on the water, the diamond she received by way of present from you, and the regale you are now preparing—all this speaks much better in favour of your passion than all the things you yourself could possibly have said to her.

M. JOURDAIN There's no expense I would not be at, if I could by that means find the way to her heart. A woman of quality has powerful charms for me, and 'tis an honour I would purchase at any rate.

MME JOURDAIN (*aside to* NICOLE) What can they have to talk of so long together? Go softly, and listen a little.

DORANTE By and by you will enjoy the pleasure of seeing her at your ease; your eyes will have full time to be satisfied.

M. JOURDAIN To be at full liberty, I have ordered matters so that my wife shall dine with my sister, where she'll pass the whole afternoon.

DORANTE You have done wisely, for your wife might have perplexed us a little. I have given the proper orders for you to the cook, and for everything necessary for the ball. 'Tis of my own invention; and provided the execution answers the plan, I am sure 'twill be—

M. JOURDAIN (*perceives that* NICOLE *listens, and gives her a box on the ear*) Hey, you're very impertinent. (*to* DORANTE) Let us go if you please.

(*Exeunt* M. JOURDAIN *and* DORANTE)

NICOLE I'faith, curiosity has cost me something; but I believe there's a snake in the grass, for they were talking of some affair which they were not willing you should be present at.

MME JOURDAIN This is not the first time, Nicole, that I have had suspicions of my husband. I am the most deceived person in the world, or there is some amour in agitation, and I am labouring to discover what it should be. But let's think of my daughter. You know the love Cléonte has for her. He is a man who hits my fancy, and I have a mind to favour his addresses and help him to Lucile, if I can.

NICOLE In truth, madame, I am the most ravished[5] creature in the world, to find you in these sentiments; for if the master hits your taste, the man hits mine no less; and I could wish our marriage might be concluded under favour of theirs.

MME JOURDAIN Go, and talk with him about it, as from me, and tell him to come to me presently, that we may join in demanding my daughter of my husband.

NICOLE I fly, madame, with joy, and I could not have received a more agreeable commission.

(*Exit* MME JOURDAIN)

I believe I shall very much rejoice their hearts.

(*Enter* CLÉONTE *and* COVIELLE)

Hah, most luckily met. I'm an ambassadress of joy, and I come—

CLÉONTE Be gone, ye perfidious slut, and don't come to amuse me with thy traitorous speeches.

NICOLE Is it thus you receive—

CLÉONTE Be gone, I tell thee, and go directly and inform thy false mistress, that she never more, while she lives, shall impose upon the too simple Cléonte.

NICOLE What whim is this? My dear Covielle, tell me a little what does this mean.

COVIELLE Thy dear Covielle, wicked minx? Away quickly out of my sight, hussy, and leave me at quiet.

NICOLE What! dost thou, too—

COVIELLE Out o' my sight, I tell thee, and talk not to me, for thy life.

NICOLE (*aside*) Hey-day! What gadfly has stung 'em both? Well, I must march and inform my mistress of this pretty piece of history.

(*Exit* NICOLE)

CLÉONTE What! treat a lover in this manner; and a lover the most constant, the most passionate of all lovers!

COVIELLE 'Tis a horrible trick they have served us both.

CLÉONTE I discover all the ardour for her, all the

[5]Delighted. Nicole wishes to marry Cléonte's servant.

tenderness one can imagine. I love nothing in the world but her, have nothing in my thoughts besides her. She is all my care, all my desire, all my joy. I speak of nought but her, think of nought but her, dream of nought but her, I breathe only for her, my heart lives wholly in her; and this is the worthy recompense of such a love! I am two days without seeing her, which are to me two horrible ages; I meet her accidentally, my heart feels all transported at the sight; joy sparkles in my face; I fly to her with ecstasy, and the faithless creature turns away her eyes, and brushes hastily by me, as if she had never seen me in her life!

COVIELLE I say the same as you do.

CLÉONTE Is it possible to see anything, Covielle, equal to this perfidy of the ungrateful Lucile?

COVIELLE Or to that, sir, of the villainous jade Nicole?

CLÉONTE After so many ardent sacrifices of sighs and vows that I have made to her charms!

COVIELLE After so much assiduous sneaking, cares, and services that I have paid her in the kitchen!

CLÉONTE So many tears that I have shed at her feet!

COVIELLE So many buckets of water that I have drawn for her!

CLÉONTE Such ardour as I have shown, in loving her more than myself!

COVIELLE So much heat as I have endured, in turning the spit in her place!

CLÉONTE She flies me with disdain!

COVIELLE She turns her back upon me with impudence!

CLÉONTE This is a perfidy worthy the greatest punishment.

COVIELLE This a treachery that deserves a thousand boxes o' the ear.[6]

CLÉONTE Prithee, never think to speak once more to me in her favour.

COVIELLE I, sir? Marry, Heaven forbid.

CLÉONTE Never come to excuse the action of this perfidious woman.

COVIELLE Fear it not.

CLÉONTE No, d'ye see, all discourses in her defence will signify nothing.

COVIELLE Who dreams of such a thing?

CLÉONTE I'm determined to continue my resentment against her, and break off all correspondence.

COVIELLE I give my consent.

CLÉONTE This same count that visits her, pleases perhaps her eye; and her fancy, I see plainly, is dazzled with quality. But I must, for my own honour, prevent the triumph of her inconstancy. I'll make as much haste as she can do towards the change which I see she's running into, and won't leave her all the glory of quitting me.

COVIELLE 'Tis very well said, and for my share, I enter into all your sentiments.

CLÉONTE Second my resentments, and support my resolutions against all the remains of love that may yet plead for her. I conjure thee, say all the ill things of her thou canst. Paint me her person so as to make her despicable; and, in order to disgust me, mark me out well all the faults thou canst find in her.

COVIELLE She, sir? A pretty mawkin, a fine piece to be so much enamoured with. I see nothing in her but what's very indifferent, and you might find a hundred persons more deserving of you. First of all she has little eyes.

CLÉONTE That's true, she has little eyes; but they are full of fire, the most sparkling, the most piercing in the world, the most striking that one shall see.

COVIELLE She has a wide mouth.

CLÉONTE Yes; but one sees such graces in it, as one does not see in other mouths, and the sight of that mouth inspires desire: 'tis the most attractive, the most amorous in the world.

COVIELLE As to her height, she's not tall.

CLÉONTE No; but she's easy, and well-shaped.

COVIELLE She affects a negligence in speaking and acting.

CLÉONTE 'Tis true; but all this has a gracefulness in her, and her ways are engaging; they have I don't know what charms that insinuate into our hearts.

COVIELLE As to her wit—

CLÉONTE Ah! Covielle, she has the most refined, the most delicate turn of wit.

COVIELLE Her conversation—

CLÉONTE Her conversation is charming.

COVIELLE She's always grave.

CLÉONTE Would you have flaunting pleasantry, a perpetual profuse mirth? And d'ye see anything more impertinent than those women who are always upon the giggle?

COVIELLE But in short, she is the most capricious creature in the world.

CLÉONTE Yes, she is capricious, I grant ye, but everything sits well upon fine women; we bear with everything from the fair.

COVIELLE Since that's the case, I see plainly you desire always to love her.

---

[6]This scene has an operatic quality, as if the master and valet are singing a duet. How does each one reflect his social class?

CLÉONTE I! I should love death sooner; and I am now going to hate her as much as ever I loved her.

COVIELLE But how, if you think her so perfect?

CLÉONTE Therein shall my vengeance be more glaring; therein shall I better display the force of my resolution in hating her, quitting her, most beautiful as she is; most charming, most amiable, as I think her. Here she is.

(*Enter* LUCILE *and* NICOLE)

NICOLE (*to* LUCILE) For my part, I was perfectly shocked at it.

LUCILE It can be nothing else, Nicole, but what I said. But there he comes.

CLÉONTE (*to* COVIELLE) I won't so much as speak to her.

COVIELLE I'll follow your example.

LUCILE What means this, Cléonte, what's the matter with you?

NICOLE What ails thee, Covielle?

LUCILE What trouble has seized you?

NICOLE What cross humour possesses thee?

LUCILE Are you dumb, Cléonte?

NICOLE Hast thou lost thy speech, Covielle?

CLÉONTE The abandoned creature!

COVIELLE Oh! the Judas!

LUCILE I see very well that the late meeting has disordered your mind.

CLÉONTE (*to* COVIELLE) O, ho! She sees what she has done.

NICOLE The reception of this morning has made thee take snuff.

COVIELLE (*to* CLÉONTE) She has guessed where the shoe pinches.

LUCILE Is it not true, Cléonte, that this is the reason of your being out of humour?

CLÉONTE Yes, perfidious maid, that is it, since I must speak; and I can tell you that you shall not triumph, as you imagine, by your unfaithfulness, that I shall be beforehand in breaking with you, and you won't have the credit of discarding me. I shall, doubtless, have some difficulty in conquering the passion I have for you: 'twill cause me uneasiness; I shall suffer for a while; but I shall compass my point, and I would sooner stab myself to the heart than have the weakness of returning to you.

COVIELLE (*to* NICOLE) As says the master, so says the man.

LUCILE Here's a noise indeed about nothing. I'll tell you, Cléonte, the reason that made me avoid joining you this morning.

CLÉONTE (*endeavouring to go to avoid* LUCILE) No, I'll hear nothing.

NICOLE (*to* COVIELLE) I'll let thee into the cause that made us pass you so quick.

COVIELLE (*endeavouring to go to avoid* NICOLE) I will hear nothing.

LUCILE (*following* CLÉONTE) Know that this morning—

CLÉONTE (*walks about without regarding* LUCILE) No, I tell you.

NICOLE (*following* COVIELLE) Learn that—

COVIELLE (*walks about likewise without regarding* NICOLE) No, traitress.

LUCILE Hear me.

CLÉONTE Not a bit.

NICOLE Let me speak.

COVIELLE I'm deaf.

LUCILE Cléonte!

CLÉONTE No.

NICOLE Covielle!

COVIELLE No.

LUCILE Stay.

CLÉONTE Idle stuff.

NICOLE Hear me.

COVIELLE No such thing.

LUCILE One moment.

CLÉONTE Not at all.

NICOLE A little patience.

COVIELLE A fiddle-stick.

LUCILE Two words.

CLÉONTE No, 'tis over.

NICOLE One word.

COVIELLE No more dealings.

LUCILE (*stopping*) Well, since you won't hear me, keep your opinion, and do what you please.

NICOLE (*stopping likewise*) Since that's thy way, e'en take it all just as it pleases thee.

CLÉONTE Let's know the subject then of this fine reception.

LUCILE (*going in her turn to avoid* CLÉONTE) I've no longer an inclination to tell it.

COVIELLE Let us a little into this history.

NICOLE (*going likewise in her turn to avoid* COVIELLE) I won't inform thee now, not I.

CLÉONTE (*following* LUCILE) Tell me—

LUCILE No, I'll tell you nothing.

COVIELLE (*following* NICOLE) Say—

NICOLE No, I say nothing.

CLÉONTE For goodness' sake.

LUCILE No, I tell you.

COVIELLE Of all charity.

NICOLE Not a bit.

CLÉONTE I beseech you.

LUCILE Let me alone.
COVIELLE I conjure thee.
NICOLE Away with thee.
CLÉONTE Lucile!
LUCILE No.
COVIELLE Nicole!
NICOLE Not at all.
CLÉONTE For Heaven's sake.
LUCILE I will not.
COVIELLE Speak to me.
NICOLE Not a word.
CLÉONTE Clear up my doubts.
LUCILE No, I'll do nothing towards it.
COVIELLE Cure my mind.
NICOLE No, 'tis not my pleasure.
CLÉONTE Well, since you are so little concerned to ease me of my pain, and to justify yourself as to the unworthy treatment my passion has received from you, ungrateful creature, 'tis the last time you shall see me, and I am going far from you to die of grief and love.
COVIELLE (*to* NICOLE) And I'll follow his steps.
LUCILE (*to* CLÉONTE, *who is going*) Cléonte!
NICOLE (*to* COVIELLE, *who follows his master*) Covielle!
CLÉONTE (*stopping*) Hey?
COVIELLE (*likewise stopping*) Your pleasure?
LUCILE Whither do you go?
CLÉONTE Where I told you.
COVIELLE We go to die.
LUCILE Do you go to die, Cléonte?
CLÉONTE Yes, cruel, since you will have it so.
LUCILE I? I have you die?
CLÉONTE Yes, you would.
LUCILE Who told you so?
CLÉONTE (*going up to* LUCILE) Would you not have it so, since you would not clear up my suspicions?
LUCILE Is that my fault? Would you but have given me the hearing, should I not have told you that the adventure you make such complaints about was occasioned this morning by the presence of an old aunt who will absolutely have it that the mere approach of a man is a dishonour to a girl, who is perpetually lecturing us upon this head, and represents to us all mankind as so many devils, whom one ought to avoid.
NICOLE (*to* COVIELLE) There's the whole secret of the affair.
CLÉONTE Don't you deceive me, Lucile?
COVIELLE (*to* NICOLE) Dost thou not put a trick upon me?
LUCILE (*to* CLÉONTE) There's nothing more true.
NICOLE (*to* COVIELLE) 'Tis the very thing, as it is.
COVIELLE (*to* CLÉONTE) Shall we surrender upon this?
CLÉONTE Ah, Lucile, what art have you to calm my passions with a single word! How easily do we suffer ourselves to be persuaded by those we love!
COVIELLE How easily is one wheedled by these plaguy animals![7]

(*Enter* MME JOURDAIN)

MME JOURDAIN I am very glad to see you, Cléonte, and you are here apropos. My husband's acoming; catch your opportunity quick, and demand Lucile in marriage.
CLÉONTE Ah, madame, how sweet is that word, how it flatters my wishes! Could I receive an order more charming? a favour more precious?

(*Enter* M. JOURDAIN)

Sir, I was not willing to employ any other person to make a certain demand of you which I have long intended. It concerns me sufficiently to undertake it in my own person; and, without further circumlocution, I shall inform you that the honour of being your son-in-law is an illustrious favour which I beseech you to grant me.
M. JOURDAIN Before I give you an answer, sir, I desire you would tell me whether you are a gentleman.
CLÉONTE Sir, the generality of people don't hesitate much on this question. People speak out bluff, and with ease. They make no scruple of taking this title upon 'em, and custom now-a-days seems to authorise the theft. For my part, I confess to you, my sentiments in this matter are somewhat more delicate. I look upon all imposture as unworthy an honest man, and that there is cowardice in denying what Heaven has made us; in tricking ourselves out, to the eyes of the world, in a stolen title; in desiring to put ourselves off for what we are not. I am undoubtedly born of parents who have held honourable employments. I have had the honour of six years' service in the army; and I find myself of consequence enough to hold a tolerable rank in the world; but for all this I won't give myself a name, which others in my place would think they might pretend to, and I'll tell you frankly that I am no gentleman.[8]

---

[7]This scene between the four lovers has been compared to a ballet because of its schematic, patterned quality. Can you imagine it danced or mimed?

[8]Cléonte, as opposed to Jourdain, accepts his station in life with neither pretense nor shame. It is a fact that many bourgeois were literally buying their way into the nobility at this time.

M. JOURDAIN Your hand, sir; my daughter is no wife for you.

CLÉONTE How?

M. JOURDAIN You are no gentleman, you shan't have my daughter.

MME JOURDAIN What would you be at then with your gentlemen? D'ye think we sort of people are of the line of St. Louis?[9]

M. JOURDAIN Hold your tongue, wife, I see you're acoming.

MME JOURDAIN Are we either of us otherwise descended than of plain citizens?

M. JOURDAIN There's a scandalous reflection for you!

MME JOURDAIN And was not your father a tradesman as well as mine?

M. JOURDAIN Plague take the woman! She never has done with this. If your father was a tradesman, so much was the worse for him; but as for mine, they are numskulls that say he was. All that I have to say to you is that I will have a gentleman for my son-in-law.

MME JOURDAIN Your daughter should have a husband that's proper for her, and an honest man who is rich and well made would be much better for her than a gentleman who is deformed and a beggar.

NICOLE That's very true. We have a young squire in our town who is the most awkward looby, the veriest driveller that I ever set eyes on.

M. JOURDAIN Hold your prate, Madame Impertinence. You are always thrusting yourself into conversation. I've means sufficient for my daughter, and want nothing but honour, and I will have her a marchioness.

MME JOURDAIN A marchioness!

M. JOURDAIN Yes, a marchioness.

MME JOURDAIN Marry, Heaven preserve me from it!

M. JOURDAIN 'Tis a determined thing.

MME JOURDAIN 'Tis what I shall never consent to. Matches with people above one are always subject to grievous inconveniences. I don't like that a son-in-law should have it in his power to reproach my daughter with her parents, or that she should have children who should be ashamed to call me grandmother. Should she come and visit me with the equipage of a grand lady and, through inadvertency, miss curtsying to some of the neighbourhood, they would not fail, presently, saying a hundred idle things. Do but see, would they say, this lady marchioness, what haughty airs she gives herself! She's the daughter of Monsieur Jourdain, who was over and above happy, when she was a little one, to play children's play with us. She was not always so lofty as she is now; and her two grandfathers sold cloth near St. Innocent's Gate. They amassed great means for their children, which they are paying for now, perhaps very dear, in the other world. People don't generally grow so rich by being honest. I won't have all these tittle-tattle stories; in one word, I'll have a man who shall be beholden to me for my daughter, and to whom I can say, Sit you down there, son-in-law, and dine with me.

M. JOURDAIN See there the sentiments of a little soul, to desire always to continue in a mean condition. Let me have no more replies; my daughter shall be a marchioness in spite of the world; and if you put me in a passion, I'll make her a duchess.

(*Exit* M. JOURDAIN)

MME JOURDAIN Cléonte, don't be discouraged by all this. (*to* LUCILE) Follow me, daughter, and come tell your father resolutely that if you have not him, you won't marry anybody at all.

(*Exeunt* MME JOURDAIN, LUCILE, *and* NICOLE)

COVIELLE You have made a pretty piece of work of it with your fine sentiments.

CLÉONTE What wouldst thou have me do? I have a scrupulousness in this case that no precedents can conquer.

COVIELLE You're in the wrong to be serious with such a man as that. Don't you see that he's a fool? And would it cost you anything to accommodate yourself to his chimeras?

CLÉONTE You're in the right; but I did not dream it was necessary to bring your proofs of nobility, to be son-in-law to Monsieur Jourdain.

COVIELLE (*laughing*) Ha, ha, ha.

CLÉONTE What d'ye laugh at?

COVIELLE At a thought that's come into my head to play our spark off and help you to obtain what you desire.

CLÉONTE How?

COVIELLE The thought is absolutely droll.

CLÉONTE What is it?

COVIELLE There was a certain masquerade performed a little while ago, which comes in here the best in the world; and which I intend to insert into a piece of roguery I design to make for our coxcomb. This whole affair looks a little like making a joke of him; but with him we may hazard everything. There's no need here to study finesse so much—he's a man who will play his part to a wonder, and will

---

[9]Louis IX, King of France 1226–1270.

easily give in to all the sham tales we shall take in our heads to tell him. I have actors, I have habits all ready, only let me alone.

CLÉONTE But inform me of it.

COVIELLE I am going to let you into the whole of it. Let's retire; there he comes.

(*Exeunt* COVIELLE *and* CLÉONTE. *Enter* M. JOURDAIN)

M. JOURDAIN What the deuce can this mean? They have nothing but great lords to reproach me with; and I for my part see nothing so fine as keeping company with your great lords; there's nothing but honour and civility among 'em, and I would it had cost me two fingers of a hand to have been born a count or a marquis.

(*Enter a* LACKEY)

LACKEY Sir, here's the count, and a lady whom he's handing in.

M. JOURDAIN Good lack-a-day, I have some orders to give. Tell 'em that I'm acoming in a minute.

(*Exit* M. JOURDAIN. *Enter* DORANTE *and* DORIMÈNE)

LACKEY My master says that he's acoming in a minute.

(*Exit* LACKEY)

DORANTE 'Tis very well.

DORIMÈNE I don't know, Dorante; I take a strange step here in suffering you to bring me to a house where I know nobody.

DORANTE What place then, madame, would you have a lover choose to entertain you in, since, to avoid clamour, you neither allow of your own house nor mine?

DORIMÈNE But you don't mention that I am every day insensibly engaged to receive too great proofs of your passion. In vain do I refuse things, you weary me out of resistance, and you have a civil kind of obstinacy which makes me come gently into whatsoever you please. Frequent visits commenced, declarations came next, which drew after them serenades and entertainments, which were followed by presents. I opposed all these things, but you are not disheartened, and you become master of my resolutions step by step. For my part, I can answer for nothing hereafter, and I believe in the end you will bring me to matrimony, from which I stood so far aloof.

DORANTE Faith, madame, you ought to have been there already. You are a widow, and depend upon nobody but yourself. I am my own master, and love you more than my life. What does it stick at, then, that you should not, from this day forward, complete my happiness?

DORIMÈNE Lack-a-day, Dorante, there must go a great many qualities on both sides, to make people live happily together; and two of the most reasonable persons in the world have often much ado to compose a union to both their satisfactions.

DORANTE You're in the wrong, madame, to represent to yourself so many difficulties in this affair; and the experience you have had concludes nothing for the rest of the world.

DORIMÈNE In short, I always abide by this. The expenses you put yourself to for me disturb me for two reasons; one is, they engage me more than I could wish; and the other is, I'm sure (no offence to you!) that you can't do this but you must incommode yourself, and I would not have you do that.

DORANTE Fie, madame, these are trifles, and 'tis not by that—

DORIMÈNE I know what I say; and, amongst other things, the diamond you forced me to take, is of value—

DORANTE Nay, madame, pray don't enhance the value of a thing my love thinks unworthy of you: and permit—Here's the master of the house.

(*Enter* M. JOURDAIN)

M. JOURDAIN (*after having made two bows, finding himself too near* DORIMÈNE) A little farther, madame.

DORIMÈNE How?

M. JOURDAIN One step, if you please.

DORIMÈNE What then?

M. JOURDAIN Fall back a little for the third.

DORANTE Monsieur Jourdain, madame, knows the world.

M. JOURDAIN Madame, 'tis a very great honour that I am fortunate enough to be so happy, but to have the felicity that you should have the goodness to grant me the favour, to do me the honour, to honour me with the favour of your presence; and had I also the merit to merit a merit like yours, and that Heaven—envious of my good—had granted me—the advantage of being worthy—of—

DORANTE Monsieur Jourdain, enough of this; my lady does not love great compliments, and she knows you are a man of wit. (*aside to* DORIMÈNE) 'Tis a downright bourgeois, ridiculous enough, as you see, in his whole behaviour.

DORIMÈNE (*aside to* DORANTE) It is not very difficult to perceive it.

DORANTE Madame, this is a very good friend of mine.

M. JOURDAIN 'Tis too much honour you do me.

DORANTE A very polite man.

DORIMÈNE I have a great esteem for him.

M. JOURDAIN I have done nothing yet, madame, to merit this favour.

DORANTE (*aside to* M. JOURDAIN) Take good care however not to speak to her of the diamond you gave her.

M. JOURDAIN (*aside to* DORANTE) Mayn't I ask her only how she likes it?

DORANTE (*aside to* M. JOURDAIN) How! Take special care you don't. 'Twould be villainous of you; and to act like a man of gallantry, you should make as if it were not you who made the present. (*aloud*) Monsieur Jourdain, madame, says that he's in raptures to see you at his house.

DORIMÈNE He does me a great deal of honour.

M. JOURDAIN (*aside to* DORANTE) How am I obliged to you, sir, for speaking to her in that manner on my account!

DORANTE (*aside to* M. JOURDAIN) I have had a most terrible difficulty to get her to come hither.

M. JOURDAIN (*aside to* DORANTE) I don't know how to thank you enough for it.

DORANTE He says, madame, that he thinks you the most charming person in the world.

DORIMÈNE 'Tis a great favour he does me.

M. JOURDAIN Madame, it's you who do the favours, and—

DORANTE Let's think of eating.

(*Enter a* LACKEY)

LACKEY (*to* M. JOURDAIN) Everything is ready, sir.

DORANTE Come, then, let us sit down to table; and fetch the musicians.[10]

(*Six cooks, who have prepared the feast, dance together for the third intermission. After this, they carry on a table covered with several dishes.*)

ACT IV

THE SCENE DORIMÈNE, MONSIEUR JOURDAIN, DORANTE, *three* MUSICIANS, LACKEYS

[10]This is a key scene of the play, prepared for in the first scene of Act I. What do we learn about the characters of Dorante and Dorimène here?

DORIMÈNE How, Dorante? Why here's a most magnificent repast!

M. JOURDAIN You are pleased to banter, madame; I would it were more worthy of your acceptance.

(DORIMÈNE, M. JOURDAIN, DORANTE *and three* MUSICIANS *sit down at the table*)

DORANTE Monsieur Jourdain, madame, is in the right in what he says, and he obliges me in paying you, after so handsome a manner, the honours of his house. I agree with him that the repast is not worthy of you. As it was myself who ordered it, and I am not so clearly sighted in these affairs as certain of our friends, you have here no very learned feast; and you will find incongruities of good cheer in it, some barbarisms of good taste. Had our friend Damis had a hand here, everything had been done by rule; elegance and erudition would have run through the whole, and he would not have failed exaggerating all the regular pieces of the repast he gave you, and force you to own his great capacity in the science of good eating; he would have told you of bread *de rive,* with the golden kissing-crust, raised too all round with a crust that crumples tenderly in your teeth; of wine with a velvet sap, heightened with a smartness not too overpowering; of a breast of mutton stuffed with parsley; of a loin of veal *de rivière,* thus long, white, delicate, and which is a true almond paste between the teeth; of your partridges heightened with a surprising *goût;* and then by way of farce or entertainment, of a soup with jelly broth, fortified with a young plump turkey-pout, cantoned with pigeons, and garnished with white onions married to succory. But, for my part, I confess to you my ignorance; and, as Monsieur Jourdain has very well said, I wish the repast were more worthy of your acceptance.[1]

DORIMÈNE I make no other answer to this compliment than eating as I do.

M. JOURDAIN Ah! what pretty hands are there!

DORIMÈNE The hands are so so, Monsieur Jourdain; but you mean to speak of the diamond, which is very pretty.

M. JOURDAIN I, madame? Marry, Heaven forbid I should speak of it; I should not act like a gentleman of gallantry, and the diamond is a very trifle.

DORIMÈNE You are wondrous nice.

[1]This speech gives us a good idea of what a seventeenth-century court meal was like. The French were already famous for their cuisine.

M. JOURDAIN You have too much goodness—

DORANTE (*having made signs to* M. JOURDAIN) Come, give some wine to Monsieur Jourdain, and to those gentlemen who will do us the favour to sing us a catch.

DORIMÈNE You give a wondrous relish to the good cheer by mixing music with it; I am admirably well regaled here.

M. JOURDAIN Madame, it is not—

DORANTE Monsieur Jourdain, let us listen to these gentlemen, they'll entertain us with something better than all we can possibly say.

FIRST AND SECOND MUSICIANS (*together, each with a glass in his hand*)

Put it round, my dear Phyllis, invert the bright glass;
Oh what charms to the crystal those fingers impart!
You and Bacchus combined, all resistance surpass,
And with passion redoubled have ravished my heart.
'Twixt him, you, and me, my charmer, my fair,
Eternal affection let's swear.

At the touch of those lips how he sparkles more bright!
And his touch, in return, those lips does embellish:
I could quaff 'em all day, and drink bumpers all night.
What longing each gives me, what gusto, what relish!
'Twixt him, you, and me, my charmer, my fair,
Eternal affection let's swear.

SECOND AND THIRD MUSICIANS (*together*)

Since time flies so nimbly away,
Come drink, my dear boys, drink about;
Let's husband him well while we may,
For life may be gone before the mug's out.
When Charon has got us aboard,
Our drinking and wooing are past;
We ne'er to lose time can afford,
For drinking's a trade not always to last.

Let your puzzling rogues in the schools,
Dispute of the bonum *of man;*
Philosophers dry are but fools—
The secret is this: drink, drink off your can.
When Charon has got us aboard,
Our drinking and wooing are past;
We ne'er to lose time can afford,
For drinking's a trade not always to last.

ALL THREE (*together*)

Why bob there! some wine, boys! come fill the glass, fill,
Round and round let it go, till we bid it stand still.

DORIMÈNE I don't think anything can be better sung; and 'tis extremely fine.

M. JOURDAIN I see something here though, madame, much finer.

DORIMÈNE Hey! Monsieur Jourdain is more gallant than I thought he was.

DORANTE How, madame! who do you take Monsieur Jourdain for?

M. JOURDAIN I wish she would take me for what I could name.

DORIMÈNE Again?

DORANTE (*to* DORIMÈNE) You don't know him.

M. JOURDAIN She shall know me whenever she pleases.

DORIMÈNE Oh! Too much.

DORANTE He's one who has a repartee always at hand. But you don't see, madame, that Monsieur Jourdain eats all the pieces you have touched.

DORIMÈNE Monsieur Jourdain is a man that I am charmed with.

M. JOURDAIN If I could charm your heart, I should be—

(*Enter* MME JOURDAIN)

MME JOURDAIN Hey-day! why here's a jolly company of you, and I see very well you did not expect me. It was for this pretty affair, then, Monsieur Husband o' mine, that you were in such a violent hurry to pack me off to dine with my sister; I just now found a play-house below, and here I find a dinner fit for a wedding. Thus it is you spend your money, and thus it is you feast the ladies in my absence, and present 'em with music and a play, whilst I'm sent abroad in the meantime.

DORANTE What do you mean, Madame Jourdain? and what's your fancy to take it into your head that your husband spends his money, and that 'tis he who entertains my lady? Know, pray, that 'tis I do it, that he only lends me his house, and that you ought to consider a little better what you say.

M. JOURDAIN Yes, Madame Impertinence, 'tis the count that presents the lady with all this, who is a person of quality. He does me the honour to borrow my house, and is pleased to let me be with him.

MME JOURDAIN 'Tis all stuff, this. I know what I know.

DORANTE Madame Jourdain, take your best spectacles, take 'em.

MME JOURDAIN I've no need of spectacles, sir, I see clear enough; I've smelt things out a great while ago, I am no ass. 'Tis base in you, who are a great lord, to lend a helping hand, as you do, to the follies of my husband. And you, madame, who are a great lady, 'tis neither handsome nor honest in you to sow dissension in a family, and to suffer my husband to be in love with you.

DORIMÈNE What can be the meaning of all this? Go, Dorante, 'tis wrong in you to expose me to the silly visions of this raving woman.

DORANTE (*following* DORIMÈNE, *who goes out*) Madame, why madame, where are you running?

M. JOURDAIN Madame—My lord, make my excuses to her and endeavour to bring her back.

(*Exit* DORANTE)

(*To* MME JOURDAIN) Ah! impertinent creature as you are, these are your fine doings; you come and affront me in the face of all the world, and drive people of quality away from my house.

MME JOURDAIN I value not their quality.

(LACKEYS *take away the table*)

M. JOURDAIN I don't know what hinders me, you plaguy hussy, from splitting your skull with the fragments of the feast you came here to disturb.

MME JOURDAIN (*going*) I despise all this. I defend my own rights, and I shall have all the wives on my side.

M. JOURDAIN You do well to get out of the way of my fury.

(*Exit* MME JOURDAIN)

She came here at a most unlucky time. I was in the humour of saying fine things, and never did I find myself so witty. What have we got here?

(*Enter* COVIELLE, *disguised*)

COVIELLE Sir, I don't know whether I have the honour to be known to you.

M. JOURDAIN No, sir.

COVIELLE I have seen you when you were not above thus tall.

M. JOURDAIN Me?

COVIELLE Yes. You were one of the prettiest children in the world; and all the ladies used to take you in their arms to kiss you.

M. JOURDAIN To kiss me?

COVIELLE Yes, I was an intimate friend of the late gentleman your father.

M. JOURDAIN Of the late gentleman my father!

COVIELLE Yes. He was a very honest gentleman.

M. JOURDAIN What is't you say?

COVIELLE I say that he was a very honest gentleman.

M. JOURDAIN My father?

COVIELLE Yes.

M. JOURDAIN Did you know him very well?

COVIELLE Certainly.

M. JOURDAIN And did you know him for a gentleman?

COVIELLE Without doubt.

M. JOURDAIN I don't know then what the world means.

COVIELLE How?

M. JOURDAIN There is a stupid sort of people who would face me down that he was a tradesman.

COVIELLE He a tradesman? 'Tis mere scandal; he never was one. All that he did was, that he was very obliging, very officious, and as he was a great connoisseur in stuffs, he used to pick them up everywhere, have 'em carried to his house, and gave 'em to his friends for money.

M. JOURDAIN I'm very glad of your acquaintance, that you may bear witness that my father was a gentleman.

COVIELLE I'll maintain it in the face of all the world.

M. JOURDAIN You will oblige me. What business brings you here?

COVIELLE Since my acquaintance with the late gentleman your father, honest gentleman, as I was telling you, I have travelled round the world.

M. JOURDAIN Round the world?

COVIELLE Yes.

M. JOURDAIN I fancy 'tis a huge way off, that same country.

COVIELLE Most certainly. I have not been returned from these tedious travels of mine but four days. And because I have an interest in everything that concerns you, I come to tell you the best news in the world.

M. JOURDAIN What?

COVIELLE You know that the son of the Great Turk is here.

M. JOURDAIN I? No.

COVIELLE How? He has a most magnificent train. All the world goes to see him, and he has been received in this country as a person of importance.

M. JOURDAIN In troth, I did not know that.

COVIELLE What is of advantage to you in this affair is that he is in love with your daughter.

M. JOURDAIN The son of the Great Turk?

COVIELLE Yes, and wants to be your son-in-law.

M. JOURDAIN My son-in-law, the son of the Great Turk?

COVIELLE The son of the Great Turk your son-in-law. As I have been to see him, and perfectly understand his language, he held a conversation with me; and after some other discourse, says he to me: "Acciam croc soler, onch alla moustaph gidelum amanahem varahini oussere carbulath." That is to say, "Have you not seen a young handsome person, who is the daughter of Monsieur Jourdain, a gentleman of Paris?"

M. JOURDAIN The son of the Great Turk said that of me?

COVIELLE Yes, as I made answer to him that I knew you particularly well, and that I had seen your daughter. Ah, says he to me, "Marababa sahem"; that is to say, "Ah! how am I enamoured with her!"

M. JOURDAIN "Marababa sahem" means: "Ah! how am I enamoured with her"?

COVIELLE Yes.

M. JOURDAIN Marry, you did well to tell me so, for as for my part, I should never have believed that "Marababa sahem" had meant, "Ah! how am I enamoured with her!" 'Tis an admirable language, this same Turkish!

COVIELLE More admirable than one can believe. Do you know very well what is the meaning of "Cacaramouchen"?

M. JOURDAIN "Cacaramouchen"? No.

COVIELLE 'Tis as if you should say, "My dear soul."

M. JOURDAIN "Cacaramouchen" means, "My dear soul"?

COVIELLE Yes.

M. JOURDAIN Why, 'tis very wonderful! "Cacaramouchen—my dear soul." Would one ever have thought it? I am perfectly confounded at it.

COVIELLE In short, to finish my embassy, he comes to demand your daughter in marriage; and to have a father-in-law who should be suitable to him, he designs to make you a Mamamouchi, which is a certain grand dignity of his country.

M. JOURDAIN Mamamouchi?

COVIELLE Yes, Mamamouchi; that is to say, in our language, a Paladin. Paladin is your ancient—Paladin, in short—there's nothing in the world more noble than this; and you will rank with the grandest lord upon earth.

M. JOURDAIN The son of the Great Turk does me a great deal of honour, and I desire you would carry me to him, to return him my thanks.

COVIELLE How? Why he's just acoming hither.

M. JOURDAIN Is he acoming hither?

COVIELLE Yes. And he brings all things along with him for the ceremony of your dignity.

M. JOURDAIN He's main hasty.

COVIELLE His love will suffer no delay.

M. JOURDAIN All that perplexes me, in this case, is that my daughter is an obstinate hussy who has took into her head one Cléonte, and vows she'll marry no person besides him.

COVIELLE She'll change her opinion when she sees the son of the Grand Turk; and then there happens here a very marvellous adventure, that is, that the son of the Grand Turk resembles this Cléonte, with a trifling difference. I just now came from him, they showed him me; and the love she bears for one may easily pass to the other, and—I hear him coming; there he is.

(*Enter* CLÉONTE, *like a Turk, and three* PAGES *holding up his gown*)

CLÉONTE Ambousahim oqui boraf, Iordina, salamalequi.[2]

COVIELLE (*to* M. JOURDAIN) That is to say, Monsieur Jourdain, "May your heart be all the year like a rose-tree in flower!" These are obliging ways of speaking in that country.

M. JOURDAIN I am His Turkish Highness's most humble servant.

COVIELLE Carigar camboto oustin moraf.

CLÉONTE Oustin yoc catamalequi basum base alla moran.

COVIELLE He says, "Heaven give you the strength of lions and the prudence of serpents!"

M. JOURDAIN His Turkish Highness does me too much honour; and I wish him all manner of prosperity.

COVIELLE Ossa binamin sadoc babally oracaf ouram.

CLÉONTE Bel-men.

COVIELLE He says that you should go quickly with him to prepare yourself for the ceremony, in order afterwards to see your daughter and to conclude the marriage.

M. JOURDAIN So many things in two words?

COVIELLE Yes, the Turkish language is much in that way; it says a great deal in a few words. Go quickly where he desires you.

(*Exeunt* M. JOURDAIN, CLÉONTE, *and* PAGES)

Ha, ha, ha. I'faith, this is all absolutely droll. What a dupe! Had he had his part by heart, he could not have played it better. O, ho!

(*Enter* DORANTE)

---

[2]This is, of course, an invented language, but Molière has made it sound somewhat like Arabic.

I beseech you, sir, lend us a helping hand here, in a certain affair which is in agitation.

DORANTE Ah! ah! Covielle, who could have known thee? How art thou trimmed out there!

COVIELLE You see, ha, ha!

DORANTE What do ye laugh at?

COVIELLE At a thing, sir, that well deserves it.

DORANTE What?

COVIELLE I could give you a good many times, sir, to guess the stratagem we are making use of with Monsieur Jourdain, to bring him over to give his daughter to my master.

DORANTE I don't at all guess the stratagem, but I guess it will not fail of its effect, since you undertake it.

COVIELLE I know, sir, you are not unacquainted with the animal.

DORANTE Tell me what it is.

COVIELLE Be at the trouble of withdrawing a little farther off, to make room for what I see acoming. You will see one part of the story whilst I give you a narration of the rest.

THE TURKISH CEREMONY

The MUFTI, DERVISHES, TURKS (*assisting the* MUFTI), SINGERS *and* DANCERS

THE SCENE *Six* TURKS *enter gravely, two and two, to the sound of instruments. They bear three carpets, with which they dance in several figures, and then lift them up very high. The* TURKS, *singing, pass under the carpets and range themselves on each side of the stage. The* MUFTI, *accompanied by* DERVISHES, *closes the march.*

Then the TURKS *spread the carpets on the ground and kneel down upon them, the* MUFTI *and the* DERVISHES *standing in the middle of them; while the* MUFTI *invokes Mahomet in dumb contortions and grimaces, the* TURKS *prostrate themselves to the ground, singing* Allah, *raising their hands to heaven, singing* Allah, *and so continuing alternately to the end of the invocation, when they all rise up, singing* Allahekber.

Then two DERVISHES *bring* MONSIEUR JOURDAIN, *clothed like a Turk, his head shaved, without a turban or sabre.*

MUFTI (*to* M. JOURDAIN)

If thou understandest,
Answer;
If thou dost not understand,
Hold thy peace, hold thy peace.

I am Mufti,
Thou! who thou art
I don't know:
Hold thy peace, hold thy peace.

(*Two* DERVISHES *retire with* M. JOURDAIN)

Say, Turk, who is this, An Anabaptist, an Anabaptist?

THE TURKS No.

MUFTI A Zwinglian?

THE TURKS No.

MUFTI A Coffite?

THE TURKS No.

MUFTI A Hussite? A Morist? A Fronist?

THE TURKS No, no, no.

MUFTI No, no, no. Is he a Pagan?

THE TURKS No.

MUFTI A Lutheran?

THE TURKS No.

MUFTI A Puritan?

THE TURKS No.

MUFTI A Brahmin? A Moffian? A Zurian?

THE TURKS No, no, no.

MUFTI No, no, no. A Mahometan, a Mahometan?

THE TURKS There you have it, there you have it.

MUFTI How is he called? How is he called?

THE TURKS Jourdain, Jourdain.

MUFTI (*dancing*) Jourdain! Jourdain!

THE TURKS Jourdain, Jourdain.

MUFTI

To Mahomet for Jourdain
I pray night and day,
That he would make a Paladin
Of Jourdain, of Jourdain.
Give him a turban, and give a sabre,
With a galley and a brigantine,
To defend Palestine.
To Mahomet for Jourdain
I pray night and day.[3]
(*to the Turks*) Is Jourdain a good Turk?

THE TURKS That he is, that he is.

MUFTI (*singing and dancing*) *Ha, la ba, ba la chou, ba la ba, ba la da.*

(*Exit* MUFTI)

THE TURKS *Ha, la ba, ba la chou, ba la ba, ba la da.*

THE SCENE *The* MUFTI *returns with the State Turban, which is of an immeasurable largeness, garnished with lighted wax candles, four or five rows deep, accompanied by two* DERVISHES, *bearing the Alcoran, with comic caps garnished also with lighted candles.*

---

[3]The resemblance of Monsieur Jourdain's name to the Jordan river is used to make him "defender of Palestine."

The two other DERVISHES *lead up* MONSIEUR JOURDAIN *and place him on his knees with his hands to the ground so that his back, on which the Alcoran is placed, may serve for a desk to the* MUFTI, *who makes a second burlesque invocation, knitting his eyebrows, striking his hands sometimes upon the Alcoran, and tossing over the leaves with precipitation, after which, lifting up his hands, and crying with a loud voice,* Hoo.

During this second invocation the assistant TURKS, *bowing down and raising themselves alternately, sing likewise,* HOO, HOO, HOO.

M. JOURDAIN (*after they have taken the Alcoran off his back*) Ouf!

MUFTI (*to* M. JOURDAIN) Thou wilt not be a knave?

THE TURKS No, no, no.

MUFTI Not be a thief?

THE TURKS No, no, no.

MUFTI (*to the* TURKS) Give the turban.

THE TURKS

Thou wilt not be a knave?
No, no, no.
Not be a thief?
No, no, no.
Give the turban.

(*The* TURKS, *dancing, put the turban on* M. JOURDAIN'S *head at the sound of the instruments*)

MUFTI (*giving the sabre to* M. JOURDAIN)
Be brave, be no scoundrel,
Take the sabre.

THE TURKS (*drawing their sabres*)
Be brave, be no scoundrel,
Take the sabre.

(*The* TURKS, *dancing, strike* M. JOURDAIN *several times with their sabres, to music*)

MUFTI
Give, give
The bastonade.

THE TURKS
Give, give
The bastonade.

(*The* TURKS, *dancing, give* M. JOURDAIN *several strokes with a cudgel, to music*)

MUFTI
Don't think it a shame,
This is the last affront.

THE TURKS
Don't think it a shame,
This is the last affront.

(*The* MUFTI *begins a third invocation. The* DERVISHES *support him with great respect, after which the* TURKS, *singing and dancing round the* MUFTI, *retire with him and lead off* MONSIEUR JOURDAIN.)

ACT V

THE SCENE MADAME JOURDAIN, MONSIEUR JOURDAIN

MME JOURDAIN Bless us all! Mercy upon us! What have we got here? What a figure! What! dressed to go a-mumming, and is this a time to go masked? Speak therefore, what does this mean? Who has trussed you up in this manner?

M. JOURDAIN Do but see the impertinent slut, to speak after this manner to a Mamamouchi.

MME JOURDAIN How's that?

M. JOURDAIN Yes, you must show me respect now I am just made a Mamamouchi.

MME JOURDAIN What d'ye mean with your Mamamouchi?

M. JOURDAIN Mamamouchi, I tell you. I am a Mamamouchi.

MME JOURDAIN What beast is that?

M. JOURDAIN Mamamouchi, that is to say, in our language, a Paladin.

MME JOURDAIN A Paladin? Are you of an age to be a morris-dancer?[1]

M. JOURDAIN What an ignoramus! I say, Paladin. 'Tis a dignity of which I have just now gone through the ceremony.

MME JOURDAIN What ceremony then?

M. JOURDAIN Mahameta per Jordina.

MME JOURDAIN What does that mean?

M. JOURDAIN Jordina, that is to say, Jourdain.

MME JOURDAIN Well, how Jourdain?

M. JOURDAIN Voler far un Paladina de Jordina.[2]

MME JOURDAIN What?

M. JOURDAIN Dar turbanta con galera.

MME JOURDAIN What's the meaning of that?

M. JOURDAIN Per deffender Palestina.

MME JOURDAIN What is it you would say?

M. JOURDAIN Dara, dara, bastonnara.

MME JOURDAIN What is this same jargon?

---

[1]In the original, "a ballet dancer." Morris dances were (and are) done in the English countryside, in costume.

[2]This "language," which resembles Italian, is used in the ceremony in the original.

M. JOURDAIN Non tener honta, questa star l'ultima affronta.

MME JOURDAIN What in the name of wonder can all this be?

M. JOURDAIN (*singing and dancing*) *Hou la ba, ba la chou, ba la ba, ba la da.* (*falls down to the ground*)

MME JOURDAIN Alas and well-a-day! My husband is turned fool.

M. JOURDAIN (*getting up and walking off*) Peace! insolence, show respect to Monsieur Mamamouchi.

MME JOURDAIN (*alone*) How could he lose his senses? I must run and prevent his going out. (*seeing* DORIMÈNE *and* DORANTE) So, so, here come the rest of our gang. I see nothing but vexation on all sides.

(*Exit* MME JOURDAIN. *Enter* DORANTE *and* DORIMÈNE)

DORANTE Yes, madame, you'll see the merriest thing that can be seen; and I don't believe it's possible, in the whole world, to find another man so much a fool as this here. And besides, madame, we must endeavour to promote Cléonte's amour and to countenance his masquerade. He's a very pretty gentleman and deserves that one should interest one's self in his favour.

DORIMÈNE I've a very great value for him, and he deserves good fortune.

DORANTE Besides, we have here, madame, an entertainment that will suit us, and which we ought not to suffer to be lost; and I must by all means see whether my fancy will succeed.

DORIMÈNE I saw there magnificent preparations, and these are things, Dorante, I can no longer suffer. Yes, I'm resolved to put a stop, at last, to your profusions; and to break off all the expenses you are at on my account, I have determined to marry you out of hand. This is the real secret of the affair, and all these things end, as you know, with marriage.

DORANTE Ah! madame, is it possible you should form so kind a resolution in my favour?

DORIMÈNE I only do it to prevent you from ruining yourself; and without this, I see plainly that before 'tis long you won't be worth a groat.

DORANTE How am I obliged to you, madame, for the care you take to preserve my estate! 'Tis entirely at your service, as well as my heart, and you may use both of 'em just in the manner you please.

DORIMÈNE I shall make a proper use of them both. But here comes your man; an admirable figure.

(*Enter* M. JOURDAIN)

DORANTE Sir, my lady and I are come to pay our homage to your new dignity, and to rejoice with you at the marriage you are concluding betwixt your daughter and the son of the Grand Turk.

M. JOURDAIN (*bowing first in the Turkish manner*) Sir, I wish you the force of serpents and the wisdom of lions.

DORIMÈNE I was exceeding glad to be one of the first, sir, who should come and congratulate you upon the high degree of glory to which you are raised.

M. JOURDAIN Madame, I wish your rose-tree may flower all the year round; I am infinitely obliged to you for interesting yourselves in the honour that's paid me; and I am greatly rejoiced to see you returned hither, that I may make my most humble excuses for the impertinence of my wife.

DORIMÈNE That's nothing at all, I can excuse a commotion of this kind in her; your heart ought to be precious to her, and 'tis not at all strange the possession of such a man as you are should give her some alarms.

M. JOURDAIN The possession of my heart is a thing you have entirely gained.

DORANTE You see, madame, that Monsieur Jourdain is none of those people whom prosperity blinds, and that he knows, in all his grandeur, how to own his friends.

DORIMÈNE 'Tis the mark of a truly generous soul.

DORANTE Where is His Turkish Highness? We should be glad, as your friends, to pay our devoirs to him.

M. JOURDAIN There he comes, and I have sent to bring my daughter to join hands with him.

(*Enter* CLÉONTE, *in a Turkish habit*)

DORANTE (*to* CLÉONTE) Sir, we come to compliment Your Highness, as friends of the gentleman your father-in-law, and to assure you, with respect, of our most humble services.

M. JOURDAIN Where's the dragoman, to tell him who you are and make him understand what you say? You shall see that he'll answer you, and he speaks Turkish marvellously. Hola! there; where the deuce is he gone? (*to* CLÉONTE)
Stref,
strif,
strof,
straf.
The gentleman is a
grande segnore, grande segnore,
grande segnore;
and madame is a
granda dama, granda dama.

(*Seeing he cannot make himself be understood*)

Lack-a-day! (*to* CLÉONTE) Sir, he be a French Mamamouchi, and madame a French Mamamouchess. I can't speak plainer. Good, here's the dragoman.

(*Enter* COVIELLE, *disguised*)

Where do you run? We can say nothing without you. (*pointing to* CLÉONTE) Inform him a little that the gentleman and lady are persons of great quality who come to pay their compliments to him, as friends of mine, and to assure him of their services. (*to* DORIMÈNE *and* DORANTE) You shall see how he will answer.

COVIELLE Alabala crociam, acci boram alabamen.

CLÉONTE Catalequi tubal ourin soter amalouchan.

M. JOURDAIN (*to* DORIMÈNE *and* DORANTE) Do ye see?

COVIELLE He says that the rain of prosperity waters, at all seasons, the garden of your family.

M. JOURDAIN I told you that he speaks Turkish.

DORANTE This is admirable.

(*Enter* LUCILE)

M. JOURDAIN Come, daughter, come nearer, and give the gentleman your hand who does you the honour of demanding you in marriage.

LUCILE What's the matter, father, how are you dressed here? What! are you playing a comedy?

M. JOURDAIN No, no, 'tis no comedy, 'tis a very serious affair; and the most honourable for you that possibly can be wished. (*pointing to* CLÉONTE) This is the husband I bestow upon you.

LUCILE Upon me, father?

M. JOURDAIN Yes, upon you. Come, take him by the hand, and thank Heaven for your good fortune.

LUCILE I won't marry.

M. JOURDAIN I'll make you; am I not your father?

LUCILE I won't do it.

M. JOURDAIN Here's a noise indeed! Come, I tell you. Your hand here.

LUCILE No, father, I've told you before that there's no power can oblige me to take any other husband than Cléonte; and I am determined upon all extremities rather than—(*discovering* CLÉONTE) 'Tis true that you are my father; I owe you absolute obedience; and you may dispose of me according to your pleasure.

M. JOURDAIN Hah, I am charmed to see you return so readily to your duty; and it is a pleasure to me to have my daughter obedient.

(*Enter* MME JOURDAIN)

MME JOURDAIN How, how, what does this mean? They tell me you design to marry your daughter to a mummer.[3]

M. JOURDAIN Will you hold your tongue, impertinence? You're always coming to mix your extravagances with everything; there's no possibility of teaching you common sense.

MME JOURDAIN 'Tis you whom there's no teaching to be wise, and you go from folly to folly. What's your design, what would you do with this flock of people?

M. JOURDAIN I design to marry my daughter to the son of the Grand Turk.

MME JOURDAIN To the son of the Grand Turk?

M. JOURDAIN Yes. (*pointing to* COVIELLE) Make your compliments to him by the dragoman there.

MME JOURDAIN I have nothing to do with the dragoman, and I shall tell him plainly to his face that he shall have none of my daughter.

M. JOURDAIN Will you hold your tongue once more?

DORANTE What, Madame Jourdain, do you oppose such an honour as this? Do you refuse His Turkish Highness for a son-in-law?

MME JOURDAIN Lack-a-day, sir, meddle you with your own affairs.

DORIMÈNE 'Tis a great honour, 'tis by no means to be rejected.

MME JOURDAIN Madame, I desire you too not to give yourself any trouble about what no ways concerns you.

DORANTE 'Tis the friendship we have for you that makes us interest ourselves in what is of advantage to you.

MME JOURDAIN I shall easily excuse your friendship.

DORANTE There's your daughter consents to her father's pleasure.

MME JOURDAIN My daughter consent to marry a Turk?

DORANTE Certainly.

MME JOURDAIN Can she forget Cléonte?

DORANTE What would one not do to be a great lady?

MME JOURDAIN I would strangle her with my own hands, had she done such a thing as this.

M. JOURDAIN Here's tittle-tattle in abundance. I tell you this marriage shall be consummated.

---

[3]An actor.

MME JOURDAIN And I tell you that it shall not be consummated.

M. JOURDAIN What a noise is here?

LUCILE Mother!

MME JOURDAIN Go, you are a pitiful hussy.

M. JOURDAIN (*to* MME JOURDAIN) What! do you scold her for being obedient to me?

MME JOURDAIN Yes, she belongs to me as well as you.

COVIELLE (*to* MME JOURDAIN) Madame.

MME JOURDAIN What would you say to me, you?

COVIELLE One word.

MME JOURDAIN I've nothing to do with your word.

COVIELLE (*to* M. JOURDAIN) Sir, would she hear me but one word in private, I'll promise you to make her consent to what you have a mind.

MME JOURDAIN I won't consent to it.

COVIELLE Only hear me.

MME JOURDAIN No.

M. JOURDAIN (*to* MME JOURDAIN) Give him the hearing.

MME JOURDAIN No, I won't hear him.

M. JOURDAIN He'll tell you—

MME JOURDAIN He shall tell me nothing.

M. JOURDAIN Do but see the great obstinacy of the woman! Will it do you any harm to hear him?

COVIELLE Only hear me; you may do what you please afterwards.

MME JOURDAIN Well, what?

COVIELLE (*aside to* MME JOURDAIN) We have made signs to you, madame, this hour. Don't you see plainly that all is done purely to accommodate ourselves to the visions of your husband; that we are imposing upon him under this disguise, and that it is Cléonte himself who is the son of the Great Turk?

MME JOURDAIN (*aside to* COVIELLE) Oh, oh?

COVIELLE (*aside to* MME JOURDAIN) And that 'tis me, Covielle, who am the dragoman?

MME JOURDAIN (*aside to* COVIELLE) Oh! in that case, I give up.

COVIELLE (*aside to* MME JOURDAIN) Don't seem to know anything of the matter.

MME JOURDAIN (*aloud*) Yes, 'tis all done, I consent to the marriage.

M. JOURDAIN Ay, all the world submits to reason. (*to* MME JOURDAIN) You would not hear him. I knew he would explain to you what the son of the Great Turk is.

MME JOURDAIN He has explained it to me sufficiently, and I'm satisfied with it. Let us send for a notary.

DORANTE 'Tis well said. And, Madame Jourdain, that you may set your mind perfectly at rest, and that you should this day quit all jealousy which you may have entertained of the gentleman your husband, my lady and I shall make use of the same notary to marry us.

MME JOURDAIN I consent to that too.

M. JOURDAIN (*aside to* DORANTE) 'Tis to make her believe.

DORANTE (*aside to* M. JOURDAIN) We must by all means amuse her a little with this pretence.

M. JOURDAIN Good, good. (*aloud*) Let somebody go for the notary.

DORANTE In the meantime, till he comes and has drawn up the contracts, let us see our entertainment, and give His Turkish Highness the diversion of it.

M. JOURDAIN Well advised; come let us take our places.

MME JOURDAIN And Nicole?

M. JOURDAIN I give her to the dragoman; and my wife, to whosoever pleases to take her.

COVIELLE Sir, I thank you. (*aside*) If it's possible to find a greater fool than this, I'll go and publish it in Rome.

(*The play ends with the "ballet des nations," a spectacle of music, singing, and dancing in which various nationalities are impersonated.*)

COMMENTS AND QUESTIONS

1. Outline the plot of this comedy. Notice its simplicity. Some elements—the young lovers who wish to marry against the father's wishes, the marriages at the end—are stock features of comedy. How does Molière maintain interest?
2. Is anything really resolved in the end? Do you wonder about M. Jourdain's future? Could Molière have ended the comedy differently? More satisfactorily?
3. Do you feel that it is appropriate for each of the acts, and the whole show, to end with ballets? Why or why not?
4. What is Molière really ridiculing here, in your opinion? The bourgeoisie? The nobility? A particular type of character or character defect? The defects of an overcivilized society? Support your answer.
5. For which character do you feel the most sympathy? The least? There has always been considerable disagreement on this point—why?

6. How does a playwright succeed in portraying a character? What makes the character of M. Jourdain memorable?

7. How does this play differ from and resemble other examples of comedy that we read in Volume I both as drama (*Lysistrata*) and as narrative ("The Miller's Tale")?

8. Could *The Would-Be Gentleman* be rewritten as a sentimental drama or as a tragedy? How and why does it make human weakness funny?

The Seventeenth Century

No historical period is more complex and contradictory than the one we have just studied. Every general statement made about seventeenth-century culture almost seems to generate an equally valid opposite. Perhaps this is because the first half of the century, at least, was a time of tremendous change, of birth and growth. By the second half of the century, Europe was established as a world power and had become more stable at home, culturally as well as politically. Let us review briefly some of the often conflicting aspects of the seventeenth century and their significance.

Religion

In the area of religion, Europe by 1650 was divided into Catholic and Protestant territories, which have more or less survived as such into the present. Protestantism evolved from a revolutionary movement into an establishment or series of establishments, each with its own set of orthodox beliefs. With the subsidence of religious warfare came a growing indifference to religion and a secular view of the world. Attempts by new reform movements among Catholics and Protestants could not halt the trend.

Science

The rapid developments in science were in part responsible for this increasingly nonreligious view of the world. First the revolutionary Copernican theory and then experiments conducted by scientists such as Newton and Galileo taught people to trust their own minds or senses rather than the decrees of authority. Bacon condemned what he conceived of as the traditional deductive approach to nature and called for a new method based on principles derived directly from observation. By use of this method, he believed, a new age of discovery could begin. Eventually human beings would be able to understand and control their surroundings. In practice, at least, many thinkers of the century treated nature itself as a self-regulating, autonomous machine: God was needed only to explain how the world came into being in the first place. But some felt uneasy about living in such a world. A few experienced a kind of terror. If earth was no longer perceived as the center of the universe, the position of humanity also had to be rethought.

Economics

The seventeenth century witnessed a new stage in the development of a highly important modern economic institution: industrial capitalism. The desire for world markets and wealth led to the exploitation of African and American cultures by Europeans. Whereas in the sixteenth century, America had furnished Europe primarily with precious metals, in the seventeenth the American colonies supplied important agricultural products and raw materials. The colonies became an important outlet for European investment. Slaves were a significant cost factor here. In its turn, trade with the New World and Africa stimulated intracontinental trade in Europe as well. The new economic interests were another influence in the growth of secularism.

Politics

The rapid accumulation of wealth allowed many middle-class people, "would-be gentlemen," literally to buy their way into the nobility. After very unsettled political conditions in the first half of the century, the European monarchs (most strikingly Louis XIV) then learned how to keep the upper classes politically subservient; royal absolutism became the political order of the day. Absolutism was the means by which strong central government was established in most of Europe. Accordingly, the modern political state owes more to absolutism than to republican or constitutional monarchical forms.

Drawing on the mechanistic model prevalent in the new sciences and terrified of anarchy, Hobbes intended to come to the aid of absolutism with his *Leviathan.* Only by surrendering their individual wills to a will jointly created through a common covenant could humankind know the peace and security sought by the life force in each person. The justification for Leviathan's absolute power was purely utilitarian: he could claim obedience only so long as he provided the security for which he had been created.

If rejected by contemporary defenders for absolutism, Hobbes's *Leviathan,* in basing political theory on enlightened self-interest, clearly predicted the direction of the modern age. For the next two centuries, self-interest became recognized generally as the basic motive in human action. Almost as a necessary counterpoise to this strong individualism, Hobbes insisted on the need for a superior will with absolute power that people, out of self-interest, must obey to keep from killing one another. Here, too, he was a harbinger of the modern world, which has witnessed a steady increase in the power wielded by the state over the lives of individuals.

The Baroque Style

The baroque style in the arts in many ways reflects the turmoil, contradictions, and dynamism of the age in which it flourished. Exuberance is perhaps its most overriding quality. We have seen in many instances that baroque art is characterized by intense sensuality combined with intense spirituality, by a realistic depiction of everyday life along with a love of fantasy and illusion, by a delight in the material aspects of life with a sense of the impermanence of life in this world. Aesthetically, we have seen that the concept *baroque* may include the neoclassical—a classicism expanded to create a sense of magnificence and grandeur. This classicism fitted well with the increase in political stability in the last half of the century.

Performing Arts

Theatricality is characteristic of much of seventeenth-century culture. The Catholic mass became more like a show as churches came to resemble theaters; Bernini transformed Rome into something like a huge theater. Louis XIV, the master showman, built a showplace and ran his court ritual like a ballet. It is not surprising that the theatrical arts rose to great importance during this period. The first theaters that we can call modern were built in Italy and influenced those in other parts of Europe. Two forms of modern stage entertainment, the opera and the ballet, came into being in the seventeenth century; Handel developed the *oratorio* into a form that could be used for a popular show. Greek and Roman tragedies were reborn in neoclassical form with the dramas of Corneille and Racine. Molière, with his ability to depict characters both everyday and universal, created the first truly modern comedies. The combined arts of dance, drama, and music make Molière's comedy-ballets enchanting spectacles as well as incisive commentaries on human nature. A stage piece like *Le Bourgeois Gentilhomme,* with its play between reality and fantasy, is another illustration of the diverse richness of seventeenth-century art.

The grandeur, magnificence, and exuberance that characterize the baroque style are nowhere more apparent than in Handel's *Messiah.* Yet many knowing musicians turn to Bach, not Handel, as the culmination of the era. In truth, both composers, and their works, were at the same time typical and extraordinary in their day and ours. Musically speaking, we have extended the limit of the seventeenth century into the mid-eighteenth because of the longer duration of musical baroque. The early eighteenth century, which saw a flowering of great religious music, was on the whole for the other humanities a most nonreligious time. We will see the secular spirit that began in the fourteenth and developed throughout the seventeenth century take a more profound hold on Western culture in the eighteenth as the larger-than-life dimensions of baroque art are reduced to a more "reasonable" level.

Part Seven

Reason, Revolution, Romanticism: The Eighteenth and Early Nineteenth Centuries

Plate XII
Pieter Brueghel the Elder, *The Harvest*. 1565. National Gallery, Prague.
(Giraudon/Art Resource, NY)

Plate XIII
El Greco, *View of Toledo.* Oil on Canvas. Height 47¾″, width 42¾″.
(The Metropolitan Museum of Art, Bequest of Mrs. H. O. Havemeyer, 1929. The H.O. Havemeyer Collection.)

Plate XIV
Caravaggio, *Calling of Saint Matthew*. San Luigi dei Francesi, Rome.
(Scala/Art Resource, NY)

Plate XV
Peter Paul Rubens, *Garden of Love*. c. 1638. Oil on canvas,
6′6″ x 9′3⅜″.
Museo del Prado, Madrid.
(Scala/Art Resource, NY)

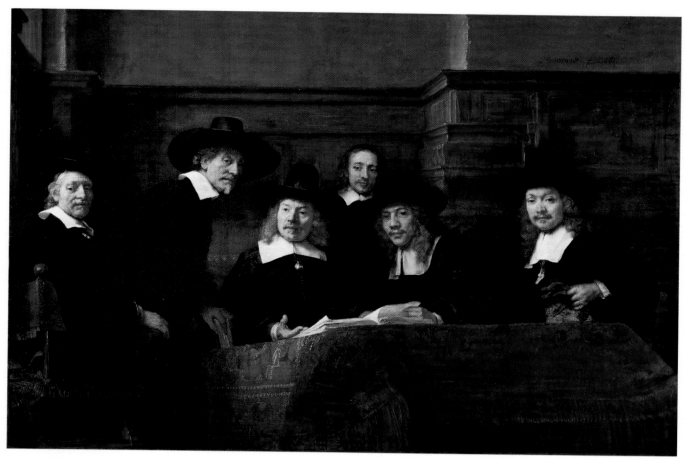

Plate XVI Rembrandt, *The Syndics of the Drapers' Guild* (after restoration). Canvas, 191.5 x 279 cm. (Rijksmuseum, Amsterdam)

Plate XVII Rembrandt, *Portrait of the Artist*, c. 1660. (The Iveagh Bequest, Kenwood/English Heritage)

Plate XVIII Rembrandt, *Return of the Prodigal Son*, c. 1669. Oil on canvas, 8′8″ x 6′8¾″. The Hermitage Museum, Leningrad. (Scala/Art Resource, NY)

Plate XIX
Jan Vermeer,
The Kitchenmaid
(after restoration).
Canvas, 45.5 x 41 cm.
(Rijksmuseum, Amsterdam)

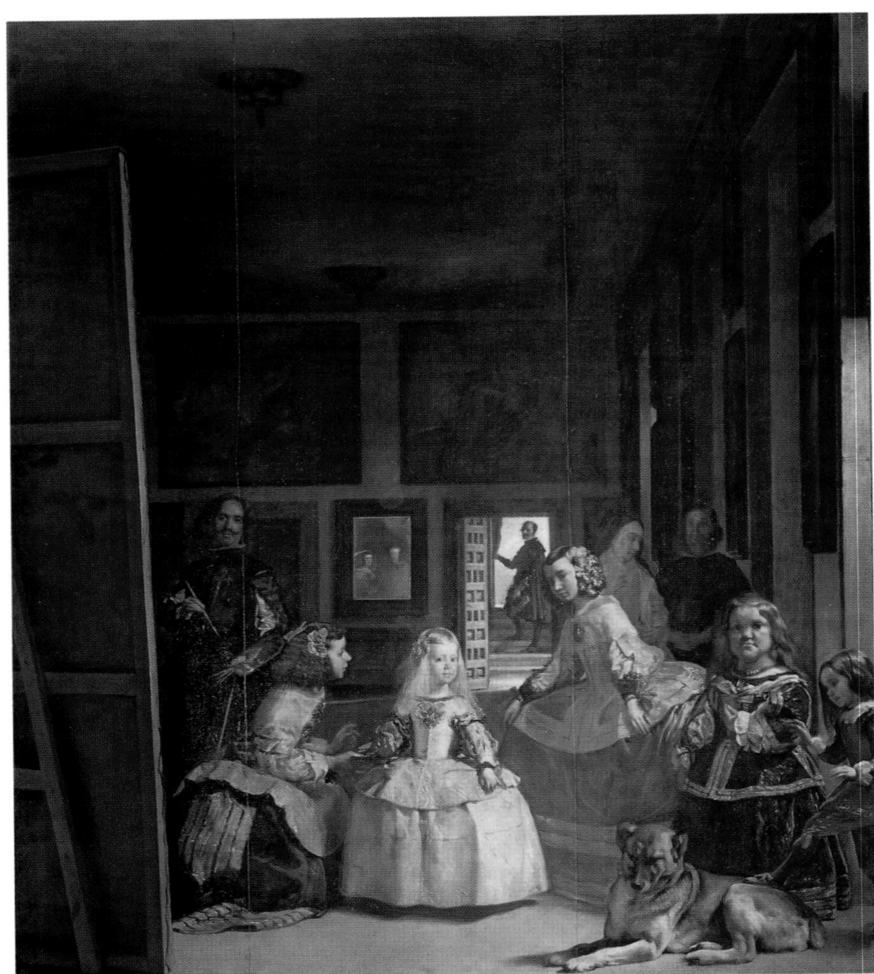

Plate XX
Diego Velazquez, *Las Meninas,* 1656. Oil on canvas, 10′5″ x 9′½″. Museo del Prado, Madrid. (Art Resource, NY)

24

The European Enlightenment

A Pre-revolutionary Movement

The thinkers formed by the Scientific Revolution taught reliance on individual experience or reason rather than on authority and tradition. Within the age of absolutism, seeds were being planted for a cultural, and eventually political, revolution that would destroy everything the age stood for. France, which dominated Europe culturally and politically throughout the eighteenth century, began the period with Louis XIV, king by the grace of God, and ended it with General Napoleon, sovereign by popular support. In the interim Louis's royal line, the Bourbon family, was swept away by the earthshaking revolution of 1789, which toppled in its turn one European crowned head after the other. The ideas originating in France also had a profound impact on the formation of a new republic across the Atlantic.

The Philosophes

The intellectual movement that came to be known as the Enlightenment was led by a group of diverse, individualistic Frenchmen who are usually labeled together as the *philosophes.* Although the word literally means "philosopher," these people were not on the whole creators of new philosophical systems. Rather, they were propagandists for a general set of ideas that they believed would bring "light" to their generation and so improve the life of the human race as a whole. Primarily middle-class, skilled and prolific writers, the philosophes reached their public through the burgeoning printed media—not only books and pamphlets but also the newly introduced weekly newspaper and monthly journal. Their mission would have

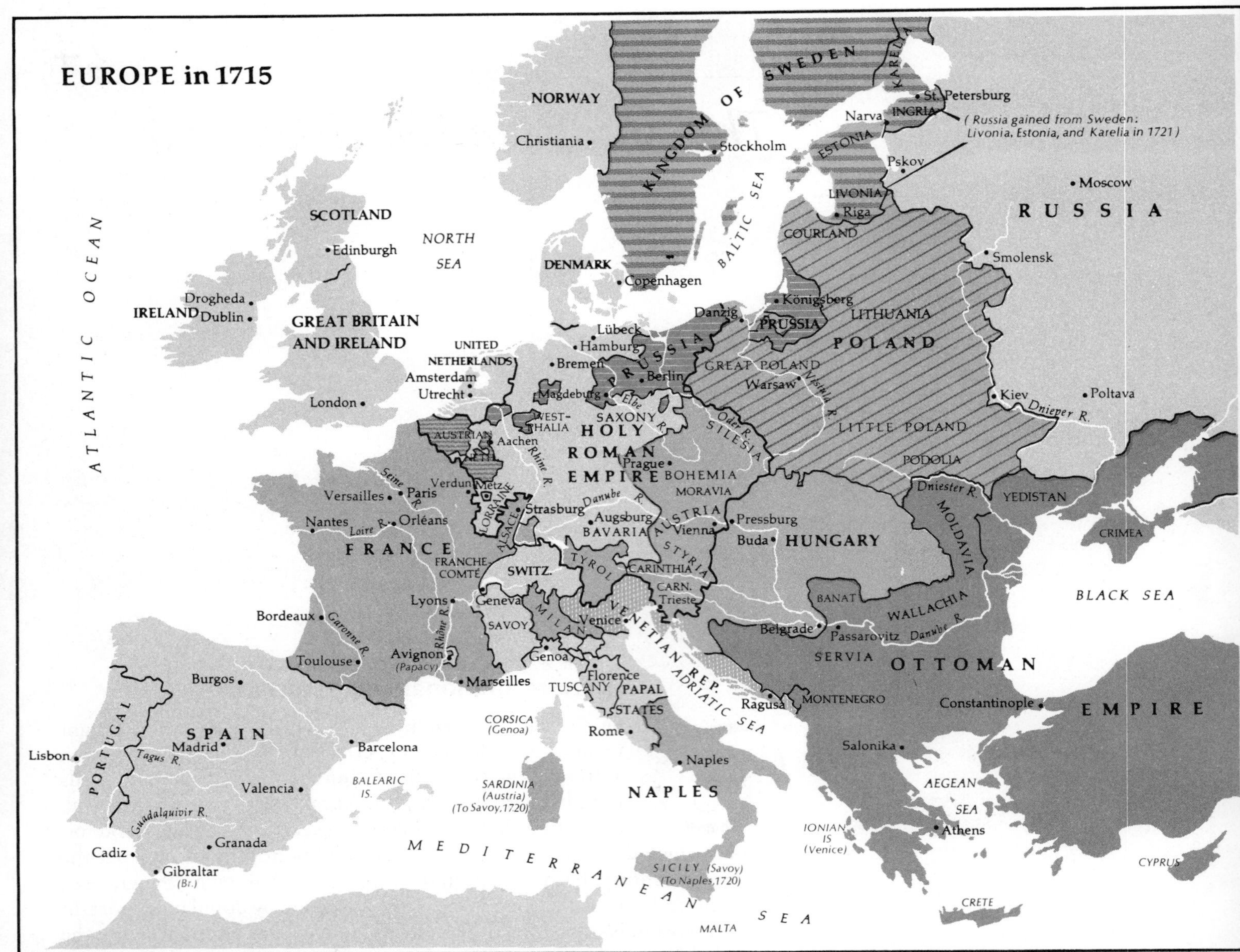

been impossible in prior centuries, when the level of literacy was low even in the upper class. The philosophes were able to reach a wide, literate upper- and middle-class public, but not the poor. The lower classes throughout the eighteenth century remained, in general, as oppressed as before, although they joined the bourgeoisie at the end to overthrow the monarchy and to enthrone the goddess of reason. The philosophes had a rather abstract, if genuine, concern for the poor, but they associated primarily with the polished, witty, urbane men and women who frequented the Parisian *salons.* Paris was now replacing Versailles as the center of cultural life.

The Salon

The Hôtel de Soubise, designed by Germain Boffrand and begun in 1732, is an example of the smaller and more intimate quarters fashioned for the nobility in Paris (Fig. 24-1). Located on small and sometimes awkwardly shaped urban sites, these buildings had a fairly simple exterior; the architects and clients concentrated on the interiors, where the salon was used for small gatherings that replaced the great festivities of the court. The salons were run primarily by women—Madame du Deffand and Madame Geoffrin were two of the most celebrated—and the sexes conversed and exchanged ideas on an equal footing. These conversations were also means for spreading ideas. As the century progressed, educated men and women everywhere strove to be recognized as "enlightened"; even the sovereigns of Europe sought to win the title of "enlightened monarch."

24-1 *Germain Boffrand, Salon de la Princesse, Hôtel de Soubise, Paris. (Giraudon/Art Resource, NY)*

Foundations of the Enlightenment: John Locke (1632–1704)

How did the Enlightenment develop, and what were its common tenets? Essentially, the French philosophes' conceptions of the sources of knowledge were confused. They claimed to be *empiricists,* deriving their ideas from experience, but they also espoused a belief in natural rights determined by examination of the human conscience. In *rationalist* fashion they used these natural rights as criteria for judging both the society and government of their time. The confusions in their thought, however, were in a sense inherited from the late-seventeenth-century English philosopher Locke, from whom they took much of the methodological approach.

John Locke was the author of two fundamental tracts, *Essay on Human Understanding* and *Essay Concerning the True Original Extent and End of Civil Government.* In the tradition of Bacon, Locke held in his *Essay on Human Understanding* that all knowledge comes from sense perception. The mind begins as a blank slate, a *tabula rasa,* and what the mind comes to know is a product of combining perceptions and reflection on those combinations. What this in effect meant was that people were products of their environment: change the environment and the person is changed. Inspired in his turn by the scientific discoveries taking place in his time, Locke attempted to establish laws of human behavior by *inductive* means.

Like his compatriot Hobbes a few decades earlier, Locke begins his *Essay Concerning Civil Government* by assuming that originally people lived in a state of nature before the existence of government. Locke had the Indians living in the New World very much in mind. Whereas Hobbes saw primitive people as locked in an endless struggle for self-preservation, isolated and hostile to one another, Locke viewed them in nowhere near such dire circumstances. For Locke, people in that state possessed by nature certain rights to life, liberty, and property. These natural rights could not be proved by experience but were deduced by an examination of the conscience. Because people are by nature sociable, society existed in the state of nature, even without government. Nonetheless, because individuals could not adequately protect all their rights without government, they created the state to guarantee them. Whereas in Hobbes's view people gave up all liberty to escape their miserable predicament, in Locke's they created a state with limited power, one whose executive was closely watched by a legislature. If, however, the state ceased to perform the express functions for which it was created and began to rob and oppress its citizens, then Locke advocated revolution and the creation of a new government.

The Philosophes' Political and Religious Doctrines

Empiricism and a rationalistic doctrine of natural rights formed the core of the Enlightenment. With a few exceptions, the philosophes believed that all people were essentially equal, in that they all possessed reason. As a creature of reason and equal to every other person by nature, every individual had the right to life, liberty, and a chance at happiness. Associated with these natural rights were others like the right to freedom of speech and to religious liberty. The philosophes deplored the intolerance to Protestants still practiced by the Catholic Church in France; in fact, they viewed the Church itself as a source of superstition, ignorance, and subservience. Priests and others in the hierarchy served to benight, rather than to enlighten, the multitudes. A philosophe motto, "Crush the infamous!" (*Écrasez l'infâme*) referred to all irrational and superstitious forces but was directed primarily against the Church.

Although the philosophes supported tolerance for Protestants, they had little respect for any Christian doctrines. They called their own form of religion *deism.* Drawing heavily on the conception of God fostered by Descartes and the Scientific Revolution, they held that God had created the world and set it running on its own, as a watchmaker makes a watch. Heaven and hell were not to be found in the hereafter but on this earth. If human beings would follow their God-given reason rather than their momentary passions, they could create a world in which everyone would enjoy felicity and peace.

Although their ideas were to influence the revolution, the majority of the philosophes politically were proponents of *despotism,* or rule by one enlightened person, harking back to Plato's notion of the philosopher-king. Turgot, a philosophe and one of Louis XV's ministers, declared, "Give me five years of despotism and I will make France free." Given the situation in France, the greatest concern was to establish a basic equality among the classes and to eliminate privilege; the only way to do this practically was to give the central government absolute control of reform. In England, where, despite the existence of classes, there was a basic equality before the law, Locke stressed constitutional monarchy; in France the worst source of oppression came from the privileged classes and groups. If there was to be toleration and freedom of the press in France, it would have to come from the king: the Church and other interest groups were violently opposed to such freedoms.

The reason that the French did not enjoy natural rights in the present was the fault of evil institutions. People are good, but corrupted institutions have damaged them. Reform the institutions and people will improve. Indeed, the philosophes believed that if the proper institutions could be designed, people might eventually perfect themselves. Thus the philosophes introduced a doctrine of progress. They placed great hope in the reform of the state because they saw it as a central means for reforming all the other institutions of society.

Diderot and the Encyclopedia

The philosophes were the first to broadcast an idea both widely accepted and under attack today: progress through education. If human beings are to be enlightened, to be able to use their reason to unmask lies and superstitions, then they must *know.* To this end one of the most intelligent and versatile of their number, Denis Diderot (1713–1784), conceived and directed the compiling of a vast encyclopedia called *Dictionnaire Raisonné des Sciences, des Arts et des Métiers.* French authorities saw the whole idea as dangerous—twice they suppressed the encyclopedia. It contained articles, written by philosophes and others, on everything from how to make wallpaper to the definition of God. It was full of information on science and technology. Eighteenth-century socialites, as well as the philosophes, were passionate amateur scientists, often performing experiments for company after dinner in their elegant salons.

Voltaire (1694–1778)

A contributor to the encyclopedia and the giant of the French Enlightenment was François-Marie Arouet, better known by his pen name Voltaire. Probably no other writer was so adored and so hated during his lifetime. Not a profoundly original thinker, he was endowed with an ability to see through hypocrisy and delusion as well as with a witty, satiric style that he used mercilessly against his enemies and anti-Enlightenment forces.

Son of a bourgeois lawyer and an aspiring poet, the young Voltaire wanted nothing so much as to ingratiate himself with the court nobility; with his wit, intelligence, and good education, he accomplished this. Becoming well known as a writer of neoclassical tragedies, he discovered that in spite of his talents he was not socially equal to aristocrats when one of them had him publicly beaten and then thrown into the infamous French prison, the Bastille. He also suffered from an inefficient censorship law, which arbitrarily swooped down on a victim and punished him with imprisonment or exile. After his release from the Bastille, Voltaire was sent into exile in England, where he found a constitutional government, an enlightened noble class that obeyed the law, a tolerant spirit, and the works of John Locke. It was Voltaire who introduced Locke's ideas into France. He also brought back to France the idea that its government and society could, indeed should, be changed. But Voltaire's *Philosophical Letters* (1734) on his impressions of England were seized by the French censors; the philosophe then sought a safe haven in northeastern France at Cirey with his friend and mistress for the next ten years, Emilie du Châtelet.

Madame du Châtelet herself deserves attention as

24-2 Mariane Loir, *Portrait de Gabrielle Emilie Ce Tonnelier de Bretevil, Marquise du Châtelet.* Bordeaux Musée des Beaux-Arts. (Cliché du M.B.A. de Bordeaux)

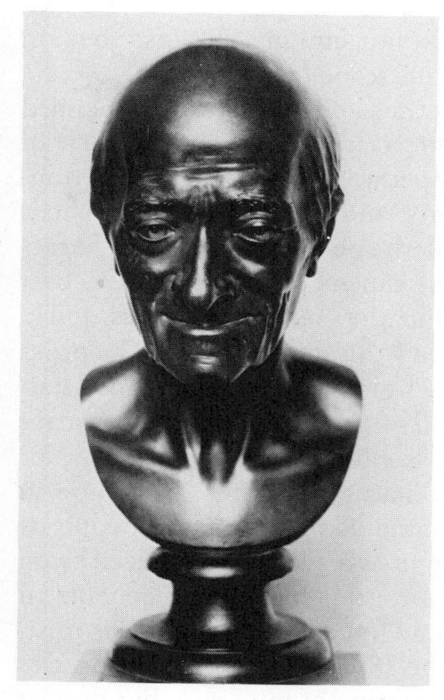

24-3 *Jean Antoine Houdon,* Bust of Voltaire, *Louvre, Paris. (Art Resource, NY)*

one of the liberated women of eighteenth-century France. Her portrait (Fig. 24-2), by a woman, Marianne Loir, reveals a subtle intelligence and love of learning coupled with a smile—typical features of the Enlightenment. Forced into an early marriage with an unintellectual nobleman, she astonished Parisian society by exiling herself to a small town to devote herself to intellectual pursuits. She was a mathematician who wrote several treatises on natural philosophy as well as mathematics. While Voltaire lived with her, they observed a rigid schedule filled with scientific experiments, studies, and theatrical performances put on by themselves and their visitors. Another of Voltaire's ambitions while at Cirey was to write history in a manner worthy of a scientific age. With the desire to create a record of the advance of civilization and to deal with all of the creations of the human mind—art, literature, science, business, and politics—Voltaire composed *The Century of Louis XIV,* still a classic of its kind.

In 1750 Voltaire left his country haven to live at the court of Frederick the Great of Prussia, a man whom many of the philosophes saw as the prototype of the "enlightened despot." Eventually he settled on an estate that he bought at Ferney, just outside Geneva but in France, where he became an enthusiastic farmer. It is there that he wrote, apparently with astounding speed, the most famous of what he called his "philosophical tales," *Candide.* One can see the influence of the satisfaction of cultivating the earth after suffering the vicissitudes of life in the tale's conclusion. Voltaire devoted the rest of his life not only to farming and writing but also to espousing various causes in the name of enlightened justice. He exposed some of the miseries of the French peasants who lived around him and took up the cause of Jean Calas, an aged French Protestant executed by torture after being falsely charged with murdering his son because he had converted to Catholicism. Voltaire exposed the facts of the scandal in his *Treatise on Toleration,* which concludes with "An Address to the Deity." A deist, Voltaire made the plea for tolerance in matters of religion, along with the demand for social justice, a constant throughout his life.

The old Voltaire, admirably portrayed in a statue by the sculptor Houdon (Fig. 24-3) was confident that he had witnessed the triumph of reason in his lifetime. "It is certain," he wrote, "that the knowledge of nature, the skeptical attitude toward old fables dignified by the name of history, a healthy metaphysic freed from the absurdities of the schools, are the fruits of that century when reason was perfected."

He was to see Paris only once more, and to die there, but because he would not "retract his errors" to a priest, his body was not allowed to be buried in consecrated ground. Thirteen years after his death, after the revolution that he did not live to see, his body was brought back to Paris and interred in the Pantheon. Skeptical and cynical as he was, he undoubtedly would not have approved of the revolution. Yet the crowds that came to honor him in 1790 inscribed on his tomb, "He taught us to be free."

Voltaire's life was thus an active one that spanned almost the entire eighteenth century. The products of his pen were many: poetry, philosophy, history, tragedies, pamphlets, essays, and the genre for which he is now best remembered, the philosophical tale. Characteristic of the Enlightenment, his talents were best suited to forms in which he could exercise his quick, sharp style and especially his gift for satire. The progress of Voltaire's thought may be roughly divided into the periods before and after 1755, when a significant event occurred. The earthquake at Lisbon on November 1, the worst natural disaster in Europe in centuries, killed an estimated fifty thousand people. If Voltaire's earlier thought had been characterized by an unshakable belief in progress and in the benefits of civilization, he was now forced to reevaluate his position. His "Poem on the Disaster of Lisbon" expresses compassion for the suffering of humanity but disgust for the proponents of the doctrine of optimism. He was to develop this vision more fully in *Candide,* written in 1758 and published in 1759.

One of the targets of Voltaire's satire in *Candide* was the doctrine of the German philosopher Gottfried Wilhelm Leibnitz (1646–1716). This doctrine, which came to be known as optimism, postulated that God, having an infinite choice of worlds to create, had decided to create a world containing evil as well as good because evil is necessary in order for certain goods, such as free will, to exist. The world that we live in is thus "the best of all possible worlds." Voltaire, who had earlier espoused this philosophy, saw it after the Lisbon earthquake as naive and distorting.

If *Candide* were only a satire on an outmoded philosophical doctrine, it would have long ago been forgotten. But it is also a great adventure story and, at the same time, because of its flagrant improbabilities, a parody of the adventure story and the romance. It contains a utopian vision—the country of El Dorado, significantly in the New World—which shows Voltaire's basic faith in human nature, but it viciously satirizes human pretensions, greed, and fanaticism. In the end it is a testimony to neither optimism nor pessimism but to the ability of the indomitable human spirit to adapt itself and to do what it can to better life on earth.

Montesquieu (1689–1755)

One of the greatest objections leveled against the philosophes by later generations is that they had no appreciation for the effect of history on humankind. Too analytical, they saw humanity in the abstract and were therefore unable to effect reform within a historical context. One perceptive critic of the eighteenth century, Charles-Louis de Secondat, the baron de Montesquieu, attacked this neglect of history on the very same grounds. His belief was that people are basically a product of history and that constitutions must be tailored to meet the conditions and historical traditions of the particular society.

Yet Montesquieu himself is usually regarded as a philosophe on the grounds that despite his historical interests he, like most of the others in the movement, was a deist, a believer in natural rights, and a reformer, especially of the penal code. Although he was also an empiricist, he included history as a vital part of the human experience; his insistence on history as an important factor when considering reforms of society and government led him to be politically conservative. A member of the privileged provincial nobility, he was both by self-interest and conviction antagonistic to political reforms predicated on the belief that the past could simply be wiped away. Frankly fearing for personal liberty in a state ruled by a despot, no matter how enlightened, he found Locke's theory of an executive checked by a legislature very appealing. Admiring English government but basically misunderstanding its constitutional machinery, Montesquieu developed a theory of separation of powers among legislative, judicial, and executive agencies; he insisted that the individual could be free only where the power of one of these branches of government was checked by the other two. Of almost no importance in France, the theory had tremendous influence in the conception of the United States Constitution.

An issue dealt with by Montesquieu in *The Spirit of the Laws,* which did not take effect in America until much later, was the question of slavery. Seventeenth-century absolutists and capitalists had accepted slavery in the course of their trade; Montesquieu and other philosophes, scrutinizing the institution under the light of reason, found it unnatural and evil. It is clear that slavery would be abhorrent to those who believe in the natural rights of human beings. (We will examine the paradox of its continuation in the new, "enlightened" United States in the next chapter.)

Rousseau (1712–1778)

Jean-Jacques Rousseau was a paradoxical figure who in some ways belongs with the philosophes and in others may be seen as a precursor of romanticism. Of humble origins, Rousseau was born in the city-state of Geneva, in Switzerland; he came to Paris at the age of thirty after fifteen years of living a vagabond existence. An insecure, unhappy man, suffering from a sense of persecution and an embarrassing urinary problem, Rousseau found the source of his difficulties in the artificiality of society. Among the many contradictions of his life was his writing in praise of the simple, virtuous life in Geneva while he continued to live in Paris.

In two essays that brought him his first literary honors, the *Discourse on the Sciences and Arts* (1749) and *On the Origin of Inequality Among Men* (1755), he attacked the corruptions of society and characterized the progress that people had made in the arts and sciences as contributing to this degeneration. Accordingly, he idealized the state of nature, the time when people were originally free. Although he did not deny the rational capacity of humanity, Rousseau believed that the deepest part of the human being was at the level of the instincts and that by nature people are loving, sympathetic, and kind. When Voltaire finished reading *On the Origins,* he commented that Roûsseau's work made him feel like getting down on four legs.

In the society of his own time Rousseau idealized the lower classes, who seemed to him to be living closest to the natural life. In works like *Émile,* a treatise on "natural" education, and his novel, *The New Heloise,* he depicted the beauties of the simple life led amid nature. So popular were these works by the last quarter of the century that all over France the upper classes, including the queen herself, entertained themselves by dressing as shepherds and peasants, picnicking and playing in the woods and fields. It became fashionable to speak of one's feelings in public, to act "naturally," and to idealize the poor.

Rousseau's most important work on political theory, *The Social Contract* (1762), reflects the contradictions found in this tortured genius who endeavored to reconcile into a system the philosophe inheritance with his own intense experience of life. Terminology like "contract" and "state of nature" is that of Locke and Voltaire. On humanity's emerging from the state of nature to set up a government, the philosophes commonly spoke of a contract being made among the members of the society and the government that they created. This contract was to stipulate the duties and limitations of the government and to afford a legal basis for destroying the government if it violated the terms.

In Rousseau's hands the language of the Enlightenment remains, but the meanings are very different. Whereas previously he had seen humanity as good in the state of nature and subsequently corrupted by evil institutions, in this work human beings in nature are depicted as brutes driven by their impulses and appetites. The individual, however, is less self-conscious and rational in Rousseau's state of nature than in Hobbes's, and the transformation of the personality once society has been formed is much greater. For Rousseau, a person becomes truly human only when living in a civil society: "By dint of being exercised, his sentiments become ennobled and his whole soul becomes so elevated that, but for the fact that misuse of the new conditions still, at times, degrades him to a point below that from which he has emerged, he would unceasingly bless the day which freed him for ever from his ancient state, and turned him from a limited and stupid animal into an intelligent being and a man." Against his own earlier view and that of earlier philosophes, Rousseau maintains that the state is not a creation of fully formed human beings, but rather that people become human only by living in a community. There is no interest in returning to a state of nature; the task is to create a better society where one's humanity can be fully realized.

Moreover, for Rousseau the contract is not an agreement between a society and its government but between the various free individuals in the state of nature to create the society itself. Driven by the desire for self-preservation, brutish and lonely people unite themselves out of fear and voluntarily surrender their natural freedom in exchange for the benefits of social life. Merging their individual wills into a "general will," they agree to obey everything that "will" decrees. Rousseau's ideal society is small enough so that the collective body of the citizens can assemble to express the general will, which rules that state. The actual government consists just of administrators who carry out its orders. Rousseau probably had in mind a society like the city-state of Geneva where he grew up. But whereas Geneva was governed by an *aristocracy,* Rousseau's ideal state was a *democracy.*

What is the general will? One thing is clear: for Rousseau it is not the will of the majority. Often the vote of the multitude reflects only the combined self-interest of every individual and not the public interest. For Rousseau the general will is mysteriously found in each citizen below the level of his individual selfish will. It is the common will that seeks the good of the whole community; when it speaks, it reflects the true interests even of those citizens who violently opposed its decision. In the case of citizens who differ with the general will, they are literally forced to be free, that is, to accept what the deepest part of their being really wants.

Voltaire and other philosophes envisaged people as atoms of rationality that were alike all over the earth. Rousseau saw human beings rather as essentially bundles of feelings and instincts determined to a large extent by the society in which they live. For Rousseau an individual's community was not simply a convenience; rather, it provided the framework in which the individual realized himself or herself. But for full personal development to occur, every member of the community had to participate in deliberations. Only in this way could the collective, or general, will be expressed and the good of all best be served. Of course, by maintaining that even the will of the majority does not necessarily express that will, he left the door open for the rise of a demagogue who knew better what the people needed than they did themselves. At various times, and with valid reasons, Rousseau has been called the father of democracy, socialism, communism, nationalism, and fascism.

Enlightenment Feminism: Mary Wollstonecraft (1759–1797)

We have seen that aristocratic and some upper-middle-class women played an influential role in the salons and other intellectual circles of eighteenth-century society, particularly in France. It is clear, however, that the educated woman who considered herself equal to men remained the exception rather than the rule and that in general women were expected to limit their education to domestic arts along with a few "accomplishments," such as singing; to interest themselves primarily in fashion, gossip, and flirtation; and not to meddle in the affairs of men. Rousseau, the radical thinker whose ideas challenged so many of the fundamental assumptions of his society, remained fundamentally conventional in his attitudes toward women. In his treatise on education entitled *Emile,* in which he proposes many of the theories that underlie modern ideas on "progressive" education with regard to boys, he maintains that women's role is to be subservient to men and that women's education should be structured accordingly:

> For this reason the education of women should always be relative to men. To please, to be useful to us, to make us love and esteem them, to educate us when young, and take care of us when grown up, to advise us, to console us, to render our lives easy and agreeable—these are the duties of women at all times, and what they should be taught in their infancy.[1]

Despite the fact that Rousseau's attitude represented the norm, the eighteenth century witnessed several challenges to the inferior status of women. In England, Lady Mary Wortley, whose pen name was "Sophia," referred to women's social position as one of "slaves" and argued for better education and more independence for her sex. The rhetoric of the French Revolution supplied fuel for the feminist fire. In France, Olympe de Gouges attempted to extend the revolution's doctrine of the Rights of Man by publishing a pamphlet entitled *Declaration of the Rights of Woman and of the Female Citizen* in 1791. Advocates for better education for women included the philosophe Condorcet, the English writer Catherine Macaulay, and Mary Wollstonecraft.

Wollstonecraft's *A Vindication of the Rights of Woman,* published in 1792, in many way prefigures some of the feminist ideas that have become common currency in our own time. A middle-class woman who shared the Enlightenment thinkers' disdain for the "decadent" aristocracy, Wollstonecraft worked as a governess and a teacher, attempted to found a school, and lived for a while in Paris, where she fell in love with an American. She eventually married her old friend, the English social thinker William Godwin, and had with him a daughter, Mary Wollstonecraft Godwin. She died of "childbed fever" at the age of thirty-eight. Wollstonecraft's stated aim in her treatise was "to persuade women to endeavour to acquire strength, both of mind and body. . . ."Incorporating revolutionary ideas, she paints a rather dismal portrayal of the lives of contemporary women while advocating both domestic virtue and educational and professional achievement.

Aspects of Painting in the Enlightenment

Many of the tendencies found in the philosophes—the movement from the nobility to the bourgeois, from the grandiose to the petite, from tragedy to satire, as well as the interests in science and in society—are reflected in the art of the early eighteenth century. An example of the new middle-class passion for science and home-made experiments may be seen in the painting *Experiment with the Air-Pump* (1768) by an Englishman, Joseph Wright (Fig. 24-4). Exhibited in London, it would have appealed to Diderot and Voltaire, for it

---

[1]Jean-Jacques Rousseau, *Emile or A Treatise on Education,* ed. W. H. Payne (New York and London, 1906), p. 263.

24-4 *Joseph Wright,* Experiment with the Air-Pump. *(Reproduced by courtesy of the Trustees, The National Gallery, London)*

records a scientific experiment in explicit detail. The air pump, on the table in the center of the composition, has been purchased by a prosperous bourgeois to entertain and to educate. The glass globe contains a dove that will die when the air is pumped from the globe to create a vacuum. The two young girls are sad, but the others, youths and elders, watch with interest. The surfaces and textures of objects are rendered with extreme *verisimilitude*—the painter is as observant as the scientist.

Paintings such as this indicate one characteristic of eighteenth-century art: the decline in importance of the art of the court. Another type, a more intimate and sensual art, replaced the neoclassicism of Le Brun and his school. Watteau's *Pilgrimage to Cythera* (Color Plate XXI) is thematically the progeny of Rubens's *Garden of Love* (Color Plate XV). Yet these couples who move through the forest of the enchanted island of Venus are not arriving, but leaving, to return to the real world. Watteau has given a sense of melancholy to the beautiful but shallow world of entertainments and parties that seemed more and more to occupy the life of the nobility.

Boucher, who followed Watteau, continued the decorative and intimate character of his art while adding a more sexual, sensuous content (Fig. 24-5). The golden colors, the flesh tones and textures, and the delightful abandon of these figures are the subject. Mythological or other themes are only an excuse for these handsome paintings that celebrate the life of the senses.

The philosophe Diderot, who also wrote essays on contemporary art, was not impressed by these frivolous objects. Diderot's taste ran rather toward *genre* painting—scenes from everyday life among the peasants and the lower classes. In particular he praised Chardin and Greuze, two painters whose work have only the most superficial elements in common. Chardin imparts to his subjects, whether a maid, a mother and child, or a still life, a monumental and quiet objectivity that recalls Vermeer (Color Plate XIX). Chardin's pictures of still-life subjects seem constructed from a careful, loving observation of nature that renders textures, surfaces, and light with verisimilitude (Color Plate XXII). Order and harmony are extracted from the simple events and objects of the middle classes. We know that Chardin meant his pictures to educate and to instruct in virtue, but the depiction of objects seems to mean as much to him as the portrayal of a moral. It was Chardin's naturalism that so appealed to Diderot; yet, in contrast to Vermeer, Chardin's paint has a creamy sensual surface that is as covertly appealing as his subjects.

Greuze's work appealed to Diderot because his scenes suggested narratives that praised virtue or had a didactic moral. Too frequently, these scenes also had a marked sentimentalizing attitude toward the event. *The Village Bride,* shown in the Salon of 1761, is a sample of his work. A youthful bride watches while the dowry is negotiated, the grandfather admonishes, the mother is pensive, the hen in the foreground protects her chicks (Fig. 24-6). These sweet, clean, honest, virtuous, natural peasants provide a vivid contrast to what we know of life. But these pictures appealed to the upper bourgeoisie of the mid-eighteenth century, who saw in these peasants natural virtue.

24-5 *François Boucher,* Diana after the Hunt. *(Musée Cognacq-Jay/Photographie Bulloz, Paris)*

24-6 *Jean-Baptiste Greuze,* The Village Bride, *1761, Louvre, Paris. (Art Resource, NY)*

Reading Selections

Voltaire

From *Candide*

(Translation by T. Smollett, revised by James Thornton; abridged)

Chapter I

How Candide Was Brought Up in a Magnificent Castle, and How He Was Driven from Thence

In the country of Westphalia, in the castle of the most noble Baron of Thunder-ten-tronckh, lived a youth whom nature had endowed with a most sweet disposition. His face was the true index of his mind. He had a solid judgment joined to the most unaffected simplicity; and hence, I presume, he had his name of Candide. The old servants of the house suspected him to have been the son of the Baron's sister, by a mighty good sort of a gentleman of the neighbourhood, whom that young lady refused to marry, because he could produce no more than threescore and eleven quarterings in his arms;[1] the rest of the genealogical tree belonging to the family having been lost through the injuries of time.

The Baron was one of the most powerful lords in Westphalia; for his castle had not only a gate, but even windows; and his great hall was hung with tapestry. He used to hunt with his mastiffs and spaniels instead of greyhounds; his groom served him for huntsman; and the parson of the parish officiated as grand almoner.[2] He was called "My Lord" by all his people, and he never told a story but every one laughed at it.

My lady Baroness weighed three hundred and fifty pounds, consequently was a person of no small consideration; and then she did the honours of the house with a dignity that commanded universal respect. Her daughter Cunegund was about seventeen years of age, fresh coloured, comely, plump, and desirable. The Baron's son seemed to be a youth in every respect worthy of his father. Pangloss the preceptor was the oracle of the family, and little Candide listened to his instructions with all the simplicity natural to his age and disposition.

Master Pangloss taught the metaphysico-theologo-cosmolo-nigology. He could prove to admiration that there is no effect without a cause; and that, in this best of all possible worlds, the Baron's castle was the most magnificent of all castles, and my lady the best of all possible baronesses.

"It is demonstrable," said he, "that things cannot be otherwise than they are; for as all things have been created for some end, they must necessarily be created for the best end. Observe, for instance, the nose is formed for spectacles, therefore we wear spectacles. The legs are visibly designed for stockings, accordingly we wear stockings. Stones were made to be hewn, and to construct castles, therefore my lord has a magnificent castle; for the greatest baron in the province ought to be the best lodged. Swine were intended to be eaten; therefore we eat pork all the year round: and they who assert that everything is right do not express themselves correctly; they should say, that everything is best."

Candide listened attentively, and believed implicitly; for he thought Miss Cunegund excessively handsome, though he never had the courage to tell her so. He concluded that next to the happiness of being Baron of Thunder-ten-tronckh, the next was that of being Miss Cunegund, the next that of seeing her every day, and the last that of hearing the doctrine of Master Pangloss, the greatest philosopher of the whole province, and consequently of the whole world.

One day, when Miss Cunegund went to take a walk in a little neighbouring wood, which was called a park, she saw, through the bushes, the sage Doctor Pangloss giving a lecture in experimental physics to her mother's chambermaid, a little brown wench, very

[1] He could not prove that he was entirely of a noble lineage.

[2] The one who officially distributes alms.

pretty, and very tractable. As Miss Cunegund had a great disposition for the sciences, she observed with the utmost attention the experiments which were repeated before her eyes; she perfectly well understood the force of the doctor's reasoning upon causes and effects. She retired greatly flurried, quite pensive, and filled with the desire of knowledge, imagining that she might be a sufficing reason for young Candide, and he for her.[3]

On her way back she happened to meet Candide; she blushed, he blushed also: she wished him a good morning in a faltering tone; he returned the salute, without knowing what he said. The next day, as they were rising from dinner, Cunegund and Candide slipped behind the screen. She dropped her handkerchief, the young man picked it up. She innocently took hold of his hand, and he as innocently kissed hers with a warmth, a sensibility, a grace—all very extraordinary; their lips met; their eyes sparkled; their knees trembled; their hands strayed. The Baron of Thunder-ten-tronckh chanced to come by; he beheld the cause and effect, and, without hesitation, saluted Candide with some notable kicks on the breech, and drove him out of doors. Miss Cunegund fainted away, and, as soon as she came to herself, the Baroness boxed her ears. Thus a general consternation was spread over this most magnificent and most agreeable of all possible castles.

Candide is impressed into the Bulgarian army, escapes, and makes his way to Holland. A kindly Anabaptist saves him from poverty and starvation and he encounters Dr. Pangloss, who has acquired syphilis from the baron's maid, Pacquette. James, the Anabaptist, pays for Pangloss's cure, and they sail together for Lisbon.

Chapter V

A Tempest, a Shipwreck, an Earthquake; and What Else Befell Dr. Pangloss, Candide, and James the Anabaptist

One half of the passengers, weakened and half dead with the inconceivable anguish which the rolling of a vessel at sea occasions to the nerves and all the humours of the body, tossed about in opposite directions, were lost to all sense of the danger that surrounded them. The other made loud outcries, or betook themselves to their prayers; the sails were blown into shivers, and the masts were brought by the board. The vessel leaked. Every one was busily employed, but nobody could be either heard or obeyed. The Anabaptist, being upon deck, lent a helping hand as well as the rest, when a brutish sailor gave him a blow, and laid him speechless; but, with the violence of the blow, the tar himself tumbled head foremost overboard, and fell upon a piece of the broken mast, which he immediately grasped. Honest James flew to his assistance, and hauled him in again, but, in the attempt, was thrown overboard himself in sight of the sailor, who left him to perish without taking the least notice of him. Candide, who beheld all that passed, and saw his benefactor one moment rising above water, and the next swallowed up by the merciless waves, was preparing to jump after him; but was prevented by the philosopher Pangloss, who demonstrated to him that the coast of Lisbon had been made on purpose for the Anabaptist to be drowned there. While he was proving his argument *à priori,* the ship foundered, and the whole crew perished, except Pangloss, Candide, and the brute of a sailor who had been the means of drowning the good Anabaptist. The villain swam ashore; but Pangloss and Candide got to land upon a plank.

As soon as they had recovered a little, they walked towards Lisbon; with what little money they had left they thought to save themselves from starving after having escaped drowning.

Scarce had they done lamenting the loss of their benefactor and set foot in the city, when they perceived the earth to tremble under their feet, and the sea, swelling and foaming in the harbour, dash in pieces the vessels that were riding at anchor. Large sheets of flames and cinders covered the streets and public places; the houses tottered, and were tumbled topsy-turvy, even to their foundations, which were themselves destroyed, and thirty thousand inhabitants of both sexes, young and old, were buried beneath the ruins.

The sailor, whistling and swearing, cried, "Damn it, there's something to be got here."

"What can be the sufficing reason of this phenomenon?" said Pangloss.

"It is certainly the day of judgment," said Candide.

The sailor, defying death in the pursuit of plunder, rushed into the midst of the ruin, where he found some money, with which he got drunk, and after he had slept himself sober, he purchased the favours of the first good-natured wench that came his way, amidst the ruins of demolished houses, and the groans of half-

---

[3] Allusions to the terminology of Leibnitz.

buried and expiring persons. Pangloss pulled him by the sleeve.

"Friend," said he, "this is not right, you trespass against the universal reason, and have mistaken your time."

"Death and zounds!" answered the other, "I am a sailor, and born at Batavia, and have trampled four times upon the crucifix in as many voyages to Japan: you are come to a good hand with your universal reason."

Candide, who had been wounded by some pieces of stone that fell from the houses, lay stretched in the street, almost covered with rubbish.

"For God's sake," said he to Pangloss, "get me a little wine and oil. I am dying."

"This concussion of the earth is no new thing," replied Pangloss, "the city of Lima,[4] in America, experienced the same last year; the same cause, the same effects: there is certainly a train of sulphur all the way under ground from Lima to Lisbon."

"Nothing more probable," said Candide; "but, for the love of God, a little oil and wine."

"Probable!" replied the philosopher, "I maintain that the thing is demonstrable."

Candide fainted away, and Pangloss fetched him some water from a neighbouring spring.

The next day, in searching among the ruins, they found some eatables with which they repaired their exhausted strength. After this, they assisted the inhabitants in relieving the distressed and wounded. Some, whom they had humanely assisted, gave them as good a dinner as could be expected under such terrible circumstances. The repast, indeed, was mournful, and the company moistened their bread with their tears; but Pangloss endeavoured to comfort them under this affliction by affirming that things could not be otherwise than they were.

"For," said he, "all this is for the very best end; for if there is a volcano at Lisbon, it could be on no other spot; for it is impossible for things not to be as they are, for everything is for the best."

By his side sat a little man dressed in black, who was one of the familiars of the Inquisition.[5] This person, taking him up with great politeness, said, "Possibly, my good Sir, you do not believe in original sin; for if everything is best, there could have been no such thing as the fall or punishment of man."

"I humbly ask your Excellency's pardon," answered Pangloss, still more politely; "for the fall of man, and the curse consequent thereupon necessarily entered into the system of the best of worlds."

"That is as much as to say, Sir," rejoined the familiar, "you do not believe in free will."

"Your Excellency will be so good as to excuse me," said Pangloss; "free will is consistent with absolute necessity; for it was necessary we should be free, for in that the will——"

Pangloss was in the midst of his proposition, when the familiar made a sign to the attendant who was helping him to a glass of port wine.

Chapter VI

How the Portuguese Made a Suberb Auto-Da-Fé[6] to Prevent Any Future Earthquakes, and How Candide Underwent Public Flagellation

After the earthquake which had destroyed three-quarters of the city of Lisbon, the sages of that country could think of no means more effectual to preserve the kingdom from utter ruin, than to entertain the people with an *auto-da-fé,* it having been decided by the University of Coimbra that burning a few people alive by a slow fire, and with great ceremony, is an infallible secret to prevent earthquakes.

In consequence thereof they had seized on a Biscayan for marrying his godmother, and on two Portuguese for taking out the bacon of a larded pullet chicken they were eating.[7] After dinner, they came and secured Dr. Pangloss, and his pupil Candide; the one for speaking his mind, and the other for seeming to approve what he had said. They were conducted to separate apartments, extremely cool, where they were never incommoded with the sun. Eight days afterwards they were each dressed in a *fanbenito,*[8] and their heads were adorned with paper mitres. The mitre and *fanbenito* worn by Candide were painted with flames reversed, and with devils that had neither tails nor claws; but Dr. Pangloss's devils had both tails and

---

[4]There had been an earthquake in Peru in 1746.

[5]The Spanish Inquisition was created by Ferdinand and Isabella in 1478 to deal with heresy especially among recently converted Jews and Moors in Spain. With the conquests in the New World agencies of the Inquisition were established there as well. "Familiars" were its police officers.

[6]Literally, "act of faith": the public execution, often by burning, of heretics by the Inquisition.

[7]Thus they were thought to be Jews. How does Voltaire satirize religious intolerance?

[8]A kind of garment worn by the prisoners of the Inquisition.

claws, and his flames were upright. In these habits they marched in procession, and heard a very pathetic sermon, which was followed by a chant, beautifully intoned. Candide was flogged in regular cadence, while the chant was being sung; the Biscayan, and the two men who would not eat bacon, were burnt, and Pangloss was hanged, although this is not a common custom at these solemnities. The same day there was another earthquake, which made most dreadful havoc.

Candide, amazed, terrified, confounded, astonished, and trembling from head to foot, said to himself, "If this is the best of all possible worlds, what are the others? If I had only been whipped, I could have put up with it, as I did among the Bulgarians; but, O my dear Pangloss! thou greatest of philosophers! that ever I should live to see thee hanged, without knowing for what! O my dear Anabaptist, thou best of men, that it should be thy fate to be drowned in the very harbour! O Miss Cunegund, you mirror of young ladies! that it should be your fate to have your belly ripped open."

He was making the best of his way from the place where he had been preached to, whipped, absolved, and received benediction, when he was accosted by an old woman, who said to him, "Take courage, my son, and follow me."

Chapter VII

How the Old Woman Took Care of Candide, and How He Found the Object of His Love

Candide followed the old woman, though without taking courage, to a decayed house where she gave him a pot of pomatum to anoint his sores, showed him a very neat bed, with a suit of clothes hanging up by it; and set victuals and drink before him.

"There," said she, "eat, drink, and sleep, and may our blessed Lady of Atocha, and the great St. Anthony of Padua, and the illustrious St. James of Compostella, take you under their protection. I shall be back tomorrow."

Candide, struck with amazement at what he had seen, at what he had suffered, and still more with the charity of the old woman, would have shown his acknowledgment by kissing her hand.

"It is not my hand you ought to kiss," said the old woman, "I shall be back to-morrow. Anoint your back, eat, and take your rest."

Candide, notwithstanding so many disasters, ate and slept. The next morning, the old woman brought him his breakfast; examined his back, and rubbed it herself with another ointment. She returned at the proper time, and brought him his dinner; and at night she visited him again with his supper. The next day she observed the same ceremonies.

"Who are you?" said Candide to her. "What god has inspired you with so much goodness? What return can I ever make you?"

The good old beldame kept a profound silence. In the evening she returned, but without his supper.

"Come along with me," said she, "but do not speak a word."

She took him by the arm, and walked with him about a quarter of a mile into the country, till they came to a lonely house surrounded with moats and gardens. The old woman knocked at a little door, which was immediately opened, and she showed him up a pair of back stairs into a small, but richly furnished apartment. There she made him sit down on a brocaded sofa, shut the door upon him, and left him. Candide thought himself in a trance; he looked upon his whole life hitherto as a frightful dream, and the present moment as a very agreeable one.

The old woman soon returned, supporting with great difficulty a young lady, who appeared scarce able to stand. She was of a majestic mien and stature; her dress was rich, and glittering with diamonds, and her face was covered with a veil.

"Take off that veil," said the old woman to Candide.

The young man approached, and, with a trembling hand, took off her veil. What a happy moment! What surprise! He thought he beheld Miss Cunegund; he did behold her, it was she herself. His strength failed him, he could not utter a word, he fell at her feet. Cunegund fainted upon the sofa. The old woman bedewed them with spirits; they recovered; they began to speak. At first they could express themselves only in broken accents; their questions and answers were alternately interrupted with sighs, tears, and exclamations. The old woman desired them to make less noise; and left them together.

"Good heavens!" cried Candide, "is it you? Is it Miss Cunegund I behold, and alive? Do I find you again in Portugal? Then you have not been ravished? They did not rip open your belly, as the philosopher Pangloss informed me?"

"Indeed but they did," replied Miss Cunegund; "but these two accidents do not always prove mortal."

"But were your father and mother killed?"

"Alas!" answered she, "it is but too true!" and she wept.

"And your brother?"

"And my brother also."

"And how did you come to Portugal? And how did you know of my being here? And by what strange adventure did you contrive to have me brought into this house?"

"I will tell you all," replied the lady, "but first you must acquaint me with all that has befallen you since the innocent kiss you gave me, and the rude kicking you received."

Candide, with the greatest submission, obeyed her, and though he was still wrapped in amazement, though his voice was low and tremulous, though his back pained him, yet he gave her a most ingenuous account of everything that had befallen him since the moment of their separation. Cunegund, with her eyes uplifted to heaven, shed tears when he related the death of the good Anabaptist James, and of Pangloss; after which, she thus related her adventures to Candide, who lost not one syllable she uttered, and seemed to devour her with his eyes all the time she was speaking.

> Cunegund tells her story. The old woman, Cunegund, and Candide manage to embark from Cadiz for South America and arrive in Buenos Aires. The governor offers to marry Cunegund. Since they have no money, the old woman advises Cunegund to do so and tells Candide he must leave.

Chapter XIV

The Reception Candide and Cacambo Met with Among the Jesuits in Paraguay

Candide had brought with him from Cadiz such a footman as one often meets with on the coasts of Spain and in the colonies. He was the fourth part of a Spaniard, of a mongrel breed, and born in Tucuman.[9] He had successively gone through the profession of a choirboy, sexton, sailor, monk, pedlar, soldier, and lackey. His name was Cacambo; he had a great affection for his master because his master was a mighty good man. He immediately saddled the two Andalusian horses.

"Come, my good master," he said, "let us follow the old woman's advice, and make all the haste we can from this place, without staying to look behind us."

Candide burst into a flood of tears.

"O my dear Cunegund, must I then be compelled to quit you, just as the Governor was going to honour us with his presence at our wedding! Cunegund, so long lost, and found again, what will become of you?"

"Lord!" said Cacambo, "she must do as well as she can; women are never at a loss. God takes care of them, and so let us make the best of our way."

"But whither wilt thou carry me? Where can we go? What can we do without Cunegund?" cried the disconsolate Candide.

"By St. James of Compostella," said Cacambo, "you were going to fight against the Jesuits of Paraguay; now, let us go and fight for them: I know the road perfectly well; I'll conduct you to their kingdom; they will be delighted with a captain that understands the Bulgarian exercise; you will certainly make a prodigious fortune. If we cannot find our account in one world, we may in another. It is a great pleasure to see new objects, and perform new exploits."

"Then you have been in Paraguay?" said Candide.

"Ay, marry, have I," replied Cacambo: "I was a scout in the College of the Assumption, and I am as well acquainted with the new government of Los Padres[10] as I am with the streets of Cadiz. Oh, it is an admirable government, that is most certain! The kingdom is at present upwards of three hundred leagues in diameter, and divided into thirty provinces; the fathers are there masters of everything, and the people have no money at all; this is that masterpiece of justice and reason. For my part, I see nothing so divine as the good fathers, who wage war in this part of the world against the King of Spain and the King of Portugal, at the same time that they hear the confessions of those very princes in Europe; who kill Spaniards in America, and send them to Heaven in Madrid. This pleases me exceedingly, but let us push forward; you are going to be most fortunate of all mortals. How charmed will those fathers be to hear that a captain who understands the Bulgarian exercise is coming among them!"

As soon as they reached the first barrier, Cacambo called to the advance guard, and told them a captain wanted to speak to my Lord the General. Notice was given to the main guard, and immediately a Paraguayan officer ran to throw himself at the feet of the Commandant to impart this news to him. Candide and Cacambo were immediately disarmed, and their two Andalusian horses were seized. The two strangers were now conducted between two files of musketeers, the Commandant was at the farther end with a three-cornered cap on his head, his gown tucked up, a sword by his side, and a half-pike in his hand; he made a sign,

[9]Part of Argentina.

[10]"The Fathers"—that is, the Jesuits.

and instantly four-and-twenty soldiers drew up round the newcomers. A sergeant told them that they must wait; the Commandant could not speak to them; and that the Reverend Father Provincial did not suffer any Spaniard to open his mouth but in his presence, or to stay above three hours in the province.

"And where is the Reverend Father Provincial?" said Cacambo.

"He is just come from mass, and is at the parade," replied the sergeant, "and in about three hours' time, you may possibly have the honour to kiss his spurs."

"But," said Cacambo, "the captain, who, as well as myself, is perishing with hunger, is no Spaniard, but a German; therefore, pray, might we not be permitted to break our fast till we can be introduced to his Reverence?"

The sergeant immediately went, and acquainted the Commandant with what he heard.

"God be praised," said the Reverend Commandant, "since he is a German, I will hear what he has to say; let him be brought to my arbour."

Immediately they conducted Candide to a beautiful pavilion, adorned with a colonnade of green and gold marble, and with trellises of vines, which served as a kind of cage for parrots, humming-birds, fly-birds, guinea-hens, and all other curious kinds of birds. An excellent breakfast was provided in vessels of gold; and while the Paraguayans were eating coarse Indian corn out of wooden dishes in the open air, and exposed to the burning heat of the sun, the Reverend Father Commandant retired to his cool arbour.

He was a very handsome young man, round-faced, fair, and fresh-coloured, his eyebrows were finely arched, he had a piercing eye, the tips of his ears were red, his lips vermilion, and he had a bold and commanding air; but such a boldness as neither resembled that of a Spaniard nor of a Jesuit. He ordered Candide and Cacambo to have their arms restored to them, together with their two Andalusian horses. Cacambo gave the poor beasts some oats to eat close by the arbour, keeping a strict eye upon them all the while for fear of surprise.

Candide having kissed the hem of the Commandant's robe, they sat down to table.

"It seems you are a German?" said the Jesuit to him in that language.

"Yes, Reverend Father," answered Candide.

As they pronounced these words, they looked at each other with great amazement, and with an emotion that neither could conceal.

"From what part of Germany do you come?" said the Jesuit.

"From the dirty province of Westphalia," answered Candide: "I was born in the castle of Thunder-ten-tronckh."

"Oh heavens! is it possible?" said the Commandant.

"What a miracle!" cried Candide.

"Can it be you?" said the Commandant.

On this they both retired a few steps backwards, then embraced, and let fall a shower of tears.

"Is it you then, Reverend Father? You are the brother of the fair Cunegund? you who were slain by the Bulgarians! you the Baron's son! you a Jesuit in Paraguay! I must confess this is a strange world we live in. O Pangloss! Pangloss! what joy would this have given you, if you had not been hanged."

The Commandant dismissed the negro slaves, and the Paraguayans who were presenting them with liquor in crystal goblets. He returned thanks to God and St. Ignatius[11] a thousand times; he clasped Candide in his arms, and both their faces were bathed in tears.

"You will be more surprised, more affected, more transported," said Candide, "when I tell you that Miss Cunegund, your sister, whose belly was supposed to have been ripped open, is in perfect health."

"Where?"

"In your neighbourhood, with the Governor of Buenos Ayres; and I myself was going to fight against you."

Every word they uttered during this long conversation was productive of some new matter of astonishment. Their souls fluttered on their tongues, listened in their ears, and sparkled in their eyes. Like true Germans, they continued a long time at table, waiting for the Reverend Father Provincial; and the Commandant spoke to his dear Candide as follows:

Chapter XV

How Candide Killed the Brother of His Dear Cunegund

"Never while I live shall I lose the remembrance of that horrible day on which I saw my father and mother barbarously butchered before my eyes, and my sister ravished. When the Bulgarians retired, we found no sign of my dear sister; but the bodies of my father, mother, and myself, with two servant maids, and three little boys with their throats cut, were thrown into a cart, to be buried in a chapel belonging to the Jesuits,

[11]Ignatius Loyola, founder of the Jesuit order.

within two leagues of our family seat. A Jesuit sprinkled us with some holy water, which was confoundedly salt, and a few drops of it went into my eyes: the father perceived that my eyelids stirred a little; he put his hand on my breast, and felt my heart beat; upon which he gave me proper assistance, and at the end of three weeks I was perfectly recovered. You know, my dear Candide, I was very handsome; I became still more so, and the Reverend Father Croust, Superior of the House, took a great fancy to me; he gave me a novice's habit, and some years afterwards I was sent to Rome. Our general stood in need of new levies of young German Jesuits. The sovereigns of Paraguay admit as few Spanish Jesuits as possible; they prefer those of other nations, as being more obedient to command. The Reverend Father General looked upon me as a proper person to work in that vineyard. I set out in company with a Pole and a Tyrolese. Upon my arrival, I was honoured with a subdeaconship and a lieutenancy. Now I am colonel and priest. We shall give a warm reception to the King of Spain's troops; I can assure you, they will be well excommunicated and beaten. Providence has sent you hither to assist us. But is it true that my dear sister Cunegund is in the neighbourhood with the Governor of Buenos Ayres?"

Candide swore that nothing could be more true; and the tears began again to trickle down their cheeks.

The Baron knew no end of embracing Candide: he called him his brother, his deliverer.

"Perhaps," said he, "my dear Candide, we shall be fortunate enough to enter the town sword in hand, and rescue my sister Cunegund."

"Ah! that would crown my wishes," replied Candide, "for I intended to marry her; and I hope shall still be able to do so."

"Insolent fellow!" replied the Baron. "You! you have the impudence to marry my sister, who bears seventy-two quarterings! I think you have an insufferable degree of assurance to dare so much as to mention such an audacious design to me."

Candide, thunder-struck at the oddness of this speech, answered, "Reverend Father, all the quarterings in the world are of no significance. I have delivered your sister from a Jew and an Inquisitor; she is under many obligations to me, and she is resolved to give me her hand. Master Pangloss always told me that mankind are by nature equal. Therefore, you may depend upon it, that I will marry your sister."

"We shall see about that, villain!" said the Jesuit Baron of Thunder-ten-Tronckh, and struck him across the face with the flat side of his sword.

Candide, in an instant, drew his rapier, and plunged it up to the hilt in the Jesuit's body; but, in pulling it out reeking hot, he burst into tears.

"Good God!" cried he, "I have killed my old master, my friend, my brother-in-law; I am the mildest man in the world, and yet I have already killed three men; and of these three two were priests."

Cacambo, standing sentry near the door of the arbour, instantly ran up.

"Nothing remains," said his master, "but to sell our lives as dearly as possible; they will undoubtedly look into the arbour; we must die sword in hand."

Cacambo, who had seen many of these kind of adventures, was not discouraged! He stripped the Baron of his Jesuit's habit, and put it upon Candide, then gave him the dead man's three-cornered cap, and made him mount on horseback. All this was done as quick as thought.

"Gallop, master," cried Cacambo; "everybody will take you for a Jesuit going to give orders; and we shall have passed the frontiers before they are able to overtake us."

He flew as he spoke these words, crying out aloud in Spanish, "Make way, make way for the Reverend Father Colonel."

Candide and Cacambo visit a tribe called the "Oreillons" (long ears). They are almost eaten, but when it is discovered that they are not Jesuits, they are treated with civility.

Chapter XVII

Candide and His Servant Arrive in the Country of El Dorado.[12] *What They Saw There*

When they got to the frontiers of the Oreillons, Cacambo said to Candide, "You see, this hemisphere is no better than the other: take my advice, and let us return to Europe by the shortest way possible."

"But how can we get back?" said Candide; "and whither shall we go? To my own country? the Bulgarians and the Abares are laying that waste with fire and sword. Or shall we go to Portugal? there I shall be burnt; and if we abide here, we are every moment in danger of being spitted. But how can I bring myself to quit that part of the world where Miss Cunegund has her residence?"

[12]The legendary "land of gold" in the New World.

"Let us turn towards Cayenne,"[13] said Cacambo; "there we shall meet with some Frenchmen; for you know those gentry ramble all over the world; perhaps they will assist us, and God will look with pity on our distress."

It was not so easy to get to Cayenne. They knew pretty nearly whereabouts it lay; but the mountains, rivers, precipices, robbers, savages, were dreadful obstacles in the way. Their horses died with fatigue, and their provisions were at an end. They subsisted a whole month upon wild fruit, till at length they came to a river bordered with cocoa-nut palms, the sight of which at once sustained life and hope.

Cacambo, who was always giving as good advice as the old woman herself, said to Candide, "You see there is no holding out any longer; we have traveled enough on foot. I see an empty canoe near the riverside; let us fill it with cocoa-nuts, get into it, and go down with the stream; a river always leads to some inhabited place. If we do not meet with agreeable things, we shall at least meet with something new."

"Agreed," replied Candide; "let us recommend ourselves to Providence."

They rowed a few leagues down the river, the banks of which were in some places covered with flowers; in others barren; in some parts smooth and level, and in others steep and rugged. The stream widened as they went further on, till at length it passed under one of the frightful rocks whose summits seemed to reach the clouds. Here our two travelers had the courage to commit themselves to the stream beneath this vault, which, contracting in this part, hurried them along with a dreadful noise and rapidity. At the end of four-and-twenty hours, they saw daylight again; but their canoe was dashed to pieces against the rocks. They were obliged to creep along, from rock to rock, for the space of a league, till at last a spacious plain presented itself to their sight, bound by inaccessible mountains. The country appeared cultivated equally for pleasure, and to produce the necessaries of life. The useful and agreeable were here equally blended. The roads were covered, or rather adorned, with carriages formed of glittering materials, in which were men and women of a surprising beauty, drawn with great rapidity by red sheep of a very large size, surpassed in speed the finest coursers of Andalusia, Tetuan, or Mequinez.[14]

"Here is a country, however," said Candide, "preferable to Westphalia."

He and Cacambo landed near the first village they saw, at the entrance of which they perceived some children covered with tattered garments of the richest brocade, playing at quoits. Our two inhabitants of the other hemisphere amused themselves greatly with what they saw. The quoits were large round pieces, yellow, red, and green, which cast a most glorious lustre. Our travelers picked some of them up, and they proved to be gold, emeralds, rubies, and diamonds, the least of which would have been the greatest ornament to the superb throne of the great Mogul.

"Without doubt," said Cacambo, "those children must be the king's sons, that are playing at quoits."

As he was uttering those words, the schoolmaster of the village appeared, who came to call them to school.

"There," said Candide, "is the preceptor of the royal family."

The little ragamuffins immediately quitted their game, leaving the quoits on the ground with all their other playthings. Candide gathered them up, ran to the schoolmaster, and, with a most respectful bow, presented them to him, giving him to understand by signs that their Royal Highnesses had forgotten their gold and precious stones. The schoolmaster, with a smile, flung them upon the ground, then having examined Candide from head to foot with an air of great surprise, went on his way.

Our travelers took care, however, to gather up the gold, the rubies, and the emeralds.

"Where are we?" cried Candide. "The king's children in this country must have an excellent education, since they are taught to show such a contempt for gold and precious stones."

Cacambo was as much surprised as his master.

They at length drew near the first house in the village, which was built after the manner of a European palace. There was a crowd of people round the door, and a still greater number in the house. The sound of the most delightful musical instruments was heard, and the most agreeable smell came from the kitchen. Cacambo went up to the door, and heard those within talking in the Peruvian language, which was his mother tongue; for every one knows that Cacambo was born in a village of Tucuman where no other language is spoken.

"I will be your interpreter here," said he to Candide, "let us go in; this is an eating-house."

Immediately two waiters, and two servant-girls, dressed in cloth of gold, and their hair braided with ribbons of tissue, accosted the strangers, and invited them to sit down to the ordinary. Their dinner consisted of four dishes of different soups, each garnished

---

[13] In French Guiana.

[14] Province of Spain and two towns in Morocco.

with two young paroquets, a large dish of bouille that weighed two hundredweight, two roasted monkeys of a delicious flavour, three hundred humming-birds in one dish, and six hundred fly-birds in another; some excellent ragouts, delicate tarts, and the whole served up in dishes of rock-crystal. Several sorts of liquors, extracted from the sugar-cane, were handed about by the servants who attended.

Most of the company were chapmen and wagoners, all extremely polite: they asked Cacambo a few questions, with the utmost discretion and circumspection; and replied to his in a most obliging and satisfactory manner.

As soon as dinner was over, both Candide and Cacambo thought they would pay very handsomely for their entertainment by laying down two of those large gold pieces which they had picked off the ground; but the landlord and landlady burst into a fit of laughing and held their sides for some time before they were able to speak.

"Gentlemen," said the landlord, "I plainly perceive you are strangers, and such we are not accustomed to see; pardon us, therefore, for laughing when you offered us the common pebbles of our highways for payment of your reckoning. To be sure, you have none of the coin of this kingdom; but there is no necessity to have any money at all to dine in this house. All the inns, which are established for the convenience of those who carry on the trade of this nation, are maintained by the government. You have found but very indifferent entertainment here, because this is only a poor village; but in almost every other of these public houses you will meet with a reception worthy of persons of your merit."

Cacambo explained the whole of this speech of the landlord to Candide, who listened to it with the same astonishment with which his friend communicated it.

"What sort of a country is this," said the one to the other, "that is unknown to all the world, and in which Nature has everywhere so different an appearance from what she has in ours? Possibly this is that part of the globe where everything is right, for there must certainly be some such place; and, for all that Master Pangloss could say, I often perceived that things went very ill in Westphalia."

Chapter XVIII

What They Saw in the Country of El Dorado

Cacambo vented all his curiosity upon the landlord by a thousand different questions.

The honest man answered him thus: "I am very ignorant, Sir, but I am contented with my ignorance; however, we have in this neighbourhood an old man retired from court, who is the most learned and communicative person in the whole kingdom."

He then directed Cacambo to the old man; Candide acted now only a second character, and attended his servant. They entered a quite plain house, for the door was nothing but silver, and the ceiling was only of beaten gold, but wrought in so elegant a taste as to vie with the richest. The antechamber, indeed, was only incrusted with rubies and emeralds; but the order in which everything was disposed made amends for this great simplicity.

The old man received the strangers on a sofa, which was stuffed with humming-birds' feathers; and ordered his servants to present them with liquors in golden goblets, after which he satisfied their curiosity in the following terms:

"I am now one hundred and seventy-two years old; and I learnt of my late father who was equerry to the King the amazing revolutions of Peru, to which he had been an eye-witness. This kingdom is the ancient patrimony of the Incas, who very imprudently quitted it to conquer another part of the world, and were at length conquered and destroyed themselves by the Spaniards.

"Those princes of their family who remained in their native country acted more wisely. They ordained, with the consent of their whole nation, that none of the inhabitants of our little kingdom should ever quit it; and to this wise ordinance we owe the preservation of our innocence and happiness. The Spaniards had some confused notion of this country, to which they gave the name of El Dorado; and Sir Walter Raleigh, an Englishman, actually came very near it, about a hundred years ago: but the inaccessible rocks and precipices with which our country is surrounded on all sides have hitherto secured us from the rapacious fury of the people of Europe, who have an unaccountable fondness for the pebbles and dirt of our land, for the sake of which they would murder us all to the very last man."

The conversation lasted some time and turned chiefly on the form of government, the customs, the women, the public diversions, and the arts. At length, Candide, who had always had a taste for metaphysics, asked whether the people of that country had any religion.

The old man reddened a little at this question.

"Can you doubt it?" said he. "Do you take us for wretches lost to all sense of gratitude?"

Cacambo asked in a respectful manner what was

the established religion of El Dorado. The old man blushed again.

"Can there be two religions then?" he said. "Ours, I apprehend, is the religion of the whole world; we worship God from morning till night."

"Do you worship but one God?" said Cacambo, who still acted as the interpreter of Candide's doubts.

"Certainly," said the old man; "there are not two, nor three, nor four Gods. I must confess the people of your world ask very extraordinary questions."

However, Candide could not refrain from making many more inquiries of the old man; he wanted to know in what manner they prayed to God in El Dorado.

"We do not pray to him at all," said the reverend sage; "we have nothing to ask of him, he has given us all we want, and we give 'im thanks incessantly."

Candide had a curiosity to see some of their priests, and desired Cacambo to ask the old man where they were.

At this he, smiling, said, "My friends, we are all of us priests; the King and all the heads of families sing solemn hymns of thanksgiving every morning, accompanied by five or six thousand musicians."

"What!" said Cacambo, "have you no monks among you, to dispute, to govern, to intrigue, and to burn people who are not of the same opinion with themselves?"

"Do you take us for fools?" said the old man. "Here we are all of one opinion, and know not what you mean by your monks."

During the whole of this discourse Candide was in raptures, and he said to himself:

"What a prodigious difference is there between this place and Westphalia, and this house and the Baron's castle! If our friend Pangloss had seen El Dorado, he would no longer have said that the castle of Thunder-ten-Tronckh was the finest of all possible edifices: there is nothing like seeing the world, that's certain."

This long conversation being ended, the old man ordered six sheep to be harnessed, and put to the coach, and sent twelve of his servants to escort the travellers to Court.

"Excuse me," said he, "for not waiting on you in person; my age deprives me of that honour. The King will receive you in such a manner that you will have no reason to complain; and doubtless you will make a proper allowance for the customs of the country, if they should not happen altogether to please you."

Candide and Cacambo got into the coach, the six sheep flew, and in less than a quarter of an hour they arrived at the King's palace, which was situated at the further end of the capital. At the entrance was a portal two hundred and twenty feet high, and one hundred wide; but it is impossible for words to express the materials of which it was built. The reader, however, will readily conceive they must have a prodigious superiority over the pebbles and sand which we call gold and precious stones.

Twenty beautiful young virgins-in-waiting received Candide and Cacambo at their alighting from the coach, conducted them to the bath, and clad them in robes woven of the down of humming-birds; after this they were introduced by the great officers of the crown of both sexes to the King's apartment, between two files of musicians, each file consisting of a thousand, according to the custom of the country. When they drew near to the presence chamber, Cacambo asked one of the officers in what manner they were to pay their obeisance to his Majesty: whether it was the custom to fall upon their knees, or to prostrate themselves upon the ground? whether they were to put their hands upon their heads, or behind their backs? whether they were to lick the dust off the floor? in short, what was the ceremony usual on such occasions?

"The custom," said the great officer, "is to embrace the King, and kiss him on each cheek."

Candide and Cacambo accordingly threw their arms round his Majesty's neck; and he received them in the most gracious manner imaginable, and very politely asked them to sup with him.

While supper was preparing, orders were given to show them the city, where they saw public structures that reared their lofty heads to the clouds; the marketplaces decorated with a thousand columns; fountains of spring water, besides others of rose water, and of liquors drawn from the sugar-cane, incessantly flowing in the great squares; these were paved with a kind of precious stone that emitted an odour like that of cloves and cinnamon. Candide asked to see the high court of justice, the parliament; but was answered that they had none in that country, being utter strangers to lawsuits. He then inquired, if they had any prisons; they replied, "None." But what gave him at once the greatest surprise and pleasure was the Palace of Sciences, where he saw a gallery two thousand feet long, filled with the various apparatus of mathematics and natural philosophy.

After having spent the whole afternoon in seeing only about the thousandth part of the city, they were brought back to the King's palace. Candide sat down at the table with his Majesty, his servant Cacambo, and several ladies of the Court. Never was entertainment more elegant, nor could any one possibly show more wit than his Majesty displayed while they were at supper. Cacambo explained all the King's *bons mots* to Candide, and although they were translated they still appeared to be *bons mots.* Of all the things that surprised Candide, this was not the least. They spent a whole month in this hospitable place, during which time Candide was continually saying to Cacambo:

"I own, my friend, once more, that the castle where I was born is a mere nothing in comparison with the place where we now are; but still Miss Cunegund is not here, and you yourself have doubtless some mistress in Europe. If we remain here, we shall only be as others are: whereas, if we return to our own world with only a dozen of El Dorado sheep, loaded with the pebbles of this country, we shall be richer than all the kings in Europe; we shall no longer need to stand in awe of the Inquisitors; and we may easily recover Miss Cunegund."

This speech pleased Cacambo. A fondness for roving, for making a figure in their own country, and for boasting of what they had seen in their travels, was so strong in our two wanderers that they resolved to be no longer happy; and demanded permission of his Majesty to quit the country.

"You are about to do a rash and silly action," said the King; "I am sensible my kingdom is an inconsiderable spot; but when people are tolerably at their ease in any place, I should think it would be their interest to remain there. Most assuredly, I have no right to detain you or any strangers against your wills; this is an act of tyranny to which our manners and our laws are equally repugnant: all men are free; you have an undoubted liberty to depart whenever you please, but you will have many difficulties in passing the frontiers. It is impossible to ascend that rapid river which runs under high and vaulted rocks, and by which you were conveyed hither by a miracle. The mountains by which my kingdom is hemmed in on all sides are ten thousand feet high, and perfectly perpendicular; they are above ten leagues over each, and the descent from them is one continued precipice. However, since you are determined to leave us, I will immediately give orders to the superintendent of machines to cause one to be made that will convey you safely. When they have conducted you to the back of the mountains, nobody can attend you further; for my subjects have made a vow never to quit the kingdom, and they are too prudent to break it. Ask me whatever else you please."

"All we shall ask of your Majesty," said Cacambo, "is a few sheep laden with provisions, pebbles, and the clay of your country."

The King smiled at the request, and said, "I cannot imagine what pleasure you Europeans find in our yellow clay; but take away as much of it as you will, and much good may it do you."

He immediately gave orders to his engineers to make a machine to hoist these two extraordinary men out of the kingdom. Three thousand good mathematicians went to work and finished it in about fifteen days; and it did not cost more than twenty millions sterling of that country's money. Candide and Cacambo were placed on this machine, and they took with them two large red sheep, bridled and saddled, to ride upon when they got on the other side of the mountains; twenty others to serve as pack-horses for carrying provisions; thirty laden with presents of whatever was most curious in the country; and fifty with gold, diamonds, and other precious stones. The King embraced the two wanderers with the greatest cordiality.

It was a curious sight to behold the manner of their setting off, and the ingenious method by which they and their sheep were hoisted to the top of the mountains. The mathematicians and engineers took leave of them as soon as they had conveyed them to a place of safety, and Candide was wholly occupied with the thoughts of presenting his sheep to Miss Cunegund.

"Now," said he, "thanks to heaven, we have more than sufficient to pay the Governor of Buenos Ayres for Miss Cunegund, if she is redeemable. Let us make the best of our way to Cayenne, where we will take ship, and then we may at leisure think of what kingdom we shall purchase."

Chapter XIX

What Happened to Them at Surinam, and How Candide Became Acquainted with Martin

Our travellers' first day's journey was very pleasant; they were elated with the prospect of possessing more riches than were to be found in Europe, Asia, and Africa together. Candide, in amorous transports, cut the name of Miss Cunegund on the trees. The second day, two of their sheep sank into a morass, and were swallowed up with their loads; two more died of fatigue some few days afterwards; seven or eight perished with hunger in a desert, and others, at different times, tumbled down precipices; so that, after travelling about a hundred days, they had only two sheep left.

Said Candide to Cacambo, "You see, my dear friend, how perishable the riches of this world are; there is nothing solid but virtue and the joy of seeing Miss Cunegund again."

"Very true," said Cacambo; "but we have still two sheep remaining, with more treasure than ever the King of Spain will be possessed of; and I espy a town at a distance, which I take to be Surinam, a town belonging to the Dutch. We are now at the end of our troubles, and at the beginning of happiness."

As they drew near the town, they saw a negro stretched on the ground with only one half of his habit, which was a pair of blue cotton drawers; for the poor man had lost his left leg, and his right hand.

"Good God," said Candide in Dutch, "what dost thou here, friend, in this deplorable condition?"

"I am waiting for my master Mynheer Vanderdendur, the famous trader," answered the negro.

"Was it Mynheer Vanderdendur that used you in this cruel manner?"

"Yes, Sir," said the negro; "it is the custom here. They give a pair of cotton drawers twice a year, and that is all our covering. When we labour in the sugar-works, and the mill happens to snatch hold of a finger, they instantly chop off our hand; and when we attempt to run away, they cut off a leg. Both these cases have happened to me, and it is at this expense that you eat sugar in Europe; and yet when my mother sold me for ten pattacoons on the coast of Guinea, she said to me, 'My dear child, bless our fetishes; adore them for ever; they will make thee live happy; thou hast the honour to be a slave to our lords the whites, by which thou wilt make the fortune of us thy parents.' Alas! I know not whether I have made their fortunes; but they have not made mine: dogs, monkeys, and parrots, are a thousand times less wretched than me. The Dutch fetishes who converted me tell me every Sunday that, blacks and whites, we are all children of Adam. As for me, I do not understand any thing of genealogies; but if what these preachers say is true, we are all second cousins; and you must allow, that it is impossible to be worse treated by our relations than we are."

"O Pangloss!" cried out Candide, "such horrid doings never entered thy imagination. Here is an end of the matter; I find myself, after all, obliged to renounce thy Optimism."

"Optimism!" said Cacambo, "what is that?"

"Alas!" replied Candide, "it is the obstinacy of maintaining that everything is best when it is worst": and so saying, he turned his eyes towards the poor negro, and shed a flood of tears; and in this weeping mood he entered the town of Surinam.

Immediately upon their arrival, our travellers inquired if there was any vessel in the harbour which they might send to Buenos Ayres. The person they addressed themselves to happened to be the master of a Spanish bark, who offered to agree with them on moderate terms, and appointed them a meeting at a public-house. Thither Candide and his faithful Cacambo went to wait for him, taking with them their two sheep.

Candide, who was all frankness and sincerity, made an ingenuous recital of his adventures to the Spaniard, declaring to him at the same time his resolution of carrying off Miss Cunegund.

"In that case," said the shipmaster, "I'll take good care not to take you to Buenos Ayres. It would prove a hanging matter to us all. The fair Cunegund is the Governor's favourite mistress."

These words were like a clap of thunder to Candide; he wept bitterly for a long time, and, taking Cacambo aside, he said to him:

"I'll tell you, my dear friend, what you must do. We have each of us in our pockets to the value of five or six millions in diamonds; you are cleverer at these matters than I; you must go to Buenos Ayres and bring off Miss Cunegund. If the Governor makes any difficulty, give him a million; if he holds out, give him two; as you have not killed an Inquisitor, they will have no suspicion of you: I'll fit out another ship and go to Venice, where I will wait for you: Venice is a free country, where we shall have nothing to fear from Bulgarians, Abares, Jews, or Inquisitors."

Cacambo greatly applauded this wise resolution. He was inconsolable at the thought of parting with so good a master, who treated him more like an intimate friend than a servant; but the pleasure of being able to do him a service soon got the better of his sorrow. They embraced each other with a flood of tears. Candide charged him not to forget the old woman. Cacambo set out the same day. This Cacambo was a very honest fellow.

Candide continued some days longer at Surinam, waiting for any captain to carry him and his two remaining sheep to Italy. He hired domestics and purchased many things necessary for a long voyage; at length, Mynheer Vanderdendur, skipper of a large Dutch vessel, came and offered his service.

"What will you take," said Candide, "to carry me, my servants, my baggage, and these two sheep you see here, direct to Venice?"

The skipper asked ten thousand piastres; and Candide agreed to his demand without hesitation.

"Oh, ho!" said the cunning Vanderdendur to himself, "this stranger must be very rich; he agrees to give me ten thousand piastres without hesitation."

Returning a little while after, he told Candide that upon second consideration he could not undertake the voyage for less than twenty thousand.

"Very well, you shall have them," said Candide.

"Zounds!" said the skipper to himself, "this man agrees to pay twenty thousand piastres with as much ease as ten."

Accordingly he went back again, and told him roundly that he would not carry him to Venice for less than thirty thousand piastres.

"Then you shall have thirty thousand," said Candide.

"Odso!" said the Dutchman once more to himself, "thirty thousand piastres seem a trifle to this man. Those sheep must certainly be laden with an immense treasure. I'll stop here and ask no more; but make him pay down the thirty thousand piastres, and then we shall see."

Candide sold two small diamonds, the least of which was worth more than all the skipper asked. He paid him before-hand, and the two sheep were put on board, and Candide followed in a small boat to join the vessel in the road. The skipper took his opportunity, hoisted his sails, and put out to sea with a favourable wind. Candide, confounded and amazed, soon lost sight of the ship.

"Alas!" said he, "this is a trick like those in our old world!"

He returned back to the shore overwhelmed with grief; and, indeed, he had lost what would have been the fortune of twenty monarchs.

Immediately upon his landing, he applied to the Dutch magistrate: being transported with passion, he thundered at the door; which being opened, he went in, told his case, and talked a little louder than was necessary. The magistrate began with fining him ten thousand piastres for his petulance, and then listened very patiently to what he had to say, promised to examine into the affair at the skipper's return, and ordered him to pay ten thousand piastres more for the fees of the court.

This treatment put Candide out of all patience: it is true, he had suffered misfortunes a thousand times more grievous; but the cool insolence of the judge and of the skipper who robbed him raised his choler and threw him into a deep melancholy. The villainy of mankind presented itself to his mind in all its deformity, and his soul was a prey to the most gloomy ideas. After some time, hearing that the captain of a French ship was ready to set sail for Bordeaux, as he had no more sheep loaded with diamonds to put on board, he hired the cabin at the usual price; and made it known in the town that he would pay the passage and board of any honest man who would give him his company during the voyage; besides making him a present of ten thousand piastres, on condition that such person was the most dissatisfied with his condition and the most unfortunate in the whole province.

Upon this there appeared such a crowd of candidates that a large fleet could not have contained them. Candide, willing to choose from among those who appeared most likely to answer his intention, selected twenty, who seemed to him the most sociable, and who all pretended to merit the preference. He invited them to his inn, and promised to treat them with a supper, on condition that every man should bind himself by an oath to relate his own history. He declared at the same time that he would make choice of that person who should appear to him the most deserving of compassion, and the most justly dissatisfied with his condition of life; and that he would make a present to the rest.

This extraordinary assembly continued sitting till four in the morning. Candide, while he was listening to their adventures, called to mind what the old woman had said to him on their voyage to Buenos Ayres, and the wager she had laid that there was not a person on board the ship but had met with some great misfortune. Every story he heard put him in mind of Pangloss.

"My old master," said he, "would be confoundedly put to it to demonstrate his favourite system. Would he were here! Certainly if everything is for the best, it is in El Dorado, and not in the other parts of the world."

At length he determined in favour of a poor scholar who had laboured ten years for the booksellers at Amsterdam, being of opinion that no employment could be more detestable.

This scholar, who was in fact a very honest man, had been robbed by his wife, beaten by his son, and forsaken by his daughter, who had run away with a Portuguese. He had been likewise deprived of a small employment on which he subsisted, and he was persecuted by the clergy of Surinam, who took him for a Socinian.[15] It must be acknowledged that the other competitors were, at least, as wretched as he; but Candide was in hopes that the company of a man of letters would relieve the tediousness of the voyage. All the other candidates complained that Candide had done them great injustice; but he stopped their mouths by a present of a hundred piastres to each.

Chapter XX

What Befell Candide and Martin on Their Voyage

The old scholar, whose name was Martin, took ship with Candide for Bordeaux. They both had seen and

[15] A heresy resembling modern Unitarianism.

suffered a great deal; and if the ship had been destined to sail from Surinam to Japan round the Cape of Good Hope, they could have found sufficient entertainment for each other during the whole voyage in discoursing upon moral and natural evil.

Candide, however, had one advantage over Martin: he lived in the pleasing hopes of seeing Miss Cunegund once more; whereas the poor philosopher had nothing to hope for. Besides, Candide had money and jewels, and, notwithstanding he had lost a hundred red sheep, laden with the greatest treasure on the earth, and though he still smarted from the reflection of the Dutch skipper's knavery, yet when he considered what he had still left, and repeated the name of Cunegund, especially after meal-times, he inclined to Pangloss's doctrine.

"And pray," said he to Martin, "what is your opinion of the whole of this system? What notion have you of moral and natural evil?"

"Sir," replied Martin, "our priests accused me of being a Socinian; but the real truth is, I am a Manichaean."[16]

"Nay, now you are jesting," said Candide; "there are no Manichaeans existing at present in the world."

"And yet I am one," said Martin; "but I cannot help it; I cannot for the soul of me think otherwise."

"Surely the devil must be in you," said Candide.

"He concerns himself so much," replied Martin, "in the affairs of this world that it is very probable he may be in me as well as everywhere else; but I must confess, when I cast my eye on this globe, or rather globule, I cannot help thinking that God has abandoned it to some malignant being. I always except El Dorado. I scarce ever knew a city that did not wish the destruction of its neighbouring city; nor a family that did not desire to exterminate some other family. The poor, in all parts of the world, bear an inveterate hatred to the rich, even while they creep and cringe to them; and the rich treat the poor like sheep, whose wool and flesh they barter for money: a million of regimented assassins traverse Europe from one end to the other to get their bread by regular depredation and murder, because it is the most gentleman-like profession. Even in those cities which seem to enjoy the blessings of peace, and where the arts flourish, the inhabitants are devoured with envy, care, and anxiety, which are greater plagues than any experienced in a town besieged. Private chagrins are still more dreadful than public calamities. In a word, I have seen and suffered so much, that I am a Manichaean."

"And yet there is some good in the world," replied Candide.

"May be," said Martin, "but it has escaped my knowledge."

While they were deeply engaged in this dispute they heard the report of cannon, which redoubled every moment. Each took out his glass, and they espied two ships warmly engaged at the distance of about three miles. The wind brought them both so near the French ship that those on board her had the pleasure of seeing the fight with great ease. At last one of the two vessels gave the other a shot between wind and water, which sank her outright. Then could Candide and Martin plainly perceive a hundred men on the deck of the vessel which was sinking, who, with hands uplifted to heaven, sent forth piercing cries, and were in a moment swallowed up by the waves.

"Well," said Martin, "you now see in what manner mankind treat each other."

"It is certain," said Candide, "that there is something diabolical in this affair."

As he was speaking thus, he saw something of a shining red hue, which swam close to the vessel. The boat was hoisted out to see what it might be, when it proved to be one of his sheep. Candide felt more joy at the recovery of this one animal than he did grief when he lost the other hundred, though laden with the large diamonds of El Dorado.

The French captain quickly perceived that the victorious ship belonged to the crown of Spain; that the other which sank was a Dutch pirate, and the very same captain who had robbed Candide. The immense riches which this villain had amassed were buried with him in the deep, and only this one sheep saved out of the whole.

"You see," said Candide to Martin, "that vice is sometimes punished: this villain, the Dutch skipper, has met with the fate he deserved."

"Very true," said Martin; "but why should the passengers be doomed also to destruction? God has punished the knave, and the devil has drowned the rest."

The French and Spanish ships continued their cruise, and Candide and Martin their conversation. They disputed fourteen days successively, at the end of which they were just as far advanced as the first moment they began. However, they had the satisfaction of disputing, of communicating their ideas, and of mutually comforting each other. Candide embraced his sheep.

[16]A believer in the doctrine (considered heretical) that good and evil are forces of equal strength in the universe.

"Since I have found thee again," said he, "I may possibly find my Cunegund once more."

Candide and Martin travel to Paris, London, and Venice. Voltaire satirizes each of these societies. In Venice they meet Pacquette, who has taken up with a monk named Friar Giroflée, and search in vain for a truly happy person.

Chapter XXVII

Candide's Voyage to Constantinople

The trusty Cacambo had already engaged the captain of the Turkish ship that was to carry Sultan Achmet back to Constantinople, to take Candide and Martin on board. Accordingly, they both embarked, after paying their obeisance to his miserable Highness. As they were going on board, Candide said to Martin:

"You see we supped in company with six dethroned kings, and to one of them I gave charity. Perhaps there may be a great many other princes still more unfortunate. For my part, I have lost only a hundred sheep, and am now going to fly to the arms of Cunegund. My dear Martin, I must insist on it, that Pangloss was in the right. All is for the best."

"I wish it may be," said Martin.

"But this was an odd adventure we met with at Venice. I do not think there ever was an instance before, of six dethroned monarchs supping together at a public inn."

"This is no more extraordinary," said Martin, "than most of what has happened to us. It is a very common thing for kings to be dethroned; and as for our having the honour to sup with six of them, it is a mere accident, not deserving our attention. What does it matter with whom one sups, provided one has good fare?"

As soon as Candide set his foot on board the vessel, he flew to his old friend and servant Cacambo; and throwing his arms about his neck, embraced him with transports of joy.

"Well," said he, "what news of Cunegund? Does she still continue the paragon of beauty? Does she love me still? How is she? You have, doubtless, purchased a palace for her at Constantinople?"

"My dear master," replied Cacambo, "Cunegund washes dishes on the banks of the Propontis, in the house of a prince who has very few to wash. She is at present a slave in the family of an ancient sovereign, named Ragotsky, whom the Grand Turk allows three crowns a day to maintain him in his exile; but the most melancholy circumstance of all is, that she has lost her beauty and turned horribly ugly."

"Ugly or handsome," said Candide, "I am a man of honour; and, as such, am obliged to love her still. But how could she possibly have been reduced to so abject a condition, when I sent five or six millions to her by you?"

"Lord bless me," said Cacambo, "was not I obliged to give two millions to Senor Don Fernando d'Ibaraa y Figueora y Mascarenas y Lampourdos y Souza, Governor of Buenos Ayres, for liberty to take Miss Cunegund away with me? and then did not a brave fellow of a pirate very gallantly strip us of all the rest? and then did not this same pirate carry us with him to Cape Matapan, to Milo, to Nicaria, to Samos, to Petra, to the Dardanelles, to Marmora, to Scutari? Cunegund and the old woman are now servants to the prince I have told you of; and I myself am slave to the dethroned Sultan."

"What a chain of terrible calamities!" exclaimed Candide. "But, after all, I have still some diamonds left, with which I can easily procure Cunegund's liberty. It is a pity she is grown so very ugly."

Then turning to Martin, "What think you, friend," said he, "whose condition is most to be pitied, the Emperor Achmet's, the Emperor Ivan's, King Charles Edward's,[17] or mine?"

"Faith, I cannot resolve your question," said Martin, "unless I had been in the breasts of you all."

"Ah!" cried Candide, "was Pangloss here now, he would have known, and satisfied me at once."

"I know not," said Martin, "in what balance your Pangloss could have weighed the misfortunes of mankind, and have set a just estimation on their sufferings. All that I pretend to know of the matter is that there are millions of men on the earth whose conditions are an hundred times more pitiable than those of King Charles Edward, the Emperor Ivan, or Sultan Achmet."

"Why, that may be," answered Candide.

In a few days they reached the Bosphorus; and the first thing Candide did was to pay a high ransom for Cacambo: then, without losing time, he and his companions went on board a galley, in order to search for his Cunegund, on the banks of the Propontis, notwithstanding she was grown so ugly.

There were two slaves among the crew of the galley, who rowed very ill, and to whose bare backs the master of the vessel frequently applied a lash of oxhide. Candide, from natural sympathy, looked at

---

[17]The deposed kings Candide and Martin met in Venice.

these two slaves more attentively than at any of the rest, and drew near them with a look of pity. Their features, though greatly disfigured, appeared to him to bear a strong resemblance with those of Pangloss and the unhappy Baron Jesuit, Miss Cunegund's brother. This idea affected him with grief and compassion: he examined them more attentively than before.

"In troth," said he, turning to Martin, "if I had not seen my master Pangloss fairly hanged, and had not myself been unlucky enough to run the Baron through the body, I could believe these are they rowing in the galley."

No sooner had Candide uttered the names of the Baron and Pangloss than the two slaves gave a great cry, ceased rowing, and let fall their oars out of their hands. The master of the vessel, seeing this, ran up to them, and redoubled the discipline of the lash.

"Hold, hold," cried Candide, "I will give you what money you ask for these two persons."

"Good heavens! it is Candide," said one of the men.

"Candide!" cried the other.

"Do I dream," said Candide, "or am I awake? Am I actually on board this galley? Is this my lord Baron, whom I killed? and that my master Pangloss, whom I saw hanged?"

"It is I! it is I!" cried they both together.

"What! is this your great philosopher?" said Martin.

"My dear Sir," said Candide to the master of the galley, "how much do you ask for the ransom of the Baron of Thunder-ten-tronckh, who is one of the first barons of the empire, and of Mr. Pangloss, the most profound metaphysician in Germany?"

"Why then, Christian cur," replied the Turkish captain, "since these two dogs of Christian slaves are barons and metaphysicians, who no doubt are of high rank in their own country, thou shalt give me fifty thousand sequins."

"You shall have them, Sir: carry me back as quick as thought to Constantinople, and you shall receive the money immediately. No! carry me first to Miss Cunegund."

The captain, upon Candide's first proposal, had already tacked about, and he made the crew apply their oars so effectively that the vessel flew through the water quicker than a bird cleaves the air.

Candide bestowed a thousand embraces on the Baron and Pangloss.

"And so then, my dear Baron, I did not kill you? and you, my dear Pangloss, are come to life again after your hanging? But how came you slaves on board a Turkish galley?"

"And is it true that my dear sister is in this country?" said the Baron.

"Yes," said Cacambo.

"And do I once again behold my dear Candide?" said Pangloss.

Candide presented Martin and Cacambo to them; they embraced each other, and all spoke together. The galley flew like lightning, and now they were got back to the port. Candide instantly sent for a Jew, to whom he sold for fifty thousand sequins a diamond richly worth one hundred thousand, though the fellow swore to him all the time, by Abraham, that he gave him the most he could possibly afford. He no sooner got the money into his hands than he paid it down for the ransom of the Baron and Pangloss. The latter flung himself at the feet of his deliverer, and bathed him with his tears: the former thanked him with a gracious nod, and promised to return him the money at the first opportunity.

"But is it possible," said he, "that my sister should be in Turkey?"

"Nothing is more possible," answered Cacambo; "for she scours the dishes in the house of a Transylvanian prince."

Candide sent directly for two Jews, and sold more diamonds to them; and then he set out with his companions in another galley, to deliver Cunegund from slavery.

Pangloss and the baron explain how they were not killed.

Chapter XXIX

In What Manner Candide Found Cunegund and the Old Woman Again

While Candide, the Baron, Pangloss, Martin, and Cacambo were relating their several adventures, and reasoning on the contingent or non-contingent events of this world; while they were disputing on causes and effects, on moral and physical evil, on free will and necessity, and on the consolation that may be felt by a person when a slave and chained to an oar in a Turkish galley, they arrived at the house of the Transylvanian prince on the coasts of the Propontis. The first objects they beheld there were Miss Cunegund and the old woman, who were hanging some table-cloths on a line to dry.

The Baron turned pale at the sight. Even the tender Candide, that affectionate lover, upon seeing his fair Cunegund all sun-burnt, with blear eyes, a withered neck, wrinkled face and arms, all covered with a red scarf, started back with horror; but, recovering himself, he advanced towards her out of good manners. She embraced Candide and her brother; they embraced the old woman, and Candide ransomed them both.

There was a small farm in the neighbourhood, which the old woman proposed to Candide to make a shift with till the company should meet with a more favourable destiny. Cunegund, not knowing that she was grown ugly, as no one had informed her of it, reminded Candide of his promise in so peremptory a manner that the simple lad did not dare to refuse her; he then acquainted the Baron that he was going to marry his sister.

"I will never suffer," said the Baron, "my sister to be guilty of an action so derogatory to her birth and family; nor will I bear this insolence on your part: no, I never will be reproached that my nephews are not qualified for the first ecclesiastical dignities in Germany; nor shall a sister of mine ever be the wife of any person below the rank of a baron of the Empire."

Cunegund flung herself at her brother's feet, and bedewed them with her tears, but he still continued inflexible.

"Thou foolish fellow," said Candide, "have I not delivered them from the galleys, paid thy ransom, and thy sister's too who was a scullion, and is very ugly, and yet I condescend to marry her? and shalt thou make claim to oppose the match? If I were to listen only to the dictates of my anger, I should kill thee again."

"Thou mayest kill me again," said the Baron, "but thou shalt not marry my sister while I am living."

Chapter XXX

Conclusion

Candide had, in truth, no great inclination to marry Cunegund; but the extreme impertinence of the baron determined him to conclude the match; and Cunegund pressed him so warmly that he could not recant. He consulted Pangloss, Martin, and the faithful Cacambo. Pangloss composed a fine memorial, by which he proved that the Baron had no right over his sister; and that she might, according to all the laws of the Empire, marry Candide with the left hand.[18] Martin concluded that they should throw the Baron into the sea: Cacambo decided that he must be delivered to the Turkish captain and sent to the galleys; after which he should be conveyed by the first ship to the Father General at Rome. This advice was found to be very good; the old woman approved of it, and not a syllable was said to his sister; the business was executed for a little money: and they had the pleasure of tricking a Jesuit and punishing the pride of a German baron.

It was altogether natural to imagine that after undergoing so many disasters, Candide, married to his mistress, and living with the philosopher Pangloss, the philosopher Martin, the prudent Cacambo, and the old woman, having besides brought home so many diamonds from the country of the ancient Incas, would lead the most agreeable life in the world. But he had been so much cheated by the Jews that he had nothing else left but his little farm; his wife, every day growing more and more ugly, became ill-natured and insupportable; the old woman was infirm, and more bad-tempered yet than Cunegund. Cacambo, who worked in the garden, and carried the produce of it to sell at Constantinople, was past his labour, and cursed his fate. Pangloss despaired of making a figure in any of the German universities. And as to Martin, he was firmly persuaded that a person is equally ill-situated everywhere. He took things with patience. Candide, Martin, and Pangloss disputed sometimes about metaphysics and morality. Boats were often seen passing under the windows of the farm fraught with effendis, pashas, and cadis,[19] that were going into banishment to Lemnos, Mytilene, and Erzeroum. And other cadis, pashas, and effendis were seen coming back to succeed the place of the exiles, and were driven out in their turns. They saw several heads very curiously stuffed with straw, being carried as presents to the Sublime Porte.[20] Such sights gave occasion to frequent dissertations; and when no disputes were carried on, the irksomeness was so excessive that the old woman ventured one day to say to them:

"I would be glad to know which is worst, to be ravished a hundred times by negro pirates, to have one buttock cut off, to run the gauntlet among the Bulgarians, to be whipped and hanged at an *auto-da-fé*, to be dissected, to be chained to an oar in a galley, and in short to experience all the miseries through which every one of us hath passed,—or to remain here doing nothing?"

"This," said Candide, "is a big question."

This discourse gave birth to new reflections, and Martin especially concluded that man was born to live in the convulsions of disquiet, or in the lethargy of idleness. Though Candide did not absolutely agree to

[18]That is, Candide would not assume his wife's rank.

[19]Turkish officials.

[20]The gate of the sultan's palace.

this; yet he was sure of nothing. Pangloss avowed that he had undergone dreadful sufferings; but having once maintained that everything went on as well as possible, he still maintained it, and at the same time believed nothing of it.

There was one thing which, more than ever, confirmed Martin in his detestable principles, made Candide hesitate, and embarrassed Pangloss. This was the arrival of Pacquette and Friar Giroflée one day at their farm. This couple had been in the utmost distress; they had very speedily made away with their three thousand piastres; they had parted, been reconciled; quarrelled again, been thrown into prison; had made their escape, and at last Brother Giroflée turned Turk. Pacquette still continued to follow her trade wherever she came; but she got little or nothing by it.

"I foresaw very well," said Martin to Candide, "that your presents would soon be squandered, and only make them more miserable. You and Cacambo have spent millions of piastres, and yet you are not more happy than Brother Giroflée and Pacquette."

"Ah!" said Pangloss to Pacquette. "It is heaven who has brought you here among us, my poor child! Do you know that you have cost me the tip of my nose, one eye, and one ear? What a handsome shape is here! and what is this world!"

This new adventure engaged them more deeply than ever in philosophical disputations.

In the neighbourhood lived a very famous dervish,[21] who passed for the best philosopher in Turkey; him they went to consult: Pangloss, who was their spokesman, addressed him thus:

"Master, we come to intreat you to tell us why so strange an animal as man has been formed?"

"Why do you trouble your head about it?" said the dervish. "Is it any business of yours?"

"But, my Reverend Father," said Candide, "there is a horrible deal of evil on the earth."

"What signifies it," said the dervish, "whether there is evil or good? When his Highness sends a ship to Egypt, does he trouble his head whether the rats in the vessel are at their ease or not?"

"What must then be done?" said Pangloss.

"Be silent," answered the dervish.

"I flattered myself," replied Pangloss, "that we should have the pleasure of arguing with you on causes and effects, on the best of possible worlds, the origin of evil, the nature of the soul, and the pre-established harmony."

At these words the dervish shut the door in their faces.

During this conversation, news was spread abroad that two viziers of the bench and the mufti[22] had just been strangled at Constantinople, and several of their friends impaled. This catastrophe made a great noise for some hours. Pangloss, Candide, and Martin, as they were returning to the little farm, met with a good-looking old man, who was taking the air at his door, under an alcove formed of orange-trees. Pangloss, who was as inquisitive as he was argumentative, asked him what was the name of the mufti who was lately strangled.

"I cannot tell," answered the good old man; "I never knew the name of any mufti or vizier breathing. I am entirely ignorant of the event you speak of; I presume, that in general, such as are concerned in public affairs sometimes come to a miserable end; and that they deserve it: but I never inquire what is happening at Constantinople; I am content with sending thither the produce of the garden which I cultivate."

After saying these words, he invited the strangers to come into his house. His two daughters and two sons presented them with diverse sorts of iced sherbet of their own making; besides *caymac,* heightened with the peel of candied citrons, oranges, lemons, pineapples, pistachio-nuts, and Mocha coffee unadulterated with the bad coffee of Batavia or the West Indies. After which the two daughters of this good mussulman perfumed the beards of Candide, Pangloss, and Martin.

"You must certainly have a vast estate," said Candide to the Turk.

"I have no more than twenty acres of ground," he replied, "the whole of which I cultivate myself with the help of my children; and our labour keeps off from us three great evils, idleness, vice, and want."

Candide, as he was returning home, made profound reflections on the Turk's discourse.

"This good old man," he said to Pangloss and Martin, "appears to me to have chosen for himself a lot much preferable to that of the six kings with whom we had the honour to sup."

"Human grandeur," said Pangloss, "is very dangerous, if we believe the testimonies of almost all philosophers; for we find Eglon, King of the Moabites, was assassinated by Ehud; Absalom was hanged by the hair of his head, and run through with three darts; King Nadab, son of Jeroboam, was slain by Baasha; King Elah by Zimri; Ahaziah by Jehu; Athaliah by Jehoiada; the Kings Jehoiakim, Jechoniah, and

[21]A Moslem friar.

[22]Officials of the Moslem legal system.

Zedekiah were led into captivity: I need not tell you what was the fate of Croesus, Astyages, Darius, Dionysius of Syracuse, Pyrrhus, Perseus, Hannibal, Jugurtha, Ariovistus, Caesar, Pompey, Nero, Otho, Vitellius, Domitian, Richard II of England, Edward II, Henry VI, Richard III, Mary Stuart, Charles I, the three Henrys of France, and the Emperor Henry IV."

"Neither need you tell me," said Candide, "that we must take care of our garden."

"You are in the right," said Pangloss; "for when man was put into the Garden of Eden, it was with an intent to dress it: and this proves that man was not born to be idle."

"Work then without disputing," said Martin; "it is the only way to render life supportable."

The little society, one and all, entered into this laudable design; and set themselves to exert their different talents. The little piece of ground yielded them a plentiful crop. Cunegund indeed was very ugly, but she became an excellent hand at pastry-work; Pacquette embroidered; the old woman had the care of the linen. There was none, down to Brother Giroflée, but did some service; he was a very good carpenter, and became an honest man. Pangloss used now and then to say to Candide:

"There is a concatenation of all events in the best of possible worlds; for, in short, had you not been kicked out of a fine castle by the backside for the love of Miss Cunegund, had you not been put into the Inquisition, had you not travelled over America on foot, had you not run the Baron through the body, and had you not lost all your sheep which you brought from the good country of El Dorado, you would not have been here to eat preserved citrons and pistachio-nuts."

"Excellently observed," answered Candide; "but let us take care of our garden."

COMMENTS AND QUESTIONS

1. Voltaire has in part followed the model of the "picaresque" tale, developed in seventeenth-century Spain, that recounts the adventures of a young man wandering through the world. How does the use of an innocent, truthful, "candid" hero allow Voltaire to satirize some of the world's follies?
2. What events in the tale are most improbable? Do these add to or detract from its effectiveness? How?
3. To what extent are the characters realistic? Why are they not as "well rounded" as those in a realistic novel, for example?
4. What are some of the specific objects of Voltaire's satire? How would you describe generally the human characteristics that he most scorns?
5. Find specific passages most representative of Voltaire's satiric technique and attempt to analyze his method.
6. What different philosophies of life are represented in the tale and by which characters? Does Voltaire side entirely with any of them? What philosophy of life emerges from *Candide?*
7. How do you interpret Candide's final sentence?

VOLTAIRE

An Address to the Deity

No longer then do I address myself to men, but to Thee, God of all beings, of all worlds, and of all ages; if it may be permitted weak creatures lost in immensity and imperceptible to the rest of the universe, to presume to petition Thee for aught, who hast given plenty of all things, and whose decrees are immutable as eternal. Deign to look with an eye of pity on the errors annexed to our natures! let not these errors prove the sources of misery to us! Thou hast not given us hearts to hate, nor hands to kill one another; grant then that we may mutually aid and assist each other to support the burden of this painful and transitory life! May the trifling differences in the garments that cover our frail bodies, in the mode of expressing our insignificant thoughts, in our ridiculous customs and our imperfect laws, in our idle opinions, and in our several conditions and situations, that appear so disproportionate in our eyes, and all are equal in Thine; in a word, may the slight variations that are found amongst the atoms called men not be made use of by us as signals of mutual hatred and persecution! May those who worship Thee by the light of tapers at noonday bear charitably with those who content themselves with the light of that glorious planet Thou hast placed in the midst of the heavens! May those who dress themselves in a robe of white linen to teach their hearers that Thou art to be loved and feared, not detest or revile those who teach the same doctrine in long cloaks of black wool! May it be accounted the same to adore Thee in a dialect formed from an ancient or a modern language! May those who, clothed in vestments of crimson or violet color, rule over a little parcel of that heap of dirt called the world, and are possessed of a few round fragments of a certain metal, enjoy without pride or insolence what they call grandeur and riches, and may others look on them without envy; for Thou knowest, O God, that there is nothing in all these vanities proper to inspire envy or pride.

May all men remember that they are brethren! May they alike abhor that tyranny which seeks to subject the freedom of the will, as they do the rapine which tears from the arms of industry the fruits of its peaceful labors! And if the scourge of war is not to be avoided, let us not mutually hate and destroy each other in the midst of peace; but rather make use of the few moments of our existence to join in praising, in a thousand different languages, from one extremity of the world to the other, Thy goodness, O all-merciful Creator, to whom we are indebted for that existence!

COMMENTS AND QUESTIONS

1. Tolerance of different beliefs and customs is more or less accepted—ideally if not in practice—in our society today, but it was quite a new idea in the eighteenth century. Could this have been written in the Middle Ages? The Reformation? The seventeenth century? Why not?
2. Is Voltaire himself really tolerant of all views and practices?
3. Define for yourself what, exactly, tolerance means and how far its limits extend.
4. What do different people who claim to practice toleration term intolerable?

MONTESQUIEU

FROM *The Spirit of the Laws*

Translation by Thomas Nugent

Of Civil Slavery

Slavery, properly so called, is the establishment of a right which gives to one man such a power over another as renders him absolute master of his life and fortune. The state of slavery is in its own nature bad. It is neither useful to the master nor to the slave; not to the slave, because he can do nothing through a motive of virtue; nor to the master, because by having an unlimited authority over his slaves he insensibly accustoms himself to the want of all moral virtues, and thence becomes fierce, hasty, severe, choleric, voluptuous, and cruel.

In despotic countries, where they are already in a state of political servitude, civil slavery is more tolerable than in other governments. Every one ought to be satisfied in those countries with necessaries and life. Hence the condition of a slave is hardly more burdensome than that of a subject.

But in a monarchical government, where it is of the utmost importance that human nature should not be debased or dispirited, there ought to be no slavery. In democracies, where they are all upon equality; and in aristocracies, where the laws ought to use their utmost endeavors to procure as great an equality as the nature of the government will permit, slavery is contrary to the spirit of the constitution: it only contributes to give a power and luxury to the citizens which they ought not to have....

Knowledge humanizes mankind, and reason inclines to mildness; but prejudices eradicate every tender disposition.

Another Origin of the Right of Slavery

I would as soon say that religion gives its professors a right to enslave those who dissent from it, in order to render its propagation more easy.

This was the notion that encouraged the ravagers of America in their iniquity. Under the influence of this idea they founded their right of enslaving so many nations; for these robbers, who would absolutely be both robbers and Christians, were superlatively devout.

Louis XIII was extremely uneasy at a law by which all the negroes of his colonies were to be made slaves; but it being strongly urged to him as the readiest means for their conversion, he acquiesced without further scruple.

Of the Slavery of the Negroes

Were I to vindicate our right to make slaves of the negroes, these should be my arguments:—

The Europeans, having extirpated the Americans, were obliged to make slaves of the Africans, for clearing such vast tracts of land.

Sugar would be too dear if the plants which produce it were cultivated by any other than slaves.

These creatures are all over black, and with such a flat nose that they can scarcely be pitied.

It is hardly to be believed that God, who is a wise Being, should place a soul, especially a good soul, in such a black, ugly body.

It is so natural to look upon color as the criterion of human nature, that the Asiatics, among whom eunuchs are employed, always deprive the blacks of their resemblance to us by a more opprobrious distinction.

The color of the skin may be determined by that of the hair, which, among the Egyptians, the best philosophers in the world, was of such importance that they put to death all the red-haired men who fell into their hands.

The negroes prefer a glass necklace to that gold which polite nations so highly value. Can there be a greater proof of their wanting common sense?

It is impossible for us to suppose these creatures to be men, because, allowing them to be men, a suspicion would follow that we ourselves are not Christians.

Weak minds exaggerate too much the wrong done to the Africans. For were the case as they state it, would the European powers, who make so many needless conventions among themselves, have failed to enter into a general one, in behalf of humanity and compassion?

QUESTIONS

1. How do you think Montesquieu's arguments would strike an eighteenth-century public?
2. Explain the use of *irony* in the last section. Is it effective?
3. How does Montesquieu turn to ridicule statements that were undoubtedly believed by many?
4. Compare Montesquieu's satire on European "civilization" to that of Montaigne in Chapter 19.

JEAN-JACQUES ROUSSEAU

FROM *The Social Contract*

Translation by Henry J. Tozer

The Social Pact

I assume that men have reached a point at which the obstacles that endanger their preservation in the state of nature overcome by their resistance the forces which each individual can exert with a view to maintaining himself in that state. Then this primitive condition can no longer subsist, and the human race would perish unless it changed its mode of existence.

Now, as men cannot create any new forces, but only combine and direct those that exist, they have no other means of self-preservation than to form by aggregation a sum of forces which may overcome the resistance, to put them in action by a single motive power, and to make them work in concert.

This sum of forces can be produced only by the combination of many; but the strength and freedom of each man being the chief instruments of his preservation, how can he pledge them without injuring himself, and without neglecting the cares which he owes to himself? This difficulty, applied to my subject, may be expressed in these terms:

"To find a form of association which may defend and protect with the whole force of the community the person and property of every associate, and by means of which each, coalescing with all, may nevertheless obey only himself, and remain as free as before." Such is the fundamental problem of which the social contract furnishes the solution.

The clauses of this contract are so determined by the nature of the act that the slightest modification would render them vain and ineffectual; so that, although they have never perhaps been formally enunciated, they are everywhere the same, everywhere tacitly admitted and recognised, until, the social pact being violated, each man regains his original rights and recovers his natural liberty, whilst losing the conventional liberty for which he renounced it.

These clauses, rightly understood, are reducible to one only, viz. The total alienation to the whole community of each associate with all rights; for, in the first place, since each gives himself up entirely, the conditions are equal for all; and, the conditions being equal for all, no one has any interest in making them burdensome to others.

Further, the alienation being made without reserve, the union is as perfect as it can be, and an individual associate can no longer claim anything; for, if any rights were left to individuals, since there would be no common superior who could judge between them and the public, each being on some point his own judge, would soon claim to be so on all; the state of nature would still subsist, and the association would necessarily become tyrannical or useless.

In short, each giving himself to all, gives himself to nobody; and as there is not one associate over whom we do not acquire the same rights which we concede to him over ourselves, we gain the equivalent of all that we lose, and more power to preserve what we have.

If, then, we set aside what is not of the essence of the social contract, we shall find that it is reducible to the following terms: "Each of us puts in common his person and his whole power under the supreme direction of the general will; and in return we receive every member as an indivisible part of the whole."

Forthwith, instead of the individual personalities of all the contracting parties, this act of association produces a moral and collective body, which is composed of as many members as the assembly has voices, and which receives from this same act its unity, its common self, its life, and its will. This public person, which is thus formed by the union of all the individual members, formerly took the name of "city" and now takes that of "republic" or "body politic," which is called by its members "State" when it is passive, "sovereign" when it is active, "power" when it is compared to similar bodies. With regard to the associates, they take collectively the name of "people," and are called individually "citizens," as participating in the sovereign power, and "subjects," as subjected to the laws of the State. But these terms are often confused and are mistaken one for another; it is sufficient to know how to distinguish them when they are used with complete precision.

QUESTIONS

1. What societies do not have a social contract? Why?
2. Why must the individual give up all his rights on entering the contract?
3. Why, after the creation of the social contract, does each individual remain as free as before?
4. What limitations are there on the actions of the community in regard to the individual? What kind of laws can the community not make?

Whether the General Will Can Err

It follows from what precedes that the general will is always right and always tends to the public advantage; but it does not follow that the resolutions of the people have always the same rectitude. Men always desire their own good, but do not always discern it; the people are never corrupted, though often deceived, and it is only then that they seem to will what is evil.

There is often a great deal of difference between the will of all and the general will; the latter regards only the common interest, while the former has regard to private interests, and is merely a sum of particular wills; but take away from these same wills the pluses and minuses which cancel one another, and the general will remains as the sum of the differences.

If the people came to a resolution when adequately informed and without any communication among the citizens, the general will would always result from the great number of slight differences, and the resolution would always be good. But when factions, partial associations, are formed to the detriment of the whole society, the will of each of these associations becomes general with reference to its members, and particular with reference to the State; it may then be said that there are no longer as many voters as there are men, but only as many voters as there are associations. The differences become less numerous and yield a less general result. Lastly, when one of these associations becomes so great that it predominates over all the rest, you no longer have as the result a sum of small differences, but a single difference; there is then no longer a general will, and the opinion which prevails is only a particular opinion.

It is important, then, in order to have a clear declaration of the general will, that there should be no partial association in the State, and that every citizen should express only his own opinion.

QUESTIONS

1. Why does Rousseau feel as he does about political parties?
2. How did most philosophes regard such organizations? Why?
3. What does Rousseau mean by natural rights? Who determines the limits of these rights in society?

MARY WOLLSTONECRAFT

FROM *A Vindication of the Rights of Woman*

Chapter IX

Of the Pernicious Effects Which Arise from the Unnatural Distinctions Established in Society

From the respect paid to property[1] flow, as from a poisoned fountain, most of the evils and vices which render this world such a dreary scene to the con-

[1]Note that Wollstonecraft shares with Rousseau the idea that social ills are caused by private property.

templative mind. For it is in the most polished society that noisome reptiles and venomous serpents lurk under the rank herbage; and there is voluptuousness pampered by the still sultry air, which relaxes every good disposition before it ripens into virtue. . . .

It is vain to expect virtue from women till they are, in some degree, independent of men; nay, it is vain to expect that strength of natural affection, which would make them good wives and mothers. Whilst they are absolutely dependent on their husbands they will be cunning, mean, and selfish, and the men who can be gratified by the fawning fondness of spaniel-like affection, have not much delicacy, for love is not to be bought, in any sense of the words, its silken wings are instantly shrivelled up when any thing beside a return in kind is sought. Yet whilst wealth enervates men; and women live, as it were, by their personal charms, how can we expect them to discharge those ennobling duties which equally require exertion and self-denial? Hereditary property sophisticates[2] the mind, and the unfortunate victims to it, if I may so express myself, swathed from their birth, seldom exert the locomotive faculty of body or mind; and, thus viewing every thing through one medium, and that a false one, they are unable to discern in what true merit and happiness consist. False, indeed, must be the light when the drapery of situation hides the man, and makes him stalk in masquerade, dragging from one scene of dissipation to another the nerveless limbs that hang with stupid listlessness, and rolling round the vacant eye which plainly tells us that there is no mind at home. . . .

To illustrate my opinion, I need only observe, that when a woman is admired for her beauty, and suffers herself to be so far intoxicated by the admiration she receives, as to neglect to discharge the indispensable duty of a mother, she sins against herself by neglecting to cultivate an affection that would equally tend to make her useful and happy. True happiness, I mean all the contentment, and virtuous satisfaction, that can be snatched in this imperfect state, must arise from well-regulated affections; and an affection includes a duty. Men are not aware of the misery they cause, and the vicious weakness they cherish, by only inciting women to render themselves pleasing; they do not consider that they thus make natural and artificial duties clash, by sacrificing the comfort and respectability of a woman's life to voluptuous notions of beauty, when in nature they all harmonize.

Cold would be the heart of a husband, were he not rendered unnatural by early debauchery, who did not feel more delight at seeing his child suckled by its mother, than the most artful wanton tricks could ever raise; yet this natural way of cementing the matrimonial tie, and twisting esteem with fonder recollections, wealth leads women to spurn. To preserve their beauty, and wear the flowery crown of the day, which gives them a kind of right to reign for a short time over the sex, they neglect to stamp impressions on their husbands' hearts, that would be remembered with more tenderness when the snow on the head began to chill the bosom, than even their virgin charms. The maternal solicitude of a reasonable affectionate woman is very interesting, and the chastened dignity with which a mother returns the caresses that she and her child receive from a father who has been fulfilling the serious duties of his station, is not only a respectable, but a beautiful sight. So singular, indeed, are my feelings, and I have endeavoured not to catch factitious ones, that after having been fatigued with the sight of insipid grandeur and the slavish ceremonies that with cumbrous pomp supplied the place of domestic affections, I have turned to some other scene to relieve my eye by resting it on the refreshing green every where scattered by nature. I have then viewed with pleasure a woman nursing her children, and discharging the duties of her station with, perhaps, merely a servant maid to take off her hands the servile part of the household business. I have seen her prepare herself and children, with only the luxury of cleanliness, to receive her husband, who returning weary home in the evening found smiling babes and a clean hearth. My heart has loitered in the midst of the group, and has even throbbed with sympathetic emotion, when the scraping of the well known foot has raised a pleasing tumult. . . .

The preposterous distinctions of rank, which render civilization a curse, by dividing the world between voluptuous tyrants, and cunning envious dependents, corrupt, almost equally, every class of people, because respectability is not attached to the discharge of the relative duties of life, but to the station, and when the duties are not fulfilled the affections cannot gain sufficient strength to fortify the virtue of which they are the natural reward. Still there are some loop-holes out of which a man may creep, and dare to think and act for himself; but for a woman it is an herculean task, because she has difficulties peculiar to her sex to overcome, which require almost superhuman powers.

A truly benevolent legislator always endeavours to make it the interest of each individual to be virtuous; and thus private virtue becoming the cement of public happiness, an orderly whole is consolidated by the tendency of all the parts towards a common centre.

---

[2]Corrupts.

But, the private or public virtue of woman is very problematical; for Rousseau, and a numerous list of male writers, insist that she should all her life be subjected to a severe restraint, that of propriety. Why subject her to propriety—blind propriety, if she be capable of acting from a nobler spring, if she be an heir of immortality? Is sugar always to be produced by vital blood? Is one half of the human species, like the poor African slaves, to be subject to prejudices that brutalize them, when principles would be a surer guard, only to sweeten the cup of man? Is not this indirectly to deny woman reason? for a gift is a mockery, if it be unfit for use.

Women are, in common with men, rendered weak and luxurious by the relaxing pleasures which wealth procures; but added to this they are made slaves to their persons, and must render them alluring that man may lend them his reason to guide their tottering steps aright. Or should they be ambitious, they must govern their tyrants by sinister tricks, for without rights there cannot be any incumbent duties. The laws respecting woman, . . . make an absurd unit of a man and his wife;[3] and then, by the easy transition of only considering him as responsible, she is reduced to a mere cypher.

The being who discharges the duties of its station is independent; and, speaking of women at large, their first duty is to themselves as rational creatures, and the next, in point of importance, as citizens, is that, which includes so many, of a mother. The rank in life which dispenses with their fulfilling this duty necessarily degrades them by making them mere dolls. Or, should they turn to something more important than merely fitting drapery upon a smooth block, their minds are only occupied by some soft platonic attachment; or, the actual management of an intrigue may keep their thoughts in motion; for when they neglect domestic duties, they have it not in their power to take the field and march and countermarch like soldiers, or wrangle in the senate to keep their faculties from rusting.

I know that, as a proof of the inferiority of the sex, Rousseau has exultingly exclaimed, How can they leave the nursery for the camp!—And the camp has by some moralists been termed the school of the most heroic virtues; though, I think, it would puzzle a keen casuist to prove the reasonableness of the greater number of wars that have dubbed heroes. I do not mean to consider this question critically; because, having frequently viewed these freaks of ambition as the first natural mode of civilization, when the ground must be torn up, and the woods cleared by fire and sword, I do not choose to call them pests; but surely the present system of war has little connection with virtue of any denomination, being rather the school of *finesse* and effeminacy, than of fortitude.

Yet, if defensive war, the only justifiable war, in the present advanced state of society, where virtue can shew its face and ripen amidst the rigours which purify the air on the mountain's top, were alone to be adopted as just and glorious, the true heroism of antiquity might again animate female bosoms.—But fair and softly, gentle reader, male or female, do not alarm thyself, for though I have compared the character of a modern soldier with that of a civilized woman, I am not going to advise them to turn their distaff into a musket, though I sincerely wish to see the bayonet converted into a pruning-hook. I only recreated an imagination, fatigued by contemplating the vices and follies which all proceed from a feculent stream of wealth that has muddied the pure rills of natural affection, by supposing that society will some time or other be so constituted, that man must necessarily fulfil the duties of a citizen, or be despised, and that while he was employed in any of the departments of civil life, his wife, also an active citizen, should be equally intent to manage her family, educate her children, and assist her neighbours.

But, to render her really virtuous and useful, she must not, if she discharge her civil duties, want, individually, the protection of civil duties, want, individually, the protection of civil laws; she must not be dependent on her husband's bounty for her subsistence during his life, or support after his death—for how can a being be generous who has nothing of its own? or, virtuous, who is not free? The wife, in the present state of things, who is faithful to her husband, and neither suckles nor educates her children, scarcely deserves the name of a wife, and has no right to that of a citizen. But take away natural rights, and duties become null.

Women then must be considered as only the wanton solace of men, when they become so weak in mind and body, that they cannot exert themselves, unless to pursue some frothy pleasure, or to invent some frivolous fashion. What can be a more melancholy sight to a thinking mind, than to look into the numerous carriages that drive helter-skelter about this metropolis in a morning full of pale-faced creatures who are flying from themselves. I have often wished, with Dr. Johnson, to place some of them in a little shop with

[3]According to English law at the time, the husband was the only legally responsible person in a family unit.

half a dozen children looking up to their languid countenances for support. I am much mistaken, if some latent vigour would not soon give health and spirit to their eyes, and some lines drawn by the exercise of reason on the blank cheeks, which before were only undulated by dimples, might restore lost dignity to the character, or rather enable it to attain the true dignity of its nature. Virtue is not to be acquired even by speculation, much less by the negative supineness that wealth naturally generates.

Besides, when poverty is more disgraceful than even vice, is not morality cut to the quick? Still to avoid misconstruction, though I consider that women in the common walks of life are called to fulfil the duties of wives and mothers, by religion and reason, I cannot help lamenting that women of a superiour cast have not a road open by which they can pursue more extensive plans of usefulness and independence. I may excite laughter, by dropping an hint, which I mean to pursue, some future time, for I really think that women ought to have representatives, instead of being arbitrarily governed without having any direct share allowed them in the deliberations of government.

But, as the whole system of representation is now, in this country, only a convenient handle for despotism, they need not complain, for they are as well represented as a numerous class of hard working mechanics, who pay for the support of royalty when they can scarcely stop their children's mouths with bread. How are they represented whose very sweat supports the splendid stud of an heir apparent, or varnishes the chariot of some female favourite who looks down on shame? Taxes on the very necessaries of life, enable an endless tribe of idle princes and princesses to pass with stupid pomp before a gaping crowd, who almost worship the very parade which costs them so dear. This is mere gothic grandeur, something like the barbarous useless parade of having sentinels on horseback at Whitehall, which I could never view without a mixture of contempt and indignation....

But what have women to do in society? I may be asked, but to loiter with easy grace; surely you would not condemn them all to suckle fools and chronicle small beer![4] No. Women might certainly study the art of healing, and be physicians as well as nurses. And midwifery, decency seems to allot to them, though I am afraid the word midwife, in our dictionaries, will soon give place to *accoucheur*,[5] and one proof of the former delicacy of the sex be effaced from the language.

They might, also, study politics, and settle their benevolence on the broadest basis; for the reading of history will scarcely be more useful than the perusal of romances, if read as mere biography; if the character of the times, the political improvements, arts, &c. be not observed. In short, if it be not considered as the history of man; and not of particular men, who filled a niche in the temple of fame, and dropped into the black rolling stream of time, that silently sweeps all before it, into the shapeless void called—eternity.—For shape, can it be called, "that shape hath none"?[6]

Business of various kinds, they might likewise pursue, if they were educated in a more orderly manner, which might save many from common and legal prostitution. Women would not then marry for a support, as men accept of places under government, and neglect the implied duties; nor would an attempt to earn their own subsistence, a most laudable one! sink them almost to the level of those poor abandoned creatures who live by prostitution. For are not milliners and mantua-makers[7] reckoned the next class? The few employments open to women, so far from being liberal, are menial; and when a superiour education enables them to take charge of the education of children as governesses, they are not treated like the tutors of sons, though even clerical tutors are not always treated in a manner calculated to render them respectable in the eyes of their pupils, to say nothing of the private comfort of the individual. But as women educated like gentlewomen, are never designed for the humiliating situation which necessity sometimes forces them to fill; these situations are considered in the light of a degradation; and they know little of the human heart, who need to be told, that nothing so painfully sharpens sensibility as such a fall in life.

Some of these women might be restrained from marrying by a proper spirit or delicacy, and others may not have had it in their power to escape in this pitiful way from servitude; is not that government then very defective, and very unmindful of the happiness of one half of its members, that does not provide for honest, independent women, by encouraging them to fill respectable stations? But in order to render their private virtue a public benefit, they must have a civil existence in the state, married or single; else we shall

[4] *Othello* II.i.160.

[5] "The birther," a male doctor.

[6] *Paradise Lost* II.666–667.

[7] Dressmakers.

continually see some worthy woman, whose sensibility has been rendered painfully acute by undeserved contempt, droop like "the lily broken down by a plow-share."

It is a melancholy truth; yet such is the blessed effect of civilization! the most respectable women are the most oppressed; and, unless they have understandings far superiour to the common run of understandings, taking in both sexes, they must, from being treated like contemptible beings, become contemptible. How many women thus waste life away the prey of discontent, who might have practised as physicians, regulated a farm, managed a shop, and stood erect, supported by their own industry, instead of hanging their heads surcharged with the dew of sensibility, that consumes the beauty to which it at first gave lustre; nay, I doubt whether pity and love are so near akin as poets feign, for I have seldom seen much compassion excited by the helplessness of females, unless they were fair; then, perhaps, pity was the soft handmaid of love, or the harbinger of lust.

How much more respectable is the woman who earns her own bread by fulfilling any duty, than the most accomplished beauty!—beauty did I say?—so sensible am I of the beauty of moral loveliness, or the harmonious propriety that attunes the passions of a well-regulated mind, that I blush at making the comparison; yet I sigh to think how few women aim at attaining this respectability by withdrawing from the giddy whirl of pleasure, or the indolent calm that stupefies the good sort of women it sucks in....

Would men but generously snap our chains, and be content with rational fellowship instead of slavish obedience, they would find us more observant daughters, more affectionate sisters, more faithful wives, more reasonable mothers—in a word, better citizens. We should then love them with true affection, because we should learn to respect ourselves; and the peace of mind of a worthy man would not be interrupted by the idle vanity of his wife, nor the babes sent to nestle in a strange bosom,[8] having never found a home in their mother's.

QUESTIONS

1. How does Wollstonecraft's concept of "unnatural distinctions" reveal Enlightenment thinking? In what respects is she a romantic?
2. Why does Wollstonecraft place so much importance on women nursing their own children?
3. What accounts for women's inferior status in society? What are Wollstonecraft's remedies?
4. Does Wollstonecraft seem too hard on the women of her own time?
5. Compare Wollstonecraft's views to those of present-day feminists.

[8]That of a wet-nurse.

25

The Enlightenment in the United States

Political events in North America in the last four decades of the eighteenth century fascinated European observers. While the French philosophes were forced to adapt their goals for improving the human condition to the circumstances of a very traditional social and political structure, English-speaking North America presented the situation of a new people in an underdeveloped land largely untrammeled by the weight of past institutions. Once the colonists had thrown off the control imposed on their society by the imperial system of the mother country, the possibilities for political creativity and experimentation seemed limitless. As the new nation emerged from the endless deliberations of the political leadership, European intellectuals watched intently for signs to determine whether the American republic, the most populous and geographically extensive republican government in the history of the world, would succeed or fail.

The history of the creation of the United States, following more than a century of colonial development, can be divided into three basic phases. The first phase began with the defeat of French armies in the New World by combined British and colonial forces, part of a worldwide struggle between rival European powers. When British officials then tried to impose increased taxes on the growing colonies to help cover the rising military and administrative costs of the empire, the colonists resisted in increasing numbers and finally declared themselves politically independent in 1776. The second phase comprises the period from the first years of the war until the creation of the Constitution in 1787, when the dominant minds in America attempted to devise some sort of lasting union among the thirteen loosely confederated states. The final period is that of the first decades after ratification of the Constitution (which went into effect in 1789) as Americans endeavored to make the new government work in the face of forces for decentralization that threatened at times to pull the new federal structure apart.

American Religion

Christianity in prerevolutionary America was the most important cultural and intellectual force in colonial life. Among whites, the predominant allegiance of the colonists was to some form of Protestantism. Even in Maryland, originally founded as a Catholic refuge, Protestants were in the vast majority. The few Jews in the colonies resided largely in the coastal towns. Missionary associations of various churches had achieved little success with the rapidly dwindling Native American population, but from the 1730s on African Americans converted in large numbers. By the revolution conversion among the enslaved population, now principally being carried out by blacks themselves, created a significant mass of black Christians in the colonies. The African American churches, however, retained many elements of religious practices from the African religious heritage.

The beginning of the conversion of blacks on a large scale in the 1730s was only one aspect of a great religious revival that swept the English colonies in that and the succeeding decade. Known as the Great Awakening, the movement started in New Jersey, was taken up by Jonathan Edwards (1703–1758), a Congregational minister in Northampton, Connecticut, and within the next few years was spread by a series of fiery preachers the entire length of the Atlantic coast.

Americans in these years were responding to a deeply felt sense that their churches were becoming too institutionalized and too committed to doctrine while the passion of belief that nourished the emotional life of the believer was draining away. By arousing religious feelings at the expense of catechisms and using emotion rather than reasoned argument, the preachers of the Great Awakening, a movement that cut across all doctrinal lines, exercised an enormous appeal, especially on those with little education. The spiritual malaise was so general, however, that large numbers from all classes were attracted to the revival movement.

Effect of the Great Awakening

The Great Awakening had a tremendously disruptive effect on established religion in the colonies, dividing congregations into Old Light and New Light groups. The activity of itinerant preachers tended to destroy the identification of churches with particular territories, and because the preachers of the Awakening were marked more by charismatic gifts than by education or status, it undermined the authority of the traditional clergy. The intensity of the Great Awakening abated after 1750, but its effects on American religion were long lasting.

This revival movement contributed to bringing into question two fundamental beliefs of traditional Christianity: that religious conformity was necessary and that the state should lend financial and other support to a particular church. Although some states continued to use tax money to support a designated church or churches, the competition for membership in the spiritual market in the second half of the eighteenth century could not be prevented, and in practice freedom of conscience for all religions became the rule. Unlike European countries, in which the established church had a guaranteed membership and religion tended to be taken for granted, in the British colonies the competition for souls fostered an almost continual spirit of revival and a rich variety of choices. Consequently, by the time of the revolution the Christian churches were highly decentralized and largely voluntary in membership, and reflected the evolution of republican feeling in a broad sector of the population.

European Influences

From the early eighteenth century the dominant stream of ideas shaping politics in America was English. The *empiricism* of English thinkers like Bacon and Newton made a strong impact on Americans, and theory was reinforced by a pioneer culture that respected labor and practical know-how. Products of a highly mobile society with a flexible social structure, the colonists worked well together at the local level in meeting their common needs. The validity of Locke's doctrine of natural rights of humankind seemed borne out by their experience. Beginning as they did in a new environment, the colonists tended to view critically any limitation on their freedom of action unless it could be justified in terms of personal advantage. With the executive power firmly in the hands of British governors, they also found Locke's emphasis on the duty of legislative assemblies to supervise the executive authority to their liking. Characteristically, the Declaration of Independence, which claimed rights to life, liberty, and the pursuit of happiness to be self-evident, justified severance with England on the grounds of George III's tyranny, not because of oppression by

Parliament. Furthermore, the Declaration of Independence and the Constitution echo Locke in their statements that governments derive their just powers from the consent of the governed and that when governments exceed their power, the people have the right to institute new governments.

French philosophes were, on the whole, ardent supporters of the American Revolution. They admired versatile diplomats like Benjamin Franklin and Thomas Jefferson, both of whom lived for long periods in France, as the kind of "enlightened" individuals that the New World could produce. People like Turgot, a *philosophe* minister of Louis XV, used their influence at court to bring the French government into the war on the rebels' side in 1778, and the French intervention was decisive. On the intellectual level, Montesquieu doubtless had the most significant influence on American political thought in the revolutionary period. His conception of a balance of power among the legislative, executive, and judicial branches of government suited the American distrust of the executive and made the Constitution more attractive to many who looked on a strong executive as a potential threat to individual freedom. In the 1780s and 1790s, however, Rousseau's democratic theories provided ammunition against elitist conceptions of political authority held by most American thinkers. For example, property qualifications for voting rights were reduced at this time.

To an extent, the ease with which Americans accepted the ideas of the philosophes stemmed from the fact that much of the philosophy of the French thinkers had been inspired by the English political experience, which Americans had inherited. But more than this, the increasingly voluntaristic character of American religion made Christianity in the colonies compatible with most of their ideas. In France, as we have seen, intellectuals attacked the privileged Church as obscurantist and as the champion of political oppression. Religion itself became tainted by association. On the other hand, in religiously pluralistic America, the Enlightenment lost its antireligious bias. Whereas in France the Enlightenment doctrine of religious toleration aimed at subverting the hold of the Catholic Church on French culture, in America this doctrine was introduced to justify a practical situation created by the existence of conflicting religious groups.

American Federalism

Federalism, perhaps the United States' most original contribution to the theory and practice of republican government, owed little to either the French or the English; it was born of necessity. Under no circumstances able to induce strong, independent state governments to become mere agencies of the central government, the writers of the Constitution established a principle of separation of powers between the central government and the states. Such a system of power division was to have a great future because it permitted unification of large areas of land and supported regional diversity while still limiting the power of local opposition.

The Heritage of Ancient Rome

No account of the ideology of the American revolutionary epoch would be complete without acknowledging the extent to which these patriots thought of themselves and were considered by their European sympathizers as the heirs to the republican tradition of ancient Rome. Since the Renaissance the educated class of the Western world had been deeply imbued with classical culture; one aspect of that culture, clearly defined since the early fifteenth century, was its *republican* tradition. The leaders of the revolution appeared to contemporaries as the simple, honest descendants of Roman leaders like Cato, or the general Cincinnatus, who left his own plow to lead an army against the enemies of the Roman Republic. Americans often signed their letters of protest against English tyranny with Roman names, and Washington and other officers of the revolutionary army took part in a controversial Society of Cincinnatus. In their struggle for liberty, the patriots (from Latin *patria*—homeland) seemed to be the modern counterparts of Roman heroes like Horatio and Brutus. The architects of the Constitution drew on words of Latin derivation like *president* and *senate,* and the Great Seal of the new nation and its coinage were marked with Latin phrases and classical emblems (Fig. 25-1). Houdon's statue of Washington in the capital at Richmond dramatically illustrates these associations of the new republic with the old. In 1786 the French sculptor represented the future president of the United States in modern dress; but he stands beside the Roman *fasces,* a bundle of rods symbolic of power and union, in a pose based on that of a classical statue (Fig. 25-2).

Thomas Jefferson (1743–1826)

The figure who best represents the American Enlightenment is Thomas Jefferson. Jefferson combined the Old World's tradition of scholarship and philosophy with the New World's practicality and readiness to

25-1 *Great Seal of the United States. (Bureau of Engraving and Printing, U.S. Department of the Treasury)*

25-2 *Jean Antoine Houdon,* George Washington, *1788–92, marble, height 74", State Capitol, Richmond. (Virginia State Library and Archives)*

experiment. Both philosopher and plantation manager, he was at home in the salons of Paris and the still untamed parts of Virginia. Like the French philosophes, he combined wide learning in the classical humanities with a lively interest in recent scientific developments. He regarded the republic of letters and ideas as an international one.

In addition to his career as a politician, Jefferson was an excellent writer, an educator, a farmer, and an architect. One of his masterpieces is his home near Charlottesville, Virginia, which he called Monticello ("little mountain"; see Fig. 25-3). The house itself is symbolic of the nature of the American Enlightenment. Jefferson used the *Palladian* Villa Rotunda as his model (Fig. 23-1), but the plan of the interior exhibits a functional adaptation of the symmetrical plan to his own particular needs. Similarly, the building, originally designed for stone execution, is rendered in red brick with white wooden trim—an elegant, rich contrast to the building's general simplicity of shape. These adaptations to use and surroundings do not, however, detract from the *portico* and *dome,* the two architectural forms that link it with those of democratic Greece and republican Rome. Facing westward, to the wilderness, dominating but sympathetic to the landscape, the house is almost a metaphor for the man—aristocratic, cosmopolitan, inventive, practical—a farmer and a philosopher.

Designing his own tomb for the grounds at Monticello, Jefferson composed the following inscription: "Here was buried Thomas Jefferson, author of the Declaration of American Independence, of the Statute of Virginia for Religious Freedom, and Father of the University of Virginia." He apparently did not consider that being the third president of the United States was among his most significant accomplishments. Those that he lists are excellent examples of the application of the principles of the Enlightenment to the American experience.

The Declaration of Independence The Declaration, written largely by Jefferson and approved by the Continental Congress on July 4, 1776, is a statement of political philosophy as well as an act of rebellion. It is in fact typical of the American Enlightenment that theory and its practical application are combined in the same document. The Declaration may be divided into two distinct parts: the first sets forth principles of democratic government and proves, in the abstract, philosophical terms of the Enlightenment, the right of the colonies to rebel. The second part is a specific list of grievances against the king of Great Britain, George III.

A close reading of the first two paragraphs of the Declaration reveals the purpose of the document and a theoretical basis for rebellion.

> When, in the course of human events, it becomes necessary for one people to dissolve the political

25-3 *Thomas Jefferson, Monticello, west front. (Thomas Jefferson Memorial Foundation Inc.)*

bands which have connected them with another, and to assume, among the powers of the earth, the separate and equal station to which the laws of nature and of nature's God entitle them, a decent respect to the opinions of mankind requires that they should declare the causes which impel them to the separation.

We hold these truths to be self-evident: That all men are created equal; that they are endowed by their Creator with certain unalienable rights; that among these are life, liberty & the pursuit of happiness; that to secure these rights governments are instituted among men, deriving their just powers from the consent of the governed; that whenever any form of government becomes destructive of these ends, it is the right of the people to alter or to abolish it, and to institute new government, laying its foundation on such principles and organizing its powers in such form, as to them shall seem most likely to effect their safety and happiness.

QUESTIONS

1. Is there any religious basis for the rebellion? Does it seem to be Christian?
2. How do the expressions "laws of nature," "nature's God," and "truths" that are "self-evident" reflect values of the Enlightenment?
3. Did the American political system in fact guarantee the "unalienable rights" that Jefferson lists? What do you think that he meant by "the pursuit of happiness"? By "all men are created equal"?
4. How do Jefferson's political ideals differ from, or resemble, those of Thucydides's? (See Chapter 4.)
5. Do the principles of the Enlightenment found here (such as self-evident truths) seem a valid basis from which to argue legal and moral questions today?

The questions raised here may be applied to the entire Declaration. The second part of the document purports to show, by the list of grievances, that George III deliberately and malevolently attempted to establish an "absolute tyranny" over the colonies. It is consistent with Jefferson's idea of a government that derives its powers from the "consent of the governed" that he blames all sorts of evils on the tyrannical will of the king. The last of Jefferson's charges, omitted by the Congress in the final draft of the Declaration, was an indictment against the enslavement of Africans.

He has waged cruel war against human nature itself, violating its most sacred rights of life and liberty in the persons of a distant people who never offended him, captivating and carrying them into slavery in another hemisphere, or to incur miserable death in their transportation thither. This piratical warfare, the opprobrium of *infidel* powers, is the warfare of the *Christian* king of Great Britain. Determined to keep open a market where MEN should be bought and sold, he has prostituted his negative for suppressing every legislative attempt to prohibit or to restrain this execrable commerce; and that this assemblage of horrors might want no fact of distinguished die, he is now exciting these very people to rise in arms among us, and to purchase that liberty of which *he* deprived them, by murdering the people upon whom *he* also obtruded them; thus paying off former crimes committed against the *liberties* of one people, with crimes which he urges them to commit against the *lives* of another.

QUESTIONS

1. How does Jefferson's application of the principles of the Enlightenment to the question of slavery differ from and/or resemble that of Montesquieu?
2. Does it make good historical sense to blame the existence of slavery and the slave trade on George III?
3. What important factors does Jefferson omit?

Jefferson's own position on slavery was fraught with ambiguity. He owned many slaves on his plantation at Monticello. He seems to have been tormented by his contradictory feelings that slavery was a moral wrong and would eventually be abolished, but that the time was not yet ripe for black Americans to be free. Recent biographies of Jefferson wrestle with this and other contradictions in this multifaceted man.

The Virginia Statute and the University of Virginia The second accomplishment on which Jefferson prided himself, the Virginia Statute of Religious Liberty (October 1785), is in the spirit of Voltaire's *Treatise on Toleration.* The statute was part of the constitution of the state of Virginia, which served as a model for other state constitutions.

Jefferson remained a nominal Anglican until the end of his life but continued to combat what he considered to be superstitions and unnecessary dogmas in Christianity. He respected Jesus as a great moral teacher but did not necessarily believe him to be divine. He made his own edition of the Bible, cutting out references to miracles. Unitarians today consider Jefferson one of their forefathers. In an "unenlightened" age a century or two earlier, he would have been arrested as a heretic.

In keeping with Jefferson's beliefs, his third monu-

25-4 *Thomas Jefferson, University of Virginia, 1856 engraving by C. Bohn. (University of Virginia Library)*

mental project, the University of Virginia, was the only early university not to be associated with a church. Jefferson viewed this "academical village" as an opportunity not only to create an ideal educational environment but also to improve the tastes of the Americans who would be educated there (Fig. 25-4).

Jefferson had always scorned the architecture of Williamsburg, where he was educated, and had tried to mold taste with his designs for the capitol of Virginia at Richmond (Fig. 25-5). He used no Renaissance models or sources. Having seen engravings of the Maison Carrée in Nîmes, he adopted the plan of that building for the new capitol.

That the pure temple form was not immediately adopted nationally can be seen by comparing the Virginia state capitol with the Massachusetts State House in Boston, designed by Charles Bulfinch in 1795 (Fig. 25-6). The sources of the State House are from the English Renaissance as well as from Rome. Both buildings, however, provided strong images of the state.

This belief, that art and architecture reinforce and perpetuate strong, appropriate images for ideals, was much in Jefferson's mind when the university was laid out. The heart of the university is a rectangular quadrangle bounded on each of its long sides by a one-story covered colonnade broken at intervals by the two-story houses of the professors. Students lived in rooms off the colonnades; professors held classes downstairs in their living quarters (Fig. 25-7). The east end of the quad is closed by the library, a domed, porticoed rotunda (Fig. 25-8). Suggested by Benjamin Latrobe, another important architect, the rotunda acted as the focus and capstone, while the west end of the campus was open to the mountains. This very regular pattern for the central campus was relieved by the dining rooms, kitchens, and other service facilities located behind the two parallel rows of colonnades. There were found gardens (which students were expected to help work), pathways, and private walks for the

25-5 *Thomas Jefferson, Capitol, Richmond. (Virginia State Library and Archives)*

25-6 *Charles Bulfinch, Massachusetts State House. (Courtesy of the Trustees of the Public Library of the city of Boston)*

students, who would participate in the educative life in the main quad but still have time for meditation, contemplation, and studies close to nature.

The rotunda and professors' houses were carefully detailed with what Jefferson considered the best forms of the classical *orders;* the Corinthian was reserved for the interior of the rotunda. All are used in correct proportion and with their correct *entablatures* and *moldings.* Jefferson drew on ancient and Renaissance treatises in his planning.

The architecture of the campus reflects the two areas in which students were supposed to grow to become successful adults—the active and the contemplative lives. Conspicuously absent is a chapel or church since religion was to be a personal, private affair. Unlike Harvard, Yale, or Princeton, this early university of the new republic was a monument to free thought.

The ideal behind the University of Virginia was, in typical Enlightenment fashion, universal. "Enlighten the people generally," Jefferson wrote, "and oppressions of body and mind will vanish like evil spirits at the dawn of day." Practically, however, because of the nature of the education planned, it could accommodate only an elite few. Women of all races, blacks, and white males from poor families were excluded. Jefferson, though he educated his daughters, held in fact very conventional ideas regarding women: they should not mix in politics or public meetings or be outspoken in any way; their proper place was in the domestic sphere. The educated elite, who alone were fit to rule the American nation in Jefferson's view, would have been limited to white men of some means if his plan had remained the pattern. Fortunately, as is the case with most important thinkers, Jefferson's ideas outgrew his era's limitations and eventually served the causes of struggles for civil rights in which we are still involved.

The product of Jefferson's old age and retirement years, the University of Virginia opened its doors in 1824, when its founder was eighty-one. It was perhaps natural that the revolutionary, politician, and diplomat should retire into creating an ideal world on a reduced scale. This edifice for the education of the New World elite stands today as a manifestation of the styles and ideals of the Enlightenment, as interpreted by the New World's best example of Enlightenment thinking.

25-7 *Thomas Jefferson, University of Virginia, Pavilion and Colonnade. (University of Virginia Library)*

25-8 *Thomas Jefferson, University of Virginia, Rotunda. (University of Virginia Library)*

Reading Selections

Jonathan Edwards

From *A Faithful Narrative of the Surprising Work of God*

In the following excerpt from *A Faithful Narrative of the Surprising Work of God* (1737), Edwards first describes the effect of his revivalist preaching on his congregation and then the diffusion of its effect to the surrounding countryside in the Connecticut Valley. Edwards tells us that he had resolved to preach from the pulpit with no ambiguity that humanity is saved by faith alone, and that human beings have absolutely no power to ensure, or even to cooperate in, their own salvation. These sermons had a dazzling and surprising effect.

Although great fault was found with meddling with the controversy in the pulpit, by such a person, at that time, and though it was ridiculed by many elsewhere; yet it proved a word spoken in season here; and was most evidently attended with a very remarkable blessing of heaven to the souls of the people in this town. They received thence a general satisfaction with respect to the main thing in question, which they had in trembling doubts and concern about; and their minds were engaged the more earnestly to seek that they might come to be accepted of God, and saved in the way of the gospel, which had been made evident to them to be the true and only way. And then it was, in the latter part of December [1734], that the Spirit of God began extraordinarily to set in, and wonderfully to work amongst us; and there were, to all appearance, savingly converted, and some of them wrought upon in a very remarkable manner.

Particularly, I was surprised with the relation of a young woman, who had been one of the greatest company keepers in the whole town: when she came to me, I had never heard that she was become in any wise serious, but by the conversation I then had with her, it appeared to me, that what she gave an account of, was a glorious work of God's infinite power and sovereign grace; and that God had given her a new heart, truly broken and sanctified. I could not then doubt of it, and have seen much in my acquaintance with her since to confirm it.

Though the work was glorious, yet I was filled with concern about the effect it might have upon others: I was ready to conclude (though too rashly) that some would be hardened by it, in carelessness and looseness of life; and would take occasion from it to open their mouths, in reproaches of religion.[1] But the event was the reverse, to a wonderful degree; God made it, I suppose, the greatest occasion of awakening to others, of any thing that ever came to pass in the town. I have had abundant opportunity to know the effect it had, by my private conversation with many. The news of it seemed to be almost like a flash of lightning, upon the hearts of young people, all over the town, and upon many others. Those persons amongst us, who used to be farthest from seriousness, and that I most feared would make an ill improvement of it, seemed greatly to be awakened with it; many went to talk with her, concerning what she had met with; and what appeared in her seemed to be to the satisfaction of all that did so.

Presently upon this, a great and earnest concern about the great things of religion, and the eternal world, became universal in all parts of the town, and among persons of all degrees, and all ages; the noise amongst the dry bones waxed louder and louder: all other talk but about spiritual and eternal things was soon thrown by; all the conversation in all companies, and upon all occasions, was upon these things only, unless so much as was necessary for people carrying

---

[1]Edwards feared that when people were told that they could do nothing to help in their own salvation, they would abandon themselves to pleasure or curse God for his injustice in robbing them of the power of their will.

on their ordinary secular business. Other discourse than of the things of religion, would scarcely be tolerated in any company. The minds of people were wonderfully taken off from the world; it was treated amongst us as a thing of very little consequence: they seem to follow their worldly business, more as a part of their duty, than from any disposition they had to it; the temptation now seemed to be on that hand, to neglect worldly affairs too much, and to spend too much time in the immediate exercise of religion: which thing was exceedingly misrepresented by reports that were spread in distant parts of the land, as though the people here had wholly thrown by all worldly business, and betook themselves entirely to reading and praying, and such like religious exercises....

This work of God, as it was carried on, and the number of true saints multiplied, soon made a glorious alteration in the town; so that in the spring and summer following, anno 1735, the town seemed to be full of the presence of God: it never was so full of love, nor so full of joy; and yet so full of distress as it was then. There were remarkable tokens of God's presence in almost every house. It was a time of joy in families on the account of salvation's being brought unto them; parents rejoicing over their children as new born, and husbands over their wives, and wives over their husbands. *The goings of God were then seen in his sanctuary, God's day was a delight, and his tabernacles were amiable.* Our public assemblies were then beautiful; the congregation was alive in God's service, every one earnestly intent on the public worship, every hearer eager to drink in the words of the minister as they came from his mouth; the assembly in general were, from time to time, in tears while the word was preached; some weeping with sorrow and distress, others with joy and love, others with pity and concern for the souls of their neighbors....

When this work of God first appeared, and was so extraordinarily carried on amongst us in the winter, others round about us, seemed not to know what to make of it; and there were many that scoffed at, and ridiculed it; and some compared what we called conversion to certain distempers. But it was very observable of many, that occasionally came amongst us from abroad, with disregardful hearts, that what they saw here cured them of such a temper of mind: strangers were generally surprised to find things so much beyond what they had heard, and were wont to tell others that the state of the town could not be conceived of by those that had not seen it. The notice that was taken of it by the people that came to town on occasion of the court, that sat here in the beginning of March, was very observable. And those that came from the neighborhood to our public lectures, were for the most part remarkably affected. Many that came to town, on one occasion or other, had their consciences smitten, and awakened, and went home with wounded hearts, and with those impressions that never wore off till they had hopefully a saving issue; and those that before had serious thoughts, had their awakenings and convictions greatly increased. And there were many instances of persons that came from abroad, on visits, or on business, that had not been long here before, to all appearance, they were savingly wrought upon, and partook of that shower of divine blessing that God rained down here, and went home rejoicing; till at length the same work began evidently to appear and prevail in several other towns in the county.

In the month of March, the people in South Hadley began to be seized with deep concern about the things of religion; which very soon became universal: and the work of God has been very wonderful there; not much, if any thing, short of what it has been here, in proportion to the bigness of the place. About the same time it began to break forth in the west part of Suffield (where it has also been very great), and it soon spread into all parts of the town. It next appeared at Sunderland, and soon overspread the town; and I believe was for a season, not less remarkable than it was here. About the same time it began to appear in a part of Deerfield, called Green River, and afterwards filled the town, and there has been a glorious work there: it began also to be manifest in the south part of Hatfield, in a place called the Hill, and after that the whole town, in the second week in April, seemed to be seized, as it were at once, with concern about the things of religion: and the work of God has been great there. There has been also a very general awakening at West Springfield, and Long Meadow; and in Enfield, there was, for a time, a pretty general concern amongst some that before had been very loose persons. About the same time that this appeared at Enfield, the Rev. Mr. Bull of Westfield informed me, that there had been a great alternation there, and that more had been done in one week there than in seven years before.—Something of this work likewise appeared in the first precinct in Springfield, principally in the north and south extremes of the parish. And in Hadley old town, there gradually appeared so much of a work of God on souls, as at another time would have been thought worthy of much notice. For a short time there was also a very great and general concern, of the like nature, at Northfield. And wherever this concern appeared, it seemed not to be in vain: but in every place God brought saving blessings with them, and his word attended with his Spirit (as we have all reason to think) returned not void. It might well be said at that time in all parts of the country, *Who are these that fly as a cloud, and as doves to their windows?...*

This remarkable pouring out of the Spirit of God, which thus extended from one end to the other of this country, was not confined to it, but many places in Connecticut have partook in the same mercy: as for instance, the first parish in Windsor, under the pastoral care of the Reverend Mr. Marsh, was thus blest about the same time, as we in Northampton, while we had no knowledge of each other's circumstances....

But this shower of Divine blessing has been yet more extensive: there was no small degree of it in some parts of the Jerseys; as I was informed when I was at New-York (in a long journey I took at that time of the year for my health), by some people of the Jerseys, whom I saw: especially the Rev. Mr. William Tennent, a minister, who seemed to have such things much at heart, told me of a very great awakening of many in a place called the Mountains, under the ministry of one Mr. Cross; and of a very considerable revival of religion in another place under the ministry of his brother the Rev. Mr. Gilbert Tennent; and also at another place, under the ministry of a very pious young gentleman, a Dutch minister, whose name as I remember, was Freelinghousen.

QUESTIONS

1. What is meant by "saved by faith alone"? Compare Luther's position in Chapter 19.
2. How does Edwards explain the spread of the "Great Awakening"?

THOMAS JEFFERSON

The Virginia Statute of Religious Liberty

An Act for Establishing Religious Freedom

I. Whereas Almighty God hath created the mind free; that all attempts to influence it by temporal punishments or burthens, or by civil incapacitations, tend only to beget habits of hypocrisy and meanness, and are a departure from the plan of the Holy author of our religion, who being Lord both of body and mind, yet chose not to propagate it by coercions on either, as was in his Almighty power to do; that the impious presumption of legislators and rulers, civil as well as ecclesiastical, who being themselves but fallible and uninspired men, have assumed dominion over the faith of others, setting up their own opinions and modes of thinking as the only true and infallible, and as such endeavouring to impose them on others, hath established and maintained false religions over the greatest part of the world, and through all time; that to compel a man to furnish contributions of money for the propagation of opinions which he disbelieves, is sinful and tyrannical; that even the forcing him to support this or that teacher of his own religious persuasion, is depriving him of the comfortable liberty of giving his contributions to the particular pastor whose morals he would make his pattern, and whose powers he feels most persuasive to righteousness, and is withdrawing from the ministry those temporary rewards, which proceeding from an approbation of their personal conduct, are an additional incitement to earnest and unremitting labours for the instruction of mankind; that our civil rights have no dependence on our religious opinions, any more than our opinions in physics or geometry; that therefore the proscribing any citizen as unworthy the public confidence by laying upon him an incapacity of being called to offices of trust and emolument, unless he profess or renounce this or that religious opinion, is depriving him injuriously of those privileges and advantages to which in common with his fellow-citizens he has a natural right; that it tends only to corrupt the principles of that religion it is meant to encourage, by bribing with a monopoly of worldly honours and emoluments, those who will externally profess and conform to it; that though indeed these are criminal who do not withstand such temptation, yet neither are those innocent who lay the bait in their way; that to suffer the civil magistrate to intrude his powers into the field of opinion, and to restrain the profession or propagation of principles on supposition of their ill tendency, is a dangerous fallacy, which at once destroys all religious liberty, because he being of course judge of that tendency will make his opinions the rule of judgment, and approve or condemn the sentiments of others only as they shall square with or differ from his own; that it is time enough for the rightful purposes of civil government, for its officers to interfere when principles break out into overt acts against peace and good order; and finally, that truth is great and will prevail if left to herself, that she is the proper and sufficient antagonist to error, and has nothing to fear from the conflict, unless by human interposition disarmed of her natural weapons, free argument and debate, errors ceasing to be dangerous when it is permitted freely to contradict them.

II. Be it enacted by the General Assembly, that no man shall be compelled to frequent or support any religious worship, place or ministry whatsoever, nor shall be enforced, restrained, molested, or burthened in his body or goods, nor shall otherwise suffer on account of his religious opinions or belief; but that all men shall be free to profess, and by argument to maintain, their opinions in matters of religion, and that the same shall in no wise diminish, enlarge or affect their civil capacities.

III. And though we well know that this Assembly, elected by the people for the ordinary purposes of legislation only, have no power to restrain the acts of succeeding Assemblies, constituted with powers equal to our own, and that therefore to declare this Act to be irrevocable would be of no effect in law; yet as we are free to declare, and do declare, that the rights hereby asserted are of the natural rights of mankind, and that if any Act shall hereafter be passed to repeal the present, or to narrow its operation, such Act will be an infringement of natural right.

QUESTIONS

1. On what basis does Jefferson seek to establish religious tolerance?
2. Is he critical of Christianity? How?
3. What does Jefferson mean by "truth," and what are his criteria for determining what is true?
4. Does his optimistic belief that truth will inevitably triumph over error strike you as typical of the Enlightenment? As typically American?
5. What specific human rights does Jefferson consider "natural"?

26

The Classical Style in Music, the Development of Opera, and Mozart's Don Giovanni

The baroque style in music, as stated earlier, lasted well into the eighteenth century, but the second half of the century saw the development of a musical style better suited to the ideals of the Enlightenment. This period of calm, lightening, balancing, and simplifying, this brief and splendid era, is one that music historians have labeled *classic*. It reached its height in the works of two towering geniuses: Josef Haydn and Wolfgang Amadeus Mozart. The music of Mozart forsook the intricate counterpoint and long-winded phrases of the baroque master Bach. The compositions of Haydn consistently employed distinct phrases and sections in new structures that achieved unity and balance through readily perceived contrasts of melodies and harmonies. Composers seemed to find a regularity in their musical language that brought a logical coherence to works both tiny and grandiose. They worked primarily with the short, articulated phrase; they strove for structural symmetry; and they contrasted the rhythmic activities of the melody and the harmony in such a way that "tune" and "harmony" became distinct entities. New instruments developed, as they always had in the past; but, more important, old instruments changed character so that eventually the piano would replace the harpsichord and clavichord and the violin would replace the viol. This came about because the new bourgeoisie created a market for music, calling it from the patron's chamber to the public concert hall. As *dynamics* became louder, the music became more appropriate for performance before large audiences. It was at this time that the symphony orchestra emerged as a primary musical medium on which compositional ideas might be sounded in concert.

We will study the form of the classical symphony in the next chapter as we look at a work that breaks the classical limits to announce the romantic style: Beethoven's Ninth Symphony. Here we intend to focus on one of the greatest works of the classical period and one of the greatest operas ever written. First, however, it is necessary to understand the development of this form combining drama, spectacle, and music.

Opera

Opera as we know it today has a long, continuous history that dates back to a group of Florentine aristocrats who met at the home of Count Giovanni de' Bardi in the late sixteenth century. He was host to a set of Italian humanists known as the Camerata, a group of friends who met as an intellectual club to discuss cultural—primarily literary—matters. However, most of the members were musical amateurs, and three—Vincenzo Galilei, Giulio Caccini, and Pietro Strozzi—were musicians of the highest order. In the Camerata's attempt to understand classical Greek drama and the power music apparently held to sway the emotions of the ancient Greeks, they laid the groundwork for the development of a music drama soon to be called *opera*. Their search for cultural roots brought them back to classical Greece, but one must not overlook the fact that there had been a continuous interest in the West in the relationship of musical matters (appropriate themes, modes, rhythms, and so forth) to textual significance and dramatic events.

Even Gregorian chants may be seen as a musical amplification and ornamentation of the drama of the liturgy. The Mass, after all, is the repeated symbolic action of the last days of Christ on earth. In the later Middle Ages, we saw that more overt musical drama developed within the Church when we studied *The Play of Daniel* (Chapter 10). Then, in the Renaissance, the development of oratorio and opera heralded the dawn of the baroque period. The music of the first opera that resulted from the efforts of the Camerata is lost, but we saw a sample of the declamatory style developed to "imitate" Greek music drama in the passage from Jacopo Peri's *Euridice*, the earliest opera (1600) for which complete music has survived (see Chapter 21). The first masterpiece in this genre followed soon after, Claudio Monteverdi's *L'Orfeo* (1607), and the next two centuries saw a rapid expansion of interest and remarkable growth, change, and development in nearly all technical aspects of the genre: libretto, scenery, costume, dance, and music—orchestration, forms, vocal virtuosity, and so on. The growth of opera took place throughout Europe, not just in Italy, and important contributors were Lully in France (for example, *Le Bourgeois Gentilhomme*, Chapter 23), Henry Purcell in England, Giovanni Pergolesi and Alessandro Scarlatti in Italy, and Handel in Germany and England (for example, *Messiah*). Even though he was German and wrote for German audiences, Handel composed Italian operas in the Italian style.

The word *opera* comes from the Italian *opera in musica* (work in music), and it may be defined as a drama, either tragic or comic, sung throughout and presented on stage with scenery and action. The emphasis is on the solo voice, and, like the oratorio, which borrowed the forms from opera, it employs arias and recitatives. Because opera, of all the musical or dramatic forms, is the most difficult and expensive to produce, it has always been associated with the upper strata of social life. Often, the satisfaction of being able to support an operatic production—that is, sponsor a big, ostentatious display—has been compensation enough for a great many noble and wealthy patrons. Likewise, to be able to understand and appreciate this art form has been, and still is, a prestige symbol with the general public.

The successful composer and producer of opera has also traditionally received special rewards because of its difficulty, expense, and elite clientele. In the second half of the eighteenth century, such a composer was Wolfgang Amadeus Mozart—child prodigy, court figure, true genius, and perhaps the most universal composer in the history of Western music. In 1769, Sigismund, count of Schrattenbach and archbishop of Salzburg, gave orders for Mozart's first opera, *La Finta Semplice*, to be performed in the palace. Wolfgang was thirteen and had written it when he was twelve! After the performance, Sigismund appointed the young Mozart Kapellmeister, an important court position. This opera was not Mozart's first stage composition, for he had composed the *Singspiel* (operetta) *Bastien und Bastienne* a year earlier. As fine as these early compositions are, they are still youthful works and only serve as a prelude to the towering monuments of his mature years. The opera *Don Giovanni* (Don Juan) is one such masterpiece.

By 1787, the year of *Don Giovanni*, opera was a popular form among the elite of Austria, and Mozart was riding on the success of *Le Nozze di Figaro* (*The Marriage of Figaro*), produced in Prague the preceding winter. The classical style in music was established, and opera as a formal structure was well defined and commonly understood. When Mozart asked his librettist, Lorenzo da Ponte, for a new opera to follow *Figaro*, da Ponte was already busy with two other commissions. It may have been for this reason that he seized on the story of Don Juan, for he could rework a well-known tale more quickly than compose a new one.

The *Don Juan* Theme

Tirso de Molina's *The Trickster of Seville* fired the imaginations of many imitators, notably in the Italian *commedia dell'arte* ("improvised theater") in which Don Juan began to appear not so much as an overconfident aristocrat but more as a wicked and scheming character, in revolt against both society and religion. His next important literary incarnation is in Molière's play *Don Juan* (1665). There the hero appears as a character type prevalent in the French neoclassical period: the libertine. Refined and sophisticated, a cynical philosopher of free love rather than an unrepentant deceiver, Molière's Don Juan apparently has no religious beliefs. The eighteenth century, a time of increased freedom between the sexes, saw portrayals of a scheming seducer who pursued women as if in a military campaign and who cared for nothing but his own pleasure. By then Don Juan had a real-life counterpart in Italy—the famous Casanova.

Da Ponte and Mozart's collaborative work was not the first opera on Don Juan (Giovanni is the Italian equivalent of John or Juan), but it is the one that has made the legend immortal. Da Ponte was able to combine the vitality and passion of Tirso's hero with the wit and scheming intelligence of the Don Juans of Molière and his successors. Although the basic story line of Tirso's play remains, da Ponte has added some characters and events, eliminated some, and changed almost everyone's name. With his development of the character of the Don's servant, now called Leporello, he was able to merge the comic with the serious in original ways (as when Leporello sings under the table during Don Giovanni's supper with the statue). It is true that, as in most operas, there are some improbable incidents and the action does not always follow smoothly. This is more than compensated for, however, by the genius of Mozart.

In *Don Giovanni* perhaps even more than in his earlier operas, Mozart shows his ability to assume the personality and state of mind of his principal characters and his genius to create music suitable to each. Indeed, the music changes mood and character, reflecting the attitude and frame of mind of the singer. In fact, Mozart creates character in musical terms in the same way that Shakespeare does with vocabulary and poetic structures. This is remarkable enough in the parts in which only one character appears on stage at a time, but his virtuosity is particularly apparent in the scenes in which several characters appear together, usually in conflict. It is at these times that the element of "symphonic development" enters as an important ingredient in Mozart's style. It is through this polyphonic interweaving of the voice and orchestra that the characterization comes to life.

Don Giovanni: The Rake Punished

A Comic Opera in Two Acts

Poetry by Lorenzo da Ponte
Music by Wolfgang Amadeus Mozart[1]

Don Giovanni (baritone) is a Spanish nobleman who is both courageous and self-indulgent. With bravado he defies convention, propriety, and established authority, and with gusto he pursues, seduces, and subsequently abandons all women who cross his path. This opera represents the end of a dazzlingly successful career of seduction. It portrays not Don Giovanni's successes but rather his failures, and it ends with a heroic rejection of compromise, along with the terrible penalty exacted for the Don's refusal of penitence.

We learn that before the story begins, *Donna Anna* (soprano) was successful in rejecting the forceful advances of Don Giovanni, but, because this event took place in the dark, she is unaware of the identity of her assailant. Don Giovanni is served by *Leporello* (bass), a resourceful but cowardly scoundrel. In contrast to Don Giovanni, Donna Anna's fiancé, *Don Octavio* (tenor), is a somewhat pale character. But *Donna Elvira* (soprano) is not. She is a lady from Burgos who truly loves Don Giovanni and vainly hopes to reform him. Even through the pain of having been loved and deserted by the Don, she tries to win him back and save his soul. Donna Elvira is almost as striking a character as the Don himself, for she refuses to accept the code of conduct laid down by society. Even though she is of the nobility and has been wronged by Don Giovanni, she considers herself to be his wife, follows him around, and tries to save him, not from the mores of society but from the evil within himself.

[1]Mozart himself conducted the first performance in Prague in 1787, and the audience responded with cheers.

Three lesser but important roles complete the cast of characters. The *Commendatore* (bass), Donna Anna's father, is killed in the first scene by Don Giovanni while trying to avenge his daughter's honor. *Zerlina* (soprano), just one more conquest for the Don, is an attractive peasant girl who is seduced on the very eve of her wedding day. *Masetto* (bass) is the country bumpkin to whom she is engaged. Mozart also gives dramatic substance to the *Chorus*, which sings and dances as peasants in Act I and which personifies devils in Act II.

The opera begins with an orchestral overture, a symphonic composition in its own right. It has a slow (andante) introduction. The massive opening chords establish the key of D minor and use a syncopated rhythm to begin the forward motion and give the listener a feeling of disquiet.

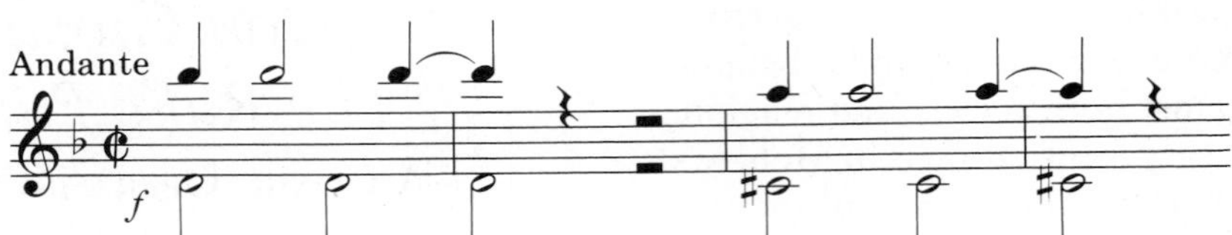

Soon the syncopations move at twice the speed, and the forward movement becomes more intense. Shifting harmonies, expressive dissonances, and the hypnotic syncopated figure help set the mood for the music that follows.

The notes are subdivided again, and the speed increases with running passages that crescendo and decrescendo (grow louder and softer) in sequence.

Suddenly the tempo changes, the mood becomes more lively as the mode shifts to major, and the principal theme is introduced. This is the exposition section, and Mozart displays his musical prowess in sonata form, a musical construction in three sections—exposition, development, and recapitulation—in which two contrasting musical ideas are pitted against each other, developed, and brought together for resolution. The rising first theme

is followed by a descending and less lyrical second theme.

The conflicting personalities of the music in this opening movement undergo a dramatic development not unlike the drama that will take place on the stage later. In music, the development involves changes of key, interworkings of themes and fragments of themes, orchestration changes, contrasts of dynamics, and the general interplay of musical elements that give life to an extended composition. The overture is a beginning, and before the final resolution it flows without pause into the opening song of Leporello. The curtain rises on the Don's servant, wrapped in his cloak and pacing back and forth in the darkness outside the house of Donna Anna.

LEPORELLO:
Notte e gionor faticar ´ ˘ ´ ˘ ´ ˘ ´ [-car]
Per chi nulla sa gradir; ˘ ˘ ´ ˘ ´ ˘ ´ [-dir]
Pioggia e vento sopportar, ´ ˘ ´ ˘ ´ ˘ ´ [-tar]
Mangiar male e mal dormir! ´ ˘ ´ ˘ ´ ˘ ´ [-mir]

Night and day I slave away
For one who's never pleased.
Through wind and rain I earn my pay
Of rotten food and troubled sleep.

Don Giovanni suddenly appears, having been forced to make a hasty exit from the house of Donna Anna. She pursues him, and the commotion wakes her father, the Commandant. He challenges Don Giovanni who, at first reluctant to duel the old man, succumbs to vanity and murders him. Others rush to the scene of the crime, but Don Giovanni and Leporello escape. The scene closes with Don Octavio promising to avenge the deed.

The scene changes to another street, where the Don and Leporello chatter about his habits. An angry Donna Elvira appears, and we learn that she pursues him because he seduced her with a promise of marriage. She sings her aria

DONNA ELVIRA:
Ah! chi mi dice mai ´ ˘ ˘ ´ ˘ ´ ˘ [-i]
Quel barbaro dov'è, ´ ´ ˘ ´ ˘ ´ ´ [-v'è]
Che per mio scorno amai ´ ˘ ˘ ´ ˘ ´ ˘ [-i]
Che mi mancò di fè? ´ ´ ˘ ´ ˘ ` [-fè]

Oh, who can tell me now
Where to find the cad I seek,
Whom, to my shame, I gave my love,
Who betrayed and left me there?

Don Giovanni slips out, leaving Leporello to explain the facts of his master's life to her. In a rollicking song he points out that, to date, his master has already seduced 2,065 women, 1,003 of them in Spain. No matter how serious the crime, the worldly audience cannot help laughing. And this is *opera buffa* at its best, a tradition reaching back to seventeenth-century Italy and forward at least as far as Gilbert and Sullivan. For those who know *The Mikado,* it becomes obvious that Leporello's aria serves as the model for Pooh Bah's "I've got a little list!" Still, the astute drama critic would realize that this gesture of open confession is somewhat out of character for the trusted servant.

LEPORELLO:

Madamina, il catalogo è questo
Delle belle che amò il padron mio:
Un catalogo egli è che ho fatt'io;
Osservate, leggete con me.
In Italia seicentoquaranta,
In Alemagna duecentotrentuna,
Cento in Francia, in Turchia novantuna,
Ma in Ispagna son già mille e tre.
V'han fra queste contadine,
Cameriere, cittadine,
V'han contesse, baronesse,
Marchesane, principesse,
E v'han donne d'ogni grado,
D'ogni forma, d'ogni età.

Little lady, this is a list
Of the beauties my master loved:
A catalogue I compiled;
Take a look, read along with me.
In Italy, six hundred and forty,
In Germany two hundred thirty-one.
One hundred in France, ninety-one in Turkey,
But in Spain, already one thousand and three.
Among these are peasant girls,
Maidservants, city girls,
Countesses, baronesses,
Noble ladies, even princesses.
Women of every rank,
Of every size, of every age.

Nella bionda egli ha l'usanza
Di lodar la gentilezza;
Nella bruna la costanza;
Nella bianca la dolcezza;
Vuol d'inverno la grassotta,
Vuol d'estate la magrotta;
È la grande maestosa,
La piccina è ognor vezzosa;
Delle vecchie fa conquista
Pel piacer di porle in lista;
Sua passion predominante
È la giovin principiante;
Non si picca se sia ricca,
Se sia brutta, se sia bella;
Purchè porti la gonnella,
Voi sapete quel che fa.

With blonds, it is his habit
To praise their kindness;
With brunettes their faithfulness;
Or the white-haired's sweetness.
In the winter he likes fat ones,
In the summer, he likes them thin.
He calls the tall ones stately,
A tiny one always dainty;
Even the elderly he seduces for
The pleasure of adding to the list.
His greatest passion
Is the young beginner;
It doesn't matter if she's rich,
If she's ugly or a beauty;
Because if she wears a skirt,
You know what he does.

The scene changes. A group of gay young country people are celebrating the forthcoming marriage of Zerlina and Masetto. When Don Giovanni and Leporello join the group, the Don loses no time in beginning his seduction of Zerlina. He promises a party at the villa and orders Masetto to lead the others there. He, of course, will escort the bride-to-be. Masetto is not fooled, but he fears disobeying the nobleman. As soon as they are gone, Don Giovanni promises to marry Zerlina in a lovely duet. Mozart's mastery of both the classical principles of formal balance and the dramatist's need to set the words of a love duet for a simple country maid in appropriate sounds is clearly demonstrated here. The duet's formal scheme of A–B–A–C is combined with simple melodies, clear harmonies, and uncomplicated rhythms.

A

DON GIOVANNI:
Là ci darem la mano,
Là mi dirai di sì
Vedi, non è lontano,
Partiam, ben mio, da qui.
There we'll hold hands,
There you'll whisper "yes,"
See, it's not far,
Let's go there, my dear.

ZERLINA:
Vorrei, e non vorrei...
Mi trema un poco il cor...
Felice, è ver, sarei:
Ma può burlarmi ancor.
I'd like to but I dare not,
My heart trembles a bit,
It's true, I would be happy:
But might he be tricking me?

B

DON GIOVANNI:
Vieni, mio bel diletto!
Come, my dearly beloved!

ZERLINA:
Mi fa pietà Masetto!
I'm sorry for Masetto!

DON GIOVANNI:
Io cangerò tua sorte.
I'll change your way of life.

ZERLINA:
Presto... non son più forte.
Quickly... I'm not very strong.

[repeat of beginning in dialogue form]

C

TOGETHER:
Andiam, andiam, mio bene,
A ristorar le pene
D'un innocente amor!
Let's go, let's go, my dearest,
To soothe the ache
Of an innocent love!

Before the two can slip away, Donna Elvira appears and exposes the Don's real intentions. She takes the girl with her, and Donna Anna and Don Octavio enter to enlist Don Giovanni's aid in the search for her father's murderer. Donna Elvira returns to expose her faithless lover again, and Donna Anna begins to suspect the possible guilt of Don Giovanni.

Donna Elvira leaves, and she is followed by a much-irritated Don Giovanni. Donna Anna confides her suspicions to Don Octavio, and they talk the circumstances through in a recitative.

DONNA ANNA:
Don Ottavio... son morta!
Don Octavio, I shall die!

DON OCTAVIO:
Cos'è stato?
What's happened?

DONNA ANNA:
Per pietà, soccorretemi.
For pity's sake, help me.

DON OCTAVIO:
Mio bene, fate coraggio.
My dearest, be brave.

DONNA ANNA:
Oh Dei! quegli è il carnefice del padre mio!
Oh God! There goes my father's executioner!

DON OCTAVIO:
Che dite?
What did you say?

DONNA ANNA:
Non dubitate più. Gli ultimi accenti, che l'empio proferì, tutta la voce richiamà nel cor mio di quell'indegno che nel mio appartamento...
There's no doubt about it. His parting words, the quality of his voice, bring back the memory of that vile beast who, in my chamber...

DON OCTAVIO:
Oh ciel! possibile che sotto il sacro manto d'amicizia...
Ma come fu, narratemi lo strano avvenimento.
Oh heaven! Could it be that under the sacred cloak of friendship...
But what happened? Describe this bizarre affair.

DONNA ANNA:
Era già alquanto avanzata la notte, quando nelle mie stanze, ove soletta mi trovai per sventura, entrar io vidi in un mantello avvolto un uom che al primo istante avea preso per voi; ma riconobbi poi che un inganno era il mio...

It was already quite late when into my room, where unluckily I happened to be alone, I saw a man enter all wrapped in a cloak. At first, I mistook him for you: But I soon found out how mistaken I was . . .

DON OCTAVIO:
Stelle; seguite.

Great heavens! Go on.

DONNA ANNA:
Tacito a me s'appressa, e mi vuol abbracciar; sciogliermi cerco, ei più mi stringe; io grido; non vien alcun; con una mano cerca d'impedire la voce, e coll'altra m'afferra stretta cosi, che già mi credo vinta.

Silently he came next to me, and drew me to him: I tried to free myself, but he only drew me closer. I screamed, but no one came: With one hand, he tried to stifle my voice, and with the other, he held me so tight I thought I must die.

DON OCTAVIO:
Perfido! E alfin?

Horrible! And then?

DONNA ANNA:
Alfine il duol, l'orrore dell'infame attentato accìrebbe sì la lena mia che a forza di svincolarmi, torcermi e piegarmi, da lui mi sciolsi.

Finally, the shame, the horror of this vile affront, so strengthened me that by struggling, twisting, and turning I was able to break loose from him.

DON OCTAVIO:
Ahimè! Respiro.

Thank God! I can breathe again.

DONNA ANNA:
Allora rinforzo i stridi miei, chiamo soccorso, fugge il fellon; arditamente il seguo fin nella strada per fermarlo, e sono assalitrice ed assalita: il padre v'accorre, vuol conoscerlo, e l'indegno che del povero vecchio era più forte, compie il misfatto suo col dargli morte.

Then I redoubled my screaming. I yelled for help, and the criminal raced out: boldly I chased him out to the street to stop him and began hitting my assailant: my father challenged him, wanting to know his identity. But the wretch, who was stronger than my poor old father, ended his night of crime by killing him.

She then cries for vengeance in a magnificent *Da capo* aria, with coda. (*Da capo* means "go back to the beginning.") Therefore, the aria, which has two musical sections (A–B), gains its classical, rounded binary form when the first section is repeated (A–B–A). Then, with a little extension (coda), it closes.

A

DONNA ANNA:
Or sai chi l'onore
Rapire a me volse:
Chi fu il traditore,
Che il padre mi tolse:
Vendetta ti chiedo,
La chiede il tuo cor.

Now you know who tried
To take from me my honor,
Who was my betrayer,
Who took my father's life:
I ask you for vengeance,
Your heart asks it too.

B

Rammenta la piaga
Del misero seno:
Rimira di sangue
Coperto il terreno,
Se l'ira in te langue
D'un giusto furor.

Remember the wound
In his poor breast:
If the wrath of a just fury
Ever weakens in you,
Remember the pool of blood
Covering the ground.

[D.C. (*da capo*—A again) and Coda]

Donna Anna
Or sai chi l'o - no - re ra - pi - re'a me vol - se,

Donna Anna leaves, and Don Octavio sings of his love for her as well as his determination to discover the truth. He must either redeem his friend, Don Giovanni, or avenge his love.

In the next scene, the Don is fully recovered and goes on as though nothing has happened. He is preparing the party for Masetto and Zerlina, and he's laying plans for his next conquest.

DON GIOVANNI:
Fin ch'han dal vino
Calda la testa,
Una gran festa
Fa preparar.
Se trovi in piazza
Qualche ragazza,
Teco ancor quella
Cerca menar.
Senza alcun ordine
La danza sia:
Chi il minuetto,
Chi la follia,
Chi l'alemanna
Farai ballar.
Ed io frattanto
Dall'altro canto
Con questa e quella
Vo' amoreggiar.
Ah! La mia lista
Doman mattina
D'una decina
Devi aumentar.

Go and prepare
A lavish affair
With plenty of wine
To make the heads spin.
If you find some young lady
Standing out in the square
Invite her too,
Try to bring her along.
Let the dancing be
Free and unrestricted:
Let them dance
Here a minuet,
Here a folia,
There an allemande.
And in the meantime,
To a different song,
I'll make love
To this one and that one.
Ah! Tomorrow morning
You will have to add
A dozen names
To my little list.

Don Giovanni
Fin ch'han dal vi - no cal - da la te - sta,

In the garden, Masetto scolds Zerlina and she begs his forgiveness. He is not thoroughly convinced of her faithfulness, but Don Giovanni turns the tables by reproaching Masetto for having left his bride. The three enter the house, and Donna Anna, Donna Elvira, and Don Octavio appear, masked. Leporello invites them to the party and then engages Masetto so that the Don can try once again to seduce Zerlina. They move into another room, but she begins to scream. The Don tries to bluff his way out by rushing from the room, sword in hand, pretending it was Leporello who was annoying her. No one believes the story this time, but the fearless Don brazens his way out through the crowd, pushing Leporello in front of him.

Act II opens with Don Giovanni and Leporello standing before the inn in which Donna Elvira is staying. The Don, who now wants to seduce Donna Elvira's maid, has a mandolin in his hand. Knowing that Donna Elvira still loves him, he disguises Leporello as himself by exchanging clothes with his servant. Leporello then leads her off, leaving him a little free time with the maid. Don Giovanni serenades her with one of the most charming songs in the opera.

DON GIOVANNI:
Deh! vieni alla finestra,
o mio tesoro.
Deh, vieni a consolar
il pianto mio.
Se neghi a me di dar
qualche ristoro,
Davanti agli occhi tuoi
morir vogl'io.

O come to the window,
  my treasure,
O come and dispel
  my tears.
If you refuse
  to save me,
I will die
  before your eyes.

Tu ch'hai la bocca dolce
  più del miele,
Tu che il zucchero porti
  in mezzo al core,
Non esser, gioia mia,
  con me crudele,
Lasciati almen vedere,
  o bell'amore!

Your lips are sweeter
  than honey,
Your heart, the essence
  of sweet,
Do not be cruel,
  my gladness,
At least let me see you,
  my love.

But the Don is doomed to yet another failure, for before she can come to him, Masetto returns with a band of armed friends. Pretending to be Leporello, the Don sends Masetto's companions off on a wild goose chase, then tricks the not-too-bright Masetto into giving him his weapons and beats him severely before making an escape. Zerlina returns, comforts her bruised fiancé, and promises never to be unfaithful again.

The scene changes to a dark courtyard before Donna Anna's house. Donna Elvira tries to make love to Leporello, whom she believes to be Don Giovanni, and Leporello seeks a way to escape. Suddenly, he is cornered by all of the Don's enemies, and he reveals his identity to save himself. They are irate at discovering that they have been tricked again, and seizing the opportunity, Leporello bolts away from them. Finally, Don Octavio promises to avenge them all and sings of his love for Donna Anna.

Although most of the drama of this scene is second rate—few in the audience really believe that Leporello can imitate Don Giovanni well enough to deceive the one woman who knows, understands, and truly loves him, or that Leporello could simply run away from this furious group of armed men—the music is not. Following a brief recitative, each of the characters, in turn, expresses his thoughts with a brief melodic line characteristic of that particular personage. Gradually, the parts begin to combine until the five—Donna Anna, Zerlina, Donna Elvira, Don Octavio, and Masetto—group their musical forces against the line of Leporello in a sextet that is excellent musical drama. As they blend together in song, each maintains a distinct musical identity.

LEPORELLO (recitative):
  Di molte faci il lume s'avvicina....
    See the light of torches coming near....

DONNA ELVIRA (1st solo in sextet):
Sola, sola in buio loco, palpitar il cor mi sento....
All alone in this dark spot I feel the beating of my heart....

LEPORELLO (2nd solo in sextet):
Più che cerco, men ritrovo
Questa porta sciaguarata?...
The more I search, the less I find.
Where is this stupid doorway?...

DON OCTAVIO (3rd solo in sextet):
Tergi il ciglio, o vita mia!
E da calma al tuo dolore....
Stop your crying, my beloved,
And calm your sadness....

In time, Zerlina and Masetto are introduced into the fabric too. When all are properly entered, the five side against Leporello.

LEPORELLO:
...
Viver lasciatemi, per carità!
...
Let me live, I beg you!

THE OTHERS:
Dei! Leporello!
Che inganno è questo?...
What? Leporello!
What trick is this?...

D. An. — sotto voce — Dei! Le-po-rel - lo!

Zer. — sotto voce — Dei! Le-po-rel - lo!

D. Elv. — sotto voce — Dei! Le-po-rel - lo!

D. Oct. — sotto voce — Dei! Le-po-rel - lo!

Mas. — sotto voce — Dei! Le-po-rel - lo!

Lep. — per ca - ri - tà, per ca - ri - tà!

Orch. — *p* — *p*

Also, when the group is about to punish Leporello, he stops the action with an aria that both seeks their pity and gives him time to move toward a convenient gate.

LEPORELLO:

Ah! Pietà signori miei!
Do ragione a voi . . . a lei . . .
Ma il delitto mio non è.
Il padron con prepotenza
L'innocenza mi rubò.
Donna Elvira! Compatite;
Già capite come andò.
Di Masetto non so nulla,
Vel dirà questa fanciulla;
E un'oretta circum circa
Che con lei girando vo.
A voi, signore, non dico niente.
Certo timore . . . certo accidente . . .
Di fuori chiaro . . . di dentro scuro. . . .
Non c'è riparo . . . la porta, il muro . . .
Io me ne vo da quel lato. . . .
Poi qui celato, l'affar si sa. . . .
Ma s'io sapeva, fuggia per qua! . . .

> Oh! Have mercy my lords!
> You are right, sir . . . and you . . .
> But the real fault is not mine.
> My master, with threats,
> Robbed me of my innocence.
> Donna Elvira! Forgive me!
> You know what happened.
> Of Masetto, I know nothing.

This lady can confirm it:
For about an hour
I've been walking with her.
To you, sir, I can say nothing.
Partly fear . . . partly chance . . .
It was light out but dark here.
No way out, the door, the wall,
I couldn't get out of here. . . .
Then I hid myself, you know all.
But had I known this, I'd have run from here! (flees)

Leporello
Ah pie - tà, Si - gno - ri miei, ah pie - tà, pie - tà di me,

Even though we are no more likely to believe that Don Octavio will live up to his word this time, since he has failed in the past, his sincerity, and his lovely tenor voice, are beautifully displayed in his aria.

DON OCTAVIO
Il mio tesoro intanto
Andate a consolar:
E del bel ciglio il pianto
Cercate d'asciugar.
Ditele che i suoi torti
A vendicar io vado;
Che sol di stragi e morti
Nunzio voglio tornar.

Meanwhile, go and console
My dearest treasure:
And from her beautiful eyes,
Try and dry the tears.
Tell her I go
To avenge her wrongs:
I will return to announce
His punishment and death.

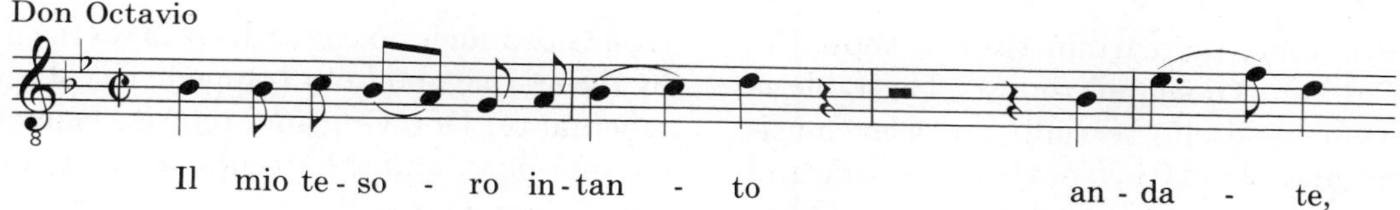
Don Octavio
Il mio te - so - ro in - tan - to an - da - te,

The scene changes to an enclosed cemetery with several equestrian statues, including that of the Commendatore. Don Giovanni enters, laughing about the night's events, and is quickly followed by a distressed Leporello. The Don chides him and tells about another escapade with a girl on his escape route. She mistook him for Leporello, showed affection, and was just about to be compromised by the Don when he heard pursuers coming and decided to run. Leporello is serious, but the Don is clever and unconcerned. Leporello says:

LEPORELLO:
Ma se fosse costei stata mia moglie?
But supposing she had been my wife?

And the Don laughingly replies:

DON GIOVANNI:
Meglio ancora!
Better still!

Then one of the most dramatic moments in the opera takes place, for the statue speaks!

COMMENDATORE:
Di rider finirai prima dell'aurora.
Your laughter will be silenced before morning.

From this moment on, the intense conflict between Don Giovanni's personal libertine philosophy and the morality of heaven and earth is personified in the struggle between the Don and the Commendatore. Leporello is frightened beyond reason when the marble statue speaks and nods, but Don Giovanni disdainfully commands his servant to invite the statue to dinner.

A brief respite takes place when the scene changes to a room in Donna Anna's house. Don Octavio tells her to calm down; the murder will be avenged. They should bow to the will of Providence, and she should soothe his longings by marrying him tomorrow. Donna Anna is affronted, Don Octavio calls her cruel, and she sets him straight in her recitative and aria.

DONNA ANNA (recitative):
Crudele? Ah no! mio bene!...

I cruel? Oh no, my dear!...

(aria)
Non mi dir, bell'idol mio,
Che son io crudel con te....

Don't tell me, my love,
That I am cruel to you....

Dramatically, there is not much point to this scene, other than providing time for a set change to Don Giovanni's dining hall. But musically, this aria gives Donna Anna an opportunity to display her coloratura vocal wares for the last time before the finale. She sings an embellished line, as follows:

DONNA ANNA:
Forse un giorno il cielo ancora
Sentirà pietà di me.

Perhaps, one day, heaven will again
Feel merciful for me.

In the next scene, the curtain rises to show the dining room in Don Giovanni's house. The table is laid, and the Don, Leporello, servants, and a few musicians await the guest. Don Giovanni begins eating and jokes with Leporello and the musicians. Donna Elvira enters, pleads her love, and asks him to change. He only mocks her. Fearful screaming outside announces the approach of the invited guest. Leporello hides under the table while the Don opens the door. He invites the Commandant to the table, and the statue slowly and grotesquely moves upstage. After a brief verbal repartee, the statue speaks.

COMMENDATORE:
Tu m'invitasti a cena:
Il tuo dovere or sai,
Rispondimi; verrai
Tu a cenar meco?

You invited me to supper;
You know what you must do,
So answer me: will you
Come and dine with me?

Don Giovanni is no coward. He takes the hand offered by the statue, and he is trapped. The statue demands repentance; Don Giovanni refuses. Flames leap up, a chasm opens, and the trombone voices of hell speak out. Before he is pulled to the torments of the underworld, Don Giovanni cries out:

DON GIOVANNI:
Chi l'anima mi lacera!
Chi m'agita le viscere!
Che strazio! ohimè! che smania!
Che inferno! che terror!

My soul is torn in agony!
My body is in torture!
What torment! Ah, what madness!
The fires of hell! The terror!

The flames rise and the chorus sings.

CHORUS:
Tutto a tue colpe è poco:
Vieni; c'è un mal peggior.
For all your sins, this is nothing:
Come! worse torments await below!

Were the opera to end here, it would have the elements of tragedy. The hero, Don Giovanni, recognizes his sins and goes to pay the price. But Mozart and da Ponte did not set out to moralize, but to entertain a pleasure-seeking audience. And with their final scene, they turn the drama from tragedy to comedy. As Don Giovanni disappears from the stage into the great abyss, all the principals emerge on the stage with officials and the entire cast. They ask for the criminal, learn of his fate, and quickly proceed to announce:

DON OCTAVIO:
I want to get married.

DONNA ANNA:
Give me a year.

DONNA ELVIRA:
I'm off to a convent.

ZERLINA AND MASETTO:
Let's go home to dinner.

LEPORELLO:
I'll go to the Inn and find a better master.

And together, everyone sings and dances the moral of the tale:

TUTTI:
Questo è il fin di chi fa mal!
E de' perfidi la morte
Alla vita è sempre ugual.
This is the evil doer's end.
Death is the payment for great sin.
Always was and always will be.

Created toward the end of the Enlightenment and on the eve of the French Revolution, *Don Giovanni* reflects the Enlightenment's reliance on reason and individual experience rather than on authority and tradition. Despite the final outcome, the opera is not without sympathy for the hero, for it balances the comic and tragic aspects of real human experience. Yet in presenting Don Giovanni as a man who lives without restraint and who views the well-being of others as incidental to the pleasure-seeking principle, Mozart and da Ponte seem to warn against the perils of supreme individualism. In keeping with the spirit of an age that could produce a treatise on toleration and the American Declaration of Independence and Constitution, the composer and the poet acknowledge the responsibilities of the individual and the possibility of retribution for acts that deny the rights of other individuals. *Don Giovanni* portrays this dilemma, a situation modern psychology would call the conflict of the id and superego, the struggle between immediate gratification and deferred pleasure for the greater good of both society and the individual. Yet it is not a sermon, but a work of art and an entertainment, a masterpiece of music and poetry by Wolfgang Amadeus Mozart and Lorenzo da Ponte.[2]

---

[2]Many fine recordings of *Don Giovanni* are, and will always be, available. One that can be recommended for both its fine performance and technical brilliance as well as the quality of the book that accompanies the set is produced by Deutsche Grammophon (419179-1 GH3; compact disc 419179-2 GH3), is conducted by Herbert von Karajan and stars Kathleen Battle. Recorded, mixed, and edited with the latest digital technology, the resulting quality of sound is exquisite. Several films of the opera are now available on videocassette, and the Glyndebourne Festival production by Peter Hall is one of the best (two cassettes, V69005, available from Media for the Arts, P.O. Box 1011, Newport, R.I. 02840).

27

Romanticism: Revolution, Individualism, Nature, and Love

The delicate balance between the demands of enlightened reason and those of passionate individualism was not to have a long supremacy in European culture. The philosophes' demands for a more just and equal society were to culminate in an upheaval of which they probably would not have approved and that was to change the face of Europe forever: the French Revolution.

The American Revolution, far less bloody, had in a sense served as a prelude to the French one. The American experiment demonstrated to Europeans that Enlightenment ideas could be realized in practice. The Declaration of Independence and the Virginia Statute of Religious Liberty were not abstract treatises but statements by a government of its official beliefs and policies. Heretofore, the principles of limited government and a system of checks endorsed by the American Constitution had been considered by most Europeans to be connected with feudal privilege and aristocratic domination. This is why many of the philosophes had espoused absolute monarchy. America seemed to prove that this kind of constitutional structure could in fact foster the freedom and equality sought by Enlightenment thinkers.

The French Revolution

Causes of the Revolution

The American example was particularly important for France. The most populous country in Europe and among the most prosperous, France in the last half of the eighteenth century was a troubled society. The death of Louis XIV in 1715 had brought to the throne a five-year-old boy, Louis XV (1710–1774). Largely unconcerned with government, Louis was primarily interested in women, eating, and lock making. His son, Louis XVI (1754–1793), although well meaning, was weak and popularly seen as dominated by his wife, Marie Antoinette.

Neither of these monarchs, consequently, played a guiding role in the political life of the nation. A succession of ministers of varying ability governed the country, and policy lacked the consistency that an active monarch could have given it. Indicative of the shift in political focus was the increasing marginalization of Versailles as the center of French culture and the return of Paris to that position.

In retrospect, historians after the French Revolution came to speak of France in the eighteenth century as the *ancien régime* (the "old order"). All phases of French life were dominated by an outmoded social structure that endured primarily because it was legally defined and protected. All French citizens except the royal family were divided into three classes: the clergy, the nobility, and the third estate, by far the largest of the three, comprising the peasants, the artisans of the towns, and the middle class or *bourgeois.* Of France's twenty-four million people, only about 2 percent belonged to the clergy and nobility. Yet in a society where land remained the greatest form of wealth, the other 98 percent owned only 60 percent of the landed property. This social group was the greatest force in causing the revolution.

But there was a greater source of discontent among the third estate. The clergy and nobility paid almost no taxes. Moreover, while giving little or nothing to support it, the nobility enjoyed all the highest offices in the government; they also constituted the officer corps of the army. As for the clergy, this class had the right to levy a tax, for its maintenance, on all agricultural goods produced by the third estate.

What made the situation volatile was that for most of the eighteenth century the economy was expanding. Bankers, merchants, and other members of the middle class had accumulated great wealth, and many of the peasants were prosperous. Traditionally, there had been various avenues by which successful members of the third estate could work their way into the nobility, but in the course of the eighteenth century these avenues had gradually been shut off by an aristocracy resolved not to dilute its membership further. The upper bourgeois, therefore, felt excluded from the social and financial privileges to which their success entitled them.

Economic prosperity also entailed rising prices and higher living costs. The nobility and clergy, barred by law from entering commerce or industry to reap the profits of the boom, increasingly came to insist on their economic rights over the third estate. Indeed, this was the heyday of lawyers employed by the upper classes to dredge up old, long-neglected rights over the peasantry. Moreover, although the bourgeoisie and the upper peasantry were profiting throughout most of the eighteenth century, the lower classes, at least in the last half of the century, saw their wages rise more slowly than prices and their standard of living fall.

The most immediate cause of the revolution, which began in the summer of 1789, was the government's financial crisis. Because some of the wealthiest elements in the country were exempt from taxation, the state could not balance its budget. An important element in the French public debt was the expense incurred by helping the Americans in their revolt against England. For years the enlightened advisers of the French king had endeavored to abolish the tax privileges of the clergy and the nobility, but these two orders had solidly resisted the effort. The king could proclaim the necessary laws, but the courts, completely controlled by the nobility, would never enforce them. Finally, in 1788, the royal government simply abolished the old court system and created a new one.

The result was an aristocratic revolt: the army officers and the king's officials at Paris and in the provinces refused to serve, and the whole state was brought to a halt. Unable to persevere in the attempt at reform, the king (Louis XVI) acceded to noble demands that, for the first time since 1614, a National Assembly be called to settle the nation's problems. The nobility clearly intended to gain more control over the king's government through an assembly that, by tradition, gave them and the clergy (dominated by the aristocracy) two votes, against one for the third estate.

Beginning of the Revolution

The Assembly met in May 1789 at Versailles, but in the months preceding the meeting, the third estate, growing conscious of its massive power, resolved to use the Assembly as a means of abolishing legal classes. Refusing their places in the Royal Assembly, where they were given one of the three votes, the delegates of the third estate declared themselves to be the Assembly of the Nation and defied the monarchy. Although Louis XVI called troops to Versailles at the end of June, he hesitated to arrest the disobedient delegates. In the atmosphere of tension prevailing over the next weeks, the common people of Paris rose on July 14, 1789, stormed and captured the Bastille (the king's prison in the city), and the revolution was on. The terrified king ordered the nobility and clergy to join with the third estate; those who had not already joined out of sympathy or gone home did so.

One of the first steps of the new one-house National Assembly was the publication of a Declaration of the Rights of Man and the Citizen on August 26, 1789. Like the American Bill of Rights, its provisions emphasized the freedom and equality of every man. Subsequently, all privilege was abolished and the Church's property confiscated; henceforth, the clergy was to receive salaries from the state. The leaders of the Assembly at this stage were determined to make France a constitutional monarchy like that of England. Before the new constitution could be approved, however, the would-be constitutional monarch, Louis XVI, fled in June 1791. Despite his capture, the position of the leadership was undercut, and the Jacobins or republicans seized power in the National Assembly in September 1791. The king, however, was not officially deposed until August 1792, when France was declared a republic.

The Jacobins

The Jacobins were interested in more than transforming the French monarchy into a republic; they also wished to topple the crowned heads all over Europe and republicanize the subcontinent. Their rise to power naturally brought on conflict with the rest of Europe, and from the spring of 1792 France was at war. When the war began badly and the politicians blamed the defeat of the army on treachery behind the lines, the pursuit of traitors was under way. Starting in May 1793, the radical Jacobins, a group of ruthless idealists, displaced the more moderate leadership.

Robespierre (1754–1794)

Whereas the moderate Jacobins had aimed at establishing a republic governed by an electorate with modest property qualifications, the radical Jacobins wanted an eventual democratic republic. Their leader, Maximilien Robespierre, believed that, before this could be brought about, a dictatorship representing Rousseau's general will must destroy all the reactionaries. His dictatorship took the form of an executive committee of twelve men called the Committee of Public Safety. He introduced the Reign of Terror, which lasted over a year. A new device, the guillotine, was introduced to expedite the execution of traitors to the revolution, including the king and queen. Nevertheless, by July 1794, France was tired of blood, and the Assembly, now called the National Convention, had Robespierre arrested and guillotined.

The government emerging from the reaction was dominated by large property owners. The fragility of its control, with radicals to the left and royalists on the right, was to an extent balanced by the success that French armies were having on the battlefield. Actually, after a bad start, the French by the fall of 1792 were having one victory after another. By mid-1794 they had occupied what is now Belgium, the Netherlands, and Germany up to the Rhine as well as parts of northern Italy. In large part their success derived from the fact that the volunteer armies were enormous as opposed to the small professional armies of their opponents. Under the command of officers who held their commissions because of merit rather than family position, highly motivated by intense patriotic zeal, the French soldiers were irresistible. Everywhere they went they were welcomed by revolutionaries opposed to the local regime of despotism and privilege. French conquest meant the abolition of a legal class system and the establishment of a more equitable law code and social system.

Napoleon Bonaparte (1769–1821)

By 1796 one of the revolutionary generals, Napoleon Bonaparte, had distinguished himself above the others by a brilliant invasion of Italy and a swift capture of most of the northern part of the peninsula. Born in 1769 of minor Corsican nobility, Napoleon would probably never have risen above the rank of captain in the old aristocratic French army, but in the new army, he was a general by the age of twenty-five. Not only a military genius but a brilliant politician as well, Napoleon in 1797 purged the leadership of the conservative government that had come in after the Reign of Terror. In 1799, after an invasion of Egypt that stirred the imagination of all Europe, Napoleon abolished the whole government and declared himself the First Consul of France.

Napoleon had been deeply influenced by the Enlightenment. He has been referred to as "the last of the Enlightened despots," and he once said of himself, "I am the revolution." Napoleon believed that the real concern of the French was not so much political liberty as social equality. Political participation was for them secondary to their desire for a society where all people were equal before the law and where advancement derived from merit. Although Napoleon's constitution provided for a parliamentary government with universal male suffrage, there could be no question that Napoleon governed France.

Napoleon established a meritocracy in the bureaucracy and army, and he reformed laws to enable more equality. His fiscal system was run by professionals, and there were no tax exemptions. On the whole, it

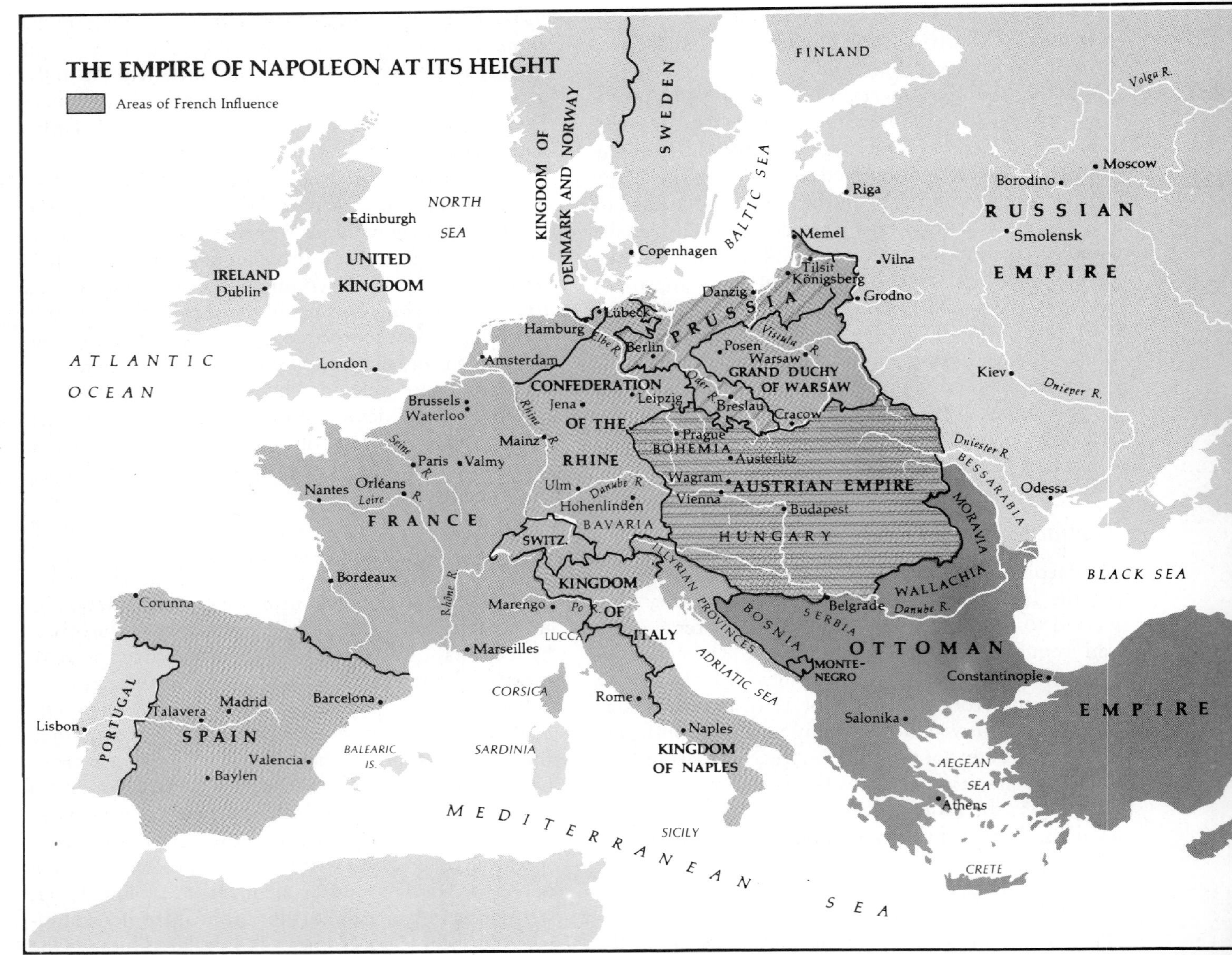

is fair to say that Napoleon realized in his government most of the goals of the Enlightenment: those dealing with political freedom had always been secondary in any case.

Between 1799 and 1814 Napoleon, who took the title of emperor of the French in 1802, almost succeeded in conquering all of continental Europe. But when he penetrated Russia as far as Moscow in 1812, the invasion cost him dearly; five hundred thousand soldiers never returned, and from this point on, his fortune waned.

With the heavy loss in troops and resistance to French war taxation growing among the subject peoples, Napoleon decided to surrender to an allied coalition of England, Austria, Russia, and Prussia. He abdicated and was sent in exile to Elba off the Italian coast in 1814. With hopes of turning the tables, he appeared again in France early in 1815. The French rallied, his old soldiers gathered again, and in the spring of 1815 he fought and lost the great battle of Waterloo. Defeated, he was exiled this time to Saint Helena in the Atlantic Ocean, and a brother of Louis XVI was made king of France by the allies.

Effects of the Revolution

The French Revolution and its aftermath, however, left a lasting mark on western Europe. No longer could rulers fight with the small professional armies of the past: the levy *en masse* was an absolute necessity in a new age of war. Rulers had to put arms in the hands of their subjects. Despite their conservative temper and fear of reform, kings, including the new French monarch, could not reimpose the old legal class structure where it had been abolished. The law codes destroying legal privilege in these areas were permanent. Moreover, French nationalism had proven infectious. At first welcomed as liberators by many in the conquered countries, the French ended by creating a national feeling directed against them in Germany, Italy, Spain, and elsewhere. Until later in the nineteenth century, however, nationalism would be considered the property of liberals wishing to imitate the French. After that time monarchs would learn how to use it for their own purposes. Although the allies reduced France to its boundaries before 1789, the French were considered the most dangerous people of Europe until 1870. The figure of Napoleon, the keen rationalist, became a symbol of the creative, mysterious, and at times demonic personality that fascinated the first generation of the nineteenth century.

The Art of the French Revolution: Jacques-Louis David (1748–1825)

Just as the leaders of the American Revolution instigated the search for a new visual and architectural language for the new republic, so the French Revolution and its aftermath profoundly affected art in France and England. The citizens of France, like those of the United States, first adopted the severe classical style of republican Rome; Napoleon, however, preferred to imitate the empire. The foremost painter of the revolutionary and Napoleonic eras was Jacques-Louis David. David revolted strongly against the sensual elegance of the court style as exemplified by the paintings of Boucher (Fig. 24-5) and Fragonard. He sought to renew art by contact with the art of Rome and the Italian High Renaissance. While in Italy he painted his first important picture in this fresh style. Displayed in his Roman studio, *The Oath of the Horatii* (1784–1785) combined qualities from the sixteenth and seventeenth centuries to convey what some saw as revolutionary sentiments. Based on a story from Livy, *The Oath* places loyalty to the state above all other concerns, even those of family. The painting shows heroic male figures in a stark architectural setting. As in the *Death of Marat* (Fig. 27-1), the figures are somewhat idealized but retain a degree of intense realism through an almost photographic rendering of

27-1 *Jacques-Louis David,* Death of Marat, *1793, oil on canvas, $63\frac{3}{4}'' \times 49\frac{1}{8}''$. (Musées Royaux des Beaux-Arts © A.C.L. Bruxelles)*

flesh and muscle. Such detail makes them highly convincing. Colors are cool; the harsh light isolates form and gesture. Crisp and clear, the figures seem like a sculpted bas-relief.

Returning to Paris, where his style was immediately recognized as revolutionary, although not necessarily politically so, David nevertheless moved away from the sentiments of the Royal Academy that had sent him to Rome. In *The Death of Socrates* (1787) he explored the theme of injustice by a government fearing the truth. This picture and others like it were celebrated as manifestos of those virtues most lacking in monarchial France, and their artist became a leading revolutionary painter.

David was commissioned by the Committee of Public Safety to make three paintings of revolutionary heroes; only one of them was finished, the *Death of Marat* (Fig. 27-1). It portrays the murder of the Jacobin Marat by Charlotte Corday, from a rival revolutionary group. Sending a note to Marat, she gained access to him while, seated in a medicinal bath, he received petitioners. She stabbed him when he could offer no resistance. An almost ludicrous scene is transformed by David into the final act of a great tragedy.

27-2 *Jacques-Louis David,* Napoleon Crossing the Alps, *Versailles Museum. (Art Resource, NY)*

The dead revolutionary still lies in his draped tub, the focus of a cold, dramatic light. His wound gapes, blood stains his drapery and the water, and his limp arm and hand fall to the floor, his pen permanently stilled. The figure is rendered with sculptural intensity. Although there is a pervasive sense of reality, the body bears no marks of the skin disease that forced him to sit in the tub. His face shows little age, no anguish. In the contrast between reality and abstraction, David creates a magnificent tension—a tension like that between reason and intuition, calculation and passion.

Recognizing this formidable talent, Napoleon made David the pageant master of the consular government and then of the empire. In his *Napoleon Crossing the Alps* (Fig. 27-2) David's abstract clarity has given way to an ideal image. The youthful general, astride a rearing horse, his cloak blowing in the wind as he gestures forward, has become a romantic hero comparable to Hannibal and Charlemagne, whose names are carved in the rocks. This is not a real general; it is how all generals might see themselves—indeed how people might envision a hero—commanding, youthful, virile, clean, shiny, and dry, in spite of cold, snow, and the hell of war.

The revolution in style begun by David would take on new forms with the birth of the sensibility called *romanticism.*

Romanticism: A Revolutionary Movement

The two great revolutions of the eighteenth century, the American and the French, were followed not only by upheavals altering the course of European politics but also by rapid changes in other spheres of life: taste, feeling, thought, behavior, and social and domestic relations. The varied, often contradictory cultural movement that swept over Europe and America and became known as romanticism had profound effects on the humanities—effects still very much felt in the contemporary world. The individualism, sense of isolation, and alienation of which we are now so aware have their roots in the Renaissance and Reformation period, but they were cultivated and brought to flower by the romantics.

Romanticism as a movement may be said to have originated in Germany, but the word *romantic* first appeared in England in the mid-eighteenth century. It originated from an association with medieval "romances," the (predominantly French) stories of knights and ladies. As the word became coined in all European languages, it took on connotations of fanciful, picturesque, rugged, spontaneous, natural, and sentimental. During the early nineteenth century it was applied to groups of rebellious young artists promoting creativity, individualism, and free expression of emotion in opposition to classical canons and the regulations and standards based on "enlightened" reason that their parents' generation had espoused. For the romantics, life and art were one: as they threw out the old standards for art, so they lived their lives with bohemian freedom, following their passions or imagination rather than their reason or the "artificial" rules of society. Artistic and political ideals also intertwined: the French writer Victor Hugo called romanticism "liberalism in literature" and proclaimed that words, like postrevolutionary human beings, were now free from tyranny. By the middle of the century, however, many romantics had grown conservative, Catholic, or nationalistic, or they had retreated into an asocial dream world. This was partly because of the political scene in Europe: many who had first adored Napoleon as the bearer of the revolution became disillusioned with Napoleon the emperor. Yet some romantics were intensely conservative from the beginning, looking back toward the Middle Ages as an ideal period of order and spirituality. (The liberals, too, liked medieval themes, but for other reasons.) It is impossible to attribute an exact beginning and end to this complex, varied, pan-European and American movement; but the French Revolution gave impetus to its latent beginnings, and it died out in most places before 1850. In Slavic countries, however, the romantic movement in literature (and in nationalistic politics) continued longer, and romantic music flourished in Germany, France, and Italy throughout the nineteenth century. It is hardly possible to attempt a global history or definition of romanticism here. We will concentrate instead on the artistic expression of some major romantic themes: revolution, the hero, nature, and love.

Enlightened Ideas, Romantic Style

The American and French revolutions fired the imaginations of the romantics as they had seemed at first to confirm the reasonableness of the philosophes. Jean-Jacques Rousseau is the single most important figure for understanding the transition between the Enlightenment and romanticism. Revered as a forefather of the revolution because of his analyses of social injustice and his "enlightened" beliefs in human dignity and freedom, Rousseau was the first in French letters to promote feeling above reason and nature above institutions. Above all, he raised the unique, individual self to a position of prime importance. The individualism propounded by Rousseau seemed to be the philosophical foundation of the new American republic, the largest territory ever ruled by a government proclaiming people to be free and equal.

Liberty, Equality, Fraternity

Liberty, equality, and fraternity, the catchwords of the French Revolution, were taken by the romantics to apply to all aspects of life. Ironically, it was outside of France that these ideals first took hold as a cultural force. It is in Germany and in England that we first see poets celebrating the ideals of the revolution, and it is there, too, that other signs of budding romanticism first show themselves. Germany's two greatest writers, Johann Wolfgang von Goethe (1749–1832) and Friedrich Schiller (1759–1805), spanned neoclassicism and romanticism in their careers. Schiller's fervent belief in human rights to dignity and freedom and his lofty hopes for universal brotherhood place him in the transition between the Enlightenment and romanticism. His poem "Ode to Joy," written on the eve of the French Revolution, is a passionate statement of those beliefs and hopes that were stirring at the time. Immortalized by Beethoven in his Ninth Symphony some thirty years later, it has become one of the great statements of romanticism.

Ludwig van Beethoven (1770–1827)

The late eighteenth and early nineteenth centuries saw the flowering of German music as well as of German literature. Beethoven, like Goethe and Schiller, is a gigantic figure whose works rise above categories like classical or romantic but include elements of both. Like many of his generation, he was at first stirred by the ideals of the French Revolution and by their embodiment in Napoleon, and later disillusioned. Beethoven had both feet firmly planted in the fertile soil of classicism but was able to reach out with both hands to grapple with the giant problems of romanticism: the meaning of life, the values of human existence, the powers of humanity, and the importance of the individual.

What does romanticism in music really mean? What are the musical features that inform our ears about the interests and ideals of Beethoven and the nineteenth-century composers who followed him? To search for answers to these questions, let us look into a single masterpiece that fuses classical and romantic styles—the values of the Enlightenment and the passions of the romantic revolutionaries. Let us try to learn from Beethoven's last and most monumental symphony, his Symphony in D Minor, opus 125, a work familiarly known as the Ninth Symphony.

Like all classical symphonies, Beethoven's Ninth is divided into four movements, and they follow a traditional pattern: the first and fourth movements are energetic, moving at a lively speed; the second and third movements offer contrast, one slow and the other a dance form related to the classical dance called the minuet. This four-movement, balanced structure developed as a means to create a large-scale work (a half hour or more) capable of capturing intellectual attention for long periods of time using musical means only. In other words, the composers were seeking an answer to a compositional problem: if we exclude extramusical ideas and effects (such as a church service, a dance, a festival, and programmatic ideas), how can we keep from losing the listener's attention if we play a continuous piece of music for a very long time? Haydn, Mozart, and their mid-eighteenth century contemporaries solved the problem by designing symphonies that had distinct movements related by key, contrasted by mood, and subdivided by various formal designs that developed contrasting melodies in a variety of ways. Their large works lasted up to thirty or even forty minutes; Beethoven's Ninth lasts almost two hours! His first movement continues as long as do most complete classical symphonies. Although Beethoven's concept of form was classical, his expansion of dimensions, his breaking of boundaries, was romantic.

Classical composers had a knack for the well-turned phrase, a neat tune of four or eight measures' duration whose shape had character and individuality and was capable of expansion or development as the piece progressed. Classical melodies had musical characteristics that allowed these tunes, usually, to be categorized as antecedent-consequent phrases; that is, the first half is answered and completed by the second half. A good example of this type of theme is Mozart's opening theme from his Symphony no. 40 in G Minor (K. 550),

where both halves are similar but different, ascending and descending, opening and closing. In fact, Mozart's sense of balance was so certain and ingrained that the entire phrase can be seen as the antecedent of the next four-measure phrase.

This analytical game can be played even further, if we choose, for the two-to-two and four-to-four measure relationships can be carried even further by viewing the first eight measures as antecedent to the second eight measures. This is possible with Mozart and his G minor symphony; it is not possible with the opening theme of Beethoven's Ninth.

Beethoven's "tune" is hardly a melody at all; it is a series of short *motives* laid out along a descending *arpeggiated* chord and a brief closing figure.

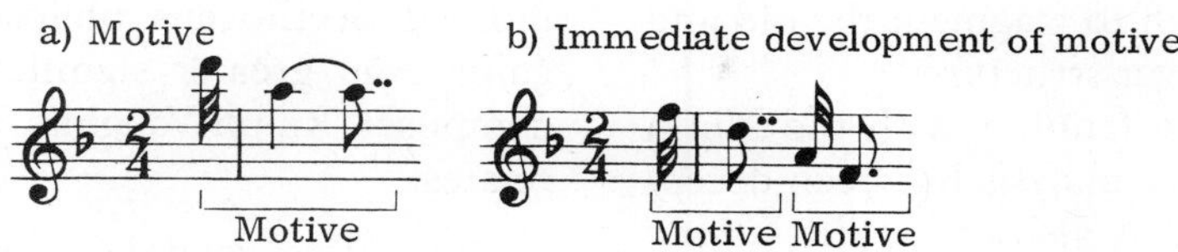

From small germinal ideas, Beethoven sculpts larger forms; from almost tuneless groups of notes, he creates tonal music of a relentless, soul-searching nature. Each fragment of melody is taken in turn, examined, dissected, synthesized, and reissued in a new shape within a fresh context at a later time. The rhythm of the closing fragment

becomes a driving melody for the bass instruments at one point

and a lyrical, sweet passage for French horn at another.

In other words, even these few processes we have discussed here sound the death knell for the ease, grace, and regularity of classical music. In time the classical forms will even be replaced or set aside, but for Beethoven it was enough to fragment the old and pile smaller blocks into larger structures.

Those who already are familiar with the Ninth Symphony will say that this analysis has been deceptive thus far, for the Ninth is also called the *Choral* Symphony and is unlike its classical predecessors if for no other reason than that. Additionally, they might add that a chorus and vocal soloists require text and that words bring extramusical ideas immediately into play. True enough, but in the Ninth Symphony of Beethoven, the vocalists do not begin their work until the last movement. An hour of instrumental music has been performed before they sing their first note. To understand the Ninth, we must first grasp the meaning of this creation on purely musical terms, for it is a complex instrumental construction with a choral and literary element added to it. Without the chorus, it would still be a classical-romantic symphony. The chorus does not make it romantic; the notes do. Without an understanding of the first three movements, the fourth would be diminished. Beethoven binds the beginning to the end, for he takes the opening motive from the beginning of the symphony to play in the introduction to the fourth, or choral, movement; likewise he takes the melody of the scherzo, or second movement, for use in the finale's introduction. The restatement of earlier ideas in a Beethoven symphony is not merely saying the same thing twice; rather, it is a reiteration of initial ideas now seen in the new light cast from all the music that has been played since the ideas were first stated. Had the remainder of the symphony not been performed—that is, had the first three movements been omitted—the music of the opening of the last movement would be extraneous and the finale reduced to a skillfully orchestrated choral piece. Beethoven's way made it the crowning gem of a symphonic career. The Ninth Symphony looks both ways—back to the past and forward into the future.

Since this work is indeed a choral symphony, we must look carefully at the poem, for surely a composer's preoccupation with text is the critical event that starts the compositional process for a choral setting. In Beethoven's case it was truly a preoccupation. From a letter of 1793 written by a Viennese admirer, Bartolomeus Fischenich, when the composer was only twenty-three years old, we learn that the young musician intended to set Schiller's *Freude* (Joy) poem stanza by stanza; the Ninth Symphony was completed in 1824. Obviously Beethoven was not actively working on this symphony for thirty-one years, but the Schiller poem seems to have been tucked within the composer's mind throughout the period of the Napoleonic exploits in France, a series of events that strongly molded Beethoven's philosophy. In fact, this poem gains even greater significance if the noted British composer, Ralph Vaughan Williams, is correct, for he relates:

> When I was young I was told that Schiller originally wrote his Ode to "Freedom" (*Freiheit*), not "Joy" (*Freude*), and that Beethoven knew of this when he composed the music. I have never been able to find any confirmation of this legend, but we may profitably keep it at the back of our minds when we play or sing or read, or hear this great Symphony.[1]

There is no doubt that Schiller's poem exemplifies the romantic spirit in Europe and was capable of holding special meaning for Beethoven.

Alle Menschen werden Brueder,
  Wo dein sanfter Fluegel weilt.

(Men throughout the world are brothers,
  In the haven of thy wings.)

Napoleon, until he named himself emperor, had been a hero for Beethoven, a leader of common people against the tyranny of the rich, the oppression of the aristocracy. Beethoven did not like his indebtedness to the patronage of the rich; recognizing personal worth and artistic genius to be far superior to accident of birth, he struggled constantly throughout his life to assert his independence, his freedom. To him freedom was the greatest joy, and Schiller's poem expressed in words what he felt in his soul and was capable of translating into music. (Only the portion of the poem used by Beethoven is printed below.)

Friedrich Schiller (1759–1805)

Hymn to Joy

Translation by Louis Untermeyer

BARITONE: O Freunde, nicht diese Toene!
Sondern lasst uns angenehmere anstimmen,
und freudenvollere.

O friends, friends, not these sounds!
Let us sing something more pleasant,
more full of gladness.
O Joy, let us praise thee!

[1] Ralph Vaughan Williams, *Some Thoughts on Beethoven's Choral Symphony with Writings on Other Musical Subjects* (London: Oxford University Press, 1953), p. 13.

BARITONE SOLO, QUARTET and CHORUS:

Freude, schoener Goetterfunken,
Tochter aus Elysium,
Wir betreten feuer-trunken,
Himmlische, dein Heiligthum!
Deine Zauber binden wieder,
Was die Mode streng getheilt;
Alle Menschen werden Brueder,
Wo dein sanfter Fluegel weilt.

Joy, thou source of light immortal,
Daughter of Elysium,
Touched with fire, to the portal
Of thy radiant shrine we come.
Thy pure magic frees all others
Held in Custom's rigid rings;
Men throughout the world are brothers
In the haven of thy wings.

Wem der grosse Wurf gelungen,
Eines Freundes Freund zu sein,
Wer ein holdes Weib errungen,
Mische seinen Jubel ein!

He who knows the pride and pleasure
Of a friendship firm and strong,
He who has a wife to treasure,
Let him swell our mighty song.

Ja, wer auch nur eine Seele
Sein nennt auf dem Erdenrund!
Und wer's nie gekonnt, der stehle
Weinend sich aus diesem Bund!

If there is a single being
Who can call a heart his own,
And denies it—then, unseeing,
Let him go and weep alone.

Freude trinken alle Wesen
An den Bruesten der Natur;
Alle Guten, alle Boesen
Folgen ihrer Rosenspur.
Kuesse gab sie uns und Reben,
Einen Freund, geprueft im Tod;
Wollust ward dem Wurm gegeben,
Und der Cherub steht vor Gott.

Joy is drunk by all God's creatures
Straight from earth's abundant breast;
Good and bad, all things are nature's,
And with blameless joy are blessed.
Joy gives love and wine; her gladness
Makes the universe her zone,
From the worm that feels spring's madness
To the angel near God's throne.

TENOR SOLO and CHORUS:

Froh, wie seine Sonnen fliegen
Durch des Himmels praecht'gen Plan,
Laufet, Brueder, eure Bahn,
Freudig, wie ein Held zum Siegen.

Glad, as when the suns run glorious
Through the deep and dazzling skies,
Brothers, run with shining eyes—
Heroes, happy and victorious.

Freude, schoener Gotterfunken,
Tochter aus Elysium,
Wir betreten feuer-trunken,
Himmlische, dein Heiligthum!
Deine Zauber binden wieder,
Was die Mode streng getheilt;
Alle Menschen werden Brueder,
Wo dein sanfter Fluegel weilt.

Joy, thou source of light immortal,
Daughter of Elysium,
Touched with fire, to the portal
Of thy radiant shrine we come.
Thy pure magic frees all others
Held in Custom's rigid rings;
Men throughout the world are brothers
In the haven of thy wings.

QUARTET and CHORUS:

Seid umschlungen, Millionen!
Diesen Kuss der ganzen Welt!
Brueder, ueber'm Sternenzelt
Muss ein lieber Vater wohnen.
Ihr stuerzt nieder, Millionen?
Ahnest du den Schoepfer, Welt?
Such ihn ueber'm Sternenzelt!
Ueber Sternen muss er wohnen.

Millions, myriads, rise and gather!
Share this universal kiss!
Brothers, in a heaven of bliss,
Smiles the world's all-loving Father.
Do the millions, His creation,
Know Him and His works of love?
Seek Him! In the heights above
Is His starry habitation!

Beethoven's chorus, singing their heads off in a "fire-drunk" jubilation, celebrate the human spirit; they are singing a great song for all peoples, nations, and languages. And as the fervor builds and the orchestral and vocal sounds sweep you away, the listener is unlikely to notice that this great romantic outpouring is framed by Beethoven's simplest, and most classical, melody.

The simplicity of the *theme,* the clarity of its form (A–A–B–A–B–A), the unpretentious nature of its harmony and rhythm, make it a song for the common person, and that it has become. The works of Beethoven live today because, in addition to their sheer beauty and historical importance, they symbolize those values that we cherish now. In the words of Romain Rolland:

> The music of Beethoven is the daughter of the same forces of imperious Nature that had just sought an outlet in the man of Rousseau's *Confessions.* Each of them is the flowering of a new season.... [Beethoven], too, like the eagle on his rock, goes into exile on an island lost in the expanse of the seas—more truly lost than that island in the Atlantic, for he does not hear even the waves breaking on the rocks. He is immured. And when out of the silence there rises the song of the Ego of the last ten years of his life, it is no longer the same Ego; he has renounced the empire of men; he is with his God.[2]

Individualism and the Romantic Hero

From the romantic version of revolutionary ideals—as from the writings of the transitional Rousseau—there developed a new sense of the value of the unique individual. Rousseau's confession "If I am not better than other men, *at least* I am different!" would be unthinkable to a classicist. Schiller, who could write a hymn to human fellowship, could also write a play, *The Robbers,* with an individualistic outlaw as hero. People like Beethoven, and for that matter Napoleon, embodied the romantic doctrine of individual, unique, "titanic" genius.

But the romantic hero could also be a forlorn individual, solitary and alienated. Although the "suffering" type of romantic hero may wander off to commune with nature or commit suicide, the "titanic" type of rebel attempts to take destiny into his own hands. Prometheus, the deity from Greek mythology who stole the secret of fire from the gods to bring it to man and who defied Zeus himself, was a favorite subject of romantic verse and drama. The romantics' Prometheus goes beyond their model, the Prometheus of the Greek tragedian Aeschylus. Prometheus combines two aspects of the romantic hero that may be separate and contradictory elsewhere: he is both a self-willed individual and a benefactor of mankind. Shelley's verse drama *Prometheus Unbound* is the most extended treatment of this theme; Byron's short lyric "Prometheus" is an early model for what came to be known as the Byronic hero. Byron's "On this day I complete my thirty-sixth year" portrays a suffering type of hero but offers a solution in dedication to revolution. But Byron was capable of mocking his own heroic types with a comic antihero, Don Juan.

The poet George Gordon, Lord Byron (1788–1824), is a good example of a romantic who lived as well as wrote his romanticism. Spectacularly handsome, he was involved in many unhappy love affairs. He wandered restlessly over Europe and finally died while fighting for a liberal cause, the war of the Greeks against their oppressors, the Turks. Byron's literary heroes, particularly his Childe Harold, Manfred, and Cain, are rebellious individuals with a passionate belief in individual freedom. They are men of powerful emotions and a genius that may at times appear satanic. There is a "dark" side to the Byronic hero that we may see in some of the characters created in his wake, such as Melville's Captain Ahab. The "gothic" hero and the mad scientist, two other romantic types,

---
[2]Romain Rolland, *Beethoven the Creator*, trans. Ernest Newman (New York: Harper & Brothers, 1929), pp. 25ff.

may be seen as offshoots of the Byronic hero. The most famous of the latter, Victor Frankenstein, was created by Mary Godwin Shelley, a close friend of Byron's. She called her novel *Frankenstein, or the Modern Prometheus.*

Perhaps the most enduring romantic hero-rebel, one who goes beyond romanticism, is Goethe's Faust, in the long dramatic poem of that title. Faust's rebellion is really against human limits, or finitude. He embarks on a quest after the absolute: absolute knowledge, power, and love, and in the process puts his soul in the hands of the devil. He refuses to accept any limits on his individuality until the end of the poem, when he also becomes a benefactor of humankind.

The various types of romantic individuals took hold of the imaginations of Americans as well as Europeans. It is possible to see in the romantic hero a kind of literary prototype for the "robber barons" of the later nineteenth century. The romantic period was the time when American literature came into its own. Ralph Waldo Emerson celebrated the heroic, "self-reliant" individual; Herman Melville and Edgar Allan Poe portrayed the darker side of the soul. A different and perhaps more typically American romantic individualism emerged in the poetry of Walt Whitman (1819–1892). In his long poem *Song of Myself* he celebrates his unique self in an attempt to break down the artificial barriers that society creates between human beings. An unheroic but no less significant sense of individual uniqueness is expressed in the extraordinary poetry of Emily Dickinson (1830–1886).

Nature and "Natural People"

For the "enlightened" European or American, the word *nature* meant essentially human nature, and the natural place of human beings was among their peers. Human institutions might be corrupt, but they could be changed for the better. Civilization brought with it many ills, but it was still humanity's greatest achievement. Yet as early as the eighteenth century, we witness a kind of disillusionment with Western civilization and urban life and a curiosity about "uncivilized" peoples that came to be known as the "noble savage" craze. With this came a yearning for unspoiled natural scenery—forests, lakes, mountains, the ocean.

Once again, Rousseau is a pivotal figure here. Just as he went beyond a doctrine of liberty to one of individuality, so he went beyond a critique of the faults of civilized society to a radical questioning of its value. The romantics who followed Rousseau eulogized the free and "natural" life of American Indians as superior to that of decadent Europeans, although few seemed to understand the social and economic threat that the new republic posed to the former. The social ideals promoted by the revolutions were also used by romantics, first British and later American, in the service of the antislavery cause that culminated in the abolitionist movement. In the romantic view, the black African was a proud, noble individual who had suffered the oppression and tyranny of the old order of Europe, an order that was now to be overthrown on all levels. The romantic liberals championed the cause of the peasant, the worker, the poor, and the oppressed; they looked with contempt on the rich bourgeois, smug and materialistic. Naturally, the champions of the oppressed tended to, as we would say, "romanticize" those that they perceived as victims, sometimes endowing them with sublime, superhuman characters. They were, in fact, more interested in lofty ideals than in everyday reality. Out of the revolution, they believed, a new order would be born that would bring with it the creative freedom of the individual and the unity of all humankind.

Rousseau influenced not only the idealization of "natural" peoples but also the tendency of the "misunderstood," unhappy, and yearning urban romantic to seek solitude and solace in the natural world. In his *Reveries of the Solitary Walker,* Rousseau describes the beauty of the Swiss landscape, its mountains and lakes, and his feeling of communion with it. He also describes his joy in abandoning himself to "pure sensation" as he experiences the lapping of a mountain lake's waves. To be able to abandon thought and feel oneself in unison with nature: a romantic ideal is born.

Ideas such as returning to nature and living a natural (that is, nonartificial, nonurban) life began in the romantic period to acquire the connotations that they have today. Changes in fashion were indicative of the trend. Partly because of Rousseau, women abandoned corsets and stiffened skirts for loose, flowing, "natural" attire, and the formal, symmetrical French garden (as at Versailles) gave way to the more luxuriant, chaotic, and "natural" English garden. Hiking and mountain climbing became for the first time popular pastimes in Europe. The vine-covered cottage replaced the palace as dream house. The life of the simple peasant was prized (at least in theory) above that of the sophisticated city dweller, and feeling, or richness of sensation, above intellectual capacity. There was even a concern for what we could call conservation and ecology. The New Englander Henry David Thoreau (1817–1862) actually carried out a solitary back-to-nature experiment, which he described both practically and emotionally in *Walden.*

The celebration of nature in romantic art took on varying aspects, corresponding to the individualistic temperaments of the artists. Romantic artists tended to depict nature as reflecting the sensations of their own souls. For some it consoled; to others it seemed indifferent. To some it was picturesque; to others, fearful and sublime. Some romantics, weary of cold and sterile eighteenth-century deism, found their religious yearnings satisfied in their relations with the natural world. Those drawn back to a devout Christianity found God's bounty and goodness reflected in nature; those who shunned organized religion tended toward a kind of pantheism, worshiping the spirit of nature itself. Coleridge's poetry emphasizes the mystical, uplifting aspects of nature. A poet like Keats (1795–1821), on the other hand, renders through language the pure sensuous feelings of an autumn day or a summer night, sensations comparable to those rendered in paint by the artist J. M. W. Turner. Emily Dickinson's close observations of natural phenomena sometimes reveal nature as a soothing mother and sometimes as a terrifying foreboder of death. In music we find composers imitating the sounds and feelings of nature with new orchestral textures. Beethoven's *Pastoral* Symphony (no. 6) renders a wide range of moods from the natural world—sublime, mysterious, joyful, humble—and it even imitates a thunderstorm. In painting, landscapes came into vogue. Like the romantic poets, romantic landscape painters often attempted to render the communion between human emotion and nature. The painters John Constable and Jean-François Millet, when juxtaposed with the poet William Wordsworth, exemplify some aspects of the romantic vision of nature common to both visual art and poetry.

John Constable (1776–1837)

Keen observers of the world around them, Constable and Wordsworth were more taken with the humble, everyday aspects of nature than with its sublime or mystical ones. Both were profoundly attached to their native countryside. Constable recorded his pleasure in simple phenomena: "The sound of water escaping from mill dams, willows, old rotten planks, slimy posts, brickwork. I love such things." The statement would have been inconceivable to a Renaissance or neoclassical artist. It reveals not only a sensitivity to the textures of ordinary objects but also (especially in the escaping water and the rotten plants) a concern with mutability, the ways in which time changes things. Constable's pursuit of a means to capture his experience of the natural world led him to study clouds, rain, light, and the weather. His early pictures are not far removed from the perpetual sunlight or storm of seventeenth- and eighteenth-century pictures; but, as his ideas and abilities mature, we see him open the landscape to capture the broken light of moving air and clouds. Colors become more intense, and the surface of paint is dense and wet. His brush strokes give trees a shimmer and clouds a sense of movement and energy. Constable painted only those things that he knew and loved. The River Stour was completely familiar to him and he took comfort and refreshment from its mossy banks, bridges, and surrounding countryside (Color Plate XXIII).

William Wordsworth (1770–1850)

A poem by Wordsworth, written on his return to a spot near the medieval ruins of Tintern Abbey, in many ways parallels Constable's painting. The primary theme of both works is humanity's relationship to nature. "Lines Composed a Few Miles Above Tintern Abbey" paints a landscape in its first stanza and meditates on the poet's interaction with it in the rest of the poem. But the landscape painted by Wordsworth is not a simple one; it is superimposed, as in a double-exposure photograph. From the first lines the reader is aware that Wordsworth is *also* viewing this scene with the memory of how he had viewed it five years previously. A sense of the passage of time is imposed on the place. Because of this dual perception, the poet is able to reexperience his feelings as they were five years before. At that time he was able to enjoy the purely sensational effects of nature; now he finds that the recollection, as well as the new vision of the natural landscape, has a profound effect on his moral and intellectual being. Both of these perceptions are conveyed to the reader. Another dimension is added as the poet looks, through the person of his sister Dorothy, into the future. The sensations from nature that they experience in the present will be sublimated and perpetuated as "lovely forms" in her mind's "mansion." In Wordsworth's mention of the possibility of his own death while his sister is still alive, we experience no sense of dread, or even sadness, but a sense of life as continuity. The life and death of the individual are part of the processes of nature. Still, it is through the individual's consciousness and judgment that nature is given meaning. Wordsworth's poem, like Constable's painting, brings out the interdependence between the human life cycle and nature.

27-3 *Jean-François Millet,* The Sower, *c. 1850, oil on canvas, 40″ × 32½″. (Courtesy, Museum of Fine Arts, Boston. Gift of Quincy Adams Shaw through Quincy Adams Shaw, Jr., and Mrs. Marian Shaw Haughton)*

Beauty, for Wordsworth, could also be found in the simple people who inhabited his countryside. One of Wordsworth's ideals was to let his poems speak for the inarticulate, to express the poetry latent in the woodsman, the peasant, or the country girl: such a poem is his "Solitary Reaper." Here again Wordsworth emphasizes the beauty to be found in the familiar and the near at hand. The young girl reaping is a part of nature, yet her song—whether of past events or eternal emotions—gives a continuity and a temporality to the natural world that it would not otherwise have. At the end the suggestion is made that the poet will perpetuate her song into the future.

Jean-François Millet (1814–1875)

A painter who saw the same poetry in simple people at their country tasks was the Frenchman Jean-François Millet. Millet portrayed the French peasantry as virtuous, humane, and monumentally enduring. In his picture *The Sower* (Fig. 27-3) the figure is huge, the gesture simple, the colors earthy and rich. Unlike the romantic hero or heroine, the romantic peasant in poem and painting is anonymous and eternal, rather than individualistic. Like Wordsworth, Millet emphasizes the harmony between the workers of the field and their natural surroundings.

Art: Revolution, Individualism, and Nature

We have seen how the painter David turned from neoclassicism to portray Napoleon as a romantic hero. The revolutionary ideals of liberty, equality, and fraternity had a profound influence on developing romanticism in the visual arts as in literature. There were also inventions and advances that affected art internally. The development of photography; the scientific study of light, color, and perception; and the opening of Japan and China to the Western world all had immediate repercussions in painting, sculpture, and the graphic arts.

Architecture was challenged by the growing diversification of life and human needs. Commissions for palaces and churches were replaced by industrial, commercial, and transportation needs. Hospitals, housing, and prisons were demanded as never before. The manufacture of iron, then steel, glass, and finally concrete provided new building possibilities and problems without precedent. Both the private individual and governments experienced the stress of a burgeoning economy and rapidly increasing population. Systems of transportation, water, waste disposal, marketing, and housing taxed cities beyond their limits, and the vast slum became a familiar reality.

Not only were the artist and architect challenged by these things, but also the systems of education and patronage experienced pressures that were either absorbed or ignored. In France the academy that had produced David and his pupils also produced a number of artists who revolted against the doctrines of Davidian classicism; they began searching for a form and content expressive of revolutionary and romantic ideals. Three painters who typify, in different ways, the search for new forms and means of expression are the Spaniard Francisco Goya; the Frenchman Eugène Delacroix; and the Englishman J. M. W. Turner.

Francisco Goya (1746–1828)

Goya was a successful and celebrated painter in the court of Charles IV. He had begun his career as a designer of tapestries whose subjects, the amusements of the court life, document the end of an era with elegance and beauty. There was, however, a toughness and tenacity about Goya that was first revealed in a

27-4 *Francisco Goya,* The Sleep of Reason Produces Monsters, *etching and aquatint, working proof. (Courtesy, Museum of Fine Arts, Boston. Gift of Mr. and Mrs. Burton S. Stern, Mr. and Mrs. Bernard S. Shapiro, and the M. and M. Karolik Fund)*

series of etchings, *Los Caprichos* (*Human Follies*), executed in 1795–1796. Of this collection perhaps the most famous is one of the first, *The Sleep of Reason Produces Monsters* (Fig. 27-4). The title is a complex one. A sleeping man dreams of horrible winged creatures who hover about his head. Reason, when she flees, permits the appearance of the dark, demonic, undisciplined self; but a rigid and inflexible Reason produces the monsters of revolution, too. Technically, Goya draws on traditional conventions but transforms them into an awful assemblage of shadow and texture.

While serving as the court painter, he experienced the horror of the French invasion of Spain with its guerrilla warfare. Spanish royalists fought the invaders, republicans fought the royalists, and the invaders and the ensuing chaos reduced the populace to a terror-filled mob. No longer reserved for armies and

27-5 *Francisco Goya,* The Disasters of War; I Saw This (Yo Lo Vi). *(Photo courtesy of the Trustees of the Public Library of the City of Boston)*

generals, war decimated the entire population. There was looting, rape, pillage, and plunder. These years are recorded in the etchings *The Disasters of War.* Probably made from scenes he witnessed, the pictures reveal the violence, brutality, and monstrous inhumanity of humankind. Figure 27-5, *I Saw This,* shows a family wrenched apart. In Figure 27-6 a man stumbles on a tumbled mass of bodies; the sight and smell make him retch.

After the war Goya was commissioned to commemorate the events of May 2 and 3, 1808, when the citizenry of Madrid had attacked the soldiers of Napoleon in the Puerta del Sol. That night and the next day citizens were rounded up and summarily shot in a gesture of reprisal. *The Third of May, 1808, at Madrid* is among the most brilliant images that Goya created (Fig. 27-7). The huddled citizens, unarmed

27-6 *Francisco Goya,* The Disasters of War; For This You Were Born (Para Eso Habeis Nacido). *(Photo courtesy of the Trustees of the Public Library of the City of Boston)*

27-7 *Francisco Goya,* The Third of May, 1808, at Madrid: The Shootings on Principe Pio Mountain, *1814, oil on canvas, 8′8¾″ × 11′3⅞″. (All rights reserved © Museo del Prado, Madrid)*

and frightened, and the anonymous rank of surging soldiery spotlighted by a flaring lamp resemble a nightmare. The open mouths and astonished faces, the blood and gore, are without precedent. The loosely handled paint is rapidly brushed, and the earthy tones, cream, and reds focus our eyes into the center foreground, where the pose of the figure with upraised arms alludes to Christ and an attitude of innocence. This is a court of no resort; no pleading protects women or children. Death is stark, awful, ignominious. The romantic revolt against tyranny is the theme, but Napoleon is the villain rather than the hero.

27-8 *Eugene Delacroix,* The Massacres of Scios, *1822–24, oil, 13′10″ × 11′7″, Louvre, Paris. (Art Resource, NY)*

Eugène Delacroix (1798–1863)

Goya's work was known in France and was not without influence. But for the French romantic painter Eugène Delacroix, considered a revolutionary by his peers and teachers, war's terrifying nature was still susceptible to the romanticizing distance of place, if not time. Delacroix's painting *The Massacres of Scios* (Fig. 27-8) recounts an event similar in nature to the

27-9 *Eugene Delacroix,* Liberty at the Barricades, *Louvre, Paris. (Art Resource, NY)*

murders in Madrid, but the event is presented as a scene from a poetic drama. The figures are drawn from Renaissance types: their deaths seem to be those of passive resignation. There is little immediate violence. The men are handsome and noble, the women are splendidly beautiful in old age or youth, the costumes are magnificent, and the horse is glorious. Yet Delacroix was condemned for the intensity of his presentation and for the looseness of his brilliant paint. Compared to the hard coldness of Jacques-Louis David and his followers, Delacroix's work was considered a direct threat to the classicism of the academy.

In his painting *Liberty at the Barricades* (Fig. 27-9), a scene from the Revolution of 1830, Delacroix uses a bare-breasted female to personify Liberty. The diagonal composition and the piled-up bodies recall Rubens and the monumental compositions of the baroque. Nevertheless, Delacroix, who painted nudes, animals, and scenes from the Bible, mythology, and the tales of Sir Walter Scott, exemplifies a romantic response to the strictures of the past. His emotion-filled canvases, brilliant in color and heavy with paint, are his attempt to make an art in response to his personal temperament and imagination.

Baudelaire, the French poet and critic, praised Delacroix for his imagination and energy, finding in his work an individual temperament given free reign to speak directly to the emotions and dreams of others. Yet Delacroix's work seems reserved and controlled when compared to the elemental passion tapped in Goya's work.

We can understand this only when we remember that Delacroix revered the art of the past, seeking to preserve it while giving it new values, whereas Goya seemed absolutely unable to incorporate his feelings and ideas in the old traditions. It is this split between reverence for the past and a passion for new ways of thinking, seeing, and feeling that characterizes the romantic period.

Delacroix drew on the images of the past as sources for form and for inspiration. He also used photographs as a means to study poses and gestures, and he developed theories about color and light that influenced his work enormously. But his interest was nevertheless in the narrative, which by its very nature depends on human figures as the *dramatis personae.*

Other painters looked at the natural world and found there the inspiration for new approaches to painting and to the landspace. In France, Corot, Millet, and others sought nature in the farmland and the forests of Barbizon. In England, J. M. W. Turner, like John Constable, drew revolutionary ideas from his observations of nature.

27-10 *J. M. W. Turner,* Mortlake Terrace: Early Summer Morning. *(The Frick Collection, New York)*

J. M. W. Turner (1775–1851)

Joseph Mallord William Turner began by painting the studied landscapes that one associates with early-nineteenth-century academic work, but even those showed an intense interest in light (Fig. 27-10). By the 1840s, however, Turner had transformed the light, air, and motion of the observed world into a visibly fragmented and energy-charged painted surface. *Rain, Steam, and Speed—The Great Western Railway* (Color Plate XXIV), painted in 1845, was, according to Turner, a literal account of an event—a train in a snowstorm—that Turner himself had witnessed. However, it was not accepted by the public, who considered the thin veils of paint "tinted steam." Untroubled by popular opinion, Turner continued to explore similar subjects—sometimes with a narrative or moral, but more often concentrating on light. The light of the sun was energy creating, and countless fluid, light-filled, and layered canvases convey an almost tragic obsession that is mitigated only by Turner's success in achieving a sense of the fluctuating, ephemeral world of light that his studies of nature revealed. Not until the impressionists—indeed, many would argue, not until the completely nonobjective paintings of the twentieth century—have there been other works similar enough to Turner's to form a basis for comparison. But he, like Constable, took his inspiration from the natural, external world, not from the internal world of the mind or from the hermetic world of paintings about painting, which was to become characteristic of the "romanticism" of the twentieth century.

The Romantic Woman and Romantic Love

Another facet of the complex romantic sensibility was its fervent interest in questions regarding the nature of women and the nature of love. In the romantic era—in life as well as in art—women undoubtedly assumed a new importance, a role more influential than in any previous cultural epoch in the West. Yet the positions assumed by women in society and as artists, and the images of women in art created by men, seem, from our modern point of view, contradictory. Liberated and autonomous, predatory and dangerous, domestic and subservient, ethereal and mystical; all are aspects of the image of romantic woman.

Romantic Women Novelists

Mary Wollstonecraft Godwin (who married the poet Shelley) followed in her mother Mary Wollstonecraft's footsteps in that she became a writer, but she typified the shift from the Enlightenment to romanticism, writing novels of fantasy rather than treatises. Her *Frankenstein*, mentioned above, has become a classic in its genre. The early nineteenth century saw a veritable outbreak of female writers, primarily novelists, struggling against restrictions imposed on them by family and society, in order to live freely as human beings and as artists. Many of them published under male pen names. In England, there were the Brontë sisters and Mary Ann Evans (George Eliot); in France, Germaine Necker (known as Madame de Staël) and Aurore Dupin (George Sand). The United States produced the outspoken Margaret Fuller and the reclusive Emily Dickinson. The two Frenchwomen were particularly concerned in their novels with the nature and destinies of women. Sand was a liberated woman in her lifestyle, which included a passionate affair with the composer Chopin; but, with typical romantic contradiction, she exalts the simple, virtuous wife in many of her works. Her *Lélia* is nonetheless an apology for free love. Madame de Staël's Corinne, in the novel of that name, is a poetic genius who suffers and dies of unrequited love. Her statement on poetic inspiration is remarkable not only for its portrayal of women but for its typically romantic exaltation of inspired genius:

> Sometimes . . . my impassioned excitement carries me beyond myself; teaches me to find in nature and my own heart such daring truths and forcible expressions as solitary meditation could never have engendered. My enthusiasm then seems supernatural: a spirit speaks within me far greater than my own; it often happens that I abandon the measure of verse to explain my thoughts in prose. . . . Sometimes my lyre, by a simple national air, may complete the effect which flies from the control of words. In truth, I feel myself a poet, less when a happy choice of rhymes, of syllables, of figures, may dazzle my auditors, than when my spirit soars disdainful of all selfish baseness; when godlike deeds appear easy to me, 'tis then my verse is at its best. I am . . . a poet while I admire or hate, not by my personal feelings nor in my own cause, but for the sake of human dignity and the glory of the world. . . . I cannot touch on any of the themes that affect me, without that kind of thrill which is the source of ideal beauty in the arts, of religion in the recluse, generosity in heroes and disinterestedness among men.

How far we are here from the neoclassical conception of the role of the artist and the composition of the work of art! Corinne's portrayal of herself is comparable to that of an allegorical figure, like Delacroix's *Liberty at the Barricades.*

Romantic Love and Female Types

Literature and the other arts continued nevertheless to be dominated by men in the romantic period, and so it is primarily woman as viewed by man that has given us the various images of woman in romantic art. These range from the idealized simple, domestic, virtuous girl and mother to the ethereal beauty, inspirer of lofty ideas, to the she-devil, temptress or *femme fatale* who seduces and ruins innocent young men. All these types may inspire romantic love, an all-consuming passion that can never be fulfilled (if it is, it usually leads to disillusionment and a new object) and often causes the hero extreme misery or even death. The romantic sufferer and the romantic lover are often one and the same, as in Goethe's romantic novel *The Sorrows of Young Werther.* Werther, a lover of nature and poetry but a misfit in society, is obsessed with love for a married woman, Charlotte. Unable to find any kind of satisfaction in this world, he finally commits suicide. Young people all over Europe identified with Werther, both in their art and in their lives. The novel actually provoked a rash of suicides. Romantic sufferers, pursuing an ideal, impossible love, felt themselves to be born in the wrong place at the wrong time, sensitive geniuses inevitably misunderstood by a crass society.

Throughout American romantic fiction—the novels of James Fenimore Cooper, Hawthorne, and Melville offer some examples—one can find examples of blond heroines who inspire the hero to noble thoughts and chaste love and brunettes who inevitably bring out his "darker" passions. In France, the type of the fatal woman, the *femme fatale,* is exemplified in Prosper Mérimée's novella *Carmen,* about a young man led to ruin by an enticing, fickle Spanish gypsy. This mythical character was developed further in the opera *Carmen* by Bizet. Romantic opera—*La Bohème* and *La Traviata* are other examples—is indeed full of free-living women who inspire consuming passions. Music, many romantics were convinced, could express the passion of love better than any other art could. Words by themselves were too limited. In the early-nineteenth-century, Germany witnessed an extraordinary cooperation between poets and composers that resulted in a new art form, the *Lied* (art song), or the song cycle. One of the best known of the cycles on the theme of love is *Dichterliebe* ("The Love of a Poet") by the poet Heinrich Heine (1797–1856) and the composer Robert Schumann (1810–1856). The culminating portrayal of romantic love in music is Richard Wagner's opera *Tristan und Isolde,* taking its subject from the literature that gave romantic love its prototype, the medieval romance. The music portrays the soaring passions of the lovers and the only climax possible—death.

27-11 Carlotta Grisi in Giselle, *from a lithograph by J. Bouvier. (Courtesy of the Board of Trustees, Victoria and Albert Museum, London)*

The Romantic Ballet

A romantic art form that gave great importance to women, both as artists and as mythical figures, and to romantic love was the ballet. The neoclassical stage ballet of the eighteenth century, like the *ballet de cour* of the seventeenth, showed an equality of roles between the sexes but gave some predominance to men in the execution of showy steps. In the romantic ballet, however, the first female dancer of the company—the *prima ballerina*—upstaged everyone. Dancing on the tips of the toes, or *pointe,* and airy tulle costumes appeared at this time. Men were sometimes reduced to machines to lift the ethereal creatures in the air. The popular notion of ballet as a woman's art, as it still is in most of the best-known ballets still performed, dates from the romantic period. Romanticism in ballet, as in the other arts, stressed exoticism, fantasy, nature, and, of course, love—an unrealizable love for an evanescent lady or a "fatal" love for a heartless temptress.

Paris, with London a close second, was the center of romantic ballet. It was there, at the opera, that the stars—the Italians Maria Taglioni and Carlotta Grisi and the Viennese Fanny Essler—became for their admirers legendary, almost goddesslike. The poet Théophile Gautier, an admirer of the art of dance, wrote the story for the greatest romantic ballet, *Giselle,* one that is still popular with modern audiences. Based on a German legend, the ballet recounts the story of a young country girl who loves to dance and falls in love with a shepherd boy. Her mother foretells her fate: "Unhappy child! You will dance forever, you will kill yourself, and, when you are dead, you will become a *Wili* (a dancing spirit)." Giselle pays no heed, but the prophecy comes true. It turns out that the shepherd whom she loves is really a duke in disguise and, when Giselle learns that he is in reality engaged to a noble lady, she kills herself. We then see the *Wilis* dancing around Giselle's grave, coaxing her spirit out to become one of them. The duke, in tears, returns to her tomb, and is almost danced to death by the *Wilis.* After a frenzied dance and a passionate love scene, Giselle returns to the grave and the duke is consoled by his noble fiancée. Carlotta Grisi, according to Gautier, danced this role "with a perfection, lightness, boldness, and a chaste and refined seductiveness, which places her in the first rank... she was nature and artlessness personified." The contemporary lithograph (Fig. 27-11) suggests an ethereal, floating creature, idealized and unearthly.

Reading Selections

Romantic Lyric Poetry

Romantic writers were prolific in all *genres*—fiction, drama, and poetry—but the movement is perhaps best remembered for its achievements in poetry. The individualistic, subjective, and emotional bent of romanticism made the *lyric* a congenial form. In contrast to the period of the Enlightenment, the romantic era was one of the great ages of lyricism. This was true all over Europe, but especially in Germany and in England. American poetry also flourished in this period. Because it is so abundant, of such greatness, and representative of the themes discussed, we have (except for the two songs by Heine) limited our literary selections to lyric poetry written in English.

William Wordsworth

From *The Prelude*

Residence in France

Oh! pleasant exercise of hope and joy!
For mighty were the auxiliars which then stood
Upon our side, we who were strong in love!
Bliss was it in that dawn to be alive,
But to be young was very heaven!—Oh! times,
In which the meagre, stale, forbidding ways
Of custom, law, and statute, took at once
The attraction of a country in romance!
When Reason seemed the most to assert her rights,
When most intent on making of herself
A prime Enchantress—to assist the work
Which then was going forward in her name!
Not favoured spots alone, but the whole earth,
The beauty wore of promise, that which sets
(As at some moments might not be unfelt
Among the bowers of paradise itself)
The budding rose above the rose full blown.
What temper at the prospect did not wake
To happiness unthought of? The inert
Were roused, and lively natures rapt away!
They who had fed their childhood upon dreams,
The playfellows of fancy, who had made
All powers of swiftness, subtilty, and strength
Their ministers,—who in lordly wise had stirred
Among the grandest objects of the sense,
And dealt with whatsoever they found there
As if they had within some lurking right
To wield it;—they, too, who, of gentle mood,
Had watched all gentle motions, and to these
Had fitted their own thoughts, schemers more mild,
And in the region of their peaceful selves;—
Now was it that *both* found, the meek and lofty
Did both find, helpers to their hearts' desire,
And stuff at hand, plastic as they could wish;
Were called upon to exercise their skill,
Not in Utopia, subterranean fields,
Or some secreted island, Heaven knows where!
But in the very world, which is the world
Of all of us,—the place where in the end
We find our happiness, or not at all!

QUESTIONS

1. Whose viewpoint of the French Revolution does Wordsworth give here?
2. What is romantic in his interpretation of the revolution?

The Solitary Reaper

Behold her, single in the field,
Yon solitary Highland Lass!
Reaping and singing by herself;
Stop here, or gently pass!
Alone she cuts and binds the grain,
And sings a melancholy strain;
O listen! for the Vale profound
Is overflowing with the sound.

No Nightingale did ever chaunt
More welcome notes to weary bands
Of travellers in some shady haunt,
Among Arabian sands:
A voice so thrilling ne'er was heard
In spring-time from the Cuckoo-bird,
Breaking the silence of the seas
Among the farthest Hebrides.

Will no one tell me what she sings?—
Perhaps the plaintive numbers flow
For old, unhappy, far-off things,
And battles long ago:
Or is it some more humble lay,
Familiar matter of to-day?
Some natural sorrow, loss, or pain,
That has been, and may be again?
Whate'er the theme, the Maiden sang
As if her song could have no ending;
I saw her singing at her work,
And o'er the sickle bending;—
I listened, motionless and still;
And, as I mounted up the hill,
The music in my heart I bore,
Long after it was heard no more.

Lines

Composed a few miles above Tintern Abbey on revisiting the banks of the Wye during a tour, July 13, 1798[1]

Five years have passed; five summers, with the length
Of five long winters! and again I hear
These waters, rolling from their mountain-springs
With a soft inland murmur. Once again
Do I behold these steep and lofty cliffs,
That on a wild secluded scene impress
Thoughts of more deep seclusion; and connect
The landscape with the quiet of the sky.
The day is come when I again repose
Here, under this dark sycamore, and view
These plots of cottage-ground, these orchard tufts,
Which at this season, with their unripe fruits,
Are clad in one green hue, and lose themselves
'Mid groves and copses. Once again I see
These hedge-rows, hardly hedge-rows, little lines
Of sportive wood run wild: these pastoral farms,
Green to the very door; and wreaths of smoke
Sent up, in silence, from among the trees!
With some uncertain notice, as might seem
Of vagrant dwellers in the houseless woods,
Or of some hermit's cave, where by his fire
The hermit sits alone.
These beauteous forms,
Through a long absence, have not been to me
As is a landscape to a blind man's eye;
But oft, in lonely rooms, and 'mid the din
Of towns and cities, I have owed to them,
In hours of weariness, sensations sweet,
Felt in the blood, and felt along the heart;
And passing even into my purer mind,
With tranquil restoration—feelings too
Of unremembered pleasure: such, perhaps,
As have no slight or trivial influence
On that best portion of a good man's life,
His little, nameless, unremembered acts
Of kindness and of love. Nor less, I trust,
To them I may have owed another gift,
Of aspect more sublime; that blesséd mood,
In which the burthen of the mystery,
In which the heavy and the weary weight
Of all this unintelligible world,
Is lightened—that serene and blesséd mood,
In which the affections gently lead us on—
Until, the breath of this corporeal frame
And even the motion of our human blood
Almost suspended, we are laid asleep
In body, and become a living soul;
While with an eye made quiet by the power
Of harmony, and the deep power of joy,
We see into the life of things.
If this
Be but a vain belief, yet, oh! how oft—
In darkness and amid the many shapes
Of joyless daylight; when the fretful stir
Unprofitable, and the fever of the world,
Have hung upon the beatings of my heart—
How oft, in spirit, have I turned to thee,
O sylvan Wye! thou wanderer through the woods,
How often has my spirit turned to thee!

And now, with gleams of half-extinguished thought,
With many recognitions dim and faint,
And somewhat of a sad perplexity,

---

[1]Wordsworth wrote this poem at the age of twenty-eight; he had first visited the ruins of the medieval abbey five years earlier while on a solitary walking tour.

The picture of the mind revives again;
While here I stand, not only with the sense
Of present pleasure, but with pleasing thoughts
That in this moment there is life and food
For future years. And so I dare to hope,
Though changed, no doubt, from what I was when first
I came among these hills; when like a roe
I bounded o'er the mountains, by the sides
Of the deep rivers, and the lonely streams,
Wherever nature led: more like a man
Flying from something that he dreads than one
Who sought the thing he loved. For nature then
(The coarser pleasures of my boyish days,
And their glad animal movements all gone by)
To me was all in all.—I cannot paint
What then I was. The sounding cataract
Haunted me like a passion; the tall rock,
The mountain, and the deep and gloomy wood,
Their colors and their forms, were then to me
An appetite; a feeling and a love,
That had no need of a remoter charm,
By thought supplied, nor any interest
Unborrowed from the eye. That time is past,
And all its aching joys are now no more,
And all its dizzy raptures. Not for this
Faint I, nor mourn nor murmur; other gifts
Have followed; for such loss, I would believe,
Abundant recompense. For I have learned
To look on nature, not as in the hour
Of thoughtless youth; but hearing oftentimes
The still, sad music of humanity,
Nor harsh nor grating, though of ample power
To chasten and subdue. And I have felt
A presence that disturbs me with the joy
Of elevated thoughts; a sense sublime
Of something far more deeply interfused,
Whose dwelling is the light of setting suns,
And the round ocean and the living air,
And the blue sky, and in the mind of man:
A motion and a spirit, that impels
All thinking things, all objects of all thought,
And rolls through all things. Therefore am I still
A lover of the meadows and the woods
And mountains; and of all that we behold
From this green earth; of all the mighty world
Of eye, and ear—both what they half create,
And what perceive; well pleased to recognize
In nature and the language of the sense
The anchor of my purest thoughts, the nurse,
The guide, the guardian of my heart, and soul
Of all my moral being.

Nor perchance,
If I were not thus taught, should I the more
Suffer my genial spirits to decay:
For thou art with me here upon the banks
Of this fair river; thou my dearest Friend,[2]
My dear, dear Friend; and in thy voice I catch
The language of my former heart, and read
My former pleasures in the shooting lights
Of thy wild eyes. Oh! yet a little while
May I behold in thee what I was once,
My dear, dear Sister! and this prayer I make,
Knowing that Nature never did betray
The heart that loved her; 'tis her privilege,
Through all the years of this our life, to lead
From joy to joy: for she can so inform
The mind that is within us, so impress
With quietness and beauty, and so feed
With lofty thoughts, that neither evil tongues,
Rash judgments, nor the sneers of selfish men,
Nor greetings where no kindness is, nor all
The dreary intercourse of daily life,
Shall e'er prevail against us, or disturb
Our cheerful faith, that all which we behold
Is full of blessings. Therefore let the moon
Shine on thee in thy solitary walk;
And let the misty mountain-winds be free
To blow against thee: and, in after years,
When these wild ecstasies shall be matured
Into a sober pleasure; when thy mind
Shall be a mansion for all lovely forms,
Thy memory be as a dwelling-place
For all sweet sounds and harmonies; oh! then,
If solitude, or fear, or pain, or grief,
Should be thy portion, with what healing thoughts
Of tender joy wilt thou remember me,
And these my exhortations! Nor, perchance—
If I should be where I no more can hear
Thy voice, nor catch from thy wild eyes these gleams
Of past existence—wilt thou then forget
That on the banks of this delightful stream
We stood together; and that I, so long
A worshiper of Nature, hither came
Unwearied in that service; rather say
With warmer love—oh! with far deeper zeal
Of holier love. Nor wilt thou then forget,
That after many wanderings, many years
Of absence, these steep woods and lofty cliffs,
And this green pastoral landscape, were to me
More dear, both for themselves and for thy sake!

---

[2]His sister Dorothy.

QUESTIONS

1. Find all the instances of the word *nature* in the poem. Does it always have the same meaning? How would you define Wordsworth's conception of nature?
2. How does the poet describe the moral effect that nature has on him?
3. With what images does he convey the differences between his present and former selves?
4. What is the role of his sister in the poem?
5. Do you find any points of comparison between this poem and Constable's painting? What are the different processes that a painter and a poet must go through to render a landscape?

GEORGE GORDON, LORD BYRON

Prometheus

I

Titan! to whose immortal eyes
 The sufferings of mortality,
 Seen in their sad reality,
Were not as things that gods despise;
What was thy pity's recompense?
A silent suffering, and intense;
The rock, the vulture, and the chain,
All that the proud can feel of pain,
The agony they do not show,
The suffocating sense of woe,
 Which speaks but in its loneliness,
And then is jealous lest the sky
Should have a listener, nor will sigh
 Until its voice is echoless.

II

Titan! to thee the strife was given
 Between the suffering and the will,
 Which torture where they cannot kill;
And the inexorable Heaven,
And the deaf tyranny of Fate,
The ruling principle of Hate,
Which for its pleasure doth create
The things it may annihilate,
Refused thee even the boon to die:
The wretched gift eternity
Was thine—and thou hast borne it well.
All that the Thunderer wrung from thee
Was but the menace which flung back
On him the torments of they rack;
The fate thou didst so well foresee,
But would not to appease him tell;
And in thy Silence was his Sentence,
And in his Soul a vain repentance,
And evil dread so ill dissembled,
That in his hand the lightnings trembled.

III

Thy Godlike crime was to be kind,
 To render with thy precepts less
 The sum of human wretchedness,
And strengthen Man with his own mind;
But baffled as thou wert from high,
Still in thy patient energy,
In the endurance, and repulse
 Of thine impenetrable Spirit,
Which Earth and Heaven could not convulse,
 A mighty lesson we inherit:
Thou art a symbol and a sign
 To Mortals of their fate and force;
Like thee, Man is in part divine,
 A troubled stream from a pure source;
And Man in portions can foresee
His own funereal destiny;
His wretchedness, and his resistance,
And his sad unallied existence:
To which his Spirit may oppose
Itself—and equal to all woes,
 And a firm will, and a deep sense,
Which even in torture can descry
 Its own concenter'd recompense,
Triumphant where it dares defy,
And making Death a Victory.

QUESTIONS

1. Look up the myth of Prometheus if you are not familiar with it. How has Byron reinterpreted it?
2. What is the *meter* of the verse used here? How would you describe the language of the poem? How are both appropriate to the subject matter?
3. Of what is Prometheus a "symbol and a sign"? What makes him a hero? Would he be a fitting heroic symbol for our times?

On This Day I Complete My Thirty-sixth Year

Missolonghi,[1] January 22, 1824

'Tis time this heart should be unmoved,
Since others it hath ceased to move:
Yet, though I cannot be beloved,
Still let me love!

My days are in the yellow leaf;
The flowers and fruits of love are gone;
The worm, the canker, and the grief
Are mine alone!

The fire that on my bosom preys
Is lone as some volcanic isle;
No torch is kindled at its blaze—
A funeral pile.

The hope, the fear, the jealous care,
The exalted portion of the pain
And power of love, I cannot share,
But wear the chain.

But 'tis not *thus*—and 'tis not *here*—
Such thoughts should shake my soul, nor *now,*
Where glory decks the hero's bier,
Or binds his brow.

The sword, the banner, and the field,
Glory and Greece, around me see!
The Spartan, born upon his shield,
Was not more free.

Awake! (not Greece—she *is* awake!)
Awake, my spirit! Think through *whom*
Thy life-blood tracks its parent lake,
And then strike home!

Tread those reviving passions down,
Unworthy manhood!—unto thee
Indifferent should the smile or frown
Of beauty be.

If thou regrett'st thy youth, *why live?*
The land of honorable death
Is here:—up to the field, and give
Away thy breath!

Seek out—less often sought than found—
A soldier's grave, for thee the best;
Then look around, and choose thy ground,
And take thy rest.

[1]Town in Greece where Byron had gone to help the Greeks in their war for independence from Turkey. Less than three months later he died there.

QUESTIONS

1. What two typically romantic states of mind does Byron contrast in this poem?
2. How is political commitment understood as individual salvation?

She Walks in Beauty

I

She walks in beauty, like the night
Of cloudless climes and starry skies;
And all that's best of dark and bright
Meet in her aspect and her eyes:
Thus mellow'd to that tender light
Which heaven to gaudy day denies.

II

One shade the more, one ray the less,
Had half impair'd the nameless grace
Which waves in every raven tress,
Or softly lightens o'er her face;
Where thoughts serenely sweet express
How pure, how dear their dwelling-place.

III

And on that cheek, and o'er that brow,
So soft, so calm, yet eloquent,
The smiles that win, the tints that glow,
But tell of days in goodness spent,
A mind at peace with all below,
A heart whose love is innocent!

QUESTIONS

1. How does the poet compare the woman to the night?
2. In what way is the portrayal of woman here "romantic"?

JOHN KEATS

Ode to a Nightingale

My heart aches, and a drowsy numbness pains
My sense, as though of hemlock° I had drunk,
Or emptied some dull opiate to the drains
One minute past, and Lethe-wards° had sunk:
'Tis not through envy of thy happy lot,
But being too happy in thy happiness,—
That thou, light-wingèd Dryad of the trees,
In some melodious plot
Of beechen green, and shadows numberless,
Singest of summer in full-throated ease.

O for a draught of vintage! that hath been
Cool'd a long age in the deep-delved earth,
Tasting of Flora° and the country-green,
Dance, and Provençal song,° and sun-burnt mirth!
O for a beaker full of the warm South,°
Full of the true, the blushful Hippocrene,°
With beaded bubbles winking at the brim,
And purple-stained mouth;
That I might drink, and leave the world unseen,
And with thee fade away into the forest dim:

Fade far away, dissolve, and quite forget
What thou among the leaves hast never known,
The weariness, the fever, and the fret
Here, where men sit and hear each other groan;
Where palsy shakes a few, sad, last grey hairs,
Where youth grows pale, and spectre-thin, and dies;
Where but to think is to be full of sorrow
And leaden-eyed despairs;
Where beauty cannot keep her lustrous eyes,
Or new Love pine at them beyond to-morrow.

Away! away! for I will fly to thee,
Not charioted by Bacchus and his pards,
But on the viewless wings of Poesy,
Though the dull brain perplexes and retards:
Already with thee! tender is the night,
And haply the Queen-Moon is on her throne,
Cluster'd around by all her starry Fays;
But here there is no light,
Save what from heaven is with the breezes blown
Through verdurous glooms and winding mossy ways.

I cannot see what flowers are at my feet,
Nor what soft incense hangs upon the boughs,
But, in embalmed darkness, guess each sweet
Wherewith the seasonable month endows
The grass, the thicket, and the fruit-tree wild;
White hawthorn, and the pastoral eglantine;
Fast-fading violets cover'd up in leaves;
And mid-May's eldest child,
The coming musk-rose, full of dewy wine,
The murmurous haunt of flies on summer eves.

Darkling° I listen; and for many a time
I have been half in love with easeful Death,
Call'd him soft names in many a mused rhyme,
To take into the air my quiet breath;
Now more than ever seems it rich to die,
To cease upon the midnight with no pain,
While thou art pouring forth thy soul abroad
In such an ecstasy!
Still wouldst thou sing, and I have ears in vain—
To thy high requiem become a sod.

Thou wast not born for death, immortal Bird!
No hungry generations tread thee down;
The voice I hear this passing night was heard
In ancient days by emperor and clown:
Perhaps the self-same song that found a path
Through the sad heart of Ruth, when, sick for home,
She stood in tears amid the alien corn;
The same that oft-times hath
Charm'd magic casements, opening on the foam
Of perilous seas, in faery lands forlorn.

Forlorn! the very word is like a bell
To toll me back from thee to my sole self.
Adieu! the fancy cannot cheat so well
As she is famed to do, deceiving elf.
Adieu! adieu! thy plaintive anthem fades
Past the near meadows, over the still stream,
Up the hill-side; and now 'tis buried deep
In the next valley-glades:
Was it a vision, or a waking dream?
Fled is that music:—Do I wake or sleep?

---

[2] A poison.

[4] Toward Lethe, the river of forgetfulness in the classical underworld.

[13] Goddess of flowers and spring. (See Botticelli's *Primavera,* Chapter 17 and Color Plate V.)

[14] Troubadour songs from southern France.

[15] Wine.

[16] Fountain of the Muses.

[51] As it grows dark.

QUESTIONS

1. What is the feeling of the poet toward the nightingale? What attractions does it represent?
2. What different sensations (tactile, visual, auditory, and so forth) are represented in the poem, and how?
3. Compare Keats's attitudes toward and representation of nature with Wordsworth's.
4. Compare Keats's sensuous expression of colors and textures to Turner's (see Color Plate XXIV).

PERCY BYSSHE SHELLEY (1792–1822)

Lines: When the Lamp Is Shattered

I

When the lamp is shattered
  The light in the dust lies dead—
When the cloud is scattered
  The rainbow's glory is shed.
When the lute is broken,
  Sweet tones are remembered not;
When the lips have spoken,
  Loved accents are soon forgot.

II

As music and splendour
  Survive not the lamp and the lute,
The heart's echoes render
  No song when the spirit is mute:—
No song but sad dirges,
  Like the wind through a ruined cell,
Or the mournful surges
  That ring the dead seaman's knell.

III

When hearts have once mingled,
  Love first leaves the well-built nest;
The weak one is singled
  To endure what it once possessed.
O Love! who bewailest
  The frailty of all things here,
Why choose you the frailest
  For your cradle, your home, and your bier?

IV

Its passions will rock thee
  As the storms rock the ravens on high;
Bright reason will mock thee,
  Like the sun from a wintry sky.
From thy nest every rafter
  Will rot, and thine eagle home
Leave thee naked to laughter,
  When leaves fall and cold winds come.

QUESTIONS

1. Describe the emotion portrayed here.
2. What *images* and rhythmic effects does the poet use to portray emotion?

HEINRICH HEINE[1]

You Are Just Like a Flower

You are just like a flower
So fair and chaste and dear;
Looking at you, sweet sadness
Invades my heart with fear.

I feel I should be folding
My hands upon your hair,
Praying that God may keep you
So dear and chaste and fair.

A Young Man Loves a Maiden

A young man loves a maiden
Whose heart for another sighed;
This other loves another
Who then becomes his bride.

The maiden takes the first man
Who happens to come her way
Just out of spite and anger;
The youth is left in dismay.

It is an old old story
And yet it's always new;
And to whomever it happens
'Twill break his heart in two.

---

[1]If possible, listen to both of Heine's lyrics set to the music of Robert Schumann in his *Dichterliebe* ("Love of a Poet") song cycle.

QUESTIONS

1. What aspects of love are portrayed in the first and the second poem?
2. How and where does the *tone* change in the second poem?

WALT WHITMAN

FROM *Song of Myself*

1

I celebrate myself, and sing myself,
And what I assume you shall assume,
For every atom belonging to me as good belongs to you.

I loafe and invite my soul,
I lean and loafe at my ease observing a spear of summer grass.

My tongue, every atom of my blood, form'd from this soil, this air,
Born here of parents born here from parents the same, and their parents the same,
I, now thirty-seven years old in perfect health begin,
Hoping to cease not till death.
Creeds and schools in abeyance,
Retiring back a while sufficed at what they are, but never forgotten,
I harbor for good or bad, I permit to speak at every hazard,
Nature without check with original energy.

24

Walt Whitman, a kosmos, of Manhattan the son,
Turbulent, fleshy, sensual, eating, drinking and breeding,
No sentimentalist, no stander above men and women or apart from them,
No more modest than immodest.

Unscrew the locks from the doors!
Unscrew the doors themselves from their jambs!

Whoever degrades another degrades me,
And whatever is done or said returns at last to me.

Through me the afflatus surging and surging, through me the current and index.

I speak the pass-word primeval, I give the sign of democracy,
By God! I will accept nothing which all cannot have their counterpart of on the same terms.

Through me many long dumb voices,
Voices of the interminable generation of prisoners and slaves,
Voices of the diseas'd and despairing and of thieves and dwarfs,
Voices of cycles of preparation and accretion,
And of the threads that connect the stars, and of wombs and of the father-stuff,
And of the rights of them the others are down upon,
Of the deform'd, trivial, flat, foolish, despised,
Fog in the air, beetles rolling balls of dung.

Through me forbidden voices,
Voices of sexes and lusts, voices veil'd and I remove the veil,
Voices indecent by me clarified and transfigur'd.

I do not press my fingers across my mouth,
I keep as delicate around the bowels as around the head and heart,
Copulation is no more rank to me than death is.

I believe in the flesh and the appetites,
Seeing, hearing, feeling, are miracles, and each part and tag of me is a miracle.

Divine am I inside and out, and I make holy whatever I touch or am touch'd from,
The scent of these arm-pits aroma finer than prayer,
This head more than churches, bibles, and all the creeds.

If I worship one thing more than another it shall be the spread of my own body, or any part of it,
Translucent mould of me it shall be you!
Shaded ledges and rests it shall be you!
Firm masculine colter it shall be you!
Whatever goes to the tilth of me it shall be you!
You my rich blood! your milky stream pale strippings of my life!
Breast that presses against other breasts it shall be you!
My brain it shall be your occult convolutions!
Root of wash'd sweet-flag! timorous pond-snipe! nest of guarded duplicate eggs! it shall be you!

Mix'd tussled hay of head, beard, brawn, it shall be you!
Trickling sap of maple, fibre of manly wheat, it shall be you!
Sun so generous it shall be you!
Vapors lighting and shading my face it shall be you!
You sweaty brooks and dews it shall be you!
Winds whose soft-tickling genitals rub against me it shall be you!
Broad muscular fields, branches of live oak, loving lounger in my winding paths, it shall be you!
Hands I have taken, face I have kiss'd, mortal I have ever touch'd, it shall be you.

I dote on myself, there is that lot of me and all so luscious,
Each moment and whatever happens thrills me with joy,
I cannot tell how my ankles bend, nor whence the cause of my faintest wish,
Nor the cause of the friendship I emit, nor the cause of the friendship I take again.

That I walk up my stoop, I pause to consider if it really be,
A morning-glory at my window satisfies me more than the metaphysics of books.

To behold the day-break!
The little light fades the immense and diaphanous shadows,
The air tastes good to my palate.

Hefts of the moving world at innocent gambols silently rising, freshly exuding,
Scooting obliquely high and low.

Something I cannot see puts upward libidinous prongs,
Seas of bright juice suffuse heaven.

The earth by the sky staid with, the daily close of their junction,
The heav'd challenge from the east that moment over my head,
The mocking taunt, See then whether you shall be master!

QUESTIONS

1. Why and how does Whitman "celebrate" and "sing" himself? In what different connections does he view the self?
2. In what sense is this a democratic poem?
3. What "unpoetic" subject matters does Whitman treat? How might he have shocked his readers?
4. Whitman was the first American poet to make extensive use of *free verse,* that is, lines that are not predetermined by any metrical scheme. Why is free verse appropriate to this poem?
5. Can you find patterns of sound and rhythms in this verse? What is their effect?
6. What seems to be Whitman's idea of his role as a poet?

EMILY DICKINSON

I

A narrow fellow in the grass
Occasionally rides;
You may have met him,—did you not?
His notice sudden is.
The grass divides as with a comb,
A spotted shaft is seen;
And then it closes at your feet
And opens further on.

He likes a boggy acre,
A floor too cool for corn.
Yet when a child, and barefoot,
I more than once, at morn,

Have passed, I thought, a whip-lash
Unbraiding in the sun,—
When, stooping to secure it,
It wrinkled, and was gone.

Several of nature's people
I know, and they know me;
I feel for them a transport
Of cordiality;

But never met this fellow,
Attended or alone,
Without a tighter breathing,
And zero at the bone.

II

The leaves, like women, interchange
Sagacious confidence;
Somewhat of nods, and somewhat of
Portentous inference,

The parties in both cases
  Enjoining secrecy,—
Inviolable compact
  To notoriety.

III

I dreaded that first robin so,
But he is mastered now,
And I'm accustomed to him grown,—
He hurts a little, though.

I thought if I could only live
Till that first shout got by,
Not all pianos in the woods
Had power to mangle me.

I dared not meet the daffodils,
For fear their yellow gown
Would pierce me with a fashion
So foreign to my own.

I wished the grass would hurry,
So when 'twas time to see,
He'd be too tall, the tallest one
Could stretch to look at me.

I could not bear the bees should come,
I wished they'd stay away
In those dim countries where they go:
What word had they for me?

They're here, though; not a creature failed,
No blossom stayed away
In gentle deference to me,
The Queen of Calvary.

Each one salutes me as he goes,
And I my childish plumes
Lift, in bereaved acknowledgment
Of their unthinking drums.

IV

I'm nobody! Who are you?
Are you nobody, too?
Then there's a pair of us—don't tell!
They'd banish us, you know.
How dreary to be somebody!
How public, like a frog
To tell your name the livelong day
To an admiring bog!

V

Wild nights! Wild nights!
  Were I with thee,
Wild nights should be
  Our luxury!

Futile the winds
  To a heart in port,—
Done with the compass,
  Done with the chart.

Rowing in Eden!
  Ah! the sea!
Might I but moor
  To-night in thee!

QUESTIONS

1. How would you describe Emily Dickinson's view of nature? Compare it to that of Wordsworth, Keats, and Whitman.
2. How, if at all, does the fact that Emily Dickinson is a woman influence her perception of individuality and of love?

From the Enlightenment to Romanticism

The two great political revolutions at the end of the eighteenth century, the French and the American, not only transformed the leading philosophies of government in the Western world but dramatically altered some basic conceptions about the nature of human beings as well. In terms of the humanities, these revolutions embodied the ideas of the Enlightenment while exciting the passions of romanticism.

Enlightenment Ideals

The primarily middle-class philosophes challenged once and for all the medieval belief that every person occupies an individual place in a hierarchical society, a belief that still held sway in the absolutist seventeenth century. Human beings, they argued, are "naturally" equal and thus entitled to certain natural rights. Thomas Jefferson, in a sense an American philosophe, defined these as life, liberty, and the pursuit of happiness. The writers and artists of the Enlightenment submitted everything—social customs and institutions, religious beliefs, passions—to the cold light of reason.

The Enlightenment belief that the human predicament was largely the product of bad institutions raised tremendous expectations regarding the possibilities of improving human beings and their society through institutional reforms. Although Voltaire's El Dorado was not intended as a model for imitation, other philosophes were deeply engaged in drawing up sketches of model societies, which they took very seriously. Within limits, this belief in human-engineered progress provided a healthy incentive to reform what were seen as present evils. But this belief could also justify something like the Reign of Terror during the French Revolution. An idealist, Robespierre felt perfectly justified in destroying thousands of human beings in the name of a brighter tomorrow. Unfortunately, he was not to be the last of this type.

Enlightenment Style

If the seventeenth century was an age for the grandiose in the arts, the eighteenth was an age for the petite and the well ordered. Neoclassicism, no longer inspired by the baroque sense of splendor, became in the Enlightenment less ornate and somewhat colder and more mechanical. Eighteenth-century artists were more interested in sensuality than in love, in humble virtues than in religious yearnings.

Classical composers such as Mozart and Haydn made use of short phrases and strived to achieve unity, balance, and symmetry, forsaking the complex fugues of the baroque era. Architecture, such as the government buildings in Washington, D.C., and Jefferson's ideal "academic village," The University of Virginia, reflected the inspiration of classical Rome and a belief in order and rationality. Like classical Rome, with Horace and Juvenal, European literature in the eighteenth century reflected a strong predilection for satire and thus for examining human folly and pretensions under the light of reason. Voltaire's *Candide,* with its short, witty, sometimes biting humor and its distrust of metaphysical abstraction, represents well the style of the Enlightenment.

In our post-Freudian era we may view the Enlightenment's understanding of human nature with some skepticism. People cannot be defined primarily as atoms of reason, as some of the philosophes seemed to suppose. We cannot share all of their optimism about progress through education and science. Yet many of the ideals formulated during the Enlightenment are still the basis of many of our society's assumptions. Toleration of the beliefs of others, human equality, basic human rights, the freedom to think for oneself, and even less widespread notions such as equal legal and social rights for women—all of these have had considerable impact on our way of thinking.

Romantic Changes

The romantics adapted the ideals of the Enlightenment to their own purposes. Rejecting the belief that reason is the primary human faculty, they developed a current of sentimentality already present in the eighteenth century. The transitional Jean-Jacques Rousseau makes the Enlightenment's belief in the natural goodness of human beings the basis for a romantic apology for feeling above reason and for the supremacy of the unique individual, thus laying the groundwork for the misunderstood romantic sufferer and the titanic romantic hero. Napoleon, the rationalistic administrator, becomes, as in David's painting, the passionate, dashing, almost superhuman general, comparable to Byron's Prometheus, the savior of humankind.

Rousseau's mature thought made an important contribution to nascent nationalism, which began to take shape in the early decades of the nineteenth century, in a sense inspired by French aggression. Whereas the Enlightenment conceived of human beings as essentially a universal race, the proponents of nationalism saw them as divided into linguistically and culturally defined groupings. Each of these groupings had its own particular characteristics and its own political will. Further, each political will had a right to self-government.

Nothing could have been more congenial to the nationalist position than Rousseau's idea that human beings become human only by virtue of membership in a particular community. To it they owe their values and the character of their intellectual and emotional lives. Moreover, created in a very real sense by their culture, human beings have, as their very essence, a general will, which they share with other members of the community. It was easy for nineteenth-century nationalists to identify this general will as the will of the nation and to envisage it as struggling for life against other general wills that would attempt to oppress it.

Romantic Style

We have seen how the rationalistic goals of liberty, equality, and fraternity became passionate statements in the hands of romantic artists. Open to the entire range of human emotions, the romantics also tended to plumb the depths as well as the heights of experience. Goya, for example, who had lived through the disasters of a brutal war rather than with the theories of revolution, portrayed the demonic side of human nature while showing an intense compassion for the victims of exploitation and tyranny. The desire to portray the extremes and varieties of human passions greatly enriched the range and textures of romantic visual, literary, and musical art. The artists' need for individuality of expression also caused them to find the neat balances and rules of neoclassical art insufficient. Beethoven expanded both classical structures and orchestration, Delacroix experimented with color and composition, the English romantic poets opened poetry to music and to the sensuous imagery of painting, Whitman abandoned the meters and vocabulary considered suitable for poetry, and Dickinson found highly personal images and rhymes.

Romantic Continuities

Romantic exuberance for social causes and for nature, as well as romantic individualism and emotionalism, is still with us. The modern concept of the artist as a supersensitive being—more likely to be misunderstood by, and at odds with, society than in harmony with it—was born with the romantics. The romantic concept of love and the romantic views of women have also, for good or ill, profoundly influenced our own.

We have seen that love, for the romantics, resembled an infinite yearning that could never really be satisfied by a finite human being. Romantic lovers in literature and life were doomed to desire the unattainable and to suffer—or to throw themselves into one passionate love affair after another. They viewed a stable marriage and family life either as too bourgeois and constricting or as a kind of dreamy ideal.

In ways that are often contradictory, women became a romantic preoccupation. A romantic lover might idealize a domestic and virtuous young girl as a mysterious and ethereal creature; he might be destroyed by a *femme fatale* or temptress. The romantic ballet, with the predominance it gave to the ballerina, reinforced the idealization of women. At the same time, women began to explore, in their own way, the romantic ideal of individual freedom. The notion of women's liberation, a philosophical ideal with Mary Wollstonecraft, became a way of life for some romantic women.

The modern reverence for unspoiled nature began in the romantic period. The romantics were particularly prone to see their own emotions reflected in the natural world or to look on nature as a mother, a consolation for their troubles. Many romantics shunned organized religions, finding a substitute in the worship of nature, but even orthodox Christians found that they could approach God through immersion in his works. As they idealized nature, the romantics idealized the simple life of the "natural" peasant, unspoiled by the corruptions of the modern world. Yet the life of peasants, with the growing industrialism of Europe, was in fact beginning to be more and more affected by the modern world. For many of them, urbanization would mean a dramatic uprooting. It would also necessitate new responses in thought and style from the humanities.

PART EIGHT

Industrialism and the Humanities: The Middle and Late Nineteenth Century

28

The Industrial Revolution and New Social Thought

By the beginning of the nineteenth century, while Keats was musing on his nightingale and Wordsworth was celebrating the English countryside and his solitary reaper, the face of rural England was in a state of transformation. Eighteenth-century country towns such as Manchester were fast becoming makeshift cities for hundreds of thousands of poor workers who sought employment in the new factories whose belching smokestacks polluted the landscape for miles around. A few years before Wordsworth's death in 1850, engineers laid down the iron rails that were to bring the first trains across the wheat fields.

The Industrial Revolution could easily be considered the most important event in the history of the human race. In all previous known societies, periods of population growth were necessarily succeeded by periods of contraction caused by disease and starvation. After 1750, however, the productive capacity of the world rapidly increased to the point where population could expand unceasingly and at the same time enjoy an improved standard of living. What the so-called revolution entailed was basically the massive substitution of machines and new techniques of production for human labor. The result was that, depending on the commodity, the output of the individual worker expanded five, fifty, a hundred, and even a thousand or more times, causing accumulations of goods undreamed of earlier. That human beings in such a world continued to live in dire poverty came to appear either as the fault of a backward regional system of production or as an unjust method of distributing the rewards—or a combination of both.

The Industrial Revolution was not, of course, an event like the political revolution in France that took place within a few years' time. It exerted its effect on different areas at different times. By 1785 clearly under way in the British Isles, significant industrial development occurred on the Continent only after 1815, and before 1900 it still remained limited to western Europe, parts of North America, and Japan. Even today certain parts of the world have yet to undergo their industrial revolution.

England in the Lead

There are a number of reasons for English precedence in industrial development. By the early eighteenth century the English (with the Dutch) had the highest standard of living in the world. After approximately a century of applying innovative techniques, English agricultural producers were able to supply food cheaply and in abundance while still making a profit. This efficiency in agriculture also liberated a large percentage of the working population for other pursuits. English government compared with continental monarchies was inexpensive, and the low tax burden left most of the money in the pockets of those who earned it. There was consequently a good deal of money available for investment and consumption. Moreover, whereas absolutist monarchies on the Continent regulated economic life closely, productive enterprise in England was relatively free; personal initiative and experimentation were encouraged. Finally, in the coming age of the machine, England was particularly favored with its enormous deposits of a cheap fuel, coal.

The breakthrough in industrialism first came in cotton, a cloth industry that, compared with wool or silk, was very new. Because of its low cost relative to that of wool and silk, the market for cotton cloth was large, and it happened that cotton could be worked more easily by machine than by hand. By the late eighteenth century the demand for cotton cloth both in England and abroad was such that the raw material came into short supply. Eli Whitney's cotton gin remedied the major bottleneck in production of raw cotton, and the plantation economy of the American South soared from the 1790s on.

The mechanization of cotton production encouraged invention and investment in other areas of the economy. By the end of the eighteenth century the English had developed a relatively efficient steam engine, were able to mine coal and manufacture steel in impressive quantities, and were increasingly using new chemical discoveries for industrial purposes. The nineteenth century in Europe was marked by the continued progress of British industry and by the desperate efforts of continental and American competitors to imitate and catch up with Britain.

Social Effects of Industrialization

The social consequences of industrialization were enormous. Within decades hundreds of thousands of workers moved into the industrial centers, overwhelming the capacity of the cities to absorb them. Shantytowns grew up on the outskirts where the new workers lived in crowded unsanitary conditions. The machines not only demanded regimentation of work but also reduced the need for skill or physical force. Especially in the cloth industry most operations involved in mechanized production could be performed by children, who were cheaper to hire than adults. By the middle 1820s a small boy working two looms could produce fifteen times more than an adult laborer working by hand.

Unable to support the family even with both mother and father working, parents were forced to send their children into the factories. Children four and five years of age worked from twelve to sixteen hours, six days a week, for pennies. Often forbidden to sit down during their hours of work, they were subject to the brutality of the overseer for the slightest infraction. In the case of babies too young to work, desperate parents, unable to pay for babysitters, resorted to "Mother's Helper" to drug the baby from early morning until late at night when they returned home. In the seething tenements of workers' quarters, twisted bodies and early death were common.

Despite the terrible conditions of life among the workers, many historians maintain that, on the whole, conditions of the laboring poor in England improved with the Industrial Revolution. Many of the poor preferred the urban slums to those in the rural districts where their misery was compounded by chronic underemployment and hunger.

Friedrich Engels and Karl Marx

In 1844, a young German socialist and friend of Karl Marx named Friedrich Engels (1820–1895) set himself the task of describing living conditions in the cities of England, the most advanced industrial country in Europe. What Engels exposed in *The Condition of the Working Class in England,* published in 1845, were urban conglomerations sharply divided into neighborhoods for the rich and the poor, the exploiters and the exploited, the high livers and the downtrodden. For Engels, these unjust social and economic conditions were a result of capitalism and could be changed only by a socialist revolution. The phenomenon of the modern city with its subhuman living conditions, its despair and alienation, as well as its teeming life, will become a theme that haunts the imaginations of late-nineteenth- and early-twentieth-century artists and writers.

Like Engels, the German philosopher Karl Marx (1818–1883), who also spent much of his life in London, felt a sense of moral outrage at a system of distribution in which millions, living on the borderline of subsistence, slaved so that a few thousand could wallow in luxury and indolence. Marx expressed his theories primarily in philosophical and economic language, most notably in *Das Kapital,* his analysis of the capitalist system and of its inevitable downfall. Along with Engels, Marx believed that bourgeois capitalism was a necessary stage in a historical development in which justice, in the form of true communism, would triumph.

Human history for Marx was characterized by a series of economic organizations, the more recent evolving out of the preceding as a result of class conflict. Slavery, the economic system of the ancient world, was brought to an end because of slave revolts. The ancient economy was replaced by a feudal one in which serfs, who were not slaves because they were tied to the land and could not be sold, worked for the benefit of the landlords. According to Marx, the continued oppression of the serf by feudal lords induced numbers of these laborers to flee. These runaways constituted the founders of the medieval merchant class. From the sixteenth century on, this merchant class, or bourgeoisie, gained increasing power until finally in England in the 1640s, in France in 1789, and in Germany in 1848, they were successful in overthrowing the feudal order and establishing themselves as the masters of the economy. The Industrial Revolution was the triumph of the new oppressors; the development of the factory brought into being a new class of oppressed, the proletariat. These were the workers, men, women, and children, who possessed nothing but the labor of their bodies.

In Marx's theory, fierce competition among the capitalists—those who control the means of production and the goods—would result in the concentration of wealth into fewer and fewer hands and the swelling of the worker ranks by bourgeois who go under. At the same time the need to keep up profit margins in a situation of limited markets encourages more intensive exploitation of the workers. Whereas formerly the oppressed classes had been widely diffused, by its very nature industrialism brings them together; then they gradually become aware of the injustice of the system and of their own power.

Marx firmly believed that the conflicts between classes were nearing a crisis point. A revolution of the masses against the exploiters was inevitable. When that occurred, Marx thought, the course of human history would change. Because the proletariat made up the vast majority of the people, this revolution would mark the end of class struggle and a new society would result, where all would live in harmony with one another.

Marx felt that the duty of communists was to help workers become more intensely conscious of their status and to weld them into a political class. Although Marx himself favored trade unions, he urged the workers not to be content with better wages and better conditions of work. Joining the system in this way would undermine the solidarity of the movement and, although improving the lot of certain individuals, would leave the mass of proletarians in their misery. The communist was dedicated to the destruction of private property, which was the primary tool in the hands of the bourgeoisie for the subjection of the lower class. Also slated for destruction was the state, which was the political means by which the bourgeois protected their property and controlled the workers. Once bourgeois property had been eliminated and the classless society achieved, social conflict would end and there would be no need for the oppressive power of the state.

Although Marx believed that certain members of the bourgeoisie, such as himself, could work themselves free from their class allegiances, on the whole he maintained that individual mentalities were determined by the economic class to which they belonged. Accordingly, the agencies of historical change were not for him individuals but rather classes. Nevertheless, Marx remained to the end a child of the Enlightenment. His final goal for humanity remained the attainment of personal liberty and equality. He was committed to the belief that once the forces of exploitation were annihilated, people would be rational enough to live as brothers and sisters, sharing the goods of their labor. Indeed, his faith in the power of rationality and the essential goodness of humanity was even greater than that of the philosophes, for he thought that people in the final stage would live in freedom and equality even without the presence of a government.

Although Marx developed his theories in more elaborate form in his later writings, *The Communist Manifesto,* composed in 1848, represents his basic positions most eloquently. Written in collaboration with Engels, the work was published in the very year when Europe was swept by a revolutionary fervor that threatened to destroy most of its major monarchies. In the long run all of the revolutions failed, and in none of them did Marx's thought serve as a platform for a significant group of revolutionaries. Marxism did not become a major ideological force until the twentieth century.

The Growth of Material Progress

Paradoxically, Marxism enjoyed its greatest success in those countries where industrialism was only getting under way and where agriculture remained the dominant occupation. This was the case in Russia in 1917 and in China in the years immediately following World War II. In western Europe and America, however, Marx's fears were realized. In the course of the century after the publication of *The Communist Manifesto,* workers proved more concerned with immediate material gains than with ultimate goals and found that these could be accomplished with greater ease and security through trade unionism and participation in the established political system than through revolution. Although the capitalist economy suffered periodic setbacks, some of great magnitude such as the Depression of the 1930s, on the whole the working population of the Western world experienced a steady increase in its standard of living. Rather than polarizing between the extremes of rich bourgeoisie and proletariat, industrial society witnessed an enormous expansion of the middle class. Large numbers of workers were drawn into its ranks, or at least many were led to believe they belonged there. Belief in progress, scientific and technological as well as economic, came to be characteristic of all social classes in the late nineteenth century.

People rich and poor flocked to the Great Exhibition in London in 1851 at the astounding Crystal Palace, which they viewed as a marvel of engineering and a symbol of an optimistic age of technological achievement. Science created new wonders in daily life at an astounding rate. The railroad, the steamship, the telegraph and telephone, electricity, and the internal-combustion engine convinced most people that scientific invention was fundamentally helpful to humankind and that continuous progress was inevitable. Workers' awareness of continuing economic inequalities and social injustices was largely overcome by a trust in future improvement and in the efficacy of political action within the system.

Liberalism

While no doubt regretting the sufferings of the poor, an important group of English and continental thinkers called *liberals* believed that these were minor evils compared with the greater good attained by industrialization. Espousing the Enlightenment values of liberty and equality, thinkers such as Adam Smith and David Ricardo argued that there was a kind of law of human nature: if individuals were allowed to follow their own enlightened self-interest, the general good and liberty of all would best be served. The state should interfere as little as possible with the exercise of individual judgment, aside from keeping order and protecting property; the economy as well as other aspects of society should be in the control of private citizens. Wages would always tend to stay at the subsistence level because, when workers rise above this, they have more children who devour the surplus, thus forcing the family income down again. However, in a free society, the liberals argued optimistically, individuals with initiative have the opportunity of leaving this condition and joining the ranks of the successful.

Although thinkers of this stamp violently opposed it, public opinion in the 1830s and 1840s finally forced the English government to pass legislation to remedy the worst abuses. As the Continent came to industrialize, government there, too, stepped in to ameliorate the condition of workers to a degree. Some of the major proponents of this legislation belonged to a new breed of liberals. These thinkers had come to realize that, if liberty and equality were truly the goals of a society, the major threats to those principles did not come so much from the government as from private pressures. A worker's freedom was essentially limited to starving or accepting the conditions offered by an employer. The role of government, as they began to conceive it, was that of a mediator, which through its laws would prevent the oppression of one individual by another. The ideal remained, as earlier, to foster individual freedom, but the experience of the first fifty years of industrialism had shown that, paradoxically, freedom had in certain respects to be restricted by legislation in order to maximize it for everyone. The new liberals also moved gradually to the position that the lower classes must also be given the vote. Political power was not, as for earlier liberals, a privilege achieved by the successful; rather, it was a basic right. Thus, the newer liberalism endeavored to incorporate the workers into the establishment.

From the opening decades of the nineteenth century, however, there were critics of the industrial economy who believed that the major source of its evils came from the fact of private property. As long as the principle of private property was regarded as sacred, no amount of legislation, even by a government in which workers participated, could guarantee a just society. To a varying degree these critics maintained that basic industry and essential services should be taken out of private hands and operated by the community for the common welfare. Some of these thinkers, like Charles Fourier (1772–1837) went further, devising utopian communities where each would do the work for which he or she was best suited and would receive the fruits of the collective labor according to need.

Women's Rights

The Seneca Falls Convention

While Marx was publishing his *Communist Manifesto* in 1848, a group of women met peacefully at Seneca Falls, New York, in an effort to organize the struggle for the rights of women. In the *Manifesto,* Marx had argued that for the bourgeois, women, including the wives of the bourgeois themselves, were merely instruments of production. In England and in the United States, some of the women and men who were active in the antislavery movement began to expand their interests to include issues involving women's rights. The abolitionist William Lloyd Garrison called attention to the injustices perpetrated on slave women, who were often subject to the sexual demands of their masters. The eloquent black woman abolitionist leader Sojourner Truth demonstrated that women could do men's work and more. Yet when the abolitionists Lucretia Mott and Elizabeth Cady Stanton attended the World Anti-Slavery Convention in London in 1840, they found that they were forced to sit in a special screened-off section. This incident was one of the factors that led Mott and Stanton to organize the Seneca Falls women's rights convention.

At the convention, the women drew up a "Declaration of Sentiments," modeled on the Declaration of Independence. Twelve resolutions were passed at the convention, although one of them—the demand for the right to vote—did not pass unanimously. Women did not receive this right until much later, and the passage of other reforms involving woman's independence from her husband in legal matters was equally slow. Still, the battle was joined.

John Stuart Mill (1806–1873)

Perhaps the most eloquent of the early writings arguing for the equality of women and against the injustice of their present status was John Stuart Mill's *The Subjection of Women,* written in 1861. One of the finest, most decent spirits of his age, the author was the son of John Mill, one of the leaders of early liberalism. A disciple of his father in his youth, John Stuart Mill gradually grew disillusioned with a philosophy that, although committed to human freedom and equality, could permit the degradation of the poor and even justify it as part of the law of nature. As a writer and later a member of Parliament, he defended the rights of individuals against the oppression of the majority but at the same time urged the government to interfere when powerful individuals inflicted injury on society as a whole by abusing those same rights. Earlier liberals for him had been too selective in their espousal of the principles of liberty and equality. Conveniently, they had stopped short of ensuring such freedoms when they would interfere with their own prejudices or economic and political interests. This respect for individual personality at all levels made Mill a vigorous opponent of slavery and, in his maturity, a champion of women's rights as well.

The struggle for equal rights for women was to last for many years. In the crucial matter of suffrage, for instance, women were not to have the vote in Canada until 1917, and in the United States and England until 1920 and 1928, respectively; in France they were denied this basic right until after World War II. This chronology follows by fifty to a hundred years the granting of voting rights to all males in the various countries of western Europe and in America. Even after voting rights were won, however, large areas remained in which women experienced discrimination. The women's movement that began around 1970 represents an ongoing determination to eliminate inequalities.

Reading Selections

Friedrich Engels

From *The Condition of the Working Class in England in 1844*

Translation by Florence Kelley Wischnewetzky

Chapter 2

The Great Towns

A Town, such as London, where a man may wander for hours together without reaching the beginning of the end, without meeting the slightest hint which could lead to the inference that there is open country within reach, is a strange thing. This colossal centralisation, this heaping together of two and a half millions of human beings at one point, has multiplied the power of this two and a half millions a hundredfold; has raised London to the commercial capital of the world, created the giant docks and assembled the thousand vessels that continually cover the Thames. I know nothing more imposing than the view which the Thames offers during the ascent from the sea to London Bridge. The masses of buildings, the wharves on both sides, especially from Woolwich upwards, the countless ships along both shores, crowding ever closer and closer together, until, at last, only a narrow passage remains in the middle of the river, a passage through which hundreds of steamers shoot by one another; all this is so vast, so impressive, that a man cannot collect himself, but is lost in the marvel of England's greatness before he sets foot upon English soil.[1]

But the sacrifices which all this has cost become apparent later. After roaming the streets of the capital a day or two, making headway with difficulty through the human turmoil and the endless lines of vehicles, after visiting the slums of the metropolis, one realizes for the first time that these Londoners have been forced to sacrifice the best qualities of their human nature, to bring to pass all the marvels of civilization which crowd their city; that a hundred powers which slumbered within them have remained inactive, have been suppressed in order that a few might be developed more fully and multiply through union with those of others. The very turmoil of the streets has something repulsive, something against which human nature rebels. The hundreds of thousands of all classes and ranks crowding past each other, are they not all human beings with the same qualities and powers, and with the same interest in being happy? And have they not, in the end, to seek happiness in the same way, by the same means? And still they crowd by one another as though they had nothing in common, nothing to do with one another, and their only agreement is the tacit one, that each keep to his own side of the pavement, so as not to delay the opposing streams of the crowd, while it occurs to no man to honour another with so much as a glance. The brutal indifference, the unfeeling isolation of each in his private interest becomes the more repellant and offensive, the more these individuals are crowded together, within a limited space. And, however much one may be aware that this isolation of the individual, this narrow self-seeking is the fundamental principle of our society everywhere, it is nowhere so shamelessly barefaced, so self-conscious as just here in the crowding of the great city. The dissolution of mankind into monads, of which each one has a separate principle, the world of atoms, is here carried out to its utmost extreme. . . .

What is true of London, is true of Manchester, Birmingham, Leeds, is true of all great towns. Everywhere barbarous indifference, hard egotism on one hand, and nameless misery on the other, everywhere social warfare, every man's house in a state of siege, everywhere reciprocal plundering under the protection of the law, and all so shameless, so openly avowed

[1]This applies to the time of sailing vessels. The Thames now is a dreary collection of ugly steamers.—F.E.

that one shrinks before the consequences of our social state as they manifest themselves here undisguised, and can only wonder that the whole crazy fabric still hangs together....

Every great city has one or more slums, where the working-class is crowded together. True, poverty often dwells in hidden alleys close to the palaces of the rich; but, in general, a separate territory has been assigned to it, where, removed from the sight of the happier classes, it may struggle along as it can. These slums are pretty equally arranged in all the great towns of England, the worst houses in the worst quarters of the towns; usually one or two-storied cottages in long rows, perhaps with cellars used as dwellings, almost always irregularly built. These houses of three or four rooms and a kitchen form, throughout England, some parts of London excepted, the general dwellings of the working-class. The streets are generally unpaved, rough, dirty, filled with vegetable and animal refuse, without sewers or gutters, but supplied with foul, stagnant pools instead. Moreover, ventilation is impeded by the bad, confused method of building of the whole quarter, and since many human beings here live crowded into a small space, the atmosphere that prevails in these working-men's quarters may readily be imagined. Further, the streets serve as drying grounds in fine weather; lines are stretched across from house to house, and hung with wet clothing.

Let us investigate some of the slums in their order. London comes first, and in London the famous rookery of St. Giles which is now, at last, about to be penetrated by a couple of broad streets. St. Giles is in the midst of the most populous part of the town, surrounded by broad, splendid avenues in which the gay world of London idles about, in the immediate neighborhood of Oxford Street, Regent Street, of Trafalgar Square and the Strand. It is a disorderly collection of tall, three or four-storied houses, with narrow, crooked, filthy streets, in which there is quite as much life as in the great thoroughfares of the town, except that, here, people of the working-class only are to be seen. A vegetable market is held in the street, baskets with vegetables and fruits, naturally all bad and hardly fit to use, obstruct the sidewalk still further, and from these, as well as from the fish-dealers' stalls, arises a horrible smell. The houses are occupied from cellar to garret, filthy within and without, and their appearance is such that no human being could possibly wish to live in them. But all this is nothing in comparison with the dwellings in the narrow courts and alleys between the streets, entered by covered passages between the houses, in which the filth and tottering ruin surpass all description. Scarcely a whole window-pane can be found, the walls are crumbling, doorposts and window-frames loose and broken, doors of old boards nailed together, or altogether wanting in this thieves' quarter, where no doors are needed, there being nothing to steal. Heaps of garbage and ashes lie in all directions, and the foul liquids emptied before the doors gather in stinking pools. Here live the poorest of the poor, the worst paid workers with thieves and the victims of prostitution indiscriminately huddled together, the majority Irish, or of Irish extraction, and those who have not yet sunk in the whirlpool of moral ruin which surrounds them, sinking daily deeper, losing daily more and more of their power to resist the demoralizing influence of want, filth, and evil surroundings.

Nor is St. Giles the only London slum. In the immense tangle of streets, there are hundreds and thousands of alleys and courts lined with houses too bad for anyone to live in, who can still spend anything whatsoever upon a dwelling fit for human beings. Close to the splendid houses of the rich such a lurking-place of the bitterest poverty may often be found. So, a short time ago, on the occasion of a coroner's inquest, a region close to Portman Square, one of the very respectable squares, was characterised as an abode "of a multitude of Irish demoralised by poverty and filth." So, too, may be found in streets, such as Long Acre and others, which, though not fashionable, are yet "respectable," a great number of cellar dwellings out of which puny children and half-starved, ragged women emerge into the light of day. In the immediate neighbourhood of Drury Lane Theatre, the second in London, are some of the worst streets of the whole metropolis, Charles, King, and Park Streets, in which the houses are inhabited from cellar to garret exclusively by poor families. In the parishes of St. John and St. Margaret there lived in 1840, according to the *Journal of the Statistical Society,* 5,366 working-men's families in 5,294 "dwellings" (if they deserve the name!), men, women, and children thrown together without distinction of age or sex, 26,830 persons all told; and of these families three-fourths possessed but one room. In the aristocratic parish of St. George, Hanover Square, there lived, according to the same authority, 1,465 working-men's families, nearly 6,000 persons, under similar conditions, and here, too, more than two-thirds of the whole number crowded together at the rate of one family in one room. And how the poverty of these unfortunates, among whom even thieves find nothing to steal, is exploited by the property-holding class in lawful ways! The abominable dwellings in Drury Lane, just mentioned, bring in the following rents: two cellar dwellings, 3s.; one room, ground-floor, 4s.; second-storey, 4s. 6d.; third-floor, 4s.; garret-room, 3s. weekly, so that the starving occupants of Charles Street alone, pay the house-owners a yearly tribute of £2,000, and the 5,336 families above mentioned in Westminister, a yearly rent of £40,000. . . .

But in spite of all this, they who have some kind of a shelter are fortunate, fortunate in comparison with the utterly homeless. In London fifty thousand human beings get up every morning, not knowing where they are to lay their heads at night. The luckiest of this multitude, those who succeed in keeping a penny or two until evening, enter a lodging-house, such as abound in every great city, where they find a bed. But what a bed! These houses are filled with beds from cellar to garret, four, five, six beds in a room; as many as can be crowded in. Into every bed four, five, or six human beings are piled, as many as can be packed in, sick and well, young and old, drunk and sober, men and women, just as they come, indiscriminately. Then come strife, blows, wounds, or, if these bed-fellows agree, so much the worse; thefts are arranged and things done which our language, grown more humane than our deeds, refuses to record. And those who cannot pay for such a refuge? They sleep where they find a place in passages, arcades, in corners where the police and the owners leave them undisturbed. A few individuals find their way to the refuges which are managed, here and there, by private charity, others sleep on the benches in the parks close under the windows of Queen Victoria. Let us hear the London *Times:*

> It appears from the report of the proceedings at Marlborough Street Police Court in our columns of yesterday, that there is an average number of 50 human beings of all ages, who huddle together in the parks every night, having no other shelter than what is supplied by the trees and a few hollows of the embankment. Of these, the majority are young girls who have been seduced from the country by the soldiers and turned loose on the world in all the destitution of friendless penury, and all the recklessness of early vice.
>
> This is truly horrible! Poor there must be everywhere. Indigence will find its way and set up its hideous state in the heart of a great and luxurious city. Amid the thousand narrow lanes and by-streets of a populous metropolis there must always, we fear, be much suffering—much that offends the eye—much that lurks unseen.
>
> But that within the precincts of wealth, gaiety, and fashion, nigh the regal grandeur of St. James, close on the palatial splendour of Bayswater, on the confines of the old and new aristocratic quarters, in a district where the cautious refinement of modern design has refrained from creating one single tenement for poverty; which seems, as it were, dedicated to the exclusive enjoyment of wealth, that *there* want, and famine, and disease, and vice should stalk in all their kindred horrors, consuming body by body, soul by soul!
>
> It is indeed a monstrous state of things! Enjoyment the most absolute, that bodily ease, intellectual excitement, or the more innocent pleasures of sense can supply to man's craving, brought in close contact with the most unmitigated misery! Wealth, from its bright saloons, laughing—an insolently heedless laugh—at the unknown wounds of want! Pleasure, cruelly but unconsciously mocking the pain that moans below! All contrary things mocking one another—all contrary, save the vice which tempts and the vice which is tempted!
>
> But let all men remember this—that within the most courtly precincts of the richest city of God's earth, there may be found, night after night, winter after winter, women—young in years—old in sin and suffering—outcasts from society—ROTTING FROM FAMINE, FILTH, AND DISEASE. Let them remember this, and learn not to theorise but to act. God knows, there is much room for action nowadays.[2] . . .

COMMENTS AND QUESTIONS

1. For Engels, the existence of slums and homeless people is a direct result of the unbridled development of industrial capitalism. What arguments can be made for and against this view?
2. What techniques of description does Engels use to elicit the reader's sympathy?
3. To what extent do the conditions that Engels describes exist today?
4. What, for Engels, are the dehumanizing characteristics of the modern city? The theme of the city will become an important one for many nineteenth- and twentieth-century writers. Keep Engels's view in mind as we study literary and artistic representations of the city in succeeding chapters.

[2] *Times,* Oct. 12th, 1843.

Karl Marx and Friedrich Engels

From *The Communist Manifesto*

Translation by Samuel Moore

Introduction

A spectre is haunting Europe—the spectre of Communism. All the powers of old Europe have entered into a holy alliance to exorcise this spectre: Pope and Czar, Metternich and Guizot, French Radicals and German political police.

Where is the party in opposition that has not been decried as communistic by its opponents in power? Where is the opposition that has not hurled back the branding reproach of Communism, against the more advanced opposition parties as well as against its reactionary adversaries?

Two things result from this fact:

1. Communism is already acknowledged by all European powers to be itself a power.

2. It is high time that Communists should openly, in the face of the whole world, publish their views, their aims, their tendencies, and meet this nursery tale of the spectre of Communism with a manifesto of the party itself.

To this end, Communists of various nationalities have assembled in London, and sketched the following manifesto, to be published in the English, French, German, Italian, Flemish and Danish languages.

Chapter I

Bourgeois and Proletarians

The history of all hitherto existing society is the history of class struggles.

Freeman and slave, patrician and plebeian, lord and serf, guild-master and journeyman, in a word, oppressor and oppressed, stood in constant opposition to one another, carried on an uninterrupted, now hidden, now open fight, a fight that each time ended, either in a revolutionary reconstitution of society at large, or in the common ruin of the contending classes.

In the earlier epochs of history, we find almost everywhere a complicated arrangement of society into various orders, a manifold gradation of social rank. In ancient Rome we have patricians, knights, plebeians, slaves; in the Middle Ages, feudal lords, vassals, guild-masters, journeymen, apprentices, serfs; in almost all of these classes, again, subordinate gradations.

The modern bourgeois society that has sprouted from the ruins of feudal society has not done away with class antagonisms. It has but established new classes, new conditions of oppression, new forms of struggle in place of the old ones.

Our epoch, the epoch of the bourgeoisie, possesses, however, this distinctive feature: it has simplified the class antagonisms. Society as a whole is more and more splitting up into two great hostile camps, into two great classes directly facing each other—bourgeoisie and proletariat.

From the serfs of the Middle Ages sprang the chartered Burghers of the earliest towns. From these burgesses the first elements of the bourgeoisie were developed.

The discovery of America, the rounding of the Cape, opened up fresh ground for the rising bourgeoisie. The East-Indian and Chinese markets, the colonization of America, trade with the colonies, the increase in the means of exchange and in commodities generally, gave to commerce, to navigation, to industry, an impulse never before known, and thereby, to the revolutionary element in the tottering feudal society, a rapid development.

The feudal system of industry, in which industrial production was monopolized by closed guilds, now no longer sufficed for the growing wants of the new markets. The manufacturing system took its place. The guild-masters were pushed aside by the manufacturing middle class; division of labour between the different corporate guilds vanished in the face of division of labour in each single workshop.

Meantime the markets kept ever growing, the demand ever rising. Even manufacture no longer sufficed. Thereupon, steam and machinery revolutionized industrial production. The place of manufacture was taken by the giant, modern industry, the place of the industrial middle class by industrial millionaires, the leaders of whole industrial armies, the modern bourgeois.

Modern industry has established the world market, for which the discovery of America paved the way. This market has given an immense development to commerce, to navigation, to communication by land. This development has, in its turn, reacted on the extension of industry; and in proportion as industry, commerce, navigation, railways extended, in the same proportion the bourgeoisie developed, increased its capital, and pushed into the background every class handed down from the Middle Ages.

We see, therefore, how the modern bourgeoisie is itself the product of a long course of development, of a series of revolutions in the modes of production and of exchange.

Each step in the development of the bourgeoisie was accompanied by a corresponding political advance of that class. An oppressed class under the sway of the feudal nobility, it became an armed and self-governing association in the medieval commune; here independent urban republic (as in Italy and Germany), there taxable "third estate" of the monarchy (as in France); afterwards, in the period of manufacture proper, serving either the semi-feudal or the absolute monarchy as a counterpoise against the nobility, and, in fact, cornerstone of the great monarchies in general, the bourgeoisie has at last, since the establishment of modern industry and of the world market, conquered for itself, in the modern parliamentary State, exclusive political sway. The executive of the modern State is but a committee for managing the common affairs of the whole bourgeoisie.

The bourgeoisie, historically, has played a most revolutionary part.

The bourgeoisie, wherever it has got the upper hand, has put an end to all feudal, patriarchal, idyllic relations. It has pitilessly torn asunder the motley feudal ties that bound man to his "natural superiors," and has left no other nexus between man and man than naked self-interest, than callous "cash payment." It has drowned the most heavenly ecstasies of religious fervour, of chivalrous enthusiasm, of Philistine sentimentalism, in the icy water of egotistic calculation. It has resolved personal worth in exchange value and in place of the numberless indefeasible chartered freedoms has set up that single, unconscionable freedom—Free Trade. In one word, for exploitation veiled by religious and political illusions it has substituted naked, shameless, direct, brutal exploitation. . . .

The need of a constantly-expanding market for its products chases the bourgeoisie over the whole surface of the globe. It must get a footing everywhere, settle everywhere, establish connections everywhere.

The bourgeoisie has through its exploitation of the world market given a cosmopolitan character to production and consumption in every country. To the great chagrin of reactionaries, it has drawn from under the feet of industry the national ground on which it stood. Old established national industries have been destroyed and are still being destroyed every day. They are dislodged by new industries, whose introduction becomes a life and death question for all civilized nations, by industries that no longer work up indigenous raw material, but raw material drawn from the remotest zones; industries whose products are consumed, not only at home, but in every quarter of the globe. In place of the old wants, satisfied by the production of the country, we find new wants, requiring for their satisfaction the products of distant lands and climes. In place of the old local and national seclusion and self-sufficiency, we have exchange in every direction, universal interdependence of nations. And as in material, so also in intellectual production. The intellectual creations of individual nations become common property. National onesidedness and narrowmindedness become more and more impossible, and from the numerous national and local literatures there arises a world literature.

The bourgeoisie, by the rapid improvement of all instruments of production, by the immensely facilitated means of communication, draws all, even the most barbarian, nations into civilization. The cheap prices of its commodities are the heavy artillery with which it batters down all Chinese walls, with which it forces the barbarians' intensely obstinate hatred of foreigners to capitulate. It compels all nations, on pain of extinction, to adopt the bourgeois mode of production; it compels them to introduce what it calls civilization into their midst, i.e., to become bourgeois themselves. In one word, it creates a world after its own image. . . .

We see then: the means of production and of exchange, on whose foundation the bourgeoisie built itself up, were generated in feudal society. At a certain stage in the development of these means of production and of exchange, the conditions under which feudal society produced and exchanged, the feudal organization of agriculture and manufacturing industry, in one word, the feudal relations of property, became no longer compatible with the already developed productive forces; they hindered production instead of promoting it; they became so many fetters. They had to be burst asunder; they were burst asunder.

Into their place stepped free competition, accompanied by a social and political constitution adapted to it, and by the economical and political sway of the bourgeois class.

A similar movement is going on before our own eyes. Modern bourgeois society with its relations of production, of exchange and of property, a society that has conjured up such gigantic means of production and of exchange, is like the sorcerer who is no longer able to control the powers of the nether world whom he has called up by his spells. For many a decade past the history of industry and commerce is but the history of the revolt of modern productive forces against modern conditions of production, against the property relations that are the conditions for the existence of the bourgeoisie and of its rule. It is enough to mention the commercial crises that by their periodical return put the existence of the entire bourgeois society on its trial, each time more threateningly. In these crises a great part, not only of the existing products, but also

Plate XXI
Jean Antoine Watteau, *Pilgrimage to Cythera,* 1717. Staatliche Schlosser und Garten, Berlin.
(Bildarchiv Preuss-ischer Kulturbesitz, Berlin)

Plate XXII
Jean-Baptiste-Siméon Chardin,*Morgontoiletten (Morning Toilet).*
(Nationalmuseum, Stockholm)

above, **Plate XXIII**
Attributed to John Constable, *Dedham Vale with the House called "Dedham Valley."* (The Tate Gallery, London)

below, **Plate XXIV**
Joseph Mallord William Turner, *Rain, Steam and Speed—The Great Western Railway,* 1844. Oil on canvas, 35¾" x 48". (Reproduced by courtesy of the Trustees, The National Gallery, London)

left, **Plate XXV**
Claude Monet,
The Bridge at Argenteuil, 1874.
60 x 81.3 cm. Bayer. Staatsgemaldesammlungen-Neue Pinakothek, München.
(Joachim Blauel/Artothek)

below, **Plate XXVI**
Claude Monet,
Impression, Sunrise,
1872. Musée Marmottan, Paris.
(Giraudon/Art Resource, NY)

Plate XXVII
Paul Cézanne,
Mont Sainte-Victoire,
1886–87.
(The Phillips Collection,
Washington, D.C.)

of the previously-created productive forces, are periodically destroyed. In these crises there breaks out an epidemic that, in all earlier epochs, would have seemed an absurdity—the epidemic of over-production. Society suddenly finds itself put back into a state of momentary barbarism; it appears as if a famine, a universal war of devastation, had cut off the supply of every means of subsistence; industry and commerce seem to be destroyed. And why? Because there is too much civilization, too much means of subsistence, too much industry, too much commerce. The productive forces at the disposal of society no longer tend to promote bourgeois civilization and bourgeois property; on the contrary, they have become too powerful for these relations, by which they are fettered, and so soon as they overcome these fetters, they bring disorder into the whole of bourgeois society, endanger the existence of bourgeois property. The conditions of bourgeois society are too narrow to contain the wealth created by them. And how does the bourgeoisie get over these crises? On the one hand by enforced destruction of a mass of productive forces; on the other, by the conquest of new markets, and by the more thorough exploitation of the old ones. That is to say, by paving the way for more extensive and more destructive crises, and by diminishing the means whereby crises are prevented.

The weapons with which the bourgeoisie felled feudalism to the ground are now turned against the bourgeoisie itself.

But not only has the bourgeoisie forged the weapons that bring death to itself; it has also called into existence the men who are to wield those weapons—the modern working class—the proletarians.

In proportion as the bourgeoisie, i.e., capital, is developed, in the same proportion is the proletariat developed—the modern class of workers, who live only so long as they find work, and who find work only so long as their labour increases capital. These workmen, who must sell themselves piecemeal, are a commodity, like every other article of commerce, and are consequently exposed to all the vicissitudes of competition, to all the fluctuations of the market.

Owing to the extensive use of machinery and to division of labour, the work of the proletarians has lost all independent character, and, consequently, all charm for the workman. He becomes a mere appendage of the machine, and it is only the most simple, most monotonous, and most easily acquired knack, that is required of him. Hence, the cost of production of a workman is restricted, almost entirely, to the means of subsistence that he requires for his maintenance, and for the propagation of his race. But the price of a commodity, and therefore also of labour, is equal to its cost of production. In proportion, therefore, as the repulsiveness of the work increases, the wage decreases. Nay, more, in proportion as the use of machinery and division of labour increases, in the same proportion the burden of toil also increases, whether by prolongation of the working hours, by increase of the work exacted in a given time, or by increased speed of the machinery, etc.

Modern industry has converted the little workshop of the patriarchal master into the great factory of the industrial capitalist. Masses of labourers, crowded into the factory, are organized like soldiers. As privates of the industrial army they are placed under the command of a perfect hierarchy of officers and sergeants. Not only are they slaves of the bourgeois class, and of the bourgeois State; they are daily and hourly enslaved by the machine, by the overlooker, and, above all, by the individual bourgeois manufacturer himself. The more openly this despotism proclaims gain to be its end and aim, the more petty, the more hateful and the more embittering it is.

The less the skill and exertion of strength implied in manual labour, in other words, the more modern industry becomes developed, the more is the labour of men superseded by that of women. Differences of age and sex have no longer any distinctive social validity for the working class. All are instruments of labour, more or less expensive to use, according to their age and sex.

No sooner is the exploitation of the labourer by the manufacturer so far at an end that he receives his wages in cash, than he is set upon by the other portions of the bourgeoisie, the landlord, the shopkeeper, the pawnbroker, etc.

The former lower strata of the middle class—the small manufacturers, traders and persons living on small incomes, the handicraftsmen and peasants—all these sink gradually into the proletariat, partly because their diminutive capital does not suffice for the scale on which modern industry is carried on and is swamped in the competition with the large capitalists, partly because their specialized skill is rendered worthless by new methods of production. Thus the proletariat is recruited from all classes of the population.

But with the development of industry the proletariat not only increases in number; it becomes concentrated in greater masses, its strength grows, and it feels that strength more. The various interests and conditions of life within the ranks of the proletariat are more and more equalized, in proportion as machinery obliterates all distinctions of labour, and nearly everywhere reduces wages to the same low level. The growing competition among the bourgeois, and the resulting commercial crises, make the wages of the workers ever more fluctuating. The unceasing improvement of machinery, ever more rapidly developing, makes their livelihood more and more precarious; the collisions between individual workmen and individual bourgeois take more and more the character of collisions between two classes. Thereupon the workers begin to form combinations against the bourgeois; they club together in order to keep up the rate of wages; they themselves found permanent associations in order to make provision beforehand for these occasional revolts. Here and there the contest breaks out into riots. Now and then the workers are victorious, but only for a time. The real fruit of their battles lies, not in the immediate result, but in the ever-expanding union of the workers. This union is helped on by the improved means of communication that are created by modern industry and that place the workers of different localities in contact with one another. It was just this contact that was needed to centralize the numerous local struggles, all of the same character, into one national struggle between classes. But every class struggle is a political struggle. And that union, to attain which the Burghers of the Middle Ages, with their miserable highways, required centuries, the modern proletarians, thanks to railways, achieve in a few years.

This organization of the proletarians into a class, and consequently into a political party, is continually being upset again by the competition between the workers themselves. But it ever rises up again, stronger, firmer, mightier. It compels legislative recognition of particular interests of the workers, by taking advantage of the divisions among the bourgeoisie itself. Thus the ten-hours' bill in England was carried.

Altogether, collisions between the classes of the old society further in many ways the course of development of the proletariat. The bourgeoisie finds itself involved in a constant battle. At first with the aristocracy; later on, with those portions of the bourgeoisie itself, whose interests have become antagonistic to the progress of industry; at all times with the bourgeoisie of foreign countries. In all these battles it sees itself compelled to appeal to the proletariat, to ask for its help, and thus, to drag it into the political arena. The bourgeoisie itself, therefore, supplies the proletariat with its own elements of political and general education, in other words, it furnishes the proletariat with weapons for fighting the bourgeoisie.

Further, as we have already seen, entire sections of the ruling classes are, by the advance of industry, precipitated into the proletariat, or are at least threatened in their conditions of existence. These also supply the proletariat with fresh elements of enlightenment and progress.

Finally, in times when the class struggle nears the decisive hour, the process of dissolution going on within the ruling class, in fact within the whole range of old society, assumes such a violent, glaring character, that a small section of the ruling class cuts itself adrift, and joins the revolutionary class, the class that holds the future in its hands. Just as, therefore, at an earlier period, a section of the nobility went over to the bourgeoisie, so now a portion of the bourgeoisie goes over to the prolatariat, and in particular, a portion of the bourgeois ideologists who have raised themselves to the level of comprehending theoretically the historical movement as a whole.

Of all the classes that stand face to face with the bourgeoisie today, the proletariat alone is a really revolutionary class. The other classes decay and finally disappear in the face of modern industry; the proletariat is its special and essential product.

The lower middle class, the small manufacturer, the shopkeeper, the artisan, the peasant, all these fight against the bourgeoisie, to save from extinction their existence as fractions of the middle class. They are therefore not revolutionary, but conservative. Nay, more, they are reactionary, for they try to roll back the wheel of history. If by chance they are revolutionary, they are so only in view of their impending transfer into the proletariat; they thus defend not their present, but their future interests; they desert their own standpoint to place themselves at that of the proletariat.

The "dangerous class," the social scum, that passively rotting mass thrown off by the lowest layers of old society, may, here and there, be swept into the movement by a proletarian revolution; its conditions of life, however, prepare it far more for the part of a bribed tool of reactionary intrigue.

In the conditions of the proletariat, those of old society at large are already virtually swamped. The proletarian is without property; his relation to his wife and children has no longer anything in common with the bourgeois family relations; modern industrial labour, modern subjection to capital, the same in England as in France, in America as in Germany, has stripped him of every trace of national character. Law, morality, religion, are to him so many bourgeois prejudices, behind which lurk in ambush just as many bourgeois interests.

All the preceding classes that got the upper hand sought to fortify their already-acquired status by subjecting society at large to their conditions of appropriation. The proletarians cannot become masters of the productive forces of society except by abolishing their own previous mode of appropriation, and thereby also every other previous mode of appropriation. They have nothing of their own to secure and to fortify; their mission is to destroy all previous securities for, and insurances of, individual property.

All previous historical movements were movements of minorities, or in the interest of minorities. The proletarian movement is the self-conscious, independent movement of the immense majority, in the interest of the immense majority. The proletariat, the lowest stratum of our present society, cannot stir, cannot raise itself up, without the whole superincumbent strata of official society being sprung into the air.

Though not in substance, yet in form, the struggle of the proletariat with the bourgeoisie is at first a national struggle. The proletariat of each country must, of course, first of all settle matters with its own bourgeoisie.

In depicting the most general phases that make up the development of the proletariat, we traced the more or less veiled civil war, raging within existing society, up to the point where that war breaks out into open revolution, and where the violent overthrow of the bourgeoisie lays the foundation for the sway of the proletariat.

Hitherto, every form of society has been based, as we have already seen, on the antagonism of oppressing and oppressed classes. But in order to oppress a class, certain conditions must be assured to it under which it can, at least, continue its slavish existence. The serf, in the period of serfdom, raised himself to membership in the commune, just as the petty bourgeois, under the yoke of feudal absolutism, managed to develop into a bourgeois. The modern labourer, on the contrary, instead of rising with the progress of industry, sinks deeper and deeper below the conditions of existence of his own class. He becomes a pauper, and pauperism develops more rapidly than population and wealth. And here it becomes evident that the bourgeoisie is unfit to rule because it is incompetent to assure an existence to its slave within his slavery, because it cannot help letting him sink into such a state that it has to feed him, instead of being fed by him. Society can no longer live under this bourgeoisie; in other words, its existence is no longer compatible with society.

The essential condition for the existence and for the sway of the bourgeois class is the accumulation of wealth in the hands of private individuals, the formation and augmentation of capital; the condition for capital is wage-labour. Wage-labour rests exclusively on competition between the labourers. The advance of industry, whose involuntary promoter is the bourgeoisie, replaces the isolation of the labourers, due to competition, by their revolutionary combination, due to association. The development of modern industry, therefore, cuts from under the feet of the bourgeoisie the very foundation on which it produces and appropriates products. What the bourgeoisie therefore produces, above all, are its own grave-diggers. Its fall and the victory of the proletariat are equally inevitable.

QUESTIONS

1. How does Marx explain the triumph of the bourgeois over the feudal aristocracy?
2. What is the function of the state under bourgeois rule?
3. Why is bourgeois supremacy antinationalistic?
4. What does Marx mean when he writes that the productive forces of society have become too powerful for the conditions of bourgeois property?
5. Why is the wage of a worker roughly equal to his or her level of subsistence?
6. In what way does the bourgeoisie produce "its own grave-diggers"?
7. In what sense are all the enemies of the bourgeoisie save the proletariat reactionary?
8. What did Marx foresee and what did he not foresee?

The "Declaration of Sentiments" of the Seneca Falls Convention

When, in the course of human events, it becomes necessary for one portion of the family of man to assume among the people of the earth a position different from that which they have hitherto occupied, but one to which the laws of nature and of nature's God entitle them, a decent respect to the opinions of mankind requires that they should declare the causes that impel them to such a course.

We hold these truths to be self-evident: that all men and women are created equal; that they are endowed by their Creator with certain inalienable rights; that among these are life, liberty, and the pursuit of happiness; that to secure these rights governments are instituted, deriving their just powers from the consent of the governed. Whenever any form of government becomes destructive of these ends, it is the right of those who suffer from it to refuse allegiance to it, and to insist upon the institution of a new government, laying its foundation on such principles, and organizing its powers in such form, as to them shall seem most likely to effect their safety and happiness. Prudence, indeed, will dictate that governments long established should not be changed for light and transient causes; and accordingly all experience hath shown that mankind are more disposed to suffer, while evils are sufferable, than to right themselves by abolishing the forms to which they were accustomed. But when a long train of abuses and usurpations, pursuing invariably the same object, evinces a design to reduce them under absolute despotism, it is their duty to throw off such government, and to provide new guards for their future security. Such has been the patient sufferance of the women under this government, and such is now the necessity which constrains them to demand the equal situation to which they are entitled.

The history of mankind is a history of repeated injuries and usurpations on the part of man toward woman, having in direct object the establishment of an absolute tyranny over her. To prove this, let facts be submitted to a candid world.

He has never permitted her to exercise her inalienable right to the elective franchise.

He has compelled her to submit to laws, in the formation of which she had no voice.

He has withheld from her rights which are given to the most ignorant and degraded men—both natives and foreigners.

Having deprived her of this first right of a citizen, the elective franchise, thereby leaving her without representation in the halls of legislation, he has oppressed her on all sides.

He has made her, if married, in the eye of the law, civilly dead.

He has taken from her all right in property, even to the wages she earns.

He has made her, morally, an irresponsible being, as she can commit many crimes with immunity, provided they be done in the presence of her husband. In the covenant of marriage, she is compelled to promise obedience to her husband, he becoming, to all intents and purposes, her master—the law giving him power to deprive her of her liberty, and to administer chastisement.

He has so framed the laws of divorce, as to what shall be the proper causes, and in case of separation, to whom the guardianship of the children shall be given, as to be wholly regardless of the happiness of women—the law, in all cases, going upon a false supposition of the supremacy of man, and giving all power into his hands.

After depriving her of all rights as a married woman, if single, and the owner of property, he has taxed her to support a government which recognizes her only when her property can be made profitable to it.

He has monopolized nearly all the profitable employments, and from those she is permitted to follow, she receives but a scanty remuneration. He closes against her all the avenues to wealth and distinction which he considers most honorable to himself. As a teacher of theology, medicine, or law, she is not known.

He has denied her the facilities for obtaining a thorough education, all colleges being closed against her.

He allows her in Church, as well as State, but a subordinate position, claiming Apostolic authority for her exclusion from the ministry, and, with some exceptions, from any public participation in the affairs of the Church.

He has created a false public sentiment by giving to the world a different code of morals for men and women, by which moral delinquencies which exclude women from society, are not only tolerated, but deemed of little account in man.

He has usurped the prerogative of Jehovah himself, claiming it as his right to assign for her a sphere of action, when that belongs to her conscience and to her God.

He has endeavored, in every way that he could, to destroy her confidence in her own powers, to lessen her self-respect, and to make her willing to lead a dependent and abject life.

Now, in view of this entire disfranchisement of one-half the people of this country, their social and religious degradation—in view of the unjust laws above mentioned, and because women do feel themselves aggrieved, oppressed, and fraudulently deprived of their most sacred rights, we insist that they have immediate admission to all the rights and privileges which belong to them as citizens of the United States.

In entering upon the great work before us, we anticipate no small amount of misconception, misrepresentation, and ridicule; but we shall use every instrumentality within our power to effect our object. We shall employ agents, circulate tracts, petition the State and National legislatures, and endeavor to enlist the pulpit and the press in our behalf. We hope this Convention will be followed by a series of Conventions embracing every part of the country.

QUESTIONS

1. What is the purpose of modeling this declaration on the Declaration of Independence?
2. Compare the views of women's oppressions

expressed here with those of Mary Wollstonecraft (Chapter 24).

3. Which of the injustices toward women listed in the declaration have been rectified today? Are there any that still prevail?

John Stuart Mill

From *The Subjection of Women*

The object of this Essay is to explain as clearly as I am able, the grounds of an opinion which I have held from the very earliest period when I had formed any opinions at all on social or political matters, and which, instead of being weakened or modified, has been constantly growing stronger by the progress of reflection and the experience of life. That the principle which regulates the existing social relations between the two sexes—the legal subordination of one sex to the other—is wrong in itself, and now one of the chief hindrances to human improvement; and that it ought to be replaced by a principle of perfect equality, admitting no power or privilege on the one side, nor disability on the other....

...It is one of the characteristic prejudices of the reaction of the nineteenth century against the eighteenth, to accord to the unreasoning elements in human nature the infallibility which the eighteenth century is supposed to have ascribed to the reasoning elements. For the apotheosis of Reason we have substituted that of Instinct; and we call everything instinct which we find in ourselves and for which we cannot trace any rational foundation. This idolatry, infinitely more degrading than the other, and the most pernicious of the false worships of the present day, of all of which it is now the main support, will probably hold its ground until it gives way before a sound psychology laying bare the real root of much that is bowed down to as the intention of Nature and the ordinance of God....

The generality of a practice is in some cases a strong presumption that it is, or at all events once was, conducive to laudable ends. This is the case, when the practice was first adopted, or afterwards kept up, as a means to such ends, and was grounded on experience of the mode in which they could be most effectually attained. If the authority of men over women, when first established, had been the result of a conscientious comparison between different modes of constituting the government of society; if, after trying various other modes of social organisation—the government of women over men, equality between the two, and such mixed and divided modes of government as might be invented—it had been decided, on the testimony of experience, that the mode in which women are wholly under the rule of men, having no share at all in public concerns, and each in private being under the legal obligation of obedience to the man with whom she has associated her destiny, was the arrangement most conducive to the happiness and well-being of both; its general adoption might then be fairly thought to be some evidence that, at the time when it was adopted, it was the best: though even then the considerations which recommended it may, like so many other primeval social facts of the greatest importance, have subsequently, in the course of ages, ceased to exist. But the state of the case is in every respect the reverse of this. In the first place, the opinion in favour of the present system, which entirely subordinates the weaker sex to the stronger, rests upon theory only; for there never has been trial made of any other: so that experience, in the sense in which it is vulgarly opposed to theory, cannot be pretended to have pronounced any verdict. And in the second place, the adoption of this system of inequality never was the result of deliberation, or forethought, or any social ideas, or any notion whatever of what conduced to the benefit of humanity or the good order of society. It arose simply from the fact that from the very earliest twilight of human society, every woman (owing to the value attached to her by men, combined with her inferiority in muscular strength) was found in a state of bondage to some man. Laws and systems of polity always begin by recognising the relations they find already existing between individuals. They convert what was a mere physical fact into a legal right, give it the sanction of society, and principally aim at the substitution of public and organised means of asserting and protecting these rights, instead of the irregular and lawless conflict of physical strength. Those who had already been compelled to obedience became in this manner legally bound to it. Slavery, from being a mere affair of force between the master and the slave, became regularised and a matter of compact among the masters, who, binding themselves to one another for common protection, guaranteed by their collective strength the private possessions of each, including his slaves. In early times, the great majority of the male sex were slaves, as well as the whole of the female. And many ages elapsed, some of them ages of high cultivation, before any thinker was bold enough to question the rightfulness, and the absolute social necessity, either of the one slavery or of the other. By degrees such thinkers did arise; and (the general progress of society assisting) the slavery of the male sex has, in all the countries of Christian Europe at least (though, in one of them, only within the last few years) been at length abolished, and that of the female sex has been gradually changed into a milder form of dependence. But this dependence, as it exists at present, is not an original institution, taking a fresh start from considerations of justice and social expediency—it is the primitive state of slavery lasting on, through successive mitigations and modifications occasioned by the same causes which have softened the general manners, and brought all human relations more under the control of justice and the influence of humanity. It has not lost the taint of its brutal origin. No presumption in its favour, therefore, can be drawn from the fact of its existence....

Some will object, that a comparison cannot fairly be made between the government of the male sex and the forms of unjust power which I have adduced in illustration of it, since these are arbitrary, and the effect of mere usurpation, while it on the contrary is natural. But was there ever any domination which did not appear natural to those who possessed it? There was a time when the division of mankind into two classes, a small one of masters and a numerous one of slaves, appeared, even to the most cultivated minds, to be natural, and the only natural, condition of the human race. No less an intellect, and one which contributed no less to the progress of human thought, than Aristotle, held this opinion without doubt or misgiving; and rested it on the same premises on which the same assertion in regard to the dominion of men over women is usually based, namely that there are different natures among mankind, free natures, and slave natures; that the Greeks were of a free nature, the barbarian races of Thracians and Asiatics of a slave nature. But why need I go back to Aristotle? Did not the slave-owners of the Southern United States maintain the same doctrine, with all the fanaticism with which men cling to the theories that justify their passions and legitimate their personal interests? Did they not call heaven and earth to witness that the dominion of the white man over the black is natural, that the black race is by nature incapable of freedom, and marked out for slavery? some even going so far as to say that the freedom of manual labourers is an unnatural order of things anywhere. Again, the theorists of absolute monarchy have always affirmed it to be the only natural form of government; issuing from the patriarchal, which was the primitive and spontaneous form of society, framed on the model of the paternal, which is anterior to society itself, and, as they contend, the most natural authority of all....

But, it will be said, the rule of men over women differs from all these others in not being a rule of force: it is accepted voluntarily; women make no complaint, and are consenting parties to it. In the first place, a great number of women do not accept it. Ever since there have been women able to make their sentiments known by their writings (the only mode of publicity which society permits to them), an increasing number of them have recorded protests against their present social condition: and recently many thousands of them, headed by the most eminent women known to the public, have petitioned Parliament for their admission to the Parliamentary Suffrage. The claim of women to be educated as solidly, and in the same branches of knowledge, as men, is urged with growing intensity, and with a great prospect of success; while the demand for their admission into professions and occupations hitherto closed against them, becomes every year more urgent. Though there are not in this country, as there are in the United States, periodical conventions and an organised party to agitate for the Rights of Women, there is a numerous and active society organised and managed by women, for the more limited object of obtaining the political franchise. Nor is it only in our own country and in America that women are beginning to protest, more or less collectively, against the disabilities under which they labour. France, and Italy, and Switzerland, and Russia now afford examples of the same thing. How many more women there are who silently cherish similar aspirations, no one can possibly know; but there are abundant tokens how many *would* cherish them, were they not so strenuously taught to repress them as contrary to the proprieties of their sex. It must be remembered, also, that no enslaved class ever asked for complete liberty at once....

All causes, social and natural, combine to make it unlikely that women should be collectively rebellious to the power of men. They are so far in a position different from all other subject classes, that their masters require something more from them than actual service. Men do not want solely the obedience of women, they want their sentiments. All men, except the most brutish, desire to have, in the woman most nearly connected with them, not a forced slave but a willing one, not a slave merely, but a favourite. They have therefore put everything in practice to enslave their minds. The masters of all other slaves rely, for maintaining obedience, on fear; either fear of themselves, or religious fears. The masters of women wanted more than simple obedience, and they turned the whole force of education to effect their purpose. All women are brought up from the very earliest years in the belief that their ideal of character is the very opposite to that of men; not self-will, and government by self-control, but submission, and yielding to the control of others. All the moralities tell them that it is the duty of women, and all the current sentimentalities that it is their nature, to live for others; to make complete abnegation of themselves, and to have no life but in their affections. And by their affections are meant the only ones they are allowed to have—those to the men with whom they are connected, or to the children who constitute an additional and indefeasible tie between them and a man. When we put together three things—first, the natural attraction between opposite sexes; secondly, the wife's entire dependence on the husband, every privilege or pleasure she has being either his gift, or depending entirely on his will; and lastly, that the principal object of human pursuit, consideration, and all objects of social ambition, can in general be sought or obtained by her only through him, it would be a miracle if the object of being attractive to men had not become the polar star of feminine education and formation of character. And, this great means of influence over the minds of women having been acquired, an instinct of selfishness made men avail themselves of it to the utmost as a means of holding women in subjection, by representing to them meekness, submissiveness, and resignation of all individual will into the hands of a man, as an essential part of sexual attractiveness. Can it be doubted that any of the other yokes which mankind have succeeded in breaking, would have subsisted till now if the same means had existed, and had been so sedulously used, to bow down their minds to it? . . .

. . . What is the peculiar character of the modern world—the difference which chiefly distinguishes modern institutions, modern social ideas, modern life itself, from those of times long past? It is, that human beings are no longer born to their place in life, and chained down by an inexorable bond to the place they are born to, but are free to employ their faculties, and such favourable chances as offer, to achieve the lot which may appear to them most desirable. Human society of old was constituted on a very different principle. All were born to a fixed social position, and were mostly kept in it by law, or interdicted from any means by which they could emerge from it. As some men are born white and others black, so some were born slaves and others freemen and citizens; some were born patricians, others plebeians; some were born feudal nobles, others commoners and *roturiers.* A slave or serf could never make himself free, nor, except by the will of his master, become so. . . .

In modern Europe, and most in those parts of it which have participated most largely in all other modern improvements, diametrically opposite doctrines now prevail. Law and government do not undertake to prescribe by whom any social or industrial operation shall or shall not be conducted, or what modes of conducting them shall be lawful. These things are left to the unfettered choice of individuals. Even the laws which required that workmen should serve an apprenticeship, have in this country been repealed: there being ample assurance that in all cases in which an apprenticeship is necessary, its necessity will suffice to enforce it. The old theory was, that the least possible should be left to the choice of the individual agent; that all he had to do should, as far as practicable, be laid down for him by superior wisdom. Left to himself he was sure to go wrong. The modern conviction, the fruit of a thousand years of experience, is, that things in which the individual is the person directly interested, never go right but as they are left to his own discretion; and that any regulation of them by authority, except to protect the rights of others, is sure to be mischievous. . . .

If this general principle of social and economical science is not true; if individuals, with such help as they can derive from the opinion of those who know them, are not better judges than the law and the government, of their own capacities and vocation; the world cannot too soon abandon this principle, and return to the old system of regulations and disabilities. But if the principle is true, we ought to act as if we believed it, and not to ordain that to be born a girl instead of a boy, any more than to be born black instead of white, or a commoner instead of a nobleman, shall decide the person's position through all life—shall interdict people from all the more elevated social positions, and from all, except a few, respectable occupations. . . .

At present, in the more improved countries, the disabilities of women are the only case, save one, in which laws and institutions take persons at their birth, and ordain that they shall never in all their lives be allowed to compete for certain things. The one exception is that of royalty. Persons still are born to the throne; no one, not of the reigning family, can ever occupy it, and no one even of that family can, by any means but the course of hereditary succession, attain it. All other dignities and social advantages are open to the whole male sex: many indeed are only attainable by wealth, but wealth may be striven for by anyone, and is actually obtained by many men of the very humblest origin. The difficulties, to the majority, are indeed insuperable without the aid of fortunate accidents; but no male human being is under any legal ban: neither law nor opinion superadd artificial obstacles to the natural ones. . . .

Neither does it avail anything to say that the *nature* of the two sexes adapts them to their present functions and position, and renders these appropriate to them. Standing on the ground of common sense and the constitution of the human mind, I deny that anyone knows, or can know, the nature of the two sexes, as long as they have only been seen in their present relation to one another. If men had ever been found in society without women, or women without men, or if there had been a society of men and women in which the women were not under the control of the men, something might have been positively known about the mental and moral differences which may be inherent in the nature of each. What is now called the nature of women is an eminently artificial thing—the result of forced repression in some directions, unnatural stimulation in others. It may be asserted without scruple, that no other class of dependents have had their character so entirely distorted from its natural proportions by their relation with their masters; for, if conquered and slave races have been, in some respects, more forcibly repressed, whatever in them has not been crushed down by an iron heel has generally been let alone, and if left with any liberty of development, it has developed itself according to its own laws; but in the case of women, a hot-house and stove cultivation has always been carried on of some of the capabilities of their nature, for the benefit and pleasure of their masters. Then, because certain products of the general vital force sprout luxuriantly and reach a great development in this heated atmosphere and under this active nurture and watering, while other shoots from the same root, which are left outside in the wintry air, with ice purposely heaped all round them, have a stunted growth, and some are burnt off with fire and disappear; men, with that inability to recognise their own work which distinguishes the unanalytic mind, indolently believe that the tree grows of itself in the way they have made it grow, and that it would die if one half of it were not kept in a vapour bath and the other half in the snow. . . .

We may safely assert that the knowledge which men can acquire of women, even as they have been and are, without reference to what they might be, is wretchedly imperfect and superficial, and always will be so, until women themselves have told all that they have to tell.

And this time has not come; nor will it come otherwise than gradually. It is but of yesterday that women have either been qualified by literary accomplishments, or permitted by society, to tell anything to the general public. As yet very few of them dare tell anything, which men, on whom their literary success depends, are unwilling to hear. Let us remember in what manner, up to a very recent time, the expression, even by a male author, of uncustomary opinions, or what are deemed eccentric feelings, usually was, and in some degree still is, received; and we may form some faint conception under what impediments a woman, who is brought up to think custom and opinion her sovereign rule, attempts to express in books anything drawn from the depths of her own nature. The greatest woman who has left writings behind her sufficient to give her an eminent rank in the literature of her country, thought it necessary to prefix as a motto to her boldest work, "Un homme peut braver l'opinion; une femme doit s'y soumettre."[1] The greater part of what women write about women is mere sycophancy to men. In the case of unmarried women, much of it seems only intended to increase their chance of a husband. Many, both married and unmarried, overstep the mark, and inculcate a servility beyond what is desired or relished by any man, except the very vulgarest. But this is not so often the case as, even at a quite late period, it still was. Literary women are becoming more free-spoken, and more willing to express their real sentiments. Unfortunately, in this country especially, they are themselves such artificial products, that their sentiments are compounded of a small element of individual observation and consciousness, and a very large one of acquired associations. This will be less and less the case, but it will remain true to a great extent, as long as social institutions do not admit the same free development of originality in women which is possible to men. When that time comes, and not before, we shall see, and not merely hear, as much as it is necessary to know of the nature of women, and the adaptation of other things to it. . . .

One thing we may be certain of—that what is contrary to women's nature to do, they never will be made to do by simply giving their nature free play. The anxiety of mankind to interfere in behalf of nature, for fear lest nature should not succeed in effecting its purpose, is an altogether unnecessary solicitude. What women by nature cannot do, it is quite superfluous to forbid them from doing. What they can do, but not so well as the men who are their competitors, competition suffices to exclude them from; since nobody asks for protective duties and bounties in favour of women;

[1]From the title page of Mme de Staël's *Delphine:* "A man can go against public opinion; a woman must submit herself to it."

it is only asked that the present bounties and protective duties in favour of men should be recalled. If women have a greater natural inclination for some things than for others, there is no need of laws or social inculcation to make the majority of them do the former in preference to the latter. Whatever women's services are most wanted for, the free play of competition will hold out the strongest inducements to them to undertake. And, as the words imply, they are most wanted for the things for which they are most fit; by the apportionment of which to them, the collective faculties of the two sexes can be applied on the whole with the greatest sum of valuable result.

The general opinion of men is supposed to be, that the natural vocation of a woman is that of a wife and mother. I say, is supposed to be, because, judging from acts—from the whole of the present constitution of society—one might infer that their opinion was the direct contrary. They might be supposed to think that the alleged natural vocation of women was of all things the most repugnant to their nature; insomuch that if they are free to do anything else—if any other means of living or occupation of their time and faculties, is open, which has any chance of appearing desirable to them—there will not be enough of them who will be willing to accept the condition said to be natural to them. If this is the real opinion of men in general, it would be well that it should be spoken out. I should like to hear somebody openly enunciating the doctrine (it is already implied in much that is written on the subject)—"It is necessary to society that women should marry and produce children. They will not do so unless they are compelled. Therefore it is necessary to compel them." The merits of the case would then be clearly defined. It would be exactly that of the slaveholders of South Carolina and Louisiana. "It is necessary that cotton and sugar should be grown. White men cannot produce them. Negroes will not, for any wages which we choose to give. *Ergo* they must be compelled." An illustration still closer to the point is that of impressment. Sailors must absolutely be had to defend the country. It often happens that they will not voluntarily enlist. Therefore there must be the power of forcing them. How often has this logic been used! and, but for one flaw in it, without doubt it would have been successful up to this day. But it is open to the retort—First pay the sailors the honest value of their labour. When you have made it as well worth their while to serve you, as to work for other employers, you will have no more difficulty than others have in obtaining their services. To this there is no logical answer except "I will not": and as people are now not only ashamed, but are not desirous, to rob the labourer of his hire, impressment is no longer advocated. Those who attempt to force women into marriage by closing all other doors against them, lay themselves open to a similar retort. If they mean what they say, their opinion must evidently be, that men do not render the married condition so desirable to women, as to induce them to accept it for its own recommendations. It is not a sign of one's thinking the boon one offers very attractive, when one allows only Hobson's choice, "that or none." And here, I believe, is the clue to the feelings of those men, who have a real antipathy to the equal freedom of women. I believe they are afraid, not lest women should be unwilling to marry, for I do not think that anyone in reality has that apprehension; but lest they should insist that marriage should be on equal conditions; lest all women of spirit and capacity should prefer doing almost anything else, not in their own eyes degrading, rather than marry, when marrying is giving themselves a master, and a master too of all their earthly possessions. And truly, if this consequence were necessarily incident to marriage, I think that the apprehension would be very well founded. I agree in thinking it probable that few women, capable of anything else, would, unless under an irresistible *entraînement*, rendering them for the time insensible to anything but itself, choose such a lot, when any other means were open to them of filling a conventionally honourable place in life: and if men are determined that the law of marriage shall be a law of despotism, they are quite right, in point of mere policy, in leaving to women only Hobson's choice. But, in that case, all that has been done in the modern world to relax the chain on the minds of women, has been a mistake. They never should have been allowed to receive a literary education. Women who read, much more women who write, are, in the existing constitution of things, a contradiction and a disturbing element: and it was wrong to bring women up with any acquirements but those of an odalisque, or of a domestic servant.

QUESTIONS

1. List the arguments that Mill says have been made in favor of the subjection of women and explain how he answers each of these.
2. Compare Mill's portrayal of women's condition and his arguments for women's equality with those of Mary Wollstonecraft.

3. What ideas of liberalism are reflected in this passage?
4. What comparisons does Mill make between the condition of women and slavery? How valid are these parallels in your opinion?
5. How do Mill's analyses of, and remedies for, an oppressed class differ from those of Marx?
6. How relevant are the injustices that Mill points out and the solutions that he offers to the condition of present-day women?

29

Art and Literature in the Industrial World: Realism and Beyond

Artists, as well as social thinkers, were forced to come to terms with the industrialization of society. The conventions and enthusiasms that had permitted an artist to create the gentle *Experiment with the Air-Pump* (Fig. 24-4) were no longer appropriate in an age in which scientific progress had produced the vast, dehumanizing factories of Leeds and Birmingham. Nor did the idealizing and exotic tendencies of romanticism deal adequately with the problems of the mid-nineteenth century. Industrialism and its social consequences necessitated profound changes in *all* the arts, but our examples will be drawn from painting and architecture.

Architecture

Nineteenth-century architects were hesitant in their attempts to create a new architectural language for their age. In 1847 Professor Donaldson, speaking at a meeting of the Architectural Association (an important English architectural school), said, "The great question is, are we to have an architecture of our period, a distinct, individual, palpable style of the 19th century?" Romanticism had produced a series of revivals: Gothic, Romanesque, Renaissance. It is difficult for us to imagine the controversies that raged as to which style was the most correct or appropriate for particular needs. By mid-century, the architect tended to elect forms based on associations with the functions of the building, hence, Gothic for churches and Italian Renaissance for banks and businesses. Yet the new functions, needs, and materials of architecture posed new problems and demanded new solutions, which were more frequently offered by engineers and builders than by architects. An example of such a new problem and a new solution is the Crystal Palace, created for the Great Exhibition of 1851 in London (Fig. 29-1).

29-1 *Crystal Palace.* (Illustrated London News, *Sept. 6, 1851*)

A call for designs for the main exhibition hall, one-third of a mile long, produced a variety of solutions that would take too long to build, were too costly, and would be impossible to light. However, Joseph Paxton, gardener of the earl of Chatworth, proposed a modular glass box made of cast and wrought iron framing and glass. All the parts could be prefabricated, shipped by rail, and erected on the site in Hyde Park. On July 16, 1850, an agreement was signed between the commissioners of the exhibition, the engineers, and the glass manufacturers. The completed hall was handed over on January 31, 1851, ready for the installation of exhibits. Lighted naturally, cooled by giant louvered windows that could be opened mechanically, the Crystal Palace was truly a marvel (although John Ruskin, the English architectural critic, refused to call it architecture). Today we see it as a modern solution to a difficulty without reliance on the visual or technical formulas of traditional architecture.

Similar requirements—limited land, money, and time; the need for adequate space and light—were the conditions that created the tall office building in Chicago in the last decades of the nineteenth century. Tall buildings had become possible with the invention of the elevator, fireproofing, and the perfection of iron and steel framing. Yet many architects tended to clothe these stacks of floors in Greek, Gothic, or Renaissance details. The problem was to decide what a skyscraper was supposed to look like. After the fire of 1871 destroyed the heart of commercial Chicago, the architects of that city were faced with problems demanding innovation.

William Le Baron Jenney (1832–1907) was one of the first architects in the city to take on the problem in his design for the Home Insurance Building (1883–1885) (Fig. 29-2). The entire surface of the building hangs on its steel and iron frame, but nothing visibly suggests the innovative nature of its design. Rather, this problem was left to many young architects who worked in Jenney's office, among them Louis Sullivan and Daniel Burnham.

Louis Sullivan (1856–1924) and the Commercial Style

One of Chicago's most influential architects of this period, Sullivan searched for the theoretical and philosophical ideas that building expressed. Sullivan was born in Boston and began his higher education in MIT's architectural program but left after a year. He then worked in Philadelphia and Chicago and finally traveled to Paris, where he studied briefly at the Ecole des Beaux Arts and worked in an architect's studio. While in Paris he absorbed the essential principles of academic architecture: functional planning, sound construction, and expressive decoration. The suc-

29-2 *William Le Baron Jenny, Chicago Home Insurance Building. (Chicago Architectural Photographing Company)*

29-3 *Louis Sullivan, Wainwright Building, St. Louis. (Missouri Historical Society, negative no. PB182)*

cessful creation of the form for the tall office building, as he called it, became one of the driving forces of his architecture.

Sullivan, in partnership with Dankmar Adler (1844–1900), produced a series of buildings that addressed the problem. Sullivan suggested that the tall office building should be articulated precisely in relation to its unique visible functions: ground-floor shops and entry, midsection offices, and topmost floors where mechanical systems were placed. Given that verticality was the essence of the building, Sullivan insisted that this element be emphasized. His ideas were demonstrated in a series of buildings of which the Wainwright in Saint Louis, Missouri (1890–1891), was one of the most successful. The Wainwright has all the elements of a modern skyscraper: the entire building is carried on a fireproofed steel frame, and its three sections can be easily read (Fig. 29-3). It should be compared with the Reliance Building (Fig. 29-4), designed by Burnham and Root. Built in the summer of 1891, it is also a self-supporting metal cage with glass infill. It was simple to erect and maintain. The walls were great expanses of glass, some fixed, some movable panels, providing light and ventilation for the offices lining each side of its central corridor. Visually, the building is a very clear expression of its function, which is to be, as Sullivan had noted, tall, economical, and useful. There are no classical orders, no pointed arches. Chicagoans pointed with pride to the development of the "Commercial Style," but some critics felt that its simple expression of function through form was too commercial, too expedient. It would not be until after World War I that the hold of tradition would be completely broken.

29-4 *Burnham & Root, Reliance Building, Chicago. (Chicago Architectural Photographing Company)*

Painting: Realism

In architecture, as in any art, it is never enough to solve a problem. Building forms have a profound effect on the quality of life; painting and sculpture reflect, comment on, and affect the future of the arts and of humanity. In mid-century what seemed most real and most important was progress and economic expansion. In painting the consequences of industrialism made the problems perceived by Delacroix, Goya, and Constable seem more acute. Again and again artists found themselves asking, what should they paint, for whom, and how? Some painters found that industrialism itself provided fascinating subject matter. The English painter J. M. W. Turner interpreted the technology that had revolutionized transportation in *Rain, Steam and Speed—The Great Western Railway* (Color Plate XXIV). Painted in 1844, it was, according to Turner, a literal account of an event that he had witnessed during a storm while riding on a train. The public, however, could not readily accept the modern, "unartistic" subject matter, and Turner's methods were not to the liking of the public, which was used to the smooth surfaces and academic perfection of most successful painting.

Gustave Courbet (1819–1877)

The questions of what one should paint and how one should paint it are issues that were central to the development of art in the nineteenth century. Turner and Constable represented one kind of revolt from the accepted academic painting that was a natural descendant of the art of the seventeenth and eighteenth centuries. Another kind of revolt was that represented by the French painter Gustave Courbet and the collection of artists who thought of themselves as realists. This group, which included landscape painters as well as figure and genre painters, succeeded in dominating trends in painting in the third quarter of the nineteenth century. In an 1855 manifesto, Courbet, the pioneer in the movement, stated his principal aims as a realist to be "to translate the customs, the ideas, the appearances of my epoch." The artist was to paint what he saw. For Courbet, this meant depicting the ugly as well as the beautiful. In his view the lower classes were more important than the upper social groups because it was on their labor that modern life was founded. Born in the French countryside, Courbet was the personification of the swaggering, tough, independent socialist. In rendering the harsh reality of his peasant subjects, Courbet depicted life in the country in a way far removed from romantic idealization of it. Courbet was a realist primarily because of his subject matter and his attitudes, but he was not concerned with rendering the details and textures of every object. For this reason he usually painted in his studio, doing only sketches out-of-doors. More traditional painters criticized his strong colors and his heavily layered paint, which he sometimes applied with a palette knife, a most unconventional process. The total effect of his work, however, was shocking only to those who preferred older styles of painting.

Ford Madox Brown (1821–1893)

In England the painter Ford Madox Brown, like Courbet, chose subjects that had philosophical or social relevance for the day. His paintings were filled with the minutiae of life. Brown, like Constable, worked out-of-doors, drawing his subjects from nature in an attempt to create an intensified illusion of reality. His large painting *Work,* 1862–1865 (Fig. 29-5), shows a sharp

29-5 *Ford Madox Brown,* Work. *(Manchester City Art Galleries)*

contrast between busy laborers and elegant passersby. To the right, watching the scene, is the English philosopher Carlyle, who wrote about the dignity of labor. Beside Carlyle is Frederick D. Maurice, who helped to found the Working Men's College, an institution dedicated to combating social ills and raising workers' status through education. *Work* is certainly more than a picture of Hampstead on a sunny day.

Compare this painting with *The Stonebreakers*, painted in 1849 by Courbet (Fig. 29-6). Begin by deciding what you consider "realism." Does it have to do with the subject matter or the way in which the subject is presented? How does the stonebreaker differ from the workers in *Work?* Which is more anonymous? Which portrays workers more authentically? Which picture rouses a greater response? Why? Does Courbet's focus on two figures intensify or detract from the scene? Do you think the two pictures have a moral? What is that moral? Are location, time of day, and condition of the weather as important as they were to Constable?

Thomas Eakins (1844–1916)

Born in Philadelphia, Eakins studied at the Pennsylvania Academy and then traveled abroad to France and Spain, where he was profoundly affected by the work of Velásquez. When he returned home in 1870 he began to produce the intense, ordered, and descriptive paintings that are characteristic of his particular style of realism. He worked out-of-doors sketching and studying light, air, and the movement of both over figures and ground. In his *Max Schmitt in a Single Scull* (Fig. 29-7) Eakins, portrayed in the far boat, pulls away from his more famous friend whose skill at racing had made him an important figure in the Philadelphia area. Schmitt is seen in the near ground, and the effort and concentration that characterize the sport have lapsed into a momentary pause that permits us to see Schmitt and the setting as if in a single moment in time. Eakins's ability to capture a moment in time should be compared with that of Monet, the French impressionist who will be considered in the next chapter.

29-6 *Gustave Courbet,* The Stonebreakers, *1849, oil on canvas, 5'3" × 8'6", formerly Gemäldegalerie, Dresden. (Staatliche Kunstsammlungen, Dresden)*

29-7 *Thomas Eakins,* Max Schmitt in a Single Scull, *oil on canvas, 32¼" × 46¼". (The Metropolitan Museum of Art, Purchase 1934, Alfred N. Punnett Fund and Gift of George D. Pratt 34.92)*

Photography

The problem with being a realist painter is no better revealed than when one compares a photograph with a painting. The social and economic forces that influenced the realists coincided with the technological revolution that produced new ways in which pictures could be made. Although Courbet, Ford Madox Brown, and Eakins might call themselves "realists," they could not compete with the ability of the camera to give an account of the thing seen. Invented in the first decades of the nineteenth century (the earliest photograph dates from c. 1826), the camera, by the 1850s, seemed able to capture more detail and information than the eye could see or the hand record. If realism was to be defined by painterly conventions that rendered everything as it was seen, then painting was in danger of being replaced. If, however, realism was an attitude that was defined by an honesty toward subject matter and a willingness to seek subject matter in the everyday life and experiences of people, then photography was much less threatening—artists could rely on their skill in creating a convincing painting. Artists responded with some of both, and some artists saw photography as a tool that they, too, might use. Eakins and the Frenchman Edgar Degas both used Eadweard Muybridge's *Studies in Animal Locomotion* (Fig. 29-8), the first important publication of both the human figure and animals in motion, as caught by time-lapse photography, as a means to study forms in action. Eventually photographers too would seek to have their work accepted as art.

Realism in Literature

Writers in the industrial world, like artists, felt the need to portray as exactly as possible real life around them. As Courbet called for realism in painting, the French critic Duranty urged writers to strive for "the exact, complete, and sincere reproduction of the social milieu in which we live." Writers who considered themselves realists reacted against the fantastic, exotic, and ideal elements in romanticism, although in many of the greatest nineteenth-century works of literature, realism and romanticism coexist. If romanticism produced great *lyrics*, realism, as might be expected, produced great *novels*, for the novel, of all literary genres, is most capable of representing the varied dimensions of a society and its characters. If the middle to late nineteenth century was the great age of

29-8 *Eadweard Muybridge,* Studies in Animal Locomotion. *(International Museum of Photography at George Eastman House)*

the realistic novel, there are still many writers who practice this art today. Although realism has been severely questioned in the twentieth century, it has not died out. Realistic novels are still popular in the United States. Until recently, "socialist realism" was the only officially accepted style for novelists in communist countries.

One reason for the success of realism as a literary style in the nineteenth century was the increase in literacy among people in the middle and lower classes and the diffusion of journalism. Many novels were published in serial form in the cheap and easily accessible newspapers and journals. The new reading public was not interested in kings, gods, or ideal types; people preferred to read about others like themselves in surroundings like their own.

Realism could be considered a literary school only in France, where it had its fervent proponents and its detractors, its practitioners and its critics. The greatest realistic novelists there were Stendhal and Balzac. The latter, in his series of novels entitled *The Human Comedy* (obviously in contrast to *The Divine Comedy*), attempted a complete portrayal of French nineteenth-century society, creating memorable characters in the process. In England, Charles Dickens, George Eliot, and William Thackeray are examples of realistic novelists. Realism in the United States began later than in Europe, but it had a considerable impact on American fiction that continues to the present day. Henry James studied the French realists for his own benefit; William Dean Howells wrote against "romantic lies" in literature in favor of realism, which portrays "men and women as they actually are, actuated by the motives and the passions in the measure we all know." Stephen Crane, who portrayed the harsher aspects of the Civil War, was another great American realist.

What are the basic characteristics of realism? As Howells's statement indicates, a belief in the possibility of realism implies a belief in an objective reality. Realism can be both material and psychological. It uses words to depict the way that things look and feel and the way that people act. Very often, the things influence or represent the people. The realist believes in "realistically" motivated characters who do not act in unexpected ways. Wishing to exclude nothing, realistic writers pay much attention to detail, especially the more sordid or shocking aspects of human life. Although nineteenth-century realists claimed to be objective in their portrayal of actual life, many of them reveal in their writings their profound convictions on contemporary social issues. The impact of industrialism on cities and on human life, especially the wretched condition of the urban poor, was a particularly apt subject for socially concerned realists. A good example of such a realist writer is Charles Dickens (1812–1870). Dickens, a great literary success through his serial novels widely diffused in journals, was one of the most vivid portrayers of the new cities, the characters of all social strata within them, and the alienating effects of industrial capitalism. Because of his improbable plots and grotesque, almost monstrous characters, he cannot be called a consistently realistic novelist; still, he does to a great extent reproduce the material, social, and psychological environment of his time.

Naturalism

One characteristic of realism was to become more and more important toward the end of the nineteenth century: the determination of human character by the material and social environment. As this belief evolved into a so-called scientific credo, the movement known as *naturalism* replaced realism. The naturalists, more interested in the new theories of Charles Darwin on human evolution than in Courbet's ideas on the reproduction of reality, tried to establish cause-and-effect laws in their novels. Certain conditions in the environment, they demonstrated, will produce certain traits in human beings. The foremost practitioner of naturalism in France was Émile Zola; he found an avid follower in the American Theodore Dreiser. As late as 1940, the black American writer Richard Wright produced a great naturalistic novel, *Native Son*, which demonstrates how a young black man becomes a criminal through the influence of the racist society in which he lives.

The Poet and the City: Baudelaire

If one poet can be said to have been the initiator of modern poetry, it is probably the Frenchman Charles Baudelaire (1821–1867). An art critic as well as a poet, Baudelaire was extremely sensitive to the achievements of the best painters of his time, particularly Eugène Delacroix (see Chapter 27). Of Edouard Manet (see page 349), he wrote (in *Esthetic Curiosities*) that he "combined with a definite taste for reality, modern reality—which is already a good sign—that ample, lively, sensitive, and daring imagination without which, it must be said, all the best faculties are only servants without a master, agents without a government." The description might be applied to Baudelaire's own poetry as well. The artist's task, for him, is to portray outward reality through an inner, spiritual vision.

When it appeared in 1857, Baudelaire's collection of poetry entitled *Les fleurs du mal* (*The Flowers of Evil*) shocked the bourgeois public. Along with Gustave Flaubert, who published his great realist novel *Madame Bovary* the same year, Baudelaire was put on trial for "offense to public and religious morality and to good morals." Six of the poems in the collection remained censored until 1949. One of the charges against both Baudelaire and Flaubert was their espousal of realism, defined by their accusers as a fascination with the ugly and evil and a negation of standards upholding the beautiful and the good. Yet many of Baudelaire's poems dealt with the concept of ideal beauty, a theme that was to influence the symbolists that followed him.

It is in his poems dealing with life in the city, his native Paris, that Baudelaire is the most "realistic." One section of *The Flowers of Evil* entitled "Tableaux parisiens" presents a haunted view of urban life, one that would influence T. S. Eliot in *The Wasteland.* Baudelaire also wrote poems in prose, although the collection entitled *Poems in Prose* or *The Spleen of Paris* was not published until 1869, two years after his death. The use of prose allows for even greater realism in poetry. In his visions of Paris, Baudelaire portrayed some of the same conditions that Engels and Dickens had observed in the industrialized cities of England: the gap between the smug, comfortable bourgeoisie and the marginalized poor, the dehumanized nature of the crowd, the alienations of modern life. But Baudelaire was a poet, not a reformer. His task was to bring "flowers from evil"; to create beauty by exploring the very depths of the ugliness of modern life. His Paris was the city recently transformed by Haussmann's majestic urban renewal, with its wide new boulevards and elegant neoclassical façades. His era was Napoleon III's Second Empire, which was dominated by materialism and greed. Baudelaire's vision of the modern city resembles that of Dante in the *Inferno* in that it becomes a symbolic representation of infinite spiritual loss. Behind the shiny new products of materialistic progress are to be found the squalor and poverty that reveal unpleasant truths about the human condition.

Late-Nineteenth-Century Thinkers and Writers

The years corresponding to the reign of Queen Victoria in England (1837–1901) produced a number of radical changes in the ways that people in the West viewed themselves and their environment. As industrialism became a fact of life, prevailing attitudes became more and more materialistic. Marx had taught human beings to see themselves as controlled by economic forces, although they could help to shape these forces for the cause of social justice. Some liberal thinkers envisaged a future time when the steady progress of capitalistic industry would create a society in which everyone would be surrounded by mechanical conveniences and physical comfort. Living in a world where every year seemed to witness dramatic technical achievements, middle-class Europeans or Americans (if they did not accept the predictions of Marx) had every reason to feel smug about themselves and their society.

Charles Darwin (1809–1882)

In the pure, as opposed to the applied, sciences, more fundamental changes were taking place. Among the most important of these were the evolutionary theories put forth by Charles Darwin. Darwin, who published his *Origin of Species* in 1859 and *The Descent of Man* in 1871, showed through his scientific observations of the "lower" animals that humankind was an integral part of their world. By evolution he meant that species are mutable: that each class of living organisms has developed through a series of gradual changes from a different one that preceded it. Species developed through mutations in inherited characteristics. Those inheriting the most useful characteristics—for fighting, food gathering, or mating—survived; the others died out. Thus life was basically a struggle for existence. The "survival of the fittest" was brought about through "natural selection." Humankind was one of those species that had evolved from the primate family and had managed to survive.

The protest against Darwin and his theories, which lasted well into the twentieth century, was very great indeed. Fundamentalist religious groups denounced him for proposing a theory of creation contrary to the one in Genesis; other moralists and religious authorities claimed that he had turned humanity into monkeys and undermined the foundations of human dignity, morality, and religion. The most upsetting concept in Darwin's theory of evolution was its concept of life as a scene of struggle and survival, of "nature red in tooth and claw." Nature could no longer be seen as the harmonious work of the Supreme Being or as the motherly source of consolation for wounded emotions. Constant flux, change,

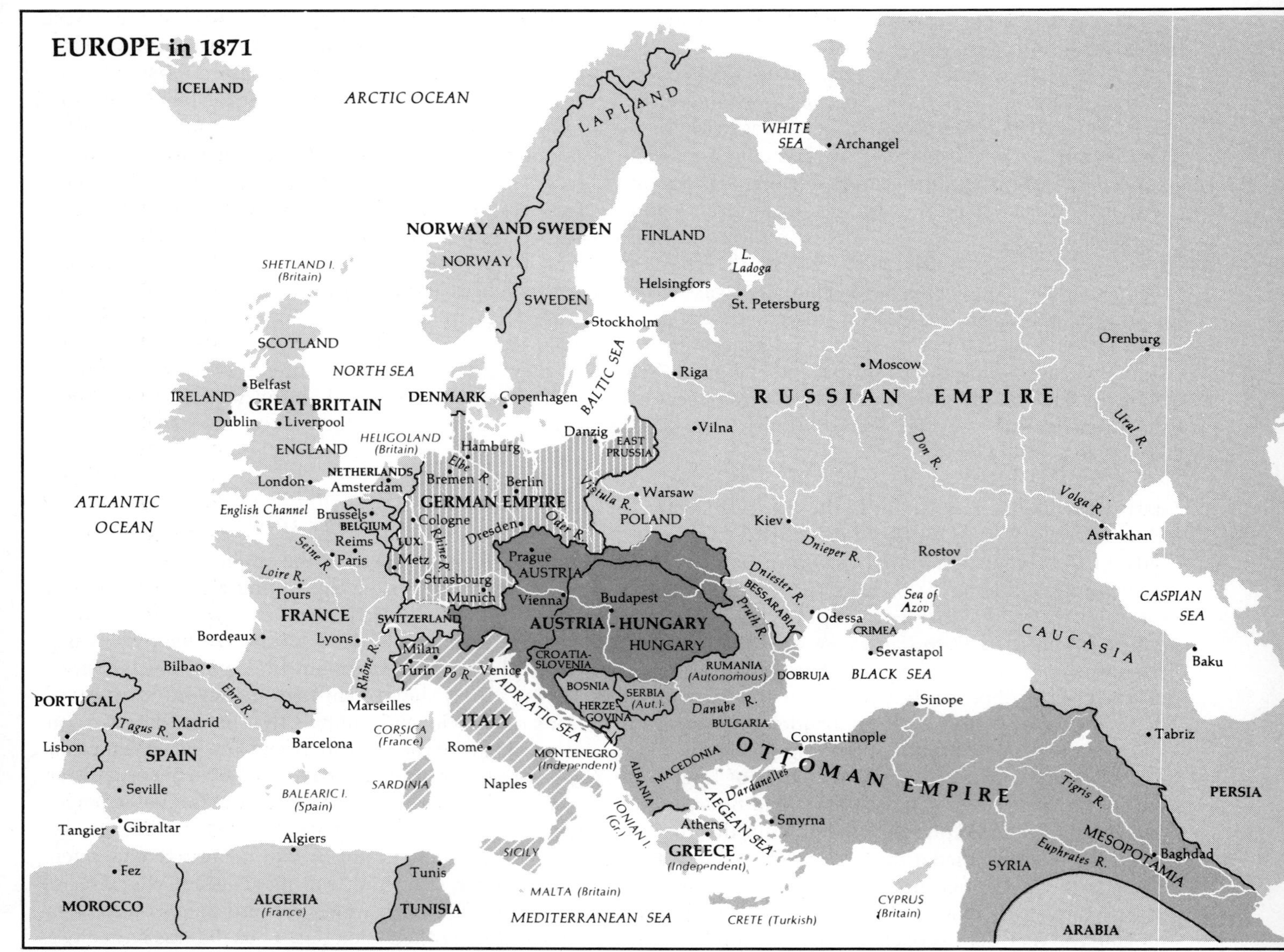

relativity of existence, and the elimination of the weak were in the natural order of things.

Herbert Spencer (1820–1903)

Nonscientific Darwin enthusiasts did not hesitate to apply his theories to human society. Herbert Spencer proclaimed a doctrine of agnosticism (the impossibility of knowing the existence of God with certainty) and what came to be known as "social Darwinism." Spencer argued that society, like the natural world, was governed by the principle of evolution. There, too, the fittest survived and the weak went under. Social evolution was headed toward the increased freedom of the individual, and governments had no business interfering in the "natural" economic processes or protecting the weak and unfit. In stressing the freedom of individual struggle in the economic process, Spencer seemed to give a scientific confirmation to the doctrines of early liberalism. His ideas had a particularly great influence in the United States, where the individualistic capitalism that led to the "robber barons" was booming. Thus the nineteenth-century bourgeois managed to assimilate even the radical theories of evolution into their materialistic, self-satisfied view of the world.

Friedrich Nietzsche (1844–1900)

Yet other philosophers and artists raised their voices loudly against this view of human nature and society. The highly influential German Nietzsche, a poetic more than a systematic philosopher, adapted evolutionary theories to purposes quite different from Spencer's. He denounced his bourgeois contemporaries for their hypocrisy, their stale morality, and their rationalism. He also saw human nature in terms of evolution toward freedom and elimination of weakness, but the freedom that interested him was spiritual and intellectual rather than economic and material. Rather than being satisfied with Western culture as he found it, he attacked not only its present state but also what we have seen to be its roots: the Greco-Roman and Judeo-Christian traditions. The Greek emphasis on reason as exemplified by Socrates worked against the healthy vitality of the instincts, according to Nietzsche. He did admire an aspect of Greek culture that, he felt, modern times had neglected—the irrational or "Dionysian" strain represented by ancient tragedy. Nietzsche advocated a revolt against the limits of reason and reasonableness and a return to greater sources of personal and cultural power in the irrational and in myth. The moral values of Jews and Christians he found to be the expressions of weaklings or of "slaves." Christian ideas such as "pity," "turning the other cheek," and "sin" were for Nietzsche notions designed to keep people in their place instead of allowing free individuals to realize themselves to their full potential.

Nietzsche's thought, interpreted in various ways, has been influential on a variety of modern doctrines. Following his profound doubts about Western culture, some thinkers turned to the Orient or to Africa in an effort to find new sources of vitality for their own times. Others, following an opposite line of thought, derived racist ideas from Nietzsche, seeing in his theory of human evolution toward the free, noble "superman" a justification for beliefs in the superiority of the white or Aryan race. The Nazis interpreted Nietzsche in this way. Nietzsche's thought has been deeply influential on the philosophical school of existentialism, in both its Christian and its atheistic forms.

Fyodor Dostoevsky (1821–1881)

Another radical critique of materialistic and rationalistic Western society came from the Russian writer Dostoevsky. Dostoevsky, who was to have a major impact on Western literature and thought in the twentieth century, considered himself as a Russian outside the traditions of western Europe and thus able to view them more critically. He envisioned a major role for Russia in the destiny of the West. History proved him right in a way that he would not have approved.

Dostoevsky began his intellectual career as a socialist, associating with one of many groups of young Russians interested in the new doctrines from Europe. For this, the tsarist regime arrested him, sending him off to imprisonment in Siberia. He was at first sentenced to death, but the sentence was commuted at the last minute. During his stay in the Siberian prison, an experience that he recounted later in *The House of the Dead*, Dostoevsky underwent a reconversion to a mystical, Russian Orthodox Christianity. He also gained insight from observing the various criminals and political prisoners around him. In his later novels Dostoevsky portrayed characters in the extremes of moral degradation on the one hand and spiritual illumination on the other. The achievement of salvation through doubt, suffering, and even crime became one of his major themes. Like Nietzsche, Dostoevsky praised the extremes of human existence and deplored the safe, smug middle road; but, unlike Nietzsche, he believed that humanity could be saved through faith in Christ.

The much-acclaimed Crystal Palace became in Dostoevsky's first major work, *Notes from the Underground* (1864), a symbol of the utopia of those who believe in the doctrines of progress through science and materialism. The kind of happiness represented by the Crystal Palace (Fig. 29-1) could, according to Dostoevsky, be achieved only through the loss of human freedom. Freedom, not political or economic but spiritual freedom of choice, is for Dostoevsky humanity's precious possession. People should be free to follow their irrational yearnings, their caprice, in order to develop their spiritual nature fully. People in Dostoevsky's view are not naturally good, as the optimists of both the eighteenth and the nineteenth centuries believed, but fallen and yet free to choose faith in Christ. Such a choice made for reasons of certainty or stability would be, however, a false one. The choice for Christ should be made irrationally, or suprarationally, through faith, taking upon oneself the burden of humanity since "everybody is guilty for all and before all." Dostoevsky came to believe that only the Russian people and the Russian church had preserved Christianity in its pure form, and he prophesied a messianic role for Russia. The West, whether materialistic or socialistic or Catholic, was for him in complete decay. Roman Catholicism he viewed as a kind of herd religion, an attempt to force belief and conformity through authority.

Dostoevsky develops these themes in his four great novels, *Crime and Punishment* (1866), *The Idiot* (1868), *The Possessed* (1871), and *The Brothers Karamazov* (1880). There his ideas are given flesh and blood through the complexity and fullness of his tortured, extremist characters and the settings in which they play out their destinies. In his ability to create living characters, Dostoevsky is in the tradition of the great European realists and indeed one of the masters of realism; yet his belief in human freedom puts him in direct opposition to the naturalists, who portrayed humanity as conditioned by social and material conditions. His supreme interest in the exploration of the human soul makes Dostoevsky break through the bounds of a style limited to everyday life and "realistic" character motivation. Influenced by Dickens, he developed aspects of the grotesque already present in the English novelist's works. For Dostoevsky, reality, in art as in life, extended beyond realism. In a letter of 1869 he wrote, "I have my own view of art, and that which the majority call fantastic and exceptional is for me the very essence of reality."

It is perhaps not too surprising, then, that at the heart of *The Brothers Karamazov*, in many ways a realistic novel about nineteenth-century Russia, lies a fantastic story recounting the return of Christ to the earth during the *Inquisition* in sixteenth-century Spain. The story is told by one of the Karamazov brothers, Ivan, to his younger brother Alyosha. Ivan, for whom Dostoevsky shows great sympathy, is an atheist, or at least one who cannot accept the revelations of Christianity though he struggles with them desperately. Alyosha, in contrast, is a novice in a monastery and a pure-souled believer. Before telling the story that he calls "The Grand Inquisitor," Ivan makes two pronouncements, both of which have been widely quoted and commented on by twentieth-century thinkers. In the first, Ivan reasons that if God and the immortality of the individual soul do not exist, "everything is permitted." Without such a foundation, there can be no universal morality, and people are free to create their own. In the second, Ivan finds the existence of human suffering a just cause for revolt against God. If God can permit innocent children to be tortured to death, Ivan asks, how can he be just? What Ivan cannot accept is the world as he finds it, the world that God has made. Ivan demands justice on his own terms.

The Grand Inquisitor in Ivan's story represents the established Church, the Roman Church, but also what Ivan would consider an authentic view of most human beings as weak, slavish, and needing authority. In the Inquisitor's view, Christ neither loved nor understood human beings because he believed them capable of freely chosen faith without the assurances of material comfort and proof. The arguments of the Grand Inquisitor are strong ones; they have caused many readers to believe that Dostoevsky, in spite of his professed intentions, was really on his side. What is at stake here are two fundamentally different conceptions of human nature and of religion that Dostoevsky has set against each other with exquisite balance.

From Realism to Symbolism in Painting

By the middle of the nineteenth century, realism was perceived by some artists as a limitation as well as an inspiration. Like the novelists and poets who came to feel that "reality" lay beyond the grasp of "realism," painters began to experiment with ways of rendering reality that went beyond the representational or photographic. The first school of painters to experiment along these lines was called, by a hostile art critic, "impressionist." Between the harsh "reality" of Courbet's *Stonebreakers* and the thrilling light of Monet's *The Bridge at Argenteuil* (Color Plate XXV) lie years of experimentation by artists, painting both out-of-doors and in the studio, trying paints, brushes, sketches, and colors to achieve the sense of momentariness that is so characteristic of the impressionist painters.

Whenever artists have to discover new ways of making the images that fascinate them, old habits first have to be broken, old ways of seeing altered. This is not easy. Often (as we shall see in the case of African art in the early twentieth century) the influence of the art of a foreign culture can be a profoundly liberating one. For Edouard Manet, Edgar Degas, and the impressionists, the printmakers of Japan provided a major source of inspiration for change. Prints came to the West as wrapping paper. Usually woodblock, in two or three colors, these prints, of everyday events, comic happenings, satire, the theater, represented a completely new way of seeing the world and accounting for it. The Japanese printmaker was essentially interested not in creating a reproduction of the experienced event but in creating an image that focused attention by simplification—thus eliminating any need to reproduce natural light and shade, space, or textures. Rhythmic patterns, flat colors, abstraction, and stylization are characteristics of these art objects. To the artists in France, these prints (see Fig. 29-9) were a complete revelation. They proved it was possible to make successful art without attempting to copy nature. Artists from Manet on looked at prints and sometimes adapted them to their particular needs. Thus as industrialization brought problems, it also

29-9 *Suzuki Harunobu (1725?–1770),* Suzumegai, *Japanese woodblock print from a poem by Basho. (Courtesy, Museum of Fine Arts, Boston, Asiatic Curators Fund in memory of Marjorie K. Hussey)*

brought information that was as new and revolutionary as technology itself.

Edouard Manet (1832–1883)

In the development of impressionism, Manet played the role of a transitional figure. Although born into the Parisian upper middle class, Manet was not a conscious rebel like Courbet, but he did approach the subject matter suggested by the realists with different artistic tools. From his studies of seventeenth-century art, particularly Velásquez, his viewing of the newly imported Japanese prints, and a knowledge of photography, Manet set out to create a personal style for recording the public and private pursuits of his milieu. Using what photography had shown him, he set his subjects in a strong, harsh light that tended to flatten them against their background, even as a photograph eliminates much three-dimensionality. Unlike the photograph, which does not discriminate among objects, however, Manet concentrated on the firm contours of his subjects. He used sharp contrasts of light and dark to create a strong sense of three-dimensionality, unlike the surface modeling or tonal adjustments of earlier pictures.

Manet's painting *Olympia* (Fig. 29-10), exhibited in the Salon of the Refused in 1863 (a countershow to the government-sanctioned Salon), typifies his emerging style. The idea of a reclining nude is a very old one in art, but this one is different. Who is this woman? What is her profession? Is Manet being critical or patronizing? Why or why not? Paris was shocked by this rather pert lady who engaged the viewer with her direct, quizzical look. It is certain that she is no Venus; she is too present and familiar. The flat white of the sheets and the creamy flat paint that delineates her body end in harsh dark edges and folds. The black servant and black cat seem to emphasize the black/white impact of the picture. The bouquet of flowers, brilliant slashes of painting, recalls the sensation of flowers seen in passing. The elimination of detail, the surface textures, the harsh contrasts, together with Olympia's direct, unself-conscious gaze, create the sensation of a scene glimpsed for an instant, but captured, arrested permanently.

These early paintings, which recall photography's impact and the culture of the past (Venus, for instance), reveal Manet's hesitancy in creating his personal style. More and more, however, he was able to compose freely, reducing gesture and pose to that which was most telling, most revelatory for a particular moment or personality. His later pictures were also coloristically richer. This later concern with color was in part due to the influence of young painters who were, properly speaking, members of the impressionist group. Manet in turn played an important role in influencing them to paint contemporary life in an appropriate way. So also did Edgar Degas, who took his subjects in the city, and who, like Manet, viewed them with detachment and objectivity, unlike the impressionists, whose chief interest was in capturing the experience of landscape.

Edgar Degas (1834–1917)

Edgar Degas was from an upper-middle-class family, and, like Manet, he never set out to be an artistic rebel. Rather he considered himself primarily a draftsman in the grand tradition of Ingres. He concentrated on human subjects and is most frequently associated with the memorable images of ballerinas, whose bodies in motion formed the basis of many of his studies and paintings and introduced a new subject into art.

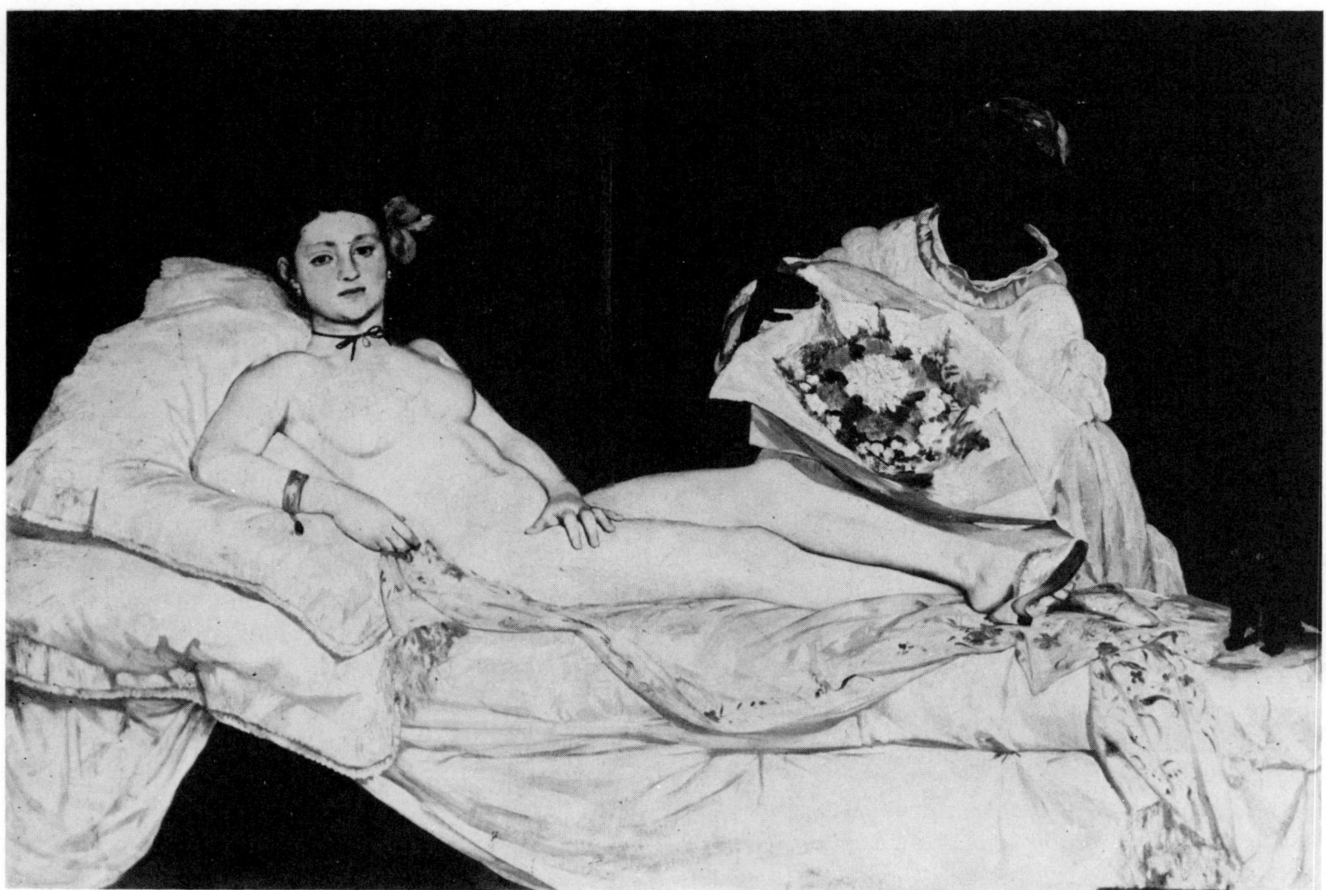

29-10 *Edouard Manet,* Olympia, *Louvre, Paris. (Scala/Art Resource, NY)*

But the qualities of observation and detachment that served Degas so well as he painted dancers derived in part from his interest in abstract form and composition. The study of Japanese prints influenced him as it had Manet and, also like Manet, Degas was fascinated by photography. He used stop motion photography to study the human form for use in his compositions. From these media Degas learned to express a sense of fleeting momentary time, like pictures glimpsed through a window or a scene witnessed when passing on the street.

The Glass of Absinthe (*L'Absinthe*) (Fig. 29-11), painted in 1876, is an excellent example of Degas's scenes drawn from café life. He organizes the picture plane to suggest the isolation and misery of the many anonymous, lower-class workers who streamed into the cities after 1870. The tops of the café tables and their front edges are flat against the picture plane and hold the viewer at a distance from the seated drinker who slouches against the banquette. The tables in the foreground are empty but for a paper and matches, and the drinker seems pushed into the corner against, but not in contact with, the man seated beside her, who is oblivious to her presence. The colors are light, muted, indoor, cool colors, and the softly rendered surfaces of forms with muted edges suggest a vision of life seen through a smoky haze. This image of a café should be compared with the one that Van Gogh painted a few years later (Fig. 29-14).

As his art matured, Degas became less interested in portraying naturalistic color and light in the manner of the younger impressionist painters and, turning to pastels—a chalklike medium that can be rubbed, scraped, and layered—he used color arbitrarily to create the patterns and surfaces that interested him. His increasingly abstract images and surfaces would, like those of Manet, influence artists for many generations.

Impressionism

Claude Monet, August Renoir, and Camille Pissarro were the chief creators of impressionism. Painting landscapes out-of-doors, these artists became com-

29-11 *Edgar Degas,* L'Absinthe, *oil on canvas, Musée d'Orsay, Paris. (Giraudon/Art Resource, NY)*

mitted to recording the illusive effects of sunlight on objects. They had some knowledge of the sciences of color and optics; but when we study their paintings made between 1860 and 1880, we observe that their search for a painterly language unfolds experimentally and unevenly. Consider your own experience of a landscape. The color is vivid; details attract your eyes as they shift, adjusting to the brightness, concentrating, shifting, focusing. Even as this occurs, the scene itself is changing, for clouds, sun, air, and people move and transform what you are seeing even as you see it. If you pause only for a moment, the light/dark contrasts give you information on the location of things; but if you stay to observe, you become aware of the vibrant, changing color and light.

To translate this experience onto the canvas, the painters first realized that they must eliminate black, brown, and gray from their palettes. Natural light is the product of the *hues* of the spectrum: red, orange, yellow, green, blue, and purple. Like Constable, the impressionists realized that a local color, such as green grass, could be made more intense by painting it not as a flat green but as a mottled combination of green and its components, blue and yellow. Moreover, they began to take into account not only the colors of objects themselves but also the fact that objects take on the colors of objects adjacent to them, reflecting some of that color back into the air. Next they realized that shadows are not simply black, brown, or gray but rather the contrasting color of light on the object. Realizing then that all objects, light, and air are reflected, refracted waves of color that the eye perceives and joins into patterns and volumes, they considered it appropriate that the brush stroke should also be fragmented and short, in commas, dots, and dashes. In addition, this kind of brush stroke gave the pictures a sense of immediacy and tension suggesting a rapid, feverish execution.

Landscapes, seascapes (Color Plate XXV), and people on boats and in gardens celebrate the apparent conquest of the momentary that is also a real experience. Monet's *Impression: Sunrise,* painted in 1873, gave the movement its name and was exhibited at the first impressionist exhibition of 1874 (Color Plate XXVI). Like Courbet and Manet, these painters met with a hostile reception: their works were "crude and unfinished." Today we see the pictures made by Monet and his colleagues in the 1870s and 1880s as monuments to the splendor of the natural world. As the impressionists continued their experiments, each of their styles changed in different ways.

Monet remained most true to impressionism's ideal of recording the fleeting transformations of sunlight on objects. Resorting to numerous canvases, each to record a different hour of the day, Monet's almost scientific obsession caused him to concentrate on a few subjects, year after year. A series of huge paintings entitled *Waterlilies,* for example, contains his impressions of a pond at different times of day. Compare a canvas of waterlilies (Fig. 29-12) with *Impression: Sunrise*. Where are Monet's references to the visual world? How are the objects of his interest defined? Does time of day make a difference in your perception of the two works? Compare the brush strokes and the surfaces. In which painting do you sense more clearly the presence of the artist? Why? Are the pond and lilies really important? It would seem that the waterlilies become known to us now only as a concept; they are our link with reality that succumbs to Monet's intensely personal way of seeing and organizing experience.

29-12 *Claude Monet,* Waterlilies, *sunrise section. (Cliché des Musées Nationaux, Paris/Art Resource, NY)*

Waterlilies represents an extremity of the artistic movement that started with realism. What began as an attempt to paint the world "as it is" has become a recording of a subjective view of the world. This approach to art will produce new, more complex, and more elaborate languages with which to apprehend and render experience.

Postimpressionism and Symbolism

With Monet's *Waterlilies* we witness a delicate balance between the need to paint what is seen and the need to paint what is felt. If the impressionists went beyond realism in their representation of the visual world, their successors broke with the tenets of realism altogether. From about 1870 onward, a growing segment of artists, along with poets and musicians, tended to think that the function of art was *not* to represent, or even to interpret, the everyday, normal world, but rather to create its own world and its own meaning. Traditional religion, most believed, was outmoded; its images were no longer valid for modern people. The philosophies of materialism—whether Marxist or liberal—failed to satisfy spiritual and aesthetic needs. Left to fill the vacuum was art—not art for or about something else, but art for its own sake. Thus art became a kind of new religion. The movement began in France with painters usually grouped together under the rubric "postimpressionist," with writers who came to be known as symbolists, and with musicians, such as Claude Debussy and Maurice Ravel, who were associated with them. This end-of-the-century trend was followed in England by aesthete and "dandies" such as Oscar Wilde and Aubrey Beardsley. Germany, Italy, and Spain produced their own symbolist, and later, decadent, schools. In the United States, where realism had taken a strong hold, symbolism, and the view of art as religion, did not have any appreciable effect until the early twentieth century. Here we will study the trend briefly through a few French paintings and poems.

Vincent Van Gogh (1853–1890) The Dutchman Vincent Van Gogh came at first to Paris to make his painting career. Oppressed by the inhumanity and materialism of city life, however, he moved to Arles in southern France. As a response to the pain and suffering that people brought into the world, Van Gogh wished to paint pictures that would be comforting and uplifting. He presents aspects of nature such as the sun, a flower, or a plowed field in a way that does not emphasize their photographic reality, but intensifies our experience of them through the use of strong, pure colors and a vigorous brush stroke. Compare Van Gogh's *The Sower* (Fig. 29-13) with that of Millet (Fig. 27-3). Pay particular attention to the differences created by tone and texture. What is the role of the bare tree? What does the sun stand for? How does it relate to the sower?

Van Gogh's *The Night Café* (Fig. 29-14) is obviously neither a realistic nor an impressionistic

29-13 *Vincent Van Gogh,* The Sower. *(Vincent Van Gogh Foundation/Van Gogh Museum, Amsterdam)*

29-14 *Vincent Van Gogh,* The Night Café, *1888, oil on canvas, 28½" × 36¼". (Yale University Art Gallery, New Haven, Connecticut, bequest of Stephen Carlton Clark, B.A. 1903)*

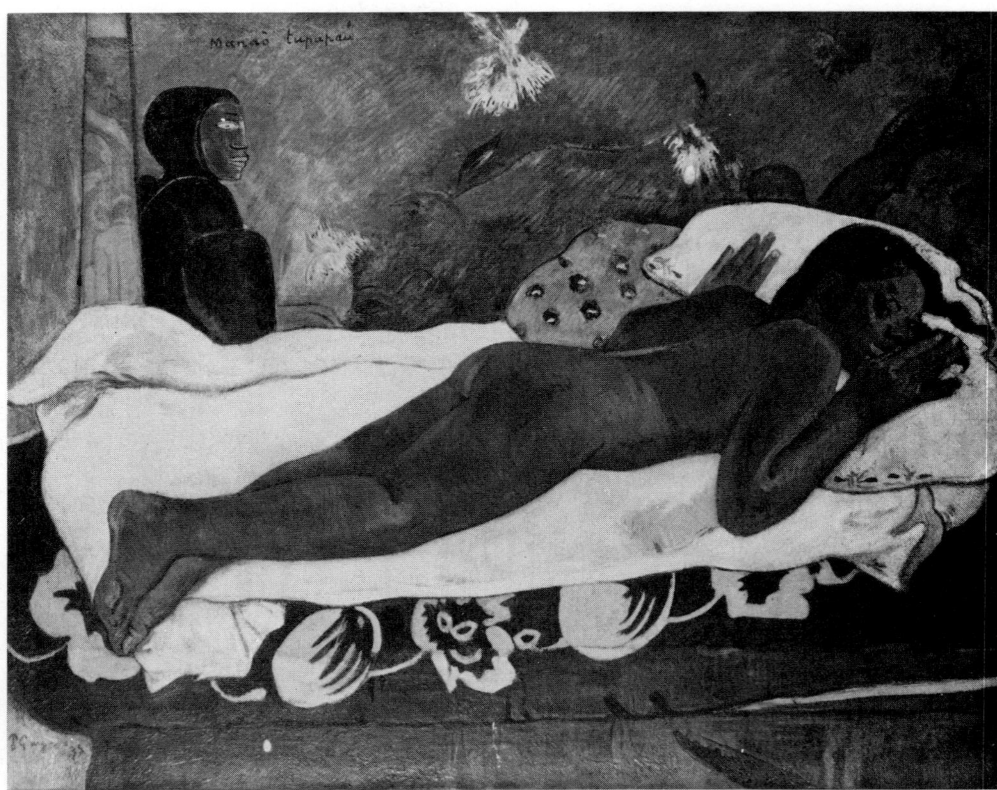

29-15 *Paul Gauguin,* Spirit of the Dead Watching, *1892, oil on burlap mounted on canvas, 28½" × 36⅜". (Albright-Knox Art Gallery, Buffalo, New York, A. Conger Goodyear Collection, 1965)*

rendering of an apparently familiar subject: a café with a billiard table, chairs and smaller tables arranged around the walls, a bar, a host. But what of this place? The space seems empty and somehow threatening; the lamps have strangely glowing halos, and the patrons are anonymous bodies. Van Gogh, unlike the impressionist painters who were primarily interested in rendering account of the surface appearance of things, wished to penetrate beneath the surface. Writing of this painting, Van Gogh said, "I have tried to express humanity's terrible passions by using red and green." This basic color scheme produces intense contrasts perceptible in the black-and-white reproduction, and heightens the emotions that seem to emanate from the scene. What are those emotions? What do they convey? How? What is humanity's plight as Van Gogh describes it here?

Although Van Gogh believed strongly in the redemptive power of art, he remained, unlike most end-of-the-century artists, a convinced Christian. His was a deep and tortured nature, not unlike that of Dostoevsky's characters. At the end of his life he went mad. The fine line between genius and madness was never more evident than in this period.

Paul Gauguin (1848–1903) Gauguin avoided both religious torments and rampant materialism by leaving his native France for Tahiti, where he found a natural, instinctive culture free from inhibitions and greed. The faraway Pacific island also provided him with an unfamiliar subject matter that forces the viewer to concentrate on the experience of the picture rather than on the familiar narrative or object. In a letter to a friend written in 1893 he explains *Spirit of the Dead Watching* (Fig. 29-15).

This letter, quoted below, reveals Gauguin's active search for an abstract pictorial language that can communicate with the viewer.

> A young Tahitian girl is lying on her stomach, showing part of her frightened face. She rests on a bed covered by a blue *pareu* and a light chrome yellow sheet. A violet purple background, sown with flowers glowing like electric sparks; a strange figure sits beside the bed.
>
> Captured by a form, a movement, I paint them with no other preoccupation than to execute a nude figure. As it is, it is a slightly indecent study of a nude, and yet I wish to make of it a chaste picture and imbue it with the spirit of the native, its character and tradition.

The *pareu* being intimately connected with the life of a Tahitian, I use it as a bedspread. The bark cloth sheet must be yellow, because in this color it arouses something unexpected for the spectator, and because it suggests lamplight. This, however, prevents me from making an actual effect of a lamp. I need a background of terror; purple is clearly indicated. And now the musical part of the picture is laid out.

What can a young native girl be doing completely nude on a bed, and in this somewhat difficult position? Preparing herself for making love? That is certainly in character, but it is indecent, and I do not wish it to be so. Sleeping? The amorous activity would then be over, and that is still indecent. I see here only fear. What kind of fear? Certainly not the fear of Susanna surprised by the elders. That kind of fear does not exist in Oceania.

The *tupapau* (Spirit of the Dead) is clearly indicated. For the natives it is a constant dread. A lamp is always lighted at night. No one ever goes out on the paths on a moonless night without a lantern, and even then they travel in groups.

Once I have found my *tupapau* I devote my attention completely to it and make it the motif of my picture. The nude sinks to a secondary level.

What can a spirit mean to a Tahitian? She knows neither the theatre nor the reading of novels, and when she thinks of a dead person she thinks necessarily of someone she has already seen. My spirit can only be an ordinary little woman. Her hand is outstretched as if to seize a prey.

My decorative sense leads me to strew the background with flowers. These flowers are the phosphorescent flowers of the *tupapau*; they are the sign that the spirit nears you. Tahitian beliefs.

The title *Manao tupapau* has two meanings, either the girl thinks of the spirit, or the spirit thinks of her.

To sum up: The musical part: undulating horizontal lines; harmonies of orange and blue, united by the yellows and purples (their derivatives) lit by greenish sparks. The literary part: the spirit of a living person linked to the spirit of the dead. Night and Day.

This genesis is written for those who must always know the *why* and the *wherefore*.

Otherwise it is simply a study of an Oceanian nude.

Although Van Gogh and Gauguin did not share identical aims, their concern with the value of line, color, and form to express a personal view of human truths demonstrates a common understanding of the power of the purely formal, abstract elements of art. This philosophy helps us to understand the rationale that will permit the painter to eliminate the familiar visual world from the canvas altogether.

Paul Cézanne (1836–1906) Among the postimpressionists was another great genius, Paul Cézanne, who was older than the other two but whose work matured in the same years. His goal was to formulate a painterly language that would give an account of nature. He distrusted the implicit subjectivism and emotionalism of Van Gogh and Gauguin, and he felt that impressionism created ephemeral works. He wanted to make art universal and independent, timeless, and free of subjectivity and emotionalism.

Cézanne liked to paint several versions of the same subject, such as Mont Sainte-Victoire in southern France. The version reproduced here (Color Plate XXVII) shows his technique of using bright, intense colors, applied in varying thicknesses, sometimes even reduced to transparency. Cézanne has alluded to the natural experience of the out-of-doors, but there is none of the transient quality of an impressionist picture. Each object—trees, housetops, road, bridge, mountain, sky—exists in space, separated by air and distance from us and from each other. Each object has weight and volume; but there is no consistent single point *perspective,* no consistent shadow pattern. Objects in the middle and background do not diminish in clarity as they do in traditional painting. Rather, the painted surface is made up of blocks of color; when the color changes, our eyes see that change as a change in direction toward or away from us. We follow the changes from a smoother foreground into a more complex middle and background. The overlapping colored blocks also establish the perception of behind and beside, which the mind tells us are sensations of distance and space, volume and weight. We can identify objects, but Cézanne does not attempt to emulate the texture of objects. Rather, he paints a characteristic contour, color, and mass, drawing on all our knowledge of, and associations with, that object. Mont Sainte-Victoire is a particular mountain made of rugged, substantial, colored blocks that suggest the concepts of height, weight, mass, and, therefore, mountain. The pine tree that spreads over the foreground surface, enveloping the mountain and sky, is not only that tree but every experience of the graceful, linear, light-filtering pine, whose branches and needles flatten against the sky and through which the sky literally shines. The same process has been applied to all objects; they are particular and universal. It is Cézanne's experience of the world, but it is made up of the experiences of seeing that may be everyone's.

Cézanne had always wanted to paint nature and to thereby portray the essential integrity of each object; yet he also wished to integrate each object into the framework that gives it meaning. The forest recedes when we concentrate on one tree, but we *know* that the other trees are there, acting with it to give it meaning. As our focus changes, the importance of one object is transferred to another object; it is this process of seeing that Cézanne has recorded, presenting an experience parallel to that in nature. Rather than creating the illusion of a window on the world, he wanted the canvas and paint to be present in their own right while acting as *abstract* equivalents for the seen world. This sounds difficult and as a painterly ideal it is; but as a convention it resembles those used by medieval or Renaissance artists to portray their world. What makes Cézanne's approach different is that he does not want to represent a medieval world of profound religious mystery or a Renaissance world of idealized and ordered harmonies, but the personal experience of seeing, in which to see is to know, because we come to know by focusing our attention from object to object. Cézanne makes us aware of the processes by which we see, and we enjoy his paintings because they are abstract arrangements of color and form that are pleasing and stimulating in their own right, without reference to the particular or specific world.

Reading Selections

Charles Dickens

From *The Old Curiosity Shop*

This selection describes the arrival of the novel's heroine, little Nell, and her grandfather in the English mill town of Birmingham.

In all their journeying, they had never longed so ardently, they had never so pined and wearied, for the freedom of pure air and open country, as now. No, not even on that memorable morning, when, deserting their old home, they abandoned themselves to the mercies of a strange world, and left all the dumb and senseless things they had known and loved, behind—not even then, had they so yearned for the fresh solitudes of wood, hillside, and field, as now; when the noise and dirt and vapour of the great manufacturing town, reeking with lean misery and hungry wretchedness, hemmed them in on every side, and seemed to shut out hope, and render escape impossible.

"Two days and nights!" thought the child. "He said two days and nights we should have to spend among such scenes as these. Oh! if we live to reach the country once again, if we get clear of these dreadful places, though it is only to lie down and die, with what a grateful heart I shall thank God for so much mercy!"

With thoughts like this, and with some vague design of travelling to a great distance among streams and mountains, where only very poor and simple people lived, and where they might maintain themselves by very humble helping work in farms, free from such terrors as that from which they fled—the child, with no resource but the poor man's gift, and no encouragement but that which flowed from her own heart, and its sense of the truth and right of what she did, nerved herself to this last journey and boldly pursued her task.

"We shall be very slow to-day, dear," she said, as they toiled painfully through the streets; "my feet are sore, and I have pains in all my limbs from the wet of yesterday. I saw that he looked at us and thought of that, when he said how long we should be upon the road."

"It was a dreary way he told us of," returned her grandfather, piteously. "Is there no other road? Will you not let me go some other way than this?"

"Places lie beyond these," said the child, firmly, "where we may live in peace, and be tempted to do no harm. We will take the road that promises to have that end, and we would not turn out of it, if it were a hundred times worse than our fears lead us to expect. We would not, dear, would we?"

"No," replied the old man, wavering in his voice, no less than in his manner. "No. Let us go on. I am ready. I am quite ready, Nell."

The child walked with more difficulty than she had led her companion to expect, for the pains that racked her joints were of no common severity, and every exertion increased them. But they wrung from her no complaint, or look of suffering; and, though the two travellers proceeded very slowly, they did proceed; and clearing the town in course of time, began to feel that they were fairly on their way.

A long suburb of red brick houses,—some with patches of garden ground, where coal-dust and factory smoke darkened the shrinking leaves, and coarse rank flowers; and where the struggling vegetation sickened and sank under the hot breath of kiln and furnace, making them by its presence seem yet more blighting and unwholesome than in the town itself,—a long, flat, straggling suburb passed, they came by slow degrees upon a cheerless region, where not a blade of grass was seen to grow; where not a bud put forth its promise in the spring; where nothing green could live but on the surface of the stagnant pools, which here and there lay idly sweltering by the black roadside.

Advancing more and more into the shadow of this mournful place, its dark depressing influence stole upon their spirits, and filled them with a dismal gloom. On every side, and as far as the eye could see into the heavy distance, tall chimneys, crowding on each other, and presenting that endless repetition of the same dull, ugly form, which is the horror of oppressive dreams, poured out their plague of smoke, obscured the light, and made foul the melancholy air. On mounds of ashes by the wayside, sheltered only by a few rough boards, or rotten pent-house roofs, strange engines spun and writhed like tortured creatures; clanking their iron chains, shrieking in their rapid whirl from time to time as though in torment unendurable, and making the ground tremble with their agonies. Dismantled houses here and there appeared, tottering to the earth, propped up by fragments of others that had fallen down, unroofed, windowless, blackened, desolate, but yet inhabited. Men, women, children, wan in their looks and ragged in attire, tended the engines, fed their tributary fires, begged upon the road, or scowled half-naked from the doorless houses. Then came more of the wrathful monsters, whose like they almost seemed to be in their wildness and their untamed air, screeching and turning round and round again; and still, before, behind, and to the right and left, was the same interminable perspective of brick towers, never ceasing in their black vomit, blasting all things living or inanimate, shutting out the face of day, and closing in on all these horrors with a dense dark cloud.

But night-time in this dreadful spot!—night, when the smoke was changed to fire; when every chimney spirted up its flame; and places, that had been dark vaults all day, now shone red-hot, with figures moving to and fro within their blazing jaws, and calling to one another with hoarse cries—night, when the noise of every strange machine was aggravated by the darkness; when the people near them looked wilder and more savage; when bands of unemployed labourers paraded in the roads, or clustered by torchlight round their leaders, who told them in stern language of their wrongs, and urged them on to frightful cries and threats; when maddened men, armed with sword and firebrand, spurning the tears and prayers of women who would restrain them, rushed forth on errands of terror and destruction, to work no ruin half so surely as their own—night, when carts came rumbling by, filled with rude coffins (for contagious disease and death had been busy with the living crops); when orphans cried, and distracted women shrieked and followed in their wake—night, when some called for bread, and some for drink to drown their cares; and some with tears, and some with staggering feet, and some with bloodshot eyes, went brooding home—night, which, unlike the night that Heaven sends on earth, brought with it no peace, nor quiet, nor signs of blessed sleep—who shall tell the terrors of the night to that young wandering child!

And yet she lay down, with nothing between her and the sky; and, with no fear for herself, for she was past it now, put up a prayer for the poor old man. So very weak and spent she felt, so very calm and unresisting, that she had no thought of any wants of her own, but prayed that God would raise up some friend for *him*. She tried to recall the way they had come, and to look in the direction where the fire by which they had slept last night was burning. She had forgotten to ask the name of the poor man, their friend, and when she had remembered him in her prayers, it seemed ungrateful not to turn one look towards the spot where he was watching.

A penny loaf was all they had had that day. It was very little, but even hunger was forgotten in the strange tranquillity that crept over her senses. She lay down very gently, and, with a quiet smile upon her face, fell into a slumber. It was not like sleep—and yet it must have been, or why those pleasant dreams of the little scholar all night long!

Morning came. Much weaker, diminished powers even of sight and hearing, and yet the child made no complaint—perhaps would have made none, even if she had not that inducement to be silent, travelling by her side. She felt a hopelessness of their ever being extricated together from that forlorn place, a dull conviction that she was very ill, perhaps dying; but no fear or anxiety.

A loathing of food, that she was not conscious of until they expended their last penny in the purchase of another loaf, prevented her partaking even of this poor repast. Her grandfather ate greedily, which she was glad to see.

Their way lay through the same scenes as yesterday, with no variety or improvement. There was the same thick air, difficult to breathe; the same blighted ground, the same hopeless prospect, the same misery and distress. Objects appeared more dim, the noise less, the path more rugged and uneven, for sometimes she stumbled, and became roused, as it were, in the effort to prevent herself from falling. Poor child! the cause was in her tottering feet.

Towards the afternoon, her grandfather complained bitterly of hunger. She approached one of the wretched hovels by the wayside, and knocked with her hand upon the door.

"What would you have here?" said a gaunt miserable man, opening it.

"Charity. A morsel of bread."

"Do you see that?" returned the man hoarsely, pointing to a kind of bundle on the ground. "That's a dead child. I and five hundred other men were thrown out of work three months ago. That is my third dead child, and last. Do you think I have charity to bestow, or a morsel of bread to spare?"

The child recoiled from the door, and it closed upon her. Impelled by strong necessity, she knocked at another: a neighbouring one, which, yielding to the slight pressure of her hand, flew open.

It seemed that a couple of poor families lived in this hovel, for two women, each among children of her own, occupied different portions of the room. In the centre stood a grave gentleman in black who appeared to have just entered, and who held by the arm a boy.

"Here, woman," he said, "here's your deaf and dumb son. You may thank me for restoring him to you. He was brought before me this morning, charged with theft; and with any other boy it would have gone hard, I assure you. But as I had compassion on his infirmities, and thought he might have learnt no better, I have managed to bring him back to you. Take more care of him for the future."

"And won't you give me back *my* son!" said the other woman, hastily rising and confronting him. "Won't you give me back *my* son, sir, who was transported for the same offence!"

"Was *he* deaf and dumb, woman?" asked the gentleman sternly.

"Was he not, sir?"

"You know he was not."

"He was," cried the woman. "He was deaf, dumb, and blind, to all that was good and right, from his cradle. Her boy may have learnt no better! where did mine learn better? where could he? who was there to teach him better, or where was it to be learnt?"

"Peace, woman," said the gentleman, "your boy was in possession of all his senses."

"He was," cried the mother; "and he was the more easy to be led astray because he had them. If you save this boy because he may not know right from wrong, why did you not save mine who was never taught the difference? You gentlemen have as good a right to punish her boy, that God has kept in ignorance of sound and speech, as you have to punish mine, that you kept in ignorance yourselves. How many of the girls and boys—ah, men and women too—that are brought before you and you don't pity, are deaf and dumb in their minds, and go wrong in that state, and are punished in that state, body and soul, while you gentlemen are quarrelling among yourselves whether they ought to learn this or that?—Be a just man, sir, and give me back my son."

"You are desperate," said the gentleman, taking out his snuff-box, "and I am sorry for you."

"I *am* desperate," returned the woman, "and you have made me so. Give me back my son, to work for these helpless children. Be a just man, sir, and for God's sake, as you have had mercy upon this boy, give me back my son!"

The child had seen and heard enough to know that this was not a place at which to ask for alms. She led the old man softly from the door, and they pursued their journey.

QUESTIONS

1. What contrast does Dickens make between the city and the country in this passage? What are the techniques that produce this contrast?
2. Is Dickens's description an entirely objective one? What subjective elements do you find in it?
3. What relationship is established between the industrial environment and the people who inhabit it? How?
4. Compare Engels's description of London in Chapter 28 with Dickens's description of Birmingham. What do the social philosopher and the novelist have in common? What differentiates them?
5. Compare this passage with Courbet's paintings. Can realistic art ever be an exact reproduction of reality? Why or why not? What conventions do realistic artists use?

Charles Baudelaire

From *Les Fleurs du Mal/ The Flowers of Evil*

A Une Passante

La rue assourdissante autour de moi hurlait.
Longue, mince, en grand deuil, douleur majestueuse,
Une femme passa, d'une main fastueuse
Soulevant, balançant le feston et l'ourlet;

Agile et noble, avec sa jambe de statue.
Moi, je buvais, crispé comme un extravagant,
Dans son œil, ciel livide où germe l'ouragan,
La douceur qui fascine et le plaisir qui tue.

Un élair... puis la nuit!—Fugitive beauté
Dont le regard m'a fait soudainement renaître,
Ne te verrai-je plus que dans l'éternité?

Ailleurs, bien loin d'ici! trop tard! *jamais* peut-être!
Car j'ignore où tu fuis, tu ne sais où je vais,
O toi que j'eusse aimée, ô toi qui le savais!

To a Passer-By

Translation by C. F. MacIntyre

Amid the deafening traffic of the town,
Tall, slender, in deep mourning, with majesty,
A woman passed, raising, with dignity
In her poised hand, the flounces of her gown;

Graceful, noble, with a statue's form.
And I drank, trembling as a madman thrills,
From her eyes, ashen sky where brooded storm,
The softness that fascinates, the pleasure that kills.

A flash . . . then night!—O lovely fugitive,
I am suddenly reborn from your swift glance;
Shall I never see you till eternity?

Somewhere, far off! too late! *never*, perchance!
Neither knows where the other goes or lives;
We might have loved, and you knew this might be!

QUESTIONS

1. Why do you think Baudelaire uses the sonnet form in this poem? Note the rhyme scheme in the original.
2. Do you recognize any aspects of romantic love in this poem?
3. What is the tone of this poem, and how does Baudelaire convey it?
4. What role does the city play in this brief "love story"?

The Swan

To Victor Hugo

Translation by Anthony Hecht

I

Andromache, I think of you. The little stream,
A yellowing mirror that onetime beheld
The huge solemnity of your widow's grief
(That other Simois your tears have swelled)[1]
Suddenly flooded the memory's dark soil
As I was crossing the new *Place du Carrousel.*[2]
The old Paris is gone (the face of a town
Is more changeable than the heart of mortal man).

I see what seem the ghosts of these royal barracks,
The rough-hewn capitals, the columns waiting to
crack,
Weeds, and the big rocks greened with standing
water,
And at the window, a jumble of bric-a-brac.

One time a menagerie was on display there,
And there I saw one morning at the hour
Of cold and clarity when Labor rises
And brooms make little cyclones of soot in the air

A swan that had escaped out of his cage,
And there, web-footed on the dry sidewalk,
Dragged his white plumes over the cobblestones,
Lifting his beak at the gutter as if to talk,

And bathing his wings in the sifting city dust,
His heart full of some cool, remembered lake,
Said, "Water, when will you rain? Where is your
thunder?"
I can see him now, straining his twitching neck

Skyward again and again, like the man in Ovid,[3]
Toward an ironic heaven as blank as slate,
And trapped in a ruinous myth, he lifts his head
As if God were the object of his hate.

II

Paris changes, but nothing of my melancholy
Gives way. Foundations, scaffoldings, tackle and
blocks,
And the old suburbs drift off into allegory,
While my frailest memories take on the weight of
rocks.

And so at the Louvre one image weighs me down:
I think of my great swan, the imbecile strain
Of his head, noble and foolish as all the exiled,
Eaten by ceaseless needs—and once again

[1] Allusion to Book III of Virgil's *Aeneid*. Andromache, the widow of the Trojan general Hector, and now a captive in Greece, weeps into the stream she calls "Simois" after a Trojan river.

[2] An interior courtyard of the Louvre palace.

[3] Allusion to Ovid's *Metamorphoses* I.85: "The creator gave man a face turned toward the sun so that he could look directly at it."

Of you, Andromache, from a great husband's arms
Fallen to the whip and mounted lust of Pyrrhus,
And slumped in a heap beside an empty tomb,
(Poor widow of Hector, and bride of Helenus)[4]

And think of the consumptive negress, stamping
In mud, emaciate, and trying to see
The vanished coconuts of hidden Africa
Behind the thickening granite of the mist;

Of whoever has lost what cannot be found again,
Ever, ever; of those who lap up the tears
And nurse at the teats of that motherly she-wolf,
  Sorrow;
Of orphans drying like flowers in empty jars.

So in that forest where my mind is exiled
One memory sounds like brass in the ancient war:
I think of sailors washed up on uncharted islands,
Of prisoners, the conquered, and more, so many
  more.

QUESTIONS

1. How does Baudelaire portray the old and the new Paris in this poem?
2. What different figures represent the theme of exile, and how?
3. What does the swan symbolize?

FROM *Poems in Prose (The Spleen of Paris)*

Translation by Arthur Symons

Windows

He who looks in through an open window never sees so many things as he who looks at a shut window. There is nothing more profound, more mysterious, more fertile, more gloomy, or more dazzling, than a window lighted by a candle. What we can see in the sunlight is always less interesting than what goes on behind the panes of a window. In that dark or luminous hollow, life lives, life dreams, life suffers.

Across the waves of roofs, I can see a woman of middle age, wrinkled, poor, who is always leaning over something, and who never goes out. Out of her face, out of her dress, out of her attitude, out of nothing almost, I have made up the woman's story, and sometimes I say it over to myself with tears.

If it had been a poor old man, I could have made up his just as easily.

And I go to bed, proud of having lived and suffered in others.

Perhaps you will say to me: "Are you sure that it is the real story?" What does it matter, what does any reality outside of myself matter, if it has helped me to live, to feel that I am, and what I am?

The Plaything of the Poor

I should like to give you an idea for an innocent diversion. There are so few amusements that are not guilty ones!

When you go out in the morning for a stroll along the highways, fill your pockets with little penny contrivances—such as the straight merryandrew moved by a single thread, the blacksmiths who strike the anvil, the rider and his horse, with a whistle for a tail—and, along the taverns, at the foot of the trees, make presents of them to the unknown poor children whom you meet. You will see their eyes grow beyond all measure. At first, they will not dare to take; they will doubt their good fortune. Then their hands will eagerly seize the gift, and they will flee as do the cats who go far off to eat the bit you have given them, having learned to distrust man.

On a road, behind the rail of a great garden at the foot of which appeared the glitter of a beautiful mansion struck by the sun, stood a pretty, fresh child, clad in those country garments so full of affectation.

Luxury, freedom from care, and the habitual spectacle of wealth, make these children so pretty that one would think them formed of other paste than the sons of mediocrity or of poverty.

Beside him on the grass lay a splendid toy, fresh as its master, varnished, gilt, clad in a purple robe, covered with plumes and beads of glass. But the child was not occupied with his favored plaything, and this is what he was watching:

On the other side of the rail, on the road, among the thistles and the thorns, was another child, puny, dirty, fuliginous, one of those pariah-brats the beauty of which an impartial eye might discover if, as the eye of the connoisseur divines an ideal painting beneath the varnish of the coach-maker, it cleansed him of the repugnant patina of misery.

Across the symbolic bars which separate two worlds, the highway and the mansion, the poor child was showing the rich child his own toy, which the latter examined eagerly, as a rare and unknown object.

[4] Pyrrhus, the Greek general, abducted Andromache to Troy and married her to Helenus.

Now, this toy, which the ragamuffin was provoking, tormenting, tossing in a grilled box, was a live rat! His parents, doubtless for economy, had taken the toy from life itself.

And the two children were laughing together fraternally, with teeth of equal *whiteness!*

QUESTIONS

1. In what sense do these poems fit the aesthetics of realism, and in what sense do they go beyond realism?
2. In your opinion, are these poems although they are written in prose? Why do you think Baudelaire chose to write them in prose?
3. Do these poems convey a social message? How?
4. Compare Baudelaire's visions of the city with those of Engels, Dickens, Van Gogh, and Degas.

FRIEDRICH NIETZSCHE

Excerpts

Although Nietzsche's works are best read in their entirety, people tend to remember his stunning aphorisms. A few of the influential ones, taken from *The Antichrist, Beyond Good and Evil, Thus Spake Zarathustra,* and *The Will to Power*, are printed below. Consider each one for its implications and possible impact on modern culture and thought.

The Christian religion grew upon a soil of such utter falsification, where the deepest instincts of the ruling factions were opposed to nature and natural values to such an extent, that Christianity became a death struggle against reality which has never been surpassed.

Nothing is more pathological in our pathological modernity than this disease of Christian pity.

What is good? All that elevates the feeling of power, the will to power, the power itself in man.

What is bad? All that proceeds from weakness.

Life is an instinct of growth, for survival, for the accumulation of forces, for power.

Morality is the best of all devices for leading mankind by the nose.

Woman was God's second mistake.

I call Christianity the one great curse, the one intrinsic depravity, . . . the one immortal blemish on the human race.

Life itself is *Will to Power;* self-preservation is only one of the indirect and most frequent results thereof.

The noble soul has reverence for itself.

The Christian faith from the beginning, is sacrifice: the sacrifice of all freedom, all pride, all self-confidence of spirit; it is at the same time subjection, self-derision, and self-mutilation.

There are no eternal facts, as there are no absolute truths.

I teach you the Superman. Man is something that is to be surpassed. What have you done to surpass him?

All the gods are dead; so we now want the superman to live.

God is dead! God remains dead! And we have killed Him!

He who must be a creator in good and evil—verily, he must first be a destroyer, and break values into pieces.

The man who has won his freedom . . . tramples ruthlessly upon that contemptible kind of comfort which tea-grocers, Christians, cows, women, Englishmen and other democrats worship in their dreams.

The world is beautiful, but has a disease called Man.

The Christian resolve to find the world evil and ugly has made the world evil and ugly.

FYODOR DOSTOEVSKY

FROM *The Brothers Karamazov*

Translation by Constance Garnett

The Grand Inquisitor

"Even this must have a preface—that is, a literary preface," laughed Ivan, "and I am a poor hand at making one. You see, my action takes place in the sixteenth century, and at that time, as you probably learnt at school, it was customary in poetry to bring down heavenly powers on earth. Not to speak of Dante, in France, clerks, as well as the monks in the monasteries, used to give regular performances in which the Madonna, the saints, the angels, Christ, and God Himself were brought on the stage. In those days it was done in all simplicity. In Victor Hugo's 'Notre

Dame de Paris' an edifying and gratuitous spectacle was provided for the people in the Hotel de Ville of Paris in the reign of Louis XI. in honour of the birth of the dauphin. It was called *Le bon jugement de la très sainte et gracieuse Vierge Marie*, and she appears herself on the stage and pronounces her *bon jugement*. Similar plays, chiefly from the Old Testament, were occasionally performed in Moscow too, up to the time of Peter the Great. But besides plays there were all sorts of legends and ballads scattered about the world, in which the saints and angels and all the powers of Heaven took part when required. In our monasteries the monks busied themselves in translating, copying, and even composing such poems—and even under the Tatars. There is, for instance, one such poem (of course, from the Greek), 'The Wanderings of Our Lady through Hell,' with descriptions as bold as Dante's. Our Lady visits Hell, and the Archangel Michael leads her through the torments. She sees the sinners and their punishment. There she sees among others one noteworthy set of sinners in a burning lake; some of them sink to the bottom of the lake so that they can't swim out, and 'these God forgets'—an expression of extraordinary depth and force. And so Our Lady, shocked and weeping, falls before the throne of God and begs for mercy for all in Hell—for all she has seen there, and indiscriminately. Her conversation with God is immensely interesting. She beseeches Him, she will not desist, and when God points to the hands and feet of her Son, nailed to the Cross, and asks, 'How can I forgive His tormentors?' she bids all the saints, all the martyrs, all the angels and archangels to fall down with her and pray for mercy on all without distinction. It ends by her winning from God a respite of suffering every year from Good Friday till Trinity day, and the sinners at once raise a cry of thankfulness from Hell, chanting, 'Thou art just, O Lord, in this judgment.' Well, my poem would have been of that kind if it had appeared at that time. He comes on the scene in my poem, but He says nothing, only appears and passes on. Fifteen centuries have passed since He promised to come in His glory, fifteen centuries since His prophet wrote, 'Behold, I come quickly'; 'Of that day and that hour knoweth no man, neither the Son, but the Father,' as He Himself predicted on earth. But humanity awaits him with the same faith and with the same love. Oh, with greater faith, for it is fifteen centuries since man has ceased to see signs from Heaven.

> No signs from Heaven come to-day
> To add to what the heart doth say.

There was nothing left but faith in what the heart doth say. It is true there were many miracles in those days. There were saints who performed miraculous cures; some holy people, according to their biographies, were visited by the Queen of Heaven herself. But the devil did not slumber, and doubts were already arising among men of the truth of these miracles. And just then there appeared in the north of Germany a terrible new heresy. 'A huge star like to a torch' (that is, to a church) 'fell on the sources of the waters and they became bitter.' These heretics began blasphemously denying miracles. But those who remained faithful were all the more ardent in their faith. The tears of humanity rose up to Him as before, awaiting His coming, loved Him, hoped for Him, yearned to suffer and die for Him as before. And so many ages mankind had prayed with faith and fervour, 'O Lord our God, hasten Thy coming,' so many ages called upon Him, that in His infinite mercy He deigned to come down to His servants. Before that day He had come down, He had visited some holy men, martyrs and hermits, as is written in their 'Lives.' Among us, Tyutchev, with absolute faith in the truth of his words, bore witness that

> Bearing the Cross, in slavish dress
> Weary and worn, the Heavenly King
> Our mother, Russia, came to bless,
> And through our land went wandering.

And that certainly was so, I assure you.

"And behold, He deigned to appear for a moment to the people, to the tortured, suffering people, sunk in iniquity, but loving Him like children. My story is laid in Spain, in Seville, in the most terrible time of the Inquisition, when fires were lighted every day to the glory of God, and 'in the splendid *auto da fé* the wicked heretics were burnt.' Oh, of course, this was not the coming in which He will appear according to His promise at the end of time in all His heavenly glory, and which will be sudden 'as lightning flashing from east to west.' No, He visited His children only for a moment, and there where the flames were crackling round the heretics. In His infinite mercy He came once more among men in that human shape in which He walked among men for three years fifteen centuries ago. He came down to the 'hot pavement' of the southern town in which on the day before almost a hundred heretics had, *ad majorem gloriam Dei*, been burnt by the cardinal, the Grand Inquisitor, in a magnificent *auto da fé*, in the presence of the king, the court, the knights, the cardinals, the most charming ladies of the court, and the whole population of Seville.

"He came softly, unobserved, and yet, strange to say, every one recognised Him. That might be one of the best passages in the poem. I mean, why they recognised Him. The people are irresistibly drawn to Him, they surround Him, they flock about Him, follow Him. He moves silently in their midst with a gentle smile of infinite compassion. The sun of love burns in His heart, light and power shine from His eyes, and their radiance, shed on the people, stirs their hearts with responsive love. He holds out His hands to them, blesses them, and a healing virtue comes from contact with Him, even with His garments. An old man in the crowd, blind from childhood, cries out, 'O Lord, heal me and I shall see Thee!' and, as it were, scales fall from his eyes and the blind man sees Him. The crowd weeps and kisses the earth under His feet. Children throw flowers before Him, sing, and cry hosannah. 'It is He—it is He!' all repeat. 'It must be He, it can be no one but Him!' He stops at the steps of the Seville cathedral at the moment when the weeping mourners are bringing in a little open white coffin. In it lies a child of seven, the only daughter of a prominent citizen. The dead child lies hidden in flowers. 'He will raise your child,' the crowd shouts to the weeping mother. The priest, coming to meet the coffin, looks perplexed, and frowns, but the mother of the dead child throws herself at His feet with a wail. 'If it is Thou, raise my child!' she cries, holding out her hands to Him. The procession halts, the coffin is laid on the steps at His feet. He looks with compassion, and His lips once more softly pronounce, 'Maiden, arise!' and the maiden arises. The little girl sits up in the coffin and looks round, smiling with wide-open wondering eyes, holding a bunch of white roses they had put in her hand.

"There are cries, sobs, confusion among the people, and at that moment the cardinal himself, the Grand Inquisitor, passes by the cathedral. He is an old man, almost ninety, tall and erect, with a withered face and sunken eyes, in which there is still a gleam of light. He is not dressed in his gorgeous cardinal's robes, as he was the day before, when he was burning the enemies of the Roman Church—at that moment he was wearing his coarse, old, monk's cassock. At a distance behind him come his gloomy assistants and slaves and the 'holy guard.' He stops at the sight of the crowd and watches it from a distance. He sees everything; he sees them set the coffin down at His feet, sees the child rise up, and his face darkens. He knits his thick grey brows and his eyes gleam with a sinister fire. He holds out his finger and bids the guards take Him. And such is his power, so completely are the people cowed into submission and trembling obedience to him, that the crowd immediately make way for the guards, and in the midst of deathlike silence they lay hands on Him and lead Him away. The crowd instantly bows down to the earth, like one man, before the old inquisitor. He blesses the people in silence and passes on. The guards lead their prisoner to the close, gloomy vaulted prison in the ancient palace of the Holy Inquisition and shut Him in it. The day passes and is followed by the dark, burning 'breathless' night of Seville. The air is 'fragrant with laurel and lemon.' In the pitch darkness the iron door of the prison is suddenly opened and the Grand Inquisitor himself comes in with a light in his hand. He is alone; the door is closed at once behind him. He stands in the doorway and for a minute or two gazes into His face. At last he goes up slowly, sets the light on the table and speaks.

"'Is it Thou? Thou?' but receiving no answer, he adds at once, 'Don't answer, be silent. What canst Thou say, indeed? I know too well what Thou wouldst say. And Thou hast no right to add anything to what Thou hadst said of old. Why, then, art Thou come to hinder us? For Thou hast come to hinder us, and Thou knowest that. But dost Thou know what will be to-morrow? I know not who Thou art and care not to know whether it is Thou or only a semblance of Him, but to-morrow I shall condemn Thee and burn Thee at the stake as the worst of heretics. And the very people who have to-day kissed Thy feet, to-morrow at the faintest sign from me will rush to heap up the embers of Thy fire. Knowest Thou that? Yes, maybe Thou knowest it,' he added with thoughtful penetration, never for a moment taking his eyes off the Prisoner."

"I don't quite understand, Ivan. What does it mean?" Alyosha, who had been listening in silence, said with a smile. "Is it simply a wild fantasy, or a mistake on the part of the old man—some impossible *quid pro quo*?"

"Take it as the last," said Ivan, laughing, "if you are so corrupted by modern realism and can't stand anything fantastic. If you like it to be a case of mistaken identity, let it be so. It is true," he went on, laughing, "the old man was ninety, and he might well be crazy over his set idea. He might have been struck by the appearance of the Prisoner. It might, in fact, be simply his ravings, the delusion of an old man of ninety, over-excited by the *auto da fé* of a hundred heretics the day before. But does it matter to us after all whether it was a mistake of identity or a wild fantasy? All that matters is that the old man should speak out, should speak openly of what he has thought in silence for ninety years."

"And the Prisoner too is silent? Does He look at him and not say a word?"

"That's inevitable in any case," Ivan laughed again. "The old man has told Him He hasn't the right to add anything to what He has said of old. One may say it is the most fundamental feature of Roman Catholicism, in my opinion at least. 'All has been given by Thee to the Pope,' they say, 'and all, therefore, is still in the Pope's hands, and there is no need for Thee to come now at all. Thou must not meddle for the time, at least.' That's how they speak and write too—the Jesuits, at any rate. I have read it myself in the works of their theologians. 'Hast Thou the right to reveal to us one of the mysteries of that world from which Thou hast come?' my old man asks Him, and answers the question for Him. 'No, Thou hast not; that Thou mayest not add to what has been said of old, and mayest not take from men the freedom which Thou didst exalt when Thou wast on earth. Whatsoever Thou revealest anew will encroach on men's freedom of faith; for it will be manifest as a miracle, and the freedom of their faith was dearer to Thee than anything in those days fifteen hundred years ago. Didst Thou not often say then, "I will make you free"? But now Thou has seen these "free" men,' the old man adds suddenly, with a pensive smile. 'Yes, we've paid dearly for it,' he goes on, looking sternly at Him, 'but at last we have completed that work in Thy name. For fifteen centuries we have been wrestling with Thy freedom, but now it is ended and over for good. Dost Thou not believe that it's over for good? Thou lookest meekly at me and deignest not even to be wroth with me. But let me tell Thee that now, to-day, people are more persuaded than ever that they have perfect freedom, yet they have brought their freedom to us and laid it humbly at our feet. But that has been our doing. Was this what Thou didst? Was this Thy freedom?' "

"I don't understand again," Alyosha broke in. "Is he ironical, is he jesting?"

"Not a bit of it! He claims it as a merit for himself and his Church that at last they have vanquished freedom and have done so to make men happy. 'For now' (he is speaking of the Inquisition, of course) 'for the first time it has become possible to think of the happiness of men. Man was created a rebel; and how can rebels be happy? Thou wast warned,' he says to Him. 'Thou hast had no lack of admonitions and warnings, but Thou didst not listen to those warnings; Thou didst reject the only way by which men might be made happy. But, fortunately, departing Thou didst hand on the work to us. Thou has promised, Thou hast established by Thy word, Thou has given to us the right to bind and to unbind, and now, of course, Thou canst not think of taking it away. Why, then, hast Thou come to hinder us?' "

"And what's the meaning of 'no lack of admonitions and warnings'?" asked Alyosha.

"Why, that's the chief part of what the old man must say.

" 'The wise and dread Spirit, the spirit of self-destruction and nonexistence,' the old man goes on, 'the great spirit talked with Thee in the wilderness, and we are told in the books that he "tempted" Thee. Is that so? And could anything truer be said than what he revealed to Thee in three questions and what Thou didst reject, and what in the books is called "the temptation"? And yet if there has ever been on earth a real stupendous miracle, it took place on that day, on the day of the three temptations. The statement of those three questions was itself the miracle. If it were possible to imagine simply for the sake of argument that those three questions of the dread spirit had perished utterly from the books, and that we had to restore them and to invent them anew, and to do so had gathered together all the wise men of the earth—rulers, chief priests, learned men, philosophers, poets—and had set them the task to invent three questions, such as would not only fit the occasion, but express in three words, three human phrases, the whole future history of the world and of humanity—dost Thou believe that all the wisdom of the earth united could have invented anything in depth and force equal to the three questions which were actually put to Thee then by the wise and mighty spirit in the wilderness? From those questions alone, from the miracle of their statement, we can see that we have here to do not with the fleeting human intelligence, but with the absolute and eternal. For in those three questions the whole subsequent history of mankind is, as it were, brought together into one whole, and foretold, and in them are united all the unsolved historical contradictions of human nature. At the time it could not be so clear, since the future was unknown; but now that fifteen hundred years have passed, we see that everything in those three questions was so justly divined and foretold, and has been so truly fulfilled, that nothing can be added to them or taken from them.

" 'Judge Thyself who was right—Thou or he who questioned Thee then? Remember the first question; its meaning, in other words, was this: "Thou wouldst go into the world, and art going with empty hands, with some promise of freedom which men in their simplicity and their natural unruliness cannot even understand, which they fear and dread—for nothing has ever been more insupportable for a man and a human society than freedom. But seest Thou these stones in this parched and barren wilderness? Turn them into bread, and mankind will run after Thee like a flock of sheep, grateful and obedient, though for ever trembling, lest Thou withdraw Thy hand and deny them Thy bread." But Thou wouldst not deprive man of freedom and didst reject the offer, thinking, what is that freedom worth, if obedience is bought with bread? Thou didst reply that man lives not by bread alone. But dost Thou know that for the sake of that earthly bread the spirit of the earth will rise up against Thee and will strive with Thee and overcome Thee, and all will follow him, crying, "Who can compare with this beast? He has given us fire from heaven!" Dost Thou know that the ages will pass, and humanity will proclaim by the lips of their sages that there is no crime, and therefore no sin; there is only hunger? "Feed men, and then ask of them virtue!" That's what they'll write on the banner, which they will raise against Thee, and with which they will destroy Thy temple. Where Thy temple stood will rise a new building; the terrible tower of Babel will be built again, and though, like the one of old, it will not be finished, yet Thou mightest have prevented that new tower and have cut short the sufferings of men for a thousand years; for they will come back to us after a thousand years of agony with their tower. They will seek us again, hidden underground in the catacombs, for we shall be again persecuted and tortured. They will find us and cry to us, "Feed us, for those who have promised us fire from heaven haven't given it!" And then we shall finish building their tower, for he finishes the building who feeds them. And we alone shall feed them in Thy name, declaring falsely that it is in Thy name. Oh, never, never can they feed themselves without us! No science will give them bread so long as they remain free. In the end they will lay their freedom at our feet, and say to us, "Make us your slaves, but feed us." They will understand themselves, at last, that freedom and bread enough for all are inconceivable together, for never, never will they be able to share between them! They will be convinced, too, that they can never be free, for they are weak, vicious, worthless and rebellious. Thou didst promise them the bread of Heaven, but, I repeat again, can it compare with earthly bread in the eyes of the weak, ever sinful and ignoble race of man? And if for the sake of the bread of Heaven thousands and tens of thousands shall follow Thee, what is to become of the millions and tens of thousands of millions of creatures who will not have the strength to forgo the earthly bread for the sake of the heavenly? Or dost Thou care only for the tens of thousands of the great and strong, while the millions, numerous as the sands of the sea, who are weak but love Thee, must exist only for the sake of the great and strong? No, we care for the weak too. They are sinful and rebellious, but in the end they too will become obedient. They will marvel at us and look on us as gods, because we are ready to endure the freedom which they have found so dreadful and to rule over them—so awful it will seem to them to be free. But we shall tell them that we are Thy servants and rule them in Thy name. We shall deceive them again, for we will not let Thee come to us again. That deception will be our suffering, for we shall be forced to lie.

"'This is the significance of the first question in the wilderness, and this is what Thou has rejected for the sake of that freedom which Thou hast exalted above everything. Yet in this question lies hid the great secret of this world. Choosing "bread," Thou wouldst have satisfied the universal and everlasting craving of humanity—to find some one to worship. So long as man remains free he strives for nothing so incessantly and so painfully as to find some one to worship. But man seeks to worship what is established beyond dispute, so that all men would agree at once to worship it. For these pitiful creatures are concerned not only to find what one or the other can worship, but to find something that all would believe in and worship; what is essential is that all may be *together* in it. This craving for *community* of worship is the chief misery of every man individually and of all humanity from the beginning of time. For the sake of common worship they've slain each other with the sword. They have set up gods and challenged one another, "Put away your gods and come and worship ours, or we will kill you and your gods!" And so it will be to the end of the world, even when gods disappear from the earth; they will fall down before idols just the same. Thou didst know, Thou couldst not but have known, this fundamental secret of human nature, but Thou didst reject the one infallible banner which was offered Thee to make all men bow down to Thee alone—the banner of earthly bread; and Thou hast rejected it for the sake of freedom and the bread of Heaven. Behold what Thou didst further. And all again in the name of freedom! I tell Thee that man is tormented by no greater anxiety than to find some one quickly to whom he can hand over that gift of freedom with which the ill-fated creature is born. But only one who can appease their conscience can take over their freedom. In bread there was offered Thee an invincible banner; give bread, and man will worship Thee, for nothing is more certain than bread.

But if some one else gains possession of his conscience—oh! then he will cast away Thy bread and follow after him who has ensnared his conscience. In that Thou wast right. For the secret of man's being is not only to live but to have something to live for. Without a stable conception of the object of life, man would not consent to go on living, and would rather destroy himself than remain on earth, though he had bread in abundance. That is true. But what happened? Instead of taking men's freedom from them, Thou didst make it greater than ever! Didst Thou forget that man prefers peace, and even death, to freedom of choice in the knowledge of good and evil? Nothing is more seductive for man than his freedom of conscience, but nothing is a greater cause of suffering. And behold, instead of giving a firm foundation for setting the conscience of man at rest for ever, Thou didst choose all that is exceptional, vague and enigmatic; Thou didst choose what was utterly beyond the strength of men, acting as though Thou didst not love them at all—Thou who didst come to give Thy life for them! Instead of taking possession of men's freedom, Thou didst increase it, and burdened the spiritual kingdom of mankind with its sufferings for ever. Thou didst desire man's free love, that he should follow Thee freely, enticed and taken captive by Thee. In place of the rigid ancient law, man must hereafter with free heart decide for himself what is good and what is evil, having only Thy image before him as his guide. But didst Thou not know he would at last reject even Thy image and Thy truth, if he is weighed down with the fearful burden of free choice? They will cry aloud at last that the truth is not in Thee, for they could not have been left in greater confusion and suffering than Thou hast caused, laying upon them so many cares and unanswerable problems.

"'So that, in truth, Thou didst Thyself lay the foundation for the destruction of Thy kingdom, and no one is more to blame for it. Yet what was offered Thee? There are three powers, three powers alone, able to conquer and to hold captive for ever the conscience of these impotent rebels for their happiness—those forces are miracle, mystery and authority. Thou hast rejected all three and hast set the example for doing so. When the wise and dread spirit set Thee on the pinnacle of the temple and said to Thee, "If Thou wouldst know whether Thou art the Son of God then cast Thyself down, for it is written: the angels shall hold him up lest he fall and bruise himself, and Thou shalt know then whether Thou art the Son of God and shalt prove then how great is Thy faith in Thy Father." But Thou didst refuse and wouldst not cast Thyself down. Oh! of course, Thou didst proudly and well like God; but the weak, unruly race of men, are they gods? Oh, Thou didst know then that in taking one step, in making one movement to cast Thyself down, Thou wouldst be tempting God and have lost all Thy faith in Him, and wouldst have been dashed to pieces against that earth which Thou didst come to save. And the wise spirit that tempted Thee would have rejoiced. But I ask again, are there many like Thee? And couldst Thou believe for one moment that men, too, could face such a temptation? Is the nature of men such, that they can reject miracle, and at the great moments of their life, the moments of their deepest, most agonising spiritual difficulties, cling only to the free verdict of the heart? Oh, Thou didst know that Thy deed would be recorded in books, would be handed down to remote times and the utmost ends of the earth, and Thou didst hope that man, following Thee, would cling to God and not ask for a miracle. But Thou didst not know that when man rejects miracle he rejects God too; for man seeks not so much God as the miraculous. And as man cannot bear to be without the miraculous, he will create new miracles of his own for himself, and will worship deeds of sorcery and witchcraft, though he might be a hundred times over a rebel, heretic and infidel. Thou didst not come down from the Cross when they shouted to Thee, mocking and reviling Thee, "Come down from the cross and we will believe that Thou art He." Thou didst not come down, for again Thou wouldst not enslave man by a miracle, and didst crave faith given freely, not based on miracle. Thou didst crave for free love and not the base raptures of the slave before the might that has overawed him for ever. But Thou didst think too highly of men therein, for they are slaves, of course, though rebellious by nature. Look round and judge; fifteen centuries have passed, look upon them. Whom hast Thou raised up to Thyself? I swear, man is weaker and baser by nature than Thou hast believed him! Can he, can he do what Thou didst? By showing him so much respect, Thou didst, as it were, cease to feel for him, for Thou didst ask far too much from him—Thou who hast loved him more than Thyself! Respecting him less, Thou wouldst have asked less of him. That would have been more like love, for his burden would have been lighter. He is weak and vile. What though he is everywhere now rebelling against our power, and proud of his rebellion? It is the pride of a child and a schoolboy. They are little children rioting and barring out the teacher at school. But their childish delight will end; it will cost them dear. They will cast down temples and drench the earth with blood. But they will see at last, the foolish children, that, though they are rebels, they are impotent rebels, unable to keep up their own rebellion. Bathed in their foolish tears, they will recognise at last that He who created them rebels must have meant to mock at them. They will say this in despair, and their utterance will be a blasphemy which will make them more unhappy still, for man's nature cannot bear blasphemy, and in the end always avenges it on itself. And so unrest, confusion and unhappiness—that is the present lot of man after Thou didst bear so much for their freedom! Thy great prophet tells in vision and in image, that he saw all those who took part in the first resurrection and that there were of each tribe twelve thousand. But if there were so many of them, they must have been not men but gods. They had borne Thy cross, they had endured scores of years in the barren, hungry wilderness, living upon locusts and roots—and Thou mayest indeed point with pride at those children of freedom, of free love, of free and splendid sacrifice for Thy name. But remember that they were only some thousands; and what of the rest? And how are the other weak ones to blame, because they could not endure what the strong have endured? How is the weak soul to blame that it is unable to receive such terrible gifts? Canst Thou have simply come to the elect and for the elect? But if so, it is a mystery and we cannot understand it. And if it is a mystery, we too have a right to preach a mystery, and to teach them that it's not the free judgment of their hearts, not love that matters, but a mystery which they must follow blindly, even against their conscience. So we have done. We have corrected Thy work and have founded it upon *miracle, mystery* and *authority*. And men rejoiced that they were again led like sheep, and that the terrible gift that had brought them such suffering, was, at last, lifted from their hearts. Were we right teaching them this? Speak! Did we not love mankind, so meekly acknowledging their feebleness, lovingly lightening their burden, and permitting their weak nature even sin with our sanction? Why hast Thou come now to hinder us? And why dost Thou look silently and searchingly at me with Thy mild eyes? Be angry. I don't want Thy love, for I love Thee not. And what use is it for me to hide anything from Thee? Don't I know to Whom I am speaking? All that I can say is known to Thee already. And is it for me to conceal from Thee our mystery? Perhaps it is Thy will to hear it from my lips. Listen, then. We are not working with Thee, but with *him*—that is our mystery. It's long—eight centuries—since we have been on *his* side and not on Thine. Just eight centuries ago, we took from him what Thou didst reject with scorn, that last gift he offered Thee, showing Thee all the kingdoms of the earth. We took from him Rome and the sword of Caesar, and proclaimed ourselves sole rulers of the earth, though hitherto we have not been able to complete our work. But whose fault is that? Oh, the work is only beginning, but it has begun. It has long to await completion and the earth has yet much to suffer, but we shall triumph and shall be Caesar's, and then we shall plan the universal happiness of man. But Thou mightest have taken even then the sword of Caesar. Why didst Thou reject that last gift? Hadst Thou accepted that last counsel of the mighty spirit, Thou wouldst have accomplished all that man seeks on earth—that is, some one to worship, some one to keep his conscience, and some means of uniting all in one unanimous and harmonious ant-heap, for the craving for universal unity is the third and last anguish of men. Mankind as a whole has always striven to organise a universal state. There have been many great nations with great histories, but the more highly they were developed the more unhappy they were, for they felt more acutely than other people the craving for world-wide union. The great conquerors, Timours and Ghenghis-Khans, whirled like hurricanes over the face of the earth striving to subdue its people, and they too were but the unconscious expression of the same craving for universal unity. Hadst Thou taken the world and Caesar's purple, Thou wouldst have founded the universal state and have given universal peace. For who can rule men if not he who holds their conscience and their bread in his hands. We have taken the sword of Caesar, and in taking it, of course, have rejected Thee and followed *him*. Oh, ages are yet to come of the confusion of free thought, of their science and cannibalism. For having begun to build their tower of Babel without us, they will end, of course, with cannibalism. But then the beast will crawl to us and lick our feet and spatter them with tears of blood. And we shall sit upon the beast and raise the cup, and on it will be written, "Mystery." But then, and only then, the reign of peace and happiness will come for men. Thou art proud of Thine elect, but Thou hast only the elect, while we give rest to all. And besides, how many of those elect, those mighty ones who could become elect, have grown weary waiting for Thee, and have transferred and will transfer the powers of their spirit and the warmth of their heart to the other camp, and end by raising their *free* banner against Thee. Thou didst Thyself lift up that banner. But with us all will be happy and will no more rebel nor destroy one another as under Thy freedom. Oh, we shall persuade them that they will only become free when they renounce their freedom to us and submit to us. And shall we be right or shall we be lying? They will be convinced that we are right, for they will remember the horrors of slavery and confusion to which Thy freedom brought them. Freedom, free thought and science, will lead them into such straits and will bring them face to face with such marvels and insoluble mysteries, that some of them, the fierce and rebellious, will destroy themselves, others, rebellious but weak, will destroy one another, while the rest, weak and unhappy, will crawl fawning to our feet and whine to us: "Yes, you were right, you alone possess His mystery, and we come back to you, save us from ourselves!"

"'Receiving bread from us, they will see clearly that we take the bread made by their hands from them, to give it to them, without any miracle. They will see that we do not change the stones to bread, but in truth they will be more thankful for taking it from our hands than for the bread itself! For they will remember only too well that in old days, without our help, even the bread they made turned to stones in their hands, while since they have come back to us, the very stones have turned to bread in their hands. Too, too well they know the value of complete submission! And until men know that, they will be unhappy. Who is most to blame for their not knowing it, speak? Who scattered the flock and sent it astray on unknown paths? But the flock will come together again and will submit once more, and then it will be once for all. Then we shall give them the quiet humble happiness of weak creatures such as they are by nature. Oh, we shall persuade them at last not to be proud, for Thou didst lift them up and thereby taught them to be proud. We shall show them that they are weak, that they are only pitiful children, but that childlike happiness is the sweetest of all. They will become timid and will look to us and huddle close to us in fear, as chicks to the hen. They will marvel at us and will be awe-stricken before us, and will be proud at our being so powerful and clever, that we have been able to subdue such a turbulent flock of thousands of millions. They will tremble impotently before our wrath, their minds will grow fearful, they will be quick to shed tears like women and children, but they will be just as ready at a sign from us to pass to laughter and rejoicing, to happy mirth and childish song. Yes, we shall set them to work, but in their leisure hours we shall make their life like a child's game, with children's songs and innocent dance. Oh, we shall allow them even sin, they are weak and helpless, and they will love us like children because we allow them to sin. We shall tell them that every sin will be expiated, if it is done with our permission, that we allow them to sin because we love them, and the punishment for these sins we take upon ourselves. And we shall take it upon ourselves, and they will adore us as their saviour who have taken on themselves their sins before God. And they will have no secrets from us. We shall allow or forbid them to live with their wives and mistresses, to have or not to have children—according to whether they have been obedient or disobedient—and they will submit to us gladly and cheerfully. The most painful secrets of their conscience, all, all they will bring to us, and we shall have an answer for all. And they will be glad to believe our answer, for it will save them from the great anxiety and terrible agony they endure at present in making a free decision for themselves. And all will be happy, all the millions of creatures except the hundred thousand who rule over them. For only we, we who guard the mystery, shall be unhappy. There will be thousands of millions of happy babes, and a hundred thousand sufferers who have taken upon themselves the curse of the knowledge of good and evil. Peacefully they will die, peacefully they will expire in Thy name, and beyond the grave they will find nothing but death. But we shall keep the secret, and for their happiness we shall allure them with the reward of heaven and eternity. Though if there were anything in the other world, it certainly would not be for such as they. It is prophesied that Thou wilt come again in victory, Thou wilt come with Thy chosen, the proud and strong, but we will say that they have only saved themselves, but we have saved all. We are told that the harlot who sits upon the beast, and holds in her hands the *mystery*, shall be put to shame, that the weak will rise up again, and will rend her royal purple and will strip naked her loathsome body. But then I will stand up and point out to Thee the thousand millions of happy children who have known no sin. And we who have taken their sins upon us for their happiness will stand up before Thee and say: "Judge us if Thou canst and darest." Know that I fear Thee not. Know that I too have been in the wilderness, I too have lived on roots and locusts, I too prized the freedom with which Thou hast blessed men, and I too was striving to stand among Thy elect, among the strong and powerful, thirsting "to make up the number." But I awakened and would not serve madness. I turned back and joined the ranks of those *who have corrected Thy work*. I left the proud and went back to the humble, for the happiness of the humble. What I say to Thee will come to pass, and our dominion will be built up. I repeat, to-morrow Thou shalt see that obedient flock who at a sign from me will hasten to heap up the hot cinders about the pile on which I shall burn Thee for coming to hinder us. For if any one has ever deserved our fires, it is Thou. To-morrow I shall burn Thee. *Dixi.*'"

Ivan stopped. He was carried away as he talked and spoke with excitement; when he had finished, he suddenly smiled.

Alyosha had listened in silence; towards the end he was greatly moved and seemed several times on the point of interrupting, but restrained himself. Now his words came with a rush.

"But... that's absurd!" he cried, flushing. "Your poem is in praise of Jesus, not in blame of Him—as you meant it to be. And who will believe you about freedom? Is that the way to understand it? That's not the idea of it in the Orthodox Church.... That's Rome, and not even the whole of Rome, it's false—those are the worst of the Catholics, the Inquisitors, the Jesuits!... And there could not be such a fantastic creature as your Inquisitor. What are these sins of mankind they take on themselves? Who are these keepers of the mystery who have taken some curse upon themselves for the happiness of mankind? When have they been seen? We know the Jesuits, they are spoken ill of, but surely they are not what you describe? They are not that at all, not at all.... They are simply the Romish army for the earthly sovereignty of the world in the future, with the Pontiff of Rome for Emperor... that's their ideal, but there's no sort of mystery or lofty melancholy about it.... It's simple lust of power, of filthy earthly gain, of domination—something like a universal serfdom with them as masters—that's all they stand for. They don't even believe in God perhaps. Your suffering inquisitor is a mere fantasy."

"Stay, stay," laughed Ivan, "how hot you are! A fantasy you say, let it be so! Of course it's a fantasy. But allow me to say: do you really think that the Roman Catholic movement of the last centuries is actually nothing but the lust of power, of filthy earthly gain? Is that Father Païssy's teaching?"

"No, no, on the contrary, Father Païssy did once say something rather the same as you... but of course it's not the same, not a bit the same," Alyosha hastily corrected himself.

"A precious admission, in spite of your 'not a bit the same.' I ask you why your Jesuits and Inquisitors have united simply for vile material gain? Why can there not be among them one martyr oppressed by great sorrow and loving humanity? You see, only suppose that there was one such man among all those who desire nothing but filthy material gain—if there's only one like my old inquisitor, who had himself eaten roots in the desert and made frenzied efforts to subdue his flesh to make himself free and perfect. But yet all his life he loved humanity, and suddenly his eyes were opened, and he saw that it is no great moral blessedness to attain perfection and freedom, if at the same time one gains the conviction that millions of God's creatures have been created as a mockery, that they will never be capable of using their freedom, that these poor rebels can never turn into giants to complete the tower, that it was not for such geese that the great idealist dreamt his dream of harmony. Seeing all that he turned back and joined—the clever people. Surely that could have happened?"

"Joined whom, what clever people?" cried Alyosha, completely carried away. "They have no such great cleverness and no mysteries and secrets.... Perhaps nothing but atheism, that's all their secret. Your inquisitor does not believe in God, that's his secret!"

"What if it is so! At last you have guessed it. It's perfectly true that that's the whole secret, but isn't that suffering, at least for a man like that, who has wasted his whole life in the desert and yet could not shake off his incurable love of humanity? In his old age he reached the clear conviction that nothing but the advice of the great dread spirit could build up any tolerable sort of life for the feeble, unruly 'incomplete, empirical creatures created in jest.' And so, convinced of this, he sees that he must follow the counsel of the wise spirit, the dread spirit of death and destruction, and therefore accept lying and deception, and lead men consciously to death and destruction, and yet deceive them all the way so that they may not notice where they are being led, that the poor blind creatures may at least on the way think themselves happy. And note, the deception is in the name of Him in Whose ideal the old man had so fervently believed all his life long. Is not that tragic? And if only one such stood at the head of the whole army 'filled with the lust of power only for the sake of filthy gain'—would not one such be enough to make a tragedy? More than that, one such standing at the head is enough to create the actual leading idea of the Roman Church with all its armies and Jesuits, its highest idea. I tell you frankly that I firmly believe that there has always been such a man among those who stood at the head of the movement. Who knows, there may have been some such even among the Roman Popes. Who knows, perhaps the spirit of that accursed old man who loves mankind so obstinately in his own way, is to be found even now in a whole multitude of such old men, existing not by chance but by agreement, as a secret league formed long ago for the guarding of the mystery, to guard it from the weak and the unhappy, so as to make them happy. No doubt it is so, and so it must be indeed. I fancy that even among the Masons there's something of the same mystery at the bottom, and that that's why the Catholics so detest the Masons as their rivals breaking up the unity of the idea, while it is so essential that there should be one flock and one shepherd. ... But from the way I defend my idea I might be an author impatient of your criticism. Enough of it."

"You are perhaps a Mason yourself!" broke suddenly from Alyosha. "You don't believe in God," he added, speaking this time very sorrowfully. He fancied besides that his brother was looking at him ironically. "How does your poem end?" he asked, suddenly looking down. "Or was it the end?"

"I meant to end it like this. When the Inquisitor ceased speaking he waited some time for his Prisoner to answer him. His silence weighed down upon him. He saw that the Prisoner had listened intently all the time, looking gently in his face and evidently not wishing to reply. The old man longed for Him to say something, however bitter and terrible. But He suddenly approached the old man in silence and softly kissed him on his bloodless aged lips. That was all his answer. The old man shuddered. His lips moved. He went to the door, opened it, and said to Him: 'Go, and come no more.... Come not at all, never, never!' And he let Him out into the dark alleys of the town. The Prisoner went away."

"And the old man?"

"The kiss glows in his heart, but the old man adheres to his idea."

"And you with him, you too?" cried Alyosha, mournfully.

Ivan laughed.

"Why, it's all nonsense, Alyosha. It's only a senseless poem of a senseless student, who could never write two lines of verse. Why do you take it so seriously? Surely you don't suppose I am going straight off to the Jesuits, to join the men who are correcting His work? Good Lord, it's no business of mine. I told you, all I want is to live on to thirty, and then ... dash the cup to the ground!"

"But the little sticky leaves, and the precious tombs, and the blue sky, and the woman you love! How will you live, how will you love them?" Alyosha cried sorrowfully. "With such a hell in your heart and your head, how can you? No, that's just what you are going away for, to join them ... if not, you will kill yourself, you can't endure it!"

"There is a strength to endure everything," Ivan said with a cold smile.

"What strength?"

"The strength of the Karamazovs—the strength of the Karamazov baseness."

"To sink into debauchery, to stifle your soul with corruption, yes?"

"Possibly even that ... only perhaps till I am thirty I shall escape it, and then."

"How will you escape it? By what will you escape it? That's impossible with your ideas."

"In the Karamazov way, again."

"'Everything is lawful,' you mean? Everything is lawful, is that it?"

Ivan scowled, and all at once turned strangely pale.

"Ah, you've caught up yesterday's phrase, which so offended Miüsov—and which Dmitri pounced upon so naïvely and paraphrased!" he smiled queerly. "Yes, if you like, 'everything is lawful' since the word has been said. I won't deny it. And Mitya's version isn't bad."

Alyosha looked at him in silence.

"I thought that going away from here I have you at least," Ivan said suddenly, with unexpected feeling; "but now I see that there is no place for me even in your heart, my dear hermit. The formula, 'all is lawful,' I won't renounce—will you renounce me for that, yes?"

Alyosha got up, went to him and softly kissed him on the lips.

"That's plagiarism," cried Ivan, highly delighted. "You stole that from my poem. Thank you though. Get up, Alyosha, it's time we were going, both of us."

QUESTIONS

1. Reconstruct, as precisely as you can, the line of argument followed by the Grand Inquisitor. How does he arrive at the conclusions that Christ has caused human beings to suffer, that he is indifferent and unconcerned toward the masses of people, and that he is a heretic?
2. Describe the Grand Inquisitor's concept of human nature. Why does he believe that human beings fear freedom?
3. Does Christ answer the arguments of the Grand Inquisitor? If so, in what way? How does his view of human nature differ?
4. Whose side is the author on, in your opinion?
5. Which view of human nature seems truer to you? Which one has history borne out?

Industrialism and the Humanities

The effects of industrialism on our modern world have been almost incalculable. In addition to restructuring the economic and social fabric of Western society, the so-called Industrial Revolution contributed significantly to the ways in which human beings perceive themselves and their world.

Social, Political, and Scientific Thought

Much of the social and political thought of the nineteenth century takes the new conditions into account by extending the egalitarian ideas of the Enlightenment into the economic sphere. Early liberal stress on individual initiative in the marketplace was clearly an outgrowth of Enlightenment principles, but the cost of laissez-faire capitalism in human suffering, as Friedrich Engels's vivid descriptions of working-class life demonstrate, had to be reckoned with. Among the various socialist thinkers, Karl Marx, whose theories have produced societies that might astound him, understood best the economic, social, and human consequences of industrialism.

Whereas most nineteenth-century socialist thought approached the problems of society from a collective viewpoint—seeing a person not so much as an individual but as a member of a group or class—the new liberalism from the middle decades of the century endeavored to foster social and economic justice while preserving an individualistic perspective. Its call for selective government intervention in the marketplace was based on the belief that such regulation would enhance the liberty of all while preventing the tyranny of the few. These newer liberals also urged extension of the suffrage to members of the lower classes in the furtherance of Enlightenment goals. John Stuart Mill maintained that this goal necessitated recognition of the rights of women as well as of men. Recent feminist movements owe much to Mill's arguments.

In any event, the pragmatic philosophy of the newer liberals, together with the preference of the lower classes for immediate economic gains, prevented the social revolution predicted by Marx and other radical thinkers. The overall tendency in Western industrial societies by the end of the century was toward the amelioration of the living conditions of the lower classes and the rapid increase in the number of middle-class families.

Scientific and technological developments also contributed to changes in human perceptions. The evolutionary theories of Charles Darwin profoundly upset traditional religious and humanistic notions of humanity's unique position in creation. The notion of life as evolutionary, together with the increasing standard of living, generally tended to support belief in inevitable progress and to encourage an overriding interest in the material aspects of life.

Realism in the Arts

Artists responded to these conditions in various ways. Although romanticism remained the dominant trend in music until the very end of the nineteenth century, the style called realism came to dominate painting and literature around 1850. Realist artists and writers felt that the times called for depicting the world as in its beauty. The invention and development of photography seemed in many ways to replace what the realists were trying to accomplish. Stressing the effects of the environment on individual characters, the realists and, even more so, the naturalists, were often harshly critical of the social and psychological consequences of industrialism.

Architects tended either to escape from the modern world by building in revival styles such as Greek classical or Gothic, or to respond enthusiastically to the new technological possibilities. Unlike the often critical realistic painting and fiction, buildings such as the Crystal Palace in London and the early skyscrapers in Chicago are testimonies to a dynamic capitalistic society, proud of itself and its accomplishments.

Beyond Realism

During the closing decades of the nineteenth century many prominent artists and thinkers were reacting against both the assurance that life could be portrayed as it seemed, "realistically," and the widespread contemporary self-satisfaction with material progress. Although still in the realist tradition, Dostoevsky maintained that reality was to be found more in the human soul than in the external environment. Nietzsche, who accepted Dostoevsky's emphasis on the irrational and spiritual but not his religious beliefs, insisted on the moral and intellectual weakness of Judaism and Christianity and proclaimed: "God is dead!" As a solution to the problems of humankind without God, he advocated the free development of all human potentialities in the individual "superman."

In painting, Edouard Manet served as a kind of bridge between realism and the style that became known as impressionism. Using the discoveries of photography and through experimenting with light, the impressionists became more interested in rendering subjective "impressions" of the visible world than in attempting to portray objective reality. The post-impressionist artists and the symbolist poets veered even more sharply from the tenets of realism. The function of art became not to reproduce the crass material world but to create a purer—and indeed *truer*—world. Extending the romantic vision, these artists imposed a personal, symbolic world of nature. By the end of the century, art seemed to many to fill the vacuum left by religion.

The City

The rapid growth of industrialism brought with it the equally rapid and unplanned development of what we have come to call urban sprawl. Cut off from the natural rhythms of rural living and from the reassurances of an ancestral homeland, millions of new city dwellers, although less likely to starve than they would have been in the country, came to experience not only the miserable living conditions but also the rootlessness and alienation endemic to city life. Social thinkers such as Engels described the sense of inhumanity present in city crowds composed of the indifferent well-off and the indigent and homeless. Novelists and poets such as Dickens, Dostoevsky, and Baudelaire expressed the hell-like nature of the city. For Baudelaire and the symbolist poets who followed him, the city became not so much a reality to be rendered objectively as an outward manifestation of the exploration of inner dreams and nightmares. The love-hate relationship with city life and the rift between ordinary external reality and poetic reality was to expand dramatically in the works of artists and writers of the early twentieth century.

PART NINE

Discontinuities: The Early Twentieth Century

30

A Culture in Self-Doubt

In 1900, continuity snapped...
HENRY ADAMS

On or about December, 1910, human nature changed.
VIRGINIA WOOLF

Developments in Science, Politics, and Economics

The study of the humanities makes it evident that change—in forms, styles, ideas, outlooks, and especially in the apprehension of the nature of reality—is inevitable. The values and the truths of one generation cannot be those of the generation that succeeds it; the children must grow away from or revolt against the parents. We have seen that in certain periods change in the humanities comes about gradually, whereas in others it seems to erupt violently. No culture in the history of the world, however, has experienced either the extent or the intensity of change as that which the West has seen in our own century. Changes in Western culture have had profound repercussions on the rest of the world, and the rest of the world has in turn challenged the West's claim to leadership.

As the quotations heading this chapter indicate, it seemed to artists and thinkers in the early 1900s that the twentieth century had broken in a new and radical way with previous tradition. A radical break in the arts became evident with a series of new styles that can all be loosely grouped under the name *modernism.* We will look at some examples of this trend shortly; first let us examine briefly some of the intellectual and social developments that contributed toward making this period one of discontinuity.

Scientific Developments

In the pure sciences, a series of astounding new discoveries altered the scientific picture of the natural world as radically as had Newtonian physics in the seventeenth century and Darwinian biology in the nineteenth. Among the more important was Max Planck's discovery at the turn of the century that atoms emit energy not with continuity but in separate units. Several years later Albert Einstein (1879–1955) initially expounded his theory of

relativity: that space, time, and motion are not absolute (as Newtonian physics had assumed), but rather that all are relative to the observer's position. The Newtonian conceptions appeared inapplicable to the atom or the universe where movement was measured at the speed of light.

There are, however, two essential differences between this scientific revolution and the two previous ones. First, whereas the intelligent layperson could read Newton and Darwin and gain a fairly good understanding of their theories, it was and is impossible for someone without scientific training to have more than a superficial understanding of the discoveries of Planck and Einstein. Second, whereas Newton offered a rational picture of the world and evolution stressed progressive continuity between one species and another, the new physics seemed to postulate a world without continuity or absolutes, a world in which nothing was certain. Even without a scientific knowledge of physics, twentieth-century human beings are well aware that a world composed of subatomic particles, a world in which matter and energy, space and time, interpenetrate, a world in which scientific laws are given names like "relativity" (Einstein) or "uncertainty" (Werner Heisenberg), is a world in which nothing is as it appears to be to the human senses.

In the social sciences, too, certainties of the past gave way to uncertainties or relativities. Developments in anthropology emphasized the relativity of cultural values. The new science of psychology (launched in the 1870s) showed, first through the work of the Russian

Ivan Pavlov, that human beings could be conditioned by their environment to elicit certain responses, thus that they did not act primarily from reason and conscious decision. Foremost in upsetting traditional notions about human nature was the work of Sigmund Freud. Freud's theories that our actions and behavior are rooted in our unconscious, rather than our conscious mind, seemed to many a more pessimistic view of human nature than Darwin's theories about our ancestry. We will examine Freud's work in more detail.

What the early twentieth century witnessed was what Nietzsche had prophesied: a radical questioning of the Greco-Roman and Judeo-Christian roots of our culture. Reason and authority, humanism and faith, the pillars of these cultures, were undermined as never before. Yet the great minds who contributed most to this upheaval, Einstein and Freud (we could add the earlier Marx), were of Jewish backgrounds and steeped in humanistic culture.

Colonialism

At the same time that Western culture appeared to be casting doubts on itself, the Western powers, particularly England and France, expanded colonization in Africa, Asia, and America. The years after 1880 witnessed an increasingly bitter competition between European powers to establish their flags over as many colonies in the world as possible.

The effect of this late colonialism was devastating for the life of those areas occupied. True, the Europeans brought with them some of the benefits of communication, transportation, and scientific advancement, but the cost in terms of the social and cultural life of Asiatic and African people was tremendous. This rapid change—the disintegration of a traditional society—is graphically chronicled by the Nigerian writer Chinua Achebe in his *Things Fall Apart.* The influence, however, was not all one-way. Especially in the visual arts in the decades before World War I, western Europeans, questioning their own culture, proved receptive to the civilization of the colonized peoples.

World War I

By the first decade of the twentieth century, after all the desirable opportunities for colonial expansion were realized, the focus of international competition came back to the European continent itself. World War I started in 1914 in an almost careless mood with plumes and full-dress parades; but within the first year it became a war fought in muddy trenches with interminable days and nights of waiting alternating with sudden attacks, sometimes costing thousands of lives for a few square yards of ground gained. The growth of industrialism had made possible an exquisite technology of destruction: the tank, the machine gun, the airplane, and poison gas. The following poem, "Dulce et Decorum Est," by Wilfred Owen (1893–1918), describes the horror of a gas attack at the front. The poem constitutes a commentary on the ancient Latin patriotic motto in the last two lines: "It is sweet and becoming to die for one's country." The poet himself was killed at age twenty-five a week before the war ended.

WILFRED OWEN

Dulce et Decorum Est

Bent double, like old beggars under sacks,
Knock-kneed, coughing like hags, we cursed through sludge,
Till on the haunting flares we turned our backs
And towards our distant rest began to trudge.
Men marched asleep. Many had lost their boots
But limped on, blood-shod. All went lame; all blind;
Drunk with fatigue; deaf even to the hoots
Of disappointed shells that dropped behind.

Gas! Gas! Quick, boys!—An ecstasy of fumbling,
Fitting the clumsy helmets just in time;
But someone still was yelling out and stumbling
And floundering like a man in fire or lime.—
Dim, through the misty panes and thick green light
As under a green sea, I saw him drowning.

In all my dreams, before my helpless sight,
He plunges at me, guttering, choking, drowning.

If in some smothering dreams you too could pace
Behind the wagon that we flung him in,
And watch the white eyes writhing in his face,
His hanging face, like a devil's sick of sin;
If you could hear, at every jolt, the blood
Come gargling from the froth-corrupted lungs,
Obscene as cancer, bitter as the cud
Of vile, incurable sores on innocent tongues,—
My friend, you would not tell with such high zest
To children ardent for some desperate glory,
The old Lie: Dulce et decorum est
Pro patria mori.

At the war's outset the Central Powers—Germany, Austria-Hungary, and Turkey—opposed the Allies: Great Britain, France, and Russia. Italy joined the latter three in 1915. The loss of Russia in 1917 because of a civil war was balanced by the entrance of the United States on the Allied side. Although the Central Powers put up a vigorous fight for more than a year, by late 1918 the Allies were victorious.

Europeans on both sides became almost immediately aware that the war had, if anything, aggravated longstanding problems. The losses in human life, land, and property were enormous, and it was difficult to say that anything had been gained. At Versailles in 1919, where the peace settlement was worked out, the major European powers, primarily France and England, intentionally set out to so cripple Germany that it could not again pose a threat to the victors. Parts of its territory were taken away, and the newly established democratic government, the Weimar Republic, was burdened with paying an astronomical reparations debt to its former enemies. Restrictions were placed on the size of the German army. While the fledgling government in Germany suffered peculiar handicaps, democracy there, as in the half-dozen new countries created out of the old Austro-Hungarian empire, also suffered from the lack of any sort of republican tradition. Most, although not all, of these governments created by the victors in the lands of the vanquished had little popular support in their own country. The weakness of these new states therefore made the whole political atmosphere unstable.

The League of Nations

To ensure that this war really had been "a war to end all wars," the victors at Versailles, led by Woodrow Wilson, the American president, drew up a covenant, or constitution, for an international organization designed to defend the independence of every member nation. Created in January 1920 at Geneva, Switzerland, the League of Nations from the very beginning was weakened by the refusal of the most powerful nation in the world, the United States, to participate in its operations. Throughout its life in the years between the two world wars, the league was further hampered by conflicting interpretations of its purposes by member nations and by its inability to take decisive action when a powerful nation was party to a dispute.

Decline of the West

Europe in the early 1920s was worn out and discouraged. Symptomatic of the weariness and sense of decline was the work of Otto Spengler (1880–1936) with its ominous title, *The Decline of the West.* For Spengler, Western culture was in old age, its ruling classes were timid and not so much governing as administrating. Without faith and self-discipline the forces of anarchy would grow in the society and, unless strong leaders arose, it would continue its path of decline.

The new governments formed out of the defeated states proved highly unstable. The war had created a cooperative spirit between workers and bosses, but, with the war over, social conflicts increased markedly. Capitalists nervously eyed developments in Russia, where a communist state came into being infused with missionary zeal. Would the workers in the capitalist countries heed the call to revolt? Many expected another dreaded war but it was felt more than likely that that war would not be an affair of nations but of classes.

The Roaring Twenties

The postwar mood in the United States contrasted starkly with that in Europe. While many Europeans looked gloomily at the future of the human race, Americans exuded optimism. Unwilling to play its role as the key power in international relations, the United States was not reluctant to assert its economic predominance. The magic word of the decade of the 1920s was *credit:* a generous policy of lending against future earnings led to an enormous expansion of production. The first generation of installment-plan buyers in America found within its reach a range of luxuries, now considered necessities, that could be had on the promise of payment later. Because the country was the leading financial and industrial power, the economic system of other nations eventually became drawn into the same upward draft. When in 1929 panic struck Wall Street, the bubble burst and the world's economy shriveled; production statistics dropped, millions were thrown out of work, and the Great Depression of the 1930s was launched.

Politics in the 1930s: Communism and Fascism

The collapse of the world economy had its effect on almost every area of the globe but nowhere was it as marked as in the highly developed economic countries of western Europe and the United States. Breadlines, starving sharecroppers, and dispossessed families constituted only the most obvious results of the financial disaster. In such circumstances, the gulf between the

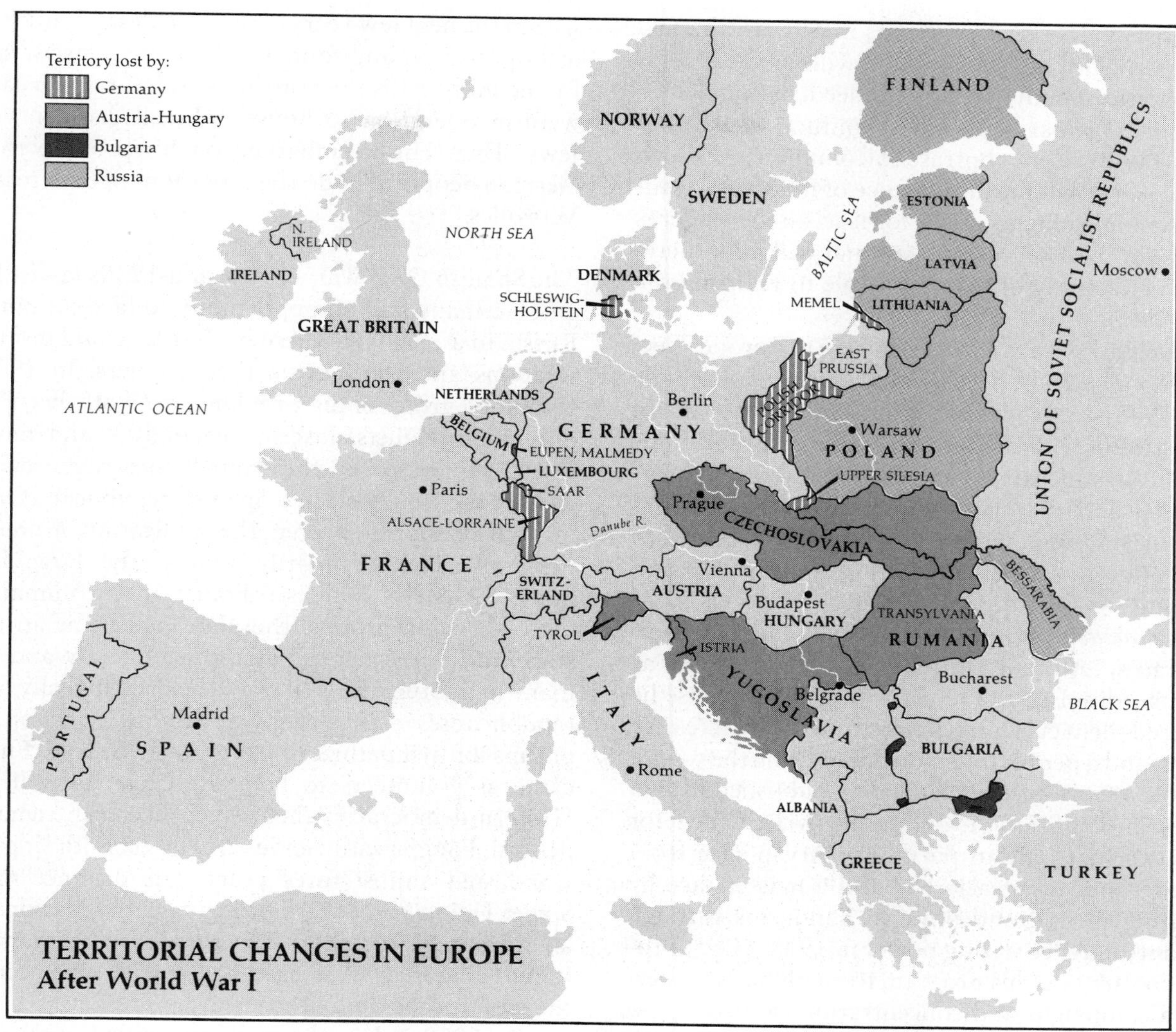

TERRITORIAL CHANGES IN EUROPE
After World War I

haves and the have-nots in society became glaringly obvious, with a corresponding intensification of social tension.

The sense of shock and dismay brought on by the economic crisis led to a broad questioning of traditional political values both in the United States and abroad. Could free enterprise and democracy survive? Almost totally independent of Western capitalism, the socialistic economy of the Soviet Union—although it had problems of its own—was insulated from the shock. In capitalistic countries millions of peasants and workers, either unemployed or threatened with unemployment, looked to communism as a way out of a depression in which they were the chief sufferers.

On the other hand, large numbers of people—many members of the middle classes as well as peasants and urban workers—turned to the radical right, especially to fascism, for a solution. Partly motivated by a fear of communism, partly by an antipathy toward big business that reduced the artisan to a laborer and threatened the shopkeeper with competition, they felt the appeal of a conservative right stressing the old values of thrift, industry, national traditions, and loyalty to the country.

Communism is similar to fascism in that it is a totalitarian political philosophy that sees the individual as having historical existence only in terms of a larger group. For the communist the larger group is the class; for the fascist it is the nation. Just as the communists declare that an individual's mentality is determined by the class to which he or she belongs, so the fascists claim that one's basic outlook derives from one's nationality. What we call reason, therefore, is relative to each nation. Like Rousseau's general will, the national will of the fascist is the deepest part of every member of the national group. Whereas the communists view class conflict as inevitable, the fascists see struggle between national wills as the central characteristic of human history. Indeed, national wills are defined primarily in their conflict with other nations. However, in contrast to communism, which tends to play down the importance of individual leaders in accomplishing its goals, for fascism the leader is the one who best senses the national will and, therefore, can effectively direct the people to realizing the nation's destiny.

In contrast with fascism elsewhere in Europe, German fascism had a peculiarly racial bias. Adolf Hitler (1889–1945), the leader of the movement in Germany from the 1920s, viewed German nationalism as a manifestation of superior Aryan culture. Many anthropologists believe that the Aryans were a large *linguistic* group originating in north-central Europe that around 3000 B.C. began migrating southward, eastward, and westward. For Hitler the Aryans constituted a *racial* group and one naturally superior to all other "races." Although he regarded all non-Aryans as inferior, he despised the Jews particularly, because he considered them cultural parasites, enemies of creative societies, and a people intent on dominating the world. His book *Mein Kampf* (*My Battle*), published in two volumes in 1925 and 1926, respectively, called for state action not only to purify the Aryan race from racial corruption but also to build a master race by eliminating mental and physical handicaps through birth control. After seizing power in 1933, Hitler proceeded to carry out his program through massive sterilization campaigns and concentration camps.

Caught between extreme movements on the right and left, European democratic political parties were hard put to deal with enemies who would not play according to the rules. Already in the early years after World War I, Benito Mussolini in Italy had successfully used the threat of communism to destroy the government and to establish a fascist state. Now, in the early 1930s, it was Germany's turn. With six million unemployed—including their families, about 40 percent of the German population was involved—Germany in 1932 was ripe for a violent change. Adolf Hitler and his National Socialist (Nazi) party used every trick in the election of that year to present the choice as one between communism and the forces of order. Particularly virulent were the Nazi attacks on the Jews as the authors of the Depression and the source of Germany's major ills. (This was a new element in fascism not found in Mussolini's Italy.) The result was a plurality for the Nazi party in the popular assembly, the Reichstag. Hitler was appointed chancellor, or prime minister, by the president of the Weimar Republic; within the next few years he acted to destroy any political opposition and to make Germany a fascist state. By the mid-1930s the notorious concentration camps were in operation to house political dissidents and Jews. Then Hitler embarked on his promise to the German people to undo the provisions of the Treaty of Versailles.

The Spanish Civil War In the mid-1930s fascist Italy and Germany had an opportunity to face communist Russia in a trial war where both sides could test their weapons and the fascists their soldiers. In 1936 a combined group of high-ranking army officers, Catholic traditionalists, fascists (Falangists) and monarchists, supported by the Church hierarchy, revolted against the legally elected Spanish republican government in an effort to prevent the application of a reform program aimed primarily against the large landholders. General Francisco Franco took command of the right-wing groups, the Nationalists, at an early stage and requested the assistance of Italy and Germany in fighting the civil war. The principal ally of the republicans, or Loyalists, was the Soviet Union, but groups of sympathizers from America and Europe came as volunteers to help the cause as well. The Western democracies themselves, however, remained neutral. Fought with vicious cruelty on both sides, the war lasted almost three years. The distance of the Soviet Union from the fighting gave the Nationalists an advantage in allies. The powerful German and Italian air forces were used for merciless bombing of the cities occupied by the enemy.

By 1939, when the civil war ended with a Nationalist victory, the hope of the Allies in World War I "to make the world safe for democracy" seemed in large part frustrated. Spain became one of the seventeen European nations out of twenty-seven to fall under the rule of a dictator. The League of Nations, essentially an international debating forum, was powerless to enforce international law and agreements. Not only were Germany and Italy aggressively menacing the remaining democratic powers, but, moreover, in August of that year Germany and Russia dumbfounded the world by signing a nonaggression pact. This meant that the burden for stopping the designs of the Axis powers (the term taken by Germany and Italy for their alliance) fell on Great Britain and France, neither of whom wanted war nor was prepared for it.

Sigmund Freud (1856–1939)

The debacle of World War I and the precarious character of peace in the postwar years led Sigmund Freud, like Spengler and others of that generation, to meditate on the nature of civilization. As a psychologist rather than a historian, Freud was primarily interested in the conflicts between individuals and their society, and reflection led him to trace the origins of civilized life back to its source in the human psyche. Freud's thought is represented in his central work on this theme, *Civilization and Its Discontents* (1930). To assess his considerable impact on modern culture, however, it is also necessary to know something of the development of his ideas before that work. We will summarize this development briefly.

Depth Psychology

A Viennese neurologist, Freud left his first vocation to develop what came to be called "depth psychology." This depth psychology claimed to furnish a key to the exploration of the unconscious mind and, through this, a renewed knowledge of the conscious mind, with wider application to the understanding of literature, art, religion, and culture. The first dynamic psychiatry had been, in the main, the systematization of observations made on hypnotized patients. With Freud's method of free association, a new approach was introduced. The patient, relaxed on a couch, was told the basic rule: to tell whatever came to mind, no matter how futile, absurd, embarrassing, or even offensive it seemed.

Three Parts of Mind

Much of Freud's understanding of the human individual rests on his contention that mental life is produced by the interaction of three psychic agencies: the ego, the id, and the superego. The *ego* was defined as "the coordinated organization of mental processes in a person." The *id* was not very different from what Freud had originally described as the unconscious, the seat of both the repressed material and the drives, to which had been added the unconscious fantasies and unconscious feelings, notably guilt feelings. The *superego* is the watchful, judging, punishing agency in the individual, the source of social and religious feelings in humankind.

The main aspects of depth psychology were Freud's dream theory and his theory of parapraxis, or faulty behavior, that is, slips of the tongue and erroneously carried-out actions. These theories were elaborated simultaneously and presented in two of his best-known books, *The Interpretation of Dreams* in 1900 and *The Psychopathology of Everyday Life* in 1904.

Dreams

Freud's theory of dreams has been told so often that it has become common knowledge. Among the many trivial events of the day, the dream chooses the one that shows some relationship to a childhood memory; and, as Freud puts it, the dream stands with one foot in the present and one foot in childhood. Thus one is led from the latent content still farther back to a childhood memory expressing an unfulfilled wish of that remote time. Here Freud introduced the notion he had found in his self-analysis and in his patients, the *Oedipus complex:* the little boy, wanting to possess his mother, wishes to get rid of his father; but he is frightened of this threatening rival and of castration as a punishment for his incestuous feelings toward the mother. Such is, Freud says, the terrible secret that every man keeps in the recesses of his heart, repressed and forgotten, and which appears in a veiled form in a dream every night. Freud named this complex from the Greek myth on which Sophocles built his tragedy. Freud postulated a similar trauma for women, the *Electra complex,* in which the little girl desires to have children by her father and to kill her mother. A great reader in the humanities, Freud was well aware that profound psychological truths had been expressed in literature and art before being formulated scientifically.

The dream, for Freud, is essentially a fulfillment of a repressed, unacceptable sexual wish. When controls of consciousness are relaxed, waking acts, too, can reveal repressed wishes or desires. Such acts include forgetting proper names, slips of the tongue and speech blunders, mistakes in reading and writing, acts of physical clumsiness, and intellectual errors.

The Pleasure Principle and Instincts

Also important in Freud's thinking are his theories of the pleasure principle and of the instincts, *Thanatos* and *Eros,* as discussed in his *Beyond the Pleasure Principle* (1920). The pleasure principle may be understood as a person's constant attempt to achieve pleasure and to avoid pain. As for his dualistic theory of instincts, Freud contended that Eros included the sexual instincts, most of the egoistic or self-preservative impulses, and those drives and forces that enhanced and unified life. Thanatos, on the other hand, included the tendency to self-punishment in the individual as well as those impulses that denied life and disrupted civilized existence. Thus Freud hypothesized that perhaps there was an innate tendency in the psychobiological makeup of people that overrides the pleasure principle. Or, expressed another way, since the aim of the instincts (according to Freud's older definition) was to diminish tension and since this was also his definition of pleasure, the ultimate pleasure was not life or Eros, but Thanatos, stasis or death. There is no doubt that the experience of World War I influenced Freud's concept of the "death wish."

Freud on Religion, Culture, and Literature

Soon after he had conceived his psychoanalytic theory, Freud expanded his reflection on the fields of religion, sociology, cultural history, art, and literature. In 1907 he compared obsessive-compulsive symptoms of neurotics with religious rituals and creeds, concluding that religion was a universal obsessional neurosis and that obsession was an individualized religion. Twenty years later, in *The Future of an Illusion,* Freud defined religion as an illusion inspired by infantile belief in the omnipotence of thought, a universal neurosis, a kind of narcotic that hampers the free exercise of intelligence, something that humanity will have to give up. With *Totem and Taboo* Freud undertook to retrace the origin not only of religion but of human culture as well, trying to find a link between the individual Oedipus complex and the prehistory of humankind.

Whereas Freud found religion harmful, he deemed art and literature beneficial to humanity. *The Interpretation of Dreams* contains two major ideas that have an impact on art and the criticism of art: the conception of the unconscious and the theory of the pleasure principle. Freud sees the work of art as the expression of a wish and the artist as a neurotic. Like the neurotic, artists yearn for honor, power, wealth, fame, and love; however, they do not have the necessary means of achieving these goals. Therefore they turn their backs on reality, transferring their interests to the expression of their wishes in fantasy as creation. Art thus becomes, in Freud's view, something like a public dream, an occasion to contemplate the unconscious. "Dostoevsky and Parricide," "Leonardo da Vinci," and "The Moses of Michelangelo" are only three of the many works by Freud that reveal this psychoanalytical approach to the work of art.

Civilization and Its Discontents

In his essay of 1930, *Civilization and Its Discontents,* Freud applies psychoanalytical methods to the study of civilization. He begins by asking the question: why do so many people blame the fact of human unhappiness on civilization and technical progress? Would we in fact be better off in a "free" primitive state? Freud analyzes the clash between individual instincts, creative and destructive, and the restrictive forces of overripe Western civilization. He nevertheless argues that all societies, even the most primitive, impose restrictions and taboos and that human cultures in fact develop through the sublimation of instinctual drives. *Eros,* the drive for individual happiness, may clash with social necessities, but it also takes the form of the urge that causes human beings to seek to bind together, first in families and then in larger social groups. The other basic instinct, *Thanatos,* conceptualized by Freud shortly after World War I, occurs both in the form of an individual "death wish" and as aggression toward others. It constantly threatens the destruction of both self and society. Freud concludes, pessimistically, that civilization of necessity had to channel and restrain people's instinctual strivings if both individuals and civilization were to survive. Unlike Marx and the tradition of Western radicalism emerging from the Enlightenment, Freud saw no possibility for a radically different future for the majority of humankind. His philosophic outlook is often thought of as a secular variant of the doctrine of original sin or as a modern version of the tragic vision.

In Freud's view, the meaning of culture is the struggle between Eros and Thanatos as it works itself out in human society. "This struggle," he says, "is what all life essentially consists of and the evolution of civilization may therefore be simply described as the struggle for the life of the human species."

Reading Selections

Adolf Hitler

From *Mein Kampf*

Translation by Ralph Manheim

The Jews

The mightiest counterpart to the Aryan is represented by the Jew. In hardly any people in the world is the instinct of self-preservation developed more strongly than in the so-called "chosen." Of this, the mere fact of the survival of this race may be considered the best proof. Where is the people which in the last two thousand years has been exposed to so slight changes of inner disposition, character, etc., as the Jewish people? What people, finally, has gone through greater upheavals than this one—and nevertheless issued from the mightiest catastrophes of mankind unchanged? What an infinitely tough will to live and preserve the species speaks from these facts!

The mental qualities of the Jew have been schooled in the course of many centuries. Today he passes as "smart," and this in a certain sense he has been at all times. But his intelligence is not the result of his own development, but of visual instruction through foreigners.

Since the Jew—for reasons which will at once become apparent—was never in possession of a culture of his own, the foundations of his intellectual work were always provided by others. His intellect at all times developed through the cultural world surrounding him.

The reverse process never took place.

For if the Jewish people's instinct of self-preservation is not smaller but larger than that of other peoples, if his intellectual faculties can easily arouse the impression that they are equal to the intellectual gifts of other races, he lacks completely the most essential requirement for a cultured people, the idealistic attitude.

In the Jewish people the will to self-sacrifice does not go beyond the individual's naked instinct of self-preservation. Their apparently great sense of solidarity is based on the very primitive herd instinct that is seen in many other living creatures in this world. It is a noteworthy fact that the herd instinct leads to mutual support only as long as a common danger makes this seem useful or inevitable. The same pack of wolves which has just fallen on its prey together disintegrates when hunger abates into its individual beasts. The same is true of horses which try to defend themselves against an assailant in a body, but scatter again as soon as the danger is past....

If the Jews were alone in this world, they would stifle in filth and offal; they would try to get ahead of one another in hate-filled struggle and exterminate one another, in so far as the absolute absence of all sense of self-sacrifice, expressing itself in their cowardice, did not turn battle into comedy here too.

So it is absolutely wrong to infer any ideal sense of sacrifice in the Jews from the fact that they stand together in struggle, or, better expressed, in the plundering of their fellow men....

Hence the Jewish people, despite all apparent intellectual qualities, is without any true culture, and especially without any culture of its own. For what sham culture the Jew today possesses is the property of other peoples, and for the most part it is ruined in his hands.

No, the Jew possesses no culture-creating force of any sort, since the idealism, without which there is no true higher development of man, is not present in him and never was present. Hence his intellect will never have a constructive effect, but will be destructive, and in very rare cases perhaps will at most be stimulating, but then as the prototype of the "force which always wants evil and nevertheless creates good." Not through him does any progress of mankind occur, but in spite of him.

The State

The folkish state[1] must make up for what everyone else today has neglected in this field. *It must set race in the center of all life. It must take care to keep it pure. It must declare the child to be the most precious treasure of the people. It must see to it that only the healthy beget children; that there is only one disgrace: despite one's own sickness and deficiencies, to bring children into the world, and one highest honor: to renounce doing so. And conversely it must be considered reprehensible: to withhold healthy children from the nation. Here the state must act as the guardian of a millennial future in the face of which the wishes and the selfishness of the individual must appear as nothing and submit. It must put the most modern medical means in the service of this knowledge. It must declare unfit for propagation all who are in any way visibly sick or who have inherited a disease and can therefore pass it on, and put this into actual practice. Conversely, it must take care that the fertility of the healthy woman is not limited by the financial irresponsibility of a state régime which turns the blessing of children into a curse for the parents. It must put an end to that lazy, nay criminal, indifference with which the social premises for a fecund family are treated today, and must instead feel itself to be the highest guardian of this most precious blessing of a people. Its concern belongs more to the child than to the adult. . . .*

In the folkish state, finally, the folkish philosophy of life must succeed in bringing about that nobler age in which men no longer are concerned with breeding dogs, horses, and cats, but in elevating man himself, an age in which the one knowingly and silently renounces, the other joyfully sacrifices and gives.

That this is possible may not be denied in a world where hundreds and hundreds of thousands of people voluntarily submit to celibacy, obligated and bound by nothing except the injunction of the Church.

Should the same renunciation not be possible if this injunction is replaced by the admonition finally to put an end to the constant and continuous original sin of racial poisoning, and to give the Almighty Creator beings such as He Himself created?

[1] A state designed to serve the needs of a race capable of culture—i.e., the Aryans.

QUESTIONS

1. How does Hitler characterize the intelligence of Jews?
2. Why could the Jews never found their own state? By implication, why does Hitler believe the Aryans capable of creating a powerful state?
3. What result has the Weimar Republic's indifference to controlling birth produced?
4. What policies for remedying the "racial poisoning" suggest themselves?

SIGMUND FREUD

FROM *Civilization and Its Discontents*

Translation by James Strachey

VI

. . . The assumption of the existence of an instinct of death or destruction has met with resistance even in analytic circles; I am aware that there is a frequent inclination rather to ascribe whatever is dangerous and hostile in love to an original bipolarity in its own nature. To begin with it was only tentatively that I put forward the views I have developed here, but in the course of time they have gained such a hold upon me that I can no longer think in any other way. To my mind, they are far more serviceable from a theoretical standpoint than any other possible ones; they provide that simplification, without either ignoring or doing violence to the facts, for which we strive in scientific work. I know that in sadism and masochism we have always seen before us manifestations of the destructive instinct (directed outwards and inwards), strongly alloyed with erotism; but I can no longer understand how we can have overlooked the ubiquity of non-erotic aggressivity and destructiveness and can have failed to give it its due place in our interpretation of life. (The desire for destruction when it is directed *inwards* mostly eludes our perception, of course, unless it is tinged with erotism.) I remember my own defensive attitude when the idea of an instinct of destruction first emerged in psycho-analytic literature, and how long it took before I became receptive to it. That others should have shown, and still show, the same attitude of rejection surprises me less. For "little children do not like it"[1] when there is talk of the inborn human inclination to "badness," to aggressiveness and destructiveness, and so to cruelty as well. God has made them in the image of His own perfection; nobody wants to be reminded how hard it is to reconcile the undeniable existence of evil—despite the protestations of Christian Science—with His all-powerfulness or His all-goodness. The Devil would be the best way out as an excuse for God; in that way he would be playing the same part as an agent of economic discharge as the Jew does in the world of the Aryan ideal. But even so, one can hold God responsible for the existence of the wickedness which the Devil embodies. In view of these difficulties, each of us will be well advised, on some suitable occasion, to make a low bow to the deeply moral nature of mankind; it will help us to be generally popular and much will be forgiven us for it.

The name "libido" can once more be used to denote the manifestations of the power of Eros in order to distinguish them from the energy of the death instinct. It must be confessed that we have much greater difficulty in grasping that instinct; we can only suspect it, as it were, as something in the background behind Eros, and it escapes detection unless its presence is betrayed by its being alloyed with Eros. It is in sadism, where the death instinct twists the erotic aim in its own sense and yet at the same time fully satisfies the erotic urge, that we succeed in obtaining the clearest insight into its nature and its relation to Eros. But even where it emerges without any sexual purpose, in the blindest fury of destructiveness, we cannot fail to recognize that the satisfaction of the instinct is accompanied by an extraordinarily high degree of narcissistic enjoyment, owing to its presenting the ego with a fulfillment of the latter's old wishes for omnipotence. The instinct of destruction, moderated and tamed, and, as it were, inhibited in its aim, must, when it is directed towards objects, provide the ego with the satisfaction of its vital needs and with control over nature. Since the assumption of the existence of the instinct is mainly based on theoretical grounds, we must also admit that it is not entirely proof against theoretical objections. But this is how things appear to us now, in the present state of our knowledge; future research and reflection will no doubt bring further light which will decide the matter.

...The inclination to aggression is an original, self-subsisting instinctual disposition in man, and... it constitutes the greatest impediment to civilization. At one point in the course of this enquiry I was led to the idea that civilization was a special process which mankind undergoes, and I am still under the influence of that idea. I may now add that civilization is a process in the service of Eros, whose purpose is to combine single human individuals, and after that families, then races, peoples and nations, into one great unity, the unity of mankind. Why this has to happen, we do not know; the work of Eros is precisely this. These collections of men are to be libidinally bound to one another. Necessity alone, the advantages of work in common, will not hold them together. But man's natural aggressive instinct, the hostility of each against all and of all against each, opposes this programme of civilization. This aggressive instinct is the derivative and the main representative of the death instinct which we have found alongside of Eros and which shares world-dominion with it. And now, I think, the meaning of the evolution of civilization is no longer obscure to us. It must present the struggle between Eros and Death, between the instinct of life and the instinct of destruction, as it works itself out in the human species. This struggle is what all life essentially consists of, and the evolution of civilization may therefore be simply described as the struggle for life of the human species. And it is this battle of the giants that our nurse-maids try to appease with their lullaby about Heaven.[2]

QUESTIONS

1. According to Freud, what evidence is there for the existence of the death instinct?
2. In what different ways does Eros manifest itself?
3. Compare Freud's notion of the "social contract" to Rousseau's.
4. Does Freud's theory of Eros and Thanatos lead to the repudiation of the Enlightenment?
5. In what way are Freud's ideas similar to traditional Judeo-Christian teachings? How are they different?

[1] A quotation from a poem by Goethe.

[2] "*Eiapopeia vom Himmel,*" a quotation from Heine's poem *Deutschland,* Caput I.

6. What are your feelings about Freud's observation that "one can hold God responsible for the existence of the Devil just as well as for the existence of the wickedness which the Devil embodies"?
7. Do you think that Freud's emphasis on sexuality is excessive? Is the libido the underlying reality of existence or merely one facet of it?
8. Do Freud's ideas perpetuate pessimism, despair, and cynicism?
9. Take any aspect of Freud's theories with which you disagree and present your own argument.

31

Modernism in the Visual Arts

In the years between 1900 and 1930 there developed a lifestyle that was self-consciously modern. The theories of Freud, often misinterpreted, led to a desire to be "liberated" from the restraints and taboos of proper Victorian society and to greater sexual freedom. Women, having finally gained the vote in England and America, began to demand greater freedoms and more of a place in society for themselves. Young women shocked their elders by wearing their hair and their skirts short and dancing modern dances such as the Charleston. Blacks in America, although suffering from Jim Crow laws in the South and limited employment possibilities in the North, nevertheless made substantial contributions to the art and culture of the new age. The most substantial of these was jazz, a totally new art form that we will discuss as music in the next chapter. The modernist age can as well be called the jazz age, for jazz seemed to express the fast, frantic, free way of life that culminated in the Roaring Twenties. Automobiles, airplanes, radio, and technology that made possible the development of another new art form—the motion picture—all contributed to the impression that life was speeding up and changing at an incredible rate and that modern values and styles had to replace old-fashioned ones.

As is often the case, the changes in lifestyle were preceded by changes in the arts. Artists, too, became self-consciously modern, aware that art had to keep pace with, or advance, a rapidly changing society. In addition to jazz, another important new art form, modern dance, was an American creation, but the cradle of modernism in the early twentieth century was really Paris. There young painters, sculptors, writers, musicians, and dancers flocked from all over the world to exchange ideas and to participate in the creation of the new. Many Americans, white and black, fled what they considered to be the culturally backward, repressive atmosphere of the United States to give free rein to their creativity in Paris.

This period of intense modernist activity in Paris, beginning shortly before World War I, is described by Roger Shattuck as "the banquet years." The French accomplishments of the late nineteenth century seemed to offer developing artists a feast on which to nourish themselves. Visual, musical, literary, and theatrical artists were conscious of the interrelationships among their arts as never before. During the first three decades of the twentieth century, there developed an astounding number of literary-artistic-musical schools, all with "-isms" attached to them. Their histories have been made, and we will only mention a few of them here. What we will attempt to grasp through the rich variety of expressions is just what it meant (and means) to be "modern."

Modernist Painting, 1900–1930

In the early years of this century two important trends can be distinguished. The first is the continuing transformation of the *figurative* tradition, in which the human body and the objects of habitual visual experience form the basis of art. The second is the complete rejection of the visual world for an attempt to communicate through the pure plastic possibilities of the formal elements of painting, sculpture, and graphics. Two prominent figures are associated with the first: a Frenchman, Henri Matisse, and a Spaniard, Pablo Picasso. A Russian, Wassily Kandinsky, and a Dutchman, Piet Mondrian, are representative of the second. We will consider representative works from these trends and look briefly at their influence in the United States. We will then turn to two important modernist developments after World War I: Dada and surrealism.

Henri Matisse (1869–1954)

Matisse emerged as an important artist in an exhibition of his work and that of some colleagues in 1905. Called Les Fauves (wild beasts) because of the large areas of strong, simplified colors, slashing brush strokes, and thick paint that characterized their work, these artists were all clearly inspired by impressionism, Gauguin, and Van Gogh. Matisse's *Portrait of Madame Matisse (The Green Stripe)* (Color Plate XXVIII), makes use of areas of strong, contrasting colors to create a sense of space and light instead of traditional shading and shadow. Matisse's ability to suggest weight, volume, and space through color juxtaposition was further enhanced by his command of the possibilities of line and contour. In 1905–1906, when Matisse painted *The Joy of Life* (Fig. 31-1), the heavy brush strokes of his earlier work gave way to flowing contours and colors, spaciously arranged on a light ground. Compared to the canvases of Van Gogh and Gauguin, this work is empty of brooding and is filled with an almost musical lyricism and optimism. This painting truly affirms life and joy, resonating with exploding vigor and sensuality that we will witness in the music and ballet of Stravinsky's *Rite of Spring.*

Pablo Picasso (1881–1973)

Matisse's joyful visions of life were not shared by Picasso. In his early works, done in Paris around the turn of the century, Picasso used as subjects clowns, acrobats, peasants, and the dregs of Parisian night life that had also been used by Manet, Degas, and Toulouse-Lautrec. Filled with melancholy and a brooding sense of alienation, they remain nineteenth-century pictures in spite of Picasso's unconventional use of color, distortion, and space (Fig. 31-2).

Among Matisse's most important predecessors had been Gauguin. Picasso, however, turned to the works of Paul Cézanne, finding in them another way to see and experience the world and to realize that experience in a painterly language. Cézanne had reduced objects to a series of visual references arranged in patterns of color and shape that created a sense of volume and space. For example, an orange would be represented as round and orange but with no reference to typical texture, surface formation, or any other transient characteristics of an orange—some are green, others are not orange all over, others have spots. Other objects on the picture surface would be reduced in the same way. A human figure, for example, would not have typical skin color, texture, even gesture. Rather, Cézanne would study the figure until he seemed to find the essence, an essential way for that figure to be represented that was convincing but not dependent on the painted form's being a direct copy of the seen and experienced human form. This process emphasized the nature of painting itself, as a process, and of seeing, as a collection of experiences summarized and encapsulated by the mind through human experience. It was this that Picasso built on in his explorations made after the turn of the century.

African and Oceanic Art

Another artistic phenomenon that had a major impact on Picasso and his friends was the art of Africa and the South Pacific. Acquaintance with such a completely

31-1 *Henri Matisse,* The Joy of Life, *1905–6, oil on canvas, 68½″ × 93¾″. (Copyright the Barnes Foundation, 1976, Merion Station, Pennsylvania)*

31-2 *Pablo Picasso,* Family of Saltimbanques, *1905, oil on canvas, 83¾″ × 90⅜″. (Copyright 1992, National Gallery of Art, Washington. Chester Dale Collection)*

different formal tradition is usually a very liberating experience to artists. It was so in the nineteenth century when Europeans became acquainted with Japanese prints. When Gauguin and others brought objects to Paris from Africa or the Pacific, interest was stimulated in what had heretofore been considered curiosities brought as memorabilia by colonists, travelers, or ethnographers. This so-called "primitive art" represented, as we saw in the chapter on African art in Volume I, completely different formal traditions. For example, in the mask in Fig. 31-3, the African artist has abstracted from reality those elements that are most important for the meaning and purpose of the mask. These have been exaggerated and combined into a strong, harmonious whole by the purely formal elements of the medium: plane, surface, texture, and shape. The existence of this tradition affirmed the belief of many artists that objects of art could speak in their own right, independent of the need to copy the familiar aspects of the visible world. At first these artists, including Picasso, copied the new forms and shapes, studying them and including them directly in their work. But very rapidly each artist adopted this influence to his or her particular uses, making the objects almost unrecognizable. Naturally, the majority of the European public did not receive either the African art or the work of artists inspired by it with enthusiasm. An apologist for both, the French poet and art critic Guillaume Apollinaire, argued persuasively for an understanding of African art. The piece that follows (translated by Susan Suleiman) was written in 1918.

31-3 *African Dan mask. (Copyright Frank Willett, Glasgow)*

> Curiosity has found a new field of exploration in the sculptures of Africa and Oceania.
>
> This new branch of curiosity, although born in France, has to this day found more commentators abroad. Since it originated in France, however, we have every reason to believe that it is here that its influence is being most deeply felt. These *fetishes,* which have not been uninfluential in modern art, are all related to the religious passion, which is the source of the purest art.
>
> The interest of these fetishes lies essentially in their plastic form, even though they are sometimes made of precious materials. This form is always powerful, very far removed from our conceptions and yet capable of nourishing the inspiration of artists.
>
> It is not a question of competing with the models of classical antiquity, but of renewing subjects and forms by bringing artistic observation back to the first principles of great art.
>
> In fact, the Greeks learned much more from the African sculptors than has been noted up to now. If it is true that Egypt exerted an appreciable influence on the very human art of Hellas (Greece), one would have to be very unfamiliar with the art of the Egyptians and of the Negro fetishes to deny that the latter provides the key to the hieraticism and the forms characteristic of Egyptian art.
>
> The enthusiasm of today's painters and collectors for the art of fetishes is an enthusiasm for the basic principles of our arts; their taste is renewed through contact with these works. In fact, certain masterpieces of Negro sculpture can compete perfectly well with beautiful works of European sculpture of the greatest periods. I remember an African head in M. Jacques Doucet's collection that can stand up perfectly against some fine pieces of Romanesque sculpture. In any case, no one today would dream of denying these evident truths, except ignorant people who do not want to take the trouble to look at things closely.

The Influence of Cézanne and African Art on Picasso

The combined influences of Cézanne and African art help us to better understand *Les Demoiselles d'Avignon,* an unfinished picture that Picasso showed his

31-4 *PICASSO, Pablo.* Les Demoiselles d'Avignon, *1907, oil on canvas, 8′ × 7′8″. (Collection, The Museum of Modern Art, New York, acquired through the Lillie P. Bliss Bequest)*

friends in 1907 (Fig. 31-4). What do we see? A large canvas is filled with female bodies. It is difficult to tell if they are seated, standing, or leaning because the space in which we would expect them to exist has been shattered. Look at the figure on the far left. Does she stand behind, beside, in front of, or in the drapery? Does it bother you that you cannot tell? Look at the center figure. Is she standing or lying down? Why is it confusing? Where are her legs? Can you explain the position of her arms? Which figure seems to be rushing into the space? How can you tell? Which figures seem to have had their faces transformed by masks? Does the seated figure in the lower left face you or sit with her back to you? How does Picasso achieve a three-dimensional effect in the faces of the three figures center and left? How have the bodies been transformed? What does the picture mean? Does it matter if you cannot tell? Why or why not?

Interpretation of this picture is difficult because it is no longer a picture with subject matter that tells a story. What is happening may be clarified by remembering how Picasso and his friends looked at African masks and sculptures. They did not know the meaning or purpose of either, but in spite of that, they could recognize human and animal forms and patterns and colors that rendered an account of everyday objects. Initially, this sense of recognition was important just because it told these Western artists that, indeed, there was more than one way to experience and give form to the world. Just as the medieval or Renaissance artist created conventions to capture experience and transmit knowledge, African artists had created their conventions. Western artists' experience of African art tended to reinforce the new (and very un-African) belief that line, color, and texture, when properly ordered in a work of art, have the power to create a personal response independent of religious or literary meaning. The problem became one of defining and understanding the limits of the power of the formal elements of art. African art, in particular, with its purposeful distortions of space, scale, and location, provided a major impetus for these artists.

Determined to free the picture from its dependence on old formulas, Picasso and his friend Georges Braque (1882–1963) worked together over a period of about four years. Like Cézanne, they considered the act of seeing to be one in which, first, we perceive what we focus on; second, what we perceive is determined by the length of time that we focus; third, we perceive by manipulating objects within our frame of reference; and fourth, we perceive by filling in information based on what we already know. For these two painters, the flat canvas became an imaginary grid with squares of equal size. Thus the canvas that one usually thinks of as having a bottom and top, left, and right sides, and whose characteristics of bottom, top, left, or right side have an established value (for example, the horizon line is usually between two-thirds and halfway down from the top of the canvas) becomes a surface that can be manipulated in any direction. All directions are of equal importance. Like the mapmaker who distills the elaborate, complex, three-dimensional world into an *abstraction* of lines and colors that convey information, the two painters distilled simple, everyday, familiar objects. They eliminated bright colors from their canvases because color itself can be emotionally powerful and evocative. They eliminated the traditional three-dimensional space invented in the Renaissance, and with it all references to fore-, mid-, and background. Objects or fragments of objects could now be placed anywhere in the shallow space. The artist could show us backs and sides of things, arranged at will on the canvas. A face is rendered in profile and full-face; we may see the side of the head and the back of the shoulder. References to specific objects are limited or reduced to familiar aspects.

31-5 *Pablo Picasso,* Man with a Violin. *(Philadelphia Museum of Art: Louise and Walter Arensberg Collection)*

31-6 *PICASSO, Pablo.* Man with a Hat. *(winter 1912–13). Cut-and-pasted papers, charcoal, and brush and ink, 24½" × 18⅝". (Collection, The Museum of Modern Art, New York. Purchase.)*

Cubism

Examine the picture *Man with a Violin* (Fig. 31-5). What parts of the man do you see? What features of the violin? How does the painter suggest space, light, and the volume and weight of the man's body? Of the violin? Picasso, instead of creating a picture to be perceived in the most habitual, traditional mode, gives us a construction, an arrangement of shapes, colors, textures, spaces, and weights that invites us to participate in the process of seeing and knowing. We are not invited completely to "find" the man and his violin but to learn how little we must know in order to see and understand. Moreover, we become more and more familiar with the purely formal qualities of the painting such as *balance, harmony, contrast* of color, *texture,* and *form* that make up the experience of looking at pictures—an experience that can be enjoyable not because the picture is of "something" but because it "is." These paintings were named "cubist" by a hostile critic who pointed to their most conspicuous aspect—the small facets or planes that intersect and appear somewhat cubelike.

Collages

Neither Picasso nor Braque was content to continue in this style. They began to try other ideas such as adding materials like sand, pasted paper, or rope to the canvas to create the first *collages* (in French, "pasting," "gluing") (Fig. 31-6). The inclusion of "real" materials in their pictures increased the potential for humor and irony. For example, a head cut out of newspaper is made to stand for a three-dimensional volume, while the lettering on the paper is intrinsically flat. It is a game in which what you see may not necessarily be what you think you see; but, above all, what you see is a *made* object that is important in its own right and not because it is a copy of the familiar, habitual visual world. (See Color Plate XXIX.)

The rational and orderly methodology of early cubism and the simplicity of the early collages were tested by the addition of color and the simplification of the *grid.* To what extent did pictures presenting more recognizable forms still maintain their identity as painted, made things? Picasso's *Three Musicians* (Fig. 31-7) is derived from the broken space and complicated, overlapping, superimposed views of *Man with a Violin.* The simple, vivid colors, along with the intersecting forms of the musicians and their instruments, create a rhythmic movement that visually echoes the syncopations of jazz.

Nonobjective and Expressionist Painting

The belief in the ability of an object to act as a means of communication is nowhere more vividly tested than in the work of the painters Wassily Kandinsky and Piet Mondrian. Here we meet canvases that are completely free of any reference to the habitual, familiar objects

31-7 *PICASSO, Pablo.* Three Musicians. *1921 (summer) oil on canvas, 6′7″ × 7′3¾″. (Collection, The Museum of Modern Art, New York. Mrs. Simon Guggenheim Fund.)*

and activities of our experience. We are left alone with arrangements of line and color that are, in Kandinsky's words, "a new world," capable of speaking to our conscious as well as our unconscious minds, if we will but permit it, asking not that it be a picture of something but that it just be.

Wassily Kandinsky (1866–1944)

Kandinsky became a painter when he saw one of Monet's *Haystacks* at an exhibition in Moscow. He tells us that he could not distinguish the subject. All that he saw was a veil of shimmering color, producing an emotional sensation like that produced when listening to great music. Stunned by this experience, Kandinsky traveled all over Europe, painting and absorbing the work of Gauguin, Van Gogh, Monet, and others. Settling in Munich, a place intellectually stimulating like Paris, Kandinsky began to experiment, seeking a method of painting that accomplished his aims. An incident recounted in his *Reminiscences* helps us to understand his concept of the idea of the nonobjective painting:

> It was the hour approaching dusk. I returned home with my paint box after making a study, still dreaming and wrapped into the work completed, when suddenly I saw an indescribably beautiful picture, imbibed by an inner glow. First I hesitated, then I quickly approached this mysterious picture, on which I saw nothing but shapes and colors, and the contents of which I could not understand. I immediately found the key to the puzzle; it was a picture painted by me, leaning against the wall, standing on its side. The next day, when there was daylight, I tried to get yesterday's impression of the painting. However, I only succeeded half-ways; on its side too, I constantly recognized the objects and the fine finish of dusk was lacking. I now knew fully well, that the object harms my paintings.
>
> A frightening abyss, a responsible load of all kinds of questions confronted me. And the most important: What should replace the missing object?...
>
> Only after many years of patient working, strenuous thinking, numerous careful attempts, constantly developing ability to purely and nonobjectively feel artistic forms, to concentrate deeper and deeper into this endless depth, I arrived at the artistic forms, with which I am now working and which, I hope will develop much further.

The process was a long and arduous one. We already know that *line, color,* and *shape* can create sensations of space, movement, weight, and volume. But what of color disassociated from an object? Red, for example, will almost always conjure up images of fire, fire truck, stoplight, or car. Try to imagine a response to "winter"—a response not made of words or images of snow and ice, but of pure shapes, lines, and colors. The process is indeed an arduous one.

Writing as he worked, Kandinsky tried to explain his ideas, particularly in *On the Spiritual in Art,* published in 1912. In this treatise Kandinsky affirms his belief in the power of art to speak to the intellect and intuition of people without benefit of the habitual, familiar objects of the material world. He also advances a philosophical basis for this belief and suggests its social implications. Western people, he felt, had become desensitized by the materialism of their society.

Only by freeing painting from the material could the painter respond to the unconscious, the spiritual, and the immaterial longings of man. Moreover, a response freed from the material world would create a more universally understood language. He warned that his work was only a beginning and that future painters would be able to play on color harmonies as musicians play on the harmonies of the scales. Kandinsky's nonobjective pictures seem to build on Einstein's theories of the relativity of time and space, which were developing at this time. Indeed, Kandinsky embraces the buzzing, booming confusion of Einstein's universe in which all matter is energy. *Painting No. 201,* 1914 (Color Plate XXX) appears as an eruption of the energy of the universe. Slashing lines of color race and run, as if to leap from the space of the canvas. Rich in possibilities for fantasy, dream, and daydream, Kandinsky's pictures offered future artists an example of a language of color, line, texture, and shape unfiltered by the material world.

Expressionism

In Munich, Kandinsky formed a group of artists called the Blue Rider. Members of this group and other German artists, writers, and musicians centered in Dresden and Berlin came to be known as expressionists. Expressionism drew on the powerful emotional quality of Van Gogh and on the bold color and line of Gauguin and Matisse. It is essentially, as the name implies, an art of self-expression or subjectivity. Influenced by Freud, expressionist artists (and the writers and musicians associated with them) wished to express the deep, hidden drives of human beings rather than surface "reality." They sensed, along with Marxists, the alienation of the individual in modern society

31-8 *KIRCHNER, Ernst.* Street, Berlin. *(1913) oil on canvas, 47½" × 35⅞". (Collection, The Museum of Modern Art, New York. Purchase.)*

and the dehumanizing effects of bourgeois capitalism. They were dissatisfied with the materialism and complacency of German society and often criticized it harshly in their works. Ernst Kirchner's (1880–1938) painting *Street, Berlin* (1913) is a good example of an expressionist work (Fig. 31-8). What is going on in the picture? What is the artist's attitude toward the way of life portrayed here? How does he express that attitude?

Mondrian and Purism

At the opposite pole from expressionism, another group of artists, centered primarily in Holland, celebrated the spirit of progress and humanity's rational and orderly faculties. The group called De Stilj was dedicated to "the devaluation of tradition,... the exposure of the whole swindle of lyricism and sentiment." In their work they stressed the need for abstraction and simplification, for clarity, certainty, and order. One, Piet Mondrian (1872–1944), began as a traditional painter, visited Paris, learned from the cubists, and returned to Holland. He began to remove all references to the familiar visual world from his canvases, concentrating on the "pure" reality of the formal plastic elements of art, which he began to confine to a linear black grid imposed on a white ground. He inserted color, usually red, yellow, or blue (the three primaries), to create contrasts that were resolved in harmonious balance (Color Plate XXXI). Compare your experience of this work with *Painting No. 201* by Kandinsky (Color Plate XXX). One is fantastic, the other orderly; both grow out of the manipulation of the essential elements of painting.

Dada and Surrealism

In 1915 a number of young people from all over Europe converged in Zurich, Switzerland, to create a movement that sought the fantastic and absurd in art, literature, and music. The movement was called Dada, a term whose origin is obscure. The most frequently quoted version is that a French-German dictionary opened at random produced the word *dada,* which means a child's hobbyhorse or rocking horse. The point is, of course, that life itself is random and uncontrolled: art should reflect the randomness and pessimism that is bred by the recognition of people's inability to control their lives. The movement in Zurich was most concerned with poetry and music, producing events that combined the two in a nonsensical manner. Ridiculing the materialism of the middle classes and the optimism of the scientifically oriented progressives, the movement seemed at first merely a destructive one that challenged not only the traditional values of art but also the most recent. Nevertheless, there was a deep seriousness about these people that encouraged the artist to look again at the irrational, the subjective, the unconstructed side of the human psyche as it responded to life in this century.

In painting, the artist who exemplifies Dada is Marcel Duchamp (1887–1968) (one of three brothers who were deeply involved in new movements in Paris), who had already created a masterpiece in his painting *Nude Descending a Staircase, No. 2,* 1912 (Fig. 31-9). For us today, familiar with time-lapse photography, film, and the multiple images of advertising, the painting is a remarkably expressive rendering of a figure walking down the stairs. Duchamp, however, was not satisfied with painting; he felt that it was a limited process, doomed to end. By attempting a startling variety of approaches, he called into the question all the processes of art. Sometimes he would reduce his subject matter to the components of a fantastic

31-9 *Marcel Duchamp,* Nude Descending a Staircase, No. 2, *1912, oil on canvas, 58″ × 35″. (Philadelphia Museum of Art: Louise and Walter Arensberg Collection)*

machine; at other times he rendered objects with a scientific accuracy that gave them a superreal and fantastic quality (Fig. 31-10). Then, denying the hand of the artist altogether, he simply chose everyday objects, designating them "art" by the application of his signature. For the Armory Show in the United States in 1913 he signed a urinal "R Mutt" and submitted it with the name *Fountain.* It was not shown in the exhibition. These "ready-mades," as Duchamp called them, were offensive to many, but others saw them as the realization and affirmation of the control of the machine and machine-made products in life. In 1915 Duchamp emigrated to New York, where he associated with the group at Stieglitz's 291. There he began a work that came to be considered exemplary of surrealism, the movement in art that emerged from Dada after World War I.

The chief spokesman for the new movement, André Breton, was a writer whose experiences in World War I convinced him of the unlimited depth of the human psyche. Impressed by the ideas of Freud, he identified the unconscious mind as the source for a new synthesis of the sometimes unpleasant concrete world with the world of rich associations created in dream and fantasy. The goal was to free individual creativity to respond positively to the conflict between the rational and the irrational, producing a heightened awareness of the vitality of life and the mind that would ameliorate its apparent emptiness. Techniques for achieving this synthesis included collage, automatic drawing, and photographic montage of images. Generally, the results were a dreamlike or hallucinatory juxtaposition of images and objects that stimulated personal free association and intense emotional responses.

In this context Marcel Duchamp's work *Large Glass; Bride Stripped Bare by Her Bachelors* (Fig. 31-11) became a seminal surrealist work. Duchamp

31-10 *Marcel Duchamp,* Chocolate Grinder, No. 2, *1913. (Philadelphia Museum of Art: Louise and Walter Arensberg Collection)*

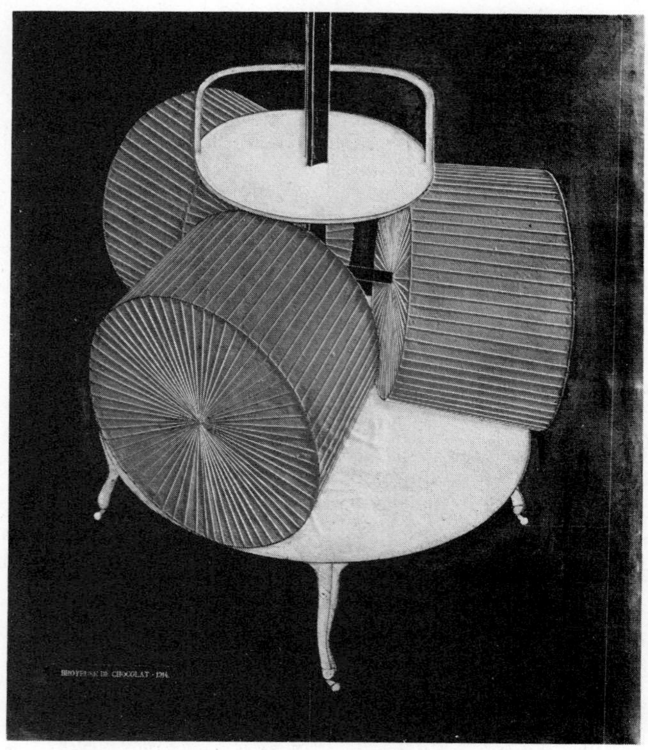

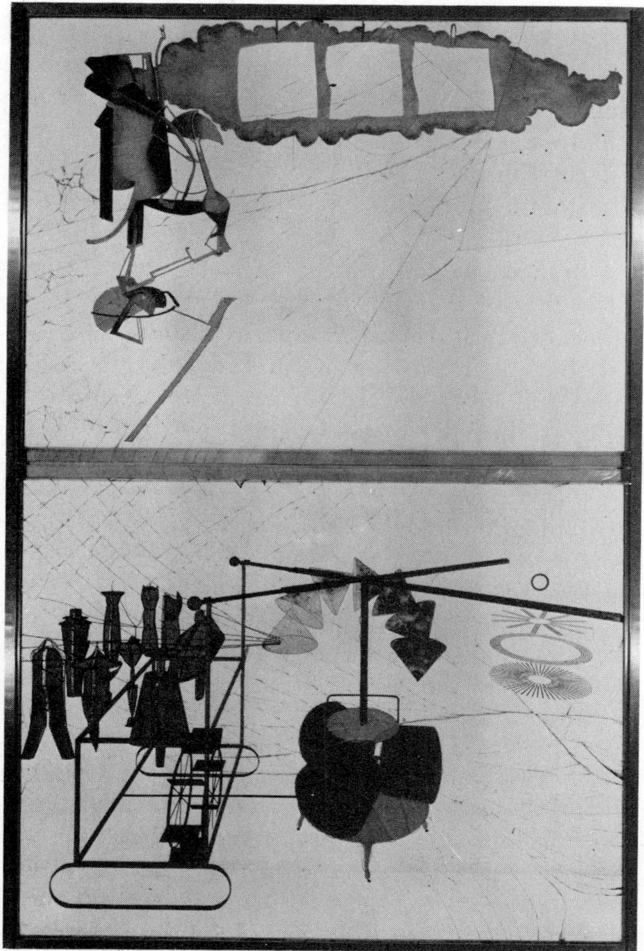

31-11 *Marcel Duchamp,* Large Glass; Bride Stripped Bare by Her Bachelors, *c. 1915, oil, lead foil, and quicksilver on plate glass, 9′1¼″ × 5′9⅛″. (Philadelphia Museum of Art: Bequest of Katherine S. Dreier)*

had worked on the idea for years, accumulating images that he transferred to a sheet of plate glass where dust, allowed to collect, had been glued in place. Other random elements, the frame, and finally the cracks in the glass itself became part of the work. According to Breton's interpretation, these images reflect the mechanization of persons and of the sexual act. Although such a representation may appear somewhat repulsive, if not inhumane, the artist intended to play on the contrast of humanity with machine and the perpetual conflict between the sexes. In so doing, he intended to enlarge our awareness of the unconscious associations that may accompany our lives.

Other artists in various media learned from surrealist techniques how to contradict our familiar and habitual perception of reality. Surrealism has been a source of inspiration not only in painting, sculpture, the graphic arts, and poetry but also in the production of motion pictures.

Salvador Dalí (1904–1989)

The tenets of surrealism were also adopted by the Spaniard Salvador Dalí. Dalí's education as an artist began traditionally, and after he emerged from the Academy of Fine Arts in Madrid he worked in a number of styles then influential—including cubism and the neoclassicism of Picasso. To these and other important twentieth-century influences he added the ability and desire to paint in a realist way, comparable to that of Vermeer.

Dalí moved to Paris in 1929, where he associated with the French surrealists. Here he formulated a theoretical basis for his art, which he described as a visionary reality created from visions, dreams, and memories with pathological or psychological distortions. He now eschewed the formalism of the cubists and the abstraction of the constructivists. His work depended on the free association of images, and his painting style became characterized by forms of violence, destruction, decay, and transformation in which familiar objects such as the human form, watches, telephones, pianos, insects, or images from other paintings appeared. These forms might be multiplied obsessively or fragmented and distorted. They were rendered with a meticulous attention, creating a frightening sense of reality captured in harsh, intense, and luminescent colors. *The Persistence of Memory,* 1931 (Fig. 31-12), in which watches collapse, melt,

31-12 *DALÍ, Salvador.* The Persistence of Memory. *1931. Oil on canvas, 9½″ × 13″. (Collection, Museum of Modern Art. Given anonymously.)*

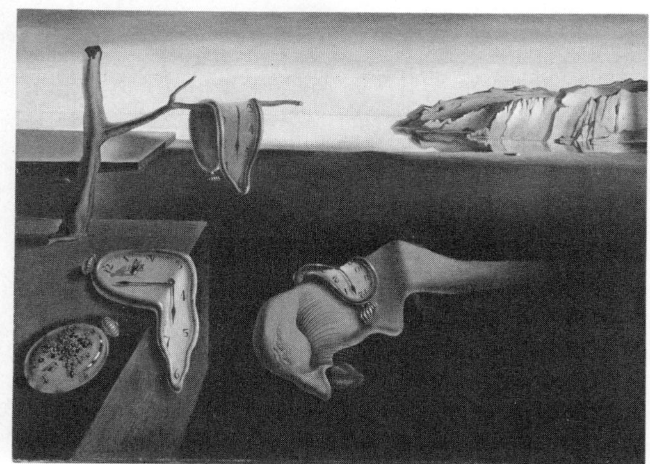

bend, and decay, is among the most famous and familiar of this period.

By the end of the decade Dalí had moved to the United States, where he achieved ready fame with his fantastic appearance and personality and his penchant for publicity. He designed jewelry, theatrical sets, books, and objets d'art. In the 1950s he began to paint serious Christian subjects, including a Crucifixion and a Last Supper.

These later paintings are as controversial as Dalí's entire career. Some consider him a gifted painter, whereas others have considered him nothing more than a facile charlatan whose pretensions to art represent surrealism at its most excessive.

Modernist Sculpture, 1900–1930

Sculpture, like painting and graphics, responded to the same ideas and impulses that had transformed art after 1900. Just as we can distinguish those artists who continue interest in the human form as a means of communication, so we can identify artists who work only in forms, shapes, and colors freed from Renaissance and baroque conventions. Similarly, we can identify cubist sculptors, expressionist sculptors, and sculptors whose work is always associated with Dada and surrealism. We will consider work by two artists, Constantin Brancusi (1876–1957) and Jacques Lipchitz (1891–1973).

Brancusi was a Romanian whose work really parallels that of the cubists rather than being directly influenced by it. He was trained in the academic manner; but, after arriving in Paris in 1904, he turned more and more toward the evocation of forms by reducing them to bare essentials. A splendid craftsman with tremendous empathy for the textures and characteristics of a given material, he described his efforts as a search for the universally expressive essence of forms. *Bird in Space* (Fig. 31-13), made in 1924, can be interpreted as the reduction of a bird's wing, its soaring power, its light gracefulness. The beautifully polished surface of the chrome form calls out to our

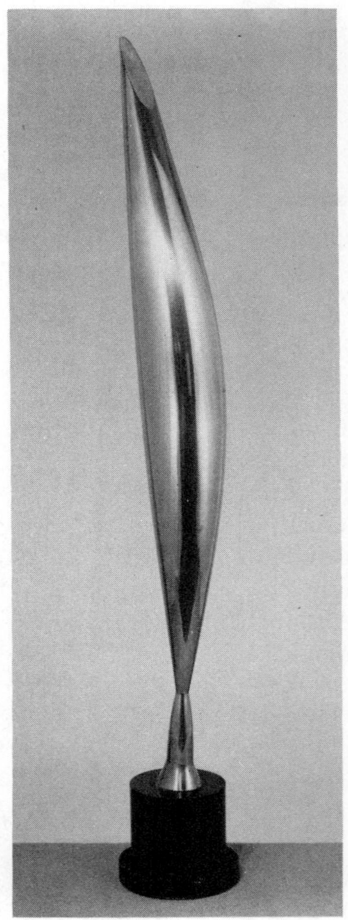

31-13 *Near right. Constantin Brancusi,* Bird in Space, *c. 1924. (Philadelphia Museum of Art: Louise and Walter Arensberg Collection)*

31-14 *Far right. LIPCHITZ, Jacques.* Figure. *1926–30. Bronze (cast 1937) 7′1¼″ × 38⅝″. (Collection, The Museum of Modern Art, New York. Van Gogh Purchase Fund.)*

31-15 *John Sloan,* Sunday, Women Drying Their Hair, *1912, oil on canvas, 26″ × 32″. (Addison Gallery of American Art, Phillips Academy, Andover, Massachusetts. All Rights Reserved)*

tactile senses, and it is possible to imagine the cool purity of the shape that a caress would produce.

The work of Jacques Lipchitz forms a strong contrast with much of that of Brancusi. Much more directly influenced by the cubist painters, he made low reliefs in stone that can be directly compared to paintings and collages by Braque and Picasso. A freestanding piece like *Figure* (Fig. 31-14), made between 1926 and 1930, is strongly suggestive of the totemic power of African figures; but the juxtaposition of side with frontal views that occurs when one moves around a figure in space is based on the orderly perception of the interrelationship of parts—a characteristic of cubism. Lipchitz modeled figures like these in clay or plasticine for bronze casting; the complex surface, which is rough and extremely tactile, was retained in the casting process. Compare this work with Brancusi's *Bird in Space.* Does *Figure* bear any relationship to other sculpture that has been considered? Why or why not? Does the interpenetration of shapes and spaces bear any relationship to painting that we have seen? Is it possible to imagine such relationships in architecture?

Modernist Painting in America

The art scene in the United States was very different from that in Europe between 1900 and the beginning of World War II. Many American artists were hostile to the art of Paris, Munich, and Berlin. The painters who constituted the "ashcan school" remained loyal to an essentially realist aesthetic, basing their work on that of Thomas Eakins (see Chapter 29), but their art was more reportorial and concerned with the life and times of the city. (It was in fact this subject matter that gave them their name.) John Sloan (1871–1951), one of the most representative painters of this group, took his subject matter from the daily activities of the ordinary, the poor, the immigrant (Fig. 31-15). The painters in this group were not convinced that European art could make a contribution to the development of a uniquely American art.

However, painters in this group helped to give modern art its first important, large exhibition in the United States. Arranged by an association of American artists, the Armory Show of February 1913, staged at the Armory of the Infantry in New York City, exhibited the work of Cézanne, Van Gogh, Gauguin,

Matisse, Kandinsky, Picasso, and Duchamp, among others. The public was generally shocked and offended, but many American artists were stimulated and attracted by these works, for a strong stream of innovation already existed. Moreover, these young artists had already found a rallying point in the figure of Alfred Stieglitz, a photographer who had studied in Berlin and returned to the United States. Stieglitz opened a gallery at 291 Fifth Avenue, where he exhibited the most advanced work from abroad and attracted artists and critics. Many important American artists were associated with the gallery and with the impact of European ideas on the American scene.

Stuart Davis (1894–1964)

For decades an acknowledged leader of American abstraction, Davis evolved his style out of the cubism of Picasso and the ordinary objects of American urban life. Choosing as subject matter cigarette packs, light bulbs, electric fans, rubber gloves, and an eggbeater, Davis subjected these ordinary items to a rigorous process of abstraction (Fig. 31-16). Using very few colors, Davis combined objects that seem caught in an energizing framework. Compare *Egg Beater No. 4* (Abstraction), 1927, with Picasso's *Man with a Violin* (Fig. 31-5) and *Three Musicians* (Fig. 31-7). Which of the two Picassos is more like Davis's work? Why? Is there a particularly American quality to Davis's work that you do not find in Picasso's? Can you be specific?

Davis's painting *House and Street* (1931) also gives a powerful portrayal of a typical American scene. The juxtaposition of close-up with distant view and the simplification of forms and colors seem almost cartoonlike, but the energy that the painter gives to the place is hard to ignore. Davis's work demonstrated that abstraction had its place in American painting.

Georgia O'Keeffe (1887–1986)

Another important painter in this group, Georgia O'Keeffe, the wife of Stieglitz, was active as a painter until the 1970s. Her work, like that of Davis, seems to be a major bridge between the American desire for a realistic imagery and the idealism implicit in European abstraction. Certainly she created a very modern, personal idiom. She could make works that completely eliminated objects, and she painted the skyscrapers of New York City (Fig. 31-17) and the barns of Lake George with a clarity and rectitude comparable to the work of Charles Sheeler and George Demuth, two of her contemporaries.

O'Keeffe is most frequently associated with two kinds of images. The first are scenes of the American Southwest. Her knowledge of the area began in the late

31-16 *Stuart Davis,* Egg Beater No. 4. *(The Phillips Collection, Washington, D.C.)*

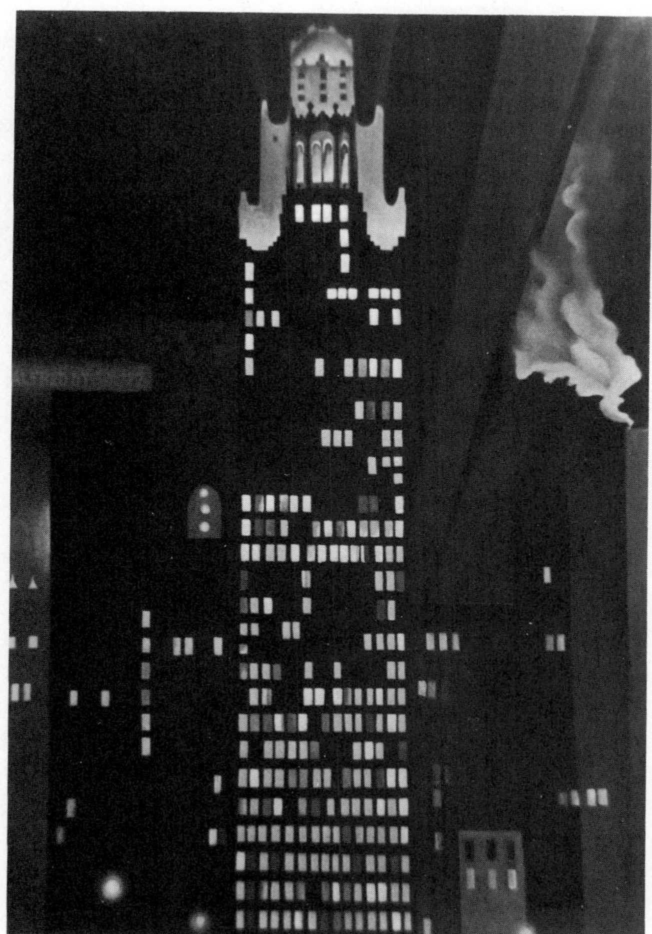

31-17 *Georgia O'Keeffe,* The Radiator Building: Night, New York, *1927, oil on canvas, 48″ × 30″. (Courtesy Fisk University, The Alfred Stieglitz Collection)*

"teens," and in the expansive New Mexican arid landscape, she identified feelings and discovered forms in light that seemed to confirm a vision and provide the means of achieving it. Bleached bones and bony mountains, solid adobe walls and cool, shadowed spaces are painted as intensely experienced but universalized in feeling. The juxtaposition of bones with blossoms and the reduction of endless sky to patterns of light were constant subjects of her last thirty-five years (Fig. 31-18; Color Plate XXXII).

Second are those in which the object, usually a flower or other plant, occupies the entire picture space. In her clear, painstaking account of the magnified flower, we find a rich ground for symbolic associations. The crisp, smooth, painterly surface, however, presents the object with a cold objectivity that contrasts with our resonating fantasies. This tension between the unavoidable presence of the object and the opportunity for free fantasy seems characteristic of American life; it is a contrast like that between our great dependence on the machine and our fear of its dehumanizing possibilities.

O'Keeffe's paintings, drawings, and watercolors of flowers have always been received with critical ambivalence—great enthusiasm counterbalanced by grave reservations because of her being a woman. Historically, "flower painting" was a "woman's art," and the complex messages conveyed by her work seemed both to challenge and make fun of the idea that art created by women should be somehow different from that made by men. Further, her artistic reputation had always been colored by her associations with the artists who represented the *avant-garde* of American painting. As Stieglitz's wife and model, she was regarded as an interesting, "bohemian" figure, not an important painter. A recent major exhibition of her

31-18 *Georgia O'Keeffe,* Cow's Skull with Calico Roses, *1932, oil on canvas, 36⁵⁄₁₆″ × 24⅛″. (Gift of Georgia O'Keeffe, 1947.712, photograph © 1992, The Art Institute of Chicago. All Rights Reserved)*

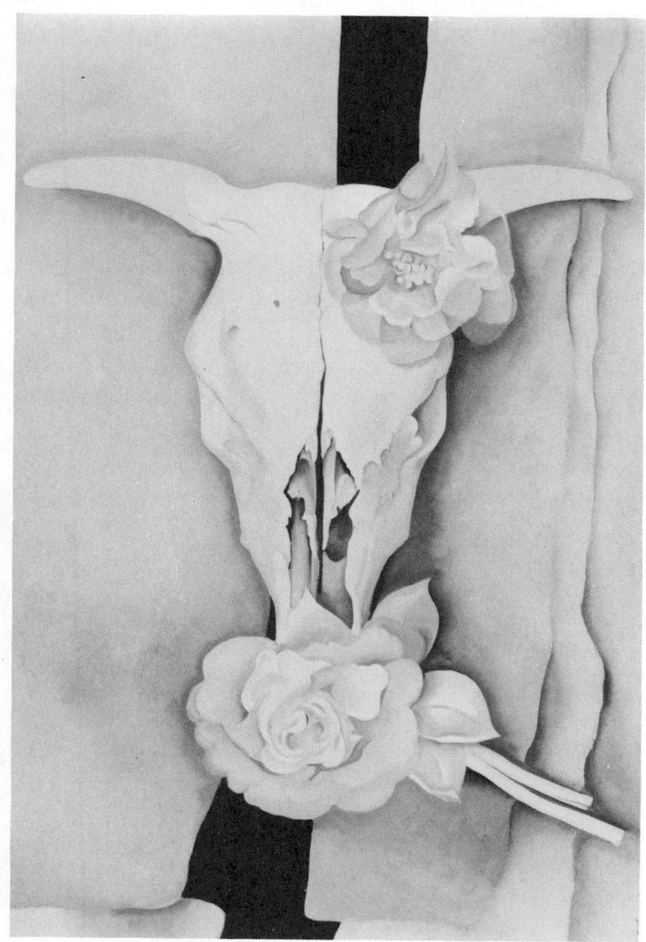

work at the National Gallery of Art takes the position that it is time for serious study because it is her work and not her personality that must withstand critical assessment.

Modernist Architecture, 1900–1930

Although it may seem that Americans had much to learn from Europe in the visual arts, they also had much to contribute. This is nowhere more apparent than in architecture and in a particular genius, Frank Lloyd Wright.

Frank Lloyd Wright (1867–1959)

Wright worked with Louis Sullivan, an architect who had made great contributions to the development of the Chicago School (see Chapter 29). Wright left Sullivan's office in 1893 to work where he lived, in a suburb of Chicago, Oak Park. He had been greatly challenged by Sullivan, but his particular interest in these early years was the single-family dwelling. The typical, two-story wood frame house of the late nineteenth century was, to Wright, a disaster. It was cramped, ugly, dark, and dank. It wasted space, had no relationship to its site, ignored innovations in mechanical systems, and separated people from the land that was their aboriginal home. Wright asked fundamental questions about architecture, beginning with the abstract idea of dwelling, of shelter. He asked what features, forms, and shapes would place people in a harmonious relationship to the earth, giving them the comfort and warmth of the aboriginal cave. He asked what materials should be used, how, and in what forms. He asked questions about the family: how does it function as a small community, and how can the dwelling provide essential privacy for each member within the context of the family? Moreover, he asked how use might be made of growing technology and machine-tooled elements to make the house more livable, comfortable, and responsive as well as less time-consuming, in terms of its upkeep, to free the family for more personal leisure and growth. The approximately thirty houses that grew up on the prairie of Oak Park were the answers to these questions.

Economical to build, dependent on the direct and simple use of wood, glass, brick, and stucco, the Oak Park houses were made for owners who were neither eccentric nor particularly rich. The plans of the houses frequently grew outward from a central core of hearth and services—plumbing, electricity, and heat. Bedrooms were confined to one area, kitchen and servants

31-19 *Frank Lloyd Wright, Robie House. (Hedrich Blessing, Chicago)*

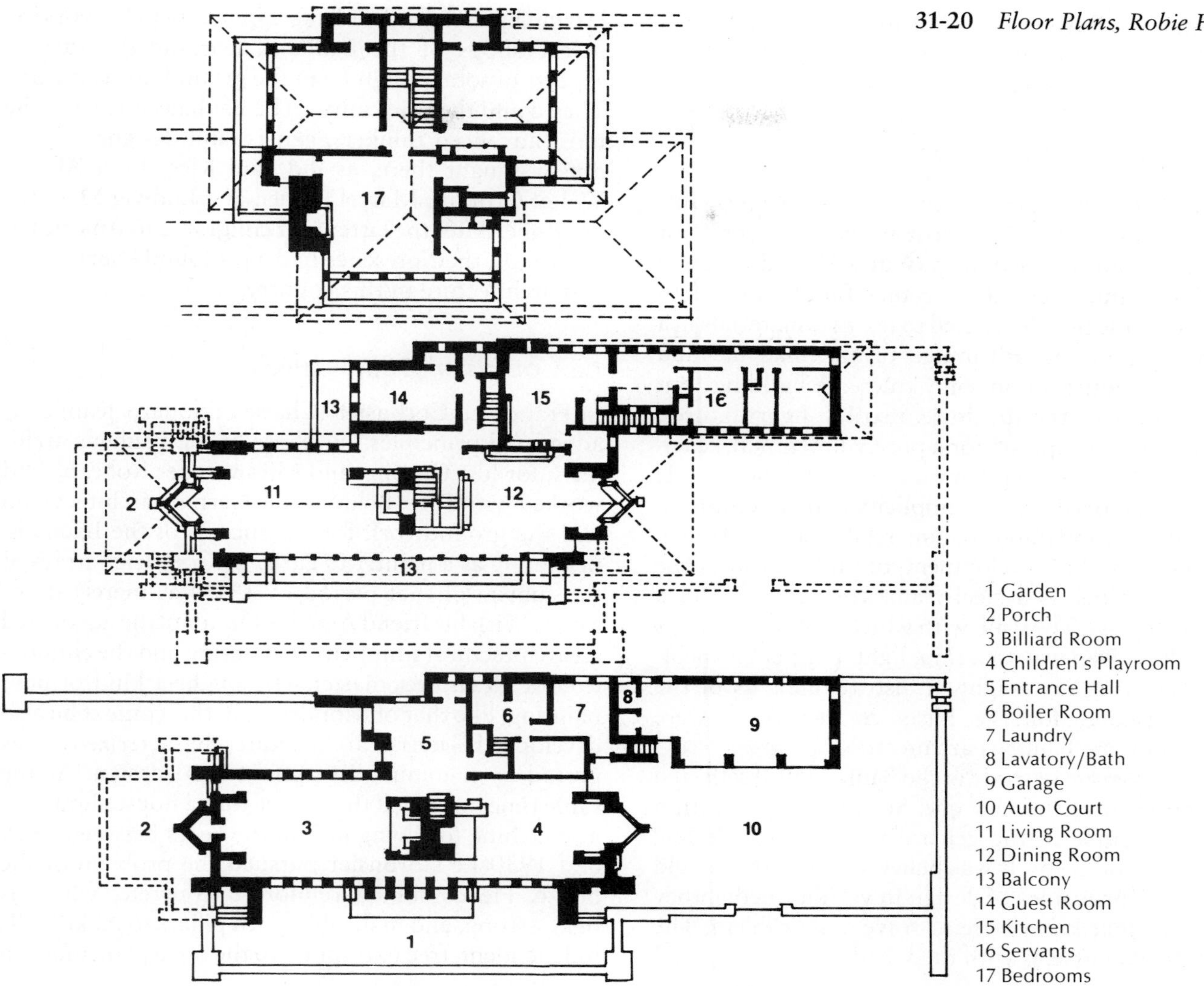

31-20 *Floor Plans, Robie House.*

to another wing; the family-oriented activities were grouped in integrated spaces around the hearth. Overhanging eaves sheltered the long windows and glass doors that opened onto patio, terrace, or balcony. Low walls of stone, brick, or shrubbery separated the houses from the intrusions of the street. The owners loved their homes. Wright's solutions were among the most innovative that this country had seen.

The Robie house in Chicago is a mature expression of Wright's ideas (Figs. 31-19, 31-20). Study the plan. Why does Wright focus the house around the hearth and fireplace? What is the effect of the deep, overhanging eaves, the long continuous lines produced by the roofs and the porches? Where does he use glass? Why does he partially conceal the house from the neighborhood streets? Does the combination of brick and concrete seem a good one? Why not simply use one or the other? The house in the "prairie style," as it came to be known, produced tremendous response from the Europeans who visited Wright in Chicago. His work became exemplary of the possibilities for an architecture that was not "in the styles."

Wright's emphasis on the orderly and rational, coupled with a deep, intuitive feeling for human nature and what would make a suitable dwelling, produced a marriage of ideas that struck strong chords in European thought. His emphasis on the use of machined materials—glass, brick, veneers, and, in the Robie house, steel members for the far-reaching eaves—seemed to combine the best of two worlds: technology and the machine, people and their imagination. But, although some of Wright's contributions were influential in Europe, many of his ideas seemed too romantic to the architects and theorists of the school known as the Bauhaus.

The Bauhaus (1919–1933)

Founded at Weimar, then moved to Dessau, Germany, the Bauhaus became the most influential center for architects who shunned the past and wanted to create a rational, functional architecture for the twentieth century. These people wanted to use new materials in a direct way, taking advantage of the machine and machine production not only to create buildings but also to produce the furniture, textiles, light fixtures, and objects appropriate for a purely functional, scientific age. The physical plant for the school (Fig. 31-21) is almost factorylike in its simplicity and directness. In fact, factories and purely commercial design had much influence on the development of these forms. The classroom block is a steel framework enclosed in a curtain of glass. The wall, with which human buildings began, has given way to a thin, light, permeable membrane carrying no weight. It also reminds us of the Crystal Palace, for the ideas created there were admired by the Bauhaus architect.

The program of study at the Bauhaus also reflected the optimism of the new age. Students began with a yearlong course in the general principles of design, materials, and color. It was believed that if they could master the principles of design in various media, they could use that knowledge to solve any problem. The analogy, of course, is with the scientific method. After learning principles, students applied them by working in the shops of the Bauhaus, learning the various aspects of total design from the ground up, as it were. They could then specialize. The Bauhaus attracted the most advanced thinkers, artists, and designers. Kandinsky taught there, as did Paul Klee, Josef Albers, Walter Gropius, Marcel Breuer, and Ludwig Miës van der Rohe. After the latter four emigrated to America in the 1930s, their presence had a profound effect on art and architecture in this country.

Le Corbusier (1887–1965)

In France Le Corbusier (Charles Édouard Jeanneret) advocated principles like those of the Bauhaus architects, for like Gropius and Miës van der Rohe, he had worked with Peter Behrens, the German architect who laid the groundwork for the success of the Bauhaus. Beginning as a painter in Paris, Le Corbusier attacked the cubism of that period (c. 1918) as merely decorative. With his friend Amédée Ozenfant, he advocated an architectural simplicity in painting and the elimination of all subject matter. He sought a kind of pure painting, like that of Mondrian; in this context he also developed his idea of architecture, characterized in this period by a minimalist approach to design. At the same time he coined the phrase that a house should be a "machine for living in." In the years between 1918 and 1930 Le Corbusier pursued the problem of the house. He combined reinforced concrete, which is light, strong, and malleable, with pillars to make walls independent, free to respond to the open plan, much in

31-21 *GROPIUS, Walter.* The Bauhaus, *Dessau, Germany. 1925–26. (Photograph courtesy, The Museum of Modern Art, New York.)*

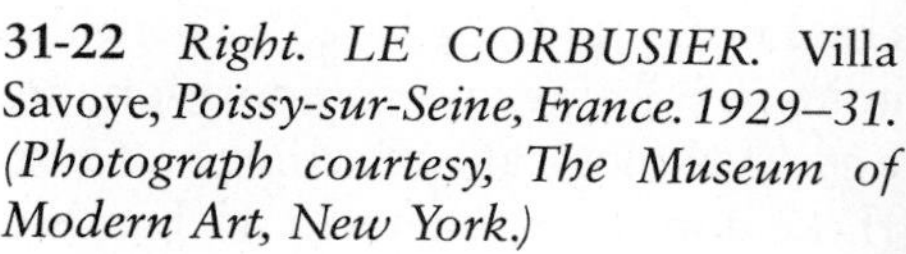

31-22 *Right.* LE CORBUSIER. Villa Savoye, *Poissy-sur-Seine, France. 1929–31. (Photograph courtesy, The Museum of Modern Art, New York.)*

31-23 *Below.* *Le Corbusier,* Villa Savoye. *(left) Plan of Ground Floor showing driveway and garage between the columns (pilotis), service areas, and guest quarters. (right) Plan of Second Floor with main living quarters and roof terrace.*

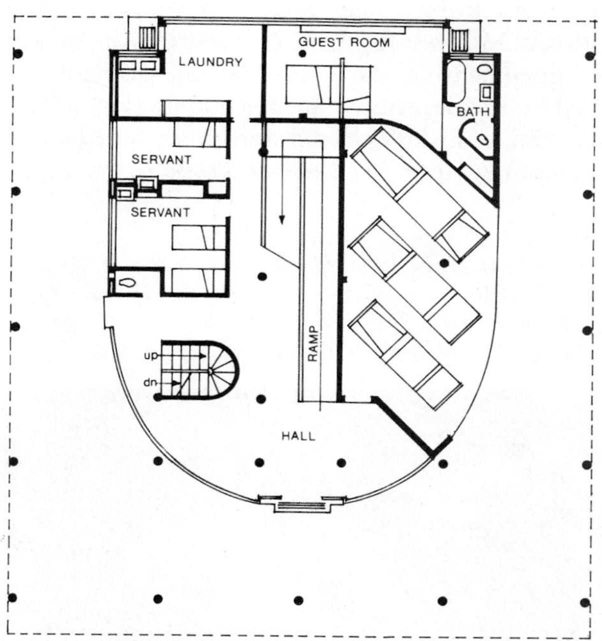

GROUND FLOOR

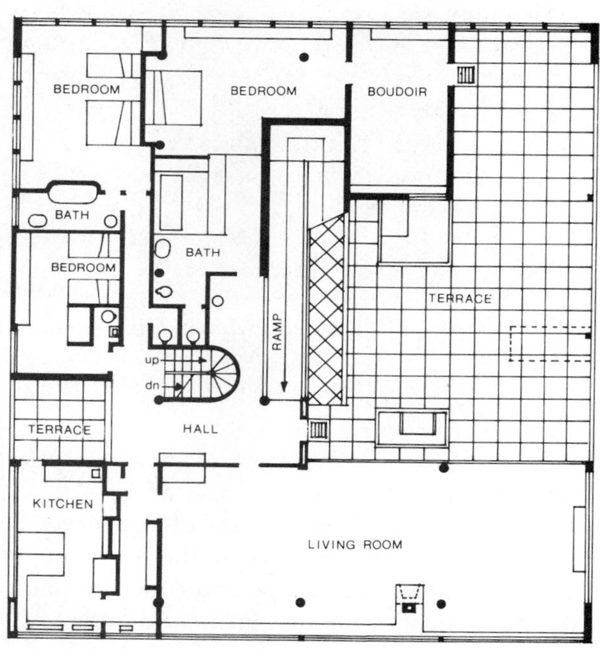

SECOND FLOOR

the same way that Wright had done. Like Wright, he was concerned with the interpenetration of spaces, but he was more inclined to separate the house from its site, turning the house inward on itself. Compare the Villa Savoye at Poissy (Figs. 31-22, 31-23), 1929–1930, with the Robie house. Notice the difference created by materials. Which house seems more in sympathy with its site? Which house seems the more "rational" and "functional"? Which would you prefer and why?

Two New Art Forms: Photography and Film

Photography began to evolve into an art form after it was discovered in France in the 1830s. Painters such as Courbet, Degas, and Eakins used their own photographs as inspiration for their paintings, and photographers such as Nadar and Eugene Atget learned to use the camera to make pictures that were meant to be seen as art and not simply as a copy of the subject represented. Photographs allowed both painters and

31-24 *STIEGLITZ, Alfred.* Winter, Fifth Avenue, *1893 from* Camera Work, *Plate 2, No. 12, 1905. Photogravure, 8⅝" × 6¹⁄₁₆". (Collection, The Museum of Modern Art, New York.)*

photographers to show viewers objects never before observed by the human eye. By the beginning of the twentieth century in Europe and America, photography had become an art form and today is fully accepted as such.

It has always been important that photographers not only expose their own film but also develop their own prints, thus controlling the many variables inherent in the process. At first, photographic subject matter was limited to carefully posed compositions such as portraits and staged dramatic scenes. The exposure of photographic film or plates was too slow to prevent anything that moved from blurring, and both photographers and their sitters had to be very patient. As the technology improved, so did the ability of photographers to record and respond to life.

Edward Steichen (1879–1973) and Alfred Stieglitz (1864–1946) are the two people most often associated with photography's development as an art form in America in the early twentieth century. Stieglitz showed photography at his New York gallery, 291, along with modern paintings and sculpture by American and European artists (Fig. 31-24). His magazine, *Camera Work,* reproduced the work of many promising artists. Both Steichen and Stieglitz chose subjects from everyday life, as well as made memorable portraits of friends and notables (Fig. 31-25). Their photographs are studies in lighting and composition, and the portraits are as psychologically revealing and emotionally rich as those done by painters. In the hands of others such as Lewis Hine and Jacob Riis, who photographed immigrants struggling to survive in the tenements of New York, photographs became a tool for promoting reform. American life in all its variety was a source for artistic inspiration (Fig. 31-26).

When the Great Depression cloaked the nation, photographers such as Walker Evans, Dorothea Lange, and Russell Lee traveled through the rural South and Midwest for the Farm Security Administration, documenting the suffering and displacement caused by the devastated farm economy (Fig. 31-27). Later, Walker Evans's photographs were joined with a text by James Agee, *Let Us Now Praise Famous Men,*

31-25 *STEICHEN, Edward.* Henri Matisse and "The Serpentine," *1910, from* Camera Work, *No. XL 11–XLIII, 1913. Photogravure, 8⅝" × 6¹³⁄₁₆". (Collection, The Museum of Modern Art, New York. Gift of William A. Grigsby.)*

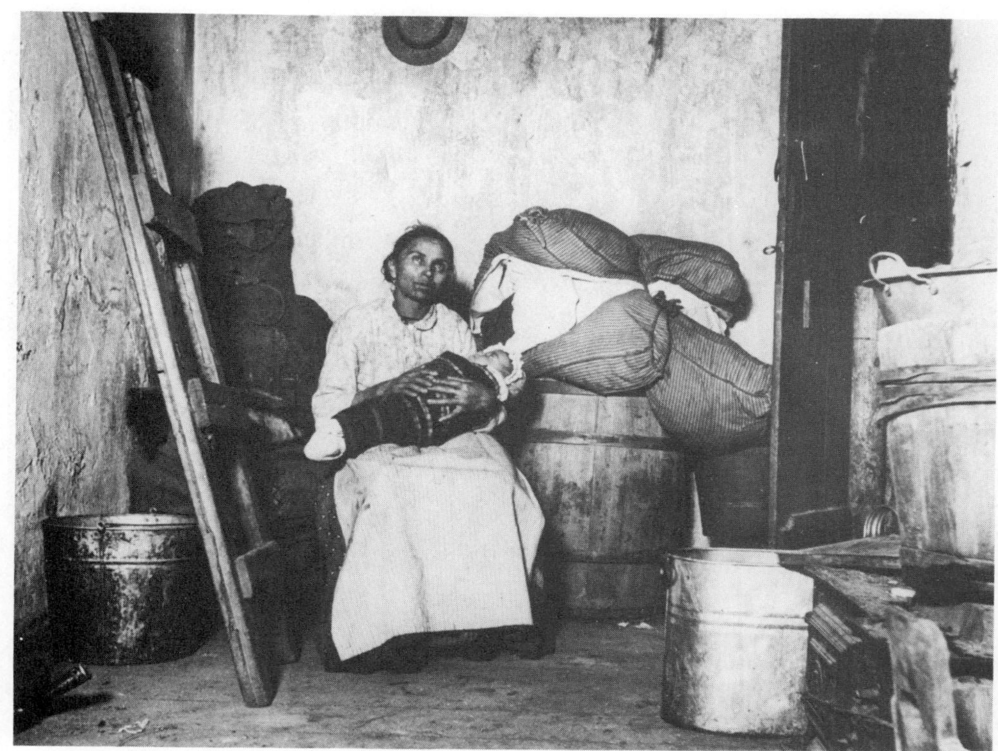

31-26 *Jacob Riis,* Home of an Italian Ragpicker, *1888. (The Museum of the City of New York)*

that successfully unites words and images to create a work of art.

In the 1920s and 1930s, a group of photographers in California were inspired by Edward Weston (Fig. 31-28). Working primarily with the cumbersome view camera, these artists studied and recorded objects—vegetables, fruit, the human body—as if they were abstract patterns of form, texture, shade, and shadow. They formed a group, F/64 (named after the setting on a view camera that brings the maximum area into sharp focus), and exhibited and published their work. Weston and Ansel Adams, also a member of F/64, emerged as two of the major figures in American photography during this period. Adams's subject, like that of W. H. Jackson and Timothy O'Sullivan before him, was the landscape of the American West (Fig. 31-29).

Photographers like Henri Cartier-Bresson and Eugene Smith showed that small 35mm cameras could be used to work quickly and intuitively, producing images of street scenes and war zones that could stimulate the mind as much as photographs made with larger equipment (Fig. 31-30).

By the mid-1950s, "art" photographs were as widely collected as the work of painters and sculptors. The still photograph, whether black and white or color, has become a particularly appropriate medium

31-27 *EVANS, Walker.* Hale County, Alabama, *1936. Gelatin-silver print, 9⅜" × 6⅝". (Collection, The Museum of Modern Art, New York. Stephen R. Currier Memorial Fund.)*

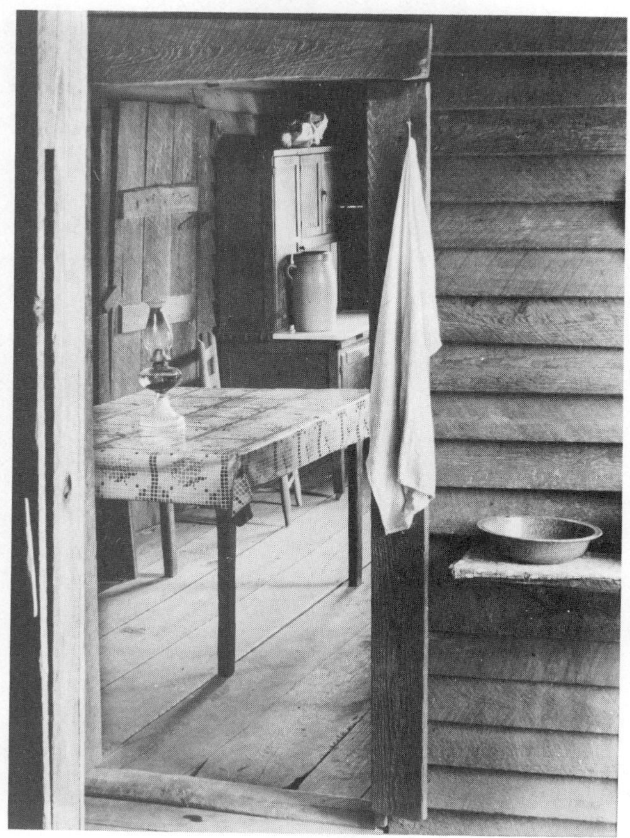

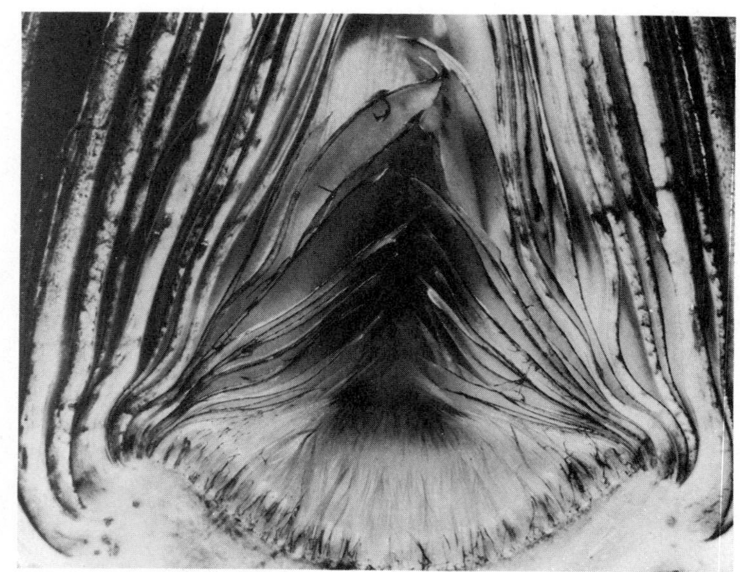

31-28 *WESTON, Edward.* Artichoke, Halved. *1930. Gelatin-silver print, 7½" × 9½". (Collection, The Museum of Modern Art, New York. Gift of David H. McAlpin. © 1981, Center for Creative Photography, Arizona Board of Regents)*

31-29 *Ansel Adams,* Mount Williamson, The Sierra Nevada, from Manzanar, California, *1944. (Copyright 1992 by the Trustees of The Ansel Adams Publishing Rights Trust. All Rights Reserved)*

31-30 *Henri Cartier-Bresson,* Children Playing in the Ruins, Spain, *1934. (Magnum Photos)*

for the art of the twentieth century but no more so than its counterpart—also a product of film—the motion picture.

Developed barely six decades after photography, the motion picture—like oral or written literature, painting, sculpture, photography, and the phonograph recording—is a cultural form of recorded memory. With the development of new technology and sound recording, human beings were for the first time able to preserve not only words and images of their culture but also its actions, sights, and sounds.

Motion pictures were at first limited to short sequences, such as a clown's trick or a locomotive seen head-on, rushing at the audience. But the silent movie, accompanied by captions and live pianists, soon developed into a genuine art form. Perhaps its most memorable figure is Charlie Chaplin (Fig. 31-31), whose portrayal of the "little tramp" baffled by modern civilization made him a true comic hero of the times.

The full-length motion picture that presents an entire drama is obviously analogous to the theater. The mechanics of producing a play, whether on stage or for filming, involve the same elements: actors, script, sets, props, costumes, makeup, lighting, sound effects, director, producer, and marketing (getting the production to audiences). Recording a play on film has both advantages and disadvantages. The principal disadvantage is that the sense of immediacy is lost, and the unspoken communication between performance and audience is missing in the film.

The advantages of cinema include the ability to make a permanent and reproducible record of what happened in front of the camera and the use of *montage,* the ability to edit the performance. Unlike the stage director, the film editor can remove and replace sequences in which an actor forgot his or her lines. The editor can also show change in a way that is nearly impossible for a stage director.

In the American film *Citizen Kane* (1941), directed by Orson Welles, there is a sequence introduced in the script by this note:

> The following scenes, which cover a period of nine years, are played in the same set with only changes in lighting, special effects outside the window, and wardrobe.

The scriptwriter could have noted that changes in makeup also occur; the actors seem to become older as the scenes progress. What happens is this: in each of the seven brief scenes, Kane and his wife are shown in the breakfast room. The first scene presents them as newlyweds—happy, in love, and just getting home after being up all night going to six parties. As the action progresses, the development of their marriage is revealed. Love turns to complacency, then to rancor, and finally to resignation. The last scene is silent—they are reading different newspapers. These scenes

31-32 *Scene from* Stagecoach, *1939. (Culver Pictures, Inc.)*

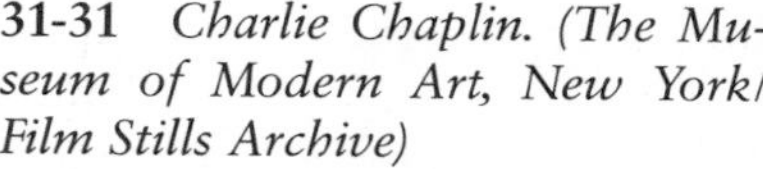

31-31 *Charlie Chaplin. (The Museum of Modern Art, New York/Film Stills Archive)*

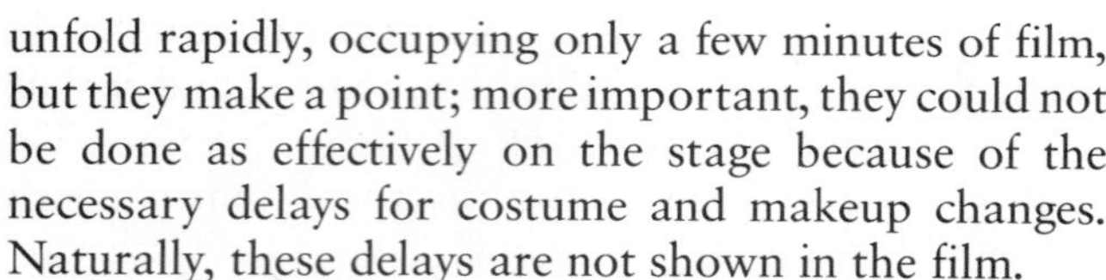

unfold rapidly, occupying only a few minutes of film, but they make a point; more important, they could not be done as effectively on the stage because of the necessary delays for costume and makeup changes. Naturally, these delays are not shown in the film.

The filmmaker can also move the camera. He or she can show close-ups of an actor, which is impossible for the stage director, as well as focus attention much more easily than the stage director can. Moreover, the camera can be taken out of the theater and moved to many different places.

These differences between plays and films are powerful artistic tools that have been exploited effectively by the greatest filmmakers. Techniques such as the flashback, dissolve, and close-up made it possible for avant-garde filmmakers to experiment with layers of time, symbolic images, or portrayal of the unconscious in ways parallel to such presentations in modernist literature and art.

Filmmaking, like photography, has attracted many practitioners. As with all other artistic endeavors, the criteria for success have varied from generation to generation. Following the establishment of the genre in early masterpieces such as *The Birth of a Nation* (1915), the Chaplin and Marx Brothers comedies, and Orson Welles's *Citizen Kane* (1941), a host of important directors have created films whose situations, heroes, and heroines have established typical

American archetypes: the honest politician in *Mr. Smith Goes to Washington* (1939), the war hero in *Sergeant York* (1941), the gentle giant in *King Kong* (1933), the displaced of the Great Depression in *The Grapes of Wrath* (1940), the cruel mobster in *Scarface* (1932), and the myth of the moviemaking genre itself, the beautiful starlet who achieves great fame in *A Star Is Born* (1937). The movies also used the great drama of nineteenth-century American western expansion as the source for the cowboy film, which presented the eternal struggle of good and evil (Fig. 31-32).

Following World War I, a host of movies dealt with the trauma of that experience. With the Great Depression came a series of lavish musicals and hilarious comedies designed to help Americans forget their terrible plight. Fred Astaire and Ginger Rogers appeared in elegantly staged and beautifully choreographed dance numbers that enthralled audiences. After World War II, American and foreign films explored new conventions and new techniques. Cinematographic epics such as *The Ten Commandments* (1923), made by Cecil B. deMille, shared the screen with the intellectually and emotionally complex films from the European, Japanese, and Indian cinema. Each country has developed its own styles and stars. The limits of the media have been stretched considerably from those in force when *Gone with the Wind* was produced in 1938. But the film, gifted with the ability to convey many ideas and images at once, vehicle of popular entertainment as well as serious art form, continues to be a source of controversy.

From Cézanne and Picasso to Wright and Le Corbusier, to Stieglitz and Welles, we have covered the ground of the watershed period of this century in the arts. We have actually touched down only in a very few places. More is omitted than included. We have tried to outline the predicament of the visual artist in these years, torn between rational optimism and irrational pessimism; between the desire for an orderly and pure art and architecture and the desire to speak to the anxiety that was given its most awful expression in World War I itself, where the fruits of science produced the gas mask, shell shock, and the romance of the airplane. On the one hand, all seems pure and promising; on the other, all life seems destined only for suffering and death. The American artist faced the years between the wars in either a self-imposed isolation or a struggle with the implications of European work. New technologies and ideas would eventually fuse developments in Europe to produce a great American school that was also truly international.

32

Modernism in Music, Dance, and Literature

Closely allied with the various modernist movements in the visual arts, artists in the fields of music, dance, theater, poetry, and prose in the opening decades of the twentieth century showed many of the same formal and thematic concerns. Modernism, however, was and is not simply a movement limited to that era. It became a new way of apprehending the world through art. Every serious artist of the twentieth century has felt the necessity either to react against modernism or to build on its innovations.

Stravinsky, the Russian Ballet, and *The Rite of Spring*

Igor Stravinsky, a Russian-born musician whose musical education and taste led him to Paris during the early years of this present century, was part of the artistic revolution that sets the music, art, and literature of the twentieth century apart from all that went before. His musical roots were planted in, and flourished amid, the fertile harmonic gardens of the nineteenth century; but his branches sought light among the complex ideas of the abstract painters, modern dancers, and revolutionary men and women of letters who worked in Europe during the first two decades of our century. Stravinsky became a part, some might say even a causal factor, of a revolution in classical music.

Stravinsky worked closely with a fellow Russian, Sergei Diaghilev, a theatrical impresario who had brought Russian ballet, opera, and painting exhibits to Paris in 1909. The Russian innovations in all these arts, but particularly in ballet, were to have an invigorating effect on western Europe.

In the mid-nineteenth century the world center of ballet had moved from Paris to Saint Petersburg; ballet in the West had become to a great extent reduced to pretty dancing girls executing mechanical movements. The imperial ballet in Russia, however, underwent a classical revival that produced the great ballets to the music of Tchaikovsky: *Sleeping Beauty, Swan Lake,* and *The Nutcracker.* A young choreographer, Mikhail Fokine, revolted against the somewhat rigid, conventionalized vocabulary of this style of ballet. In a manifesto written in 1904, Fokine called for a greater unity of composition in ballet, more integration with the other arts, and gestures "built on the laws of natural expressiveness" to enable dance to "regain its spiritual forms and qualities." Fokine, whose ideas influenced Diaghilev, became the first choreographer for the latter's Russian Ballet troupe. Fokine's training also produced the troupe's greatest male dancer, Vaslav Nijinsky. The extraordinary innovations of the Diaghilev ballets in Paris sprang from the combined talents of composers such as Stravinsky; dancers and choreographers; artists who designed the sets (Picasso among them); and, later, writers such as Jean Cocteau, all under the masterful direction of Diaghilev.

In the section on the African Gelede festival in Chapter 14, we attempted to show that the unification of dance with the other arts, for the purpose of expressing the basic values or spiritual needs of a community, is typical of African artistic expression. European artists, seeking new ways to combine the arts through dance, were in a sense trying to recover a means of expression that they felt had been lost in their own society. Their search may be viewed as belonging to the "discontents" with "civilization" in the early twentieth century. It was in fact often combined with what is called primitivism, or an attempt to find fresh artistic sources in cultures less intellectualized and less specialized. Painters and sculptors, as we have seen, turned to the arts of Africa and Polynesia. But Stravinsky, with the other Russians in Paris, looked for inspiration to his native land, where folkloric traditions were still rich and "civilization" only recent. Both the primitivist dream and the desire to re-create the unity of the arts were instrumental in the conception of Stravinsky's great musical composition *Le Sacre du Printemps* (*The Rite of Spring*) and its ballet.

Stravinsky himself has described the sources of his inspiration. He remembered the "violent Russian spring" that seemed to begin suddenly and to set the whole earth cracking as the most exciting yearly event of his childhood. The memory of this natural event was no doubt linked to a vision that he had while in the midst of completing *The Firebird,* another ballet score.

> I saw in imagination a solemn pagan rite: sage elders, seated in a circle, watched a young girl dance herself to death. They were sacrificing her to propitiate the god of spring. Such was the theme of the *Sacre du Printemps.* I must confess that this vision made a deep impression on me, and I at once described it to my friend, Nicholas Roerich, he being a painter who had specialized in pagan subjects. He welcomed my inspiration with enthusiasm, and became my collaborator in this creation. In Paris I told Diaghileff [Diaghilev] about it, and he was at once carried away by the idea.[1]

Diaghilev chose the revolutionary Nijinsky to do the choreography; Roerich did the sets, and the entire new production was presented to the Parisian public at the opening of the Théâtre des Champs-Elysées in the spring of 1913.

The subject matter of *The Rite of Spring,* if Russian in inspiration, is in fact universal. In searching for the cultural roots of this piece, we might consider that the prehistoric origins of all modern peoples hide pagan and barbaric customs that we would now find repulsive and dreadful. Stravinsky's *Rite* is no figment of the imagination. The ritual of human sacrifice to appease angry gods seems to reappear in every mythology, and factual evidence proving the existence of terrifying practices by humans of more recent vintage only serve to remind us that Abraham's intended sacrifice of his son Isaac or the jungle headhunter's devouring of enemies are not entirely fairy tales of another time, place, and people. In early Greece it would appear that the Dionysian festival helped ensure a bountiful harvest in the succeeding season by sacrificing the festival king. With the growth of civilization, real sacrifice is replaced by ritual or symbolic sacrifice, but the need to communicate and propitiate one's god or gods seems to remain in some form a part of human nature. It is the human desire to communicate with elemental forces that challenged Stravinsky's creativity, bringing forth one of the most remarkable musical compositions of the twentieth century.

The scenario, or story line, deals with the veneration of spring by primitive peoples, a process viewed as a mystical rebirth of the earth. The decay of vegetation during the winter was considered to be a weakening of nature's fertility, and the rejuvenation of nature called for a sacrifice in spring, *le sacre du printemps.* A female is chosen, and she pays homage for her people with her life. To show this on the stage, Stravinsky set his music in parts, each section with a self-explanatory title. The

[1]Igor Stravinsky, *An Autobiography* (New York: Simon & Schuster, 1936; reprinted New York: M. & J. Steuer, 1958), p. 31.

music is continuous in each part, and the episodes follow each other without pause.

PART I

Adoration of the Earth

1. Introduction
2. Dance of the Adolescents
3. Dance of Seduction
4. Rounds of Spring
5. Games of the Rival Communities
6. Entrance of the Celebrant
7. Consecration of the Earth
8. Dance of the Earth

PART II

The Sacrifice

1. Introduction
2. Mysterious Circle of the Adolescents
3. Glorification of the Chosen One
4. Evocation of the Ancestors
5. Ritual of the Ancestors
6. Sacrificial Dance of the Chosen One

The Music

The music Stravinsky composed to set these ritual dances to had, and still has, a shocking effect on its audiences. Peculiar chords assault the ears. Not only were the combinations of notes unfamiliar to all but to the most avant-garde listeners of the day; they did not progress through familiar chord patterns that concert patrons had come to expect in music for the ballet. The music was loud, so loud; and it seemed to repeat discord after discord in irregular and jagged rhythms. Worst of all, there were no lovely, singable melodies that the music-loving French might whistle or hum as they left the theater. In fact, the first audience found this music so distasteful that they literally started a riot. Jean Cocteau describes the scene thus:

> The public played the role that it had to play. It laughed, spat, hissed, imitated animal cries. They might have eventually tired themselves of that if it had not been for the crowd of esthetes and a few musicians, who, carried by excess of zeal, insulted and even pushed the public of the boxes (the very wealthy in the box seats). The riot degenerated into a fight. Standing in her box, her diadem askew, the old Countess de Pourtales brandished her fan and shouted all red in the face: "It is the first time in sixty years that anyone has dared to make a fool of me!"

What was happening in music in 1913 that could cause such a hostile reaction in Paris? Basically, all the musical values of the past were being questioned and replaced with new, experimental ideas. Stravinsky was not alone in working toward a new tonal idiom, although his solutions differed from those of his important contemporaries—Claude Debussy, Erik Satie, Alexander Scriabin, Arnold Schönberg, and Anton von Webern. But whereas music to this time had been building on the past—adding to and depending on tradition—the new music of these composers, Stravinsky included, negated the validity of the past and imposed a new order on the sounds of music. *Harmony,* in the traditional sense of the word, was discarded; so were the notions of *melody* and *rhythm* that prevailed at the time. New orchestral effects were pried out of the instruments, and new types of heroes, or antiheroes, were sought for the songs and scenarios of the rebellious avant-garde composers.

Stravinsky opens his work with a bassoon solo that is "too high." Traditional composers would never have spotlighted a bassoon in that register because, they thought, it sounds strange. Stravinsky needed a primeval sound, and he found it in the bassoon. He also needed a new harmonic sound, which he found by pitting two chords against each other at the same time, an F-flat chord and an E-flat chord (an E♭7).

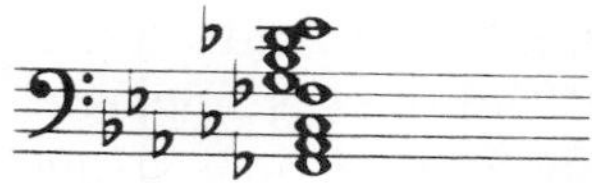

Needing something to replace *harmonic progression,* he chose to discard progression and substitute repetition. He would take one dissonant cluster of notes, hammering them over and over until he felt that a change was called for aesthetically. Then another cluster of notes would follow; but the choice of pitches for the second set was determined not by the old laws of harmony and chordal resolution, but by the laws of Stravinsky's ear. Like the painter Picasso, Stravinsky had all the training and technique necessary to create masterpieces in the old style. His was not the frenetic searching of an ignorant musician but the conscious decision of a master. The values of the twentieth century were not the same as those that held sway a few short years before. And the change in values demanded the changes that took place in artistic expression.

Of all the innovative changes that Stravinsky demonstrated in his new composition of 1913, nothing captured the hearts of practicing musicians more emphatically than his use of rhythm. In *The Rite of Spring* we hear irregular series of pulses, changing *meters,* groupings of five and seven where multiples of two and three had been the norm. The effect is a sense of discontinuity and terror: a new style is introduced into twentieth-century music. The rhythm is similar to that of jazz in its energy and very different from the fluctuating pulse-beat of the late romantic composers.

At once both regular and irregular, at once both orderly and chaotic, *The Rite of Spring* communicates in the music basic conflicts between the barbaric and the civilized, the controlled and the ecstatic, the conflict of *id* and *superego.* The people of Paris were shocked by what they heard in 1913, but today this work must be called tame in comparison with those of our contemporaries. And as a commentary on how brazen we have become since Stravinsky crashed his orchestra about the ears of his public, we should note that in 1940 Walt Disney used *The Rite of Spring* as background music for a full-length cartoon, *Fantasia,* in which mesozoic monsters fight and die amid the primordial slime and volcanic dust.

But once one has overcome the effects of the novelty of the sounds themselves, one discovers that order and design are present. Reason prevails, and the artistic laws of unity and variety are still operative. The orchestration is a unifying factor; so is the dance and the story line. Rhythmic elements from earlier sections reappear at later times, sometimes transformed or disguised and sometimes not. The types of melodic units that Stravinsky employs are similar and seem to fit within a discernible style. Contrast is apparent and seems to be used judiciously. Slow sections are interspersed among the fast; heavy orchestration is balanced with solo performance and light accompaniment; chordal writing is matched with linear composition.

For all its newness, *The Rite of Spring* does not abandon *tonality,* which is the basic feature of the harmonic language of the nineteenth century. However, Stravinsky is called on to use different means to establish a feeling of tonal center for our ears; for, if he cannot use standard chord progressions, cadences, and tonal melodies, what can he employ to lend tonal stability to his composition? Repetition. By repeating a chordal sound over and over, the lowest-sounding pitches assume the functions of chordal roots. They spell out the "key" of the moment. He reinforces this by choosing clusters of tones that can be grouped into familiar chords, sounds that a layperson's ear can organize rather quickly. Nor does Stravinsky actually abandon melody. He simply uses lines of notes that do not fit easily into our common practice major-minor tonal system; he chooses intervals that are hard to sing; he sometimes calls on instruments to play them in manners that are difficult and therefore sound strained; and he does not develop them in the way that a nineteenth-century romantic composer might. Still we can analyze the piece and discern the most important "tunes" or motives of the various sections.

So what are the features that one needs to study before a comprehension of the work is possible? Strangely enough, the answer is probably "none." Stravinsky's *Rite* is music of our time: once the scenario has been digested, the sounds are accepted naturally. We all have the experience of today's television, movie, and radio music to help us, and the common sounds of today are not so different from what was novel in 1913. Stravinsky helped bridge our musical experience to the past or, more properly, connect the past with the music of the present. *The Rite of Spring* is perhaps the single most important composition of the twentieth century for its impact on all the music that followed.

The Ballet

What kind of dance could be created to accompany this music of tones and rhythms unrecognizable to the public of 1913? Certainly, the movements on stage were as shocking to the public as the sounds. In *101 Stories of the Great Ballets* George Balanchine, Diaghilev's last choreographer (who later became director of the New York City Ballet), describes the action of the dance and its relationship with the music. The thematic link between dance and death in this ballet recalls that in *Giselle.*

GEORGE BALANCHINE AND FRANCIS MASON

The Rite of Spring

First Tableau—Adoration of the Earth

A musical prelude recalls man's first relations with the world about him. The curtain rises. In a wasteland scene dominated by great masses of stone, young girls and boys sit in separate groups. They do not move, they wait and watch, as if expecting some sign from the stone shafts they revere. The girls rise, as if drawn by the abundance of Nature to which the music calls their attention. A wise man stands among the dancers; the girls rush around and around him. Now he moves toward the sacred mound of the enclosure. The girls follow and bow before him. The opening phrase of the ballet—the quiet, plaintive cry of man against all-powerful Nature—is repeated.

The strings sound strong, persistent chords that rouse the young men. To the virile beat of the music, they begin to dance, their movements accelerating at its demand, their feet stamping, stamping the earth. The girls join in the dance, the music becomes joyous, and the adolescents abandon themselves to the swift, exuberant rhythms of the orchestra.

This music changes sharply. A new, penetrating melody shrieks warningly and disturbs the young people. The happiness of the boys and girls shifts abruptly to fierce savagery. They split into different groups; the boys face the girls and move toward them. The boys seem bent on attack, but at the last minute they hesitate; they move back and forth in an almost helpless effort, ignorant of their own true intent. The rhythmic crescendos give place to the soft trilling of flutes. Now the boys break their formation, and each carries a girl away.

Four boys remain on the scene. They choose four girls, lift them up on their backs, and dance slowly, bending low under the weight of their burdens in imitation of the plodding chords of the music. This "Round Dance of Spring" gradually increases in volume, and all the adolescents participate. All the dancers step back as the trilling flutes repeat their love call.

Drums herald the beginning of a contest between two rival tribes. Groups of men from each tribe engage in vigorous games. In the midst of their activity, the wise man, represented in the orchestra by a portentous melody on the tuba, tries to interrupt the games. The stronger theme of the games at first drowns out the wise man's theme, then recedes. The men turn to the wise man. There is a brief, taut silence, then all the men fall to the ground and worship the earth.

The drum rolls loudly, and all rise to dance, as if they had felt the pulse of the earth and been renewed by its power. The dance grows frenzied in its intensity. The curtain falls.

Second Tableau—The Sacrifice

Night is about to fall as this second scene begins; the setting sun has turned the sky scarlet. The girls sit near the wise man at a fire. One of these girls must be chosen by the others to make the sacrifice to the earth: this girl must dance herself to death. The music is calm; the figures on stage are quiet and they are unafraid. The girls regret what they have to do, but they are resigned to it with a kind of physical tiredness that the music reflects. They do not feel that they are victimized by Nature, but rather that they must obey what they believe to be its rules.

Soon the girls rise and move in the patterns of the "Dance of the Mysterious Circles." Their movements are trancelike, as if they themselves were not to make their dreadful decision. Their inspiration arrives, and they rush to the periphery of the scene; the chosen one stands alone in the center of the stage.

Now begins the dance that glorifies the victim. The chosen one remains motionless as the girls and men of the tribe whirl around her. All are transfixed at her power. They invoke the spirit of their ancestors, terrified anew by the force of Nature. Marking the relentless, sharp rhythms of the music with their feet, their dance reaches an ultimate expression of uncontrolled glory in sacrifice.

All the tribe members retire to watch the chosen one. The orchestra sounds strong, militant chords, trumpets blare harshly, cutting the air. The dance of the chosen one begins. The brutal savagery of the demanding music compels her to imitate it. Brief moments of comparative quiet, which seem at first to be periods of rest and release, are in reality more deadly because of the thrashing force that follows them. The girl is now wholly a part of the music, part of the earth. Hypnotized by her movements, the tribe joins in the violent dance. The chosen one begins to lose her strength, but—forced on by the convulsive violence of the music—is endowed with a new, superhuman compulsion. When it seems that Nature can demand no more, the girl is pushed into a fresh frenzy. Then she falls. She is dead.

The men of the tribe catch her up in their arms and hold her high over their heads before the sacred mound. The people of the tribe rush around her, holding up their arms. At the last slapping crescendo of the music, they fall to the earth.

(Dame Marie Rambert, who had been Nijinsky's choreographic assistant, describes the nature of his choreography and the audience's reaction.)

"Nijinsky again first of all established the basic position: feet very turned in, knees slightly bent, arms held in reverse of the classical position, a primitive, prehistoric posture. The steps were very simple: walking smoothly or stamping, jumps mostly off both feet, landing heavily. There was only one a little more complicated, the dance for the maidens in the first scene. It was mostly done in groups, and each group has its own precise rhythm to follow. In the dance (if one can call it that) of the Wisest Elder, he walked two steps against every three steps of the ensemble. In the second scene the dance of the sacrifice of the Chosen Virgin was powerful and deeply moving. I watched Nijinsky again and again teaching it to Maria Piltz. Her reproduction was very pale by comparison with his ecstatic performance, which was the greatest tragic dance I have ever seen.

"The first night of that ballet was the most astonishing event . . . at the first sounds of the music, shouts and hissing started in the audience, and it was very difficult for us on the stage to hear the music, the more so as part of the audience began to applaud in an attempt to drown the hissing. We all desperately tried to keep time without being able to hear the rhythm clearly. In the wings Nijinsky counted the bars to guide us. Pierre Monteux conducted undeterred, Diaghilev having told him to continue to play at all costs.

"But after the interlude things became even worse, and during the sacrificial dance real pandemonium broke out. That scene began with Maria Piltz, the Chosen Virgin, standing on the spot trembling for many bars, her folded hands under her right cheek, her feet turned in, a truly prehistoric and beautiful pose. But to the audience of the time it appeared ugly and comical.

"A shout went up in the gallery:

"'*Un docteur!*'

"Somebody else shouted louder:

"'*Un dentiste!*'

"Then someone else screamed:

"'*Deux dentistes!*'

"And so it went on. One elegant lady leaned out of her box and slapped a man who was clapping. But the performance went on to the end.

"And yet now there is no doubt that, musically and choreographically, a masterpiece had been created that night. The only ballet that could compare with it in power was Bronislava Nijinska's *Les Noces,* created in 1923. She, like her brother, produced a truly epic ballet—so far unexcelled anywhere."

32-1 *Auguste Rodin,* Nijinsky, *1912, bronze, 17.5 × 9.7 cm. (Musée Rodin, Paris/Photo copyright Bruno Jarret)*

Nijinsky's sister Nijinska was in fact a better choreographer than he, although the importance of his innovations is undeniable. Stravinsky was not particularly pleased with Nijinsky's choreography for *The Rite of Spring*, and the ballet has been redone many times since. Yet Nijinsky himself, a stunning dancer with great powers of characterization and capable of amazing leaps (Fig. 32-1), has become a legend in our cultural history. He and Anna Pavlova, another Russian who also danced for Diaghilev, are still for many the greatest dancers of the twentieth century. In Nijinsky as in Nietzsche, however, genius bordered on madness. For several years he was confined to an asylum in Switzerland; in 1950 he killed himself in London by leaping out of a window.

Modern Dance

While Mikhail Fokine was working to revitalize ballet in Russia, an American woman from California named Isadora Duncan began an entirely new approach to dance. Duncan, who made a deep impression on Fokine during a visit to Russia in 1905, wanted to free dance entirely from the restrictions of steps, poses, and attitudes. For her, dance meant individual spontaneity and Dionysian contact with nature. She admired classical Greek art for its simplicity and natu-

32-2 *Isadora Duncan. (Harvard Theatre Collection)*

ral forms and believed, like the Greeks, that the human body, without artificial decoration, is the noblest form in art. Yet she was very American in her daring defiance of tradition and reliance on individual feeling. Her dances, she declared, were inspired by her native California; her first dancing masters were "wind and wave and the winged flight of bird and bee." Since every dance she performed was spontaneous and new, she left no school and no choreography behind her. What she did leave was the impression of a soul in movement (Fig. 32-2) on those who watched her, and her re-creation of dance as self-expression left a heritage of complete freedom to those who followed her.

The great innovators in dance in the early twentieth century shared with modernists in the other arts a desire for freedom of expression; an experimental attitude toward the use of elements such as space, texture, and time; and a need to return to primitive and archaic modes of expression. Some of the leaders in the modern dance movement, such as Ruth St. Denis and Louis Horst, sought to recapture both the primitive expressivity of the body and the relationship between dance and religion.

Modern dance differs from ballet in that it abandons not only the traditional steps but also *pointe* (toe-dancing) and the frothy tulle costumes. The portrayal of woman in most modern dances differs considerably from that in the romantic ballet (as we saw it in *Giselle*) or that in the Russian neoclassical ballet. The most important innovator in this aspect, as in other, more technical ones, is Martha Graham. In her major works from the 1930s through the 1950s, Graham presented woman not as ethereal and ideal, but as earthy, passionate, and complex. Her choreography probes the psychic depths of her characters. She reworked classical and biblical myths for dance so that they appeared told from the woman's viewpoint; for example, she re-created the Oedipus story as the experience of Jocasta. Graham developed a technique built on the principle of contraction and release of the muscles that continues to be taught in schools of dance. The Martha Graham Company is still a major force in the American dance world.

Modern dance and ballet have remained separate art forms, but they have borrowed from and influenced each other extensively. Fokine, as we have noted, was influenced by Duncan. Martha Graham danced the leading role in the American premiere of *The Rite of Spring* (with new choreography by Massine) in 1930. The choreographer Kurt Jooss in Germany composes in an idiom that is partly ballet and partly modern dance. The United States remains the world leader in modern dance and shares the honors in ballet with Russia and Britain.

African American Dance

African American dance, although closely allied with the modernist movement, has sought its own directions by exploring its African roots. The black dancer and choreographer could draw on a rich folkloric tradition in African America itself, on European and white American innovations in ballet and modern dance, and on his or her own observations and knowledge of African (as well as Caribbean) dance. The talents that have made use of these elements have created a truly unique idiom in dance.

There is no doubt that American blacks managed to preserve an African style of dance. This developed into social dances like the cake walk and performing

32-3 Revelations, *Mari Kajiwara, Melvin Jones, Judith Jamison. (Alvin Ailey American Dance Theater. Photo, Fred Fehl)*

dances like the tap dance. Blacks performed in minstrel shows touring the United States from the 1840s to the beginning of World War I. In spite of the often negative way in which whites took minstrels, these shows helped to establish blacks as entertainers and influenced the development of the American musical comedy.

The two dancers who did most to establish African American dance as an art form were Katherine Dunham and Pearl Primus, both active in the 1930s and 1940s. Pearl Primus, who studied with Martha Graham, established herself as a serious concert dancer although she also performed in night clubs. Becoming interested in African dance, she went to Africa to do research, particularly in the (then) Belgian Congo (now Zaire). She used this knowledge, as well as African American themes, in her choreography. One of her most moving compositions is "The Negro Speaks of Rivers," based on the Langston Hughes poem.

Black dance companies today continue to adapt African and African American styles and themes to modern dance. Alvin Ailey, until his death in 1989, was perhaps the most acclaimed black choreographer. His company, now headed by the great dancer Judith Jamison, continues to be one of the best and most successful on the New York scene (Fig. 32-3). Ailey's works such as *Revelations,* set to spirituals, and *Roots of the Blues* interpret the African American musical experience in dance. *Cry* is a tribute to black women. The company doing most to bring African dance to the American stage is that of Chuck Davis. Davis, who has studied in Africa, presents authentic African dances and his own compositions based on African movements.

Modernist Movements in Literature

We have temporarily stepped out of chronology to explore briefly the impact of modernist innovations on dance in our own era. Let us return now to the early twentieth century to examine experiments and changes taking place in literature as they relate to those in the other arts.

A Literature of Exiles

Most of the great modernist writers lived, at one time or another, in Paris. Besides the native French writers associated with the Dada, surrealist, and other artistic-literary modernist movements, there were German expressionists, Italian futurists, and other Europeans.

Plate XXVIII
Henri Matisse, *Portrait of Madame Matisse (The Green Stripe)*, 1905. Statens Museum for Kunst, Copenhagen.
(Copyright 1992 Succession H. Matisse/ARS, N.Y.)

Plate XXIX
Georges Braque, *Musical Forms*, 1918. 30⅜″ x 37⅜″. Pasted paper, corrugated cardboard, charcoal and gouache on cardboard.
(Philadelphia Museum of Art: The Louise and Walter Arensberg Collection)

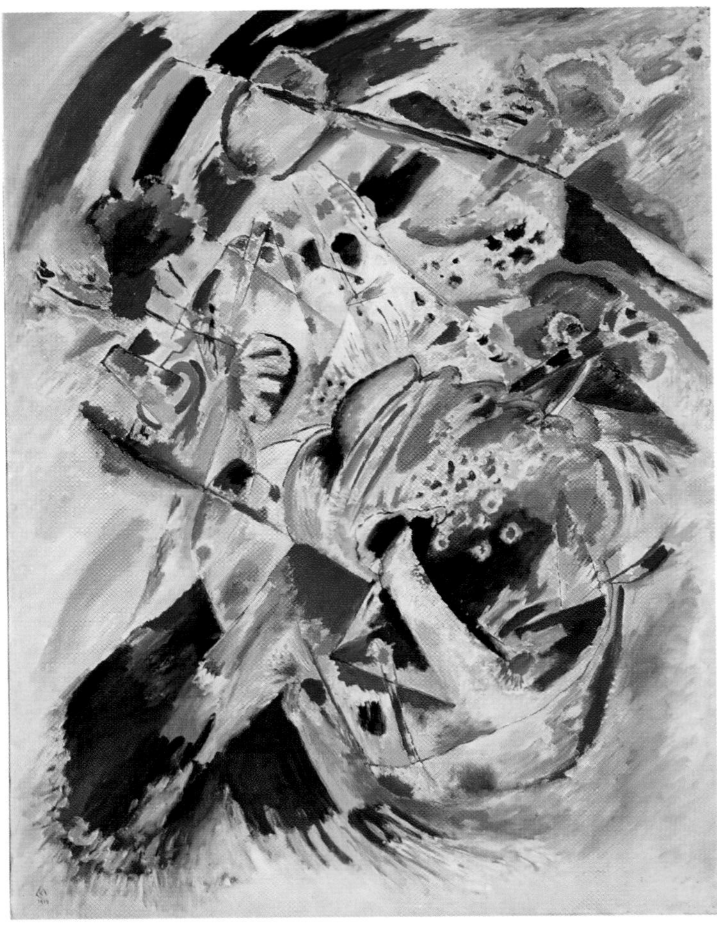

Plate XXX
KANDINSKY, Vasily,
Painting No. 201,
1914.Oil on canvas,
64¼″ x 48¼″.
(Collection, The Museum of Modern Art, New York. Nelson A. Rockefeller Fund. By exchange.)

Plate XXXI
Mondrian,
Composition with Red, Blue, and Yellow, 1921.
(Collection Haags Gemeentemuseum, The Hague)

Plate XXXII
Georgia O'Keefe,
American, 1887–1986,
Sky Above Clouds IV.
Oil on canvas, 1965,
243.8 x 731.5 cm.
(Restricted gift of the Paul and Gabriella Rosenbaum Foundation and gift of Georgia O'Keefe, 1983. 821. Copyright 1992 The Art Institute of Chicago. All rights reserved.)

Plate XXXIII
Jacob Lawrence,
Forward, 1967.
(North Carolina Museum of Art, Raleigh. Purchased with funds from the State of North Carolina.)

Plate XXXIV
WARHOL, Andy,
Gold Marilyn Monroe,
1962. Synthetic polymer paint, silkscreened, and oil on canvas, 6′11¼″ x 57″.
(Collection, The Museum of Modern Art, New York. Gift of Philip Johnson.)

Plate XXXV
Judy Chicago,
Mary Wollstonecraft
place setting from *The Dinner Party*.
(Copyright Judy Chicago 1979. Photograph by Donald Woodman.)

Paris was also the cradle for a dynamic new African literature written in French by intellectuals from the French African colonies, some of whom were involved with the surrealist movement. It is no exaggeration to say that Paris in the early twentieth century was a fermenting center of British and American letters. James Joyce, the Irish novelist and poet who became one of the greatest and most original stylists in the English language, found as his first publisher an American in Paris—Sylvia Beach, who managed the bookstore Shakespeare and Co. American expatriates such as Gertrude Stein, Ezra Pound, F. Scott Fitzgerald, and Ernest Hemingway also gathered at Beach's bookstore. Gertrude Stein was a close associate and supporter of Picasso and other modern painters, who were highly influential on her style. Stein coined the phrase "the lost generation" to describe these Americans who had fled their country for Europe. Common among them was the feeling that a crass, philistine American public was incapable of understanding or sustaining them and that they needed to turn elsewhere for intellectual and aesthetic nourishment.

The rift between artist and public, first sensed by the romantics and intensified by the symbolists, was, for the modernists, a fact of life. It is not surprising that a literature of expatriates, a literature responsible to no one, is a literature characterized by a sense of exile and by an extreme subjectivity. The lack of contact with a public, except for a small coterie, gives the writer great freedom to experiment but also encourages esotericism. Many of the modernist writers who did not join the expatriates in Paris experienced some sort of exile. The American T. S. Eliot did live briefly in Paris but emigrated to England. Those who were not in physical exile often experienced an inner exile. Franz Kafka (1883–1924), in his own words a "triple exile" as a German-speaking Jew living in Czechoslovakian Prague under the Austro-Hungarian empire, produced the most innovative prose in modern German and some of the most influential modernist images. Kafka's three unfinished novels—*Amerika, The Trial,* and *The Castle*—deal with the modern sense of anguish and alienation in the face of a civilization characterized by a faceless bureaucracy and a cosmos that no longer offers answers to metaphysical questions. Perhaps his best-known work is the long story *The Metamorphosis,* which deals with an ordinary salesman who awakens one morning to find himself transformed into a giant beetle. Unlike many modernists, Kafka wrote in an apparently logical order, with clear sentences and close attention to external details. It is only after reading for a while that we realize that we are in a grotesque world in which our ordinary values and logic do not apply, a world that conveys the nightmarish quality of everyday life. In some ways Kafka's stories resemble dreams, and the surrealist exploration of the dream world. Like the expressionist painters, Kafka presents distorted, shocking images that represent some of our deepest unconscious fears.

Exploration of the Unconscious and Technical Experimentation

In spite of their sense of exile and their feeling of being misunderstood, the modernists on the whole maintained a strong belief in the saving power of art, a continuation of the late nineteenth century's adherence to the religion of art. In a declining, empty civilization, art appeared as a refuge, a form of salvation. Many of the new ideas and concerns of the twentieth century seemed to writers, as well as to artists, composers, and choreographers, to necessitate a radical breakup of traditional forms. Einstein's theories and the general sense of a breach in continuity after World War I surely had their impact, but perhaps the greatest influence was Freud's discovery of the unconscious. The most important experiments in rendering psychological states were done by novelists. The Frenchman Marcel Proust, in his monumental *Remembrance of Things Past,* found a new language for the expression of his characters' most subtle feelings and an inner, as opposed to a chronological, sense of time. The inner sense of time was also explored by the German Thomas Mann in *The Magic Mountain.* The Englishwoman Virginia Woolf experimented with language and time to convey inner reality in novels such as *To the Lighthouse* and *Mrs. Dalloway;* the American William Faulkner used extremely long, "ungrammatical" sentences to express a world below the surface of appearance. The most radical experiments in this vein were done by James Joyce (1880–1941). The unconscious or semiconscious part of the mind, as Freud showed, functions outside the logical order and time frame established by reason. It works rather by association, by summoning images that merge past, present, and future. To convey this state, Joyce used the device of the "interior monologue" or "stream of consciousness," abandoning rules of grammar and syntax, even inventing new words. The effect is similar to the abandonment of perspective and the juxtaposition of planes and of images in modernist painting. Joyce's *Ulysses,* published in 1922, although a long novel, takes place in the course of one day in Dublin. Because of the interior monologue technique, however, the novel can actually span all of the time within the characters' memories. In addition, the day in Dublin loosely parallels the events in Homer's *Odyssey* (hence the title), thus opening up a mythic dimension.

Visual Aspects of Literature

Other experimental modernist writers, especially poets, became interested in attempting to do with words something comparable to what modernist painters were doing in their medium. Rendering startling, concrete images as opposed to vague, loose, "romantic" sentiments in poetry became a preoccupation of Ezra Pound (1885–1972), another American exile and founder of the "imagist" school of poetry. Pound studied Chinese and Japanese, as well as medieval French and Italian poets, in a search for "visual" poetry on which to model his own work. Gertrude Stein, through a kind of word painting, attempted to bring cubism into literature.

Poetry of the City and the Theme of Spiritual Emptiness

A certain world-weariness invades much of modernist writing. The devastations of World War I seemed to confirm already-present philosophical assumptions about the futility and fragility of humankind's existence. With traditional religion and other sustaining myths dead, the individual was often left only with questions. Politics, to most moderns, did not offer a substitute for religion; even love, or any form of real communication between individuals, seemed to many extremely problematic in the modern world. One of the best chroniclers of this state of emotional vacuum was T. S. Eliot (1888–1965). Eliot, who was born in Saint Louis, Missouri, studied at Harvard, and moved to London in 1915. His most ambitious poem, *The Waste Land,* portrays the spiritual desolation of a modern city, London, through references to ancient literature, oriental mythology, and modern poets such as Baudelaire. The influence of Baudelaire and of other French symbolist poets was in fact a decisive one for Eliot. It enabled him to throw off conventionally poetic language and imagery and to depict modern reality in all its sordidness through a language that is both dense and everyday and through images that reflect the dinginess and the futility of modern city life. Eliot sought to eliminate abstract language and explanations of feelings from his poetry and instead to convey emotion through images evoked from the external world—what he called the "objective correlative."

One of Eliot's most influential poems is "The Love Song of J. Alfred Prufrock," written in 1915. The city it depicts is probably Boston, but the details recall as well Baudelaire's Paris, and the monotonous rhythms of urban life that are its subject matter could be found in any big city. The dingy city portrayed in the first two stanzas is reminiscent of "Preludes" (and the "yellow fog" quotes Baudelaire's "The Seven Old Men"); the setting of the rest of the poem moves to London interiors inhabited by upper-class English society. Prufrock is a typically "modern" man, unable to make decisions, to act, or even to feel—an overcivilized human being in an overcivilized society. The irony with which Eliot depicts his character has become a stable feature of much other twentieth-century literature. It may be of interest to note that Eliot is also the author of *Old Possum's Book of Practical Cats,* the basis of the book for Andrew Lloyd Webber's musical *Cats,* and that "Preludes," as well as some of Eliot's other early poems, are quoted in the song "Memory."

Eliot eventually solved his personal problems with meaninglessness and emptiness by converting to the Anglican Church and, in 1927, becoming a loyal British subject. Still, for many, the spiritual anguish at the core of modernism has remained a central fact of twentieth-century existence. The great Irish poet W. B. Yeats seems to sum up this state: "Things fall apart, the centre cannot hold. . . ."

Virginia Woolf and Modern Feminism

Along with her work as a novelist, Virginia Woolf (1882–1941) was profoundly interested in the feminist movement that had flourished in England since the days of John Stuart Mill and had assumed renewed importance in the 1920s. Women in England received full voting rights in 1928, the year in which Woolf composed her most widely read feminist work, *A Room of One's Own.* The book grew out of a series of lectures that she gave on "women and fiction." It eventually became a mixture of an essay and a first-person fiction with a narrator called Mary Seton. It begins with the narrator's account of her visit to "Oxbridge," a college for men, and to "Fernham," a recently established college for women. At the first she was served an abundant luncheon of sole and partridge, at the second a meager dinner of boiled beef, prunes, and custard. The two scenes evoke the wealth of the male establishment and the fundamental poverty and dependence of women.

Woolf contends that economic independence and equal opportunity for education and experience are even more important than the vote to the feminist cause. As to the question of women and fiction, she says that, in order to write, "a woman must have money and a room of her own." Few women have created great works of art because they have been denied opportunities to develop their talents. After examining the question historically and critically, Woolf makes a plea for an "androgynous" literature. The greatest creations will come through a fusing of male and female elements without sacrificing one to the other.

One part of *A Room of One's Own,* which reads like a complete story in itself, has been called "Shakespeare's sister." Here, the memory of a remark by an old bishop, that "it was impossible for any woman—past, present, or to come—to have the genius of Shakespeare," leads Woolf (or the narrator) to a kind of historical musing on what might have happened to a talented woman of Shakespeare's era who wanted to write for the theater.

Reading Selections

Franz Kafka

A Country Doctor

I was in great perplexity; I had to start on an urgent journey; a seriously ill patient was waiting for me in a village ten miles off; a thick blizzard of snow filled all the wide spaces between him and me; I had a gig, a light gig with big wheels, exactly right for our country roads; muffled in furs, my bag of instruments in my hand, I was in the courtyard all ready for the journey; but there was no horse to be had, no horse. My own horse had died in the night, worn out by the fatigues of this icy winter; my servant girl was now running around the village trying to borrow a horse; but it was hopeless, I knew it, and I stood there forlornly, with the snow gathering more and more thickly upon me, more and more unable to move. In the gateway the girl appeared, alone, and waved the lantern; of course, who would lend a horse at this time for such a journey? I strode through the courtyard once more; I could see no way out; in my confused distress I kicked at the dilapidated door of the yearlong uninhabited pigsty. It flew open and flapped to and fro on its hinges. A steam and smell as of horses came out from it. A dim stable lantern was swinging inside from a rope. A man, crouching on his hams in that low space, showed an open blue-eyed face. "Shall I yoke up?" he asked, crawling out on all fours. I did not know what to say and merely stooped down to see what else was in the sty. The servant girl was standing beside me. "You never know what you're going to find in your own house," she said, and we both laughed. "Hey there, Brother, hey there, Sister!" called the groom, and two horses, enormous creatures with powerful flanks, one after the other, their legs tucked close to their bodies, each well-shaped head lowered like a camel's, by sheer strength of buttocking squeezed out through the door hole which they filled entirely. But at once they were standing up, their legs long and their bodies steaming thickly. "Give him a hand," I said, and the willing girl hurried to help the groom with the harnessing. Yet hardly was she beside him when the groom clipped hold of her and pushed his face against hers. She screamed and fled back to me; on her cheek stood out in red the marks of two rows of teeth. "You brute," I yelled in fury, "do you want a whipping?" but in the same moment reflected that the man was a stranger; that I did not know where he came from, and that of his own free will he was helping me out when everyone else had failed me. As if he knew my thoughts he took no offense at my threat but, still busied with the horses, only turned around once toward me. "Get in," he said then, and indeed: everything was ready. A magnificent pair of horses, I observed, such as I had never sat behind, and I climbed in happily. "But I'll drive, you don't know the way," I said. "Of course," said he, "I'm not coming with you anyway, I'm staying with Rose." "No," shrieked Rose, fleeing into the house with a justified presentiment that her fate was inescapable; I heard the door chain rattle as she put it up; I heard the key turn in the lock; I could see, moreover, how she put out the lights in the entrance hall and in further flight all through the rooms to keep herself from being discovered. "You're coming with me," I said to the groom, "or I won't go, urgent as my journey is. I'm not thinking of paying for it by handing the girl over to you." "Gee up!" he said; clapped his hands; the gig whirled off like a log in a freshet; I could just hear the door of my house splitting and bursting as the groom charged at it and then I was deafened and blinded by a storming rush that steadily buffeted all my senses. But this only for a moment, since, as if my patient's farmyard had opened out just before my courtyard gate, I was already there; the horses had come quietly to a standstill; the blizzard had stopped;

moonlight all around; my patient's parents hurried out of the house, his sister behind them; I was almost lifted out of the gig; from their confused ejaculations I gathered not a word; in the sickroom the air was almost unbreathable; the neglected stove was smoking; I wanted to push open a window; but first I had to look at my patient. Gaunt, without any fever, not cold, not warm, with vacant eyes, without a shirt, the youngster heaved himself up from under the feather bedding, threw his arms around my neck, and whispered in my ear: "Doctor, let me die." I glanced around the room; no one had heard it; the parents were leaning forward in silence waiting for my verdict; the sister had set a chair for my handbag; I opened the bag and hunted among my instruments; the boy kept clutching at me from his bed to remind me of his entreaty; I picked up a pair of tweezers, examined them in the candlelight, and laid them down again. "Yes," I thought blasphemously, "in cases like this the gods are helpful, send the missing horse, add to it a second because of the urgency, and to crown everything bestow even a groom——" And only now did I remember Rose again; what was I to do, how could I rescue her, how could I pull her away from under that groom at ten miles' distance, with a team of horses I couldn't control. These horses, now, they had somehow slipped the reins loose, pushed the windows open from outside, I did not know how; each of them had stuck a head in at a window and, quite unmoved by the startled cries of the family, stood eyeing the patient. "Better go back at once," I thought, as if the horses were summoning me to the return journey, yet I permitted the patient's sister, who fancied that I was dazed by the heat, to take my fur coat from me. A glass of rum was poured out for me, the old man clapped me on the shoulder, a familiarity justified by this offer of his treasure. I shook my head; in the narrow confines of the old man's thoughts I felt ill; that was my only reason for refusing the drink. The mother stood by the bedside and cajoled me toward it; I yielded, and, while one of the horses whinnied loudly to the ceiling, laid my head to the boy's breast, which shivered under my wet beard. I confirmed what I already knew; the boy was quite sound, something a little wrong with his circulation, saturated with coffee by his solicitous mother, but sound and best turned out of bed with one shove. I am no world reformer and so I let him lie. I was the district doctor and did my duty to the uttermost, to the point where it became almost too much. I was badly paid and yet generous and helpful to the poor. I had still to see that Rose was all right, and then the boy might have his way and I wanted to die too. What was I doing there in that endless winter! My horse was dead, and not a single person in the village would lend me another. I had to get my team out of the pigsty; if they hadn't chanced to be horses I should have had to travel with swine. That was how it was. And I nodded to the family. They knew nothing about it, and, had they known, would not have believed it. To write prescriptions is easy, but to come to an understanding with people is hard. Well, this should be the end of my visit, I had once more been called out needlessly, I was used to that, the whole district made my life a torment with my night bell, but that I should have to sacrifice Rose this time as well, the pretty girl who had lived in my house for years almost without my noticing her—that sacrifice was too much to ask, and I had somehow to get it reasoned out in my head with the help of what craft I could muster, in order not to let fly at this family, which with the best will in the world could not restore Rose to me. But as I shut my bag and put an arm out for my fur coat, the family meanwhile standing together, the father sniffing at the glass of rum in his hand, the mother, apparently disappointed in me—why, what do people expect?—biting her lips with tears in her eyes, the sister fluttering a blood-soaked towel, I was somehow ready to admit conditionally that the boy might be ill after all. I went toward him, he welcomed me smiling as if I were bringing him the most nourishing invalid broth—ah, now both horses were whinnying together; the noise, I suppose, was ordained by heaven to assist my examination of the patient—and this time I discovered that the boy was indeed ill. In his right side, near the hip, was an open wound as big as the palm of my hand. Rose-red, in many variations of shade, dark in the hollows, lighter at the edges, softly granulated, with irregular clots of blood, open as a surface mine to the daylight. That was how it looked from a distance. But on a closer inspection there was another complication. I could not help a low whistle of surprise. Worms, as thick and as long as my little finger, themselves rose-red and blood-spotted as well, were wriggling from their fastness in the interior of the wound toward the light, with small white heads and many little legs. Poor boy, you were past helping. I had discovered your great wound; this blossom in your side was destroying you. The family was pleased; they saw me busying myself; the sister told the mother, the mother the father, the father told several guests who were coming in, through the moonlight at the open door, walking on tiptoe, keeping their balance with outstretched arms. "Will you save me?" whispered the boy with a sob, quite blinded by the life within his wound. That is what people are like in my district.

Always expecting the impossible from the doctor. They have lost their ancient beliefs; the parson sits at home and unravels his vestments, one after another; but the doctor is supposed to be omnipotent with his merciful surgeon's hand. Well, as it pleases them; I have not thrust my services on them; if they misuse me for sacred ends, I let that happen to me too; what better do I want, old country doctor that I am, bereft of my servant girl! And so they came, the family and the village elders, and stripped my clothes off me; a school choir with the teacher at the head of it stood before the house and sang these words to an utterly simple tune:

> Strip his clothes off, then he'll heal us,
> If he doesn't, kill him dead!
> Only a doctor, only a doctor.

Then my clothes were off and I looked at the people quietly, my fingers in my beard and my head cocked to one side. I was altogether composed and equal to the situation and remained so, although it was no help to me, since they now took me by the head and feet and carried me to the bed. They laid me down in it next to the wall, on the side of the wound. Then they all left the room; the door was shut; the singing stopped; clouds covered the moon; the bedding was warm around me; the horses' heads in the open windows wavered like shadows. "Do you know," said a voice in my ear, "I have very little confidence in you. Why, you were only blown in here, you didn't come on your own feet. Instead of helping me, you're cramping me on my deathbed. What I'd like best is to scratch your eyes out." "Right," I said, "it is a shame. And yet I am a doctor. What am I to do? Believe me, it is not too easy for me either." "Am I supposed to be content with this apology? Oh, I must be, I can't help it. I always have to put up with things. A fine wound is all I brought into the world; that was my sole endowment." "My young friend," said I, "your mistake is: you have not a wide enough view. I have been in all the sickrooms, far and wide, and I tell you: your wound is not so bad. Done in a tight corner with two strokes of the ax. Many a one proffers his side and can hardly hear the ax in the forest, far less that it is coming nearer to him." "Is that really so, or are you deluding me in my fever?" "It is really so, take the word of honor of an official doctor." And he took it and lay still. But now it was time for me to think of escaping. The horses were still standing faithfully in their places. My clothes, my fur coat, my bag were quickly collected; I didn't want to waste time dressing; if the horses raced home as they had come, I should only be springing, as it were, out of this bed into my own. Obediently a horse backed away from the window; I threw my bundle into the gig; the fur coat missed its mark and was caught on a hook only by the sleeve. Good enough. I swung myself onto the horse. With the reins loosely trailing, one horse barely fastened to the other, the gig swaying behind, my fur coat last of all in the snow. "Gee up!" I said, but there was no galloping; slowly, like old men, we crawled through the snowy wastes; a long time echoed behind us the new but faulty song of the children:

> O be joyful, all you patients,
> The doctor's laid in bed beside you!

Never shall I reach home at this rate; my flourishing practice is done for; my successor is robbing me, but in vain, for he cannot take my place; in my house the disgusting groom is raging; Rose is his victim; I do not want to think about it anymore. Naked, exposed to the frost of this most unhappy of ages, with an earthly vehicle, unearthly horses, old man that I am, I wander astray. My fur coat is hanging from the back of the gig, but I cannot reach it, and none of my limber pack of patients lifts a finger. Betrayed! Betrayed! A false alarm on the night bell once answered—it cannot be made good, not ever.

COMMENTS AND QUESTIONS

1. This story was probably to some extent based on the experience of Kafka's uncle, who was a country doctor. What realistic elements do you find in it?
2. At what point do you realize that this story has left the domain of the realistic and entered into the fantastic or grotesque? What effect does this have on the reader?
3. "To write prescriptions is easy, but to come to an understanding with people is hard," observes the doctor. Can this phrase be used as a key to the experience the doctor undergoes in the story?
4. It is important to realize that there is no one "right" way to interpret Kafka. His stories are open-ended parables, although in some sense representative of the dilemmas of modern individuals. Give your own interpretation of the nature of the experience the doctor undergoes, along with the meaning of symbols such as the pigsty, the groom, the horses, the wound, and so on. Compare them with those of your classmates.

James Joyce

From *Ulysses*

The central character of the book is Leopold Bloom; the selection reprinted below is part of a half-dreaming monologue of Bloom's wife, Molly. Molly has been unfaithful to her husband, but in these final pages of the novel she recalls their early love together and ends the novel with a life-affirming "Yes!"

. . . a quarter after what an unearthly hour I suppose theyre just getting up in China now combing out their pigtails for the day well soon have the nuns ringing the angelus theyve nobody coming in to spoil their sleep except an odd priest or two for his night office the alarmclock next door at cockshout clattering the brains out of itself let me see if I can doze off 1 2 3 4 5 what kind of flowers are those they invented like the stars the wallpaper in Lombard Street was much nicer the apron he gave me was like that something only I only wore it twice better lower this lamp and try again so as I can get up early Ill go to Lambes there beside Findlaters and get them to send us some flowers to put about the place in case he brings him home tomorrow today I mean no no Fridays an unlucky day first I want to do the place up someway the dust grows in it I think while Im asleep then we can have music and cigarettes I can accompany him first I must clean the keys of the piano with milk whatll I wear shall I wear a white rose or those fairy cakes in Liptons I love the smell of a rich big shop at 7½d. a lb or the other ones with the cherries in them and the pinky sugar 11d. a couple of lbs of course a nice plant for the middle of the table Id get that cheaper in wait wheres this I saw them not long ago I love flowers Id love to have the whole place swimming in roses God of heaven theres nothing like nature the wild mountains then the sea and the waves rushing then the beautiful country with fields of oats and all kinds of things and all the fine cattle going about that would do your heart good to see rivers and lakes and flowers all sorts of shapes and smells and colours springing up even out of the ditches primroses and violets nature it is as for them saying theres no God I wouldnt give a snap of my two fingers for all their learning why dont they go and create something I often asked him atheists or whatever they call themselves go and wash the cobbles off themselves first then go howling for the priest and they dying and why why because theyre afraid of hell on account of their bad conscience ah yes I know them well who was the first person in the universe before there was anybody that made it all who ah that they dont know neither do I so there you are they might as well try to stop the sun from rising tomorrow the sun shines for you he said the day we were lying among the rhododendrons on Howth head in the grey tweed suit and his straw hat the day I got him to propose to me yes first [I gave him the bit of seedcake out of my mouth and it was leapyear like now yes 16 years ago my God after that long kiss I near lost my breath yes he said I was a flower of the mountain yes so we are flowers all a womans body yes that was one true thing he said in his life and the sun shines for you today yes that was why I liked him because I saw he understood or felt what a woman is and I knew I could always get round him and I gave him all the pleasure I could leading him on till he asked me to say yes] and I wouldnt answer first only looked out over the sea and the sky I was thinking of so many things he didn't know of Mulvey and Mr Stanhope and Hester and father and old captain Groves and the sailors playing all birds fly and I say stoop and washing up dishes they called it on the pier and the sentry in front of the governors house with the thing round his white helmet poor devil half roasted and the Spanish girls laughing in their shawls and their tall combs and the auctions in the morning the Greeks and the jews and the Arabs and the devil knows who else from all the ends of Europe and Duke street and the fowl market all clucking outside Larby Sharons and the poor donkeys slipping half asleep and the vague fellows in the cloaks asleep in the shade on the steps and the big wheels of the carts of the bulls and the old castle thousands of years old yes and those handsome Moors all in white and turbans like kings asking you to sit down in their little bit of a shop and Ronda with the old windows of the posadas glancing eyes a lattice hid for her lover to kiss the iron and the wineshops half open at night and the castanets and the night we missed the boat at Algeciras the watchman going about serene with his lamp and O that awful deepdown torrent O and the sea the sea crimson sometimes like fire and the glorious sunsets and the figtrees in the Alameda gardens yes and all the queer little streets and pink and blue and yellow houses and the rosegardens and the jessamine and geraniums and cactuses and Gibraltar as a girl where I was a Flower of the mountain yes when I put the rose in my hair like the Andalusian girls used or shall I wear a red yes and how he kissed me under the Moorish wall and I thought well as well him as another and then I asked him with my eyes to ask again yes and then he asked me would I yes to say yes my mountain flower and first I put my arms around him yes and drew him down to me so he could feel my breasts all perfume yes and his heart was going like mad and yes I said yes I will Yes.

QUESTIONS

1. How long does it take you, as a reader, to "get into" this text and discover what is going on? How do you react to it initially?
2. Does Joyce's technique effectively represent a state of semiconsciousness? Why or why not?
3. Show from the text how time is "flattened out" here; that is, how past, present, and future are superimposed. In what sense is this representation of psychic reality more "real" than a realistic text?
4. Trace the *motif* of the flower in this text. How does it function?

EZRA POUND

The River-Merchant's Wife: A Letter

(after Rihaku)[1]

While my hair was still cut straight across my
 forehead
I played about the front gate, pulling flowers.
You came by on bamboo stilts, playing horse,
You walked about my seat, playing with blue plums.
And we went on living in the village of Chokan:
Two small people, without dislike or suspicion.

At fourteen I married My Lord you.
I never laughed, being bashful.
Lowering my head, I looked at the wall.
Called to, a thousand times, I never looked back.

At fifteen I stopped scowling,
I desired my dust to be mingled with yours
For ever and for ever and for ever.
Why should I climb the look out?

At sixteen you departed,
You went into far Ku-to-yen, by the river of swirling
 eddies,
And you have been gone five months.
The monkeys make sorrowful noise overhead.

[1]Japanese name for an eighth-century Chinese poet, Li Po.

You dragged your feet when you went out.
By the gate now, the moss is grown, the different
 mosses,
Too deep to clear them away!

The leaves fall early this autumn, in wind.
The paired butterflies are already yellow with
 August
Over the grass in the West garden;
They hurt me. I grow older.
If you are coming down through the narrows of the
 river Kiang,
Please let me know beforehand,
And I will come out to meet you
As far as Cho-fu-Sa.

In a Station of the Metro[1]

The apparition of these faces in the crowd;
Petals on a wet, black bough.

QUESTIONS

1. Do you find "In a Station of the Metro" effective as poetry? Can you compare the technique used to a technique in modern painting?
2. How does "The River-Merchant's Wife" render visual images in poetry?
3. Can you compare the influence of the Orient on European painting (see Chapter 29) to its influence on poetry?

[1]Of this poem Pound writes in *Gaudier-Brzeska: A Memoir* (1916): "Three years ago in Paris I got out of a 'metro' train at La Concorde, and saw suddenly a beautiful face, and then another and another, and then a beautiful child's face, and then another beautiful woman, and I tried all that day to find words for what this had meant to me, and I could not find any words that seemed to me worthy, or as lovely as that sudden emotion. And that evening... I was still trying and I found, suddenly, the expression. I do not mean that I found words, but there came an equation... not in speech, but in little splotches of colour.... The 'one-image poem' is a form of super-position, that is to say, it is one idea set on top of another. I found it useful in getting out of the impasse in which I had been left by my metro emotion. I wrote a thirty-line poem, and destroyed it.... Six months later I made a poem half that length; a year later I made the following *hokku*-like sentence."

T. S. Eliot

Preludes

I

The winter evening settles down
With smell of steaks in passageways.
Six o'clock.
The burnt-out ends of smoky days.
And now a gusty shower wraps
The grimy scraps
Of withered leaves above your feet
And newspapers from vacant lots;
The showers beat
On broken blinds and chimney-pots,
And at the corner of the street
A lonely cab-horse steams and stamps.
And then the lighting of the lamps.

II

The morning comes to consciousness
Of faint stale smells of beer
From the sawdust-trampled street
With all its muddy feet that press
To early coffee-stands.
With the other masquerades
That time resumes,
One thinks of all the hands
That are raising dingy shades
In a thousand furnished rooms.

III

You tossed a blanket from the bed,
You lay upon your back, and waited;
You dozed, and watched the night revealing
The thousand sordid images
Of which your soul was constituted;
They flickered against the ceiling.
And when all the world came back
And the light crept up between the shutters
And you heard the sparrows in the gutters,
You had such a vision of the street
As the street hardly understands;
Sitting along the bed's edge, where
You curled the papers from your hair,
Or clasped the yellow soles of feet
In the palms of both soiled hands.

IV

His soul stretched tight across the skies
That fade behind a city block,
Or trampled by insistent feet
At four and five and six o'clock;
And short square fingers stuffing pipes,
And evening newspapers, and eyes
Assured of certain certainties,
The conscience of a blackened street
Impatient to assume the world.
I am moved by fancies that are curled
Around these images, and cling:
The notion of some infinitely gentle
Infinitely suffering thing.

Wipe your hand across your mouth, and laugh;
The worlds revolve like ancient women
Gathering fuel in vacant lots.

QUESTIONS

1. What sights and sounds of the city has Eliot included in his poem? What is their effect?
2. In what respects is this poem consciously "modern," in contrast to, for example, a romantic poem?
3. Identify the tone and the main sentiment of the poem.

The Love Song of J. Alfred Prufrock

S'io credessi che mia risposta fosse
a persona che mai tornasse al mondo,
questa fiamma staria senza più scosse.
Ma per ciò che giammai di questo fondo
non tornò vivo alcun, s'i'odo il vero,
senza tema d'infamia ti rispondo.[1]

[1]Epigraph from Dante's *Inferno,* Canto 27: "If I thought that my answer was to someone who would ever return to the world, this flame would shake no more. But since no one has ever returned alive from this place [hell], if I hear rightly, without fear of infamy I will answer you."

Let us go then, you and I,[2]
When the evening is spread out against the sky
Like a patient etherised upon a table;
Let us go, through certain half-deserted streets,
The muttering retreats
Of restless nights in one-night cheap hotels
And sawdust restaurants with oyster-shells:
Streets that follow like a tedious argument
Of insidious intent
To lead you to an overwhelming question...
Oh, do not ask, "What is it?"
Let us go and make our visit.

In the room the women come and go
Talking of Michelangelo.

The yellow fog that rubs its back upon the window-panes,
The yellow smoke that rubs its muzzle on the window-panes,
Licked its tongue into the corners of the evening,
Lingered upon the pools that stand in drains,
Let fall upon its back the soot that falls from chimneys,
Slipped by the terrace, made a sudden leap,
And seeing that it was a soft October night,
Curled once about the house, and fell asleep.

And indeed there will be time
For the yellow smoke that slides along the street
Rubbing its back upon the window-panes;
There will be time, there will be time
To prepare a face to meet the faces that you meet;
There will be time to murder and create,
And time for all the works and days of hands
That lift and drop a question on your plate;
Time for you and time for me,
And time yet for a hundred indecisions,
And for a hundred visions and revisions,
Before the taking of a toast and tea.

In the room the women come and go
Talking of Michelangelo.
And indeed there will be time
To wonder, "Do I dare?" and, "Do I dare?"
Time to turn back and descend the stair,
With a bald spot in the middle of my hair—

[2]Prufrock and a companion (or his own alter ego?) are going to make a visit to a woman.

(They will say: "How his hair is growing thin!")
My morning coat, my collar mounting firmly to the chin,
My necktie rich and modest, but asserted by a simple pin—
(They will say: "But how his arms and legs are thin!")
Do I dare
Disturb the universe?
In a minute there is time
For decisions and revisions which a minute will reverse.

For I have known them all already, known them all—
Have known the evenings, mornings, afternoons,
I have measured out my life with coffee spoons;
I know the voices dying with a dying fall
Beneath the music from a farther room.
So how should I presume?

And I have known the eyes already, known them all—
The eyes that fix you in a formulated phrase,
And when I am formulated, sprawling on a pin,
When I am pinned and wriggling on the wall,
Then how should I begin
To spit out all the butt-ends of my days and ways?
And how should I presume?

And I have known the arms already, known them all—
Arms that are braceleted and white and bare
(But in the lamplight, downed with light brown hair!)
Is it perfume from a dress
That makes me so digress?
Arms that lie along a table, or wrap about a shawl.
And should I then presume?
And how should I begin?

. . . . .

Shall I say, I have gone at dusk through narrow streets
And watched the smoke that rises from the pipes
Of lonely men in shirt-sleeves, leaning out of windows?...

I should have been a pair of ragged claws
Scuttling across the floors of silent seas.

. . . . .

And the afternoon, the evening, sleeps so peacefully!
Smoothed by long fingers,

Asleep . . . tired . . . or it malingers,
Stretched on the floor, here beside you and me.
Should I, after tea and cakes and ices,
Have the strength to force the moment to its crisis?
But though I have wept and fasted, wept and prayed,
Though I have seen my head (grown slightly bald)
  brought in upon a platter,[3]
I am no prophet—and here's no great matter;
I have seen the moment of my greatness flicker,
And I have seen the eternal Footman hold my coat,
  and snicker,
And in short, I was afraid.

And would it have been worth it, after all,[4]
After the cups, the marmalade, the tea,
Among the porcelain, among some talk of you and
  me,
Would it have been worth while,
To have bitten off the matter with a smile,
To have squeezed the universe into a ball
To roll it toward some overwhelming question,
To say: "I am Lazarus, come from the dead,
Come back to tell you all, I shall tell you all"—
If one,[5] settling a pillow by her head,

  Should say: "That is not what I meant at all.
  That is not it, at all."

And would it have been worth it, after all,
Would it have been worth while,
After the sunsets and the dooryards and the
  sprinkled streets,
After the novels, after the teacups, after the skirts
  that trail along the floor—
And this, and so much more?—
It is impossible to say just what I mean!
But as if a magic lantern threw the nerves in patterns
  on a screen:
Would it have been worth while
If one, settling a pillow or throwing off a shawl,
And turning toward the window, should say:
  "That is not it at all,
  That is not what I meant, at all."

No! I am not Prince Hamlet, nor was meant to be;
Am an attendant lord, one that will do
To swell a progress,[6] start a scene or two,
Advise the prince; no doubt, an easy tool,
Deferential, glad to be of use,
Politic, cautious, and meticulous;
Full of high sentence, but a bit obtuse;
At times, indeed, almost ridiculous—
Almost, at times, the Fool.

I grow old . . . I grow old . . .
I shall wear the bottoms of my trousers rolled.[7]

Shall I part my hair behind? Do I dare to eat a
  peach?
I shall wear white flannel trousers, and walk upon
  the beach.
I have heard the mermaids singing, each to each.

I do not think that they will sing to me.

I have seen them riding seaward on the waves
Combing the white hair of the waves blown back
When the wind blows the water white and black.

We have lingered in the chambers of the sea
By sea-girls wreathed with seaweed red and brown
Till human voices wake us, and we drown.

QUESTIONS

1. This poem presents itself as a *narrative*, but the action that occurs is very slight. Tell what it is.
2. Describe the character of Prufrock. What images does Eliot use to tell us about him?
3. Does Prufrock's problem seem to you a particularly modern one? Why?
4. In what sense, if any, is this a "love song"?
5. Is there any justification for the quotation from Dante's *Inferno?*

[3]Refers to the head of John the Baptist, brought to Salome, the stepdaughter of King Herod.

[4]The use of the past tense here suggests that the moment for Prufrock to speak has passed.

[5]Prufrock's woman friend.

[6]A royal journey.

[7]The latest fashion.

Virginia Woolf

From *A Room of One's Own*

. . . I could not help thinking, as I looked at the works of Shakespeare on the shelf, that the bishop was right at least in this; it would have been impossible, completely and entirely, for any woman to have written the plays of Shakespeare in the age of Shakespeare. Let me imagine, since facts are so hard to come by, what would have happened had Shakespeare had a wonderfully gifted sister, called Judith, let us say. Shakespeare himself went, very probably—his mother was an heiress—to the grammar school, where he may have learnt Latin—Ovid, Virgil and Horace—and the elements of grammar and logic. He was, it is well known, a wild boy who poached rabbits, perhaps shot a deer, and had, rather sooner than he should have done, to marry a woman in the neighbourhood, who bore him a child rather quicker than was right. That escapade sent him to seek his fortune in London. He had, it seemed, a taste for the theatre; he began by holding horses at the stage door. Very soon he got work in the theatre, became a successful actor, and lived at the hub of the universe, meeting everybody, knowing everybody, practising his art on the boards, exercising his wits in the streets, and even getting access to the palace of the queen. Meanwhile his extraordinarily gifted sister, let us suppose, remained at home. She was as adventurous, as imaginative, as agog to see the world as he was. But she was not sent to school. She had no chance of learning grammar and logic, let alone of reading Horace and Virgil. She picked up a book now and then, one of her brother's perhaps, and read a few pages. But then her parents came in and told her to mend the stockings or mind the stew and not moon about with books and papers. They would have spoken sharply but kindly, for they were substantial people who knew the conditions of life for a woman and loved their daughter—indeed, more likely than not she was the apple of her father's eye. Perhaps she scribbled some pages up in an apple loft on the sly, but was careful to hide them or set fire to them. Soon, however, before she was out of her teens, she was to be betrothed to the son of a neighbouring wool-stapler. She cried out that marriage was hateful to her, and for that she was severely beaten by her father. Then he ceased to scold her. He begged her instead not to hurt him, not to shame him in this matter of her marriage. He would give her a chain of beads or a fine petticoat, he said; and there were tears in his eyes. How could she disobey him? How could she break his heart? The force of her own gift alone drove her to it. She made up a small parcel of her belongings, let herself down by a rope one summer's night and took the road to London. She was not seventeen. The birds that sang in the hedge were not more musical than she was. She had the quickest fancy, a gift like her brother's, for the tune of words. Like him, she had a taste for the theatre. She stood at the stage door; she wanted to act, she said. Men laughed in her face. The manager—a fat, loose-lipped man—guffawed. He bellowed something about poodles dancing and women acting—no woman, he said, could possibly be an actress. He hinted—you can imagine what. She could get no training in her craft. Could she even seek her dinner in a tavern or roam the streets at midnight? Yet her genius was for fiction and lusted to feed abundantly upon the lives of men and women and the study of their ways. At last—for she was very young, oddly like Shakespeare the poet in her face, with the same grey eyes and rounded brows—at last Nick Greene the actor-manager took pity on her; she found herself with child by that gentleman and so—who shall measure the heat and violence of the poet's heart when caught and tangled in a woman's body?—killed herself one winter's night and lies buried at some cross-roads where the omnibuses now stop outside the Elephant and Castle.

That, more or less, is how the story would run, I think, if a woman in Shakespeare's day had had Shakespeare's genius. But for my part, I agree with the deceased bishop, if such he was—it is unthinkable that any woman in Shakespeare's day should have had Shakespeare's genius. For genius like Shakespeare's is not born among labouring, uneducated, servile people. It was not born in England among the Saxons and the Britons. It is not born today among the working classes. How, then, could it have been born among women whose work began, according to Professor Trevelyan, almost before they were out of the nursery, who were forced to it by their parents and held to it by all the power of law and custom? Yet genius of a sort must have existed among women as it must have existed among the working classes. Now and again an Emily Brontë or a Robert Burns blazes out and proves its presence. But certainly it never got itself on to paper. When, however, one reads of a witch being ducked, of a woman possessed by devils, of a wise woman selling herbs, or even of a very remarkable man who had a mother, then I think we are on the track of a lost novelist, a suppressed poet, of some mute and inglorious Jane Austen, some Emily Brontë who dashed her brains out on the moor or mopped and mowed about the highways crazed with the torture that her gift had put her to. Indeed, I would venture to guess that Anon, who wrote so many poems without signing them, was often a woman. It was a woman Edward Fitzgerald, I think, suggested who made the ballads and the folk-songs, crooning them to her children, beguiling her spinning with them, or the length of the winter's night.

This may be true or it may be false—who can say?—but what is true in it, so it seemed to me, reviewing the story of Shakespeare's sister as I had made it, is that any woman born with a great gift in the sixteenth century would certainly have gone crazed, shot herself, or ended her days in some lonely cottage outside the village, half witch, half wizard, feared and mocked at. For it needs little skill in psychology to be sure that a highly gifted girl who had tried to use her gift for poetry would have been so thwarted and hindered by other people, so tortured and pulled asunder by her own contrary instincts, that she must have lost her health and sanity to a certainty. No girl could have walked to London and stood at a stage door and forced her way into the presence of actor-managers without doing herself a violence and suffering an anguish which may have been irrational—for chastity may be a fetish invented by certain societies for unknown reasons—but were none the less inevitable. Chastity had then, it has even now, a religious importance in a woman's life, and has so wrapped itself round with nerves and instincts that to cut it free and bring it to the light of day demands courage of the rarest. To have lived a free life in London in the sixteenth century would have meant for a woman who was poet and playwright a nervous stress and dilemma which might well have killed her. Had she survived, whatever she had written would have been twisted and deformed, issuing from a strained and morbid imagination. And undoubtedly, I thought, looking at the shelf where there are no plays by women, her work would have gone unsigned. That refuge she would have sought certainly. It was the relic of the sense of chastity that dictated anonymity to women even so late as the nineteenth century. Currer Bell,[1] George Eliot, George Sand, all the victims of inner strife as their writings prove, sought ineffectively to veil themselves by using the name of a man. Thus they did homage to the convention, which if not implanted by the other sex was liberally encouraged by them (the chief glory of a woman is not to be talked of, said Pericles, himself a much-talked-of man), that publicity in women is detestable. Anonymity runs in their blood. The desire to be veiled still possesses them. They are not even now as concerned about the health of their fame as men are, and, speaking generally, will pass a tombstone or a signpost without feeling an irresistible desire to cut their names on it, as Alf, Bert or Chas. must do in obedience to their instinct, which murmurs if it sees a fine woman go by, or even a dog, Ce chien est à moi. And, of course, it may not be a dog, I thought, remembering Parliament Square, the Sieges Allee and other avenues; it may be a piece of land or a man with curly black hair. It is one of the great advantages of being a woman that one can pass even a very fine negress without wishing to make an Englishwoman of her.

That woman, then, who was born with a gift of poetry in the sixteenth century, was an unhappy woman, a woman at strife against herself. All the conditions of her life, all her own instincts, were hostile to the state of mind which is needed to set free whatever is in the brain. But what is the state of mind that is most propitious to the act of creation, I asked. Can one come by any notion of the state that furthers and makes possible that strange activity? Here I opened the volume containing the Tragedies of Shakespeare. What was Shakespeare's state of mind, for instance, when he wrote *Lear* and *Antony and Cleopatra?* It was certainly the state of mind most favourable to poetry that there has ever existed. But Shakespeare himself said nothing about it. We only know casually and by chance that he "never blotted a line." Nothing indeed was ever said by the artist himself about his state of mind until the eighteenth century perhaps. Rousseau perhaps began it. At any rate, by the nineteenth century self-consciousness had developed so far that it was the habit for men of letters to describe their minds in confessions and autobiographies. Their lives also were written, and their letters were printed after their deaths. Thus, though we do not know what Shakespeare went through when he wrote *Lear,* we do know what Carlyle went through when he wrote the *French Revolution;* what Flaubert went through when he wrote *Madame Bovary;* what Keats was going through when he tried to write poetry against the coming of death and the indifference of the world.

And one gathers from this enormous modern literature of confession and self-analysis that to write a work of genius is almost always a feat of prodigious difficulty. Everything is against the likelihood that it will come from the writer's mind whole and entire. Generally material circumstances are against it. Dogs will bark; people will interrupt; money must be made;

[1]The pseudonym for Charlotte Brontë.

health will break down. Further, accentuating all these difficulties and making them harder to bear is the world's notorious indifference. It does not ask people to write poems and novels and histories; it does not need them. It does not care whether Flaubert finds the right word or whether Carlyle scrupulously verifies this or that fact. Naturally, it will not pay for what it does not want. And so the writer, Keats, Flaubert, Carlyle, suffers, especially in the creative years of youth, every form of distraction and discouragement. A curse, a cry of agony, rises from those books of analysis and confession. "Mighty poets in their misery dead"—that is the burden of their song. If anything comes through in spite of all of this, it is a miracle, and probably no book is born entire and uncrippled as it was conceived.

But for women, I thought, looking at the empty shelves, these difficulties were infinitely more formidable. In the first place, to have a room of her own, let alone a quiet room or a sound-proof room, was out of the question, unless her parents were exceptionally rich or very noble, even up to the beginning of the nineteenth century. Since her pin money, which depended on the good will of her father, was only enough to keep her clothed, she was debarred from such alleviations as came even to Keats or Tennyson or Carlyle, all poor men, from a walking tour, a little journey to France, from the separate lodging which, even if it were miserable enough, sheltered them from the claims and tyrannies of their families. Such material difficulties were formidable; but much worse were the immaterial. The indifference of the world which Keats and Flaubert and other men of genius have found so hard to bear was in her case not indifference but hostility. The world did not say to her as it said to them, Write if you choose; it makes no difference to me. The world said with a guffaw, Write? What's the good of your writing? Here the psychologists of Newnham and Girton might come to our help, I thought, looking again at the blank spaces on the shelves. For surely it is time that the effect of discouragement upon the mind of the artist should be measured, as I have seen a dairy company measure the effect of ordinary milk and Grade A milk upon the body of the rat. They set two rats in cages side by side, and of the two one was furtive, timid and small, and the other was glossy, bold and big. Now what food do we feed women as artists upon? I asked, remembering, I suppose, that dinner of prunes and custard.

QUESTIONS

1. Is the story of "Shakespeare's sister" convincing? What does it say about women and creativity?
2. What is the point of the account of the scientific experiment at the end of the passage?
3. To what extent have conditions for the intellectual or creative woman changed since 1928?

33

New Americans on the World Cultural Scene: The Rise of African American and Latin American Cultures

As the aftermath of World War I contributed to a certain skepticism toward traditional Western humanistic values along with a revived interest in non-Western and so-called primitive cultures on the part of Euro-Americans and Europeans, cultural traditions that had previously appeared peripheral in global terms began to attract attention and to flourish on their own. Participation in the war effort was in large part responsible for a new self-awareness displayed by black U.S. citizens during the years between the wars. The Mexican revolutionary era (1910–1916) stimulated a growth of cultural awareness not only on the part of Mexicans but of all Latin Americans. African American and Latin American artists and writers of the interwar years were, in varying degrees, influenced both by the innovations of European modernism and by their rediscovery and reevaluation of their own cultural traditions.

The Rise of African American Culture

Although consciousness of emancipation from racial and racist stereotypes, such as the minstrel clown, into what was called the "New Negro" had its origin in the prewar years, changes in American society after World War I intensified the process. Economic opportunities produced by the war brought blacks to northern cities in great numbers. The war dislodged blacks not only from the South but also from other countries throughout the world, as blacks from the French and British West Indies and Africa all gathered in northern cities, New York in particular. But while many blacks developed and articulated their racial consciousness in New York, others from Martinique, Haiti, and Senegal delivered radical racial manifestos from Paris and London. The result was that Pan-Africanism, the quest for black unity throughout the world, became a dominant attitude and ideology.

In addition to making African Americans conscious of the international dimension of their racial struggle, the war stimulated their eagerness to produce racial peace and equality in the United States. If they could march and fight alongside white Americans to make the world "safe for democracy," then the same, they reasoned, could be done for racial harmony in the United States. As the shift in black leadership changed from the accommodationist policy of Booker T. Washington to the radical protest of the intellectual W. E. B. Du Bois, African Americans became more racially conscious and self-assertive, proclaiming themselves to be human beings worthy of respect. Du Bois states the case in *The Souls of Black Folks*:

> The history of the American Negro is the history of this strife,—this longing to attain self-conscious manhood, to merge his double self into a better and truer self. In this merging he wishes neither of the older selves to be lost. He would not Africanize America, for America has too much to teach the world and Africa. He would not bleach his Negro soul in a flood of white Americanism, for he knows that Negro blood has a message for the world. He simply wishes to make it possible for a man to be both a Negro and an American, without being cursed and spit upon by his fellows, without having the doors of Opportunity closed roughly in his face.

This determined quest for racial equality and America's insistence on racial segregation produced the "bloody summer" of 1919, when race riots erupted in more than twenty-five U.S. cities. In reaction to this outburst of violence, the poet Claude McKay, born in Jamaica and later part of the Harlem Renaissance, wrote his now well-known poem "If We Must Die."

CLAUDE MCKAY (1890–1948)

If We Must Die

If we must die, let it not be like hogs
Hunted and penned in an inglorious spot,
While round us bark the mad and hungry dogs,
Making their mock at our accursed lot.
If we must die, O let us nobly die,
So that our precious blood may not be shed
In vain; then even the monsters we defy
Shall be constrained to honor us though dead!
O kinsmen! we must meet the common foe!
Though far outnumbered let us show us brave,
And for their thousand blows deal one deathblow!
What though before us lies the open grave?
Like men we'll face the murderous, cowardly pack,
Pressed to the wall, dying but fighting back!

The inability to produce rapid racial equality caused many blacks to become disillusioned with life in America altogether. One such person, Marcus Aurelius Garvey, also from the Caribbean island of Jamaica, attempted to alleviate this problem by initiating a "back to Africa" movement. Many middle-class African Americans fought Garvey's idea. Some genuinely felt that African Americans should work out their destiny in America, not Africa. For others, Garvey's term *Afro-American* was itself a source of shame. The hyphen represented for them not a source of pride but rather bondage to a dark, backward country and brutal past they wanted to forget. Garvey was thus shunned by the bourgeoisie and laughed at by many of the intellectuals for his antics. Even so, he was an important influence on the image that African Americans shaped for themselves after World War I. He is reported to have had a following of anywhere between half a million and six million. The black masses apparently loved him.

The essence of Garvey's "back to Africa" message was that black was superior to white and that the destiny of African Americans lay in Africa, not America. Garvey's efforts, however, were not confined to getting blacks back to Africa, a place Garvey himself was never to see. He also attempted to produce African American pride and self-help through a program of black capitalistic enterprise that anticipated the work and ideas of Elijah Muhammad and his Nation of Islam. The Universal African Legion, Black Cross Nurses, the Universal African Motor Corps, the Black Eagle Flying Corps, and the Black Star Line represent only a few of his efforts. Although these programs and organizations largely failed, Garvey was most instrumental in strengthening African Americans' sense of racial pride and in encouraging them to think about their heritage, roots, and racial past.

The Harlem Renaissance

The Harlem Renaissance, a florescence of creative activity in art, music, dance, poetry, drama, and fiction, was a logical extension of the African American's new racial, cultural, and political thinking. We have already discussed some of the movement's achievements in dance (Chapter 32). The movement started around 1919, reached its peak in the years 1925 to 1928, and tapered off in 1932. As an artistic, cultural, and social journey of self-discovery, it was an important time for all African Americans. As Alain Locke, one of the movement's cultural mentors, expressed it in 1925:

> The pulse of the Negro world has begun to beat in Harlem. . . . Hope rests in the revaluation by white and black alike of the Negro in terms of his artistic endowments and cultural contributions, not only in his folk-art, music especially, which has always found appreciation, but in larger, though humbler and less acknowledged ways. . . . A second crop of the Negro's gifts promises still more largely. He now becomes a conscious contributor and lays aside the status of a beneficiary and ward for that of a collaborator and participant in American civilization. The great social gain in this is the releasing of our talented group from the arid fields of controversy and debate to the productive fields of creative expression.

Locke, who often compared the African American's cultural reawakening to the national movements of folk expression that were taking place in Ireland, Czechoslovakia, Yugoslavia, India, China, Egypt, Russia, Palestine, and Mexico, later edited an anthology called *The New Negro*. Designed specifically to register the inner life of African Americans and to document them culturally and socially, *The New Negro* reflected the idealism and optimism of most American progressive reformers, black and white. For Locke, Du Bois, James Weldon Johnson, Charles S. Johnson, Carl Van Vechten, and other Harlem Renaissance leaders and participants, the creative expressions of African Americans were viewed as a means toward racial peace and as adequate proof of their ability to participate in American life.

Although such hopes were not immediately realized, the Harlem Renaissance did witness an unprecedented amount of interracial activities and cooperation. By 1920 the "coon" shows had given way to the talented performances of such black actors and musicians as Josephine Baker, Charles Gilpin, Paul Robeson, Frank Wilson, Noble Sissle, and Eubie Blake. In both Europe and America interest in the New Negro was focused around jazz, African art, and the cult of the primitive. African Americans were in vogue, as their lifestyle had become a fad.

Langston Hughes (1902–1967) Of the many writers who began to flourish in Harlem during the 1920s and 1930s, Langston Hughes was undoubtedly the best known. Two basic impulses sustaining Hughes's drive to write about the common black folk were his genuine love for his race and his attachment to his town, Harlem. The Simple stories (with the folk commentator, Jessie B. Simple) make clear Hughes's recognition of the common plight of all blacks and the vital spark of African life and culture.

Jean Toomer (1894–1967) A lesser-known but highly talented and interesting writer of the Harlem Renaissance was Jean Toomer, a man of mixed race who described himself as "French, Dutch, Welsh, Negro, German, Jewish, and Indian . . . inevitably an American." Spiritually, however, Toomer considered himself to be black, for his need for artistic expression pulled him "deeper and deeper into the Negro group." Although Toomer wrote prolifically during his lifetime, he published only one book, entitled *Cane*. Published in 1923, *Cane* is a collection of poems and prose sketches, many in highly original, experimental styles, adapting modernist techniques to evoke the African American experience.

Assessments of the accomplishments of the Harlem Renaissance differ markedly. Most historians and literary critics agree, however, that its major significance lies in its contribution to African Americans' consciousness of their blackness and their African heritage, their search for black values, and their quest for a new beginning in America.

Jazz

The writer F. Scott Fitzgerald justly labeled the decades of the 1920s and 1930s "The Jazz Age." Indeed, the end of World War I marks the emergence of jazz music as a national rage. Spawned in the urban poverty of African America, and born of the mingling of sacred and secular, African, European classical, and American folk music sources, this all-American art form spread from New Orleans to Kansas City, Chicago, and New York with lightning speed and ultimately found enthusiastic adherents and vociferous critics all across the land and in Europe as well. Jazz came of age at the same time the radio and recording industries did, and the networks were soon bringing the new sounds of the 1920s into nearly every home in America.

Jazz is an improvisatory art. Every great performer transforms the basic materials, re-creates them. In a very real sense, every jazz performance is a new work, and through live performances, recordings, and radio, musicians everywhere learned from each other. The amateurs and hacks borrowed what they could imitate; the great talents assimilated what they heard only to move forward in an evolving art form. As early as January 1917, musicians from New Orleans, the Original Dixieland Jazz Band, were playing in New York, and it was not long before they were in the recording studios. The hot music from New Orleans was soon heard in parlors from Maine to California. It might be said that the history of the jazz age is etched in the grooves of ten-inch, three-minute-play, shellac discs.

Jazz is also a performance art. Its giants have been first and foremost virtuoso performers, whether vocalists or instrumentalists. The most successful of them knew how to combine a constantly high level of musical inventiveness with crowd-pleasing showmanship. One man exemplifies all the traits of the great jazz artist. Born into the abject poverty of black uptown New Orleans on August 4, 1900, Louis "Satchmo" Armstrong apprenticed in local bands for several years, emulating his idol, Joe "King" Oliver. When the call came in 1922 to join King Oliver's Creole Jazz Band in Chicago, Louis was not only ready but soon became the star. Throughout those years he developed a brilliant trumpet technique that not only made him the leading jazz virtuoso of the day, but allowed him to turn new musical ideas into sound in some of the most creative jazz solos ever known.

Before long, as leader of his own groups, he began to temper the "hot" New Orleans style with elements of the New York ensemble sound of Fletcher Henderson and even a little of the "sweet" dance sounds of Guy Lombardo's Royal Canadians. The new synthesis can be heard on his recordings of "Cakewalking Babies" or the later "Struttin' with Some Barbeque." Louis's recordings with his Hot Five and Hot Seven are classics, outstanding accomplishments even compared to the great flurry of jazz activity of the time. (See note on page 469.)

Throughout his career, Louis Armstrong suffered, like all African American musicians, from the racism and segregation of his native country, even as his extraordinary improvisatory skills and his ebullient personality as an entertainer brought him worldwide recognition and honor. In the later years, when his highly acclaimed European tours had won him the official title of America's Ambassador of Jazz, his style still combined virtuoso trumpet playing and the "scat-singing" that had become his trademark (that is, vocal performances that are instrumentally conceived and vocalized on nonsense syllables) with large doses of "cornball" showmanship. Most would agree that he was protecting his ego with humor, but for a time this great man even had to suffer the rejection of many of his own people who interpreted such antics as selling out, playing Uncle Tom. Louis Armstrong carried his burden well, but he knew the meaning of "Black and Blue."

Many first-class musicians were associated over the years with Louis Armstrong, and one of the most important was Earl "Fatha" Hines. Their association, beginning in 1927, produced a major change in Louis's style as well as in the role the piano was to take in jazz ensembles. Some of the most extraordinary virtuoso pieces of the day were recorded when these two men collaborated. "Weather Bird," a duet for trumpet and piano, is unmatched as a combination whose sum is greater than the parts. It is a perfect example of how the working jazz musician draws on a finite set of musical phrases and then reworks, reshapes, and develops them under the impetus of the creative moment and the muses. During the performance he seeks a new sound, a clever turn of phrase, or an exciting rhythmic innovation. Through this process of reshaping a limited number of musical ideas within the solo, improvisational composition comes about. Structural unity and invention are developed partially through conscious thought, but a stronger determinant is the subconscious interplay of stored mental structures and habitual, reflexive lip and finger patterns. "Satch" and "Fatha" put it all together.

Duke Ellington (1899–1974) The economic gloom that resulted from the stock market crash of 1929 created a taste for dreamy, sentimental, and blindly optimistic popular songs. Hot jazz began to lose its audience, and a number of new substyles began to develop. Also, for purely musical reasons, the emergence of the big-band concept brought a shift in jazz styles. Throughout the decade of the 1930s, a new jazz orchestra sound was taking over, a smooth, swinging music featuring mellow moods and a new sense of ensemble, interspersed with improvised solos, some hot and others not. One of the giants of the new swing music was Edward Kennedy "Duke" Ellington. Starting out as a pianist and bandleader in the late 1920s, Duke soon began to explore the possibilities of the new musical territory in his own compositions. One of his notable accomplishments was the introduction of his own brand of chromatic harmonic thinking into jazz; another was his exploration of a broader timbral palette; and a third was the concept of writing and orchestrating music for particular jazz soloists, the members of his orchestra. Through his piano explorations he broke out of the traditional mold of simple triadic harmony to an expanded harmonic vocabulary. An excellent example is his composition "Sophisticated Lady" with its sliding, chromatic chords. His ear for sound per se (timbre) led him to score for muted brass, slides and growls, percussion effects, and winds from low baritone sax to high clarinet. Almost every recording of Ellington's orchestra illustrates a range of tonal color. The blend of composed music and swinging jazz, of arrangement and solo performance, gives the music of Duke Ellington its special appeal. "East St. Louis Toodle-Oo" or "Harlem Airshaft" or "Mood Indigo" are both jazz compositions and jazz performances, pieces of music and social commentary. As the titles reflect the world of Duke Ellington, so does the music. Duke and his orchestra also became examples and models for black America as well. They were successful, even in poverty. They were people of accomplishment and respect, even though their personal fortunes were, to a large extent, dependent on the health of the larger society and frustrated by their race. But in spite of difficulty and hostility, the Ellington orchestra rode out the storm.

African American Art

The period following World War I marked the emergence of African American art on the national and international levels just as it did for African American writing. The art of African America had been a varied conglomeration of many interests, schools of thought, and modes of expression. The works of early African American artists such as Edward M. Bannister, Edmonia Lewis (the first black female sculptor), R. S. Duncanson, and Henry O. Tanner were for the most part academic in treatment, cosmopolitan in theme, and lacking in race consciousness. These artists viewed themselves primarily as artists and only incidentally as black. As a result of this attitude, they were considered pretentious by both blacks and whites, since the fine arts were generally associated with security, leisure, wealth, and "high culture."

Picasso and the other artists who discovered African art in Paris helped to stimulate interest in it in the United States. Although some black artists in America rejected identification with African art, as they did with Africa itself, others spoke of the need to develop an African American art idiom based on African forms. Thus the decades of the 1920s and 1930s witnessed racially conscious African American artists who dealt with many of the themes that were articulated in the New Negro movement: the celebration of the beauty of black people, the illumination of the history of the African American experience, and the search for identity and roots.

Aaron Douglas (1898–1979) One of the most successful artists to emerge from the Harlem Renaissance was Aaron Douglas. Known for his geometric forms, stylized figures, patterns of mystical light, and exoticism, Douglas is rightly regarded as the pioneer of African style among African American painters. He led the way into a new field of African American art with wall decorations in Nashville (Fisk University), Harlem, Chicago, and elsewhere. Two of his well-known murals in the Countee Cullen Branch of the New York Public Library are reproduced here (Figs. 33-1, 33-2). The murals, entitled *Aspects of Negro Life,* depict the cultural and historical background of African Americans.

Jacob Lawrence (b. 1927) Another important African American painter whose work has been associated with arousing consciousness of black history and experience is Jacob Lawrence, who was among the many young artists supported by the WPA Artists Relief Program. American scene painting, and American responses to European modernism, combine with his experience as a black to form his art. Lawrence has always dealt with American themes, particularly work and the urban experience. He also painted several important series that narrate major events in African American history. Perhaps the best known is the series on the life of Harriet Tubman, a black woman who helped slaves gain access to freedom on the underground railway. The painting illustrated here, *Forward* (Color Plate XXXIII), is executed in Lawrence's typical manner. The surface is very flat and matte, like a Renaissance wall mural. The abstracted figures are carefully arranged in a compressed space, and the narrative is described through strong bodily gestures. The colors are also strong, flat, and limited to a few hues. This kind of work may be compared with the work of a number of other American artists, such as Milton Avery, who were also active in this period. Lawrence, like some other black artists who were deeply influenced by European modernism, experienced hostility not only toward his race but also toward his manner of painting. However, this did not deter him from creating a remarkable body of work, which can be associated not only with the African American past but also with the shared and universal themes of freedom and repression, human life, and work.

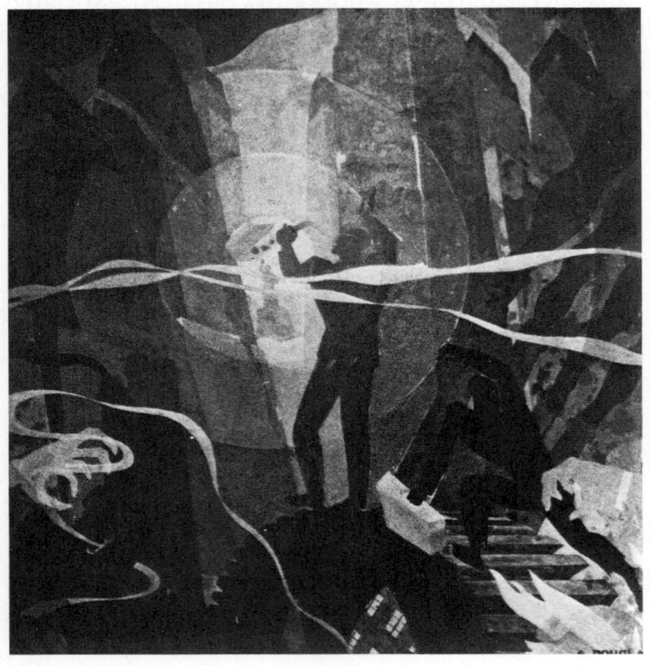

33-1, 33-2 *Aaron Douglas,* Aspects of Negro Life, From Slavery Through Reconstruction, *1934. (Art & Artifacts Division, Schomburg Center for Research in Black Culture, The New York Public Library, Astor, Lenox and Tilden Foundations)*

African American Sculpture It was in sculpture that a consciously African style was most clearly expressed. The works of Richmond Barthé and Sargent Johnson offer the best examples of such sculpture. Sargent Johnson's bust *Chester* (Fig. 33-3) and Barthé's *African Dancer* (Fig. 33-4) are both particularly striking for their African qualities. Using your knowledge from the section on African art in Chapter 14, what African qualities can you identify?

The works of Barthé and Johnson, like those of Douglas, differ from each other and from African art. The forces that motivated artists in America in the 1930s and 1940s cannot be the same as those that motivated the artist of the Benin head or the Dogon votive figure. Yet the search for roots, as surely as the presence of successful artists, exerted a profound influence on the black artists in America who reached maturity after World War II. The recognition that the past, as well as the present, is profoundly different and tremendously rich is liberating.

Modernism and the Rise of Latin American Culture

The Rediscovery of Indigenous Civilizations

While blacks in the United States were rediscovering their African heritage and attempting to integrate it with their American experience, Americans in the heterogeneous cultural and geographical area south of the Rio Grande and in the Caribbean islands were rediscovering the importance of their native American, African, and European heritages. When the thirty-five-year dictatorship of Porfirio Díaz was overthrown in 1911 in Mexico, not only the social fabric but eventually the entire cultural orientation of the

33-3 *Sargent Johnson,* Chester, *1931. Terra cotta, 10⅞" × 6¾" × 6⅜". (San Francisco Museum of Modern Art, Albert M. Bender Collection, Gift of Albert M. Bender)*

33-4 *Richmond Barthé,* African Dancer, *1933, plaster, height (including base), 42¾" (108.6 cm). (Collection of Whitney Museum of American Art, New York. Purchase 33.53)*

country underwent a profound alteration. This upheaval, combined with the general disillusionment among the intellectuals caused by World War I, shifted the emphasis from a slavish imitation of European, essentially French, patterns to a renaissance of the Mayan, Aztec, and Olmec heritages of the country. These and other indigenous cultures, so long considered inferior by many of the elite, became by the 1920s a fertile source of serious study and artistic inspiration. José Vasconcelos, then minister of education, stimulated art and literature in immediate and direct ways. He commissioned a group of young artists to paint murals on new and old public buildings. Orozco, Siqueiros, Rivera, and others created paintings representing and interpreting Mexico's rich Indian and colonial past and, in allegories, its revolutionary present and future. José Clemente Orozco's *Cortés y La Malinche* (Figure 33-5) illustrates the origin of Mexico's mixed racial heritage by its depiction of Cortés the conqueror and La Malinche, his Indian mistress, as a kind of Mexican Adam and Eve, but one must not fail to note the dead or dying figure at their feet. *Tenochtitlán* (Figure 33-6) depicts Rivera's idealized vision of the Indian past before the arrival of the Spanish invaders. Mural paintings were meant to instruct a public largely illiterate and ignorant of the social and cultural forces of the nation's past. Then, to combat this illiteracy more directly, Vasconcelos undertook a campaign to teach everyone to read and write, and, as a logical ancillary, he established a government printing press in order to make available inexpensive editions of world classics and works by Mexico's own writers. In one sense he created a public and a general interest for national writers. Mariano Azuela (1873–1952), one of the first and most important chroniclers of the chaos of the Mexican revolution, saw his masterpiece, *Los de abajo* (*The Underdogs*), republished in 1925.

Vasconcelos also encouraged the formation of a national symphony orchestra under the genial leadership of Jorge Chávez, who introduced significant indigenous elements into classical musical forms. Chávez, in such works as *Sinfonia India* (*Indian Symphony*) successfully proved that Indian and folk music and instruments constituted a worthy base for serious symphonic music. Eventually the world-famous *Ballet folklórico de México* evolved from his efforts.

Many writers, musicians, artists, and architects from other nations in Latin America and even from Europe came to Mexico to observe, learn, and participate during the 1920s and 1930s. Mexico's success was contagious, and indigenous movements soon flourished throughout Latin America. In the Caribbean and Brazil, the large black populations provided a rich source of vital, genuine innovation. In Brazil, for example, Gilberto Freyre's sociological studies of the significance of the black slave in Brazil's history inspired writers and poets to distill their own direct

33-5 *José Clemente Orozco,* Cortés y La Malinche. *(Art Museum of The Americas, OAS, Washington, D.C.)*

33-6 *Diego Rivera,* Tenochtitlán. *(Art Museum of The Americas, OAS, Washington, D.C.)*

experiences into literature. In addition to the past as artistic stimulus, there also coexisted the "futurity" of what Latin America could or would become.

Modernism in Latin America

Latin America as a land of the future, coupled with the gathering clouds of the Spanish Civil War (1936–1939) and of World War II, brought many Europeans to rediscover America. In 1936 under the influence of Le Corbusier, Lúcio Costa and Oscar Niemeyer designed and built the now historically significant Ministry of Education Building in Rio. The building represented a unique and stunning adaptation to local climatic needs. The great Brazilian painter Cándido Portinari, like his fellow muralists in Mexico, contributed a series of murals for the building's interior depicting the agricultural and mineral wealth of Brazil and glorifying the anonymous men and women who labor in these pursuits. He also created an impressive abstract mural executed in ceramic tiles for the building's exterior. This same painter, again like his Mexican colleagues, evidenced a strong social commitment in both his easel and mural painting. The dramatic and poignant *Os retirantes* (*The Migrants*) (Fig. 33-7) portrays the plight of the landless, rural poor who flee the drought-plagued Brazilian Northeast in order to seek the chimera of a better life in the burgeoning urban areas.

33-7 *Candido Torquato Portinari, (Brodosqui, SP, 1903–Rio de Janeiro, 1962)* Os retirantes, *oil on canvas, 192 × 181 cm. (Collection Museu de Arte de São Paulo, photo by Luiz Hossaka)*

In a very real sense, the past, present, and future fused together in Latin America. Stone Age Indians coexisted with Bauhaus, the primitive with the cosmopolitan. Time mixes created magical, surrealistic conditions. The magical, which had been absent from the European tradition since the Middle Ages, thrived here. America, in the Hispanic sense of the word, represented a vital, authentic superreality. This startling blend of cultures, along with the ever-present impact of the great artistic experiments of European and North American modernism, gave birth to the movement known as *la vanguardia*, the *avant-garde* or "vanguard." The Spanish term *modernismo* had been used to define an earlier movement more akin to French symbolism. In Spanish America, *la vanguardia* surfaced in art, music, and literature during the first years of the 1920s. In Portuguese-speaking Brazil, the new modernism boldly manifested itself in "*una semana de arte moderna*," an important "modern" art exhibit held in São Paulo in April 1922.

In the literature of what we might call the Latin American modernist period, some of which was not "discovered" by the northern world until much later, three types of writers flourished: those who sought only inspiration and aesthetic values in indigenous themes expressed in realist-naturalist modes; those who pursued cosmopolitan and universal themes adapting the avant-garde and European "-isms" to their literary requirements; and those who combined the search for the truly autochthonous with avant-garde techniques.

Among the writers of the first group are Mariano Azuela, Ciro Alegria, the Peruvian novelist who dealt with the life of the Andean Indians and the *mestizos*, and José Lins do Rego, who re-created the life of the Brazilian plantation societies of the Northeast. None of these writers rooted in the traditions of the past and the present made stylistic innovations a priority. They wrote simply and straightforwardly of what they had known and lived. Their writings are often infused with a marked moral or social concern for their disinherited compatriots. In the second group of writers and poets, an interest or desire to join with the rest of the world is evident. Jorge Luis Borges (1899–1986) of Buenos Aires, "vast suburb of the world," Julio Cortázar, also of Argentina, and Clarice Lispector of Brazil are representative. In the third group, Miguel Angel Asturias (1899–1974) of Guatemala and Pablo Neruda (1904–1973) of Chile (both Nobel laureates) attempted to reconcile indigenous themes with vanguard techniques. They sought to give an American voice to the American reality.

Reading Selections

Jean Toomer—USA

Karintha

Her skin is like dusk on the eastern horizon,
O cant you see it, O cant you see it,
Her skin is like dusk on the eastern horizon
. . . When the sun goes down.

Men always wanted her, this Karintha, even as a child, Karintha carrying beauty, perfect as dusk when the sun goes down. Old men rode her hobby-horse upon their knees. Young men danced with her at frolics when they should have been dancing with their grown-up girls. God grant us youth, secretly prayed the old men. The young fellows counted the time to pass before she would be old enough to mate with them. This interest of the male, who wishes to ripen a growing thing too soon, could mean no good to her.

Karintha, at twelve, was a wild flash that told the other folks just what it was to live. At sunset, where there was no wind, and the pine-smoke from over by the sawmill hugged the earth, and you couldnt see more than a few feet in front, her sudden darting past you was a bit of vivid color, like a black bird that flashes in light. With the other children one could hear, some distance off, their feet flopping in the two-inch dust. Karintha's running was a whir. It had the sound of the red dust that sometimes makes a spiral in the road. At dusk, during the hush just after the sawmill had closed down, and before any of the women had started their supper-getting-ready songs, her voice, high-pitched, shrill, would put one's ears to itching. But no one ever thought to make her stop because of it. She stoned the cows, and beat her dog, and fought the other children. . . . Even the preacher, who caught her at mischief, told himself that she was as innocently lovely as a November cotton flower. Already, rumors were out about her. Homes in Georgia are most often built on the two-room plan. In one, you cook and eat, in the other you sleep, and there love goes on. Karintha had seen or heard, perhaps she had felt her parents loving. One could but imitate one's parents, for to follow them was the way of God. She played "home" with a small boy who was not afraid to do her bidding. That started the whole thing. Old men could no longer ride her hobby-horse upon their knees. But young men counted faster.

Her skin is like dusk,
O cant you see it,
Her skin is like dusk,
When the sun goes down.

Karintha is a woman. She who carries beauty, perfect as dusk when the sun goes down. She has been married many times. Old men remind her that a few years back they rode her hobby-horse upon their knees. Karintha smiles, and indulges them when she is in the mood for it. She has contempt for them. Karintha is a woman. Young men run stills to make her money. Young men go to the big cities and run on the road. Young men go away to college. They all want to bring her money. These are the young men who thought that all they had to do was to count time. But Karintha is a woman, and she has had a child. A child fell out of her womb onto a bed of pine-needles in the forest. Pine-needles are smooth and sweet. They are elastic to the feet of rabbits. . . . A sawmill was nearby. Its pyramidal sawdust pile smouldered. It is a year before one completely burns. Meanwhile, the smoke curls up and hangs in odd wraiths about the trees, curls up, and spreads itself out over the valley. . . . Weeks after Karintha returned home the smoke was so heavy you tasted it in water. Some one made a song:

Smoke is on the hills. Rise up.
Smoke is on the hills, O rise
And take my soul to Jesus.

Karintha is a woman. Men do not know that the soul of her was a growing thing ripened too soon. They will bring their money; they will die not having found it out. . . . Karintha at twenty, carrying beauty, perfect as dusk when the sun goes down. Karintha . . .

> Her skin is like dusk on the eastern horizon,
> O cant you see it, O cant you see it,
> Her skin is like dusk on the eastern horizon
> . . . When the sun goes down.
>
> Goes down . . .

QUESTIONS

1. Through what specific linguistic effects does Toomer create this portrait of a black woman?
2. Compare the techniques used in this word portrait with those in the portrait of Molly Bloom by Joyce.

LANGSTON HUGHES—USA

"The Weary Blues," which epitomizes "jazz" or "blues" poetry, displays most of the qualities that dominated Hughes's poetry throughout the Harlem Renaissance: it is loose in form, songful, and idiomatic in vocabulary. In "The Negro Speaks of Rivers," Hughes expresses his sense of the cultural roots of African Americans in ancient African civilizations.

The Weary Blues

Droning a drowsy syncopated tune,
Rocking back and forth to a mellow croon,
  I heard a Negro play.
Down on Lenox Avenue the other night
By the pale dull pallor of an old gas light
  He did a lazy sway. . . .
  He did a lazy sway. . . .
To the tune o' those Weary Blues.
With his ebony hands on each ivory key
He made that poor piano moan with melody.
  O Blues!
Swaying to and fro on his rickety stool
He played that sad raggy tune like a musical fool.
  Sweet Blues!
Coming from a black man's soul.
  O Blues!
In a deep song voice with a melancholy tone
I heard that Negro sing, that old piano moan—
  "Ain't got nobody in all this world,
  Ain't got nobody but ma self.
  I's gwine to quit ma frownin'
  And put ma troubles on de shelf."
Thump, thump, thump, went his foot on the floor.
He played a few chords then he sang some more—
  "I got de Weary Blues
  And I can't be satisfied.
  Got de Weary Blues
  And can't be satisfied—
  I ain't happy no mo'
  And I wish that I had died."
And far into the night he crooned that tune.
The stars went out and so did the moon.
The singer stopped playing and went to bed.
While the Weary Blues echoed through his head
He slept like a rock or a man that's dead.

The Negro Speaks of Rivers

I've known rivers!
I've known rivers ancient as the world and older than the flow of human blood in human veins.
My soul has grown deep like the rivers.

I bathed in the Euphrates when dawns were young,
I built my hut near the Congo and it lulled me to sleep,
I looked upon the Nile and raised the pyramids above it.

I heard the singing of the Mississippi when Abe Lincoln went down to New Orleans,
And I've seen its muddy bosom turn all golden in the sunset.

I've known rivers:
Ancient, dusky rivers,
My soul has grown deep like the rivers.

QUESTIONS

1. How and where does Hughes imitate jazz rhythms in "The Weary Blues"?
2. What different connotations does the word "rivers" carry in the second poem?

Mariano Azuela—Mexico

From *Los de abajo*

Translation by E. Munguía, Jr.

Chronologically the first to deal with the Mexican revolution, Mariano Azuela's vision is, nevertheless, unrevolutionary. In *Los de abajo* and subsequent novels, he undertook to criticize those who corrupted the goals of the revolution and took advantage of its chaos to enrich themselves or gain power. In this selection from the concluding chapter of Part I, two major, allegorical characters—Luis Cervantes, the urban middle-class opportunist, and Alberto Solís, the disaffected revolutionary—meet. While observing the devastated town below, Solis and Cervantes discuss the nature of the revolution and its impact on its people.

The firing lessened, then slowly died out. Luis Cervantes, who had been hiding amid a heap of ruins at the fortification on the crest of the hill, made bold to show his face. How he had managed to hang on, he did not know. Nor did he know when Demetrio and his men had disappeared. Suddenly he had found himself alone; then, hurled back by an avalanche of infantry, he fell from his saddle; a host of men trampled over him until he rose from the ground and a man on horseback hoisted him up behind him. After a few moments, horse and riders fell. Left without rifle, revolver, or arms of any kind, Cervantes found himself lost in the midst of white smoke and whistling bullets. A hole amid a debris of crumbling stone offered a refuge of safety.

"Hello, partner!"

"Luis, how are you!"

"The horse threw me. They fell upon me. Then they took my gun away. You see, they thought I was dead. There was nothing I could do!" Luis Cervantes explained apologetically. Then:

"Nobody threw me down," Solís said. "I'm here because I like to play safe."

The irony in Solís' voice brought a blush to Cervantes' cheek.

"By God, that chief of yours is a man!" Solís said. "What daring, what assurance! He left me gasping—and a hell of a lot of other men with more experience than me, too!"

Luis Cervantes vouchsafed no answer.

"What! Weren't you there? Oh, I see! You found a nice place for yourself at the right time. Come here, Luis, I'll explain; let's go behind that rock. From this meadow to the foot of the hill, there's no road save this path below. To the right, the incline is too sharp; you can't do anything there. And it's worse to the left; the ascent is so dangerous that a second's hesitation means a fall down those rocks and a broken neck at the end of it. All right! A number of men from Moya's brigade who went down to the meadow decided to attack the enemy's trenches the first chance they got. The bullets whizzed about us, the battle raged on all sides. For a time they stopped firing, so we thought they were being attacked from behind. We stormed their trenches—look, partner, look at that meadow! It's thick with corpses! Their machine guns did that for us. They mowed us down like wheat; only a handful escaped. Those Goddamned officers went white as a sheet; even though we had reinforcements they were afraid to order a new charge. That was when Demetrio Macías plunged in. Did he wait for orders? Not he! He just shouted:

"'Come on, boys! Let's go for them!'

"'Damn fool!' I thought, 'What the hell does he think he's doing!'

"The officers, surprised, said nothing. Demetrio's horse seemed to wear eagle's claws instead of hoofs, it soared so swiftly over the rocks. 'Come on! Come on!' his men shouted, following him like wild deer, horses and men welded into a mad stampede. Only one young fellow stepped wild and fell headlong into the pit. In a few seconds the others appeared at the top of the hill, storming the trenches and killing the Federals by the thousand. With his rope, Demetrio lassoed the machine guns and carried them off, like a bull herd throwing a steer. Yet his success could not last much longer, for the Federals were far stronger in numbers and could easily have destroyed Demetrio and his men. But we took advantage of their confusion, we rushed upon them and they soon cleared out of their position. That chief of yours is a wonderful soldier!"

Standing on the crest of the hill, they could easily sight one side of the Bufa peak. Its highest crag spread out like the feathered head of a proud Aztec king. The three-hundred-foot slope was literally covered with dead, their hair matted, their clothes clotted with grime and blood. A host of ragged women, vultures of prey, ranged over the tepid bodies of the dead, stripping one man bare, despoiling another, robbing from a third his dearest possessions.

Amid clouds of white rifle smoke and the dense black vapors of flaming buildings, houses with wide doors and windows bolted shone in the sunlight. The streets seemed to be piled upon one another, or wound picturesquely about fantastic corners, or set to scale the hills nearby. Above the graceful cluster of houses, rose the lithe columns of a warehouse and the towers and cupola of the church.

"How beautiful the revolution! Even in its most barbarous aspect it is beautiful," Solís said with deep feeling. Then a vague melancholy seized him, and speaking low:

"A pity what remains to do won't be as beautiful! We must wait a while, until there are no men left to fight on either side, until no sound of shot rings through the air save from the mob as carrion-like it falls upon the booty; we must wait until the psychology of our race, condensed into two words, shines clear and luminous as a drop of water: *Robbery! Murder!* What a colossal failure we would make of it, friend, if we, who offer our enthusiasm and lives to crush a wretched tyrant, became the builders of a monstrous edifice holding one hundred or two hundred thousand monsters of exactly the same sort. People without ideals! A tyrant folk! Vain bloodshed!"

Large groups of Federals pushed up the hill, fleeing from the "high hats." A bullet whistled past them, singing as it sped. After his speech, Alberto Solís stood lost in thought, his arms crossed. Suddenly, he took fright.

"I'll be damned if I like these plaguey mosquitoes!" he said. "Let's get away from here!"

So scornfully Luis Cervantes smiled that Solís sat down on a rock quite calm, bewildered. He smiled. His gaze roved as he watched the spirals of smoke from the rifles, the dust of roofs crumbling from houses as they fell before the artillery. He believed he discerned the symbol of the revolution in these clouds of dust and smoke that climbed upward together, met at the crest of the hill and, a moment after, were lost....

"By heaven, now I see what it all means!"

He sketched a vast gesture, pointing to the station. Locomotives belched huge clouds of black dense smoke rising in columns; the trains were overloaded with fugitives who had barely managed to escape from the captured town.

Suddenly he felt a sharp blow in the stomach. As though his legs were putty, he rolled off the rock. His ears buzzed.... Then darkness... silence... eternity....

QUESTIONS

1. Why and how did the two find themselves on the hilltop?
2. What specific criticisms does Solís make? On what are they based?
3. In what kinds of words and images is the revolution described?
4. What tone pervades these final pages, and how does it apply to the author's message?

Jorge Luis Borges—Argentina

Death and the Compass

Translation by Donald A. Yates

Borges may prove to be this century's most important and influential writer. The dissemination of his works worldwide since the late 1950s and their impact on readers and other writers have virtually canonized him. His name has become adjectivized: "Borgesian," like Proustian or Joycean, denotes a content and writing style that is unique but for which modernist precedents such as Kafka were important. Most of his major "fictions" were written and published before 1952, but it was only with his "discovery" in French translation in the late 1950s and early 1960s that he became internationally acclaimed. Although initially an excellent poet and essayist, his reputation rests on a hybrid somewhere between the essay and the short story. Metaphysical ruminations about time, reality, philosophies, religions, and humankind's place in the universe provide the stimulus and basis for his work. "Death and the Compass," a classic detective mystery first published in the magazine *Sur* in 1942, provides the framework for an examination of the patterns of time, space, and humanity. As Borges has written in an English commentary to the story, "A triangle is suggested but the solution is really based on a rhombus.... The killer and the slain, whose minds work in the same way, may be the same man."

Of the many problems which exercised the reckless discernment of Lönnrot, none was so strange—so rigorously strange, shall we say—as the periodic series of bloody events which culminated at the villa of Triste-le-Roy, amid the ceaseless aroma of the eucalypti. It is true that Erik Lönnrot failed to prevent the last murder, but that he foresaw it is indisputable. Neither did he guess the identity of Yarmolinsky's luckless assassin, but he did succeed in divining the secret morphology behind the fiendish series as well as the participation of Red Scharlach, whose other nickname is Scharlach the Dandy. That criminal (as countless others) had sworn on his honor to kill Lönnrot, but the latter could never be intimidated. Lönnrot believed himself a pure reasoner, an Auguste Dupin, but there was something of the adventurer in him, and even a little of the gambler.

The first murder occurred in the Hôtel du Nord—that tall prism which dominates the estuary whose waters are the color of the desert. To that tower (which quite glaringly unites the hateful whiteness of a hospital, the numbered divisibility of a jail, and the general appearance of a bordello) there came on the third day of December the delegate from Podolsk to the Third Talmudic Congress, Doctor Marcel Yarmolinsky, a gray-bearded man with gray eyes. We shall never know whether the Hôtel du Nord pleased him; he accepted it with the ancient resignation which had allowed him to endure three years of war in the Carpathians and three thousand years of oppression and pogroms. He was given a room on Floor R, across from the suite which was occupied—not without splendor—by the Tetrarch of Galilee. Yarmolinsky supped, postponed until the following day an inspection of the unknown city, arranged in a *placard* his many books and few personal possessions, and before midnight extinguished his light. (Thus declared the Tetrarch's chauffeur who slept in the adjoining room.) On the fourth, at 11:03 A.M., the editor of the *Yidische Zaitung* put in a call to him; Doctor Yarmolinsky did not answer. He was found in his room, his face already a little dark, nearly nude beneath a large anachronistic cape. He was lying not far from the door which opened on the hall; a deep knife wound had split his breast. A few hours later, in the same room amid journalists, photographers and policemen, Inspector Treviranus and Lönnrot were calmly discussing the problem.

"No need to look for a three-legged cat here," Treviranus was saying as he brandished an imperious cigar. "We all know that the Tetrarch of Galilee owns the finest sapphires in the world. Someone, intending to steal them, must have broken in here by mistake. Yarmolinsky got up; the robber had to kill him. How does it sound to you?"

"Possible, but not interesting," Lönnrot answered. "You'll reply that reality hasn't the least obligation to be interesting. And I'll answer you that reality may avoid that obligation but that hypotheses may not. In the hypothesis that you propose, chance intervenes copiously. Here we have a dead rabbi; I would prefer a purely rabbinical explanation, not the imaginary mischances of an imaginary robber."

Treviranus replied ill-humoredly:

"I'm not interested in rabbinical explanations. I am interested in capturing the man who stabbed this unknown person."

"Not so unknown," corrected Lönnrot. "Here are his complete works." He indicated in the wall-cupboard a row of tall books: a *Vindication of the Cabala; An Examination of the Philosophy of Robert Fludd;* a literal translation of the *Sepher Yezirah;* a *Biography of the Baal Shem;* a *History of the Hasidic Sect;* a monograph (in German) on the Tetragrammaton; another, on the divine nomenclature of the Pentateuch. The inspector regarded them with dread, almost with repulsion. Then he began to laugh.

"I'm a poor Christian," he said. "Carry off those musty volumes if you want; I don't have any time to waste on Jewish superstitions."

"Maybe the crime belongs to the history of Jewish superstitions," murmured Lönnrot.

"Like Christianity," the editor of the *Yidische Zaitung* ventured to add. He was myopic, an atheist and very shy.

No one answered him. One of the agents had found in the small typewriter a piece of paper on which was written the following unfinished sentence:

The first letter of the Name has been uttered

Lönnrot abstained from smiling. Suddenly become a bibliophile or Hebraist, he ordered a package made of the dead man's books and carried them off to his apartment. Indifferent to the police investigation, he dedicated himself to studying them. One large octavo volume revealed to him the teachings of Israel Baal Shem Tobh, founder of the sect of the Pious; another, the virtues and terrors of the Tetragrammaton, which is the unutterable name of God; another, the thesis that God has a secret name, in which is epitomized (as in the crystal sphere which the Persians ascribe to Alexander of Macedonia) his ninth attribute, eternity—that is to say, the immediate knowledge of all things that will be, which are and which have been in the universe. Tradition numbers ninety-nine names of God; the Hebraists attribute that imperfect number to magical fear of even numbers; the Hasidim reason that that hiatus indicates a hundredth name—the Absolute Name.

From this erudition Lönnrot was distracted, a few days later, by the appearance of the editor of the *Yidische Zaitung*. The latter wanted to talk about the murder; Lönnrot preferred to discuss the diverse names of God; the journalist declared, in three columns, that the investigator, Erik Lönnrot, had dedicated himself to studying the names of God in order to come across the name of the murderer. Lönnrot, accustomed to the simplifications of journalism, did not become indignant. One of those enterprising shopkeepers who have discovered that any given man is resigned to buying any given book published a popular edition of the *History of the Hasidic Sect*.

The second murder occurred on the evening of the third of January, in the most deserted and empty corner of the capital's western suburbs. Towards dawn, one of the gendarmes who patrol those solitudes on horseback saw a man in a poncho, lying prone in the shadow of an old paint shop. The harsh features seemed to be masked in blood; a deep knife wound had split his breast. On the wall, across the yellow and red diamonds, were some words written in chalk. The gendarme spelled them out... That afternoon, Treviranus and Lönnrot headed for the remote scene of the crime. To the left and right of the automobile the city disintegrated; the firmament grew and houses were of less importance than a brick kiln or a poplar tree. They arrived at their miserable destination: an alley's end, with rose-colored walls which somehow seemed to reflect the extravagant sunset. The dead man had already been identified. He was Daniel Simon Azevedo, an individual of some fame in the old northern suburbs, who had risen from wagon driver to political tough, then degenerated to a thief and even an informer. (The singular style of his death seemed appropriate to them: Azevedo was the last representative of a generation of bandits who knew how to manipulate a dagger, but not a revolver.) The words in chalk were the following:

The second letter of the Name has been uttered

The third murder occurred on the night of the third of February. A little before one o'clock, the telephone in Inspector Treviranus' office rang. In avid secretiveness, a man with a guttural voice spoke; he said his name was Ginzberg (or Ginsburg) and that he was prepared to communicate, for reasonable remuneration, the events surrounding the two sacrifices of Azevedo and Yarmolinsky. A discordant sound of whistles and horns drowned out the informer's voice. Then, the connection was broken off. Without yet rejecting the possibility of a hoax (after all, it was carnival time), Treviranus found out that he had been called from the Liverpool House, a tavern on the rue de Toulon, that dingy street where side by side exist the cosmorama and the coffee shop, the bawdy house and the bible sellers. Treviranus spoke with the owner. The latter (Black Finnegan, an old Irish criminal who was immersed in, almost overcome by, respectability) told him that the last person to use the phone was a lodger, a certain Gryphius, who had just left with some friends. Treviranus went immediately to Liverpool House. The owner related the following. Eight days ago Gryphius had rented a room above the tavern. He was a sharp-featured man with a nebulous gray beard, and was shabbily dressed in black; Finnegan (who used the room for a purpose which Treviranus guessed) demanded a rent which was undoubtedly excessive; Gryphius paid the stipulated sum without hesitation. He almost never went out; he dined and lunched in his room; his face was scarcely known in the bar. On the night in question, he came downstairs to make a phone call from Finnegan's office. A closed cab stopped in front of the tavern. The driver didn't move from his seat; several patrons recalled that he was wearing a bear's mask. Two harlequins got out of the cab; they were of short stature and no one failed to observe that they were very drunk. With a tooting of horns, they burst into Finnegan's office; they embraced Gryphius, who appeared to recognize them but responded coldly; they exchanged a few words in Yiddish—he in a low, guttural voice, they in high-pitched, false voices—and then went up to the room. Within a quarter hour the three descended, very happy. Gryphius, staggering, seemed as drunk as the others. He walked—tall and dizzy—in the middle, between the masked harlequins. (One of the women at the bar remembered the yellow, red and green diamonds.) Twice he stumbled; twice he was caught and held by the harlequins. Moving off toward the inner harbor which enclosed a rectangular body of water, the three got into a cab and disappeared. From the footboard of the cab, the last of the harlequins scrawled an obscene figure and a sentence on one of the slates of the pier shed.

Treviranus saw the sentence. It was virtually predictable. It said:

The last of the letters of the Name has been uttered

Afterwards, he examined the small room of Gryphius-Ginzberg. On the floor there was a brusque star of blood, in the corners, traces of cigarettes of a Hungarian brand; in a cabinet, a book in Latin—the *Philologus Hebraeo-Graecus* (1739) of Leusden—with several manuscript notes. Treviranus looked it over with indignation and had Lönnrot located. The latter, without removing his hat, began to read while the inspector was interrogating the contradictory witnesses to the possible kidnapping. At four o'clock they left. Out on the twisted rue de Toulon, as they were treading on the dead serpentines of the dawn, Treviranus said:

"And what if all this business tonight were just a mock rehearsal?"

Erik Lönnrot smiled and, with all gravity, read a passage (which was underlined) from the thirty-third dissertation of the *Philologus: Dies Judacorum incipit ad solis occasu usque ad solis occasum diei sequentis.*

"This means," he added, "'The Hebrew day begins at sundown and lasts until the following sundown.'"

The inspector attempted an irony.

"Is that fact the most valuable one you've come across tonight?"

"No. Even more valuable was a word that Ginzberg used."

The afternoon papers did not overlook the periodic disappearances. *La Cruz de la Espada* contrasted them with the admirable discipline and order of the last Hermetical Congress; Ernst Palast, in *El Mártir*, criticized "the intolerable delays in this clandestine and frugal pogrom, which has taken three months to murder three Jews"; the *Yidische Zaitung* rejected the horrible hypothesis of an anti-Semitic plot, "even though many penetrating intellects admit no other solution to the triple mystery"; the most illustrious gunman of the south, Dandy Red Scharlach, swore that in his district similar crimes could never occur, and he accused Inspector Franz Treviranus of culpable negligence.

On the night of March first, the inspector received an impressive-looking sealed envelope. He opened it; the envelope contained a letter signed "Baruch Spinoza" and a detailed plan of the city, obviously torn from a Baedeker. The letter prophesied that on the third of March there would not be a fourth murder, since the paint shop in the west, the tavern on the rue de Toulon and the Hôtel du Nord were "the perfect vertices of a mystic equilateral triangle"; the map demonstrated in red ink the regularity of the triangle. Treviranus read the *more geometrico* argument with resignation, and sent the letter and the map to Lönnrot—who, unquestionably, was deserving of such madnesses.

Erik Lönnrot studied them. The three locations were in fact equidistant. Symmetry in time (the third of December, the third of January, the third of February); symmetry in space as well... Suddenly, he felt as if he were on the point of solving the mystery. A set of calipers and a compass completed his quick intuition. He smiled, pronounced the word Tetragrammaton (of recent acquisition) and phoned the inspector. He said:

"Thank you for the equilateral triangle you sent me last night. It has enabled me to solve the problem. This Friday the criminals will be in jail, we may rest assured."

"Then they're not planning a fourth murder?"

"Precisely because they *are* planning a fourth murder we can rest assured."

Lönnrot hung up. One hour later he was traveling on one of the Southern Railway's trains, in the direction of the abandoned villa of Triste-le-Roy. To the south of the city of our story, flows a blind little river of muddy water, defamed by refuse and garbage. On the far side is an industrial suburb where, under the protection of a political boss from Barcelona, gunmen thrive. Lönnrot smiled at the thought that the most celebrated gunman of all—Red Scharlach—would have given a great deal to know of his clandestine visit. Azevedo had been an associate of Scharlach; Lönnrot considered the remote possibility that the fourth victim might be Scharlach himself. Then he rejected the idea... He had very nearly deciphered the problem; mere circumstances, reality (names, prison records, faces, judicial and penal proceedings) hardly interested him now. He wanted to travel a bit, he wanted to rest from three months of sedentary investigation. He reflected that the explanation of the murders was in an anonymous triangle and a dusty Greek word. The mystery appeared almost crystalline to him now; he was mortified to have dedicated a hundred days to it.

The train stopped at a silent loading station. Lönnrot got off. It was one of those deserted afternoons that seem like dawns. The air of the turbid, puddled plain was damp and cold. Lönnrot began walking along the countryside. He saw dogs, he saw a car on a siding, he saw the horizon, he saw a silver-colored horse drinking the crapulous water of a puddle. It was growing dark when he saw the rectangular belvedere of the villa of Triste-le-Roy, almost as tall as the black eucalypti which surrounded it. He thought that scarcely one dawning and one nightfall (an ancient splendor in the east and another in the west) separated him from the moment long desired by the seekers of the Name.

A rusty wrought-iron fence defined the irregular perimeter of the villa. The main gate was closed. Lönnrot, without much hope of getting in, circled the area. Once again before the insurmountable gate, he placed his hand between the bars almost mechanically and encountered the bolt. The creaking of the iron surprised him. With a laborious passivity the whole gate swung back.

Lönnrot advanced among the eucalypti treading on confused generations of rigid, broken leaves. Viewed from anear, the house of the villa of Triste-le-Roy abounded in pointless symmetries and in maniacal repetitions: to one Diana in a murky niche corresponded a second Diana in another niche; one balcony was reflected in another balcony; double stairways led to double balustrades. A two-faced Hermes projected a monstrous shadow. Lönnrot circled the house as he had the villa. He examined everything; beneath the level of the terrace he saw a narrow Venetian blind.

He pushed it; a few marble steps descended to a vault. Lönnrot, who had now perceived the architect's preferences, guessed that at the opposite wall there would be another stairway. He found it, ascended, raised his hands and opened the trap door.

A brilliant light led him to a window. He opened it: a yellow, rounded moon defined two silent fountains in the melancholy garden. Lönnrot explored the house. Through anterooms and galleries he passed to duplicate patios, and time after time to the same patio. He ascended the dusty stairs to circular antechambers; he was multiplied infinitely in opposing mirrors; he grew tired of opening or half-opening windows which revealed outside the same desolate garden from various heights and various angles; inside, only pieces of furniture wrapped in yellow dust sheets and chandeliers bound up in tarlatan. A bedroom detained him; in that bedroom, one single flower in a porcelain vase; at the first touch the ancient petals fell apart. On the second floor, on the top floor, the house seemed infinite and expanding. *The house is not this large*, he thought. *Other things are making it seem larger: the dim light, the symmetry, the mirrors, so many years, my unfamiliarity, the loneliness.*

By way of a spiral staircase he arrived at the oriel. The early evening moon shone through the diamonds of the window; they were yellow, red and green. An astonishing, dizzying recollection struck him.

Two men of short stature, robust and ferocious, threw themselves on him and disarmed him; another, very tall, saluted him gravely and said:

"You are very kind. You have saved us a night and a day."

It was Red Scharlach. The men handcuffed Lönnrot. The latter at length recovered his voice.

"Scharlach, are you looking for the Secret Name?"

Scharlach remained silent, indifferent. He had not participated in the brief struggle, and he scarcely extended his hand to receive Lönnrot's revolver. He spoke; Lönnrot noted in his voice a fatigued triumph, a hatred the size of the universe, a sadness not less than that hatred.

"No," said Scharlach. "I am seeking something more ephemeral and perishable, I am seeking Erik Lönnrot. Three years ago, in a gambling house on the rue de Toulon, you arrested my brother and had him sent to jail. My men slipped me away in a coupé from the gun battle with a policeman's bullet in my stomach. Nine days and nine nights I lay in agony in this desolate, symmetrical villa; fever was demolishing me, and the odious two-faced Janus who watches the twilights and the dawns lent horror to my dreams and to my waking. I came to abominate my body, I came to sense that two eyes, two hands, two lungs are as monstrous as two faces. An Irishman tried to convert me to the faith of Jesus; he repeated to me the phrase of the *goyim:* All roads lead to Rome. At night my delirium nurtured itself on that metaphor; I felt that the world was a labyrinth, from which it was impossible to flee, for all roads, though they pretend to lead to the north or south, actually lead to Rome, which was also the quadrilateral jail where my brother was dying and the villa of Triste-le-Roy. On those nights I swore by the God who sees with two faces and by all the gods of fever and of the mirrors to weave a labyrinth around the man who had imprisoned my brother. I have woven it and it is firm: the ingredients are a dead heresiologist, a compass, an eighteenth-century sect, a Greek word, a dagger, the diamonds of a paint shop.

"The first term of the sequence was given to me by chance. I had planned with a few colleagues—among them Daniel Azevedo—the robbery of the Tetrarch's sapphires. Azevedo betrayed us: he got drunk with the money that we had advanced him and he undertook the job a day early. He got lost in the vastness of the hotel; around two in the morning he stumbled into Yarmolinsky's room. The latter, harassed by insomnia, had started to write. He was working on some notes, apparently, for an article on the Name of God; he had already written the words: *The first letter of the Name has been uttered.* Azevedo warned him to be silent; Yarmolinsky reached out his hand for the bell which would awaken the hotel's forces; Azevedo countered with a single stab in the chest. It was almost a reflex action; half a century of violence had taught him that the easiest and surest thing is to kill... Ten days later I learned through the *Yidische Zaitung* that you were seeking in Yarmolinsky's writings the key to his death. I read the *History of the Hasidic Sect;* I learned that the reverent fear of uttering the Name of God had given rise to the doctrine that that Name is all powerful and recondite. I discovered that some Hasidim, in search of that secret Name, had gone so far as to perform human sacrifices... I knew that you would make the conjecture that the Hasidim had sacrificed the rabbi; I set myself the task of justifying that conjecture.

"Marcel Yarmolinsky died on the night of December third; for the second 'sacrifice' I selected the night of January third. He died in the north; for the second 'sacrifice' a place in the west was suitable. Daniel Azevedo was the necessary victim. He deserved death; he was impulsive, a traitor; his apprehension could destroy the entire plan. One of us stabbed him; in order to link his corpse to the other one I wrote on the paint shop diamonds: *The second letter of the Name has been uttered.*

"The third murder was produced on the third of February. It was, as Treviranus guessed, a mere sham. I am Gryphius-Ginzberg-Ginsburg; I endured an interminable week (supplemented by a tenuous fake beard) in the perverse cubicle on the rue de Toulon, until my friends abducted me. From the footboard of the cab, one of them wrote on a post: *The last of the letters of the Name has been uttered.* That sentence revealed that the series of murders was *triple.* Thus the public understood it; I, nevertheless, interspersed repeated signs that would allow you, Erik Lönnrot, the reasoner, to understand that the series was quadruple. A portent in the north, others in the east and west, demand a fourth portent in the south; the Tetragrammaton—the name of God, JHVH—is made up of *four* letters; the harlequins and the paint shop sign suggested *four* points. In the manual of Leusden I underlined a certain passage: that passage manifests that Hebrews compute the day from sunset to sunset; that passage makes known that the deaths occurred on the *fourth* of each month. I sent the equilateral triangle to Treviranus. I foresaw that you would add the missing point. The point which would form a perfect rhomb, the point which fixes in advance where a punctual death awaits you. I have premeditated everything, Erik Lönnrot, in order to attract you to the solitudes of Triste-le-Roy."

Lönnrot avoided Scharlach's eyes. He looked at the trees and the sky subdivided into diamonds of turbid yellow, green and red. He felt faintly cold, and he felt, too, an impersonal—almost anonymous—sadness. It was already night; from the dusty garden came the futile cry of a bird. For the last time, Lönnrot considered the problem of the symmetrical and periodic deaths.

"In your labyrinth there are three lines too many," he said at last. "I know of one Greek labyrinth which is a single straight line. Along that line so many philosophers have lost themselves that a mere detective might well do so, too. Scharlach, when in some other incarnation you hunt me, pretend to commit (or do commit) a crime at A, then a second crime at B, eight kilometers from A, then a third crime at C, four kilometers from A and B, half-way between the two. Wait for me afterwards at D, two kilometers from A and C, again halfway between both. Kill me at D, as you are now going to kill me at Triste-le-Roy."

"The next time I kill you," replied Scharlach, "I promise you that labyrinth, consisting of a single line which is invisible and unceasing."

He moved back a few steps. Then, very carefully, he fired.

QUESTIONS

1. In the text, there is an almost constant juxtaposition of things associated with the numbers three and four. What are these, and how do they pertain to the story?
2. Borges likes to play with words, preferring the denotation, or the strictly literal meaning of a word, to the connotation, or the affective and sometimes equivocal, ambiguous meaning of the word. For example, he describes the first murder scene as occurring in "that tall prism," the Hôtel du Nord. What is the precise definition of the word *prism,* and how does this fit into the story?
3. What kinds of time are evident in the story?
4. The characters' names are important to the structure of the story, as well as to the erasure of their individuality. What associations exist among Red, Scharlach, Lönnrot, and Erik? Are there any others?
5. At the conclusion of the story, Lönnrot ironically proposes a single-line labyrinth for the final murder in some future cycle of time. This "labyrinth" is based on Zeno's paradox (the Eleatic paradox). What is this paradox, and how does it apply to "Death and the Compass"?

MIGUEL ANGEL ASTURIAS—GUATEMALA

Tatuana's Tale

Translation by Patricia Emigh and Frank MacShane

In 1967 Asturias was awarded the Nobel Prize in literature. For most of his adult life, he had fought the repressive dictatorships of his country, distilling his experiences into masterworks such as *El Señor Presidente* and *Week-end-en Guatemala*. The selection here is from *Leyendas de Guatemala*, written while Asturias was a student in Paris and published in 1930. These "legends," a blend of dream, story, myth, and poetry, represented his first efforts at recreating the rich Maya-Quiché[1] world he knew so profoundly. In "Tatuana's Tale," a magical, mythical world is portrayed.

[1]The Quiché Maya are an ancient Mayan people who originated in Guatemala and eventually expanded into Mexico.

Father Almond Tree, with his pale pink beard, was one of the priests who were so richly dressed that the white men touched them to see if they were made of gold. He knew the secret of medicinal plants, the language of the gods that spoke through translucent obsidian, and he could read the hieroglyphics of the stars.

One day he appeared in the forest, without being planted, as though brought there by spirits. He was so tall he prodded the clouds, he measured the years by the moons he saw, and was already old when he came from the Garden of Tulan.

On the full moon of Owl-Fish (one of the twenty months of the four-hundred-day year), Father Almond Tree divided his soul among the four roads. These led to the four quarters of the sky: the black quarter, the Sorcerer Night; the green quarter, Spring Storm; the red quarter, Tropical Ecstasy; the white quarter, Promise of New Lands.

"O Road! Little Road!" said a dove to White Road, but White Road did not listen. The dove wanted Father Almond Tree's soul so that it would cure its dreams. Doves and children both suffer from dreams.

"O Road! Little Road!" said a heart to Red Road, but Red Road did not listen. The heart wanted to distract Red Road so it would forget Father Almond Tree's soul. Hearts, like thieves, don't return what others leave behind.

"O Road! Little Road!" said a vine trellis to Green Road, but Green Road did not listen. It wanted the Father's soul to get back some of the leaves and shade it had squandered.

How many moons have the roads been traveling?

The fastest, Black Road, whom no one spoke to along the way, entered the city, crossed the plaza and went to the merchants' quarter, where it gave Father Almond Tree's soul to the Merchant of Priceless Jewels in exchange for a little rest.

It was the hour of white cats. They prowled back and forth through the streets. Wonder of rosebushes! The clouds looked like laundry strung across the sky.

When Father Almond Tree found out what Black Road had done, he once again took on human form, shedding his tree-like shape in a small stream that appeared like an almond blossom beneath the crimson moon. Then he left for the city.

He reached the valley after a day's travel, just at evening time when the flocks are driven home. The shepherds were dumbfounded by this man in a green cloak and pale pink beard. They thought he was an apparition and answered his questions in monosyllables.

Once in the city, he made his way to the western part of town. Men and women were standing around the public fountains. The water made a kissing sound as it filled their pitchers. Following the shadows to the merchants' quarter, he found that part of his soul Black Road had sold. The Merchant of Priceless Jewels kept it in a crystal box with gold locks. He went up to the Merchant, who was smoking in a corner, and offered him two thousand pounds of pearls for the piece of soul.

The Merchant smiled at the Father's absurd suggestion. Two thousand pounds of pearls? No, his jewels were priceless.

Father Almond Tree increased his offer. He would give him emeralds, big as kernels of corn, fifty acres of them, enough to make a lake.

The Merchant smiled again. A lake of emeralds? No, his jewels were priceless.

He would give him amulets, deer's eyes that bring rain, feathers to keep storms away, marijuana to mix with his tobacco.

The Merchant refused.

He would give him enough precious stones to build a fairy-tale palace in the middle of the emerald lake!

The Merchant still refused. His jewels were priceless—why go on talking about it? Besides, he planned to exchange this piece of soul for the most beautiful slave in the slave market.

It was useless for Father Almond Tree to keep on making offers and show how much he wanted to get his soul back. Merchants have no hearts.

A thread of tobacco smoke separated reality from dream, black cats from white cats, the Merchant from his strange customer. As he left, Father Almond Tree banged his sandals against the doorway to rid himself of the cursed dust of the house.

After a year of four hundred days, the Merchant was returning across the mountains with the slave he had bought with Father Almond Tree's soul. He was accompanied by a flower bird who turned honey into hyacinths, and by a retinue of thirty servants on horseback.

The slave was naked. Her long black hair, wrapped in a single braid like a snake, fell across her breasts and down to her legs. The Merchant was dressed in gold and his shoulders were covered with a cape woven from goat hair. His thirty servants on horseback stretched out behind like figures in a dream.

"You've no idea," said the Merchant to the slave, reining in his horse alongside hers, "what your life will be like in the city! Your house will be a palace, and all my servants will be at your call, including me, if you like." His face was half lit by the sun. "There," he continued, "everything will be yours. Do you know I refused a lake of emeralds for the piece of soul I exchanged for you? We'll lie all day in a hammock and have nothing to do but listen to a wise old woman tell stories. She knows my fate and says that it rests in a gigantic hand. She'll tell your fortune as well, if you ask her."

The slave turned to look at the countryside. It was a landscape of muted blues, growing dimmer in the distance. The trees on either side formed so fanciful a design it might have appeared on a woman's shawl. The sky was calm, and the birds seemed to be flying asleep, winglessly. In the granite silence, the panting of the horses as they went uphill sounded human.

Suddenly, huge solitary raindrops began to spatter on the road. On the slopes below, shepherds shouted as they gathered their frightened flocks. The horses stepped up their pace to find shelter, but there wasn't enough time. The wind rose, lashing the clouds, and ripping through the forest until it reached the valley, which vanished from sight under blankets of mist, while the first lightning bolts lit up the countryside like the flashes of a mad photographer.

As the horses stampeded, fleeing in fear, reins broken, legs flying, manes tangled in the wind and ears pressed back, the Merchant's horse stumbled and threw the man to the foot of a tree which at that instant, split by lightning, wrapped its roots about him like a hand snatching up a stone and hurled him into the ravine.

Meanwhile Father Almond Tree, who had remained in the city, wandered the streets like a madman, frightening children, going through garbage, talking to donkeys, oxen and stray dogs, which, like men, are all sad-eyed animals.

"How many moons have the roads been traveling?" he asked from door to door, but the people were dumfounded by this man in a green cloak and pale pink beard, and they slammed them shut without answering as though they'd seen a specter.

At length Father Almond Tree stopped at the door of the Merchant of Priceless Jewels and spoke to the slave, who alone had survived the storm.

"How many moons have the roads been traveling?"

The answer which began to form froze on her lips. Father Almond Tree was silent. It was the full moon of Owl-Fish. In silence their eyes caressed each other's faces like two lovers who have met after a long separation.

They were interrupted by raucous shouts. They were arrested in the name of God and the King, he as a warlock and she as his accomplice. Surrounded by crosses and swords, they were taken to prison, Father Almond Tree with his pale pink beard and green cloak, the slave displaying flesh so firm it seemed to be made of gold.

Seven months later, they were condemned to be burned alive in the Plaza Mayor. On the eve of the execution, Father Almond Tree tattooed a little boat on the slave's arm with his fingernail.

"Tatuana, by means of this tattoo," he said, "you will be able to flee whenever you are in danger. I want you to be as free as my spirit. Trace this little boat on a wall, on the ground, in the air, wherever you wish. Then close your eyes, climb aboard and go . . .

"Go, my spirit is stronger than a clay idol.

"My spirit is sweeter than the honey gathered by bees sipping from the honeysuckle.

"As my spirit, you'll become invisible."

At once, Tatuana did what Father Almond Tree said: she drew a little boat, closed her eyes, and, as she got in, the boat began to move. So she escaped from prison and death.

On the following morning, day of the execution, the guards found in the cell only a withered tree, whose few almond blossoms still retained their pale pink color.

QUESTIONS

1. When do you think "Tatuana's Tale" occurs? On what do you base your answer?
2. How do Mayan elements manifest themselves, and for what purpose?
3. What meanings or interpretations does the legend have?
4. Do you see any points of comparison between this retelling of a Mayan legend and the African legends in Chapter 13?

Pablo Neruda—Chile

Ode to Broken Things

Translation by Malcolm J. Parr

The poetry of Neruda, another Nobel laureate, evolved from symbolism into some of the richest, most innovative free verse and imagery of this century. People, and those things touched by, made by, or affecting them, are his subjects. Neruda is the poet of *cosalismo* ("thing-ism"), which transforms some of the most humble plants, minerals, and animals into subjects of beautiful poems. His poetry ranges from the profound, hermetic, and complex works of *Residencia en la tierra I, II* (*Residence on Earth, Parts I and II*) and *Canto general* (*General Song*), in which appears his renowned "Heights of Macchu Picchu," to the simple and touching odes to a variety of subjects. The selection here is from *Navegaciones y regresos* (*Voyages and Homecomings*), first published in 1959, and is representative of his *cosalismo* and humanism.

Things keep breaking
in the home
as though impelled
by an unseen and willful brute:
not my hands,
not yours,
not the girls
with the hard nails
and starry feet:
it wasn't anything or anyone,
it wasn't the wind,
it wasn't the orange noon,
or the earth's shadows,
it wasn't a nose, an elbow,
a curving hip,
an ankle
or the air:
the plate split, the lamp slipped
and all the flowerpots toppled
one by one,
in the middle of October,
crimson-heaped,
weighed down with violets,
and one other pot, empty,
spinning, spinning, spinning,
through the winter
until all that was left
was powder,
a shattered memory, a glowing dust.

And the clock
from which the sound
was
our life's voice,
the hidden
thread
of the weeks,
joining
so many hours
one by one
to honey and silence,
to so many births and tasks
even that clock
fell and among
the broken pieces of glass
its delicate blue entrails
throbbed
and its long heart
spun out.

Life goes on grinding
glasses, wearing out clothes,
destroying,
pulverizing
patterns,
and what time lets last is as it were
an island or a ship at sea,
passing,
locked in by brittle dangers,
and the menaces of relentless waters.

Let's put everything at once,
clocks, plates, wineglasses carved in ice,
in one sack and carry
our treasures down to the sea:
and all our possessions
will be lost
smashing and roaring
like a river bursting its banks;
and may the sea
in its toiling tides
bring back for us
all those useless things
that nobody breaks
but were broken nevertheless.

QUESTIONS

1. What is an "ode"? Why does Neruda employ this form?
2. What structural and lexical devices are used to make this poetry?
3. What is the ode's theme, and how is it developed?

The Early Twentieth Century: New Traditions

Western Cultural Doubt

There is no doubt that the early twentieth century marked a deep cleft in the Western humanistic tradition. The expectations for an increasingly civilized world based largely on immense accomplishments in the material realm were dashed by World War I. Not only did the war starkly reveal the well of irrationality and violence present in human nature, but technological progress allowed these forces to express themselves with lethal effect. For many thinkers, artists, and writers, the Greco-Roman reliance on reason, the Judeo-Christian hope in God, and, more immediately, the nineteenth century's optimistic materialism no longer seemed valid cultural centers. The titles of two important early-twentieth-century books sum up the state of affairs: Freud's *Civilization and Its Discontents* and Spengler's *The Decline of the West.*

The peace treaty of 1919 finally brought hostilities to a halt, but for the next two decades, Western culture was haunted by the fear of another war. The Great Depression of the early 1930s further exacerbated the situation. For many, Marxism offered an attractive alternative to traditional capitalism. That the next war would be one of classes rather than nations became a real possibility. In Germany and Italy, leaders arose—embodiments of an irrational nationalism—who promised to squelch class conflict by violent measures. The Western democracies felt trapped between the extremism of both left and right. Given such instability, it is surprising that the next war did not finally erupt until 1939.

Influence of Africa

The weariness with their own cultural roots led Western artists of the early twentieth century to look elsewhere for inspiration. It is at this point that the African cultural root really makes it entry into the Western humanities. European and American painters and sculptors experimenting with abstraction found that African artists, who had long been creating in this style, had much to teach them. African writers who had been educated in the Western tradition turned toward their native cultures for fresh subject matter and stylistic innovation. Dancers and choreographers saw in the African union of dance with religious rites and other forms of cultural expression an art form more meaningful than the stylized, artificial ballet. African rhythms and tonalities entered into Western music in the form of jazz and profoundly altered its course. Finally, African American writers, thinkers, artists, musicians, and dancers began to turn back toward their African heritage, seeking ways of combining it with their American experience and in the process creating an important new voice on the world cultural scene.

Influence and Emergence of Other Cultures

Africa was not the only culture to which discontented Westerners turned. Some were attracted to what they viewed as the spirituality of the Orient as opposed to the materialism of the Occident. Writers such as Ezra Pound found the brilliant imagery in Chinese and Japanese poetry a source for experimentation. Other artists and writers turned to the arts of Southeast Asia and Polynesia, or to whatever seemed primitive or at least not overcivilized. Igor Stravinsky found in the rites of his native Russia energizing sources for creating new musical sounds. Choreographers and dancers such as Nijinsky and Duncan tried to express a new "primitive" wholeness in their dance. Frank Lloyd Wright looked even farther away toward the aboriginal cave for a basis for his innovations in architecture. In Latin America, artists and intellectuals looked to the heritage of pre-Columbian as well as European civilizations, fusing cultural roots in new forms and creations. Writers such as Borges would rise to world prominence as inheritors of European modernism.

Breakup in the Arts

The sense of breaking with tradition as well as contact with new traditions gave artists in this period an exhilarating sense of freedom; so did new discoveries in the sciences, such as Freud's concept of the unconscious and Einstein's relativity theory. The term *modernism* covers a variety of experimental movements in the arts, only a few of which we have mentioned in this section. The breaking apart of traditional forms—of traditional ways of perceiving space, time, and reality—and the synthesizing of elements in new ways are perhaps the essential characteristics of modernism. In literature this included Joyce's abandonment of syntax, mixture of time frames, and portrayal of the unconscious and Kafka's and Borges's stark, fantastic realism. Painting shows Picasso's experiments with abstractions of the human figure and Kandinsky's total abandonment of subject matter for the portrayal of an inner world of form and color. The music of Stravinsky demonstrates a reorganization of the elements of rhythm, harmony, and melody. Dance does away with the "classical" steps of ballet to create new forms. The new arts of photography and film reorganize traditional ways of viewing time and space.

Feminism

The new sense of freedom and of breaking with tradition, particularly after World War I, affected customs, manners, and ways of life, as well as the arts. One of the most important legacies of this new vision was the growing concern over equality for women, culminating in the women's rights and suffragette movements and, ultimately, the vote, in England and the United States. Virginia Woolf's *A Room of One's Own* is one of the most eloquent statements on the needs and rights of the modern creative woman. Contemporary feminism owes a great deal to its precursors in the modernist era.

Connections with Cultural Roots

We should perhaps stress at this point that, although modernism makes a radical break with tradition, it does not make a total break. Its innovations would not be possible without a cultural tradition to react against and, in some sense, to continue. Joyce's radically experimental novel is based on one of the oldest narratives in the Greco-Roman tradition, Homer's *Odyssey*. Distortion in art for expression of the unseen was a characteristic of medieval art and part of the inheritance of the modernists. Modern poetry, modern cinema, and modern dance are incomprehensible without the prior forms of lyric, drama, and ballet. Modernism, in the form of ongoing experimentation, is very much still with us. In the late twentieth century, we will witness a proliferation of cultural plurality.

Part Ten

Cultural Plurality: The Middle and Late Twentieth Century

34

Absurdity and Alienation: The Second World War and the Postwar Period

World War II

World War II, beginning in 1939, only twenty years after the Treaty of Versailles, seemed like a continuation of World War I. Great Britain and France, two of the victors in World War I, wearily faced the prospect of having to do battle again with their old enemy Germany, now allied with Italy. Encouraged by fascist successes in the Spanish Civil War, Germany and Italy were eager to demonstrate their military prowess on a large scale. Unprepared for war, the two democracies had tried appeasement the year before at Munich. In September 1938 they delivered up the German-speaking part of Czechoslovakia to Hitler, who claimed to be contented with this settlement. In March 1939, however, he incorporated most of what was left of Czechoslovakia into Germany. Now France and England would not back down, and when in September Hitler invaded Poland, they went to war.

World War II was to last four years and involve fighting on every continent of the globe. Having already gobbled up half of China, Japan joined the Axis in 1941 in the hope of being able to annex some of the colonial possessions of the Western democracies in Asia. Both Russia and the United States entered the war in 1941 on the side of Great Britain; by this time France was under German domination. In the early stages of the war the Axis powers had the initiative, but by late 1942 the Allies were slowly moving to the offensive. The Allies gradually took over the whole of North Africa from the Italians and Germans and in the spring of 1943 invaded Sicily. At the same time the Russians, despite a terrible loss of life, outlasted the Germans at Stalingrad, their farthest point of penetration in Russia, and began pushing the Germans back toward the west. In the Pacific the Americans initiated their campaign of island hopping, defeating one Japanese garrison after the other until by early 1945 they were within three hundred miles of Japan itself. In 1944, while the Russians continued their advance all along the eastern front, the Allied armies invaded France; by the spring of 1945 Germany was invaded from both east and west. On May 8, 1945, Germany surrendered unconditionally. The dropping of the atomic bomb on two Japanese cities in August terrified the Japanese into surrendering officially on September 2, 1945.

In contrast with World War I, civilians suffered more casualties than did the military. The systematic extermination of populations by the Germans and the intensive bombing of cities by both sides explain the large losses. The introduction of the atomic bomb at the very end of the war dramatically illustrated what would occur in the event of a third world war. The apprehension was only increased by the introduction of an arms race in nuclear weapons, which began with the Soviet Union's development of its own atomic bomb in 1946.

The Postwar Period

After World War II, the center of power moved out of Western Europe, and the United States became potentially the most powerful country in the world. However, the power configuration was a bipolar one, with the United States and the Soviet Union attempting to attract the other powers into their respective spheres of influence. The dissolution of the colonial empires of the European powers, either with or without the latter's consent, produced scores of new nations and furnished a fertile field for propaganda activities on both sides.

The hope of the Allies during the war had been for an international peace-keeping institution after the war; in 1945 at San Francisco the United Nations was created for that purpose. Like the League of Nations, however, the United Nations was crippled from the start by the reluctance of nations to give up any of their sovereignty. Although it provided a means for direct communication between the world powers, the organization could not prevent the reinstitution of hostile alliance systems. The United States sought its security in a number of European and Asian alliances with democratic and right-wing governments, whereas the Soviet Union fortified its position by a tight alliance with communist satellite countries in Eastern Europe and active support for sympathetic political factions elsewhere. The communist conquest of China in 1949 seemed especially alarming to the West, and in the United States itself a fear of subversion inspired a series of investigations to ferret out spies and communist sympathizers. By the early 1950s, moreover, the United States was waging war in Korea, endeavoring to stop the spread of communism in that area. Many feared that the hostility between the two superpowers, known as the Cold War, would soon reach a point of open conflict.

It did not. The closest the United States and the Soviet Union came to direct confrontation in the years immediately following the termination of the Korean War in 1953 came in 1962. In that year President Kennedy, declaring that Soviet shipments of missiles to Cuba constituted a threat to American security, placed a naval blockade around the island. At almost the last hour before contact between Soviet freighters and American warships, Soviet premier Khrushchev backed down and agreed to remove the missiles on the island. Clearly the stakes were too high, and neither people would risk a war by interfering directly in the sphere of influence of the other.

World War II and its aftermath left the humanities in a crisis situation. The attempted genocide of the Jews, the large-scale death camps, and finally the use of the atomic bomb raised terrifying questions about the extreme possibilities of people's inhumanity to others. The role of the humanities as a humanizing force, the ideal of traditional humanism, had to be put seriously in doubt. Were there not S.S. men who listened to their Bach or read their Goethe after a day's work at the gas chambers? The possibility of instant extermination through nuclear war made many of the traditional forms and values seem obsolete.

European Literature

Literature and the Holocaust: Primo Levi (1919–1987)

Because of the unprecedented cruelty experienced in the nightmarish world of the Nazi concentration camps, many intellectuals, both Jews and non-Jews, declared that this was a subject unfit for "literature" or for "art" because the horror of it was inexpressible in artistic terms and that either silence or direct, nonartistic testimony was the only possible reaction. In spite of this opinion, a flood of novels, poems, films, and other documents dealing with the experience of Jewish, gypsy, and other "racial" concentration camp inmates, as well as with that of those interned or deported for political reasons, has seen and continues to see publication. Many of the accounts emphasize the unspeakable horrors perpetrated by the Nazis, apparently with the goal of forcing the prisoners to abandon their humanity. Reduced through deprivation to elementary feelings of hunger, thirst, cold, and fear, presented with a constant image of themselves as objects, it is hardly surprising that some prisoners abandoned themselves to a subhuman existence. There are numerous stories of inmates stealing bread from weaker fellow prisoners, of trafficking in gold teeth or in prostitution with the Nazis, even of cannibalism. Other renderings of the experience, however, stress that inmates reduced through suffering to the barest state humanly possible either abandoned their humanity or acceded to a higher spiritual life. On the part of deeply religious Jews and Christians and even of fervently committed Marxists, this is perhaps not surprising. But this type of spiritual experience was possible even for those whose faith was more humanistic than religious.

Perhaps the most sensitive writer to have succeeded in communicating the experience to those who did not undergo it was Primo Levi, an Italian Jew who survived a year in the most infamous of all the Nazi camps, Auschwitz. Levi's *Se questo è un uomo,* published in 1958 and translated into English as *If This Is a Man* in 1979, is a horrifying and yet extremely sober and artistic account of the literal hell of the camp. One of the discoveries that Levi makes in Auschwitz is the strangely vital, fundamental value of his profound knowledge of the humanities. There is irony but real edification in the fact that Levi, a nonreligious Jew, rediscovers what it is to be human through his memory of Dante's *Divine Comedy,* the supreme poem of Roman Catholicism but also the great cultural monument for all Italians.

Sartre and Existentialism

The most influential philosophical and literary movement to grow out of the war years became known as existentialism. As a philosophy, existentialism had actually been developed much earlier, through the influence of Nietzsche and the work of Martin Heidegger and Karl Jaspers in Germany. It was, however, the French intellectual Jean-Paul Sartre (1905–1980) who did most to bring existentialism into the arts and into a search for an authentic way of life on the part of many of the disaffected youth of Europe and America. Sartre's seminal philosophical work, *Being and Nothingness* (1943), was born not only of his readings in German philosophy but through his experiences in the war years as well. As a soldier, Sartre experienced combat as well as confinement in a German prisoner-of-war camp, where he wrote his first play. Back in Paris, he lived through the years of the German occupation of France, a humiliating and often nightmarish experience of defeat and captivity that lasted from 1940 until the liberation of Paris in 1944. It seemed to Sartre and to other French intellectuals at that time that the choice before the French was clear: collaborate with the enemy (and doing nothing was in itself a form of collaboration) or resist the enemy by participating in the resistance movement. Resistance could take many forms: joining the *maquis* (underground military groups) to blow up bridges or trains used by the Nazis; hiding Jews or helping them to escape; writing for the underground press; helping to recruit and organize for the movement. Being captured by the Gestapo and identified as a member of the Resistance often meant imprisonment, torture, deportation, or execution. The extremity of the situation and the tests to which it put human choice were crucial to Sartre's development as an artist and a thinker.

At the heart of Sartrean existentialism is a sense of limitless and therefore anxiety-producing human freedom. Life for each human being is a series of situations requiring choices and acts; the acts that one chooses determine what one *is.* According to Sartre, humanity is not given *being,* but only *existence.* There is no God; there are no absolute standards of morality or of truth. Each person must forge his or her own morality and truth, must indeed create his or her own being out of existence. First, however, people must be aware of the dreadful state of freedom that is their true state of existence. Something like a Nietzschean "re-valuation of all values" is needed, but there is no superman to give guidance, only the individual. Sartre's words "life begins on the other side of despair" express the necessity for recognition of one's freedom. His "man is the sum of his acts" indicates that one's self is to be created through the use of this freedom.

Sartre found philosophy too limiting a vehicle with which to express the fundamental concerns of human beings. In a novel, *Nausea,* written before the war, he had already treated the theme of the absurdity (or, as he called it, the "contingency") of life and the outmoded hollowness of moralities such as traditional humanism. The main character of the novel, an intellectual named Roquentin, experiences an "existential crisis" as he confronts the meaninglessness of his existence.

During the war Sartre turned to the theater, which was better adapted to illustrating his theory that each situation in human life is like a trap. One works one's way out of the trap by exercising one's freedom, making a choice, and acting on it. One of Sartre's best plays, the one-act *No Exit,* portrays three dead characters trapped in a hell that they themselves created because they were unable to exercise their freedom during their lifetime.

Sartre's essays, collected in several volumes called *Situations,* treat a wide range of cultural and political topics. One of the central themes is the German Occupation of France. For Sartre, the awareness of being in a situation limited by death and the necessity to choose a course of action made life under the Occupation represent the existentialist situation with a clarity that the complexities of postwar life obscured.

Camus (1913–1960)

The war and postwar literature of existentialism must include not only the fiction and theater of Sartre but also that of Albert Camus, who, nonetheless, refused to call himself an existentialist. In his novel *The Stranger,* written on the eve of the war and published in 1942, as well as in his essay *The Myth of Sisyphus,* Camus demonstrates his concept of the "absurd"—the fundamental meaninglessness of human life and traditional beliefs. Camus's concept of the absurd is perhaps clearest in the following quotation from *The Myth of Sisyphus:*

> A world that can be explained by reasoning, however faulty, is a familiar world. But in a universe that is suddenly deprived of illusions and of light, man feels a stranger. His is an irremediable exile, because he is deprived of memories of a lost homeland as much as he lacks the hope of a promised land to come. This divorce between man and his life, the actor and his setting, truly constitutes the feeling of Absurdity.

Thus the human mind demands reason, logic, order, and an explanation for the way things are, but the world offers none. Individuals must then create their own morality, their own way of resisting the "absurd."

Yet for Camus there was always "another side of the coin." His native continent being North Africa rather than Europe, he retained a belief in the regenerative value of nature—sea and sun—that is absent from Sartre's work. His postwar novel *The Plague* (1948) is about the effects of an imaginary plague on the Algerian city of Oran, but it is often read as an allegory of the German occupation of Paris. Camus, like Sartre, portrays human beings making choices in the face of an extreme situation. But Camus's values are finally closer to those of traditional humanism than Sartre's are. His heroes choose, in the face of death, in the face of absurdity, simply to do what they can, to help each other, to fight the plague. Friendship and love are in the end more important than political commitment. The revolt against the absurd becomes a way of reaffirming one's humanity. *The Plague* and Camus's philosophical work *The Rebel* precipitated a break between the two men who had become intellectual leaders in Western culture. The reasons were complex, but basically Sartre was critical of what he felt was Camus's compromise with humanism and liberalism.

Sartre himself later moved toward a radically Marxist position, modifying considerably his view of human beings as totally free. Camus, who died in an "absurd" automobile accident in 1960, had retained his faith in the individual rebel, shunning all forms of totalitarian belief systems.

If the philosophical essay *The Myth of Sisyphus* constitutes Camus's most developed statement of "the absurd," Sisyphus himself is not mentioned until the very end. Camus's "absurd hero" is a figure from Greek mythology who represents the condition of modern humanity. Rewritings of ancient Greek myths were common in French literature around the time of World War II. It seemed that those who lived through tragic situations could seek truth or at least guidance through a reevaluation of a fundamental root of Western culture. Camus's Sisyphus braves his superiors, the gods, states by his choice the value he places on earthly life, and, paradoxically, through his very consciousness of the meaninglessness of his condition, forges his own liberty and happiness.

The Influences of Existentialism

Existentialism as a lifestyle in Europe and America in the postwar years produced a group of young people who rebelled against the traditional values of their parents and sought to assert their freedom in a meaningless world. In France they gathered in cafés for discussions with Sartre and his friends, to hear the "existentialist" songs of Juliette Greco, or to listen to American jazz. In the United States, somewhat later, they went "on the road" or "dropped out," running away from what they perceived to be meaningless and false in American life. "Beatniks" and "hippies" were, indirectly at least, influenced by popularized existentialism.

The French existentialists' consciousness of the absurdity of human life was balanced by the pressing need for social and political commitment. In exercising one's freedom by choosing to resist Nazi control, anguish and despair could, in some limited way at least, end in triumph. In the years following the war, however, such extreme situations, or clear opportunities for commitment, did not often present themselves. One could, of course, commit oneself to a Marxist revolution, but the rise of Stalin in the Soviet Union made that solution seem much less attractive. The terrible knowledge of the concentration camps and the nuclear bomb made life seem precarious and individual human efforts vain. The sense of despair, gloom, and absurdity in existentialism seemed more relevant than its more heroic side.

Postwar American Literature

Much of the literature of the 1940s and 1950s, in the United States as well as in Europe, shows a direct or indirect influence of existentialism. Jack Kerouac's runaways and bums, Norman Mailer's heroes, and even many of Hemingway's lonely figures in his later works struggle with their existence in a world devoid of meaning. As in the "lost generation" of the 1920s, many American writers went to live in Europe, especially in France, during this period. Europe, and its literary themes of alienation and despair, seemed particularly attractive to African American intellectuals, discouraged with the continuing segregation and racism in the United States.

Richard Wright (1908–1960)

One important African American writer who left the United States to live in France was Richard Wright. A product of the Deep South, of the Depression, and of poverty, Wright was born near Natchez, Mississippi, and, because of the instability of his family, was reared in a number of Mississippi towns. After graduating from high school in 1925 and working for a while in Memphis, he went to Chicago, where he joined the Communist party in the 1930s and became a member of the Federal Writers' Project. In 1937 he went to New York, where, among other things, he edited a Communist party literary journal called the *New Challenge.* In the early 1940s he wrote his best-known books, *Native Son* and *Black Boy.* After World War II Wright left the United States for Paris, where he lived and wrote under the influence of Sartre, Camus, Merleau-Ponty, Koestler, and other European writers until his death in 1960.

James Baldwin (1924–1987)

Wright's powerful naturalistic, existentialist, and Marxist novel, *Native Son*, inspired an entire generation of African American writers. Under his influence, a movement described by one critic as "urban realism" developed in post–World War II America and was called the "Wright School." Although not considered a member of the Wright School, James Baldwin met Richard Wright, his "idol since childhood," in the winter of 1944–1945. Born illegitimate and later oppressed by a tyrannical stepfather who was a storefront preacher, Baldwin spent his childhood in Harlem. Teachers in his high school soon recognized his literary gifts, and after graduation he moved to Greenwich Village in the hopes of living as a writer. He felt estranged, however, both from the black world in which he had grown up and from the white artist-intellectual establishment. After meeting Wright, who obtained some grant money for him, Baldwin, like Wright, went to live in Paris, where he stayed for nine years and where he wrote his first novel, *Go Tell It on the Mountain.* His stay in France involved an intense struggle with Wright as a new father figure and a search for his own identity. On his return to the United States in the 1960s, Baldwin was to become an articulate spokesman for the civil rights movement. His later essays, such as *The Fire Next Time,* predict "the shape of the wrath to come" if the vestiges of American racism are not eradicated.

Ralph Ellison (b. 1914)

Unlike many of the prominent African American writers of the 1930s and 1940s, Ellison did not leave the United States to live in Europe, nor did he join the Communist party. Nevertheless, in the mid-1950s Ellison did lecture widely in Germany and Austria, and he does acknowledge a number of European influences on his art, Dostoevsky among them. Also, like Baldwin and many others of the time, he came under the strong influence of Richard Wright, having been introduced to him by Langston Hughes. Again like Baldwin, Ellison later broke away from that influence to establish his own unique style and vision.

Ellison was born in Oklahoma City, majored in music at Tuskegee Institute, was a jazz trumpeter, and originally intended to be a musician before he established himself as a writer. Ultimately, it is music, African American "blues" especially, that becomes the aesthetic mainspring of his writing. In 1952, *Invisible Man,* his only novel to date, was honored with the National Book Award and, in a *Book Week* poll, was judged "the most distinguished single work" published in America between 1945 and 1965.

In the course of a journey from the Deep South to Harlem, the protagonist of *Invisible Man* assumes a variety of roles to fit the larger society's definition of a "Negro." As a young high school boy in the South, he is a "Tom," something of a "darky" entertainer; in college, a Booker T. Washington accommodationist. When he moves north, he flirts for a while with communism. Finally, he becomes a Rinehart, Ellison's word for the alienated urban black who deliberately tries to manipulate the desires and fantasies of whites and blacks to his own advantage. Although the protagonist believes in most of these roles at the time, each one disappoints him since they fail to take into account the complexity of his individual existence. Chaos and violence are often the result of the protagonist's failure to live out the roles others have assigned to him: barroom brawls, factory explosions, street fights, and race riots. At the end of the novel, hidden away in a forgotten basement room in an apartment building, the protagonist comes to no true resolution of his predicament except the realization that he—that is, his humanity—is invisible to most people, black and white, and that he must discover for himself what his existence is to be.

The Prologue to *Invisible Man* is perhaps the best introduction to Ellison's literary world. It describes the protagonist in his secret basement room announcing his intention to narrate the absurd and catastrophic events of his life. He has rigged up along the walls 1,369 electric lights, whose power he has somehow managed, illegally, to acquire from the Monopolated Light and Power Company, in order to shed light on his invisibility. He has been playing a Louis Armstrong record, the punning refrain of which runs: "What did I do/To be so black/And blue?" This refrain represents the blues motif that runs throughout each major episode of the novel. As his attempts to play out the dehumanizing roles that whites have assigned him end in disaster, the invisible man in effect feels compelled to ask himself Armstrong's question. Each episode thus serves, in a sense, as an extended blues verse, with the protagonist serving as the singer. And just as the last verse of a blues song is frequently the same as the first, the novel's epilogue brings the reader back to the present, to the secret basement room in the Prologue, with the protagonist singing his story.

Postwar Music

What was the effect of World War II on music in America? In general, it served as a watershed that separated the traditions of the past from the new music of the day, a barrier that both protected the old traditions on one side and sped the waters of the *avant-garde* down the other. The advanced technology of the war effort gave classical music the computers, tape recorders, and electronic equipment developed for military purposes as new instruments for composition and performance. Popular music was likewise affected, and jazz was popular music. The Special Services units of the armed forces employed thousands of young musicians full time to entertain the troops. Soldiers on duty listened to recorded jazz, and soldiers on leave frequented nightclubs in which live jazz was the rule. The music of the Swing Era remained popular, but a new style of jazz was also created, partially in reaction to the musical restrictions of swing, and partially as a result of the emerging freedoms and greater equality of black Americans.

Charlie Parker (1920–1955)

"Yardbird" or "Bird," as the trumpeter Charlie Parker was known, was in a sense the embodiment of all the pent-up frustrations of black America after the war, a man who represented the crowning achievement of African American genius but was rejected and ignored by society at large. Wasted by drugs, alcohol, and a self-abusive life, he died at thirty-five. Yet his music continued to speak—the walls of Harlem, the underpasses of Chicago, and the blackboards of Los Angeles read "Bird lives!" The style he created, bebop, or bop, as it became known, broke with the tradition that had kept jazz tied to dance music and to popular songs. Jazz continued to evolve as the country emerged from World War II, and the higher technical competence of the swing soloists had created a breed of virtuoso who could improvise at breakneck speed. Bebop introduced continually shifting accents, new, rude sounds, unexpected harmonies—and its adepts improvised at speeds that set them apart from, and above, other jazz musicians. The bop musicians, or "hipsters," developed their own private language, their own style of dress, and even an antisocial performance style (turning their backs on audiences, walking off stage when they had finished their solos) that set them apart. More important, they also developed a free way of treating the standard harmonic and melodic materials that allowed them to transform popular ballads into totally new jazz compositions. In his recording of "Koko," for example, Bird imposes a new tune over the changes (the pattern of harmonies) of the popular and innocuous song "Cherokee (Indian Love Song)."

Another good example of Bird's style is in "Parker's Mood."[1] It is a music of freedom unfettered by the rules of popular music. The melodies are not regular, they are asymmetric. A fanfarelike flourish that opens and closes it demands attention. A laid-back phrase or two followed by a torrent of cascading sounds makes the listener struggle to follow the old, familiar blues pattern. It is a song without words, it is defiant, it is self-assured and fragile at the same time. In 1940, Charlie Parker was unknown; in 1948, when he recorded "Parker's Mood," he was famous; and in 1955, he was dead. So much energy, suffering, and vision became focused and supercharged in this one man, and only through his horn was he able to speak to and for a people. Through his music he would show the way to a freedom he himself never had. His voice and presence in the 1940s and 1950s was a penetrating cry for the social awakening that America experienced in the 1960s.

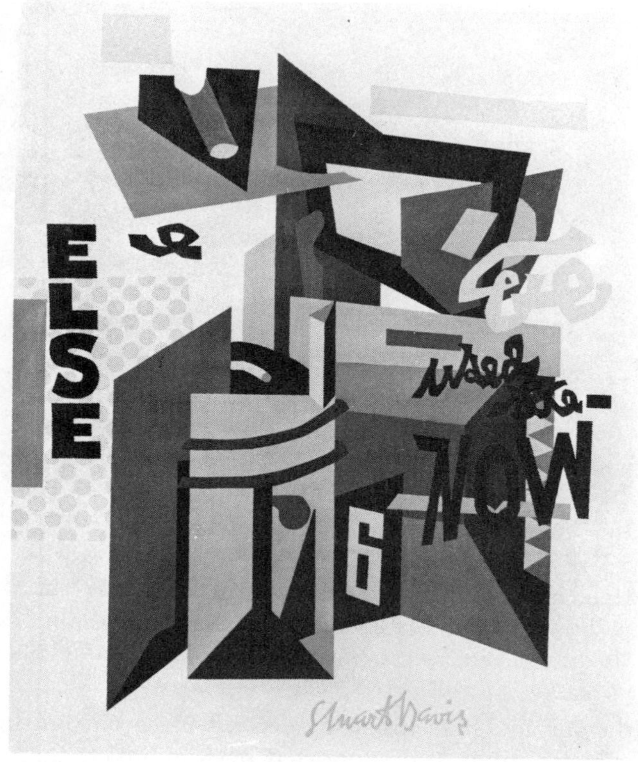

34-1 *Stuart Davis,* Owh! in San Pao, *1951, oil on canvas, 52¼" × 41¾" (132.7 cm × 106 cm). (Collection of Whitney Museum of American Art, New York. Purchase 52.2)*

Painting After World War II

The sense of the absurd, the feeling of alienation from society, and the emphasis on individual self-expression that were manifest in writing and in jazz music appeared also in the visual arts. In painting, the ferment that fed the Armory Show of 1913 continued, and by the late 1940s a large number of painters reached maturity. Stuart Davis, for example, had followed the lines of development suggested by the abstraction process of cubism and, influenced by jazz, made larger canvases filled with vaguely familiar objects, rhythmically charged with energy derived from distortion and intense color. "Owh! in San Pao" (Fig. 34-1), painted in 1951, is a careful arrangement of interlocking, overlapping forms that create a busy swirl of front, back, beside, and behind kaleidoscopic patterns held against the vibrant yellow surface by words, letters, and dots. Davis's signature is an active part of the design and punctuates the space as sharply as the bright sounds of the jazz musician fill the air. Georgia O'Keeffe moved to the Southwest, where she created haunting visions based on the desert. These and other American artists provided the strong background against which a new style appeared in the years following World War II.

Abstract Expressionism

This style, called abstract expressionism, or action painting, was the product of many factors—America, the emigration of many artists from Europe during the war years, and the confluence of an almost obsessive individualism with the desire to make original and deeply serious paintings. In retrospect, the painters whose work is commonly described by the term were a most heterogeneous group of individuals, and lumping them together seems superficial and presumptuous. Nevertheless, it is possible to discern enough similarities to explain the name. Consider the canvas by Jackson Pollock (Fig. 34-2). First, it is a very large painting, wall-size in fact. Second, it reminds us of a work by Kandinsky in that it has no identifiable subject matter except the formal one that is the product of the combination of shapes, forms, and colors on

---

[1] Charlie Parker recorded over 175 blues performances, and the availability of specific recorded performances is difficult to predict. "Parker's Mood" was recorded in New York in September 1948 and is available on Savoy MGV-12009. It has been reissued many times, and most college libraries will have it in the *Smithsonian Collection of Classic Jazz* (P6 11891), record side 8, cut number 3 (available from W. W. Norton & Co., 500 Fifth Avenue, New York, NY 10110).

34-2 *Jackson Pollock,* Blue Poles, *1952, oil, enamel, and aluminum paint, glass on canvas, 210.4 cm × 486.8 cm. (Collection: Australian National Gallery, Canberra. Copyright 1992 Succession J. Pollock/ARS, N.Y.)*

the surface. It seems to be derived in part from the cubist notion, also supported by Kandinsky, that a painting is good because it *is,* not because it represents something. But we also know from Kandinsky, the cubists, and the surrealists (as well as from Van Gogh and Gauguin) that lines, colors, and shapes are capable of communicating directly with the viewer, through the unconscious and the intuition. By appealing to these faculties rather than the rational, intellectualizing ones, the artist involves the spectator in a dialogue with the pure elements of the painting.

We also know, particularly from Kandinsky, how very difficult it is to create a picture outside of the habitual and familiar, so we might ask how Pollock has created such seemingly random patterns on the canvas. Pollock created his paintings by dripping, pouring, and splashing paint on a canvas laid out on the floor. It was his belief that in this uninhibited way of working, he surrendered control of his rational processes; the work produced would be a reflection of interior, personal drives and motivations. He also believed that in this way his paintings would speak directly to the unconscious, therefore allowing the viewer to apprehend a shared universality existing beyond the habitual and familiar. In this painting we seem to have the unification of a number of ideas that had already emerged in the early twentieth century. The large scale of this work, however, gives it unrelieved energy and an overwhelming appeal to the emotional and subjective, capable of creating an environment that is one with the viewer.

Not all the painters who were a part of the abstract expressionist school made paintings that had no recognizable objects. But all the painters involved gave primacy to the unconscious and to the physical act, the gesture of making the work. The two aims are, in a way, almost mutually exclusive. If the painter is to be uninhibited and have gestures as free from conscious motivation as possible, then from the moment that the first bit of paint is laid down, the painter becomes involved in an emotionally charged situation.

You can demonstrate this for yourself. Take a piece of paper. Put down a random line. Now you must decide, will the first line determine the placement of the second, or will you attempt to let the second line be as random as the first? Once two lines are down you are forced, almost unconsciously, to make some kind of decision about the placement of a third line, or form. Imagine how complicated this would become if you were working not only with a black line but with colored lines. The factors that are unconsciously forcing you into a decision-making situation are first, the sheet of paper, which acts as a kind of frame; second, there is your natural orientation to the world: top, bottom, left, right, front, back, beside, behind. Then there is an unconscious need to make the arrangement "look right," to produce a sense of balance and rhythm, order and harmony. Whether these needs are inborn or the product of culture does not matter in this instance. What is clear is the need to make "sense" of the thing; to find a personal structure and to impose it on the experience. Thus, on the one hand, the struggle is for a decisive subjective statement; on the other, it is a struggle with the powerful forces generated by the familiar knowledge of seeing, knowing, and experiencing both the painterly world and the habitual world.

It is this ambiguity between ends and means that makes abstract expressionist paintings so strong, enduring, and powerful. Drawn into the dialogue that the painter carries on with the canvas and paint, the viewer experiences the emotionally charged event of which the canvas is a record. At the same time it was this ambiguity that made this kind of painting a difficult act to sustain. Like Monet, who sought more and more transient effects in the landscape, these painters were forced to greater and greater personal and emotional extremes to sustain creative energy; otherwise, their gestures ran the risk of becoming hollow and repetitive. According to one abstract expressionist painter, the need for simplicity, clarity, order, and objectivity becomes overwhelming in the face of spending so much emotional energy.

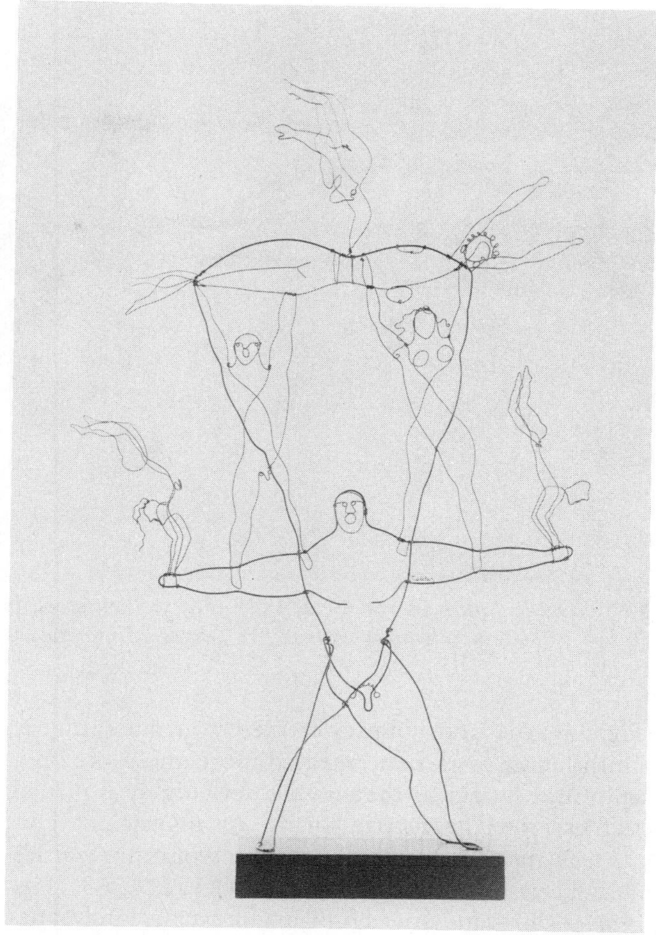

34-3 *Alexander Calder,* The Brass Family, *1929, wire, height 64". (Collection of Whitney Museum of American Art, New York, gift of artist)*

Sculpture After World War II

By the end of World War I, constructed sculpture—that is, work made from metal, wood, and other materials welded, bolted, or wired together—began to assume great importance as a way of working, in addition to the traditional methods of cast bronze or carved stone. During the 1930s Alexander Calder (1898–1976), an American influenced by European surrealism, began to produce wire and wood constructions that have some of the same energy and whimsy of the Stuart Davis pieces of the same period (Fig. 34-3). As Calder matured in the postwar years his work assumed more heroic proportions in which the components of these constructed works not only decorated but animated the architectural spaces in which they were placed. The mobiles (constructions suspended from a framework with moving parts) and stabiles (large-scale metal plate constructions) used forms that appeared to be derived from the natural world but were machined and carefully painted to create vigorous, aerodynamic, energetic sculptures whose machinelike components seemed to echo the sleek surfaces and large scale of International Style architecture (Fig. 34-4).

34-4 *Alexander Calder,* Hello Girls, *painted metal mobile, 8′9″ × 15″ × 22′11″. (Los Angeles County Museum of Art, Art Museum Council Fund)*

David Smith (1906–1965)

David Smith's early constructed works originated in surrealism's emphasis on the unconscious and on dreams as a source for forms. *The Royal Bird,* 1948

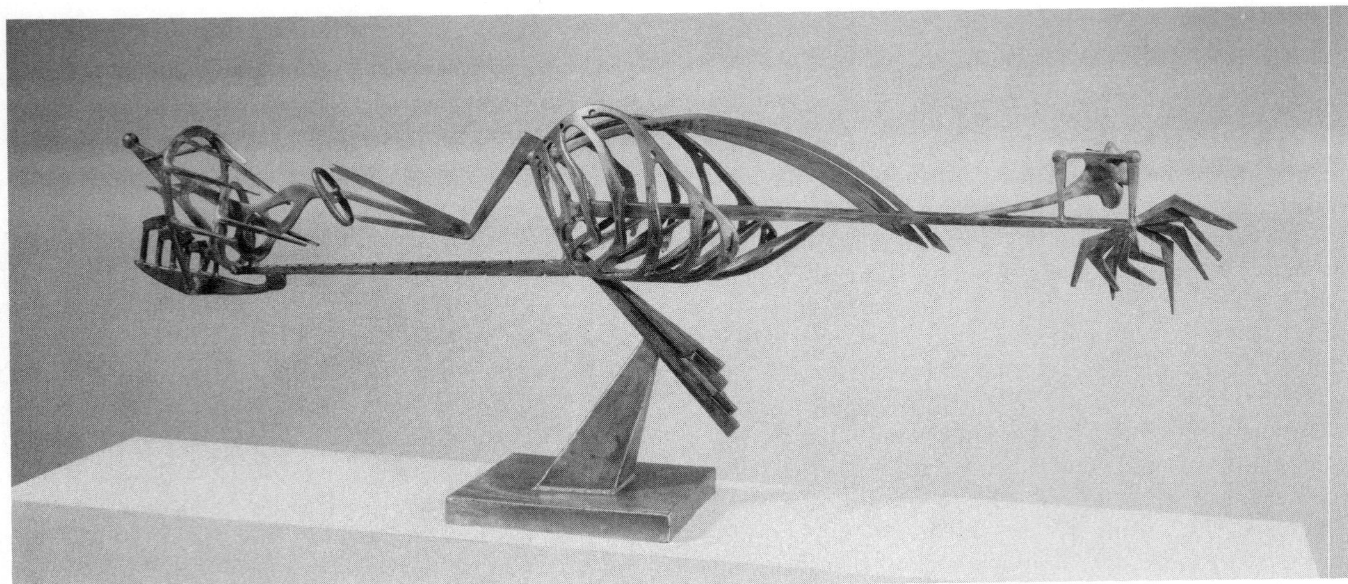

34-5 *David Smith,* Royal Bird, *1947–48, welded steel, bronze, and stainless steel, 22⅛" × 59 13/16" × 8½". (Collection Walker Art Center, Minneapolis, gift of the T.B. Walker Foundation, 1952)*

(Fig. 34-5), is a bird of prey created from a nightmare. Smith's later work concentrated more and more on a sculptural language that used a few highly polished stainless steel geometric forms. As monumental as Calder's mobiles and stabiles, the works in Smith's Cubi Series—for example, *Cubi XVII,* 1963 (Fig. 34-6)—can stand powerfully in almost any landscape, rendering the space around it a frame and the distance or the building seen through its openings as a picture.

Calder and Smith represent possibilities for the sculptor that were opened by the nonobjective and expressive language that began with Kandinsky and evolved into constructivism in Europe and abstract expressionism in America following World War II. Both men relied on the power of form to draw the viewer into a dialogue with the work; both assumed, like Kandinsky and the abstract expressionist painters, that color and form speak directly. But other artists continued to rely on the human form to act as a carrier of meaning.

34-6 *David Smith,* Cubi XVII, *1963, stainless steel, height 9'. (Dallas Museum of Fine Arts)*

Alberto Giacometti (1901–1966)

Giacometti, a Swiss-Italian artist who lived in Paris and was a friend of Sartre's, created a memorable figure-type that seemed to epitomize the human condition as viewed by the existentialist. The gouged, stretched, attenuated human form, whether male or female, adult or child, presents an image that contrasts vividly with the heroic scale and optimistic power of Smith's or Calder's work. Giacometti creates lonely

34-7 *GIACOMETTI, Alberto.* Chariot, *1950 Bronze, 57" × 26" × 26⅛". (Collection, The Museum of Modern Art, New York. Purchase.)*

individuals who suffer their fate and fear as they live in, but aloof from, the modern society (Fig. 34-7).

The architecture of the postwar period presents a very different picture and will be discussed in the next chapter in conjunction with more recent developments.

The Theater of the Absurd

The 1950s saw an important revival of writing for the theater, a new type of drama that the British critic Martin Esslin baptized "the theatre of the absurd." Although they have never formed a school and are in many respects highly different one from the other, the "absurdist" playwrights, many of whom are still writing, do share a radically new vision of the theatrical medium. Several of them came to Paris from other countries but adopted French as their language of expression. These include the Irishman Samuel Beckett, the Romanian Eugène Ionesco, and the Spaniard Fernando Arrabal. The French ex-convict Jean Genet (1910–1985), brought to prominence by Sartre, was in a sense an exile in his own country. Esslin also grouped the English playwright Harold Pinter, the American Edward Albee, and the Czech (now turned politician) Vaclav Havel among the practitioners of theater of the absurd. In a sense, these playwrights have developed Camus's philosophy of the absurd into a literary form. Their theatrical world is one in which traditional elements like plot and character are almost abandoned, and language is freed from its everyday, logical restraints. Their experimentation grows out of both modernism and existentialism, but they tend to lack both the modernist belief in the redemptive value of art and the existentialist credo that humanity can create meaning in a meaningless world.

Fernando Arrabal (b. 1932)

Fernando Arrabal, whose work shows many of the absurdist tendencies, began his career alone and independent of any movement. Born in Spain at the beginning of the civil war, he grew up in the repressive atmosphere of the Franco dictatorship. By his early twenties, when he moved to France, he had already written several plays, although he knew very little about the work of other absurdist writers. The institutions that supported Franco—the army, the police, and the Church—appear in a grotesque form in all of Arrabal's plays. His characters, those who are not allied with the forces of repression, are childlike, spontaneous people, alienated from but often crushed by society. Arrabal's plays often present tragic situations with a comic treatment. Theater, for him, should be seen more in its ancient function as a ceremony than as a realistic portrayal of life. Totally opposed to the classical aesthetic of unity of tone and *verisimilitude,* Arrabal is closer to the baroque in his claim that a theatrical performance can and should mix tragedy with farce and sublime poetry with sordid vulgarity.

Picnic on the Battlefield, Arrabal's most often performed play, is clearly centered on the theme of the total absurdity of war. The situation, particularly the ending, is potentially tragic, but Arrabal's puppetlike characters and their preposterous actions make the effect on the spectator a comic one. Written in 1952, the play was perhaps directly inspired by the Korean War, but its impact extends to the phenomenon of war in general.

Primo Levi

If This Is a Man

Translation by Stuart Woolf

In the eleventh chapter of *If This Is a Man,* Levi attempts to teach Italian and Dante to a French fellow prisoner by reciting what he remembers of Canto 26 of the *Inferno,* the canto of Ulysses. In the context, the words of the poet take on a new meaning. To appreciate this passage fully, the reader is advised to reread Canto 26 of the *Inferno.*

Chapter 11

The Canto of Ulysses

There were six of us, scraping and cleaning the inside of an underground petrol tank; the daylight only reached us through a small manhole. It was a luxury job because no one supervised us; but it was cold and damp. The powder of the rust burnt under our eyelids and coated our throats and mouths with a taste almost like blood.

The rope-ladder hanging from the manhole began to sway: someone was coming. Deutsch extinguished his cigarette, Goldner woke Sivadjan; we all began to vigorously scrape the resonant steelplate wall.

It was not the *Vorarbeiter,*[1] it was only Jean, the Pikolo of our Kommando.[2] Jean was an Alsatian student; although he was already twenty-four, he was the youngest Häftling of the Chemical Kommando. So that he was given the post of Pikolo, which meant the messenger-clerk, responsible for the cleaning of the hut, for the distribution of tools, for the washing of bowls and for keeping record of the working hours of the Kommando.

Jean spoke French and German fluently: as soon as we recognized his shoes on the top step of the ladder we all stopped scraping.

"Also, Pikolo, was gibt es Neues?"[3]

"Qu'est ce qu'il-y-a comme soupe aujourd'hui?"[4]

. . . in what mood was the Kapo? And the affair of the twenty-five lashes given to Stern? What was the weather like outside? Had he read the newspaper? What smell was coming from the civilian kitchen? What was the time?

Jean was liked a great deal by the Kommando. One must realize that the post of Pikolo represented a quite high rank in the hierarchy of the Prominents: the Pikolo (who is usually no more than seventeen years old) does no manual work, has an absolute right to the remainder of the daily ration to be found on the bottom of the vat and can stay all day near the stove. He "therefore" has the right to a supplementary half-ration and has a good chance of becoming the friend and confidant of the Kapo, from whom he officially receives discarded clothes and shoes. Now Jean was an exceptional Pikolo. He was shrewd and physically robust, and at the same time gentle and friendly: although he continued his secret individual struggle against death, he did not neglect his human relationships with less privileged comrades; at the same time he had been so able and persevering that he had managed to establish himself in the confidence of Alex, the Kapo.

Alex had kept all his promises. He had shown himself a violent and unreliable rogue, with an armour of solid and compact ignorance and stupidity, always excepting his intuition and consummate technique as convict-keeper. He never let slip an opportunity of proclaiming his pride in his pure blood and his green triangle, and displayed a lofty contempt for his ragged and starving chemists: *"Ihr Doktoren! Ihr Intel-*

[1] *Vorarbeiter:* the foreman, a prisoner.

[2] *Kommando:* a unit of workers within the camp.

[3] "What's new, little one?"

[4] "What kind of soup is there today?"

ligenten!"[5] he sneered every day, watching them crowd around with their bowls held out for the distribution of the ration. He was extremely compliant and servile before the civilian *Meister* and with the SS he kept up ties of cordial friendship.

He was clearly intimidated by the register of the Kommando and by the daily report of work, and this had been the path that Pikolo had chosen to make himself indispensable. It had been a long, cautious and subtle task which the entire Kommando had followed for a month with bated breath; but at the end the porcupine's defence was penetrated, and Pikolo confirmed in his office to the satisfaction of all concerned.

Although Jean had never abused his position, we had already been able to verify that a single word of his, said in the right tone of voice and at the right moment, had great power; many times already it had saved one of us from a whipping or from being denounced to the SS. We had been friends for a week: we discovered each other during the unusual occasion of an air-raid alarm, but then, swept by the fierce rhythm of the Lager, we had only been able to greet each other fleetingly, at the latrines, in the washroom.

Hanging with one hand on the swaying ladder, he pointed to me: "*Aujourd'hui c'est Primo qui viendra avec moi chercher la soupe.*"[6]

Until yesterday it had been Stern, the squinting Transylvanian; now he had fallen into disgrace for some story of brooms stolen from the store, and Pikolo had managed to support my candidature as assistant to the "*Essenholen,*" the daily corvée of the ration.

He climbed out and I followed him, blinking in the brightness of the day. It was warmish outside, the sun drew a faint smell of paint and tar from the greasy earth, which made me think of a holiday beach of my infancy. Pikolo gave me one of the two wooden poles, and we walked along under a clear June sky.

I began to thank him, but he stopped me: it was not necessary. One could see the Carpathians covered in snow. I breathed in the fresh air, I felt unusually lighthearted.

"*Tu es fou de marcher si vite. On a le temps, tu sais.*"[7] The ration was collected half a mile away; one had to return with the pot weighing over a hundred pounds supported on the two poles. It was quite a tiring task, but it meant a pleasant walk there without a load, and the ever-welcome chance of going near the kitchens.

We slowed down. Pikolo was expert. He had chosen the path cleverly so that we would have to make a long detour, walking at least for an hour, without arousing suspicion. We spoke of our houses, of Strasbourg and Turin, of the books we had read, of what we had studied, of our mothers: how all mothers resemble each other! His mother too had scolded him for never knowing how much money he had in his pocket; his mother too would have been amazed if she had known that he had found his feet, that day by day he was finding his feet.

An SS man passed on a bicycle. It is Rudi, the *Blockführer.* Halt! Attention! Take off your beret! "*Sale brute, celui-là. Ein ganz gemeiner Hund.*"[8] Can he speak French and German with equal facility? Yes, he thinks indifferently in both languages. He spent a month in Liguria, he likes Italy, he would like to learn Italian. I would be pleased to teach him Italian: why not try? We can do it. Why not immediately, one thing is as good as another, the important thing is not to lose time, not to waste this hour.

Limentani from Rome walks by, dragging his feet, with a bowl hidden under his jacket. Pikolo listens carefully, picks up a few words of our conversation and repeats them smiling: "*Zup-pa, cam-po, acqua.*"[9]

Frenkl the spy passes. Quicken our pace, one never knows, he does evil for evil's sake.

... The canto of Ulysses. Who knows how or why it comes into my mind. But we have no time to change, this hour is already less than an hour. If Jean is intelligent he will understand. He *will* understand—today I feel capable of so much.

... Who is Dante? What is the Comedy? That curious sensation of novelty which one feels if one tries to explain briefly what is the Divine Comedy. How the Inferno is divided up, what are its punishments. Virgil is Reason, Beatrice is Theology.

Jean pays great attention, and I begin slowly and accurately:

> "Then of that age-old fire the loftier horn
> Began to mutter and move, as a wavering flame
> Wrestles against the wind and is over-worn;
> And, like a speaking tongue vibrant to frame
> Language, the tip of it flickering to and fro
> Threw out a voice and answered: 'When I
> came...'"

[5] "You doctors, you intellectuals."

[6] "Today it's Primo who will come with me for the soup."

[7] "You're crazy to walk so fast. We have time, you know."

[8] "Dirty beast, that one. A common dog."

[9] Soup, field, water.

Here I stop and try to translate. Disastrous—poor Dante and poor French! All the same, the experience seems to promise well: Jean admires the bizzare simile of the tongue and suggests the appropriate word to translate "age-old."

And after "When I came?" Nothing. A hole in my memory. "Before Aeneas ever named it so." Another hole. A fragment floats into my mind, not relevant: "... nor piety To my old father, not the wedded love That should have comforted Penelope...," is it correct?

> "... So on the open sea I set forth."

Of this I am certain, I am sure, I can explain it to Pikolo, I can point out why "I set forth"[10] is not *"je me mis,"* it is much stronger and more audacious, it is a chain which has been broken, it is throwing oneself on the other side of a barrier, we know the impulse well. The open sea: Pikolo has travelled by sea, and knows what it means: it is when the horizon closes in on itself, free, straight ahead and simple, and there is nothing but the smell of the sea; sweet things, ferociously far away.

We have arrived at Kraftwerk, where the cable-laying Kommando works. Engineer Levi must be here. Here he is, one can only see his head above the trench. He waves to me, he is a brave man, I have never seen his morale low, he never speaks of eating.

"Open sea," "open sea," I know it rhymes with "left me": "... and that small band of comrades that had never left me," but I cannot remember if it comes before or after. And the journey as well, the foolhardy journey beyond the Pillars of Hercules, how sad, I have to tell it in prose—a sacrilege. I have only rescued two lines, but they are worth stopping for:

> "... that none should prove so hardly
> To venture the uncharted distances..."

"to venture":[11] I had to come to the Lager to realize that it is the same expression as before: "I set forth." But I say nothing to Jean, I am not sure that it is an important observation. How many things there are to say, and the sun is already high, midday is near. I am in a hurry, a terrible hurry.

Here, listen Pikolo, open your ears and your mind, you have to understand, for my sake:

> "Think of your breed; for brutish ignorance
> Your mettle was not made; you were made men,
> To follow after knowledge and excellence."

As if I also was hearing it for the first time: like the blast of a trumpet, like the voice of God. For a moment I forget who I am and where I am.

Pikolo begs me to repeat it. How good Pikolo is, he is aware that it is doing me good. Or perhaps it is something more: perhaps, despite the wan translation and the pedestrian, rushed commentary, he has received the message, he has felt that it has to do with him, that it has to do with all men who toil, and with us in particular; and that it has to do with us two, who dare to reason of these things with the poles for the soup on our shoulders.

> "My little speech made every one so keen..."

... and I try, but in vain, to explain how many things this "keen" means. There is another lacuna here, this time irreparable. "... the light kindles and grows Beneath the moon" or something like it; but before it?... Not an idea, "*keine Ahnung*" as they say here. Forgive me, Pikolo, I have forgotten at least four triplets.

"*Ça ne fait rien, vas-y tout de même.*"[12]

> "... When at last hove up a mountain, grey
> With distance, and so lofty and so steep,
> I never had seen the like on any day."

Yes, yes, "so lofty and so steep," not "very steep,"[13] a consecutive proposition. And the mountains when one sees them in the distance... mountains... oh, Pikolo, Pikolo, say something, speak, do not let me think of my mountains which used to show up against the dusk of evening as I returned by train from Milan to Turin!

Enough, one must go on, these are things that one thinks but does not say. Pikolo waits and looks at me.

I would give today's soup to know how to connect "the like on any day" to the last lines. I try to reconstruct it through the rhymes, I close my eyes, I bite my fingers—but it is no use, the rest is silence. Other verses dance in my head: "... The sodden ground belched wind...," no, it is something else. It is late, it is late, we have reached the kitchen, I must finish:

---

[10] "Misi me" [translator's note].

[11] "Si metta" [translator's note].

[12] "It doesn't matter, go ahead anyway."

[13] "Alta tanto," not "molto alta" [translator's note].

"And three times round she went in roaring smother
With all the waters; at the fourth the poop
Rose, and the prow went down, as pleased Another."

I keep Pikolo back, it is vitally necessary and urgent that he listen, that he understand this "as pleased Another" before it is too late; tomorrow he or I might be dead, or we might never see each other again, I must tell him, I must explain to him about the Middle Ages, about the so human and so necessary and yet unexpected anachronism, but still more, something gigantic that I myself have only just seen, in a flash of intuition, perhaps the reason for our fate, for our being here today...

We are now in the soup queue, among the sordid, ragged crowd of soup-carriers from other Kommandos. Those just arrived press against our backs. "*Kraut und Rüben? Kraut und Rüben.*" The official announcement is made that the soup today is of cabbages and turnips: "*Choux et navets. Kaposzta és répak.*"

"And over our heads the hollow seas closed up."

QUESTIONS

1. Why does Levi choose the Ulysses canto to teach to his friend?
2. What new meanings do the recited lines take on in this context? How do they differ from those intended by Dante in the context of the *Divine Comedy?*
3. What does this brief passage convey to you about the concentration camp experience?

Jean-Paul Sartre

The Republic of Silence

We have never been so free as under German occupation. We had lost every right, and above all the right of speech: we were insulted every day and we had to remain silent; we were deported as laborers, as Jews, as political prisoners; everywhere, on the walls, in the newspapers, and on the screen, we saw the foul and listless face which our oppressors wanted to give us. Because of all this we were free. Since the Nazi venom penetrated our very thoughts, every true thought was a victory. Since an all-powerful police tried to force us to be silent, each word became as precious as a declaration of principle. Since we were hounded, every one of our movements had the importance of commitment. The often atrocious circumstances of our struggle had at last put us in a position to live our life without pretenses—to live in this torn, unbearable condition which we call the human condition. Exile, captivity, and above all death, which is ably disguised in periods of happiness, became the perpetual object of our concern; we discovered that they were not inevitable accidents or even constant but external threats: they had become our *lot,* our destiny, the source of our reality as men. Each second we fully realized the meaning of the trite little phrase "All men are mortal." And the choice which each man made on his own was genuine, since he made it in the presence of death, since he would always have been able to express it in terms of "better death than..." And I'm not talking of the elite formed by the true resistants, but of every Frenchman who, at every hour of the day and night, for four years, said no. The cruelty of the enemy pushed us to the extremes of our condition by forcing us to ask these questions which we avoid in peacetime: each of us—and what Frenchman did not at one point find himself in this position?—who knew certain details concerning the Resistance wondered anxiously: "If I were tortured, would I hold out?" Thus the question of liberty was raised and we were on the brink of the deepest knowledge that man can have of himself. Because man's secret is not his Oedipus complex or his inferiority complex, it is the limit of his freedom, it is his power to resist torture and death. To those who were active in the underground, the circumstances of this struggle were a new experience: they did not fight in the open, like soldiers; they were hunted in solitude, arrested in solitude, and it was all alone that they resisted torture: alone and naked before well-shaved, well-fed, well-dressed executioners who laughed at their wretched flesh, who with clean consciences and unlimited power, looked as though they were in the right. And yet at the depths of this solitude it was the others, all the others, all the comrades of the Resistance whom they defended. One word was enough to cause ten, a hundred arrests. Is not total responsibility in total solitude the revelation of our liberty? The need, the solitude, the enormous risk were the same for everybody, for the leaders and the men. For those who carried messages and did not know what they contained as for those who organized the whole Resistance, there was only one sentence: imprisonment, deportation, death. There is no army in the world with such equal risks for the soldiers and the general. And that is why the Resistance was a real democracy: for the soldier and for the leader there was the same danger, the same responsibility, the same absolute liberty in discipline. Thus, in darkness and in blood, the strongest republic was formed. Each of its citizens knew that he owed himself to everyone and could only count on himself; each one performed his historic part in total solitude. Each one, in defiance of the oppressor, undertook to be himself; irremediably and by freely choosing himself, he chose freedom for everybody. This republic without institutions, without army or police, had to be conquered by each Frenchman and established at every moment against Nazism. We are now on the brink of another Republic:[1] can't we preserve by day the austere virtues of the Republic of Silence and Night?

QUESTIONS

1. How does Sartre see the situation of the Occupation as a microcosm of the human condition?
2. In what way does individual liberty entail responsibility for Sartre?

ALBERT CAMUS

FROM *The Myth of Sisyphus*

The gods had condemned Sisyphus to ceaselessly rolling a rock to the top of a mountain, whence the stone would fall back of its own weight. They had thought with some reason that there is no more dreadful punishment than futile and hopeless labor.

If one believes Homer, Sisyphus was the wisest and most prudent of mortals. According to another tradition, however, he was disposed to practice the profession of highwayman. I see no contradiction in this. Opinions differ as to the reasons why he became the futile laborer of the underworld. To begin with, he is accused of a certain levity in regard to the gods. He stole their secrets. Aegina, the daughter of Aesopus, was carried off by Jupiter. The father was shocked by that disappearance and complained to Sisyphus. He, who knew of the abduction, offered to tell about it on condition that Aesopus would give water to the citadel of Corinth. To the celestial thunderbolts he preferred the benediction of water. He was punished for this in the underworld. Homer tells us also that Sisyphus had put Death in chains. Pluto could not endure the sight of his deserted, silent empire. He dispatched the god of war, who liberated Death from the hands of her conqueror.

It is said also that Sisyphus, being near to death, rashly wanted to test his wife's love. He ordered her to cast his unburied body into the middle of the public square. Sisyphus woke up in the underworld. And there, annoyed by an obedience so contrary to human love, he obtained from Pluto permission to return to earth in order to chastise his wife. But when he had seen again the face of this world, enjoyed water and sun, warm stones and the sea, he no longer wanted to go back to the infernal darkness. Recalls, signs of anger, warnings were of no avail. Many years more he lived facing the curve of the gulf, the sparkling sea, and the smiles of earth. A decree of the gods was necessary. Mercury came and seized the impudent man by the collar and, snatching him from his joys, led him forcibly back to the underworld, where his rock was ready for him.

You have already grasped that Sisyphus is the absurd hero. He *is*, as much through his passions as through his torture. His scorn of the gods, his hatred of death, and his passion for life won him that unspeakable penalty in which the whole being is exerted toward accomplishing nothing. This is the price that must be paid for the passions of this earth. Nothing is told us about Sisyphus in the underworld. Myths are made for the imagination to breathe life into them. As for this myth, one sees merely the whole effort of a body straining to raise the huge stone, to roll it and push it up a slope a hundred times over; one sees the face screwed up, the cheek tight against the stone, the shoulder bracing the clay-covered mass, the foot wedging it, the fresh start with arms outstretched, the wholly human security of two earth-clotted hands. At the very end of his long effort measured by skyless space and time without depth, the purpose is achieved. Then Sisyphus watches the stone rush down in a few moments toward that lower world whence he will have to push it up again toward the summit. He goes back down to the plain.

It is during that return, that pause, that Sisyphus interests me. A face that toils so close to stones is

[1]The Fourth Republic, France's new government after the liberation.

already stone itself! I see that man going back down with a heavy yet measured step toward the torment of which he will never know the end. That hour like a breathing-space which returns as surely as his suffering, that is the hour of consciousness. At each of those moments when he leaves the heights and gradually sinks toward the lairs of the gods, he is superior to his fate. He is stronger than his rock.

If this myth is tragic, that is because its hero is conscious. Where would his torture be, indeed, if at every step the hope of succeeding upheld him? The workman of today works every day in his life at the same tasks, and this fate is no less absurd. But it is tragic only at the rare moments when it becomes conscious. Sisyphus, proletarian of the gods, powerless and rebellious, knows the whole extent of his wretched condition: it is what he thinks of during his descent. The lucidity that was to constitute his torture at the same time crowns his victory. There is no fate that cannot be surmounted by scorn.

If the descent is thus sometimes performed in sorrow, it can also take place in joy. This word is not too much. Again I fancy Sisyphus returning toward his rock, and the sorrow was in the beginning. When the images of earth cling too tightly to memory, when the call of happiness becomes too insistent, it happens that melancholy rises in man's heart: this is the rock's victory, this is the rock itself. The boundless grief is too heavy to bear. These are our nights of Gethsemane. But crushing truths perish from being acknowledged. Thus, Oedipus at the outset obeys fate without knowing it. But from the moment he knows, his tragedy begins. Yet at the same moment, blind and desperate, he realizes that the only bond linking him to the world is the cool hand of a girl. Then a tremendous remark rings out: "Despite so many ordeals, my advanced age and the nobility of my soul make me conclude that all is well." Sophocles' Oedipus, like Dostoevsky's Kirilov, thus gives the recipe for the absurd victory. Ancient wisdom confirms modern heroism.

One does not discover the absurd without being tempted to write a manual of happiness. "What! by such narrow ways—?" There is but one world, however. Happiness and the absurd are two sons of the same earth. They are inseparable. It would be a mistake to say that happiness necessarily springs from the absurd discovery. It happens as well that the feeling of the absurd springs from happiness. "I conclude that all is well," says Oedipus, and that remark is sacred. It echoes in the wild and limited universe of man. It teaches that all is not, has not been, exhausted. It drives out of this world a god who had come into it with dissatisfaction and a preference for futile sufferings. It makes of fate a human matter, which must be settled among men.

All Sisyphus' silent joy is contained therein. His fate belongs to him. His rock is his thing. Likewise, the absurd man, when he contemplates his torment, silences all the idols. In the universe suddenly restored to its silence, the myriad wondering little voices of the earth rise up. Unconscious, secret calls, invitations from all the faces they are the necessary reverse and price of victory. There is no sun without shadow, and it is essential to know the night. The absurd man says yes and his effort will henceforth be unceasing. If there is a personal fate, there is no higher destiny, or at least there is but one which he concludes is inevitable and despicable. For the rest, he knows himself to be the master of his days. At that subtle moment when man glances backward over his life, Sisyphus returning toward his rock, in that slight pivoting he contemplates that series of unrelated actions which becomes his fate, created by him, combined under his memory's eye and soon sealed by his death. Thus, convinced of the wholly human origin of all that is human, a blind man eager to see who knows that the night has no end, he is still on the go. The rock is still rolling.

I leave Sisyphus at the foot of the mountain! One always finds one's burden again. But Sisyphus teaches the higher fidelity that negates the gods and raises rocks. He too concludes that all is well. This universe henceforth without a master seems to him neither sterile nor futile. Each atom of that stone, each mineral flake of that nightfilled mountain, in itself forms a world. The struggle itself toward the heights is enough to fill a man's heart. One must imagine Sisyphus happy.

QUESTIONS

1. What, exactly, is Sisyphus' condition, and how, in Camus's vision, is it representative of the human condition?
2. What seems to be the relationship between tragedy and happiness for Camus?
3. How does Camus's style differ from Sartre's? How does this style reflect Camus's view of the human condition?
4. Can you relate the myth of Sisyphus to the experiences of the concentration camp and the Occupation?

RALPH ELLISON

PROLOGUE TO *Invisible Man*

I am an invisible man. No, I am not a spook like those who haunted Edgar Allan Poe; nor am I one of your Hollywood-movie ectoplasms. I am a man of substance, of flesh and bone, fiber and liquids—and I might even be said to possess a mind. I am invisible, understand, simply because people refuse to see me. Like the bodiless heads you see sometimes in circus sideshows, it is as though I have been surrounded by mirrors of hard, distorting glass. When they approach me they see only my surroundings, themselves, or figments of their imagination—indeed, everything and anything except me.

Nor is my invisibility exactly a matter of a biochemical accident to my epidermis. That invisibility to which I refer occurs because of a peculiar disposition of the eyes of those with whom I come in contact. A matter of the construction of their *inner* eyes, those eyes with which they look through their physical eyes upon reality. I am not complaining, nor am I protesting either. It is sometimes advantageous to be unseen, although it is most often rather wearing on the nerves. Then too, you're constantly being bumped against by those of poor vision. Or again, you often doubt if you really exist. You wonder whether you aren't simply a phantom in other people's minds. Say, a figure in a nightmare which the sleeper tries with all his strength to destroy. It's when you feel like this that, out of resentment, you begin to bump people back. And, let me confess, you feel that way most of the time. You ache with the need to convince yourself that you do exist in the real world, that you're a part of all the sound and anguish, and you strike out with your fists, you curse and you swear to make them recognize you. And, alas, it's seldom successful.

One night I accidentally bumped into a man, and perhaps because of the near darkness he saw me and called me an insulting name. I sprang at him, seized his coat lapels and demanded that he apologize. He was a tall blond man, and as my face came close to his he looked insolently out of his blue eyes and cursed me, his breath hot in my face as he struggled. I pulled his chin down sharp upon the crown of my head, butting him as I had seen the West Indians do, and I felt his flesh tear and the blood gush out, and I yelled, "Apologize! Apologize!" But he continued to curse and struggle, and I butted him again and again until he went down heavily, on his knees, profusely bleeding. I kicked him repeatedly, in a frenzy because he still uttered insults though his lips were frothy with blood. Oh yes, I kicked him! And in my outrage I got out my knife and prepared to slit his throat, right there beneath the lamplight in the deserted street, holding him in the collar with one hand, and opening the knife with my teeth — when it occurred to me that the man had not *seen* me, actually; that he, as far as he knew, was in the midst of a walking nightmare! And I stopped the blade, slicing the air as I pushed him away, letting him fall back to the street. I stared at him hard as the lights of a car stabbed through the darkness. He lay there, moaning on the asphalt; a man almost killed by a phantom. It unnerved me. I was both disgusted and ashamed. I was like a drunken man myself, wavering about on weakened legs. Then I was amused: Something in this man's thick head had sprung out and beaten him within an inch of his life. I began to laugh at this crazy discovery. Would he have awakened at the point of death? Would Death himself have freed him for wakeful living? But I didn't linger. I ran away into the dark, laughing so hard I feared I might rupture myself. The next day I saw his picture in the *Daily News,* beneath a caption stating that he had been "mugged." Poor fool, poor blind fool, I thought with sincere compassion, mugged by an invisible man!

Most of the time (although I do not choose as I once did to deny the violence of my days by ignoring it) I am not so overtly violent. I remember that I am invisible and walk softly so as not to awaken the sleeping ones. Sometimes it is best not to awaken them; there are few things in the world as dangerous as sleepwalkers. I learned in time though that it is possible to carry on a fight against them without their realizing it. For instance, I have been carrying on a fight with Monopolated Light & Power for some time now. I use their service and pay them nothing at all, and they don't know it. Oh, they suspect that power is being drained off, but they don't know where. All they know is that according to the master meter back there in their power station a hell of a lot of free current is disappearing somewhere into the jungle of Harlem. The joke, of course, is that I don't live in Harlem but in a border area. Several years ago (before I discovered the advantages of being invisible) I went through the routine process of buying service and paying their outrageous rates. But no more. I gave up all that, along with my apartment, and my old way of life: That way based upon the fallacious assumption that I, like other men, was visible. Now, aware of my invisibility, I live rent-free in a building rented strictly to whites, in a section of the basement that was shut off and forgotten during the nineteenth century, which I discovered when I was trying to escape in the night from Ras the Destroyer. But that's getting too far ahead of the story, almost to the end, although the end is in the beginning and lies far ahead.

The point now is that I found a home—or a hole in the ground, as you will. Now don't jump to the conclusion that because I call my home a "hole" it is damp and cold like a grave; there are cold holes and warm holes. Mine is a warm hole. And remember, a bear retires to his hole for the winter and lives until spring; then he comes strolling out like the Easter chick breaking from its shell. I say all this to assure you that it is incorrect to assume that, because I'm invisible and live in a hole, I am dead. I am neither dead nor in a state of suspended animation. Call me Jack-the-Bear, for I am in a state of hibernation.

My hole is warm and full of light. Yes, *full* of light. I doubt if there is a brighter spot in all New York than this hole of mine, and I do not exclude Broadway. Or the Empire State Building on a photographer's dream night. But that is taking advantage of you. Those two spots are among the darkest of our whole civilization—pardon me, our whole *culture* (an important distinction, I've heard)—which might sound like a hoax, or a contradiction, but that (by contradiction, I mean) is how the world moves: Not like an arrow, but a boomerang. (Beware of those who speak of the *spiral* of history; they are preparing a boomerang. Keep a steel helmet handy.) I know; I have been boomeranged across my head so much that I now can see the darkness of lightness. And I love light. Perhaps you'll think it strange that an invisible man should need light, desire light, love light. But maybe it is exactly because I *am* invisible. Light confirms my reality, gives birth to my form. A beautiful girl once told me of a recurring nightmare in which she lay in the center of a large dark room and felt her face expand until it filled the whole room, becoming a formless mass while her eyes ran in bilious jelly up the chimney. And so it is with me. Without light I am not only invisible, but formless as well; and to be unaware of one's form is to live a death. I myself, after existing some twenty years, did not become alive until I discovered my invisibility.

That is why I fight my battle with Monopolated Light & Power. The deeper reason, I mean: It allows me to feel my vital aliveness. I also fight them for taking so much of my money before I learned to protect myself. In my hole in the basement there are exactly 1,369 lights. I've wired the entire ceiling, every inch of it. And not with fluorescent bulbs, but with the older, more-expensive-to-operate kind, the filament type. An act of sabotage, you know. I've already begun to wire the wall. A junk man I know, a man of vision, has supplied me with wire and sockets. Nothing, storm or flood, must get in the way of our need for light and ever more and brighter light. The truth is the light and light is the truth. When I finish all four walls, then I'll start on the floor. Just how that will go, I don't know. Yet when you have lived invisible as long as I have you develop a certain ingenuity. I'll solve the problem. And maybe I'll invent a gadget to place my coffee pot on the fire while I lie in bed, and even invent a gadget to warm my bed—like the fellow I saw in one of the picture magazines who made himself a gadget to warm his shoes! Though invisible, I am in the great American tradition of tinkers. That makes me kin to Ford, Edison and Franklin. Call me, since I have a theory and a concept, a "thinker-tinker." Yes, I'll warm my shoes; they need it, they're usually full of holes. I'll do that and more.

Now I have one radio-phonograph; I plan to have five. There is a certain acoustical deadness in my hole, and when I have music I want to *feel* its vibration, not only with my ear but with my whole body. I'd like to hear five recordings of Louis Armstrong playing and singing "What Did I Do to Be So Black and Blue"—all at the same time. Sometimes now I listen to Louis while I have my favorite dessert of vanilla ice cream and sloe gin. I pour the red liquid over the white mound, watching it glisten and the vapor rising as Louis bends that military instrument into a beam of lyrical sound. Perhaps I like Louis Armstrong because he's made poetry out of being invisible. I think it must be because he's unaware that he *is* invisible. And my own grasp of invisibility aids me to understand his music. Once when I asked for a cigarette, some jokers gave me a reefer, which I lighted when I got home and sat listening to my phonograph. It was a strange evening. Invisibility, let me explain, gives one a slightly different sense of time, you're never quite on the beat. Sometimes you're ahead and sometimes behind. Instead of the swift and imperceptible flowing of time, you are aware of its nodes, those points where time stands still or from which it leaps ahead. And you slip into the breaks and look around. That's what you hear vaguely in Louis' music.

Once I saw a prizefighter boxing a yokel. The fighter was swift and amazingly scientific. His body was one violent flow of rapid rhythmic action. He hit the yokel a hundred times while the yokel held up his arms in stunned surprise. But suddenly the yokel, rolling about in the gale of boxing gloves, struck one blow and knocked science, speed and footwork as cold as a well-digger's posterior. The smart money hit the canvas. The long shot got the nod. The yokel had simply stepped inside of his opponent's sense of time. So under the spell of the reefer I discovered a new analytical way of listening to music. The unheard sounds came through, and each melodic line existed of itself, stood out clearly from all the rest, said its piece, and waited patiently for the other voices to speak. That night I found myself hearing not only in time, but in space as well. I not only entered the music but descended, like Dante, into its depths. And *beneath the swiftness of the hot tempo there was a slower tempo and a cave and I entered it and looked around and heard an old woman singing a spiritual as full of Weltschmerz as flamenco, and beneath that lay a still lower level on which I saw a beautiful girl the color of ivory pleading in a voice like my mother's as she stood before a group of slaveowners who bid for her naked body, and below that I found a lower level and a more rapid tempo and I heard someone shout:*

"Brothers and sisters, my text this morning is the 'Blackness of Blackness.'"

And a congregation of voices answered: "That blackness is most black, brother, most black . . ."

"In the beginning . . ."

"At the very start," they cried.

". . . there was blackness . . ."

"Preach it . . ."

". . . and the sun . . ."

"The sun, Lawd . . ."

". . . was bloody red . . ."

"Red . . ."

"Now black is . . ." the preacher shouted.

"Bloody . . ."

"I said black is . . ."

"Preach it, brother . . ."

". . . an' black ain't . . ."

"Red, Lawd, red: He said it's red!"

"Amen, brother . . ."

"Black will git you . . ."

"Yes, it will . . ."

"Yes, it will . . ."

". . . an' black won't . . ."

"Naw, it won't!"

"It do . . ."

"It do, Lawd . . ."

". . . an' it don't."

"Halleluiah . . ."

". . . It'll put you, glory, glory, Oh my Lawd, in the WHALE'S BELLY.*"*

"Preach it, dear brother . . ."

". . . an' make you tempt . . ."

"Good God a-mighty!"

"Old Aunt Nelly!"

"Black will make you . . ."

"Black . . ."

". . . or black will un-make you."

"Ain't it the truth, Lawd?"

And at that point a voice of trombone timbre screamed at me, "Git out of here, you fool! Is you ready to commit treason?"

And I tore myself away, hearing the old singer of spirituals moaning, "Go curse your God, boy, and die."

I stopped and questioned her, asked her what was wrong.

"I dearly loved my master, son," she said.

"You should have hated him," I said.

"He gave me several sons," she said, "and because I loved my sons I learned to love their father though I hated him too."

"I too have become acquainted with ambivalence," I said. "That's why I'm here."

"What's that?"

"Nothing, a word that doesn't explain it. Why do you moan?"

"I moan this way 'cause he's dead," she said.

"Then tell me, who is that laughing upstairs?"

"Them's my sons. They glad."

"Yes, I can understand that too," I said.

"I laughs too, but I moans too. He promised to set us free but he never could bring hisself to do it. Still I loved him . . ."

"Loved him? You mean . . . ?"

"Oh yes, but I loved something else even more."

"What more?"

"Freedom."

"Freedom," I said. "Maybe freedom lies in hating."

"Naw, son, it's in loving. I loved him and give him the poison and he withered away like a frost-bit apple. Them boys woulda tore him to pieces with they homemade knives."

"A mistake was made somewhere," I said, "I'm confused." And I wished to say other things, but the laughter upstairs became too loud and moan-like for me and I tried to break out of it, but I couldn't. Just as I was leaving I felt an urgent desire to ask her what freedom was and went back. She sat with her head in her hands, moaning softly; her leather-brown face was filled with sadness.

"Old woman, what is this freedom you love so well?" I asked around a corner of my mind.

She looked surprised, then thoughtful, then baffled. "I done forgot, son. It's all mixed up. First I think it's one thing, then I think it's another. It gits my head to spinning. I guess now it ain't nothing but knowing how to say what I got up in my head. But it's a hard job, son. Too much is done happen to me in too short a time. Hit's like I have a fever. Ever' time I starts to walk my head gits to swirling and I falls down. Or if it ain't that, it's the boys; they gits to laughing and wants to kill up the white folks. They's bitter, that's what they is . . ."

"But what about freedom?"

"Leave me 'lone, boy; my head aches!"

I left her, feeling dizzy myself. I didn't get far.

Suddenly one of the sons, a big fellow six feet tall, appeared out of nowhere and struck me with his fist.

"What's the matter, man?" I cried.

"You made Ma cry!"

"But how?" I said, dodging a blow.

"Askin' her them questions, that's how. Git outa here and stay, and next time you got questions like that, ask yourself!"

He held me in a grip like cold stone, his fingers fastening upon my windpipe until I thought I would suffocate before he finally allowed me to go. I stumbled about dazed, the music beating hysterically in my ears. It was dark. My head cleared and I wandered down a dark narrow passage, thinking I heard his footsteps hurrying behind me. I was sore, and into my being had come a profound craving for tranquility, for peace and quiet, a state I felt I could never achieve. For one thing, the trumpet was blaring and the rhythm was too hectic. A tom-tom beating like heart-thuds began drowning out the trumpet, filling my ears. I longed for water and I heard it rushing through the cold mains my fingers touched as I felt my way, but I couldn't stop to search because of the footsteps behind me.

"Hey, Ras," I called. "Is it you, Destroyer? Rinehart?"

No answer, only the rhythmic footsteps behind me. Once I tried crossing the road, but a speeding machine struck me, scraping the skin from my leg as it roared past.

Then somehow I came out of it, ascending hastily from this underworld of sound to hear Louis Armstrong innocently asking,

What did I do
To be so black
And blue?

At first I was afraid; this familiar music had demanded action, the kind of which I was incapable, and yet had I lingered there beneath the surface I might have attempted to act. Nevertheless, I know now that few really listen to this music. I sat on the chair's edge in a soaking sweat, as though each of my 1,369 bulbs had everyone become a klieg light in an individual setting for a third degree with Ras and Rinehart in charge. It was exhausting—as though I had held my breath continuously for an hour under the terrifying serenity that comes from days of intense hunger. And yet, it was a strangely satisfying experience for an invisible man to hear the silence of sound. I had discovered unrecognized compulsions of my being—even though I could not answer "yes" to their promptings. I haven't smoked a reefer since, however; not because they're illegal, but because to *see* around corners is enough (that is not unusual when you are invisible). But to hear around them is too much; it inhibits action. And despite Brother Jack and all that sad, lost period of the Brotherhood, I believe in nothing if not in action.

Please, a definition: A hibernation is a covert preparation for a more overt action.

Besides, the drug destroys one's sense of time completely. If that happened, I might forget to dodge some bright morning and some cluck would run me down with an orange and yellow street car, or a bilious bus! Or I might forget to leave my hole when the moment for action presents itself.

Meanwhile I enjoy my life with the compliments of Monopolated Light & Power. Since you never recognize me even when in closest contact with me, and since, no doubt, you'll hardly believe that I exist, it won't matter if you know that I tapped a power line leading into the building and ran it into my hole in the ground. Before that I lived in the darkness into which I was chased, but now I see. I've illuminated the blackness of my invisibility—and vice versa. And so I play the invisible music of my isolation. The last statement doesn't seem just right, does it? But it is; you hear this music simply because music is heard and seldom seen, except by musicians. Could this compulsion to put invisibility down in black and white be thus an urge to make music of invisibility? But I am an orator, a rabble rouser—Am? I *was,* and perhaps shall be again. Who knows? All sickness is not unto death, neither is invisibility.

I can hear you say, "What a horrible, irresponsible bastard!" And you're right. I leap to agree with you. I am one of the most irresponsible beings that ever lived. Irresponsibility is part of my invisibility; any way you face it, it is a denial. But to whom can I be responsible, and why should I be, when you refuse to see me? And wait until I reveal how truly irresponsible I am. Responsibility rests upon recognition, and recognition is a form of agreement. Take the man whom I almost killed: Who was responsible for that near murder—I? I don't think so, and I refuse it. I won't buy it. You can't give it to me. *He* bumped *me, he* insulted *me.* Shouldn't he, for his own personal safety, have recognized my hysteria, my "danger potential"? He, let us say, was lost in a dream world. But didn't *he* control that dream world—which, alas, is only too real!—and didn't *he* rule me out of it? And if he had yelled for a policeman, wouldn't *I* have been taken for the offending one? Yes, yes, yes! Let me agree with you, I was the irresponsible one; for I should have used my knife to protect the higher interests of society. Some day that kind of foolishness will cause us tragic trouble. All dreamers and sleepwalkers must pay the price, and even the invisible victim is responsible for the fate of all. But I shirked that responsibility; I became too snarled in the incompatible notions that buzzed within my brain. I was a coward...

But what did *I* do to be so blue? Bear with me.

COMMENTS AND QUESTIONS

1. In a satire titled *Black No More,* George Schuyler, a Harlem Renaissance novelist, conceived of a plot in which the "Negro Problem" was solved by "electrical nutrition," a process that changed the texture of the hair, the skin color, and other facial features of black people, thereby making them all white. Douglas Turner Ward's *Day of Absence* is a play about the same subject: the disappearance of blacks from a Southern town. Is the disappearance and resulting "invisibility" of African Americans by means of assimilation, isolation, or destruction an event that may one day come to pass?
2. The protagonist acknowledges that he is in hiding, but describes his state as "hibernation." What type of life do you foresee for him after his state of hibernation?
3. In what sense is the protagonist's dilemma an "existential" one? How would Sartre analyze it?
4. The Prologue to *Invisible Man* clearly employs the blues motif. What role, if any, does jazz play?

FERNANDO ARRABAL

Picnic on the Battlefield

CHARACTERS

ZAPO, *a soldier*
MONSIEUR TÉPAN, *the soldier's father*
MADAME TÉPAN, *the soldier's mother*
ZÉPO, *an enemy soldier*
FIRST CORPSMAN
SECOND CORPSMAN

THE SCENE. *A battlefield. Barbed wire stretches from one end of the stage to the other, with sandbags piled against it. Battle is in full swing. We hear bombs bursting, rifle shots and machine-gun fire.*

Alone on stage, hidden flat on his belly among the sandbags, ZAPO *is very frightened.*

The fighting stops. Silence.

From a knitting-bag, ZAPO *takes out a ball of wool, knitting needles, and starts knitting a sweater that is already quite well along. The field telephone beside him suddenly rings.*

ZAPO Hello... hello... yes, sir, Captain.... Yes, this is the sentry in Section 47.... Nothing new, Captain.... Excuse me, Captain, when are we going to start fighting again?... and what am I supposed to do with the grenades? Should I send them on up front or to the rear?... Don't get annoyed, I didn't say that to upset you.... And, Captain, I'm really feeling pretty lonesome. Couldn't you send me a companion out here?... Even the goat. (*Evidently the Captain gives him a good dressing down.*) Yes sir, Captain, yes sir! (ZAPO *hangs up. We hear him grumbling to himself. Silence.*)

(*Enter* MONSIEUR *and* MADAME TÉPAN, *carrying baskets as though they are off on a picnic. Their son, who is sitting with his back turned, does not see them arriving.*)

M. TÉPAN (*ceremoniously*) My boy, get up and kiss your mother on the forehead.

(*Taken by surprise,* ZAPO *gets up and, with a great deal of respect, gives his mother a kiss on the forehead. He is about to speak, but his father beats him to it.*)

Now give *me* a kiss.

ZAPO My dear sweet parents, how did you ever dare come all the way out to a dangerous spot like this? You must leave here right away.

M. TÉPAN Are you trying to tell your father what war and danger are all about? For me, all this is only a game. How many times do you think I've jumped off the subway while it was still moving?

MME TÉPAN We thought you were probably bored, so we came to pay you a little visit. After all, this war business must get pretty tiresome.

ZAPO It all depends.

M. TÉPAN I know perfectly well what goes on. In the beginning it's all new and exciting. You enjoy the killing and throwing grenades and wearing a helmet; it's quite the thing, but you end up bored as hell. In my day, you'd have really seen something. Wars were a lot livelier, much more colorful. And then best of all, there were horses, lots of horses. It was real pleasure: If the Captain said "Attack!" before you could shake a stick we were all assembled on horseback in our red uniforms. That was something to see. And then we'd go galloping forward, sword in hand, and suddenly find ourselves hard against the enemy. And they'd be at their finest too, with their horses—there were always loads and loads of beautifully round-bottomed horses and their polished boots, and their green uniforms.

MME TÉPAN No, the enemy uniform wasn't green. It was blue. I remember perfectly well it was blue.

M. TÉPAN And I say it was green.

MME TÉPAN When I was little I went out on the balcony any number of times to watch the battle, and I'd say to the little boy next door, "I'll bet you a gumdrop the Blues win." And the Blues were our enemies.

M. TÉPAN All right, so you win.

MME TÉPAN I always loved battles. When I was little, I always said that when I grew up I wanted to be a Colonel in the Dragoons. But Mama didn't want me to. You know what a stickler she is.

M. TÉPAN Your mother's a real nincompoop.

ZAPO Forgive me, but you've got to leave. You can't go walking into a war when you're not a soldier.

M. TÉPAN I don't give a damn. We're here to have a picnic with you in the country and spend a nice Sunday.

MME TÉPAN I even made a lovely meal. Sausage, hard-boiled eggs, I know how much you like them! Ham sandwiches, red wine, some salad and some little cakes.

ZAPO O.K., we'll do whatever you say. But if the Captain comes along he'll throw a fit. Plus the fact that he doesn't go for the idea of visiting the battlefront. He keeps telling us: "War calls for discipline and grenades, but no visits."

M. TÉPAN Don't you worry about it, I'll have a few words with your Captain.

ZAPO And what if we have to start fighting again?

M. TÉPAN You think that scares me, I've seen worse. Now if it was only cavalry battles! Times have changed, that's something you don't understand. (*A pause.*) We came on motorcycle. Nobody said anything.

ZAPO They probably thought you were arbitrators.

M. TÉPAN We did have some trouble getting through, though. With all those jeeps and tanks.

MME TÉPAN And the very minute we arrived, you remember that bottleneck because of the cannon?

M. TÉPAN During wartime, you've got to be prepared for anything. Everybody knows that.

MME TÉPAN Well now, we're ready to start eating.

M. TÉPAN Right you are, I could eat a horse. It's the smell of gunpowder that does it.

MME TÉPAN We'll eat sitting down on the blanket.

ZAPO All right to eat with my rifle?

MME TÉPAN Let your rifle alone. It's bad manners to bring your rifle to the table. (*A pause.*) Why, child, you're filthy as a little pig. How did you manage to get in such a mess? Let's see your hands.

ZAPO (*Ashamed, he shows them.*) I had to crawl along the ground during maneuvers.

MME TÉPAN How about your ears?

ZAPO I washed them this morning.

MME TÉPAN That should do then. Now how about your teeth? (*He shows them.*) Very good. Now who's going to give his little boy a great big kiss for brushing his teeth so nicely? (*To her husband.*) Well, give your son a kiss for brushing his teeth so nicely. (M. TÉPAN *gives his son a kiss.*) Because, you know, one thing I just won't allow is not washing, and blaming it on the war.

ZAPO Yes, Mama.

(*They eat.*)

M. TÉPAN Well, my boy, have you been keeping up a good shooting score?

ZAPO When?

M. TÉPAN Why, the last few days.

ZAPO Where?

M. TÉPAN Right here and now. After all, you *are* fighting a war.

ZAPO No, no great shakes. I haven't kept up a very good score. Practically no bull's-eyes.

M. TÉPAN Well, what have you been scoring best with in your shooting, enemy horses or soldiers?

ZAPO No, no horses. There aren't any horses any more.

M. TÉPAN Well, soldiers then?

ZAPO Could be.

M. TÉPAN Could be? Aren't you sure?

ZAPO It's just that I . . . I fire without taking aim (*a pause*) and when I fire I say an *Our Father* for the guy I shot.

M. TÉPAN You've got to show more courage. Like your father.

MME TÉPAN I'm going to put a record on the phonograph. (*She puts on a record: a Spanish pasodoble. Sitting on the ground, they all three listen.*)

M. TÉPAN Now that's real music. Yes, ma'am. I tell you. *Olé!*

(*As the music continues, an enemy soldier,* ZÉPO, *enters. He is dressed like* ZAPO. *Only the color of his uniform is different.* ZÉPO *wears green;* ZAPO *wears gray. Standing unseen behind the family, his mouth agape,* ZÉPO *listens to the music. The record comes to an end.* ZAPO, *getting up, spots* ZÉPO. *Both raise their hands in the air, while* M. *and* MME TÉPAN *look at them startled.*)

M. TÉPAN What's going on?

(ZAPO *seems about to act, but hesitates. Then, very decisively, he points his rifle at* ZÉPO.)

ZAPO Hands up!

(ZÉPO, *more terrified than ever, raises his hands still higher.* ZAPO *doesn't know what to do. All of a sudden, he hurriedly runs toward* ZÉPO *and taps him gently on the shoulder, saying*)

ZAPO You're it! (*Pleased as punch, to his father.*) There you are! A prisoner!

M. TÉPAN That's fine. Now what are you going to do with him?

ZAPO I don't know. But could be they'll make me a corporal.

M. TÉPAN In the meantime, tie him up.

ZAPO Tie him up? What for?

M. TÉPAN That's what you do with prisoners, you tie 'em up!

ZAPO How?

M. TÉPAN By his hands.

MME TÉPAN Oh yes, you've definitely got to tie his hands. That's the way I've always seen it done.

ZAPO All right. (*To the prisoner.*) Please put your hands together.

ZÉPO Don't do it too hard.

ZAPO Oh, no.

ZÉPO Ouch! You're hurting me.

M. TÉPAN Come on now, don't mistreat your prisoner.

MME TÉPAN Is that the way I brought you up? Haven't I told you over and over again that you've got to be considerate of your fellow man?

ZAPO I didn't do it on purpose. (*To* ZÉPO.) Does it hurt the way it is now?

ZÉPO No, like this it doesn't hurt.

M. TÉPAN Speak right up and tell him if it does. Just pretend we're not here.

ZÉPO This way it's O.K.

M. TÉPAN Now his feet.

ZAPO His feet too? How long does this go on?

M. TÉPAN Didn't they teach you the rules?

ZAPO Sure.

M. TÉPAN Well?

ZAPO (*to* ZÉPO, *very politely*) Would you kindly be good enough to please sit down on the ground?

ZÉPO All right, but don't hurt me.

MME TÉPAN See! Now he's taking a dislike to you.

ZAPO No. No he's not. I'm not hurting you, am I?

ZÉPO No, this is fine.

ZAPO (*out of nowhere*) Papa, suppose you took a snapshot with the prisoner down there on the ground and me standing with my foot on his stomach?

M. TÉPAN Say, yes! That'll look classy.

ZÉPO Oh, no you don't. Not that!

MME TÉPAN Let him. Don't be so stubborn.

ZÉPO No. I said no and mean no.

MME TÉPAN Just a little old snip of a snapshot. What difference could that possibly make to you? Then we could put it in the dining room right next to the Lifesaving Certificate my husband got thirteen years ago.

ZÉPO No, you'll never talk me into it.

ZAPO But why should you refuse?

ZÉPO I've got a fiancée. And if she ever sees the snapshot, she'll say I don't know how to fight a war.

ZAPO No, all you have to do is tell her it isn't you at all, it's a panther.

MME TÉPAN C'mon, say yes.

ZÉPO All right, but I'm only doing it to please you.

ZAPO Stretch all the way out.

(ZÉPO *stretches all the way out.* ZAPO *puts one foot on his stomach and grabs his rifle with a military air.*)

MME TÉPAN Throw your chest out more.

ZAPO Like this?

MME TÉPAN Yes, that's it. Don't breathe.

M. TÉPAN Make like a hero.

ZAPO How do you mean a hero, like this?

M. TÉPAN It's a cinch. Make like the butcher when he was telling us what a lady-killer he is.

ZAPO Like so?

M. TÉPAN Yes, that's it.

MME TÉPAN Just be sure your chest is puffed way out, and don't breathe.

ZÉPO Are you about finished?

M. TÉPAN Have a little patience. One . . . two . . . three.

ZAPO I hope I'll come out all right.

MME TÉPAN Oh yes, you looked very military.

M. TÉPAN You were fine.

MME TÉPAN That makes me want to have my picture taken, too.

M. TÉPAN Now there's a good idea.

ZAPO All right. I'll take it if you want me to.

MME TÉPAN Give me your helmet so I'll look like a soldier.

ZÉPO I don't want any more pictures. Even one was too much.

ZAPO Don't feel that way. Come right down to it, what difference could it make?

ZÉPO That's my final say.

M. TÉPAN (*to his wife*) Don't push him. Prisoners are always very touchy. If we keep it up, he'll get mad and spoil all our fun.

ZAPO Well now, what are we going to do with him?

MME TÉPAN We could ask him to eat with us. What do you think?

M. TÉPAN I don't see any reason why not.

ZAPO (*to* ZÉPO) All right then, how'd you like to eat with us?

ZÉPO Uh...

M. TÉPAN We brought along a nice bottle of wine.

ZÉPO Well, in that case O.K.

MME TÉPAN Make yourself right at home. Don't be afraid to ask for things.

ZÉPO Fine.

M. TÉPAN Well now, how about you, have you been keeping up a good shooting score?

ZÉPO When?

M. TÉPAN Why, the last few days.

ZÉPO Where?

M. TÉPAN Right here and now. After all, you *are* fighting a war.

ZÉPO No, no great shakes. I haven't kept up a very good score. Practically no bull's-eyes.

M. TÉPAN Well, what have you been scoring best with in your shooting, enemy horses or soldiers?

ZÉPO No, no horses. There aren't any horses any more.

M. TÉPAN Well, soldiers then?

ZÉPO Could be.

M. TÉPAN Could be? Aren't you sure?

ZÉPO It's just that I...I fire without taking aim (*a pause*) and when I fire I say a *Hail Mary* for the guy I shot.

ZAPO A *Hail Mary?* I'd have thought you'd say an *Our Father.*

M. TÉPAN Come, my boy, you have to be courageous.

ZÉPO No. Always a *Hail Mary.* (*A pause.*) It's shorter.

MME TÉPAN (*to* ZÉPO) If you like, we can untie you.

ZÉPO No, leave me this way. It doesn't matter.

M. TÉPAN You're not going to start putting on airs with us? If you want us to untie you, just say the word.

MME TÉPAN Please feel free.

ZÉPO Well, if you really mean it, untie my feet. But it's just to please you people.

M. TÉPAN Zapo, untie him.

(ZAPO *unties him.*)

MME TÉPAN Well now, feel better?

ZÉPO Sure do. But listen, maybe I'm causing you too much trouble.

M. TÉPAN Not at all. Make yourself right at home. And if you want us to undo your hands, just say so.

ZÉPO No, not my hands, too. I don't want to overdo it.

M. TÉPAN Not at all, my boy, not at all. I tell you, you don't disturb us one bit.

ZÉPO All right, go ahead and untie my hands then. But just while we eat, huh? I don't want you to think when you give me an inch I'm going to take a mile.

M. TÉPAN Untie his hands, sonny.

MME TÉPAN Well, since our honorable prisoner is so nice, we're going to have a lovely day here in the country.

ZÉPO Don't call me "honorable" prisoner. Just say "prisoner" plain and simple.

MME TÉPAN You're sure that won't make you feel bad?

ZÉPO No, not at all.

M. TÉPAN Well, you're certainly unpretentious, anyway.

(*Sound of airplanes.*)

ZAPO Airplanes. They're going to bomb us for sure.

(ZAPO *and* ZÉPO *dive for the sandbags and hide.*)

ZAPO (*to his parents*) Run for cover! The bombs are going to land right on you.

(*The sound of the planes drowns out everything. Immediately bombs start falling. Shells explode nearby. Deafening racket.* ZAPO *and* ZÉPO *are crouching among the sandbags.* M. TÉPAN *goes on calmly talking to his wife, who answers him with equal calm. Because of the bombardment we cannot hear their conversation.*

MME TÉPAN *heads for one of the picnic baskets, from which she takes an umbrella. She opens it. The* TÉPANS *take shelter under the umbrella as though it were raining. Standing there, they shift from one foot to the other, in rhythm, all the while discussing personal matters. The bombardment continues. At last, the airplanes take off. Silence.*

M. TÉPAN *stretches one arm out from under the umbrella to make certain there is no longer anything coming down from the sky.*)

M. TÉPAN You can close your umbrella now.

(MME TÉPAN *closes it. Together they go over to their son and prod him on the behind a couple of times with the umbrella.*)

M. TÉPAN All right, come on out. The bombing's over.

(ZAPO *and* ZÉPO *come out of their hiding place.*)

ZAPO They didn't get you?

M. TÉPAN You don't expect anything to happen to your father, do you? (*Proudly.*) Little bombs like that? Don't make me laugh.

(*From the left, a pair of Red Cross* CORPSMEN *enter, carrying a stretcher.*)

FIRST CORPSMAN Any bodies?

ZAPO No, none here.

FIRST CORPSMAN You're sure you took a good look?

ZAPO Absolutely.

FIRST CORPSMAN And there's not one single body?

ZAPO Didn't I just say so?

FIRST CORPSMAN Not even someone wounded?

ZAPO Not even.

SECOND CORPSMAN Well, we're really up the creek! (*To* ZAPO, *persuasively.*) Take a good look all around here, see if you don't turn up a stiff someplace.

FIRST CORPSMAN Don't press the issue. They told you once and for all there aren't any.

SECOND CORPSMAN What a lousy deal!

ZAPO I'm really very sorry. I swear I didn't plan it that way.

SECOND CORPSMAN That's what they all say. That there aren't any corpses, and that they didn't plan it that way.

FIRST CORPSMAN So let the man alone!

M. TÉPAN (*obligingly*) If we can help you at all, we'd be delighted to. At your service.

SECOND CORPSMAN Well, I don't know. If we keep on like this, I really don't know what the Captain's going to say to us.

M. TÉPAN What seems to be the trouble?

SECOND CORPSMAN Just that the others are all getting sore wrists carrying out the dead and wounded, while we still haven't come up with anything? And it's not because we haven't been looking.

M. TÉPAN I see. That really is a bore. (*To* ZAPO.) You're quite sure there are no corpses?

ZAPO Obviously, Papa.

M. TÉPAN You looked under the sandbags?

ZAPO Yes, Papa.

M. TÉPAN (*angrily*) Why don't you come right out and say you don't want to have any part in helping these good gentlemen?

FIRST CORPSMAN Don't jump on him like that. Leave him alone. We'll just hope we have better luck in some other trench where maybe everybody'll be dead.

M. TÉPAN I'd be delighted for you.

MME TÉPAN So would I. Nothing pleases me more than to see people who take their work seriously.

M. TÉPAN (*indignantly, to anyone within hearing*) Well, isn't anyone going to do anything for these gentlemen?

ZAPO If it was up to me, it'd be good as done.

ZÉPO Same here.

M. TÉPAN Look here now, isn't one of you at least wounded?

ZAPO (*ashamed*) No, not me.

M. TÉPAN (*to* ZÉPO) What about you?

ZÉPO (*ashamed*) Me either. I never was lucky.

MME TÉPAN (*delighted*) I just remembered! This morning, while I was peeling onions, I cut my finger. How's that?

M. TÉPAN Why of course! (*Really in the swing of things.*) They'll put you on the stretcher and carry you right off!

FIRST CORPSMAN Sorry, it's no good. Women don't count.

M. TÉPAN Well, that didn't get us anywhere.

FIRST CORPSMAN It doesn't matter.

SECOND CORPSMAN Maybe we can get our fill in the other trenches. (*They start to go off.*)

M. TÉPAN Don't you worry, if we find a corpse we'll hang onto it for you. There's not a chance we'd give it to anybody but you.

SECOND CORPSMAN Thank you very much, sir.

M. TÉPAN It's nothing, my boy. It's the very least I could do.

(*The* CORPSMEN *make their goodbyes. All four of the others reply in kind. The* CORPSMEN *exit.*)

MME TÉPAN That's what's so pleasant about spending Sunday out in the battlefield. You always run into such nice folks. (*A pause.*) Come to think of it, why is it you're enemies?

ZÉPO I don't know. I'm not too well educated.

MME TÉPAN I mean is it from birth, or did you become enemies after?

ZÉPO I don't know. I don't know a thing about it.

M. TÉPAN Well then, how did you come to go to war?

ZÉPO One day I was home fixing my mother's iron and a man came by and said to me: "Are you Zépo?" ... "Yes." ... "Good, you've got to go to war." So I asked him, "What war?" And he said to me: "Don't you read the newspapers? You are a hick!" So I told him yes I did, but not all that war stuff...

ZAPO That's just what happened to me; exactly what happened to me.

M. TÉPAN Sure, they came after you, too.

MME TÉPAN No, it's not the same. You weren't fixing the iron that day, you were repairing the car.

M. TÉPAN I was talking about the rest of it. (*To* ZÉPO.) Go on. Then what happened?

ZÉPO Well, then I told him that I had a fiancée, and if I didn't take her to the movies on Sunday, she wouldn't know what to do with herself. He said that that didn't matter.

ZAPO Same as me. Exactly the same as me.

ZÉPO Well, then my father came down and he said I couldn't go to war because I didn't have a horse.

ZAPO Like my father said.

ZÉPO The man said they didn't use horses any more, and I asked him if I could take along my fiancée. He said no. Then I asked him could I take along my aunt to make me custard every Thursday. I like custard.

MME TÉPAN (*realizing that she has forgotten something*) Oh! The custard!

ZÉPO Again he said no.

ZAPO The way he did to me.

ZÉPO And ever since then, here I am, nearly always all alone in the trench here.

MME TÉPAN As long as you're so much alike, and both so bored, I think you and your honorable prisoner might play together this afternoon.

ZAPO Oh no, Mama! I'm too scared. He's an enemy.

M. TÉPAN Oh come on now, don't be scared.

ZAPO If you knew what the general told us about the enemy.

MME TÉPAN What did he tell you?

ZAPO He said the enemy soldiers are very mean. When they take prisoners, they put pebbles in their socks so it hurts when they walk.

MME TÉPAN How horrible! What savages!

M. TÉPAN (*indignantly, to* ZÉPO) Aren't you ashamed to be part of an army of criminals?

ZÉPO I didn't do anything. I'm not mad at anybody.

MME TÉPAN He's trying to put one over on us, acting like a little saint.

M. TÉPAN We should never have untied him. Probably all we have to do is have our backs turned for him to go putting pebbles in our socks.

ZÉPO Don't be so mean to me.

M. TÉPAN How do you expect us to be? I'm shocked. I know just what I'm going to do. I'm going to find the Captain and ask him to let me go into battle.

ZAPO He won't let you. You're too old.

M. TÉPAN Well then I'll go buy a horse and a saber and I'll go to war on my own.

ZÉPO Please, madame, don't treat me like this. Besides, I was just going to tell you, *our* general said the same thing about you people.

MME TÉPAN How could he dare tell such a lie?

ZAPO The very same thing, honest?

ZÉPO Yes, the very same thing.

M. TÉPAN Maybe it's the same one who talked to both of you.

MME TÉPAN Well, if it is the same general, the least he could do is use a different speech. Imagine telling everybody the same thing.

M. TÉPAN (*to* ZÉPO, *changing his tone*) Can I fill your glass again?

MME TÉPAN I hope you enjoyed our little lunch.

M. TÉPAN It was better than Sunday, anyway.

ZÉPO What happened then?

M. TÉPAN Well, we went out to the country and laid all our chow out on the blanket. While we had our backs turned, a cow came along and ate the whole lunch, including the napkins.

ZÉPO What a glutton, that cow!

M. TÉPAN Yes, but then to get even, we ate the cow.

(*They laugh.*)

ZAPO (*to* ZÉPO) I bet they weren't hungry after that.

M. TÉPAN To your health!

(*They all drink.*)

MME TÉPAN (*to* ZÉPO) Tell me something, what do you do for amusement in the trenches?

ZÉPO Just to pass the time and keep myself amused, I take odds and ends of rags and make little flowers out of them. See, I get bored a lot.

MME TÉPAN And what do you do with these rag flowers?

ZÉPO At first I used to send them to my fiancée, but one day she told me that the cellar and the greenhouse were already filled with them, that she didn't know what to do with them any more, and would I mind sending her something else for a change?

MME TÉPAN And what did you do?

ZÉPO I tried learning something else, but I couldn't do it. So, to pass the time, I just go on making my rag flowers.

MME TÉPAN And then do you throw them away?

ZÉPO No, now I've found a way to make use of them: I furnish one flower for each of my buddies who dies. That way, I know that even if I make a whole lot, there'll never be enough.

M. TÉPAN You found a good way out.

ZÉPO (*timidly*) Yes.

ZAPO Well, you know what I do so's not to get bored is knit.

MME TÉPAN But tell me, do all the soldiers get bored the way you two do?

ZÉPO That depends on what they do for relaxation.

ZAPO Same thing over on our side.

M. TÉPAN Well then, let's stop the war.

ZÉPO But how?

M. TÉPAN Very easy. You tell your buddies that the enemy doesn't want to fight, and you tell the same thing to your comrades. And everybody goes home.

ZAPO Terrific.

MME TÉPAN That way you can finish fixing the iron.

ZAPO How come nobody ever thought of that before?

MME TÉPAN It takes your father to come up with ideas like that. Don't forget he's a Normal School graduate, and a philatelist, too.

ZÉPO But what will all the field-marshals and the corporals do?

M. TÉPAN We'll give 'em guitars and castanets to keep 'em quiet.

ZÉPO Excellent idea.

M. TÉPAN See how easy it is? It's all settled.

ZÉPO We'll wow 'em.

ZAPO Boy, will my buddies be glad!

MME TÉPAN What do you say we celebrate and put on that pasodoble we were listening to before?

ZÉPO Wonderful!

ZAPO Yes, put on the record, Mama.

(MME TÉPAN *puts on the record. She winds the phonograph and waits. Not a sound is heard.*)

M. TÉPAN You can't hear anything.

MME TÉPAN (*going to the phonograph*) Oh! . . . I made a boo-boo! Instead of putting on a record, I put on a beret.

(*She puts the record on. A lively pasodoble is heard.* ZAPO *dances with* ZÉPO; MME TÉPAN *with her husband.*

The field telephone rings. None of the group hears it. They go on dancing in a lively manner.

The phone rings again. The dancing continues. Battle breaks out once more with a great din of bombs, rifle fire, and the crackle of machine-guns. Having noticed nothing, the two couples keep on dancing gaily.

A sudden machine-gun blast mows them all down. They fall to the ground, stone dead. One bullet seems to have nicked the phonograph: the music keeps repeating the same strain over and over, like a record with a scratch in it. We hear this repeated strain for the remainder of the play.

From the left, the two CORPSMEN *enter, carrying the empty stretcher.*)

FAST CURTAIN

QUESTIONS

1. Describe the characters in the play. How developed are they? To what extent are you as reader/spectator involved with them?
2. How are the similarities between Zapo and Zépo brought out? What is the effect of this?
3. How does Mr. Tépan's "idea" come about?
4. Is the comic tone maintained throughout or does the play ever become serious?
5. What is your opinion of the ending?
6. Does "theater of the absurd" seem an apt description of this play? Why or why not?

35

Toward a Postmodern Culture

To define trends while they are still occurring is a particularly risky enterprise, especially when one is trying to characterize the direction in which a whole society is moving. Nonetheless, the consistency with which contemporary thinkers tend to characterize recent decades gives some assurance that they are on the right track. These thinkers commonly speak of our age as one of postindustrialism, postmodernism, posthumanism, and the like—language suggesting an awareness that a significant period of historical time has ended but that no label for the present age as yet seems adequate. The *age of the computer,* the *electronic age,* the *television age,* and the *nuclear age* have been suggested, but none of these seems comprehensive enough. This final chapter endeavors to give some outline to the shape of the new age.

From the 1960s into the 1990s

America's large-scale involvement in Vietnam, beginning in 1964 and lasting until the recall of troops in 1972, marked a watershed in the political life of the United States. In a sense fought daily on the evening-news television screen, the Vietnam War was for the U.S. government as much a battle for citizens' support as it was a struggle against the Viet Cong and the North Vietnamese. Secret invasions, exaggerated body counts, claims of winning belied repeatedly by striking enemy victories, and beneath these phenomena the burning issue of whether American troops ought to be engaged in such a war at all—all this evoked a degree of protest unknown in American history since the Civil War. With the protests came the countercharges regarding the motives of the protesters and the effect of demonstrations on the course of the war. Many feared that the United States was losing the basic consensus needed to keep a political body alive. Protests directed against the war in many cases developed into a critique of the entire fabric of American society. The "counterculture" attracted more and more of the disaffected young, many of whom lost faith in all the basic institutions of society—government, family, church, and work.

The humiliation in 1973 of the president who had become closely associated with the war served perhaps to help America close the book on one of the most politically disruptive periods in its history, but the shock of the great oil shortage in the winter of 1973–1974 made Americans painfully aware again that they could no longer control the world and that a group of Middle Eastern powers could, if they wished, bring the country to economic ruin. As a whole, the decade of the 1970s was a period of renewed talk of the "decline of the West" and of skepticism about the ability of political leaders to make more than superficial improvements in society. The 1970s were also the decade that Tom Wolfe characterized as that of the "me generation," with the attentions of the young and the not-so-young turned less toward revolutionizing society than toward self-fulfillment by means of encounter groups, yoga, charismatic and other nonmainstream religions, or by freewheeling life-styles, drugs, and sexual liberation. The considerable expansion of the women's movement and the gay liberation movement, however, brought out the links between the personal and the political.

American optimism reasserted itself in the 1980s, choosing to overlook a rapidly increasing national debt, an enormous trade imbalance, and the onslaught of foreign investors eager to buy up American assets. Until the last part of the decade, moreover, the effects of these factors on the daily life of most Americans were almost imperceptible. On the other hand, the Reagan administration's policy of low taxes, a minimal inflation rate, and a buoyant stock market created something of a capitalistic idyll. The counterparts of the 1980s to the hippies of the 1960s were the yuppies—young men and women whose goals in life consisted of a pursuit of financial well-being and the latest physical comforts. Nevertheless, the drastic fall in the stock market in October 1987 chastened investor optimism while the country increasingly confirmed its status as the world's biggest debtor nation.

The early 1990s witnessed the onset of an economic recession accompanied by widespread unemployment among white-collar as well as blue-collar workers and a serious loss of consumer confidence. For the first time in history Americans were coming to believe that the next generation would not enjoy the prosperity enjoyed by their parents. Traditional means of intervention by the federal government to reverse economic trends through work projects were seriously hampered by fear of augmenting a federal budget already of colossal proportions. Whatever action public powers took to engineer economic recovery in the short run, all agreed that in the final analysis only a per capita increase in productivity could keep Americans' standard of living high. Key elements in any plan to achieve this long-term goal would involve greater investment in research and development and in a higher level of public education in general.

The 1980s and early 1990s witnessed a return of conservatism on many fronts and radical changes in others. Mainstream religions saw a rise in membership, but so did the "electronic church," at least until the discovery that some of its prominent leaders had been involved in sexual and financial scandals. The sudden and dramatic spread of the killer disease AIDS caused a serious reevaluation of the sexual revolution and the drug culture. Although we have not "gone back" to the 1950s—domestic arrangements now on the whole recognize more autonomy and equality for women—there has been a noticeable return to matrimony, monogamy, and the family. At the same time, human interventions in the reproductive process, such as artificial insemination, freezing embryos, "test-tube" babies, surrogate motherhood, and abortion, constantly force us to rethink ethical questions and the nature of the family. The nature of community, until only recently primarily defined in terms of neighborhood and family, must also be constantly redefined. With a plethora of information from all parts of the world more and more readily available through the electronic media of computers and television, our participation in what Marshall McLuhan twenty-five years ago called the "global village" has greatly expanded.

The New World Order

In 1989 the political system ruled by two superpowers, which had maintained an enduring, if unstable, international balance since the end of World War II, began rapidly to disintegrate. The next two years witnessed the reunification of Germany under democratic rule, the replacement of communist regimes by democratic ones in most of Eastern Europe, and then the breakup of the Soviet Union itself into fifteen independent republics, many of them established on an ethnic basis.

Despite the general euphoria that followed the death of communist regimes in the heartland of the European-Asian landmass, Western leaders were apprehensive. The old dual superpower arrangement had become institutionalized, and the two sides had established complex arrangements for preventing the outbreak of massive international conflict. On the other hand, no one could predict what shape the new world order would assume. Could the Eastern European republics and the fifteen states formed out of the USSR successfully adapt their economies to capitalism? Could ethnic and religious rivalries within and between the new states be kept under control? Would supervision of the vast Soviet nuclear arsenal be given to responsible authorities?

The United States emerged in the early 1990s as the single great superpower, yet its capacity for policing the world and supplying economic assistance abroad was severely limited by economic concerns and the disposition of its own people. At the same time, with the disappearance of the Soviet threat to Western Europe, American influence there diminished. Western Europeans, eager to create a more integrated union among themselves making them more competitive economically with and more politically independent of the United States, felt less need of America's protective umbrella. The soaring economic power of Japan, largely unburdened with military expenses, and Japanese penetration of American markets led Americans to question their government's priorities. If military power blocs were replaced by economic ones, how would the United States fare?

The "Other" Half

What relationship will leading economic areas such as Canada, Japan, Western Europe, and the United States, all in the Northern Hemisphere, have with their poorer neighbors to the south? By the early 1990s economic and demographic differences between the two hemispheres were becoming ever sharper. Whereas in much of Latin America, Africa, and southern Asia population was growing about 1.5 percent per year, populations in North America, Europe, and northern Asia barely reproduced themselves. In many areas of the Caribbean and Africa gross national products, rising in the 1960s and 1970s, have not only leveled off but, in some cases, fallen steeply.

Paradoxically, in an era of the "global village," the horizons of "have" nations seem to have narrowed to focus largely on domestic concerns. Granted, American interest in developing poorer nations since 1945 had been in part motivated by competition with the United States' military rival, the Soviet Union. Nevertheless, in the decades of great American prosperity after World War II, U.S. foreign policy reflected a genuine willingness on the part of Americans to share wealth with less fortunate countries. To what extent will this tendency to look inward continue and the gap between rich and poor nations widen?

Increasingly reluctant to fund ambitious projects for international development, the United States, however, has continued to reaffirm one of its greatest traditions, that of the "open door." The aftermath of the Vietnam War brought about an exodus of Southeast Asians, the "boat people," to the United States. So extensive was the influx that the racial balance in a number of America's cities was radically altered. As in the past, American society was prepared to absorb the costs of educating these new citizens in the expectation that they would add their talents to the common pool. More recently, the number of immigrants, both legal and illegal, from Mexico, Central and South America, and the Caribbean has also dramatically increased. Spanish is now the main language in several U.S. communities, and the question of the desirability of bilingual education (with Spanish and oriental languages the "second language") continues to be hotly debated. It is clear that American society is becoming more and more culturally pluralistic. With the rise in diverse ethnic groups has come an increased demand for social and economic justice and for recognition of cultural identity. Groups demanding greater rights and recognition include native Americans, African Americans, Hispanics, and Asian Americans.

The New Utopia?

With about one-fourth of the people of the planet, a billion Chinese, still living under a Marxist regime, communism cannot yet be written off. Nonetheless, despite survivals, the feasibility of embodying communist theories in a practical form of government has largely been discredited. Believers in the secular religion, committed to creating the perfect society on this earth, may defend their position by arguing that actual communist regimes failed to live up to Marxist ideals, but in all probability the future of Marxism lies largely in the theoretical domain as a methodology of social criticism.

In contrast with communism, liberal democracy has no religious pretensions. Indeed, it cannot, by definition. Pragmatic, theoretically committed to rational debate, majority rule, and strict separation between church and state, liberal democracy claims only to govern the limited area of human life that by common consent has been entrusted to public authority. Such an approach to political power intrinsically frustrates those with totalitarian views of society who wish to use government to integrate all aspects of society around specific goals.

The current rise of regimes with an Islamic orientation suggests that for many the fragmented authority endorsed by liberal democrats proves unsatisfactory. Beginning with the establishment of an Islamic regime in Iran in the 1970s, Islam as a political force has revived political passions in a vast area stretching from North Africa to Indonesia. Its doctrines have found adherents in the United States, especially among African and Arab Americans. Significantly, its most intense appeal is found among the populations of the extensive buffer areas lying between the Northern and Southern hemispheres. The degree to which Islamic utopianism will appeal to the downtrodden masses of the depressed south, instilling in them a spirit of cohesion against the economic and political domination of the north, remains a vital question.

Black Liberation

The most longstanding and perhaps most representative of the minority movements in the United States is the black liberation movement. It can be dated back to the slave revolts and the Civil War, but it has become an established, if diversified, force primarily in the years since World War II. In 1954, however, the decision of the Supreme Court in *Brown* v. *Board of Education of Topeka* that compulsory segregation in the public schools denied equal protection under the law marked the real beginning of an all-out struggle for equality in American society. Almost immediately, African Americans, impatient with the slow-moving court system, took matters into their own hands. In 1955, blacks in Montgomery, Alabama, under the leadership of Martin Luther King, Jr., boycotted a local bus line when a black woman, Rosa Parks, was arrested for refusing to give her seat to a white passenger. The ultimate success of the boycott showed the power that united action could produce, and succeeding years witnessed the organization of "sit-ins" and "freedom rides" throughout the South as well as protests in the North against the more subtle kind of segregation prevalent there. This phase of the civil rights movement was crowned with success by the passage of the Civil Rights Act of 1964, which had among its more important provisions the prohibition against segregation in public places and discrimination in employment. With this accomplished, King, by now the leading national figure in the movement, struck out at discrimination in voting rights, an effort that led up to the passage of the Voting Rights Act of 1965.

The middle years of the 1960s marked the rise of more militant black groups, led by people such as Stokely Carmichael and Floyd McKissick. Their slogan was "Black Power," which meant the creation of separate economic and social institutions as power bases for black communities. At the same time, these leaders expressed a willingness to meet the traditional violence the white community inflicted on blacks with violence of their own. More conservative leaders like King and Leroy Wilkins could not accept this militant stance, and the civil rights movement clearly became divided.

Through the years, the movement has had its martyrs, such as Medgar Evers, the NAACP field secretary killed in Mississippi in 1963, and Viola Liuzzo, a white civil rights worker killed in Alabama in 1965. But the most stunning loss came in 1968, when Martin Luther King was assassinated in Memphis, Tennessee. His last effort was focused on economic disparity between blacks and whites, a problem of inequality far more difficult to resolve politically than those of segregation and voting rights.

The death of King, the apostle of nonviolence, was followed by a series of violent riots in major American cities such as Los Angeles, Detroit, and Washington, D.C. A period of "white backlash" including major "white flight" from cities to suburbs and the formation of racist groups followed the riots. During the 1970s and 1980s, certain whites became increasingly resentful of what they viewed as the excesses of affirmative action and welfare programs. The ascent of a political figure such as David Duke, ex-Klansman and neo-Nazi, demonstrated the growth of the backlash sentiment. But the black urban riot, which many considered a relic of the 1960s, surfaced again in Los Angeles in the spring of 1992 after an all-white jury found four policemen not guilty of using excessive force on a black motorist, Rodney King. The fact that millions had witnessed what appeared to be a savage beating on a televised videotape triggered not only the riot, but national and international reaction to the verdict. The events brought to national consciousness latent social problems: the gaps between rich and poor as well as between black and white were still enormous, and Martin Luther King's vision of a society based on equality and harmonious race relations remained a dream.

The Black Aesthetic, Afrocentricity, and Négritude

The 1980s witnessed a resurgence of interest in Africa and things African among African Americans. Known as "Afrocentricity" or "Afrocentrism," the movement seeks to place African experiences, values, ideals, and perspectives at the center of education and other areas of African American life. Afrocentricity is, in large part, a reenactment of the black aesthetic movement and its quest for black pride during the 1960s. Influenced by the Harlem Renaissance of the 1920s and the idea of *négritude* during the 1930s, African Americans in the 1960s began to affirm their culture and identify with blacks around the world.

First coined as a concept in Aime Césaire's poem "Cahier d'un retour au pays natal" ("Return to My Native Land"), *négritude* is essentially a revolt against colonialism and an effort toward self-definition and self-appraisal. It emphasizes traditional African beliefs, their survival throughout the diaspora, the African's "sense of the divine," and the ability to perceive the supernatural within the natural, in order to create and define a Pan-African cultural universe.

The writings of the Algerian Frantz Fanon served as major revolutionary statements for third world thinking during the 1960s. In *Les Damnés de la terre* (*The Wretched of the Earth*) Fanon examined the psychological consequences of colonialism, and in *Black Skin, White Masks,* he explored what he called the "master-slave" relationship between the black colonized and the white colonizer. Although politics was an explicit part of the *négritude* movement for writers like Fanon, for others the movement remained primarily cultural and intellectual. Léopold Sédar Senghor of Senegal, West Africa, defined *négritude* as the "sum total of African values." He spoke of a special spiritual endowment of the African, of a "Negro soul," that was shared by blacks of African descent throughout the world. The African approach to the world was said to constitute "intuitive reason," as opposed to the Greek (thus Western) approach of "logical reason." Whereas logical reason involves a confrontation of subject and object, intuitive reason involves a kind of participation and communion, in which subject and object become one. In Senghor's words, "Emotion is African, as Reason is Hellenic."

Although the movement was popular among French-speaking black intellectuals, many African and African American writers looked on it with skepticism and suspicion. English-speaking Africans, such as Ezekiel Mphalele, James Ngugi, and Nobel prize winner Wole Soyinka, criticized *négritude* because of its "romanticization" of Africa and celebration of the past. Black writing, according to Soyinka and others, should serve a more critical function by dealing with social problems and other realities. Among African American writers, many, including Ralph Ellison and James Baldwin, insisted that the culture of the African American was as much American as it was African. Others, however, saw *négritude* as the way toward a worldwide spiritual unity of blacks and a polemic against the dominant values and ideals of Western civilization. Malcolm X, Ron Karenga, LeRoi Jones (Amiri Baraka), and other black nationalists were instrumental in convincing many African Americans that in the time of revolutionary struggle, traditional Western ideals are irrelevant and therefore must be abolished. As a result, one of the central missions of the black aesthetic movement (also known as the black arts movement) became what the literary critic Addison Gayle, Jr., called the de-Americanization of black people.

This de-Americanization of black people, along with the hostility and protest literature that often accompanied it, constituted only one phase of the movement's development. Its members soon came to the conclusion that protest literature and other modes of speaking to an unsympathetic American society were all futile. Consequently, they began to address themselves to other blacks by investing their work with the distinctive styles, rhythms, and colors of the ghetto as found, for instance, in the music of Aretha Franklin, Otis Redding, Nina Simone, and James Brown. Thus, as an artistic style, the black aesthetic may be viewed as an attempt to develop an idiom, symbolism, imagery, mythology, and iconology that reflect the uniqueness of the African American experience. The following list of seven black aesthetic categories offered by Don L. Lee is a good example of this effort:

1. polyrhythmic, uneven, short, and explosive lines
2. intensity; depth, yet simplicity; spirituality, yet flexibility
3. irony; humor; signifying
4. sarcasm—a new comedy
5. direction; positive movement; teaching, nation building
6. subject matter—concrete; reflects a collective and personal lifestyle
7. music: the unique use of vowels and consonants with the developed rap demands that the poetry be read, and read out loud.

35-1 *Dana Chandler,* Knowledge is Power, Stay in School. *Street Mural, Roxbury, Mass. (Copyright 1988 Mark Diamond)*

Implicit in these categories is the notion that the rules of grammatical form may be suspended and that poetry needs to be taken away from the academic level and written according to the realities of the black masses—to express their joys, sorrows, and concerns.

Black Aesthetic Art

Black aesthetic art was, like the literature and music of the movement, considered functional, collective, and didactic. Whereas the dominant trend of art before the 1960s was to illustrate the frustration, oppression, and domination of African Americans, the new art centered on positive and determined cultural enrichment. Like Mexican and other Latin American artists before them, black artists of the 1960s chose outdoor murals for their high visibility to everyone in black neighborhoods. In these murals, the artists sought to give form and color to everyday black life, to create new images and heroes, and to provide positive teachings. In the mural *Knowledge Is Power, Stay in School* (Fig. 35-1), Dana Chandler instructs his viewers in the value of knowledge and education. Erect and sturdy black men and women are depicted freeing both children and adults from the egg (visibly white) of oppression and racism. The dominant colors of the black revolution movement—red, black, and green—stand for blood, skin color (or Africa), and renewed life, respectively.

Jazz of the Sixties: Ornette Coleman (b. 1930)

The career of one leading jazz musician exemplifies the cultural and social upheavals that took place in America beginning in the 1960s. The changes in his music and in his public image reflect transformations taking place in American society among all races and socioeconomic groups. In many ways, jazz saxophonist Ornette Coleman was and is as much a social leader as he is a musical artist of the first rank, and his struggles with both music and society tell us much about ourselves and our country.

The significance of Coleman's contribution can be measured accurately only against a broad spectrum of music history. Jazz has many great figures—men and women of extraordinary musical talent, artistic acumen, and virtuosic technique, whose legacy of refined creation is loved, respected, replayed, re-created, imitated, and built on. In this regard, jazz is like all other serious art musics of the world. But Coleman's contribution to jazz was unlike the achievements of Oscar Peterson, Duke Ellington, Louis Armstrong, or Mary Lou Williams; even those of Charlie Parker, Thelonious Monk, and Miles Davis were essentially different, in that each built on the tradition handed to them by their musical predecessors. Ornette Coleman changed the nature of the language itself.

How many times in the history of Western music have there been changes in conception so pronounced that the musicians themselves, at the time the first events occurred, actually noticed a radical shift and designated a new style? In the last thousand years in the West, one can count these events on the fingers of both hands. This rarity is in itself a measure of the attainment, as well as the daring and fortitude, of the jazz artist Ornette Coleman. By way of comparison, one might look to the beginning of the fourteenth century, when Philippe de Vitry declared that the then-new music with duple rhythms, new notation, and pervasive secular interests constituted an *Ars nova* (new art).

Around 1960, Ornette Coleman revolted against the restraints of jazz harmonies and traditional rhythm sections and replaced the standard monodic and harmonic style of jazz with a complicated tapestry of atonal polyphony. In so doing, he incorporated into jazz the *free form* concept that is pivotal to his thinking and the new style.

Surely the environment surrounding Coleman in the late 1950s did not lack jazz explorers paddling furiously against the current of the mainstream. Saxophonist Sonny Rollins experimented with time signatures uncommon in jazz and recorded "Valse Hot" and "Blue Seven"; Teo Macero incorporated electronic sounds and electronically distorted sounds into his music and recorded his "Sounds of May"; the exciting John Coltrane moved quickly toward "sheets of sound" and rapid harmonic changes with his "Giant Steps" album; and Miles Davis ushered in "modal" jazz when he recorded "Kind of Blue."

These examples alone represent experiments in rhythm, form, timbre, instrumental technique, harmonic progression, and modal improvisation, but they all fit within the mainstream techniques of jazz of the 1950s. This is the backdrop that set the stage for the dramatic entrance of Ornette Coleman.

Born in Texas in 1930, Ornette Coleman had little formal musical training, but by 1944, at the age of fourteen, he was playing with rhythm-and-blues bands in the Fort Worth area. In the 1940s, the black community of America lacked the cohesion and unity of purpose that it developed in the 1960s. Just after World War II, the United States was not an integrated society, especially in the South. Hostility between races was prevalent, and even within the black community racial tension and unrest were rife. Coleman, although only one among many admirable black leaders, was an important and noteworthy catalyst in the process that first cemented the black community and later demanded and won recognition, respect, and equality for an oppressed minority. But it required of him a personal struggle that was both conscious and painful.

To illustrate, in 1949 when Coleman was nineteen, he visited a musician in New Orleans, the cornetist Melvin Lastie, and accompanied his friend to a job in nearby Baton Rouge. Ornette's personal manner, even then, was free rather than conventional; he wore long, straightened hair and a beard at a time when polite male blacks were clean shaven and wore a "razor cut." Both his playing and his appearance were put on the line. Coleman relates:

> And I was sittin' there listening to the band and all of a sudden a guy came in and said some musicians wanted to meet me outside. So I went outside and there were these really big guys, six or seven of them. I said, "How you doin'?" And one of them said, "Where you from?" And I said, "Oh, I'm from Fort Worth." And they were all black guys.... They started using "nigger" and all this, and "You're not from Texas with your beard like that and your long hair. You must be one of those Yankee kind of niggers!" And all of a sudden a guy kicked me in my stomach and then he kicked me in the ass and I had my horn cradled in my arms and I blacked out 'cause blood was everywhere.... They were just beating me to death. One guy took my tenor and threw it down the street. Then Melvin and the band came out and discovered I was beat up and they took me to the police department. The cops said, "What you doing with that long hair?" And they started calling me nigger and they told me that if them other niggers didn't finish me, *they were gonna.*
>
> So I went back to Melvin's house, and I was thinking just like my mother had told me, that the tenor was bad luck. David had an alto, and he said, "I'll let you borrow my alto."[1]

From this anecdote we gain insight into the society in which Coleman matured, the society that would undergo a social revolution in the succeeding years, especially the period following the appearance of the record album *Free Jazz.* Coleman's role in this societal

---

[1]Interview with Ornette Coleman by Jonathan Foose, November 6, 1981, quoted in Jason Berry et al., *Up from the Cradle: New Orleans Music Since World War II* (Athens: University of Georgia Press, 1986), pp. 43ff.

change was not direct, but the music that sprang from the horns of Ornette's followers in the 1960s—people such as Archie Shepp, Sun Ra, John Coltrane, and groups such as the Art Ensemble of Chicago—became the music of black Americans on the rise. It became a significant voice of dissent, drawing to itself the symbolism of individual and minority rights, people power, nonconformity, and freedom of expression. To say that this music answered this need innocently and by chance would be to ignore the statements and lives of its musicians, their choices of titles for the compositions, the venue of its performance, the mode of its expression, the emotion and content of its words, and the blackness of its performers.

The essence of free jazz is its liberation from tradition, the environment that restricts expression and inhibits change. *Tomorrow Is the Question, Change of the Century,* and *Free Jazz*[2] are all prophetic statements, especially when one considers that they were produced in 1959 and 1960. But Ornette Coleman did not overtly seek social change. What transpired on a national and international level, and the role he and his music played in that development, resulted from releasing the frustrations of an entire race. He played his part by expressing his individuality in his music and letting his music exert its power on others. He did not say that music should underpin or accompany a revolt. He was and is first and foremost a musician who is primarily concerned with *The Shape of Jazz to Come.*

Society changed, in a somewhat free-form movement, to the sound of his jazz. Shortly after the incident in Louisiana, Coleman was working in California and developing his style. It was there that he met Donald Cherry, a trumpeter of like mind and extraordinary technique. In 1959, Coleman attended the Lenox School of Jazz in Massachusetts, where he interacted with John Lewis, Gunther Schuller, and other musicians thoroughly grounded in the European classical traditions, both ancient and modern. At the same time, he was reevaluating his own life and declared, along with the literary followers of the black aesthetic, "Black is beautiful." *Change of the Century,* recorded in 1959, foreshadows the revolution that is about to erupt. Long solo lines, enormous bursts of notes, and semi-unisons that gather the form together at oddly spaced points are some of the noteworthy characteristics. One might say that this work exemplifies and marks the end of Coleman's first period—the years of learning, growth, development, and change.

Free Jazz (1960) is the masterpiece that broke with tradition, set the standard, influenced other musicians, and truly moved jazz in a new direction. Here one finds improvisation on a grand scale and a unique sound never employed in jazz before. This effort represents a true penetration into a new frontier. One will look in vain for harmonies, recognizable melodies, rhythms to tap one's foot to. The ensemble is different—a double quartet—and the sound is harsh, strident, penetrating, and loud. Where traditional jazz dealt with well-shaped melodic units (often singable) and well-ordered harmonic progressions, this jazz employs the near total freedom of action and reaction among musicians of like mind. The importance of the soloist is lessened as the total blend of the entire ensemble is attenuated. Instrumental virtuosity, in the old sense of the word, holds little value here, where fast notes and slow notes vie equally for the listener's attention. The production of the music becomes a communal action, very much an African characteristic. The blending of ancient and modern, traditional and experimental, into an artistic cluster is a signal accomplishment.

Surrounded by creative musicians, Ornette Coleman continued to search not only for the sound of the future but also for clues to the past. For a while, he returned to the tenor sax, an instrument of his youth, which, in his quest for roots, he hoped might provide him with a "real" black voice. He also experimented with additional sounds from his instruments and even with the syntactical value of silence in a time art. This can be heard in "Silence" (1965), which he recorded in Europe because of the lack of enthusiasm for his music at home.[3]

Coleman is still searching for new frontiers. "Harmolodic Bebop" from the *Caravan of Dreams*[4] album was recorded in 1985 by his group Prime Time. This work shows Coleman's new interest in electronic instruments and his continuing mastery of his free jazz style. "Song X"[5] with Pat Metheny was also recorded in 1985. This is exciting music by two masters at home in a natural surrounding.

Today, *Free Jazz* is over a quarter of a century old, and in retrospect, we might ask: "How significant was the change?" "What effect has it had on other jazz

[2]Contemporary S7569, Atlantic 1327, and Atlantic 1364, respectively.

[3]"Silence," from *The Great London Concert* (Arista 1900).

[4]"Harmolodic Bebop" from *Opening the Caravan of Dreams* (Caravan of Dreams 85001).

[5]"Song X" from *Song X* (Geffen 24096-2)

musicians and their music?" "Has it played a role in influencing the composition and performance of music beyond the world of jazz?" and "Has this music affected society at large, and in what way?"

Ornette Coleman's music led other jazz musicians to question their values and sent many of these musicians on musical and spiritual quests of their own. He is a significant artist, and we can observe his influence on the music of John Coltrane, Muhal Richard Abrams and the Association for the Advancement of Creative Musicians, the Art Ensemble of Chicago, Archie Shepp, Anthony Braxton, Cecil Taylor, and even Miles Davis. *Free Jazz* is a classic, a classic of jazz dating from the 1960s.

Feminism

Issues involving women's rights seem to come to the forefront and then subside at various times throughout Western history. We have seen various feminist questions addressed in Mary Wollstonecraft's *Vindication of the Rights of Women,* in John Stuart Mill's *On the Subjection of Women,* in the women's suffrage movement, and in Virginia Woolf's *A Room of One's Own.* In the decades following the suffrage movement of the 1920s, once women had obtained the vote in England and America, feminist issues gave way to the more immediately urgent problems posed by the Depression and the war. And yet the movement was launched. Women who took over men's jobs while the men were fighting in the war learned that they could do "men's work." In 1948, just three years after the end of the war and after women obtained the vote in France, a ground-breaking work of feminist theory appeared: Simone de Beauvoir's *The Second Sex.*

Beauvoir (1908–1986), author of many works of fiction and philosophical essays, was an important figure in the French existentialist movement. The lifelong companion of Jean-Paul Sartre—both of them eschewed marriage as a repressive institution—she developed her own brand of existentialism, most importantly applying existentialist ideas to feminism. *The Second Sex* is a long and ambitious treatise that views the phenomenon of woman from historical, biological, psychological, sociological, and philosophical points of view. One of Beauvoir's major points is that woman has always been treated as "the Other," "the second sex," something less than a full human being. Growing up in a patriarchal and repressive society, women have always encountered barriers to the assertion of their individuality and freedom. Like Virginia Woolf, Beauvoir sees women's economic dependence on men as a major obstacle. At the end of her book, she calls for a "liberation" of women, including equal opportunity in the work force.

The first reaction to *The Second Sex* was hostility, especially in France, Beauvoir's native country. French men and women alike did not like the attack they perceived on woman's traditional role as wife, homemaker, and mother. The book was more enthusiastically received in the United States, but even there by only a handful of people. The decade of the 1950s, on both sides of the Atlantic, in fact saw a return, on the part of the majority of women, to the traditional roles and the ideal of the "nurturer" of husband and children. To be "feminine" was to stay in one's place, not to be assertive. It is this conception of femininity that Betty Friedan was to attack in another ground-breaking work, *The Feminine Mystique* (1963).

In the radicalized atmosphere of the 1960s, many young women did step out of the traditional bounds of "femininity," but even there they were often treated as auxiliaries—the ones to make coffee and sandwiches while the men discussed radical politics. It was not until the 1970s that the women's movement really mushroomed, profoundly affecting the lives of women of all ages and social classes. "Consciousness-raising" groups were formed to help women clarify what oppressed them and to liberate themselves, women's studies programs were organized at universities, the National Organization for Women with Betty Friedan as president was founded, and other women's groups all along the political spectrum sprang up. Legal and political battles against various types of discrimination and for the continuation of abortion rights continue. A great many works of feminist theory, too numerous and too diverse to be discussed here, have appeared since that time. Although the movement has been accused by some as being too white and middle class in orientation, African American, Hispanic, and native American women have made important contributions. Feminism has had and continues to have significant repercussions in all of the arts, as well as in theory and in politics. One important black feminist is the writer Alice Walker (b. 1944), author of the Pulitzer prize–winning novel *The Color Purple.*

Postindustrialism

At least some of the talk current in the 1970s of the decline of the West was the product of a partial vision of social and economic change. The depressed state of the American automobile and steel industries, and the growing number of workers who, once laid off, would probably never return to full-time employment, were only symptomatic of the passing away of America's industrial age and the beginning of postindustrialism. It is difficult to provide a chronology for the development, but by the early 1970s white-collar workers outnumbered blue-collar workers in the country by five to one.[6] By this time a majority of the American working population was engaged not in agriculture and industry, but in some kind of service work—that is, in areas such as health, education, government, transportation, utilities, and finance. Among the white-collar workers, moreover, the fastest-growing segments were professionals and technicians, especially scientists and engineers.

The rapid increase in these latter occupations provides evidence of the centrality, in a postindustrial society, of theoretical knowledge and its transformation into abstract systems of symbols designed to control innovation and make social planning possible. Advancement in technological areas no longer lies with the tinkerers like Henry Ford or Thomas A. Edison but rather with the masters of highly intricate bodies of theoretical knowledge. Through the use of computers, society has the capacity to organize and use vast quantities of data, which allows for informed investigation of major problems, such as cleaning up the environment and defense strategy. These new statistical and logical techniques, focused on defining rational action and the means to achieve it, are replacing the intuitive judgments founded on immediate cause-and-effect relationships, which are often deceptive.

The new heroes in this age are the scientists and engineers, and the creative centers of intellectual technology are the universities and research laboratories of government and industry. The massive interest of today's students in acquiring computer literacy and technological and scientific training represents a response to the fact that the world has changed and that for many, such knowledge is a guarantee of places in the forefront of the future society. American industry is bound to suffer in the new age but, if postindustrial America successfully meets the challenges to its leadership in research and development, the loss in industry will be more than balanced.

[6]Daniel Bell, *The Coming of Post-Industrial Society: A Venture in Social Forecasting* (New York: Basic Books, 1973), p. 17. The above account is based on Bell's analysis.

Postmodernism in Culture and the Arts

Three important aspects of postindustrial society seem to affect everyone in some way:

1. the dominant role of the mass media, especially television, in politics, in advertising, and in our general awareness of the world
2. the control exercised by the information networks and the increasing dependence on computer technology
3. a pervasive consumerism that encourages the acquisition of more and more goods and services.

All of these have helped to create a new popular culture, worldwide rather than local or regional, and based on the consumption of images rather than on contact with people, events, and live performance. Yet previous cultural modes continue to survive alongside and within the new. If we look at the incredible array of artifacts and information easily available—fat romantic narratives lining shelves at the airport, piped music juxtaposing a baroque concerto on original instruments with the latest rap, instant telephonic or electronic communication with almost any place in the world, instant (and instantly forgotten) celebrities made by television, American soap operas eagerly awaited by people of widely divergent backgrounds and nationalities, a screen ethic of instant sexual gratification along with reminders of the menace of AIDS, the continuing proliferation of books and newspapers along with expanding types and amounts of information available from computers—we might well believe ourselves to be living in several temporal and spatial dimensions at once. This is precisely what we might call the *postmodern scene.*

Where does this situation leave the artist and the arts? We have seen that, since the romantic period, there has developed a gradually widening cleavage between popular or mass culture on one hand and "high" or elitist culture on the other. The cleavage was recognized as an inescapable fact of life during the heyday of modernism. Six hundred people, according to Ezra Pound, are all that it takes to make a culture. Taking their art very seriously, exploring new frontiers in the use of language, sound, and visual forms, the modernist artists knew that they were creating only for the few who had the leisure and the sophistication to understand their works. Modernism in the arts is far from dead, and for many, the notion of the artist as an individual struggling to express his or her highly individual view of the world still obtains. Yet new currents have entered the cultural stream.

Modernism	*Postmodernism*
• urbanism, city as cosmos	• destruction of the city; the world as "global village" or as "spaceship earth"
• "alienation" from industrialism and technology	• use of media and of computer as extension of consciousness
• individualism, expression of self	• fragmentation of the individual; impersonality, "cool"
• emphasis on form, purpose, design	• antiform or open form; play, chance
• art object/finished work	• process/performance/happening
• use of material (outpouring of words, paint, sound)	• fascination with reproduction of images and surfaces; use of silence
• emphasis on craft, technique, seriousness of art	• irony toward "work of art," anti–"deep meaning," playful
• consciousness of historic evolution	• mixing of different styles and genres, pastiche
• common cultural tradition	• decanonization

Critics in the 1960s, sensing a turning away from the tenets of modernism, began to speak of "postmodern" architecture and art, dance, music, and literature. Since then, the term has caught on and been extended to characterize culture in general. Initially, the term was used in a negative sense. Some literary critics, for example, felt that the legacy of the great modernists such as Eliot, Joyce, and Kafka, with their intense devotion to high art and their essentially humanistic faith in human intelligence and human language, was being abandoned. Others welcomed the turning away from a type of art that seemed out of touch with the realities of mass, electronic culture. The critic Leslie Fiedler embraced the art that he saw emerging from the anti-intellectual, antiestablishment trends in the counterculture. The "postmodern" sensibility was, he claimed, apocalyptic, antirational, and joyous, capable of absorbing "pop" culture.

Another critic, Ihab Hassan, who has written extensively about postmodernism, characterizes it as an "art of silence." The artists and writers he chooses to represent postmodernism are not necessarily less difficult or obscure than the modernists, but they lack the modernist faith in the saving power of the work of art and therefore produce an art that tends to be playful and to mock itself. The list of contrasts above, taken primarily from Hassan's book *The Dismemberment of Orpheus* and his 1986 essay entitled "Pluralism in Postmodern Perspective," identifies some contrasts between the modernist and postmodernist sensibilities.

The 1980s and early 1990s have seen a proliferation of theorizing on the phenomenon of postmodernism. Fredric Jameson, in a seminal essay entitled "Postmodernism, or the Cultural Logic of Late Capitalism" (1984), defines the phenomenon as a culture of the "simulacrum" or "spectacle." Techniques of mass reproduction have made everything appear to be reproducible; society has lost, or radically redefined, its sense of historical time and space. Whereas modernist avant-gardes had the power to offend or to challenge society's norms, postmodern spectacle society absorbs everything as just another image. Others, however, see movements such as ecology, multiculturalism, and feminism as indications of a postmodern resistance. If the white male bourgeois subject is "dead" or no longer the culture's central point of reference, previously marginalized voices now seem to speak with more authority. One of the major repercussions of this has been the intense debate over the "canon" in schools and colleges. Is there still a common core of great books of Western civilization that every educated individual should have read, or will the humanities courses of the future replace most of these with texts by non-western, women, and other writers outside of the canon?

Postmodern Music and Dance

Not everyone, by any means, accepts the label "postmodern" as a valid description of, or even a tendency in, contemporary culture. Yet if used with an awareness of the difficulties of describing one's own era, it may be a helpful guide. A few brief examples from music and dance may serve as illustrations before we go on to study some examples from architecture, visual art, and literature.

John Cage, a composer considered by many to be a kind of apostle of the postmodern, published in 1961 a work called *Silence.* His idea was to have the audience listen to the random sounds around them, to consider these as art. He told them:

nothing is accomplished by writing a piece of music
nothing is accomplished by hearing a piece of music
nothing is accomplished by playing a piece of music
our ears are now in excellent condition

Cage continued to experiment with random sound and silence, and his thought and work have affected a whole generation of composers. Ruth Schonthal, whose early works are masterfully crafted compositions of neoclassical character, composed in 1967 an aleatoric (random) work for piano entitled *Nachklänge* (*Reverberations*) in which she was trying to "create the impression of something broken that once was very beautiful evoking the image of a bombed-out cathedral."[7] Seven years later (1974), presumably after random explorations on and in the piano, she settled on a fixed form of the piece that calls for wood and metal objects placed on the lower strings and glass, plastic, and wood objects located in the middle register. In this manner, the "prepared piano," when played as indicated in the musical score, reacts to hammer strokes on the strings with sounds inconceivable for music in the times of Bach, Mozart, Beethoven, or Brahms. The ears of the postmodern listener are able to accept a much-expanded palette of sonorities from the instrument and relate them to a global and interplanetary experience unavailable even to their grandparents. In her piece, Schonthal explains,

> there are echoes freely reminiscent of a Bach chorale. A section, entitled "Nostalgia," is followed by a section, entitled "War," which remains aleatory (the out-of-control element of war). The next section uses the melody from the German soldier's song, "Ich Hatt' einen Kameraden," that bemoans the loss of a comrade. . . . It all ends with the Nostalgic theme coming to some kind of peace from within.

Thus the postmodern composer incorporates substantive issues of the surrounding culture together with experimental devices, unusual sounds, and traditional elements into an artwork that consciously "makes a statement." In quite another vein, the music of composers such as Miles Davis and Ornette Coleman, who mix jazz, popular rock, "serious" electronic music, and African music, may also be considered postmodern. In dance, the choreographer Merce Cunningham, who collaborated extensively with Cage, is generally considered the progenitor of postmodernism. Cunningham broke away from the modern dance of Martha Graham, with its symbolism and psychological exploration, to create a dance of pure movement, with the dancers often dancing to silence. Younger contemporary choreographers have tended to do away with dance as "art," having untrained performers sweep the floor, lie still, or deliver a monologue, calling everything "dance." Others, such as Laura Dean, use repetitious geometric patterns—for example, whirling in continuous circles. Twyla Tharp, in one postmodern vein, incorporates social dances from the 1920s through the 1950s into her choreography, as well as experiments with ordinary "non-dance" movements and nonstage environments. In recent years, "performance artists" have mixed dance movements with verbal improvisation and media, adding another multidimensional form to the postmodern scene.

An Example of Postmodern Jazz

Jane Ira Bloom is a soprano saxophonist whose performance career blends music, dance, electronics, and current phenomena into works of art. Recently commissioned by NASA to compose music inspired by the starburst liftoffs at Cape Canaveral, she sculpts sound into musical structures that seem to pulsate, bend, weave, twist, and dance. On stage her performance is a form of dance, for the sounds she creates are partially made by the physical motion of her instrument around the microphone. Connected to an electronic synthesizer that is operated partly by foot pedals, controlled partly by the notes played on her saxophone, and directed partly by signals received from the microphone (which is sensitive to the Doppler effect), Jane Ira Bloom reacts live in real time with her fellow musicians and the electronic gadgetry of this age. The result is music with spirit, spontaneity, and great creativity. On her album *Modern Drama,*[8] one needs only to listen to the track dedicated to female race driver Shirley Muldowney, "The Race," to realize that the

[7]From the liner notes of *Ruth Schonthal: Compositions for Piano,* Orion Records ORS 81413.

[8]Columbia FC 40755.

opening swirl of sound, the layers of sound on sound, the high-speed chase of saxophone after piano after drum, and the fluid harmonies are evocations of today's genius, this decade's technology, this generation's concerns. It is like the past in neither substance nor nature, but it is music, it is jazz, it is a postmodern sound art.

Architecture from the International Style to Postmodernism

The term *postmodern* has been used more consistently in architecture than in any other art form. To approach it, we will first have to review developments in architecture since the onset of modernism.

Although the abstract principles of the style could be applied to any architectural problem, probably the one that seemed to cry out most for a new kind of realization was the skyscraper. The Lever Building (Fig. 35-2), the first important skyscraper in the International Style, was designed by Skidmore, Owings, and Merrill for Lever Brothers' headquarters site on Park Avenue in New York City. The glass-curtain wall of the tower, the tower separated from the ground and from the entrance floor, the courtyard with green trees and open space, create an image of the best of technology and progress. The only decoration is that provided by the materials, by reflections, and by the spaces themselves. The tall office building is elegant and crisp, and makes a very powerful corporate image. Buildings like these began to proliferate.

35-2 *The Lever Building, New York. (Ezra Stoller copyright ESTO)*

When the Seagram Building, designed by Miës van der Rohe, was erected on Park Avenue, it seemed to be the final statement about the potentialities of the International Style. Constructed of bronze-anodized steel and dark glass, isolated on the edge of its impersonal plaza, outfitted with sumptuous interiors of wood veneers, bronze, and marble, the Seagram Building was the epitome of corporate wealth and success, and of the unabated technological and economic progress, indeed, hegemony of America in the early 1960s.

The International Style was the "progressive" style. Apartment complexes, colleges, private housing, grocery stores, fire and police stations, hotels, motels, hospitals—whatever was to appear new, modern, and up-to-date—was built in this mode. The box might be of splendid marble, bronze, and dark glass, or of plain stucco and concrete, or of brick with plate-glass windows, but the sameness began to suggest that perhaps this formal language, this style, had limitations, and that there might be other forms for building and more appropriate sources of inspiration for the contemporary age.

In 1967 the Museum of Modern Art again published a book perhaps as important in the history of architecture as the International Style. *Complexities and Contradictions in Architecture* was written by Robert Venturi, a young graduate of the Yale School of Architecture. The book summed up an evolutionary process that had already begun and would continue for decades. *Complexities and Contradictions* said exactly what some architects had already demonstrated and what would prove challenging to many more: architecture need not be confined to the cool, rational box of the International Style. Architecture should be humorous, contextual, traditional, personal, and emotional. Venturi's book constituted a statement of the failure of confidence that many in the architectural profession had in the forms, ideas, and logic of the International Style.

The late work of some of the great masters of the International Style in the 1960s reflects the beginnings of such a change in taste. In his only building built in America, the Carpenter Center at Harvard University (Fig. 35-3), completed in 1963, Le Corbusier turned away from the pure geometry of his early work to use concrete and steel-reinforced concrete as a malleable sculptural medium. Frank Lloyd Wright's Guggenheim

35-3 *Le Corbusier, Carpenter Center, Cambridge, Mass. (Harvard University News Office)*

Museum (Fig. 35-4) at Fifth Avenue and 89th Street in New York, built in 1959, is a highly personal, controversial building, both for a city and as an art museum. Centrifugal and vertiginous, at times the building seems to be better for people than for art. Eero Saarinen worked in a variety of forms and materials, attempting to give symbolic expression and imagery to building. The Dulles Airport outside Washington, D.C. (Fig. 35-5), shows his use of reinforced concrete and steel with a glass curtain to create a building expressive of the idea of flight, movement, and energy.

The disenchantment with the International Style encouraged journalists and architectural critics to seek out a deliberately "postmodern" non–International Style building that would establish, if not the vocabulary, at least the ideas that would form the inspiration for a truly postmodern architecture. This building has usually been identified as the 1978 design for the AT&T headquarters building in New York by Philip Johnson, once a chief practitioner and propagator of the International Style. The building, with its crowning parapet—a swan-necked, broken-pedimented top similar to that of an eighteenth-century Chippendale highboy (as it is sometimes derisively described)—makes a stunning addition to the New York skyline (Fig. 35-6). At street-entry level, a barrel vault cuts into

35-4 *Frank Lloyd Wright, Solomon R. Guggenheim Museum, New York City. (Courtesy of the Guggenheim Museum)*

35-5 *Eero Saarinen, Dulles Airport. (Photo copyright 1962 Dandelet)*

35-6 *Philip Johnson and John Burgee, AT&T Headquarters Building, New York City, 1980. (Copyright 1988 Peter Mauss/ESTO)*

a columnar screen, and the entry portico looks like a Roman triumphal arch moved to the building base. Smooth, butt-jointed granite slabs face walls with almost negligible windows. The contrast with Miës van der Rohe's Seagram glass box building is stark and deliberate.

The historical allusions of Johnson's building are also deliberate and are the consequence not only of dissatisfaction with the International Style but also of renewed interest in historical architecture for its own sake. Academic interest in the architecture of the past received validation from exhibitions such as *The Architecture of the Ecole des Beaux-Arts* (October 1975–January 1976) at the Museum of Modern Art, which revealed a great deal about the difference in ideals, training, and understanding that created the scorned neoclassical architecture of the past.

Of almost equal importance to this changed attitude has been the growth of the historic preservation movement, which began as an elite movement to save buildings associated with great people and great

35-7 *South Street Seaport, New York City. The top photo was taken before restoration work began, the bottom one after it was finished. As in other historic preservation and rehabilitation efforts, an attempt has been made to recreate the original atmosphere of the area. Note the original or authentically reproduced building facades, cobblestone paving, lampposts, and signs. (Top: Courtesy of Benjamin Thompson & Associates, Inc., Architects and Planners, Cambridge, Mass. Bottom: Copyright 1984 Peter Aaron/ESTO)*

35-8 *Richard Meier, Hartford Seminary, Hartford, CT (Ezra Stoller Copyright ESTO)*

deeds and broadened at the grass-roots level in towns and cities across America as urban renewal and road building threatened the historic fabric of many places. In response to public pressure, the federal government, through the Department of the Interior, established the National Register of Historic Places. This project established standards for the listing, care, and restoration of historic structures and sites and encouraged local and state governments to survey, identify, photograph, research, and preserve sites of local, regional, or national significance. The existing fabric of many residential, commercial, and industrial neighborhoods has been saved because their presence records important moments and events in American history. Today many of these buildings are being preserved because it is realized that they are part of the total complex that characterized Big City or Small Town, USA (Fig. 35-7).

This movement was joined by architects who for many years had insisted that good design should be based on the context, with ideas drawn from the existing fabric and built with local materials and in concert with local traditions. So strident and successful had been the popularizers of the International Style that many important architects in America were overlooked for years while they quietly and successfully practiced architecture sympathetic to their regions in California, or the Midwest, or the South. Now teachers, critics, and practitioners consider this architecture truly "American," because it relates directly to the place where it was built rather than being based on an abstract canon of rules.

Certainly, the new corporate and institutional architecture of the past twenty years has been more complex, varied, controversial, and contradictory in appearance than that of the International Style. Three examples of recent work that have attracted attention are Louis Kahn's Mellon Center for British Studies at Yale University, Charles Moore's Piazza d'Italia in New Orleans, and Richard Meier's Hartford Seminary (Fig. 35-8). Each building represents a different approach to design.

Louis Kahn's Mellon Center, which combines an art museum and library, derives its forms from the function of the building and from its location in a complex urban neighborhood. The building itself seems somewhat self-effacing. The exterior is fairly plain and fits into the low-rise collection of small commercial buildings in which it sits. The interior, however, is a rich, complex space that serves the user and the art displayed inside.

In contrast, Charles Moore's Piazza d'Italia derives its forms from classicism and the world of neon and advertising. Challenged to provide a lively focus for this part of New Orleans, Moore has taken the architectural vocabulary that one would find in the streets of an Italian city. Columns, architraves, and arches were built using a lightweight construction technique employing neon decoration that contributes to the liveliness and movement of the fountains. The Piazza inspires a feeling of gaiety and fun.

Richard Meier's Hartford Seminary is a late-twentieth-century reinterpretation of the vocabulary of Le Corbusier with high-tech materials. The stunning bright, white building sits in a much older neighborhood, but it does not seem out of place. Its scale and the elegance of the design make it welcoming and friendly.

Thus each building represents a way of designing that accounts for the past and gives consideration to its site and to the uses for which it is designed. Each architect has interpreted the demands of the problem with different results. This variety may be much more significant than any style name because these buildings may indicate that in architecture, as in art, pluralism is good for design.

Postmodern Visual Art: The Example of Judy Chicago

The postmodern culture of the simulacrum, or reproducible image, was perhaps announced in the "pop art" of the 1960s by artists such as Andy Warhol. Warhol, who also made "underground" films, was perhaps best known for his serial images of popular figures such as the movie star Marilyn Monroe (Color Plate XXXIV) or his giant reproductions of advertising images such as the Campbell's soup can (Fig. 35-9). Such images triggered a new awareness of the relationships between art and advertising and the potential irony and humor of the relationship. A postmodern art form that may only be classified loosely as sculpture is environmental art.

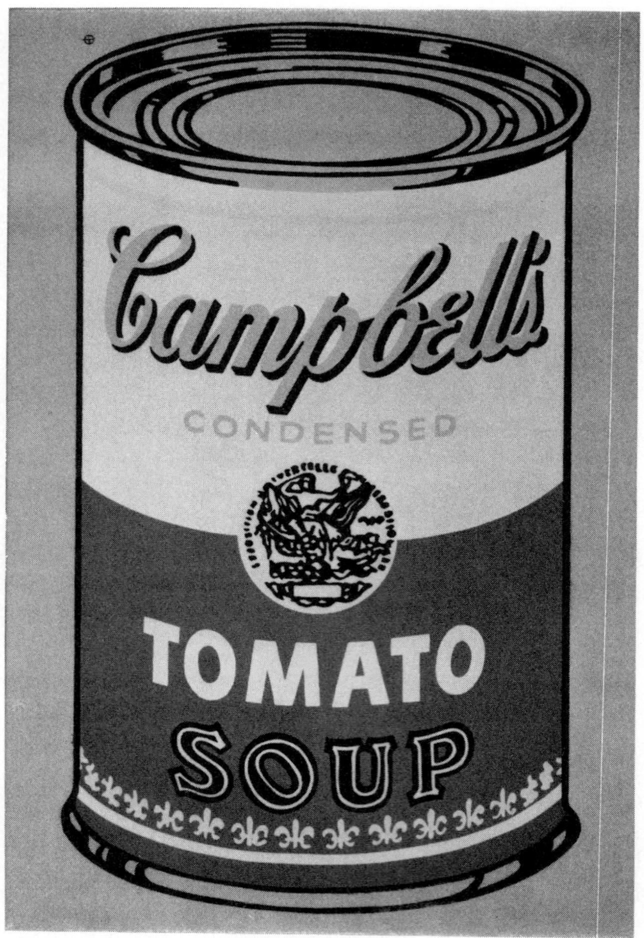

35-9 *WARHOL, Andy.* Campbell's Soup. *(1965). Oil silkscreened on canvas, 36⅛" × 24". (Collection, The Museum of Modern Art, New York. Philip Johnson Fund.)*

The earthworks that the sculptor Michael Heizer constructed in southern Nevada (Fig. 35-10), the curtain that Christo hung in Rifle Gorge, Colorado (Fig. 35-11), the beams of Corten steel that Richard Serra planted in the earth—all make fun of art in an ironic way while calling attention to the natural environment, attempting to make a kind of peace with it through imaginative uses of technology, and engaging the viewer in an active relationship with the situation. Environmental pieces, whether created for a museum or installed in urban, institutional, or natural sites, are capable of altering the viewer's understanding of both the site and the object, giving new life and interest to both, and to the viewer as well.

Although artists continue to work in painting, sculpture, and other traditional forms, some postmodern artists are experimenting with new media or art forms previously considered "minor." Such an artist is the feminist Judy Chicago, who set out to celebrate the traditional achievements and creativity of women in her monumental work *The Dinner Party.* In the spring of 1979 *The Dinner Party* went on exhibit at the San Francisco Museum of Modern Art. The work took five years to complete and involved about four hundred people. It is supposed to symbolize the history of women in Western civilization but might also be understood as a symbol of the controversies that surround the feminist movement in art (Fig. 35-12) and Color Plate XXXV).

On a large table shaped like an equilateral triangle are arranged thirty-nine place settings (thirteen to a side) of porcelain plate, goblet, and cutlery on elaborate embroidered and appliquéd runners whose decorations identify the individual mythical or historical

35-10 *Michael Heizer,* Double Negative, *1969–70, 1500′ × 50′ × 30′, 240,000 tons of rhyolite and sandstone displaced, Virgin River Mesa, Nevada. (Collection, Virginia Dwan. Photo courtesy Xavier Fourcade, Inc., New York)*

35-11 *Christo,* Valley Curtain, *Rifle Gorge, Colorado, 1970–72, width 1250–1368 feet, height 185–365 feet, 200,000 square feet of nylon polyamide; 110,000 pounds of steel cable; 800 tons of concrete. (Photo by Harry Shunk. Copyright Christo 1972)*

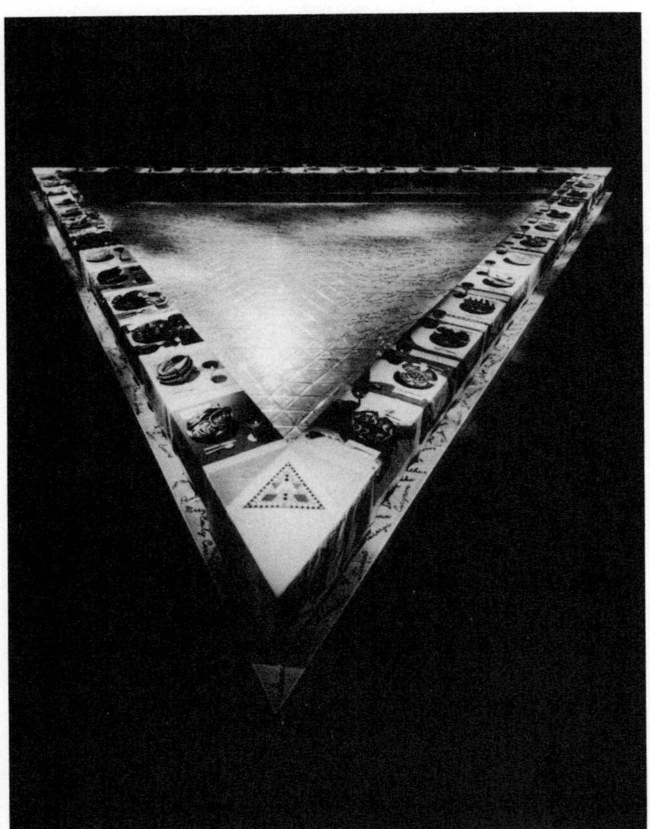

35-12 *Judy Chicago,* The Dinner Party, *1979, 48′ on each side. (Photograph copyright Michael Alexander/Through the Flower Corp.)*

figure symbolized by the plate. The predominant motif of most of the plates is the female genitalia, abstracted and represented in lustrous forms and colors in the technique of modern hand-painted china.

The table is placed on a ceramic floor whose tiles are covered with the names of another 999 women from past to present. The first wing of the table, "Pre-History to Rome," includes a primordial goddess (the earth mother, the matriarchical society), Sophia (wisdom), Hatshepsut (queen of Egypt), Sappho (the Greek Lesbian poet), and Boadicea, the Briton warrior queen who fought the Roman invaders. The second wing, "From the Beginning of Christianity to the Reformation," has settings for St. Bridget, Theodora (wife of Justinian and empress of Byzantium), Eleanor of Aquitaine, Christine de Pisan (the poet), Elizabeth I, and the Italian painter Artemisia Gentileschi. The third wing, "From the American Revolution to the women's revolution," seats Anne Hutchinson, Sacajawea, Caroline Herschel, Mary Wollstonecraft, Sojourner Truth, Susan B. Anthony, Elizabeth Blackwell, Emily Dickinson, Ethel Smyth, Margaret Sanger, Natalie Barney, Virginia Woolf, and Georgia O'Keeffe.

Controversy has arisen regarding the choice of dinner guests, but much more was provoked by Chicago's focus on the female genitalia as the major representative motif for the dinner plates. Some critics have called her work insulting, others simplistic (is that the *only* symbol of woman?), and still other critics have not questioned the motif but noted that the plates are simply not good art but rather are uninspired and banal. Almost unanimous approval, however, has been given to the needlework of the thirty-nine runners and the white linen tablecloths. This work elevates and inspires because it is of such high quality and because it recalls the exquisite needlework that has adorned the rich, powerful, and priestly in Western society for millennia. Both china painting and needlework, minor arts always associated with women, were treated as high or fine arts by Chicago. This idea in itself is an important one. *The Dinner Party* also attracted many audiences and stimulated much thinking.

Art, propaganda, or both? *The Dinner Party,* like other feminist enterprises—the Museum of Woman's Art in Washington, D.C., for example, or the masked, anonymous Gorilla Girls, whose advertisements in art magazines have tried to prove that a white male establishment controls art exhibitions and juries in the major museums, and thus access to galleries, patrons, power, and profit—have raised both the ire and the consciousness of many people. *The Dinner Party* attracted large crowds in Houston, Boston, Atlanta, San Francisco, and New York City. Many people were deeply moved, others scoffed, and still others have decried the deliberate separation of women from men. But none would deny that the feminist movement has brought a new energy and self-confidence to artists who are also women while contributing to the growing pluralism of art in general, in which no particular school or movement holds sway.

Postmodern Literature and Theory

As postmodern architecture plunders the whole repertoire of past styles, and postmodern visual art makes pastiches while calling into question the very notion of "art," so do certain postmodern writers comment ironically on the literary canon of the past while questioning the possibility of still writing "literature." The traditional genres that we have observed throughout this book—lyric poetry, drama, prose fiction—tend to become blurred, mixed, or done away with entirely in postmodern writing. Street theater and happenings abandoned the stage; new journalists such as Tom Wolfe and Norman Mailer in his later writings, mixed subjective impressions with straight reporting; lyric poetry does not hesitate to comment on political and social questions; pop culture appears alongside high culture. Along with this blurring of genres has come a newfound eminence for what used to be called literary criticism and is now referred to simply as "theory."

The field of theory is far too complex and vast to summarize here, but one point, however simplified, needs to be made: the importance of the nature of language in understanding literature and other cultural phenomena. For a critic and theorist such as Roland Barthes (1915–1980), language is in the last analysis about itself: that is, a text is self-referential, and we should not confuse it with some hypothetical "outside reality." Thus, in an influential essay published in 1968, Barthes announced the "death of the author." Michel Foucault (1926–1984), who called himself an "archeologist of knowledge," spoke about language in the following terms:

> Having become a dense and consistent historical reality, language forms the locus of tradition, of the unspoken habits of thought, of what lies hidden in a people's mind.... Expressing their thoughts in words of which they are not the masters, enclosing them in verbal forms whose historical dimension they are unaware of, men believe that their speech is their servant and do not realize that they are submitting themselves to its demands.

And so we are caught in the prison house of language. There is no sovereign subject, no great author who meant to say something; there are only texts made of words on which we can write commentaries of commentaries. What Foucault proclaims is nothing less than the death of classical humanism. We have gone from a God-centered world to a human-centered world, to a world without center, a world as text.

This view of language is also reflected in a literature that appears to be about itself or about the infinite possibilities of language. Although we discussed the Argentinian Jorge Luis Borges in the section on modernism, where he belongs in many ways, his stories that consist of commentaries on commentaries on texts may be considered postmodern. Postmodern in their concern with language as well as in their use of media are the works of two other Argentinians: Julio Cortazar, who experimented with the limits and limitations of the short story and novel in *Hopscotch* and in *Blowup and Other Short Stories,* and Manuel Puig, who in works such as *Betrayed by Rita Hayworth* and *The Kiss of the Spider Woman* portrays the increasing incursions of the fictional world of the mass media, particularly of Hollywood films, into the "real" world. The Cuban fiction writer Guillermo Cabrera Infante and the Nicaraguan poet Ernesto Cardenal with his use of parody, puns, and spoken language, exemplify other aspects of postmodernism. While Latin American literature since the period in the late 1960s called *el boom* has been one of the major forces in postmodernism, many North American and European writers are often grouped under the rubric "postmodern" as well. Among them are the German Peter Handke, the Italian Italo Calvino, and the Irish-French writer Samuel Beckett. African American writers such as Ishmael Reed, John Edgar Wideman, Clarence Major, and the later works of Toni Morrison (e.g., *Beloved*) are often considered postmodernist. Also included among the North American postmodernists are Donald Barthelme, Ronald Sukenick, and John Barth.

Reading Selections

Sonia Sanchez (b. 1934)

present

this women vomiten her
hunger over the world
this melancholy woman forgotten
before memory came
this yellow movement bursten forth like
Coltrane's melodies all mouth
buttocks moven like palm trees,
this honeycoatedalabamianwoman
raining rhythms of blue / blk / smiles
this yellow woman carryen beneath her breasts
pleasures without tongues
this woman whose body weaves
desert patterns,
this woman, wet with wanderen,
reviven the beauty of forests and winds
is tellen u secrets
gather up yo odors and listen
as she sings the mold from memory

there is no place
for a soft / blk / woman
there is no smile green enough or
summertime words warm enough to allow my
growth
and in my head
i see my history
standen like a shy child
and i chant lullabies
as i ride my past on horseback
tasten the thirst of yesterday tribes
hearen the ancient / blk / woman
me singen hay-hay
hay-hay-hay-ya-ya-ya
hay-hay-hay
hay-hay-ya-ya-ya
like a slow scent
beneath the sun
and i dance my
creation and my grandmothers gatheren
from my bones like great wooden birds
spread their wings
while their long / legged / laughter /
stretches the night.
and i taste the
seasons of my birth. mangoes. papayas
drink my woman / coconut / milks
stalk the ancient grandfathers
sippen on proud afternoons
walk with a song round my waist
tremble like a new / born / child troubled
with new breaths
and my singen
becomes the only sound of a
blue / blk / magical / woman. walken.
womb ripe. walken. loud with mornings. walken
maken pilgrimage to herself. walken.

COMMENTS AND QUESTIONS

1. Black aesthetic poetry is noted for its bold images and figures of speech. Identify some of them, and explain how they relate to the poem's overall theme.
2. How effective is Sanchez's decision to ignore the standard rules of grammatical form? What ideological statement is she making?
3. What, for Sanchez, gives the black woman a privileged place in African American history?
4. Is there a "maternal instinct"? Discuss the claim that black women are more maternal than white women.

ALICE WALKER

"*Really,* Doesn't *Crime Pay?*"

In this short story, taken from her collection entitled *In Love and Trouble,* Walker deals with modern woman's preoccupation with beauty, rebellion against male authority, and struggle for personal freedom.

(Myrna)

September, 1961

page 118

I sit here by the window in a house with a thirty-year mortgage, writing in this notebook, looking down at my Helena Rubenstein hands . . . and why not? Since I am not a serious writer my nails need not be bitten off, my cuticles need not have jagged edges. I can indulge myself—my hands—in Herbessence nailsoak, polish, lotions, and creams. The result is a truly beautiful pair of hands: sweet-smelling, small, and soft. . . .

I lift them from the page where I have written the line "Really, *Doesn't* Crime Pay?" and send them seeking up my shirt front (it is a white and frilly shirt) and smoothly up the column of my throat, where gardenia scent floats beneath my hairline. If I should spread my arms and legs or whirl, just for an instant, the sweet smell of my body would be more than I could bear. But I fit into my new surroundings perfectly; like a jar of cold cream melting on a mirrored vanity shelf.

page 119

"I have a surprise for you," Ruel said, the first time he brought me here. And you know how sick he makes me now when he grins.

"What is it?" I asked, not caring in the least.

And that is how we drove up to the house. Four bedrooms and two toilets and a half.

"Isn't it a beauty?" he said, not touching me, but urging me out of the car with the phony enthusiasm of his voice.

"Yes," I said. It is "a beauty." Like new Southern houses everywhere. The bricks resemble cubes of raw meat; the roof presses down, a field hat made of iron. The windows are narrow, beady eyes; the aluminum glints. The yard is a long undressed wound, the few trees as bereft of foliage as hairpins stuck in a mud cake.

"Yes," I say, "it sure is a beauty." He beams, in his chill and reassured way. I am startled that he doesn't still wear some kind of military uniform. But no. He came home from Korea a hero, and a glutton for sweet smells.

"Here we can forget the past," he says.

page 129

We have moved in and bought new furniture. The place reeks of newness, the green walls turn me bilious. He stands behind me, his hands touching the edges of my hair. I pick up my hairbrush and brush his hands away. I have sweetened my body to such an extent that even he (especially he) may no longer touch it.

I do not want to forget the past; but I say "Yes," like a parrot. "We can forget the past here."

The past of course is Mordecai Rich, the man who, Ruel claims, caused my breakdown. The past is the night I tried to murder Ruel with one of his chain saws.

May, 1958

page 2

Mordecai Rich

Mordecai does not believe Ruel Johnson is my husband. "*That* old man," he says, in a mocking, cruel way.

"Ruel is not old," I say. "Looking old is just his way." Just as, I thought, looking young is your way, although you're probably not much younger than Ruel.

Maybe it is just that Mordecai is a vagabond, scribbling down impressions of the South, from no solid place, going to none . . . and Ruel has never left Hancock County, except once, when he gallantly went off to war. He claims travel broadened him, especially his two months of European leave. He married me because although my skin is brown he thinks I look like a Frenchwoman. Sometimes he tells me I look Oriental: Korean or Japanese. I console myself with this thought: My family tends to darken and darken as we get older. One day he may wake up in bed with a complete stranger.

"He works in the store," I say. "He also raises a hundred acres of peanuts." Which is surely success.

"That many," muses Mordecai.

It is not pride that makes me tell him what my husband does, is. It is a way I can tell him about myself.

page 4

Today Mordecai is back. He tells a funny/sad story about a man in town who could not move his wife. "He huffed and puffed," laughed Mordecai, "to no avail." Then one night as he was sneaking up to her bedroom he heard joyous cries. Rushing in he found his wife in the arms of another woman! The wife calmly dressed and began to pack her bags. The husband begged and pleaded. "Anything you want," he promised. "What *do* you want?" he pleaded. The wife began to chuckle and, laughing, left the house with her friend.

Now the husband gets drunk every day and wants an ordinance passed. He cannot say what the ordinance will be against, but that is what he buttonholes people to say: "I want a goddam ordinance passed!" People who know the story make jokes about him. They pity him and give him enough money to keep him drunk.

page 5

I think Mordecai Rich has about as much heart as a dirt-eating toad. Even when he makes me laugh I know that nobody ought to look on other people's confusion with that cold an eye.

"But that's what I am," he says, flipping through the pages of his scribble pad. "A cold eye. An eye looking for Beauty. An eye looking for Truth."

"Why don't you look for other things?" I want to know. "Like neither Truth nor Beauty, but places in people's lives where things have just slipped a good bit off the track."

"That's too vague," said Mordecai, frowning.

"So is Truth," I said. "Not to mention Beauty."

page 10

Ruel wants to know why "the skinny black tramp"—as he calls Mordecai—keeps hanging around. I made the mistake of telling him Mordecai is thinking of using our house as the setting for one of his Southern country stories.

"Mordecai is from the North," I said. "He never saw a wooden house with a toilet in the yard."

"Well maybe he better go back where he from," said Ruel, "and shit the way he's used to."

It's Ruel's pride that is hurt. He's ashamed of this house that seems perfectly adequate to me. One day we'll have a new house, he says, of brick, with a Japanese bath. How should I know why?

page 11

When I told Mordecai what Ruel said he smiled in that snake-eyed way he has and said, "Do *you* mind me hanging around?"

I didn't know what to say. I stammered something. Not because of his question but because he put his hand point-blank on my left nipple. He settled his other hand deep in my hair.

"I am married more thoroughly than a young boy like you could guess," I told him. But I don't expect that to stop him. Especially since the day he found out I wanted to be a writer myself.

It happened this way: I was writing in the grape arbor, on the ledge by the creek that is hidden from the house by trees. He was right in front of me before I could put my notebook away. He snatched it from me and began to read. What is worse, he read aloud. I was embarrassed to death.

"No wife of mine is going to embarrass me with a lot of foolish, vulgar stuff," Mordecai read. (This is Ruel's opinion of my writing.) *Every time he tells me how peculiar I am for wanting to write stories he brings up having a baby or going shopping, as if these things are the same. Just something to occupy my time.*

"If you have time on your hands," he said today, "why don't you go shopping in that new store in town."

I went. I bought six kinds of face cream, two eyebrow pencils, five nightgowns and a longhaired wig. Two contour sticks and a pot of gloss for my lips.

And all the while I was grieving over my last story. Outlined—which is as far as I take stories now—but dead in embryo. My hand stilled by cowardice, my heart the heart of a slave.

page 14

Of course Mordecai wanted to see the story. What did I have to lose?

"Flip over a few pages," I said. "It is the very skeleton of a story, but one that maybe someday I will write."

"The One-Legged Woman," Mordecai began to read aloud, then continued silently.

> The characters are poor dairy farmers. One morning the husband is too hung over to do the milking. His wife does it and when she has finished the cows are frightened by thunder and stampede, trampling her. She is also hooked severely in one leg. Her husband is asleep and does not hear her cry out. Finally she drags herself home and wakes him

> up. He washes her wounds and begs her to forgive him. He does not go for a doctor because he is afraid the doctor will accuse him of being lazy and a drunk, undeserving of his good wife. He wants the doctor to respect him. The wife, understanding, goes along with this.
>
> However, gangrene sets in and the doctor comes. He lectures the husband and amputates the leg of the wife. The wife lives and tries to forgive her husband for his weakness.
>
> While she is ill the husband tries to show he loves her, but cannot look at the missing leg. When she is well he finds he can no longer make love to her. The wife, sensing his revulsion, understands her sacrifice was for nothing. She drags herself to the barn and hangs herself.
>
> The husband, ashamed that anyone should know he was married to a one-legged woman, buries her himself and later tells everyone that she is visiting her mother.

While Mordecai was reading the story I looked out over the fields. If he says one good thing about what I've written, I promised myself, I will go to bed with him. (How else could I repay him? All I owned in any supply were my jars of cold cream!) As if he read my mind he sank down on the seat beside me and looked at me strangely.

"*You* think about things like this?" he asked.

He took me in his arms, right there in the grape arbor. "You sure do have a lot of heavy, sexy hair," he said, placing me gently on the ground. After that, a miracle happened. Under Mordecai's fingers my body opened like a flower and carefully bloomed. And it was strange as well as wonderful. For I don't think love had anything to do with this at all.

page 17

After that, Mordecai praised me for my intelligence, my sensitivity, the depth of the work he had seen—and naturally I showed him everything I had: old journals from high school, notebooks I kept hidden under tarpaulin in the barn, stories written on paper bags, on table napkins, even on shelf paper from over the sink. I am amazed—even more amazed than Mordecai—by the amount of stuff I have written. It is over twenty years' worth, and would fill, easily, a small shed.

"You must give these to me," Mordecai said finally, holding three notebooks he selected from the rather messy pile. "I will see if something can't be done with them. You could be another Zora Hurston[1]—" he smiled—"another Simone de Beauvoir!"[2]

Of course I am flattered. "Take it! Take it!" I cry. Already I see myself as he sees me. A famous authoress, miles away from Ruel, miles away from anybody. I am dressed in dungarees, my hands are a mess. I smell of sweat. I glow with happiness.

"How could such pretty brown fingers write such ugly deep stuff?" Modecai asks, kissing them.

page 20

For a week we deny each other nothing. If Ruel knows (how could he not know? His sheets are never fresh), he says nothing. I realize now that he never considered Mordecai a threat. Because Mordecai seems to have nothing to offer but his skinny self and his funny talk. I gloat over this knowledge. Now Ruel will find that I am not a womb without a brain that can be bought with Japanese bathtubs and shopping sprees. The moment of my deliverance is at hand!

page 24

Mordecai did not come today. I sit in the arbor writing down those words and my throat begins to close up. I am nearly strangled by my fear.

page 56

I have not noticed anything for weeks. Not Ruel, not the house. Everything whispers to me that Mordecai has forgotten me. Yesterday Ruel told me not to go into town and I said I wouldn't, for I have been hunting Mordecai up and down the streets. People look at me strangely, their glances slide off me in a peculiar way. It is as if they see something on my face that embarrasses them. Does everyone know about Mordecai and me? Does good loving show so soon? . . . But it is not soon. He has been gone already longer than I have known him.

page 61

Ruel tells me I act like my mind's asleep. It is asleep, of course. Nothing will wake it but a letter from Mordecai telling me to pack my bags and fly to New York.

---

[1]African American novelist (1891–1960).

[2]French feminist writer (1908–1986).

page 65

If I could have read Mordecai's scribble pad I would know exactly what he thought of me. But now I realize he never once offered to show it to me, though he had a chance to read every serious thought I ever had. I'm afraid to know what he thought. I feel crippled, deformed. But if he ever wrote it down, that would make it true.

page 66

Today Ruel brought me in from the grape arbor, out of the rain. I didn't know it was raining. "Old folks like us might catch rheumatism if we don't be careful," he joked. I don't know what he means. I am thirty-two. He is forty. I never felt old before this month.

page 79

Ruel came up to bed last night and actually cried in my arms! He would give anything for a child, he says.

"Do you think we could have one?" he said.

"Sure," I said. "Why not?"

He began to kiss me and carry on about my goodness. I began to laugh. He became very angry, but finished what he started. He really does intend to have a child.

page 80

I must really think of something better to do than kill myself.

page 81

Ruel wants me to see a doctor about speeding up conception of the child.

"Will you go, honey?" he asks, like a beggar.

"Sure," I say. "Why not?"

page 82

Today at the doctor's office the magazine I was reading fell open at a story about a one-legged woman. They had a picture of her, drawn by someone who painted the cows orange and green, and painted the woman white like a white cracker, with little slit-blue eyes. Not black and heavy like she was in the story I had in mind. But it is still my story, filled out and switched about as things are. The author is said to be Mordecai Rich. They show a little picture of him on a back page. He looks severe and has grown a beard. And underneath his picture there is that same statement he made to me about going around looking for Truth.

They say his next book will be called "The Black Woman's Resistance to Creativity in the Arts."

page 86

Last night while Ruel snored on his side of the bed I washed the prints of his hands off my body. Then I plugged in one of his chain saws and tried to slice off his head. This failed because of the noise. Ruel woke up right in the nick of time.

page 95

The days pass in a haze that is not unpleasant. The doctors and nurses do not take me seriously. They fill me full of drugs and never even bother to lock the door. When I think of Ruel I think of the song the British sing: "Ruel Britannia"! I can even whistle it, or drum it with my fingers.

September, 1961

page 218

People tell my husband all the time that I do not look crazy. I have been out for almost a year and he is beginning to believe them. Nights, he climbs on me with his slobber and his hope, cursing Mordecai Rich for messing up his life. I wonder if he feels our wills clashing in the dark. Sometimes I see the sparks fly inside my head. It is amazing how normal everything is.

page 223

The house still does not awaken to the pitter-patter of sweet little feet, because I religiously use the Pill. It is the only spot of humor in my entire day, when I am gulping that little yellow tablet and washing it down with soda pop or tea. Ruel spends long hours at the store and in the peanut field. He comes in sweaty, dirty, tired, and I wait for him smelling of Arpège, My Sin, Wind Song, and Jungle Gardenia. The women of the community feel sorry for him, to be married to such a fluff of nothing.

I wait, beautiful and perfect in every limb, cooking supper as if my life depended on it. Lying unresisting on his bed like a drowned body washed to shore. But he is not happy. For he knows now that I intend to do nothing but say yes until he is completely exhausted.

I go to the new shopping mall twice a day now; once in the morning and once in the afternoon, or at night. I buy hats I would not dream of wearing, or even owning. Dresses that are already on their way to Goodwill. Shoes that will go to mold and mildew in the cellar. And I keep the bottles of perfume, the skin softeners, the pots of gloss and eye shadow. I amuse myself painting my own face.

When he is quite, quite tired of me I will tell him how long I've relied on the security of the Pill. When I am quite, quite tired of the sweet, sweet smell of my body and the softness of these Helena Rubenstein hands I will leave him and this house. Leave them forever without once looking back.

QUESTIONS

1. In "Really, *Doesn't* Crime Pay?" Walker employs the tale-within-a-tale technique. In what way does the theme of the inner story, "The One-Legged Woman," enlarge or mirror the narrator's predicament?
2. What is the narrator's attitude toward her body? Do you think that such an attitude points to a significant flaw in the modern woman?
3. What does the narrator mean when she says, "I fit into my new surroundings perfectly; like a jar of cold cream melting on a mirrored vanity shelf"?
4. Why does the narrator continue to live with her husband, Ruel Johnson? Why does she try to slice off his head with a chain saw?
5. Discuss the similarities and differences between Mordecai Rich and Ruel Johnson. Which, if either, of the two is more tolerable as a male companion?
6. What techniques of rebellion or resistance to male domination are employed by the narrator?
7. Can this story be characterized as "postmodern"?

ADRIENNE RICH (1929–)

A longtime activist in the women's movement, as well as an important contemporary American poet, Rich develops feminist themes in both poetry and prose.

Translations

You show me the poems of some woman
my age, or younger
translated from your language

Certain words occur: enemy, oven, sorrow
enough to let me know
she's a woman of my time

obsessed

with Love, our subject:
we've trained it like ivy to our walls
baked it like bread in our ovens
worn it like lead on our ankles
watched it through binoculars as if
it were a helicopter
bringing food to our famine
or the satellite
of a hostile power

I begin to see that woman doing things: stirring rice
ironing a skirt
typing a manuscript till dawn
trying to make a call
from a phonebooth

The phone rings unanswered
in a man's bedroom
she hears him telling someone else
Never mind. She'll get tired—
hears him telling her story to her sister
who becomes her enemy
and will in her own time
light her own way to sorrow

ignorant of the fact this way of grief
is shared, unnecessary
and political

The Ninth Symphony of Beethoven Understood at Last as a Sexual Message

A man in terror of impotence
or infertility, not knowing the difference
a man trying to tell something
howling from the climacteric
music of the entirely
isolated soul
yelling at Joy from the tunnel of the ego
music without the ghost
of another person in it, music
trying to tell something the man
does not want out, would keep if he could

gagged and bound and flogged with chords of Joy
where everything is silence and the
beating of a bloody fist upon
a splintered table

QUESTIONS

1. Define Rich's conception of love in "Translations." What is the effect of the *similes* in the stanza beginning "with Love..."?
2. What is the meaning of "political" in "Translations"? Why do you think that the poem ends with this word?
3. Describe the rhythm in "The Ninth Symphony." Do you see any relationship to Beethoven's music?
4. What is the "sexual message"?
5. What kind of dialogue is established here between a contemporary poet and a major monument of Western culture?

Motherhood: The Contemporary Emergency and the Quantum Leap

One of the most powerful social and political catalysts of the past decade has been the speaking of women with other women, the telling of our secrets, the comparing of wounds and the sharing of words. This hearing and saying of women has been able to break many a silence and taboo; literally to transform forever the way we see. Let this be a time, then, for hearing and speaking together, for breaking silences, not only within yourselves but among all our selves: the daughter and the mother; the black woman and the white; the lesbian mother and the married housewife; the woman who has chosen single or communal motherhood and the woman who has chosen to use her life in ways which do not include the raising of children; the woman who has given up custody of her children and the woman who is fighting to keep hers; the stepdaughter, the foster-mother, the pregnant woman; the daughter who has never known her mother, the mother who has no daughters. What we all, collectively, have lived, as the daughters of women, as the mothers of children, is a tale far greater than any three or four of us can encompass: a tale only beginning to be told. I hope that here, speaking to and hearing one another, we can begin to fling cables of recognition and attention across the conditions that have divided us. And so I begin . . . by urging each of you to take responsibility for the voicing of her experience, to take seriously the work of listening to each other and the work of speaking, whether in private dialogue or in larger groups. In order to change what is, we need to give speech to what *has been,* to imagine together what *might be.*

I have seen massive sculpturelike weavings, of jute, hemp, and wool, in which many varicolored strands are quickly visible like vines or striations; but when you come closer and try to touch this or that strand, your hand enters a dense, bristling mesh, thick with knotted and twisted filaments, some harsh and rough to the fingers, others surprisingly silky and strong. In writing *Of Woman Born,* and in thinking about motherhood ever since, I have felt a similar sensation, of elemental exploration and of complex discovery. Let us try then to do justice to the complexity of this immense weaving, even as we single out particular strands or finger particular knots that seem to account for the whole. For motherhood is the great mesh in which all human relations are entangled, in which lurk our most elemental assumptions about love and power.

If we speak of motherhood at all, we are inevitably speaking of something far more than the relationship of a woman with her children. And even this relationship has been shaped long before the first child's birth. All women are daughters of women—is this an obvious, a simple-minded statement? or does it reach through the layers of the weaving to inner chambers only now beginning to be explored by women? It has been suggested by Margaret Mead that possibly a deep chemical affinity exists, of which we as yet know nothing, between the body of the mother and her still unborn female child. It has been affirmed by Nancy Chodorow, that through the intense mother-daughter relationship women come into a deeper and richer inner life than men, and, even when heterosexual, tend to be more deeply attached to women than to men, and more capable than men of relationship.[1] Both Chodorow and Dorothy Dinnerstein feel strongly that the solution to sexual inequality would be a radical change in the system of parenting, that is, that parenting must be shared equally between women and men. I wish here to suggest other forces which sit in wait in

[1] *The Reproduction of Mothering* (Berkeley: University of California Press, 1978), p. 198.

the birth-chamber as a woman completes her first nine months of mothering.

Historically, cross-culturally, a woman's status as childbearer has been the test of her womanhood. Through motherhood, every woman has been defined from outside herself: mother, matriarch, matron, spinster, barren, old maid—listen to the history of emotional timbre that hangs about each of these words. Even by default motherhood has been an enforced identity for women, while the phrases "childless man" and "nonfather" sound absurd and irrelevant to us.

And so this woman in labor is on the one hand, even perhaps in terror and pain, doing what history has told her it was her duty and destiny to do; while at the same time doing what her mother did, reenacting a scene, which both separates her from her own mother (for now she is, supposedly, herself a woman and no longer a child) and creates her more intensely in her mother's image....

Motherhood, the family, are still too often relegated to the realm of the "private and personal." "For love," women are assumed to provide unflagging emotional care, not only to children but to men; while in terms of the physical work we do, our enormous, unpaid contribution to every economy is everywhere dismissed as only the natural service of women to men and children. We would rightly be skeptical of a feminism which denied the value and dignity of traditional women's work in the home. But in fact it is not feminists who have belittled and devalued the work of the housewife and mother: It is the statisticians, the political scientists, the economists, the image-makers of television and other advertising, the professionals, who depict the woman at home as "not working," as invisible, as an empty-headed consumer. Listen to the idiotic baby-voices allotted to women in canned radio commercials, look at the grimacing smiles of housewives and mothers as depicted on television, observe the obscene patronizing of women on game shows, read the childraising and sex manuals, equally patronizing, written by the male doctor experts.[2] The feminist movement has from the first demanded choice as each women's right, respect for each woman's being; feminist artists, historians, anthropologists have been the first to show concern and respect for the crafts of the midwives and grandmothers, the anonymous work of women's hands, the oral culture of women sitting in kitchens, the traditional arts and remedies passed on from mother to daughter, the female culture never granted the reverence accorded to "high art." A recognition of women's unquenchable creativity—contained so often within domestic limits, yet astounding in its diversity—has been one of the deep perceptions of a feminism which looks with fresh eyes on all that has been trivialized, devalued, forbidden, or silenced in female history. And so we can both take pride in all that women have done for "love"—including the resourceful, heroic coping of ordinary women everywhere—and also ask: "Why should women, and women only, work for love only? And what kind of love is this, which means always to be for others, never for ourselves?"

[2]For a detailed documentation and analysis of the creation of "the woman problem" by postindustrial science, especially medicine, see B. Ehrenreich and D. English, *For Her Own Good: 150 Years of the Experts' Advice to Women* (New York: Doubleday/Anchor, 1978), a brilliant study marred only by its failure to deal with heterosexuality itself as a primary mandate to women.

QUESTIONS

1. Define Rich's concept of motherhood. How does it resemble and differ from traditional concepts? What is your opinion of it?
2. Compare Rich's ideas on female creativity in the arts with the work of Judy Chicago.

Roland Barthes (1915–1980)

The Death of the Author

Translation by Richard Howard

In his tale *Sarrasine,* Balzac, speaking of a castrato disguised as a woman, writes this sentence: "She was Woman, with her sudden fears, her inexplicable whims, her instinctive fears, her meaningless bravado, her defiance, and her delicious delicacy of feeling." Who speaks in this way? Is it the hero of the tale, who would prefer not to recognize the castrato hidden beneath the "woman"? Is it Balzac the man, whose personal experience has provided him with a philosophy of Woman? Is it Balzac the author, professing certain "literary" ideas about femininity? Is it universal wisdom? Romantic psychology? We can never know, for the good reason that writing is the destruction of every voice, every origin. Writing is that neuter, that composite, that obliquity into which our subject flees, the black-and-white where all identity is lost, beginning with the very identity of the body that writes.

No doubt it has always been so: once a fact is *recounted*—for intransitive purposes, and no longer to act directly upon reality, i.e., exclusive of any function except that exercise of the symbol itself—this gap appears, the voice loses its origin, the author enters into his own death, writing begins. However, the effect of this phenomenon has been variable; in ethnographic societies, narrative is never assumed by a person but by a mediator, shaman, or reciter, whose "performance" (i.e., his mastery of the narrative code) can be admired, but never his "genius." The *author* is a modern character, no doubt produced by our society as it emerged from the Middle Ages, inflected by English empiricism, French rationalism, and the personal faith of the Reformation, thereby discovering the prestige of the individual, or, as we say more nobly, of the "human person." Hence, it is logical that in literary matters it should be positivism, crown and conclusion of capitalist ideology, which has granted the greatest importance to the author's "person." The *author* still reigns in manuals of literary history, in biographies of writers, magazine interviews, and in the very consciousness of litterateurs eager to unite, by means of private journals, their person and their work; the image of literature to be found in contemporary culture is tyrannically centered on the author, his person, his history, his tastes, his passions; criticism still largely consists in saying that Baudelaire's oeuvre is the failure of the man Baudelaire, Van Gogh's is his madness, Tchaikovsky's his vice: *explanation* of the work is still sought in the person of its producer, as if, through the more or less transparent allegory of fiction, it was always, ultimately, the voice of one and the same person, the *author,* which was transmitting his "confidences."

Though the Author's empire is still very powerful (the new criticism has quite often merely consolidated it), we know that certain writers have already tried to subvert it. In France, Mallarmé, no doubt the first, saw and foresaw in all its scope the necessity to substitute language itself for the subject hitherto supposed to be its owner; for Mallarmé, as for us, it is language which speaks, not the author; to write is to reach, through a preliminary impersonality—which we can at no moment identify with the realistic novelist's castrating "objectivity"—that point where not "I" but only language functions, "performs": Mallarmé's whole poetics consists in suppressing the author in favor of writing (and thereby restoring, as we shall see, the reader's place). Valéry, entangled in a psychology of the ego, greatly edulcorated Mallarmean theory, but led by a preference for classicism to conform to the lessons of Rhetoric, he continued to cast the Author into doubt and derision, emphasized the linguistic and "accidental" nature of his activity, and throughout his prose works championed the essentially verbal condition of literature, as opposed to which any resort to the writer's interiority seemed to him pure superstition. Proust himself, despite the apparently psychological character of what is called his *analyses,* visibly undertook to blur by an extreme subtilization the relation of the writer and his characters: by making the narrator not the one who has seen or felt, or even the one who writes, but the one who is *going to write* (the young man of the novel—but, as a matter of fact, how old is he and *who* is he?—wants to write but cannot, and the novel ends when writing finally becomes possible), Proust has given modern writing its epic: by a radical reversal, instead of putting his life into his novel, as is so often said, he made his life itself a work of which his own book was the model, so that it is quite clear to us that it is not Charlus who imitates Montesquiou, but Montesquiou, in his anecdotal, historical reality, who is only a secondary, derived fragment of Charlus. Finally Surrealism, to keep to this prehistory of modernity, could doubtless not attribute a sovereign place to language, since language is system, and what this movement sought was, romantically, a direct subversion of the codes—an illusory subversion, moreover, for a code cannot be destroyed, only "flouted": yet, by constantly striving to disappoint expected meanings (this was the famous surrealist "shock"), by urging the hand to write as fast as possible what the head was unaware of (this was automatic writing), by accepting the principle and the experiment of collective writing, Surrealism helped desacralize the image of the Author. Last, outside literature itself (in fact, such distinctions are becoming quite dated), linguistics furnishes the destruction of the Author with a precious analytic instrument, showing that the speech-act in its entirety is an "empty" process, which functions perfectly without its being necessary to "fill" it with the person of the interlocutors: linguistically, the author is nothing but the one who writes, just as *I* is nothing but the one who says *I:* language knows a "subject," not a "person," and this subject, empty outside of the very speech-act which defines it, suffices to "hold" language, i.e., to exhaust it.

The removal of the Author (with Brecht, we might speak here of a veritable *distancing,* the Author diminishing like a figure at the far end of the literary stage) is not only a historical fact or an act of writing: it utterly transforms the modern text (or—which is the same thing—the text is henceforth produced and read so that the author absents himself from it at every level). Time, first of all, is no longer the same. The Author, when we believe in him, is always conceived as the past of his own book: book and author are voluntarily placed on one and the same line, distributed as a *before* and an *after:* the Author is supposed to *feed* the book, i.e., he lives before it, thinks, suffers, lives for it; he has the same relation of antecedence with his work that a father sustains with his child. Quite the contrary, the modern *scriptor* is born *at the same time* as his text; he is not furnished with a being which precedes or exceeds his writing, he is not the subject of which his book would be the predicate; there is no time other than that of the speech-act, and every text is written eternally *here* and *now.* This is because (or it follows that) *writing* can no longer designate an operation of recording, of observation, of representation, of "painting" (as the Classics used to say), but instead what the linguists, following Oxfordian philosophy, call a performative, a rare verbal form (exclusively found in the first person and in the present), in which the speech-act has no other content (no other statement) than the act by which it is uttered: something like the *I declare* of kings or the *I sing* of the earliest poets; the modern *scriptor,* having buried the Author, can therefore no longer believe, according to the pathos of his predecessors, that his hand is slower than his passion and that in consequence, making a law of necessity, he must emphasize this delay and endlessly "elaborate" his form; for him, on the contrary, his hand, detached from any voice, borne by a pure gesture of inscription (and not of expression), traces a field without origin—or at least with no origin but language itself, i.e., the very thing which ceaselessly calls any origin into question.

We know now that a text consists not of a line of words, releasing a single "theological" meaning (the "message" of the Author-God), but of a multi-dimensional space in which are married and contested several writings, none of which is original: the text is a fabric of quotations, resulting from a thousand sources of culture. Like Bouvard and Pécuchet, those eternal copyists, at once sublime and comical, whose profound absurdity *precisely* designates the truth of writing, the writer can only imitate an ever anterior, never original gesture; his sole power is to mingle writings, to counter some by others, so as never to rely on just one; if he seeks to *express himself,* at least he knows that the interior "thing" he claims to "translate" is itself no more than a ready-made lexicon, whose words can be explained only through other words, and this ad infinitum: an adventure which exemplarily befell young Thomas De Quincey, so versed in his Greek that in order to translate certain absolutely modern ideas and images into this dead language, Baudelaire tells us, "he had a dictionary made for himself, one much more complex and extensive than the kind produced by the vulgar patience of purely literary themes" (*Les Paradis artificiels*); succeeding the Author, the *scriptor* no longer contains passions, moods, sentiments, impressions, but that immense dictionary from which he draws a writing which will be incessant: life merely imitates the book, and this book itself is but a tissue of signs, endless imitation, infinitely postponed.

Once the Author is distanced, the claim to "decipher" a text becomes entirely futile. To assign an Author to a text is to impose a brake on it, to furnish it with a final signified, to close writing. This conception is quite suited to criticism, which then undertakes the important task of discovering the Author (or his hypostases: society, history, the psyche, freedom) beneath the work: once the Author is found, the text is "explained," the critic has won; hence, it is hardly surprising that historically the Author's empire has been the Critic's as well, and also that (even new) criticism is today unsettled at the same time as the Author. In multiple writing, in effect, everything is to be *disentangled,* but nothing *deciphered,* structure can be followed, "threaded" (as we say of a run in a stocking) in all its reprises, all its stages, but there is no end to it, no bottom; the space of writing is to be traversed, not pierced; writing constantly posits meaning, but always in order to evaporate it: writing seeks a systematic exemption of meaning. Thereby, literature (it would be better, from now on, to say *writing*), by refusing to assign to the text (and to the world-as-text) a "secret," i.e., an ultimate meaning, liberates an activity we may call countertheological, properly revolutionary, for to refuse to halt meaning is finally to refuse God and his hypostases, reason, science, the law.

To return to Balzac's sentence. No one (i.e., no "person") says it: its source, its voice is not the true site of writing, it is reading. Another very specific example will help us here: recent investigations (J.-P. Vernant) have shed some light on the constitutively ambiguous nature of Greek tragedy, whose text is "woven" of words with double meanings, words which each character understands unilaterally (this perpetual misunderstanding is precisely what we call the "tragic"); there is, however, someone who understands each word in its duplicity, and further understands, one may say, the very deafness of the characters speaking in his presence: this "someone" is precisely the reader (or here the listener). Here we discern the total being of writing: a text consists of multiple writings, proceeding from several cultures and entering into dialogue, into parody, into contestation; but there is a site where this multiplicity is collected, and this site is not the author, as has hitherto been claimed, but the reader: the reader is the very space in which are inscribed, without any of them being lost, all the citations out of which a writing is made; the unity of a text is not in its origin but in its destination, but this destination can no longer be personal: the reader is a man without history, without biography, without psychology; he is only that *someone* who holds collected into one and the same field all of the traces from which writing is constituted. That is why it is absurd to hear the new writing condemned in the name of a humanism which hypocritically claims to champion the reader's rights. Classical criticism has never been concerned with the reader; for that criticism, there is no other man in literature than the one who writes. We are no longer so willing to be the dupes of such antiphrases, by which a society proudly recriminates in favor of precisely what it discards, ignores, muffles, or destroys; we know that in order to restore writing to its future, we must reverse the myth: the birth of the reader must be requited by the death of the Author.

QUESTIONS

1. What, exactly, does Barthes mean by the "death of the author"?
2. In what sense is the concept of "author" a modern, Western one?
3. What implications does the idea that there is "no final meaning" to a text have for interpretation and commentary in the humanities?
4. What do you understand by "the birth of the reader"?

JOHN BARTH (1930–)

Autobiography: A Self-Recorded Fiction

You who listen give me life in a manner of speaking.

I won't hold you responsible.

My first words weren't my first words. I wish I'd begun differently.

Among other things I haven't a proper name. The one I bear's misleading, if not false. I didn't choose it either.

I don't recall asking to be conceived! Neither did my parents come to think of it. Even so. Score to be settled. Children are vengeance.

I seem to've known myself from the beginning without knowing I knew; no news is good news; perhaps I'm mistaken.

Now that I reflect I'm not enjoying this life: my link with the world.

My situation appears to me as follows: I speak in a curious, detached manner, and don't necessarily hear myself. I'm grateful for small mercies. Whether anyone follows me I can't tell.

Are you there? If so I'm blind and deaf to you, or you are me, or both're both. One may be imaginary; I've had stranger ideas. I hope I'm a fiction without real hope. Where there's a voice there's a speaker.

I see I see myself as a halt narrative: first person, tiresome. Pronoun sans ante or precedent, warrant or respite. Surrogate for the substantive; contentless form, interestless principle; blind eye blinking at nothing. Who am I. A little *crise d'identité*[1] for you.

I must compose myself.

Look, I'm writing. No, listen, I'm nothing but talk; I won't last long. The odds against my conception were splendid; against my birth excellent; against my continuance favorable. Are yet. On the other hand, if my sort are permitted a certain age and growth, God help us, our life expectancy's been known to increase at an obscene rate instead of petering out. Let me squeak on long enough, I just might live forever: a word to the wise.

My beginning was comparatively interesting, believe it or not. Exposition. I was spawned not long since in an American state and born in no better. Grew in no worse. Persist in a representative. Prohibition, Depression, Radicalism, Decadence, and what have you. An eye sir for an eye. It's alleged, now, that Mother was a mere passing fancy who didn't pass quickly enough; there's evidence also that she was a mere novel device, just in style, soon to become a commonplace, to which Dad resorted one day when he found himself by himself with pointless pen. In either case she was mere, Mom; at any event Dad dallied. He has me to explain. Bear in mind, I suppose he told her. A child is not its parents, but sum of their conjoined shames. A figure of speech. Their manner of speaking. No wonder I'm heterodoxical.

[1] *Crise d'identité* is French for "identity crisis."

Nothing lasts longer than a mood. Dad's infatuation passed; I remained. He understood, about time, that anything conceived in so unnatural and fugitive a fashion was apt to be freakish, even monstrous—and an advertisement of his folly. His second thought therefore was to destroy me before I spoke a word. He knew how these things work; he went by the book. To expose ourselves publicly is frowned upon; therefore we do it to one another in private. He me, I him; one was bound to be the case. What fathers can't forgive is that their offspring receive and sow broadcast their shortcomings. From my conception to the present moment Dad's tried to turn me off; not ardently, not consistently, not successfully so far; but persistently, persistently, with at least half a heart. How do I know? I'm his bloody mirror!

Which is to say, upon reflection I reverse and distort him. For I suspect that my true father's sentiments are the contrary of murderous. That one only imagines he begot me; mightn't he be deceived and deadly jealous? In his heart of hearts he wonders whether I mayn't after all be the get of a nobler spirit, taken by beauty past his grasp. Or else, what comes to the same thing, to me, I've a pair of dads, to match my pair of moms. How account for my contradictions except as the vices of their versus? Beneath self-contempt, I particularly scorn my fondness for paradox. I despite pessimism, narcissism, solipsism,[2] truculence, word-play, and pusillanimity, my chiefer inclinations; loathe self-loathers *ergo me;*[3] have no pity for self-pity and so am free of that sweet baseness. I doubt I am. Being me's no joke.

I continued the tale of my forebears. Thus my exposure; thus my escape. This cursed me, turned me out; that, curse him, save me; right hand slipped me through left's fingers. Unless on a third hand I somehow preserved myself. Unless unless: the mercy-killing was successful. Buzzards let us say made brunch of me betimes but couldn't stomach my voice, which persists like the Nauseous Danaid.[4] We... monstrosities are easilier achieved than got rid of.

In sum I'm not what either parent or I had in mind. One hoped I'd be astonishing, forceful, triumphant—heroical in other words. One dead. I myself conventional. I turn out I. Not every kid thrown to the wolves ends a hero: for each survivor, a mountain of beast-baits; for every Oedipus, a city of feebs.[5]

So much for my dramatic exposition: seems not to've worked. Here I am, Dad: Your creature! Your caricature!

Unhappily, things get clearer as we go along. I perceive that I have no body. What's less, I've been speaking of myself without delight or alternative as self-consciousness pure and sour; I declare now that even that isn't true. I'm not aware of myself at all, as far as I know. I don't think... I know what I'm talking about.

Well, well, being well into my life as it's been called I see well how it'll end, unless in some meaningless surprise. If anything dramatic were going to happen to make me successfuller... agreeabler... endurabler ... it should've happened by now, we will agree. A change for the better still isn't unthinkable; miracles can be cited. But the odds against a wireless *deus ex machina*[6] aren't encouraging.

Here, a confession: Early on I too aspired to immortality. Assumed I'd be beautiful, powerful, loving, loved. At least commonplace. Anyhow human. Even the revelation of my several defects—absence of presence to name one—didn't fetch me right to despair: crippledness affords its own heroisms, does it not; heroes are typically gimpish, are they not. But your crippled hero's one thing, a bloody hero after all; your heroic cripple another, etcetcetcetcetcet. Being an ideal's warped image, my fancy's own twist figure, is what undoes me.

I wonder if I repeat myself. One-track minds may lead to their origins. Perhaps I'm still in utero,[7] hung up in my delivery; my exposition and the rest merely foreshadow what's to come, the argument for an interrupted pregnancy.

Womb, coffin, can—in any case, from my viewless viewpoint I see no point in going further. Since Dad among his other failings failed to end me when he should've, I'll turn myself off if I can this instant.

---

[2]Narcissism is the love of one's self; solipsism is the philosophical position that nothing exists but the contents of one's own mind.

[3]*Ergo me* is Latin for "therefore me."

[4]A Danaid is one of the mythical fifty daughters of Danaus, ruler of Argus, who ordered his daughters to murder their husbands on their wedding night.

[5]Oedipus, the mythical ruler of Thebes (rhymes with "feebs") unknowingly killed his father and married his mother. Oedipus was left out on a hillside (exposed) when born because his father, Laïos, wished to avoid the prophecy that he would be slain by his son. Oedipus was saved by shepherds, who raised him. See Sophocles' tragedy *Oedipus Rex* in Volume I.

[6]*Deus ex machina* literally means "god from a machine," a stage device used in Greek drama that would lower an actor, dressed up as a god, to unravel complicated plots and bring about a happy ending.

[7]*In utero* is a medical term for "in the womb."

Can't. *Then if anyone hears me, speaking from here inside like a sunk submariner, and has the means to my end, I pray him do us both a kindness.*

Didn't. Very well, my ace in the hole: *Father, have mercy, I dare you! Wretched old fabricator, where's your shame? Put an end to this, for pity's sake! Now! Now!*

So. My last trump, and I blew it. Not much in the way of a climax; more a climacteric. I'm not the dramatic sort. May the end come quietly, then, without my knowing it. In the course of any breath. In the heart of any word. This one. This one.

Perhaps I'll have a posthumous cautionary value, like gibbeted corpses,[8] pickled freaks. Self-preservation, it seems, may smell of formaldehyde.[9]

A proper ending wouldn't spin out so.

I suppose I might have managed things to better effect, in spite of the old boy. Too late now.

Basket case. Waste.

Shake up some memorable last words at least. There seems to be time.

Nonsense, I'll mutter to the end, one word after another, string the rascals out, mad or not, heard or not, my last words will be my last words.

QUESTIONS

1. Who is the speaker in this story?
2. Who is the speaker's father?
3. How does the speaker call attention to the structure of the story?
4. In what ways is the relationship between a protagonist and its author an example of narcissism? Of solipsism?
5. How is the Oedipus story a model of the relationship between an author and his protagonist?
6. How are the puns appropriate to this story?

[8]Gibbeted corpses were dead persons left hanging on the gallows.

[9]Formaldehyde is a chemical used for preserving dead bodies.

ISHMAEL REED (1938–)

beware: do not read this poem

tonite, *thriller* was
abt an ol woman, so vain she
surrounded her self w/
   many mirrors

it got so bad that finally she
locked herself indoors & her
whole life became the
   mirrors

one day the villagers broke
into her house, but she was too
swift for them. she disappeared
      into a mirror
each tenant who bought the house
after that, lost a loved one to
      the ol woman in the mirror:
      first a little girl
      then a young woman
      then the young woman/s husband

the hunger of this poem is legendary
it has taken in many victims
back off from this poem
it has drawn in yr feet
back off from this poem
it has drawn in yr legs
back off from this poem
it is a greedy mirror
you are into this poem. from
   the waist down
nobody can hear you can they?
this poem has had you up to her
         belch
this poem aint got no manners
you cant call out frm this poem
relax now & go w/ this poem
move & roll on to this poem
do not resist this poem
this poem has yr eyes
this poem has his head
this poem has his arms
this poem has his fingers
this poem has his fingertips

this poem is the reader & the
reader this poem

statistic: the us bureau of missing persons reports
that in 1968 over 100,000 people
disappeared
leaving no solid clues
nor trace only
a space in the lives of their friends

QUESTIONS

1. What is the significance of the "mirror" as a central postmodern image? What does it say about the postmodern view of reality?
2. Explain the meaning of the expression "this poem is the reader & the/reader this poem." What does it suggest about the postmodern attitude toward authorship?
3. What postmodern linguistic and stylistic techniques are evident in Reed's poem?
4. The fantastic, irrationality, and entropy are common themes of postmodern literature. Identify each element in the poem and discuss its function.

ERNESTO CARDENAL (1925–)

This poet priest, like so many other Latin Americans before him, has lived in Nicaragua under the harsh oppression of a long-term dictatorship. He combines Christian and biblical forms with themes of social protest and revolution. His is the voice of the voiceless. An echo of liberation theology can be heard in much of his profoundly religious poetry. Since the overthrow of the Somozas he has become an active participant in the formation of a new Nicaragua. Poetic works such as *Hora cero* (*Zero Hour*), *Epigramas,* and *Oración por Marilyn Monroe* (*A Prayer for Marilyn Monroe*) reflect both postmodern themes and a pervasive tone of imminent social upheaval.

Epigrama 18

De pronto suena en la noche una sirena
de alarma, larga, larga,
el aullido lúgubre de la sirena
de incendio o de la ambulancia blanca de la muerte
como el grito de la cegua en la noche,
que se acerca y se acerca sobre las calles
y las casas y sube, sube, y baja
y crece, crece, baja y se aleja
creciendo y bajando. No es incendio ni muerte:
Es Somoza[1] que pasa.

Epigram 18

Translation by Thomas Merton

Suddenly in the night the sirens
sound their long, long, long alarm,
the siren's miserable howl
of fire, or death's white ambulance
like a ghost wailing in the night,
coming closer and closer above the streets
and the houses, it rises, rises, and falls,
and it grows, grows, falls and goes away
growing and dying. It's neither a fire nor a death:
Just the Dictator flashing by.

Salmo 5

Escucha mis palabras oh Señor
Oye mis gemidos
Escucha mi protesta
Porque no eres tú un Dios amigo de los dictadores
ni partidario de su política
ni te influencia la propaganda
ni estás en sociedad con el gángsters

No existe sinceridad en sus discursos
ni en sus declaraciones de prensa

Hablan de paz en sus discursos
mientras aumentan su producción de guerra

Hablan de paz en las Conferencias de Paz
y en secreto se preparan para la guerra

Sus radios mentirosos rugen toda la noche
Sus escritorios están llenos de planes criminales
y expedientes siniestros
Pero tú me salvarás de sus planes

Hablan con la boca de las ametralladoras
Sus lenguas relucientes
son las bayonetas...

[1]Dictator of Nicaragua from 1967 to 1984.

Castígalos oh Dios
malogra su política
confunde sus memorándums
impide sus programas

A la horna de la Sirena de Alarma
tú estarás conmigo
tú serás mi refugio el día de la Bomba

Al que no cree en la mentira de sus anuncios comerciales
ni en sus campañas publicitarias ni en sus campañas politicas
tú lo bendices
Lo rodeas con tu amor
como con tanques blindados

Psalm 5

Translation by John R. Kelly

Listen to my words oh Lord
Hear my cries
Listen to my protest
Because you are not a God friendly to dictators
nor party to their politics
nor does their propaganda influence you
nor are you in league with the gangster

No sincerity exists in their speeches
nor in their press releases

They talk of peace in their speeches
While they increase their war production

They talk of peace at Peace Conferences
and secretly they prepare for war

Their lying radios roar all night
Their desks are full of criminal plans
and sinister files
But you will save me from their plans

They speak with the mouth of machine guns
Their glistening tongues
are the bayonets...

Punish them oh God
wreck their politics
Confuse their memoranda
hinder their programs

At the hour of the Alarm Siren
You will be with me
You will be my refuge on the day of the Bomb

He who does not believe in the lie of their commercials
nor their advertising campaigns nor in their political campaigns
You bless him
You surround him with your love
like an armored tank

Prayer for Marilyn Monroe

Translation by Robert Pring-Mill

Lord
accept this girl called Marilyn Monroe throughout the world
though that was not her name
(but You know her real name, that of the orphan raped at nine,
the shopgirl who tried to kill herself aged just sixteen)
who now goes into Your presence without make-up
without her Press Agent
without her photographs or signing autographs
lonely as an astronaut facing the darkness of outer space.
When she was a child, she dreamed she was naked in a church
(according to *Time*)
standing in front of a prostrate multitude, heads to the ground, and had to walk on tiptoe to avoid the heads.
You know our dreams better than the psychiatrists.
Church, house, or cave all represent the safety of the womb
but also something more....
The heads are admirers, so much is clear (that
mass of heads in the darkness below the beam to the screen).
But the temple isn't the studio of 20th-Century Fox.
The temple, of gold and marble, is the temple of her body
in which the Son of Man stands whip in hand
driving out the money-changers of 20th-Century Fox
who made Your house of prayer a den of thieves.

Lord,
in this world defiled by radioactivity and sin,

surely You will not blame a shopgirl
who (like any other shopgirl) dreamed of being a star.
And her dream became "reality" (Technicolor reality).
All she did was follow the script we gave her,
that of our own lives, but it was meaningless.
Forgive her Lord and forgive all of us
for this our 20th Century
and the Mammoth Super-Production in whose making we all shared.

She was hungry for love and we offered her tranquilizers.
For the sadness of our not being saints they recommended Psychoanalysis.
Remember Lord her increasing terror of the camera
and hatred of make-up (yet her insistence on fresh make-up
for each scene) and how the terror grew
and how her unpunctuality at the studios grew.

Like any other shopgirl
she dreamed of being a star.
And her life was as unreal as a dream an analyst reads and files.

Her romances were kisses with closed eyes
which when the eyes are opened
are seen to have been played out beneath the spotlights and the spotlights are switched off

and the two walls of the room (it was a set) are taken down
while the Director moves away notebook in hand, the scene being safely canned.
Or like a cruise on a yacht, a kiss in Singapore, a dance in Rio,
a reception in the mansion of the Duke and Duchess of Windsor viewed in the sad tawdriness of a cheap apartment.

The film ended without the final kiss.
They found her dead in bed, hand on the phone.
And the detectives never learned who she was going to call.
It was as
though someone had dialed the only friendly voice
and heard a prerecorded tape just saying "WRONG NUMBER";
or like someone wounded by gansters, who
reaches out toward a disconnected phone.

Lord, whoever
it may have been that she was going to call
but did not (and perhaps it was no one at all
or Someone not in the Los Angeles telephone book),
Lord, You pick up that phone.

QUESTIONS

1. For what reasons does Cardenal employ such traditional modes as the epigram, prayer, and psalm?
2. What relationship does Cardenal's "Psalm 5" have to the Old Testament's Psalm 5? Why has he used this form and what is its theme?
3. What postmodernist themes appear in "Prayer for Marilyn Monroe"? Why has the poet employed a prayer as his vehicle here?
4. Compare the image of Marilyn Monroe in this poem to that used by Andy Warhol in his silkscreen (Color Plate XXXV).

Middle and Late Twentieth-Century Humanities

The human creations of the present day exhibit a discontinuity with tradition in appearance even more radical than did those of the early twentieth century. The great systems of the past that once served as intellectual frameworks "fell apart," as we have seen, at that time. As yet, no dominant system of belief has arisen to restore to Western culture its lost unity. Our own time is rather one of searching, of experimentation, and of multiplicity in morality and ideology as well as in the arts. The artistic freedom for which the great modernist innovators struggled has been achieved, or overachieved. Whereas the artists who made the first break with the representation of the real world shocked their public by challenging its cultural assumptions and traditions, contemporary artists confront a public that is virtually shockproof. The necessity to innovate seems constant; indeed styles, trends, and schools appear and disappear within periods of a few years. The fact that they also coexist makes the contemporary scene one characterized by a bewildering but exhilarating plurality of forms.

The explanation of this state of affairs lies not only in the evolution of the humanities themselves but also in the economic, political, and social environment in which the changes have taken place. In contrast to ancient Greece or to traditional Africa, support for arts and letters in the West has been until recently in the keeping of a well-educated, relatively small class of individuals, who had both leisure and wealth to devote to such pursuits. During the past century, with the beginnings of redistribution of income and the rise in the standards of living and literacy in the lower classes, this cultural hegemony has gradually diminished. In addition, the rise in immigration to the West from non-Western countries, along with the spread of Afrocentric and feminist movements, has made multiculturalism a force to be reckoned with. Mass communications, too, have increased the facility and speed with which cultural products can be distributed. But mass communications also change the nature of these products. A play seen on television or a symphony heard on compact disc offers a different experience from one seen and heard in a theater or concert hall. As more and more cultural material is communicated to us electronically, the question of whether the forms we call "literature," "art," and "music" will survive as such is a legitimate one.

Mass communication has also vastly increased our awareness of the cultures outside the one in which we live and has made Marshall McLuhan's prediction of a "global village" a reality. This in turn has tended to make our sense of cultural relativity deeper and more pervasive than it was in the days of Montaigne or Voltaire. The shifting balance of the West's position in international politics has also had its effect here. Western culture, which has imposed its values on the rest of the planet, at least since the seventeenth century, is no longer an unquestioned leader in cultural matters. The "boom" in Latin American arts and the importance of writers from south of the Rio Grande on the postmodern literary scene may be symptomatic. More remote cultures become constantly more accessible. In the course of a few days, we may watch a program on tribal life in the South Pacific, attend a performance of a touring company doing Chinese dances, hear a lecture on Islam and the Middle East, listen to Japanese music or to medieval European music on authentic instruments reproduced by Japanese technology, see a film on native Americans, and look through a newly published novel by an African writer. As the third world continues to adopt Western technology, some Europeans and Americans, sensing a spiritual vacuum in the West, turn toward non-Western philosophies, religions, and healing arts.

The feeling of being able to exist in several temporal, spatial, and cultural zones at once is, as we have seen, characteristic of the postmodern era. Expressing this sense of pluralism, postmodern architects, for example, play with elements of various styles. In the humanities in general, the new pluralism has led to a movement toward opening up the canon, or the "sacred texts," of the tradition. Feminists have called attention to the neglect of the study of creative works by women and also propose fresh approaches to the reading of old texts. African Americans and other minorities have succeeded in legitimizing their formerly neglected contributions.

In the postmodern arts, popular and high culture, less distinct than formerly, blend and exchange forms. Contemporary serious composers learn from and incorporate pop, rock, and jazz; painters and advertisers share some of the same visual language; films and television programs speak to cultured and uncultured alike. Still, it is possible to make at least one basic distinction between the true artist and the producer of mass entertainment. The former demands from his or her public an *active* participation—an involvement of the mind, spirit, and senses—very much, as we have seen, within the humanistic spirit. The latter, in accord with many other aspects of modern life, encourages passive consumption.

Rather than luring or spellbinding their audiences with a smooth, finished product, many artists today like to show the wheels in their machines. People in the theater are constantly reminded that they are witnessing a play, an artifice, and not a window on the world. The actors may even enter into a dialogue with the audience. Similarly, novelists, poets, and filmmakers tend to say, in effect, "I am writing a novel," "I am trying to create a poem," "I am making a film." Visual artists, taking their work out of the museum and into the environment, emphasize both the differences between their creations and the natural world, and the dialogue that must take place between them. Architects are not afraid to expose things such as wiring and plumbing. Musicians make compositions of *sounds,* not pure music, using tape recorders and electronic synthesizers along with acoustic instruments.

Our acceptance of an art without bounds is closely related to the growing tendency to integrate the arts into society. The elitist quality, characteristic of Western art since the Renaissance, might in a sense be viewed as a deviation from the history of the humanities not only in other areas of the world but even in Europe itself. Our present vision of art as a form of relating to the world and to other human beings seems to echo John Donne's words, "No man is an island." Although modern Americans lack the cohesive, unitary vision of the ancient Greeks or the traditional Africans, they, too, are coming to treat the humanities as playing a vital role in the life of the community and to see the artist as making a social contribution.

Although in some ways postmodern expressions are more accessible and more in tune with popular culture than were their modernist counterparts, in other ways they are more remote. They may use electronics, advertising images, and other modes, but postmodern artists may nonetheless be making a violent critique of bland, passive mass culture. The whole domain of "theory" is certainly difficult for the average reader and even for many highly educated readers to access. Yet in their demonstrations of our dependence on images, our imprisonment in "textuality" or systems of language, the "death of the author," and the collapse of traditional Western notions of reality, the theorists have formulated some of the important underpinnings of contemporary culture.

Everyone is aware that our world today is characterized by increased bureaucracy and regimentation. Data banks, computers, and officials intervene constantly in daily life. This regimentation is in large part motivated by the belief that fairness to everyone requires governmental order and supervision, but it often has the effect of making individuals feel that they are being reduced to automatons. This phenomenon, certainly a threat to humanistic values from many points of view, seems, however, to have led to a widespread awareness of the need for creative expression, and for the humanities generally, in modern life. One of the most important tasks before those dedicated to the humanities today is to help prevent the vital, creative being from being replaced by a passive, docile consumer.

Naturally, if the humanities are to be relevant to contemporary problems, they must keep pace with the rapid changes in contemporary life. What is called for are forms and thoughts oriented toward the future, not a self-satisfied idealization of the past. Yet, paradoxically, the humanist who would be future-oriented must be well versed in the past. Human beings are not islands in time, just as they are not islands in space—their modes of feeling and thinking, as well as their material way of life, are to a great extent shaped by what took place before they existed. It is only through awareness of cultural roots, as we have tried to emphasize throughout this book, that men and women can be equipped to understand and to shape the humanities of the future. Of course, every generation will conceive of its roots in slightly different ways and will find that certain works or periods from the past speak to it more urgently than do others. We are at last beginning to understand the African contribution to our cultural heritage and to envision ourselves as a multicultural society. We also understand more fully how Western culture is itself a child of Africa and the Near East—of Egypt and Mesopotamia. Yet, the Western humanities, with their roots in the Greco-Roman and Judeo-Christian traditions, are still present in all our forms of expression. Even if artists see Beethoven's Ninth Symphony as a sexual message or the *Mona Lisa* as a computer printout, if they work with laser beams rather than gold paint, if they decry the cultural hegemony of the monuments of the Western world, they affirm a certain kind of continuity by the very force of their reaction. In the midst of change and diversity, we can be fairly certain that if we manage not to destroy our planet, people centuries from now will still be reading Dostoevsky, visiting Versailles, and listening to Beethoven. They will react to these works with their intelligence and sensibility, absorbing them as part of their individual and collective cultures. North Americans and Europeans will also, with increasing frequency, integrate aspects of African, Asian, Latin American, and other artistic and philosophical creations into their culture. It is possible that we will eventually witness the evolution of a world culture with forms of artistic communication accessible to everyone. The ways in which the tradition of the humanities will be carried forward into the future will be determined by its present students.

Glossary

Italics are used within the definitions to indicate terms that are themselves defined elsewhere in the glossary and, in a few cases, to distinguish titles of works or foreign words.

ABA Form MUSIC: A particular organization of parts used in a musical *composition* in which there are three units, the first and third of which are the same. See *Da capo aria.*

Abbey Religious body governed by an abbot or abbess, or the collection of buildings themselves, also called a monastery.

Absolutism The theory that all political power in a society is derived from one authority, normally a monarch.

Abstract VISUAL ARTS: Not representational or *illusionistic.* Describes painting or sculpture that simplifies or distills figures from the material world into *forms,* lines, *colors.*

Affect MUSIC: The production of emotional reactions in the listener by certain musical sounds, according to a theory from the baroque period. For example, sorrow should be characterized by slow-moving music, hatred by very repulsive harmonies.

African Survival A specific form or function of an institution, ritual, belief, language, or art that is clearly identifiable with an African origin, although adapted to the situation of African descendants in the New World.

Allegory LITERATURE, VISUAL ARTS: The technique of making concrete things, animals, or persons represent abstract ideas or morals. A literary allegory usually takes the form of a *narrative* which may be read on at least two levels; for example, Dante's *Divine Comedy.* Medieval sculptures often have allegorical significance.

Altarpiece VISUAL ARTS: A painted or sculptured decoration on canvas or panels placed behind or above an altar.

Ambulatory ARCHITECTURE: A covered passageway for walking. In a church, the semicircular passage around the main altar.

Anaphora (ah-na'fo-rah) LITERATURE: A rhetorical figure which uses the repetition of the same word or phrase to introduce two or more clauses or lines of verse.

Animism The belief that parts of nature, such as water, trees, etc., have souls and can influence human events. The term is used by Westerners to describe African religions.

Antiphon MUSIC: In Gregorian chant, a short text from the Scriptures or elsewhere set to music in a simple *style,* and sung before and after a Psalm or a canticle.

Antiphonal MUSIC: See *Antiphony.*

Antiphony (an-ti'fo-ny) MUSIC: The sound produced by *choirs* or instruments "answering" one another. For instance, one choir will sing, and then it is "answered" by another choir.

Antithesis LITERATURE: The balance of parallel word groups conveying opposing ideas.

Apse (aap'ss) ARCHITECTURE: A large semicircular or polygonal *niche, domed* or *vaulted.* In a Roman *basilica* the apse was placed at one or both ends or sides of the building. In a Christian church it is usually placed at the east end of the *nave* beyond the *choir.*

Arcade ARCHITECTURE: A covered walk made of *arches* on *piers* or *columns,* rather than *lintels.*

Arch ARCHITECTURE: 1. Commonly, any curved structural member that is used to span an opening. 2. Specifically, restricted to the spanning members of a curved opening that are constructed of wedge-shaped stones called *voussoirs.* Arches may be of many shapes, basically round or pointed. See Roman Architecture (Ch. 7) and Gothic Architecture (Ch. 10).

Archaic 1. Obsolete. 2. In its formative or early stages.

Architrave (ahr'kuh-trave) ARCHITECTURE: A *beam* that rests directly on the *columns;* the lowest part of the *entablature.*

Aria (ah'ree-ah) MUSIC: An elaborate *composition* for solo voice with instrumental accompaniment.

Aristocracy Form of government from Greek word meaning "rule by the few for the common good."

Arpeggiated MUSIC: Describes a rippling effect produced by playing the notes of a chord one after another instead of simultaneously. See *Chord.*

Asantehene (a-sahn'tee-hee-nee) The Akan term for the King of the Ashanti state.

Ase (ah-say') Yoruba word meaning power, authority, potential energy.

Atmospheric Perspective See *Perspective.*

Atonal MUSIC: Describes music written with an intentional disregard for a central keynote (or tonal center). This style of composition was developed after World War I by Arnold Schoenberg and his followers.

Aulos (ow'los) MUSIC: The most important wind instrument of the ancient Greeks. It is not a flute (as is often stated), but a shrill-sounding oboe. It originated in the Orient and was associated with the orgiastic rites of the god Dionysus.

Axis VISUAL ARTS: The imaginary line that can be passed through a building or a figure, around which the principal parts revolve. See *Balance.*

Balance VISUAL ARTS: The creation of an apparent equilibrium or *harmony* between all the parts of a *composition,* be it a building, painting, or sculpture.

Ballad A narrative poem or song in short stanzas, usually with a refrain, often handed down orally.

Balustrade ARCHITECTURE: A rail or handrail along the top edge of a roof or balcony, made up of a top horizontal rail, a bottom rail, and short *columns* between.

Baptistry ARCHITECTURE: The building or room for performing the rite of baptism. Contains a basin or pool.

Baroque Term first applied to the visual arts and later to the music and literature of the 17th and 18th centuries to designate a style characterized by energy, movement, realism, and violent contrasts. The baroque style is often set in opposition to the orderly and formal "classical" style of the High Renaissance.

Barrel Vault See *Vault.*

Base ARCHITECTURE: 1. The lowest visible part of a building. 2. The slab on which some *column* shafts rest. See *Orders.*

Basilica (bah-sil'i-cah) ARCHITECTURE: A large, rectangular hall with a central space surrounded by aisles on the sides and an *apse* at one or each end or side. The basilica was used as a court of justice by the Romans and adopted by the early Christians as a church.

Bay ARCHITECTURE: One of a series of regularly repeated spaces of a building marked off by vertical elements.

Beam ARCHITECTURE: A large piece of squared timber, long in proportion to its breadth and thickness, used for spanning spaces. A *lintel* is a specific kind of beam.

Blank Verse LITERATURE: Unrhymed lines in *iambic pentameter.* A common form for dramatic verse in English. See Shakespeare (Ch. 19).

Boss ARCHITECTURE: The circular *keystone* at the crossing of diagonal *ribs.* May be richly carved and decorated.

Buttress ARCHITECTURE: The vertical exterior mass of masonry built at right angles into the *wall* to strengthen it and to counteract the lateral *thrust* of a *vault* or *arch.* Architecture of the Gothic period developed this *form* into the flying buttress, which is a combination of the regular or *pier*-like buttress and the arched buttress. See *Chartres* (Ch. 10).

Cadence MUSIC: A formula or cliché that indicates a point of repose. The cadence is one of several possible melodic, rhythmic, or harmonic combinations that signal a slowing down or stopping of the forward motion.

Candace Title of the Queen Mother in Nubia.

Cantilever ARCHITECTURE: 1. A horizontally projecting member, sometimes called a bracket, used to carry the cornice or eaves of a building. 2. A beam or slab, projecting beyond the wall or supporting column, whose outward thrust or span is held down at one end only. See Robie House (Ch. 31).

Capital ARCHITECTURE: The uppermost or crowning member of a *column, pilaster,* or *pier* that forms the visual transition from the post to the *lintel* above. See *Orders.*

Caryatid (kahr'ee-ah-tid) ARCHITECTURE: The name given a *column* when it is disguised as a female figure.

Casting SCULPTURE: A method of reproducing sculpture through the use of a mold that is the receptacle for a liquid which hardens when cooled. The method may be used to produce solid or hollow cast *forms.*

Cathedral Principal church of a diocese, literally the location of the bishop's throne, or cathedra.

Cella ARCHITECTURE: The principal chamber of a Greek or Roman temple, housing the cult image.

Centering ARCHITECTURE: The temporary wooden *structure* that supports an *arch* or dome while it is being erected.

Chapel ARCHITECTURE: 1. A small church. 2. A separate compartment in a large church that has its own altar.

Choir ARCHITECTURE: The part of the church reserved for clergy and singers, usually the space between the crossing and the *apse.* MUSIC: A group of singers in a church.

Chord MUSIC: The simultaneous sounding of three or more usually harmonious *tones.*

Chordal MUSIC: Characterized by the employment of *chords* in a logical progression of harmonies.

Choreographer DANCE: Person responsible for the *choreography* of a dance.

Choreography DANCE: The design and arrangement of the movements of a ballet or modern dance.

Chromatic MUSIC: Describes a scale progressing by halftones instead of the normal degrees of the scale; e.g., in C major: c-c#-d-d#-e instead of c-d-e. VISUAL ARTS: Refers to the visual spectrum of hues. See *Color.*

Cire Perdu (seer pehr-doo') SCULPTURE: French expression meaning "lost wax." Technique for making bronze sculpture that involves molding wax over a clay mold, encasing it with another clay mold, heating the mold, then allowing the wax to drain out and replacing it with molten bronze.

Classic, Classical ALL ARTS: Recognized generally to be excellent, time-tested. LITERATURE AND VISUAL ARTS: 1. From ancient Greece or Rome. 2. From "classical" (fifth century B.C.) Greece or having properties such as *harmony, balance,* moderation and magnitude characteristic of art of that period. MUSIC: The musical *style* of the late 18th century. Leading composers in the classical style are Haydn, Mozart, and the early Beethoven.

Clerestory (clear'story) ARCHITECTURE: An upper story in a building that carries windows or openings for the transmission of light to the space beneath.

Coda MUSIC: A passage of music added to the end of a piece to confirm an impression of finality.

Coffer, Coffering ARCHITECTURE: Originally a casket or box, later, a recessed ceiling panel. Coffering is a technique for making a ceiling of recessed panels.

Collage (kohl-lahzh') VISUAL ARTS: From the French, *coller,* "to glue." A technique for creating *compositions* by pasting or in some way attaching a variety of materials or objects to a flat surface or canvas.

Colonnade ARCHITECTURE: A series of regularly spaced *columns* supporting a *lintel* or *entablature.*

Color VISUAL ARTS: A quality perceived in objects by the human eye that derives from the length of the light waves reflected by individual surfaces. The visible spectrum is divided into six basic hues: red, orange, yellow, green, blue, and violet. Red, yellow and blue are called the *primary colors;* the others, which result from mixing adjacent primary colors, are called *secondary colors.* White, black, and grays result from mixing these six hues and are not *chromatic:* they cannot be distinguished by hue, only by value. Value is the property of a color that distinguishes it as light or dark. Colors that are "high" in value are light colors; those that are "low" in value are dark colors. Adding white to a color will raise its value to make a *tint;* adding black to a color will lower its value to make a *shade.* Saturation is the property of a color by which its vividness or purity is distinguished. See also *Complementary Colors, Cool Colors, Warm Colors.*

Column ARCHITECTURE: A cylindrical, upright post or pillar. It may contain three parts: *base, shaft,* and *capital.*

Comedy LITERATURE: A drama that ends happily, intended to provoke laughter from its audience. Comedy often includes *satire* on types of characters or societies.

Complementary Colors VISUAL ARTS: Hues that form a neutral gray when mixed but, when juxtaposed, form a sharp contrast. The complementary of any *primary color* (red, yellow, or blue) is made by mixing the other two primaries. Example: The complementary of red is green, obtained by mixing yellow with blue.

Composition VISUAL ARTS: The arrangements of elements within the work in order to create a certain effect based on a variety of principles and conventions: e.g., *balance, color, contour, focal point,* proportion, scale, *symmetry, volume.* MUSIC: The putting together of elements such as *melody, harmony, rhythm,* and orchestration into a musical *form.* The term may be used similarly to denote a putting together of elements in a dance or film. LITERATURE: The act of composing an oral or written work.

Compound Pier ARCHITECTURE: A *pier* or post made up of attached *columns.* See *Chartres* (Ch. 10).

Concerto (con-chair'toe) MUSIC: A composition for one or more solo instruments and an orchestra, each competing with the other on an equal basis.

Content ALL ARTS: What the *form* contains and means. Content may include subject matter and theme. The quality of a work of art is often judged by the appropriateness, or apparent inseparability, of form and content.

Continuo MUSIC: In the scores of baroque composers (Bach, Handel) the bass part, performed by the harpsichord or organ, together with a viola da gamba or cello. The continuo, during the baroque era, provided the harmonic structure of the pieces being performed.

Contour PAINTING, DRAWING: The visible edge or outline of an object, *form* or shape, used especially to suggest volume or mass by means of the distinctness, thickness, or color of the edge or line.

Contrapuntal (con-tra-pun'tal) MUSIC: In a *style* that employs *counterpoint.*

Cool Colors VISUAL ARTS: Blues, greens, and associated hues. Cool colors will appear to recede from the viewer in a picture, while *warm colors* will tend to project.

Cornice ARCHITECTURE: 1. The horizontal projection that finishes the top of a *wall.* 2. In classical architecture, the third or uppermost horizontal section of an *entablature.* See *Orders.*

Counterpoint MUSIC: Music consisting of two or more *melodies* played simultaneously. The term is practically synonymous with *polyphony.*

Couplet LITERATURE: Two lines of poetry together, of the same meter and rhyme.

Crossing In a church, the intersection of the *nave* and *transept* in front of the *apse.*

Cuneiform Writing system used in Mesopotamia, based on wedge shapes.

Da Capo Aria (dah cah'poh ahr'ee-ah) MUSIC: A particular type of *aria* that developed in the baroque period (17th and 18th centuries). It consists of two sections, the first of which is repeated after the second. The result is the *ABA form.* See *Aria, ABA Form.*

Deduction PHILOSOPHY: Reasoning from a general principle to a specific fact or case, or from a premise to a logical conclusion.

Democracy From the Greek word meaning "rule by the people." A form of government in which the electorate is coincident with the adult population (sometimes only the adult males) of a community.

Demotic The most simplified, "popular" Egyptian writing system.

Despotism Government by a ruler with unlimited powers.

Dialectic PHILOSOPHY: 1. Platonic—A method of logical examination of beliefs, proceeding by question and answer. 2. Hegelian and Marxian—A logical method that proceeds by the contradiction of opposites (thesis, antithesis) to their resolution in a synthesis.

Dome ARCHITECTURE: A curved or hemispherical roof structure spanning a space and resting on a curved, circular, or polygonal *base.* Theoretically, a dome is an *arch* rotated 360 degrees around a central *axis.* See *Pantheon* (Ch. 7).

Drapery SCULPTURE: The clothing of a figure or *form* in a usually nonspecific but *tactile* and responsive material.

Drum ARCHITECTURE: The cylindrical or polygonal *structure* that rises above the body of a building to support a *dome.*

Duration MUSIC: The time-value assigned to a musical note; that is, how long it is to be played or sung.

Dynamics MUSIC: Words or signs that indicate the varying degrees of loudness in the music. For instance, *forte* (loud), *piano* (soft, quiet), *diminuendo* (decrease *volume* gradually).

Ego In Freudian theory, one of the three parts of the mind. The ego is the conscious, controlling, self-directed part.

Egungun (eh-goon-goon) Yoruba masqueraders concerned with mediating between the community of the living and that of the recently dead.

Elevation ARCHITECTURE: 1. Generally, a term that refers to one of the sides of a building. 2. Specifically, a drawing or graphic representation showing one face or side of a building. It can be of the interior or exterior.

Empiricism PHILOSOPHY: The theory that knowledge is derived from observation of nature and by experiment.

Entablature ARCHITECTURE: The upper section of a classical *order* resting on the capitals of the columns and including architrave, frieze, *cornice,* and pediment.

Epic LITERATURE: A long *narrative* poem that recounts an event of importance in a culture's history and presents a hero of that culture. See section on Homer (Ch. 3).

Episode LITERATURE: In Greek tragedy, a section of action between two choruses. In drama and fiction generally, a group of events having unity in itself. A story is created from a series of related episodes. A fiction is said to be episodic if the episodes fall into no logical relationship.

Epithet LITERATURE: A short phrase used to modify a noun by pointing out a salient characteristic. Epithets (e.g., Homer's "swift-footed Achilles") are often used in epic poetry.

Eros In Greek mythology, son of Aphrodite and god of sexual love, called "Cupid" by the Romans.

Ethics PHILOSOPHY: The branch of philosophy dealing with problems of good and bad, right and wrong, in human conduct.

Façade (fa-sahd') ARCHITECTURE: A face of a building.

Fetish Statue or other object believed to embody supernatural power.

Figurative VISUAL ARTS: Describes painting or sculpture in which the human body and the objects of habitual visual experience are clearly recognizable in the work.

Fluting ARCHITECTURE: The grooves or channels, usually parallel, that decorate the shafts of *columns.* Fluting may run up and down a shaft or around the shaft in various directions.

Focal Point VISUAL ARTS: The place of major or dominant interest on which the eyes repeatedly focus in a painting, drawing, or architectural arrangement.

Foreshortening PAINTING: The method of representing objects or parts of objects as if seen from an angle so that the object seems to recede into space instead of being seen in a frontal or profile view. The technique is based on the principle of continuous diminution in size along the length of the object or figure. See *Perspective* and *Vanishing Point.*

Form ALL ARTS: The arrangement or organization of the elements of a work of art in space (visual arts) or time (literary, musical, performing arts). A form may be conventional or imposed by tradition (the Greek temple, the sonnet, the sonata, the five-act play) or original with the artist. In the latter case, form is said to follow from, or adapt itself to, *content.*

Free Verse LITERATURE: Poetic lines with no conventional meter or rhyme.

Fresco PAINTING: The technique of making a painting on new, wet plaster. Fresco painting was particularly favored it Italy from Roman times until the eighteenth century. See Ch. 17.

Frieze ARCHITECTURE: 1. Middle horizontal element of the classical *entablature.* See *Orders.* 2. A decorative band near the top of an interior wall that is below the *cornice* molding.

Frontality (adj. frontally) Artistic device used by the Egyptians whereby part of the body appears frontally and part in profile.

Fugal MUSIC: Characteristic of the *fugue.*

Fugue (fewg) MUSIC: A *composition* based on a *theme* (known as the *subject*) that is stated at the beginning in one voice part alone and is then restated by the other voice parts in succession. The theme reappears at various places throughout the composition in one voice part or another in combination with forms of itself.

Gable ARCHITECTURE: The triangular space at the end of a building formed by the slopes of a pitched roof, extending from the *cornice* or eaves to the *ridge.* In classical architecture the gable is called a *pediment.*

Gallery ARCHITECTURE: A long, covered area, usually elevated, that acts as a passageway on the inside or exterior of a building.

Genre (john'ruh) LITERATURE: A literary type or form. Genres include *tragedy, comedy, epic, lyric, novel,* short story, essay.

Greco-Roman Belonging to the cultures of ancient Greece and Rome.

Grid VISUAL ARTS: A pattern of vertical and horizontal lines forming squares of uniform size on a chart, map, drawing, etc.

Griot (gree-oh') African oral poet, musician, and historian.

Groin Vault See *Vault.*

Groundplan ARCHITECTURE: A drawing of a horizontal *section* of a building that shows the arrangement of the *walls,* windows, supports and other elements. A groundplan is used to produce blueprints.

Ground Plane PAINTING: In a picture, the surface, apparently receding into the distance, on which the figures seem to stand. It is sometimes thought of as comparable to a kind of stage space.

Harmonic Modulation MUSIC: The change of key within a composition. Modulations are accomplished by means of a *chord* (or chords) common to the old key as well as the new one.

Harmony MUSIC: The chordal structure of music familiar to most Western listeners in popular music accompanied by guitars, in Romantic orchestral music, etc.

Hebraic Belonging to the Hebrews, Jews, or Israelites. Refers primarily to the culture of the ancient Hebrews of biblical times.

Hebraism Hebrew culture, thought, institutions.

Hellenic Greek. Usually refers to the "classical" period of Greek culture; i.e., the fifth and fourth centuries B.C.

Hellenism The culture of ancient Greece.

Hellenistic Literally, "Greek-like." Refers to Greek history and artistic style from the third century B.C.

Hieratic Egyptian writing system; a simplified cursive form of hieroglyphics. See *Hieroglyphic.*

Hieroglyphic Egyptian writing system, originally based on pictures.

Homophonic (hawm-o-fon'ic) Characteristic of *homophony.*

Homophony (hoh-maw'foh-nee) MUSIC: A single *melody* line supported by its accompanying *chords* and/or voice parts. See *Monophony, Polyphony, Chord,* and Texture.

Hubris (hyoo'bris) A Greek word meaning arrogance or excessive pride.

Hue See *Color.*

Hyperbole (high-purr'boh-lee) LITERATURE: A figure of speech that uses obvious exaggeration.

Iamb (eye'amb) LITERATURE: A metrical "foot" consisting of one short (or unaccented) syllable and one long (or accented) syllable. Example: hĕllō.

Iambic Pentameter (eye-am'bic pen-tam'eh-ter) LITERATURE: The most common metrical line in English verse, consisting of five *iambs.* Example, from Shakespeare: "Shăll Ī cŏmpāre thĕe tō ă sūmmĕr's dāy?"

Id In Freudian theory, one of the three parts of the mind. The id is the instinctive, non-controlled part.

Ifa (ee'fah) A Yoruba system of divination in which a priest advises his clients of proper courses of behavior based upon the casting of palm kernels and the interpretation of poems chosen for their numerical links to the patterns of thrown kernels.

Illusionism VISUAL ARTS: The attempt by artists to create the illusion of reality in their work. Illusionism may also be called realism. It is important to remember that illusionism is not the motivating intention of all works of art.

Image ALL ARTS: The representation of sense impressions to the imagination. Images are a fundamental part of the language of art. They differ from the abstract terminology of science and philosophy in that they are a means whereby complex emotional experience is communicated. Images may be tactile, auditory, olfactory, etc., but the word is ordinarily used for visual impressions.

Imagery LITERATURE: Patterns of images in a specific work or in the entire works of an author. May refer to a specific type (animal imagery, garden imagery). VISUAL ARTS: The objects, *forms* or shapes depicted by the artist in a particular work.

Impasto (em-pah'stoh) PAINTING: Paint that has the consistency of thick paste, used for bright highlights or to suggest *texture.* Examples: Rembrandt and Van Gogh.

Improvisation MUSIC: The art of performing spontaneously rather than recreating written music.

Induction PHILOSOPHY: Reasoning from particular facts or cases to a general conclusion.

Inflection MUSIC: The shaping or changing of a musical passage in a way that is unique to the individual performer of the music.

Initiation Ceremonies or rites by which a young person is brought into manhood or womanhood, or an older person is made a member of a secret society, brotherhood, etc.

Inquisition A former tribunal in the Roman Catholic Church directed at the suppression of heresy.

Irony LITERATURE: A manner of speaking by which the author says the opposite of what he means, characteristically using words of praise to imply scorn. Dramatic or tragic irony means that the audience is aware of truths which the character speaking does not understand.

Iwi (ee'wee) Yoruba poems sung by Egungun masqueraders.

Jamb ARCHITECTURE: A vertical member at either side of a door frame or window frame. When sculpture is attached to this member it is called a jamb sculpture or jamb figure. See *Chartres* (Ch. 10).

Kente (ken'teh) Large ceremonial cloth from Ghana made of narrow strips sewn together and distinguished by elaborate, multicolored geometric designs of silk.

Keystone ARCHITECTURE: The central wedge-shaped stone of an *arch* that locks together the others.

Komos Greek word for a revel. Root of the word *comedy.*

Kouros (koo'rohs), **Kore** (koh'ray) SCULPTURE: Greek for a male nude votive figure, female votive figure.

Labarai (lah-bah-rye') Hausa tales told by old men, involving cultural, family, and group history.

Lantern ARCHITECTURE: The windowed turret or tower-like form that crowns a *dome* or roof.

Libretto (lih-bret'toe) MUSIC: The text of an opera, *oratorio,* or other dramatic musical work.

Linear Perspective See *Perspective.*

Lintel ARCHITECTURE: The horizontal member or *beam* that spans an opening between two upright members, or posts, over a window, door, or similar opening.

Lyric LITERATURE: A short poem or song characterized by personal feeling and intense emotional expression. Originally, in Greece, lyrics were accompanied by the music of a lyre.

Matrilineal System of descent in which inheritance of goods, access to land, and group leadership pass to the children through the family of the mother.

Medium (pl. media) ALL ARTS: 1. The material or materials with which the artist works. Examples from VISUAL ARTS: paint, stone, wood, bronze, plaster, concrete. MUSIC: sound. LITERATURE: language. CINEMA: film. DANCE: human body. DRAMA: language, costume, lighting, actors, sound, etc. 2. Modern means of communication (television, radio, newspapers). 3. PAINTING: A substance such as oil, egg, or water with which *pigment* is mixed.

Melodic Elaboration MUSIC: The ornamentation of *melody* by one or more of a number of possible musical devices, such as added notes, interval changes, etc.

Melody MUSIC: A succession of musical *tones.* Often the melody is known as the "tune," and is not to be confused with the other accompanying parts of a song. See *Homophony.*

Metaphor LITERATURE: A figure of speech that states or implies an analogy between two objects or between an object and a mental or emotional state. Example: "My days are in the yellow leaf;/The flowers and fruits of love are gone" (Byron) makes an analogy between the poet's life and the seasonal changes of a tree.

Metaphorical Describing statements or representations to be taken as analogy, not to be taken literally.

Meter POETRY: A regularly recurring rhythmic pattern. Meter in English is most commonly measured by accents, or stresses, and syllables. The most common metric "foot" in English is the *iamb.* The most common verse line is the *iambic pentameter* (five iambs). MUSIC: A pattern of fixed temporal units. For example, ¾ meter means one beat to a quarter note and three beats to a measure. In a musical *composition* meter is the basic grouping of notes in time.

Metope (meh'toh-pay) ARCHITECTURE: The blank space of block between the *triglyphs* in the Doric *frieze,* sometimes sculpted in low *relief.* See *Orders.*

Modal MUSIC: Describes a type of music conforming to the scale patterns of the medieval Church *modes.* See *Modes.*

Modeling VISUAL ARTS: 1. The creation of a three-dimensional *form* in clay or other responsive material, such as wax, soap, soft bone, ivory, etc. 2. By analogy, in painting and drawing, the process of suggesting a three-dimensional *form* by the creation of *shade* and shadow.

Modernism Generic name given to a variety of movements in all the arts, beginning in the early 20th century. Promotes a subjective or inner view of reality and uses diverse experimental techniques.

Modes MUSIC: Melodic scales used for church music of the Middle Ages. The modes are organized according to *pitches* similar to our modern major and minor scales, yet different enough to set them apart from the modern scales.

Molding ARCHITECTURE: A member used in construction or decoration that produces a variety in edges or contours by virtue of its curved surface.

Monastery The dwelling place of a community of monks. See *Abbey.*

Monasticism A way of life assumed by those who voluntarily separate themselves from the world to contemplate divine nature. See *Monastery.*

Monophonic (mo-no-fohn'ic) Characteristic of *monophony.*

Monophony (mo-nof'o-nee) MUSIC: A simple *melody* without additional parts or accompaniment, such as the music of a flute playing alone or of a woman singing by herself. See *Homophony, Polyphony, Texture.*

Mosaic VISUAL ARTS: A *form* of surface decoration made by inlaying small pieces of glass, tile, enamel, or varicolored stones in a cement or plaster matrix or ground.

Motet (moh-tette') MUSIC: Usually an unaccompanied choral composition based on a Latin sacred text. The motet was one of the most important forms of *polyphonic* composition from the thirteenth through the seventeenth centuries.

Motif (moh-teef'), **Motive** (moh-teev') LITERATURE: A basic element that recurs, and may serve as a kind of foundation, in a long poem, fiction, or drama. A young woman awakened by love is the motif of many tales, such as *Sleeping Beauty.* VISUAL ARTS: An element of design repeated and developed in a painting, sculpture, or building. MUSIC: A recurring melodic phrase, sometimes used as a basis for variation.

Mural PAINTING: Large painting in oil, fresco, or other *medium* made for a particular *wall,* ceiling, or similar large surface.

Myth Stories developed anonymously within a culture that attempt to explain natural events from a supernatural or religious point of view.

Mythology The body of myths from a particular cultural group.

Naos (nah'ohs) ARCHITECTURE: Greek word for the *cella* or main body of a Greek temple.

Narrative LITERATURE: 1. (noun) Any *form* that tells a story or recounts a sequence of events (novel, *tale,* essay, article, film). 2. (adj.) In story form, recounting.

Narthex ARCHITECTURE: The entrance hall or porch that stands before the *nave* of a church.

Naturalism LITERATURE, VISUAL ARTS: Faithful adherence to the appearance of nature or outer reality.

Nave ARCHITECTURE: In Roman architecture, the central space of a *basilica;* in Christian architecture, the central longitudinal or circular space in the church, bounded by aisles.

Nave Arcade ARCHITECTURE: The open passageway or screen between the central space and the *side aisles* in a church.

Nemesis (neh'ma-sis) Greek goddess of Fate. Word means retribution, punishment.

Neoclassicism ALL ARTS: A movement that flourished in Europe and America in the late seventeenth and eighteenth centuries, heavily influenced by the classical style of Greece and Rome. Neoclassical art and literature is characterized by sobriety, balance, logic, and restraint. The corresponding musical style (18th century) is usually called *classical.*

Neolithic The stage in the evolution of human societies when peoples began systematic cultivation and the domestication of animals.

Niche (nish) ARCHITECTURE: A semicircular or similarly shaped recess in a wall designed to contain sculpture, an urn, or other object. It is usually covered by a half*dome.*

Nonobjective VISUAL ARTS: Not representing objects in the material world.

Novel LITERATURE: A lengthy prose narrative, traditionally spanning a broad period of time, containing a plot and developing characters. The modern European novel took form in the eighteenth century.

Oba Name for the chief ruler of Benin.

Oculus (ock'you-luhs) ACHITECTURE: Circular opening at the crown of a *dome.* See *Pantheon* (Ch. 7).

Odu (oh'doo) A secret body of poetry used in the Yoruba *Ifa* divination process.

Oil Painting The practice of painting by using *pigments* suspended in oil (walnut, linseed, etc.).

Oligarchy (oh'lih-gar-key) Greek word meaning "rule by the few." Rule by the few where the state is primarily utilized to serve the interest of the governors. Traditionally contrasted with *aristocracy,* rule by the few for the common good.

Olorun (oh-low'roon), **Oludumare** (oh-loo-doo-mah'ray) The Yoruba term for the supreme high deity.

Open Fifths MUSIC: *Chords,* normally made of three sounds, with the middle *pitch* absent.

Oratorio MUSIC: An extended musical setting for solo voices, chorus, and orchestra, of a religious or contemplative nature. An oratorio is performed in a concert hall or church, without scenery, costumes, or physical action. One of the greatest examples is Handel's *Messiah.*

Orchestration MUSIC: Orchestration is the art of writing music for the instruments of the orchestra that will bring out desired effects of the various instruments. Indeed, it is the art of "blending" the voices of the orchestra so that a pleasing sound is the end result.

Orders ARCHITECTURE: Types of *columns* with *entablatures* developed in classical Greece. The orders are basically three: Doric, Ionic, and Corinthian. They determine not only the scale and therefore dimensions of a temple but also the experience generated by the building, or its *style.* See section on Greek Architecture and diagram of the orders (Ch. 4).

Oriki (ohr-ee'key) Yoruba term meaning praise poems based on names given to gods, places, rulers, and important persons.

Orisha (ohr-ee'sha) In Yoruba religion, lesser gods (below the chief god) and sometimes ancestor figures, ancient kings, and founders of cities who have been deified.

Ostinato (aw-stee-nah'stoe) MUSIC: Italian for obstinate or stubborn; the persistent repetition of a clearly defined *melody,* usually in the same voice. This device is often used in a bass part to organize a *composition* for successive variations.

Oxymoron (ock-see-mohr'on) LITERATURE: A figure of speech that brings together two contradictory terms, such as "sweet sorrow."

Palazzo (pa-laht'so) ARCHITECTURE: Italian for palace, or large, impressive building.

Palladian ARCHITECTURE: Designating the Renaissance architectural style of Andrea Palladio.

Panel Painting A painting made on a ground or panel of wood, as distinguished from a *fresco* or a painting on canvas.

Parapet ARCHITECTURE: In an exterior *wall,* the part entirely above the roof. The term may also describe a low wall that acts as a guard at a sudden edge or drop, as on the edge of a roof, battlement, or wall.

Parody LITERATURE: A work that exaggerates or burlesques another, serious one. Often a parody pokes fun at an author and his style. The parody may be compared to a visual caricature or cartoon.

Pathos (pay'thaws) ALL ARTS: A quality that sets off deep feeling or compassion in the spectator or reader.

Patrilineal System of descent in which inheritance of goods, access to land, and group leadership passes to the children through the family of the father.

Pediment ARCHITECTURE: In classical architecture the triangular space at the end of a roof formed by the sloping ridges of the roof. The pediment was often filled with decoration which could be painted or sculpted or both.

Pentatonic Scale MUSIC: Five-note scale that occurs in the music of nearly all ancient cultures. It is common in West African music and is found in jazz.

Perspective VISUAL ARTS: Generally, the representation of three-dimensional objects in space on a two-dimensional surface. There are a variety of means to achieve this. The most familiar is that of "linear perspective" developed in the fifteenth century and codified by Brunelleschi, in which all parallel lines and edges of surfaces recede at the same angle and are drawn, on the picture plane, to converge at a single *vanishing point.* The process of diminution in size of objects with respect to location is very regular and precise. Other techniques, often used in combination with linear perspective, include: (a) vertical perspective—objects further from the observer are shown higher up on the picture, (b) diagonal perspective—objects are not only higher but aligned along an oblique *axis* producing the sensation of continuous recession, (c) overlapping, (d) *foreshortening,* (e) *modeling,* (f) *shadows,* and (g) atmospheric perspective, the use of conventions such as blurring of outlines, alternation of hue toward blue, and decrease of *color* saturation.

Philosophe (fee-low-soph') Eighteenth-century French intellectual and writer; not usually a systematic philosopher.

Phrase MUSIC: A natural division of the *melody;* in a manner of speaking, a musical "sentence."

Picture Plane PAINTING: The surface on which the picture is painted.

Picture Space PAINTING: The space that extends behind or beyond the picture plane; created by devices such as *linear perspective.* Picture space is usually described by foreground, middleground, and background.

Pier ARCHITECTURE: A *column,* post, or similar member designed to carry a great load; may also refer to a thickened vertical mass within the *wall* designed to provide additional support.

Pigment PAINTING: The grains or powder that give a *medium* its *color.* Can be derived from a variety of sources: clays, stones, metals, shells, animal and vegetable matter.

Pilaster (pih'lass-ter) ARCHITECTURE: A flattened engaged *column* or *pier* that may have a *capital* and *base.* It may be purely decorative or it may reinforce a *wall.*

Pitch MUSIC: A technical term identifying a single musical sound, taking into consideration the frequency of its fundamental vibrations. Some songs, or instruments, are pitched high and others are pitched low.

Plan See *Groundplan.*

Plane A flat surface.

Plasticity VISUAL ARTS: The quality of roundness, palpability, solidity, or three-dimensionality of a *form.*

Plinth A block or slab on which a statue, pedestal, or column is placed, and, by extension, the base on which a building rests or appears to rest.

Podium ARCHITECTURE: The high platform or *base* of a Roman temple, or any elevated platform.

Polis (poh'liss) The ancient Greek city-state.

Polyphonic (paul-ee-fon'ick) Characteristic of *polyphony.*

Polyphony (paul-if'o-nee) MUSIC: Describes *composition* or *improvisations* in which more than one *melody* sounds simultaneously—that is, two or more tunes at the same time. Polyphony is characterized by the combining of a number of individual melodies into a harmonizing and agreeable whole. See *Homophony, Monophony,* and *Texture.*

Portico ARCHITECTURE: Porch or covered walk consisting of a roof supported by *columns.*

Post-and-Lintel ARCHITECTURE: an essential system of building characterized by the use of uprights—posts—which support horizontal *beams*—*lintels*—in order to span spaces. Used as supports for a window or door, the posts are the *jambs* and the *lintel* is the window head.

Primary Colors Red, Yellow, Blue—the three primary hues of the spectrum. See *Color.*

Pronaos (pro'nah-ohs) ARCHITECTURE: In classical architecture, the inner *portico* or room in front of the *naos* or *cella.*

Prose LITERATURE: Generally, may mean any kind of discourse, written or spoken, which cannot be classified as poetry. More specifically, prose refers to written expression characterized by logical, grammatical order, *style,* and even *rhythm* (but not *meter*).

Proverb A saying that succinctly and effectively expresses a truth recognized by a community or a wise observation about life. Proverbs are most often transmitted orally.

Rationalism PHILOSOPHY: The theory that general principles are essentially deductive; i.e., deducible from an examination of human reason. Reason, not the senses, is the ultimate source of basic truths.

Realism LITERATURE, VISUAL ARTS: A movement which began in the mid-nineteenth century and which holds that art should be a faithful reproduction of reality and that artists should deal with contemporary people and their everyday experience.

Recitative (reh-see-tah-teev') MUSIC: A vocal style used to introduce ideas and persons in the musical *composition,* or to relate a given amount of information within a short period of time. The recitative has practically no melodic value. This device is employed extensively in Handel's *Messiah.*

Relief Sculpture Sculpture that is not freestanding but projects from a surface of which it is a part. A slight projection is called low relief (bas-relief); a more pronounced projection, high relief.

Republic A form of government in which ultimate power resides in the hands of a fairly large number of people but not necessarily the entire community. This power is exercised through representatives. The word derives from Latin meaning "public thing."

Response MUSIC: A solo-chorus relationship in which the soloist alternates performance with the chorus. The response is a particularly noteworthy device in traditional African music as well as in Gregorian chant.

Responsorial MUSIC: Describing the performance of a chant in alternation between a soloist and a chorus. (It is unlike antiphonal music, where alternating choruses sing.)

Rhythm ALL ARTS: An overall sense of systematic movement. In music, poetry, and dance this movement may be literally felt; in the visual arts it refers to the regular repetition of a *form,* conveying a sense of movement by the contrast between a form and its interval.

Rib ARCHITECTURE: Generally a curved structural member that supports any curved shape or panel.

Ribbed Vault ARCHITECTURE: A *vault* whose sections seem to be supported or are supported by slender, curved structural members that also define the sections of the vault. The ribs may run either transversely, that is from side to side, or diagonally, from corner to corner of the vault.

Riddle A form of popular, usually oral, literature that asks an answer to a veiled question. Riddles often make use of striking *images* and *metaphors.*

Ridge ARCHITECTURE: The line defined by the meeting of the two sides of a sloping roof.

Romance LITERATURE: A long narrative in a *Romance language,* presenting chivalrous ideals, heroes involved in adventures, and love affairs from medieval legends.

Romance Language One of the languages that developed from popular Latin speech during the Middle Ages, and that exist now as French, Italian, Spanish, Portuguese, Catalan, Provençal, Romanic, and Rumanian.

Romanesque An artistic movement of the eleventh and twelfth centuries, primarily in architecture. The name comes from similarities with Roman architecture.

Romanticism A movement in all of the arts as well as in philosophy, religion, and politics that spread throughout Europe and America in the early nineteenth century. The romantics revolted against the Neoclassical emphasis on order and reason and substituted an inclination for nature and imagination. See Ch. 27.

Rose Window ARCHITECTURE: The round ornamental window frequently found over the entrances of Gothic cathedrals.

Sarcophagus (sahr-cough'a-gus) A large stone coffin. It may be elaborately carved and decorated.

Satire A mode of expression that criticizes social institutions or human foibles humorously. The Roman invented the verse satire, but satire may appear in any literary *genre,* in visual art, in film, mime, and dance.

Satyr (say'ter) **Play** LITERATURE: A light, burlesque play given along with *tragedies* and *comedies* at the festival of Dionysus in ancient Athens.

Scholasticism PHILOSOPHY: A way of thought that attempted to reconcile Christian truth with truth established by natural reason. Originating in the early Middle Ages, it reached its height in the thirteenth century in response to the recovery of Aristotle's scientific and philosophical writings.

Secondary Colors See *Color.*

Section ARCHITECTURE: The drawing that represents a vertical slide through the interior or exterior of a building, showing the relation of floor to floor.

Shade PAINTING: A *color* mixed with black. Mixing a color with white produces a *tint.*

Shading VISUAL ARTS: The process of indicating by graphics or paint the change in *color* of an object when light falls on its surface revealing its three-dimensional qualities. Shading can be produced not only by a change of color, but also by the addition of black, brown, or gray, or by drawing techniques.

Shadow VISUAL ARTS: The *form* cast by an object in response to the direction of light.

Shed Roof ARCHITECTURE: A roof shape with only one sloping *plane,* such as the roof of a lean-to, or that over the *side aisle* in a Gothic or Romanesque church.

Side Aisle ARCHITECTURE: The aisles on either side of, and therefore parallel to, the *nave* in a Christian church or Roman *basilica.*

Simile (sim'eh-lee) LITERATURE: A type of *metaphor* which makes an explicit comparison. Example: "My love is like a red, red rose."

Sonata MUSIC: An important form of instrumental music in use from the baroque era to the present. It is a *composition* usually with three or four movements, each movement adhering to a pattern of contrasting tempos. Example: Allegro, Adagio, Scherzo, Allegro.

Sonnet LITERATURE: A *lyric* poem of fourteen lines, following one of several conventions. The two main types of sonnet are the Italian (Petrarchan) which divides the poem into octave (eight lines) and sestet (six lines) and the English (Shakespearean) which divides the poem into three quatrains of four lines each and a final rhyming couplet.

Span ARCHITECTURE: The interval between two posts, *arches, walls,* or other supports.

Stained Glass ARCHITECTURE: Glass to which a *color* is added during its molten state, or glass which is given a hue by firing or otherwise causing color to adhere to the glass.

Stele (stee'lee) ARCHITECTURE: In classical Greece a stone upright or slab used commemoratively; it may mark a grave or record an offering or important event.

Stretto MUSIC: The repetition of a *theme (subject)* that has been collapsed by diminishing the time values of the notes. As a result, the listener is literally propelled to the dramatic end or climactic conclusion of the music. Handel used this *fugal* device effectively in the last chorus of his *Messiah.*

Structure ALL ARTS: The relationship of the parts to the whole in a work of art. A structure may be mechanical (division of a play into acts, a symphony into movements) or may be more concealed and based on such things as the inter-relationships of *images, themes, motifs, colors,* shapes. In a *narrative* the structure usually refers to the arrangement of the sequence of events. In architecture structure may refer either to the actual system of building or to the relationships between the elements of the system of building.

Style ALL ARTS: Characteristics of *form* and technique that enable us to identify a particular work with a certain historical period, place, group, or individual. Painters in Florence in the 15th and 16th centuries used *perspective, color,* etc., in ways that allow us to identify a Renaissance style, but within that group we may distinguish the individual style of Leonardo from that of Raphael. The *impressionist* painters in France at the end of the nineteenth century used light and *color* in a particular way: a painting in which this technique is followed has an impressionistic style. But the use of certain *forms, colors,* design and *composition* enables us to distinguish within this group the style of Renoir from that of Monet. Afro-European *rhythms* and *improvisation* distinguish a jazz style, but within that general category are many schools of jazz or even different styles of one individual, such as Duke Ellington. Literary style is determined by choices of words, sentence *structure* and syntax *rhythm,* figurative language, rhetorical devices, etc. One may speak of an ornate, simple, formal, or colloquial style; of a period style such as *Neoclassical, romantic, realist;* or of an individual's style. Style is sometimes contrasted with *content.*

Subject ALL ARTS: What the work is about. The subject of the painting "Mont Ste Victoire" is that particular mountain; the subject of Richard Wright's *Native Son* is a young black man in Chicago. MUSIC: The *melody* used as the basis of a *contrapuntal composition* (e.g., the subject of a *fugue*).

Suite MUSIC: An important instrumental form of baroque music, consisting of a grouping of several dancelike movements, all in the same key.

Superego In Freudian theory, one of the three parts of the mind. The superego is the censuring faculty, replacing parents or other authorities.

Symbol VISUAL ARTS, LITERATURE: An *image* that suggests an idea, a spiritual or religious concept, or an emotion beyond itself. It differs from *metaphor* in that the term of comparison is not explicitly stated. Symbols may be conventional; i.e., have a culturally defined meaning such as the Christian cross or the Jewish star of David. Since the nineteenth century, symbols have tended to denote a variety or an ambiguity of meanings.

Symbolism 1. The use of symbol in any art. 2. A literary school which began in France in the late nineteenth century, characterized by the use of obscure or ambiguous *symbols.*

Symmetry VISUAL ARTS: The balance of proportions achieved by the repetition of parts on either side of a central *axis.* The two sides may be identical, in which case we can speak of bilateral symmetry.

Syncopation MUSIC: A rhythmic device characterized as a deliberate disturbance of a regularly recurring pulse. Accented offbeats or irregular *meter* changes are two means of achieving syncopation.

Tactile VISUAL ARTS, LITERATURE: Refers to the sense of touch. In the visual arts, tactile *values* are created by techniques and conventions that specifically stimulate the sense of touch in order to enhance suggestions of weight, *volume* (roundness), visual approximation, and therefore three-dimensionality. Writers may also create tactile effects, as in the description of cloth or skin.

Tale LITERATURE: A simple *narrative,* whose subject matter may be real or imaginary, and whose purpose is primarily to entertain. Tales may also make use of "morals" to instruct.

Tatsuniyoyi (taht-soon-yoh'yee) Hausa tales about animals and people told by old women to entertain and instruct young children.

Tempera (tehm'per-ah) PAINTING: Technique in which the *pigment* is suspended in egg, glue, or a similar soluble *medium,* like water. Tempera paint dries very quickly and does not blend easily, producing a matte (flat, nonreflective) surface, because, unlike *oil paint,* it is essentially an opaque medium.

Texture VISUAL ARTS: Surface quality (rough, smooth, grainy, etc.) LITERATURE: Elements such as *imagery,* sound patterns, etc. apart from the *subject* and *structure* of the work. MUSIC: The working relationship between the *melody* line and the other accompanying parts, or the characteristic "weaving" of a musical *composition.* There are three basic musical textures: *Monophonic* (a single line), *Homophonic* (a melody supported by *chords*), and *Polyphonic* (multiple melodic lines).

Thanatos Greek word for death. For Freud, the death-wish or death-force, opposed to Eros, the life force.

Theme VISUAL ARTS: A *color* or pattern taken as a subject for repetition and modification. Example: a piece of sculpture may have a cubical theme. MUSIC: A *melody* which constitutes the basis of variation and development. Example: "The Ode to Joy" song in the last movement of Beethoven's *Ninth Symphony.* LITERATURE AND PERFORMING ARTS: An emotion or idea that receives major attention in the work. A novel or film may contain several themes, such as love, war, death. A dance may be composed on the theme of struggle, joy, etc. Theme is sometimes used in this sense for visual arts and music as well.

Threnody (threh'no-dee) MUSIC: A song of lamentation, a very mournful song.

Through-Composed MUSIC: Describes a type of song in which new music is provided for each stanza. A through-composed song is thus unlike most modern hymns, folk, and popular songs, which use the same tune for each stanza.

Thrust ARCHITECTURE: The downward and outward pressure exerted by a *vault* or *dome* on the *walls* supporting it.

Timbre (taam'bruh) MUSIC: The quality of "color" of a particular musical *tone* produced by the various instruments. For instance, the very "nasal" sound of the oboe is markedly different from the very "pure" sound of the flute.

Tint VISUAL ARTS: The *color* achieved by adding white to a hue to raise its *value,* in contrast to a *shade,* which is a hue mixed with black to lower its value.

Tonal MUSIC: Organized around a pitch center. A tonal *composition* is one in which the *pitches* of all the various *chords* and *melodies* relate well to one another. Tonal music has a recognizable beginning, middle, and end. See *Chord, Melody, Pitch.*

Tonality MUSIC: The specific *tonal* organization of a composition.

Tone ALL ARTS: The creation of a mood or an emotional state. In painting, tone may refer specifically to the prevailing effect of a *color.* Thus, a painting may be said to have a silvery, bluish, light, or dark tone as well as a wistful, melancholy, or joyful tone. The term may also refer to *value* or *shade* (see *Color*). In literature, tone usually describes the prevailing attitude of an author toward his material, audience, or both. Thus a tone may be cynical, sentimental, satirical, etc. In music, "tone color" may be used as a synonym for *timbre.* Tone in music also means a sound of definite *pitch* and duration (as distinct from noise), the true building material of music. The notes on a written page of music are merely symbols that represent the tones that actually make the music.

Tornada (tore-nah'dah) MUSIC: In troubadour songs, a short stanza added at the end as a "send-off."

Tracery ARCHITECTURE: The curvilinear or rectilinear pattern of open stonework or wood that supports the glass or other transparent or translucent material in a window or similar opening. May also be used generally to refer to decorative patterns carved similarly on wood or stone.

Tragedy LITERATURE: A serious drama that recounts the events in the life of a great person which bring him or her from fortune to misfortune. Tragedies usually meditate on the relation between human beings and their destiny. Tragedies first developed in ancient Greece; other great periods of tragedy include Elizabethan England and France under Louis XIV. The word is sometimes used to describe a novel or story.

Transept ARCHITECTURE: The transverse portion of a church that crosses the central *axis* of the *nave* at right angles between the nave and *apse* to form a cross-shaped (cruciform) planned building.

Triglyph (try'glif) ARCHITECTURE: The block carved with three channels or grooves that alternates with the *metopes* is a classical Doric *frieze.* See *Orders.*

Triumphal Arch ARCHITECTURE: The monumental urban gateway, invented by the Romans, set up along a major street to commemorate important military successes. It may have one or three arched openings and is usually decorated with inscriptions, *reliefs,* and freestanding sculpture on the top.

Trope MUSIC: Lengthened musical passage or elaboration on the Mass used during the Middle Ages. LITERATURE: 1. Verbal amplification of the text of the Mass. 2. A figure of speech.

Troubadour A lyric poet and singer, including wandering minstrels, originating in Provence in the eleventh century and flourishing throughout southern France, northern Italy, and Eastern Spain during the twelfth and thirteenth centuries.

Truss ARCHITECTURE: Originally a wooden structural member composed of smaller, lighter pieces of wood joined to form rigid triangles and capable of spanning spaces by acting as a *beam.*

Tympanum (tihm'pah-nuhm) ARCHITECTURE: The triangular or similarly shaped space enclosed by an *arch* or *pediment.*

Tyranny In ancient Greece, meant "rule of the strong man." Historically, came to mean arbitrary rule of one, but generally taken to mean arbitrary political rule of any kind.

Value See *Color.*

Vanishing Point PAINTING: The point or points of convergence for all lines forming an angle to the *picture plane* in pictures constructed according to the principles of linear *perspective.*

Vault ARCHITECTURE: The covering or spanning of a space employing the principle of the *arch* and using masonry, brick, plaster, or similar malleable materials. The extension of an arch infinitely in one plane creates a barrel or tunnel vault. The intersection of two barrel vaults at right angles to each other produces a cross or groin vault. *Ribs* are sometimes placed along the intersections of a groin vault to produce a *ribbed vault.*

Veneer VISUAL ARTS: A thin layer of precious or valuable material glued or otherwise attached to the surface of another, less expensive, or less beautiful material. The Romans, for example, applied thin layers of marble to the concrete and rubble fill surfaces of their buildings to produce a more splendid effect. In this century, valuable woods like walnut or mahogany are applied as veneers to the surfaces of plywood.

Verisimilitude Literally, "true-seeming." LITERATURE: A doctrine prevalent in the *Neoclassical* period, which hold that elements in a story must be so arranged that they seem to be true or that they could actually occur. VISUAL ARTS: The effect of near-perfect emulation or reproduction of objects in the visual world. Not to be confused with *realism.*

Vernacular The common daily speech of the people; nonliterary language. During the Middle Ages, any language that was not Latin.

Viewpoint The position or place from which the viewer looks at an object or the visual field.

Vizier A chief administrator.

Volume ARCHITECTURE: Refers to the void or solid three-dimensional quality of a space or *form* whether completely enclosed or created by the presence of forms which act as boundaries. Compare the "volume" of the *Parthenon* with the "volume" of the *Pantheon.*

Volute A spiral or scroll-like ornamental form, which may be used either as a purely decorative or as a supporting member in an architectural ensemble. The curvilinear portion of an Ionic capital is a volute, and by extension a portion of such a shape is a volute.

Voussoir (voo-swahr′) ARCHITECTURE: The wedge-shaped stone or masonry unit of an *arch,* wider at the top and tapering toward the bottom.

Wall ARCHITECTURE: A broad, substantial upright slab that acts as an enclosing *form* capable of supporting its own weight and the weight of *beams* or *arches* to span and enclose space.

Warm Colors VISUAL ARTS: The hues commonly associated with warmth—yellow, red, and orange. In *compositions* the warm colors tend to advance, in contrast to the *cool colors,* which tend to recede from the viewer.

Watercolor PAINTING: Technique using water as the *medium* for very fine *pigment.* Watercolor dries very fast and can be extremely transparent.

Ziggurat ARCHITECTURE: The Mesopotamian temple-tower.

Credits

J M Dent & Sons From *Candide* by Voltaire, translated by T. Smollett: Revised by James Thornton, copyright 1937. Reprinted by permission of J M Dent & Sons Ltd.

Doubleday From *101 Stories of the Great Ballets* by George Balanchine and Francis Mason. Copyright © 1975 by Doubleday, a division of Bantam Doubleday Dell Publishing Group, Inc. Used by permission of Doubleday, a division of Bantam Doubleday Dell Publishing Group, Inc.

"Autobiography: A Self-Recorded Fiction" by John Barth, first appeared in the *North American Review, #2.* From the book *Lost in the Funhouse.* © 1968 by John Barth. Reprinted by permission of Doubleday, a division of Bantam, Doubleday, Dell Publishing Group, Inc.

Farrar, Straus & Giroux, Inc. "The Death of the Author" from *The Russell of Language,* by Roland Barthes. Translated by Richard Howard. Translation copyright © 1986 by Farrar, Straus & Giroux, Inc. Reprinted by permission of Hill and Wang, a division of Farrar, Straus & Giroux, Inc.

Editions Gallimard "The Republic of Silence" from *Defeat and Beyond: An Anthology of French Wartime Writing (1940–1945)* by Jean Paul Sartre, ed. by Germaine Bree and George Bernauer. Copyright © 1949 by Editions Gallimard. Used by permission of the publisher.

Alan A. Gonzalez Poem "Liama de Amor Viva" and sonnet "Inscription for the Tomb of Dominico Greco," translated by Alan A. Gonzalez.

Grove Press *Picnic on the Battlefield* by Fernando Arrabal is reprinted by permission of Grove Press, Inc. These translations copyright © 1967 by Calder & Boyars, Ltd., London.

Harcourt Brace Jovanovich, Inc. "Preludes" and "The Love Song of J. Alfred Prufrock" from *Collected Poems 1909–1962* by T. S. Eliot, copyright 1936 by Harcourt Brace Jovanovich, Inc., copyright © 1964, 1963 by T. S. Eliot, reprinted by permission of the publisher.

Excerpt from *A Room of One's Own* by Virginia Woolf, copyright 1929 by Harcourt Brace Jovanovich, Inc. and renewed 1957 by Leonard Woolf, reprinted by permission of the publisher.

"Really, Doesn't Crime Pay?" from *In Love & Trouble* copyright © 1973 by Alice Walker, reprinted by permission of Harcourt Brace Jovanovich, Inc.

Harvard University Press Reprinted by permission of the publishers from *Petrarch's Lyric Poems* by Robert M. Durling, Cambridge, Mass.: Harvard University Press. Copyright © 1976 by Robert M. Durling.

Anthony Hecht "The Swan" by Baudelaire, translated by Anthony Hecht, from the bilingual edition of Baudelaire's *Les Fleurs du Mal,* edited by Marthiel and Jackson Matthews, published by New Directions.

Houghton Mifflin Company From *Mein Kampf* translated by Ralph Manheim. Copyright 1943 and copyright © renewed 1971 by Houghton Mifflin Company. Reprinted by permission of Houghton Mifflin Company.

Liveright Publishing Corporation "Karintha" is reprinted from *Cane* by Jean Toomer, by permission of Liveright Publishing Corporation. Copyright 1923 by Boni & Liveright. Copyright renewed 1951 by Jean Toomer.

Macmillan Publishing Company Excerpt from Montesquieu's *Spirit of the Laws,* translated by Thomas Nugent, copyright 1949. Reprinted by permission of Macmillan Publishing Company, Inc.

"beware: do not read this poem" by Ishmael Reed. Reprinted with permission of Atheneum Publishers, an imprint of Macmillan Publishing Company, from *New and Collected Poems* by Ishmael Reed. Copyright © 1972 by Ishmael Reed.

New Directions Publishing Corporation "Dulce et Decorum Est" by Wilfred Owen, *Collected Poems.* Copyright © 1963 by Chatto & Windus, Ltd. Reprinted by permission of New Directions Publishing Corporation.

Ezra Pound, "The River Merchant's Wife" and "In a Station of the Metro" from *Personae.* Copyright 1926 by Ezra Pound. Reprinted by permission of New Directions Publishing Corporation.

"Death and the Compass" by Jorge Luis Borges, *Labyrinths.* Copyright © 1964 by New Directions Publishing Corporation.

Ernesto Cardenal, *Apocalypse and Other Poems.* Copyright © 1960, 1963 by the Trustees of the Merton Legacy Trust. Copyright © 1977 by Ernesto Cardinal and Robert Pring-Mill. Reprinted by permission of New Directions Publishing Corporation.

University of Pittsburgh Press Reprinted from *Heinrich Heine: Lyric Poems and Ballads* by Heinrich Heine, translated by Ernst Feise, by permission of the University of Pittsburgh Press. © 1961 by University of Pittsburgh Press.

Random House, Inc. From *The Penal Colony* by Franz Kafka, trans. by Willa and Edwin Muir. Translation copyright 1948 and renewed 1976 by Schocken Books, Inc. Reprinted by permission of Schocken Books, published by Pantheon Books, a division of Random House, Inc.

From *Ulysses* by James Joyce. Copyright 1934 and renewed 1962 by Lucia and George Joyce. Reprinted by permission of Random House, Inc.

"The Weary Blues" and "The Negro Speaks of Rivers" from *Selected Poems* by Langston Hughes. Copyright 1926 by Alfred A. Knopf, Inc. and renewed 1954 by Langston Hughes. Reprinted by permission of the publisher.

Excerpt from *The Myth of Sisyphus and Other Essays* by Albert Camus, translated by Justin O'Brien. Copyright © 1955 by Alfred A. Knopf, Inc. Reprinted by permission of Alfred A. Knopf, Inc.

From *Invisible Man* by Ralph Ellison. Copyright © 1952 by Ralph Ellison. Reprinted by permission of Random House, Inc.

RCA Records The English text of "Hymn to Joy" is a free translation by Louis Untermeyer. Copyright 1952 by RCA Records. Reprinted by permission of RCA and Bryna Untermeyer.

Sonia Sanchez "Present" by Sonia Sanchez from *I've Been a Woman: New and Selected Poems,* Third World Press, 1985. Reprinted by Permission of Sonia Sanchez.

Triquarterly "Ode to Broken Things" by Pablo Neruda from *Navagaciones y Regresso* (Voyages and Homecomings), copyright © 1969 *Triquarterly.* Reprinted by permission.

Twayne Publishers "If We Must Die" from *The Selected Poems of Claude McKay,* copyright 1981 and reprinted with the permission of Twayne Publishers, a division of G. K. Hall & Co., Boston.

University of California Press Excerpt from "Manao Tupapau" from the manuscript "Cahier pour Aline" as translated by Herschel B. Chipp in *Theories of Modern Art.* Copyright © 1968 The Regents of the University of California. Reprinted by permission of the University of California Press.

"To a Passer-By" by Baudelaire, translated by C. F. MacIntyre from *100 Poems from Les Fleurs du Mal,* copyright 1947 by University of California Press. Reprinted by permission of the publisher.

Viking Penguin, Inc. From *If This is a Man* by Primo Levi. Translation, copyright © 1959 by Orion Press. Reprinted by permission of Viking Penguin, Inc.

W. W. Norton "Translations" and "The Ninth Symphony of Beethoven Understood at Last as a Sexual Message." Reprinted from *The Fact of A Door Frame, Poems Selected and New, 1950–1984,* by Adrienne Rich, by permission of W. W. Norton & Company, Inc. Copyright © 1984 by Adrienne Rich. Copyright © 1975, 1978 by W. W. Norton & Company, Inc. Copyright © 1981 by Adrienne Rich.

Selection from "Motherhood: The Contemporary Emergency and the Quantum Leap" from *On Lies, Secrets, and Silence, Selected Prose, 1966–1978* by Adrienne Rich, by permission of the author and W. W. Norton & Company, Inc. Copyright © 1979 by W. W. Norton & Company, Inc.

Freud selection is reprinted from *Civilization and Its Discontents* by Sigmund Freud, translated and edited by James Strachey, by permission of W. W. Norton & Company, Inc. Copyright © 1961 by James Strachey.

Index

Page numbers in boldface type indicate black and white illustrations.